T0391948

THE OXFORD HANDBOOK OF

W. B. YEATS

THE OXFORD HANDBOOK OF

W. B. YEATS

Edited by
LAUREN ARRINGTON
and
MATTHEW CAMPBELL

OXFORD
UNIVERSITY PRESS

Great Clarendon Street, Oxford, OX2 6DP,
United Kingdom

Oxford University Press is a department of the University of Oxford.
It furthers the University's objective of excellence in research, scholarship,
and education by publishing worldwide. Oxford is a registered trade mark of
Oxford University Press in the UK and in certain other countries

Published in the United States of America by Oxford University Press
198 Madison Avenue, New York, NY 10016, United States of America

British Library Cataloguing in Publication Data
Data available

Library of Congress Control Number: 2022943508

ISBN 978–0–19–883467–0

DOI: 10.1093/oxfordhb/9780198834670.001.0001

Printed and bound in the UK by
TJ Books Limited

Preface

....

'*What then?*' the ghost of Plato asks in a late poem that surveys a life very much like that of Yeats himself: friends, family, a house and garden. But the interrogation that persists above all is of the poet's legacy. He declares, ' "Let the fools rage, I swerved in naught, / Something to perfection brought;" / *But louder sang that ghost: "What then?"*' Nearly a century later, scholars and everyday readers alike continue to be drawn to the reiterated question posed by Plato's ghost when offered a short four-stanza litany of the seeming achievements of the artist, impresario, public figure, historical thinker. Did Yeats use his fame and public voice with responsibility in tumultuous times? Did his work vindicate the friendship he had won among a fraternity of artists and thinkers and public women and men? Was he a good father, husband, lover? Did he ever manage to produce the perfection of great art? All of these questions remain open to literary criticism and history as generations of scholars and students continue to pore over the legacy of Yeats's seventy-three-year life.

Yeats's work covers a publishing history which began in 1885 and spanned Victorianism to modernism. He had a career as writer and director for the stage which began in 1892 and continued through decades of theatrical experiment. His life as a writer of critical and esoteric prose was surmounted by the two complete versions of a world and art-historical system, *A Vision* written in collaboration with his wife, George. By middle age, the Nobel Prize-winning Yeats was 'A sixty-year-old smiling public man', a senator who took an active part in everyday politics in the new Irish Free State, a performer whose lectures and readings could fill Carnegie Hall.

Above all, Yeats remains a figure whose work intersects at multiple points with the story of world literature. His voice is at once regional—the County Sligo family origins to which his writing returned throughout his career and to which his body was (probably) returned for burial; national—occupied in the political struggles and petty disputes of a small country at the western seaboard of Europe; international—a writer whose audiences, interlocutors, and interests spanned Asia and the Americas as well as European literature from Plato through Dante to Blake and Shelley; and otherworldly—both in terms of an emerging new Einsteinian science and astronomy and the less tangible worlds of communicators, astrologers, and the tarot.

The forty-two chapters in this book consider Yeats's early toil, his practical and esoteric concerns as his career developed, his friends and enemies, how he was and is understood. This book brings together critics and writers who have considered what Yeats wrote and how he wrote, moving between texts and their contexts in ways that leads the reader through Yeats's multiple selves as poet, playwright, public figure, and mystic. The book cannot be encyclopaedic and neither can it ever be wholly consistent, but among the virtues of the Oxford Handbook series is that volumes like this can bring together a variety of views, establish a dialogue, and in this instance add to the Yeatsian sense of dialogue, the antinomial or deliberately divided way of thinking that Yeats relished and encouraged. Wedded to the questioning of certainty in a poem like 'What then?' is the deliberate 'Vacillation' of another late work. This book aims to put that sense of a living dialogue in tune both with the history of Yeatsian criticism and with contemporary critical and ethical debate, not shirking the complexities of Yeats's more uncomfortable political positions or personal life. It is hoped that the book will speak of Yeats's life and work from the times in which we find ourselves, and provide one basis from which future Yeats scholarship can continue to participate in the fascination of all the contributors here in the satisfying difficulty of this great writer.

Our collaboration as editors and contributors grew out of other collaborations and networks, especially the many gatherings at the Yeats International Summer School, where we served as co-directors. Many of the contributors in this book met in Sligo, and while it is invidious to mention individuals, we would like to thank Jonathan Allison, Meg Harper, Anne Margaret Daniel, and James Pethica for their invitations to be inducted into the community of the Summer School. For more than half a century the work of the Yeats Society Sligo has been a model for a cultural community which links the work of local and international expertise. We would like to thank those in Sligo who unconditionally shared their knowledge along with their hospitality, among them Martin and Maura McTighe, Damien and Paula Brennan, Susan O'Keeffe, and the inestimable Martin Enright. The International Yeats Society has done tremendous work in expanding the boundaries of where and how W. B. Yeats is read, and we would like to acknowledge the work of those who have organized conferences and edited the journal, including Sean Golden, Catherine Paul, Alexandra Poulain, Charles Armstrong, and Rob Doggett. We owe many thanks to all three of these organizations for the opportunities they continue to provide for scholars to embark on an enterprise such as this book.

We are grateful to Jacqueline Norton at OUP for commissioning this volume and to Aimee Wright and others at OUP for bringing it to publication. The valuable comments of a number of anonymous readers refined the initial plan considerably. We express our thanks to the Department of English and Related Literature at the University of York and Maynooth University Department of English for research support, the F. R. Leavis Fund at the University of York and the National University of Ireland for supporting costs associated with production. Stephen Grace did immense work with the initial task of standardizing the referencing throughout a very big book indeed.

Matthew Campbell would like to thank Valerie Cotter for her unconditional support—and for her willingness to spend at least an annual fortnight for five years in the (admittedly beautiful) county of Sligo. Maeve and Hannah Campbell got dragged along too sometimes and might have had fun. Lauren Arrington would like to thank Ali Shah for learning to tolerate the Irish weather.

Lauren Arrington
Matthew Campbell

Contents

PART II IN AND THROUGH HISTORY

PART III FROM THE GLOBAL TO THE INTERPLANETARY

PART IV GENRES AND MEDIA

PART V PLAYING YEATS

PART VI READING YEATS

POSTSCRIPT

LIST OF ILLUSTRATIONS

List of Abbreviations

Au	*Autobiographies.* London: Macmillan, 1955.
ARGYV	Neil Mann, *A Reader's Guide to Yeats's 'A Vision'* (Clemson, SC: Clemson University Press, 2019).
BC	*The Book of the Courtier*, trans. Thomas Hoby, Everyman's Library (London: J. M. Dent, 1928).
CL InteLex	*The Collected Letters of W. B. Yeats*, gen. ed. John Kelly, Oxford University Press (InteLex Electronic Edition), 2002. Letters cited by aAccession number.
CL1	*The Collected Letters of W. B. Yeats: Volume I, 1865–1895*, ed. John Kelly and Eric Domville. Oxford: Clarendon Press, 1986.
CL2	*The Collected Letters of W. B. Yeats: Volume II, 1896–1900*, ed. Warwick Gould, John Kelly, and Deirdre Toomey. Oxford: Clarendon Press, 1997.
CL3	*The Collected Letters of W. B. Yeats: Volume III, 1901–1904*, ed. John Kelly and Ronald Schuchard. Oxford: Clarendon Press, 1994.
CL4	*The Collected Letters of W. B. Yeats, Volume IV, 1905–1907*, ed. John Kelly and Ronald Schuchard. Oxford: Clarendon Press, 2005.
CL5	*The Collected Letters of W. B. Yeats, Volume V, 1908–1910*, ed. John Kelly and Ronald Schuchard. Oxford: Oxford University Press, 2018.
CW1	*The Poems*, second edition, ed. Richard J. Finneran. New York: Scribner, 1997.
CW2	*The Plays,* ed. David R. Clark and Rosalind E. Clark. New York: Scribner, 2001.
CW3	*Autobiographies,* ed. William H. O'Donnell and Douglas N. Archibald, assisted by J. Frasier Cocks III and Gretchen Schwenker. New York: Scribner, 1999.
CW4	*Early Essays,* ed. Richard J. Finneran and George Bornstein. New York: Scribner, 2007.
CW5	*Later Essays,* ed. William H. O'Donnell, with assistance from Elizabeth Bergmann Loizeaux. New York: Scribner, 1994.
CW6	*Prefaces and Introductions: Uncollected Prefaces and Introductions by Yeats to Works by Other Authors and to Anthologies edited by Yeats,* ed. William H. O'Donnell. London: Macmillan, 1988.

CW7	*Letters to the New Island,* eds. George Bornstein and Hugh Witemeyer. London: Macmillan, 1989.
CW8	*The Irish Dramatic Movement,* eds. Mary FitzGerald and Richard J. Finneran. New York: Scribner, 2003.
CW9	*A Vision* (1925), ed. Catherine E. Paul and Margaret Mills Harper. New York: Scribner, 2008.
CW10	*Later Articles and Reviews: Uncollected Articles, Reviews, and Radio Broadcasts written after 1900,* ed. Colton Johnson. New York: Scribner, 2000.
CW12	*John Sherman and Dhoya,* ed. Richard J. Finneran. New York: Macmillan Publishing Company, 1991.
CW13	*A Vision: The Original 1925 Version,* ed. Catherine E. Paul and Margaret Mills Harper. New York: Scribner 2008.
CW14	*A Vision: Tthe Rrevised 1937 Eedition,* ed. Margaret Mills Harper and Catherine E. Paul. New York: Scribner, 2015.
E&I	*Essays and Introductions.* London and New York: Macmillan, 1961.
Ex	*Explorations,* selected by Mrs W. B. Yeats. London: Macmillan, 1962; New York: Macmillan, 1963.
Life 1	*W. B. Yeats: A Life, I: The Apprentice Mage,* by R. F. Foster. Oxford and New York: Oxford University Press, 1997.
Life 2	*W. B. Yeats: A Life, II: The Arch-Poet,* by R. F. Foster. Oxford and New York: Oxford University Press, 2003.
Mem	*Memoirs: Autobiography—First Draft Journal,* transcribed and edited by Denis Donoghue. London: Macmillan, 1972; New York: Macmillan, 1973.
MNY	B. L. Reid, The Man from New York: John Quinn and his Friends (New York: Oxford University Press, 1968).
Myth 2005	*Mythologies,* ed. by Warwick Gould and Deirdre Toomey. Houndmills, Basingstoke: Palgrave Macmillan, 2005.
NLI	National Library of Ireland.
QC	John Quinn Memorial Collection, New York Public Library.
SS	Senate Speeches. *The Senate Speeches of W. B. Yeats,* ed. Donald R. Pearce. Bloomington, IN: Indiana University Press, 1960; London: Faber and Faber, 1961.
VP	*The Variorum Edition of the Poems of W. B. Yeats,* ed. Peter Allt and Russell K. Alspach. New York: Macmillan, 1957.
VPl	*The Variorum Edition of the Plays of W. B. Yeats,* ed. Russell K. Alspach, assisted by Catharine C. Alspach. New York: Macmillan, 1966.
YA	Yeats Annual.
YAACTS	*Yeats: An Annual of Critical and Textual Studies,* ed. Richard J. Finneran (publishers vary, 1983–1999).
YGYL	*W. B. Yeats and George Yeats: the Letters,* ed. Ann Saddlemyer. Oxford: Oxford University Press, 2011.

Notes on Contributors

Nicholas Allen is the director of the Willson Center and holds a Professorship in Humanities in the department of English at UGA. He has published several books on Ireland and its literature, has been the Burns Visiting Scholar at Boston College, and has received many grants and awards, including from the Mellon Foundation, the National Endowment for the Humanities, and the Irish Research Council.

Charles Armstrong is a Professor of English at the University of Agder. He is currently co-director of the Yeats International Summer School, vice president of the International Yeats Society, and president of the Nordic Association of English Studies. He is the author of *Reframing Yeats: Genre, Allusion and History*, *Figures of Memory: Poetry, Space and the Past*, and *Romantic Organicism: From Idealist Origins to Ambivalent Afterlife*, and has also co-edited five essay collections.

Lauren Arrington is Professor of English at Maynooth University, where she also serves as Head of Department. She is the author of three monographs, most recently *The Poets of Rapallo: How Mussolini's Italy shaped British, Irish, and U.S. Writers*. She has held visiting fellowships at Boston College, Trinity College Dublin's Long Room Hub, the Harry Ransom Center, Cambridge University's CRASSH, and the New York Public Library. She was founding editor of the journal *International Yeats Studies*. Her writing has appeared in popular and scholarly publications including the *TLS*, *Public Books*, *LARB* and *LitHub*.

Zsuzsanna Balázs is Assistant Professor of Communication at Óbuda University in Budapest. Her PhD research at National University Ireland, Galway explored queer structures of feeling in W. B. Yeats's and Gabriele D'Annunzio's drama, focusing on unorthodox representations of gender, power, and desire in light of the playwrights' queer and feminist networks.

Fran Brearton is Professor of Modern Poetry at Queen's University Belfast. Her books include *The Great War in Irish Poetry*, *Reading Michael Longley*, and, as co-editor, *The Oxford Handbook of Modern Irish Poetry* and *Incorrigibly Plural: Louis MacNeice and his Legacy*.

Stephanie Burt is Professor of English at Harvard. Her work has appeared in *ELH*, *Essays in Criticism*, the *London Review of Books*, and many other journals in Britain, Canada, Ireland, New Zealand, and the US. Her latest books are *After*

Callimachus: Poems and Translations and *For All Mutants*, a chapbook of poems about superheroes.

Matthew Campbell is Professor of Modern Literature at the University of York. He is the author *of Irish Poetry under the Union* and *Rhythm and Will in Victorian Poetry*. He has edited or co-edited five other books, including *The Cambridge Companion to Contemporary Irish Poetry* and *Irish Literature in Transition, 1830–1880*. He was the Director of the Yeats International Summer School from 2014 to 2019.

Wayne K. Chapman is Professor Emeritus of English at Clemson University, founding director of Clemson University Press (2000–2016), and editor of *The South Carolina Review* (1996–2016). He has written or edited numerous books on Yeats, including *Yeats and English Renaissance Literature*; *The Countess Cathleen: Manuscript Materials*, with Michael Sidnell; *Yeats's Collaborations: Yeats Annual* 15, with Warwick Gould; 'Dreaming *of the Bones' and 'Calvary': Manuscript Materials*; *The W. B. and George Yeats Library: A Short-title Catalog*; *Yeats's Poetry in the Making: 'Sing Whatever Is Well Made*; *Rewriting* The Hour-Glass: *A Play Written in Prose and Verse Versions*; *W. B. Yeats's Robartes–Aherne Writings: Featuring the Making of His 'Stories of Michael Robartes and His Friends'*, and '*Something that I read in a book': W. B. Yeats's Annotations at the National Library of Ireland*, 2 volumes.

David Dwan is Professor of English Literature and Intellectual History at the University of Oxford. His books include *The Great Community: Culture and Nationalism in Ireland*, *The Cambridge Companion to Edmund Burke* (co-edited with Chris Insole), and *Liberty, Equality and Humbug: Orwell's Political Ideals*. He is also the author of several essays on Yeats.

Katherine Ebury is Senior Lecturer in Modern Literature at the University of Sheffield. She is the author of *Modernism and Cosmology: Absurd Lights* and *Modern Literature and the Death Penalty, 1890–1950*, and the editor, with James Fraser, of *Joyce's Nonfiction Writing: Outside His Jurisfiction*. She has written articles and chapters on topics including science and technology, representations of law and justice, and animal studies, with questions about Yeats and modernism often central to her critical practice.

R. F. Foster is Emeritus Professor of Irish History at Oxford and of Irish History and Literature at Queen Mary University of London. His many prizewinning books include *Modern Ireland 1600–1972, Paddy and Mr Punch, The Irish Story: telling tales and making it up in Ireland*, the two-volume authorized biography of W .B. Yeats, *Vivid Faces: the revolutionary generation in Ireland 1890–1923*, and *On Seamus Heaney*. A Fellow of the British Academy, an Honorary Member of the Royal Irish Academy, and the holder of several honorary degrees, he is also a well-known cultural commentator and critic.

Alan Gillis is from the North of Ireland, and teaches English at The University of Edinburgh. His most recent poetry collection, *The Readiness*, was published by Picador in 2020, following four collections with The Gallery Press: *Scapegoat, Here Comes the Night, Hawks and Doves*, and *Somebody, Somewhere*. As a critic he is the author of *Irish*

Poetry of the 1930s and co-editor of *The Oxford Handbook of Modern Irish Poetry*, both published by Oxford University Press. From 2010 to 2015 he was editor of *Edinburgh Review*.

Warwick Gould FRSL, FRSA, FEA is Emeritus Professor of English Literature in the University of London, and Senior Research Fellow of the Institute of English Studies (in the School of Advanced Study), of which he was Founder Director 1999–2013. He is co-author of *Joachim of Fiore and the Myth of the Eternal Evangel in the Nineteenth and Twentieth Centuries*, and co-editor of *The Secret Rose, Stories by W. B. Yeats: A Variorum Edition*, *The Collected Letters of W. B. Yeats, Volume II, 1896–1900*, and *Mythologies*. He has edited *Yeats Annual* for thirty years.

Nicholas Grene is Emeritus Professor of English Literature at Trinity College Dublin and a Member of the Royal Irish Academy. His books include *The Politics of Irish Drama*), *Yeats's Poetic Codes*, *Home on the Stage*, *The Theatre of Tom Murphy: Playwright Adventurer*, and *Farming in Modern Irish Literature*.

Vona Groarke is a poet and Senior Lecturer at the University of Manchester. Her *Selected Poems* won the 2017 Pigott Prize for Best Irish Poetry Collection and her eighth poetry collection, *Link,* was published by The Gallery Press in 2021. Former Editor of *Poetry Ireland Review* (where she edited Issue 116, a special issue dedicated to W. B. Yeats), she lives in south County Sligo, nowhere near Innisfree.

Adam Hanna is a Lecturer in Irish Literature in the English Department of University College Cork, Ireland. He joined University College Cork as an Irish Research Council Government of Ireland Postdoctoral Fellow in 2015. Before this, he taught in the English departments of Trinity College Dublin, the University of Bristol, and the University of Aberdeen. He has trained and practised as a solicitor and is a co-founder of the Irish Network for the Legal Humanities. He is the author of *Northern Irish Poetry and Domestic Space* and the co-editor (with Jane Griffiths) of *Architectural Space and the Imagination: Houses in Art and Literature from Classical to Contemporary*. His second monograph, *Poetry, Justice, and the Law in Modern Ireland*, was published in 2022.

Margaret Mills Harper is Glucksman Professor in Contemporary Writing in English at the University of Limerick. She was Director of the Yeats International Summer School 2013–2015 and was President of the International Yeats Society. She regularly contributes to the *Yeats Annual* and has a huge number of publications on Yeats with Clemson, Oxford, and Cambridge University Presses. She published on Joyce with Palgrave Macmillan and contributed major articles on contemporary Irish literature to several outstanding journals of Irish literature. In September 2015 her long-awaited study on *A Vision* came out, co-edited with Catherine Paul as *Volume 14* of *The Collected Works of W. B. Yeats*.

Susan Cannon Harris is Professor in the Department of English and the Keough Naughton Institute for Irish Studies at the University of Notre Dame. Her book *Irish Drama and the Other Revolutions: Playwrights, Sexual Politics, and the International*

Left, 1892–1964 considers modern Irish drama in the context of the international dramatic, sexual, and socialist revolutions that shaped the late nineteenth and early twentieth centuries. Her first book, *Gender and Modern Irish Drama* was awarded the Donald Murphy Prize for a Distinguished First Book and the Robert Rhodes Prize for Books on Literature by the American Conference for Irish Studies. Her scholarship on Irish literature has also appeared in *Modern Drama, Theatre Journal, Eire-Ireland, The James Joyce Quarterly*, and *The Cambridge Companion to J. M. Synge.*

Joseph Hassett is a graduate of Canisius College and Harvard Law School, holds a PhD in Anglo-Irish Literature from University College Dublin, and was a visiting scholar at St John's College, Oxford. His most recent book is *Yeats Now: Echoing into Life*. Other books include *W. B. Yeats and the Muses* and *The Ulysses Trials: Beauty and Truth Meet the Law*. He lives and practises law in Washington, DC.

Hugh Haughton is Emeritus Professor of Modern Literature at the University of York. He is the author of *The Poetry of Derek Mahon* and the editor of *The Chatto Book of Nonsense Poetry, The Letters of T. S. Eliot*, Vols 1 and 2, *Second World War Poems*, and Freud, *The Uncanny*. He has written numerous essays on twentieth-century British and Irish poetry, including recently on Thomas Kinsella, Michael Longley and Eiléan Ni Chuilleanáin.

Seán Hewitt is Teaching Fellow in Modern British and Irish Literature at Trinity College Dublin. He is the author of *J.M. Synge: Nature, Politics, Modernism, Tongues of Fire*, and *All Down Darkness Wide*, and is Poetry Critic for *The Irish Times.*

Geraldine Higgins is Associate Professor of English at Emory University and Director of Emory's Irish Studies Program. Her publications on Irish literature include *Brian Friel, Heroic Revivals from Carlyle to Yeats*, and her editorship of *Seamus Heaney in Context*. She is the curator of the National Library of Ireland's exhibition 'Seamus Heaney: Listen Now Again'.

Susan Jones is Emeritus Professor of English Literature at the University of Oxford and Fellow of St Hilda's College. She writes on modernism, women's writing, Joseph Conrad, and the history and aesthetics of dance. She has published many articles, and books on Joseph Conrad and on *Literature, Modernism, and Dance* appeared with Oxford University Press. She is Director of Dance Scholarship Oxford and is currently writing a book for Oxford University Press on *Samuel Beckett and Choreography.*

Elizabeth Bergmann Loizeaux is Professor of English emerita, Special Assistant to the Provost, and Past Associate Provost for Undergraduate Affairs at Boston University. She is the author of *Yeats and the Visual Arts, Twentieth-Century Poetry and the Visual Arts*, and numerous essays on modern poetry. With Neil Fraistat, she co-edited *Reimagining Textuality: Textual Studies in the Late Age of Print*. Beth has served on the faculty of the Yeats International Summer School, and with fellow faculty member, actor Sam McCready, wrote and performed *Yeats's Gallery*, a multimedia performance of Yeats's poems with commentary, first presented at the Folger Shakespeare Theatre, Washington,

DC. Before moving to BU, Beth taught at the University of Maryland, College Park, where she is Professor of English emerita.

Patrick Lonergan is Professor of Drama and Theatre Studies at National University of Ireland, Galway, and a member of the Royal Irish Academy. He has edited or written *Theatre and Globalization* (winner of the 2008 Theatre Book Prize), *The Theatre and Films of Martin McDonagh*, *Theatre and Social Media*, and *Irish Drama and Theatre Since 1950* (Bloomsbury, 2019). Forthcoming publications include a study of Shakespeare and the modern Irish theatre, and a short book on Irish theatre histories and the Anthropocene.

Edna Longley is a Professor Emerita at Queen's University Belfast. She is the author of *Yeats and Modern Poetry* and *Under the Same Moon: Edward Thomas and the English Lyric*.

Claire Lynch is Professor of English and Irish Literature at Brunel University London. She is the author of *Irish Autobiography*, *Cyber Ireland: Text, Image, Culture*, and several articles and chapters on modern and contemporary Irish writing. Claire's first book of creative non-fiction, *Small: On Motherhoods*, was published by Hachette in 2021.

Lucy McDiarmid is the author or editor of eight books. Her most recent monographs are *At Home in the Revolution: what women said and did in 1916* and *Poets and the Peacock Dinner: the literary history of a meal*; she is completing a book on recent Irish poetry. *The Vibrant House: Irish Writers and Domestic Space* (edited with Rhona Richman Kenneally) was published in 2017. She has received fellowships from the Guggenheim Foundation, the Cullman Center for Scholars and Writers at the New York Public Library, and the National Endowment for the Humanities, and is Marie Frazee-Baldassarre Professor of English at Montclair State University.

Peter McDonald is the editor of *The Poems of W.B. Yeats* for the Longman Annotated English Poets series: Volume 1 (1882–1889) and Volume 2 (1890–1898) were published in 2020, and Volume 3 (1899–1910) is forthcoming in 2023. He is an Irish poet and critic: his eight books of poetry include *Collected Poems* and *The Gifts of Fortune*, and his volumes of literary criticism include *Mistaken Identities: Poetry and Northern Ireland*, *Serious Poetry: Form and Authority from Yeats to Hill*, and *Sound Intentions: The Workings of Rhyme in Nineteenth-Century Poetry*. He is the editor of *Louis MacNeice: Collected Poems*, and the translator of *The Homeric Hymns*. He is a Student of Christ Church, and Professor of British and Irish Poetry, in the University of Oxford.

Akiko Manabe is Professor of English at Shiga University, Japan. She specializes in American and Irish modernist poetry and drama. She has recently focused on the Japanese influence on European and American modernism, especially in relation to the traditional theatre of Noh and *kyogen*. Recent publications include the co-authored *Hemingway and Ezra Pound in Venezia* and the co-edited *Cultural Hybrids of (Post) Modernism: Japanese/Western Literature, Art and Philosophy*; and articles on Yeats, Pound, Hemingway, and Hearn in *Etudes Anglaises*, *Yeats and Asia*, and *International*

Yeats Studies. Since 2017 she has produced a series of performances of new *kyogen* based on the works of Yeats and Hearn in Ireland and Japan.

Neil Mann has written extensively on Yeats's esoteric interests and *A Vision*, contributing articles to the *Yeats Annual* and elsewhere, creating the website YeatsVision.com in 2002, and co-editing two collections of essays, *Yeats's* A Vision: *Explications and Contexts* with Matthew Gibson and Claire Nally, and *Yeats, Philosophy, and the Occult* with Matthew Gibson. His *A Reader's Guide to Yeats's A Vision* came out in 2019.

Emilie Morin is Professor of Modern Literature at the University of York. She has published widely on Irish modernism. Her articles on Yeats have appeared in the *Yeats Annual* and the *Historical Journal of Radio, Film and Television*, and she has recently edited a special issue of *International Yeats Studies* on Yeats and mass communications with David Dwan. Her most recent book is *Beckett's Political Imagination*.

Claire Nally is an Associate Professor of Modern and Contemporary Literature at Northumbria University, where she researches Irish Studies, Neo-Victorianism, Gender, and Subcultures. She is the author of *Envisioning Ireland: W. B. Yeats's Occult Nationalism* and *Selling Ireland: Advertising, Literature and Irish Print Culture 1891–1922* (written with John Strachan). She has co-edited a volume on Yeats, and two volumes on gender, as well as the international library series 'Gender and Popular Culture' for Bloomsbury (with Angela Smith). She has written widely on a number of modern and contemporary topics, and her most recent monograph is *Steampunk: Gender, Subculture and the Neo-Victorian*.

Francis O'Gorman has written widely on English and Irish literature, 1780 to 1920. He retired as Saintsbury Professor of English Literature at the University of Edinburgh in 2022.

Cóilín Parsons is Associate Professor of English and Director of Global Irish Studies at Georgetown University. He is the author of *The Ordnance Survey and Modern Irish Literature* and has co-edited *Relocations: Reading Culture in South Africa* and *Science, Technology, and Irish Modernism*. He is currently completing a monograph on astronomy and modernist literature.

Geraldine Parsons is a Senior Lecturer in Celtic and Gaelic at the University of Glasgow. Her primary interests are in medieval Irish literature and language. Her work on *fiannaíocht*/the Finn Cycle expands her temporal range, with eighteenth-century reflexes of the tradition another focus of research.

Adam Piette is Professor of Modern Literature at the University of Sheffield. He is the author of *Remembering and the Sound of Words: Mallarmé, Proust, Joyce, Beckett*; *Imagination at War: British Fiction and Poetry, 1939–1945*; and *The Literary Cold War, 1945 to Vietnam*. He co-edited *The Edinburgh Companion to Twentieth-Century British and American War Literature* with Mark Rawlinson and co-edits the international poetry journal *Blackbox Manifold* with Alex Houen.

Jack Quin is a British Academy postdoctoral fellow in the Department of English Literature at the University of Birmingham. He has articles on literature and the visual arts published or forthcoming in *Modernism/modernity, Modernist Cultures, Irish Studies Review,* and *New Hibernia Review.* His monograph *W. B. Yeats and the Language of Sculpture* was published by Oxford University Press in 2022.

Justin Quinn is Associate Professor at the University of West Bohemia. He is the author of several studies of poetry, including *Between Two Fires: Transnationalism and Cold War Poetry.* With Gabriela Kleckova he edited *Anglophone Literature in Second-Language Teacher Education: Curriculum Innovation through Intercultural Communication.*

Jahan Ramazani is University Professor and Edgar F. Shannon Professor of English at the University of Virginia. He is the author of *Poetry in a Global Age; Poetry and Its Others: News, Prayer, Song, and the Dialogue of Genres; A Transnational Poetics, The Hybrid Muse: Postcolonial Poetry in English; Poetry of Mourning: The Modern Elegy from Hardy to Heaney,* and *Yeats and the Poetry of Death: Elegy, Self-Elegy, and the Sublime.* He is the editor of 'Poetry and Race,' a special issue of *New Literary History,* and of *The Cambridge Companion to Postcolonial Poetry;* a co-editor of the most recent editions of *The Norton Anthology of Modern and Contemporary Poetry* and *The Norton Anthology of English Literature* (2006, 2012, 2018); and an associate editor of *The Princeton Encyclopedia of Poetry and Poetics.*

Nathan Suhr-Sytsma is Associate Professor of English at Emory University in Atlanta. His publications focus on poetry in the contexts of African, Irish, and postcolonial studies, as well as literary engagements with religion and with climate crisis. The author of *Poetry, Print, and the Making of Postcolonial Literature,* he is completing a book about twenty-first-century African poetry and literary institutions.

Tom Walker teaches in the School of English at Trinity College Dublin. His publications on various aspects of Irish writing and modern poetry include *Louis MacNeice and the Irish Poetry of his Time,* which was awarded the Robert Rhodes Prize for Literature by the American Conference for Irish Studies.

PART I

SUCH FRIENDS

Predecessors and Collaborators

CHAPTER 1

SELF-MAKING

CLAIRE LYNCH

In March 1921, W. B. Yeats finished the first draft of his memoir, sealed it in an envelope, and marked it, 'Private. Containing much that is not for publication now, if ever.'[1] Yeats's envelope, for all it requests privacy, also equivocates. There is, it seems, an imagined future where publication *might* be possible, a future self who *may* come to read the contents as no longer private. The envelope, even more so than the manuscript it contained, expresses the central dilemma of autobiography: how should a writer balance the desire to *reveal* the self, with the instinct to *conceal* it?

One of the most prolific and, arguably, the most influential Irish autobiographer of the twentieth century, Yeats published a series of major autobiographies between 1915 and 1935. Throughout his career, Yeats's life-writing was self-consciously concerned with constructing a distinctive sense of individual identity alongside a portrait of Irish literary and political life, as he observed it. The extensive scope of his autobiographical work allows us to chart the simultaneous evolution of the individual and the nation; or, as his biographer Roy Foster has it, the way in which Yeats 'adapted his public persona in order to emerge as a founding father of the new nation in 1922'.[2] We find his life story in numerous biographies, in literary histories of the Irish Revival and modernism, in the memoirs and fictions of his peers, in his own extensive autobiographical writing, and in so much of his poetry, political speeches, and dramatic writing. Indeed, so much has been written by and about Yeats on the subject of his personality and sense of self that, far from remaining a discreetly 'private' memoirist, his biography has come to be read as 'the history of his country'.[3] At times, the overwhelming scale of Yeats studies threatens to overshadow the accounts he left of himself, in his own words. As Foster writes, in his definitive biography of the poet, Yeats's 'life has been approached over and over again,

---

[1] The anecdote is recounted on the dust jacket of Denis Donoghue's edition of W. B. Yeats, *Memoirs: autobiography – First Draft Journal* (London: Macmillan, 1972).

[2] R. F. Foster, *The Irish Story: Telling Tales and Making it up in Ireland* (London: Penguin, 2001), 59.

[3] Foster, *The Irish Story*, 59.

for the purpose of relating it to his art'.[4] If Foster sees his biography of Yeats as uniquely shifting the focus from 'principally about what he wrote' to 'principally about what he did', he cannot avoid the conclusion that our interest in Yeats is bound up in his 'capacity to transmute the events of a crowded life ... into art'.[5] Art is at the centre of the discussion here since, as I will argue, fiction, artifice, and construction are essential elements of Yeats's autobiographical writing. As Marjorie Perloff observes with some despair, Yeats's autobiographies have often been taken as just a 'source of information on the poet's life'.[6] To read Yeats's autobiographies as literal, or as no more than supporting evidence, ignores—at the very least—his own attitude towards them.

In August of the same year he marked his memoir as 'Private', Yeats wrote to Olivia Shakespear: 'I find this memoir writing makes me feel clean, as if I had bathed and put on clean linen. It rids me of something and I shall return to poetry with renewed simplicity'.[7] At this stage at least, Yeats saw writing poetry and writing memoir as refreshingly different activities which, nonetheless, produce powerfully symbiotic work. Writing memoir is cathartic, cleansing work for Yeats. Yet memoir is hardly valued for its own sake at all, seen rather as a catalyst for reinvigorated poetry. There is in this an implicit power imbalance between memoir and poetry. On the one hand, poetry: inherently public, arch, high art. On the other, memoir: private, self-reflective, and, by comparison, inevitably quotidian. If writing memoir 'rids' Yeats of something, we might be forgiven for assuming that this early manuscript was marked 'Private' because it contained the results of the purge. Yeats sealed his memoirs in an envelope because it contained the dirty linen not suitable for his poetry.

In his letter to Shakespear, Yeats presents memoir and poetry as distinct modes, not only of writing but of thinking. While he was clear in his view that 'a poet writes always of his personal life', Yeats also understood that the 'person' and the 'poet' were not wholly synonymous beings.[8] In his own terms, 'the bundle of accident and incoherence that sits down to breakfast' had to be recast through the act of writing in order to be 'reborn as an idea, something intended, complete'.[9] Yeats's metaphor here is a revealing one. Writing poetry untangles, orders, even creates the poet. Writing poetry, Yeats suggests, is always, among other things, an act of self-discovery. It is, undoubtedly, tempting to read Yeats's poetry in this way. In isolation, each poem might easily be read as a fresh act of Yeats's witnessing and self-reflection. As a whole, his oeuvre is often recast as a portrait of the poet's perspective as it shifted and evolved across the course of his lifetime. More than this, many of Yeats's poems seem to invite an autobiographical reading, particularly those which employ the first

---

[4] *Life 1*, xxvi–xxvii.

[5] *Life 1*, xxvi.

[6] Marjorie Perloff, '"The Tradition of Myself": The Autobiographical Mode of Yeats', *Journal of Modern Literature*, 4:3 (1975), 537.

[7] Quoted 'Editors' Preface', *CW3*, 21.

[8] *CW3*, 21.

[9] *CW3*, 9.

person, linguistically, at least, blurring the line between the protagonist within the poem and the poet who creates it.

According to Marjorie Perloff, 'The Wild Swans at Coole' is the first of Yeats's great autobiographical poems. In the poem, Perloff reads the protagonist as 'a projection of the poet himself', a figure who '*recalls* and implicitly *judges* those experiences in his past which reveal something essential about his personality as it responds to the out-side world'.[10] Crucially, Perloff notes, it is not just the poet as protagonist that gives 'The Wild Swans at Coole' autobiographical value; rather, it is the protagonist's reflection of past selves. This is not a protagonist who exists only within the poem but, rather, steps outside it in an attempt to make sense of the larger project of self-making. The idea that a poem inevitably 'reveal[s] something essential' about the poet is perennially appealing. Indeed, to read 'The Wild Swans at Coole' without an autobiographical lens might seem deliberately obtuse. Nevertheless, readers resist simplistic interpretations in which a poem is 'about' the poet because we understand that poetry is more than that. By the same token, we must look at Yeats's autobiographical writing as more than useful his-torical source material. As in poetry, life-writing gains its meaning as much from the text's form and style as from its content. Among the most intriguing of these aspects, of course, is what aspects ought to be made public, and what might best be kept 'Private'.

Yeats's envelope, so evocative and provocative, is the starting point here because it invites us to wonder what, precisely, he was so keen to keep from public view. With the publication of Denis Donoghue's edition of the complete draft of Yeats's Autobiography and Journal under the title *Memoirs* in 1972, one might argue that the idea of public and private versions of the text hardly remains a meaningful distinction. Donoghue's painstaking work of transcription and editing maps the evolution of Yeats's early drafts, allowing readers to compare the apparently private 'memoir' manuscript with the un-apologetically public *Autobiographies* as they would later emerge. It surely goes without saying that writing changes between the first draft and the final publication proofs. Significant editing is, perhaps, particularly understandable in autobiographical writing when a mature author might easily be tempted to rework the personal indiscretions or technical weaknesses of an earlier draft. Yet what Yeats does in 1921 is quite different: he knows from the point of writing that the manuscript contains material he does not feel ready to publish. What was it about the first draft that he considered so unsuitable?

Certainly, Yeats writes with some candour about his adolescent sexual discoveries in the manuscript of *Memoirs*, as well as the failures and frustrations he encounters in his early sexual relationships. While these reflections might have been embarrassing in the form they take in the first draft, they were probably not damning. Perhaps, then, the request for privacy was not for the sake of the author himself, but in deference to the people he writes about. In their published form, Yeats's early volumes of autobiog-raphy offer a detailed survey of Irish literary society. He was wise to be cautious about how his portraits might be received. If nothing else, the books were written in a time of

---

[10] Perloff, 'The Tradition of Myself', 531.

libel; Yeats often reflected on Wilde's case in his autobiographical writing. Yeats's un-certainty about whether or not an appropriate time for publication would occur might be attributed to sensitivity over representing friends and lovers, or, at the very least, sufficient self-awareness not to publish while his most litigious peers were still alive. While plausible, this is hardly consistent with Yeats's willingness to publicly express his opinions of others. In the end, it seems that Yeats's desire to delay, if not wholly forbid, publication of the memoir was due neither to prudery nor the desire to preserve the dig-nity of others. His memoir was marked as 'not for publication' because it was unfinished.

By the time he came to seal up the first draft in 1921, Yeats had long been concerned with the project of self-making, establishing habits of life-writing that were at once crip-plingly introspective and grandly self-conscious. Although, as Gerald Levin argues, the autobiographies 'were neither written nor planned as a whole', their publication history presents them as a coherent project, completed over the course of a lifetime.[11] Whether intended to be read in this way or not, the sheer extent of Yeats's autobiographical output acts as a testament to his long-term interest in the genre. According to David Wright, Yeats's 'interest in explicit autobiography was strong as early as 1908'.[12] His reports of reading the genre can be traced in his letters from as early as 1910, becoming more concentrated when George Moore's *Hail and Farewell* was published in 1911. As a writer, Yeats embraced life-writing in multiple forms, reflecting on his own lived experiences at varying degrees of temporal distance and experimenting with forms that best reflected the role of memory. The journal format, for example, allowed Yeats to report his thoughts and experiences with immediacy. In a letter to Florence Farr in March 1909, Yeats describes what he designates 'the Journal' as the site of his hidden life-writing, the repository of the 'amusing parts' that could not, he felt, be published in his lifetime. 'The Autobiography', by contrast, written some twenty-five years after the events described, 'required not merely an act of memory on Yeats's part, but an approach to the meaning of the lives it recited, not least his own'.[13] Both forms, the daily reporting and the considered retrospective, shared a common goal. Despite the differences in these forms of autobio-graphical practice, both were intimately tied up with Yeats's focus on legacy-building. Both in terms of scale and scope, Yeats can be considered a dedicated, if not compulsive, memoirist. It is clear across both his private and published writing that he understood his reflections to have artistic and national significance. When Yeats thought and wrote about himself, it was never solely as an act of self-reflection. Yeats wrote memoir because he was preoccupied with a unique sense of responsibility. How was he to present him-self, not merely as a singular individual but also as an agent of Irish history?

Yeats's commitment to the autobiographical form in the early decades of the twen-tieth century was consistent with the political and literary zeitgeist. As Nicholas Allen

[11] Gerald Levin, 'The Yeats of the Autobiographies: A Man of Phase 17', *Texas Studies in Literature and Language*, 6:3 (1964), 398.

[12] David G. Wright, 'The Elusive Self: Yeats's Autobiographical Prose', *Canadian Journal of Irish Studies*, 4:2 (1978), 42.

[13] Donoghue, 'Introduction', in *Mem*, 9.

puts it, 'Revelation was the Revival's key mode and autobiography a central form of its aesthetic.'[14] There was, it seemed, something uniquely relevant about autobiography as a means of both recording and constructing an age of revolution. More so than poetry and drama, prose autobiography offered the perfect confluence of form and subject, inviting the personal story to be mapped onto the national one. Yeats, like so many others, was intent on creating 'an autobiographical art which would assert the place of his own tradition in Ireland, as the country moved toward apparent independence'.[15] For this generation of Irish writers, the parallels were irresistible. Autobiography invited a narrative arc that moved from subjugated childhood to a rebirth into adult independence. Even more helpfully, it relied on a protagonist with an inherent sense of destiny and self-determination. If the Irish Literary Revival can be characterized as a period of identity crises on both personal and national scales, the writer's life story may well be taken as its anthem. In their readiness to represent their own lives as symbolic of Ireland's journey to independence, Yeats and his peers demonstrated a remarkable combination of arrogance and vision. As Declan Kiberd observes, 'no [Irish] generation before or since lived with such conscious national intensity or left such an inspiring (and, in some ways, intimidating) legacy'.[16] This 'intimidating legacy' can be read across all forms of Irish cultural and artistic expression. Yet it was autobiography that had the unique advantage of allowing an author to present him- or herself as both witness and agent of the period of momentous change. As popular among nationalist autodidacts as members of the Anglo-Irish establishment, autobiography emerged in twentieth-century Ireland in a number of rich and varied forms. Far from being unique, Yeats formed part of a generation engaged in acts of self-making that were always, also, acts of tradition building.

Yeats, along with George Moore, Sean O'Casey, and many others, formed a generation of 'compulsive self-interrogators whose mastery of multi-volume autobiography' set the standard for autobiography in modern Ireland.[17] For Yeats and other Anglo-Irish writers, the work of self-reflection also meant acknowledging a way of life in decline. As Elizabeth Grubgeld explains, the internal revolutions of identity politics that Anglo-Irish autobiographers engaged in, alongside the public 'struggle' of the nation, made ideal subject matter. These writers represented themselves as torn between two conflicting influences, the past, often seen through the lens of 'family histories', and the present, 'their place within the Irish nation'. As Grubgeld observes:

> Anglo-Irish autobiographers draw from their family histories a sense of continuity and dissolution, influence and irrelevance, identity and nothingness. They rail against their own class, and they defend its attitudes and actions; they assert their

---

[14] Nicholas Allen, 'Autobiography and the Irish Revival', in Liam Harte, *A History of Irish Autobiography* (Cambridge: Cambridge University Press, 2018), 149.

[15] *Life 1*, 492.

[16] Declan Kiberd, *Inventing Ireland: The Literature of the Modern Nation* (London: Vintage, 1996), 3.

[17] Liam Harte, 'Introduction', in *A History of Irish Autobiography* (Cambridge: Cambridge University Press, 2018), 2.

place within an Irish nation, and they question its legitimacy. In every text, they query the nature of their identity and question the nature of their true home, and against an overwhelming narrative of cultural decline, they engage in the struggle of self-making that is autobiography.[18]

Yeats's fellow autobiographers, including Tynan, Bowen, and Moore, were similarly preoccupied with the sociocultural specifics of the era. As Grubgeld goes on to note, 'the vast majority of Anglo-Irish autobiographies appeared during the decades following the establishment of the Irish Free State and the beginning of the Second World War'.[19] As with Yeats, their autobiographies capture the confluence of individual lives and a national narrative in transition, an attempt to capture both the time before and time since.

Arguably more so than any writer of his generation, Yeats lived with a pressing understanding of 'the importance of life-writing within the larger project of Irish cultural nationalism'.[20] Yeats was convinced of the value of an autobiographical legacy, famously arguing that 'the power of our epoch on Ireland in the next generation will greatly depend on the way its personal history is written'.[21] In part, at least, it is Yeats's own determination to connect the personal to the national, the desire to make the singular life symbolic and symptomatic, that keeps him at the core of contemporary studies of Irish autobiography. For Liam Harte, Yeats's influence on the Irish autobiographical tradition is unparalleled, at least to the extent that 'no Irish autobiographer's work has been more extensively studied than his'.[22] James Olney goes as far as to argue that Yeats's life became 'the great reference for the lives of the other autobiographers, and his voice, as heard by each of the others, echoes through their books in an endless string of anecdotes'.[23] There is in all of this veneration a distinct difficulty in separating the reputation of the man from the literary value of the work. Are Yeats's autobiographies being judged by the metrics we apply to other texts: form, style, the author's capacity to reflect and reveal something of himself? Or, are they simply taken as significant because they are written by Yeats?

Not least among the obstacles for readers is the challenge of pinning down what we might think of as the definitive text. After all, Yeats's multivolume *Autobiographies,* as readers would now typically access it, is, in fact, an assemblage of multiple texts based on the 1932 and 1936 Macmillan proofs, the last version to be approved by the author.[24] According to William H. O'Donnell, when it came to preparing the final manuscript, Yeats chose not to work directly from the 'First Draft', apparently continuing to view it

[18] Elizabeth Grubgeld, *Anglo-Irish Autobiography: Class, Gender, and the Forms of Narrative* (New York: Syracuse University Press, 2004), xi.

[19] Grubgeld, *Anglo-Irish Autobiography,* xx.

[20] Harte, *History of Irish Autobiography,* 2.

[21] Cited in *Life 1,* 492.

[22] Harte, *History of Irish Autobiography,* 3.

[23] James Olney, *Metaphors of Self: The Meaning of Autobiography* (Princeton, NJ: Princeton University Press, 1993), 117.

[24] 'Editors' Preface', *CW3,* 13.

as not suitable for publication.[25] The 'First Draft', subsequently published as *Memoirs*, was suppressed once more, partly because of the content (the 'amusing parts'), but also because of a lack of form. For publication, the writing needed to be restructured into plotted moments rather than subject to the whims of abstract memory. As Marjorie Perloff observes, Yeats reworked his autobiography in order 'to present his friends in climactic, dramatic moments, revelatory of character, while he himself remains in the background—the calm, mature observer who ponders the crises in the lives of his friends'.[26] Whether or not Yeats referred back to his 1921 draft when preparing his published autobiographies, its influence remains clear. Both types of first draft are essential for writers—those that act as templates, and those that act as a model of what not to do. In autobiography, however, redrafting raises issues we might be tempted to couch in ethical terms. That is, if an autobiographer entirely rewrites or ignores a previous account of their life, is the newer version fundamentally 'dishonest'?

In his essay 'Yeats'. Autobiography as Myth', Sean O'Faolain claims that Yeats wrote autobiographically in order to clarify 'to himself the ideal image of himself that he had been building up during a half century which he intermittently calls his Image, or his Mask or his Myth'.[27] For O'Faolain, Yeats does not write and rewrite to get closer to his true sense of self, but, rather, to more clearly hone an artfully constructed image. As O'Faolain continues, 'in the end Yeats's mask became second nature; in that belief I frankly admit that I find his *Autobiographies* more informative by what they leave out or underwrite than by what they leave in and overwrite'.[28] Taken separately, the volumes of Yeats's *Autobiographies* bear out O'Faolain's theory, offering up not only various experiments in form but also a range of 'masks' adopted by Yeats at different points in his life. In *Reveries over Childhood and Youth* (published by Cuala Press in 1915), Yeats's first attempt at constructing a full-scale autobiographical portrait of his early life, he draws himself as gradually emerging 'from the restrictions imposed upon him by the adults who dominate his childhood world'.[29] By contrast, *Dramatis Personae* (Cuala, 1935) might be considered 'more properly a memoir than an autobiography for its focus is on other people rather than on their influence on the poet'.[30] Both *The Trembling of the Veil* (1922) and *The Death of Synge: and other passages from an old diary* (1928) not only expressly focus on insights into the life of the poet but also provide significant records of the early years of modern Ireland. As a consequence, these volumes provide an invaluable contribution to our understanding of Yeats's role in the political and cultural

---

[25] *CW3*, 18. See 'Textual Introduction' (13–29) for a full history of *Autobiographies* manuscript development and publication history.

[26] Perloff, 'The Tradition of Myself', 537.

[27] Sean O'Faolain, 'Yeats'. Autobiography as Myth', 1. National Library of Ireland John Jordan Papers, 1945–1988, MS NLI Collection, List 45, 35,057/5: Scripts intended for broadcasting in the RTE radio series 'Autobiographies' (1976). The series was broadcast on Sunday nights 30 July–15 October 1976 and was produced by Kieran Sheedy.

[28] O'Faolain, 'Yeats'. Autobiography as Myth', 5

[29] Perloff, 'The Tradition of Myself', 554.

[30] Perloff, 'The Tradition of Myself', 556.

development of the nation, told from his own perspective. The question is, what do they tell us about the man himself?

When Yeats's collection appeared under the title *The Autobiography* in 1938, it was contrary to the author's preference for the plural *Autobiographies*, which 'seemed to Yeats a better description of the portions published in 1926'.[31] As Wright puts it, the 'single title expresses a wish for unity rather than designating a unity actually achieved', hence the restoration of the plural title for the standard 1955 Macmillan edition.[32] The publication history of Yeats's autobiographical writing, the collated volumes, multiple rewrites, suppressed drafts, and so on is telling in so far as it testifies to the author's apparent inability to settle on a consistent sense of self. Equally, the collation of the separate works, all composed under necessarily different personal and political circumstances and later represented as a unified project, can be taken as an explanation of its unique character. As O'Donnell explains in the Editors' Preface to the volume in the *Collected Works*:

> *Autobiographies* is an allusive and illusive book. Yeats is not careful about details, dates, and references. It is difficult to escape the impression that he is wholly dependable about what is happening to and in his imagination, and how exciting it is, and not fully dependable about anything else.[33]

O'Donnell's scepticism about whether Yeats can be considered a 'dependable' narrator is echoed by Roy Foster, who has similarly described the way in which Yeats 'takes sweeping liberties with chronology and personnel in order to build his pattern'.[34] Their observations, or perhaps they are frustrations, point to one of the principal debates in life-writing. If autobiography is considered largely to be a form of personal history, then we might indeed hope for accuracy over 'details, dates, and references'. If, on the other hand, we think of it as a work of literature, we ought to expect it to be as subject to the work of the imagination as any other text. As Paul John Eakin sensibly claims, 'it is as reasonable to assume that all autobiography has some fiction in it as it is to recognize that all fiction is in some sense necessarily autobiographical'.[35] If Yeats's autobiographical writing takes 'liberties' in order to enhance the narrative, so be it. Life-writing theorists have long discarded the view that an autobiography that is objectively 'true' is either possible or desirable.

In his infamous disclaimer, in the Preface to *Reveries over Childhood and Youth,* Yeats writes:

> I have changed nothing to my knowledge; and yet it must be that I have changed many things without my knowledge; for I am writing after many years and have consulted neither friend, nor letter, nor old newspaper.[36]

[31] Wright, 'The Elusive Self', 42.
[32] Wright, 'The Elusive Self', 42.
[33] O'Donnell and Archibald, 'Editors' Preface', *CW3*, 10.
[34] Foster, *The Irish Story*, 67.
[35] Paul John Eakin, *Fictions in Autobiography: Studies in the Art of Self-Invention* (Princeton, NJ: Princeton University Press, 2014), 10.
[36] *Au*, 3.

In what Denis Donoghue describes as Yeats's 'charming excuse', the poet simultaneously takes responsibility for all errors in the *Autobiographies* while sidestepping
the very idea that errors are possible. As Donoghue puts it, 'If he is proved wrong,
he has not claimed to be right.'[37] This acknowledgement of unconscious change—
from experience to page, via memory—presents a sophisticated sense of the
possibilities inherent in autobiography. Not all autobiographical writing accepts
ambiguity so readily. Yeats had encouraged his father to write his own life, and although J.B. died before completing the work, it was published in 1923 as *Early
Memories, Some Chapters of Autobiography*. Marjorie Perloff has a less than flattering
opinion of *Early Memories*, describing it as 'an interesting book, if only because it
teaches us what autobiography should *not* be'.[38] Perloff criticizes J.B.'s account for
lacking literary value, and its many inconsistencies, but also on the grounds that it
is, frankly, boring. J. B. Yeats was victim to the assumption that an interesting life
is enough for an interesting book, prioritizing content at the expense of form. For
Perloff, *Early Memories* 'violates the fundamental requisite of autobiography: that
it must be a *shaping* of the past'.[39] In contrast to his father, W.B. understood from
the start the conventions of form but also, most crucially, the necessity of balancing
past and present selves. Autobiography, although drawn from the author's life
and his or her efforts to capture that in writing, is far from unmediated. Work is
required in bringing life to the page, and in that process, as Yeats understood, 'the
autobiographer must sometimes distort events or characters in the interest of
narrative design'.[40]

Ostensibly a study of the self, autobiography is also—inevitably and essentially—
an account of the people who bear the most influence on the author. While Yeats's
autobiographies offer up numerous portraits of friends and contemporaries, some
'characters' take a telling priority. When Yeats recounts his meeting Maud Gonne, for
example, in the now infamous phrase 'the troubling of my life began', he marks her as
central to both his life and the 'narrative design' of his autobiography.[41] While Yeats
presents Gonne in an 'emblematic but ... ambivalent manner' symbolized by her caged
birds as simultaneously 'grand and striking' but also 'trivial and pretentious', he creates
her in his own terms.[42] Just as O'Faolain points to the absences in Yeats's autobiographies
as the most telling parts, so too we might read his reflections of others for what they
tell us about his own sense of self. In the simplest terms, we learn far more about Yeats
than we do Gonne when we read his accounts of her. For Robert Peterson 'the poet's
self-dramatisation—at times narcissism, at others ironic—is one key to understanding

---

[37] *Mem*, 11.
[38] Perloff, 'The Tradition of Myself', 534.
[39] Perloff, 'The Tradition of Myself', 534.
[40] Perloff, 'The Tradition of Myself', 536.
[41] *Mem*, 40.
[42] Wright, 'The Elusive Self', 47.

his work'.[43] Yeats's portrayal of his infatuation with Gonne, particularly as it appears in *Memoirs,* is far from flattering, suggesting self-awareness as much as self-delusion on his part. Still the balance is hard to tread. As argued above, memoir is not exempt from the expectations of fiction to provoke and entertain. Style and, crucially for Yeats, symbolism are essential components of a successful text. When his techniques are less effective, for example in sections of *The Trembling of the Veil,* Wright claims, 'We see him performing aspects of Yeats's life, but we do not feel his responses to experience'.[44] Yeats, like all autobiographers, must find a way to shape his life into a narrative. Just as this requires converting real people, like Gonne, into the characters who populate the text, he must also construct 'a dramatic image of himself'.[45] This 'image', however, is not to be understood as entirely equivalent to the protagonist in, for instance, a poem. The self as expressed in an autobiography serves a different function: 'this image is the truth about himself, as he understood that truth at the time of writing'.[46] Throughout his autobiographies, Yeats creates clearly distinct versions of himself to enact the different stages of his life and observes the development of his personality using an identity parade of his past selves.[47] This multiple perspective is characteristic of literary autobiographies, as writers often approach the autobiographical act with a greater self-consciousness in regard to the potential complexity of the text. Their awareness of the intricacy of concepts such as truth in autobiography often results in a narrator who explicitly acknowledges the author's dilemma as Yeats did. His acceptance that he must have changed many things without his 'knowledge' would later be regarded as the norm for late twentieth-century writers who engaged overtly with the problems of memory and fiction in autobiographical texts.

For all he accepted the need to craft his memories and experiences into readable and meaningful narratives, Yeats held fast to the idea that his autobiographies were, at their core, true. Yeats's commitment to this ideal can be mapped across the multiple volumes produced over decades of work on the genre. As Wright has observed, *Autobiographies* 'becomes less subjective as it proceeds' (noting the exception of Yeats's portrayal of George Moore).[48] Yeats's belief that his autobiographical writing was verifiable was supported, in part, by his working practices. So confident was he in his capacity to achieve this, Yeats approached those he wrote about, forming a sort of ethics committee in advance of publication. Writing to George Russell (AE), Yeats promised:

---

[43]   Robert C. Peterson, 'Yeats the Autobiographer: A Dialogue of Self and Soul', *English Literature in Translation, 1880–1920,* 26:2 (1983),143.

[44]   Wright, 'The Elusive Self', 50.

[45]   Wright, 'The Elusive Self', 50.

[46]   Levin, 'The Yeats of the Autobiographies', 398.

[47]   The numerous 'versions' of Yeats which his multiple autobiographies produce are joined by those created by his biographers. These include 'The Arch-Poet' of Roy Foster's *Life 2* and Richard Ellmann's *The Man and the Masks* (London: Macmillan, 1949), which promote Yeats's alter egos and disguises.

[48]   Wright, 'The Elusive Self', 48.

I will submit to you whatever I write about yourself and publish nothing that you dislike. I wish to be able to say in my preface that wherever I have included a living man I have submitted my words for his correction.[49]

Yeats's apparent willingness to collaborate and 'correct' later drafts of his autobiography differs dramatically from his earlier reluctance to 'consult' or, indeed, his instinct to seal his first draft in an envelope marked 'Private'. Yet the fact is, his sense of what was 'true' about himself, his sense of what mattered most in the story of his life, changed. The most controversial aspects of Yeats's first attempts at writing autobiographically, the omissions and the emissions, were a testing ground, a place for the author to measure out his own ethical limits. When he rewrote his life in the polished volumes later collected as *Autobiographies*, he honed the fictional mask, the 'image' that was to take his place in the text. For many critics, the changes that can be traced between the early and final drafts signify a weakening in Yeats's impulse to write 'truthfully'. Where the early drafts are candid about Yeats's personal insecurities, his sexual frustration (and masturbation habits), the published works lack the 'the candour found in the original 1909 diary'.[50] As Wright explains, noting the contrasts between Yeats's private and public texts, '[H]e never did achieve such candour in public (this is not to imply that he should have, merely that he contemplated the attempt and changed his mind), and references to his sexuality in *Autobiographies* sometimes seem evasive.'[51]

There is in this a valuable distinction between private and public life-writing. Yeats's journal and other private efforts at life-writing may have informed his later autobiographies, but they were not, by default, templates for them. The candour of the private writing is not, necessarily, an initial attempt at the public text, but it holds a value in its own right. One might, in fact, argue that Yeats's instinct to edit and censor offers a more telling insight into his personality than the texts themselves. More than anything, Yeats sees writing autobiographically as a never-ending drafting process requiring multiple versions, new techniques, and careful reworking of previous efforts. Writing autobiographically, in other words, is not a question of remembering, but a process of editing. Yeats's draft manuscript, sealed up in 1921, takes on a different meaning in this context. Rather than viewing these pages as a preliminary attempt, we might think of them as the final autobiography's alter ego. As Wright wonders, it is possible that Yeats 'intended to write a text too frank for publication in order to clarify in his own mind the kinds of omissions he would need to make before he did publish'.[52] This alternative autobiography, containing elements that are, presumably, definitive to the author but deemed unsuitable for the public view, points to Yeats's

---

[49] WBY To George Russell (AE), 1 July [1921], *CL InteLex* #3935; Allan Wade, ed., *The Letters of W. B. Yeats* (London: Macmillan, 1955), 670.

[50] Wright, 'The Elusive Self', 46.

[51] Wright, 'The Elusive Self', 46.

[52] Wright, 'The Elusive Self', 46.

awareness of the essential futility of autobiographical writing. For all Yeats's attempts to fix himself to the page, the impermanent self refuses to stay still. Yeats's multiple volumes of autobiography are not simply a reflection of an uncommonly full life; they are a testament to his ongoing experiment in self-making. It is for this reason that the texts are most properly understood as simultaneously private and public, both fragmented volumes and a complete collection. The contradictions are vital since, in Harte's terms, Yeats's 'serial acts of self-portraiture emanate from an understanding of autobiography as process, as performative act —a continually renewed attempt to create the self at the time of writing'.[53]

Reviewing the Macmillan publication of *Autobiographies* in 1955, Lennox Robinson, advocated that these texts be read alongside Yeats's poetry, plays, and letters, as a component part in Yeats's lifelong project of self-expression. Yet if the book's function is clear, its form is not, and as Robinson continues,

> It is quite impossible to appraise this book, it is so many things. It is not a history of literature nor of Irish nationality, it is not this, it is not that and yet it is all these things; it is, in short, the history of the mind of a man of genius.[54]

In this collated and published form, Yeats's autobiographical writing does, indeed, defy traditional definitions. It is, in places, as much about other people as himself. In some volumes, the focus is turned so squarely outwards that it reads precisely like a history of 'Irish nationality'. What is certain is that Yeats's autobiographical writing provided both respite from his other work and further impetus to it. As Perloff puts it so clearly, 'the writing of autobiography taught Yeats two major things: how to invent an effective structure for the longer lyric poem, and how to make a drama out of his own personal life'.[55] Yeats's autobiographical writing is not an aside from his poetry or drama; it is the foundation that supports them. Yet above all else, these texts offer, as Robinson notes, not just an account of Yeats's life but, more importantly, a history of his mind. In December 1920, a few months before he sealed his draft memoir in an envelope, Yeats wrote to Lady Gregory: 'I think it will influence young Irishmen in the future, if for no other reason than it shows how seriously one lived and thought. I know from my own memory of my youth in Dublin how important biography can be in Ireland.'[56] From the start, Yeats held a clear vision of the community of readers his work would reach and its intended purpose. For Yeats, this form of writing and the ongoing effort to understand the self was 'sufficiently fruitful, or intriguing, or inescapable' that he felt compelled 'to repeat it in various modes at various times'.[57] The repetition of the task did not, however, bring

[53] Harte, *History of Irish Autobiography*, 3.
[54] Lennox Robinson, 'On "Autobiographies" by W. B. Yeats', *Library Review*, 15:3 (1955),164.
[55] Perloff, 'The Tradition of Myself', 532.
[56] Berg Collection, New York Public Library, cited in Foster, *The Irish Story*, 74.
[57] Wright, 'The Elusive Self', 44.

Yeats closer to a complete representation of his unique sense of self. Instead, the more he worked at interrogating his own life, the more it became apparent that the process, not the product, was the point. The final consequence is that, far from getting closer to a definitive self-portrait, 'at times a reader senses that Yeats has come dangerously close to refining himself out of existence altogether'.[58]

---

[58] Wright, 'The Elusive Self', 50–1.

CHAPTER 2

···

FAIRY AND FOLK TALES
OF BEDFORD PARK

···

SEÁN HEWITT

In early 1888, W. B. Yeats found himself at 17 Lansdowne Road, Holland Park, the residence of Madame Blavatsky, in the company of the great theosophist and a man who claimed second sight. Blavatsky had been 'abusing' Yeats over an embarrassing affair that occurred at a seance in Dublin, at which he had experienced a violent nervous shock and (in his fright) recited the opening lines of *Paradise Lost* by way of a prayer. The man with second sight, after telling Yeats 'true things' about himself (such as that he 'had rheumatism in the arms & shoulders lately'), proceeded to attempt to mesmerize the poet, but had no effect. Yeats, perhaps, was the centre of attention for reasons more than just his ailments and his jittery reaction to mediumship. 'They all look to Ireland', Yeats later wrote to John O'Leary, 'to produce some great spiritual teaching. The ark of the covenant is at Tara, says the second-sighted person, but he's a fool.'[1] Back in South Kensington, Yeats sat down to finish an article on folklore, and a few weeks later he received a letter from Ernest Rhys commissioning him to edit a book of selected folklore for his 'Camelot Classics' series. Though he may have dismissed the 'second-sighted person' as a fool, the prediction of some 'spiritual teaching' from Ireland was soon to be fulfilled by the young poet, who would position Irish fairy lore and folklore as a corrective to the limiting world of nineteenth-century materialism.

Folklore was, for Yeats, 'at once the Bible, the Thirty-nine Articles, and the Book of Common Prayer'.[2] It constituted a sort of primitive, and importantly *living*, text. It was proof of the primacy of the symbolic, the importance of the anti-rational, and the reality of spiritism. Although Mary Catherine Flannery has suggested that the events which Yeats regarded as most important during the pivotal four years between 1887 and 1891 'did not concern Irish myth but rather Eastern thought, especially Theosophy,

---

[1] Yeats to John O'Leary (after 26 January 1888), *CL InteLex*; *CL1*, 45–6.
[2] *UP1*, 284.

Indian thought, and Cabbalism', such a formulation presents a false dichotomy.[3] For Yeats, on his search for unity, his spiritual-philosophical pursuits and his interest in Irish myth and folklore were inextricable. In fact, the concomitant revivals of popular interest in magic and Irish folklore no doubt encouraged him to make connections between the two fields. In 1887, Lady Wilde's *Ancient Legends, Mystic Charms, and Superstitions of Ireland* (a book much favoured by Yeats) was published, marking 'the end of a long hiatus of general interest in Irish folklore'.[4] In the same year, MacGregor Mathers published his translation of *Kabbala Denudata*, or *The Kabbalah Unveiled*, a book which acted as a source text for the majority of the doctrines of what would become the Hermetic Order of the Golden Dawn. Yeats also met Blavatsky in 1887, and her lengthy theosophical tome *The Secret Doctrine* was published in 1888. That the fin de siècle enthusiasm for magic and occult spirituality coincided with 'the harvest-time of folk-lore' was, for Yeats at least, no mere coincidence.[5]

Yeats moved with his father, his brother Jack, and his sister Lolly to 3 Blenheim Road, Bedford Park, on 24 March 1888. His mother and his sister Lily joined a few weeks later, in mid-April. The suburb, which was planned as a self-contained village, had been ready for occupation since the early avenue was completed in the autumn of 1876, and since then had developed a reputation as 'Arcadian, Aesthetic, Bohemian ... an unconscious example of a romantic Socialist Co-operative'.[6] The painter Edward Abbey observed that entering Bedford Park was like 'walking into a water colour'.[7] Yeats himself described the 'crooked ostentatiously picturesque streets' as being like 'the Pre-Raphaelite movement at last affecting life'.[8]

By the time the Yeatses arrived, however, the suburb had already lost some of its shine. For Yeats, though he initially described it to Katharine Tynan as 'a silent tree filled place where every thing is idyllic', it later 'lost the romance'[9] he had imbued it with on his first sightings as a boy. The public house, named The Tabard after Chaucer's inn, was too ordinary for his tastes, and he was disappointed to find that the sign of a trumpeter which hung above the doorway, though originally painted by a Pre-Raphaelite, had been 'freshened by some inferior hand'.[10] The Yeats family, certainly, did not have an easy time at Bedford Park. Money was always an issue, and the Yeatses often found it necessary to 'borrow' food from neighbours, who also gave gifts of clothing to Lily and Lolly.[11] Over time, debts multiplied. W.B. recalled that he had 'lived upon bread

---

[3] Mary Catherine Flannery, *Yeats and Magic: The Earlier Works* (Gerrards Cross: Colin Smythe, 1977), 21–2.

[4] Frank Kinahan, *Yeats, Folklore, and Occultism* (Boston: Unwin Hyman, 1988), 2.

[5] *UP1*, 187.

[6] Ian Fletcher, 'Bedford Park: Aesthete's Elysium?', in Ian Fletcher, ed., *Romantic Mythologies* (London: Routledge & Kegan Paul, 1967), 169–208, 170.

[7] Quoted in Fletcher, 'Bedford Park', 171.

[8] *Au*, 113.

[9] Yeats to Katharine Tynan, 14 March [1888], *CL InteLex*; *CL1*, 56; *Au*, 113.

[10] *Au*, 113.

[11] William M. Murphy, *Prodigal Father: The Life of John Butler Yeats (1839–1922)* (Ithaca, NY: Cornell University Press, 1978), 157–8.

and tea', and had learnt to ink his socks so that they did not show through his worn-out shoes.[12] This meant that practical work was a necessity. W.B. took whatever writing he could get, though his father was concerned that such hack work might dull his creativity. From December 1888, Lily worked on embroidery under May Morris (William Morris's daughter), bringing in a regular salary.

That is not to say that Yeats agreed to edit an anthology of Irish folklore for the money, though no doubt the extra cash was welcome. Originally, as Yeats's letters to Tynan attest, the book that became *Fairy and Folk Tales of the Irish Peasantry* (1888) was envisioned as an edited version of Thomas Crofton Croker's *Fairy Legends and Traditions of the South of Ireland* (1825–8), designed to be a mid-price addition to Ernest Rhys's 'Camelot Classics' series. As it happened, the final version of Yeats's anthology included a dozen extracts from Croker's collections, alongside the works (extracted and edited) of other nineteenth-century Irish folklorists. Yeats recalls being paid £12 for the work of editing the anthology. Though not a small sum, the work required of Yeats a great deal of time and research. Later, however, he noted: 'I did not think myself badly paid, for I had chosen the work for my own purposes.'[13]

Critics such as Foster, Thuente, Kinahan, and Garrigan Mattar have emphasized the pivotal importance for Yeats of this early anthology, which was the first book to have his name on the cover. As Thuente notes, 'a great deal of time and effort' was expended by Yeats on sourcing his materials for the book, and in his close editing of many of them.[14] Indeed, *Fairy and Folk Tales* was not merely compiled by Yeats but *edited* by him, often with a rigorous hand. By 1889, Yeats could claim, with likely accuracy, to have read 'most, if not all' of the recorded Irish fairy tales which had by that time been translated into English.[15] His 'own purposes', however, are revealed in the editorial decisions he made over the course of his work on the book, which establishes a canon of Irish folklore that is anti-rational, visionary, and occult. As Warwick Gould succinctly puts it, 'one of the most enduring aspects of Yeats's occultism is its Irishness, and one of the most determined aspects of his sense of his Irishness is his occultism.'[16] The origins of such a formulation can be traced in *Fairy and Folk Tales*, his first book.

The suburb of Bedford Park (where Yeats lived whilst collating and editing his anthology) was an enclave of experimental theatre, Morrisian arts and crafts, socialism, and, importantly, spiritism. A number of its inhabitants (including Yeats) were instrumental in the establishment of the Chiswick Lodge of the Theosophical Society in 1891, and many were involved in the Hermetic Order of the Golden Dawn. Yeats was admitted to the Order in 1890, along with Florence Farr and Annie Horniman, and those with

[12] *Au*, 154.
[13] *Au*, 149.
[14] Mary Helen Thuente, *W. B. Yeats and Irish Folklore* (Dublin: Gill & Macmillan, 1980), 75.
[15] *UP1*, 139; Frank Kinahan suggests that, on balance, Yeats was likely justified in making this claim; Kinahan, Yeats, Folklore, and Occultism, 42–3.
[16] Warwick Gould, 'Frazer, Yeats, and the Reconsecration of Folklore', in Robert Fraser, ed., *Sir James Frazer and the Literary Imagination* (Basingstoke: Macmillan, 1990), 121–53, 125.

Bedford Park connections also included Dorothea Hunter (née Butler), her husband Edmund Arthur Hunter, and the theosophist Isabelle de Steiger.[17] Of course, Yeats was already steeped in occult interests before he moved to Bedford Park. His aunt Isabella Pollexfen Varley had sent him a copy of A. P. Sinnett's *Esoteric Buddhism* in 1884, and, no doubt influenced by his close friendship with Charles Johnston, he had begun his spiritual explorations in the early 1880s. The pair studied sacred objects in a museum in order to detect the 'odic force' that might be emanating from them. Later, thought transference and the possibility of astral travel attracted him greatly. In June 1885, he was instrumental in the formation of the Dublin Hermetic Society (which, in 1886, became the Dublin Theosophical Society), and became familiar with the works of H. P. Blavatsky and the teachings of Mohini Chatterjee. In particular, Yeats was excited by experiments in magic and spiritism, which sought occult knowledge and relied on control and training to yield results.[18] Though Yeats's theosophical interests were in place before he moved to Bedford Park, they were no doubt solidified there.

It is clear from his introduction to the book that Yeats's presentation of the Irish peasantry would emphasize their spirituality and their adherence to pre-modern modes of thought that saw little distinction between the real and the ideal, the physical and the spiritual. He saw folklore, in James Pethica's words, as 'a storehouse of uncanny phenomena.'[19] That the peasantry had a direct apprehension of the supernatural, and that their folklore was evidence that 'mankind in its primitive state was a vessel of revealed religion and not the first link in an evolutionary chain', were primary concerns for Yeats and testament to the fact that his early folklore anthologies should be seen as the gathering of a set of texts that might hold clues in the battle against the tide of nineteenth-century scientism, positivism, and materialism.[20] The chief purpose of his editing, as Sinéad Garrigan Mattar argues, was 'to assert the seriousness of Celtic supernaturalism.'[21] In order to achieve this, Yeats chose tales that were marked by an imaginative folk extravagance—quick corpses, changelings, pookas, merrows, and times when the Celt is dreaming, or thinking 'on the soul and on the dead.'[22] Whereas earlier collectors and compilers might have downplayed the 'irrationality' of the peasantry, belittling or chastising them for their credulity and superstition, Yeats proudly asserted that, in his editorial apparatus, he had 'not rationalised a single hobgoblin.'[23]

Thus, Yeats pitched his anthology in opposition to the 'scientific' folklorists, anthropologists, and ethnologists whose work was comparative and analytical. After

---

[17] See Alex Owen, *The Place of Enchantment: British Occultism and the Culture of the Modern* (Chicago and London: University of Chicago Press, 2004), 61.

[18] For more on these early years, see *Life 1*, 45–52.

[19] James Pethica, 'Yeats, folklore, and Irish legend', in Marjorie Howes and John Kelly, eds., *The Cambridge Companion to W. B. Yeats* (Cambridge: Cambridge University Press, 2006), 129–143, 129.

[20] Sinéad Garrigan Mattar, *Primitivism, Science, and the Irish Revival* (Oxford: Clarendon Press, 2004), 42.

[21] Mattar, *Primitivism, Science, and the Irish Revival*, 46.

[22] *FFTIP*, 7.

[23] *FFTIP*, 8.

reading the organ of the English Folklore Society, the *Folk-Lore Journal*, he complained that 'scientific people cannot tell stories'.[24] But it was not only the lack of 'the needful subtle imaginative sympathy' in these scientific presentations of folklore that Yeats objected to.[25] Rather, it was the treatment of folklore and myth as the product of a corrupted reason, the rationality of which could be remade if motifs and symbols were subject to large-scale comparative study. The German philologist Max Müller had argued that myths, and religious mythography, were the result of a 'disease of language': early mankind had used metaphors and proper names to describe natural phenomena, but over time the rationale behind this language had been forgotten, so that the original poetic vision degenerated into a structured religious faith. As Andrew Lang succinctly summarized, 'the *nomina* developed into *numina*, the names into gods, the descriptions of elemental processes into myths'.[26] Later, this degenerationist model was replaced by an explanation modelled on evolutionary theory, so that, rather than through a 'disease of language', religion was developed through a progression from animism and magic, through organized religion, and into scientific knowledge. The concept of 'survivals', a clear example of cultural evolution in late nineteenth-century anthropology, referred to the fragments or clues of earlier cultures that remained even though their rationale was lost. For an anthropologist such as Lang, 'folklore illustrates survivals as narratives'.[27] Thus, the method of comparative folklore is to recontextualize the irrational in order to recover its rationale. In Lang's words,

> The method is, when an apparently irrational and anomalous custom is found in any country, to look for a country where a similar practice is found, and where the practice is no longer irrational and anomalous, but in harmony with the manners and ideas of the people among whom it prevails.[28]

Admitting that the global corpus of myth and folklore was too complex to decode fully, he argued that it was possible to recover 'an historical condition of the human intellect to which the elements in myths, regarded by us as irrational, shall seem rational enough'.[29] Though the 'irrationality' of folklore is not due to a 'disease of language', it is still viewed as a displaced remnant, something that might, with the proper scientific method, be rationalized.

In his introduction to *Fairy and Folk Tales*, Yeats decisively pits the anthology against such scientific pursuits. Rather than telling us 'of the primitive religion of mankind, or whatever else the folk-lorists are on the gad after', the tales selected here are in sympathy with the Celt, and present irrationality without seeking explanation.[30] This is a

---

[24] Yeats to Douglas Hyde, 11 July [1888], *CL InteLex*; *CL1*, 81.
[25] Yeats to the editor of *The Academy*, 2 October 1890, *CL InteLex*; *CL1*, 229.
[26] Andrew Lang, *Myth, Ritual and Religion*, Vol. 1 (London: Longmans, Green & Co., 1913), 25.
[27] Sarah Hines, 'Collecting the Empire: Andrew Lang's Fairy Books (1889–1910)', *Marvels & Tales: Journal of Fairy-Tale Studies*, 24:1 (2010), 39–56, 47.
[28] Andrew Lang, *Custom and Myth* (London: Longmans, Green & Co., 1884), 47.
[29] Lang, *Myth, Ritual and Religion*, Vol. 1, 8.
[30] *FFTIP*, 6

slightly disingenuous remark from Yeats, who (as his own anthology attests) was particularly interested in 'primitive' religion and what folklore might reveal about the proper and original spirituality of mankind. However, his sleight of hand is perhaps a necessity. In presenting folklore as occult, and as evidence of Celtic supernaturalism, he felt it necessary to reject the methods of nineteenth-century anthropology which, through its evolutionary underpinnings, might reduce a real spirituality into a 'survival', its comparativism relegating the supernatural to its position as a superstitious hangover from a less enlightened time, or from less enlightened people.

In her theosophical teachings, Madame Blavatsky argued that 'no traditional event in the folk-lore of a people has ever been, at any time, pure fiction'.[31] In *The Secret Doctrine*, published in the same year as *Fairy and Folk Tales*, Blavatsky strongly opposed Müller's degenerative theory of myth and folklore, quoting Gerald Massey (poet, Egyptologist, and spiritualist), whose lecture on 'Luniolatry; Ancient and Modern' offered the following riposte:

> They [Müller and others] have portrayed the primitive myth-maker for us as a sort of Germanised-Hindu metaphysician, projecting his own shadow on a mental mist, and talking ingeniously concerning smoke, or, at least, *cloud*, the sky overhead becoming like the dome of dreamland, scribbled over with the imagery of aboriginal nightmare. ... The original and meaning of mythology have been missed altogether by these solarites and weather-mongers. Mythology was a primitive mode of *thinking* the early thought. It was founded on natural facts, and is still verifiable in phenomena. ... Mythology is the repository of man's most ancient science, and what concerns us chiefly is this – when truly interpreted once more, it is destined to be the death of those false theologies to which it has unwittingly given birth.[32]

The call for a 'true interpretation' of folklore and myth was echoed by Yeats, who positioned himself as a potential interpreter, equipped with both occult knowledge and a supposed intimacy with the peasantry. In an article published in the theosophical journal *Lucifer*, shortly after the appearance of *Fairy and Folk Tales*, Yeats closely paralleled the introductory materials to his anthology in detailing the 'Irish Fairies, Ghosts, Witches, etc.' for an occultist readership. 'It has occurred to me', Yeats writes, rather coyly, 'that it would be interesting if some spiritualist or occultist would try to explain the various curious and intricate spiritualistic beliefs of peasants. When reading Irish folk-lore, or listening to Irish peasants telling their tales of magic and fairyism and witchcraft, more and more is one convinced that some clue there must be.'[33] If, for Gerald Massey, a true interpretation of folklore might be the death knell of the 'false theologies' of modernity, for Yeats Irish folklore was a textual corpus which might reveal

---

[31] H. Blavatsky, *The Secret Doctrine: The Synthesis of Science, Religion, and Philosophy*, Vol. 1: *Cosmogenesis* (London: Theosophical Publishing Co., 1888), 303.

[32] Quoted in Blavatsky, *The Secret Doctrine*, Vol. 1, 303–5. Massey's lecture was privately published as *Luniolatry; Ancient and Modern, a Lecture* (Villa Bordighiera, London, 1887).

[33] *UP1*, 130.

'clues' to the reality of the supernatural. Occult knowledge and the study of folklore thus went hand in hand.

In preparing his volume for Rhys, Yeats came across 'much strange literature', including an early nineteenth-century Dublin magazine devoted to ghost stories, and 'several histories of Magic'.[34] He also specifically sought out texts that would bolster his evidence of Celtic supernaturalism. Writing to Father Matthew Russell, editor of the *Irish Monthly*, in July of 1888, Yeats was in search of additional material for his book: 'I have many stories about the fairies but am hard up for Banshee and Pooka stories and also for stories of the "headless coach" type.' Indeed, Yeats had little room for (or, perhaps less avid interest in) the sort of folk tales classified as *Märchen* or 'household tales' ('that is to say stories about kings & queens and fair princesses'), preferring instead 'stories of the Croker type'[35]. Croker's *Fairy Legends* was published in two 'series', the first in 1825 and the second in 1828. In both, he drew primarily on material that focused on the supernatural, producing a collection designed for the popular market, appealing to a popular readership with an appetite for the sort of tales being published by the Brothers Grimm.[36]

When Yeats wrote to Douglas Hyde on 11 July 1888, he copied out the divisions of his book, which was to appear in ten sections, with stories categorized accordingly (the spellings are Yeats's own):

1. Fairies
2. Changlings
3. Leprehauns
4. Banshee
5. Ghosts, headless horsemen, etc
6. Tier-na-oge
7. Witches
8. Fairy docters
9. Saints
10. The devil.[37]

In what must have been a slight panic, Yeats wrote again a little later in the month, having just discovered that his book was '60 to 70 pages short'. Enclosing a revised list of contents, he had added a final two sections, the first being 'Giants' and the second 'Kings Queens Princesses & Other Tales'.[38] Both of these sections were noted as 'incomplete', while the other ten sections had lists of tales which Yeats intended to include. These less

[34] Yeats to Father Matthew Russell, 5 July [1888], *CL InteLex*; *CL1*, 80.
[35] Yeats to Father Matthew Russell, 5 July [1888], *CL InteLex*; *CL1*, 78–9.
[36] See Anne Markey, 'The Discovery of Irish Folklore', *New Hibernia Review / Iris Éireannach Nua*, 10:4 (Winter, 2006), 21–43, 26.
[37] Yeats to Douglas Hyde, 11 July [1888], *CL InteLex*; *CL1*, 81–2.
[38] Yeats to Douglas Hyde [mid-July 1888], *CL InteLex*; *CL1*, 83–6.

overtly 'supernatural' pieces, then, were likely added out of haste. Certainly, they were not initially envisioned to be in the remit of Yeats's book. In many of the tales collected in *Fairy and Folk Tales*, the dead exist alongside the living. Thus, not only was Yeats attracted to Croker, but also to William Carleton, whose *Traits and Stories of the Irish Peasantry* (like Croker's *Fairy Legends*) was published in two series in 1830 and 1834. Carleton's style was different—he blended folklore and fiction in order to 'illuminate aspects of the Irish psyche'—but his fictionalizing tendencies were forgiven by Yeats, who no doubt was attracted to his supernaturalism, his 'aesthetic of horror'.[39] Likewise, when he selected tales from Patrick Kennedy's *Legendary Fictions of the Irish Celts* and *The Fireside Stories of Ireland*, Yeats opted for those with the strangest subjects, such as shape-shifting.[40] Indeed, Yeats chose folk stories that could (when placed together) centralize an Irish occult tradition, and which might position the Irish peasant as visionary.

These were not Yeats's only criteria in choosing stories, nor were they the only benchmark by which he set out editing his materials. Mary Thuente (whose work on finding a list of sources for *Fairy and Folk Tales* is an invaluable contribution to our understanding of Yeats's processes) suggests that the poet rejected any story which sought to draw moral conclusions. 'Without the moral', Ken Monteith observes, 'the tales appear historical, rather than allegorical, and become part of an oral ... tradition, rather than a code of conduct.'[41] Yeats also did not use stories which contained religious or political propaganda, and he deleted anti-Catholic references from Carleton's texts. He cut all extraneous authorial commentary from his source texts, and excised superfluous literary atmosphere. He also chose not to use any stories that centred solely on earthly matters, including only those with a supernatural element.[42]

In doing so, Yeats was creating a canon of fairy lore and folklore that positioned Irishness and occult thought as central. That said, he was not alone or unprecedented in envisioning accounts of fairies as important to the revival of alternative spiritualities and esoteric thought. A. E. Waite, who lived not far from the Yeatses, on the edge of Bedford Park in Gunnersbury, would become familiar to Yeats both through his involvement in the formation of the Golden Dawn and through his earlier translations of the works of the French occultist and magician Éliphas Lévi. Waite was later a master of his own order, the Fellowship of the Rosy Cross, and is primarily remembered today for his work with Pamela Colman Smith on the Rider–Waite tarot deck. In *The Mysteries of Magic* (1886), Waite's first major contribution to esoteric literature, the author compiled a digest of Lévi's longer, more unwieldy works, popularizing them for a British audience. Later, in 1888, Waite published *Elfin Music: An Anthology of English Fairy Poetry*, a compendium of English verse, including Keats, Poe, and Shakespeare alongside not a few Irish writers (notably Allingham, Lover, Mangan, and Ferguson). Yeats's copy

---

[39] Markey, 'Discovery of Irish Folklore', 30; R. F. Foster, *Words Alone: Yeats and His Inheritances* (Oxford: Oxford University Press, 2012), 150.
[40] See Thuente, *W. B. Yeats and Irish Folklore*, 90.
[41] Ken Monteith, *Yeats and Theosophy* (London and New York: Routledge, 2008), 177.
[42] Thuente, *W. B. Yeats and Irish Folklore*, 92.

of the anthology bears his signature and is dated 4 August 1888. Though this dating suggests that Waite's book arrived in Yeats's hands too late to affect his own anthology, Frank Kinahan suggests that the introductory materials to *Fairy and Folk Tales* demonstrate Yeats's familiarity with his fellow occultist's work, perhaps through an earlier copy.[43] Certainly, Waite's introduction to *Elfin Music* would have piqued Yeats's interest. Waite hoped that his volume was opportune, being published 'during the initial signs of a revival of that romantic or supernatural element which is the first characteristic of primitive song-craft in every nation'.[44] However, many of the poems Waite collected, by his own admission, 'fall below the general level of their writers'. This is symptomatic of 'the unserious spirit with which the subject has been too frequently approached by our English poets, who have generally represented a class superior to the superstitions and sometimes to the faiths of the time'.[45] A clear point of difference for Yeats, such an observation would have stoked the conviction behind his editorial decision to remove any sense of the writer of the tale looking down on their material, or attempting to rationalize or excuse the folk exuberance therein. If Waite presented his fairy poetry in the hope that it might chime with revived interest in the supernatural, though admitted that the poems in his anthology might not have been written from a genuine belief in the reality of fairies, Yeats's *Fairy and Folk Tales*, which asserts a firm faith in the supernatural, can act as both a literary anthology and a book of evidence.

Though they were 'utterly opposed to each other … in all things occult', Waite and Yeats nevertheless occupied similar territory in their thought and held each other in mutual respect.[46] Yeats drew on Waite's *Mysteries of Magic* in his editorial apparatus for *Fairy and Folk Tales*, referring to Lévi's divisions of the nature spirits as being in line with other occultists, notably Paracelsus[47]. Yeats's familiarity with Waite's books, and his interest in fairies as popular evidence of supernatural phenomena, show the precedent in occult thought for Yeats's own line of thinking. In Lévi's work on 'the great magical arcanum', which Waite translated in *The Mysteries of Magic*, the magician writes that 'When the adepts in alchemy speak of a great and unique Athanor which all can make use of, which is within the grasp of all, and which all men possess without knowing it, they allude to the philosophic and moral alchemy'.[48] The athanor (a type of furnace used by alchemists) is used not only to signify a piece of physical equipment but also to signal the properly trained mind of the adept. Drawing attention to this 'philosophic and moral alchemy' of knowledge and training, Waite took the opportunity in his editorial

---

[43] F. Kinahan, 'Armchair Folklore: Yeats and the Textual Source of *Fairy and Folk Tales of the Irish Peasantry*', *Proceedings of the Royal Irish Academy: Archaeology, Culture, History, Literature*, Vol. 83C (1983), 255–67, 264.

[44] Arthur Edward Waite, *Elfin Music: An Anthology of English Fairy Poetry* (London: Walter Scott, 1888), ix.

[45] Waite, *Elfin Music*, xxxiii.

[46] R. A. Gilbert, '"The One Deep Student": Yeats and A. E. Waite', *YA*, No. 3 (1985), 3–14, 9.

[47] *FFTIP*, 287

[48] Arthur Edward Waite, *The Mysteries of Magic: A Digest of the Writings of Éliphas Lévi* (London: George Redway, 1886), 90.

notes to make a comparison that benefited his own interest in fairy poetry, and Yeats would certainly have been interested in such a connection. The 'risen and emancipated mind' of the alchemist is comparable to the 'light proceeding from the Translucid' seen by the 'fairy-gifted poet'.[49] Though J. Patrick Pazdziora suggests that 'it is not without the realm of possibility that Waite understood the 'fairy-gifted poet' to mean a magically initiated poet and mystic, a study of the text to which the note is attached makes it clear that this was certainly Waite's meaning.[50] Taken in the context of his later anthology of fairy poetry, such a comment sets an illuminating precedent. This direct connection between alchemy, occult initiation, and fairy lore aided Yeats in his search for a unity between the two movements in which he took the keenest interest in this period, namely the revival of occultism and the revived interest in folklore and the land of faery.

Not only do Irish fairy and folk tales shed light on the truth of supernatural phenomena, but theosophy is also presented as proving the truth of Irish fairy lore. Just as later Yeats would link Irish peasant beliefs and Swedenborg's visionary accounts of the dead in *Swedenborg, Mediums and the Desolate Places*, the long essay appended to the second edition of Lady Gregory's *Visions and Beliefs in the West of Ireland* (1920), in 1890 he was suggesting that Irish peasants were visionary in the same manner that theosophists were. 'Some of the beliefs about ghosts' amongst the Irish peasantry,' Yeats notes in an article for *Lucifer*, 'are theosophical'.[51] Giving reference to Adolphe d'Assier's *Posthumous Humanity: A Study of Phantoms*, which sought to use positivist methodologies to 'bring within the compass of the laws of time and space the phenomena of the posthumous order', Yeats asserts the commonality between Irish peasant belief and the beliefs and theories handed down through occult writings, all the while underscoring their actuality.[52] In many other instances, Yeats bolsters his readings of Irish folklore by recourse to the writings of Paracelsus. In the same year that Yeats wrote his article on 'Irish Fairies, Ghosts, Witches, etc.' for *Lucifer*, he wrote elsewhere that 'Tradition is always the same. The earliest poet of India and the Irish peasant in his hovel nod to each other across the ages, and are in perfect agreement.'[53] Thus, Irish folklore is theosophical and ancient, primitive and spiritual, and able to cross gulfs of time and geography with apparent ease. Ireland is positioned by Yeats as the living past, both temporally and spiritually. In being thus, Ireland is also a vital antidote to modernity, its rationalism and its secularism. Folklore is made kin with occultism, and both are made part of that 'greater renaesence [*sic*] – the revolt of the soul against the intellect'.[54]

---

[49] Waite, *Mysteries of Magic*, 344.
[50] J. Patrick Pazdziora, 'Cynical Mysticism: The Role of the Fairies in Late-Victorian Esotericism', *Literature & Theology*, 31:3 (2017), 285–304, 296.
[51] *UP1*, 131
[52] Adolphe d'Assier, *Posthumous Humanity: A Study of Phantoms*, trans. Henry S. Olcott (London: Redway, 1887), xiv.
[53] *CW7*, 97.
[54] Yeats to John O'Leary [week ending 23 July 1892], *CL InteLex*; *CL1*, 303.

Bearing in mind his metropolitan readership, Yeats appealed to a trend for Celticism in the city by positioning the Irish peasant, and the Celtic race more generally, as being the torchbearers of an ancient and still living spirituality that would counter the sterility of modern culture. If Morris and other aesthetic socialists were looking to reinstate the link between mankind and their work by returning to a pastoral utopia, Yeats sought to re-enchant modernity through the reality of fairy lore and occult thought. What Yeats classifies as the 'trooping fairies', as opposed to the 'solitary fairies', are perhaps earth spirits, or 'gods of the earth'. He comments,

> Many poets, and all mystic and occult writers, in all ages and countries, have declared that behind the visible are chains on chains of conscious beings, who are not of heaven but of the earth, who have no inherent form but change according to their whim, or the mind that sees them. You cannot lift your hand without influencing or being influenced by hoards. The visible world is merely their skin. In dreams we go amongst them, and play with them, and combat with them.[55]

This accords with a later assertion, in an article written for the *Irish Theosophist* on 'Invoking the Irish Faeries', that 'their world is very different from ours, and they can but appear in forms borrowed from our limited consciousness'. Only a mind trained in 'the correspondence of sensuous form and supersensuous meaning' can read the significance of the shapes the faeries appear in.[56] This idea of a lost but recoverable link between sensuous and supersensuous, between natural and supernatural, is central to Yeats's project of reinstating a world of revealed religion.

Writing for a London audience in *The Leisure Hour* magazine, in a piece written in 1887 but not published until 1890, Yeats was more tempered in his assertions. Whereas his articles for theosophical journals took the reality of faeries as a given, his works for popular audiences were more guarded. *The Leisure Hour*, published by the Religious Tract Society, sought to address a general readership, printing articles on diverse topics treated 'in the light of Christian truth'.[57] Though there is no way to tell whether Yeats edited the piece specifically for publication in *The Leisure Hour* (he sent it to many publications over the span of two years), the magazine's Christian persuasion would certainly have precluded some of the more outlandish theosophical and occult interpretations he offered elsewhere. Yeats's call for a spiritualized world view, however, would have been welcome to a magazine attempting to counter encroaching secularism. Noting that he is often doubted when making the claim that the Irish peasantry still believe in faeries, Yeats addresses his metropolitan readership, who 'think that I am merely trying to weave a forlorn piece of gilt thread into the dull grey worsted of this century'.[58]

---

[55] *FFTIP*, p.11.
[56] *UP1*, 247.
[57] Stephanie Olsen, *Juvenile Nation: Youth, Emotions and the Making of the Modern British Citizen, 1880–1914* (London and New York: Bloomsbury, 2014), 23.
[58] *UP1*, 175.

Arguing that the rational philosophies of the urban centres 'soon grow silent' outside of their institutional and geographical homes, Yeats concludes that

> There are worse things after all than to believe some pretty piece of unreason, if by doing so you keep yourself from thinking that the earth under your feet is the only god, and that the soul is a little whiff of gas, or some such thing.
>
> The world is, I believe, more full of significance to the Irish peasant than to the English. The fairy populace of hill and lake and woodland have helped to keep it so. It gives a fanciful life to the dead hillsides, and surrounds the peasant, as he ploughs and digs, with tender shadows of poetry.[59]

Thus, Yeats cleverly splays the positioning of his text, opening up multiple interpretative channels for his readership. What to his theosophical readership is presented as absolute fact is given here in a more equivocal tone, with Yeats suggesting that even if faeries are 'some pretty piece of unreason', a belief in them remains valuable, even vital. By adapting the significance of fairy lore and folklore to different metropolitan audiences, Yeats was able to appeal to a popular view of the Celts as spiritual, whilst also promoting an occult revival and a re-enchanted landscape.[60] The message of the folklorist, as Yeats wrote in a long review of T. F. Thiselton-Dyer's *The Ghost World*, was a knitting of the material and the spiritual in this way: 'All these stories are such as unite man more closely to the woods and hills and waters about him, and to give him types and symbols for those feelings and passions which find no adequate expression in common life.'[61]

The folk tales collected by Yeats in *Fairy and Folk Tales* and in later anthologies during the 1890s are 'suggestive of a series of relations between the things of this world and their parallels in an "other" world', though what constituted this 'other' world could be subtly adapted to suit Yeats's reading audience.[62] Though *Fairy and Folk Tales of the Irish Peasantry* is a resolutely Irish book (it contains no work by English writers or collectors, and all of the selected tales take place in Ireland), it is clearly presented both to a wider metropolitan readership and to a more niche audience of occultists who were looking to Ireland, through a trend for Celticism, for spiritual teaching. Yeats's first book, as with all his later work, was adapted to suit his purposes. In this case, it worked to provide evidence to 'this city of the Sassenach' that 'everyone is a visionary, if you scratch him deep enough. But the Celt is a visionary without scratching.'[63]

---

[59] *UP1*, 181–2.

[60] For a fuller exploration of Yeats's 're-enchantment' of the natural world, see my article 'Yeats's Re-Enchanted Nature', *International Yeats Studies*, Vol. 2, Issue 2, Article 2 (2018).

[61] *UP1*, 287.

[62] Sinéad Garrigan Mattar, 'Yeats, Fairies, and the New Animism', *New Literary History*, 43:1 (Winter 2012), 137–57, 150.

[63] *FFTIP*, 7, 4.

CHAPTER 3

'NEVER TO LEAVE THAT VALLEY'

Sligo

PETER MCDONALD

IN a short novel published in 1891 by the author 'Ganconagh', the town of 'Ballah' is the setting for an opening chapter in which a young Anglican curate encounters an acquaintance on a bridge over a river. The out-of-town clergyman is preparing to leave, but has a certain regard for the place; as he smokes his cigarette and gazes over the water, he reflects 'How pleasantly conscious of his own identity it made him when he thought how he and not those whose birthright it was, felt most the beauty of these shadows and this river'. This reverie, which supplies him with 'a tumult of images',[1] is interrupted by the arrival of his Ballah-born friend, who sets up his fishing equipment on the bridge. He, too, thinks of leaving, but professes a reason for doing so which is much less troubled by the kinds of romantic reverie that feed the curate's ambitions. To the question, 'Do you mean to stay here … till your mind rots?', he gives a confident—and distinctly worldly—response:

> 'No, no! To be quite frank with you,' replied the other, 'I have some good looks and shall try to turn them to account by going away from here pretty soon and trying to persuade some girl with money to fall in love with me. I shall not be altogether a bad match, you see, because after she has made me a little prosperous my uncle will die and make me much more so. I wish to be able always to remain a lounger. Yes, I shall marry money. My mother has set her heart on it, and I am not, you see, the kind of person who falls in love inconveniently.'

---

[1] This phrase, by the time Yeats had very likely forgotten it, was to reappear in section VI of 'Nineteen Hundred and Nineteen' (*The Tower* (1928)).

Once the two men part company, this hard-headed (if lazy) native of Ballah passes the tobacconist's shop, eliciting from its keeper only the thought, 'There goes that *gluggerabunthaun* and Jack o'Dreams; been fishing most likely. Ugh!'[2]

'Ballah' is not a real place, any more than 'Ganconagh' is a real name; for it is the thinly disguised town of Sligo, just as the author is an easily identified W. B. Yeats. The novel itself, *John Sherman*, which was published in 1891, remains something of a shadowy presence in the Yeatsian oeuvre, revised and collected by its author in 1908 but dropped thereafter. While there was never to be further mention of 'Ballah' in Yeats's work, there was plenty of attention paid there to Sligo—though largely to County Sligo rather than the town. It is worth pausing over this semi-obscured fictional setting and its two characters, though: the romantic eye for part-other-worldly glamour is that of the curate, who is no native (either geographically or religiously speaking) of the place, while the actual native, John Sherman, professes to be both unromantic and (in financial terms) acquisitive. If either of these two men is going to become a poet, it is the Protestant clergyman.

It is also worth remembering that the Sligo of Yeats's poetry is largely County Sligo, especially in his successful early work, which includes poems such as 'The Lake Isle of Innisfree', 'The Stolen Child', 'The Man Who Dreamed of Faeryland', and 'The Fiddler of Dooney'. Much of Yeats's earlier prose work, too, depends heavily on County Sligo for its settings and sources: before he was Augusta Gregory's co-worker in folkloric field research in County Galway, the poet had plenty of experience in collecting and recycling stories from the Sligo area. Apart from that glimpse—a prolonged one, but isolated—of 'Ballah', Sligo town is notable in the early writing mainly for its absence. And yet, in biographical terms, Yeats's lived experience had been in and around Sligo town rather than the countryside. Furthermore, this experience was not quite so extensive for the child and young man as the older author allowed it to appear. David Fitzpatrick's calculation that in the poet's early life 'perhaps seven years all told were spent in Sligo' offers a useful figure, and much of this time was in effect holiday (more accurately, visits to relatives with the effect of lessening the costs of family upkeep for a hard-up John Butler Yeats). But of course the significance of time cannot be measured simply in terms of its duration, and Fitzpatrick notes how, although Yeats 'never truly resided' in Sligo 'except for the two years and four months spent with his indulgent grandparents in 1872–4', it was nevertheless 'during these months of childhood, when he had just mastered reading and was beginning to make sense of the clamour and

---

[2] All the quotations are from 'Ganconagh', *John Sherman and Dhoya* (London: T. Fisher Unwin, 1891), Ch.1 (pp. 9, 12, 15–16). This 1891 text is reprinted in G.J. Watson (ed.), *W.B. Yeats: Short Fiction* (London: Penguin Books, 1995), and the text as revised for Yeats's *Collected Works in Verse and Prose* (1908) is printed in *CW12*. The apparently Irish term '*gluggerabunthaun*', which Yeats removed from his 1908 text, is examined at length in a note in *CW12*, where it 'might be interpreted as "person-with-a-rattling-arse" or "rattle-arse" or "rattle-prolapsed-fundament" or "rattle-prolapsed-fundament-ist"'; moreover, 'the notion of farting is perhaps not absent' (xxxiii).

colour of the outside world, and to imagine magical links with an invisible world, that Yeats incurred his deepest debts to Sligo'.[3]

Those 'deepest debts' were not extensively articulated until the child had become a middle-aged man, when Yeats published his *Reveries Over Childhood and Youth* (1916). Here, the first place of memory to be named is London, but next (and still on the first page) comes Sligo, 'where I live with my grandparents', and a first Irish memory is recorded without commentary: 'I am sitting on the ground looking at a mastless toy boat with the paint rubbed and scratched, and I say to myself in great melancholy, "It is further away than it used to be", and while I am saying it I am looking at a long scratch in the stern, for it is especially the scratch which is further away.'[4] The toy boat is particularly at home here, for Yeats remembers being in the house of the Pollexfens, his mother's family, for whom the business of seagoing was commercially central; and the material that follows in these reminiscences is accordingly full of boats, ships, sailors for pleasure, and professional sea captains. Not everything in this recollection is pristine: the toy boat is both 'mastless' and 'rubbed and scratched', and the child's memory is conditioned by an apparently inevitable slow loss of the play object. The first Sligo of infancy, then, is Pollexfen Sligo, marked by both the consciousness of loss and the perception of flaws—that 'long scratch in the stern', which is forever 'further away'.

There is a contrast to be noticed here between the early memory and one of the early poems, Yeats's Sligo-centred 'The Stolen Child'.[5] In the poem (a work of youth though not of childhood, composed probably in the summer or autumn of 1886), it is the child who is going away, taken by fairies: 'Away with us he's going, / The solemn-eyed'; whereas, in the older Yeats's memory of a time earlier even than the poem, it is the damaged toy that is going away from the child. While the poem is located outside urban and commercial Sligo, it is careful to name Sligo locations such as 'Sleuth Wood' (Slish Wood, more accurately, though WBY's inaccuracy here is probably deliberate), 'furthest Rosses', and 'Where the wandering water gushes / From the hills above Glen-Car'. The poem—one of Yeats's early (and lasting) popular successes—oddly combines a call away from the world to its 'human child' with a depiction of the world to be abandoned as itself a kind of child: 'the world is full of troubles / And is anxious in its sleep'. The repeated refrain, '*For the world's more full of weeping than you can understand*', maintains this transference of 'weeping' from the child to the 'world'. 'The world' is Sligo; but the other world to which the 'human child' is being enticed is Sligo also, though Sligo in its 'fairy' dimension, of 'the waters and the wild'.

---

[3] David Fitzpatrick, 'Sligo', in David Holdeman and Ben Levitas, eds., *W. B. Yeats in Context* (Cambridge: Cambridge University Press, 2010), 74.

[4] *CW3*, 41. *Reveries Over Childhood and Youth* (written in 1914) was first published by Cuala Press in 1915, then by Macmillan in 1916: the sentence quoted here is on the opening page of text in both versions, but it is preceded by a single page with a short 'Preface' which faces the title-page in 1915, and follows it (as p.vii) in 1916.

[5] *CW1*, 18–19.

This formulation is itself a revealing one, for Yeats puts 'waters' first, and eschews any more conventional expression of poetic countryside—not (for example) 'the woods and waters wild', where the actual landscape would be adequately accounted for, but 'the waters' first and above all, then 'the wild' of which they form their part. The poem has itself begun with Lough Gill, and maintains throughout a supernatural course that is decidedly watery: the 'water-rats' on the 'leafy island' where the 'faery vats' of berries are hidden; 'the wave of moonlight' at Rosses Point, and its 'frothy bubbles'; 'the wandering water' with its 'pools above the rushes' at Glencar and the 'ferns that drop their tears / Over the young streams'; and finally, perhaps, even the water in the domestic 'kettle on the hob' suggests an other-worldly incursion into a site of human peace. Much of Yeats's earlier Sligo-centred supernatural verse gravitates towards the water—notable examples include 'The Man Who Dreamed of Faeryland', 'The Host of the Air', and, most centrally, 'The Lake Isle of Innisfree'.[6] In very broad terms, it is possible to understand water as the element of escape in Yeats's youthful imaginative chemistry; though, seen from another angle, it is the element of abduction and separation.

To return to the later memory of *Reveries*, the question is whether the toy boat is or is not 'further away than it used to be', and whether the imperfections of its surfaces can be lost in the distance. And children were, after all, 'stolen' from the poet's immediate family:

> My realization of death came when my father and mother and my two brothers and my two sisters were on a visit [to Sligo, where the young WBY was living with his Pollexfen grandparents]. I was in the library when I heard feet running past and heard somebody say in the passage that my younger brother, Robert, had died. He had been ill for some days. A little later my sister and I sat at the table, very happy, drawing ships with their flags half-mast high. We must have heard or seen that the ships in the harbour had their flags at half-mast. Next day at breakfast I heard people telling how my mother and the servant had heard the banshee crying the night before he died. It must have been after this that I told my grandmother I did not want to go with her when she went to see old bed-ridden people because they would soon die.[7]

This remembers events of March 1873, when the poet was 7 years old. Its 'realization of death' is not a memory of grief—or of Yeats's grief, at least; instead, it comes close to a memory of a sudden disappearance that could still leave the young siblings capable of being 'very happy' in their play. At the same time, it is followed by the story of the adults' hearing of the banshee—the supernatural harbinger of family deaths—which places the uncanny side by side with the everyday. The result of all this is an aversion on the part of an infant Yeats to the visible mortality of the old people, the Sligo Pollexfens and their circle: it is not so much a wish for eternal youth as a belief (there and then) in its reality.

---

[6] For detailed discussion of the significance of Sligo waters (both inland and coastal) for the poet's earlier poetry, including 'The Lake Isle of Innisfree', see Peter McDonald, 'Yeats's Early Lake Isles', *Review of English Studies*, 70:294 (April 2019), 312–31.

[7] *CW3*, 55.

Like the fairies in Yeats's accounts of them, these children have an aversion to vulgar mortality. The immediate world of the Pollexfen house in Sligo in 1873 is indeed more full of weeping than either Yeats or his younger sister can understand.

Supernatural Sligo—a place which has little to do with Sligo town—figures in Yeats's imagination as a place (perhaps a dimension) where escape and loss are fused. As such, it stands at an oblique angle to the Pollexfens and their world of respectable commerce. Around the time of his composition of 'The Stolen Child', the poet was staying with an uncle, George Pollexfen, a little way off from older and sterner relatives, at Rosses Point. Fresh from ending his time at Dublin's Metropolitan School of Art, Yeats was in waiting for a career of any kind, but he was able to watch men working on the Sligo coast, and even make a poem from what he gleaned there. 'The Meditation of the Old Fisherman' has a refrain for its speaker, '*When I was a boy with never a crack in my heart*', which may be a counterpoint to the refrain of 'The Stolen Child'.[8] The child the fisherman once was has gone; the man's heart (we assume) has had its share of cracks; and the story told in the poem (and told to its poet) commemorates what has been lost. Yeats's later notes insist on the Sligo provenance for all of this: from 1895 onwards, he let readers know that 'This poem is founded upon some things a fisherman said to me when out fishing in Sligo Bay', and in 1925 he claimed to have written the poem by adding 'a few lines' to 'the words of a not very old fisherman at Rosses Point'.[9] In the poem's very first line, the fisherman addresses 'You waves', who 'dance by my feet like children at play', and this association between water and playing children is one that points up the losses brought about by time. If this gives the poem's first stanza some tincture of the Sligo supernatural—awareness of a watery realm where children always play, but into which they have also been taken away—then the second (and central) stanza strikes out in a much more realistic—indeed, commercial—direction:

> The herring are not in the tides as they were of old;
> My sorrow! for many a creak gave the creel in the cart
> That carried the take to Sligo town to be sold,
> *When I was a boy with never a crack in my heart.*[10]

Here, too, the burden is that things are not as they were; and the fishing industry in this part of Sligo can hardly stand comparison with the shipping business of, say, the Pollexfens. It took Yeats until 1895 to arrive at this level of specificity, though, and on the poem's first three appearances in print these fish were carried 'for the sale in the far-away town' (the literary Irishism of 'My sorrow!' also came to replace the more dully poetic 'Ah woe!' and 'Ah me!' at this point). Nevertheless, it is modernity which joins in the attrition process, the putting of cracks on the heart, that the speaker is lamenting;

---

[8] *CW1*, 21.
[9] W.B. Yeats's note in *Poems* (1895) and thereafter; and his note to the poem in *Early Poems and Stories* (1925).
[10] *CW1*, 19.

and the voicing of 'Sligo town' as a place name is part of this, a reminder of the reality standing in front of imaginative longing and regret. In the last of its three stanzas, the fisherman looks askance at a contemporary 'proud maiden' in favour of the women lost to time (or lost in time), 'Who paced in the eve by the nets on the pebbly shore'. In the whole poem, there is not a fairy to be seen; yet it establishes, just as clearly as other more obviously supernatural poems in Yeats's early work, the Sligo beyond 'Sligo town' as a location where loss is to be restored through memory, and in that sense more emotionally compelling and important than the modern world of business and work.

It is the same—or at least a very nearby—location that features a few years later in 'The Man Who Dreamed of Faeryland' (composed in 1890 or 1891), when a man who is busy with the concerns of a career finds his ambition undone by forces beyond himself:

> As he went by the sands of Lisadill,
> His mind ran all on money cares and fears,
> And he had known at last some prudent years
> Before they heaped his grave under the hill;
> But while he passed before a plashy place,
> A lug-worm with its gray and muddy mouth
> Sang that somewhere to north or west or south
> There dwelt a gay, exulting, gentle race;
> And how beneath those three times blessed skies
> A Danaan fruitage makes a shower of moons,
> And as it falls awakens leafy tunes:
> And at that singing he was no more wise.[11]

Again, other-worldly Sligo puts itself in the way of worldly Sligo, this time in the form of a 'lug-worm' (of the kind to be found in the sands, and much used for fishing bait). 'Money cares and fears' are eclipsed by the 'shower of moons' belonging to the realms of what Yeats is now calling the 'Danaan' people, who can steal even the respectable man of the world away from that world. The precise location of the 'gay, exulting, gentle race' is a matter of profound imprecision, for they are 'somewhere to the north or west or south', and yet this is in other respects something of a topographical Sligo poem, covering Dromahair, Lissadell, 'the well of Scanavin', and 'the hill of Lugnagall'.[12]

---

[11] The poet altered this stanza for printings in his *Selected Poems* (1929) and after; the text quoted here is from the 1924 edition of his *Poems*. 'Lissadill' became the more familiar 'Lissadell' in *Poems* (1927): it refers at this point not in particular to Lissadell House and its demesne, owned by the Gore-Booth family, but to three coastal townlands on the Co. Sligo peninsula of Magherow, to the west of Ben Bulben.

[12] Dromahair is in fact (just) in Co. Leitrim, and about 10 miles from Sligo town; the village of Tubberscanavin is a mile south of Collooney in Co. Sligo, and its name means the well of *Sceanmhan*, 'the place of fine shingle'; Lugnagall is a townland at the foot of Copes Mountain, and near Glencar Lough, in Co. Sligo: Yeats understood the Irish name to mean 'steep place of the strangers', and referred to this in his uncollected poem 'The Protestants' Leap' (1887), with a note saying "Lug-na-Gall is a very grey cliff overlooking that Glencar lake, where Dermot and Grania had once a crannóg (whereof the remnants were found some years back)".

It is as though Yeats's poem maps a landscape of the invisible, or of the visible imaginatively transformed, in order to surround and undermine the surface realities of contemporary life. And this life, which is in fact one life lived by one man, is being rejected and perhaps condemned. It may be the life a Sligo Pollexfen could live, but not one to be lived by a Yeats.

In the 1890s, Sligo was often the setting of Yeats's short fiction, which appeared in numerous British periodicals, as well as in the books *The Celtic Twilight* (1893) and *The Secret Rose* (1897). This is the County Sligo of folklore and supernatural phenomena, populated by both fairies and a fairy-conscious peasantry. Poems drift into and out of this material, spoken or sung in the stories, then exported into collections of Yeats's verse. A case in point is 'The Hosting of the Sidhe', a poem in Yeats's *The Wind Among the Reeds* (1899), which was previously (as 'The Host') a prefatory poem to *The Celtic Twilight*. Its opening line launches a Sligo place name at the reader, following this with names of a legendary woman, a Fenian warrior, and a supernatural figure drawn from the poet's own earlier work:

> *The host is riding from Knocknarea,*
> *And over the grave of Clooth-na-bare;*
> *Caolte tossing his burning hair,*
> *And Niam calling, 'Away, come away';*[13]

Knocknarea is solidly physical in terms of its geographical identity—the high limestone hill that overlooks Sligo town—but it carries invisible as well as visible meanings. For Sir Samuel Ferguson (whose work the young Yeats had completely absorbed) it was 'haunted Knocknarea', and Yeats's poem renders the place more haunted than ever.[14] 'The grave of Clooth-na-bare' is a place not of earth (as might be supposed) but of water, as is explained in one chapter of *The Celtic Twilight*:

> Such a mortal too was Clooth-na-Bare, who went all over the world seeking a lake deep enough to drown her faery life, of which she had grown weary, leaping from hill to lake and lake to hill, and setting up a cairn of stones wherever her feet lighted, until at last she found the deepest water in the world in little Lough Ia, on the top of the Birds' Mountain at Sligo.[15]

[13] W. B. Yeats, 'The Host', *The Celtic Twilight: Men and Women, Dhouls and Faeries* (London: Lawrence & Bullen, 1893), viii.

[14] Sir Samuel Ferguson, *Congal* (1872), III, 211–13 (where the Washer of the Ford is speaking): 'my cave / For sleep is in the middle of the well-shaped Cairn of Maev, / High up on haunted Knocknarea'.

[15] W. B. Yeats, 'The Untiring Ones', in *The Celtic Twilight* (1893), 133. In a footnote, Yeats provides more information, though in doing so, offers perhaps less clarity: 'Doubtless Clooth-na-Bare should be Cailleac Beare, which would mean the old woman Beare. Beare or Bere or Verah or Dera or Dhera was a very famous person, perhaps the Mother of the Gods herself. Standish O'Grady found her, as he thinks, frequenting Lough Leath, or the Grey Lake on a mountain in the Fews. Perhaps Lough Ia is my mishearing, or the story-teller's mispronunciation of Lough Leath, for there are many Lough Leaths.'

'Little Lough Ia' (which is most likely Lough Daeane, situated on Slieve Daeane (*Sliabh Da Ean*, the mountain of two birds) to the south of Sligo town, above Lough Gill) is close enough to Knocknarea to make a leap from there by Clooth-na-bare plausible in mythic narrative. In the poem, such information is (at the very least) packed away; but what the reader is encountering is a radically different Sligo to that of the earlier writing, its place names now alienating rather than comfortably familiar. The same could be said for the characters of Caolte and Niam, though here the reader may find the easiest access by way of the already published poetry of W. B. Yeats, and in particular his 'The Wanderings of Oisin' (1889), where both appear. The call of '*Away, come away*' is the keynote of this poem: in a sense, it is an invitation to leave one (contemporary) Sligo for another (supernatural and legendary) version of the place. It is in the nature of this departure that it is not without its cost; indeed, it is very much a matter of cost. As the 'host' declare, '*if any gaze on our rushing band, / We come between him and the deed of his hand, / We come between him and the hope of his heart*'. Other-worldly enchantment entails worldly unsuccess.

As far as Yeats's familial Sligo connections are concerned, the message is not exactly in keeping with the way in which things were done. Both the Pollexfens and the Middletons, the poet's mother's side of the family, were on the whole clear-eyed and earnest about business matters and social standing. This was—even as early as the poet's early boyhood—all too evidently not the case for his father, John Butler Yeats, whose profession as a barrister was abandoned for the calling of art, but whose artistic career was slowed by the ease with which things came between him and the portrait-painting deeds of his hand. Though there were Yeats family links with Sligo, it was for the young poet at least primarily a place of maternal relations. Not that all the Pollexfens and Middletons were deaf to various callings '*Away*'; some had gone, or were going, mad; and the poet's uncle George, after all, was an astrologer, and to some degree an occultist. Yet to be called out of Pollexfen Sligo to the Sligo of faery entailed more than being allured from a modern empirical world to a place of old stories and folk-belief; for this other Sligo was also a place of anciently Irish sentiment and—by the 1890s—of active nationalist political sentiments. The Pollexfens and Middletons were—perfectly unsurprisingly—Unionists, members of the Church of Ireland, and affiliated with both the Masons and the Orange Order.

In another poem formed in the creative crucible of his 1890s short fiction, Yeats stamps Sligo with emphatically nationalist meanings. A story published in 1894, 'Kathleen-Ny-Hoolihan', incorporated a poem which Yeats modelled loosely on an eighteenth-century poem in Irish by William Heffernan the Blind, known to him through translations by James Clarence Mangan and Edward Walsh. In Yeats's treatment, the longish poem shrinks to three five-line stanzas, each one recording an act of devotion to the Kathleen figure. As before, things start with Knocknarea:

> Veering, fleeting, fickle, the winds of Knocknarea,
> When in ragged vapour they mutter night and day,
> Veering, fleeting, fickle, our loves and angers meet:

> But we bend together and kiss the quiet feet
> Of Kathleen-Ny-Hoolihan.[16]

After this, a second stanza has 'Weak and worn and weary the waves of Cummen Strand, / When the wind comes blowing across the hilly land', and a third 'Dark and dull and earthy the stream of Drumahair / When the rain is pelting out of the wintry air'. As before, this is a whirlwind tour of Sligo (Cummen Strand is the beach and townland west of Sligo, and on the south of Sligo harbour towards Strandhill), but each stop on the journey is a place to pay homage to Kathleen, the quasi-Marian embodiment of aboriginal nationality. In one of the earliest drafts, Yeats includes not Drumahair but the river in Sligo town itself:

> Dull and dark and earthy the Garavogue goes by,
> When the keen rains are slanting across the winter sky,
> Dull and dark and earthy our souls and bodies be,
> But pure as any white in the home of the Trinity
> Is our Kathleen Ni Houlihan.[17]

This is where John Sherman had set his fishing lines dreaming, not of a Virgin-like national goddess, but of a well-dowried future wife. And though Yeats is here trying his best to incorporate the town's river in the poem's overall vision, in the end it must give way to the 'dark and dull and earthy' element as found in the countryside. When he rewrote this poem for *The Secret Rose* a couple of years later, Yeats introduced 'the Green Land' (more usually 'the Green Lands', the fields along the coastline at Rosses Point), as well as Ballysodare, the small County Sligo town where the Pollexfens had their mill buildings, and where the poet claimed to have heard the song that he recycled as 'Down by the Salley Gardens'. By now, the place has taken a fully other-worldly cast:

> O heavy swollen waters, brim the Fall of the Oak trees,
> For the Grey Winds are blowing up, out of the clinging seas!
> Like heavy swollen waters are our bodies and our blood:
> But purer than a tall candle before the Blessed Rood
> Is Kathleen the Daughter of Hoolihan.[18]

As though the name 'Ballysodare', being in common currency, simply would not do, Yeats reaches for a version of its name in Irish, *Baile Easa Dara*, 'town of the oak-tree falls'. It is not until 1904 that the poem reaches a final form, as 'Red Hanrahan's Song About Ireland'; here, though, Ireland is entirely Sligo—Cummen Strand comes

---

[16] W. B. Yeats, in his story 'Kathleen-Ny-Hoolihan', *The National Observer*, 4 August 1894.

[17] These lines are found among several pages of drafts made by Yeats in a manuscript book begun in 1893, now in the collections of Boston College.

[18] W. B. Yeats, in his story 'Kathleen the Daughter of Hoolihan and Hanrahan the Red', in *The Secret Rose* (London: Lawrence & Bullen, 1897). *CW1*, 81.

back, now at the poem's beginning, where 'The old brown thorn trees break in two', Knocknarea returns with its own name (in 1897 it had been refigured as 'the high Cairn of Maive'), and the final stanza goes to where 'The yellow pool has overflowed high up on Clooth-na-Bare', and 'the wet winds are blowing out of the clinging air'.[19] A reader who recalls 'the Hosting of the Sidhe' now encounters this last location as a mountain rather than a person; but Yeats's topography remains decidedly Sligonian in either case.

'Red Hanrahan's Song About Ireland', though long in the gestation, proved to be the culmination of Yeats's specifically Sligo-centred verse, at least for the time being. As far as Irish localities and mythic locations were concerned, the early twentieth century saw the poet's concentration shift towards the County Galway of Lady Gregory, and away from the landscape of (at least part of) his youth. But instead of Sligo topography, Yeats continued to take imaginative possession of a family history that he associated especially with Sligo. This is made abundantly clear, of course, in the prose of *Reveries Over Childhood and Youth*, but it is a significant element in the poetry written by Yeats around the time of the First World War and afterwards. The best-known instance from these years is probably the introductory verses for the volume *Responsibilities*.[20] The poem effects a marriage between the Yeats and Pollexfen strands in the poet's lineage, and is ambitious in the extent of its backward reach towards ancestors in the Williamite Wars, but the last in its roll call of ancestors is the poet's grandfather, William Pollexfen, addressed as a 'silent and fierce old man'. Like the other family ghosts, Pollexfen is being asked for 'Pardon' in the poem, on the general grounds of the poet's lack of offspring in middle age, but also on the more specific matter of something said by his 'boyish lips': 'Only the wasteful virtues earn the sun'. Taking the measure of any retrospective embarrassment here is difficult, but there is no doubting the extent to which this sentiment is understood to outrage Pollexfen sensibilities ('wasteful virtues' were hardly likely to have featured in a family motto). Yet what is—and what isn't—'wasteful' is always close to the nub of Yeats's relationship with Sligo: not least, in the fictional John Sherman's adventures in—then away from, and finally back again to—Sligo town. In the County Sligo of folklore and mythic history, Yeats's fairies are determinedly 'wasteful' in relation to the world of modernity and commerce; and there is a sense, too, in which writing is feared to be as 'wasteful' of the poet Yeats's early life, as the profession of artist was in the life of his father (a father who, when he had to be in Sligo, preferred to hide away from the Pollexfens as much as possible).[21]

The discomfort of all this is not utterly left behind, even in the triumphalism of the introductory verses to *Responsibilities*; it can be, for Yeats, an essential element

---

[19]   *CW1*, 82.

[20]   'Pardon, old fathers ... ', *CW1*, 101.

[21] See remarks about the Pollexfens made by John Butler Yeats in a letter to his son of 25 April 1915: 'When they were all at home, as on Sundays, I always slipped away and spent the day at my uncles, taking care not to get home till they were all in bed. They all hated each other. How could it be otherwise, since they were not permitted by their strange code of morals to like each other?' (Richard J. Finneran, George Mills Harper, and William M. Murphy, eds., *Letters to W. B. Yeats* (London: Macmillan, 1977), Vol. 2, 312.

in the conditions that make for some of his best poetry. What is not immediately visible in the poems—not hidden from view exactly, but kept at work somewhere in the background—is often the autobiographical matter which Yeats spent an entire career processing. Once he was an established writer, he was aware that part at least of his poetry was understood to be about County Sligo; and his most famous poem remained, stubbornly, the early 'The Lake Isle of Innisfree' (somewhat to his irritation). Beyond the public dimension of Yeats's Sligo, though, and not (for the poet anyway) ever to be wholly dissociated from the meaning of Sligo, were his maternal relatives. Above all, Yeats's mother, Susan Yeats née Pollexfen, dead after years of illness in 1900, was a figure who offered the poet very little in the way of direct imaginative accessibility; instead, she stood behind the radically different mother figures (from Kathleen ni Houlihan to Lady Gregory) who could be spoken of and addressed in the medium of his lyric verse.[22] Great maker of elegies though he was, Yeats did not compose an elegy for his mother.

Yet this may not be completely true; for if there is a Yeatsian elegy for Susan Pollexfen, it is one in which she is not named. Instead, it is the poem that was eventually entitled 'In Memory of Alfred Pollexfen'; this poem (composed in 1916) is also, as it happens, the single lyric of Yeats's most intensely occupied with Sligo town.[23] Like much of his Sligo-centred work, this was written far away from the place it remembers: Yeats composed the poem while staying with Maud Gonne in the Normandy town of Colleville-sur-Mer (overlooking the stretch of French coast that would become better known, five years after the poet's own death, as Omaha Beach). Those who *are* named in the poem are the poet's grandfather William Pollexfen and his grandmother Elizabeth Pollexfen (both d.1892), his uncle George Pollexfen (d.1910), another uncle, John Pollexfen (d.1900), and—for ten lines of this thirty-nine-line poem—his uncle Alfred Pollexfen (d.1916).[24] The poem's first title (in both manuscript and print) was simply 'In Memory', and it does read as something of a group elegy, where the ranks of the departed have in common the town of Sligo.[25] Elizabeth is laid to rest with grandfather William 'In the grey stone tomb he made' (in St John the Baptist's Church, Sligo), where in due course Uncle George joins the pair, seen off with a ritual scattering of 'Acacia spray' by Masons who 'drove from miles

---

[22] An essential account of Susan Yeats's role in her son's writing and thought is Deirdre Toomey, 'Away', in Deirdre Toomey, ed., *Yeats and Women* (Basingstoke: Macmillan, 1997), 135–67.

[23] *CW1*, 156–7.

[24] A pioneering examination of the full Pollexfen cast in this poem (and beyond it) is William M. Murphy, "In Memory of Alfred Pollexfen': W. B. Yeats and the Theme of Family', *Irish University Review* 1/1 (Autumn, 1970), 30–47.

[25] Yeats was initially uncertain about the title for this poem: the earliest extant manuscript, which is dated 'August 1916' by Yeats, has 'In Memory Alfred Pollexfen', with the name heavily deleted to produce 'In Memory' (NLI, 13,587). A later manuscript, given to John Quinn, is initially entitled 'In Memory', but with 'Alfred Pollexfen' added later alongside (New York Public Library, Berg Collection). For *The Little Review* of June 1917 and *The Sphere* of 18 August 1917, the title is 'In Memory', and the poem retains this title in the Cuala Press *The Wild Swans at Coole* (1917). It appears as 'In Memory of Alfred Pollexfen' in *The Wild Swans at Coole* (London: Macmillan, 1918) and all subsequent printings.

away'. George is mourned as 'a melancholy man / Who had ended where his breath began'; but this is not the case for other departed Pollexfens:

> Many a son and daughter lies
> Far from the customary skies,
> The Mall and Eades's grammar school,
> In London or in Liverpool[.][26]

Liverpool locates the place where John Pollexfen, 'the sailor John', ended his days; but London locates a Pollexfen not named in the poem, Yeats's mother, Susan, who died there and is buried in Acton Cemetery. This, with the mention of a 'daughter', is the extent of the explicit mark made by Susan on the poem itself; yet the mark is there, and it is important. As the poem moves onwards, lamenting the 'sailor John', Yeats twice asks the rhetorical question of where his uncle is 'laid' (disingenuous as well as rhetorical, for the poet knows it is John who was laid to rest in Liverpool), before at last speaking of Alfred Pollexfen:

> Yesterday in the tenth year
> Since he who had been contented long,
> A nobody in a great throng,
> Decided he would journey home,
> Now that his fiftieth year had come,
> And 'Mr. Alfred' be again
> Upon the lips of common men
> Who carried in their memory
> His childhood and his family.

Uncle Alfred was 56 when he moved back to Sligo (it was the poet himself whose 'fiftieth year', by August of 1916, had come and gone). Imagining the return from wandering, Yeats conjures up a peaceful version of Odysseus's return to Ithaca, and to recognition by those 'common men' upon whose lips he keeps his name. The conjunction of 'childhood' and 'family' is telling and is in keeping with a central tenet of the poem, which is that the place of childhood is the true point of return as well as departure. In the poem's concluding lines, the 'family' expands to include women again, granting to them the ability to perceive and voice the 'cry' of the supernatural:

> At all these deathbeds women heard
> A visionary white sea-bird
> Lamenting that a man should die;
> And with that cry I have raised my cry.

It is here that Yeats identifies the 'cry' of his own elegiac voice with that heard by Pollexfen women (including in fact his own sister Lily (her proper name was that of

---

[26] *CW1*, 156.

their mother, Susan Mary, who had heard this banshee-like phenomenon shortly before Alfred's death). It is useful to recall how the incident of Yeats's infant brother's death in *Reveries Over Childhood and Youth*—a book completed only some eighteen months before the poem—is brought to a conclusion with the recollection that 'Next day at breakfast I heard people telling how my mother and the servant had heard the banshee crying the night before he died'.

By 1919, Yeats was able to dramatize an Alfred Pollexfen-like return for himself to Sligo—though this is in the medium of poetry only, and therefore in the nature of a 'reverie' rather than any reported fact. Again, though, there is the idea that return means recognition—recognition of family, and therefore recognition of the once lost and now returned child of that family:

> You heard that labouring man who had served my people. He said
> Upon the open road, near to the Sligo quay –
> No, no, not said, but cried it out – 'You have come again,
> And surely after twenty years it was time to come.'
> I am thinking of a child's vow sworn in vain
> Never to leave that valley his fathers called their home.[27]

'That valley' is perfectly specific, even though the context here makes it sound like the setting of some tale from folklore. As long ago as 1889, Yeats had written about 'wide, green Drumcliff valley, lying at the foot of Ben Bulben',[28] and this is also, of course, the locale in which, in his confident self-elegy 'Under Ben Bulben' (1938), the poet marks out his own grave.[29] But whereas the late poem finds a male Yeats ancestor to adduce when 'An ancestor was rector there / Long years ago', the valley was much more—and more productively, in imaginative terms—for the poet a place full of Pollexfens and Middletons, of women as well as men.

Sligo, too, was more generally for Yeats a place of early loss as well as late restitution. Some losses were straightforwardly familial—the poet's grandparents, his mother, and his brother—but others were more complex, functioning in the poetry as areas of reticence, and places known about but not straightforwardly faced or examined. Much as they have been received as pieces of marketable folklore and scenery, the best known of Yeats's earlier Sligo poems carry with them a burden of anxiety, of not-quite-belonging, as well as a feeling for fragility and precariousness. The supernatural is never far away, but neither is the world of commerce, of manufacture, of scratched toy ships, and of working ships at sea: beyond Sligo quay are London and

---

[27] Yeats, 'Under Saturn', *CW1*, 179–80.

[28] W. B. Yeats, 'Columkille and Rosses', *The Scots Observer*, 5 October 1889, reprinted in *The Celtic Twilight* (1893) as 'Drumcliff and Rosses'.

[29] W. B. Yeats, 'Under Ben Bulben', *Last Poems and Two Plays* (Dublin: Cuala Press, 1939), *CW1*, 333. David Fitzpatrick's comment is pertinent: 'In choosing Drumcliff, Yeats affirmed his link to a paternal ancestor he never knew, while sidestepping the awkward mercantile associations of his maternal lineage' (Fitzpatrick, 'Sligo', 78).

Liverpool, Indians and Japanese, even 'a ragged hat in Biscay Bay'.[30] Nevertheless, it is the Pollexfen women who hear the banshee in the form of 'a visionary white sea-bird', the harbinger of loss.

Even at the end of his career, Yeats could write a poem voiced for his mother's cousin, Henry Middleton, who occupied a house called 'Elsinore' at Rosses Point, which the poet knew well from his own childhood. Middleton's voice ends this poem with a boast:

> When every Sunday afternoon
> On the Green Lands I walk
> And wear a coat in fashion,
> Memories of the talk
> Of henwives and of queer old men
> Brace me and make me strong[.][31]

Here is perhaps the familial near miss for Yeats himself, the playmate of his youth who had never left home, and ended up in a holiday house behind a locked gate. Yeats's own family believed that Henry had been the model for the character of John Sherman, and it is true that the early novel already senses danger in too unquestioning an attachment to place, existing with no concern about being thought a '*gluggerabunthaun* and Jack o'Dreams'. Joseph Hone (whose source will have been a conversation either with the poet or with George Yeats) preserves an incident from 1919 (the same year as 'Under Saturn'):

> Henry was very good-looking, as dark as Willie, but with very blue eyes, and he had the poet's taste for a little colour in dress. He became a noted eccentric, and when Yeats visited Sligo with his young wife in 1919, he was living entirely alone at Elsinore behind a locked gate. Yeats climbed the wall and walked into the sitting room, littered with cheap novels, with a butter-churn in the middle. His cousin was there, beautifully dressed in a summer suit of white. 'You see,' he said, after they had exchanged a few words, 'that I am too busy to see anyone.'[32]

The absurdity is comic, if not wholly so. And the question Yeats voices for Henry Middleton in this poem, 'The wisdom of the people's gone, / How can the young go straight?', offers a glimpse of the final reduction to flatness of concerns of the Pollexfens and Middletons in the 'wide, green Drumcliff valley'. In his 1930s poetry, Yeats transforms this kind of grumbling into something altogether more arresting, original, and disturbing. And even in his early work the young poet had presented his relatives in Sligo town with a world antipathetic to both their values and their happiness, which was an other world of the young, and not the society of the old. As the 'One Burden' to

---

[30] Yeats, introductory lines to *Responsibilities*: 'Old merchant skipper that leaped overboard / After a ragged hat in Biscay Bay', *CW1*, 101.

[31] Yeats, 'Three Songs to the One Burden', *CW1*, 329.

[32] Joseph Hone, *W.B. Yeats: 1865–1939* (1943, 2nd edn 1962), 21–2.

the three songs of which the Henry Middleton poem is a part puts it, '*From mountain to mountain ride the fierce horsemen*': County Sligo, in all the depth and power of its mythic past, waits beyond the seaside villas of Rosses Point and the townhouses around the Garavogue. Yeats could do little about being known persistently as the poet of Sligo; but he was also, and more consequentially, the poet who left Sligo and who (at least until his eventual burial in Drumcliff churchyard) did not return there to stay.

CHAPTER 4

···

AMONG THE VICTORIANS

···

FRANCIS O'GORMAN

'No poet, no artist of any art, has his complete meaning alone.'[1] Imagine that this poem was read aloud in 1889, just after it was published. Who might the listener have thought its author? It begins:

> Autumn is over the long leaves that love us,
> And over the mice in the barley sheaves;
> Yellow the leaves of the rowan above us,
> And yellow the wet wild-strawberry leaves. (*CW1*, 14–15)

The two quatrains (however irregular) have, perhaps, something of the atmosphere of a Rossetti painting—*Veronica Veronese* (1872) or *The Roman Widow* (1874), it might be? The lines have a Pre-Raphaelite eye for natural detail ('the wet wild-strawberry leaves') and a fin de siècle sense of the falling of things, the waning of love. This could be another end-of-the-century poetic transformation of entropic fears, of which Thomas Hardy's 'The Darkling Thrush' (1900) is perhaps the most memorable. Rhythmically, some word clusters sound like Algernon Charles Swinburne (1837–1909) with his favoured anapaests ('of the wan[ing]', 'ere the sea[son]', 'With a kiss and a tear'), and the weaving together of lines through alliteration is not un-Swinburnian either ('the long leaves that love us' and, in the next stanza, 'weary and worn are our sad souls now'). Could this be a follower of the author of *Atalanta in Calydon* (1865)? Or maybe Swinburne himself? Perhaps there is something more generally Tennysonian about the decay and fall, the autumnal melancholy?

Who is it?

The answer, of course, is that 'The Falling of the Leaves' is by William Butler Yeats. The poem was included in the first printing of *The Wanderings of Oisin and Other Poems*,

---

[1] T. S. Eliot, 'Tradition and the Individual Talent', in *The Sacred Wood: Essays on Poetry and Criticism* (London: Methuen, 1960 [first published 1920]), 47–59 (49).

published in London by the English publisher Charles Kegan Paul (1828–1902) in 1889 and since 1895 presented as part of the *Crossways* section of Yeats's ordering of his early poetry. The poem's charm is in its rhythm and its convincing harmony between the season and the state of mind. Hardly does 'The Falling of the Leaves' seem a young man's poem with its sense of loss (Yeats was 24 years old), though that burden of failure, incompletion, and ending would remain with Yeats throughout his life, culminating in the extraordinary image of himself in 'The Circus Animals' Desertion' (1939) lying down where all the ladders start. Yet at the same time the voice here, in 1889, belongs to Yeats among the Victorians—to Yeats the Victorian.

By the point of the 'Introduction' to *The Oxford Book of Modern Verse* (1936), Yeats was telling his readers that the great movement of poets from 1900 onwards was one of rejection of 'Victorianism', a word that the OED records as first used in print in 1905. Emblematically, he said, this rejection involved spurning absinthe with black coffee. Aesthetically it meant, not least, 'a revolt against irrelevant descriptions of nature, [and] the scientific and moral discursiveness of *In Memoriam*'.[2] In one respect, the rather tangled and gestural 'Introduction'—in many ways a very peculiar piece of work—is a *réchauffé* of a feature of literary history, aired for instance in G. K. Chesterton's *The Victorian Age in Literature* (1913), which is now open to much qualification: that modern literature in the first half of the twentieth century came into existence as a rejection of that which was labelled 'Victorian'. But at least Yeats, at the age of 71, gave this argument some specificity. 'Victorianism', he proposed, involved too much 'rhetoric', an insufficient attention to the poet's personal vision and passion, and too many ideas. He was particularly clear on this last point. The poetry of opinion, like opinions in general, was never really to be Yeats's territory, a position he inherited from his father, John Butler Yeats (1839–1922). Once JBY had said in print that 'clamorous and confident argument are the resources of the intellectual half-breed',[3] and he was assured such argument was not, whatever else was true, the business of poetry: '[I]deas in poetry', JBY said in a firm letter to his son, 'must never be expressed, they can only be implied'. Ideas proper were the territory of 'mathematical precision', in turn 'forbidding alike eloquence and poetry'.[4] Although WBY had many complaints against his father, most recently analysed sympathetically by Colm Tóibín, he did not resist this parental view that opinions were accursed.[5] As far as Victorian poets were concerned, Matthew Arnold and Robert Browning (as well as Tennyson's scientific interests) were problematic; Rudyard Kipling

---

[2] 'Introduction', W.B. Yeats, ed., *The Oxford Book of Modern Verse, 1892–1935* (Oxford: Oxford University Press, 1936), ix.

[3] 'Why the Englishman is Happy', in John Butler Yeats, *Essays Irish and American, With an Appreciation by Æ* (Dublin: Talbot, 1918), 37–50 (48).

[4] *J. B. Yeats: Letters to His Son W.B. Yeats and Others*, ed. Joseph Hone (London: Faber, 1944), letter of '1906' to WBY, 91.

[5] See Colm Tóibín, *Mad, Bad, Dangerous to Know: The Fathers of Wilde, Yeats and Joyce* (London: Penguin, 2018).

was 'full of opinions' too, 'of politics, of impurities'.[6] Yeats in that Oxford 'Introduction' appeared to regard those nouns, where poetry was involved, as synonyms. The Victorians used poetry for discussions, he declared. What poetry *was about* was more important than the poetry. And using poetry for discussion, so far as Yeats rather oddly saw it in 1936, was what the moderns had not done.

Yet the values and assumptions of childhood and early youth, the patterns of reading and thought, the tastes and intellectual habits cannot be so easily set to one side. This is as true of Yeats as of others. For all his differences with so-called 'Victorianism', and for all the *statement* of his differences, Yeats found in some features of his youth assumptions about aesthetics that remained with him. This is not simply a matter of 'influence' but of an environment that brings out and confirms pre-existing inclinations and temperaments or provides a set of values that constitutes an intellectual and aesthetic foundation. The Victorian artists and writers among whom Yeats grew up coincided in important ways with exactly that which the young poet, dramatist, and champion of the Irish Literary Revival was coming to believe.

The most obvious point is what Yeats made of the Pre-Raphaelites. His father was a man of groups—indeed, an early artistic group in London comprising JBY, the animal painter John Trivett Nettleship (1841–1902), the poet and illustrator Edwin John Ellis (1848–1916), and the illustrator and journalist Sydney Hall (1842–1922), was called 'The Brotherhood'. JBY disliked the misleading name, as it happens, because The Brotherhood did not, unlike the Pre-Raphaelite Brotherhood, have fixed principles (however inconsistent the Pre-Raphaelites really were). But JBY's mutually supportive set of freethinking writers and artists must have helped the young Yeats recognize the importance of circles. And as far as the real Pre-Raphaelite Brotherhood was concerned, WBY had a broad admiration for what he thought their commitment to the beautiful image and to their Blake-like combination, especially for Dante Gabriel Rossetti (1828–82), of poetry and visual art. Rossetti, it might be added, twice invited JBY to call on him, but, always his own man, Yeats's father never went.[7] WBY, in *Autobiographies* (1926), remembered, nevertheless, his own youth as one that 'longed for pattern, for Pre-Raphaelitism, for an art allied to poetry' (p. 81). The Pre-Raphaelite Brotherhood's enchantment, particularly Rossetti's enchantment, with idealized beauty appealed. But the Ruskinian dimension of some of the Brotherhood's members, including John Everett Millais (1829–96) and William Holman Hunt (1827–1910)—an exactness of fidelity to the natural world—did not. Yeats would rarely be a writer interested in the sharply delineated presence of the real, for image and symbol had (almost) all his mind.

---

[6] Introduction to *The Oxford Book of Modern Verse*, xii.

[7] See William M. Murphy, *Prodigal Father: The Life of John Butler Yeats (1839–1922)* (Ithaca and London: Cornell University Press, 1978), 76.

Early Yeats translates something of (his version of) Pre-Raphaelitism into verse. *The Wanderings of Oisin* (1889), for example, is rich with a species of Pre-Raphaelite melancholy and is the medievalist poetry of high purposes clinched in exquisite visual images:

> We danced to where in the winding thicket
> The damask roses, bloom on bloom,
> Like crimson meteors hang in the gloom.
> And bending over them softly said,
> Bending over them in the dance,
> With a swift and friendly glance
> From dewy eyes: 'Upon the dead
> Fall the leaves of other roses,
> On the dead dim earth encloses:
> But never, never on our graves,
> Heaped beside the glimmering waves,
> Shall fall the leaves of damask roses.
> For neither Death nor Change comes near us,
> And all listless hours fear us,
> And we fear no dawning morrow,
> Nor the grey wandering osprey Sorrow'. (*CW1*, 363)

Yeats remembers in *Autobiographies* the modern decor of the Arts and Crafts Movement and of late Pre-Raphaelitism, which they used for the house in Bedford Park. 'We were to see De Morgan tiles, peacock-blue doors and the pomegranate and the tulip pattern of Morris' (p. 43), he recalled. Those wonders made the family realize how awful mid-Victorian interior design had been. *Oisin*, on paper, was another version of a similar aesthetic, with its patterns, attractive visuality, and sense of a higher world above the ordinary.

The search for ideal beauty, and the centrality of art as one's life's pursuit, were also what the young Yeats found in William Morris (1834–96), whose tulips and pomegranates were setting the fashion for modern middle-class urban taste. It was literally underneath a version of what WBY called 'Rossetti's *Pomegranate*'[8] that Yeats first met Morris properly, in Hammersmith after lectures for the Socialist League. (Yeats meant one of the versions of Rossetti's *Proserpine*.) Morris asked his young companion, with his striking appearance and deep commitment to writing, to contribute something on the Irish question for his socialist magazine *The Commonweal* (edited by Morris between 1885 and 1890), though nothing came of that plan.[9] An unlikely socialist, Yeats was nevertheless attracted to Morris's aesthetic priorities—plainly put, the making of beautiful things—and soon there was another family connection that involved a more literal sharing of the world of Morris's aesthetic. By the end of 1888, Lily Yeats was nearly every

[8] *CL1*, 22n.
[9] *CL1*, 23 and n.

day seeing May Morris (1862–1938), William's daughter, who was gradually becoming one of the country's leading embroiderers. Lily, a gifted embroiderer too, 'is to be a kind of assistant of hers', Yeats told Katharine Tynan on 4 December.[10] Lolly would presently join her. That was a connection that mattered for Lily's professional life, though it is true that the six years Lily worked for May were not easy. Miss Morris was demanding. Lily in due course would found the embroidery section of the Cuala Industries and, additionally, create many independent works. Her mature pieces were not Morrisian in any merely imitative sense but, for example, Lily's attentive figuring of the patterns of plants in 'Landscape at Night' (c.1934?) for the Cuala project (a silk embroidery that sold most recently at Whyte's on 29 September 2008), is a modern, even modernist, version of the same attentiveness to natural pattern that had helped make William Morris's name.

The shared ground between Yeats's poetry of the image, extended into emblem and symbol, and the Pre-Raphaelite Brotherhood's making of beautiful things, including poetic and visual images, never significantly changed. Yeats remained a poet, to use Sir Frank Kermode's terms, of the Romantic image to the end.[11] With the words commanded for his tombstone in Drumcliff churchyard and included in the very late 'Under Ben Bulben' (dated 4 September 1938), Yeats transformed the ordinary passer-by into a grand near-mythological figure in a final rendering of his magnificent drama of Ireland: 'Cast a cold eye / On Life, on death. / Horseman, pass by!' (CW1, 328). What readers leave the poem, and the grave, with is a powerful visual image, an attitude of mind summed up in a deed, the act of passing by. Here is at once the unmissable voice of late Yeats, yet also a final reinterpretation of what Yeats had, long ago, understood William Morris and some of the Pre-Raphaelites to have been doing: bringing poetry and the visual together, clinching a meaning beyond the merely material in a telling image.

One poet in the Rossetti circle troubled Yeats. And once, he troubled his father more. JBY did not mince words about Algernon Charles Swinburne, a poet who still divides opinion and peculiarly invites it. 'I detest the kind of man Swinburne is',[12] JBY wrote to his son in an undated letter of 1906—though it might be doubted that Swinburne could ever be thought to represent a 'kind' of man at all. Earlier, JBY had spotted an article in *The Athenæum* that quoted Swinburne's attack on Yeats's reading of Blake. The article, a review of the new edition of Swinburne's *William Blake*, first published in 1868, thought Swinburne 'needlessly petulant' in mentioning 'Some Hibernian commentator on Blake, if I remember a fact so insignificant'.[13] He was objecting to Yeats's (and Ellis's) assertion in *The Works of William Blake: Poetic, Symbolic, and Critical* (1893) that Blake's family was Celtic. The assertion was wrong—but that wasn't the point. JBY was outraged

[10] *CL1*, 111. For the Yeats sisters' embroideries, see Elizabeth Bergmann Loizeaux's 'Family Business at Dun Emer and Cuala: Collaboration, Contention, and Creativity', Chapter 30 in this volume.

[11] See Frank Kermode, *Romantic Image* (New York: Macmillan, 1957).

[12] *J. B. Yeats: Letters to His Son*, 96.

[13] 'William Blake: A Critical Essay', *The Athenæum*, 4111 (11 August 1906), 149–50 (149). There is something peculiar about this letter because JBY, writing on 2 July, asks, 'Have you seen this week's *Athenaeum*?' But the article in question only appeared in the edition of five weeks later.

by Swinburne's lofty dismissal of WBY: 'Byron's mantle of vulgarity', he told his son apparently on 2 July that year, after mischievously drawing his attention to the offending piece, 'has descended on Swinburne, for it is a kind of aristocratic insolence.'[14] It cannot have helped that Swinburne had been so violently Unionist, and generally anti-Irish, particularly after the Home Rule crisis that split the Liberals.[15]

About Swinburne's poetry itself, Yeats did not, nevertheless, leave much of a clue. He told Katharine Tynan, who was Irish, on 1 August 1887 that Morris and Rossetti as well as Swinburne were 'neo romantic London poets', who drew heroines that were 'powerful in conception[,] shadowy and unreal in execution'. These were, he added, men's rather than women's heroines, 'with no sep[a]rate life of their own'.[16] These are valuable comments. But it might be thought that this criticism, in addition, was Yeats talking obliquely of himself, since he was beginning seriously to work through what kind of character poetry should present—and if character was itself poetry's proper subject. Yeats's initial conclusions were not so different from his view of Swinburne. *Oisin*, after all, a couple of years later, certainly made the most of characters who were 'powerful in conception[,] shadowy and unreal in execution'. And, besides, the musical chiming of the Pre-Raphaelite Yeats—as in the poem with which I began this chapter—was not entirely, as I have said, unlike Swinburne. The charm of congruent sounds, adroitly configured, bound them. Yeats, it might be, felt more of a connection with Swinburne's conception of poetry than he could admit—perhaps because of Swinburne's oddness, his unclubbability, his notoriety after *Poems and Ballads* (1866), or his anti-Irishness? But that undeclared proximity between WBY and Swinburne would certainly explain what was going on in the episode that Lily recorded of meeting her brother on what is now O'Connell Street on 10 April 1909. She announced that Swinburne had died that very day. 'I know', Willie replied, 'and now I am king of the cats.'[17] '*King of the cats*'? WBY's sense of his Victorian precursors could be decisively competitive—and amusingly domestically phrased.

John Butler Yeats, his son reminded the reader of *Autobiographies*, 'disliked the Victorian poetry of ideas' (p. 66). But some Victorian ideas had, all the same, attracted Yeats's father. Indeed, shaped him: those of the scientific revolution. JBY was not only a committed reader of Auguste Comte, Charles Darwin, and T. H. Huxley; he was an evangelist for them. JBY had even tried, improbably, to persuade the Revd John Dowden (1840–1910)—brother of his friend Edward and later the Bishop of Edinburgh—of their merits.[18] Certainly, these were the writers that JBY associated with the origins of his own secularity and freethinking. Those evolutionists and Comte, the positivist, together with a host of other names, had, as for many Victorian readers, killed off any chance of the lawyer-become-painter turning (back?) to Christianity, even though JBY's own father

---

[14] J. B. Yeats: *Letters to His Son*, 92.
[15] See Francis O'Gorman, 'Swinburne and Ireland', *Review of English Studies*, 64 (2013), 454–74.
[16] *CL1*, 30, 31.
[17] J. B. Yeats: *Letters to His Son*, 51.
[18] See Murphy, *Prodigal Father*, 44.

had been a Church of Ireland minister. Susan Pollexfen's efforts to encourage her children to pray were rebuked by their father and church attendance vetoed in a manner that must have been exceptionally trying for Yeats's beleaguered mother.[19] And so Yeats himself had little living connection with his Sligo family's ancestral faith.

In *Autobiographies*, Yeats presents his reader with a portrait of the young artist as a Victorian scientist. It is a remarkable period piece. 'I had read Darwin and Wallace, Huxley and Haeckel,' Yeats recalls,

> and would spend hours on a holiday plaguing a pious geologist, who, when not at some job in Guinness's brewery, came with a hammer to look for fossils in the Howth cliffs. 'You know', I would say, 'that such-and-such human remains cannot be less, because of the strata they were found in, than fifty thousand years old.' 'O!' he would answer, 'they are an isolated instance.' And once when I pressed hard my case against Ussher's chronology, he begged me not to speak of the subject again. 'If I believed what you do', he said, 'I could not live a moral life.' (*CW*3, 77)[20]

Yeats is partly showing off his precociousness. And he is accidentally revealing his lack of sensitivity, which apart from anything else dogged his relationship with his father. But the poet, among the Victorians, is also framing himself in near-clichéd cultural terms: the secular, scientifically informed, and geologically aware assailer of biblical chronology. It is a story repeated across many lives in the age of Victoria. And the intellectual move recounted here is of its time too: Yeats perceives in the failure of evidence to confirm that the Genesis narration is historically reliable grounds to dispense with Judaeo-Christianity altogether. It is a familiar narrative of nineteenth-century religion in relation to science (though not, of course, the only one).

Yeats, in his own mind a child of the Darwinian turn, had other reasons, for sure, to dispose of Christianity. His Protestant Ascendancy background and the fact that JBY was an absentee landlord hardly made him the most obvious of individuals to become associated, however changefully, with Irish nationalism; to fall in love with Maud Gonne; to write, say, *Cathleen ni Houlihan* (1902) with Lady Gregory; or to involve himself with the preparations for the '98 centenary. A major advantage to becoming absorbed by magical thinking and, among other things, the Hermetic Order of the Golden Dawn, was that they allowed Yeats, and others, to bypass both Protestantism and Catholicism (while retaining some sense of the other-worldly). And so, bypassing the doctrinally divided Christianity, WBY could avoid the often limiting political assumptions both denominations inevitably involved in an Ireland unfree.[21]

---

[19] Ibid., 71–2.

[20] James Ussher was Bishop of Armagh, then Primate of All Ireland, and the author of *Annales Veteris Testamenti, a prima mundi origine deducti, una cum rerum Asiaticarum et Aegyptiacarum chronico, a temporis historici principio usque ad Maccabaicorum initia product* (1650), which offered an account of the age of the earth and its early history deduced from scripture.

[21] This statement does not mean to overlook Catholic loyalism or Protestant nationalism.

And yet that absorption with magical thinking, theosophy, and the occult was not only politically enabling. It was in part a Victorian story too. In one sense the history of Yeats's spiritual life—a placeholder term that is in many ways open to objection—is a version of a familiar Victorian narrative. The poet grew up without Christianity, which Comte, Huxley, and Darwin had extinguished for his father and continued to make impossible for him. But Yeats struggled, thereafter, to live a wholly secular, materialist life, because his inclinations were to recognize something more than materiality in experience, to believe in something above the simply empirical. The spiritually unsatisfied Yeats turned, as a result, to mystical symbols, the occult, esoteric religious practice, and magical thinking. These filled the gap, or tried to, left by the scientific revolution, and were affirmed by others Yeats cared about including Maud Gonne and George Russell (AE)—and eventually by George, his wife, who would prove to be a medium by which the unknown instructors contacted him. Others in a not-unrelated theological situation to Yeats—Sir Arthur Conan Doyle, Sir Oliver Lodge, Ruskin for a short while, Alfred Russel Wallace, and many far less distinguished names—had turned not to the hermetic societies but more plainly to spiritualism. In trying to fill in the space left by what they perceived as a now discredited Christianity, they had populated the remarkable number of late-century spiritualist societies, libraries, and private seances in London and beyond. But the direction of travel was related. Victorian secularism needed, from those who espoused versions of it but could not be wholly satisfied with what they espoused, other faiths and hopes. Part of the history of Christianity in the nineteenth century, for those who could—to whatever extent—no longer believe, is one of substitution: whether George Eliot's duty, Arnold's doctrine of conduct, Huxley's mitigation of human pain, Frederic Harrison's religion of humanity, the commitment of many to the seance, or Yeats's theosophy. WBY was unusual, perhaps, only in that he took his magical thinking *so* seriously and to the extent in which it dominated, even determined, his life and art. But in essence it was a Victorian period narrative.

There is another way of thinking about Yeats among the Victorians. That is to return to the topic with which I began and to consider more fully how reading Yeats in the nineteenth century might have felt. New poems usually invite as their first, though not only, comparison the work of others writing at the same time. Picking up a volume of new verse, the alert reader's first question is unlikely to be: is this going to be as good as Milton? Even less is it likely to be: will Milton's cultural and aesthetic context be the first environment in which to place this new volume? First judgements—both in terms of evaluation and interpretation—normally belong to their moment, though that is naturally not to say that exceptional writing, the luminous individual talent, does not require the reader to make comparisons with the tradition. But taking as a working assumption the fact that most new poetry is first assessed, and understood, in relation to what others are doing at the same time, Yeats emerges, among the Victorians, in a way that is distinctive. Some of his early poetry was first written and read in relation to a small circle in part of 1890s London, one that left behind it a material trace. And so it becomes possible to ask: how might first readers have received, how understood, Yeats as the poet who contributed to Elkin Mathews's *The Book of the Rhymers' Club* (1892), and its successor, *The Second Book of the Rhymers' Club*, in 1894? How, in those specific publishing contexts, does Yeats appear?

The Rhymers' Club had neither a fixed membership nor a fixed location. Sometimes known as the Rhymers of the Cheshire Cheese, the members met often in the historic Fleet Street inn The Cheshire Cheese, as had Charles Dickens and, allegedly, Dr Johnson before them (Johnson's house in Gough Square is only a few metres away). Sometimes the Club met in the Café Royal on Regent Street and at other times in private houses. The members kept no minutes, had no formal constitution, and composed no formal manifesto. In these respects, the Club was comparable to JBY's Brotherhood: it was not defined by an official statement of purpose. But its informal purpose, beyond being a dining club, was clear enough: poetry. Private, occasional, unofficial, the Club nonetheless published two volumes of poetry, one from Elkin Mathews, and the other from the merged Mathews & Lane.

The membership of the Club as recorded in the first volume of poetry—*The Book of the Rhymers' Club*—was made up of the poet and fiction writer Ernest Dowson (1867–1900); Edwin Ellis; the translator and civil servant G. A. Greene (1853–1921); the poet and critic Lionel Johnson (1867–1902); the writer and poet Richard Le Gallienne (1866–1947); the poet and librarian Victor Plarr (1863–1929); the poet and socialist Ernest Radford (1857–1919); the Anglo-Welsh writer and editor Ernest Rhys (1859–1946); the Irish poet and translator T. W. Rolleston (1857–1920); the poet and editor Arthur Symons (1865–1945); the Irish playwright and poet John Todhunter (1839–1916); and William Butler Yeats. Others were there on and off too, as Yeats remembered in *Autobiographies*: the Scottish poet John Davidson (1857–1909); the Arts and Crafts designer and writer Selwyn Image (1849–1930); and the designer and editor Herbert Horne (1864–1916). The poet William Watson (1858–1935), WBY said, 'joined but never came', while 'Francis Thompson [poet, 1859–1907] came once but never joined' (p. 165). Oscar Wilde, whose parents were acquainted with JBY, occasionally attended the private house meetings, as *Autobiographies* recounts.

John Sloan observes that the Club was 'essentially a gathering of Celts'.[22] But it was not consistently. There were Irish members, if largely London-based, and representation from Scotland and Wales. But the Rhymers was not a group, as it grew, to be defined by national/cultural identities. Neither was it, as the dates above reveal, quite a 'tragic generation', as Yeats would call the Rhymers in the title of Book IV of *Autobiographies*, though some of its members did indeed suffer early death or ill health.[23] The description tells us more about Yeats's preference for thinking of himself in relation to movements, generalities, and, indeed, generations than about a consistent feature of a group of

---

[22] John Sloan, *John Davidson: First of the Moderns: A Literary Biography* (Oxford: Clarendon Press, 1995), 59.

[23] On this topic, see Robert B. Shaw, 'Tragic Generations', *Poetry*, 175 (2000), 210–19, and Karl Beckson, 'The Legends of the Rhymers' Club: A Review-Article', *Victorian Poetry*, 19 (1981) 397–412. The latter is a review of the significant book by Norman Alford, *The Rhymers' Club: Poets of the Tragic Generation* (Victoria BC: Cormorant, 1980).

diverse men. Although the membership was fluid and the Club not exclusive, the publications were solid things. And it might be that, for some readers, *The Book of the Rhymers' Club* was their first meeting with Yeats.

How, then, might he have looked? A first answer would be that the volume makes Yeats feel pensive with the melancholy of the late Pre-Raphaelites, his poetry freighted with the sadness of lonely, deracinated wanderers. There is something of the London, late-century reinterpretation of the flâneur here, recast as a kind of sad homelessness. The Yeats poems for the first book, I need to say, are: 'A Man who dreamed of Faeryland'; 'Father Gilligan'; 'Dedication of "Irish Tales" '; 'A Fairy Song'; 'The Lake Isle of Innisfree'; and 'An Epitaph'. This is a volume, as a whole, with recurrent motifs of isolated individuals, night skies, far-off stars, tragic ends. And those elements of early Yeats feel peculiarly accented by their context. Lionel Johnson's 'By the Statue of King Charles the First at Charing Cross' famously presents, with austere clarity, a memory of Hubert Le Sueur's equestrian statue in Trafalgar Square in the depth of a London night: fair, fatal, alone, with but the stars for company. 'Sombre and rich, the skies', Johnson begins,

> Great gloom, and starry plains.
> Gently the night wind sighs;
> Else a vast silence reigns. (p. 4)[24]

This kind of haunting emptiness, a sense of precious things past, is a consistent feature of *The Book of the Rhymers' Club*. Richard Le Gallienne, whose 'What of the Darkness?' is the first poem in the anthology, had already set the scene of isolation and aloneness: 'What of the darkness? Is it very fair?' he asked; 'Are there great calms and find ye silence there?'[25] Other poems added more metaphorical darkness, including George Greene's 'The Pathfinders', with its further apprehension of the enormousness and enormity of the vacant skies. 'Full of world-weariness,' Greene writes, in a version of the *In Memoriam* stanza,

> and of the sense
> Of unachievement, lies the toiler down
> Who hath made smooth the way, but sees the crown
> Fade in the sunset far through depths immense …[26] (p. 18)

Clearly, the discussions in The Cheshire Cheese involved the exchange of ideas about this kind of exhaustion, of energies faltering and failing. Yeats's contribution to this

---

[24] *The Book of the Rhymer's Club* (London: Elkin Mathews, 1892), 4.The relationship between this poem and central London is discussed in Francis O'Gorman, 'Lionel Johnson and Charing Cross', *Journal of Pre-Raphaelite Studies*, 24 (2015), 78–96.

[25] *Book of the Rhymers' Club*, 3.

[26] *Book of the Rhymers' Club*, 18.

strand of thinking, which was not confined to the Club, was erotic. 'I dreamed that one had died in a strange place', Yeats wrote in 'An Epitaph' (elsewhere 'A Dream of Death'):

>Near no accustomed hand,
>And they had nailed the boards above her face,
>   The peasants of that land,
>And, wondering, planted by her solitude
>   A cypress and a yew.
>I came, and wrote upon a cross of wood,
>   —Man had no more to do—
>'She was more beautiful than thy first love,
>   This lady by the trees,'
>And gazed upon the mournful stars above
>   And heard the mournful breeze.[27]

Extracted from its Rhymers context (it had already been published in *The National Observer* on 12 December 1891), the poem reads like Yeats thinking of Maud Gonne, whom he had first met on 30 January 1889, projecting himself—as in 'When you are old' (1892)—into a future of mournful retrospection. But in *The Book of the Rhymers' Club*, the poem reads more as Yeats's contribution to the circle's melancholy note of loss and bereavement, his own version of solitude, his own account of Victor Plarr's 'small strange touch of human pain' ('Twilight-Piece') or of Richard Le Gallienne's 'Sunset in the City'. That is a poem which ends:

>… Within the town the lamps of sin are flaring,
>   Poor foolish men that know not what ye are!
>Tired traffic still upon his feet is faring—
>   Two lovers meet and kiss, and watch a star.[28]

The reading context places Yeats as part of a club: a shared enterprise or conversation, in which each poet has a distinctive version of the theme, and a mood, which is not merely their own.

Loneliness, empty skies, star-watching, and loss are one thing, but elected solitude is another. That too is a feature of *The Book of the Rhymers' Club*, with its flirtations with being out of time. And, in this context, one of Yeats's most memorable early poems, 'The Lake Isle of Innisfree', reads differently in its Cheshire Cheese environment (it was first published in *The National Observer* on 13 December 1890). Peter McDonald has written engagingly of the poetic and intellectual frame of 'The Lake Isle', of which we have a recording of the poet reading.[29] But, in his exploration of the literary significance of other

---

[27] *Book of the Rhymers' Club*, 88, and *CW1*, 42.
[28] *Book of the Rhymers' Club*, 86 and 87.
[29] See Peter McDonald, 'Yeats's Early Lake Isles', *Review of English Studies*, 70:294 (2019),https://doi. org/10.1093/res/hgy128 (accessed 18 Feb. 2019). Also see https://www.bbc.co.uk/news/av/uk-northern-ireland-32814695/archive-wb-yeats-reads-the-lake-isle-of-innisfree (accessed 19 Feb. 2019).

lake poems, McDonald does not mention how the poem might have seemed when it was read in *The Book of the Rhymers' Club*. Assuming for a moment that a reader would have taken each poem consecutively, how does 'The Lake Isle' seem?

First, the *Book* has a cluster of 'retreat' poems in multiple forms. 'By the Statue of King Charles' is an example: the poet, encountering Le Sueur's work, is out of the diurnal, safe from others, just as the King is elevated both literarily, on the pedestal, and, figuratively, as riding above time and within the stars. There is, here, an envisaging of a haven. And there are others. Ernest Dowson's 'Carmelite Nuns of the Perpetual Adoration' contemplates other-worldly detachment in a Catholic sorority: 'These heed not time', Dowson writes, 'their nights and days they make / Into a long, returning rosary.'[30] The poem is a strikingly static recollection of those who have left the quotidian world, becoming enclosed in a new order of being (puns intended). And, more closely to Yeats's imagining of being out of mainstream time, is George Greene's sonnet 'Arts Lough, Glenmalure, Co. Wicklow'. This reads, in its entirety, as follows:

> Lone lake half lost amidst encircling hills,
>   Beneath the imprisoning mountain-crags concealed;
>   Who liest to the wide earth unrevealed;
> To whose repose the brief and timorous rills
>
> Bring scarce a murmur:—thou whose sight instils
>   Despair; o'er whom his dark disdainful shield
>   Abrupt Clogherna 'gainst the sun doth wield,
> And thy dim face with deepening shadow fills:
>
> O poet soul! companionless and sad,
>   Tho' half the daytime long a death-like shade
>   Athwart thy depths with constant horror lies,
>
> Thou art not ever in dejection clad,
>   But showest still, as in a glass displayed,
>   The limitless unfathomable skies.[31]

A different kind of lake from Innisfree, this is still a remote place that Greene is imagining, a space out of the ordinary world where they marry in churches. Here is a land, or rather a water, that is living its own private life and reflecting, literally, the depths of great skies, part of the common imaginative currency of *The Book of the Rhymers' Club* more generally. There is, for sure, a political dimension that is not WBY's (or any nationalist's). That is because the valley was the location of the Battle of Glenmalure in 1580, where Irish Catholic forces defeated an English army under the 14th Baron Grey de Wilton, and of bloody events in 1798: the constant horror of the deep, the shield, the dejection, and death mark a violent past the lake still remembers beneath its unruffled surface.

---

[30] *Book of the Rhymers' Club*, 10.
[31] *Book of the Rhymers' Club*, 62.

The pattern of withdrawal from the present moment, though, is sustained. The next poem in the volume, that which begins on the recto page to Greene's 'Arts Lough' on the verso, only adds to this accumulating sense of isolated places and isolated people: Lionel Johnson's 'In Falmouth Harbour'. Not about a now tranquil lake with a bloody history but a retreat of calm water on the south Cornish coast, Johnson's conception of the harbour is, rather like Gerard Manley Hopkins's 'Heaven-Haven' (1864), of a guarded, protected place. 'A charm is on the silent bay,' Johnson writes, 'Charms of the sea, charms of the land. / Memories of open wind convey / Peace to this harbour strand.'[32] Whether the Rhymers felt themselves, in the wood-panelled first floor room of The Cheshire Cheese, in respite from the world outside, their first volume ranged through imagined spaces, out of ordinary life, just as they were literally detached, when in the pub, from the commercial vibrancy of Fleet Street, just outside the door.

It was Fleet Street itself, and its commerce, that provided Yeats, he said later in 1932, with the prompt for 'The Lake Isle of Innisfree'. A little fountain in a shop window, Yeats told the BBC, reminded him of how far he was from Sligo. In his first draft, in a letter to Katharine Tynan on 21 December 1888, however, he did not mention this; only a man who, whenever in trouble, dreamt of going away 'to live alone on that Island'.[33] Perhaps, as John Kelly remarks, the poem was partly a response to Tynan's own 'To Inishkea' (1891), beginning 'I'll arise and go to Inishkea, / Where many a one will weep with me …'.[34] But if Yeats's 'The Lake Isle of Innisfree' began in a conversation with her, the poem was later to read as a conversation with others. Published first on 13 December 1890 in *The National Observer*, Yeats's 'The Lake Isle', in *The Book of the Rhymers' Club*, read as another version of the volume's enchantment with withdrawal, with escape from daily life and private spaces out of time. It ceases to be merely an independent poem but becomes legible, as perhaps it began, as one that belongs in a circle, as part of a group—a club poem—speaking to, as well as listening to, Johnson's Falmouth, Dowson's convent, and Greene's lough (which WBY takes out of history and politics).

No wonder, taking all of this into account, *The Saturday Review* remarked in its review of *The Book of the Rhymers' Club* on 19 March 1892 that 'there is no need to individualize the claims of the Rhymers. They sing in good accord, to the avoidance of sharp lines of diversity, adopting, as it were, a deep autumnal tone, "sweet though in sadness".'[35] Despite their lack of official programme, the Rhymers had a clear identity and connection between themselves after all.

And there is one further, and surprising, element of reading Yeats in the first book of the Rhymers' Club. And that is, despite what I have said about Yeats's substitution of his family's Christianity for theosophy, his appearance among the company of the Rhymers as—a Christian poet. Dowson and Johnson gave to *The Book of the Rhymers'*

[32] *Book of the Rhymers' Club*, 64.

[33] *CL1*, 121.

[34] *CL1*, 121 n. See Katharine Tynan, *Ballads and Lyrics* (London: Kegan Paul, Trench, Trübner, 1891), 60–1.

[35] 'Recent Verse', *Saturday Review*, 73 (19 March 1892), 341–2 (342).

Club its notable strand of devotional, sometimes obviously Catholic, or Anglo-Catholic, Christianity: Dowson's 'The Nuns of the Perpetual Adoration', Johnson's 'By the Statue of King Charles' and 'A Burden of Easter Vigil', Victor Plarr's wistful memory of a Church more dedicated to the suffering of the ordinary. 'For once', Plarr ends this sharp-edged poem,

> 'twas thought the Gates of Pearl
> Best opened to the poor that trod
> The paths of the meek peasant girl
> Who bore the Son of God.[36]

And immediately after Plarr's 'In a Norman Church', as the reader turns from page 37 to 38, he or she finds W. B. Yeats's 'Father Gilligan (A legend told by the people of Castleisland, Kerry)', first published in *The Scots Observer* on 5 July 1890, and more usually called 'The Ballad of Father Gilligan' (*CW1*, 46–7).

At one level, this moving poem is a part of Yeats's Celtic Twilight project: an effort to record the folk tales, memories, and legends of rural Ireland. 'Father Gilligan' is another old song resung—and so much so, in fact, that Yeats was accused of plagiarism.[37] But in the context of *The Book of the Rhymers' Club*, the poem feels different because it cannot be detached from the other Christian texts constellated around it. An old priest, in Yeats's ballad, is summoned to the deathbed of a parishioner, but he is wearied by his pastoral demands. He remains in his chair and falls asleep. Waking, the priest realizes with dismay that he has not fulfilled his clerical responsibilities and rushes to the old man's house, only to be greeted with surprise that he has come once more. The old man died at peace, he is told, after Father Gilligan had left. The last two stanzas are the revelation, as the priest speaks:

> 'He who hath made the night of stars
>   For souls who tire and bleed
> Sent one of His great angels down
>   To help me in my need.
>
> 'He who is wrapped in purple robes,
>   With planets in His care,
> Had pity on the least of things
>   Asleep upon a chair.'[38]

There is more of the volume's concentration on solitary experience and more, again, of the night sky, the stars. Yet Yeats here, in the context of *The Book of the Rhymers' Club*, is also a writer we do not entirely recognize: not the theosophist or occultist but the poet

---

[36] *Book of the Rhymers' Club*, 37.
[37] See 'Father Gilligan' by 'A Lover of Originality', *The Academy*, 12 March 1892, 255.
[38] *Book of the Rhymers' Club*, 40. The minor differences in later versions are recorded in *VP*, 134.

enchanted, so it seems, by the benign care for a Catholic priest of the God of Jehovah. And this Yeats—so different from the magical-thinking representative of the Protestant Ascendency—is all the more apparent because of the other Christian or at least ecclesiastical texts that are beside him in Elkin Mathews's volume. The Yeats of the Rhymers' Club, talking about poetry in the company of other men, was writing, as his father had drawn and painted, in an atmosphere of mutual debate, and the sense he makes in 1892 is in part the sense his companions make.

There is, of course, a difference between how Yeats might have been read in 1892 and the Yeats that we know beyond that local moment. But reading happens in time and place, and meanings are partly dependent on both. Yeats seems most peculiarly in Victorian company in the wood-panelled room of The Cheshire Cheese. Alongside his complicated and changing relationship with Irish nationalism (placed at different times on the long line between Isaac Butt, his father's friend, and physical force Fenianism); alongside the young Yeats in Holland Park yearning to hold something from Sligo in his hand (see *Autobiographies*, p. 31), there is also Yeats on Fleet Street. It is one of the best ways of understanding Yeats among the Victorians, where the ladder started.

CHAPTER 5

....

LADY GREGORY

Patronage, collaboration, mythopoeia

....

NICHOLAS GRENE

'I have lost the friend who was my sole adviser for the greater part of my life, ... the one person who knew all that I thought and did.'[1] Yeats's reaction to the death of Lady Gregory in 1932 was no mere hyperbole of bereavement. The thirty-six years of his unbroken relationship with her was indeed one of the deepest friendships and the most important working partnership of his life. When he first contemplated the possibility of her dying, after she had suffered a cerebral haemorrhage in 1909, he recorded his feelings in a much-quoted passage in his journal:

> She has been to me mother, friend, sister and brother. I cannot realize the world without her – she brought to my wavering thoughts steadfast nobility. All day the thought of losing her is like a conflagration in the rafters. Friendship is all the house I have.[2]

The metaphor of the house threatened with destruction by fire is multiply suggestive. For Yeats, Gregory was always associated with Coole, with the shelter and peace he found in extended summer visits there, the sense of assured and supported intimacy in gracious surroundings. At a literal level, it provided him with a comfortable home very different from his cheerless rented rooms in Euston. The house was eventually to become a key icon within his poetic imaginary, the epitome of culture grounded in tradition. But it was the relationship with Gregory that animated all that and gave it meaning.

---

[1] W. B. Yeats to Shri Purohit Swami, 6–7 June [1932], *CL InteLex* #5683; *Life* 2, 4 38.

[2] *Mem*, 160–1. The final phrase supplies the title for John Kelly's detailed and illuminating essay, '"Friendship is All the House I Have": Lady Gregory and Yeats', in Ann Saddlemyer and Colin Smythe, eds., *Lady Gregory: Fifty Years After* (Gerrards Cross: Colin Smythe, 1987), 179–257.

They had met first in 1894 at the London home of Lord Morris, Gregory's Galway neighbour, but their friendship only began in 1896, when she invited Yeats and Arthur Symons to lunch at Coole, when they were staying with Edward Martyn at nearby Tillyra.[3] From then on, Yeats was a frequent guest at Queen Anne's Mansions, Gregory's London pied-à-terre, and several months of each summer from 1897 up to his marriage in 1917 were spent at Coole. The two collaborated initially on the folklore which Gregory collected in the neighbourhood around Coole and gave to Yeats for editing and publication. And, of course, they worked together on the Irish Literary Theatre project from its first inception to its development into the Abbey Theatre, of which they were lifelong directors. Apart from the running of the theatre, Yeats and Gregory collaborated on a whole series of the plays staged by the national theatre movement in its first years, most famously *Cathleen ni Houlihan* (1902). Most of these were published as Yeats's work, but they were more or less jointly authored. Already in 1900, the dedicatory poem to *The Shadowy Waters*, addressed to Gregory, celebrated the Seven Woods of Coole as the inspiring environment for his spirit drama. She was to appear as addressee and subject of many later poems, as an unnamed 'friend'. Coole, with its proximity to Yeats's own tower at Ballylee, was made the subject of the two great anticipatory elegies, 'Coole Park, 1929', and 'Coole and Ballylee, 1931'. After Gregory's death she was incorporated into the retrospective celebration of their shared cultural enterprise, 'The Municipal Gallery Re-visited'.

Their relationship was never exactly that of equals but existed within a complex and shifting power dynamic of status and authority. When they first met, Gregory had an established social position: as the widow of Sir William Gregory, former Governor of Ceylon, she moved at ease in London among titled civil servants, politicians, and writers. She was thirteen years senior to Yeats, and in taking up her 'young countryman' she could promote him and his work by introducing him into her own circles.[4] At the same time, his genius as a writer (of which she was convinced) gave him a sort of superiority; her patronage was given in the cause of his work and to this she was prepared to subordinate her own interests. That may have been one of the reasons she did not claim full credit for her share of the writings she co-authored with him. It was his career, his reputation which was all important. They were most nearly on equal terms in the management of the Abbey, in constant contact over the day-to-day running of the theatre, negotiating their differences of opinion with full acknowledgement of the other's position. In later years, when Yeats was (relatively) rich and famous, Gregory struggling with illness and the increasingly unviable Coole estate, it was he who took on the supportive role. In his poetry, however, she was monumentalized as the presiding spirit of Coole, doyenne of the Revival. The aim of this chapter is to track the changing pattern of relationship between Yeats and Gregory from patronage through collaboration to mythopoeia.

---

[3] For details, see *Diaries*, 32, 118.
[4] *Diaries*, 131

POOR BOY

Gregory, as Yeats's patron in the 1890s, set about caring for him and feeding him, acting as his promoter and agent, adviser and confidante: 'Poor boy, he has had a hard struggle.'[5] The tone of tender protective compassion here places the poet in the position of surrogate son, like Paul Harvey, also a 'poor boy' in the *Diaries*.[6] The orphaned Harvey had been semi-adopted by Gregory with the help of Henry James, and assisted into government service where he had a highly successful diplomatic career. Gregory steered him away from an unwise early marriage and, by judicious invitations to Coole, managed to set him up with an appropriate bride instead, her own niece Ethel Persse. He was a constant companion to her in the years immediately after Sir William's death—'Paul is very dear to me'—and even after his marriage he would drop in to her late in the evening when 'very tired & depressed' after a long day at the War Office during the Boer War.[7] Yeats, only four years older than Harvey, invited the same sort of quasi-maternal care.

It was obvious to Gregory that the poet was in need of material help before anything else. She was appalled by his living conditions: 'He makes his own fire in the morning & cooks eggs & bacon – & has a chop for dinner.' And she records with gratification after his first extended stay with her in Galway, 'I am bound to say that his healthiness of mind & body increased while at Coole'.[8] That was also no doubt one of the motives for inviting him to lunch and dinner so often when in London; in one period, for instance, February to March 1899, he ate with her no less than twelve times.[9] When back at Coole she sent him hampers, port, pheasants, unaccustomed luxuries for Woburn Buildings, all gratefully acknowledged—'No body has ever shown me such kindness'.[10] In London, also, she did her best to improve his life, having curtains made up for his rooms, making his breakfast, and lighting his fire when he was ill.[11]

It was, however, the promotion of his work that was paramount. Gregory began collecting folklore originally at least in part inspired by his interests in the area. When they first met in 1894, she had already read *The Celtic Twilight* and thought it 'the best thing he has done'.[12] In 1897 she gifted him with the substantial body of material she had collected and typed up, and helped him to get the articles based on it published. Characteristically, when pressed by the editor of *The Nineteenth Century* for a folklore article of her own, she stepped aside and had one by Yeats taken instead. Having the

---

[5] *Diaries*, 150–1.

[6] 'Poor boy, he has come out of his troubles with a kind of gentleness, rectitude & goodness quite uncommon' (*Diaries*, 37). For the comparison of Harvey to Yeats as surrogate sons for Gregory, see also Kelly, 'Friendship is All the House I Have', 194-5.

[7] *Diaries*, 14, 236.

[8] *Diaries* 151.

[9] See John Kelly, *W. B. Yeats a Chronology* (Basingstoke: Palgrave Macmillan, 2003), 56–7.

[10] WBY to Lady Gregory [1 November 1897], *CL InteLex*; *CL2*, 137.

[11] *Diaries*, 160, 237.

[12] *Diaries*, 327.

right connections no doubt helped. Yeats was pleased to have the piece accepted, '& has been told that there is no use in approaching the XIXth Century unless you have a title yourself or are introduced by someone with a title'.[13] All those dinner invitations, as well as a way of feeding Yeats, were occasions to make the poet known to her well-placed London friends. She was, of course, involved in the plans for the Irish Literary Theatre (ILT) from the start, but those plans might not have got off the ground without the as- sistance of W. E. H. Lecky, 'a very good and sincere friend' of Gregory who was one of the first guarantors of the ILT and, as a Unionist MP for Dublin University, promoted the clause in the 1898 Local Government Bill which allowed its performances to go ahead.[14]

Yeats, from very early in their acquaintance, poured out his heart to Gregory about his love for Maud Gonne. She was wise enough to realize that there was no means of deflecting this passion, as she had managed to reroute Harvey's affections away from an unsuitable love object, but she registered her disapproval in her diaries: 'he talked much of Miss Gonne – all the old story – poor boy, it interferes sadly with his work'; 'Poor boy – he is in a tangle'; 'I am afraid she is playing with him, from selfishness – & vanity'.[15] She did strongly counsel him not to get involved in Gonne's agitations in famine-stricken Mayo and read him a lecture on the wickedness of urging the hungry people to steal.[16] Many years later, she was to listen sympathetically to Yeats's tale of love for Iseult Gonne, and her approval was important in his decision to marry George Hyde-Lees. Her re- ward came in the terms in which Yeats, after a rocky start to the marriage, expressed his new-found happiness: 'My wife is a perfect wife, kind, wise, and unselfish. I think you were such another young girl once. She has made my life serene and full of order.'[17] This echoes a heartfelt tribute from 1898 to Gregory's 'great kindness, your most watchful & patient goodness. You have been to me a well of peace and happiness.'[18] The right wife had been found for Yeats at last, and she turned out to be a young Gregory lookalike.

Gregory not only supplied him with material comforts, actively promoted his work, and listened sympathetically to the troubles of his love life; she also gave him sums of money through the early years of their friendship. He had made a number of efforts to return these 'loans', and was taken aback to discover the total was £500: 'It was a shock to find I owed so much.'[19] It was indeed no small amount for a woman whose annual income was £800. When he did return it, in 1914 on the proceeds of an American lec- ture tour, it represented something of a tipping point in their relationship as patron and protégé, something made clear in her moving letter of response:

> As to that money, I am rather sad – I was much happier in giving it than I shall be in getting it back ... I am all the more touched by this because you have worked hard for

[13] *Diaries*, 156.
[14] *Diaries*, 180; *CL2*, 253–4.
[15] *Diaries*, 161, 177, 203.
[16] *Diaries*, 167.
[17] WBY to Lady Gregory, 16 December [1917], *CL InteLex* #3375; see also *L*, 634.
[18] WBY to Lady Gregory, 21 December [1898], *CL InteLex*; *CL2*, 322–3.
[19] *Au*, 408.

it & for me … even now, if you have any feeling at all that the payment would cloud our friendship or your thoughts of me … I would far rather keep that friendship & affection that have meant so much to me.[20]

The friendship continued unbroken, with Gregory offering advice and supporting Yeats in his personal and professional life. But with his acquisition of the tower in Ballylee and his marriage in 1917, the relationship necessarily changed. The Yeatses visited Coole as a couple, Yeats spent time there without George, and there were constant communications between the two households. Still, Gregory missed 'those years of close companionship'. 'When I am too long without a friend at hand to talk with I feel, not lonely, but insincere – never speaking my whole mind.'[21]

In terms of money and position, their situation was reversed. Yeats, with his Civil List pension of £150 a year obtained in 1910 with considerable help from Gregory, was earning substantial amounts from his writings by the 1920s, even before the award of the lucrative Nobel Prize. By contrast, Coole was in trouble and had to be sold to the Forestry Commission in 1927; by 1930, Gregory was 'selling off personal possessions such as her books to raise money, and Yeats had long been a paying guest during his stays at Coole'.[22] When in Dublin, Gregory stayed with the Yeatses in their comfortable house in Merrion Square, recuperating there after her operations for cancer. When the Merrion Square house was being sold in 1928, Yeats reassured Gregory that she would always have a room in their new flat: 'perhaps', he said, 'we can take the place of Lady Layard'.[23] Lady Layard was Gregory's close friend in London with whom she frequently stayed in the 1890s when she did not have a rented flat of her own. It is Yeats who was now the generous host, offering hospitality at need.

Gregory, at least privately, was disposed to resent the figure she cut in Yeats's mind in this period of his ascendancy. In 1924 she bridled at his evocation of her in a draft of 'The Bounty of Sweden' as ' "An old woman sinking into the infirmities of age" – not even fighting against them!'[24] When showed the proofs of the first edition of A Vision, she was not reassured by Yeats telling her that phase 24 of A Vision, in which she was placed, was 'a very good one'. She commented drily in her journal: 'I don't know that I like being classed as a "certain friend" (as well as with Galsworthy) with Queen Victoria!! … I don't think she could have written Seven Short Plays.'[25] Still they remained the closest of friends and colleagues. During Gregory's last illness in the winter of 1931–2, Yeats was in

[20] Letter to W. B. Yeats, 8 April 1914, quoted in James Pethica, 'Patronage and Creative Exchange: Yeats, Lady Gregory and the Economy of Indebtedness', YA, 9 (1992), 60–94 [82–3]. I owe a great deal to this pioneering essay.

[21] Lady Gregory, Journals, vol. 2, ed. Daniel J. Murphy (Gerrards Cross: Colin Smythe, 1987), 94, cited as LGJ2.

[22] Pethica, 'Patronage and Creative Exchange', 94.

[23] WBY To Lady Gregory [24 February 1928], CL InteLex #5081; L, 738.

[24] Lady Gregory, Journals, vol. 1, ed. Daniel J. Murphy (Gerrards Cross: Colin Smythe, 1978), 514, cited as LGJ1.

[25] LGJ2, 45.

residence in Coole practically all the time. Over the years, it had been Gregory's habit to read aloud to Yeats to spare his eyes—Spenser, Chaucer, and Tolstoy at different times.[26] In the evenings in Coole, she often read fiction to him as a means of relaxation, one author after another. Earlier it was George Sand, in the last years it was Trollope. Right through until months before her death, the journal entries record Gregory '[r]eading Trollope to Y. evenings'.[27] When she believed she was dying, she wrote a note of farewell to Yeats, paying tribute to his friendship and their work together: 'I thank you ... for these last months you have spent with me – your presence has made them pass quickly and happily in spite of bodily pain, as your friendship has made my last years – from first to last fruitful in work, in service'.[28] Work and service were all-important to Gregory, and as much as their personal relationship meant to her, it was their 'fruitful' collaboration that she most valued.

A YEATS–GREGORY SHOW

In February 1908, Gregory wrote to Yeats, then hard at work in the Abbey taking rehearsals for the first production of *The Golden Helmet* (later to be revised as *The Green Helmet*), saying that she would 'be so very glad if Golden Helmet is a real success, for you did it quite alone, & it will give you courage to go on & start another play'.[29] The tone of sympathetic encouragement is characteristic but perhaps a little surprising addressed to the author of (by then) some ten produced plays. The explanation may come in the key phrase, 'you did it quite alone'. Gregory is congratulating Yeats on bringing a play to the stage without her assistance. It seems likely that, apart from the early plays *The Land of Heart's Desire* and *The Countess Cathleen*, Gregory had a hand in every one of Yeats's plays before 1908. James Pethica, in the Introduction to the Cornell Yeats volume covering the manuscripts of the four one-act plays they are known to have written together—*Cathleen ni Houlihan*, *The Pot of Broth*, *The Country of the Young* (later rewritten as Gregory's *The Travelling Man*), and the unpublished political satire *Heads or Harps*—says that they 'collaborate[d] on at least a dozen plays between 1901 and 1908'.[30]

The nature and level of input from the two authors varied considerably. At times it was a matter of Gregory making suggestions while taking dictation from Yeats. *Where There is Nothing* was written in haste in the summer of 1902, to pre-empt George Moore's claims on it as the original author of the scenario. In his dedication to Gregory in the first published edition, Yeats offers her 'a book which is in part your own': 'I never did

[26] *LGJ2*, 201.
[27] *LGJ2*, 628.
[28] Quoted by Foster in *Life 2*, 437.
[29] *CL5*, 83 n.7.
[30] W. B. Yeats and Lady Gregory, *Collaborative One-Act Plays, 1901–1903, Manuscript Materials*, ed. James Pethica (Ithaca and London: Cornell University Press, 2006), xxvii.

anything that went so easily and quickly, for when I hesitated, you had the right thought ready, and it was always you who gave the right turn to the phrase and gave it the ring of daily life'.[31] That was to be a continuing feature of their work together; as late as his 1927 version of *Oedipus at Colonus*, Yeats 'said my help made a great difference in it, getting it into natural speech'.[32] At times, there seems to have been a clash of styles and attitudes. Yeats gave up on *The Country of the Young* after the failure of his attempt to turn it into a pagan fable and left it to be completed by the more orthodox Christian Gregory as *The Travelling Man*. Gregory had the principal responsibility for rewriting *Where There is Nothing* as *The Unicorn from the Stars*, and the critics felt that 'the work of the two writers is hopelessly incongruous and never fits together'.[33] However, while Yeats acknowledged that *The Unicorn from the Stars* was 'a play almost wholly hers in handiwork' and 'she does not wish to include it in her own works', it was published under his name alone.[34] This is one of a number of instances where Gregory refused the credit of joint authorship with Yeats, the most notorious case being *Cathleen ni Houlihan*.

As early as 1898, Yeats had suggested to Gregory that they collaborate on a 'big book of folk lore'. The form of the offer, which Gregory turned down, was suggestive: 'One hand should do the actual shaping & writing – apart from peasant talk – & I would wish to do this'.[35] No doubt as to who was to be the senior author here, but the exception is telling: Yeats was already quite aware that he could not reproduce 'peasant talk'. In the case of *Cathleen ni Houlihan*, where Yeats began with his dream 'of a cottage where there was well-being and firelight and talk of a marriage' interrupted by the old woman who 'was Ireland herself', he confesses, 'I could not get down out of that high window of dramatic verse' because 'I had not the country speech'.[36] He needed Gregory's help to write the play. She marked the extent of her contribution on the manuscript—'All this mine alone A.G', on the foot of the page on which Cathleen enters—and, since the publication of Pethica's definitive study, Gregory's co-authorship has been widely acknowledged.[37] There remains the issue of why Gregory did not claim her part in the play but allowed Yeats to appropriate it as his own. Her own answer to that question was that she did not want to 'take from [Yeats] any part of what had proved, after all, his one real popular success'. Pethica, who quotes this, comments on its 'inscrutable mixture of magnanimity, self-aggrandizement, and snideness'.[38] That is certainly one way of reading it; however, it is also no more than the literal truth. Gregory was always keen to support Yeats's

---

[31] WBY to Lady Augusta Gregory, 19 September 1902, *CL InteLex*; *CL*3, 226–7.

[32] *LGJ*2, 171.

[33] *CL*4, 775 n.3.

[34] *CW*2, 688.

[35] WBY to Lady Gregory, 22 December [1898], *Cl InteLex*; *CL*2, 323.

[36] *VPl*, 232.

[37] Yeats and Gregory, *Collaborative One-Act Plays*, 22; see James Pethica, '"Our Kathleen": Yeats's Collaboration with Lady Gregory in the Writing of *Cathleen ni Houlihan*', *YA*, 6 (1988), 3–31. The play is included as *Kathleen ni Houlihan*, Gregory's preferred spelling, in Lady Gregory, *Selected Writings*, ed. Lucy McDiarmid and Maureen Waters (London: Penguin, 1995).

[38] Yeats and Gregory, *Collaborative One-Act Plays*, xlii.

reputation, and she was fully aware of the nationalist credentials accorded to him as the playwright of *Cathleen ni Houlihan*. He would hardly have won cheers from the noisy critics of *The Playboy* by shouting, 'the co-author (with Lady Gregory) of "Kathleen ni Houlihan" appeals to you.'[39]

Yeats and Gregory worked together on the plays through the summers in Coole, but, once back in London, he was inclined to keep tinkering with them as the incorrigible reviser he was. Gregory, who evidently regarded their joint work as complete, did not approve. 'I am afraid you will be sorry to hear', Yeats writes nervously, 'I propose to put certain parts of "The Hour Glass" into verse.'[40] Gregory deprecated Yeats's unwillingness to leave well alone: 'What frightens me is your joy of creation, you are like Puppy after a chicken, when you see a new idea cross the path, tho' it may but end in a mouth full of feathers after all.'[41] Whatever each contributed to the collaboration, Gregory evidently regarded the plays as a joint creation. This comes out most strikingly when it appeared that Yeats had promised Annie Horniman, his alternative patron and Gregory's bitter rival, free use of his plays when the Abbey patent expired. Gregory wrote in anguished protest at what she felt was a personal betrayal: 'I am taking it to heart very much. Those plays were our own children, I was so proud of them, and loved them, and now I cannot think of them without the greatest pain.'[42] She might not have wanted formal credit as co-author, but the plays they had written together were not Yeats's to give away.

Yeats and Gregory were the anchors of the national theatre movement. They shed their early colleagues in the Irish Literary Theatre, George Moore and Edward Martyn; in establishing the National Theatre Society as a limited company to run the Abbey, they took charge with J. M. Synge as co-director, with their associates from the cooperative Irish National Theatre Society dropping away. Within the Yeats/Gregory/Synge triumvirate, there were tensions arising from the obvious mutual loyalties of the two older directors. Even at a time when Synge and Gregory were allied in resisting Yeats's desire to bring in an external manager of the Abbey, she affirmed her main commitment in a letter to Synge: 'I feel very much bound to him [Yeats], besides personal friendship, because we are the only survivors of the beginning of the movement. I think his work more important than any other (you must not be offended at this) and I think it our chief distinction.'[43] Synge suspected the other two directors of promoting their own work at his expense and at one point felt inclined to 'clear away to Paris and let them make it a Yeats-Gregory show in name as well as in deed'.[44] In Dublin it was

---

[39] See James Kilroy, *The 'Playboy' Riots* (Dublin: Dolmen Press, 1971), 87.

[40] WBY to Lady Augusta Gregory [3 January 1903], *CL InteLex*; *CL3*, 294.

[41] *CL3*, 268 n.6.

[42] Ann Saddlemyer, ed., *Theatre Business* (Gerrards Cross: Colin Smythe, 1982), 202, n. 1.

[43] Ibid., 197.

[44] John Millington Synge, *Collected Letters*, I *1871–1907*, ed. Ann Saddlemyer (Oxford: Clarendon Press, 1983), 318.

commonly maintained that Yeats and Gregory promoted their own work at the expense of more popular authors.[45] This may have been in part true of Gregory's insistence on the production of Yeats's verse plays, which were largely unpopular, but hardly of her own short comedies, which were highly reliable audience draws.[46] Rather than being motivated by self-interest, Gregory and Yeats's selection of the Abbey repertoire was determined by their own aesthetic values, according to which very successful playwrights like William Boyle or even George Fitzmaurice were found wanting. It was on the same basis that, much later in the 1920s, they controversially turned down both Denis Johnston's *The Old Lady Says 'No!'* and Sean O'Casey's *The Silver Tassie*.

They ruled the Abbey with a strong hand, even if Yeats positively relished the rows— 'We must get these people afraid of us. I am really rather enjoying the game'[47]—while Gregory generally sought compromise and negotiation. They were conscious of their position as management, the actors as employees, with class difference adding an extra dimension. 'I have always considered that the class we draw our actors from an essential part of our success,' Yeats wrote to Gregory, explaining his reluctance to take on a Trinity graduate: 'A young man from Trinity College would be very unlikely to join us, to continue with us. A living wage to [J. M.] Kerrigan [a regular member of the Abbey company] would not be a living wage to him.'[48] The actors, not surprisingly, were resentful of this emphasis on their plebeian origins, often publicly stated by the Directors.[49] Though Yeats was to become disenchanted with the Abbey, it was in an open letter to Lady Gregory that he voiced his unhappiness with the 'people's theatre' that they had succeeded in creating together.[50] But neither of them was about to give up control. When, as part of the deal that brought the Abbey a state subsidy in 1925, they had to have a government nominee on the directorate, they set up a system of majority voting by which they could always have their way.[51] When Yeats in 1925 unexpectedly proposed that Lennox Robinson should be made 'Managing Director', Gregory told him firmly, 'as long as I have responsibility as a Director I will keep it all – not delegate it'.[52] And keep it she did, in spite of increasing illness, to the point of her death, as Yeats was to continue in place until his. The Abbey remained, as Gregory had called it in her 1913 book, *Our Irish Theatre*.

[45] For details, see *CL4*, 834–5 n.8.
[46] Synge told F. J. Fay that on tour 'Lady G. protested very strongly ... against, our ever going to important towns without some of Yeats' verse plays, the production of which she considers the most important part of our work'. Synge, *Collected Letters*, I, 347.
[47] WBY to Lady Gregory, 3 January 1906, *CL InteLex* #301; *CL4*, 277.
[48] WBY to Lady Gregory, 2 February 1910, *CL InteLex* #1284; *CL5*, 707.
[49] *CL5*, 707 n.5.
[50] See W. B. Yeats, 'A People's Theatre: A Letter to Lady Gregory', in *Ex*, 244–59.
[51] *LGJ2*, 39.
[52] *LGJ2*, 13

AUGUSTA GREGORY

There is an odd asymmetry in the way Gregory and Yeats addressed one another. From as early as 1898, Gregory had taken to calling Yeats 'Willie' in her letters.[53] However, the salutations of his letters to her continue to be 'My dear Lady Gregory' throughout, though sometimes varied as 'My dear Friend', notably in a letter acknowledging the embarrassing gift of money.[54] It is only years after her death that she acquires a first name, and in 'The Municipal Gallery Re-visited' she is identified three times as 'Augusta Gregory' (*CW1*, 3319–21). That personal naming is the last example of the mythopoeic shaping of her as a figure within his poetry that began in 1900, commemorating their personal friendship, their shared values, and the cultural ambiance of Coole of which she was the centre.

Yeats was habitually discreet in not identifying living people in his poems. So, for instance, Maud Gonne is never named until the 1938 'Beautiful Lofty Things'—'Maud Gonne at Howth Station waiting a train.'[55] Similarly, Gregory is often referred to allusively, and often as antitype to Gonne. In 'The Folly of Being Comforted' she is 'one that is every kind' who tries to persuade the poet that '[t]ime can but make it easier to be wise' as his beloved grows older and less beautiful (*CW1*, 76); a rational argument, no doubt, but a single glance from Gonne will prove its uselessness. In 'Friends' she appears with Olivia Shakespear and Gonne as one of '[t]hree women that have wrought / What joy is in my days'. As against Gonne who 'took / All till my youth was gone / With scarce a pitying look', Gregory gave purpose to the poet, unbinding 'youth's dreamy load' so that 'I live labouring in ecstasy' (*CW1*, 124). Gregory's caring maternalism, from which a romantic relationship is excluded, serves as contrast to the torment of desire for the unattainable love object.

This role of Gregory is associated with her home; Coole, from the first naming of its Seven Woods, stands as other to a troubled world elsewhere:

> I have heard the pigeons in the Seven Woods
> Make their faint thunder, and the garden bees
> Hum in the lime-tree flowers; and put away
> The unavailing outcries and the old bitterness
> That empty the heart.

And it is not only the miseries of unrequited love that are stilled in the Seven Woods. There the poet can temporarily forget the distractions of public life: 'Tara uprooted, and new commonness / Upon the throne', the vandalism of excavations on the Hill of Tara, and the vulgarities associated with the coronation of Edward VII.[56] Coole becomes the

---

[53] *Diaries*, 241 n.85.
[54] WBY to Lady Gregory, 8 December [1898], *CL InteLex*; *CL2*, 314.
[55] *CW1*, 303.
[56] *CW1*, 77.

imaginative territory occupied by Sligo in the earlier poetry, a place of magic where mystical revelation may well up from a landscape suffused with mystic traces. The Seven Woods, named one after another in the prologue to *The Shadowy Waters* addressed to Gregory, are the natural spaces where the folklore of Biddy Earley, the local wise woman, is suggestive of older, unnameable beings, '*immortal, mild, proud shadows*' (*CW1*, 405). Yeats, who lived for most of the year a life driven by the immediate needs of his work— journals, publishers and reviews, the quarrels and alliances of literary politics—found in Coole, as earlier in Sligo, a nurturing environment supporting not only his imagination but his deepest beliefs.

Folklore was one of the shared interests that brought them together, Gregory providing Yeats the stories she had gathered round Gort for a series of articles. But the attractions of Coole and its mistress developed into a new ideal of the landed estate first adumbrated in 'Upon a House shaken by the Land Agitation', when the Coole rents were threatened by an application of tenants to the Land Court.[57] There is a new defiant elitism in the poem's celebration of the house '[w]here passion and precision have been one / Time out of mind'. As against the '[m]ean roof-trees' of the tenants, the great house is the centre of a culture born of tradition—'Time's last gift, a written speech—Wrought of high laughter, loveliness and ease' (*CW1*, 95–6). By the late 1920s, with Coole already sold and Gregory terminally ill, these qualities are mourned in elegiac retrospect. In 'Coole Park, 1929' the poet looks back to the cultural achievement of the Revival, over which Gregory presided—'Thoughts long knitted into a single thought, / A dance-like glory that these walls begot'—and to the future, '[w]hen all these rooms and passages are gone', invoking a tribute to the memory of 'that laurelled head'.[58] In the companion poem 'Coole Park and Ballylee, 1931' the tone is even more plangent, as Yeats mourns not only Gregory's coming death and the destruction of the house but the passing of the artistic vision they shared: 'We were the last romantics – chose for theme / Traditional sanctity and loveliness.'

It is hard not to be impatient with some of Yeats's gestural rhetoric here: 'all is changed, that high horse riderless, / Though mounted in that saddle Homer rode.'[59] What on earth does Homer have to do with the studied complexity of Yeats's highly wrought poetry or Gregory's dialect ventriloquism? The memorializing in 'The Municipal Gallery Revisited' is different because it takes in a whole generation, and Gregory is no longer identified primarily as the mistress of Coole. 'Augusta Gregory', as she is here repeatedly called, is connected to the others whose portraits hang in the Gallery, her 'son; her sister's son, / Hugh Lane'. Even as she is monumentalized in the contemplation of her portrait by Mancini, it is her very self that is missed:

> But where is the brush that could show anything
> Of all that pride and that humility?

[57] See *Life 1*, 411–12, for the background.
[58] *CW1*, 243.
[59] *CW1*, 249.

> And I am in despair that time may bring
> Approved patterns of women or of men
> But not that selfsame excellence again.

Synge is included with the poet and Gregory in one last summation of their aesthetic:

> We three alone in modern times had brought
> Everything down to that sole test again.
> Dream of the noble and the beggar-man. (*CW1*, 327–8)

Whatever about Synge, this is expressive of the vision Yeats believed he had in common with Gregory—Gregory who put him in touch with the voice and thought of the people, Coole that gave him an ideal of gracious, cultured life.

It was an unbroken, but not an untroubled, friendship. Gregory was often anxious to appease Yeats, worried if she found herself at odds with him. At the end of 1906, when she had been resisting his Abbey Theatre plans, she wrote imploring him to accept the present of a travelling rug: 'I haven't given you anything "worth while" for a long time, except annoyance, obstinacy, exasperation & their kin—so let me wind up the old year with something better.'[60] She always needed his approval of her work, and resented his slighting of it. When Yeats abruptly turned down Lennox Robinson's proposal for an Abbey revival of *The Image* in 1924, she wrote in her journal: '[r]ather a shock to me, my chief play, and one made much of in London and elsewhere.'[61] She suspected, probably rightly, that Yeats undervalued her writing, hence her tart comment about being placed with Queen Victoria in Phase 24 of *A Vision*. On the other hand, she could be fierce enough with Yeats when she felt he let her down personally, as in the incident in 1910 when she received an insulting letter from Edmund Gosse. The letter was shown to Yeats, who was staying at Coole, and his initial response was to send a 'milk-and-water' letter; she 'said that if he hadn't any sense of dignity or self-respect he should remember that he was her guest, and she insisted on a stronger reply.'[62] The strong reply was duly written, but Gregory did not finally let Yeats send it, aware how dependent he was on Gosse for the negotiation of his Civil List pension. Again, in 1921, when Yeats wrote 'Reprisals', capitalizing on the dead figure of Robert Gregory for an attack on the atrocities of the Black and Tans, Gregory was horrified: 'I cannot bear the dragging of R., from his grave to make what I think a not very sincere poem'; at her insistence the poem was never published.[63]

However, these were but minor strains in a deep-rooted, long-lasting friendship. Mary Lou Kohfeldt, one of Gregory's biographers, takes a sceptical view of her relationship with Yeats: 'There was ... an emptiness at the heart of their union; they were using

---

[60] *CL4*, 559 n.8.
[61] *LGJ1*, 585.
[62] *CL5*, 859 n.3.
[63] *LGJ1*, 207–8.

one another.'[64] John Kelly, who quotes this statement, comments that it is 'too reductive and simplistic'.[65] One might go further and say it is just not true. The relationship did no doubt develop initially on the basis of mutual need. Yeats, living in poor conditions in the late 1890s, always hard up, dependent to a large extent on paid journalism, evidently benefited from the material comforts of his extended stays at Coole, as well as Gregory's support in cash and kind. But still more important was the sympathetic ear she was prepared to offer the poet, whose disastrous emotional life left him always close to nervous collapse. Gregory, already a published author, with a growing interest in Irish cultural nationalism, was looking for a new outlet for her considerable energies. But the needs that brought them together soon grew into a relationship that meant much to both of them. While Gregory gave shape and purpose to Yeats's career so that he found himself 'labouring in ecstasy', he provided her with the confidence to go on as a writer. Looking back at what she had achieved by 1909, she wrote in her diary, 'I owe to him [WBY] what I have done of late years – he gave me belief in myself.'[66]

Their writing collaboration was a deep source of satisfaction and acknowledged as such. The testimony of Yeats, quoted earlier, about their work on *Where There is Nothing*—'I never did anything that went so easily and quickly'—is striking coming from a writer who habitually composed with such laborious difficulty. If Gregory was devastated at the idea that Yeats had assigned rights to Horniman in their jointly authored plays, it was because they were 'our own children'. The Abbey, for all the sniping of Dublin critics and the occasional suspicion of Synge that it was just a 'Yeats-Gregory show', was not primarily designed to promote their own work. Yeats might chafe at the demands of '[t]heatre business, management of men' (*CW1*, 92), which kept him from writing poems, but he and Gregory made that often irksome, time-consuming, and difficult task a lifelong commitment, for little or no reward. Coming though they did from different political viewpoints, they were both patriots, serving what they believed were the best interests of Ireland. There is no doubting the sincerity of the famous passage of Yeats's letter to Gregory reacting to the news of the Easter Rising: 'The Dublin tragedy has been a great sorrow and anxiety. ... I had no idea that any public event could so deeply move me – and I am very despondent about the future. At the moment I feel that all the work of years has been overturned, all the bringing together of classes, all the freeing of Irish literature and criticism from politics.'[67] The extraordinarily voluminous correspondence between the two, sustained over thirty-five years, stands as a record not only of a working partnership but of a friendship that was staunch, intimate, and fully reciprocal. For Gregory he was the friend to whom she could speak her 'whole mind'; for Yeats she was 'the one person who knew all that I thought and did'.

---

[64] Mary Lou Kohfeldt, *Lady Gregory: the Woman Behind the Irish Renaissance* (London: Andre Deutsch, 1984), 118.

[65] Kelly, 'Friendship is All the House I Have', 181.

[66] *Diaries*, 316.

[67] WBY to Lady Gregory [11 May 1916], *CL InteLex* #2950; *L*, 612–13.

CHAPTER 6

W. B. YEATS, JOHN QUINN, AND THE LITERARY MARKETPLACE

JOSEPH HASSETT

In the summer of 1921, New York lawyer John Quinn paid the overdue rent for the room occupied by W. B. Yeats's father, John Butler Yeats, in a boarding house several miles up-town from Quinn's Wall Street office. Quinn complained to Ezra Pound that the younger Yeats had written 'that he couldn't send any money and if I would make the payments he would pay me in MSS, as though I was a MS sewer or a MS dealer, or a book agent or a broker or some other kind of "whore"'.[1] Quinn's outburst may be explained by his conscious or unconscious realization that he was, in fact, a manuscript dealer. He had purchased manuscripts from various authors and then sold a group of them in 1912 to Henry E. Huntington for the library he was establishing in California, thus functioning as a dealer between the authors and a permanent cultural institution.[2] Further sales were on the horizon. As discussed below, within three years of his outburst to Pound, Quinn arranged the sale of all of his manuscripts. The criticism he would receive for realizing a tenfold profit on manuscripts purchased from Joseph Conrad focused uncomfortably on the commercial aspect of Quinn's acquisition of manuscripts.[3] That focus had

---

[1] Letter from John Quinn to W. B. Yeats, 1 May 1921 (hereafter in this chapter Q to Y or Y to Q). John Quinn Memorial Collection, New York Public Library ('QC'). Quinn letters not identified by source are from QC. Quinn's letters to W. B. Yeats are collected in *LJQ*. The author greatly appreciates the professionalism and courtesy of the staff of the John Quinn Memorial Collection, Manuscripts and Archives Division, New York Public Library, Astor, Lenox, and Tilden Foundations, especially Tal Nadan and Maurice Klapwald; and the Henry W. and Albert A. Berg Collection, New York Public Library, especially Lyndsi Barnes.

[2] B. L. Reid, *The Man from New York: John Quinn and his Friends* (New York: Oxford University Press, 1968) (hereafter 'MNY'), 123.

[3] *MNY*, 603–5.

been foreshadowed in 1919 when Conrad sold a manuscript to someone else after Quinn hesitated at Conrad's asking price.[4]

Quinn had been a supportive patron of W. B. Yeats, but the mercenary character of buying and selling manuscripts threatened the self-image urged on him by Pound's blandishment that a patron 'creates' and, indeed, by acts of patronage, 'makes himself equal to the artist'. Conflicts of this kind stoked the tensions that lay beneath the many roles played by Quinn in W. B. Yeats's life, including agent, lawyer, promoter, lecture tour organizer, publicist, would-be editor, advisor, friend, and rival. The conflicts are flashpoints that illuminate aspects of Quinn's highly productive role in the literary marketplace for Yeats's work.

When Quinn first met Yeats on a visit to Ireland in 1902, the 37-year-old poet was not yet the imposing figure known globally as WBY. The degree of self-invention that remained to be accomplished is apparent from the fact that when Yeats's collected poems were published by Macmillan in New York and London in 1906 and 1907, the two volumes were entitled *The Poetical Works of William B. Yeats*. Yeats's biographer Roy Foster places 'the years of making "WBY"' in the period leading up to completion of *Reveries over Childhood and Youth* in 1914.[5]

Quinn contributed significantly to the creation of WBY and the marketing of his work in the US. The 32-year-old lawyer's first proffered assistance involved American copyright law, which protected domestic printers and their employees to the detriment of foreign authors. The US had denied copyright to foreign authors until the statute was amended in 1891 to grant them protection if, no later than publishing a book elsewhere, they published in the US and filed in Washington two copies of the book that were manufactured from type set in the US or from plates made from such type. Although Quinn's practice was highly specialized in bank, taxation, and commercial matters,[6] upon his return to New York from Ireland in 1902, he offered to obtain US copyright for the play, *Where There Is Nothing*, that he and WBY (as we shall call him) had discussed in Ireland. His letter of 27 September 1902, which enclosed a colleague's memorandum on US copyright law, suggested that WBY protect his US copyright by publishing all of his work simultaneously in England and the US and depositing in Washington two copies of the work that were printed in the US. There seems never to have been any mention of WBY paying for Quinn's services.

Quinn was soon at work as agent. On 13 May 1903, he sent George Brett, the president of Macmillan in New York, the contract for *Where There Is Nothing* as executed by WBY. Quinn the promoter was not far behind. Enthusiastically acting to create a readership, Quinn organized the Irish Literary Society of New York, and wrote to Brett on 15 May telling him of the Society's goal of 'making known in this country the fine work that is being done in Ireland'. Quinn threw himself into having the Society stage three of WBY's short plays, *Cathleen ni Houlihan*, *A Pot of Broth*, and *The Land of Heart's Desire*.

---

[4] *MNY*, 361–2; 378–84.
[5] *Life 1*, xv.
[6] Letter from Quinn to Joseph Conrad, 30 June 1920.

Following the performances, Quinn wrote to WBY on 26 June 1903, emphasizing an important accomplishment: 'You are known now to a great many who before the Irish Literary Society of New York was started and the plays given did not know what you stood for.' However, it was already apparent that the society had too narrow an outlook to carry the banner of the WBY brand. Objections by members of the society to an honorary office for WBY on the grounds that he was anticlerical convinced Quinn that the next foray into the American market should aim for an audience less subject to clerical influence.[7]

Quinn wasted no time starting. On 13 July 1903, before leaving for Dublin, where he would obtain WBY's agreement to an American lecture tour, Quinn advised Brett that 'Mr. Yeats expects to lecture here in October or November and will lecture at Harvard, Columbia, Chicago University and other colleges and universities and before various societies in the large cities of the country ... and I am sure there will be a very prompt and good demand for his books, and it would be a pity not to have such a fine book as his volume of "Poems" on sale here'.

Upon returning to New York, Quinn frantically importuned his circle of successful Irish-American businessmen and political figures to help create the schedule he had proleptically outlined to Brett. With the help of a friend, he arranged a lecture for WBY at Yale and then leveraged that prestigious appearance in missives to other institutions. He supported his letters with self-made circulars and pamphlets describing the projected lectures and incorporating critical commentary on WBY's work. Quinn's letters were not tepid boilerplate sent to random addressees. Rather, they were personal and highly informed pleas to people in a position to make things happen. In a study of the literary marketplace, they merit attention in some detail.

Quinn's letter of 13 October 1903 to Sligo native Bourke Cochran, a six-term Tammany-backed Democratic congressman from New York, exemplifies his approach. Forwarding copies of his promotional material and touting the Yale lecture, Quinn urged, 'If you know the Presidents of any colleges in New York or anywhere in the country or the professors of English literature, I should be glad if you can send them the circulars and try to obtain an invitation or two for him to lecture before the college.' Quinn's anxiety is apparent as he confides that his request is 'rather cheeky' but explains that he 'is driven ... to make it a personal matter' because 'time is short before his arrival and I am so anxious to have at least ten or a dozen dates fixed before he starts'.

Another letter of 13 October—this one to James Byrne, a New York lawyer and a trustee of the College of the City of New York—sought help in reaching influential people among trustees, faculty, and alumni at Princeton, Columbia, and Harvard.[8] The letter explains that lining up such appearances 'will make the other institutions more anxious to hear him'. He reports reluctance by the famous reforming president of Columbia, Nicholas Butler, to invite WBY and notes that 'Mr. Butler, I feel quite sure,

---

[7] 26 June 1903, Q to Y.
[8] *Harvard Graduates' Magazine*, vol. XXVIII (Boston, 1920), 723–4.

knows practically nothing about the Irish movement or about Yeats's writings'. Quinn distils the message to be conveyed: WBY 'is one of the foremost literary writers in Europe today [and] is as well known in Paris as he is in London ...'.

The range of Quinn's reach is apparent in his letter of 22 October 1903 to Colonel Thomas Wentworth Higginson, Emily Dickinson's correspondent and confidant, famous abolitionist, Unitarian minister, and colonel in the 1st South Carolina Volunteers, the first federally authorized black regiment in the Civil War. 'You of course do not recall me,' wrote Quinn,' but I had the pleasure of meeting you at the Harvard Union in the winter of 1894–1895 when you lectured for the young men.' Quinn's letter assures Higginson that 'Mr. Yeats is not only an eloquent speaker but his lectures are bound in passages of singular beauty and literary grace and style'. He tells Higginson that Mr Roche of *The Boston Pilot* 'has written to me stating that he has forwarded to you some of the circulars announcing' WBY's forthcoming visit; he reports that Professor Frederick Robinson of Harvard had invited WBY to deliver one lecture at Harvard; and he asks Higginson if he can get Harvard to invite WBY for four lectures as originally requested. He encloses the circulars for good measure.

Writing on the same date to James D. Phelan, a prominent lawyer and banker who had been Mayor of San Francisco and would become US senator from California, Quinn, perhaps gilding the lily, says that Colonel Higginson 'personally arranged' for WBY to be invited to Harvard, and asks Phelan to secure engagements at Stanford and Berkeley on terms sufficient to support the cost of travel to the West Coast. Again vouching personally for WBY, Quinn insists, 'I cannot make it too strong that Yeats has a gift for oratory and you need not at all fear to assure your friends in San Francisco that his oratory will not disappoint them.' Quinn had already sounded a recurring theme in a letter of 15 October 1903 that assured Phelan that WBY's lectures will 'do a great deal to explain a part of Irish life to Irishmen in America which is little explained, the more prominent Irishmen having talked of the political and parliamentary side only and having dwelt little on the intellectual, spiritual, and artistic aspects of Irish life and of the Irish literary revival of the last fifteen years', of which WBY 'has been the real leader'.

Quinn did not confine himself to organizing the lectures. He worked to make them succeed. An accomplished 'spin artist' *avant la lettre*, he cultivated a group of literary journalists attentive to his views, arranged press interviews, and planted stories designed to maximize public impact and minimize controversy. For example, he invited James Gibson Huneker to dinner with WBY early in the tour.[9] Although Huneker was unable to dine, he was receptive to Quinn's critique of a review by Paul Elmore Moore in *The New York Evening Post* that criticized WBY's recent work for showing evidence of 'decadence'.[10] Quinn's letter to Huneker refuting the characterization of decadence reflected its author's lawyerly frame of mind and detailed knowledge of WBY's work. For example, it ridiculed Moore for thinking that 'The Old Age of Queen Maeve' predated

---

[9] Letter of 15 December 1903.
[10] Letter of 15 December 1903.

The Wind Among the Reeds. Huneker came through with a long article in *The Sun* on 27 December 1903 that had a good chuckle at Moore's thinking that 'The Old Age of Queen Maeve' pre-dated *The Wind Among the Reeds*, and declared that to call WBY's 'work decadent, meaning that it is false, artificial, morbid or immoral, is not to say the truth'.

Throughout the tour, which extended from 11 November 1903 until 9 March 1904, Quinn spent an enormous amount of time making arrangements and guiding WBY, reminding him, for example, to have his linen washed, and dictating detailed instructions as to how to ship a trunk. He also arranged a lunch at the White House with President Theodore Roosevelt, and mailed $4 in bills at WBY's request to Harvard Professor Frederick Robinson, who had made a loan to the cash-strapped itinerant poet.[11]

The tour was an enormous success. WBY earned $3,230.40, the largest sum of money he had ever had.[12] Importantly, the tour and attendant publicity expanded his potential market, a fact he was quick to emphasize to George Brett of Macmillan, with whom he was negotiating American publication of his work. WBY's 8 March 1904 letter to Brett shows his savvy translation of the tour into a compelling marketing message. He pointed out that he had spoken at more than sixty-four colleges and literary societies and drawn large crowds, citing an audience of more than 2,000 in San Francisco and a packed house of 4,000 to 4,500 people at the New York Academy of Music. Overall, WBY concluded, 'Mr. Quinn estimates that I have spoken to between twenty-five and thirty thousand and people while I have been here.' Driving home the market impact, WBY emphasized that since he had 'spoken on literary themes alone, it is impossible to believe that there is not an awakened interest in Irish Literature . . .'. Concluding with a show of strength, WBY said that if they could not reach an agreement he would like to discuss the terms on which Macmillan would release its rights to three of his books because a prominent publishing house had approached him about taking over all of his books in the US, but Macmillan's rights in the three books were a stumbling block.[13] Buoyed by the success of the tour, progress with Brett, and Quinn's £75 commitment to the Abbey Theatre, WBY wrote to Quinn on 18 March 1904, 'I am facing the world with great hopes & strength & I owe it all to you & I thank you & shall always be grateful.'[14]

Engaging directly with Brett, WBY arranged for a Macmillan collected edition and advised Quinn on 15 April 1905 that he had done so and that Brett had accepted Quinn's suggestion that the edition be in two volumes, one devoted to poems and one to plays.[15] The agreement was signed, effective 26 June 1905.[16] The Macmillan two-volume collected edition was published in New York in 1906 and in London in 1907.

---

[11] Letter of 3 December 1903.
[12] *MNY* 19; Yeats to Jeanne Robert Foster, 10 August [1924], *CL InteLex* #4617.
[13] Yeats to George P. Brett, 8 March 1904, *CL InteLex*; *CL3*, 554
[14] Y to Q [18 March 1904], *CL InteLex*; *CL3*, 557–8.
[15] Y to Q, 15 April [1905], *CL InteLex* #147; *CL4*, 74–5.
[16] Agreement with The Macmillan Company (New York), 26 June 1905, *CL InteLex* #174; *CL4*, 121–3.

The success of his American tour encouraged WBY to contemplate another. Intending to use the Pond Bureau, a lecture agency to which Quinn had introduced him, on 5 December 1905 WBY sent a letter to Quinn to be forwarded to Pond saying he would like to arrange a lecture tour by himself and, 'if possible, I should very much desire that Miss Florence Farr should be engaged in conjunction with me, or for some lectures in conjunction with me and for others on her own account, to illustrate my theories by recitations of poetry to musical notes'.[17] Farr and WBY shared many theatrical and esoteric interests, toured widely, performing together in England and Scotland in the spring of 1905.[18] Ostensibly seeking to protect the WBY brand in America, Quinn ignored WBY's letter about a joint tour until finally announcing in a 13 July 1906 letter, 'Now for a confession: I did not show your letter to the Pond Bureau.' In purported explanation, couched in brand protection terms, Quinn lectured WBY: 'It wouldn't do for you and Miss Farr to come here together. This is after all a provincial people.' Quinn told Yeats that he was known in the most dignified way in America 'and can lecture here again, especially at the Women's Colleges. But coming here with a woman it would be entirely different.' Farr toured America on her own for four months in 1907, lecturing on 'Speaking to the Psaltery'. Quinn likely became Farr's lover during the solo tour on which Quinn had insisted, while Yeats wrote to Farr from Florence, where he was visiting with Augusta and Robert Gregory, lamenting her silence.[19] When Quinn sold his library in 1923–4, he sold three books inscribed to Farr by WBY.[20]

Farr had apparently spoken to Quinn about WBY's plan for the handsomely produced final text of all of his work that he had been planning with the English publisher A. H. Bullen. Referring to Farr by her formal name as the ex-wife of the actor Frederick Emery, Quinn's letter to WBY of 23 August 1907 asked, 'What about a collected edition of your writings that Mrs. Emery spoke about?' The question was timely. As WBY told Bullen in a letter of 8 July 1907, he was 'devoting myself for a year to making a final text of all my works'.[21] The *Collected Works* ('*CW*') would contain both earlier work that was extensively revised for the new edition, new material such as two plays, *The Unicorn from the Stars* and *The Golden Helmet*, and new prose such as *Discoveries*.[22] WBY thought that *CW* would be frequently consulted as an authoritative source and would, as he said in a letter to Farr of 14 April 1908, 'greatly strengthen my position—for my work is far stronger when put all together [*sic*]. I have been myself surprised by the unity of it all & by its general elevation of style as I think.'[23]

---

[17] Y to Q, 5 December 1905, *CL InteLex* #264; *CL4*, 237–9.

[18] Joseph M. Hassett, *W. B. Yeats and the Muses* (Oxford: Oxford University Press, 2010), ch. 2.

[19] See *CL4*, 630 n.14; Yeats to Florence Farr [mid-April 1907], *CL4*, 651; *CL InteLex* #587.

[20] The Anderson Galleries, *Complete Catalogue of the Library of John Quinn* (New York, 1924, repr. Lemma Publishing), ('Quinn Sale Catalogue') items 11482, 11484, and 11490.

[21] *Life 1*, 371; Yeats to A. H. Bullen, 8 July 1907, *CL InteLex* #627; *CL4*, 692.

[22] *CL4*, 978–90.

[23] Yeats to Florence Farr [14 April 1908], *CL InteLex* #857; *CL5*, 173. The footnotes and a detailed appendix (by editors John Kelly and Ronald Schuchard) in this volume are extraordinarily illuminating respecting the *CW*. The author is grateful to John Kelly for his astute observations respecting the *CW*, to

Quinn's 23 August 1907 letter also asked whether Brett was 'going to do an edition here'. Quinn's question about a US edition reflected his view that distribution of the *CW* would advance WBY's reputation in the US.[24] Additionally, as Quinn had made clear in his initial letter to WBY of 27 September 1902, printing in the US was a prerequisite to obtaining US copyright. Moreover, US law barred importation of any book copyrighted in the US or any plates of the same not made from type set within the US. There was an exception for importation, subject to tariff, for use and not for sale, of not more than two copies at any one time. Quinn's reference to Brett made sense because Macmillan's 26 June 1905 agreement with WBY precluded US publication of any collected edition except through Macmillan. WBY had told Brett about the projected *CW* in 1905 and asked him (unsuccessfully) to 'make some arrangement by which this edition could be taken up by you in America'.[25]

Correctly anticipating that he would not be able to sell the entire projected 1,000-copy print run of *CW*,[26] Bullen contacted Quinn on 20 November 1907, asking him to try to induce Brett 'to be friendly' to the *CW*, explaining that he thought Brett 'could easily [sell] 250 sets without doing a dollar's worth of damage to his own editions'.[27] Bullen suggested to Quinn that 'a few persuasive words from you may soften' any hostility Brett might have to the *CW*. Bullen's interest in ridding himself of 250 surplus sets of the English *CW* was different from WBY's interest in an edition of *CW* printed and copyrighted in the US by Macmillan or with Macmillan's consent. Such an edition would comply with WBY's contract with Macmillan and protect US copyright in the new material in *CW*. Moreover, it would avoid the risk that violating the bar against importing material copyrighted in the US would be seen as circumventing the domestic printing policy of the US statute and thus jeopardize WBY's existing US copyrights. Quinn did not raise the potential conflict of interest or any of the substantive questions with WBY. Rather, he simply told WBY by letter of 8 December that he would comply with Bullen's request, and on 10 December wrote to Brett urging him 'to make some arrangement with Bullen by which you could offer 200 or 300 sets of this edition to the American public'.[28]

Brett replied to Quinn on 13 December 1907 that he wished that 'it might be possible to handle this charming edition in this country', but that American copyright law precluded it. He said there were no clear legal decisions but thought that the statute meant 'that books cannot be imported in quantity for sale if they contain matter which has been duly copyrighted on this side'.[29]

Robert Spoo for his sage comments on copyright law, and to Warwick Gould for his typically generous sharing of his detailed knowledge of all things Yeatsian.

[24] Quinn letter to Bullen, 20 November 1907.
[25] Yeats to George P. Brett, 31 March [1905], *CL InteLex* #137; *CL4*, 64–6.
[26] In the four years following publication only half of the thousand sets were sold. (*Life 1*, 396.)
[27] QC.
[28] *CL4*, 811 n.32.
[29] *CL4*, 811. Brett also wrote directly to Bullen on 20 December 1907, who copied out Brett's letter and included it in a 23 December 1907 letter to Quinn (QC).

This was the moment for launching a cooperative approach by recognizing that there was risk for both Macmillan and WBY but also an opportunity to get the definitive *CW* into the hands of US educational and cultural institutions and other opinion-makers who could enhance WBY's reputation and drive sales of Macmillan's more modestly priced volumes. A cooperative approach required that Quinn recognize, and convey to WBY, the validity of the risk identified by Brett, and propose ways of managing or compensating for the risk. Quinn was the wrong choice for that task. As his biographer observed in another context, 'his was a temperament which required to dominate'.[30] Ignoring both the idea of a friendly approach to Brett and the risk to WBY's existing US copyrights, Quinn's 5 February 1908 reply to Brett asserted flatly that 'it seems to me plain ... that the prohibition [against importation] is for the benefit and protection of the owner or holder of the copyright, and that if, as provided in [the section creating a civil action for damages] he consents in writing ... to the importation of the works in question, all or part of which he may hold the American copyright of, the prohibition falls and the penalty provided to be recovered in the civil action referred to falls with it'.[31]

Quinn sent Bullen a copy of what he called his 'rather carefully worked out opinion' and assured him that 'Brett hasn't a leg to stand on with his legal objection ...'.[32] In fact, Brett *did* have a leg to stand on. As Quinn himself told Lady Gregory a few months later, 'all the American publishers agree here that if a publisher here copyrights a work and then later on imports English copies not printed from plates made in America or typeset in America, they might invalidate their own copyright'. He explained that this view was based on the protectionist spirit and text of the American law, and advised against selling sheets from an Irish edition in the US.[33]

In his 6 February 1908 response to Quinn, Brett repeated the position he had expressed to Bullen.[34] Rather than exploring a collaborative approach, Quinn closed discussions with Brett by telling him that he disagreed with his interpretation but recognized this as 'a business question for you to determine'.[35] He then told WBY, by letter of 28 February 1908, 'I have done the best I can to induce Brett to take 200 or 250

---

[30] *MNY* 174. Quinn's need to dominate also manifested itself at about this time in his efforts on WBY's behalf to prevent William Fay and his company from representing themselves in America as the 'Irish National Theatre Company of Dublin', which WBY regarded as injurious to the Abbey Theatre's reputation. Quinn energetically and successfully pursued Fay, but, as the editors of *CL5* recount, Lady Gregory thought Fay 'was being bullied by Quinn, and there is much to be said for her view' (*CL5*, lxii).

[31] The 'all or part of' language was an effort to write around the fact that Yeats did not hold a US copyright on all of the material in the *CW*.

[32] Letter of 6 February 1908 (QC).

[33] Letter of 5 June 1908, quoted in *CL5*, 61 n.2.

[34] *CL5*, 49. Although Brett did not spell out his thinking in detail, Bullen's 19 February letter to Quinn pointed out that Brett's position would make sense with regard to a very popular book where an English publisher printed only a few copies in the US and a great many outside the country. Bullen thought such reasoning was 'wholly absurd' as applied to *CW*, but his recognition of the soundness of the principle should have prompted Quinn to recommend to WBY that he pursue a collaborative approach with Brett. (QC; *CL5*, 78 n.1.)

[35] Letter of 10 February 1908.

sets of the limited edition. He raised some legal objections at first and I gave him a very exhaustive opinion, a copy of which I sent to Mr. Bullen. Bullen has probably told you about it.'[36]

There is no record of a letter from Quinn to Yeats and Bullen telling them what he told Gregory. The fact that Quinn did not apprise WBY of the risk identified by Brett is confirmed by WBY's letter of 4 March 1908 to Bullen, pointing out, 'you have never told me something which I learned from [Dublin publisher George] Roberts that you have found out, that owing to a new law you cannot import in bulk into the states. I had thought that this was a fable of Brett's.'[37] Quinn's unrescinded advice that Brett didn't have a leg to stand on remained an obstacle to objective assessment of the situation. As late as 27 October 1912 Bullen insisted to WBY that a principal cause of *CW*'s commercial failure was that Brett and Macmillan had refused to take the book or let another publisher handle it despite Quinn's 'legal opinion in which he clearly showed that Macmillan ran no risk of endangering their American copyright by taking up my edition ...'.[38]

By then Bullen had long been resigned to 'stalk[ing] Yeats's American admirers singly.'[39] The *CW* was published in England over the second half of 1908. There was no American edition of the work that WBY regarded as the foundation of his reputation. Bullen's meagre efforts to sell copies singly in America are reflected in Quinn's letter to WBY of 23 May 2008, advising that Bullen had asked him for a list of potential American buyers of the collected edition and that he would try to 'prepare a list of 50 or 75 likely persons ...'.

Even though *CW* was not published in the US, Quinn contributed to it in a variety of ways. In a gesture of serious scholarship, he prepared a detailed twenty-nine-page bibliography of American editions of WBY's works and sent it to Bullen by letter of 5 August 1908 for use in the *CW*. Quinn the patron was an important source of support for *CW*. For example, he facilitated two distinctive features of *CW*, the oil portrait of WBY by Charles Shannon, which appeared as the frontispiece to Volume 3, and a charcoal drawing of WBY by John Singer Sargent, which took a similar place of honour in the first volume. Shannon offered to do an oil portrait for £100, one-third of his normal rate, expecting Quinn to buy the original.[40] Quinn did so, and wrote twice to WBY saying he was 'very much obliged to you about the Shannon portrait.'[41] The portrait was sold by Quinn's estate in 1927 for $625,[42] netting a profit of approximately $141. Gregory lined up Sargent for the charcoal drawing, hoping Quinn would purchase it.[43] He did so, and was

---

[36] By letter of 19 February 1908, Bullen asked Brett to reconsider his decision in view of Quinn's opinion, but Brett replied on 3 March that he did not believe Quinn's view was 'so well taken or with knowledge of all the trade questions attaching thereto' (QC; *CL5*, 78–9, 99).

[37] Yeats to A. H. Bullen, 4 March 1908, *CL InteLex* #814; *CL5*, 102.

[38] *CL5*, 50 n.1.

[39] Bullen letter to Quinn, 23 December 1907 (QC).

[40] Q to Y, 8 December 1907.

[41] Letters of 21 February and 23 May 1908 (QC).

[42] *New York Times*, 20 February 1927.

[43] *Life 1*, 373, citing Sargent to Gregory, 17 May 1908 (Emory) and Gregory to Quinn, 28 March 1908 (Berg).

delighted to have it, writing to WBY on 20 December 1908 that 'It looks like a piece of marble. It is a magnificent drawing and I am very glad to have it.'

Quinn's support as patron included his purchase of five sets of *CW*. Patronage elided into promotion when Quinn sent an extra set to James Huneker, who responded with a good review in the 25 July 1908 *New York Sun*.[44] His patronage of *CW* overlapped into collecting when Quinn asked WBY to autograph or write a verse or a paragraph in each volume, telling WBY, 'It won't take you 1/10 of the time … that it will take me to prepare the list of possible American subscribers that I am going to get up for Bullen, and so, as the phrase is, "we'll break even at that".'[45] Yeats signed four of the volumes, sometimes writing out an excerpt from the volume or a comment, and Bullen copied short excerpts and signed the other four volumes. Quinn sold his embellished set of the *CW* for $125 ($1,857 in 2020 values) at his library sale on 17 March 1924.[46]

Patronage had already meandered into collecting. In the course of communicating with WBY over the *CW*, Quinn had written on 8 December 1907 that he already owned three 'fine manuscripts' by other writers and would be delighted to have the manuscript of WBY's play *Deirdre*. Two days later he wrote to Bullen, 'I have been collecting some interesting MSS. recently and I should be very glad to add some Yeats MSS. to my collection.' Neither of these overtures had borne fruit by the time the relationship between Quinn and WBY ruptured in August 1909.[47] Quinn's biographer attributes the break to Quinn's belief that WBY had been gossiping about—and trying to emulate—his relationship with his mistress, Dorothy Coates.[48] Again exhibiting a personality that needed to dominate, Quinn ceased communication with WBY from the time he exchanged bitter words with him about Coates in mid-August 1909 until the urging of the terminally ill Coates led him to reconcile with WBY in March 1914.[49]

By the time of his break with WBY, Quinn had sent Bullen a standard list of libraries and similar institutions that might purchase the *CW*, and indicated he would send something more detailed, but he never made a comprehensive effort to open doors to the network enlisted for the 1903–4 book tour.[50] The *CW* never benefited from the momentum of WBY's initial foray into the US market. Nonetheless, WBY's own keen grasp of the worlds of publishing and public relations enabled him to retain his position in the American market following Quinn's departure. Others assisted in carrying on work

[44] *MNY*, 75.

[45] 16 June 1908. He had sent a similar letter to Bullen on 26 May.

[46] Quinn sale catalogue, item 11495.

[47] The *Deirdre* manuscript was not sold in Quinn's library sale or in the sale of manuscripts by Quinn's estate on 8 and 9 February 1927 at American Art Association (sale records in QC). On the other hand, papers given to NLI by Michael Yeats include a carbon typescript of *Deirdre* with corrections (MS 30,150).

[48] *MNY*, 74–5; see *Life 1*, 408.

[49] *MNY*, 176. Y to Q, 11 March [1914], *CL InteLex* #2415; Yeats to Lady Gregory, 14 March [1914], *CL InteLex* #2417. Quinn nonetheless supported the Abbey Theatre in various ways during its 1911–12 American tour featuring *The Playboy of the Western World* (*MNY* 114–18).

[50] E.g. Quinn to Bullen, 26 May 1908 (QC).

in which Quinn had been involved. For example, WBY's London agent, A. P. Watt, prepared contracts with Macmillan of New York (of which George Brett was still president) for *The Green Helmet and Other Poems* and *J. M. Synge and Other Essays* in 1911 and prepared an agreement with the Little Theatre in Chicago for performances of *The Shadowy Waters* in 1912.[51] James Pond's Lyceum Agency arranged WBY's 1914 US tour,[52] during which WBY and Quinn reconciled.

By 1914, the renowned poet had less need of Quinn's services than at the outset of their relationship. Quinn's greatest contribution to WBY between the resumption of their relations and Quinn's death from stomach cancer at age 54 in 1924 was the attention and friendship he provided to the poet's father, who had moved to New York in 1907 and remained there until his death in 1922. Quinn's principal involvement in WBY's relationship to the literary marketplace from and after 1914 was his acquisition of WBY's manuscripts. At the outset of the resumed relationship, Quinn, who had built a substantial collection of manuscripts, wrote to WBY, noting 'I think you know that I collect manuscripts', advising that he had sold many of his to the founder of the Huntington Library, and proposing an arrangement to acquire WBY's manuscripts.[53] He suggested paying a certain amount yearly, 'say seventy-five or eighty pounds', or purchasing piecemeal or in groups. Yeats declined the proposal of an annual sum but offered to 'send you all I have & you can give me a price for it according to the measure'.[54] Quinn found this 'quite satisfactory'.[55]

Reid's biography of Quinn, which does not mention Quinn's pre-1914 interest in WBY's manuscripts, describes subsequent dealings in general terms that leave room for the impression that Quinn's purchases were primarily a way of creating funds to pay the debt that JBY regularly ran up with his landladies, the Petitpas sisters.[56] A detailed review shows that Quinn began buying WBY's manuscripts for the pleasure of owning them and because he thought they were a good investment. WBY was in no hurry to part with his manuscripts, and it was Quinn who initiated the idea of using funds from manuscript sales to pay JBY's rent debt. As shown below, JBY's rent debt became the recurring reason for bringing manuscript sales to the fore, but WBY remained responsible for JBY's debts and suggested that the purchase of manuscripts be decoupled from the payment of JBY's rent. Initially, it was Quinn who kept them linked, but eventually WBY found it necessary to rely on the linkage to satisfy the gap between the ageing JBY's increasing debt and his diminished income.

WBY did not follow up on the summer 1914 understanding that he would send manuscripts to Quinn. The subject was revived when, during Lady Gregory's visit to the US in 1919, WBY asked her to look into his father's finances.[57] Gregory, who stayed

---

[51] The agreements are included in *CL InteLex* at accession numbers #1846 and #2028.
[52] *Life 1*, 510.
[53] Letter of 3 June 1914.
[54] Y to Q, 9 July [1914], *CL InteLex* #2482.
[55] Letter of 25 July [1914].
[56] *MNY* 178–9.
[57] WBY to Lady Gregory, 29 January [1915], *CL InteLex* #2592.

with Quinn during part of the visit, replied to WBY on 15 March that JBY's income from sketching and writing was drying up, that he could probably earn enough for his petty cash needs, but that his bills to the Petitpases would need to be paid. She advised they be paid through Quinn's office, adding that 'he tells me to say that he could pay something in advance on your MS—if you liked'. WBY wrote Quinn on 19 April 1915 saying that Lady Gregory 'thinks you would be so kind as to let me pay the Petitpas through you', and that 'She says also that you offered to give something on account of the MSS'.[58] WBY enclosed a cheque in an amount approximating $479 and asked Quinn to pay off JBY's debt and let him know if there was any additional amount due. Quinn paid the debt of approximately $530 but told WBY not to worry about the shortfall because that amount 'may be considered as a small payment on account of manuscripts that you are to send me'.[59] Thus began the linkage between manuscripts and rent.

WBY sent the manuscript of *Reveries over Childhood and Youth* the following July. By letter of 16 July 1915, Quinn wrote that it was 'difficult to put a price on MSS' but offered £50 and suggested that if WBY agreed to the price, he would pay himself for the small advance to the Petitpases, and then either hold the balance for JBY's account at Petitpas or send it to WBY. WBY found the price 'generous' and agreed that Quinn should hold the balance as suggested.[60] Acting on WBY's request that he be informed when JBY needed funds, Quinn wrote to WBY on 26 February 1916 saying £20 or £30 would come in handy, and offering to advance it on manuscripts. WBY responded on 26 February that he could send the money soon and asked Quinn to make it up out of 'manuscript money' in the interim.[61] WBY sent £40 on 1 August.[62] Except for a brief exchange in 1916,[63] all was quiet on the manuscript front until 16 May 1917, when WBY wrote to Quinn that he had 'been waiting the stoppings of submarines' to send manuscripts, but 'wonder[ed] if you could give [JBY] the value of some MSS of mine (my ready money is not very abundant in war time)'. He mentioned particular manuscripts, but didn't send them. Quinn was silent.

About to undergo surgery for intestinal cancer, Quinn nonetheless found time to attend to JBY's affairs. He wrote to WBY on 3 February 1918 that he could not value the manuscripts without receiving them, but that he was advancing $200 for JBY's rent. In letters of 8 February and 4 September 1918, WBY offered to decouple the rent from the manuscripts, then enquired about JBY's finances and offered to send manuscripts when

[58] Y to Q [9 April 1915], *CL InteLex* #2626.

[59] Q to Y, 24 April 1915, #153.

[60] Y to Q, 12 September 1915, *CL InteLex* #2760. Quinn sought to add the role of editor to that of owner by sending WBY a letter suggesting detailed improvements to the text (Q to Y, 16 July 1915). These were generally ignored or expressly rejected (Y to Q, 19 December [1915], *CL InteLex* #2831). Quinn had previously made minor editorial suggestions that were accepted by WBY.

[61] Y to Q, 2 April [1916], *CL InteLex* #2923.

[62] Y to Q, 1 August [1916], *CL InteLex* #3012.

[63] Q to Y 26 February 1916; and Y to Q, 2 April [1916], *CL InteLex* #2923, and 1 August [1916], *CL InteLex* #3012.

he got 'to Oxford this winter when the censor might not interfere and the war might be over'. Quinn asked that WBY send the manuscripts when he got to London.[64]

JBY's bout of pneumonia in November 1918 (brought on by the Spanish flu pandemic) elicited generous time and money from Quinn for JBY's care. In letters of 13 and 16 January 1919, Quinn summarized the costs of JBY's care and the status of WBY's manuscript account. WBY sent £234 and suggested, 'I think this is better than our arrangement about MSS', adding that he would send manuscripts and 'You can then give me what you think right for it' and 'you'll know what you are getting'.[65] However, WBY muddied the waters by writing on 11 July 1919 that he had the manuscripts of what became *The Wild Swans at Coole* and *Per Amica Silentia Lunae*.[66] Quinn put matters on hold pending receipt of the manuscripts.[67] After the manuscripts were returned to WBY for lack of a consular declaration, WBY suggested he would bring the manuscripts to New York when he made a planned visit in January.[68] The paper trail fades and vanishes at this juncture, but we know that WBY brought the two manuscripts on his 1920 visit because Quinn sold them in 1924, noting in the catalogue that they were set in order for John Quinn by WBY on 27 May 1920, the last day WBY stayed with Quinn before departing New York.[69]

With JBY's debt mounting, WBY wrote to Quinn on 9 November 1920 that his wife was looking for a manuscript that would pay JBY's expenses if Quinn could dispose of it, but if it did not prove sufficient, 'I must ask you to trust me until I have given my lectures', adding, 'If you will tell me the name of a dealer I can send the MSS to him and save you the trouble.'[70] This prompted the outburst about being a manuscript whore in Quinn's 1 May 1920 letter to Pound. WBY's 22 May letter advised Quinn that JBY had told him that Quinn had paid his rent, and assured Quinn that his bank was sending £176 to Quinn as part payment. WBY acknowledged the insufficiency of this amount and advised that he was redeeming a war note and intending to sell a manuscript to the Pierpont Morgan Library, which, he reminded Quinn, had expressed interest in acquiring one.[71] Quinn replied by asking WBY to send manuscripts to him rather than the Morgan, and saying that he 'could put a better price on them … and perhaps will get one or two dealers bidding for them and will be a good agent for you'.[72] In essence, a less harried Quinn recognized that he was, in fact, a dealer.

---

[64] Letter of 15 September 1918.

[65] WBY later explained to his father by letter of 1 September 1919 that 'it struck me of late that [past manuscript arrangements] might not be fair to Quinn, who might not really want the MSS, so I sold out my Sligo legacy or most of it & paid Quinn up-to-date'. Yeats to J. B. Yeats, 1 September [1919], *CL InteLex* #3648.

[66] Y to Q [11 July 1919], *CL InteLex* #3632.

[67] Letter of 7 August 1919.

[68] Y to Q, 9 August [1919], *CL InteLex* #3643; Y to Q 31 December [1919], CL InteLex #3696.

[69] Quinn sale catalogue, items 11564, 11569, and 11574.

[70] Y to Q, 9 November 1920, *CL InteLex* #3806.

[71] Y to Q, 22 May 1921, *CL InteLex* #3914.

[72] Letter of 5 June 1921.

By the spring of 1923, Quinn had decided to sell the bulk of his books and manuscripts, and the sale took place from 12 November 1923 to 20 March 1924.[73] Although Quinn wrote in the sale catalogue that expiration of the lease for his apartment necessitated the sale, he wrote to Henry Sinclair that he had determined to exit '*the business of collecting old or rare first editions or manuscripts*' and 'to limit myself to modest purchases of modern art'.[74] His self-conception as a dealer is even more apparent in his explanation to Pound that the underlying reason for the sale was 'that I wanted to salt down some money in investments which would bring in something while I slept. I am working toward independence, toward getting to the point where I can be freer'.[75]

Quinn's mindset had so firmly become that of a dealer clearing his inventory that he seems to have given no thought to transferring his remarkable collection of Irish books and manuscripts to a cultural institution that could have preserved the collection intact. He wrote to Dr Joseph Dunn on 1 March 1924 that his Irish books 'were slaughtered ...'. In effect, they were sold for about 14 per cent of what he paid for them.[76] He observed, 'It would have been a great chance for some club or university or library to have made an Irish collection or to have added to its collection,' but he did nothing to make that happen. John Quinn's role in the relationship of W. B. Yeats to the literary marketplace had begun with a bang set off by Quinn's tremendous energy and his belief in WBY as a writer and as an expression of Irish culture. It ended with the whimper of a dealer shutting down a business.

[73] *MNY* 589, 600.
[74] Letter to Henry A. Sinclair, 22 January(?) 1924, emphasis supplied.
[75] Quinn letter to Pound, 10 December 1923.
[76] Extrapolating from Quinn's statement to Dunn that 'books that cost me ten and twelve pounds sold for six and eight dollars ...'.

CHAPTER 7

··

GEORGE YEATS

··

MARGARET MILLS HARPER

In early March 1920, a photographer working for the *Chicago Daily News* took a series of photographs of W. B. Yeats, who was on a four-month American lecture tour.[1] The images, shot on location at the Auditorium Hotel (with its iconic modern design by Louis Sullivan and Dankmar Adler), show the famous visitor at his ease. One pose, featuring his greying hair neatly combed back and his signature pince-nez held loosely in his lap, is more formal than the other, where his hair is loose, his suit rumpled. A large ring on the baby finger of his left hand has been turned around to face the viewer in the second photo.[2] Obviously, the aim was to give an editor two options to accompany a story: more distinguished or more 'arty'.[3]

Two images from this same shoot feature Yeats's wife.[4] One image shows GY in profile, sitting leaning forward in a chair. She is wearing a turban-like hat that looks as if it is made from feathers, a loose-fitting tunic, an ankle-length skirt, a beaded purse hanging from the left hand laid lightly on her knee. The second image (Figure 7.1) is the more striking of the two. She looks directly at the camera, with a less sombre expression than

---

[1] I am grateful to Joseph Sobol for drawing my attention to these photographs.

[2] The ring with emblems of a hawk and butterfly, designed by Edmund Dulac, was commissioned by Mrs. Yeats shortly after their marriage. Both she and her husband were delighted with it. Aside from one occasion, when W. B. mentions in a notebook entry from 1921 that the Control Dionertes 'felt for it on my hand & missed it' after 'I had given George her ring before sleap [*sic*]', he seems to have worn it always. According to Ann Saddlemyer, one of GY 'last gestures at his death was to remove it from his left hand' (*Becoming George: The Life of Mrs. WBY* (Oxford: Oxford University Press, 2002), 140). See also *Life 2*, 125; Saddlemyer, *Becoming George*, 139–141; and a photograph of the ring itself in *YGYL*, facing p. 290.

[3] The titles of the stories indicate that the less formal image might have been a good match, especially the ones repeating his remarks about prohibition or about Chicago women: see, for example, 'Chicago Women Lead the World Says Poet Yeats', *Chicago Evening Post*, 1 Mar. 1920, 1, col. 1; and 'Poet Yeats Here Finds No Beer Is H—L, Old Dear', *Chicago Daily Tribune*, 1 Mar. 1920, section 2, 1, col. 2.

[4] Henceforward, I will abbreviate the names William Butler Yeats as WBY and George (Hyde Lees) Yeats as GY.

FIGURE 7.1 Mrs William Butler Yeats; public domain.

in the other pose. Indeed, an enigmatic half-smile softens her strong chin and prominent nose. She stands a little awkwardly, arms at her sides, the strings of a small purse hanging from her left hand. Her silk tunic can be seen more clearly in this image. Its straight cut is very modern, with embroidery on its yoke, hem, and sleeves in angular shapes and very large stitching, in an art deco (perhaps even verging on cubist) style. The silk might indicate it came from Liberty in London or from a craftswoman emulating its famous style. Liberty, founded to create a London-based challenge to Parisian fashion, specialized in imported fabrics, simple style, and embroidery. It promoted Indian silks and other oriental goods and championed so-called 'aesthetic dress', offering practical, healthy alternatives to corsets and stiff garments. Liberty also specialized in embroidery and patterns for home embroiderers. In general, the style, as George Bernard Shaw noted, enabled women to 'solve the problem of looking well on ARTISTIC lines—on LIBERTY

LINES—on simple, sensible lines'.[5] GY's additional ornamentation takes the form of two necklaces, a long strand of artisan-looking beads and a shorter, very striking medallion in an abstract-looking design, as well as a delicate bracelet and a ring on the ring finger of her left hand. Her hair is cut short but not sharply edged. Her total appearance is one of individual style in a mode generally avant-garde.[6]

If the two images of WBY from this shoot signal *publicity photo of famous writer*, those of GY show a self-expressed modern woman, unconventional and perhaps even a little ahead of her time but with an appreciation for the rational or aesthetic styles, emphasizing comfort and utility over constraint. She seems at once unpretentious and self-possessed, conscious of her appearance but not dramatic. The eyes are by far the most compelling aspect of the image. They are clear and sharp under definite brows and in a slightly square face. The photographer seems to have recognized the power of this gaze: he has framed his subject with her face just above the centre of the lens, equidistant from right and left, so that she seems almost to be capturing the viewer rather than the other way around.

Beginning with attention to a photograph seems as good a way as any to try to come to terms with GY, about whom many stories swirl but who did not write or speak much for public consumption. In the last several decades, this least known of the women in WBY's circle has received an increasing amount of scholarly attention, and her massive contributions to her husband's life and work are more appreciated than has been true for the longer part of the history of Yeats studies. For the first generation or two of scholarship after his death, GY was mentioned publicly and frequently in acknowledgements and copyright pages of works by and about her husband. These were plentiful, from duty but also clearly in genuine gratitude. She was often generous with her time and access to resources in her possession in the years after her long widowhood began in 1939 and before her death in 1968, especially to the more intelligent of the 'seekers' or 'Mincing Machines', as she called them.[7] Important books by scholars like Jon Stallworthy and Richard Ellmann contain expressions of gratitude like the first sentence of Ellmann's influential literary biography, *Yeats: The Man and the Masks* (1948): 'This book is based in part on published materials and in part on some 50,000 pages of unpublished manuscripts of W. B. Yeats which Mrs. Yeats, unbounded in her generosity, permitted me to examine in Dublin.'[8] Stallworthy's incisive study of genetic materials, *Behind the Lines: Yeats's Poetry in the Making* (1961), mentions on its first page that 'Many rough drafts [WBY] actually tore up, and these have only survived through the vigilance of

---

[5] Bonnie English, *A Cultural History of Fashion in the 20th and 21st Centuries*, (2nd edn, London: Bloomsbury, 2013), 112. Shaw is quoted in Barbara Morris, *Liberty Design 1897–1914* (London: Pyramid, 1989), 54.

[6] I am indebted to my colleague Síle de Cléir (Léann na Gaeilge, University of Limerick) for sharing her expertise on historical fashion.

[7] As reported in Saddlemyer, *Becoming George*, 616–17. For an account of her friendly relations with one of these scholars, see Curtis B. Bradford, 'George Yeats: Poet's Wife', *Sewannee Review*, 77 (1969): 385–404.

[8] Richard Ellmann, *Yeats: The Man and the Masks* (New York: Norton, 1948), vii.

Mrs. Yeats, who rescued them from the waste-paper basket' (one of those many swirling stories about GY). Stallworthy thanks her 'above all', since her 'generosity provided me with a cargo which alone justifies the voyage'.[9] In 1986, for a collection reprinting essays written over two decades, Kathleen Raine movingly praises GY:

> I had already met Mrs. Yeats, whom I had visited during the writing of my *Blake and Tradition* ... My pretext was to consult Yeats's Blake books, in which there were marginalia relevant to my work. But Mrs. Yeats received me as a poet, and in fact left me after her death one of the books I had gone to consult. Therefore it is with more than formal thanks that I acknowledge her help ... I have since returned on many occasions to consult Yeats's library (now in the possession of Miss Anne Yeats), and always with the sense of being in the presence of Yeats and Mrs. Yeats ... .[10]

GY did produce thousands of pages of written texts, most in the form of automatic writing, occult notebooks of varying types, and private letters. She also consulted with publishers to edit much of WBY's poetry, drama, and prose. She was a brilliant woman who led a long and active life. Yet convincing narratives about her remain few. Explanations for this state of affairs are, by and large, threefold, though related. First, GY was an intensely private person and discouraged public attention. Second, her magnum opus, as it were, consists of the records of the Yeatses' occult experiments that led to the philosophical treatise *A Vision*. These texts are designed to be cryptic even to the few people who were meant to see them. And third, these writings, as well as the large body of correspondence herself and WBY, remained unpublished until well after the main outlines of narratives about him were well established.[11] Moreover, many of those who talked and wrote about her were creative and opinionated people, with their own reasons for telling their truths slant. These tellers very much include WBY him-self, who created coded figures expressing his feelings for and experiences with GY at a dramatized distance, in poetry, drama, and the prose of *A Vision*.

As the many dedications to her in almost all scholarly work from the some thirty years of her management indicate, GY was the shaper of powerful narratives, though not often in her own words. Almost immediately after her husband's death, she was called on to approve the choice of his official biographer. As she tactfully phrased it in a letter to Harold Macmillan, 'Joe Hone' had produced a book WBY had found 'good, thorough if unimaginative', and that was what she wanted for this one:

> It would have, I think, to be written by an Irishman, and it would also have to be written by a man with whom I could personally work because there is a vast amount of material

---

[9] Jon Stallworthy, *Between the Lines: W. B. Yeats's Poetry in the Making* (Oxford: Oxford University Press, 1963), ix, x.

[10] Kathleen Raine, *Yeats the Initiate: Essays on Certain Themes in the Work of W. B. Yeats* (Mountrath: Dolmen Press; London: George Allen & Unwin, 1986), xvii.

[11] The *'Vision' Papers*, presenting the vast majority of the automatic script, related notebooks, and early versions of *A Vision*, were published in 1992 (vols 1–3) and 2001 (vol. 4). Henceforward they will be abbreviated as *YVP* followed by volume and page number. It is also telling that GY's definitive biography, by Ann Saddlemyer, only appeared in 2002.

for biography which, I think, should in recent years be used with some discrimination. I am not destroying any of this material, it will be at the free use of his biographer, I merely do not wish it to be used as sensational literature.[12]

Obviously, the material requiring 'discrimination' included accounts of WBY's late affairs with other women and the automatic writing and related papers, but GY was in general extremely conscious of her ability to shape discourse about the man who had become his admirers, in Auden's phrase.[13] Richard Ellmann, remembering his friendship with her ten years after her death, recalled something she mentioned but he had not noted in his biography: '[WBY's] extraordinary sense of the way things would look to people later on.' She was clearly describing not merely one aspect of WBY that 'never ceased to astonish her' but also giving Ellmann a window into her own motivations.[14]

In her role as literary executor GY worked with others to bring out several important collections, notably *Last Poems & Plays* (1940) and a new version of the 1933 *Collected Poems*, which, as R. F. Foster notes, was for ten years after WBY's death the only book of his in print.[15] Despite her good sense in reconstructing WBY's wishes, reading his hand, making emendations, and ordering poems, and the careful work of Thomas Mark, the publisher's reader at Macmillan, some of their choices have inspired much debate amongst textual scholars.[16] Before the death of her husband, GY had been one-third of what Warwick Gould has called WBY's 'primary editorial team', along with his publisher Harold

---

[12] Letter from GY to Harold Macmillan, 13 February 1939, quoted in Saddlemyer, *Becoming George*, 571.

[13] W. H. Auden, 'In Memory of W. B. Yeats', in *Collected Poems*, ed. Edward Mendelson (New York: Random House, 1976), 197.

[14] Richard Ellmann, *Yeats: The Man and the Masks* (rev. edn, New York: Norton, 1979), xxvii. The final words of Ellmann's preface to this edition are a moving tribute to GY's 'independence, her astuteness, her humour'. Ellmann concludes, 'Marriage to Yeats was as problem-ridden as it was magnificent. She lived through it with self-possession, with generosity, with something like nobility' (xxvii).

[15] *Life* 2, 654. An earlier posthumous volume, *Last Poems and Two Plays*, was published by the Cuala Press in July 1939. Its ordering of the poems follows a manuscript table of contents drawn up by WBY before his death, presumably to guide his sister Susan Mary ('Lily') Yeats in setting up the book. This ordering of poems and plays, which is different from the 1940 Macmillan volume, has played an important role in the editorial controversies mentioned below. See Curtis Bradford, 'The Order of Yeats's Last Poems', *Modern Language Notes* 76:6 (June 1961): 515–16; 'Last Poems Again', in *The Dolmen Press Yeats Centenary Papers*, ed. Liam Miller (Dublin: Dolmen Press, 1966); and Philip L. Marcus, 'Yeats's "Last Poems": a Reconsideration' *YA*, 5 (1987), ed. Warwick Gould, 3–14.

[16] Although GY and Mark made a number of small to substantive changes to individual texts, perhaps the most vexed issues concern the incorporation of *New Poems* (the Cuala collection published in 1938) with those of *Last Poems and Two Plays* (Cuala, 1939), and with the addition of three poems from *On the Boiler* (1939), to create *Last Poems & Plays* (Macmillan, 1940). The new ordering was continued for the hugely influential *Poems of W. B. Yeats* (Macmillan, 1949). Curtis Bradford first drew widespread attention to these issues in 1961. Given that newer standard editions have had to choose sides, as it were, with regard to ordering especially, much scholarly ink was expended for several decades on these and related textual cruxes. See James Pethica's introduction to his edition of *Last Poems* in the Cornell Yeats series for an overview. It is interesting to consider that GY continued to generate energetic conflict in the Yeatsian world for decades after her husband had become his books, a state of affairs one imagines he would have relished.

Macmillan and Mark.[17] And for the rest of her life GY carefully rescued drafts and kept manuscripts in what one scholar called 'usable disarray', politely offered or withheld access to materials, guiding scholarship and public discourse directly or through instructions to WBY's agent, A. P. Watt. She was to a large degree the curator of 'Yeats', and her achievements may be considered in the company of the many gifted interpretations of his work.[18]

The silk blouse featured in many of the photographs of GY from the early 1920s was obviously a favourite. The largest of the designs in its embroidery is a circle divided horizontally into blocks of what must have been two brightly contrasting colours with a third block closer to the colour of the background between them. A smaller circular space is left unfilled at the centre. The circle, which falls just below the waist at the centre front, is repeated at the edges of the three-quarter sleeves. It is ringed by shapes that are curved on the outside, enabling them to encircle the central image, but straight-sided and sharply angled on their inner edges. They echo triangles and quadrilateral shapes on the yoke of the tunic and draw the eye to the central circle, giving an effect that is boldly geometric, suggesting but also withholding meaning.

It makes sense that GY found appealing a garment that (in addition to looking at once comfortable and visually striking) suggests symbolic geometries. Shapes divide into twos and threes around a circle, leading this viewer at least to imagine the secret work she was pursuing intensely during the American tour, as she did wherever the Yeatses happened to be in the early years of their lives together. The revelations that began on the couple's troubled honeymoon continued almost daily (and exhaustingly, more for her than her husband) for several years, then intermittently for many more. The Yeatses worked together on the bewildering torrent of bits of information about human nature and history, over multiple incarnations, as well as cosmic forces, and eventually came to understand them as part of a symbolic 'system' that functions as a sort of unified field theory of the universe, culture, and the soul. The documents that comprise the 'Vision' papers are less a system than the record of a highly complex collaboration between the Yeatses and a number of other beings whose claim to status as 'real' was part of the research.[19] The automatic script, records of dreams, and notebooks and cards sorting and

---

[17] Warwick Gould, 'W. B. Yeats and the Resurrection of the Author', *The Library*, 16:2 (June 1994), 101–34, 110.

[18] See Saddlemyer's overview of GY's engagements with scholars in the last period of her life, including her subtle examinations and evaluations of them (*Becoming George*, 615–18).

[19] The history of the Yeatses' troubled courtship, marriage, and honeymoon can become almost irresistible for popular biographical accounts. In the midst of it all, GY attempted and succeeded at producing automatic writing. For the best account of the start of what Terence Brown calls 'one of the strangest acts of imaginative collaboration in all literary history' (*The Life of W. B. Yeats* [Oxford: Blackwell, 1999], 252), see Saddlemyer, *Becoming George*, 102–3. For a clear analysis of its meaning, see Catherine E. Paul: 'George Yeats's initial plan was interrupted by sentences that are not exactly disjointed, not exactly startling, and almost illegible, almost beyond the horizon of what can be communicated. That this forceful interruption—redirecting, repurposing—is enacted by sentences it itself interesting: the script is embodied, a conjunction of intention and product, something George Yeats produces even as it controls her. And so, too, did Yeats assent, to George Yeats, to the sentences, to

interpreting data, not to mention horary charts and natal horoscopes they cast to help understand issues and guide activities, are the documentary evidence for an extraordinary adventure in lived philosophy. Until the end of his life, WBY spoke and wrote about the deep convictions that came through a welter of detail clothed in the language of spiritualism and psychic science, astrology, symbols, diagrams, art, history, philosophy, and comparative religion.

The theories that drive the two versions of *A Vision* as well as much of WBY's work from 1917 to the end of his life cluster around geometric symbols, circles and triangles and squares. Late poems, plays, and prose frequently express propositions of endless conflict paradoxically also expressed as a single circular, or spherical, whole. These elaborations on a theme that WBY once called 'a certain myth that was itself a reply to a myth' have GY as their source, though in enigmatic ways that are themselves part of the message. They form a constantly receding horizon. As WBY put it many years later,

> Where got I that truth?
> Out of a medium's mouth,
> Out of nothing it came,
> Out of the forest loam,
> Out of dark night where lay
> The crowns of Ninevah.[20]

The long narrative poem 'The Gift of Harun Al-Rashid', an obvious allegory of the marriage and automatic experiments, appears in the first version of *A Vision*, as do several other equally fictional accounts of the automatic script. The poem, one of the first versions through which WBY told the story of his life-changing experience, anticipates the lines from the posthumously published poem 'The Statues' about what wisdom knows: 'That knowledge increases unreality, that / Mirror on mirror mirrored is all the show'.[21] 'The Gift of Harun Al-Rashid' does reveal the poet's gratitude for the dominant miracle of his later years. GY's mediumistic communications, and the Yeatses' mutual psychic experiments, are figured as a mysterious voice coming from a young bride given to an ageing scholar:

> The voice has drawn
> A quality of wisdom from her love's

---

the script and whatever or whoever dwelled behind it. Their decision to believe and their willingness to surrender enabled experiences, understanding, and writing otherwise impossible' ('W. B. Yeats and the Problem of Belief' [*YA*, 21, 2018], 308).

[20] The phrase 'a certain myth that was itself a reply to a myth' occurs in WBY's notes to his play *The Resurrection*, as do these lines, which form the second stanza of the poem 'Fragments' (*CW2*, 722, *CW1*, 218).

[21] *CW1*, 345.

> Particular quality. The signs and shapes;
> All those abstractions that you fancied were
> From the great Treatise of Parmenides;
> All, all those gyres and cubes and midnight things
> Are but a new expression of her body
> Drunk with the bitter sweetness of her youth.[22]

This risky presentation of an old man claiming that all his knowledge was 'but a new expression' of a young woman's body is complicated somewhat by following the clue of the one specific text mentioned in this description: 'the great Treatise of Parmenides'.

At the start of the poem, the narrator, a Christian scholar in the court of the eighth-century Caliph Harun Al-Rashid named Kusta Ben Luka, asks the old friend to whom he is writing, now the Caliph's treasurer, to hide his letter (that is, the poem) in the 'books of learning' in the Caliph's collection. Kusta has, he says, nearly suggested slipping the letter into the 'great book of Sappho's song'[23] but decides that Parmenides's Treatise would be a better choice. Amongst the many framing layers and displacements of the poem is the enticing suggestion that this Treasure House contained both the complete works of Sappho and Parmenides. Both now exist only as fragments and a good deal of speculation. WBY mentions this detail in notes he appended to the poem's first appearance, in the Cuala Press volume *The Cat and the Moon and Certain Poems* (1924). After telling the story of the poem as recounted in a letter from Owen Aherne (a fictional character), which contains several further alternate versions as befits an old tale kept in oral tradition, WBY writes, 'I do not think it too great a poetical licence to describe Kusta as hesitating between the poems of Sappho and the treatise of Parmenides as hiding places. Gibbon says the poems of Sappho were still extant in the twelfth century, and it does not seem impossible that a great philosophical work, of which we possess only fragments, may have found its way into an Arab library of the eighth century.'[24] In other words, this story of the automatic writing occurs in a fictional, supposedly ancient, and oriental setting, told by a witness to a friend to hide in a book that no longer exists—and not the book of Western history's most famous ancient woman poet but that of a pre-Socratic Greek philosopher, whose work is famously difficult, paradoxical, and profound. The secret is not one to be hidden in love lyrics, though that would be a possibility, but in metaphysical wisdom.

WBY knew of Parmenides not only through Plato's dialogue by that title, which depicts a fictional encounter between Parmenides and Zeno, but also through the scholarly anthology *Early Greek Philosophy* by John Burnet. When trying to piece together the shards of data coming every day in the automatic sessions and composing *A Vision*, WBY used this book extensively.[25] According to Burnet, Parmenides influences the

---

[22] *CW1*, 456.
[23] *CW1*, 451.
[24] *VP*, 829.
[25] For information about the personal library of WBY and GY, see Edward O'Shea's *Descriptive Catalogue* (New York and London: Garland, 1985), and the more recent *W. B. and George Yeats Library: A*

development of Western philosophy not only by his ideas but also by his method: 'The great novelty in the poem of Parmenides', Burnet writes, 'is the method of argument', and it is this 'thoroughgoing dialectic of Parmenides that made progress possible'.[26] WBY was not a systematic reader of philosophy, but his eye was drawn to Parmenides's assertions that reality must be ultimately spherical, or that 'there is not, and never shall be, any time other than that which is present', passages WBY marked in his copy.[27] But WBY would also have found immediately relevant how Parmenides insisted that new knowledge arrive through dialectic, one concept giving rise to and pushing against another, two viewpoints or voices. One of Parmenides's famous commentators, the fifteenth-century philosopher Pico della Mirandola, claims that Plato's dialogue mirrors Parmenides's own method of finding truth: 'But I shall first say this about the *Parmenides*. Nothing in the whole dialogue is positively asserted. ... That book is ... nothing but a dialectical exercise. ... [N]owhere is anything affirmed, but everywhere it is merely asked.'[28]

Parmenides, whose Treatise exists only in poetic fragments but whose method was hidden in the pages of *A Vision*, may also have been known to GY years before WBY pored over the pages of Burnet. As a young woman she read deeply in philosophy and esoteric religion. By 1914, the year of her initiation into the Hermetic Order of the Golden Dawn,[29] she was expert enough in the works of Pico to record in a notebook the thirty-one of his 900 theological theses that treat the mystical *Hymns of Orpheus* and magic.[30] She even purchased a handsome sixteenth-century copy of Pico's *Heptaplus* translated into Italian.[31] According to Saddlemyer, Pico's eccentric thinking 'would engross [GY] for at least the next decade' afterwards.[32] Her husband seems to have been particularly impressed by her ability to translate a thinker known for his audacious erudition, though WBY admits he knows little.[33] Once the proofs for the first version of

Short-title Catalog compiled by Wayne K. Chapman (Liverpool: Liverpool University Press, 2019). On WBY's marginalia in his copy of Burnet, see also Wayne K. Chapman, 'Authors in Eternity: Some Sources of Yeats's Creative Mysticism', *YA*, 15, and *Yeats's Collaborations*, ed. Wayne K. Chapman and Warwick Gould (Basingstoke: Palgrave Macmillan, 2002), 295–8.

[26] John Burnet, *Early Greek Philosophy* (London and Edinburgh: Adam & Charles Black, 1892), 191.

[27] Burnet, *Early Greek Philosophy*, 186–7. Beside the latter passage, WBY wrote, 'Time as illusion'. O'Shea, *Descriptive Catalog*, 308.

[28] Pico della Mirandola, *Of Being and the One*, trans. Paul J. W. Miller, in *On The Dignity of Man, Of Being and the One, Heptaplus* (Englewood Cliffs, NJ: Prentice Hall, 1985), 39–40.

[29] Notably, she was sponsored by W. B. Yeats, or, as he would have been known in the Order, Demon Est Deus Inversus. Her chosen motto was 'Nemo Sciat', 'let no one know'. See Saddlemyer, *Becoming George*, 66, and my own *Wisdom of Two* (Oxford: Oxford University Press, 2006), 104–7.

[30] These audacious theses, which Pico published when he was about GY's age, included claims of the truths of distinctly heterodox sources. They were suppressed by the Church in Pico's time but revered in the theosophical and magical circles in which both GY and WBY moved centuries later. *NLI*, 36, 281/4; see Saddlemyer, *Becoming George*, 60.

[31] Pico della Mirandola, Giovanni, *Le sette sposizioni del S. Giovanni Pico De La Mirandola, intitolate Heptaplo* (Florence, 1555).

[32] Saddlemyer, *Becoming George*, 60.

[33] Soon after the marriage began, WBY wrote to Lady Gregory that GY 'is working now at a big Latin edition of Pica della Mirandola & finds there much profound astrology', characteristically vague

A Vision arrived, he recalled later, he could at last abandon the promise made to the instructors not to read philosophy. He began with Berkeley, he says, and then 'I took down from my wife a list of what she had read, two or three volumes of Wundt, part of Hegel's *Logic*, all Thomas Taylor's *Plotinus*, a Latin work of Pico della Mirandola, and a great deal of mediaeval mysticism. I had to ignore Pico, for I had forgotten my school Latin and my wife had burnt her translation when she married me, "to reduce her luggage" '.[34] If the book WBY 'had to ignore' was the beautiful copy GY kept, even if she destroyed her translation, not only his poor Latin stood in the way: the book is in Italian (more precisely, sixteenth-century 'Tuscan', as its title page announces).

How does all this help us understand GY? A winding trail begins with a curious reference to a pre-Socratic philosopher occurring at significant points in one of WBY's more unusual poems, a long dramatic monologue set in eighth-century Persia with more affinities to the *Arabian Nights* than Irish legend. The philosopher is known for his insistence on truth arriving only through ideas coming from two directions. This reference leads to a confrontational esoteric fifteenth-century philosopher who is the founder of Christian Kabbalistic tradition, and a massive and elegant sixteenth-century Italian translation of his most important text. That book was purchased by a young Englishwoman (21 at the time), who probably intended to produce an English translation and was a much more systematic scholar than the man she married. That text contains cryptic readings of sacred verses, words, and even letters, revealing the secrets of God to those few who can decipher the signs and allegories in which they lay hidden. WBY writes out the story of how he and his wife received information from a number of disembodied instructors in automatic writing and dreams, including the detail that his wife destroyed her translation, for no other reason than to lighten her luggage (even in the era of regulations for carry-on items on flights, this explanation strains the imagination). He appends this story to the second version of the book explaining the public part of the complex occult system they received and created together. Incidentally, the first version of *A Vision*, published a dozen years earlier, had explained the reception of the system by means of outlandish tales of a mysterious book owned by Michael Robartes (another fictional character) and an Arabian tribe that danced patterns on the desert sand.

A few other mythologized semi-versions of GY exist, notably in several poems including the figures of Solomon and the Queen of Sheba. These biblical characters have enjoyed a long textual and artistic history, from Josephus and Origen to depictions and discussions in Talmudic, Coptic, Ethiopian, and Aramaic texts, in the Quran, medieval wisdom literature, and throughout the Italian Renaissance. The poems 'Solomon to Sheba' and 'Solomon and the Witch' recount or represent dialogues (though the first gives no actual speech to the female speaker) between Solomon and Sheba, the latter

---

on details: he misspells the name of the author, misstates the language of the book, and also muddles numerology and astrology (25 November [1917], *CL InteLex* #3364).

[34] *AVB*, 15.

a racialized and eroticized woman (with 'dusky face' and 'Arab eyes'[35]), matching wits and engaging in sexual play. The position of Solomon as the embodiment of wisdom is now shared. Layers of feints and veils overlay these narratives, which link conjugal love and desire with the progress of the soul towards the infinite as well as arcane realms of learning, over history and across cultures. It is not clear who is the lover and who the beloved, where agency resides and how much is determined or inflicted, how Chance and Choice (two poles discussed in 'Solomon and the Witch') operate for each or both.

Other poems and plays present similarly complex representations of such forces. Two in particular, which follow 'Solomon to Sheba' in the volume *Michael Robartes and the Dancer*, register the intense emotion accompanying the Yeatses' marriage. Read together, 'An Image from a Past Life' and 'Under Saturn' inevitably suggest a wife's jealousy at the after-effects of 'some lost love' in her husband's past.[36] Yet they can be read as more general fear and anxiety on the part of both partners embarking on a powerful commitment. The poems represent a state that joins not just two people but families and ancestral history, as well as the whole powerful collective store of images that appear in dreams. 'An Image from a Past Life', a dialogue poem between voices labelled *He* and *She*, does not make it clear whose 'sweetheart from another life' is terrifying *She*. When *She* describes the 'image of my heart that is smitten through', *He* assumes the female image is of a former lover of his. But it is the woman who had imagined 'Youth's bitterness being past' and that her heart had 'learned its lesson'.[37] Is the mysterious image a sweetheart from one of his former lives, or one of hers? The evocative poem is the stronger, I think, for its ambiguity. Metamorphoses of emotion into images in dreams are rarely stable. The point of the poem has to do with the transference of dream truth between the two new partners. They are linked even in their subconscious lives.

The larger point of all the smokescreens WBY's work throws up in front of the figure of GY is that she quickly became too close and too important for her talkative and confessional writer-husband to 'write it out in a verse'. Few if any depictions of any family members exist in WBY's work: GY is named in the short poem written 'To be Carved on a Stone at Thoor Ballylee', each child has one dedicatory poem marking their birth, and readers search in vain for portraits of parents, siblings, or children. Again, the silk blouse may come to our aid in tracing another large area of GY's significance, besides that of primary caretaker of the Yeats industry after his death, and partner and co-creator in his intellectual life—including being an incisive sounding board for drama and theatre business. She was of immense daily and material support.

That support was far greater than her skills at being gracefully capable in wifely and motherly roles, though these were considerable. For example, from the start she was a

---

[35] *CW1*, 138.

[36] *CW1*, 179. In 'Under Saturn', the original phrase 'some lost love', which the saturnine speaker asks his new lover not to imagine as coming between them, is 'unassailable / Being a portion of my youth'. The phrase was later revised to a slightly more mollifying description of 'lost love, inseparable from my thought / Because I have no other youth'.

[37] *CW1*, 178–9.

favourite with WBY's family. After first meeting her, his sister Lily wrote their father a description:

> We like George *greatly*. There is no doubt at all in our minds. She fitted in at once delightfully—is very quiet but sparkles now and again in an engaging way. And she and Willie seemed in such perfect accord. I never saw him look better, so young looking and so handsome. She looks older than her years. I think it is the marked features—a very large nose, her hair a reddish brown, very wavy and curling, and worn low over her ears. She has a good deal of colour, and very nice eyes, really beautiful eyes, blue, a charming expression. You feel that she has plenty of personality but that her disposition is so amiable that she does not often assert herself—not from inertness, but because she is happiest in agreement with the people about her. This is the impression she gave us. She has gaiety, and is I am sure intuitive. She would fit in anywhere.[38]

When GY married, she had some capital, about the same amount as her bridegroom (*pace* the persistent gossip that WBY married her for money),[39] and she was happy to use it, not only for projects like the renovation of the romantic but fund-draining Thoor Ballylee but also for WBY's family members, including his 'prodigal father' and her sisters-in-law. When Lily Yeats's health crisis forced her to stop working in 1923, GY essentially took over the embroidery wing of the Cuala enterprise. WBY wrote to his friend Sturge Moore that GY was not only managing the finances but also modernizing the style. Her taste, as shown in the Chicago photograph, had moved on from Arts and Crafts design:

> Have you heard that as a result of my sister's illness my wife has taken charge of the Cuala embroidery and that the whole industry is moving into 82 Merrion Square? My wife is full of energy of mind and body and will I think greatly improve the work. She knows what people wear and has seen modern art. My sister's work had become too sere[?] a ghost of long past colours and forms.[40]

Events in the early years of the Yeatses' lives together included caring for Iseult Gonne, restoring a distinctly uncomfortable Norman tower down the road from one of WBY's most formidable friends, Lady Gregory, travelling across the Atlantic for a major American tour a few months after giving birth, and moving his sister's craft business into her home. In the background of everything were the ongoing automatic sessions and the emotional and theoretical work of constructing the system, which emphatically joined mind, heart, and physical life.

When GY married, she did not expect a peaceful life. The character Emer in the play *The Only Jealousy of Emer*, the much-betrayed wife of the mythic hero Cuchulain, longs

---

[38] *NLI*, 31, 113; see also Saddlemyer, *Becoming George*, 157.
[39] Saddlemyer, *Becoming George*, 99.
[40] Letter from WBY to T. Sturge Moore, 18 August [1923], *CL InteLex* # 4359; *TSMC*, 49.

for such a future. The climax turns on the impossible choice Emer is offered by the im-mortal trickster Bricriu, between saving her husband's life and retaining 'the hope that some day somewhere / We'll sit together at the hearth again'.[41] This play was much discussed in the automatic script and presents a quaternity of characters with analogues in both the system of *A Vision* and in the personal lives of its co-creators. The plot bears obvious affinities to the situation in which WBY found himself at the time of his marriage, caught at a crossroads between one life and another and involved with three women. Emer yearns for her husband to grow old comfortably with her alone.

Such may have been what GY's bridegroom imagined for himself, as he wrote pri-vately to Lady Gregory shortly before the marriage:

> I am longing for all to be over that a new life of work and common interest may give Georgie & myself one mind & drive away after a time these wild gust[s] of feeling. I beleive [*sic*] that in spite of all I shall make her happy and that in seeking to do so I shall make myself happy. She has great nobility of feeling.[42]

It may also have been what he imagined GY wanted, at least at this early stage in their relationship. But I doubt she did. In June 1919, a new control arrived in the automatic script, a spirit named Ameritus. Who is this, WBY asked the two communicators for the session. In backward writing, GY gave Thomas's and Eurechtha's reply: 'interpreters daimon'. The next day, Ameritus guided the session and gave the Yeatses more informa-tion: WBY asked, 'Are you a guide giving expression to interpreters Daimon' and was informed, 'Yes that which is <u>sweet in bitterness</u>.' Is her daimon bitter, then? WBY wanted to know. No, Ameritus answered, 'That is my inscription. I am a personality,' before plunging the couple into complex discussions about vulnerable areas of their mutual lives.[43] Years later, in the 1930s, amongst the many annotations GY made to her copy of WBY's 1933 *Collected Poems* is one that echoes this sense of sweetness and bitterness to-gether. She wrote this comment in the margin at the line, from WBY's poem 'Vacillation', 'Let all things pass away'[44]:

> Homer was wrong in saying 'would that strife might perish from gods and men.' He did not see that he was praying for the destruction of the universe; for, if his prayers were heard, all things would pass away.' Heraclitus.[45]

Far from longing for escape from difficulty, GY, I suspect, found her complicated life well worth the troubles she took on by marrying WBY, even if the costs were at times considerable. Her sense of humour and good company may not be prominent in the

---

[41] *CW2*, 320.
[42] Letter from WBY to Lady Gregory, 13 October [1917], *CL InteLex* #3340.
[43] *YVP* 2:300–2 and following.
[44] *CW1*, 251–2.
[45] Annotation by GY, W. B. Yeats, *The Collected Poems* (London: Macmillan, 1933), 285; item 2323 in O'Shea's *Descriptive Catalog* and 2344 in Chapman's *Short-title Catalog*.

exotic figures in the narratives WBY created to represent her and their lives together, but they are more than evident in the letters they exchanged. WBY wrote to her frequently, more regularly and with more ease than any other of his tremendous number of correspondents. She wrote to him as well, in letters that are informative (even gossipy), incisive, sometimes moving, with a keen eye for detail and sense of the comic. Their correspondence, scrupulously edited by Ann Saddlemyer, is the second important trove of documents through which we can make sense of this astonishing woman. If the automatic experiments with their complex mythic patterns illuminate her symbolically, the correspondence gives an opposite pole: to use the symbolic terms of *A Vision*, it is solar to the lunar revelations of the occult papers. The correspondence between the Yeatses was carried out whenever they were apart, as was frequently the case; it is obviously the record of a companionship that stimulated and pleased them both. Reading the letters, one has the sense that WBY traded writing *about* her for writing *to* her. The ring she gave him represented both of them equally: hawk of intellect and butterfly of wisdom were both in motion over the twenty years of their lives together, and in further flight during the thirty years in which she lived alone as 'Mrs W. B'. The double symbol did indeed represent the answer to WBY's question, 'Were George & I chosen for each other.'[46] She wore no such ring. Her chosen symbols and patterns, like her personal style, are more abstract expressions of the encounter of oppositions: silk with angular embroidery, bright circles enclosing centres left unadorned.

---

[46]   Card S44, *YVP*, 3, 400. Following the question, the card quotes from a very early automatic script of November 1917: 'one needs material protection one emotional protection—the eagle & the butterfly' 'In her seen [as] distrust of self' 'Butterfly her & another thing'. It is far from clear which member of the couple needed, was offered, or received both sorts of protection. GY was not shielded from some of the negative effects of ongoing mediumship, despite an early instructor warning them that 'The automatic script will only continue for a time because it will be too bad for her—that side of the anti should not be developed too greatly' (10 Nov 1917, *YVP*, 1, 72).

CHAPTER 8

....

THE WRITINGS
OF JACK YEATS

....

NICHOLAS ALLEN

BESIDES his many oil paintings, illustrations, and constant sketching, Jack Yeats wrote novels, plays, and children's entertainments, collected scrapbooks, and made toy boats throughout his long life. The diversity of his art, and its interconnection, is still in need of exploration, as are its cultural underpinnings.[1] Yeats's uncertain early life was less migrant than that of his brother, the poet, the family leaving him in the care of his Sligo grandparents for longer, an attachment that secured his love of ships and the sea. One of the young boy's abiding memories was standing on the bridge over the Garavogue, watching the water run into the western ocean, from where his imagination ran to pirates, treasure, and the eventual homeward turn.[2] This setting is important because it confirms a central reality in the understanding of Jack Yeats's many subtle arts, which is their mental setting in the late British imperial world. For, however he declared himself against all forms of force and coercion, which explains in turn his reluctance to reduce, as he saw it, his art from abstraction to explanation, he lived in the cultural disruptions that this global experiment in capital and exchange brought even to the periphery of Sligo.

It was possible there to read penny dreadfuls of adventure and experience, as it was also to see the constant stream of migration from the west coast of Ireland to Boston, New York, Liverpool, and London. These transits shape Jack's brother William Butler Yeats's early novel of an unhappy shipping clerk, *John Sherman*, just as they speak to Jack's professional beginnings as an illustrator for commercial presses. Jack's first

---

[1] Much of the foundational work on the literary significance of Jack Yeats can be read in Robin Skelton, *The Collected Plays of Jack B. Yeats* (London: Secker & Warburg, 1971), John Purser, *The Literary Works of Jack B. Yeats* (London: Rowan & Littlefield, 1991), and Norah McGuinness, *The Literary Universe of Jack B. Yeats* (Washington DC: Catholic University of America Press, 1992).

[2] I discuss these maritime influences on Yeats's work more in a chapter on his scrapbooks in *Ireland, Literature and the Coast: Seatangled* (Oxford: Oxford University Press, 2020).

public writings are the short captions that accompanied his drawings of London life; here too, however, there is diversion, as many such illustrations also adorn his private letters, much as they also feature in his scrapbooks, where he was wont to add words and images to newspaper and magazine cuttings. Later again there is Yeats's marginal life in Strete, Devon, far from the metropolis of London where he made his living, the paintings beginning to sell, but only ever in modest numbers. The style of this work is well known, and documentary in a way the later hallucinatory oils of the later 1920s and after are not. Returning to Ireland, he lived outside Dublin but kept a studio in it, where he was visited by the likes of Thomas McGreevy, Louis MacNeice, and Ernie O'Malley[3].

This same period saw an increase in Jack Yeats's writing for the stage, and in fantasies that can only loosely be described as novels. For all the strangeness of books like *Sligo* and *The Amaranthers*, a representation of the multimodal world that shaped Jack Yeats from his earliest imagination to his last offers a method of approach to his written work that, if not intent on decoding that which is beyond deconstruction because it is made from the fabric of suggestion, can improve our quality of attention to his words beyond identifications like the surreal and the eccentric. Bemusement, on the other hand, has long been a common reaction to Jack Yeats's writing, even as it was first published. The challenge to the reader was that each represented a narrative with little sense of a beginning or end, but rather a delight in the assembly of words presented. His imagistic style has suggested a synchronicity between his writing, his art, and the wider panorama of modernism, which is itself shorthand for a diverse set of aesthetic forms that so populate literature in Ireland across the first half of the twentieth century. This prescription, again, tells only part of the story. In one respect the inscrutability of modernist experiment, in which form takes precedence over meaning, and image over narrative, is true to the absolute resistance of Yeats's writing to critical decoding, by whatever kind of reading. What this formation elides, however, are the deeper roots of this fantastic art in late nineteenth-century archipelagic cultures of childhood and expression[4]. By the 1930s, Jack Yeats's writing was at once archaic and contemporary, impossibly old-fashioned and apparently futuristic. That he so veiled his works in visual and textual suggestion does not mean that they were produced without context. It does invite the thought, however, that his residual insistence on the untranslatability of his art to expressive forms other than those he himself proposed in the reception of his work can itself become a point of reference from which to make connections across his illustrations, paintings, and books.

---

[3] There are amusing and insightful accounts of their interactions in both Martha Dow Fehsenfeld and Lois More Overbeck, eds., *The Letters of Samuel Beckett: Volume One, 1929–1940* (Cambridge: Cambridge University Press, 2009), and Cormac O'Malley and Nicholas Allen, eds., *Broken Landscapes: Selected Letters of Ernie O'Malley, 1924–1937* (Dublin: Lilliput, 2011).

[4] For further discussion of early twentieth-century literature in these terms read John Brannigan's excellent study, *Archipelagic Modernism: Literature in the Irish and British Isles, 1890–1970* (Edinburgh: Edinburgh University Press, 2015).

Jack Yeats was an artist of sequence. Sometimes his threads of association tangled with the contemporary moment, and sometimes they did not. Sometimes his work was made of memory and dreams, and sometimes of experience and concern for his contemporary world. Often these sequences run like threads beside each other in a text, some finishing abruptly, only to be taken up later, others consistent all the way through. The literary analogue might be Yeats's constant delight in speech, which he often captured in short snippets to accompany the sketches he drew in his letters to John Masefield. Jack Yeats loved talk, which is the motor of many of his literary works, from the children's plays to the novels. Relatedly, he was a good companion to Synge in their sometimes uncomfortable forays into the remoter areas of the western seaboard in the expedition that became *Life in the West of Ireland*. Like his brother the poet, Jack Yeats visited Lady Gregory at Coole Park, where he sketched the lake and its birdlife, even if he was at a tangent to the literary revival of which WBY was the public face, appearing most frequently in the intervals in which his sisters needed illustrations for the Cuala Press publications.

Jack Yeats inhabited a late imperial world in which these various attachments were commonplace and in no need of reconciliation. There were moments in his life, as I have argued before, that a suggestion can be made of some forms of radical dissent in his art. Whatever the merits of that discussion, Jack Yeats's writing maintains a persistent, and a never-ending, commitment to the idea of the author as a medium who tells stories to himself. This is the oddity of his enterprise, and its innovation, even as it chimes with modernist practices of narrative dissociation. The titles of even his most public works, his plays, give a clue as to his inward turn, *Ah Well* and *La La Noo* among them. The only moments where he approaches any kind of clarity are in his instructions to children, both in the plays and in the short books that tell of ships upon the main, and including detailed directions as to the best method by which to flick sand onto a paper stage in imitation of a pirate digging for treasure. *A Little Fleet* is a manual for children to build toy boats to designs that he created in his own Devon backyard. Each vessel has a name and a history, and the book shares the accounts of their voyages on the River Gara, which is the author's nod to his childhood Garavogue. The hand-drawn map of this Devon river fantasia suggests some abiding coordinates for Yeats's later prose, in shipwreck, snags, and gallows. The five craft of this flotilla are *The Monte*, *The Moby Dick*, *The Theodore*, *The Pasear*, and *The New Corinthian*, which was the name also of a book then famous for its promotion of small-boat sailing, a copy of which Erskine Childers also kept aboard his own yacht. *The Monte* was a fore-and-aft schooner made of wood, with paper sails and a stone for ballast. It met its end after a hard turn into Safety Cove, its demise marked by a poem from Yeats's close friend John Masefield:

> There, where the stones are gleamin',
>   A passer-by can hark
> To the old drowned 'Monte' seamen
>   A-singing through the dark ...
>
> Down in the pebbled ridges
>   Our old bones sing and shout;

> We see the dancing midges,
>   We feel the skipping trout.
>
> Our bones are green and weeded,
>   Our bones are old and wet;
> But the noble deeds that we did
>   We never can forget.[5]

This miniature drama bears some comparison to the transitional hydroscapes of the Revival, inland waters as the portal to other worlds, as they are in a poem like WBY's 'The Lake Isle of Innisfree'. One source for that poem is recognized as the poet's observation of a fountain in a window display in a London shop. The proximity between the cultural privileges of bourgeois life and a yearning for poetic release by rural waters brings Masefield and the Yeats brothers into a circuit that the distance between children's literature and poetry otherwise obscures. There is symmetry too in their shared formation in cultures of late Victorian masculinity and adventure, as the song of the burning *Theodore* extols:

> And let no landsman doubt it,
>   She was a gallant ship;
> And her Cap. (brave man) throughout it
>   Kept a stiff upper lip.[6]

These plays for children are the very stuff of Yeats's archipelagic attachments, which extended from the mid to late nineteenth century into the early and middle twentieth. They are archaic and modern in equal measure, the miniature mechanics of their production a choreography of all the elements that went into the imagination of what had been the home countries before Ireland broke partially free. Within the audiences that kept to the traditions of the toy theatre, Yeats was received in a line that went back through Robert Louis Stevenson to Skelt, Pollock, and Redington, the dramatists and shopkeepers who furnished children's imaginations with the theatre of oceanic empire, drawn to intimate scale. In his *Memoirs and Portraits* Stevenson recognized the synchronicity between his own childhood fascination for the little theatre and the fabric of England itself. To him, 'England, the hedgerow elms, the thin brick houses, windmills, glimpses of the navigable Thames … England, when at last I came to visit it, was only Skelt made evident: there was the inn-sign, and there the horse trough, all foreshadowed in the faithful Skelt.'[7]

Jack Yeats did something more again, which was to commit himself to the technical reimagination of these small-scale productions as a way, perhaps, of reordering that larger material world that Stevenson saw so clearly. There is in this a premonition of the

---

[5] Jack Yeats, *A Little Fleet* (London: Elkin Matthews, 1902), 14–15.

[6] Ibid., 26.

[7] Dorothy Nevile Lees, 'Robert Louis Stevenson and the Drama of Skelt', *The Mask: A Quarterly Journal of the Art of the Theatre*, 5:1 (July 1912), 78.

questions Yeats would ask again and again in his prose, of what is real and what is fancy, and of what does it matter if we cannot divide the two. Understood through the medium of the toy plays, this becomes a social as much as an aesthetic question, and points to the heightened awareness Yeats always had for an audience, however much he insisted on the integrity of his own individual ability to communicate with it. This push-me-pull-you gives the later prose an unevenness that can make it difficult to read. In the compact scenarios of the plays it gives the least movement the most purchase, the fewer words the more drama.

Jack Yeats arrived at this reduction by way of the greatest extravagances of the nineteenth-century stage, as he observed in his memory of the 'old "Penny Plain and Tuppence Coloured" plays', which 'were adapted from full grown plays like "Three fingered Jack, the terror of Jamaica," or "Paul Clifford" or "Mazeppa", plays which were full of sword fights and pistollings, swoonings of ladies and poisonings of cups'.[8] This was impossible to replicate with cardboard figures. Instead he approached the staging of his little dramas with careful stagecraft. For the coloured fires of pirates, gunpowder, and cannon he used red and green matches, 'used them good and plenty!'[9] Rather than hand-painted backgrounds he used sheets of coloured paper to show sea, land, or sky. Lighting was the shining of a light onto blue paper behind a zigzag cut in the black cloth that draped the offstage, and footlights were the reflectors from domestic night lights. The whole points to a seriousness with regard to stage and scene, and to an awareness of the ways in which small variations in the production can frame larger meanings, and, sometimes, create spectacle.

By Yeats's later career in the theatre this aesthetic architecture is harder to see. A play like *La La Noo*, which was first produced by Ria Mooney in the Abbey Theatre on 3 May 1942, is a study of a publican, a stranger, and seven women who meet by coincidence in a pub 'in a remote part of the country close to the sea'.[10] The play has no plot. Things happen, but in consequence of lives lived before any character takes the stage. The stage directions could be those of any peasant play for which the Abbey had then become too well known, except that Yeats's attention to sheets of colour gives the drabness of the public house a painterly frame:

> Green outside shutter standing against wall. Open doorway, green door to right of centre. Outside, scene of sandy road, bent grass, sea islands near, and high islands distant. Ocean horizon ...[11]

The characters themselves are barely sketched, except that they share a way-worn quality in their manner and their dress. The play begins with the publican and the stranger

[8] Jack B. Yeats, 'How Jack B. Yeats Produced his Plays for the Miniature Stage, by the Master Himself', *The Mask: A Quarterly Journal of the Art of the Theatre*, 5:1 (July 1912), 49.
[9] Ibid., 50.
[10] Jack Yeats, *La La Noo* (Dublin: Cuala, 1943).
[11] Ibid.

talking about the townland sports on the beach. The echo of Synge is obvious, but Yeats had his own long-standing interest in horses, about which he collected all kinds of ephemera throughout his life. The women appear in the pub as they have missed the bus to take them home. The stranger consoles them on their travelling late with a vision of the west coast that suggests the circumference of his own travel. 'You'll have a beautiful view on the ocean and the sun setting as you go up the road', he says, leaving 'the Bay of Naples and Sydney Harbour and Rio looking like a bunch of faded flowers before you'.[12] This word picture is framed by a fading light offstage, much as the younger Yeats created light and shade with his matches and reflections. The women too have travelled, and have an easy familiarity with America. There are other hints of faraway places, as when the rain begins to fall in Act II and the Stranger asks the Publican:

STRANGER   (to the Publican) Has the Mem Sahib any dry clothes to lend them?
PUBLICAN   Mem Sahib? Who's that?
STRANGER   The Missus—your wife.[13]

The tattoo of other languages, and the half-phrases that circulate through Ireland in the wake of its attachment to a once global empire, inform a literary technique that continues through all of Jack Yeats's writing.

It is an archaic register that survives in the literature as an indigestible remnant of the island's former bonds, which were cultural as much as, and perhaps even more than, political, if the two can be separated. Yeats lived always in the byways of these formations, and never abandoned them; however, his sympathies were for an idea of Ireland that was only barely imaginable by the mid-twentieth century. Sometimes this anachronism allowed the expression of forms of dissidence that were aside from the constitutional questions that had divided Ireland physically and psychologically, even as they pointed to the damage these compromises caused in the social sphere. The repressions of post-independence Ireland were real and dreadful, as were the realities of poverty, institutionalization, and emigration. Yeats's dialogue of the publican and the stranger is differently suggestive when thought of in these larger contexts. As the two men smoke, they worry about the women, who were soaked as they waited for the bus that has still not come:

PUBLICAN   They'll be glad to get their clothes again. The unfortunate creatures! . . .
STRANGER   And why should they worry, good dry hay and there's a fashion for it now—the nude . . .
PUBLICAN   What's that? . . .
STRANGER   The Nude, the Naked. The English pronounce it nude, the Yankees say Nood—it sounds fatter to me—the French say Le Nu.
PUBLICAN   La Noo.
STRANGER   Le Nu.

---

[12] Ibid., 5.
[13] Ibid,, 25.

PUBLICAN   La Noo. La La Noo. French That's French! ... It must be a gorgeous thing
to be able to speak maybe two or three languages. So that you could be entertaining
two or three persons with in yourself 'the nude' says he 'the nood' is that right? 'The
Nood' says he 'La La Noo' says I.[14]

Jack Yeats was not one for manifestos. Instead he drew in his words, his characters, and
his stage directions an atmosphere that was of the world, if not always in it.

It is here that a play like *La La Noo* intersects with a work like Beckett's *Waiting for
Godot*, which also has a cast waiting by a road for something that does not happen. Like
Yeats, Beckett attended carefully to stagecraft and to the capacity of fewer words to carry
more freight. Beckett departed from Jack Yeats in his jettison of the folk-drama, but
there is a common, or perhaps better a continuing, panorama in both artists' orches-
tration of experience through the suggestion of sensation. The stranger, for example,
advises the publican that he should take more pleasure in his life. 'I suppose I should', he
answers.

I have the broad ocean before me, and the clouds rushing over my head all day long
and in the night, only it's so black I can't see them, unless there was a moon. Well,
anyway, thank God for the moon, I suppose people in the distant places, if they knew
I was here, would say 'That man has the wealth of the world in the air and the sea and
his health.'[15]

This is a first instance of the inner self as the territory of multiple voices, which might be
another way to express an experience of modernity. Jack Yeats veiled these transitions in
the most hackneyed of settings and speech, the pub by the west of Ireland as a theatre for
the emotions a long-established cliché even by the mid-twentieth century. *La La Noo* is
a simulacrum of these received forms rather than a reiteration, its gesture to other styles
of expression signalled in the care Yeats gives to the offstage, where the stranger dies
when he tries to drive the bus himself down a bog road. The abrupt and bloody ending is
an old feature of the toy theatre. Now it is an opportunity for Yeats to close the play with
sense impressions that depend on the interplay between words and light. The play closes
with the body of the stranger laid out in the pub:

(Exit Third and Sixth Woman, passing window on left. Publican goes behind bar, gets
matches and lights lamp. Behind bar is now dimly lit up, and front of bar in shadow
and across to right of scene. Publican comes round ... to front of bar and sits down
in chair. Distant noise of lorry starting and going away. The sky is darkening—the
streaks of red sinking.)[16]

---

[14] Ibid., 29.
[15] Ibid., 31.
[16] Ibid., 52.

Fitting for a play of many languages and places, *La La Noo* has several endings, of the stranger, of the day, and, perhaps, of the folk-drama of sports and drink, crumpled up and thrown away like the newspaper the publican uses to wipe the counter. The fade of light from the sky suggests closure too, even if Yeats will not entirely give up the flare of red as a visual impression.

La La Noo was not a commercial success and was first printed only in a limited edition of 250 copies for the Cuala Press in January 1943, at the height of a world war whose shadows John Purser reads into the play. All of Yeats's literary work is shaped by the backward look, the prose in particular constructed from chains of association whose links are all of the past. The aesthetic effect of their connection is in consequence the key register of his experimentation, which is signalled most strongly in the gaps these fabrications leave between the text and the reader, who is caught constantly between the materiality of places that the books describe and the operations of individual memory that recall them. The book where this process works most consistently is *Sligo*, which was first published in 1930, and which is somewhere between a reverie and a memoir. *Sligo* begins with a sketch of the west coast in view of its woods, its waterways, and its islands, 'a deep broad country, with a magnificent sea-coast, and Mountains stooping to the beaches, and lakes, and bogs, and Inland Towns; and a fine sea port. Fine to me.'[17] This balladic repetition is a typical form, as is his attention to fair days and sports 'at low water spring tide, when there is a flat plain of sand like a country so large it dwarfs the little brown and black turf-coloured crowd about the tents and the winning post, with the green flag flapping in the ocean air'.[18] Yeats drew these meetings in his sketchbooks and loved the gaudy flares of posters and flags, first among which was the

> Star Spangled Banner. And without any political or international meaning at all, I say now, that, for style and effect, if I were denationalised, I would hand the gold staff to the Stars and Stripes as the finest show flag in the world. At those strand races there was always the Stars and Stripes flying not far from the Harp without the Crown.[19]

It has been commonplace to read Yeats as an artist without politics; however, that use of 'denationalized' suggests familiarity with certain forms of radical literature. The suggestion continues in the ballad Yeats recalls an old man singing as the fair wraps up, 'Remember Mitchelstown', a rebuke to the killing of three men in a dispute during the Land War in 1887, as in the popular song, 'Remember Mitchelstown, / Where they shot the people down'.[20]

The folk traditions of the Land War were one function of Yeats's cultural memory. Another includes his love of sensational stories like *The Knight of the Black Flag* and *The Trail of the Avenger*, as well as a tolerance for Charles Dickens (and Yeats's attachment

---

[17]   Jack Yeats, *Sligo* (London: Wishart, 1930), 8.
[18]   Ibid., 16.
[19]   Ibid., 16–17.
[20]   Ibid., 17.

to late nineteenth-century London is worthy of a study in itself). The arrangement of these concerns into some larger pattern was fundamental to Yeats's interest in the act of writing, which by the time of *Sligo* was his major artistic output. There is synchronicity between the prose and Yeats's visual style in his assembly of a series of scrapbooks over the years; the process of accumulation and sequencing of each is analogous to Yeats's attention to words and their meanings. In *Sligo* he approaches this issue by typically roundabout means:

> I suppose a good many people know that Master McGrath was a grey hound who won the Waterloo Cup. There was a dance called after him, I know, for I saw the lithographed cover of the music in a curiosity shop along the Quays of Dublin. It is probably now pigeon-holed in some Collector's artificial brain. At least I suppose collectors of curios are an attempt at a manufactured brainfull of memories. The real brain, soaked, indexed and counter indexed with memories, is handier and can be carried about with you; carried along too much perhaps, and that is why I am writing this book. To jettison some memories. Everyone must read this book with deep respect and a slightly mournful affection. Because it is likely it will be the last book ever written.[21]

For all his reserve, Yeats was fond of these provocations, which have at first sight more in common with the claims of a carnival barker than a writer of serious literature, for serious people. Tagged on to follow, however, is one iteration of Yeatsian style, which is as close as he ever got to stating his literary principles:

> About this memory business. Buy or steal your memories instead of stuffing yourself with your own. Other people's memories are easier got rid of: other people's thoughts can be used quickly and discarded. Everything I break's my own, as the man said when he broke his word. But it is very difficult to break up your thoughts and keep them apart. We are nearly all chain thinkers. And if anyone ever succeeded in working his thoughts in independent jolts, he would soon find himself seeking a specialist in these things. And I don't believe they understand the little jokers.[22]

This chain-thinking describes Yeats's process perfectly, however, he stretches the metaphor with his magpie memory, half his own and half fancy. In contrast, any moments of absolute clarity in the book are brief, epigrammatic, and Wildean (the best a choice between the observation that 'no heart was ever absolutely in the right place all the time' and the admission that 'There is no padding in this book except the padding of the hoof', which is only partly true).[23]

If the word chain suggests a certain iron logic to the books, this is misleading. Rather, the fabric that joins the imagery together is gossamer-thin, and proceeds from a full

---

[21] Ibid., 27–8.
[22] Ibid., 28.
[23] Ibid., 39.

utility of the senses. Smell is as consequent to observation as sight in *Sligo*, which triggers memories of the past, and what is gone, through the summons of a particular network of associations, such as the material of the town before the motor car, when '[h]alf the world then seemed to smell of horses, old harness, hay, oats, bran mashes, old stables and hub grease'[24]. These scents invite the abiding impression of Yeats's view of the world, which was established in childhood and which informs all his work, that life is a process of constant motion. Just as horses give way to sailing boats and steam packets, Yeats remembers the Dublin Quays, where every night the Isle of Man boat left the city to the serenade of a woman singing 'The Agricultural Irish Girl'.[25] Sea traffic brought the 'realization that the element which lips against one sea step in one country, without a break, except for the little hills and hollows, lips against all the sea steps of all countries'[26]. The liquidity of Yeats's imagination, by which the practice of observation becomes a flood of memory, shapes much of what remains of *Sligo*, as Yeats arranges his prose like a shop window or street scene, the text arranged like the game 'I remember', which he played as a child. The rivers of detail that follow are tributaries to the single governing idea that literature might provoke individual feeling if only its summons of the world is not freighted with description. The issue is critical to a novel, if that is the word, like *The Amaranthers*. In *Sligo*, there follow pages of sense impressions, each a miniature map for the reader to assemble according to the configuration of their senses, such as when:

> I remember seeing a Boxer's belt of true lion's skin with silver paws to it. I remember seeing in one shop window a harp, a sword, a wooden leg, a bookmaker's bag, and a pair of field-glasses, and in the next window a can of Coffin Varnish. I remember seeing a square of red sand with a curled edge to it laid in the road way in front of a public-house in Piccadilly: dappled red roses at the ears of a hansom cab horse, a Diving-Bell. An electric light bulb unbroken floating up on a stony sea beach.[27]

The abiding idea, which Yeats himself found difficult to hold to, was that these

> things remembered should not have so much description. So I remember simply
> A Ship in a bottle.
> A fiddle made out of a corn-beef tin.
> A bunch of roses made of beetroots and turnips.
> A snow storm inside a glass ball.[28]

Yeats's attention to the materiality of the world and its objects is at odds with the image of his being detached from lived reality, which his attitude to childhood and fancy might otherwise suggest. His attitude is that of a radical, engaged in society but not conditioned

---

[24] Ibid., 65.
[25] Ibid., 82.
[26] Ibid., 86.
[27] Ibid., 99–100.
[28] Ibid., 100.

by it, possessed of a late nineteenth-century modernity resilient in the twentieth. Yeats's archaic futurity led him to moments of real innovation in his prose writing, especially given his attention to nature, which he had walked through in all weathers as a younger man. His advice for walking in the wet still stands, for 'there can be great encouragement in rain once you meet it, as it were, in its own mood'.[29] Remembering the fair day at Carricknagat, he pictured 'the tossing streams, and twisty eddies, of horses', there for trade.[30] The fair was a place to look from, as much as to look at, an attention to the position of his easel that came from his practice of painting:

> From the rock of Carricknagat you can see the sea: you can see the weather rolling about the sky and the Ox Mountains rolling to the west, and you can see the roads to Sligo and to Ballina, and you can see the rivers and the falls. At least I believe you can see all these things, and I wouldn't mind seeing them this moment. I would like to be smelling a little rushy field, wrapped in my old clothes. It is a good thing perhaps to keep your old clothes, but keep your old skin anyway.[31]

The temptation to gloss memory with description is too much for Yeats to resist, whatever his claims to be able to create a picture from sense impressions alone. The books would be poorer if he had, and a large part of the pleasure in reading them comes from his digressions, some of which happen upon clusters of words that emerge from the text in striking forms of imagistic association. One short passage where he describes a stream by its smells, which Yeats declares are different for every waterway, is both poetic and new, a forerunner of contemporary writing about place that is attentive to the particular detail of the closely observed location. So, following floods of words and memories, the book banks into:

> a little stream which smelt separately of
> moss,
> wild garlic,
> rocks,
> rushes,
> clay,
> mud,
> gravel,
> water
> wagtails' feathers ...[32]

Yeats's prose is built on a scale that connects the organic and the particular to the material and the social. Place is less an absolute location than a site of reformation, a staging

[29] Ibid., 117.
[30] Ibid., 111.
[31] Ibid., 111.
[32] Ibid., 121.

post in longer cycles of making and decay. This idea holds true in his observation of the natural world, as it does for politics, or anything else, as two short closing passages from *Sligo* suggest. In one, Yeats remembers a scrapyard in north-west London, which he passed for years on the train. Among its refuse of old carts and cabs 'there was one, and one only, Irish outside car, an Exile of Erin', slowly returning to 'honourable rust, dust, and green earth'.[33] In the other, which closes *Sligo*, Yeats remembers reading a book by an American journalist, which

> spoke of the Irish and their determined bent for freedom and he quoted the old Song:
> 'As well forbid the grasses from growing as they grow,'
> and so do I.[34]

Yeats's declaration of the Irish attitude to liberty is strangely late given the publication of *Sligo* eight years and more after the foundation of the new, partitioned state. I have written elsewhere of the political possibilities that his art suggests; for now, however, consider the cultural implications of an aesthetic that is anchored in the late imperial world of the Irish and British isles of the nineteenth and early twentieth centuries, and which persists in conditions transformed by the break-up of that previous arrangement. Instead of melancholy and alienation, Yeats applied a practice of persistent, individual attention to his subjects, which led him, sometimes surprisingly, to moments of collective representation. These moments hold together so much of what was otherwise broken that they orchestrate networks of association, meaning, and belonging that exist in no other of his contemporaries' works, except perhaps for Joyce. This is not to say that Jack Yeats created a singular literature, as Joyce, WBY, Beckett, and others did, but to argue that these post-independence textual works illustrate forms of observation and record that are unimaginable otherwise; and being imaginable, they are also loosely contextual and material, opening the possibility that I have followed here, of their playful fancy being those histories of exchange and circulation that are otherwise unthinkable.

The closest this style comes to the construction of anything recognizable as a novel is in *The Amaranthers*, which was published first in 1936. It features many of the same strategies by which memory and sense impressions combine to suggest meaning to the reader as did *Sligo*, except that instead of negotiating the author's personal reveries the reader now faces the challenge of engaging with a narrator whose last task is to tell a story straight. The basic outline of the text is the removal of the four members of the Amaranth Club from a city to an island. The organization may have taken its name from a Masonic order that had a revival in the late nineteenth century. Late 1920s and 1930s Dublin was awash with little clubs and societies, and the amaranthers have an air of the Fenians about them. Brenner, Fagan, Dowd, and MacGann are fugitive figures, hounded out of the city by the suspicions of its governing authorities, and hidden on the island behind the façade of a skyscraper, whose unlikely operations are hidden until

---

[33] Ibid., 156.
[34] Ibid., 158.

the book's last moments. The reader discovers then that the amaranthers had no revolutionary intent, at least as it applies to politics. Or perhaps their revolutionary intent, being aesthetic, had political implications that remain a suggestion rather than become a statement. This prospect is visible in the novel's intermixture of the textures of painting to the practice of writing. This, for example, is a cup of tea, 'little waves tossing on its surface', and this a man lifting a window shade, the incoming light 'so yellow against the sour green of the sky'.[35] The amaranthers represent a refuge for this visionary capacity, which otherwise has no place in society. Guarded by quicksands,

> they made of the Island a tranquil picture more tranquil than the reality. The dream laid on the bright colours with tranquil strokes. The camel's hair of fancy laid out the oleograph of memory's hanging ornament, flat and high on the wall, held in the crab-like grasp of the Tierra del Fuegonian gold-licked frame.[36]

Common to all of Jack Yeats's writing is the history of the sea as the major site of human interaction, as in the world map here of objects common to the painter's art. The amaranthers' furnishings bear a similar imprint, as does the table they acquire from an islander, whose siblings are now all abroad or drowned, all lost to 'Japan, Burmah, Liverpool, Birkenhead, Crossmolina, the Isle of Wight, New York, New Jersey, the China Seas, the Canary Islands, Cardiff, Brooklyn'.[37] This network is made from a variety of sources: from novels, the toy theatre, advertisements, Yeats's life in Ireland and England. Unusually, the representation of the artist's attendant sensations is not the fundamental business of the narrative. Rather, the traces a reader might attach to the words that represent these places themselves create the potential for the text to generate a vision of life that holds the real and the abstract in temporary harmony. An analogy might be the architectural plans that the amaranthers draw for their new club, which 'were rough, ready and gay, and acknowledged no difficulty, but the difficulty of visualisation'. 'Once visualised it was,' he writes, and 'if it wasn't, you visualised again.'[38]

It is suggestive to think that part of his devotion to the art of writing in the later part of his career, even at the expense of his painting, was because a sentence can be turned to new purpose quicker than a canvas. Yeats's eddying style required the reader to assemble the composition, much as his miniature plays involved children in their staging, and much as the amaranthers require a local to execute their plans in reality. Mr Mahone is a carpenter of few words, who 'had travelled large on all seas and many lands', and whose equipment was a 'saw, a gimlet, a knife and piece of old fishing line, and putty'. 'He could handle a paint brush as if he had an extension on the Crack of Doom', and represents a medium between the inner world of the amaranthers, the outer world of island society, and the embodiment of Jack Yeats's translational aesthetic.[39] The dual perspective

---

[35] Jack Yeats, *The Amaranthers* (London: Heinemann, 1936), 17.
[36] Ibid., 40.
[37] Ibid., 65.
[38] Ibid.
[39] Ibid., 67.

required to keep the small and the large in mind is a problem of literature, and of visual art, and is one of the novel's abiding concerns. Its resolution in *The Amaranthers* proceeds from catastrophe, which suggests the radical dimensions that such a realignment might provoke if applied on the wider scale. After a hurricane rips through the island, the side of the skyscraper falls away, to reveal 'the fall of Lilliput':

> The toy railways, the toy ships, the toy canal broken and the water dripping out of it. The great tank was unharmed. The masts moving and churning about could be seen, above tank sides. The miniature world was in view, through the trick of the floors falling forward so that the slant showed all the systems of the grown children's play. The slanting floors also let slip, and slither, any toy that was not made fast. Railway engines and portable cranes, trucks and coaches. But a canal boat tipped out of the canal, hung swaying by the rope that moored it, outside the lock.[40]

A composite understanding of Jack Yeats's art across all its dimensions requires a constant adjustment of the terms by which literary, dramatic, and visual works were constructed, produced, and consumed in the turbulent decades between the nineteenth and the twentieth centuries. If there are synchronicities between Jack Yeats's aesthetic practices and those of his contemporaries, the particularities of his formation in a late imperial world, shaped by the intimate attachments of his family to a migrant Ireland of the west coast and sea anchor his art in contexts that are obscure to any reader since. This chapter has drawn some of the coordinates by which the literary works might be approached, through attention to form, sequence, and the suggestive correspondence of memory with time and event. Thinking of how these coordinates might apply to larger questions again, of modernism, literature, history, and perhaps of ideas of Ireland itself, suggests the necessity of reading Jack Yeats's literary works, which are themselves part of a wider network of aesthetic experiments that attend the fragmentation of the late British imperial world into broken forms of still uncertain meaning.

---

[40] Ibid., 267.

PART II

IN AND THROUGH HISTORY

CHAPTER 9

ANCIENT IRELAND

GERALDINE PARSONS

'AND ancient Ireland knew it all.'[1] Thus, a retrospective W. B. Yeats in 1939. The immediate context is a meditation on immortality in his poem 'Under Ben Bulben', but this phrase could be excised from its poetic frame and understood as an assertion of a guiding principle of Yeats's remarkable artistic and intellectual endeavours. It is well known that Yeats explored the Ulster Cycle—a web of prose and poetry set in Iron Age Ireland—at some length.[2] His particular interest was in that corpus's key protagonist, Cú Chulainn, the greatest warrior of the Ulaid (Ulstermen): Yeats produced five plays, eight poems, and a prose drama centred on this 'violent and famous' figure.[3] It has long been suggested that Cuchulain, as Yeats tended to spell the name, functioned as something of an avatar for the poet and playwright: they aged together and, in his final weeks, Yeats produced two treatments of Cuchulain's death.[4] While no other character from Irish-language tradition operated on Yeats's imagination so completely, an impressive array of comparable figures, and the stories that they populate, occupied him. Prominent among these was the material known collectively as the Finn, or Ossianic, Cycle, that relates the deeds of the warband, or *fían* (later *fianna*) of Finn mac Cumaill (later Fionn Mac Cumhaill/McCool).[5] Set in the third century AD, much of the corpus relates the

---

[1] *CW1*, 325. I wish to acknowledge with gratitude the teaching of Yeats by Fr B. McKenna OP, formerly of Newbridge College, at Leaving Certificate level.

[2] There is no book-length overview of the Ulster Cycle specifically. See, most recently, Mícheál B. Ó Mainnín and Gregory Toner (eds,), *Ulidia 4: Proceedings of the fourth international conference on the Ulster Cycle of tales, Queen's University Belfast, 27–9 June, 2013* (Dublin: Four Courts Press, 2017).

[3] See Geraldine Higgins, *Heroic Revivals from Carlyle to Yeats* (New York, NY: Palgrave Macmillan, 2012), 108. The allusion is to 'Cuchulain Comforted'.

[4] A. N. Jeffares, *A New Biography of W. B. Yeats* (London: Hutchinson, 1988), 149. Outwith quotations, 'Cuchulain' is used for Yeats's depictions of the character and 'Cú Chulainn' for other realizations of the character. Where Yeats's spellings of other characters' names differ from the standard medieval Irish forms, the same distinction will be observed, but other significant spellings will be noted on first reference.

[5] See Kevin Murray, *The Early Finn Cycle* (Dublin: Four Courts Press, 2017), and Joseph J. Flahive, *The Fenian Cycle in Irish and Scots-Gaelic literature*, Cork Studies in Celtic Literatures, 1 (Cork: Cork University Press, 2017).

extraordinary survival of some of these warriors, including Oisín (Yeats's Oisin) and Caílte (later Caoilte, Yeats's Caolte), into the mid-fifth century, at which point they encountered St Patrick. Other works are set wholly in the heyday of the *fían*, such as the story of Diarmaid and Gráinne's elopement.[6] The places and times to which Cuchulain and Oisin alike belonged were conceptualized by Yeats as 'ancient Ireland'. This chapter seeks to illuminate some sources underpinning Yeats's long and fruitful engagement with—as he saw it—the literary output of ancient Ireland, born of his desire to forge a national, anglophone literature for Ireland.

The belief that Irish literature set in the distant past is the product of the period it describes was an enduring one. In 1964, in the fullest working out of the idea that Ulster Cycle works set in the Iron Age derived from that period, Kenneth Jackson argued that the corpus's central saga, *Táin Bó Cúailnge* ('The Cattle Raid of Cooley'), was composed orally in the fourth century AD. He envisaged it being transmitted orally until the advent of Christianity in Ireland in the mid-fifth century, and the associated establishment of book culture and growth of literacy allowed it to be written down.[7] Jackson's theory was rejected conclusively within thirty years, but it is not surprising that many of Yeats's contemporaries accepted such works as pre-Christian compositions.[8] Yeats did likewise, although he also entertained the possibility that the 'whole history' of 'Old Celtic Ireland' was a fiction that had been 'sung out of the void by the harps of the great bardic order'.[9] Indeed, he confessed that while he believed that these works had a factual base, he cared little if that could be disproved. This he argued in an essay on 'Finn MacCool' published by the Fenian leader John O'Leary in *The Gael*, 23 April 1887, which has been partially reconstructed by John S. Kelly and which offers valuable insights into the young poet's thinking about Ireland's early literature and culture:

> A nation's history is not in what it does, this invader or that other; the elements or destiny decides all that; but what a nation imagines that is its history, there is its heart; than its legends, a nation owns nothing more precious.[10]

---

[6] Nessa Ní Shéaghdha, ed. and trans., *Tóruigheacht Dhiarmada agus Ghráinne: The pursuit of Diarmaid and Gráinne*, Irish Texts Society 48 (Dublin: Irish Texts Society, 1967). Yeats's play, written with George Moore, *The Pursuit of Diarmaid and Gráinne* (1901), treats this story, and see John S. Kelly, 'Aesthete among the athletes: Yeats's contributions to *The Gael*', in Richard J. Finneran, ed., *Yeats: An Annual of Critical and Textual Studies*, II (Ithaca, NY: Cornell University Press, 1984), 95–115.

[7] Kenneth Hurlstone Jackson, *The Oldest Irish Tradition: A window on the Iron Age*, Rede Lecture 1964 (Cambridge: Cambridge University Press, 1964).

[8] See, for example, James P. Mallory, 'The world of Cú Chulainn: the archaeology of the *Táin bó Cúailnge*', in James P. Mallory, ed., *Aspects of the Táin* (Belfast: December Publications, 1992), 103–59; John T. Koch, 'Windows on the Iron Age: 1964–1994', in Mallory and Stockman, eds., *Ulidia*, 229–37.

[9] 'Bardic Ireland', from *The Scots Observer* (1890), cited from W. B. Yeats, *Writings on Irish Folklore, Legend and Myth*, ed. Robert Welch (London: Penguin, 1993), 50-4, at 52.

[10] *CW* 9, 49–50, cited from Kelly, 'Aesthete', 91. A minor aspect of Kelly's essay relating to Yeats's conception of the history of ancient Ireland that requires correction is the statement on p. 83 that 'By the time

At any rate, he embraced pre-modern Irish-language sources, especially those from the Old and Middle Irish periods (*c.* AD 700–900 and AD 900–1200 respectively) as windows through which an ancient Irish past, however understood, could be glimpsed. In reality, of course, no written literature survives from Ireland's ancient— pre-Christian, pre-medieval—past. Yet, in the second half of the nineteenth century, even the careful pioneers of *Keltologie,* or Celtic Studies, as an academic discipline rooted in the scrutiny of medieval Ireland's documentary sources, could not resist the attractions of the adjective 'ancient'.[11] This is easily illustrated with reference to the term's usage by Eugene O'Curry, who by the 1850s was the foremost authority on Irish manuscript culture.[12] Over just two pages of an article published in 1858, he used 'ancient' to invoke the fuzzy, prehistorical hinterlands of individual medieval literary works and also to denote datable medieval evidence (a twelfth-century manuscript; a homily that he dated to AD 763–90; Old Irish grammatical forms and more).[13] His landmark publications on the contents of Ireland's medieval manuscripts, moreover, were entitled *Lectures on the manuscript materials of ancient Irish history* and *On the manners and customs of the ancient Irish*.[14] Modern oral tradition also fed into Yeats's imagining of ancient Ireland; he was a well-informed and enthusiastic collector and anthologist of folklore at the start of his career.[15] The folding of modern Irish-language folklore into a medieval and early modern mix can be explained with reference to the continuity of some protagonists and settings across more than a millennium of storytelling: the Ulster Cycle, for example, has claimed a place in the collective imagination of Irish speakers from at least the seventh century into modern times. Yet this approach also testifies to an inability or unwillingness to differentiate between different temporal layers of Irish-language tradition. By virtue of being part

he came to write the introduction to *Gods and Fighting Men* ... Yeats had realized his historical mistake and knew that Finn came before Cuchulain'. Although that may have been Yeats's interpretation of the evidence, medieval scholars located the main events of the Ulster Cycle to the period around the lifetime of Christ, whereas the events of the Finn Cycle were understood as occurring in the third century AD.

[11] On the emergence of Celtic Studies, see, for instance, Mark Williams, *Ireland's Immortals: A history of the gods of Irish myth* (Princeton, 2016), 293–4.

[12] Diarmaid Ó Catháin, 'O'Curry (Curry, Ó Comhraí), Eugene (Eoghan)', in James McGuire and James Quinn, eds., *Dictionary of Irish Biography*, (Dublin and Cambridge: Royal Irish Academy and Cambridge University Press, 2009) online edn, http://dib.cambridge.org (accessed 18 Nov. 2020).

[13] Eugene Curry, ed. and trans., 'The sick-bed of Cú Chulainn and the only jealousy of Emer, quoted from the Yellow Book of Slane in Leabhar na h-Uidhre', *Atlantis*, 1 (1858), 362–92; 2 (1859), 98–124, at 1, 366–7.

[14] Eugene O'Curry, *Lectures on the manuscript materials of ancient Irish history, delivered at the Catholic University of Ireland during the sessions of 1855 and 1856* (Dublin: James Duffy, 1861); Eugene O'Curry, *On the manners and customs of the ancient Irish: A series of lectures*, ed. W. K. Sullivan, 3 vols (London: Williams & Norgate, 1873).

[15] See Mary Helen Thuente, *W. B. Yeats and Irish Folklore* (Totowa, NJ: Barnes & Noble, 1981). Also helpful are James Pethica's remarks on Yeats as folklorist within international Romantic thought: 'Yeats, folklore and Irish legend', in Marjorie Howes and John Kelly, eds., *The Cambridge Companion to W. B. Yeats* (Cambridge: Cambridge University Press, 2006), 129–43 at 131 ff.

of Irish-language tradition at the close of the nineteenth century, then, a tale, poem, or character was invested with an attractively paradoxical status: it was both timeless and ancient. Irish-language tradition as a whole was exoticized as more primitive, and more noble, than Ireland's anglophone culture. Two stalwarts of this literary continuum, Cú Chulainn and Oisín, provide convenient case studies through which to approach the questions of how Yeats understood and accessed pre-modern Irish-language literary sources, knowledge of which expanded dramatically across his lifetime, and used them as a tool to fashion his own creative output.

THE DEATHS OF CUCHULAIN

Yeats was occupied with Cuchulain across almost the whole of his career: Cuchulain appeared in works produced by him between 1892 and 1939, the year of his death.[16] A general pattern of the loosening of Yeats's ties to his source material can be observed in the presentation of the warrior's death, something that figured in Yeats's earliest and latest envisagings of Cuchulain. It is perhaps not surprising to find that the idea of Cuchulain's death held a particular and enduring fascination for Yeats. It is, after all, a convention of heroic literature—understanding that often ambiguous label to signify pre-modern literature consciously concerned with 'heroes' who are by default martial men—that it is in death that heroism is confirmed. Just as the idea of old age exercised him from his earliest writings about Oisin on, so the idea of the emotional and physical frailty of the martial hero seems to have had a draw for Yeats from his first grapplings with Cuchulain's potential.[17]

The poem 'The Death of Cuchulain' was published in 1892. In this first appearance of Cuchulain, a devastating iteration of the heroic dilemma provides the subject matter: his killing of his son. The concluding lines have a grief-stricken Cuchulain 'warr[ing] with the bitter tide' until 'the waves flowed above him and he died'. In the play *On Baile's Strand* (1904, and revised in 1906) too, Cuchulain's death follows on rapidly from the filicide. His fate is conveyed by the Fool to the Blind Man: 'He has killed kings and giants, but the waves have mastered him, the waves have mastered him!'[18] The poem 'The Death of Cuchulain' was among those that Yeats revised, 'to express better what I thought and felt when I was a very young man.'[19] The reworked poem, retitled 'Cuchulain's Fight with the Sea' and published in 1925, saw the reference to Cuchulain's death removed. This particular change, however, is less a clarification of Yeats's original intentions than a recognition of the

---

[16] On Yeats and Cuchulain, see, for example, John V. Kelleher, 'Yeats's use of Irish materials', *Tri-Quarterly*, 4 (1965), 115–25.

[17] On the young Yeats's fascination with old age, for example, see Richard Ellmann, *Yeats: The Man and the Masks* (New York, NY: W.W. Norton, 1948), 54.

[18] *CW2*, 174.

[19] *VP*, 842.

creative—and potentially commercial—advantages of extending Cuchulain's life. For instance, the play *The Only Jealousy of Emer*, completed in 1919, follows roughly the narrative
of the Old Irish tale *Serglige Con Culainn* ('The wasting-sickness of Cú Chulainn') and
explores Cuchulain's life in the aftermath of his killing of his son.[20] Another factor was
his growing familiarity with works translated from Irish. Lady Gregory had published her
version of the ninth- or tenth-century prose tale *Aided Óenfhir Aífe* ('The violent death of
Aífe's only son') as 'The Only Son of Aoife', in *Cuchulain of Muirthemne* in 1902, in which
she hesitated over the canonicity of Cú Chulainn's drowning.[21] By 1925, then, Yeats had
disentangled Cuchulain's death from the image of his struggle with 'the ungovernable sea',
but the latter topos affords some useful insights into Yeats's sources.

Positioning his work relative to Lady Gregory's publications, Yeats asserted that his
presentations of Oisin, Maeve (Medb, later Méadhbh or Méabh), Baile and Aillin, and
Angus (Óengus, later Aonghas) and his 'fellow-immortals', the Túatha Dé Danann,
had been 'literally translated, though with much condensation and selection, from the
old writings'.[22] The translation alluded to, however, was not Yeats's own work: he never
mastered any phase of the Irish language, and such condensing and selecting as he did
was from the translations into English that appeared in the second half of the nineteenth
century (with increasing frequency across its closing two decades) and on into the
new century. 'Cuchulain killing his son and fighting the sea' was among the characters
invoked by Yeats in the notes just mentioned. Yet Yeats found the image of Cuchulain's
elemental battle in Jeremiah Curtin's *Myths and Folk Tales of Ireland* (1890), the Irish-
language source material for which had been collected in 1887; whatever Yeats's sense of
the antiquity of this orally collected story, it was not an instance of 'old writing'.[23] Curtin
gives a single, busy narrative about Cú Chulainn that ends with him slaying a boy,
Conlán. Only when the fatal blow has been dealt, does the hero learn that the boy is his
son. At this juncture, Finn magically binds Cú Chulainn to fight the sea on Baile's Strand
rather than expend his anger on his companions. Curtin provided no background information for his 'Cuculín' tale, but, whatever its origins, this account is notable for its combination of apparently innovative elements and those that resonate with a millennium's
worth of literary tradition. Cú Chulainn's killing of his son had been a productive element of Irish literature since the composition of *Aided Óenfhir Aífe*. Likewise, the fear
experienced by Finn and his companions—that Cú Chulainn, deranged with grief,
would harm them—has an early precursor: it recalls a famous scene from the medieval saga *Táin Bó Cúailnge* wherein the young Cú Chulainn's violent excesses have to

---

[20] A convenient translation of *Serglige Con Culainn* is Jeffrey Gantz (trans.), *Early Irish Myths and Sagas* (Harmondsworth: Penguin, 1981), pp 153–78.

[21] Lady Gregory, *Cuchulain of Muirthemne: The story of the men of the Red Branch of Ulster arranged and put into English by Lady Gregory with a preface by W.B. Yeats and a foreword by Daniel Murphy*, 5th edn (Gerrards Cross: Colin Smythe, 1975), 241. For *Aided Óenfhir Aífe*, see Gantz, *Early Irish myths and sagas*, 147–52.

[22] *VP*, 843.

[23] *VP*, 799.

be controlled lest he kill his own people.[24] By contrast, that Finn should be the one who shields the Ulaid from Cú Chulainn's erratic violence was unmistakably new. Although characters from the Ulster and Finn Cycles interact in some modern sources, including James Macpherson's Ossianic publications from the 1760s, Finn and Cú Chulainn were traditionally confined to discrete corpora, as Yeats knew: he replaced Curtin's Finn with a druid in his poem. The fight with the sea and Cú Chulainn's drowning constitute the other modern additions to the traditional tale.

Yeats knew that Curtin's folk tale was 'very different' to 'bardic tradition' about the death of Cú Chulainn, and by 1919 he was exploring the potential of the alternative story.[25] In *The Only Jealousy of Emer* he had Cuchulain survive his fight with the sea, even if the possibility of his death pervades the play (it presents his ghost and an embodied 'figure', as well as the still-living but mostly unconscious Cuchulain on stage, and the 'Figure of Cuchulain' predicts the true manner of his death). By Christmas 1938, in his play *The Death of Cuchulain*, Yeats was envisaging Cuchulain's death in ways that complemented pre-modern sources more clearly than before. A death tale for Cú Chulainn exists from as early as about the mid-eighth century, known variously as *Brislech Mór Maige Muirthemne* ('The great rout at Mag Muirthemne') and *Aided Con Culainn* ('The violent death of Cú Chulainn'). As well as this Old Irish account, an Early Modern Irish version, *Oidheadh Con Culainn* ('The violent death of Cú Chulainn'), is extant. The later version of the tale extends beyond the narrative of Cú Chulainn's death to consider the attempts by Conall Cernach (later Conall Cearnach) to avenge that loss, as well as including a long poem known as *Laoidh na gceann* ('The lay of the heads') occasioned by Conall's return to Emer with the heads of Cú Chulainn's enemies. Yeats's immediate source was Lady Gregory's 'Gathering at Muirthemne and Death of Cuchulain' from *Cuchulain of Muirthemne* (1902), which had drawn on printed and manuscript texts of the Old Irish and Early Modern Irish versions. These were Whitley Stokes's edition and translation of the earlier *Brislech Mór Maige Muirthemne*, published in 1878, Standish Hayes O'Grady's translation of an extract of the early modern *Oidheadh Con Culainn*, published in 1898, John Hogan and J. H. Lloyd's edition and translation of all but the *Laoidh na gCeann* portion of the early modern work, and a manuscript version of the early modern work then owned by Douglas Hyde.[26] *The Death of Cuchulain* shows the greatest level of creative engagement with source materials yet considered. It proclaims itself to be 'the last of a series of plays which has for theme [Cuchulain's] life and death', and its recapitulatory function has it ranging across Cuchulain's biography in a way unlike any one

---

[24] Cecile O'Rahilly, ed. and trans., *Táin Bó Cúalnge from the Book of Leinster* (Dublin: Dublin Institute for Advanced Studies, 1984), 32–3 and 170–1.

[25] *VP*, 799.

[26] Whitley Stokes, ed. and trans., 'Cuchulainn's death (abridged from the Book of Leinster, ff. 77a1–78b2)', *Revue celtique*, 3 (1876–8), 175–85; Standish Hayes O'Grady (trans.), 'The great defeat on the plain of Muirthemne before Cuchullin's death', in Eleanor Hull, ed., *The Cuchullin saga in Irish literature: being a collection of stories relating to the hero Cuchullin*, Grimm Library, 8 (London: David Nutt, 1898), 236–49; John Hogan and J. H. Lloyd, ed. and trans., 'Brislech mhór Mhaighe Mhuirtheimhne', *Gaelic Journal*, 11 (1901), 1–3, 17–19, 33–8, 49–52, 65–7, 81–3, 123–7, 128, 132–5, 145–7, 161–4, 177–80; 17 (1907), 305–83.

early source. Its form and setting owed little to the 'antiquated romantic stuff the thing is made of'; one allusion to its contemporary setting comes by way of a mention of the statue of the dying Cú Chulainn in the Post Office '[b]y Oliver Sheppard done', that was installed in the GPO in 1935. Sheppard's statue captures what is also the central image of the play: the dead Cú Chulainn, upright, strapped to a pillar-stone, so that his enemies' fear of him would outlast his life. Although Lady Gregory's account follows the early modern narrative overall, she drew very closely on Stokes's translation of the eighth-century text for that scene. Thus, she gave her readers the gravely wounded Cú Chulainn seeking a dignified and dutiful death. He stuffs his entrails back into his mutilated body, drinks and bathes himself, and calls on his enemies to come forth to meet him. Then he

> went to the pillar-stone, and he tied himself to it with his breast-belt, the way he would not meet his death lying down, but would meet it standing up. Then his enemies came round about him, but they were in dread of going close to him, for they were not sure but he might be still alive.[27]

Yeats, however, chose not to replicate this, the oldest evidence for Cú Chulainn's death, but instead sanitized what Lady Gregory had carried over from the earliest account. Cuchulain's wounding happens offstage. There is no gaping wound, no gathering up of his bowels. But, curiously, there is greater physical weakness in Yeats's hero. Cuchulain reveals his vulnerability to Aoife, come to avenge his past crimes against her: 'I have put my belt / About this stone and want to fasten it / And die upon my feet, but am too weak.' Lady Gregory, again drawing on Stokes, details the warrior Lugaid's decapitation of Cú Chulainn; Cuchulain's head, however, is taken by the Blind Man of *On Baile's Strand*. Even in death, the early Cú Chulainn could mete out punishment: his sword falls from his lifeless hand and severs Lugaid's hand. Cuchulain, by contrast, submits to the ignominy of the Blind Man groping for his neck and gloating over the reward for his head. Emer's dance among the severed heads ends the play's action in ancient Ireland; dance substitutes for the 'complaint' of Emer in Lady Gregory's version, which in turn corresponds to the *Laoidh na gCeann* section of the early modern *Oidheadh Con Culainn*. It is hardly necessary to show that Yeats, at the end of his career, privileged his own artistic vision over fidelity to his sources but, should proof be needed, this play offers ample evidence. It is striking too that here Yeats demonstrated no particular loyalty to the oldest layers of tradition.

The final stage in Yeats's treatment of Cuchulain's death is the poem 'Cuchulain Comforted'. Conceived of by Yeats as 'a kind of sequel' to *The Death of Cuchulain*, he saw it as 'strange too, something new'.[28] Yeats was now untethered from his source material: his setting of Cuchulain striding among the dead and sewing his own shroud has no precursors. Critics have sought Dantean or classical antecedents instead of Irish

---

[27] Lady Gregory, *Cuchulain of Muirthemne*, 256.
[28] *Life* 2, 646.

ones; theme and form—based on terza rima—make clear those channels of influence.[29] Yet, in its arresting image of the dead singing like birds, Yeats gestures towards medieval Irish sources generally, if not to any treatment of the death of Cú Chulainn. This image inverts the idea found in the eighth-century Hiberno-Latin *Navigatio Sancti Brendani* that souls who took on the bodies of birds retained the voices of men, and alludes too to the wider use of birds as supernatural markers, in works such as *Serglige Con Culainn*.[30]

ACCESSING THE 'OLD WRITINGS'

Notes on his poem 'The Secret Rose', which were included in *The Wind among the Reeds* (1899), prove instructive in terms of Yeats's access routes to the 'old writings'.[31] Lady Gregory is credited, as is Standish O'Grady. References to 'his fine imagination' make Standish James O'Grady the obvious candidate here; the young Yeats saw O'Grady as the 'one historian who is anything of an artist … rising above dates and dialects', and the latter's *History of Ireland: The heroic period*, published in 1878, exerted a significant influence on the former.[32] There is, however, another Standish O'Grady whose influence should not be discounted. Yeats knew Standish James O'Grady's cousin, Standish Hayes O'Grady, who edited and translated a large number of medieval and early modern Irish works. His early work included an edition and translation of *Tóruigheacht Dhiarmada agus Ghráinne* ('The Pursuit of Diarmaid and Gráinne'), which was published in 1857.[33] It was not well received and O'Grady abandoned his interests in Celtic Studies for a long period, before publishing *Silva Gadelica*, an anthology of editions and translations, in 1892.[34] Yeats publicly defended *Silva Gadelica* against criticism by Robert Atkinson, Professor of Romance Languages and latterly Professor of Sanskrit at Trinity College Dublin. Although also a scholar of the Irish language, Atkinson considered that 'Irish contains much that is not fit for general publication', and testified to a commission on secondary education

---

[29] *Life 2*, 647.

[30] On the *Serglige*, see above, n. 20. For Yeats's knowledge of the soul-in-bird-form topos, which he saw as folkloric, see 'A literary causerie' from the *Speaker* (1893), cited from Yeats, *Writings*, 189–200, at 196.

[31] *VP*, 812 ff.

[32] *Life 1*, 147. For brief discussion of O'Grady's *History of Ireland: The heroic period*, 2 vols (Dublin: E. Ponsonby, 1878) as an influence on Yeats, see Pethica, 'Yeats, folklore and Irish legend', 140.

[33] Standish Hayes O'Grady, ed. and trans., *Toruigheacht Dhiarmada agus Ghrainne; or, the pursuit after Diarmuid O'Duibhne, and Grainne, the daughter of Cormac Mac Airt, King of Ireland in the third century*, Transactions of the Ossianic Society, 3 (Dublin: John O'Daly, 1857).

[34] Lesa Ní Mhunghaile, 'O'Grady, Standish Hayes', in McGuire and Quinn, *Dictionary of Irish biography*, online edition, http://dib.cambridge.org (accessed 18 Nov. 2020); Standish H. O'Grady, ed. and trans., *Silva Gadelica (I-XXXI): a collection of tales in Irish*, 2 vols (London: Williams & Norgate, 1892).

in Ireland in 1899 that he would allow no daughter of his, 'of any age, to read the story of Diarmaid and Gráinne'.[35]

Yeats's knowledge of *Silva Gadelica* was in keeping with his wider reading in English-language Celtic Studies scholarship at the turn of the twentieth century. His lack of German and French meant that he was unable to absorb a significant proportion of the emerging scholarship, although Marie Henri d'Arbois de Jubainville's monumental *Cycle mythologique irlandais et la mythologie celtique* (1884) was drip-fed to him in extempore translation by Maud Gonne in the 1890s.[36] Yet he read John Rhŷs, and Kuno Meyer's edition and translation of *Immram Brain* ('The voyage of Bran') that was published with an essay by Alfred Nutt on 'the Celtic doctrine of rebirth'.[37] That being the case, the large-scale, English-language *Lectures* (1861) by O'Curry might be assumed to have been a core text for Yeats. O'Curry is not regularly mentioned as a source for Yeats's writings: he merits only a single reference across the two volumes of Roy Foster's biography, for example.[38] Yeats did acknowledge O'Curry as the source underpinning 'The Madness of King Goll', composed 1886–7, albeit that he recorded his frustration with O'Curry's 'unarranged and uninterpreted history'.[39] Peter McDonald has considered it 'unlikely that [he] made an especially close study of O'Curry's volumes'.[40] Certainly, Yeats passed over O'Curry when he recommended Standish James O'Grady and other popular writers to readers who could not themselves tackle Old and Middle Irish texts.[41] Yeats's use of O'Curry's writings, from *Lectures* and elsewhere, was greater than it might appear, however. It seems that Yeats drew on *Lectures* in the notes on 'The Secret Rose'.[42] Discussing the death tale of Conchobar, king of the Ulaid, for instance, he invoked the witness to the text preserved in the twelfth-century *Book of Leinster* and the seventeenth-century account by Geoffrey Keating; this knowledge must have derived from the editions and translations given together by O'Curry.[43] Moreover, in these notes Yeats described his imagining of a scene involving Cuchulain and his lover, Fand; by 1899, O'Curry's was the only English-language version available of the medieval tale of Cú Chulainn and Fand, *Serglige Con Culainn*.[44]

[35] David Greene, 'Robert Atkinson and Irish studies', *Hermathena*, 102 (1966), 6–15, at 7, 10, 11.

[36] Williams, *Ireland's immortals*, 297.

[37] W. B. Yeats, 'Celtic beliefs about the soul', from the *Bookman* (1898), cited from Yeats, *Writings*, 201–2; John Rhŷs, *Lectures on the origin and growth of religion as illustrated by Celtic heathendom*, Hibbert Lectures, 1886 (London and Edinburgh: Williams & Norgate, 1888); Kuno Meyer, ed. and trans., *The voyage of Bran, son of Febal to the land of the living with an essay upon the Irish vision of the happy Otherworld and the Celtic doctrine of rebirth by Alfred Nutt*, 2 vols (London: David Nutt, 1895).

[38] *Life 1*, 196.

[39] *CW5*, 205. See also Frank Kinahan, 'A source note on "The Madness of King Goll"', in Warwick Gould, ed., *Yeats Annual No. 4* (Basingstoke: Macmillan, 1986), 189–94, at 189.

[40] Peter McDonald, ed., *The Poems of W.B. Yeats, vol. 1: 1882–1889* (Abingdon: Routledge, 2021), 460–2.

[41] 'Bardic Ireland', cited from Yeats, *Writings*, 50.

[42] *VP*, 813–14.

[43] O'Curry, *Lectures*, 636–43.

[44] Curry, 'The sick-bed'.

Yeats was content to present his use of Cuchulain and Fand as a creative response to the prompting of 'one of the most beautiful of our old tales'. Yet he was diffident in noting that he 'unintentionally' changed a key detail of Conchobar's death tale. As the notes progress, his inner *Quellenkritiker* became increasingly disapproving of the taking of such liberties. Of an allusion to Fergus mac Róich, another Ulster Cycle figure, he said: 'I only knew him in Mr Standish O'Grady, and my imagination dealt more freely with what I did know than I would approve of to-day.' There is a defensive element to his note about a reference to Caolte: 'I am writing away from most of my books and have not been able to find the passage: I certainly read it somewhere.' His notes suggest that it was not his habit to keep track of the sources of specific allusions made to medieval Irish sources. For example, he described the character Orchil as 'A Fomorah and a sorceress, if I remember rightly. I forget whatever I may have once known about her.'[45] Overall, though, these notes suggest that Yeats held in tension academic explorations of early sources and his personal responses to them.

THE EVIDENCE OF OISIN: YEATS AS PSEUDOTRANSLATOR

Although valedictory, 'Cuchulain Comforted' was not Yeats's final poem. That was 'The Black Tower', which depicted soldiers awaiting their call to arms. The men are never identified, but that this was Yeats's realization of a common folkloric presentation of Finn's *fían* is not in doubt. As early as 1887, Yeats outlined that idea:

> now [Finn] sleeps in the centre of a mountain in Donegal, his hound and his steed beside him, awaiting, like another Barbarossa, the time of his country's greatest need, when he will awake and sound his dreadful horn.[46]

This came two years after Katharine Tynan's use of the same story, which she termed 'a legend well known among the peasantry of the north of Ireland', in her poem 'Waiting'.[47]

Foster has argued that the scenario of 'The Black Tower' comes 'straight from [Standish James] O'Grady's *The Masque of Finn*, a play [Yeats] had seen at Patrick Pearse's school thirty years before'.[48] Yeats attended a performance of *The Coming of Fionn*, part of O'Grady's *The Masque of Finn*, at St Enda's in March 1909; the story derived from O'Grady's *Finn and his companions* (1892). Undoubtedly these works did much to fix this motif in Yeats's memory, but his knowledge of it predates both O'Grady's book and the performance of the play. In his last poem, then, Yeats returned to a font of

---

[45] *VP*, 796.
[46] *CW*9, 49.
[47] See McDonald, *Poems, vol. 1*, 533–4.
[48] *Life* 2, 648.

inspiration from which he had been drawing in the late 1880s, and which gave rise to his first published poem as well as the one he wrote last.

Composed in 1886–7 and published in 1889, *The Wanderings of Oisin*, in Richard Ellmann's words, 'was to set the tone for the Irish literary revival'.[49] It represents a fortuitous meeting of Yeats's new Irish interests with his grounding in Romantic poetry. The gestation of this long narrative poem coincided with his most intense interest in Irish folklore: he worked on the anthology *Fairy and Folk Tales of the Irish Peasantry* between July 1887 and September 1888.[50] This was, of course, a period in which oral tradition about Finn, Oisín, and their companions was still vibrant. Beyond his own folklore collection, also available to Yeats were printed accounts of Oisín's journey to Tír na nÓg ('The Land of the Young') that were published in the period 1866–78. These were Patrick Kennedy's *Legendary Fictions of the Irish Celts*, Aubrey de Vere's *Legends of St Patrick*, which includes a poem put in the mouth of the warrior as he embraces Christianity gladly, and Standish James O'Grady's *History of Ireland: The Heroic Period*, which has an account of Oisín's railing against St Patrick at the end of his life.[51] In addition, he could have consulted discussion of the story in O'Kearney's introduction to the first volume of the Transactions of the Ossianic Society published in 1853.[52] About a decade after Yeats wrote *The Wanderings*, George Sigerson, who had also formed part of the literary and intellectual circle around O'Leary, articulated what was surely one the factors that motivated Yeats's composition.[53] Sigerson quoted O'Curry's *Lectures* on the singing of Ossianic lays in the latter's boyhood in Co. Clare, and then launched a spirited defence of the artistry and importance of this material:

> How noble and astonishing would such statements seem if they related to the peasantry of other countries! If the Venetian boatmen were heard singing Dante from their gondolas, the Norman peasants the Romance of Roland, the Spanish the lays of the Cid Campeador, the German the Nibelungenlied, the Norse the Eddas – if the English peasants assembled to sing the verse of Chaucer, Layamon's 'Brut,' or the 'Battle of Brunanburh,' there would be just and general praise, with wise and generous encouragement. A different policy directed the extinction of the intellectual inheritance of the Gael, because pigmy prejudice ruled where large intelligence would have guided.[54]

[49] Ellmann, *Yeats*, 48.

[50] See W. B. Yeats, 'The Celtic element in literature', from *Cosmopolis* (1898), cited from Yeats, *Writings*, 196. A helpful and concise account of knowledge of Finn Cycle literature and folklore during the Revival is Natasha Sumner, 'Fionn mac Cumhaill in twenty-first-century Ireland', *North American Journal of Celtic Studies*, 1:1 (2017), 82–106, at 84–9.

[51] McDonald, *Poems, vol. 1*, 529–32, and see his discussion of other creative treatments of the Tír na nÓg story available to Yeats, 536–8.

[52] Nicholas O'Kearney, *The Battle of Gabhra, Garristown in the County of Dublin, fought A.D. 283*, Transactions of the Ossianic Society, 1 (Dublin: John O'Daly, 1853), 20–7.

[53] *Life 1*, 41–2. On O'Leary and Yeats, see, for example, Kelly, 'Aesthete'.

[54] George Sigerson, *Bards of the Gael and Gall: Examples of the poetic literature of Erinn, done into English after the metres and modes of the Gael* (London: T. Fisher Unwin, 1897), 404.

The long shadow cast by Macpherson's Ossianic poems must also be acknowledged: as well as indirectly influencing many Irish folklorists of Yeats's generation, who inherited the eighteenth-century concern with establishing Irish claims to the stories of Finn, Macpherson's publications exerted a direct influence on the young poet.[55] Samuel Ferguson's influence too has been detected.[56] Of course, the story of *The Wanderings* has its roots in two medieval Irish genres—not only the Finn Cycle but also the voyage tale. The latter had already penetrated the English poetic mind. Alfred Tennyson had composed a version of the Middle Irish *Immram Curaig Maíle Dúin* ('The Voyage of Máel Dúin's currach'), 'The Voyage of Maeldune', in 1880, and *The Wanderings* is 'full of inescapably Tennysonian echoes'.[57] Moreover, Kelly has drawn attention to the young Yeats's affinity with the sea in poems composed contemporaneously with *The Wanderings*, noting that they date from a time when he 'could be sure of neither the geographical or the psychological hinterland of Ireland'.[58] *The Wanderings*, then, represents the confluence of a number of powerful external influences and personal priorities.

The Wanderings of Oisin has been subjected to detailed source criticism.[59] Yeats had indicated his sources, but vaguely. In a letter responding to a review published in *The Spectator* of 27 July 1889, he stated that his poem was a development of 'a most beautiful old poem written by one of the numerous half-forgotten Gaelic poets who lived in Ireland in the last century' and that he 'used suggestions from various ballad Dialogues of Oisin and Patrick, published by the Ossianic Society'.[60] The poem's foundations were formulated elsewhere as 'the middle Irish dialogues of St. Patrick and Usheen and a certain Gaelic poem of the last century'.[61] *Laoidh Oisín ar Thír na nÓg* ('The Lay of Oisín in the Land of the Young') is the eighteenth-century source referenced. According to Yeats's source, the edition and translation by Bryan O'Looney (Brian Ó Luanaigh), for the Ossianic Society, *Laoidh Oisín*, was composed by Michael Comyn (Mícheál Coimín), but that ascription is no longer considered secure.[62] At any rate, *Laoidh Oisín*

[55] G. J. Watson, 'Yeats, Macpherson and the cult of defeat', in Fiona Stafford and Howard Gaskill (eds), *From Gaelic to Romantic: Ossianic Translations* (Amsterdam: Rodopi, 1998), 216–25. See also McDonald, *Poems*, vol. 1, 538–9, and Russell K. Alspach, 'Some sources of Yeats's *The Wanderings of Oisin*', *PMLA*, 58 (1943), 849–66, at 865 n.78.

[56] Alspach, 'Some sources', 859.

[57] *Life 1*, 82. See too Matthew Campbell, *Irish Poetry under the Union, 1801-1924* (Cambridge: Cambridge University Press, 2013), 144–5; Matthew Campbell, 'Poetry in the four nations', in Richard Cronin et al., eds., *A Companion to Victorian Poetry* (Oxford: Blackwell, 2002), 438–56.

[58] Kelly, 'Aesthete', 130.

[59] See McDonald, *Poems*, vol. 1, 527–44. Alspach's comprehensive 'Some sources' article remains valuable. See too discussion in Daniel Gomes, 'Reviving Oisin: Yeats and the conflicted appeal of Irish mythology', *Texas Studies in Literature and Language*, 56 (2014), 376–99.

[60] Cited from McDonald, *Poems*, vol. 1, 273.

[61] *VP*, 793.

[62] Bryan O'Looney, ed. and trans., 'Tír na nÓg: the land of youth', in John O'Daly, ed., *Laoithe Fiannuigheachta, or Fenian poems*, Transactions of the Ossianic Society, 4 (Dublin: John O'Daly, 1859), 227–79; Máirtín Ó Briain, 'Some material on Oisín in the Land of Youth', in Donnchadh Ó Corráin, Liam Breatnach, and Kim R. McCone, eds., *Sages, saints and storytellers: Celtic studies in honour of Professor*

ANCIENT IRELAND 127

was followed closely by Yeats for a portion of his poem. Máirtín Ó Briain's summary of the source text can be usefully invoked here:

> The whole poem is cast in the framework of a dialogue between Oisín and Patrick. In the first verse the saint asks Oisín how he lived so long after the Fianna. Oisín describes how the Fenian survivors of the battle of Gabhair were hunting one foggy morning by the shores of Loch Léin when their hounds gave chase to a hornless deer. Soon afterwards they were approached by a beautiful lady on a white steed. She greeted Fionn and in reply to his question who she was, she told him that she was Niamh Chinn Óir, the daughter of Rí na nÓg ['the King of the Young']. She was in love with Oisín and she puts him under *geasa* [taboos] to go with her to Tír na nÓg. She then describes this place, and her description agrees in general with what we know of the traditional Irish concept of the happy otherworld. They took their leave of Fionn and the Fianna on the back of the white steed, heading towards the sea which parted before them. They saw marvels on their journey ... and Oisín managed to rescue the daughter of the king of Tír na mBeo ['the Land of the Living'] from a Fomhar ['Fomorian, giant'] on their way. Finally, when they arrive in Tír na nÓg, Oisín is greeted by Rí na nÓg and told that he will enjoy everlasting life and perpetual youth there. Oisín and Niamh are married, have children ... Oisín, however, having spent more than three hundred years there, becomes homesick, and asks permission to return home. This is granted reluctantly, and Oisín sets off home on the same horse that brought him to Tír na nÓg, having been warned by Niamh not to dismount, telling him that if he does so he will suddenly age and never return. She also tells him that Fionn and the Fianna are no more. Nevertheless, Oisín sets off, reaches Ireland, fails to find Fionn, visits Almhain [the Hill of Allen, Co. Kildare, the chief residence of Fionn] to find it overgrown with weeds and nettles. While he was going through Gleann an Smóil he saw three hundred men trying to raise a marble slab. They ask his assistance and when he throws it seven perches away the girth breaks and he falls off the horse which immediately heads off to Tír na nÓg leaving Oisín a blind old man. The whole narrative is interspersed with dialogue between Patrick and Oisín.[63]

Yeats acknowledged that the part of *The Wanderings* 'dealing with the three islands' was 'wholly [his] own', though rooted in folk tradition about Tír na nÓg. Where the *Laoidh* presented two otherworldly destinations for Oisín and Niamh, Tír na mBeo and Tír na nÓg, Yeats introduced a third for Oisin and Niam. In addition to his Isles/Islands of Victories and of Youth, the Island of Forgetfulness appears, from which Oisin returns to Ireland.[64] Once in Ireland, he sees not the *Laoidh*'s crowds trying to move a marble slab but 'two men struggling to lift a sackful of sand', although his attempt to assist the pair

James Carney, Maynooth Monographs 2, (Maynooth: An Sagart, 1989), 181–99, at 181–3; Brian Ó Dálaigh, 'Mícheál Coimín: Jacobite, Protestant and Gaelic poet 1676–1760', *Studia Hibernica*, 34 (2006-7), 123–50, at 147–50.

[63] Ó Briain, 'Some material', 183–4.
[64] Alspach, 'Some sources', 851.

ends in the same way as in the *Laoidh*.[65] This passage displays Yeats's supplementing of his main textual source, the *Laoidh*, with oral tradition: his sack-of-sand motif was drawn from modern Scottish and Irish folklore about Oisín's trip to Tír na nÓg.[66] Further illustration of Yeats's mingling of literary and folklore sources comes neatly by way of Oisín's characterization of the characters whom he saw on the Island of Forgetfulness, in Book III of *The Wanderings*, as 'all who are winter tales'. The figures named populate pre-modern literature and modern folklore alike, but this designation may allude to their being the subjects of oral tales traditionally told *ó Shamhain go Bealtaine* ('from November to May').

Russell K. Alspach demonstrated that what Yeats referred to as 'middle Irish dialogues' between St Patrick and Oisín were also likely to have been sourced in volumes of the Transactions of the Ossianic Society.[67] For example, the volume that contains *Laoidh Oisín* also presents the poem beginning *A Oisín, is fada do shúan* ('Oisín, long is thy slumber'), as well as further examples of the early modern and modern lays now known collectively as *Agallamh Oisín agus Phádraig* ('The dialogue between Oisín and Patrick').[68] A tradition of dialogues between Patrick and Oisín was initiated in the late Middle Irish period, notably in the lengthy saga *Acallam na Senórach* ('The colloquy of the ancients'), composed in the early thirteenth century.[69] No edition or translation of the tale was available until Standish Hayes O'Grady's publication in his *Silva Gadelica* in 1892, but Yeats may have known the discussion of the work in O'Curry's *Lectures* as he wrote *The Wanderings*. After the *Acallam*, the narrative of which is mostly expressed in prose, however, it was the lay that became the characteristic form of these dialogues, and such poems were popular from the late Middle Irish period down to modern times. The conversation of the long-lived pagan warrior and saint in the *Acallam* is congenial, but in the later realizations of this storyline, the interlocuters find little common ground. The animosity towards the Church on the part of Oisin in *The Wanderings*—Oisin tells Patrick that 'Two things that 'fore all things I hate / Fasting and prayers'—has been seen as a major departure from *Laoidh Oisín*.[70] It is in fact entirely in keeping with Finn Cycle mores, including many of the dialogue texts drawn on by Yeats.

---

[65] Alspach, 'Some sources', 851.

[66] Ó Briain, 'Some material', 188–9. Note that the prose version of this story told by P. W. Joyce, which Yeats knew, contains the image of the marble slab: *Old Celtic Romances Translated from the Gaelic* (London: Kegan Paul, 1879), 398. See *Life I*, 82.

[67] Alspach, 'Some sources', 853–5.

[68] John O'Daly, ed. and trans., 'Agallamh Oisín agus Phátraic', in his *Laoithe Fiannuigheachta, or Fenian poems*, Transactions of the Ossianic Society, 4 (Dublin: John O'Daly, 1859), 2–63. See also further examples of such lays in John O'Daly, ed., *Laoithe Fiannuigheachta, or Fenian poems. Second series*, Transactions of the Ossianic Society, 6 (Dublin: John O'Daly, 1861).

[69] Whitley Stokes, ed., 'Acallamh na senórach', in Ernst Windisch and Whitley Stokes, eds., *Irische Texte mit Wörterbuch*, 4 vols, iv:1 (Leipzig: S. Hirzel, 1900), 1–438; Ann Dooley and Harry Roe trans., *Tales of the elders of Ireland: Acallam na senórach* (Oxford: Oxford University Press, 1999). Note that McDonald is mistaken in his assertion that 'the Irish Oisin is found first' in the thirteenth-century *Acallam* (*Poems*, vol. 1, 539): Oisín is a major character in texts composed from the eighth century on.

[70] Gomes, 'Reviving Oisin', 388. See Alspach, 'Some sources', 854, and McDonald, *The poems, vol. 1*, 552, on the contemporary resonance of 'a confrontation between paganism and the Church'.

Yeats went beyond his acknowledged sources to allude to the substance of a number of other medieval and early modern works in *The Wanderings*. For instance, that the island he introduced induced forgetfulness can be attributed to the influence of Tennyson's *The Lotos-Eaters* (1832) and, through it, the *Odyssey*, as well as being a response to a wider interest in the *immram*, or medieval Irish voyage tale, in Victorian poetry.[71] Yeats, however, may also have been alluding to the 'drink of forgetfulness' motif that occurs across medieval works, based on his own reading of those works in translation. It appears in association with the sea god Manannán in *Serglige Con Culainn*, which, it has already been suggested, he appears to have read in O'Curry's translation by 1899.[72] That Manannán appears in *The Wanderings* is itself a significant departure from *Laoidh Oisín* and the dialogue texts that Yeats acknowledged as his textual sources; the same is true of the appearances in *The Wanderings* of Aengus and Edain (Étaín), Balor, and several Ulster Cycle, or 'Red Branch', characters including Conor Mac Nessa (Conchobar mac Nessa), Cuchul[a]in, and Fergus. Yeats made Aengus and Edain the parents of Niam—an idea that has no basis in Irish-language tradition. His bringing together of some of the Ulster Cycle's most prominent characters with those of the Finn Cycle is likewise untraditional, although anticipated by Macpherson and present too in Irish oral tradition around the time that Yeats was writing, as is evidenced by Curtin's folk tale, already discussed, published in 1890. Another aspect of Yeats's free association of characters from different parts of Irish tradition is his inclusion of Grania (Gráinne) in *The Wanderings*, albeit that she appears only in Oisin's dreams: she finds no place in the *Laoidh* or in the dialogue poems, although prominent elsewhere in Finn Cycle works. Although known from the Old Irish period, Gráinne is not depicted at any length until the early modern *Tóruigheacht Dhiarmada agus Ghráinne*.[73] Grania draws attention to the fact that Yeats does not draw on any particularly early Finn Cycle works: the *Laoidh* is eighteenth-century and the dialogue poems are early modern, like the *Tóruigheacht*. Yet the essay published by Yeats in *The Gael* in 1887 demonstrates a depth of research into the Finn Cycle that a reading of *The Wanderings* and of Yeats's discussion of his sources does not make apparent.[74] Yeats centred his essay on Finn on the twelfth-century *Macgnímartha Finn* ('The Boyhood Deeds of Finn'); he had read the translation of the story published in the Transactions of the Ossianic Society by John O'Donovan, a close associate of O'Curry and the inspiration for the character Owen in Brian Friel's *Translations*.[75] As well as illuminating Yeats's research into the medieval phase of the Finn Cycle, this essay is suggestive of Yeats's identification with the fledgling poet Finn at this early point in his

[71] See Campbell, *Irish Poetry under the Union*, 144–56.

[72] Curry, 'The sick-bed', *Atlantis*, 2 (1859), 122–4.

[73] See above n. 6.

[74] Kelly, 'Aesthete'.

[75] Brian Friel, John Andrews, and Kevin Barry, 'Translations and a paper landscape: Between fiction and history', *The Crane Bag*, 7:2 (1983), 118–24, at 123; John O'Donovan, ed. and trans., 'Macgnímartha Finn Mac Cumaill: The boyish exploits of Finn Mac Cumhaill', in John O'Daly, ed., *Laoithe Fiannuigheachta, or Fenian poems*, Transactions of the Ossianic Society, 4 (Dublin: John O'Daly, 1859), 281–304.

poetic career. In addition, it raises questions about Yeats's engagement with the Irish-language original underlying his essay that are of direct relevance to a consideration of *The Wanderings*.

Macgnímartha Finn survives in fragmentary form, but, as it is preserved, its dramatic climax is Finn's composition of his first poem; he has added poetic training to the warrior and hunting skills gained earlier in the narrative. The poem's climactic status is even more pronounced in the version that Yeats read, which breaks off midway through the poem.[76] The ability to compose poetry is bound up in the tale with the acquisition of supernatural knowledge; this association is likely to have been attractive to Yeats, who, in 1887, was deeply interested in the occult.[77] The poem, which is known by its opening word, *Cétamon* ('Mayday'), functions, 'to prove that [Finn] has the power of sight, to prove he possesses the skill of divination, wisdom, knowledge, and the craft of a poet-seer'.[78] Yeats provided his own 'hasty, though fairly literal version of it, in rhyme'.[79] McDonald, who has commented that the form of this poem—'a lyric variation on the fourteener couplets to be found in George Chapman's translation of Homer's *Iliad*'—was 'probably intended to give the verses an air of antiquity', has seen it as Yeats's transformation of 'O'Donovan's halting version ... into an effective poem'.[80] Kelly has been prepared to judge Yeats's version 'a distinct improvement upon the original translation'.[81] The first stanza of the poem gives a sense of the two versions. O'Donovan had:

> May-day delightful time! how beautiful the colour!
> The blackbirds sing their full lay, would that Laighaig were here.[82]

Yeats transformed those lines into

> How beautiful thy colours are, oh marvellous morn of May,
> The black-birds pour their copious lays; would Leigha were here.[83]

Yeats's version of the poem is certainly more successful as a stand-alone work: by imposing rhyme and avoiding the Irish word *suaill* that O'Donovan carried over from the original text, Yeats produced something that feels complete. Yet, this is not the sole, or most important, criterion in evaluating success in translation, and, of course,

---

[76] O'Donovan was reliant on an inexperienced transcriber, who could read no further. See Kuno Meyer, ed., 'Macgnímartha Find', *Revue celtique*, 5 (1882), 195–204 and 508, at 195–7.

[77] *Life* 1, 28–58.

[78] Maria Tymoczko, '"Cétamon": Vision in early Irish seasonal poetry', *Éire-Ireland*, 18:4 (1983), 17–39, at 22.

[79] Kelly, 'Aesthete', 87.

[80] McDonald, *Poems,* vol. 1, 470–1.

[81] Kelly, 'Aesthete', 87 n.15.

[82] O'Donovan, 'Mac-gnímartha Finn', 303.

[83] Kelly, 'Aesthete', 87.

O'Donovan's purpose, the provision of an academic translation centred on the meaning of the original, was not Yeats's. Yeats's poem evidences no understanding of the original text, and it is also the case that it makes no attempt to replicate its metre, rhyme, pattern of alliteration, or line breaks.

It is useful to bear this brief example in mind when contemplating Yeats's mode of engagement with *The Wanderings*. Critics of that poem have been apt to confer onto that work the status of translation. Alspach, for instance, judged that in the first part of the poem Yeats '[had] taken passage after passage from Comyn with but little change'.[84] Even allowing for 'Comyn' to mean here *Laoidh Oisín*, this is a problematic assertion; what Alspach demonstrated was Yeats's debt to O'Looney's translation. In positing a direct relationship between Yeats and the Irish-language text, in putting Yeats's response to a translation on an equal footing with it, the true nature of Yeats's use of sources is occluded. Maria Tymoczko has sought greater transparency by labelling *The Wanderings* an act of pseudotranslation.[85] Pseudotranslation refers to a literary work's claim to be a translation of a source that in fact never existed as presented; in Macpherson's Ossianic works, Yeats was familiar with this mode of writing, and he became one of a number of Anglo-Irish writers to use 'Irish material to cloak or fuel their creative literary impulses'.[86] This pseudotranslation was part of a complex system of engagement with Irish-language material, particularly medieval texts, in the late nineteenth century. Translation proper necessitated a knowledge of the source language, and had as its object the elucidation of the text, chiefly for a scholarly audience; readability and accessibility for the general public were not primary motivating factors. Literary translation, meanwhile, was 'directed to the needs of the receptor (i.e. anglophone Irish) literary system and the receptor culture'. Its target was not the original work's elucidation but its deployment to serve the needs of the author.[87] As Tymoczko underlines, literary translation was engaged in by individuals with a range of abilities in Irish, from those with little or no knowledge of the language, such as James Clarence Mangan, to people with a good grasp of the language, such as Jeremiah J. Callanan, who learned Irish in order to discharge his duties as a priest among a largely Irish-speaking population.[88] Pseudotranslation from Irish, therefore, could be undertaken by those competent in the language; this echoed the situation in Gaelic Scotland in the eighteenth century. Macpherson is likely to have

---

[84] Alspach, 'Some sources', 851. See also Gomes, 'Reviving Oisin', 387: '[I]t would seem Yeats is doing little more than recasting Comyn's lay into his own poetic diction and style.'

[85] Maria Tymoczko, *Translation in a Postcolonial Context: Early Irish Literature in English Translation* (Manchester: St Jerome), 1999, 134.

[86] Tymoczko, *Translation*, 135.

[87] Tymoczko, *Translation*, 135–6.

[88] See Sean Ryder, 'Mangan, James Clarence', in James McGuire and James Quinn (eds), *Dictionary of Irish Biography* (Dublin and Cambridge: Royal Irish Academy and Cambridge University Press, 2009), online edition, http://dib.cambridge.org (accessed 12 June 2021); Diarmaid Breatnach and Máire Ní Mhurchú, 'Callanan, Jeremiah Joseph (1795–1829)', in Breatnach and Ní Mhurchú, eds., *Ainm.ie*, https://www.ainm.ie (accessed 12 June 2021).

had reasonably good Gaelic but nonetheless made little attempt to replicate his sources in his 'translations'.[89] All this complicated a contemporary understanding of what translation from Irish really entailed. Yeats's brand of pseudotranslation comprised the reworking and adaptation of works that had already moved out of their original language, and his presentation of this work as a primary act of translation was a fiction. The identification of pseudotranslation as his modus operandi at the outset of his career helps to make sense of his later claim to be working directly with 'old writings'—simultaneously offering literal translations but also condensing them and selectively engaging with them.

CONCLUSION

Yeats's use of sources for his construction of 'ancient Ireland' is most helpfully approached as early practice rooted in pseudotranslation, that gave rise to *The Wanderings of Oisin*, giving way over time to the loose invocation of only the outlines of traditional material in 'Cuchulain Comforted'. John V. Kelleher argued that Yeats

> did not employ a great number of Irish themes or borrow characters and incidents from many Irish tales and sagas. He used only a small and, on the whole, not very rich selection, mostly taken from books he had read in the late 'eighties and in the 'nineties. During the remainder of his lifetime the amount and variety and richness of the material available to him in scholarly translation increased dramatically, and a number of tales were published for the first time, which one might think he would have seized on, so close were they to the tone of his later work; yet he seemed unaware of them or indifferent to them.

The ignorance or indifference posited by Kelleher might be explained in terms of Yeats's decreasing need to pay close attention to source material as his attachment to the pseudotranslation mode weakened. Indeed, Kelleher himself offered the provocative suggestion that Yeats, writing about Cuchulain later in his career, worked precisely as the 'bards' that he celebrated had:

> [w]ithout explanation or apology he assumed exactly the same freedom that had been assumed twelve or thirteen hundred years ago by the man or men who first wrote of Cú Chulainn; and so he achieved a somewhat comparable result. They had taken God knows what drifting fragments of outmoded pagan mythology, tribal history, ancient hero-tales ... re-imagined the whole, and so created an epic and an epic hero ... It was reworked continually ... [Yeats's] creation can I believe teach us more

---

[89] Derick S. Thomson, *The Gaelic Sources of Macpherson's Ossian*, Aberdeen University Studies, 130 (Edinburgh: Oliver & Boyd, 1952).

about the Cú Chulainn of medieval and pre-medieval Irish literature than we could ever learn through mere scholarship.[90]

The counterparts to the early medieval 'drifting fragments' envisaged by Kelleher were translations into English of core texts and some English-language scholarship. Yeats's preference for modern iterations of Irish tradition—the nineteenth-century account of Cú Chulainn's death collected by Curtin, the eighteenth-century *Laoidh Oisín*—over older material has emerged, even if they were presented by him as 'old writings'. Yet a greater reading knowledge of nineteenth-century writing about medieval Irish literature than has sometimes been credited to Yeats has also come into focus. O'Curry's influence on Yeats, for example, is rarely cited—including by Yeats himself—but is clearly discernible. Yeats's ancient Ireland was certainly built on foundations laid by him in the 1880s and 1890s, using materials from the 1850s and 1860s, but those foundations were broader than is sometimes acknowledged.

[90] Kelleher, 'Yeats's use of Irish materials', 115 and 124.

CHAPTER 10

··

THE GHOST OF PARNELL

··

R. F. FOSTER

Conor Cruise O'Brien memorably defined the history of the generation before we were born as 'a twilit zone of time', never quite belonging to the larger historical experience. Rather, it is a site of impressions and assumptions acquired from supposed 'memories' which are actually derived from our parents' recollections, and a sense of continuity dependent upon 'the personality, opinions, and talkativeness of our elder relations'. This is perhaps a particularly Irish syndrome, as Colm Tóibín has pointed out, and Cruise O'Brien went on specifically to relate this form of historical consciousness to the imagination of certain Irish writers.[1] He concentrated upon the novelist and short-story writer Sean O'Faolain, in whose attitudes to politics, sex, and individual freedom O'Brien discerned a theme which he called 'parnellism' (as distinguished from the political faith of 'Parnellism'). O'Faolain was born in 1900, a decade after Charles Stewart Parnell's fall from the leadership of the Home Rule party following a divorce scandal, and his sudden death less than a year later. In a feline and rather destructive assessment of the Cork writer's work to date, O'Brien argued that he was inhibited by the received memory of what the deposed Chief supposedly represented, trapping O'Faolain in a sterile traditionalism which necessitated evasive flight.[2]

Elsewhere, O'Brien referred to Parnell's mysterious but charismatic persona posthumously 'deviating from politics into literature', a process particularly manipulated by W. B. Yeats.[3] This is true, but the manner in which Yeats absorbed and used the memory of Parnell—very different from the case of O'Faolain—is at once more direct and more distanced than first appears. The subject of what F. S. L. Lyons long ago christened 'The

---

[1] Colm Tóibín, *Mad, Bad, Dangerous to Know: the fathers of Wilde, Yeats and Joyce* (London: Viking, 2018), 152.

[2] Donat O'Donnell [Conor Cruise O'Brien], *Maria Cross: imaginative patterns in a group of modern Catholic writers* (London: Chatto and Windus, 1953), 95–100.

[3] Conor Cruise O'Brien, *Parnell and his Party 1880–90* (Oxford: Clarendon, 1957; 2nd edn, 1964), 356. For Parnell's afterlife see Roy Foster and Alvin Jackson, 'Men for All Seasons? Carson, Parnell and the limits of heroism in modern Ireland', *European History Quarterly*, 39:3 (July 2009), 414–38.

Parnell Theme in Literature' is a suggestive one, but in Yeats's case evaluating the influence of literary Parnellism requires a careful examination of chronology, omission,
and political context.[4] Yeats, born in 1865, was much nearer than O'Faolain to the era
of Parnell's supremacy: an adolescent living in Dublin during the era of the Land War
and the Phoenix Park Murders, a young man moving in Home Rule circles in London
during Parnell's political ascendancy in the late 1880s, a 25-year-old published poet at
the time of Parnell's shattering fall in 1890 and his sudden death in October 1891. From
comments in his letters, and his sister's memories, we know that the Yeats children
sometimes attended debates in the House of Commons, and that the bohemian circles
in which they moved supported Home Rule.[5] Yet the paucity of Yeats's comments on
Parnell and politics during this era is striking, as is—apart from one polemical poem,
later disowned—his reaction to Parnell's sudden extinction. His preoccupation with the
dead Chief would come later, and for specific and present-minded reasons.

Political opinions in the Yeats household in late-Victorian Bedford Park were
influenced by the fact that Parnell's predecessor Isaac Butt, the founder of the Home Rule
movement, had been a family friend. John Butler Yeats, who nurtured a lifelong love for
Butt's daughter Rosa, constantly adverted to her father's failure in politics, attributing it
to the loveable weakness of his character as well as the political circumstances of the day,
but he adhered to the opinion that Butt was the last Irish 'statesman', whereas Parnell
was merely an 'archpolitician'.[6] Parnell had ruthlessly supplanted the older man in 1877,
and led the Irish party in a more radical and confrontational direction—not a process
which JBY found entirely appealing. Later he would write that Butt, unlike Parnell, was
incapable of being either calculating or selfish, and this led to his downfall: 'He stood
outside a world where these are the springs that mostly operate – selfishness would have
made him a peer, rich, the founder of a family, hatred would have made him the idol of
Irishmen frenzied with hatred – they were all waiting for Parnell.'[7]

As a small-scale Irish landlord JBY also had his reasons to feel ambivalent about the
Land League which Parnell headed, despite his own background as an Ascendancy land-
owner. The League challenged the landed elite in Ireland, mobilized tenants through
mass meetings, and threatened rent strikes in the Land War of 1879–82, calling for
enhanced leasehold rights (and eventually a transfer of proprietorship) and precipitating
a drastic decline in rental incomes. JBY's eldest son's attitude to Parnell and his party
was influenced by different factors. From the mid-1880s he was closely involved in the
circles around the old Fenian John O'Leary, and while Parnell had made some overtures

---

[4] F. S. L. Lyons, 'The Parnell theme in literature', in Andrew Carpenter, ed., *Place, Personality
and the Irish Writer: Irish Literary Studies I* (Colin Smythe: Gerrards Cross, 1977), 69–96; also see
John Kelly, 'Parnell in Irish literature', in D. George Boyce and Alan O'Day, eds., *Parnell in Perspective*
(London: Routledge, 1991), 242–83.

[5] See my *Life 1*, 61–2.

[6] William M. Murphy, *Prodigal Father: the life of John Butler Yeats (1839-1922)* (London: Cornell
University Press, 1978), 126.

[7] JBY to Frank MacDonagh, 16 Apr. 1913, transcript in William Murphy Papers, Union College
Schenectady.

towards the 'physical force party' (particularly in the USA) during the heady days of the Land War, from 1886 the Home Rule Party's interests were firmly attached to the Gladstonian Liberal party, who in a dramatic volte-face had adopted their cause.

It seems clear that, for Yeats in his early twenties, the romantic Fenian tradition in Irish politics was more alluring. The Young Ireland Societies, in which he was involved from the mid-1880s, formed a kind of nursery for neo-Fenians, as Matthew Kelly has shown.[8] In the same era, compiling anthologies of nineteenth-century Irish writing provided him with a crash course in Romantic nationalist literature, arousing an enduring admiration for writers such as James Clarence Mangan and John Mitchel. While he viewed Thomas Davis's less distinguished literary efforts with a severe eye, the ideas and energy focused by Young Ireland a half-century before remained a pre-occupation.[9] This grounding in nineteenth-century Irish literature, no less than the company he kept in the Southwark Literary Society and Dublin's Contemporary Club, looked—however platonically—to more stirring traditions of resistance than Parnell's and Gladstone's 'Union of Hearts'.[10] And, though he might already have taken the Irish Republican Brotherhood (IRB) oath, from 1889 his politics were further radicalized by the revolutionary and Anglophobic opinions embraced by Maud Gonne. He would later admit that when he met the mailboat at Kingstown Pier on 10 October 1891, his priority was to greet her; the fact that the boat was carrying Parnell's coffin meant far less to him at the time.[11] And the mourning clothes which Gonne wore were not (as assumed) in honour of the dead Chief but for her secret child Georges, who had died of meningitis in Paris the week before.

It is nonetheless striking that Yeats managed to be there, with his sixth sense for being at the right place at the right time. The next day would see 200,000 people crowding Dublin's streets for Parnell's funeral, which Yeats would recur to decades later in a key political poem. He had just published 'Mourn- and then Onward' in the Parnellite journal *United Ireland* on 10 October 1891, but this seems to have been a mechanical exercise. Lecturing in America many years later, he would blench at the reproduction of this banal juvenilia on the stage backdrop, mistaking it at first for a biblical quotation; and he was equally infuriated when an Irish newspaper reprinted it after the death of Arthur Griffith in 1922.[12] After Parnell's death Yeats's political stance ricocheted through a phase of revolutionary radicalism in the 1890s, reverted before World War

---

[8] See Matthew Kelly, *The Fenian Ideal and Irish Nationalism 1882–1916* (Woodbridge: Boydell, 2006), especially ch. 3.

[9] See David Dwan, *The Great Community: culture and nationalism in Ireland* (Dublin: Field Day, 2008).

[10] See my *Words Alone: Yeats and his inheritances* (Oxford: Oxford University Press, 2011), ch. 2.

[11] 'I was expecting a friend but met what I thought much less of at the time, the body of Parnell.' Commentary on 'A Parnellite at Parnell's Funeral', *VP*, 832. The coincidence is also mentioned in *Mem*, 47.

[12] As Augusta Gregory told Lennox Robinson in a letter of 23 August 1922 (Morris Library, Southern Illinois University at Carbondale). It had also been reprinted by the *Irish Weekly Independent* on 20 May 1893, when a Home Rule Bill was passing through the House of Commons, later to be rejected by the Lords.

I to supporting the Home Rule movement led by Parnell's successor John Redmond, rediscovered radical nationalism after the 1916 Rising, and supported the Treaty which ended the Anglo-Irish War in 1921.

Back in the 1890s, however, Parnellism sustained a complicated relationship to neo-Fenianism, and Yeats's political odyssey duly reflected the process. The once-powerful Irish Parliamentary Party had split over the issue of retaining Parnell as leader, and the Parnellite rump was led by the unglamorous figure of John Redmond. In the last desperate months of his career, fighting and losing by-elections, Parnell had invoked the Fenian tradition in Irish politics; it was part of a rhetorical swerve into Anglophobia, jettisoning the alliance with the Liberal Party, since Gladstone's withdrawal of support for his leadership had precipitated the Irish Party's split. Parnell's endorsement of a separatist agenda was adventitious and inconsistent, but it brought Fenian elements onside, as was evident at his funeral. Where Yeats stood in relation to this was uncertain. Thirty-odd years later, constructing the great myth of his life in his autobiographies, the date of Parnell's fall and death would be enshrined as an occasion of decisive change—a caesura cutting across the development of Irish history, a tolling bell which announced both death and renewal. But things were less clear-cut at the time.

In the rancorous split which followed the O'Shea divorce case Yeats was unequivocally pro-Parnell, as were many of his Irish friends such as Katharine Tynan. After Parnell's death, his image went through many shifts; during the internecine bickering of the 1890s, several of Yeats's Ascendancy friends and collaborators moved from inimical disapproval of a class traitor to nostalgia for a lost leader who seemed able to impose unity on the fissile elements of Irish politics. This was the course followed by Augusta Gregory, Standish O'Grady, and Douglas Hyde, who admitted that he had never valued the Chief until he was no longer alive.[13] There may also have been a certain nostalgia for someone from the 'gentry' who could impose order on his squabbling followers—a theme which would surface in several dramatic works of this era such as Edward Martyn's *The Heather Field* (1899), George Moore's *The Bending of the Bough* (1900), and Gregory's *The Deliverer* (1911). During the 1890s improbable expectations were entertained for Parnell's political heir to appear, in reconciliatory figures such as Sir Horace Plunkett and Lord Castletown. These were the political impulses which would briefly peak in the efforts towards compromise on the land question, and even political devolution, during the early 1900s.

However, in the 1890s Yeats's inclinations lay towards more distinctly 'advanced' politics. Fenian circles were also riven by splits and factions, but there was little evident wish among them for a Parnell *redivivus*. Yeats and Gonne inclined towards the Irish National Association (INA) faction, which had little to do with Redmond's more cautious course (and which led to the glamorous pair featuring in a number of slightly bemused police reports). In the culture wars prosecuted by Yeats during the 1890s, notably his attempts

[13] As pointed out in Kelly, 'Parnell in Irish Literature', 252–6. The Hyde quote comes from a letter to John O'Leary.

to found a series of publications of canonical Irish texts, he took a stance which allied him with neo-Fenian political agendas and made an enemy of Sir Charles Gavan Duffy, whose ideas were very different, and who won out in the end.[14] In a more obviously political enterprise, Yeats also became heavily invested in the plans for celebrating the centenary of the 1798 Rising, which—as Deirdre Toomey has demonstrated—aligned him yet more closely with Fenianism and involved him in murky intrigues to which he responded with confusion and ambivalence. Matters were all the more complicated by the fact that during the late 1890s he was also forming his great alliance with Augusta Gregory and raising support for the Irish Literary Theatre, an enterprise which involved a very different kind of politicking.[15]

As it turned out, during the 1898 celebrations Redmond and the constitutionalist politicians finally managed to grasp the initiative and take a prominent role in the com-memoration proceedings, with the result that Gonne and her associates were relegated to the sidelines. It was the kind of manoeuvre at which the Parnellite leader excelled; he would similarly outflank the extreme elements in the Volunteer movement in 1913. In both cases, his victory would prove to be short-term, and the future lay with the 'advanced' elements, though this was not immediately obvious. The 1898 centenary was in fact a fulcrum on which the revival of Fenian fortunes would later be seen to turn. But this was not evident at the time, and when the Irish Parliamentary Party reunited in 1900 it was under Redmond as its leader, and the divisive ghost of Parnell seemed to be laid to rest.

'Mourn- and then Onward' notwithstanding, it is questionable how much the dead Chief had ever meant to the young Yeats. In the early 1900s— the very years when Joyce was creating canonical works of literary Parnellism such as 'Ivy Day in the Committee Room' and the Christmas dinner scene in *A Portrait of the Artist as a Young Man*—the figure of Parnell does not seem to have figured large in Yeats's im-agination. He had also begun to distance himself from the Fenian politics of Gonne and her circle. Her marriage to the prominent Fenian John MacBride in 1903, and its traumatic collapse, helped to crystallize the process; Gonne was swiftly frozen out by MacBride's advanced-nationalist friends, exacerbating Yeats's repudiation of extreme politics.[16] He was prepared to invoke his own neo-Fenian past when addressing Irish-American gatherings, or defending his patriotic credentials to hos-tile Abbey audiences, but his politics had reverted to solid support for Home Rule— which advanced once more into focus after the Liberals' return to power in 1906, and their declining majorities from 1910, restored the influence of the Irish Party at Westminster.

[14] Discussed in my *Life 1*, 115–27.

[15] See Deirdre Toomey, 'Who Fears to Speak of 'Ninety-eight?', in Warwick Gould, ed., *Yeats and the Nineties: Yeats Annual no 14, A Special Number* (London, 2001), 209–64.

[16] See my *Life 1*, 330–4, and Caoimhe Nic Dháibhéid, '"This is a case in which Irish national considerations must be taken into account": The Breakdown of the Gonne-MacBride Marriage 1904–1908', *Irish Historical Studies*, 37:146 (Nov. 2010).

However, the first decade of the twentieth century, when the Irish Parliamentary Party seemed to represent a bourgeois establishment-in-waiting preparing for the Home Rule future, also saw the uncertain but significant rise of the Sinn Fein party under Arthur Griffith—and a hardening mood of generational change below the surface.[17] Meanwhile for Yeats, increasingly famous, living much of his time in London, and preoccupied by the issues of administration, maintenance, and intrigue swirling around the Abbey Theatre, Irish politics were relegated to a small niche in one of the many compartments of his life. Parnell was a distant memory. What brought the Chief back to mind was an increasing sense of elitism and a repudiation of what he would later term the values of the 'mob', a process charted by John Kelly in a classic essay.[18] This was focused by the controversy over Hugh Lane's campaign to found a gallery of modern art in Dublin; Lane and his supporters (prominent among them Gregory and Yeats) were opposed by the newspaper magnate William Martin Murphy, whose journals *The Irish Catholic* and the *Irish Independent* comprehensively denounced the project. This helped sway opinion on Dublin Corporation against endorsing Lane's gallery plan at a key meeting on 8 September 1913.[19]

Murphy had also been a prominent anti-Parnellite, and in the poem 'To a Shade' Yeats made the connection by addressing Parnell's ghost directly. The poem was written at Coole Park and the manuscript is inscribed '29 September 1913', a date carefully reproduced in the printed version; two days later Lane would remove thirty-nine modern French paintings from Dublin to London, starting a dispute still not resolved. The poet imagines the revenant Parnell drifting through the streets of Dublin, observing the monument erected in his memory, breathing the salty air and listening to the seagulls—but warns him that the kind of people who hounded him to his death are 'at their old tricks yet', whipped up against Hugh Lane's enterprise by 'Your enemy, an old foul mouth'—William Martin Murphy:

> Go, unquiet wanderer
> And gather the Glasnevin coverlet
> About your head till the dust stops your ear,
> The time for you to taste of that salt breath
> And listen at the corners has not come:
> You had enough of sorrow before death –
> Away, away! You are safer in the tomb. (*CW1*, 110)

---

[17] See my *Vivid Faces: the revolutionary generation in Ireland 1890–1923* (London: Penguin, 2014), *passim*.

[18] John S. Kelly, 'The Fifth Bell: race and class in Yeats's political thought', in Okifumu Komesu and Masaru Sekine, eds., *Irish Writers and Politics: Irish Literary Studies 36* (Colin Smythe: Gerrards Cross, 1989), 109–75.

[19] See my ' "A Family Affair": Lane, Gregory, Yeats and educating the nation', in Barbara Dawson, ed., *Hugh Lane: founder of a gallery of modern art for Ireland* (London: Scala, 2008), 15–18, and Lucy McDiarmid, 'Hugh Lane and the Decoration of Dublin, 1908-" in McDiarmid, *The Irish Art of Controversy* (Dublin: Lilliput, 2005), 10–49.

The poem appeared later that year in *Poems Written in Discouragement*, and then in *Responsibilities* (1914), where it was embellished by a remarkable commentary defining the Lane affair as one of 'three public controversies' which had stirred the poet's imagination about Irish affairs, the others being the furore over the first production of *The Playboy of the Western World* and the Parnell split. The 1914 note ended with a striking summation:

> Religious Ireland – and the pious Protestants of my childhood were signal examples – thinks of divine things as a round of duties separated from life and not as an element that may be discovered in all circumstance and emotion, while political Ireland sees the good citizen but as a man who holds to certain opinions and not as a man of good will. Against all this we have but a few educated men and the remnants of an old traditional culture among the poor. Both were stronger forty years ago, before the rise of our new middle class which made its first public display during the nine years of the Parnell split, showing how base at moments of excitement are minds without culture. (*VP*, 819)

Thus Parnell re-entered Yeats's imaginative life as embodying yet another proud Ascendancy figure who, like Gregory and Lane, worked for Ireland's salvation but received abuse and contempt from Catholic demos in return. Shortly after the appearance of 'To a Shade', Joyce would give 'Literary Parnellism' a published voice in *Dubliners* and *A Portrait of the Artist*; while George Moore had already presented in *Hail and Farewell* an audacious conflation of himself and Parnell as Wagnerian heroes attempting to pull the sword of liberation from the gnarled and recalcitrant tree trunk of Ireland.[20] And Yeats's view of Parnell as an exemplar of Anglo-Irish pride and solitude, as well as his own growing contempt for bourgeois Catholic pieties, was reinforced by a different kind of publication around this time: Katharine (O'Shea) Parnell's memoir of her life with the great man, *Charles Stewart Parnell: his love story and political life*, which was published to a scandalized reception in 1914.[21]

Yeats, like other readers, was struck by the incontrovertible evidence in the book (from original letters, often reproduced in facsimile), that Parnell's attitude towards many of his Party colleagues was contemptuous, and that he was periodically prepared to throw everything up and leave politics, taking refuge in uxorious bliss with Mrs O'Shea. Yeats was also drawn to the passionate portrait of her lover created by Katharine, particularly the episode where Parnell suggested, while witnessing a storm battering Brighton's Chain Pier, that they leap into the raging sea and end it all forever. Yeats dwelt on this incident, and what it signified about Parnell's character, in an important section of *A Vision*. In this occult gazetteer of archetypes, Parnell is the exemplary figure for Phase

---

[20] See Lyons, 'The Parnell theme in Irish literature', 78.

[21] Discussed at length in my 'Love, Politics and Textual Corruption: Mrs O'Shea's Parnell', in *Paddy and Mr Punch: Connections in Irish and English History* (London: Penguin, 1993), 123–38.

Ten, 'The Image Breaker': 'He accepts what form (*Mask* and *Image*) those about him admire and, on discovering that it is alien, casts it away with brutal violence, to choose some other form as alien.' If true to his phase, he 'creates some code of personal conduct' and 'becomes proud, masterful and practical'. His 'Body of Fate' is characterized by 'enforced emotion' and 'a kind of burning restraint, a something that suggests a savage statue to which one offers sacrifice'. This image of godlike impassivity concealing powerful emotion persists throughout the analysis—as does that of sacrifice, and Mosaic deliverance ('Perhaps Moses when he descended the mountain-side had a like stony *Mask*, and had cut out of the one rock *Mask* and table'). In the concluding paragraph of this section, Yeats writes directly about Parnell, indirectly referencing Barry O'Brien's biography and Katharine Parnell's memoir:

> He made upon his contemporaries an impression of impassivity, and yet after a speech that seemed brutal and callous, a follower has recorded that his hands were full of blood because he had torn them with his nails. One of his followers was shocked during the impassioned discussion in Committee Room No. 15, that led to his abandonment, by this most reticent man's lack of reticence in allusion to the operation of sex, an indifference as of a mathematician dealing with some arithmetical quantity, and yet Mrs Parnell tells how upon a night of storm on Brighton pier, and at the height of his power, he held her out over the waters and she lay still, stretched upon his two hands, knowing that if she moved, he would drown himself and her.[22]

By the early 1920s, when this was written, Parnell had become a far more dominating figure in Yeats's poetic imagination than he had ever been in the years of his political heyday during the 1880s, or his posthumous magnetism during the years of the Parnell Split in the 1890s. The seismic change brought by the 1916 Rising now seemed part of a phase inaugurated by the loss of Parnell's powerful hand on the national tiller twenty-five years before. Accordingly, when Yeats began during the summer of 1917 to draft the section of his autobiography which covered these years, he promoted Parnell's rise and fall to a position of immense symbolic importance—an interpretation which he does not seem to have subscribed to at the time. This would be immortalized in the version of his autobiography published as *The Trembling of the Veil* in 1922, and—yet more decisively—in his speech on the Irish Dramatic Movement delivered on the occasion of his receiving the Nobel Prize in 1923:

> The modern literature of Ireland, and indeed all that stir of thought which prepared for the Anglo-Irish war, began when Parnell fell from power in 1891. A disillusioned and embittered Ireland turned from parliamentary politics; an event was conceived; and the race began, as I think, to be troubled by that event's long gestation.[23]

---

[22] *CW* 13, 49.
[23] *CW* 3, 410.

This determinedly retrospective version played fast and loose with chronology, notably regarding the development of the cultural 'revival', whose origins were clearly in place during the years of Parnell's ascendancy rather than his collapse.[24] But the project of placing Yeats and his generation of artists and avatars at the centre of a revolution in consciousness, which would nurture a culture of political independence, was too important to be diverted by mere dates. In the conclusion to the autobiographical essay *Four Years* (published by Cuala in 1921), ending neatly in 1891, the significance of Parnell had been stressed yet again:

> Nations, races and individual men are unified by an image, or bundle of related images, symbolical or evocative of the state of mind which is, of all states of mind not impossible, the most difficult to that man, race or nation: because only the greatest obstacle that can be contemplated without despair rouses the will to full intensity ... I had seen Ireland in my own time turn from the bragging rhetoric and gregarious humour of O'Connell's generation and school, and offer herself to the solitary and proud Parnell as to her anti-self, buskin followed hard on sock, and I had begun to hope, or to half hope, that we might be the first in Europe to seek unity as deliberately as it had been sought by theologian, poet, sculptor, architect, from the eleventh to the thirteenth century. Doubtless we must seek it differently, no longer considering it convenient to epitomize all human knowledge, but find it we well might could we first find philosophy and a little passion.[25]

Parnell and O'Connell respectively donning the masks of Tragedy and Comedy provided a trope that would endure. As originally drafted, *Four Years* was combined with the main outline of *The Trembling of the Veil*, but Yeats decided to publish it separately and emphasize Parnell's fall and death in 1891 as a closure.[26] He would begin the subsequent volume (published hard on its heels in 1922) with a section called 'Ireland after Parnell': a resonant title, and a significant decision. By 1922 the 1890s as an era of transition had been established in his historicizing world view: emblematized by the *maudit* literary culture of his companions in the Rhymers' Club (to the discomfiture of several respectable survivors), the challenging avant-garde drama of *Axel* and *Ubu Roi,* and the search for occult illumination along the way of the chameleon. Later he would write flippantly that in 1900 'everybody got down off his stilts', but in 1922 he was creating a pattern of the past where (as in *A Vision*) cultural history and individual fates were intertwined.[27]

And for the purposes of Irish history the significance of Parnell's repudiation by Ireland was central. The experience of civil war, the violence of intimate hatreds, the sharpness of the weasel's tooth pervade Yeats's great sequences 'Nineteen Hundred and

---

[24] See my 'Thinking from Hand to Mouth: Anglo-Irish literature, Gaelic nationalism and Irish politics in the 1890s', in *Paddy and Mr Punch*, 262–80.

[25] *CW* 3, 167–8.

[26] This is demonstrated by the MS in NLI, 30, 536.

[27] W. B. Yeats, ed., *The Oxford Book of Modern Verse 1892–1935* (Oxford: Oxford University Press, 1936), xi

'Nineteen' and 'Meditations in Time of Civil War'. Particularly in the latter poems, the historical inheritance of Anglo-Ireland, with all its arrogance, ruthlessness, and violence, is keyed to the disruptions of the present, a theme also central to 'Blood and the Moon' (written in August 1927). The search for 'unity', so passionately evoked in the conclusion to *Four Years*, dominated his memoirs. But the Civil War recalled memories of the last occasion when savage divisions had rent the Irish body politic, in 1891: a chasm which persisted—like the divisions of 1922–3—for a generation and more. In a creatively misremembered quotation, Yeats would recur to Goethe's comment that the Irish continually reminded him of a pack of hounds dragging down a noble stag.[28] The betrayal of a leader by the mob was becoming an intrinsic part of his view of Irish history.

Also from the 1920s, Yeats's preoccupation with Georgian Ireland was taking hold, and Swift and Berkeley were advancing into importance in his personal myth of intellectual descent. A little paradoxically, the resolutely unintellectual Parnell was also enlisted in this Yeatsian pantheon of Ascendancy exemplars. The Chief's characteristics of pride, solitude, and contempt for demos were emphasized in a number of publications during this era, as his old lieutenants such as T. M. Healy, Justin McCarthy, and T. P. O'Connor produced copious volumes of memoirs—works in which the ghost of Parnell is broodingly omnipresent, while the authors attempt to rationalize their repudiation of him. In a spectacular instance of having it both ways, Parnell had also been co-opted into the Fenian apostolic succession, included there by no less an authority than Patrick Pearse in his powerful polemic *Ghosts* (1916):

> Parnell was less a political thinker than an embodied conviction: a flame that seared, a sword that stabbed. He did the thing that lay nearest his hand … His instinct was a Separatist instinct; and, far from being prepared to accept Home Rule as a 'final settlement between two nations', he was always careful to make it clear that, whether Home Rule came or did not come, the way must be left open for the achievement of the greater thing.[29]

Thus, though Joyce had Leopold Bloom reflecting in 1904 that Parnellism was dead and 'Ivy Day dying out', by the time *Ulysses* was published in 1922 the dead Chief's mystique was firmly established in other spheres.[30] Whether remembered as the austere Uncrowned King in his Home Rule heyday, or an uncompromising inspiration to the 'hillside men' of extreme nationalism, Parnell's ghost insistently hovered around the imagination of newly independent Ireland. This could take unexpected forms: in 1922 the pioneer Freudian Ernest Jones provided a psychoanalytical diagnosis of Irish nationalism in which Parnell's animosity towards England was traced to a castration

[28] Tactfully omitting the word 'Catholics', which Goethe had actually employed. See *Au*, 319 and 360–1, on divisiveness and nationalism.

[29] *Collected Works of Padraic H. Pearse: Political Writings and Speeches* (Dublin, 1922), 241.

[30] James Joyce, *Ulysses* (Paris, 1922; London, 1992 edn), 146

complex caused by the police impounding a sword from his mother's house during his childhood.[31]

For Yeats, disillusioned with the bourgeois moralizing of the Free State and in search of various kinds of excitement, the Chief's Anglo-Irish descent added to the potency. There was also an alluring supernatural dimension: both Standish O'Grady and Katharine Tynan had recorded that at Parnell's funeral (which meant so little to Yeats at the time) a star had fallen from the sky in a meteoric surge. Also in the 1890s, on the 1896 visit to Galway which brought him into Gregory's orbit, Yeats had been vouchsafed a vision which he never forgot, and constantly interrogated: a dream where a woman of marvellous beauty shot an arrow at a star, revealing an allegory of death and birth.[32]

In 1932–3, after a long period when writing poetry had been extremely difficult, Yeats drafted a poem called 'A Parnellite at Parnell's Funeral', conflating this occult vision with the death and inheritance of Parnell, and reflecting on initiation, sacrifice, and rebirth in images strongly influenced by James Frazer's *The Golden Bough*. (He was further inspired, very possibly, by the images he had been studying on classical coins and reliefs for the Commission on Ireland's new coinage, which he chaired in the late 1920s.) The theme of the poem was the 'national humiliation' of Parnell's fall: 'From that national humiliation,' Yeats wrote elsewhere, 'from the resolution to destroy all that made the humiliation possible, from that sacrificial victim I derive almost all that is living in the imagination of Ireland today.'[33] The poem opens with O'Connell as 'comedian', as the poet conjures up the drama of Parnell's funeral played out under his predecessor's tomb: before moving on to consider the fate—yet again—of an aristocratic hero (and donor) martyred by the crowd,

> … But popular rage,
> *Hysterica passio* dragged this quarry down.
> None shared our guilt; nor did we play a part
> Upon a painted stage when we devoured his heart. (*CW* 1, 279)

Later he added a coda, reflecting his brief flirtation with Eoin O'Duffy's parafascist 'Blueshirt' party in the early 1930s.[34]

> The rest I pass, one sentence I unsay.
> Had de Valera eaten Parnell's heart
> No loose-lipped demagogue had won the day.
> No civil rancour torn the land apart.
> …

[31] 'The Island of Ireland: a psychoanalytic contribution to political psychology', in Ernest Jones, *Essays in Applied Psycho-Analysis* (London and Vienna, 1922).

[32] *CW* 3, 280–2.

[33] 'Modern Ireland', a lecture printed in *Massachusetts Review*, 5:1 (1964), 258. This lecture (first given in America in 1932) is closely linked to 'Parnell's Funeral'.

[34] This was published in *The Spectator* (19 Oct. 1934) and titled 'Forty Years Later'; it was published without that title in 'Commentary on a Parnellite at Parnell's Funeral'. See *VP*, 542.

> Had even O'Duffy - but I name no more -
> Their school a crowd, his master solitude;
> Through Jonathan Swift's dark grove he passed, and there
> Plucked bitter wisdom that enriched his blood. (*CW* 1, 280)

Thus Parnell's fall not only inaugurated an era of petty squabbling among inadequate Irish politicians; their successors, who brought about first revolution and then civil war, proved equally unable to rise to the aura of the Uncrowned King, leaving Irish politics infected by their inadequacy. Parnell's ghost is dispatched—yet again—back to his Glasnevin grave, this time via a detour through Swiftian disillusionment.

During the 1930s Parnell's image continued potent for Yeats, not just as the sacrificial aristocratic hero, nor an inheritor of Anglo-Irish solitude, but also as a figure whose sexual transgression challenged the bourgeois Catholic modes of the new state. This had already been made mischievously clear in Yeats's celebrated Senate speech against the bill to outlaw divorce in 1925, when he drew attention to the fact that three major monuments in central Dublin commemorated famous adulterers:

> I have said that this is a tolerant country, yet, remembering that we have in our principal streets certain monuments, I feel it necessary that it would be wiser if I had said this country is hesitating.
>
> I have no doubt whatever that, when the iceberg melts, it will become an exceedingly tolerant country. The monuments are on the whole encouraging. I am thinking of O'Connell, Parnell and Nelson. We never had any trouble about O'Connell. It was said about O'Connell, in his own day, that you could not throw a stick over a workhouse wall without hitting one of his children, but he believed in the indissolubility of marriage, and when he died his heart was very properly preserved in Rome. I am not quite sure whether it was in a bronze or marble urn, but it is there, and I have no doubt the art of that urn was as bad as the other art of the period. We had a good deal of trouble about Parnell when he married a woman who became thereby Mrs Parnell.
>
> *An Cathaoirleach* [SPEAKER OF THE SENATE}:   Do you not think we might leave the dead alone?
> DR YEATS: I am passing on. I would hate to leave the dead alone.[35]

The same satirical thought is enshrined in his poem 'The Three Monuments', which he had already written, though it did not appear until 1927.[36]

> They hold their public meetings where
> Our most renownèd patriots stand,
> ...
> The three old rascals laugh aloud. (*CW* 1, 227)

---

[35] *SS*, 97–8.
[36] A. N. Jeffares, *A New commentary on the Poems of W .B. Yeats* (London: Macmillan, 1984), 262.

And in 1936 Yeats read *Parnell Vindicated: the lifting of the veil*, Henry Harrison's analysis of the Parnell divorce case, first published in 1931. Harrison examined Captain O'Shea's complaisance in his wife's long association with Parnell, and showed that the tawdry tale of deception presented in the divorce court travestied a long, passionate, and utterly committed relationship. (The revelation that all parties avoided regularizing it for fear of jeopardizing a large inheritance expected by Katharine from her wealthy aunt, while not ethically admirable, clarified things further.) The book, and a meeting with Harrison, stimulated further Yeatsian reflections on Parnell as mould-breaker, and a jaunty ballad encapsulating the situation and celebrating the world well lost for love, published in a 'Broadside' pamphlet with a long note attached. This commentary described meeting Henry Harrison, the revelations of his book, and Yeats's wish to write a poem that 'might suggest to somebody that there was nothing discreditable in Parnell's love for his mistress and his wife'. For good measure, he remarked that Parnell's ménage was long obvious to Gladstone and others, who hypocritically pretended not to know about it ('I was once enough of a politician to contemplate politics ever since with amusement'). Public insincerity, he added, had brought democracy into such disrepute that all over the world people were turning to dictators.[37]

Parnell's own marked tendency to dictatorship is ignored in the accompanying poem, 'Come Gather Round Me Parnellites', illustrated by a Jack Yeats sketch of topers raising their glasses to the dead Chief—possibly an echo of Joyce's lugubrious stout-drinkers in 'Ivy Day in the Committee Room'. In a more cheerful mode than the brilliantly manipulated doggerel that ends that short story, Yeats's ballad celebrates Parnell as a hero who 'fought the might of England, / And saved the Irish poor', doubly worth commemorating because of his arrogance: 'And a proud man's a lovely man, / So pass the bottle round.' Finally:

> The Bishops and the Party
> That tragic story made,
> A husband that had sold his wife
> And afterwards betrayed;
> But stories that live longest
> Are sung above the glass,
> And Parnell loved his country
> And Parnell loved his lass. (*CW* 1, 309)

By this stage of Yeats's life, Parnell had mutated from a Frazerian sacrificial god into another version of the Don Juan whom Yeats had once imagined riding through hell, while eunuchs gazed enviously at his muscular thighs. In the later 1930s his love affair with Edith Shackleton Heald brought him often to her house at Steyning in Sussex, where Parnell's and Katharine's brief marriage had taken place; Edith's aged gardener

---

[37] *CW* 5, 86.

remembered seeing the couple emerge from the registry office, to Yeats's delight.[38] In these last years of his astonishing life, his preoccupation with the conflicts and cycles of history, so brilliantly explored in poems such as 'Meditations in Time of Civil War', 'Nineteen Hundred and Nineteen', 'Lapis Lazuli', and 'The Statues', faded into the background when faced with the simple but heartbreaking memory of love and desire:

> How can I, that girl standing there,
> My attention fix
> On Roman or on Russian
> Or on Spanish politics? (*CW* 1, 348)

The epigraph to 'Politics' ironically invokes Thomas Mann's statement that 'in our time the destiny of man presents its meanings in political terms', clearly in order to disagree.

Love and the sacrifices enjoined by it may indeed be the 'story that lives longest', but throughout Yeats's creative life he summoned the ghost of Parnell for different purposes and in different guises. 'Ghosts are troublesome things in a house or in a family, as we knew even before Ibsen taught us', wrote Patrick Pearse in the preface to his famous pamphlet. 'There is only one way to appease a ghost. You must do the thing it asks you. The ghosts of a nation sometimes ask very big things; and they must be appeased, whatever the cost.'[39] Yeats's traffic with ghosts took a subtler and more manipulative route, treating the spectre of Parnell as a shape-changer who reflected the spirit and context of the times in which he was summoned. In this, the visionary poet may have been much closer than the revolutionary martyr to the enduringly ambiguous spirit and message of the Uncrowned King.

[38] *Life*2 587.
[39] Pearse, *Political Writings and Speeches*, 221.

CHAPTER 11

....

YEATS AND RENAISSANCE ITALY

'Courtly images'

....

EDNA LONGLEY

Here is a collage of quotations from Yeats's poetry: 'Urbino's windy hill', 'Michelozzo's latest plan / For the San Marco Library', 'the green shadow of Ferrara wall', 'The chief imagination of Christendom, / Dante Alighieri', 'A mind Michael Angelo knew', 'Quattrocento put in paint / ... Gardens where a soul's at ease'.[1] As sound and rhythm relish the Italian names, Yeats associates Italy with cities, books, art, architecture, mind, soul, and imagination: with all that 'renaissance' means. The English Renaissance, much entwined with Italy, equally fired Yeats's ambitions for Ireland (and for himself): Wayne K. Chapman's *Yeats and English Renaissance Literature* (1991) lays out a large field of study. But it was Renaissance Italy, in the shape of princely patrons like Cosimo de' Medici, that entered Yeats's poetic rhetoric when Dublin Corporation refused to provide a gallery for Hugh Lane's collection of modern French paintings. During this culture war (1912–13) it would not have been politic to invoke English exemplars. Yeats particularly began to uphold, as models of enlightened patronage, Ercole I d'Este (1431–1505), Duke of Ferrara, and Guidobaldo da Montefeltro (1472–1508), Duke of Urbino. The 'Wealthy Man', who required proof that 'the People wanted Pictures', is asked:

> What cared Duke Ercole, that bid
> His mummers to the market-place,
> What th'onion-sellers thought or did ...
> And Guidobaldo, when he made
> That grammar school of courtesies

---

[1] Quotations from 'To a Wealthy Man who promised a second Subscription to the Dublin Municipal Gallery if it were proved the People wanted Pictures', 'The People', 'Ego Dominus Tuus', 'An Acre of Grass', 'Under Ben Bulben', *CW* 1, 107, 150, 160, 302, 326.

> Where wit and beauty learned their trade
> Upon Urbino's windy hill,
> Had sent no runners to and fro
> That he might learn the shepherds' will ...[2]

Ercole and Guidobaldo are not just plucked out of the air. Beyond or behind rhetorical purposes, Renaissance Italy is becoming more and more essential to Yeats's whole poetic make-up. It's no accident that, thirty-six years later in 'Under Ben Bulben', the command 'Irish poets learn your trade' would echo his lines about Urbino.

The focus of this chapter will be Renaissance Italy as a model for art, for society, and for relations between the two. Yeats did not speak Italian. The two Italian writers most important to him, Dante Alighieri (1265–1321) and Count Baldassare Castiglione (1478–1529), author of *Il Libro del Cortegiano* (*The Book of the Courtier*) (1528), he read in translation. Again, unlike James Joyce and Ezra Pound, Yeats spent comparatively little time in Italy. In May 1907, with Lady Gregory and her son Robert, he visited Ravenna, Urbino, Ferrara, Venice, and Florence. (See the portrait of Lady Gregory, Figure 11.1.) In January–February 1925 he toured southern Italy and Sicily, where he absorbed the Byzantine mosaics in Monreale Cathedral, and completed *A Vision*. From 1928 to 1930 he wintered in Rapallo, where Pound had settled. But Yeats's very distance from contemporary Italy, apart from (or exemplified by) his erratic gestures towards Mussolini, may have protected the mythic presence of older 'Italies' in his work.[3] His 1907 visit inspired two brief epiphanic essays, 'A Tower on the Apennines' and 'The Thinking of the Body'. Published in autumn 1907, these essays laid down aesthetic foundations, at once symbolic and theoretical, for Yeats's future poetry. The former evokes a walk 'towards Urbino', setting of Castiglione's *Book of the Courtier*; the latter arrives at images from that book. In 'A Tower on the Apennines' Yeats recalls being 'alone amid a visionary, fantastic, impossible scenery', and seeing on one peak 'a mediæval tower' that 'rose into the clouds'. This leads to an impression 'in the mind's eye' of 'an old man ... standing in the door of the tower': 'He was the poet who had at last, because he had done so much for the word's sake, come to share in the dignity of the saint.' 'The Thinking of the Body', in which Yeats rejects abstraction and affirms that art 'bids us touch and taste and hear and see the world', ends by grounding that affirmation in Castiglione's scenario. Art is said to approve 'before all men those that talked or wrestled or tilted under the walls of Urbino, or sat in those great window-seats discussing all things, with love ever in their thought, when the wise Duchess ordered all, and the Lady Emilia gave the theme'.[4]

---

[2] See n. 1. The 'Wealthy Man' is presumed to be Lord Ardilaun.

[3] See R. F. Foster, 'Fascism', in David Holdeman and Ben Levitas (eds)., *W. B. Yeats in Context* (Cambridge: Cambridge University Press, 2010), 213–23; see also Lauren Arrington's 'Yeats in Fascist Italy', Chapter 16 in this volume.

[4] *CW* 4, 211–13.

FIGURE 11.1 Antonio Mancini, Augusta Gregory, courtesy of the Hugh Lane Gallery, Dublin.

Duke Guidobaldo had continued the endeavour of his father, Federico, to make Urbino a hub for art and learning. From 1504 to 1508 Castiglione served under Guidobaldo. His service often took the form of diplomacy, as it did under Guidobaldo's successor, Francesco Maria della Rovere, until the latter was deposed by Pope Leo X in 1516. Castiglione spent fifteen years transmuting his Urbino experiences into *The Book of the Courtier*, which became a European bestseller.[5] An influential English translation, by Sir Thomas Hoby, was published in 1561—the translation that Yeats first encountered, and from which most quotations below are taken. A new edition, with a scholarly and enthusiastic introduction by the academic critic Walter Raleigh, had appeared in 1900. Hoby's language, which Raleigh places on the cusp between 'homely' vernacular and the more elaborate diction of the later Elizabethan period, may have had Irish resonances for Yeats.[6] Castiglione himself, in his dedicatory letter, discusses the relation between speech and writing with reference to the shifting language of Italian literature: 'it is

[5] It was translated into Latin, French, and Spanish.
[6] Raleigh refers to Hoby's English as the speech of 'the age that made Shakespeare possible'; *The Book of the Courtier* (London: David Nutt, 1900), lvii–ix.

alwayes a vice to use words that are not in commune speach'.[7] Constructed as an informal symposium at the Urbino court, *The Book of the Courtier* presents after-dinner conversations over a four-day period. These conversations, which involve nobles and thinkers attached to the court, centre on the education of the ideal public servant: the qualities of mind and body, the blend of intellectual and social powers, the cultivation of arms and arts (music, dancing, painting, poetry) that will best serve the courtier's master.[8] The participants themselves exemplify the all-important skill of speech. Although they are mainly men, two women (as Yeats notes in 'The Thinking of the Body') have prominent roles: Guidobaldo's Duchess, Elisabetta Gonzaga, and her sister-in-law, Emilia Pia. Because Guidobaldo was an invalid, Elisabetta had assumed unusual authority at court, while Emilia 'seemed the maistresse and ringleader of all the company [*compagnia*]'.[9] Hoby announces his translation as 'very necessary and profitable for yonge gentilmen and gentilwomen'. It has been claimed that 'the *Courtier* asserts the dignity of woman and their essential equality with men'; and that 'among [its] many influences on later European civilisation, its contribution to an increasing recognition of, and respect for, women might be traced'.[10] Yeats's phrase 'wit and beauty' (which unite in poetry) does not necessarily divide the sexes.

Critics argue about the overall thrust and genre of the *Courtier*. For instance, is it primarily a political treatise, to be ranked with Niccolò Machiavelli's *Il Principe* (*The Prince*) (1532) as a key political testament of the sixteenth century? Political readings represent Castiglione as aiming to provide a 'functional ... handbook for survival' in 'that very uncertain political period'.[11] But other commentators stress the book's philosophical concern with larger questions of human existence: with self-realization, imagination, and salvation. For instance, the climax of the final night is a Neoplatonic discourse, spoken by the humanist Pietro Bembo, on 'the most holy mysteries of love', on beauty and the soul, on the relation between spiritual love and the divine order.[12] The editors of *Castiglione: The Ideal and the Real in Renaissance Culture* (1983) may resolve the argument by characterizing the *Courtier* as a dialectical work, which moves between practice and theory; which presents 'multiple viewpoints without advancing any one as definitive'; and which ultimately, perhaps, resists categorization. They credit Castiglione with bequeathing 'the truest, because most complex, reflection of the complicated cultural phenomenon and historical moment we call the High Renaissance'.[13] That includes

[7] *The Book of the Courtier*, trans. Thomas Hoby, Everyman's Library (London: J. M. Dent, 1928), 11: henceforward *BC*.

[8] They include Francesco Maria della Rovere (Guidobaldo's heir), Giuliano de' Medici (son of Lorenzo), Pietro Bembo (humanist scholar), and Bernardo Accolti (courtier-poet).

[9] *BC*, 20.

[10] Dain A. Trafton, 'Politics and the Praise of Women', in Robert W. Hanning and David Rosand, eds., *Castiglione: The Ideal and the Real in Renaissance Culture* (New Haven and London: Yale University Press, 1983), 33.

[11] J. R. Woodhouse, *Castiglione: A reassessment of* The Courtier (Edinburgh: Edinburgh University Press, 1978), 3.

[12] *BC*, 312.

[13] Hanning and Rosand, *Castiglione*, viii.

his contribution to aesthetics, the book's own 'wit and beauty', its value as literature. For Thomas M. Greene, the *Courtier* 'involves at once subdued drama and slightly risky play'.[14] It seems a proof of multiplicity, complexity, and 'play' that Castiglione meant so much to Yeats.

Yeats's Italian epiphanies, with their medieval-Renaissance coordinates, might be understood as revelations of 'tradition'. His essay 'Poetry and Tradition', published a year later, takes further the ideas kindled by his visit. After asserting that three 'types of men'—aristocrats, countrymen, artists—'have made all beautiful things', he says: 'If we would find a company of our own way of thinking, we must go backward to turreted walls, to courts, to high rocky places, to little walled towns'.[15] Like Pound and T. S. Eliot, Yeats seeks to connect his poetry with 'tradition'. But, for him, tradition is less textual, more holistic and metaphysical, inspirational rather than aspirational. He sums up his poetic career in the sentence, 'I must choose a traditional stanza, even what I alter must seem traditional'; his poetic origins, in recalling how, his faith destroyed by Darwinism, he 'made a new religion, almost an infallible Church, of poetic tradition, of a fardel of stories, and of personages, and of emotions, inseparable from their first expression, passed on from generation to generation by poets and painters with some help from philosophers and theologians'.[16] Tradition, thus defined, would help to shape Yeats's unclassifiable work *A Vision* (1925), which he conceived as a philosophy of history and a history of the soul, but which is, broadly, a psycho-aesthetic self-portrait. And to this portrait other writers and artists, from antiquity to the present, contribute more than a frame. They represent points on the antinomial force field that underpins his poetry. Yeats's 'doctrine of "the mask" ' had convinced him that 'every passionate man ... is, as it were, linked with another age, historical or imaginary, where alone he finds images that rouse his energy'.[17] Italy is central to two ages which crucially 'roused' both Yeats's poetry and *A Vision*. One age is largely imaginary: the age on which *A Vision* pivots, the age figured by Italy's Byzantine religious artworks. The second, more historical (though also imaginary) age is the Renaissance. For Yeats, the writer who most completely personifies that era is its late medieval progenitor, Dante, whose role in begetting Italian literature he sought to emulate. Steven Paul Ellis shrewdly comments: '[Yeats's] response to Dante is at once more profound and more superficial than Pound's or Eliot's: more profound because he regarded Dante's personal history as an exemplar; more superficial because his acquaintance with Dante's writing was remote and highly selective'.[18]

Yeats's relation to Dante is discussed elsewhere in this volume. What concerns the current chapter is how his interest in Dante coalesces with his interest in Castiglione to provide Italian Renaissance backing for the 'unities' (and European reach) of his mature

---

[14] Thomas M. Greene, '*Il Cortegiano* and the Choice of a Game', Renaissance Quarterly, 32:2 (Summer 1979), 173–86.

[15] *CW4*, 184.

[16] *CW5*, 213; *CW3*, 115.

[17] *CW3*, 139.

[18] Steven Paul Ellis, 'Yeats and Dante', *Comparative Literature*, 33:1 (Winter 1981).

aesthetic. Thus in consecutive paragraphs of *A Vision*, which hark back to the epiphanies of 1907, Yeats refers to 'that "perfectly proportioned human body" which had seemed to Dante unity of being symbolised', and to 'that kind of bodily beauty which Castiglione called "the spoil or monument of the victory of the soul"'.[19] The 'perfect Courtier' must also achieve what we might call 'unity of action': being required to 'make one bodie of [his] good qualities, so that every deede of his may bee compact and framed of all the vertues'.[20] Dante exemplifies Phase 17 of 'The Twenty-Eight Embodiments' set out in *A Vision*: the phase where 'Unity of Being', whether as a philosophical or aesthetic concept, is maximized:

> Dante, who laments his exile [from Florence] ... and sighs for his lost solitude ... was such a partisan ... that if a child, or a woman, spoke against his party he would pelt this child or woman with stones. Yet Dante, having attained, as poet, to Unity of Being, as poet saw all things set in order, had an intellect that served the *Mask* alone, that compelled even those things that opposed it to serve, was content to see both good and evil.[21]

Here Yeats, who has long moved between poles of solitude and partisanship, uses Dante as a mask—partly by making Dante himself a mask-user. The 'Mask', which can accommodate all conflicts, owes something to Castiglione, as we shall see below. Insofar as *A Vision* is an oblique work of aesthetic theory, Dante and Castiglione seem closely aligned with Yeats's thinking about the dialectics of poetic structure, the symmetries of poetic form.

Evidently, there are masks within masks. A poem of intricate layers, which epitomizes 'Yeats and Renaissance Italy', is not by Yeats himself. Or, rather, it is a 'found poem' by Yeats (who may have inaugurated this genre). It is also his only *vers libre* poem. 'Mona Lisa' sets out as verse a passage from Walter Pater's *The Renaissance* (1873/1893). Placed first in Yeats's *Oxford Book of Modern Verse* (1936), 'Mona Lisa' is a provocative start to a generally provocative anthology: a way of asserting that 'modern poetry' had begun, not with Pound or Eliot, but with Yeats's school of the 1890s, with poets much indebted to Pater's ideas. In his Introduction to the anthology Yeats claims, accurately, that Pater's account of Leonardo's portrait 'dominated a generation'. He also cites the famous Conclusion to *The Renaissance* where Pater extols 'the poetic passion, the desire of beauty, the love of art for its own sake'. This core gospel of Pater's 'religion of art', his emphasis on 'life lived as "a pure gem-like flame"', played into the lyric intensity which implicitly still defines Yeats's aesthetic.[22] Yet Pater's subject matter also had/has aesthetic and cultural meaning for him. On the cusp of the twentieth century, Pater's theory so influenced British and Irish writers that critics tend to pass over the central concern of

[19] *CW13*, 167–8.
[20] *BC*, 13, 94.
[21] *CW13*, 65.
[22] See *OBMV*, viii–ix.

his most influential work: the Italian Renaissance. Pater interprets that Renaissance in terms that surely fed Yeats's ideals for Ireland:

> There come … from time to time, eras of more favourable conditions, in which the thoughts of men draw nearer together than is their wont, and the many interests of the intellectual world combine in one complete type of general culture. The fifteenth century in Italy is one of these happier eras, and what is sometimes said of the age of Pericles is true of that of Lorenzo [de' Medici]: – it is an age productive in personalities, many-sided, centralised, complete. Here, artists and philosophers and those whom the action of the world has elevated and made keen, do not live in isolation, but breathe a common air, and catch light and heat from each other's thoughts. There is a spirit of general elevation and enlightenment in which all alike communicate. The unity of this spirit gives unity to all the various products of the Renaissance …[23]

'Mona Lisa' represents Leonardo's artwork as drawing together many historical and conceptual sources:

> She is older than the rocks among which she sits;
> Like the Vampire,
> She has been dead many times,
> And learned the secrets of the grave;
> And has been a diver in deep seas,
> And keeps their fallen day about her;
> And trafficked for strange webs with Eastern merchants;
> And, as Leda,
> Was the mother of Helen of Troy,
> And, as St Anne,
> Was the mother of Mary;
> And all this has been to her but as the sound of lyres and flutes,
> And lives
> Only in the delicacy
> With which it has moulded the changing lineaments,
> And tinged the eyelids and the hands.[24]

Just before this passage, Pater has referred to the portrait as unifying '[a]ll the thoughts and experience of the world … the animalism of Greece, the lust of Rome, the mysticism of the middle age … the return of the Pagan world, the sins of the Borgias'.[25]

Yeats's found poem marks the impact of Pater's extraordinary sentence (a quintessence of 'Renaissance') on his own art and thought. Here we find an ancient human

---

[23] Donald L. Hill, ed., Walter Pater, *The Renaissance: Studies in Art and Poetry*: the 1893 text (Berkeley, Los Angeles, and London: University of California Press, 1980), xxiv.

[24] *OBMV*, 1.

[25] Pater, *Renaissance*, 98–9.

spirit and the idea of its reincarnation, which includes the idea of tradition renewed. We find Eastern webs, a hint of esoteric secrets. We find mystical births inaugurating an era, as in 'The Second Coming' and 'Leda and the Swan', the Christian era being merely one of a series. Further, as an ekphrastic poem, a poem about a painting, 'Mona Lisa' prefigures or confirms the shuttle between poetry and the visual arts, which characterizes Yeats's Renaissance 'images'. The subtitle of *The Renaissance* is *Studies in Art and Poetry*, and one chapter is called 'The Poetry of Michelangelo': a chapter that sets no boundary between sculpture and sonnets. Pater had more generally influenced 1890s thinking about links between all the arts, as in his writings on Pre-Raphaelite poetry.[26] The poem ends, indeed, by situating Mona Lisa in the 1890s, by attaching the Renaissance to the fin de siècle. All her incarnations are subsumed into 'the sound of lyres and flutes', into lyric intensity and formal 'delicacy', into a fusion of art, music, and poetry. The histories suggested by 'Mona Lisa' include the Italian landscape's age-old presence in art and literature. Italy, more than Ireland, could immerse Yeats in deep Europe. Once, when about to visit Scotland, he complained: 'no art, no stimulus for all its beauty, too barren of man's pilgrimage ... I crave like a lover for Italy'.[27] He wrote the 'Dedication' to *A Vision* at Capri, where he had been 'wander[ing] upon the cliffs where Augustus and Tiberius wandered':

> Yesterday when I saw the dry and leafless vineyards at the very edge of the motion-less sea, or lifting their brown stems from almost inaccessible patches of earth high up on the cliff-side, or met at the turn of the path the orange and lemon trees in full fruit ... I murmured, as I have countless times, 'I have been part of it always and there is maybe no escape, forgetting and returning life after life, like an insect in the roots of the grass'.[28]

A perennial Italian scene validates the ancient 'roots' of Yeats's *Vision*. He later wrote of Rapallo: 'Mountains that shelter the bay from all but the south wind, bare brown branches of low vines ... [t]he little town described in the *Ode on a Grecian Urn*'.[29]

'Dedication' also stresses Dante's significance as model for poets seeking a unified world view:

> I wished for a system of thought that would leave my imagination free to create as it chose and yet make all that it created, or could create, part of the one history, and that the soul's. The Greeks certainly had such a system, and Dante ... and I think no man since.[30]

---

[26]   Such as his essays 'Aesthetic Poetry' (1868), 'Dante Gabriel Rossetti' (1883).
[27]   *Letters on Poetry from W. B. Yeats to Dorothy Wellesley* (London: Oxford University Press), 92.
[28]   *CW* 13, lvi.
[29]   W. B. Yeats, *A Vision*, 2nd edn (London: Macmillan, 1937), 3.
[30]   *CW* 13, lv.

'Ego Dominus Tuus' (1915),[31] a poem with close ties to *A Vision*, both features Dante and alludes to Castiglione. It's here that Dante is called 'The chief imagination of Christendom': Yeats wanted to be the chief imagination of something else. Indeed, his invocations of Dante tend to relegate 'Christendom'. In 1896, discussing William Blake's illustrations to the *Divine Comedy*, he had asserted: 'to us one-half of the philosophy of Dante is less living than his poetry'; and he unfavourably contrasted Dante's reliance on 'a complex external law, a complex external Church' with Blake's 'scorn' for 'the whole spectacle of external things', his preaching of 'the cultivated life, the internal Church, which has no laws but beauty, rapture and labour'.[32] A subtext here may be Blake's and Yeats's Protestantism. In any case, Yeats identifies Blake's 'internal Church' with Symbolist 'interiority', with the religion of art. Nineteen years later, 'Ego Dominus Tuus' effectively recruits Dante for a more advanced form of that religion, along with Yeatsian dialectics. The poem is itself dialectical: a dialogue in which 'Hic' and 'Ille' argue about aesthetic priorities. Its title comes from Dante's *La Vita Nuova* (1294), where the 'dominus' is Amore, who personifies the pure love for Beatrice that governs his poetry. With dubious historical warrant, Yeats makes Dante's dominus an earthy 'opposite': a 'lecherous' anti-self who resists his poetry's transcendental drive. Both Steven Paul Ellis and George Bornstein see Yeats as turning Dante into a 'Romantic poet', as when this poem highlights Dante's 'hollow face', his 'spectral image'.[33] Yeats's 'Dante' markedly differs from Eliot's 'Dante'. Eliot assigns Dante a 'universal' or 'classic' status because Dante's theology, as well as his Latin-derived language, places him at 'the centre of Europe': the quasi-papal omphalos for which Eliot himself yearned.[34] Since Dante's imagination matters more to Yeats than his Christendom, he now elides the 'external Church', the fact that Dante did not invent his 'system of thought', his debt to St Thomas Aquinas. And, when 'Ego Dominus Tuus' represents Dante's work as ever-conflicted, a 'tragic war', Yeats also elides the paradisal finale of the *Divine Comedy*—let alone *Comedy*. In 'Ego Dominus Tuus', Dante 'fashion[ing] from his opposite / An image' doubles for Yeats as a subjective Romantic or modern poet, but one who seeks to objectify his aesthetic—to parallel the seemingly effortless craft skills of medieval and early Renaissance art. 'Ille' says: 'By the help of an image / I call to my own opposite.' 'Hic' counters: 'And I would find myself and not an image.' Then 'Ille', who becomes the dialogue's main voice, says:

> That is our modern hope, and by its light
> We have lit upon the gentle, sensitive mind
> And lost the old nonchalance of the hand;
> Whether we have chosen chisel, pen or brush,
> We are but critics, or but half create . . .[35]

---

[31] *CW1*, 160–2.
[32] *CW4*, 100–1.
[33] For Ellis, see n. 18 above; George Bornstein, 'Yeats's Romantic Dante', *Colby Quarterly*, 15:2 (June 1979), 93–113.
[34] T. S. Eliot, 'Dante', in *Selected Prose of T. S. Eliot* (London: Faber, 1975), 209.
[35] *CW1*, 160.

'The old nonchalance of the hand' brings Castiglione into the poem, while also fusing poetry with the visual arts. Early in the *Courtier* Castiglione introduces his coinage and keyword *sprezzatura*: translated as 'nonchalance' in Leonard Eckstein Opdycke's translation (1903), which Yeats knew. Also translated as 'reck-lessness' (Hoby) and 'casualness', this word has generally 'given ... endless trouble to translators'.[36] *Sprezzatura*, from which all grace (*grazia*) springs, is a quality that should inform the courtier's other qualities: the ability 'to practise in everything a certain nonchalance that shall conceal design and show that what is done and said is done without effort and almost without thought' (Opdycke).[37] *Sprezzatura* has been interpreted both politically (as a mode of diplomatic deviousness) and aes-thetically (as a concept akin to *ars est celare artem*). Difficulty of translation is compounded by the logical inference that *sprezzatura* has a structural as well as the-matic role in the *Courtier*: that it informs Castiglione's educational strategy in ways that his readers may not always detect. For Yeats, *sprezzatura* is wholly about style, which transfers from personal style to the demeanour of artist or artwork. In 1936 he told Dorothy Wellesley: 'Those little poems of yours are nonchalant, & noncha-lance is declared by Castiglione essential to all true courtiers – so it is to warty lads & poets'.[38] 'Nonchalance' appears prominently at the end of 'Art and Ideas' (1913), an essay from which 'Ego Dominus Tuus' takes some elements, including visual–verbal links. Here Yeats revisits and revises certain principles of the Pre-Raphaelite poets/painters who had influenced his youthful thinking. The Pre-Raphaelite Brotherhood, founded in 1848, looked to the early Renaissance period before Raphael (1483–1520), for instance, had established certain 'classical' painterly tropes. Raphael was a con-temporary and friend of Castiglione, whose 'admirable conversationalists' Yeats depicts in Pre-Raphaelite terms: that is, as knowing 'that the old spontaneous life had gone' and seeking 'to retain unity of being' by following the *Courtier* play-book.[39] In 'Art and Ideas', as through 'Ille' in 'Ego Dominus Tuus', Yeats reconfigures his own aesthetic with Dante and Castiglione in view. He rejects 'sedentary medita-tion', which has replaced 'the flow of flesh under the impulse of passionate thought', and envisages 'rediscovering, by our re-integration of the mind, our more profound Pre-Raphaelitism, the old abounding, nonchalant reverie'.[40] 'Nonchalant reverie' is an oxymoron that wants to be a tautology. Yeats proposes to reconnect 'hand' with 'mind': the unselfconscious craft of medieval-Renaissance objectivity with modern Symbolist interiority. The dialogic 'Ego Dominus Tuus', in which 'Hic' and 'Ille' debate at night and nonchalantly talk of 'nonchalance' near Yeats's 'old wind-beaten tower', may itself reprise Castiglione's symposium. Apennine towers and turrets undergo a

---

[36] Edward Saccone, '*Grazia, Sprezzatura, Affettazione* in the *Courtier*', in Hanning and Rosand, *Castiglione*, 45–67 (57).

[37] *The Book of the Courtier*, trans. Leonard Eckstein Opdycke (London: Duckworth, 1902), 35.

[38] Yeats to Dorothy Wellesley, 22 May [1936], *CL InteLex* #6560.

[39] *CW5*, 234.

[40] *CW4*, 255–6.

west-of-Ireland makeover. Another *Vision*-related poem, 'The Phases of the Moon', has a similar structure and setting.

In her seminal study *Yeats and Castiglione* (1965), Corinna Salvadori shows that Yeats refers to Castiglione throughout his career; and that he 'integrated the theories of Castiglione into his own philosophy':

> One could not understand fully Yeats's theories of reincarnation, of the human personality, his philosophy of history, his writings that deal with the beauty of the soul, without Castiglione's book. One must turn to it also, if one wishes to understand Yeats's ideas on the poet's training, on the discipline of style, on poetic creation.[41]

Yeats and Castiglione has a chapter called 'Coole: An Irish Urbino', and subtitled 'The Patron and the Court-Poet'. Remarkably, Lady Gregory read Hoby's translation aloud to Yeats when he was suffering from poor eyesight at Coole Park in 1903. Perhaps this reading constituted a double whammy. Yeats began to identify Gregory with the 'wise' presiding Duchess, whom Castiglione adored, and who survived her husband. Castiglione calls her 'a chaine that kept all linked together in love' and says: 'the verye sober moode and greatnes that did knit together all the actes, woordes and gestures of the Dutchesse in jesting and laughing, made them all that had never seene her in their lyfe before, to count her a verie great Ladie'. Castiglione's dedicatory letter, which mourns the dead people who live in his book, insists: 'But the thinge that should not be rehersed without teares is, that the Dutchesse she is also dead.'[42] In 1909, when Lady Gregory was gravely ill, Yeats spent a terrible day with 'Castiglione's phrase ringing in my memory'.[43] The scholar and critic Herbert Grierson further nudged Yeats towards Italian Renaissance courts, when he recommended a book by Edmund Gardner: *Dukes & Poets in Ferrara* (1904). Gardner's title must have been irresistible to Yeats, as must the sentence, 'From the beginning of their rule in Ferrara, a halo of poetry had shone round the Court of the Estensi.'[44] He also read Gardner's follow-up book: *The King of Court Poets: A Study of the Life and Times of Lodovico Ariosto* (1906). Yeats told Grierson, 'It was my conversation with you some time ago that sent me to Italy for it started me reading books about Ferrara, and in the end sent me to Ferrara.'[45]

As Salvadori stresses, Castiglione's perfect courtier is not some flattering flunkey but that humanist ideal, 'Renaissance Man'. A laudatory sonnet by Thomas Sackville, which prefaces Hoby's translation, represents the courtier's qualities (and Castiglione's) as outclassing the worldly power of kings or dukes. This may have played well with Yeats's sense of the power balance between poet and patron:

---

[41] Corinna Salvadori, *Yeats and Castiglione* (Dublin: Alan Figgis, 1965), 2.
[42] *BC*, 20, 10.
[43] *Mem*, 163.
[44] Edmund G. Gardner, *Dukes and Poets in Ferrara* (London: Constable, 1904), 24.
[45] Yeats to H. J. C. Grierson, 28 June [1907], *CL InteLex* #618.

> No proude, ne golden Court doth he set forth
> But what in Court a Courtier ought to be.
> The prince he raiseth huge and mighty walles,
> Castilio frames a wight of noble fame:
> The king with gorgeous Tissue clads his halles,
> The Count with golden virtue deckes the same ...

The golden virtues, which Yeats attributes to Gregory's son in 'In Memory of Major Robert Gregory',[46] are essentially those advocated by Castiglione. The perfect courtier joins 'the ornament of letters with prowesse of arms'.[47] Yeats hails Gregory as 'Soldier, scholar, horseman', as a potentially 'great painter', as 'Our Sidney and our perfect man', a line that bridges the Italian and English Renaissances, while 'our' brings them home to Ireland. Further, Gregory has not simply been killed in war but has suffered 'that *discourtesy* of death' (my italics)[48]. Yeats's salutes to Coole/Urbino ultimately merge artist and aristocrat. In 1909 he had written of the artist: 'We come from the permanent things and create them ... and we carry in our head that form of society which aristocracies create now and again at some brief moment at Urbino or Versailles.'[49] Yeatsian masks span duke and poet, Ercole and 'mummer', patron and practitioner of art. At a reflexive level, the 'Unity of Being' personified by Robert Gregory affirms unity of art: the 're-integrated' aesthetic posited in 'Art and Ideas'.

Yet, however deeply Yeats had internalized 'Renaissance', he remained wary of applying that term to Ireland, and even the more usual 'Revival'. Horatio Sheafe Krans's *William Butler Yeats and the Irish Literary Revival*, a book Yeats disliked,[50] was published in 1905; Ernest A. Boyd's *Ireland's Literary Renaissance*, a genuinely foundational study, in 1916. But Yeats prefers the neutrality and specificity of 'movement': 'literary movement', 'intellectual movement', 'dramatic movement'.[51] This is partly to deflect mockery of his claims; partly to avoid offending other Irish movements, especially the language 'revival'. (Boyd interchangeably refers to 'renaissance', 'revival', and 'movement'.) Latter-day critics have coined the totalizing terms 'Revivalism' and 'Revivalists', as if describing evangelical Christians in a tent. These terms are sometimes used positively—to conjoin disparate Irish political and cultural 'movements' of the early twentieth century; sometimes negatively—to attack a supposedly impure ideological project.[52] But 'Revivalism', however applied, simplifies what might be meant by an Irish 'Renaissance'. Certainly, the idea, if not the term, recurred in Yeats's thought, as when he won the Nobel Prize

---

[46] *CW1*, 132–5.

[47] *BC*, 69.

[48] *CW1*, 133

[49] *Mem*, 156.

[50] Yeats called it 'an absurd little book'; *CL3*, 475 n.

[51] E.g. Yeats's essay 'The Literary Movement in Ireland' (1899); Lady Gregory's 'service to the Irish intellectual movement' (*CW3*, 285); the title of his Nobel lecture, 'The Irish Dramatic Movement'.

[52] For a positive, if unhistorical, use of the term 'Revivalist', see Introduction to Declan Kiberd and P. J. Matthews, eds., *Handbook of the Irish Revival* (Dublin: Abbey Theatre Press, 2015).

in 1923. His memoir 'The Bounty of Sweden' praises the Swedish royal court, once again celebrates Urbino, and recalls Lady Gregory reading Castiglione aloud. He also quotes Ben Jonson's eulogy of the Elizabethan court for supporting art and learning. Yet, despite his own honour and the honour he gives to 'fellow-workers' Gregory and J. M. Synge, Yeats considers that Sweden has come closer than Ireland to a modern form of Renaissance. He says of the collective effort behind Stockholm's splendid new City Hall: 'These myth-makers and mask-makers worked as if they belonged to one family'; 'No work comparable in method or achievement has been accomplished since the Italian cities felt the excitement of the Renaissance.' But, in this dark post-war period, Yeats represents himself and his cohorts as 'seeking foundations for an Ireland that can only come into existence in a Europe that is still but a dream'.[53]

In 1910 Yeats had distinguished his cultural vision from political nationalism by saying, 'I always rouse myself to work by imagining an Ireland as much a unity in thought and feeling as ancient Greece and Rome and Egypt.' When such ambitions seem thwarted, he consoles himself with the idea that literature plays a long game: 'Literature created for its own sake or for some eternal spiritual need can be used by politicians – Dante is said to have unified Italy – but it seldom can be used at once.'[54] In 'The Tower', where Yeats assumes a posture of abdication, of retirement from Irish struggles (not that he did retire), he sets his poetry and cultural legacy in a Renaissance vista:

> I have prepared my peace
> With learned Italian things
> And the proud stones of Greece,
> Poets' imaginings
> And memories of love,
> Memories of the words of women,
> All those things whereof
> Man makes a superhuman
> Mirror-resembling dream …[55]

A subsequent vow (which repeats 'learned') to 'make my soul, / Compelling it to study / In a learned school' further attaches Yeats to the non-Christian mode of Renaissance humanism or superhumanism. The related idea, that not God but 'we' create 'Translunar Paradise', may be a smack at Dante—or a tribute to the *Paradiso*. 'The Tower' certainly takes a smack at the un-renascent Ireland of 1925. In this abdication mode, Yeats returns to a central theme of his Lane Gallery poems: the theme of generosity spurned. He self-praises Protestant Ireland as 'The people of Burke and of Grattan / That gave, though free to refuse'. 'The People' (1915) had involved a similar trope, but a more inclusive Irish 'people' (if set against Urbino's elite 'people'). This poem presents a conversation with

---

[53] *CW3*, 406–7.
[54] *Mem*, 251, 247.
[55] *CW1*, 199.

Maud Gonne, in which the would-be courtier-poet tells the political activist that he might have avoided Dublin's 'daily spite', and lived

> Where every day my footfall should have lit
> In the green shadow of Ferrara wall;
> Or climbed among the images of the past –
> The unperturbed and courtly images –
> Evening and morning, the steep street of Urbino
> To where the Duchess and her people talked
> The stately midnight through until they stood
> In their great window looking at the dawn …[56]

To which Gonne 'answer[s] in reproof' that, although she too has been ungratefully attacked, 'Yet never have I, now nor any time, / Complained of the people'. In 'The Tower', as in other poems of the 1920s, the poet-speaker is less likely to be 'abashed' by such a rebuke. Irish and European events have brought devastation to 'courtly images', to Renaissance ideals. Salvadori[57] suggests that Yeats alludes to Guidobaldo's father, Duke Federico, in 'Meditations in Time of Civil War', when the speaker questions whether the architecture of European civilization can be restored, yet admits that civilization itself may be complicit in, or enabled by, violence:

> Some violent bitter man, some powerful man
> Called architect and artist in, that they,
> Bitter and violent men, might rear in stone
> The sweetness that all longed for night and day,
> The gentleness none there had ever known …[58]

Yeats knew that, from the Italy of Dante to the Italy of Castiglione, conflict, violence, and war were normative. Consecutive chapter titles in *Dukes & Poets in Ferrara* are 'The War of Ferrara' and 'In the Lull before the Storm'. Roy Foster refers to Yeats's 'historical fantasies of Renaissance city-states'.[59] But Dante's exile from Florence in 1302 is a point of identification, as is Cosimo de' Medici's in 1433. 'To a Wealthy Man' portrays exile as a chance for Cosimo, 'Indifferent how the rancour ran', to concentrate on 'Michelozzo's latest plan / For the San Marco Library'. Yeats goes on to associate Renaissance with peacemaking: the library being a means whereby 'turbulent Italy should draw / Delight in Art whose end is peace', along with philosophical and scientific learning, by 'sucking at the dugs of Greece'.[60] Italian 'rancour' and 'turbulence' may have helped Yeats to assuage or armour his own disappointments with thoughts of how Florence, Urbino,

---

[56] *CW1*, 150–1.
[57] Salvadori, *Yeats and Castiglione*, 30.
[58] *CW1*, 200.
[59] Foster, 'Fascism', 214.
[60] *CW1*, 107.

and Ferrara had, for a few decades, defied the odds. Castiglione justifies setting the *Courtier* in Urbino by explaining that 'now a long time it hath always bene governed with very good princes, in the common calamities of the wars of Italie it remained also a season without any at all'.[61] That 'season' had ended (with Francesco Maria's deposition) as he began to write his book, which can itself be seen as an exercise in nostalgia, a consolation for calamity. Yeats may thereby idealize an idealization. Yet he understands that Castiglione's symposium marks a 'brief moment' (see above)—a political lull and cultural opportunity—like that which he had himself grasped in Ireland after Parnell. While those moments occurred, both authors also construct or reconstruct them for their own purposes. As for Ferrara: in Gardner's second book, Ariosto (1474–1533), the best poet associated with Ferrara, endures capricious patronage; narrowly escapes a papal death threat; and is forced to spend three years as governor of a fractious province. Chapter titles here are 'From Freedom to Servitude' and 'Put Not Your Trust in Princes'. The book ends on a depressing vision of the future, which must have struck home to Yeats. Gardner laments that, with the deaths of Ariosto and (in 1534) his kinder patron, Duke Alfonso I d'Este, 'The era of the Renaissance was over; the Reformation and the Catholic Reaction were to fight for the possession of the world.'[62]

Perhaps 'unperturbed' is not always the best condition for artistic creation. Poetry may need the people, warts and all. The Latin root 'turba' (crowd or commotion) plays 'unperturbed' in 'The People' against 'turbulent' in 'To a Wealthy Man'. The earlier poem claims that art and learning can pacify turbulent politics, even if the poem is itself an angry political intervention. Yeats sharpens his point by representing renaissance—'rebirth'—in vigorously physical terms: 'sucking at the dugs of Greece'. He introduces a loftier, more strategic birth metaphor, when the 'Wealthy Man' is finally urged to give 'not what they would, / But the right twigs for an eagle's nest'. The first chapter of *Dukes & Poets in Ferrara* is named after the standard of the ducal family, 'The White Eagle of Este'. Similarly, in 'The People', the quasi-oxymoronic 'green shadow' (an allusion to the trees that fringe 'Ferrara wall') symbolizes the city's cultural legacy being reanimated as a utopian locus for the Irish poet. The passage from *The Book of the Courtier*, to which Yeats most often returns, provides another symbol of 'Renaissance': windows open to the dawn. Castiglione's penultimate paragraph begins: 'When the windowes then were opened on the side of the Pallaice that hath his prospect towarde the high top of Mount Catri, they sawe already in the East a faire morning like unto the colour of roses … .'[63] In 'The People', 'the Duchess and her people' are 'looking at the dawn', having seen 'the wicks grow yellow in the dawn'.[64]

Yeats's 'courtly images', including the phrase itself, often have a reflexive dimension. For him, *The Book of the Courtier* is ultimately an *ars poetica*. Castiglione's 'grammar

---

[61] *BC*, 17.
[62] Edmund G. Gardner, *The King of Court Poets: A Study of the Life and Times of Lodovico Ariosto* (London: Archibald Constable, 1906), 366–7.
[63] *BC*, 324.
[64] *CW1*, 151.

school of courtesies' (a reflexive précis) helped him to integrate his thinking about the mask with his thinking about form. He wrote in 1909:

> There is a relation between discipline and the theatrical sense. If we cannot imagine ourselves as different from what we are and try to assume that second self, we cannot impose a discipline upon ourselves, though we may accept one from others. Active virtue as distinguished from the passive acceptance of a current code is therefore theatrical, consciously dramatic, the wearing of a mask.[65]

Here the mask transfers between life and art. It might be worn by a Castiglione-educated courtier: 'Active virtue'. Yeats's involvement with Irish public life had brought oratory into his poetry; his involvement with the literary theatre had made his lyric dramatic. But the bracing support he takes from Castiglione is that oratory and masking are performative skills, skills that can be learned. As a 'school', the *Courtier* combines theory with eloquent performances by 'the Duchess and her people talk[ing]'. It's a key text of what Stephen Greenblatt has termed 'Renaissance self-fashioning'.[66] (Hoby translates Castiglione's verb *formar* as 'fashion'.) To quote Sackville again, 'Castilio frames a wight of noble fame: / The king with gorgeous Tissue clads his halles, / The Count with golden virtue deckes the same': the verbs 'frame' and 'deck'. Castiglione interestingly worries that the perfect courtier might be received as a self-portrait, a portrait of his own self-fashioning: 'Some ... say that my meaning was to facion my self, perswading my self that all suche qualities as I appoint to the Courtier are in me.'[67] Long before Greenblatt, Yeats understood Renaissance self-fashioning: witness Dante 'fashion[ing] from his opposite / An image' in 'Ego Dominus Tuus'. Later, the speaker of 'An Acre of Grass' either asks or insists: 'Myself must I remake / Till I am Timon and Lear ...'[68] As in the syntactical and rhythmic crescendo of that poem, mask-making is ultimately inextricable from style, from formal 'fashioning': Castiglione's verb, after all, is *formar*. In 'Poetry and Tradition', after conceiving his Urbino-like 'company of our own way of thinking', Yeats goes on to say: 'In life, courtesy and self-possession, and in the arts style, are the sensible impressions of the free mind, for both arise out of a deliberate shaping of all things ... style ... is but high breeding in words and in argument.' Then, stressing that 'the mastery of unlocking words' is not just about studying 'the great Masters', Yeats reaches for *sprezzatura*: 'the "recklessness" Castiglione thought necessary in good manners is necessary in this likewise'.[69] Thus 'courtesy' becomes a metaphor for the poetic 'shaping' essential to the unified aesthetic which Yeats, in 'The People', calls 'mixing / Courtesy and passion into one'[70]. 'Courtesy' reappears, with its full Renaissance meaning, in 'A

---

[65] *Mem*, 151.

[66] Stephen Greenblatt, *Renaissance Self-Fashioning: From More to Shakespeare* (Chicago: University of Chicago Press, 1980).

[67] *BC*, 14.

[68] *CW1*, 301.

[69] *CW4*, 185-7.

[70] *CW1*, 151

Prayer for my Daughter' (1919), a prospectus for fashioning a perfect woman and, re-flexively, a perfect poem. Here it joins 'custom' and 'ceremony' as indispensable to both art and society: 'In courtesy I'd have her chiefly learned.'[71] The words 'learn' and 'school' recur when Yeats invokes Renaissance Italy.

Yeats's version of Renaissance self-fashioning includes fashioning Renaissance masks for himself: Dante, Castiglione's dramatis personae, Timon of Athens, King Lear, and ultimately Michael Angelo. If Dante backs up Yeats's need for a 'system of thought', and Castiglione the linked disciplines of mask and style, Michael Angelo exemplifies the creative principle itself—and its stamina. The crescendo of 'An Acre of Grass' ends with the aspiration to become: 'A mind Michael Angelo knew / That can pierce the clouds ... / An old man's eagle mind' (per-haps another Ferraran 'Eagle'). In *The Renaissance* Pater celebrates Michaelangelo's 'convul-sive energy'. He says that the 'creation of life' is 'the motive of all his work'; and writes of the Sistine Chapel ceiling, 'The brooding spirit of life itself is there.'[72] Similarly, Yeats gives his Michael Angelo mask quasi-godlike powers. In the later 1930s he was rereading Nietzsche as well as Pater. Among Nietzsche's prototypes for the *Übermensch* are Michaelangelo and Julius Caesar. Earlier, Yeats's sonnet 'Leda and the Swan', a response to Michaelangelo's painting of this subject, had conjured up a god-swan whose procreative force is mirrored by the poem's own energy: 'A sudden blow.'[73] In 'Long-legged Fly' (1938), which also involves Julius Caesar, Michael Angelo rather than God seems to create Adam. Here Yeats returns with a vengeance to the 1890s axiom that life imitates art; perhaps to the humanist idea that mankind creates 'Translunar Paradise'. One reason why he was so compelled by the Italian Renaissance, as by Italy's Byzantine mosaics, is because the visual arts give poetry a rhetoric for its own dur-ability. Since it's more difficult to represent Dante's words concretely, 'Ego Dominus Tuus' dwells on his 'hollow face' and 'spectral image.'[74] In Yeats's ekphrastic poems the word 'image' moves reflexively between poem and visual artefact. 'Long-legged Fly' is partly an ekphrastic poem: that rarer mode of ekphrasis which engages with work in progress. The last stanza draws the reader into an act of present-tense 'creation':

> That girls at puberty may find
> The first Adam in their thought,
> Shut the door of the Pope's chapel,
> Keep those children out.
> There on that scaffolding reclines
> Michael Angelo ...
>
> Like a long-legged fly upon the stream
> His mind moves upon silence.[75]

---

[71] *CW1*, 189.

[72] Pater, *Renaissance*, 57–60.

[73] *CW1*, 214.

[74] The nineteenth century favoured 'portraits' of Dante, which rendered him Romantically soulful rather than magisterial.

[75] *CW1*, 339.

Michael Angelo, who seems to be creating sex as well as Adam, is once again associated with 'mind'. In the preceding stanzas, 'mind' has characterized Caesar as man of action, Helen of Troy as woman of beauty. The poem's refrain gives all its 'minds' the power of God moving upon the face of the waters. Michael Angelo does not come last by accident. This is another Renaissance vista: Roman 'civilization' and Europe's foundational Greek epic propel us towards early sixteenth-century Rome and a line that simply names 'Michael Angelo'. All Yeats's feeling for Renaissance Italy culminates in 'Long-legged Fly' (a counterpart to 'Mona Lisa'), with its refrain of the 'mind moving', its rhythm that suggests a movement of mind. His 'Michael Angelo' line is the climax of a poem which both affirms and manifests the utmost artistic concentration allied to the utmost conceptual scope.

'Coole Park, 1929' has similar layers:

> I meditate upon a swallow's flight,
> Upon an aged woman and her house . . .
> Great works constructed there in nature's spite
> For scholars and for poets after us,
> Thoughts long knitted into a single thought,
> A dance-like glory that those walls begot . . . [76]

'Courtly images' from Castiglione underlie the last-quoted line, while the previous line virtually condenses Pater's summation of the Renaissance, quoted above:

> Here, artists and philosophers and those whom the action of the world has elevated and made keen do not live in isolation, but breathe a common air, and catch light and heat from each other's thoughts. There is a spirit of general elevation and enlightenment in which all alike communicate. The unity of this spirit gives unity to all the various products of the Renaissance . . . [77]

The poem goes on to define the Irish literary movement as a 'company' (Castiglione and Yeats repeat this word)[78] of writers, thinkers, and patrons. Like the Sistine Chapel ceiling, 'Coole' is a creation of mind. The Renaissance unity of 'Thoughts long knitted into a single thought' reflexively applies to the poem's form, as does another image of the company: 'half a dozen in formation there, / That seemed to whirl upon a compass-point'. In the first quotation, 'knit' echoes Hoby's translation of Castiglione's verb (*componere*) for the Duchess's unified, unifying qualities.[79] In the second, Yeats celebrates the similarly centripetal force of Lady Gregory's 'powerful character'. Further echoes of Castiglione/Hoby include allusions to dance, a sword, and theatre; an

---

[76] *CW1*, 242–3.

[77] See n. 23.

[78] Yeats also repeats 'companions' in such poems as 'At Galway Races', 'The Grey Rock', and '*While I, from that reed-throated whisperer*', *CW1*, 97, 103, 128.

[79] See p. 163 above.

'intellectual sweetness' (*dolcezza*) that embraces poets and scholars; the poem's status as memorial to a collective conversation. In effect, this 'scene well set and excellent company' is a scene of Renaissance self-fashioning. The self-fashioning Yeats figures as 'one that ruffled in a manly pose / For all his timid heart'. 'Ruffled' conjures up an Elizabethan ruff as well as a mask stylishly worn, a successful performance, the performance of this poem. In some of Yeats's last poems ('Under Ben Bulben', for instance), the speaker adopts an autocratic tone or monotone, which forgets 'That grammar school of courtesies'; abandons *sprezzatura* as an educational and poetic strategy; and betrays the aesthetic unities for which Yeats so often adduces Renaissance models. By contrast, 'Long-legged Fly' and 'Coole Park, 1929' imply poetry's true power as intricate cognitive and rhythmic dynamics: a 'mind mov[ing] upon silence', a whirling 'formation', 'A dance-like glory', a 'scene' of complex masking. Perhaps Renaissance Italy did most for an Irish Renaissance by influencing the deep structures of Yeats's poetry. Two lines in 'Coole Park, 1929' hint that 'Coole' could light the future like the Urbino palace windows opening upon dawn: 'A sycamore and lime tree lost in night / Although that western cloud is luminous...'[80].

---

[80] *CW1*, 242.

....

CHAPTER 12

TRADITION AND PHANTASMAGORIA

Dante and Shakespeare

....

HUGH HAUGHTON

In his essay on 'Dante', T. S. Eliot claimed magisterially that 'Dante and Shakespeare divide the modern world between them. There is no third.'[1] On this reading, if we discount the classical poets, Dante and Shakespeare are the most charged avatars of poetic tradition. This was equally true for W. B. Yeats, a poet with a comparable sense of spiritual belatedness and whose Irish background put him at a fraught angle to European tradition.

Eliot's negotiations with these predecessors underline the distinctiveness of Yeats's engagements with them. In 'Tradition and the Individual Talent' (1919), Eliot argued for the importance of 'the historical sense' for poetry, an awareness not only of 'the pastness of the past, but of its presence' as played out in the poet's 'relation to the dead poets and artists' who came before him. Eliot notes that 'Shakespeare acquired more essential history from Plutarch than most men could from the whole British Museum' and dwells with intensity on Canto XV of Dante's *The Inferno* when he claims that the poet is a 'medium' for whom 'poetry' is not 'the expression of personality, but an escape from personality'.[2] Eliot went on to write critical essays on both writers—the 1930 'Dante' essay as well as 'The Problem of Hamlet' and 'Shakespeare and the Stoicism of Seneca'— texts that helped shape the twentieth-century critical reception of each.[3] Dante and Shakespeare haunt Eliot's poetry too, with the Dantean 'I had not thought death had

[1] T. S. Eliot, 'Dante', in *Selected Essays* (London: Faber, 1932), 265.

[2] T. S. Eliot, 'Tradition and the Individual Talent', in *Selected Essays*, 13–22.

[3] For short accounts of Eliot, see Massimo Bacigalupo, 'Dante', and Hugh Haughton, 'Allusion: The Case of Shakespeare', in Jason Harding, ed., *T. S. Eliot in Context* (Cambridge: Cambridge University Press, 2011), Steven Ellis, *Dante and English Poetry* (Cambridge: Cambridge University Press, 1985), and Charles Warren, *T. S. Eliot on Shakespeare* (Ann Arbor: University of Michigan Press, 1987).

undone so many' and 'Shakespeherian rag' of *The Waste Land* followed by the overtly Dante-inspired music of *Ash Wednesday* (1930) and Shakespearean music of 'Marina' and the 'Coriolan' poems. In 'Little Gidding', Shakespeare and Dante converge in the uncanny episode of the 'familiar compound ghost' in war-torn London. Based on the Brunetto Latini episode in *Inferno*, Eliot's take on the Florentine's terza rima describes the spectre 'faded on the blowing of a horn', subliminally blending Dante with the ghost in *Hamlet* who 'faded on the crowing of the cock'.

Yeats is also a crucial presence in Eliot's compound spook. In 1943 Eliot admitted he was alluding to 'a late poem of Yeats' ('The Spur'), while in 1961 he recalled he was 'thinking primarily of William Yeats'.[4] Yeats, who had only recently died, was another poet absorbed by tradition, religion, ghosts, mediums, poetic impersonality, and 'the historical sense'. For him too Shakespeare and Dante were charged sources and resources. Though he never wrote orthodox 'critical essays' on them like the Harvard-trained Eliot, the Irish poet also wrestled in verse and post-Paterian prose with these two titanic predecessors.[5] The ways he did so were central to his heterodox but equally historicist constructions of poetic tradition, coloured both by his Irish nationalism and the eclectic religious nostalgia that fired his occult affiliations.

In *Yeats's Shakespeare* (1971), Rupin Desai documents Yeats's lifelong engagement with the English Renaissance dramatist, claiming a little hyperbolically that Yeats is 'one of the major twentieth-century critics of Shakespeare'.[6] Similarly, in *Yeats, Shakespeare and Cultural Nationalism* (2014) Oliver Hennessey argues that 'the story of Yeats's Shakespeare' embodies 'the convergence of fascinating chapters in the history of Shakespearian reception and Irish cultural nationalism', identifying 'a nexus of literary, nationalist and occultist ideas … in Yeats's references to Shakespeare'. Hennessey identifies three chronological 'primary modes of Shakespeare appropriation by Yeats: de-Anglicization, nation building, and a later, reactionary phase responding to the sociocultural life of the Irish state post-Treaty'.[7] However, neither Desai's patient review of the poet's innumerable Shakespearean allusions nor Hennessey's more ideologically driven approach quite capture the vertiginous and protean incarnations of Shakespeare in Yeats's texts.

Yeats's 'A General Introduction to My Work' (1938) is an autobiographically inflected riposte to Eliot's 'Tradition' essay that also invokes Dante and Shakespeare. In it, Yeats claims memorably that 'I owe my soul to Shakespeare, to Spenser, and to Blake … and to the English language in which I think, speak and write'.[8] This certainly reflects Yeats's

---

[4] *The Poems of T. S. Eliot: Volume I*, ed. Christopher Ricks and Jim McCue (London: Faber, 2015), 1012.

[5] Reviewing Yeats's *The Cutting of an Agate* in 'A Foreign Mind' in 1919, Eliot said, 'It is a style of Pater, with a trick of the eye and a hanging of the nether lip that come from across the Irish Channel, all the more seductive'; *The Complete Prose of T. S. Eliot: Vol. 2: The Perfect Critic 1919–1926*, ed. Anthony Cuda and Ronald Schuchard (Baltimore: Johns Hopkins University Press, 2014).

[6] W. Rupin W. Desai, *Yeats's Shakespeare* (Evanston: Northwestern University Press, 1971), 132.

[7] Oliver Hennessey, *Yeats, Shakespeare and Irish Cultural Nationalism* (Madison, NJ: Fairleigh Dickinson University Press, 2014), 19, 89, 108.

[8] *CW*5, 211.

conflicted nationalism with the emphasis on his 'soul' insisting on the spiritual dimension of his poetics, aligning himself with Stephen Dedalus in *A Portrait of the Artist
as a Young Man* aspiring 'to forge within the smithy of my soul the uncreated conscience of my race.'[9] Yeats also declares that 'the natural and supernatural are wed together', and imagines that 'Europeans may find something attractive in a Christ posed
against a background not of Judaism but of Druidism', affirming that 'I was born into
this faith, have lived in it, and shall die in it; my Christ, a legitimate deduction from
the Creed of St Patrick as I think, is that Unity of Being Dante compared to a perfectly
proportioned body.'[10] No one has convincingly traced the origin of Yeats's presiding idea
of 'Unity of Being' in Dante, but his transnational vision could not be more different
from Eliot's take on 'the mind of Europe' in 'Tradition' or his definitely non-Druidic
appeal to Christendom in 'The Idea of the Classic'. Yeats claims that he owes his soul to
Shakespeare and English Romantics but is committed to St Patrick's Creed and Dante's
Unity of Being, weaving both authors into an idiosyncratic tapestry that combines
multicultural religious traditions.

Yeats here offers a version of history and the poet that is more politically contradictory
as well as more overtly autobiographical than Eliot's. It is rooted in his self-identification
as an Irishman writing in English ('everything I love comes to me through English; my
hatred tortures me with love, my love with hate'). Against Eliot's version of 'impersonality', Yeats configures Dante, Shakespeare, and tradition in terms that are both 'personal' and national, while also dynamically reconfiguring European culture:

> A poet writes always of his personal life … he never speaks directly as to someone
> at the breakfast table, there is always a phantasmagoria. Dante and Milton had
> mythologies, Shakespeare the characters of English history or of traditional ro-
> mance … he is never the bundle of accident and incoherence that sits down to break-
> fast; he has been reborn as an idea, something intended, complete … He is Lear,
> Romeo, Oedipus, Tiresias; he has stepped out of a play, and even the woman he loves
> is Rosalind, Cleopatra, never the Dark Lady. He is part of his own phantasmagoria
> and we adore him because nature has grown intelligible, and by so doing a part of our
> creative power.[11]

Tiresias, who looms large in *The Waste Land* ('And I, Tiresias, have fore-suffered all'),
looks different here in the Dantean and Shakespearean company of Lear, Romeo, and
Cleopatra. Yeats recasts Eliot's poetic 'tradition' as a 'phantasmagoria', setting Dante's and
Milton's 'mythologies' beside Shakespearean history and romance as creative resources
available to the after-breakfast poet. In other words, he casts Dante and Shakespeare
into figures in his own turbulent phantasmagoria. For him, the poet is 'reborn'—or
reinvented—out of material thrown up from national and international tradition. From

---

[9] James Joyce, *A Portrait of the Artist as a Young Man* (New York: Knopf, 1991), 318.
[10] *CW5*, 210.
[11] *CW5*, 204.

among the dead, Yeats commandeers Shakespeare and Dante to play starring roles in his historical and global psychodrama. This is most evident in *A Vision* (1925 and 1937) and the poetry of his final phase, as we will see.

'VAST WORLDS MOULDED BY THEIR OWN WEIGHT'

The two poets are often twinned. In 'Rosa Alchemica' (1897), the narrator speaks of having on his bookshelf 'Shakespeare in the orange of the glory of the world, Dante in the dull red of his anger'.[12] In the same story, Michael Robartes speaks of 'divinities' who become 'spiritual bodies in the minds of the modern poets', conjuring 'Lear, his head still wet with the thunderstorm' and 'Beatrice, with her lips half parted in a smile'.[13] In a brief history of poetry in 'The Autumn of the Body' (1898), Yeats says that, after Virgil, 'Dante added to poetry a dialectic which, although he made it serve his laborious ecstasy, was the invention of minds trained by the labour of life', while 'Shakespeare shattered the symmetry of verse and of drama that he might fill them with things and their accidental relations to one another'. In 'The Symbolism of Poetry' (1900), Yeats portrays Shakespeare as drawing on 'emotional symbols' that evoke 'our sympathy' with 'the spectacle of the world', but argues that 'if one is moved by Dante, or by the myth of Demeter, one is mixed into the shadow of God or of a goddess', prefiguring the 'intellectual symbolisms in our time, a foreshadower of the new sacred book'.[14] Here Dantean and Shakespearean figures are reconfigured within a quasi-sacred *Symboliste* order that prefigures *A Vision*.

In 'Art and Ideas' (1913) Yeats once more brackets Dante and Shakespeare under his magical term 'reverie', arguing that 'it remains for some greater time, living once more in passionate reverie, to create a *King Lear*, a *Divine Comedy*, vast worlds moulded by their own weight like drops of water'.[15] Yeats's words suggest his charged consciousness of both writers as working in a way no longer possible on a cosmological scale ('vast worlds') but with minute Blakean particulars (those 'drops of water'). In 'Per Amica Silentia Lunae' (1917), he twins them in biographical terms, when he argues that 'in all great poetical styles there is saint or hero, but when it is over Dante can return to his chambering and Shakespeare to his 'pottle-pot' (a reference to *Henry IV Part II* where Bardolph talks of drinking 'in a pottle-pot').[16] According to this new dialectical reading, the two writers 'sought no impossible perfection but when they handled paper or parchment'. The

---

[12] *Myth 2005*, 268.
[13] 'Rosa Alchemica', *Myth 2005*, 268, 275.
[14] 'The Symbolism of Poetry', *CW4*, 119.
[15] *CW4*, 256.
[16] *Myth 2005*, 333. A 'pottle-pot is a drinking vessel containing two quarts' (*A Shakespeare Glossary*).

search for 'saint or hero' in both writers and Yeats's sense of the cosmic and historical psychodrama they helped script gives Yeats's reinventions of Dante and Shakespeare an intransigence that resists recuperation in conventional terms of critical 'reception'. They have become characters in Yeats's dialectical phantasmagoria.

YEATS AT STRATFORD-UPON-AVON, OR SHAKESPEARE IN DUBLIN

Richard Halpern's *Shakespeare Among the Moderns* makes only a fleeting reference to Yeats, but the tragic Shakespeare returns again and again in his work, not only in his thinking about his own theatre but in relation to history, poetics, and aesthetics. Though Yeats names Dante in the poem 'Ego Dominus Tuus', he never names 'Shakespeare' in his verse. He does, however, work the adjective 'Shakespearean' into a telegrammatic history of poetry entitled 'Three Movements':

> Shakespearean fish swam the sea, far away from land;
> Romantic fish swam in nets coming to the hand;
> What are all those fish that lie gasping on the strand?[17]

Annotating this, A. Norman Jeffares quotes Yeats's prose draft: 'Passion in Shakespeare was a great fish of the sea, but from Goethe to the end of the Romantic movement the fish was in the net. It will soon be dead upon the shore.'[18] If the draft foregrounds 'Passion' and a singular fish, the poetic vignette attributes an oceanic multiform freedom to the Shakespearean imagination that subsequently became diminished and exhausted. Like Eliot's, Yeats's view of Shakespeare is historicist and anti-progressivist, a view elaborated in his near contemporary essay on 'Bishop Berkeley' which Denis Donoghue sets beside the poem:

> Imagination, whether in literature, painting, or sculpture, sank after the death of Shakespeare; supreme intensity had passed to another faculty; it was as though Shakespeare, Dante, Michelangelo, had been reborn with all their old sublimity, but speaking a harsh, almost unintelligible language. Two or three generations hence, when men accept the inventions of science as a commonplace . . . no educated man will doubt that the movement of philosophy from Spinoza to Hegel is the greatest of all works of intellect.[19]

---

[17] *CW1*, 240. See also Denis Donoghue, 'Yeats's Shakespeare: "There is a Great Deal of My Father in it"', in *The Living Stream: Yeats Annual No. 18*, ed. Warwick Gould (Cambridge: Open Book Publishers, 2013), 69 ff.

[18] A. Norman Jeffares, *A New Commentary on the Poems of W.B. Yeats* (London: Macmillan, 1984), 279–80.

[19] *CW5*, 102.

In Yeats's historical retrospect Dantean and Shakespearean art is displaced by the philosophy of Spinoza, the historicism of Hegel, and 'the inventions of science', a movement which represents everything Yeats pits himself against.

In 1934 Yeats, when asked to name his favourite six books, named four authors, saying, 'First comes Shakespeare' (followed by *The Arabian Nights*, William Morris, and Balzac).[20] Looking back on his life in 'Tomorrow's Revolution' (1934), Yeats records that his father had taught him to 'admire Balzac' and 'set certain passages in Shakespeare above all else in literature'.[21] Though his constructions of Shakespeare changed over time, his investment in Shakespeare's symbolically charged characters never dimmed from the time his father read to him in childhood. *Autobiographies* records that, though he had 'seen Coriolanus played a number of times', whenever he sees the scene where Coriolanus tells the insolent servants that his home is under the canopy, 'it is my father's voice I hear and not Irving's or Benson's'.[22]

Eliot's Prufrock says, 'I am not Prince Hamlet, nor was meant to be', but, according to *Autobiographies*, the young Yeats liked to think he *was* meant to be Hamlet. After seeing Henry Irving's Hamlet at the age of 12, he thought of the Danish prince as 'myself'. He said that, though his father admired Ellen Terry's Ophelia, 'For many years Hamlet was an image of heroic self-possession for the poses of youth and childhood to copy, a combatant of the battle within myself'. He later describes 'walking with an artificial stride in memory of Hamlet and stopping at shop-windows to look at my tie' and quotes Wilde's claim that 'Schopenhauer has analysed the pessimism that characterises the modern world, but Hamlet invented it'.[23] According to Yeats, Shakespeare foreshadowed 'a change in the whole temperament of the world, for, though he called his Hamlet 'fat' and even 'scant of breath', he thrust between his fingers agile rapier and dagger'. While Yeats gave such weapons to his Irish stage heroes, he says he himself 'walked the Dublin streets when nobody was looking' with Irving's 'strut', making 'the characters I created speak with his brooding, broken wildness'.[24] That 'strut' returns when in old age in 'Lapis Lazuli' he announces that 'There struts Hamlet'.[25]

Though he may have identified with Hamlet, Yeats's first sustained critical engagement with Shakespeare was on the threshold of the twentieth century in 'At Stratford-on-Avon' (1901), when he wrote in a letter that 'I feal that I am getting deeper into Shakespeare'[s] mystery than ever before'.[26] Yeats records that his father thought his article 'the best article he'd ever read', and William Murphy claims that Yeats's views of Shakespeare in the essay are 'completely his father's'.[27] In it Yeats takes issue with the

---

[20] *CW5*, 129.

[21] *CW5*, 226.

[22] *Au*, 65.

[23] *Au*, 47, 83, 135.

[24] *CW10*, 62.

[25] *CW1*, 294.

[26] Yeats to Augusta Gregory [25 April 1901], *CL3*, 62.

[27] William M. Murphy, *Prodigal Father: The Life of John Butler Yeats* (Ithaca and London: Cornell University Press, 1978), 563. See also Donoghue, 'Yeats's Shakespeare', 69 ff.

'habit of mind of the Shakespearian critics' in the era of George Eliot and utilitarianism, in which 'Shakespearian criticism became a vulgar worshipper of success'. He took particular issue with Edward Dowden, Ireland's most distinguished Shakespearean, whose book he claims he once 'read carefully'. To Yeats's horror Dowden treated *Henry V* as 'the model Shakespeare held up before England', and, because 'He lived in Ireland, where everything had failed', treated Shakespeare as the exponent of 'Success', even noting that Shakespeare 'was making a large fortune while he was writing about Henry's victories'. Against such a view, Yeats sees Shakespeare as an incarnation of Blakean 'Forgiveness of Sin', arguing that, far from being critical of the moral and political failings of heroes like Hamlet, Timon, and Richard II, as Dowden and others inferred, Shakespeare was aware that 'men are made useless to the State as often by abundance as by emptiness, and that a man's business may at times be revelation, and not reformation'. Steering clear of Dowden's Protestant, success-worshiping, patriotic Shakespeare, Yeats argues (without any evidence) that 'Shakespeare cared little for the State', and (more convincingly) that he 'meditated as Solomon, not as Bentham meditated, upon blind ambitions, untoward accidents, and capricious passions, and the world was almost as empty in his eyes as it must be in the eyes of God'.[28]

The essay was a response to watching Benson's performance of Shakespeare's history plays at Stratford, 'played in their right order, with all the links that bind play to play unbroken'. It builds on the idea that there is a 'myth for every man' and that 'Shakespeare's myth' portrays 'a wise man who was blind for very wisdom, and an empty man who thrust him from his place', calling this 'the story of Hamlet, who saw too great issues everywhere to play the trivial games of life' as well as of 'Richard II, that unripened Hamlet', a 'vessel of porcelain' created as a 'complement' of the 'vessel of clay', Henry V. Yeats brings together his interest in theatrical tradition, history, and national culture, treating Stratford as a blueprint for an Irish National Theatre:

> That strange procession of kings and queens, of warring nobles, of insurgent crowds, of courtiers, and of people of the gutter has been to me almost too visible, too audible, too full of an unearthly energy. I have felt as I have sometimes felt on grey days on the Galway shore, when a faint mist has hung over the grey sea and the grey stones, as if the world might suddenly vanish and leave nothing behind, not even a little dust under one's feet.[29]

Historically, Yeats presents Shakespeare writing 'at a time when solitary great men were gathering to themselves the fire that had once flowed hither and thither among all men', and when the common people were no longer sustained 'by the myths of Christianity'.[30] This is a Shakespeare modelled on Greek tragedy and a Nietzschean myth of solitary heroic energy, but relocated to a misty Galway shore. Oblivious to the conditions of

---

[28] *CW4*, 78–80.
[29] *E&I*, 96–7.
[30] *E&I*, 110.

Elizabethan theatre or Shakespeare's complex political imaginary, it is patently modelled on Yeats's developing personal mythology.

In *Samhain* (1904), Yeats's vision of Shakespearean drama is polemically pitted against the Ibsenism espoused by his countrymen Shaw and Joyce. In the Joycean year of 1904, Yeats portrays Shakespeare adopting Richard II in his contest with Bolingbroke as a 'good image' for the 'impracticable lyricism in his own mind'. As a result, 'The historical Richard has passed away for ever and the Richard of the play lives more intensely, it seems, than did ever living man.' This leads Yeats to ask:

> How can we create like the ancients, while innumerable considerations of external probability or social utility destroy the seeming irresponsible creative power that is life itself? Who to-day could set Richmond's and Richard's tents side by side on the battlefield, or make Don Quixote, mad as he was, mistake a windmill for a giant in broad daylight?[31]

In line with this idea of 'irresponsible creative life', Yeats develops an exhilarating Nietzschean theory of drama as above all 'a moment of intense life', involving 'an activity of the souls of the characters', before asking whether art has 'nothing to do with moral judgements?' His answer is an eloquent defence of poetic drama itself as a 'higher court':

> The character whose fortune we have been called in to see, or the personality of the writer, must keep our sympathy, and whether it be farce or tragedy, we must laugh and weep with him ... This character who delights us may commit murder like Macbeth, or fly the battle for his sweetheart as did Antony, or betray his country like Coriolanus, and yet we will rejoice in every happiness that comes to him and sorrow at this death as if it were our own. It is no use telling us that the murderer and the betrayer do not deserve our sympathy ... we are caught up into another code, we are in the presence of a higher court .... If the poet's hand had slipped, if Antony had railed at Cleopatra in the monument, if Coriolanus had abated that high pride of his in the presence of death, we might have gone away muttering the Ten Commandments ... but the subject of all art is passion ... aroused into a perfect intensity by opposition with some other passion, or it may be with the law, that is the expression of the whole, whether Church or Nation.[32]

Happy in 1904 to identify with a Coriolanus who 'betrayed his nation', by 1933 in the heyday of O'Duffy's neo-fascist movement, Roy Foster records that Yeats's 'political excitement took the characteristic form of wondering whether the Abbey should stage *Coriolanus* in Blueshirt uniform'.[33] At this earlier moment, no less contentiously, Yeats was wrestling to shape his ethically heterodox idea of a National Theatre. This was the year of the first production of *On Baile's Strand*, where, despite its lean blank verse and

---

[31] *Ex*, 150.
[32] *Ex*, 154–5.
[33] *Life 2*, 473.

sinewy prose, his heroic Cuchulain, as Desai argues, shares 'salient attributes that Yeats detected in Shakespeare's Richard' as well as momentarily calling up Othello ('Put up your swords') and Coriolanus ('I whose mere name has kept the country safe'), while the play's song-prone Fool and blind man recall *King Lear* and its Norn-like prophetic women and knocking at the door remember *Macbeth*.[34] Looking back in *On the Boiler*, Yeats says he 'gave certain years to writing plays in Shakespearean blank verse about Irish kings about whom nobody cared a farthing' but also that he had 'greater luck than any English-speaking dramatist' in that he had aimed at 'tragic ecstasy' and that here and there he had 'seen it greatly played', citing William Fay's acting at the end of *On Baile's Strand*.[35] He also praised Frank Fay for his knowledge that 'Ireland had preserved longer than England the rhythmical utterance of the *Shakespearean* stage', intimating that Ireland was better placed than England for a new Shakespearean theatre.[36] Or in other words, a new Yeatsian theatre.

As both Desai and Hennessey note, Yeats's views of Shakespeare's relation to history are changeable and conflicted (he places him in two different historical moments in the two versions of *A Vision*, as if undecided whether Shakespeare writes before or after the end of 'Unity of Being'). In *Autobiographies* he sees 'traditional doctrine' as already under threat in the Renaissance: 'Had not Europe shared one mind and heart, until both mind and heart began to break into fragments a little before Shakespeare's birth?'[37] Discussing the 'noble' tradition of Noh in 1916, Yeats rather snobbishly situates Shakespeare as caught between two audiences, with moments of 'occasional humorous realism' like 'Cleopatra's old man with an asp' aimed at 'the common citizen', while 'the great speeches' were written for 'patrons in the galleries'. Yeats felt only the latter grasped that a 'poetical passage cannot be understood without a rich memory, and like the older school of painting, appeals to a tradition', as when Hamlet in Act I speaks of 'Lethe's wharf' or Lorenzo in Act V of *Merchant of Venice* speaks of 'Dido on the wild sea banks' but also 'in rhythm and vocabulary', where the audience needs to recognize 'slight variation on old cadences and customary words'.[38]

In *A Vision* (1925) Yeats elaborates his historical argument in 'Dove or Swan', where he offers a more dialectical account of Shakespeare as 'a man in whom human personality, hitherto restrained by its dependence upon Christendom or by its own need for self-control, burst like a shell'. If this looks like a celebration of Shakespearean humanism, Yeats continues in more critical vein to imagine a more 'antithetical' than 'realist' Shakespeare:

> Perhaps secular intellect, setting itself free after five hundred years of struggle has made him the greatest of dramatists, and yet because an *antithetical* art could create

---

[34] Desai, *Yeats's Shakespeare*, 161; *CW2*, 163, 157.
[35] *CW5*, 226.
[36] 'An Introduction to My Plays', *CW2*, 24.
[37] *Au*, 191.
[38] 'Certain Noble Plays of Japan' (1916), *CW4*, 167.

a hundred plays which preserved ... the unity of a painting or a Temple pediment, we might, had the total works of Sophocles survived – they too born of a like struggle though with a different enemy – not think him the greatest. Do we not feel an unrest like that of travel itself when we watch those personages, who are so much more living than ourselves, amidst so much that is irrelevant and heterogenous, amid so much *primary* curiosity, are carried from Rome to Venice, from Egypt to Anglo-Saxon England, or in the one play from Roman to Christian mythology.[39]

We could argue that the 'unrest like that of travel' which disturbs Yeats is precisely what gives Shakespeare his unsettling, dynamic, and transnational force. Yeats, like Eliot, often seems to regret that Shakespeare was not a contemporary of Dante and was too caught up in the volatile political world of his time—the place from where the Irish poet imagined sailing back in time to Byzantium.

Yeats sets Shakespeare beside Balzac and Napoleon in Phase 20, where 'Unity of Being' is replaced by 'a unity of the creative act' and the figure 'no longer seeks to unify what is broken through conviction ... but by projecting a dramatisation or many dramatisations'.[40] As a theatrical Proteus, Shakespeare's 'actual personality seemed faint and passionless', keeping out of 'quarrels in a quarrelsome age', but nonetheless he is 'the greatest of modern poets' because he 'created always from the *Mask* and *Image*, reflected in a multiplying mirror'. In this 'phase of ambition', where Napoleon embodies 'the dramatist's own ambition', in Shakespeare it is 'that of the persons of his art ... a creative energy'.[41] In 'The Statues' Yeats contrasts Hamlet and Buddha, where 'Mirror on mirror mirrored is all the show',[42] and this Shakespearean 'multiplying mirror' is a dizzying spin-off from Hamlet's claim that the aim of 'playing' is to 'hold, as 'twere, the mirror up to nature', providing an apotheosis of theatricality itself.[43]

THE CHIEF IMAGINATION OF CHRISTENDOM

David Wallace notes that, unlike scholarly Italianists such as Joyce, Eliot, and Beckett, 'Yeats knew little Italian and probably never read any translation of the *Commedia* from cover to cover.' For Wallace, nonetheless, though Yeats admitted he was 'no Dante scholar' and 'but read him in Shadwell or in Dante Rossetti',[44] he was partly responsible for establishing a 'Dante that is almost always at odds with that of Eliot and Pound: the Irish Dante of Yeats, Joyce, Beckett and Heaney'.[45] Commenting on Yeats's invocation in

---

[39] *CW13*, 169.
[40] *CW13*, 70.
[41] *CW13*, 72.
[42] *CW1*, 337.
[43] Shakespeare, *Hamlet* III.ii.
[44] 'Anima Hominis', *Myth 2005*, 329.
[45] David Wallace, 'Dante in English', in Rachel Jacoff, ed., *The Cambridge Companion to Dante* (Cambridge: Cambridge University Press, 1993), 252. See also Piero Boitani, 'Irish Dante: Yeats, Joyce, Beckett', in Manuele Gragnolati, Fabio Camilletti, and Fabian Lampart, eds., *Metamorphosing*

'Ego Dominus Tuus' of Dante as 'the chief Imagination of Christendom', Seamus Heaney observes that, 'when poets turn to the great masters of the past, they turn to an image of their own creation, one which is likely to be a reflection of their own imaginative needs'.[46]

In his early essay, 'William Blake and the Imagination', Yeats says that Blake 'was a symbolist who had to invent his symbols', but, 'Had he been a Catholic of Dante's time he would have been well content with Mary and the angels' or 'gone to Ireland and chosen for his symbols the sacred mountains' and native Irish 'divinities which have not faded' from belief, coincidentally reflecting the imaginative needs of the young Yeats.[47] T. S. Eliot in 1920 negatively compared Blake's home-made mythology to Dante's Christian world view, saying this was why 'Dante is a classic, and Blake only a poet of genius'. By contrast, the Blakean Yeats had no time for the 'impersonal reason' or 'the objectivity of science' that Eliot found wanting in Blake.[48] As George Bornstein notes, the young Yeats 'made his soul out of Blake, Shelley and Dante Gabriel Rossetti rather than Dante, and, his early Dantean allusions view him through the lens of these elected predecessors'.[49] If Yeats's Pre-Raphaelite-style cult of Maud Gonne and Olivia Shakespear in *The Wind Among the Reeds* is an oblique reflex of Rossetti's *Vita Nuova*, he went on to forge a heterodox Dante of his own, leading Steven Ellis to claim that Yeats came to view his own life and work 'between 1915 and 1925, as a kind of *Imitatio Dantis*'. According to Ellis, his 'response to Dante is at once more profound and more superficial than Pound's or Eliot's ... more profound because he regarded Dante's personal history as an exemplar; more superficial because his acquaintance with Dante's writing was remote and highly selective'.[50]

It was in his self-exploratory dialogue poem 'Ego Dominus Tuus' of 1915, which takes its title from Dante's *La Vita Nuova*, that Yeats calls the Italian poet 'the chief imagination of Christendom' and makes him a pivotal figure in his debate about poetics and identity, imagination and belief. In *Per Amica Silentiae Lunae* (1917), he wrote of the apparition of 'elaborate, brightly lighted buildings and sceneries' seen 'between sleep and waking', saying they must 'come from above me and beyond me'.[51] In the poem named after this Dantean moment, it is Dante the man who Yeats's two protagonists engage with rather than the poet:

> And yet
> The chief imagination of Christendom,
> Dante Alighieri, so utterly found himself

Dante: Appropriations, Manipulations, and Rewritings in the Twentieth and Twenty-First Centuries, Cultural Inquiry, 2 (Vienna: Turia & Kant, 2011), 37–59.

[46] Seamus Heaney, 'Envies and Identifications', *Irish University Review*, 15:1 (Spring 1985), 5.
[47] CW4, 86.
[48] Eliot, *Selected Essays*, 322.
[49] George Bornstein, 'Yeats's Romantic Dante', *Colby Review*, 15:2 (June 1979), 93–113. See also Giorgio Melchiori, 'Yeats and Dante', *English Miscellany*, 19 (1968), 153–79, and Thomas Vance, 'Yeats, Dante and Unity of Being', *Shenandoah*, 17:2 (Winter 1966), 73–85.
[50] Steven Ellis, 'Yeats and Dante', *Comparative Literature*, 33:1 (Winter 1981), 1.
[51] CW5, 4.

> That he made that hollow face of his
> More plain to the mind's eye than any face
> But that of Christ.[52]

When 'Ille', after naming him, calls Dante 'the chief imagination of Christendom', he gives him a quasi-papal poetic status, foregrounding Yeats's profoundly heterodox take on Christianity and poetic tradition. Placing his 'hollow' mask-like face beside Christ's turns the Florentine into a poetic icon, and the 'chief imagination of Christendom' gives him an almost Christlike status. Nevertheless, 'Ille' speculates that his face is the product of an Adamic 'hunger for the apple on the bough / Most out of reach'. Yeats insists the poet is not the man who was 'mocked by Guido for his lecherous life', and who, when 'driven out / To climb the stair and eat that bitter bread', was compelled to find 'the unpersuadable justice' and 'most exalted lady loved by a man'.[53] Yeats quotes Boccaccio on the biographical Dante's investment in 'the virtues of lechery', showing some of the homework behind the claim that 'the work is the man's flight from his entire horoscope'.[54] Nevertheless, in the poem 'Hic' questions 'Ille's assumption that men always make their art out of 'tragic war', arguing instead that 'A style is found by sedentary toil / And by the imitation of great masters'. It is Ille who gets the best and last lines, saying he seeks 'an image, not a book' and developing his theory of art as anti-self, double, image, or fictional counterpart of the 'blind, stupefied hearts' of the writer.[55] Despite this, we really only know 'Dante' through his books, and the literary world created by his 'sedentary toil'. It is striking that, for both interlocutors in Yeats's meditation, the argument is built around his reading of Dante in contrast to Keats (the only poets named, apart from Guido), with Keats playing the antithetical role Blake plays for Eliot in his version of an 'orthodox' Dante.

After 'Ego Dominus' and *Per Amica Silentia Lunae* Yeats's engagement with Dante plays out with greatest intensity in *A Vision* (1925), a text hammered out from his wife George's automatic writings. The importance of Dante in Yeats's heterodox cosmology may be partly attributable to George, who, as Margaret Mills Harper and Catherine Paul point out, knew Dante and Cavalcanti well, and whose Temple Classics edition of the *Commedia*, *Vita Nuova*, and Latin works 'contain her own translations as well as marginalia in French, Italian, German and English'.[56] Before resuming the automatic script on 13 October 1919, Yeats was instructed by his 'Collaborators' 'to read the whole of Dante's Convito', perhaps 'only a little every day', illustrating the collaborative nature of the

---

[52] *CW1*, 162.

[53] *CW1*, 162.

[54] *CW5*, 7, 6.

[55] *CW1*, 162–3.

[56] *CW13*, 241. See Margaret Mills Harper, 'The Medium as Creator: George's Role in the Automatic Script', *YAACTS*, 6 (1988).

process.[57] In 1922, he had agreed to revise his commentary on Blake's illustrations to Dante for T. S. Eliot, and told George, 'We shall have to read Dante in the evenings.'[58] This added a new inwardness to the Yeatsian Dante. Amid the complex paratextual apparatus of the 1925 edition Yeats speaks of wishing 'for a system of thought that would leave my imagination free to create as it chose and yet make all that it created, or could create, part of the one history, and that the soul's'. He says, 'the Greeks certainly had such a system, and Dante – though Boccaccio thought him a bitter partisan and therefore a modern abstract man – and I think no man since.'[59] In other words, Dante is the last to have the kind of system based on 'Unity of Being' that Yeats aspired towards. In fact, Yeats also claims Dante was 'the first to substitute for Biblical or mythological figures, historical movements and actual men and women.'[60] In a sense, then, Yeats's *A Vision* is an 'antithetical' equivalent of Dante's Thomist *Commedia*, made up, like Dante's epic, of historical personae caught up in a cosmic vision of history. In it, Yeats and Dante are neighbours in the same phase of the moon. In the 1925 version, Yeats returns to the *Convito* to argue for a paradoxically daimonic rather than Thomist Dante:

> In the *Convito* Dante speaks of his exile, and the gregariousness it thrust upon him, as a great misfortune for such as he; and yet as a poet he must have accepted, not only that exile, but his grief for the death of Beatrice as that which made him *Daimonic*, not a writer of poetry alone like Guido Cavalcanti.[61]

Yeats also says Dante wrote 'the first sentence of modern autobiography and in the *Divine Comedy* imposes his own personality upon a system and a phantasmagoria hitherto impersonal; the King everywhere has found his kingdom.'[62] This is very much a Dante in his own image, as he works on constructing his systematically phantasmagoric text, *A Vision*. Yeats speaks of 'that art discovered by Dante of marshalling into a vast *antithetical* structure *antithetical material*' before 'the public certainty that sufficed for Dante and St Thomas' disappeared. Neither Dante nor St Thomas, I imagine, would have recognized this description.

In the 1937 *A Vision* Yeats set Dante against his own earlier visionary avatar Shelley, who, out of phase, 'writes pamphlets and dreams of converting the world' but 'lacked the Vision of Evil' and could not 'conceive of the world as a continual conflict'.[63] There is certainly a stronger vision of political evil in Yeats's later text, where, speaking of Dante

---

[57] George Mills Harper, *The Making of Yeats's A Vision: A Study of the Automatic Script* Vol. 2 (London: Macmillan, 1987), 329.

[58] Ann Saddlemyer, ed., *W. B. Yeats and George Yeats: The Letters* (Oxford: Oxford University Press, 2011), 97.

[59] *CW13*, lv.

[60] *CW13*, lv

[61] *CW13*, 26.

[62] *CW13*, 165.

[63] *CW14*, 143–4.

lamenting his exile and sighing for 'his lost solitude', he says he 'could never keep from politics, and was ... such a partisan that if a child, or a woman, spoke against his party he would pelt this child or woman with stones'. Nevertheless, 'Dante', having attained, as poet, to Unity of Being, 'saw all things set in order, had an intellect that served the *Mask* alone, that compelled even those things that opposed it to serve, and was content to see both good and evil'. As in 'Ego Dominus', having 'suffered injustice and the loss of Beatrice', Yeats's Dante 'found divine justice and the heavenly Beatrice'.[64] As Eliot's speaker in *The Waste Land* wonders whether he should 'set my lands in order', Yeats is another Dantean poet who wants to 'set all things in order', but, 'in part because of the age' (as he says of Shelley), his own attempt to 'hold in a single thought reality and justice', however dazzling its historical and aesthetic insights, stands on the frailest of epistemological and ethical foundations.

'Myself Must I Remake'

Both Dante and Shakespeare acquire a more dynamic, Nietzschean afterlife in Yeats's late poetry in the wake of *A Vision*. In 'Meditations in Time of Civil War', he superimposes Shakespeare's civil war play on contemporary Ireland when he describes an 'affable Irregular' as 'A heavily-built Falstaffian man', while in 'Why Should Not Old Men be Mad' he sardonically recalls 'A girl who knew all Dante once' but who lives 'to bear children to a dunce', giving this as a reason for going crazy in old age.[65] In his later verse drama Yeats brings Shakespearean blank verse to bear on a vision of the afterlife comparable to Dante's but woven out of a blend of occult philosophy, Irish mythology, and Japanese Noh theatre that is the antithesis of Dante's (or Eliot's) 'Christendom'.

Eliot and Yeats allude to the two poetic avatars in profoundly different ways. Yeats usually conjures the biographical Dante (as in 'Ego Dominus Tuus') rather than echoing his poetry as Eliot does, in *The Waste Land*'s 'so many, / I had not thought death had undone so many' in the metropolis, across *Ash Wednesday*, and in 'Little Gidding', with its terza-rima-inflected Dantean ghost speaking to him in war-torn London. As for their allusions to Shakespeare, Eliot's Prufrock famously announces, 'I am not Prince Hamlet, nor was meant to be', as *The Waste Land* conjures both Ariel's song and a 'broken Coriolanus', while Yeats, in 'An Acre of Grass', prays for 'an old man's frenzy', saying 'Myself must I remake / Till I am Timon and Lear / Or that William Blake / Who beat upon the wall / Till Truth obeyed his call.'[66] *Hamlet* recurs in an even more unlikely context in 'The Statues', a vertiginous, Paterian poem that conjures cultural history in the mode of *A Vision*, beginning with the sculpture of classical Greece and concluding with

---

[64] *Ibid.*
[65] *CW1*, 301–2.
[66] *CW1*, 308.

Pearse summoning Cuchulain in the GPO. In it Yeats briefly conjures up Shakespeare's archetypally brooding Dane before 'Grimalkin crawls to Buddha's emptiness':

> One image crossed the many-headed, sat
> Under the tropic shade, grew round and slow,
> No Hamlet thin from eating flies, a fat
> Dreamer of the Middle Ages.[67]

Caricaturing Hamlet as a type of the anxious European Renaissance intellectual, Yeats sets him against the plump Buddha, who is associated surrealistically with the image of the witches' cat in Act I of *Macbeth* ('I come, Grimalkin'). This is one of many moments where Yeats polemically sets Shakespearean characters in a larger panoptic theatre. In *On the Boiler*, Yeats wrote that 'masterpieces, whether of the stage or study, excel in their action, their visibility – who can forget Odysseus, Don Quixote, Hamlet, Lear, Faust, all figures in a peep-show – and we are not coherent to ourselves through thought but because our visible image changes slowly.'[68] This pantomimic 'peep show' is a cut-price version of the Yeatsian 'phantasmagoria'.

As early as his 1910 essay on 'The Tragic Theatre', Yeats touched on Hamlet in relation to tragedy and gaiety, at that time setting up an opposition between them:

> In writers of tragi-comedy (and Shakespeare is always a writer of tragi-comedy) there is indeed character, but … it is in moments of comedy that character is defined, in Hamlet's gaiety, let us say; while amid the great moments, when Timon orders his tomb, when Hamlet cries to Horatio 'Absent thee from felicity awhile', when Antony names 'Of many thousand kisses the poor last,' all is lyricism, unmixed passion, 'the integrity of fire'.[69]

Yeats's Shakespeare is always a mosaic of 'great moments', as here. In the second stanza of his late poem 'Lapis Lazuli', a poem about poetry, art, civilization, age, and cultural transience, Yeats homes in on the 'tragic theatre' once again, using both the adjective and the noun, now combining Hamlet's 'gaiety' with 'the great moments':

> All perform their tragic play,
> There struts Hamlet, there is Lear,
> That's Ophelia, that Cordelia;
> Yet they, should the last scene be there,
> The great stage curtain about to drop,
> If worthy their prominent part in the play,
> Do not break up their lines to weep.
> They know that Hamlet and Lear are gay;
> Gaiety transfiguring all that dread.
> All men have aimed at, found and lost;

---

[67] *CW1*, 337.
[68] *CW5*, 345.
[69] *CW4*, 175.

> Black out; Heaven blazing into the head:
> Tragedy wrought to its uttermost.
> Though Hamlet rambles and Lear rages,
> And all the drop scenes drop at once
> Upon a hundred thousand stages,
> It cannot grow by an inch or an ounce.[70]

Yeats's lines insist on the theatricality of tragedy, focusing on *Hamlet* and *Lear*, naming both their protagonists and the tragic women at the centre of the dramas, but also foregrounding the element of sheer performance, with the first line's 'tragic play' harvesting the ambiguity between a generic script and a form of tragic playfulness. Though Yeats generally undervalues Shakespearean comedy, the plausibility of the 'gay' knowledge he ascribes to Hamlet and Lear partly depends on Shakespeare's protean commitment to 'antic' wit. The verb 'struts' here echoes another Act V scene, where Macbeth conjures a vision of life as 'a poor player / That struts and frets his hour upon the stage', which, with the reference to a 'last scene', 'the great stage curtain', 'lines', 'part', 'drop scenes', 'Black out', and 'a hundred thousand stages' keeps us squarely among actors and in the theatre. Yeats's opening context in the poem is late 1930s politics under the shadow of 'Aeroplane and Zeppelin' and 'bomb-balls', but he goes on to set this part-Nietzschean, part-Brechtian theory of tragic performance in a panoptic historical and aesthetic theatre of 'Old civilisations put to the sword'[71], the now lost classical sculptures of Callimachus, and Yeats's lapis lazuli sculpture of three Chinese figures climbing a holy mountain. The poem attributes the same 'gaiety transfiguring all that dread' to them all, affirming defiantly that 'All things fall and are built again / And those that build them again are gay'.[72]

Dante is a less palpable linguistic presence than Shakespeare in late Yeats, despite the Irish poet's comparable commitment to a *Commedia*-like poetry and drama of the afterlife. Nevertheless, the ghost of Dantean verse haunts 'Cuchulain Comforted', written a couple of weeks before the poet's death. It is the poem where Yeats draws closest poetically to Dante, adopting as he does so, the terza rima form which braces the all-embracing cosmic architecture of the *Commedia* and brings it to bear on Cuchulain, the heroic subject of his many plays about 'Irish kings'. The poem opens by conjuring a visionary world caught between battlefield and Dantean afterlife:

> A man that had six mortal wounds, a man
> Violent and famous, strode among the dead;
> Eyes stared out of the branches and were gone.
>
> Then certain Shrouds that muttered head to head
> Came and were gone. He leant upon a tree
> As though to meditate on wounds and blood.

[70] *CW1*, 294.
[71] *CW1*, 294.
[72] *CW1*, 295.

> A Shroud that seemed to have authority
> Among those bird-like things came, and let fall
> A bundle of linen. Shrouds by two and three
>
> Came creeping up because the man was still.

The man is told to 'Obey our ancient rule and make a shroud' and that all these figures are 'Convicted cowards, all by kindred slain'. At the close of this eerie post-human scene, we are told:

> They sang, but had nor human tunes nor words,
> Though all was done in common as before;
>
> They had changed their throats and had the throats of birds.[73]

Scholars have traced some of the imagery of this bewildering scene to Dante—A. C. Wilson suggesting the Valley of Negligent Rulers in *Purgatorio* and T. R. Henn the parallel between Yeats's shades threading 'needles' eyes' with Dante's account of the Sodomites in Inferno 15, knitting 'their brows at us, as an old tailor does at the eye of a needle'.[74] I don't hear such specific allusions, finding in the poem instead an uncanny resurrection of Dante's afterworld poetic in modern form. It enables Yeats to give body to his own lyric work of shroud-weaving for Cuchulain and, by analogy, himself. Writing of its terza rima, Heaney notes that it is 'the only time Yeats used the form, but the proper time, when he was preparing his own death by imagining Cuchulain's descent among the shades'.[75] Last acts, final scenes, first and last things: in his final decade the shades of Shakespeare and Dante were crucial for Yeats as he approached the boundary of that country from whose bourn Hamlet says no traveller returns. Those posthumous Dantean singing-shrouds join the Shakespearean company whose 'gaiety' transfigures 'all that dread' in the last act of Yeats's unique poetic phantasmagoria.

---

[73] *CW1*, 332–3.

[74] See George Bornstein, 'Yeats's Romantic Dante', in Stuart Y. McDougal, ed., *Dante Among the Moderns* (Chapel Hill, NC: University of North Carolina Press, 1985).

[75] Seamus Heaney, 'Yeats as an Example', in *Finders Keepers: Selected Prose 1971–2001* (London: Faber, 2002), 111.

CHAPTER 13

TALKING BACK TO HISTORY

From 'September 1913' to 'Easter, 1916'

GERALDINE HIGGINS

All that I have said and done,
Now that I am old and ill,
Turns into a question till
I lie awake night after night
And never get the answers right.

W. B. Yeats, 'Man and the Echo' (*CW1*, 345)

Was Yeats fond of rhetorical questions?

(Quiz question in *Poetry Ireland Review*, 2015)[1]

THE period bookended by Yeats's two poems 'September 1913' and 'Easter, 1916' saw Ireland militarized and on the brink of civil war, Dublin devastated by a brutal stand-off between workers and their employers, and 200,000 Irishmen enlisted to fight on the Allied side in the Great War. Of course, the politics and protagonists of this foreshortened time period help to contextualize Yeats's poetry, but, to paraphrase Brian Friel, we don't go to Yeats for 'history'.[2] Although a keen observer of some of the seminal events of twentieth-century Irish history, Yeats was neither an active participant nor even a witness to the key events he writes about. Indeed, if we relied upon Yeats's historical poems for our understanding of these events, we would have a very eccentric idea about 'what happened'. If we think of the imperatives of writing history as aligned with accuracy and evidence, and the predominant historical style as aligned with narrative realism, then Yeats is an anti-historical poet.

---

[1] Spare Ribh, 'HOW YEATS ARE YOU?' *Poetry Ireland Review*, 116 (2015), 59–60, http://www.jstor.org/stable/26509664.

[2] Brian Friel used the phrase 'You don't go to *Macbeth* for history' to defend his play *Translations* (1980) against charges of historical inaccuracy. Pointing out that 'drama is first a fiction with the authority of fiction', he insisted that 'the imperatives of fiction are as exacting as the imperatives of cartography and historiography'. See Brian Friel, 'A Reply to J. H. Andrews', in Christopher Murray, ed., *Brian Friel, Essays, Diaries, Interviews 1964-1999* (Faber & Faber, 1999), 118–19.

When we turn to the representation of history in Yeats's work, we reach first for the poems that announce their topicality or attachment to current events such as 'September 1913', 'Easter, 1916', 'Meditations in Time of Civil War', and 'Nineteen hundred and Nineteen'. As this list confirms, Yeats's dates with history are both personal and political, not, as Nicholas Grene says, 'mere matters of record' but 'movable markers to be included or withheld, rendered accurately or falsified, depending on the literary purpose in hand'.[3] Yeats's manipulation of dates per se mirrors the way he engages with the complexity of 'history' as a topic of examination in his poetry and as a protagonist or subject of history himself. Although Yeats is often regarded as a poet who memorializes (or even monumentalizes) the past, in fact he uses the instability of poetry to destabilize history and to shoot it through with ambiguity.

So, what does Yeats make legible about the Irish history he made and experienced? 'History' for Yeats is personal, not simply in the sense that he sees his own biography and that of the nation as intertwined but also in his belief that the writer reshapes history itself.[4] Famously a poet who constantly remakes himself, Yeats also fashions useable versions of the past that inform his symbolic historical schema. Rejecting the poetry of witness, he sometimes inhabits the role of prophet, but rarely, if ever, can he be said to be a reliable historical chronicler.[5] How then has he come to be known as the poet without whom the age cannot be understood?[6] As I argue here, Yeats's status as a poet of history rests on the key questions embedded in his best-known public poems. These questions talk back to received ideas about the past, to political bromides about history and to Yeats's own earlier work.

Readers of Yeats have been trying to answer his most famous questions for decades: 'Was there another Troy for her to burn?', 'Did she put on his knowledge with his power? / Before the indifferent beak could let her drop?', 'And what rough beast, its hour come round at last, / Slouches towards Bethlehem to be born?'.[7] This chapter focuses on three rhetorical questions that reveal different aspects of Yeats's attitude to history—'Was it for this?' ('September 1913'), 'Was it needless death after all?' ('Easter, 1916'), and 'Did that play of mine send out certain men the English shot?' ('Man and the Echo').[8] Yeats stages his historical awareness in these poems in the form of rhetorical

---

[3] Nicholas Grene, *Yeats's Poetic Codes* (Oxford: Oxford University Press, 2008), 8.

[4] Describing Yeats's completion of *Reveries*, the first volume of his *Autobiographies*, Roy Foster writes, 'But he knew he was making history, and that his own experience was essential for understanding that. More questionably, he thought history was firmly shaped in 1914; the creation of a Home Rule Ireland had been paralleled by the construction of the poet's self.' *Life 1*, 531.

[5] In early versions of 'Pardon Old Fathers', Yeats gets his own family history wrong. At first, he believed that his Butler ancestors fought on the Jacobite side in the 1690 Battle of the Boyne before discovering that they were in fact defenders of William of Orange. See Daniel Albright, *W. B. Yeats, The Poems* (London: Dent, 1990), 519.

[6] T. S. Eliot, in his inaugural lecture at the Abbey Theatre in 1940, called Yeats 'one of those few whose history is the history of their own time, who are a part of the consciousness of an age which cannot be understood without them'. 'The First Annual Yeats Lecture', delivered to the Friends of the Irish Academy at the Abbey Theatre, Dublin, 30 June 1940, in *On Poetry and Poets* (London: Faber & Faber, 1957), 252.

[7] 'No Second Troy', *CW1*, 91; 'Leda and the Swan', *CW1*, 214; 'The Second Coming', *CW1*, 187.

[8] *CW1*, 108, 181, 345.

questions that insert notes of ambiguity and deniability into the historical record and air the poet's own doubts about the events themselves.

Beginning with two of Yeats's best-known poems 'in conversation' with history ('September 1913' and 'Easter, 1916') and ending with 'that play', *Cathleen ni Houlihan*, this chapter shows how Yeats questions history in the making and in the remembering, addressing his readers 'now and in time to be' in order to project his own authority as a 'prophet facing backwards'.[9] Featuring dates, historical figures, and time-stamped events, these texts are situated at the crossroads between art and politics but intersect with history in different ways. While including specific dates as titles (1913, 1916) and as backdrop (1798) might seem to anchor such works in history, Yeats in fact uses dates as embarkation ports for time travel. For example, although written and first performed in 1902, *Cathleen ni Houlihan* is a time-travelling play. It reaches out from its historical setting in 1798 via Maud Gonne's performance as the Old Woman in 1902 to its prophetic moment in 1916.[10] Reappearing in 'Man and the Echo' in 1938, this unruly play refuses to stay in its historical moment or its theatrical space.

Similarly, 'September 1913' is really a '1798 poem' disguised as an occasional poem, the occasion being the debate about approving public funds for a gallery in Dublin to house Hugh Lane's gift of thirty-nine Impressionist paintings. The poem's topicality is foregrounded by its initial publication in *The Irish Times*, and by its original title, 'Romance in Ireland (on reading much of the correspondence against the Art Gallery)'.[11] However, lacking any direct references to Lane, the gallery, or the paintings, the poem— in subsequent publications as 'September 1913'—reads as a generalized indictment of modern Ireland for its materialism and philistinism. The title and date with which we now identify the poem misleadingly shift the focus from the occasion of the Gallery controversy and from the historical figures invoked by Yeats as representatives of Romantic Ireland. 'September 1913' becomes a 'state of the nation' address anchored by its title to calendrical time but really devoted to the mythical timeline of heroic history.

If 'September 1913' can claim its greatest impact from its first appearance in *The Irish Times* under a different title, 'Easter, 1916' accumulates historical significance through its distance from the event it commemorates. In many ways, the most historically accurate aspect of the poem is its title. Completed five months after the Rising of April 2016 but not published until 1920, 'Easter, 1916' lacks the polemical purpose of 'September 1913' but talks back with hindsight to its portrayal of history. As Grene points out, the two

---

[9] Roy Foster, *Words Alone: Yeats and his Inheritances* (Oxford: Oxford University Press, 2011), 59.

[10] Ed Mulhall illuminates another important date in the performance history of the play in March 1919 when Lady Gregory stepped into the title role, writing in her journal, 'After all what is wanted but a hag and a voice'. In the audience for this performance were Maud Gonne and her daughter Iseult. Mulhall points out that, earlier that week, Lady Gregory had witnessed the crowds welcoming Countess Markievicz's release from prison after her election to the British parliament in 1918. Yeats himself had just become a father and, the day after this performance, brought his wife and baby daughter home to their new rented house in Dundrum, where he began work on 'A Prayer for my Daughter'. https://www.rte.ie/centuryireland/index.php/articles/the-fathers-prayers-wb-yeats-in-1919.

[11] W. B. Yeats, 'Romance in Ireland (on reading much of the correspondence against the Art Gallery)', *Irish Times*, 8 September 1913.

poems are poised almost symmetrically on either side of 1914, the midpoint of Yeats's writing life, one marking the end of the first phase of Yeats's belief in the possibility of cultural revival and the other heralding the renewal of 'a new, if distressing, epoch'.[12] David Lloyd adds 1919 to what he calls (after Benjamin) this 'constellation' of dates in which possibilities in the past that remain unrealized might become readable again.[13] While accounting for the significance of the date in the titles of these time-stamped poems, my focus is on how Yeats's public poems enact the tension between historical event and event as art by giving us access to a past that is not available to history.

WAS IT FOR THIS?

'September 1913' presents Yeats at his crankiest. Its direct opening address to the people of Ireland sounds like a question but isn't one, and sets the stage for his interrogation of modern mores and failings:

> What need you, being come to sense,
> But fumble in a greasy till
> And add the halfpence to the pence
> And prayer to shivering prayer, until
> You have dried the marrow from the bone;
> For men were born to pray and save:
> Romantic Ireland's dead and gone,
> It's with O'Leary in the grave.[14]

Understanding the poem requires contextual information from Yeats's other poems (the group later published as *Poems Written in Discouragement, 1912–1913*) and from *The Irish Times* of 8 September 1913 in which it first appeared. Prominently displayed alongside coverage of the Dublin strike and lockout as well as the aforementioned Gallery, the immediacy of the poem's appearance in the newspaper is matched by Yeats's bluntness of tone and the poem's editorializing refrain. Critics such as George Bornstein and Nicholas Grene have drawn attention to the 'thick political codings' surrounding its original publication as part of Yeats's protracted intervention on behalf of the Hugh Lane pictures.[15] These codings underline the polemical purpose of 'Romance in Ireland' to berate those who would deny funds to the project unless it 'were proved the people wanted pictures'.

---

[12] Grene, *Yeats's Poetic Codes*, 6.
[13] David Lloyd, '1913–1916–1919', in *Modernist Cultures*, 13.3 (2018), 445–64. Another significant reading of these poems influenced by Benjamin is Jahan Ramazani's *Poetry and its Others* (Chicago: University of Chicago Press, 2014), 81–8.
[14] *CW1*, 108
[15] George Bornstein, *Material Modernism: The Politics of the Page* (Cambridge: Cambridge University Press, 2001), 55–8.

This becomes even more apparent when we read the gallery poems as a cluster of poems about the Lane affair. The juxtaposition of material crassness and lofty patronage is sustained across all five poems, even when the locations shift from Ireland to Renaissance Italy and back again. The unwieldy 'To a Wealthy Man who promised a Second Subscription to the Dublin Municipal Gallery if it were proved the People wanted Pictures' supplies the context and acts as a preface to 'Romance in Ireland' in its title alone.[16] Bornstein shows that subsequent reprintings ensure that the poem 'becomes an artifact talking about politics rather than incarnating them'.[17] The particularities of the cultural betrayal of the Gallery and the 1913 strike and lockout are transposed to a general betrayal of the ideals of 1798, invoking the heroic Anglo-Irish lineage of Emmet, Fitzgerald, and Tone as well as the Fenian leader, John O'Leary. As in 'To a Shade', the later Gallery poem addressed to Parnell, rather than historicizing these figures, Yeats summons them to pass judgement on contemporary Ireland.

Yeats's enemies are those who would 'pray and save', the materialist, uncultured Catholic middle classes, and their representative, William Martin Murphy (proprietor of the *Irish Independent*). Neither Murphy nor his competitor, John Edward Healy, editor of *The Irish Times*, is mentioned in the poem, but the politics and readership of their respective papers are central to its meaning.[18] Murphy, enemy of Parnell, Larkin, and Lane, represents Catholic philistinism to Yeats. His constituency, the 'you' plural of the first line, consists of the Paudeens and Biddies cowed by what Yeats called 'a priest created terror of culture'.[19] The first and second stanzas of the poem scornfully assert the decisive differences between 'you' and 'yours' and the heroic 'they' of Romantic Ireland, culminating in the first rhetorical question of the poem, 'And what, God help us, could they save?' The implied answer is that the penny-pinching prayers and savers of the materialist, uncultured Catholic middle classes are unworthy either of salvation or rescue by the heroic names unleashed in the third stanza.

The central question of the poem, 'Was it for this', appears only once, and Yeats withholds the question mark until he intensifies his outrage by repeating 'for this':

> Was it for this the wild geese spread
> The grey wing upon every tide;
> For this that all that blood was shed,
> For this Edward Fitzgerald died,
> And Robert Emmet and Wolfe Tone,
> All that delirium of the brave?

[16] *CW1*, 107–8.
[17] Bornstein, *Material Modernism*, 55.
[18] Daniel Albright's edition of Yeats's poems notes Murphy's article in the *Irish Independent* from 17 January 1913: 'Speaking for myself I admire good pictures and I think I can appreciate them but as a choice between the two, I would rather see in the city of Dublin one block of sanitary houses at low rents replacing a reeking slum than all the pictures Corot and Degas ever painted.' See W. B. Yeats, *The Poems* (London: Dent, 1990), 529.
[19] Quoted in *Life 1*, 482.

'Was it for this?' is a rhetorical question, like the four questions detonated in the final stanza of 'Easter, 1916' (which will be examined later). It recalls the opening lines of Wordsworth's *Prelude*: 'Was it for this / That one, the fairest of all rivers, loved / To blend his murmurs with my Nurse's song?'[20] In Wordsworth's case, the implicit answer is that yes, it *was* for this: the fairest of all rivers and nature herself calls forth 'this' effusion, Wordsworth's poetry. In Yeats's poem, the emphasis falls on the specificity of the demonstrative 'this' and the answer to the same rhetorical question is a resounding no. 'This' draws our attention to the present moment of the poem's publication, the prevailing cultural and political conditions that have incurred the poet's wrath. But the demonstrative 'this' is also a sweeping gesture of scorn, perhaps even with the American inflexion that accompanies questions—was it for THIS? Yeats's 'this' is the Ireland born of 'huckster's loins', the Ireland in which Paudeen fumbling in a 'greasy till' has triumphed.

Although 'Romance in Ireland' seems to imagine a deterritorialized Ireland, an Ireland from which the heroes have fled and the heroic ideal has been betrayed, the subtitle 'on reading much of the correspondence against the Art gallery' locates the poem in the politics of space. In fact, it was Hugh Lane's insistence that only a purpose-built gallery across the Liffey would secure his thirty-nine Impressionist paintings for Dublin that most exercised his supporters and opponents. In *The Irish Art of Controversy*, Lucy McDiarmid draws attention to the materiality of the paintings and their status as talismanic objects, 'slightly magic and oddly vulnerable'.[21] Her lively account of the spatial politics of 1913 focuses on the paintings as shifting signifiers of cultural nationalism, cosmopolitan ambition, and class warfare. As she shows, ultimately Yeats's gallery poems present a polarized Dublin where Paudeen and Biddy reject the elevating condescension of their betters. Consequently, Yeats's strategic placement of his poem in support of the Lane Gallery in *The Irish Times* alongside Joseph Hone's article on 'Art and Aristocracy' calls on its readers to build the gallery with 'the right twigs for an eagle's nest'. The poem is not a call to arms but a call to cultural activism.

John O'Leary, deployed as the representative of Romantic Ireland in the poem, is an example of Yeats's changing relationship with the Ireland of his time. Despite his undoubted influence on the young Yeats, by the time that Yeats wrote 'September 1913' O'Leary's reputation and Yeats's relationship to him had changed. Although admired for his rebellious past, by the turn of the century O'Leary was described in the nationalist press as 'A tory, a social shoneen, a fossil', and by a detective from Dublin Castle as an 'old crank full of whims and honesty'.[22] For Yeats, the Romantic Ireland that is buried in the grave with O'Leary is a form of nationalism connected to *noblesse oblige* rather than revolution. To O'Leary's famous statement that there are things a man must not do to save a nation, we might add his sentiment that 'Patriotism is of no class or creed, and hearts may beat as warmly for Ireland in a castle as in a cabin, and I think are more likely to beat

---

[20] William Wordsworth, *The Prelude: the Four Texts 1798, 1799, 1805, 1850*, ed. Jonathan Wordsworth (London: Penguin Books, 1995), 8.

[21] Lucy McDiarmid, *The Irish Art of Controversy* (Ithaca, NY: Cornell University Press, 2005), 11.

[22] *Life I*, 43.

warmly in either than in a farmhouse or a shop.'[23] Yeats did not actually attend O'Leary's funeral in 1907, but here he effectively stands at the graveside of his idealized Romantic Ireland and delivers a funeral oration.

Of course, Yeats's hasty consignment of 'Romantic Ireland' to the grave in 1913 was necessarily revised by the events of 1916. His changing perspective on the historical relevance of the poem's chorus is evident in the 'Note' he added in July 1916 to the group of five Gallery poems:[24]

> 'Romantic Ireland's dead and gone' sounds old-fashioned now. It seemed true in 1913, but I did not foresee 1916. The late Dublin Rebellion, whatever one can say of its wisdom, will long be remembered for its heroism. 'They weighed so lightly what they gave,' and gave too in some cases without hope of success.[25]

In allowing that 'September 1913' sounds 'old-fashioned' in the light of the grand heroic gesture of the 1916 Rising, Yeats invokes the different temporal frameworks of history at play in his own work—historical acts, current events, and the sense of posterity claimed by future memory. Even as he time-stamps the poem 'September 1913' and thus broadens its reference to the state of the nation at a particular historical moment, Yeats talks back to the assumptions of historical thinking and writing. The note attached to his group of 'Gallery' poems recognizes that events have overtaken the poem.

The central question of the poem, 'Was it for this?', time-travels in a different direction. When Yeats asked this question, the men of the 1916 Rebellion had not yet risen or been executed. However, as I have discussed elsewhere, Yeats's 'Was it for this?' has become detached from the social, cultural, and political controversies of 1913.[26] Instead, it has become affixed to the Rising itself and to the anticipated future proclaimed in the GPO to which we now turn. As in 'September 1913', a poem ostensibly about a gallery that doesn't exist and paintings that never appear, Yeats approaches the Rising with his own set of coordinates.

WAS IT NEEDLESS DEATH AFTER ALL?

Yeats's 'Easter, 1916' is ambiguously attached to the historical event it describes. The historical, the poetic, and the political meet in a poem that has become a barometer not just of literary responses to Yeats but also of political responses to the Rising itself.

---

[23] John O'Leary, *Recollections of Fenians and Fenianism*, Vol. I (London: 1896; repr. Irish University Press, 1969), 32.

[24] This group is comprised of 'To a Wealthy Man', 'September 1913', 'To a Friend whose Work has come to Nothing', 'Paudeen', and 'To a Shade'.

[25] *VP*, 820.

[26] See my *Heroic Revivals* (London: Palgrave Macmillan, 2012), 141–7, and 'News that Stays New: The Future Life of W. B. Yeats', in *Poetry Ireland Review*, 116 (Fall 2015), 183–92.

Yeats's words conjure up the date, the setting, the players, the transformation, as well as the questions and doubts, the memory, and the names inscribed in history. Better known for its refrain than its questions, the poem is a meditation on time, change, and the transformative effect of this violent event on Irish history and memory. According to Edna Longley, 'Irish history can prevent a poem from making history in its own way. Yeats's "Easter, 1916" remains live history and live poetry, because it qualifies commemoration, because it doubts its bardic duty.'[27] However, as I suggested at the outset, if we turned to Yeats's poem as our only source of information or evidence about the 1916 Rising, we would have a very idiosyncratic sense of what happened. The ambiguity of the refrain, 'A terrible beauty is born', is matched by a curious lack of historical specificity which underscores Yeats's equivocal response to the event.

Textual scholars focus attention on the two dates that frame Yeats's poem—Easter 1916 (the event) and 25 September 1916 (the date of the poem's completion).[28] As every Irish schoolchild knows, the rebels chose Easter for their uprising because of its symbolic and religious overtones of resurrection, renewal, and rebirth. For an event that is both fixed as the moment when Ireland declared independence and flexible in terms of the myths and meanings that have been attached to it in the subsequent century, it is appropriate that Easter is a 'moveable feast', that is an annual religious event celebrated on a different date every year. (In fact, Easter won't fall on 24 April again until the year 2095.)

The poem also uniquely encodes the date of the Rising (24 April 1916 or 24/4/16) in its very form of four stanzas alternating between sixteen and twenty-four lines. Helen Vendler notes that Yeats does not use alternating stanza lengths in any other poem and goes on to say,

> As far as we know, Yeats never mentioned the poem's emblematic form: it was his own secret, long unobserved, like his other structural inventions. He must have felt that embedding the date of the Rising in his poem about it guaranteed the fit of the work to its subject.[29]

Vendler points out that such a complex historical event is beyond the expected scope of lyric poetry and praises Yeats's expansive inclusion of the characters, phases, and abstract symbols that make the Rising intelligible in the schema of the poem. Yet what of the idea that Yeats's aim is to 'fit the work to its subject?' How does this lyric poem represent the event it describes?

'Easter, 1916' (*CW1*, 180–2) is the opposite of a site-specific piece—indeed, it is a remarkably site-unspecific poem. Despite the prominence of the event in the title of the poem, it does not include any of the locations or buildings that are still so prominent

---

[27] Edna Longley, 'An ABC of Reading Contemporary Irish Poetry', in *Princeton University Library Chronicle*, LIX:3, (Spring, 1998) 517–45.

[28] See in particular Grene, *Yeats's Poetic Codes*, 14–20, and Matthew Campbell, 'Dating "Easter, 1916"', *International Yeats Studies*, Vol. 1, Article 7 (2016), https://doi.org/10.34068/.01.01.06.

[29] Helen Vendler, *Our Secret Discipline* (Oxford: Oxford University Press, 2007), 25.

in the historic national imaginary. The narrative of the Rising is embedded in the buildings anchoring each phase—the march from Liberty Hall to the GPO, the retreat from Dublin Castle to City Hall, the tenements in Moore Street where Pearse surrendered, the hasty trials in Richmond Barracks and the stonebreakers' yard in Kilmainham Gaol. Remarkably, the Rising's most important building, the GPO, appears nowhere in the poem. Absent too is that other vital location—Kilmainham Gaol—where the rebels were executed just over a week after their surrender. Given the historical, even emotional, significance that has accrued in these locations in the century since the Rising happened, it is extraordinary that they are absent as landmarks in Yeats's poem. Yeats expects his readers to know what happened and where it happened and charts instead his own shifting opinion of the participants and his doubts about the efficacy of their sacrifice.

For Yeats, the Rising is personal before it is political—his letters to Lady Gregory express his fear that 'all the work of years has been overturned', and to John Quinn he wonders if he 'could have done anything to turn these young men in some other direction'.[30] The poem opens with an assertion of Yeats's own presence ('I have met them at close of day') as he strolls around the city. The 'grey eighteenth-century houses' of the first stanza obviously indicate that the setting is Georgian Dublin, but the only building mentioned is 'the club' where Yeats escapes with his mocking tales while those with the 'vivid faces' remain outdoors and outsiders.

It is worth pausing to note the two locations (Normandy and Coole Park) and the two women (Maud Gonne and Lady Gregory) who accommodated Yeats while he conceived and finished the poem. Yeats began to work on the poem in the summer of 1916 at Maud Gonne's house in France after proposing to her once more in the wake of her husband's execution. Ben Levitas points out that Maud Gonne's house in Normandy was 'closer to the Western Front than to Sackville Street' and reminds us that when Yeats proposed again to Gonne on 1 July 1916, the Battle of the Somme was raging only 150 miles away.[31] Yet the Somme, the war, and the political context for the rebellion itself are hidden from view in Yeats's most public poem. Hidden too is the turmoil of Yeats's personal circumstance after failing to convince Gonne or her daughter Iseult to marry him. Describing Yeats's dejection on his return to Coole, James Pethica convincingly argues that Lady Gregory's opinions, letters, and writings on the Rising are in the ascendant when Yeats completes and dates the poem 25 September 1916.[32] The occlusion of these personal and political contexts in the poem itself again signals Yeats's distance from—even antipathy to—documentary history. Indeed, in Lady Gregory's autobiography, she recalls Yeats's comments on her chapter on the Rising:

---

[30] *CL InteLex* #2950 and #2960.

[31] Ben Levitas, 'War 1914–1923', in David Holdeman and Ben Levitas, eds., *W. B. Yeats in Context* (Cambridge: University Press, 2010), 48.

[32] James Pethica, "Easter, 1916' at its Centennial: Maud Gonne, Augusta Gregory and the Evolution of the Poem, *International Yeats Studies*, Vol. 1, Article 5 (2016). Pethica emphasizes the importance of an unpublished essay by Lady Gregory, 'What was their Utopia?', another rhetorical question.

You have given us the most important part of history, its lies. ... I don't believe that events have been shaped so much by the facts as by the lies that people believed about them. ... I was in London during the Rising, I had not foreseen it, though I remember saying, 'Pearse is a dangerous man; he has the vertigo of self-sacrifice.'[33]

Nothing of Pearse's 'vertigo of self-sacrifice' or his revolutionary fervour is represented in the poem. Subsumed under the seven lines devoted to Constance Markievicz, he appears only as the keeper of a school who 'rode our winged horse', an oddly outdated cliché that conveys none of the danger confided to Lady Gregory. Markievicz, as Elizabeth Cullingford has argued, 'stands in' for Maud Gonne in the poem, her femininity lost to political fanaticism and 'ignorant good will'.[34] Grouped together in the descriptive second stanza, Yeats describes but does not name the rebels who have been (passively) transformed by the revolutionary event—'that woman' (Markievicz), 'this man' (Pearse), 'this other' (MacDonagh), and 'this other man' (MacBride). We might not expect to read about all seven signatories of the proclamation, but Connolly is absent until the final stanza, and Clarke, Ceannt, and Plunkett are not named at all. Although John MacBride is 'numbered in the song' and 'transformed utterly', since the transfiguration remains unrealized it is as a 'drunken vainglorious lout' that he is remembered.[35] In fact none of the unnamed figures seem equal to the task of the heroic gesture that has transformed them and the Ireland they would create. Their instability as heroic figures is heightened by the strategies of displacement (Markievicz for Gonne), omission (Clarke, Ceannt, and Plunkett), and deferral (the heroic names) underpinning the poem.

This disorientation is heightened in the third stanza, in which Yeats abandons the urban present of the Rising for an unspecified time and place. Here, he meditates on the opposing claims of the 'stone' of 'one purpose' and the flux of living things—horse, rider, birds, moorhens, and moorcocks. The implacability of the stone is contrasted to the mutability of the changing clouds and the vulnerability of living things, 'Minute by minute they live: / The stone's in the midst of all'. Maud Gonne herself objected to the stone, and remembered that Yeats 'implored [her] to forget the stone and its inner fire for the flashing, changing joy of life'.[36] Of the draft that Yeats sent shortly after the execution of her husband, John MacBride, she wrote, 'My dear Willie, No, I don't like your poem, it isn't worthy of you & above all it isn't worthy of the subject ... you who

---

[33] Lady Isabella Augusta Gregory, *Seventy Years:1852–1922*, ed. Colin Smythe (Gerrards Cross: Colin Smythe, 1974), 549.

[34] Elizabeth Butler Cullingford, *Gender and History in Yeats's Love Poetry* (Cambridge: Cambridge University Press, 1993), 121–5. Declan Kiberd also argues that ' "Easter, 1916" is a covert love-lyric, written to soften an unrelenting woman', in *Inventing Ireland* (London: Jonathan Cape, 1995), 214. For Terence Brown, 'Though she is not mentioned in the poem, in several complex, even confusing ways, Gonne is a presiding spirit in "Easter, 1916" ', *The Life of W. B. Yeats*, (Dublin: Gill & Macmillan, 2001), 229.

[35] Yeats's support for Maud Gonne after the breakdown of her marriage (and initiation of divorce proceedings) informs his continued antipathy to MacBride here.

[36] Maud Gonne, 'An Account of Yeats', cited in *Life 2*, 62.

have studied philosophy & know something of history know quite well that sacrifice has never yet turned a heart to stone though it has immortalized many.'[37]

The stone remains immovable in the turn from the third to the fourth and final stanza, separating the half-rhyme of 'sacrifice' and 'suffice' in the poem's first question:

> Too long a sacrifice
> Can make a stone of the heart.
> O when may it suffice?

These four questions—'O when may it suffice?', 'What is it but nightfall?', 'Was it needless death after all?', 'And what if excess of love / Bewildered them till they died?'—undercut the poem's final capitulation to the ritualistic naming of the dead, 'as a mother names her child'. The heroic status of the rebels is troubled (mirroring the poem's other most important verb, 'changed') by these questions interrogating the deed and the motivation of the dead. Of the four questions, the final two reach out or talk back beyond the frame-work of the poem—was this rebellion necessary to win Ireland's freedom and does it matter if the rebels were motivated or 'bewildered' by nationalist fervour? The ambi-guity of the final question, 'what if?', asking either 'is it possible that?' or 'what does it matter?', heightens the uncertainty of the speaker as he verbalizes these doubts before the final drum roll of the poem. Yeats's doubts about the 'bewilderment' of unthinking nationalism remain to trouble his own conscience in the last years of his life.

In the years since his death, Yeats has been much mocked for this self-aggrandizing question.

Did that play of mine send out / Certain men the English shot?

With Paul Muldoon, we might chorus, 'Certainly not!', but Yeats's sense of responsibility is not merely (or even crassly) rhetorical.[38] The question has become a litmus test for the hotly debated relationship between art and historical action, confirming Yeats's belief in the power of his art to effect historical change. The power of *Cathleen ni Houlihan* as theatrical spectacle is largely attributed to the Old Woman's call to blood sacrifice and its transformational power—'They shall be remembered forever, the people shall be speaking of them forever.' Clair Wills notes that George Morrison's 1959 film *Mise Eire* intercuts photographs of Yeats and Pearse, 'suggesting in visual form the standard line that Yeats's *Cathleen ni Houlihan* had acted as a catalyst for revolutionary action'.[39]

---

[37] Maud Gonne MacBride, *Always Your Friend. The Gonne-Yeats Letters*, ed. Anna MacBride White and A. Norman Jeffares (London: Hutchinson, 1992), 384.

[38] Paul Muldoon, '7, Middagh Street', in *Poems 1968–1998* (New York: Farrar, Straus & Giroux, 2001), 178.

[39] Clair Wills, *Dublin 1916: The Siege of the GPO* (London, Profile Books, 2010), 195.

Yet, despite the widespread testimony to what Nicholas Grene calls the 'kinetic' impact of *Cathleen ni Houlihan*, no one really believes that Yeats or his play caused the Easter Rising.[40] Moreover, the question itself becomes more mundane when read alongside another from the same poem, 'Could my spoken words have checked / That whereby a house lay wrecked?'[41] Written in 1938, a few months before his death, 'Man and the Echo' manipulates repetition and circularity in its subject matter and form (rhyming couplets), suggesting that Yeats is playing with the causation conundrum he raises in the poem.

Rather than rehearsing again the vexed question about cause and effect in history and art, I want to turn now to Yeats's staging of what I have called 'time-stamped' history in *Cathleen ni Houlihan*. The play invokes a real historical event (the 1798 rebellion) and real places (Killala, Ballina, Enniscrone) alongside the mystical transformation of the Old Woman into a young girl 'with the walk of a queen' offstage.[42] Maud Gonne has long been considered the authorizing figure of the play, her performance as Cathleen making the final transformation of the Old Woman not only credible but possible.[43] Patrick Pearse describes his own credulity as typical: 'When I was a child, I believed in the actual existence of a woman called Erin and had Mr. Yeats's 'Kathleen ni Houlihan' been then written and had I seen it, I should have taken it not as an allegory, but as a representation of a thing that might happen any day in any house.'[44] Writing in 1916, Pearse imagines himself into the 1902 audience of the play (when he was 22) as a child. His desire to bridge the gap between his childlike belief and his adult recognition of allegorical meaning is achieved by temporal compression. Pearse's tenses work hard to position *Cathleen ni Houlihan* in the nationalist historical trajectory from 1798 to 1916, and to remove it from the frame of the proscenium arch. He wants it to function as a 'proclamation' rather than a play.

This tension between proclamation (as historical action) and play (as dramatic event) informs the historiography of the Rising itself. From William Irwin Thompson's 1966 book *The Imagination of an Insurrection* through Declan Kiberd's 1995 *Inventing Ireland*[45] to Roy Foster's discussion of play-acting in his 2014 *Vivid Faces: The*

---

[40] Nicholas Grene, *The Politics of Irish Drama* (Cambridge: Cambridge University Press, 1999), 69–70. Grene quotes Lennox Robinson's statement that the play (along with Lady Gregory's *The Rising of the Moon*) 'made more rebels in Ireland than a thousand political speeches or a hundred reasoned books', as well as George Bernard Shaw's reaction, 'When I see that play I feel it might lead a man to so something foolish'; and Grene concludes, 'Again and again the testimony was to the extraordinary kinetic impact of the play'.

[41] *CW1*, 345.

[42] See my *Heroic Revivals*, 123–7.

[43] See Antoinette Quinn, "*Cathleen ni Houlihan* Writes Back: Maud Gonne and Irish National Theatre", in Anthony Bradley and Maryann Gialanella Valiulis, eds., *Gender and Sexuality in Modern Ireland* (Amherst: University of Massachusetts Press and American Conference for Irish Studies, 1997), 39–59. See also, Elizabeth Brewer Redwine, *Gender, Performance, and Authorship at the Abbey Theatre* (Oxford: Oxford University Press, 2021), 18–52.

[44] Patrick H. Pearse, *Political Writings and Speeches* (Dublin: Talbot Press, 1952), 300–1.

[45] Colm Tóibín's 1996 review of Kiberd's *Inventing Ireland* vehemently rejects this treatment of the Rising as text: 'Kiberd is prepared to treat the Rising in the terms in which some of its leaders sought

Revolutionary Generation in Ireland 1890–1923, the Rising is consistently described as a form of street theatre:

> The Rising is often called a revolution of poets; in fact playwrights and actors were far more prominent. Appropriately, when the insurrection broke out, several people mistook the manoeuvres for street theatre; Constance Markievicz was asked by passers-by at Liberty Hall if she was rehearsing a play for children, and Joseph Holloway, encountering a copy of the 'Proclamation of the Irish republic', took it at first for a playbill.[46]

As Foster's book demonstrates, the revolutionary generation were people of vision, energy, and naïve idealism. They wrote plays, founded theatres, edited papers and journals, as well as teaching and organizing cultural events. The artist Sarah Purser observed that they were all like a stage army marching round and round, acting every part required of them. Nevertheless, they also numbered political activists and military strategists within their ranks. Lionel Pilkington points out that the persistent comparison of the Rising to theatre serves both to denigrate it and to erase its radical elements. Certainly, then as now, comparing these rebels and activists to a 'stage army' and reading the Rising as street theatre only carries us as far as opening night. When the curtain rises on Easter Monday 1916 and, more importantly, descends on the offstage executions just over a week later, it is harder to interpret the event as a 'casual comedy'. The idea persists because of the way in which the historical and the mythological, the spilled blood and the theatrical play-acting, the real First World War and the phony rebellion are juxtaposed in historical and literary accounts of the event.

In fact, the Proclamation of the Republic itself, also omitted from Yeats's poem, is the textual antithesis to 'Easter, 1916' and to *Cathleen ni Houlihan.* Despite the fact that it was mistaken for a playbill and also claims its authority by appealing to the 'dead generations', the proclamation does not display any doubts through ambiguous figures of speech. A proclamation by definition has no question marks. Yeats's poem and the Proclamation share certain performative elements from 'I write it out in a verse' to 'we hereby proclaim the Irish Republic as a Sovereign Independent State', but there is an important distinction between writing and signing in each text. When Yeats bows to the bardic convention of heroic naming, he claims the right to curate the present of the Rising and to guard its future meaning:

> I write it out in a verse–
> MacDonagh and MacBride
> And Connolly and Pearse,

---

to present it. But it was not a text: it involved the burning of buildings, the execution of prisoners, the shooting of soldiers, the murder of civilians. And it also used the idea of theatre and text – Kiberd calls it a performance – to create a cult of violence. I loathe everything about it; every single moment of it'. Colm Tóibín,'Playboys of the GPO', https://www.lrb.co.uk/the-paper/v18/no8/colm-toibin/playboys-of-the-gpo.

[46] Roy Foster, *Vivid Faces: The Revolutionary Generation in Ireland 1890–1923* (Norton, 2014), 112.

> Now and in time to be,
> Wherever green is worn
> Are changed, changed utterly:
> A terrible beauty is born.

But Yeats is not the only custodian of the mythically charged names of the rebels. In nationalist memory, their names are emblazoned as signatories of the Proclamation, which serves also as their death warrant. In other words, the signing of the Proclamation is a performative act only completed on Easter Monday when Pearse reads aloud the document that calls the republic into being. These signatures condemn the rebels to death and convey them to the martyrdom of nationalist memory portrayed by Yeats in 'that play': 'They shall be remembered forever / They shall be alive forever / They shall be speaking forever / The people shall hear them forever' (CW2, 92). The difference between the written signatures and the performed 'signatories' is reflected in the difference between the theatre of history and the Rising as 'play-acting'.

Much attention has been paid in Yeats studies to the delayed publication of 'Easter, 1916' as evidence of Yeats's manipulation of political and historical circumstances to his own advantage. Most provocative is Tom Paulin's 1992 essay 'Yeats's Hunger-strike poem', which connects the publication to the death of Cork Mayor Terence MacSwiney in October 1920, a moment which united nationalist Ireland in the final months of the war of independence.[47] Subsequent scholarship has shown that Yeats was more likely to have held back his 'rebellion poem' to protect the ongoing negotiations about the Lane pictures in deference to Lady Gregory.[48] However, Paulin's interpretation insists on widening the focus from the personal considerations of Yeats and his circle to contemporary political conditions. His attention to McSwiney's death and the timing of Yeats's push to revive his play 'The Revolutionist' at the Abbey releases the poem from the constrictions of the Gallery controversy and into the messy contingency of Yeats's historical moment.

Less noted are the contemporary conditions in which Yeats's poems are read today. A case in point is South African poet Sally-Ann Murray's poem 'Easter 1989', which begins in a Durban classroom in the era of apartheid as the students yawn through the heat and their teacher's lecture on 'Easter, 1916'.[49] Borrowing the language of the third

---

[47] Tom Paulin, 'Yeats's Hunger Strike Poem', in *Minotaur: Poetry and the Nation State* (Cambridge, MA: Harvard University Press, 1992), 134.

[48] Yeats wrote to Clement Shorter in March 1917, 'Please be very careful with the Rebellion poem. Lady Gregory asked me not to send it you until we had finished our dispute with the authorities about the Lane pictures. She was afraid of it getting about & damaging us & she is not timid' (*CL InteLex* #3204). Matthew Campbell reveals that the Shorter pamphlet was in fact available to read in the British Library since 1917. See Matthew Campbell, 'Dating "Easter, 1916"', *International Yeats Studies*, Vol. 1, Article 7 (2016), https://doi.org/10.34068/.01.01.06.

[49] See Nicholas Meihuizen, '"Easter 1916" in the 1990s: A South African Perspective', in *Tumult of Images: Essays on W. B. Yeats and Politics, Proceedings of the Leiden IASIL Conference: Vol. 3* (Amsterdam and Atlanta, GA: Rodopi, 1995), 211–20. 'Easter 1989' is published as an addendum to this article.

stanza of Yeats's poem, Murray repeats the phrase 'minute by minute' before introducing Sandile Thusi, a prisoner on hunger strike:

> A sky that tumbles the sun,
> a sea that plashes the beach:
> minute by minute Durban
> streams into the room as I speak
> of metaphor and history,
> romantic myths and Irish pride.
> Minute by minute while Sandile
> Thusi dies.

The poem intercuts the privileged setting of the Durban classroom with details about Thusi's life and imprisonment. The Romantic refrain 'A terrible beauty is born' is replaced by blue uniforms, yellow police vans, and a litany of injustice. Thusi's weary mother, caught by the glare of 'press and politics', does not easily release him into the prescribed heroic narrative:

> To murmur his name
> is rash comfort: all must face the danger
> that this awkward fame
> may fashion for the cause a martyred stranger.

Throughout 'Easter 1989', Murray implicitly challenges the idea that heroic sacrifice is transformative in the manner of Yeats's poem. She cuts through 'the mess of history' in order to acknowledge the minute by minute of the here and now streaming into the room. The poem ends, 'But what has changed so utterly? The students ask. / Yeats has no real answers for the class'.

What historical knowledge or experience of history do we expect from Yeats, given that his poetry never allows history to settle into a stable literary form? Yeats's work acknowledges the shifting terrains of perspective, mediation, and mood that make up what any particular moment in time was, is, or will be. His work floats free of the temporal and spatial markers of conventional history in order to question the certainties of his own time and to fashion our future memory of these events. If it is true that we do not go to Yeats for history, then it is also true that we do not go to Yeats for answers. Instead, we would do better to ask another important Yeatsian question, '*What then cried Plato's ghost? What then?*'[50]

---

[50] *CW1*, 302.

CHAPTER 14

....

'KNIGHTS OF THE AIR'

Yeats, flight and modernity

....

FRAN BREARTON

Set all your mind upon the steep ascent …

W. B. Yeats[1]

Those magnificent men in their flying machines …

Ron Goodwin[2]

IN the summer of 1927, a young American named Horace Reynolds visited Ireland, determined, as Roy Foster puts it, to 'plumb literary Dublin to its depths'. Reynolds attached himself to Oliver St John Gogarty and 'indefatigably transcribed his impressions into a diary'.[3] Later, he also records some of those experiences in his introductory essay to Gogarty's 1933 *Selected Poems*. In particular, he describes a hair-raising drive to the west with Gogarty in a 'shell-shaped Mercedes, all yellow hood and mahogany trimmings, shiningly sinister', in which Gogarty averaged 70–80 miles an hour down narrow country lanes. 'I had seen my share', writes Reynolds, 'of the speed that is born of gasoline and gin, but never had I such a ride.'[4] During the road trip to and from Renvyle in Connemara, Gogarty regaled him with tales of his numerous acquaintances, spoke of his ambition to travel to his Loch Tully island by seaplane, and talked much of Yeats. 'Gogarty loves to peer into the folds of Yeats's mind,' Reynolds tells us, 'and he loves particularly to excite him into action':

'I decided to take Yeats swimming,' said Gogarty, 'but in order to stir Yeats out of dream into action, I must appeal to his imagination. So I talked of the swimming match of

---

[1] 'A Dialogue of Self and Soul', *CW1*, 234.
[2] 'Those Magnificent Men in their Flying Machines', words and music by Ron Goodwin; arr Gwyn Arch. (1966; Faber Music Ltd, 2006).74
[3] *Life 2*, 340.
[4] Horace Reynolds, 'Gogarty in the Flesh', in Oliver St. John Gogarty, *Selected Poems* (New York: Macmillan, 1933), xxv.

Beowulf and Breca, of Swinburne's love of mixing with "the great sweet mother",
"Clothed with the green and crowned with the foam"; of Byron's fondness for bathing
in the jasper sea. And his imagination thus excited, Yeats reluctantly agreed to go.'

He did not, however, succeed in his ambition to get Yeats on horseback:

> 'I knew,' said Gogarty, 'that if I could get Yeats on a horse I could put a new rhythm
> into English lyric verse.' And so he began to speak of the noble and benevolent
> Marcus Aurelius, who rides in bronze on the Capitoline Hill . . . of the Centaurs, who
> thundered headlong down the roadway of excess – surrounding horseback riding
> with the tradition that Yeats loves to see about the things he does and thinks of. Again
> Yeats succumbed, but this time Mrs Yeats put her foot down. New rhythm or no, she
> was not going to allow her famous husband to get on a horse.[5]

Both tales of Yeats pave the way for Gogarty's update to Reynolds six years later. Meeting
him in Cambridge, Massachusetts, when Gogarty came to give a lecture at Harvard,
Reynolds tells us:

> Of course he had a new story about Yeats; baffled by Mrs Yeats's watchfulness in his plan
> to put Yeats upon a horse, he had succeeded in taking him up in his plane, for Gogarty
> is now a licensed pilot and, his Mercedes garaged, he now wings his way to the West,
> singing, like the beautiful Swan-Children of Lir. He had taken up A.E. too, but that had
> necessitated a new safety strap – 'the ordinary strap was too small for the God'.[6]

The story, with slight variation, is repeated in Ulick O'Connor's 1964 biography of
Gogarty: 'he [Gogarty] was enthusiastic about his new hobby and tried to induce his
friends to take part in it. Yeats was taken up in an aeroplane and so was A.E. A problem
was, would A.E.'s beard have to fit inside or outside his air helmet? Loyally, Gogarty
never revealed the precise fate of his friend's whiskers when subjected to the hazards
of flying gear.'[7] It is never, to my knowledge, mentioned by Yeats, and the temptation
to consider it a tall tale is reinforced by Reynolds himself, who, although he repeats the
story in apparent good faith, also tells us at the outset that Gogarty was introduced to
him as 'Dublin's arch-mocker', that he was the 'crowned arch-ollave of joke and jest'.[8]
AE's essay for the same volume—'The Poetry of my Friend'—also describes Gogarty as
having 'the wildest wit in Ireland from which nothing in heaven or earth was immune,
though often I had reverence for the things he assailed'.[9] That wit might account for
the mischief, the affectionate mockery inherent in both accounts, and the jokes at AE's

[5] Ibid., xxviii–xxx.
[6] Ibid., xxxi.
[7] Ulick O'Connor, *Oliver St John Gogarty: A Poet and his Times* (1964; Dublin: O'Brien Press, 2000),
229. The source appears to be a verbal anecdote, told to the biographer by Gogarty or one of his friends/
family.
[8] Reynolds, 'Gogarty in the Flesh', xv.
[9] A.E. (George Russell), 'The Poetry of my Friend', in Gogarty, *Selected Poems*, ix.

expense. Surely (unless the strap had been on the helmet) the anecdotal inconsistency here renders the details potentially as mischievous as the story itself. (One might also note, however, that AE doesn't appear to have contradicted the tale as told in a book to which he contributed.[10])

Although the notion that Yeats was persuaded to take a spin in Gogarty's plane, sometime between 1928 and 1932, appears somewhat fantastical in its improbability, it is by no means impossible; nor was an informal trying-out of flight in this period so unusual. Yeats's serious illnesses in the winters of 1928–9 and 1929–30, along with the months spent in Rapallo, might seem to militate against the likelihood of such a venture.[11] (If Yeats never flew, his temporary cat in Rapallo—he describes it as 'white . . . with a very fluffy tail and blue eyes'—certainly did: its permanent owner brought it initially to Rapallo by aeroplane, thereby, Yeats notes, avoiding Italian customs.[12]) On the other hand, and on either side of those illnesses, there are the many weeks spent at Renvyle or Coole—or indeed in Dublin—often without the watchful presence of Mrs George Yeats to foil any aerial plan. That might also account for Yeats's never mentioning the experience, although there is also perhaps no reason why he should have done so anyway: his experience of motor car travel was relatively early—referenced in 1908 but more probably dating back to his American tour in 1903–4—yet never a matter of note. By the mid to late 1930s, flight too was a more usual form of travel for those who could afford it, and one he notes as an option (seemingly for George, not himself) in 1937.[13] Gogarty, by the end of 1928, was a prolific flier, who had flown himself to Paris for an overnight stop; to London and back 'to perform operations in London hospitals', sometimes in the same day; from Dublin to the west of Ireland—for the most part without incident.[14] Only on a flight with Lady Heath from Renvyle to Galway, Lady Heath having decided to stop for a bathe at Thallabawn Strand, Co. Mayo, did they become temporarily stranded in the quicksands.[15] Added to an early morning horse-ride along Sandymount Strand were early morning visits to Baldonnel aerodrome, where friends in the Irish Air Force, many of whom had served in the Royal Flying Corps, would oblige him with a quick gallop across the skies too.[16] He believed flying to be good for one's physical health and

---

[10] I am grateful to Edna Longley, Peter McDonald, and Warwick Gould for their advice on Yeats, planes, and automobiles. Errors, assumptions, and speculations are my own.

[11] For a discussion of his illness and Rapallo, see *Life 2*, 378–401.

[12] W. B. Yeats, 'To Oliver St John Gogarty', 20 Mar. 1930. *CL Intelex* #5338.

[13] Yeats, telegram to George Yeats, 21 June 1937: 'Does McCartan return home at once if so wire go to Dublin by aeroplane and return to rehearse broadcast would see Doctor first. YEATS.' *CL Intelex* #6975.

[14] See O'Connor, *Oliver St John Gogarty*, 228–9.

[15] Lady Heath was piloting her light aeroplane; in this apparently 'thrilling experience' they were assisted by fishermen; and the plane, which was sinking, was pulled to 'a patch of solid strand 100 yards away'. 'Landed on Quicksands', *The Liberator (Tralee)*, Tue., 4 September 1928, 6; On Lady Heath see also n. 29 below. Thallabawn Strand and Mweelrea have a rather more poetic presence in the work of Michael Longley.

[16] See O'Connor, *Oliver St John Gogarty*, 229–30. O'Connor also here notes that in the 1930s Gogarty 'landed and killed a sheep'. Baldonnel aerodrome was first established in 1917 and used by the RFC; it then became (and remains) an Irish Air Force base; it was renamed Casement Aerodrome in honour of Roger Casement in 1965.

espoused this view, along with the other virtues of flying, in AE's *Irish Statesman* in 1927–8.[17] And, in August 1928, Gogarty was the proposer of the new Irish Aero Club—which was described by meeting chair Col. J. C. Fitzmourice as 'the first step in the development of civil aviation in the Irish Free State'.[18]

The Irish Aero Club was set up in part to capitalize on the fact that, when the British 'vacated Ireland', they 'left behind … a large number of first-class aerodromes'; but even more to capitalize on Ireland's 'geographical position' (the 'real and natural route of communication by air to America was from Ireland to Newfoundland and down the coast to New York'). Flying was also viewed as a 'sport' in which Irish youth (the Christy Mahons of the future) could and should excel, alongside their proven skills in horse riding and motor racing. It was also posited that Ireland–America air travel might redress some of the economic deprivation in the west of Ireland.[19] Demand for Aero Club flights far exceeded the number which could be offered; dozens trained for 'A' pilot licences; and in a February 1932 progress report it was noted that in the previous nine months alone, 'approximately 4000 flights' were made 'without the slightest accident', and 'more than 2000 people from all over the Free State' had flown that year.[20] Pathé News footage showed Osmond Grattan Esmonde, the Cumman na nGaedheal TD, on an Aero Club inaugural flight piloted by Captain Crossley in January 1929.[21] President Cosgrave, who had flown once or twice already in Army machines, took a lift to Cork and back in the new Gypsy Moth which had been acquired by Esmonde in April 1929.[22] Irish aviators, including J. P. Saul (navigator for the first east–west Atlantic crossing, from Baldonnel to Labrador in April 1928[23]), attended Mussolini's 'International Conference of Transatlantic Aviators' in Rome, in the spring of 1932.[24] A brief check on these years of aviation enthusiasm, and the end of the Irish Aero Club's hundred per cent safety record came only in 1933 when a Gypsy Moth on an evening pleasure flight, piloted by ex-RFC officer Major Dunckley, and with a London commercial traveller on board, fell into the sea at Dalkey.[25]

This is to suggest that although the Irish literary and cultural revival had been described at one time as possessing 'certain ardent ideas and high attitudes of mind which were the nation itself',[26] by the late 1920s it possessed a certain amount of

---

[17] See O'Connor, *Oliver St John Gogarty*, 233–4, and Nicholas Allen, *George Russell (AE) and the New Ireland, 1905–30* (Dublin: Four Courts Press, 2003), 222–3.

[18] 'New Irish Aero Club', *Drogheda Independent*, Saturday, 25 August 1928, 5.

[19] Ibid.

[20] 'Flying in Free State', *Irish Press*, Tuesday, 16 February 1932, 4.

[21] https://www.britishpathe.com/video/irish-aero-club-1 (accessed 26 June 2020).

[22] 'Mr Cosgrave to Fly to Cork', *Irish Times*, 24 April 1929, 7; 'Aeroplanes in the Free State', *Irish Times*, Wednesday, 17 April 1929, 5.

[23] https://www.irishtimes.com/opinion/april-13th-1928-the-first-east-west-atlantic-crossing-by-air-1.744179 (accessed 1 July 2020).

[24] https://timeandnavigation.si.edu/research/the-transoceanic-fliers-conference-of-1932 (accessed 1 July 2020).

[25] Both pilot and passenger died in the crash. 'Two Victims of Irish Air Disaster', *Irish Independent*, 25 May 1933, 9.

[26] *CW4*, 181.

'air-mindedness' and a high altitude of mind too. 'Flying in Free State' was neither metaphor nor existential condition, but a typical newspaper headline and a lived experience—and with a complex imperialist versus nationalist politics attached. AE, bearded mystic, had by the end of the 1920s, as Nicholas Allen observes, 'developed an obsession with the possibility of Ireland's becoming a flight centre for the developing aviation industry', seeing in the development of Europe–America flights from 1927 onwards 'a means by which even the remotest parts of the Free State might be exposed to global influence'.[27] That *The Candle of Vision* (1918) author was also a keeper of the aviation flame was recognized in Russell's 'enormous public funeral', which included 'aeroplane fly-pasts and a mile-long procession'.[28] (The 'small fleet of aeroplanes rising & dipping in salute' were, Yeats tells us, those of 'Lady Heath & her pupils: the devotion of the sinner to the poet even when the poet is a saint'.[29]) But apart from a fleeting enthusiasm for motor racing shown in 1929, largely because of his interest in Mussolini (there were Italian cars in the race and, according to Lennox Robinson, Yeats was 'as excited as a boy that Italy should win'),[30] Yeats, unsurprisingly, shows no interest in the growing air-mindedness of the 1920s, either in life or literature. Unlike Gogarty, who embraced the new and the modern, and unlike many other modernist and futurist writers who delighted in this new technology of flight (among them, and most obviously perhaps, Marinetti, who 'foregrounds the automobile and the aeroplane as experiential models for describing new artistic forms'[31]), Yeats eschewed the presence of technology in his poetry, even if he did not find it personally abhorrent. Asked if the machine should feature in poetry, his answer was unequivocal:

> Nothing new is good as a subject for poetry. The spade is ancient; it has become a symbol. But the sewing-machine has not had time to become a symbol. ... [T]he substance of poetry is a mass of symbol which has been passed on from age to age, slightly enlarged, but only slightly, as time goes on. It is a slow process because human experience is capable of taking in only a little at a time. In three or four generations perhaps, the machine may be a proper subject for poetry ....[32]

---

[27] Allen, *George Russell (AE)*, 222.

[28] Frances Flanagan, *Remembering the Irish Revolution: Dissent, Culture, and Nationalism in the Irish Free State* (Oxford: Oxford University Press, 2015), 123.

[29] WBY to Dorothy Wellesley, 26 July 1935; *CL InteLex* #6300. The 'scandalous aviatrix' (*Life* 2, 524), Lady Mary Heath, whom Yeats had met, and who was Ireland's foremost female flier in the latter half of the 1920s, was suffering some moral reputational decline at this point, as Yeats's letter goes on to show: 'She once came to me to borrow the Abbey Theatre to get up some performance for the entertainment of her pupils. A woman friend commented "not her pupils — O no — her lovers." I said "Impossible she cannot have 300 lovers." The answer was "You dont [*sic*] know her. She can easy".'

[30] *Life 2*, 390.

[31] Alex Goody, *Technology, Literature and Culture* (Cambridge: Polity Press, 2011), 16.

[32] Yeats, interview with Louise Morgan [1931], repr. in E. H. Mikhail, ed., *Interviews and Recollections* (London: Macmillan, 1977), vol. 2, 201.

(The year before Reynolds was disturbed by Gogarty's 'shiningly sinister' Mercedes, Yeats had famously recorded the 'nightmare' in which he was 'haunted by a sewing-machine, that clicked and shone'.)[33]

And yet, alone of his Revival or air-minded contemporaries, Yeats has had an influential afterlife in the world of flight literature because of a single poem, the elegy for Robert Gregory 'An Irish Airman Foresees His Death', written in the last year of the First World War. He featured in the 1938 anthology *Icarus: An Anthology of Poems about Flight*; the poem is often identified as a 'classic', alongside World War II fighter pilot John Gillespie Magee's 'High Flight'; it is frequently included in war anthologies alongside other 'flying corps' poems; and it has a lively, sometimes unlikely, internet aviation presence.[34] 'An Irish Airman', as a relatively early example of aviation poetry, is one of the few in the subgenre written in first person without direct experience of flight; its elements can be traced back to long-standing Yeatsian aesthetic principles; and its legacy is visible in the poetry of flying which followed—particularly in the 1930s and early 1940s:

> I know that I shall meet my fate
> Somewhere among the clouds above;
> Those that I fight I do not hate,
> Those that I guard I do not love;
> …
> Nor law, nor duty bade me fight,
> Nor public man, nor cheering crowds,
> A lonely impulse of delight
> Drove to this tumult in the clouds;
> I balanced all, brought all to mind,
> The years to come seemed waste of breath,
> A waste of breath the years behind
> In balance with this life, this death.[35]

The poem, as I have argued elsewhere, is stylistically distinguished from those poems in which we see what Yeats called the 'quarrel with ourselves' as central to their diction and syntax. In its balanced tetrameter, perfect rhymes, end-stopped lines, and reliance on monosyllabism, 'An Irish Airman' suggests, if deceptively, a surface clarity and simplicity—along with a certainty of 'vision' and an absence of internal conflict. It is driven by what it doesn't say as much as by what it does—and its expression in the negative (in the repeated 'do not', 'nor') already indicates as much: the 'all' that is

---

[33] *CW3*, 222.

[34] See Rupert de la Bère et al., eds., *Icarus: An Anthology of the Poetry of Flight* (London: Macmillan, 1938); Helmut H. Reda, ed., *Because I Fly: A Collection of Aviation Poetry* (New York: McGraw Hill, 2002); Brian Gardner, ed., *Up the Line to Death: The War Poets 1914–1918* (1964; London: Methuen, 1976); I. M. Parsons, ed., *Men Who March Away; Poems of the First World War* (1965; London: Chatto & Windus, 1987). See also https://www.wingsofwar.org/forums/showthread.php?4843-Aviation-Poems or https://sierrahotel.net/pages/aviation-poetry (accessed 8 July 2020).

[35] *CW1*, 135.

'brought ... to mind' is left unspoken. 'An Irish Airman' elides Gregory's politics, which were antithetical to Yeats's own: Gregory's hostility to Sinn Fein is transmuted instead into a localized altruism towards Kiltartan's 'poor'; by implication, as Foster notes, the poem also attributes to Gregory 'an alienation from empire for which there is little evidence'.[36] It negates Gregory's apparent enthusiasm for the war: he joined the 4th Connaught Rangers in 1915—a volunteer at the age of 34—and transferred to the Royal Flying Corps the following January, telling Bernard Shaw that his six months at the flying station 'had been the happiest of his life'.[37] James Pethica notes that he had 'come close to signing up immediately after the start of the war on 4 August 1914', but that in the end he was precipitated into doing so in September 1915 because of an 'explosive personal drama' (an extramarital affair with the artist Nora Summers) and its 'fallout'.[38] Either way, elision in 'An Irish Airman' seems to be—whether from personal discretion or felt political necessity on Yeats's part—the order of the day.

There are some other subtle absences in this poem too (one of them a plane). Terence Brown has perceptively argued that its formal control mirrors the controlled 'exhilaration' of piloting a small plane, with a 'carefully managed rhythmic equilibrium'.[39] But at the same time the poem is also, when compared to the continual movement inherent in Yeats's post-1917 *Vision*, extraordinarily static, holding still as much as it might be read as holding steady. Other aerial poems laud the experience of flight as enabling the pilot's (and poet's) transcendence through an uninhibited freedom of movement: the sky has— or had—no 'borders'. Magee's 1941 'High Flight' opens with 'Oh, I have slipped the surly bonds of Earth / And danced the skies on laughter-silvered wings'; O. C. Chave declares, in another World War II poem, that 'There are no frontiers in the sky'.[40] For Magee, it is the 'untrespassed sanctity of space' that allowed him to touch 'the face of God'. Magee here echoes, as David Pascoe notes, an earlier poem also in the 1938 *Icarus* anthology, 'The Blind Man Flies' by Cuthbert Hicks—'For I have danced the streets of heaven, / and touched the face of God'[41]—and, indeed, echoes a number of other writers and phrases,

---

[36] *Life* 2, 119.

[37] Colin Smythe, 'Introduction', in *Robert Gregory 1881-1918: A Centenary Tribute*, (Gerrards Cross: Colin Smythe, 1981), 10. Gregory's commanding officer in summer 2016 was Robert Loraine, 'pre-war aviator celebrity and well-known actor' who was a close friend of Shaw's. See Joe Gleeson, *Irish Aces of the RFC and RAF in the First World War: The Lives behind the Legends* (Stroud: Fonthill Media, 2015), 72.

[38] James Pethica, 'Yeats's "perfect man"', *Dublin Review*, Summer 2009, https://thedublinreview.com/article/yeatss-perfect-man/ (accessed 8 July 2020). See also Gleeson, *Irish Aces*, 72–3.

[39] Terence Brown, 'Writing the War', in *Our War: Ireland and the Great War* (Dublin: Royal Irish Academy, 2008), 242.

[40] Both Magee and Chave died in World War II, Magee in an air collision over England in 1941, Chave in operational flying in 1943. The poems are included in Ian Gentle, ed., *Spirit of Flight: Poems of Aviation* (Edinburgh: NMS Publishing, 1999), 46, 16. See also, for further discussion of both poets, Gary Campion, *The Good Fight: Battle of Britain Propaganda and the Few* (Basingstoke: Macmillan, 2009), 294–7.

[41] David Pascoe, 'Warplane', in Adam Piette and Mark Rawlinson, eds., *The Edinburgh Companion to Twentieth-Century British and American War Literature* (Edinburgh: Edinburgh University Press, 2012), 370.

some but not all from the 1938 *Icarus* anthology.[42] Yeats's bedfellows in wartime or aviation anthologies, or online collections, are typically little-known young pilots, many killed in action, for whom it is primarily the experience of flying, the ground-to-air transformation, the awareness of the horizontal as well as vertical axis, that generate the poetic impulse: 'A sudden roar, a mighty rushing sound, / a jolt or two, a smoothly sliding rise / a tumbled blur of disappearing ground …'.[43] But in 'An Irish Airman' the 'flight' is not the experience of flying; rather, it is the flight of the mind, the perspective that brings both past and future, life and death—or as Yeats had it in *A Vision*, premised as it is on dualities, 'reality and justice'[44]—into a single 'thought': invisible gyres (geometric wings?) are captured at the moment of tension where these states intersect, and are projected onto and held within the 'airman'. The air and the breath behind and in front are the 'waste' of air; the body is in metaphorical flight through life but, in the poise of the poem, seemingly suspended infinitely in its revolving gyres.

Robert Gregory's 1915 enlistment meant that Yeats had, perforce, to become rather more conscious both of the Great War's effect on those close to him, and the nature of its aerial warfare, than he would perhaps have chosen to be. As the close of Lady Gregory's autobiography makes clear, she wrote frequently to Yeats from 1916 to 1918 with news about Gregory's air battles, aerodrome inspections, and details of the 'new aeroplanes': 'The machines are single-seated, he will be alone, with a machine gun.'[45] But, with the exception of the later 'Reprisals', all three elegies for Robert Gregory—'An Irish Airman Foresees His Death', 'Shepherd and Goatherd', and 'In Memory of Major Robert Gregory'—almost wilfully, it seems, eliminate any breath of modernity and strive for continuity with Yeats's earlier themes and symbols. 'Shepherd and Goatherd', the stylized pastoral elegy in which Gregory the shepherd, who excelled at 'country sport / And every country craft' and 'died in the great war beyond the sea', possesses a form and diction which might warrant the term 'timeless'; but it might also jar with the reader as anachronistic, not only in elegizing one of the First World War dead with a singing goatherd.[46] 'In Memory of Major Robert Gregory' applauds him as 'our Sidney and our perfect man', but his qualities never lift him out of the century in which he was born (or indeed, the Elizabethan Age) into the one in which he died; nor is there any recognition of his delight in aviation and in the 'companions' of his wartime service. 'Soldier, scholar, horseman, he', Gregory is here in company with Lionel Johnson, J. M. Synge, and George Pollexfen; his implied progenitor is the model gentleman, poet, soldier, and statesman

---

[42] Also in evidence are debts to Wilde, the earlier Yeats, and Hopkins. In addition, for a perceptive, though fictionalized, account of Magee's 'kind of palimpsestic plagiarism that moves through bodies and time', see Ben Lerner's *10:04: A Novel* (London: Granta, 2015).

[43] Jeffery Day, 'On the Wings of the Morning', in Brian Gardner, ed., *Up the Line to Death*, 53. Day was killed in action in 1918. The poem immediately follows 'An Irish Airman Foresees His Death' in the anthology.

[44] *CW14.*

[45] Lady Augusta Gregory, *Seventy Years*, ed. Colin Smythe (Gerrards Cross; Colin Smythe, 1974), 50–1.

[46] *CW1*, 141–2.

Sir Philip Sidney.[47] And in 'An Irish Airman', there is no hint of a machine or aircraft, nor of the harmony between man and machine often referenced by other fliers: Gregory might well be in the 'clouds' of his own volition, since anything other than individual agency and interiorized thought—the 'tumult' of the mind—is cast out. An exhibition of contemporary artistic responses to the poem at the Hamilton Gallery, Sligo, 'An Irish Airman Foresees his Death', marked the hundredth anniversary of the end of the First World War in 2018: although aeroplanes understandably proliferated, several of the artists who responded to the poem depicted only man, or bird, or mythological figure suspended in the air, or descending like Icarus to earth.[48]

As for 'An Irish Airman's' own inspiration, the poem is in dialogue both with the pre-war Yeats and, as so often in this period, with Wordsworth as well as Shelley. The elegy for Lady Gregory's son looks back to Yeats's long 'dramatic poem' 'The Shadowy Waters', dedicated to her in 1906, with its souls in the guise of birds:

> And now they all wheel suddenly and fly
> To the other side, and higher in the air.
> And now a laggard with a woman's head
> Comes crying, 'I have run upon the sword.
> I have fled to my beloved in the air,
> In the waste of the high air, that we may wander
> Among the windy meadow of the dawn.'[49]

The 'waste of the high air' (waste in its sense of 'empty space or untenanted regions of the air') mutates in 'An Irish Airman' from space into time—'the waste of breath' that is past and future; the intense holding of the moment where both become an infinity, yet with the anticipation of 'fate' never realized in the poem itself. Only in 'The Wild Swans at Coole' is that 'balance' disturbed in the self-elegiac anticipation of Yeats's own death: 'I saw, before I had well finished, / All suddenly mount / And scatter wheeling in great broken rings / Upon their clamorous wings.'[50]

The 'lonely impulse of delight' that takes the Irish airman to the clouds is also continuous with the Wordsworth who 'wandered lonely as a cloud / That floats on high o'er vales and hills', and where perspective is vital to the experience, with the speaker able to see 'Ten thousand ... at a glance'.[51] If the 'tumult in the clouds' of Yeats's poem evokes aerial warfare for the reader, through the commotion and confusion most immediately associated with 'tumult', that the term can be associated with strong emotion and particularly with joy is also implied in the 'impulse of delight'. That Wordsworth's daffodils are 'Fluttering and dancing in the breeze' renders them almost birdlike. The essentially Romantic underpinnings to (more derivative) poems about flight—'I ... have

---

[47] *CW1*, 133–5.

[48] *An Irish Airman Foresees His Death*, exhibition catalogue, Hamilton Gallery, Sligo, 2018.

[49] *CW1*, 418.

[50] *CW1*, 131.

[51] William Wordsworth, *Poems, Volume I*, ed. John O. Hayden (London: Penguin, 1977), 619–20.

danced the skies on laughter-silvered wings'—carry echoes of this famous poem's close too: 'And then my heart with pleasure fills, / And dances with the daffodils'. An even more powerful influence on Yeats's 'flight' is Shelley, whose 'Ode to the West Wind' was among Yeats's favourite poems,[52] and whose 'clouds', 'sky's commotion', and 'tumult of ... mighty harmonies' echo in 'An Irish Airman', as does its metaphorically flying poet.[53] The elevation of thought through heightened perspective is a Romantic preoccupation evident in Yeats's imagination too—in what one might term an aesthetics of ascent. Simon Bainbridge reminds us 'how novel and extraordinary a view from 3,000 feet would be for ... Romantic-period climbers, unfamiliar with air-travel, aerial photography ... '.[54] In Shelley's 'Mont Blanc', merely to gaze upon crag and ravine is to 'seem as in a trance sublime', and he was, Bainbridge notes, 'keen to present himself as a mountaineer in both senses of the word', albeit he 'overstated' the case: 'Danger, which sports upon the brink of precipices, has been my playmate. I have trodden the glaciers of the Alps ...'.[55] Climbing enabled poets such as Coleridge, Wordsworth, and Keats ('I will clamber through Clouds and exist') to 'see new things, prospects on an unprecedented scale and colours of unsurpassable beauty. Ascent also produced new ways of seeing ... allied to a disposition on the climber's part for a transformation of vision'. Bainbridge goes on to argue that, for the Romantics, 'A change in altitude could produce a change in the self, and physical elevation could lead to spiritual elevation ... [C]limbing becomes an almost instantaneous means of elevating not only the body but also the soul, a development of the discourse of the sublime'.[56]

The Romantic mountaineering pioneers have something in common with the 'Knights of the Air' who were the early pioneers of flight.[57] Cecil Lewis, a World War I pilot who enlisted in the RFC at the age of 17, makes the link explicitly, in typically romanticized terms: 'Hitherto only gallant men with rope and axe had struggled (challenging the last crazy crags) to attain summits to whose heights we rose daily ... From this exalted eminence we surveyed the earth ...'.[58] In *Mountains of the Mind*, Robert Macfarlane shows some of the ways in which mountains 'have been *imagined* into existence down the centuries'. He notes too that 'What makes mountain-going peculiar among leisure activities is that it demands of some of its participants that they die'—and, moreover, that 'people are willing to die for love of them'.[59] As a 'sport' in

---

[52] Adele M. Dalsimer lists Yeats's most frequently quoted Shelley poems, and notes the claim that Shelley is mentioned seventy-seven times in Yeats's writing—second only to Shakespeare. *The Unappeasable Shadow: Shelley's Influence on Yeats* (1988; Abingdon: Routledge, 2017), 1 n.1.

[53] Percy Bysshe Shelley, *The Major Works*, ed. Zachary Leader and Michael O'Neill (Oxford: Oxford University Press, 2003), 412–14.

[54] Simon Bainbridge, 'Romantic Writers and Mountaineering', *Romanticism*, 18:1 (2012), 1–15, 6

[55] Bainbridge, 'Romantic Writers and Mountaineering', 2; Shelley, 'Mont Blanc', *Major Works*, 120–1.

[56] Bainbridge, 'Romantic Writers and Mountaineering', 3, 6, 7.

[57] See Peter King, *Knights of the Air* (London: Constable, 1989), for a history of the life and times of the early pioneers of aviation and the aviation industry in Britain.

[58] Cecil Lewis, *Sagittarius Rising* (1963), Kindle edn, 85–6.

[59] Robert Macfarlane, *Mountains of the Mind: A History of a Fascination* (London: Granta, 2003), 7, 9.

its early days, a 'leisure activity' (for the wealthy) as much as a commercial, industrial, or military enterprise, the compulsion to fly has also demanded such sacrifice; it is an enterprise where the investment was made as much by the mind as with money. Roland Garros, sportsman turned professional aviator and World War I flying ace, describes the compulsion to fly as the urge 'to live a beautiful adventure, even at the price of death'.[60] Flying became an obsession which also necessitated that some must die, balancing (as, presumably, did Robert Gregory himself) the risk with the reward. As Robert Wohl notes, 'the invention of the airplane was at first perceived by many as an *aesthetic* event with far-reaching implications for the new century's artistic and moral sensibility'. He also points to the 'compulsion that people felt to transform, through the play of their imagination, the most mechanical of events—the invention and development of the flying machine—into a form of spiritual creation'. The 'achievements of aeronautical technology', he emphasizes, 'acted as mere catalysts for an explosion of cultural creativity whose essential elements were already in place ... [T]he Western imagination had already invented the airplane and the aviator long before the Wrights succeeded in making their first machines leave the ground'.[61]

The compulsion towards ascent is evident in Yeats's aesthetic, alongside his being drawn, at particularly intense moments in contemplation of death or apocalypse, to images of flight. Yeats's 'Fisherman' is imagined 'Climbing up to a place / Where stone is dark under froth'; to 'climb' is, as in 'The Tower', associated with 'upstanding young men' who 'inherit my pride'; to 'climb to the tower-top' enables the vision of 'Phantoms of Hatred and of the Heart's Fullness and of the Coming Emptiness'; the 'Chinamen' of 'Lapis Lazuli' 'climb towards' the 'half-way house' and 'There, on the mountain and the sky / On all the tragic scene they stare'; and it is, in 'The Statues', anticipated by 'The Fisherman', 'We Irish ... thrown upon this filthy modern tide' who 'Climb to our proper dark'.[62] The moon, his dreams, and the soul 'take flight' at various points across his oeuvre; flight itself is an elegiac motif, from the 'swallow's flight' and 'aged woman' of 'Coole Park, 1929' to the 'wheeling' birds with 'clamorous wings' who 'climb the air' in 'The Wild Swans at Coole'.[63] The image of the swan in flight is central to his war poem 'Nineteen Hundred and Nineteen', where the soul, like the airman, is poised between two states: 'The wings half spread for flight, / The breast thrust out in pride / Whether to play, or to ride, / Those winds that clamour of approaching night'.[64] In the subsequent 'Meditations in Time of Civil War', indeed, the mechanization creeping into the 'senseless tumult' (his only other use of the word in this 1918–23 period), and the rise of the 'indifferent multitude', compromise the soul's flight with 'innumerable clanging wings that have put out the moon'.[65] In revisiting 'An Irish Airman', both in 'Reprisals'

---

[60] Quoted in Robert Wohl, *A Passion for Wings: Aviation and the Western Imagination 1908–1918* (New Haven and London: Yale University Press, 1994), 207.

[61] Wohl, *A Passion for Wings*, 1–2.

[62] *CW1*, 148, 194, 205, 294, 336.

[63] *CW1*, 242, 131.

[64] *CW1*, 206.

[65] *CW1*, 200.

(of which more anon), and in 'Meditations', 'flight' and 'tumult' show their destructive element too: Yeats's work, like that of his Romantic forebears, informs those 'essential elements' that make up the Western imagination's conception of flight and altitude; but, unlike theirs, it encompasses some awareness post 1918 of how the actuality and potentiality of flight might be other than they were once perceived to be.

Nevertheless, Yeats's 'lonely impulse of delight', while it may have little or nothing to do with the actual logistics of flying and repudiates the 'machine', resonates with the way fliers themselves conceived of, or tried with varying degrees of success between the 1910s and 1940s to articulate, an experience of flight in elevated rather than destructive terms. It is not without irony that the necessary avoidance of politics in 'An Irish Airman', given the complex and conflicting loyalties at work, has become a reason for the poem's influence, and for the perception that Yeats 'captured one of the most elusive aspects of the ace's mentality when he wrote … "Nor Law, nor duty bade me fight, / Nor public men, nor cheering crowds …".'[66] That flight experience is as much one of the mind as of the body, brought into being through centuries' literary imaginings of the body (and soul) in flight. For Cecil Lewis, his RFC enlistment meant he belonged to a 'fellowship of daring and loneliness'.[67] In Jeffery Day's 'On the Wings of Morning', quoted earlier, a poem which contains a plane, an ascent, a descent, and a 'landing ground', he also notes that, once the airman has ascended, 'all sense of motion slowly dies' and 'silence reigns'.[68] Herbert Thompson, a captain in the newly designated RAF in 1918, describes climbing in a Sopwith Triplane to 23,000 feet: 'I was probably the highest person in the world at that moment. … I remember looking at this beautiful blue sky, and singing. I didn't want to come down; I could have stayed up there forever.'[69] For Howard Nemerov, a World War II pilot, the dead in 'The War in the Air' 'stayed away out there / In the clean war, the war in the air … stayed up there in the relative wind, / Shades fading in the mind'; they remain perpetually 'In the air, in the empty air'.[70]

Yeats's general views on the First World War are now notorious enough, from his 1915 suggestion that 'in times like these / A poet's mouth be silent', and his stated intention to 'keep the neighbourhood of the seven sleepers of Ephesus, hoping to catch their comfortable snores till bloody frivolity is over',[71] to his 1936 observation that 'some blunderer has driven his car on to the wrong side of the road—that is all. If war is necessary, or necessary in our time and place, it is best to forget its suffering as we do the discomfort of fever ….'[72] His harsh response to O'Casey's *The Silver Tassie* affirms that position ('The

---

[66] Wohl, *A Passion for Wings*, 250.

[67] Lewis, *Sagittarius Rising*, 22.

[68] Gardner, *Up the Line to Death*, 53–5.

[69] Anna Malinovska and Mauriel Joslyn, *Voices in Flight: Conversations with Air Veterans of the Great War* (Barnsley: Pen & Sword Aviation, 2006), 6.

[70] Reda, *Because I Fly*, 3–4.

[71] *CW1*, 155. WBY to Henry James, 20 Aug. [1915], *CL Intelex* #2749. For further discussion of the poem and Yeats's response to the First World War, see Peter McDonald, 'Yeats and Remorse', in *Serious Poetry* (Oxford: Clarendon Press, 2002).

[72] *CW5*, 199.

mere greatness of the world war has thwarted you; it has refused to become mere back-ground, and obtrudes itself upon the stage as so much dead wood that will not burn with the dramatic fire'[73]), as does his insistence that 'In all the great tragedies, tragedy is a joy to the man who dies'.[74] His tendency to view the war primarily as part of the English not the Irish story, associated as it was for him with industrialization, mass production, imperialism, and propaganda, also led him to eschew, albeit misleadingly, any claim to the war's profound effect on his own writing.[75] He elegizes only one victim of the Great War; and he makes only one comment directly concerning wartime operations. But that comment is noticeably idiosyncratic, in ways which bear upon his view of heroism and heroic action. In one of the more repellent passages in *On the Boiler* (1938) he writes:

> If some financial reorganisation ... enable everybody without effort to procure all necessities of life and so remove the last check upon the multiplication of the uneducatable masses, it will become the duty of the educated classes to seize and control one or more of those necessities. The drilled and docile masses may submit, but a prolonged civil war seems more likely, with the victory of the skilful, riding their machines as did the feudal knights their armoured horses. During the Great War Germany had four hundred submarine commanders, and sixty per cent of the damage done was the work of twenty-four men.[76]

The point, taken out of its original context, is rather misinterpreted: 'In surface vessels', Admiral Hall explains in 1930, 'there are several factors which may bring success. ... In submarines none of these count. One man only, the commanding officer, can see, and he only with one eye. No one can help him. Germany had some four hundred submarine captains during the war, but over sixty percent of the damage they did was accomplished by but twenty-two of these four hundred officers. The inference is obvious. The one and great difficulty in submarine warfare is to find a sufficiency of officers ... who will rise superior to the incidental intricacies of these complicated vessels ... '.[77] Yeats's slightly different inference (more along the lines of 'we few, we happy few', and we only *need* a few) supports a pattern of thinking in which the eschewal of what is mass-produced, of that which constitutes mass action or mass opinion, is the hallmark of the 'skilful'—those whose 'creative power' is 'wrought to the highest pitch'.[78] The impulse is towards celebration of men and women both 'passionate and solitary'.[79] It is in not dissimilar terms that he wrote of Gregory immediately after his death: 'I think he had genius ... His

---

[73] 'To Sean O'Casey', 10 Apr. 1928, *Letters*, ed. Wade, 741.

[74] *CW*5, 199.

[75] See Fran Brearton, 'W. B. Yeats: Creation from Conflict', in *The Great War in Irish Poetry* (Oxford: Oxford University Press, 2000), 43–82.

[76] *CW*5, 231. See also 431 n.52: Yeats takes the point from Raymond B. Cattell's eugenics text, *The Fight for our National Intelligence*, published in 1937, rather than its original context (see n. 77 below).

[77] S. S. Hall, 'Preface' to William Guy Carr, *By Guess and By God: The Story of British Submarines in the War* (1930; London: Dauphin Publication, 2016), ix–x.

[78] *CW*5, 241.

[79] *CW*5, 226.

paintings had majesty and austerity and at the same time sweetness. He was the most accomplished man I have ever known. I mean that he could do more things well than any other. He had proved himself a most daring airman, having been particularly successful in single combat with German planes. What brought him to his end is not known.'[80]

As noted above, Yeats's symbols are ones which had been proven over time—the spade not the sewing machine; the sword not the gun. There is no place, then, for telegrams, telephones, typewriters, and certainly not for bicycles or motor cars; there is one mention of a train—although by the time he invokes it, the passenger train had a history going back more than a century. Horses and horsemen are, of course, a vital presence, notably in the 1920s and 1930s—even to the extent of becoming the defining self-authored epitaph for Yeats himself: 'Cast a cold eye / On life, on death. Horseman, pass by!'[81] Both Zeppelin and aeroplane do find their way into his lexis, but not as symbols, in the way 'flight' or Yeats's swans operate symbolically; rather, they suggest fear of the way in which a new technological age, with its horrific capabilities, might compromise a proper understanding of aesthetic value. If the military potential of flight had not been fully understood by most in 1914–15, who had still the expectation that the cavalry would break through to end the Western Front stalemate, Yeats was certainly one of those who saw the threatening as well as liberating aspect of flight. He had been, James Longenbach notes, genuinely frightened by the Zeppelin raids in London in 1915; but at the same time he intensely disliked the 'mob' who 'cheered … every shot from an anti-aircraft gun'.[82] In 'Lapis Lazuli' (1936), it is 'hysterical women' who implicitly voice a need for the 'poets who are always gay' to rethink their priorities:

> For everybody knows or else should know
> That if nothing drastic is done
> Aeroplane and Zeppelin will come out,
> Pitch like King Billy bomb-balls in
> Until the town lie beaten flat.[83]

The fear of towns 'beaten flat' by aerial attack was justified as it turned out, but the prescience is not really the point: as Edna Longley writes, it is a 'critical position' that is under attack here, 'the Marxist demand for *engagé* art; also, perhaps, the 1930s mood and mode of waiting for the end'. She notes that his opinion of Wilfred Owen and war poetry, as expressed in his *Oxford Book of Modern Verse* (that 'certain distaste' for the trench lyric with its 'passive suffering'[84]), contributes to the tone here too; and that ' "if nothing drastic is done" mocks the urgent voice of all politics'. Instead, the poem

---

[80] WBY to John Quinn, 8 Feb. 1918. *CL InteLex* #3407.

[81] *CW1*, 328.

[82] James Longenbach, *Stone Cottage: Pound, Yeats and Modernism* (New York: Oxford University Press, 1988), 180. See also WBY to Lady Gregory, 13 Oct. 1915, *CL Intelex* #2777, for his description of a Zeppelin raid.

[83] *CW1*, 328.

[84] *CW5*, 199.

affirms an 'aesthetic credo'.[85] Yeats by its close is the 'I' who 'Delight[s]' to imagine the 'Chinamen … seated … on the Mountain and the sky', staring 'On all the tragic scene', his perspective combining high attitude with altitude. In 'Reprisals', Yeats clarifies for the first time the nature of Gregory's calling, locating him firmly in the time, space, and technology of the First World War ('Some nineteen German planes, they say / You had brought down before you died …'[86]); he also repudiates the 'fine affair'. But it is the recognition of atrocity on his own doorstep that motivates a 'protest' poem he himself feels to be such. Writing to Lady Gregory, he says, 'I send you with this a new poem to Robert. I am sending it at once to "The Times" & if they will not have it I will send it to "The Nation". I have not asked your leave, *as I think one must make what appeal one can now & at once*. I think the poem is good & *good for its purpose*' (emphasis added). The original draft as sent to Gregory with the letter of 26 November 1920 opens:

> To Major Robert Gregory, airman.
> Considering that before you died
> You had brought down some nineteen planes
> I think that you were satisfied,
> <For> And life at last seemed worth the pains.
> 'I have had more happiness in one year
> Than in all other years' you <had> said;
> And battle joy may be so dear
> A memory even to the dead
> It chases common thought away,
> Yet rise from your Italian tomb,
> Flit to Kiltartan Cross and stay
> Till certain second thoughts have come
> Upon that cause you served, that we
> Imagined such a fine affair–:[87]

It is the context of Gregory's sacrifice that is called into question, not the action itself. The poem begins, indeed, by recording that individual achievement; but the disquiet arises from its having been made for unworthy cause—in support of the 'soldiery' then 'murdering' in Ireland—and the intent is, it seems, primarily to make a political point. He is, in effect, asking Gregory to come down to earth to reflect on the 'cause', whilst at the same time acknowledging ('we / Imagined') the role of the imagination in generating 'battle joy'.

How Yeats might have elegized a Robert Gregory whose war was trench-bound, and how he might have reconciled such 'experience' with his own aesthetic, is hard to imagine (in *On the Boiler* Yeats says that 'observed facts do not mean much until I can make them part of my experience'[88]). Whether the hundreds of planes that traversed the sky

---

[85] Edna Longley, *Yeats and Modern Poetry*, (New York: Cambridge University Press, 2013), 63–4, 66.
[86] *VP*, 791.
[87] WBY to Lady Gregory, 26 November [1920], *CL InteLex* #3813.
[88] *CW5*, 233.

in terrifying formation in World War II, and which he didn't live to see, might have cast his sewing-machine nightmare into the shade is only speculation. But that Gregory flew in the pioneering age of flight lifts him above the mass-produced and the mundane. The men who died in their hundreds of thousands in the trenches were not an 'indifferent multitude', but Yeats showed little other than indifference towards them—artistically that is. Yet from the beginning of the war aviators were lauded as heroic, individuals of daring and skill. The popular valorization of the pioneering 'Knights of the Air' before 1914 took on new resonance in the First World War, where explorers and adventurers striving for altitude of body and (it was inferred) of mind, became, in perception if not reality, the chivalric warriors of old. As Wohl notes, '[i]n 1914 the dominant image of the aviator was the "sportsman"; after 1915 it became the flying "ace", an airborne knight armed with a machine-gun who jousted in the sky'.[89]

In World War I, the 'knights of the sky', even though they were a new departure that eventually transformed the nature of modern warfare, were also perceived to be traditional—evidence of the last vestiges of a more 'noble' warfare. Often they knew each other by name and reputation—those at least who survived the shockingly brief survival rate to become experienced fliers; they engaged in one-to-one combat; and some perpetuated belief in a glorious death. Lewis, describing such combat, writes of his opponent: 'And if at last he went down, a falling rocket of smoke and flame, what a glorious and heroic death! ... For what have I been spared? To die, diseased, in a bed! Sometimes it seems a pity'.[90] The French press, celebrating Garros's achievements prior to his April 1915 capture, stressed the 'lonely nature' of his exploits (and treated the plane as a horse): 'Roland Garros mounted alone this machine ...'.[91] Herbert Thompson. RFC veteran, describes the First World War aces as 'the last of the Knight Errants'. They were, he implies, driven not so much by hate but—as Yeats would surely approve—by joy: 'We were gay and light-hearted, and there wasn't really a hatred of the Hun'.[92] 'The majesty of the heavens', said Lewis, 'gave us ... a spirit unknown to sturdier men who fought on earth. Nobility surrounded us'.[93] However inaccurate the myth of the ace might be, fliers captured the public and literary imagination; their individuality and individual actions were celebrated during and after the war—not least, on occasion, by them-selves. Wohl notes that '[f]or years after the Armistice, Rickenbacker and other aviators supplemented their income with popularizations of their adventures during the war that had little to do with what had actually happened'.[94] David Lloyd George affirmed the myth in October 1917 in a speech to the House of Commons:

> The heavens are their battlefield; they are the cavalry of the clouds. ... Every flight is
> a romance, every record is an epic. They are the knighthood of this war, without fear

---

[89] Wohl, *A Passion for Wings*, 203.
[90] Lewis, *Sagittarius Rising*, 48.
[91] Quoted in Wohl, *A Passion for Wings*, 210.
[92] Malinovska and Joslyn, *Voices in Flight*, 8–9.
[93] Lewis, *Sagittarius Rising*, 85.
[94] Wohl, *A Passion for Wings*, 249.

and without reproach. They recall the old legends of chivalry, not merely by daring individually, but by the nobility of their spirit, and, among the multitudes of heroes, let us think of the chivalry of the air.[95]

Yeats did not create the chivalric, heroic, or 'lonely' myth of the airman. But he captured its essence in 'An Irish Airman'; and he understood the compulsion even if he disapproved of the 'cause' in 'Reprisals'. He did so because the 'myth' emerged in part from pre-existing Romantic conceptions of warfare and flight that were shared by him, thereby enabling an absorption of Gregory's wartime death into an aesthetic always committed to the ideals embodied in individual 'ascent' and heroic action. In the eschewal of modernity and machine, Yeats captures two of the key elements associated with early flight, and Great War flying in particular: the loneliness—and sublimity—of the enterprise; the 'joy' in battle that was retained in the air after it had been lost on the ground. If indeed Yeats was persuaded into a plane ten years after the war, one might reasonably guess the ways in which Oliver St John Gogarty could have 'appeal[ed] to his imagination' and inspired him to such 'action'.

---

[95] David Lloyd George, *War Memoirs*, vol. II (1938), Arcole Publishing, Kindle edn. (2017), Loc 1277/ 22153.

CHAPTER 15

··

REVOLUTION AND COUNTER-REVOLUTION

··

DAVID DWAN

FEW concepts are more central to Yeats's oeuvre than the idea of revolution. This may partly reflect the fact that the idea was fundamental to the self-understanding of his own epoch. As Wyndham Lewis complained in 1926, 'Every one today, in everything is committed to revolution'—a fact that had led, he thought, to the thorough banalization of the concept. In Lewis's eyes, 'Revolutionary politics, revolutionary art, and, oh, the revolutionary mind, is the dullest thing on earth. When we open a "revolutionary" review, or read a "revolutionary" speech, we yawn our heads off. … Everything is correctly, monotonously, dishearteningly "revolutionary". What a stupid word! What a stale fuss!'[1] Lewis had a point about the exhaustion of the concept; nonetheless, it is hard to make sense of Yeats without the idea of revolution. It is the context, theme, and—as Yeats would suggest himself—the possible effect of his own art. He often distinguished between a revolution in art and in politics and could entertain disapproving views of both, but he also wondered if that rousing play of his *Cathleen Ni Houlihan* had helped to foment rebellion in his own country.[2] Prior to posing as its ostensible cause, Yeats had presented himself as a troubled witness of an Irish revolution—one that exploded onto the Dublin streets in 1916 and would ultimately lead to the establishment of a Free State in 1922. Even before that revolution turned upon itself in the Irish Civil War of 1922–3, Yeats had condemned the fanaticism that it had spawned. Confronted by such violence 'and the growing murderousness of the world', Yeats was increasingly inclined to play the role of a counter-revolutionary, a stern defender of some notional sense of 'order'.[3]

---

[1] Wyndham Lewis, *The Art of Being Ruled*, ed. Reed Way Dasenbrock (Santa Rosa: Black Sparrow Press, 1989), 17, 32.

[2] Both the distinction and an element of disapproval are detectable in his assessment of T. S. Eliot— 'the most revolutionary man of poetry during [his] lifetime, though his revolution was stylistic alone' (*CW5*, 95).

[3] *CW3*, 166

He roundly denounced the 'revolutionary simpleton' and all his dangerous dreams. But Yeats would also admit to being a 'revolutionist' himself—a figure all too susceptible to the extremism that he professed to indict. He too had a 'fanatic heart'.[4] The object of this chapter is to study this ambivalence and the great ferment it produced in his art.

IDEAL REPUBLICS, DESPOTIC FACTS

The differences between revolution and counter-revolution are sometimes difficult to spot in Yeats—not least because the revolution he initially envisaged for Ireland was often conceived as a 'revival'. Here and elsewhere the poet appears to wage a counter-revolution against the concept of revolution itself, turning away from a modern tendency to regard it as a radical break from the past, and restoring its older meaning: after all, for many ancient republicans, revolution implied a complete turn of history's wheel towards some earlier dispensation.[5] In this schema, all revolutions are conservative: they are attempts to recover a pristine past from a corrupt present. This is revolution as virtuous repetition—a second or third coming of some foundational moment—and Yeats will often think through the implications of revolution through the technique of repetition itself.[6] But it is an ambiguous technique—not least because Yeats's art can never wholly escape from a modern interpretation of revolution as a radical beginning or total break in history.

The revolution he initially sponsored was a fairly esoteric one. He yearned, as he put it, for 'a great revolution of thought ... an insurrection against everything which assumes that the external and the material are the only fixed things, the only standards of reality'.[7] Ireland, he felt, was fertile ground for this spiritual insurrection. Drawn to Matthew Arnold's nostrums on Celtic idealism, Yeats declared his country to be engaged in 'a futile revolt against the despotism of fact or ... a necessary revolt against moral and political materialism'.[8] Here and elsewhere Yeats appeared to be in revolt from modernity and took refuge in the fact that Ireland remained a 'primitive country'.[9] He famously reviewed this sociological assessment in later life—Ireland had not escaped 'the filthy

---

[4] Yeats to Lady Gregory, 1 April (1928), *CL Intelex* #5097; *CW14*, 6; *CW1*, 259.

[5] As Machiavelli maintained in the *Discorsii*, republics require renewal and 'the method of renewing them is ... to bring them back to their beginnings'. Niccolò Machiavelli, *Discourses on Livy*, trans. Julia Conaway Bondanella and Peter Bondanella (Oxford: Oxford University Press, 2008), 246.

[6] This modern conception of revolution is often traced back to the French Revolution. Edmund Burke was on the same side as many of its fomenters when he described it as a 'total revolution' or a 'schism with the whole universe'. See Edmund Burke, *The Writings and Speeches of Edmund Burke*, ed. Paul Langford (Oxford: Clarendon, Press, 1981–2015), vol. 8, 338; vol. 9, 249.

[7] *CW9*, 340.

[8] *CW9*, 389. In 1867 Arnold provided an ambiguous celebration of the Celt's resistance to 'the despotism of fact'. See Matthew Arnold, *On The Study of Celtic Literature* (London: Smith, Elder, & Co., 1867), 102, 152, 155–6.

[9] *CW6*, 73.

modern tide' and was, in fact, 'wrecked' by it—yet he initially believed that the country housed an ancient idealism that might serve as a basis for the spiritual regeneration of Europe.[10] As Seamus Deane observed, Yeats's, Ireland was a 'revolutionary country', even if the revolution he yearned for was very much conceived as a restoration.[11] If history was a film, narrating a fall into division and a loss of social cohesion, then Yeats hoped to 'reverse the cinematograph'.[12]

Yeats's spiritual revolution—his bold insurrection against moral and political materialism—might seem to preclude anything so crudely material as physical action, not to mention organized violence. Though he is reported to have joined the Irish Republican Brotherhood (IRB) under Maud Gonne's influence, the nationalism of his early poetry is a pretty tepid affair: Yeats hopes 'to sweeten Ireland's wrong', not to reverse or avenge it. Moreover, the 'measure' that Arnold felt the Celt so palpably lacked is something that Yeats seems to endorse—for political as much as for aesthetic reasons. His conclusions in 'To Ireland in the Coming Times'—'may the thoughts of Ireland brood / Upon a measured quietude'—are hardly an incitement to riot.[13] Cast against this mild green background, the pugnacity of *Cathleen Ni Houlihan* is striking. The play is an exultant celebration of violent revolution and the nobility of blood sacrifice. As Yeats's Old Woman puts it, 'They that had red cheeks will have pale cheeks for my sake, and for all that, they will think they are well paid'.[14] All the Abbey plays were 'revolts against something or other', according to one contemporary, but *Cathleen Ni Houlihan*—first performed in St Teresa's Hall in Dublin in 1902 and frequently restaged at the Abbey— packed a particular punch.[15] The shocked responses of the play's initial audiences have become part of the play's legend.[16]

It is hard to know if it was remorse or pride which triggered Yeats's late question to himself—'Did that play of mine send out / Certain men the English shot?'—though perhaps the self-questioning advertises his difference from those all too 'Certain men'.[17]

[10] *CW*1, 337.

[11] See Seamus Deane, 'Yeats, Ireland and Revolution', *The Crane Bag*, Vol.1(2) (1 January 1977), 56–64, 56.; repr. as 'Yeats and the Idea of Revolution', in *Celtic Revivals: Essays in Modern Irish Literature, 1880– 1980* (London: Faber, 1985), 38–50, 57.

[12] *CW*3, 166.

[13] *CW*1, 50. As Arnold put it, 'Balance, measure, and patience, these are the eternal conditions ... of high success; and balance, measure, and patience are just what the Celt has never had.' Arnold, *Celtic Literature*, 102. For more on 'measure' in Yeats and its relationship to violence, see Matthew Campbell, *Irish Poetry Under the Union, 1801–1924* (Cambridge: Cambridge University Press, 2013), 184–210.

[14] *CW*2, 92

[15] S. O'Hegarty, 'Art and the Nation', *Irish Freedom* (March, 1912). Quoted in Ben Levitas, *The Theatre of Nation: Irish Drama and Cultural Nationalism 1890-1916* (Oxford, 2002), 198.

[16] The constitutional nationalist Stephen Gwynn wondered 'if such plays should be produced unless one was prepared for people to go out and shoot and be shot', while those who were prepared to take a shot—like Constance Markievicz—proclaimed the play a kind of 'gospel'. Stephen Gwynn, *Irish Literature and Drama in the English Language: a Short History* (London and New York: T. Nelson, 1936), 158. Maire Nic Shiubhlaigh, *The Splendid Years: Recollections of Maire Nic Shiubhlaigh as told to Edward Kenny* (Dublin: James Duffy, 1955), 100.

[17] *CW*1, 345.

However he might claim to be its origin, the Rising of 1916 took him entirely by surprise. His initial response—a mixture of shock ('the whole thing bewilders me') and awed sadness at its 'tragic, heroic lunacy'—provides some indication of the distance he had travelled from the most 'advanced' forms of nationalism.[18] But on one point Yeats seemed certain: the Rising was a very modern kind of revolution, a radical rupture from everything that preceded it. As he put it in a letter to St John Ervine, 'as yet one knows nothing of the future except that it must be very unlike the past'.[19]

The anxious repetitions of his poem 'Easter, 1916' both confirm and resist this terrible novelty. The famous line—'All changed, changed utterly'—seems to revolt against its own content by repeating itself. The speaker struggles to come to terms with the enormity of what has happened; indeed, it is the silence of the line's caesura, punctuating all the volubility about change, which perhaps best communicates both the event's significance and unfathomability. This is a poem that seems to mistrust the power of words or at least 'Polite meaningless words'—a phrase that is itself repeated to signify the banal repetitiousness of everyday life. All talk can seem like small talk when cast against the revolutionary deed.[20]

The repetitions of 'Easter, 1916' also occur against a background theory in which 'Life is never the same twice'.[21] This is the cosmological outlook that is used to calibrate the political and moral significance of the Rising. Though drawn to Nietzsche's invitation to regard the universe as an endless recurrence of itself, Yeats was equally attracted to the philosopher's conception of life as radical flux—a theory which Nietzsche was sometimes inclined to trace back to Heraclitus.[22] Indeed, the Heraclitean river into which you can never step twice is—given its unrepeatability—ironically revived in Yeats's poem in the form of the 'living stream'. Moreover, the stream is enlisted into a symbolic landscape where fixed principles and unwavering beliefs stand in brutal opposition to the beautiful mutability of all living things. He had intimated in 1910 that the *idées fixes* of nationalism were turning minds to stone, but in 1916 they appear to have taken hold of the heart:[23]

> Hearts with one purpose alone
> Through summer and winter seem
> Enchanted to a stone
> To trouble the living stream.[24]

The much-commented-upon stone stands in marked contrast to the mobility of its surroundings—not only 'the living stream' but the living creatures that populate it: 'the

[18] Yeats to Elizabeth Corbet Yeats (30 April 1916), *CL InteLex* #2935; Yeats to Lady Gregory [9 May 1916], *CL InteLex* #2945.

[19] Yeats to St John Ervine, (8 May 1916), *CL InteLex* #2944.

[20] *CW1*, 180.

[21] Yeats to J. B. Yeats, (7 August 1910), *CL InteLex* #1403.

[22] Friedrich Nietzsche, *Human all too Human: A Book for Free Spirits*, trans. R. J. Hollingdale (Cambridge: Cambridge University Press, 1986), 268.

[23] On the petrification of minds and the ill effects of nationalist monomnia see, Yeats's 'J.M. Synge and the Ireland of his Time', *CW4*, 228.

[24] *CW1*, 181.

horse that comes from the road', 'the rider', 'the birds that range', 'the long-legged moor-hens'. As the definite articles suggest, these things are richly particular; they are also mo-bile and mutable: 'Minute by minute they change'. Once again mutability is captured and eludes capture through a fraught form of repetition. The rhyming pattern ('one', 'alone', 'stone') is also a form of repetition, enacting its own kind of chant or *enchant*ment. Further repetitions appear downstream, though they also mutate: 'Minute by minute they live'.[25] The substitution of the verb from 'change' to 'live' helps to make the point that life *is* change though once again, the various repetitions resist such change in the very act of emphasizing it, attesting to the poem's deep uncertainty about what it seeks to extol or reprove.

Yeats's sudden recourse to the natural world in a poem ostensibly about a largely urban revolution has puzzled some readers. Maud Gonne—one of the first to read the poem—was aware of the confusion it was liable to generate ('Even Iseult reading it didn't understand your thought till I explained your ... theory of constant change & becoming in the flux of things'). But Maud did not miss the point and was alert to the political entailments of the poem's natural imagery: in particular, that stone in the midst of all. The image could connote an admirable fixity of purpose re-enacted in the poem's own repetitions, but it could also communicate a dangerous fundamentalism. As Gonne complained, 'you could never say that MacDonagh & Pearse & Conally [*sic*] were sterile fixed minds'.[26] But Yeats did say that, though he also said more. His poem concedes to the paradox that fixed principles have produced a form of radical novelty, while also suggesting that steadfastness may not be such a bad thing. The stone might even stand as a monument to the patriots, showing how they have achieved a kind of im-mortality that exists above and outside the normal flow of history or the casual comedy of everyday life. Like the deed it commemorates, the stone is a total exception, which is how revolutions—and the Rising itself—were often conceived.[27] The exceptional event may be the origin of a new set of norms, but it is not assimilable to any pre-existing standards.[28] This is what makes it so hard to judge or to write about.

'Easter, 1916' is an exercise in ambivalence, as its most quoted line makes clear ('A terrible beauty is born').[29] If the emotions of tragedy are conveyed here, so too are the ambiguous sentiments of the sublime. While Edmund Burke distinguished between the sublime and the beautiful, Yeats's 'terrible beauty' seems to provoke the same cognitive dissonance that Burke found in sublime events: the Rising is simply too big, too excep-tional, too new, for minds to appropriate—a difficulty partly attested to by the dazed and

[25] *CW1*, 181.

[26] *G-YL*, 384.

[27] As James Connolly put it in 1915, 'We believe in constitutional action in normal times; we believe in revolutionary action in exceptional times. These are exceptional times.' James Connolly, *Collected Works*, 2 vols. (Dublin: New Books Publications), vol. 2, 117.

[28] On this theory of the exception—albeit used to sanction a theory of sovereignty and not a revolution against the sovereign—see Carl Schmitt, *Political Theology: Four Chapters on the Concept of Sovereignty*, trans. George Schwab (Chicago and London: Chicago University Press, 1985), 10–15.

[29] *CW1*, 180.

dizzying repetitiousness of the poem.[30] In the end Yeats is consigned to an ambiguous incantation—a murmuring of 'name upon name'.[31] This type of jabber may once again point to the emptiness of words, although it can also feel as if words have left behind their representational or semantic function in order to aspire towards something more behavioural: they no longer function as mere description but play host to a kind of practice or commemorative ritual.[32] The performative quality of the final sentence—'I write it out in a verse'—allows the poem to enact its own content and attain something like the dignity of a deed.[33] The speech act may even vie with the event it commemorates. Whatever the patriots might have done, it is now that poem that's in the midst of all—or so the poet may like to think.

Yet Yeats's poem can still communicate a wistfulness that concedes to the belatedness and derivativeness of its own enterprise. In the beginning was the deed, and everything that follows after, including representation itself, is merely a pale echo. The poem's lack of confidence in itself is conceded by the hand-me-down quality of its Easter imagery: after all, it is inherited from the organizers of the Rising itself. The feeling of déjà vu is also evident in the poem's use of intertextuality—another form of repetition. Yeats's reflections on a mother and her rebel child as well as the theory of commemoration as ritual naming are a clear nod to Pearse's poem 'The Mother'. Of course, in 'The Rose Tree' the capitulation to Pearse's sense of the Rising—and the glories of blood sacrifice—is even more explicit. As the resurrected Pearse declares, 'There's nothing but our own red blood / Can make a right Rose Tree'. In this second coming of Pearse, Yeats concedes to his own sense of having come second. Once again, the poem attests to the frivolousness of speech ('"O words are lightly spoken," / Said Pearse to Connolly,') when measured against the brute power of the deed.[34]

MOB AND PEOPLE

Yeats may have been a troubled celebrant of the Easter Rising, but he had long insisted that the artist must turn his back on the 'the passion of revolution'.[35] Indeed, he initially saw the Rising as a terrible check to his plans to uncouple art from politics. He had pursued that policy very imperfectly himself; however, he had also sharply distinguished

---

[30] As Burke put it, 'In this case the mind is so entirely filled with its object, that it cannot entertain any other, nor by consequence reason upon that object which employs it.' Burke, *Writings and Speeches*, vol. 1, 230.

[31] *CW1*, 181.

[32] Alert to this ambition, Maud Gonne insisted that Yeats had failed to create 'a living thing which our race would treasure & repeat'—a particularly tough judgement, given that this is what the poem so clearly aspires to be. See *G-YL*, 384.

[33] *CW1*, 182.

[34] *CW1*, 183.

[35] *CW8*, 60.

his own cultural project from that of the political revolutionary. The distinction itself was politically suggestive, as a letter from 1911 reveals:

> As long as ten years ago I said to myself 'I must not commit the mistake of the political revolutionists, which, as far as I can see, every theatrical reformer is ready to commit. The political revolutionist always thinks "The people are uncorrupt, are noble, it is only the Governments that are corrupt." He stakes his life upon that belief, and loses it. On the contrary, the people are no wiser than their education. Let us have no faith in the people. ...'[36]

Yeats's declining faith in the people marked the souring of the spiritual or cultural revolution that he had hoped to effect in Ireland. Misquoting Victor Hugo, he had announced that in the theatre a mob becomes a people, but in the response to *The Playboy of the Western World* in 1907, some people had behaved like a mob, triggering Yeats and the Abbey authorities to call in the police—a decidedly unrevolutionary gesture that many nationalists found hard to forgive.[37]

The furious reception of Synge's play convinced Yeats that Ireland had undergone a sad transformation. This was in part a social revolution in the poet's eyes—the rise into prominence of a new middle class that combined a craven piety with an exultant philistinism.[38] Moreover, the bad confidence of this class was boosted by a democratic revolution that had overtaken the country. In the debates surrounding the *Playboy* riots Yeats proclaimed that the structure and ethos of modern nationalism had been radically transformed:

> Some seven or eight years ago the National movement was democratised and passed from the hands of a few leaders into those of large numbers of young men organised in clubs and societies. These young men made the mistake of the newly-enfranchised everywhere; they fought for causes worthy in themselves with the unworthy instruments of tyranny and violence.[39]

Yeats often couched his opposition to democracy on broadly liberal grounds: majorities and their representatives easily tyrannized in the name of the popular will. However, Yeats had no illusions about the righteousness of the people. Having misquoted Hugo, he now misquoted Conrad: 'In a novel, by Conrad, which I have just read, a revolutionist says—"The people are always pure." No—that is the way to lose one's life'.[40] Alongside this patrician mistrust of the people, Yeats entertained a Nietzschean hatred

---

[36] Yeats to Edward Gordon Craig (16 November 1911), *CL InteLex* #1762.

[37] *CW10*, 88.

[38] As he had already put it in 1908, 'Power passed to small shopkeepers, to clerks ... to men who had risen above the traditions of the countryman, without learning those of cultivated life or even educating themselves, and who because of their poverty, their ignorance, their superstitious piety are much subject to all kinds of fear' (*CW4*, 189–90).

[39] *CW8*, 111.

[40] Yeats to Edward Gordon Craig (16 November 1911), *CL InteLex* #1762.

of egalitarian mores: they amounted to a repudiation of all noble values, indeed of the very concept of value itself.[41] Like Nietzsche, he believed that equality was often a cloak for a corrosive resentment. Ireland had succumbed to a 'democratic envy and jealousy', which made it incapable of acknowledging the supremacy of certain artists.[42] Synge's detractors, for instance, were consumed by a peevish hatred of the noble few: 'They hate the presence of a mind that is superior to their own & so invent & even beleive [sic] the cry of immorality & slander.'[43] His misgivings about Ireland's social and democratic revolution are recorded throughout *The Green Helmet* collection (1910)—not least of all in 'These are the Clouds'. Here we learn that 'all things at one common level lie': as the play on 'lie' suggests, democracy may be a social fact, but the equality it presupposes is also a corrupt fiction.[44]

Yeats's anti-democratic animus led him increasingly to adopt the position of a counter-revolutionary. His aim, in other words, was 'to reverse the process of revolution' in Ireland and to restore some hierarchical system of rule.[45] Moreover, this attitudinal shift—already in evidence in his various defences of Synge—was accompanied by a strengthened sense of his own Protestantism and a more strident identification with an ascendancy class—most winningly epitomized by his 'most true friend', Lady Gregory.[46] The power of that class had been sapped by the democratization of politics in the nineteenth century; a series of land reforms also weakened its economic base. Members of this class often compared their own declining fortunes in Ireland to the fate of the French noblesse during the Revolution of 1789—a trend that would continue under Lady Gregory herself.[47] Yeats also viewed contemporary events through a French prism, becoming a vocal critic of the social and cultural effects of the French Revolution in Ireland. As he put it in 1934, 'The influence of the French Revolution woke the peasantry from their medieval sleep, gave them ideas of the social justice and equality, but prepared a century disastrous to the national intellect.'[48] When accounting for that disaster, the poet drew enthusiastically on the writings of Edmund Burke (the great scourge of the French Revolution), as well as his beloved Nietzsche—a figure who had roundly denounced the Revolution as the culminating event in the slave revolt against noble values.[49]

---

[41] In the 1930s he supplied the following question and answer in a draft of a song: 'What's equality? – Muck in the yard' (*VP*, 547).

[42] *Mem*, 168–9.

[43] Yeats to T. Sturge Moore (4 October 1907), *CL InteLex* #669.

[44] *CW1*, 96.

[45] *CW5*, 224.

[46] Yeats to Lady Gregory (15 December 1898), *CL2*, 321.

[47] Spotting trespassers in her wood in 1920, Lady Gregory was reminded of the French Revolution, as well as the more recent one in Russia. See Judith Hill, *Lady Gregory: An Irish Life* (London: Collins, 2011), 320. For other invocations of revolutionary France, see David Dwan, *The Great Community: Culture and Nationalism in Ireland* (Dublin: Field Day, 2008), 114–15.

[48] *VP*, 833.

[49] Friedrich Nietzsche, *On the Genealogy of Morality*, ed. Keith Ansell-Pearson (Cambridge: Cambridge University Press, 2006), 33.

ABSTRACTION AND HATRED

One of the key motifs that Yeats derived from Burke was a deep suspicion of abstraction in moral and political life. The French practised this abstraction, according to Burke, when they made a series of absolute rights—the celebrated rights of man—the necessary conditions of legitimacy for government. Burke maintained that all workable notions of right were specific to a particular historical context—contexts that were produced piecemeal over time and were embodied in established legal structures, existing moral practices, and informal codes of manners. To elaborate one's notion of right independently of these frameworks—or to force our established practices to justify themselves in the light of such abstract rights—was to engage in a very dangerous form of inversion. It forced all existing reality to become accountable to a theory, when in fact our theories were answerable to our actual practices and made little sense without them. But the 'aeronauts of France' were in thrall to an abstract rationalism, which refused to be bound by historical norms.[50] It yielded, he argued, a dangerous fundamentalism that rode roughshod over ancient forms of life.

Yeats gradually became convinced that the Jacobin mindset had wreaked havoc in Ireland and throughout the world. Writing in the light of the Russian Revolution and guerrilla war in his own country, he declared: 'Logic is loose again, as once in Calvin and Knox, or in the hysterical rhetoric of Savonarola, or in Christianity itself in its first raw centuries, and because it must always draw its deductions from what every dolt can understand, the wild beast cannot but destroy mysterious life.'[51] Like Burke, Yeats drew a connection between religious fanaticism and political fundamentalism: both communicated a simplistic confidence in the attainability of truth through some flash of intuition or some abstract process of reasoning. However, the straight lines of logic made few allowances for the crooked timber of life—a point that Yeats would make over and over again when accounting for the intolerance of his own countrymen. As he recorded in his diaries in 1909, 'Ireland is ruined by abstraction.'[52]

Yeats's criticisms of Irish abstraction could themselves seem fairly abstract—applying decontextualized fragments of Burke and Nietzsche (in particular, Nietzsche's criticisms of a Platonic 'ideomania') to very different social circumstances.[53] Nonetheless, they mark an intriguing reversal of his earlier account of Irish virtue. Yeats, as we have seen, had lauded the Celts' resistance to the despotism of fact in their principled pursuit of absolute ideals. In a speech commemorating the 1798 rebellion, for instance, he had commended a Celtic 'passion for abstract right', 'abstract ideas', 'abstract law', and 'abstract emotion', but even in the midst of such celebrations he was aware that there may

---

[50] Burke, *Writings and Speeches*, vol. 8, 293.
[51] *CW5*, 44.
[52] *Mem*, 186.
[53] Nietzsche, *Genealogy of Morals*, 160.

be an unforgiving side to this pure-mindedness.[54] 'The very inhumanity of Irish jour-nalism and of Irish politics', he proclaimed, 'comes from a tendency to judge men not by one another, not by experience of the degree of excellence one may hope to meet in life and in politics, but by some abstract standard.'[55]

Over time Yeats focused more and more on this inhumanity and its political manifestations. He now became convinced that the 'French and the Irish democracies follow a logical deduction to its end, no matter what suffering it caused', not because they were Celtic and were constitutionally disposed to pursue the absolute, but rather because they had lost all sense of history and had allowed themselves to become fatally severed from the past.[56] In 1910 Yeats found himself 'planning a lecture on the Irish democrasy & its love of coarse logic'[57]—a predilection that also accounted for its philis-tinism, since art communicated through a rich suggestiveness and not through logical argument. Here he was drawn to Tocqueville's claim—reiterated by Edward Dowden and Yeats's own father—that democracies were drawn to abstraction and generaliza-tion, because individuals within them felt obliged to vindicate their own beliefs and values through an appeal to a general will.[58] Yeats was convinced that these generalizing habits were hostile to life and to great art. The superb generalizations of his own poetry ('This is no country for old men', 'The best lack all conviction'), as well as his wonderfully self-undermining opinions ('Opinion is not worth a rush'), don't bear this theory out. Indeed, while he continued to regard abstract ideas as a curse, he also conceded that 'in some curious way they are connected with poetry or rather with passion, one half its life & yet its enemy'.[59]

This uncertainty about abstraction—passion's enemy and child—appears in 'Easter, 1916'. As we have seen, the stone of abstract principle is at odds with life, yet we may feel there are few things more concrete than stone. Yeats certainly entertained the idea that the efforts of the revolutionaries were the opposite of abstract. After all, 'those that love the world serve it in action'—or so Ille declares in 'Ego Dominus Tuus'—and the rebels of 1916 had at least acted.[60] Terence MacSwiney—whose death from hunger strike occasioned the eventual publication of 'Easter, 1916'—had always maintained that the Irish revolution did not need to vindicate itself through abstract argument ('The Revolution does not need to be argued; it justifies itself').[61] Yeats certainly took up this notion of self-justifying action in 'Sixteen Dead Men'. Here the revolutionaries speak a

---

[54] *CW9*, 331.

[55] *CW9*, 331.

[56] *Mem*, 206.

[57] Yeats to Lady Gregory (12 November 1910), *CL InteLex* #1460.

[58] See Alexis de Tocqueville, *Democracy in America*, ed. Alan Ryan (London: Everyman, 1994), book 2, 15; Edward Dowden, *New Studies in Literature* (London: Trench, Trubner & Co., 1895), 9; J. B. Yeats, *Letters to his Son and Others, 1869–1922*, ed. Joseph Hone (London: Faber & Faber, 1944), 135.

[59] *CW1*, 197, 189, 177; Yeats to John Quinn (12 September 1915), *CL InteLex* #2760.

[60] *CW1*, 161.

[61] Terence MacSwiney, 'Literature and Freedom: Art for Art's Sake', in *Principles of Freedom* (New York: Dutton & Co., 1921), 159.

very concrete kind of language—they 'converse bone to bone'—and it is their critics who are condemned to abstractions: belated and counterfactual what-ifs. Surveying these critics, his speaker asks, 'is their logic to outweigh / MacDonagh's bony thumb?'[62] The sheer incommensurability of abstract logic and the material body makes the question rhetorical: these very different things can't measure up, let alone outmeasure the other. Logic—or the logic of comparison—is already routed by Yeats's bewildering question.

There may be no gainsaying MacDonagh's bony thumb, but Yeats often chose to mediate his criticisms of the Irish revolution through female personalities. Constance Markievicz is the only named revolutionary not ennobled by sacrifice in 'Easter, 1916', and in 'On a Political Prisoner' we learn that her mind has become 'a bitter, an abstract thing'.[63] In 'A Prayer for my Daughter' Maud Gonne has also suffered a sad transformation: hatred has wilted her beauty, just as it did for Constance Markievicz. In a letter to Gonne in 1927, Yeats advocated a credo for himself and made an implicit recommendation to Maud: 'To day I have one settled conviction "create, draw a firm strong line & hate nothing what ever not even … Satan himself"'.[64] This was yet another counterrevolution waged against his own previous beliefs. After all, Yeats had once dreamed of 'enlarging Irish hate' and believed—in his more metaphysical moments—that a hatred of every material thing might lead one beyond the despotism of fact into the airy kingdom of the absolute.[65] But in later years he rounded on the nihilistic energies of hatred, seeing a fundamental connection between this rancour and the love of abstraction.

THE IRISH FOR NO

Yeats suspected that 'to be choked with hate / May well be of all evil chances chief', but he also recognized that he was vulnerable to choking himself.[66] As he meekly admitted to Maud Gonne, 'I hate many things but I do my best'.[67] However, it was the nihilistic tendencies of his own 'Jacobin rage' that worried him the most.[68] Different diagnoses had been offered of Jacobin nihilism for well over a century. According to de Maistre, the French Revolution was negative because it was evil and evil was a radical form of non-being: 'it cannot create, since its power is purely negative'.[69] The negativity of the Revolution, for Burke, derived more from the emptiness of the abstractions that drove it; all historical life, he conceded, would be found wanting in the face of absolute

---

[62] *CW1*, 182.
[63] *CW1*, 183.
[64] Yeats to Maud Gonne McBride (29 September 1927), *CL InteLex* #5033.
[65] *CW4*, 182.
[66] *CW1*, 189.
[67] Yeats to Maud Gonne McBride (29 September 1927), *CL InteLex* #5033.
[68] *Mem*, 157.
[69] Joseph de Maistre, *Considerations on France*, ed. and trans. Richard A. Lebrun (Cambridge: Cambridge University Press, 1994), 38.

ideals. Hegel also related the 'fury of destruction' under the Revolution to its abstract or excessively formal idea of freedom: 'only in destroying something' did this sense of freedom ever feel real.[70] In Nietzsche's estimate, the French Revolution was a product of *ressentiment*—a historical enactment of a slave psychology that says 'no on principle to everything that is "outside", "other", "non-self"': and this "no" is its creative deed'.[71]

Yeats gave an enthusiastic 'yes' to these accounts of the revolutionary 'no'. It is possible to detect Nietzsche's shadow, for instance, in Yeats's account of Irish 'democratic envy' and resentment. 'There is no public emotion in the country, but resentment', he complained in 1924—a fact that he put down to Ireland's long history of servitude: it had bred a desire 'to enslave and be enslaved'.[72] Moreover, he had a very visceral understanding of the negative effects of Irish hatred: it was 'the intellectual equivalent to the removal of the genitals' and made truly creative thought impossible.[73] Like Burke and Hegel, Yeats was also inclined to relate the negativity of Irish politics to its fundamentally abstract or utopian character. In dreams begin irresponsibilities—or so it would appear:

> We had fed the heart on fantasies,
> The heart's grown brutal from the fare;
> More substance in our enmities
> Than in our love ...[74]

Faced with the task of putting out a revolution, while also being the product of one, Free State officials often criticized republican rebels for allowing a fundamentalism about sovereignty to produce extreme suffering. As one government journal declared, 'For an abstract political formula they are killing the living Ireland'.[75] This was a paraphrase of Piaras O'Béaslaí's speech in the Dáil directed against those that opposed the Anglo-Irish Treaty—'They are more concerned with dry political formulas than with the living nation'—but it was also an echo of Yeats's sentiments in 'Easter, 1916' and an anticipation of his 'Meditations'.[76] Though Yeats was made Senator of the Free State in December 1922, and would prove to be an enthusiastic defender of its right to defend itself with brutal force, he also strove to be inclusive in his critique of Irish abstraction in 'Meditations'. Moreover, he was prepared to admit to his own susceptibility to Jacobin rage in the final poem of the cycle. Here revolutionary monomania communicates itself through a relentless repetition. The cry for vengeance is repeated—just as vengeance itself might appear to be a bad repetition of some prior injury:

[70] G. W. F. Hegel, *Elements of the Philosophy of Right*, ed. Allen W. Wood, trans. H. B. Nisbet (Cambridge: Cambridge University Press, 1991), 38.
[71] Nietzsche, *On the Genealogy of Morality*, 21.
[72] *CW10*, 172.
[73] *Mem*, 176.
[74] *CW1*, 205.
[75] *An tÓglách*, 22 July 1922.
[76] Dáil Debates, 3 January 1922.

'Vengeance upon the murderers,' the cry goes up,
'Vengeance for Jacques Molay.' In cloud-pale rags, or in lace,
The rage-driven, rage-tormented, and rage-hungry troop,
Trooper belabouring trooper, biting at arm or at face,
Plunges towards nothing, arms and fingers spreading wide
For the embrace of nothing; and I, my wits astray
Because of all that senseless tumult, all but cried
For vengeance on the murderers of Jacques Molay.[77]

Revolution is self-cannibalizing and culminates in a series of repeated nothings. Here, of course, Irish rancour is given so broad a context that it almost seems to disappear. By invoking the murder of the Grand Master of the Templars in 1314—and the fantasies of vengeance it triggers—Yeats recycles the old conspiracy theory that the Freemasons were enabling agents of the French Revolution—an event or set of events that has been sometimes viewed as a civil war in its own right. The English Civil War might also be tacitly referenced in Yeats's repeated use of the word 'trooper'—a term that came into circulation during that conflict. His meditations may even trigger thoughts about Russia, whose own civil war was drawing to a close when Yeats was writing the poem. The murdered Romanovs, after all, had haunted the first drafts of 'A Second Coming', though once again they were seen through a French lens: 'Marie Antoinette has most brutally died, & no Burke has cried With his voice No pit (PITT?) arraigns revolution.'[78]

There was at least Yeats to arraign revolution—and much more explicitly in 'Meditations' than in 'The Second Coming'. Whatever the origins of revolutionary rancour—Irish, English, French, or Russian—its extreme negativity is its most striking note. Nothing, it seems, comes from nothing—or at least nothing very nice. In his Neoplatonic moments, Yeats had been inclined to suggest that where there is nothing there is God—since the absolute resembled nothing in its lack of any discernible borders or material determination—but in his portrait of the Irish *enragés* he seems to contend that where there is nothing there is evil—or there is simply a hatred so complete that it becomes an absolute nihilism.

ANCIENT REGIMES

In 1919 Yeats asked his spiritual instructors the following question: 'What is the opposite of the abstraction which produces the rage to destroy?' Yeats's instructors could be tricky—in August of that year they had told him that he was the reincarnation of the bastard son of the revolutionary Camille Desmoulins and the Duchess of Orleans, only

[77] *CW1*, 205–6.
[78] W. B. Yeats, *Michael Robartes and the Dancer: Manuscript Materials*, ed. Thomas Parkinson and Anne Brannen (Ithaca: Cornell University Press, 1994), 151.

to withdraw that remark when pressed for detail—but here they seemed to come up with an answer that Yeats could live with: 'family love'.[79] This was apt advice to someone who had recently fathered a child—and was coming to terms with the fact that it was not the Messiah—but it also chimed with key themes of his intellectual life. Yeats had begun to cast family as a key social unit and a counterforce to the individualistic, rationalistic, and ahistorical predisposition of his age (moreover, he would trace many of these vices to the French Revolution). Membership of a family, as Burke had suggested, was not the product of individual choice or rational deliberation—which is why he proposed it as a fitting metaphor for how political association should be conceived. Burke also insisted that political rights should be viewed as a kind of familial inheritance passed down through the generations. They had history as their source and justification and did not require a more abstract notion of right to establish their validity. This idea of inheritance—often viewed on a crudely biological basis—would prove vital to Yeats. Moreover, his definition of family would remain capacious: it stood for any association that derived its conditions of unity 'not by a logical process, but by historical association'.[80] Yeats's counter-revolution was waged in defence of these ancient regimes, though it would prove to be yet another futile revolt against the despotism of facts.

Yeats's 'A Prayer for my Daughter' is a paean to 'family love' where it appears as the counterforce to abstraction and rage. 'An intellectual hatred is the worst,' the speaker opinionatedly declares, before drawing the inference for his daughter: 'So let her think opinions are accursed'.[81] However, Yeats also tries to abstain from cursing, committed as he is to the value of good manners—those beautiful illusions that kept power gentle and obedience liberal in Burke. Indeed, the mannered quality of the poem's form—the decorous elegance of its ottava rima—communicates its fidelity to those illusions. Burke had identified beauty with sociability and gave both a highly gendered form: they had the soft and unthreatening quality of the delicate female form. Yeats's poem continues in this vein: indeed, his daughter's beauty will be so sociable that it will also be self-limiting. No one should be troubled or reduced to staring: 'May she be granted beauty and yet not / Beauty to make a stranger's eye distraught'.[82] This accommodating charm is a far cry from Yeats's terrible beauty or the wild energies of the sublime. The poet reiterates the links between beauty and sociability in the poem's final stanza. Here custom and ritual appear as a kind of greenhouse for the beautiful and the good:

> How but in custom and in ceremony
> Are innocence and beauty born?
> Ceremony's a name for the rich horn,
> And custom for the spreading laurel tree.[83]

---

[79] See George Mills Harper, *The Making of Yeats's A Vision: A Study of the Automatic Script*, 2 vols. (Carbondale and Edwardsville: Southern Illinois University Press, 1987), vol. 2, 362.

[80] *CW5*, 41.

[81] *CW1*, 189.

[82] *CW1*, 188.

[83] *CW1*, 190.

One may well wonder if this hypostatized sense of 'custom' communicates a distance from it—a sense that custom is no longer quite customary. So studied a sense of tradition might already concede to its loss. This problem would haunt Yeats's various defences of an *ancien régime* and the aristocratic virtues he felt it embodied. Significantly, in 'A Prayer from my Daughter', it is only Gregory's wood which provides protection from the roof-levelling wind (storms in Yeats often seem to possess disturbingly democratic pretensions). But in other contexts—most notably 'In a House Shaken by the Land Agitation'—it is Coole demesne which seems to require the poet's protection, leading him to emphasize what the world would lose by its disappearance.

Yeats cast the aristocracy or at least the Protestants of Ireland as 'the people of Burke'.[84] Yet it's worth recalling that Burke considered the Protestant aristocracy in Ireland to be little more than a 'plebeian oligarchy'.[85] Moreover, he condemned the perversity of their historical sense: the traditions to which they appealed were often little more than traditions of religious persecution, and they prevented time from drawing its 'oblivious veil over the unpleasant modes by which lordships and demesnes have been acquired' in Ireland, namely, through acts of conquest.[86] For Yeats, however, the Irish ascendancy was an aristocracy in a very literal sense—a structure of power featuring the 'best knit to the best'. Here virtue functions as a form of inheritance ('wings have memory of wings'), and those who participate in an aristocratic tradition find themselves with an intuitive orientation in moral space.[87] Yeats often felt that he lacked this instinct of honour—a fact he attributed to his over-reflective disposition, though it may have also had something to do with his unpromisingly bourgeois origins—but he believed it was beautifully embodied by Lady Gregory herself. In 'Coole Park, 1929' she appears as a swallow or a home for swallows, lending certainty and shape to the lives of others.

These are fond thoughts, but they were conducted against a background in which aristocratic power in Ireland and Europe was in severe decline. Indeed, the War of Independence and the civil war in Ireland would see widespread destruction of aristocratic houses. The tone of 'Ancestral Houses'—the first poem of 'Meditations in Time of Civil War'—is therefore a very beleaguered one, however it may affect a certain nonchalance:

> Surely among a rich man's flowering lawns,
> Amid the rustle of his planted hills,
> Life overflows without ambitious pains;
> And rains down life until the basin spills,
> And mounts more dizzy high the more it rains
> As though to choose whatever shape it wills
> And never stoop to a mechanical
> Or servile shape, at others' beck and call.[88]

84 Yeats, Seanad Debates, 11 June 1925.
85 Burke, *Writing and Speeches*, vol. 9, 600.
86 Ibid., 653.
87 *CW1*, 95.
88 *CW1*, 200.

Yeats may have been a critic of individualism, but here and elsewhere he credited the aristocracy with a radical independence. Since classical times this independence was often attributed to material factors—aristocrats had sufficient wealth and power to protect themselves from another's 'beck and call'. Freed from menial tasks, they had sufficient leisure to optimize their freedom. But Yeats's account of this self-delighting freedom also owes something to Nietzsche's descriptions of master morality: a radical form of autonomy or 'saying yes' to oneself which he juxtaposed to the slave's malignant and heteronomous 'no'.[89] Master morality, in Nietzsche's books, is 'self-glorification'—a claim that is clearly underlined in Yeats's own copy of Nietzsche's works.[90]

The 'fountain' in 'Ancestral Houses' is an image of this independence—its bounty captured by the repeated 'Ands' and its self-sustaining quality embodied in the rhyme, sound returning to its own source on a repeated basis, never stooping to anything external to itself. But there is also something embattled about this verse. The opening word—'Surely'—anticipates the very doubt it seeks to quash. So strident a sense of certainty can appear all too uncertain; indeed, the speaker will later declare his own confidence to be false ('mere dreams'). If the voice of the poem is aggressively imposing, so too is its form. Like the 'planted hills' of the demesne—which seem organic and yet are artificially transplanted—the ottava rima can function like an imposition. The ten-syllable lines enact a strenuous discipline, but the stanza's very exactitude may supply it with a mechanical shape (indeed, the rhyme on 'call' and 'mechanical' arguably emphasizes its machine-like action). Such verse is not without its ambitious pains. Yeats's Augustan personifications—'slippered Contemplation' and 'Childhood'—may communicate a sense of ancestral tradition, but they are also ostentatiously anachronistic. Indeed, the poem's form is a kind of carapace—just like the aristocratic independence it celebrates. The best image for the aristocracy, Yeats admits, may not a be a fountain but an 'empty sea-shell'.[91]

If there is something wilful about poetic form in 'Ancestral Houses', this is part of the point. Aristocratic culture, Yeats suggests, is a triumph of the will—a brutal imposition of order that is not without its violence. Yeats's 'planted hills', after all, bear the trace of the plantations and the violence that accompanied them. As Yeats envisages it, the founder of the great house was a 'violent and bitter man'. Burke may have criticized the Anglo-Irish for keeping alive the spirit of a conquest from which their privileges derived, but it is hard to know if Yeats is actively keeping it alive or simply owning up to its historical role in 'Ancestral Houses'. These houses may now be under attack, but they owe their origins, he admits, to brute force. Nonetheless, there is a troublesome ambiguity

---

[89] Nietzsche, *Genealogy of Morality*, 20.

[90] On the underlining, see Otto Bohlmann, *Yeats and Nietzsche: An Exploration of Major Nietzschean Echoes in the Writings of William Butler Yeats* (London: Macmillan, 1982), 101.

[91] *CW1*, 200.

in Yeats request: 'But take our greatness with our violence'.[92] It may be a plea for a more balanced assessment of what the aristocracy have achieved: people should take note of its 'greatness' before they punish its historical violence. Or the line may emphasize the co-dependency of both properties: if violence is taken away, greatness too will perish—a claim that would seem to defend not only the ancient regime but those who now assault it. There is an obvious darkness to all this magnanimity. 'I am a timid man,' Yeats wrote to Olivia Shakespear in the early months of the civil war—a figure easily spooked by the sound of gunshots in a Dublin street.[93] But Yeats was increasingly drawn to the idea of violence. As he would put it in his song for the Blueshirts, 'good strong blows are delights to the mind'—at least to the mind of the later Yeats.[94]

LEGITIMACY AND VIOLENCE

In the midst of the civil war in Ireland, Yeats yearned for a conservative revolution— a term that functions both as a tautology and an oxymoron when read in the light of the poet's other pronouncements about revolution. As he fervently wrote to Herbert Grierson in November 1922:

> We are preparing here, behind our screen of bombs & smoke, a return to conservative politics as else where in Europe. Or at least to a substitution of the historical sense for logic. The return will be painful & perhaps violent, but many educated men talk of it & must soon work for it & perhaps riot for it.[95]

The opposition between logic and the historical sense had been an *idée fixe* for some time, but he had begun to court violence with a new boldness. Of course, violence in Yeats's letter is gaily rendered as 'riot'—as if his counter-revolution would issue black eyes rather than death penalties; however, he was increasingly drawn to a sense of order whose ultimate guarantee was lethal force. Not only would Yeats accept the legitimacy of State executions during the civil war; he cast such violence as the source of legitimacy itself. As he put it in 1932, 'The Government of the Free State has been proved legitimate by the only effective test; it has been permitted to take life.'[96]

Yeats takes permissions with the word 'permitted', conflating the fact of taking life with a right to do so. He may have simply assumed that the 'permission' derived from a broader democratic mandate to rule—a position certainly adopted by the Minister of Home Affairs, Kevin O'Higgins ('the man who kills without a mandate from his people,

---

[92] *CW1*, 201.

[93] Yeats to Olivia Shakespear (May 1922), *CL InteLex* #4118.

[94] *VP*, 544.

[95] Yeats to H. J. C. Grierson (6 November 1922), *CL InteLex* #4202.

[96] *CW10*, 231. See also 'On the Boiler', *CW5,* 241: 'A government is legitimate because some instinct has compelled us to give it the right to take life in defence of its laws and its shores.'

without a constitutional democratic mandate, is a murderer,' O'Higgins declared, while insisting that his government had that mandate).[97] O'Higgins certainly advertised how illiberal democracies could be—which may explain why he was so admired by Yeats—but what impressed Yeats about the civil war was that it seemed to undermine the legitimacy of democracy itself. Like many backers of the Free State, Yeats interpreted the civil war as 'a revolt against democrasy [sic] by a small section', and though he supported the brutal suppression of that section, he also seemed to have been cheered by the implications of such revolt: it was encouraging evidence of democracy's decline.[98] As he exultantly wrote in December 1922, 'Democracy is dead & force claims its ancient right.'[99]

Since 1916 Yeats had been nervously drawn to the idea of a foundational violence that exceeded any ordinary moral or legal norms, though it might become a new source of those norms. This was the idea of the 'exception' that James Connolly had used to justify revolution against the British State; it was also the logic used to crush revolution in the name of an Irish State.[100] Such a climate of exceptions could produce feelings of moral anarchy on all sides. As the IRB man P. S. O'Hegarty declared in 1924, 'We derided the Moral Law and said there was no Law but force', a view that was almost conceded to by O'Higgins himself in the Dáil during the civil war ('We have no talisman except force').[101] This is the atmosphere that haunts poems like 'Leda and the Swan'—written just after the end of the civil war, though Yeats also had a broader context of European tumult in mind.

The act of divine rape in 'Leda and the Swan' might seem to cast derision on the moral law, or it may suggest that there is no law but violence itself. Force comes first even on a syntactical level—'A sudden blow' initiates the poem—just as rape will function as the origin point for a new kind of civilization. Moreover, the poem seems to reel from that blow more than it condemns it—like Leda herself, whose resistance to her rapist is notoriously equivocal or 'vague'. The intimation that the new order will ultimately succumb to the violence that engendered it may point to a moral law—that violence will be punished by its own hand—though this could also be viewed as further evidence of the law of force:

> A shudder in the loins engenders there
> The broken wall, the burning roof and tower
> And Agamemnon dead.[102]

[97] Dáil Debates, 19 May 1922.

[98] Yeats to Olivia Shakespear (9 October 1922), *CL InteLex* #4184.

[99] Yeats to Olivia Shakespear (18–21 December 1922), *CL InteLex* #4236.

[100] Connolly, *Collected Works*, vol. 2, 117. Defending state executions during the civil war, Eoin MacNeill declared, 'When emergencies of extreme necessity arise there is no limit.' See Dáil Debates, 8 December 1922.

[101] Patrick Sarsfield O'Hegarty, *The Victory of Sinn Féin* (Dublin: Talbot Press, 1924), 125. Ireland, according to O'Higgins, was in a state of war, and war was a form of anarchy in which 'there are no rules and no laws to guide men'. Or there was only one law, he contended, that law which Cicero had stood by: '*Salus populi suprema lex*'. Dáil Debates, 8 December 1922.

[102] *CW1*, 214.

All may not end well for Troy or for Clytemnestra's husband, but Yeats would be repeatedly drawn to the fecundity of violence. In 'Blood and the Moon' he champions his own tower as a symbol of authority—an authority that is construed as 'a bloody, arrogant power'. Force once more is constitutive: the tower, we are told, 'Rose out of the race / Uttering, mastering it'. The building may owe its origins to some pre-existing race, but it also produces and dominates that race through a kind of performative utterance. Once more a mob becomes a people through an aggressive poetics of power.[103] Yeats indicated that the poem was written in response to O'Higgins's assassination in 1927—a politician who had made no bones of the fact that 'all government is based upon force'.[104]

'He that is a Tyrant will be a Rebel,' Burke once proposed, for neither figure can accept an authority higher than their own capricious will.[105] Yeats's politics lend some weight to Burke's remark. While he admitted to being a 'revolutionist'[106]—often revolting from and revolted by his own epoch—he also recognized his own tyrannical instincts. As he told Laura Riding in 1936, 'I am a despotic man, trying to impose my will upon the times'.[107] The wilfulness may reflect his sense that there was no longer any moral or political order to be found in the world and that he lived in anarchic climes—a key theme of 'The Second Coming'. His response to such chaos was increasingly uncompromising. He became a firm believer in what he called ' "the strong line"—a line drawn upon the fluctuating chaos of human nature'. In 'Easter, 1916' he had invoked the fluctuating chaos of nature as a coded repudiation of the rigid lines of revolutionary nationalism, but by the 1920s he wished to put chaos to bed in the name of 'authoritative government'.[108] Though there was always something revolutionary about the authoritarianism to which he was drawn—consider Mussolini's march on Rome or Franco's bloody coup—Yeats continued to present himself as a firm critic of revolution. In his late lyric fragment 'The Great Day' he mocked the entire notion of a revolutionary new beginning, while also communicating a waning faith in authority. The verse is as repetitious as the history it commemorates:

> Hurrah for revolution and more cannon shot;
> A beggar upon horseback lashes a beggar upon foot;
> Hurrah for revolution and cannon come again,
> The beggars have changed places but the lash goes on.[109]

Here tyrants and rebels swap places in the merry-go-round of history. Of course, in the circular conception of time that we see in *A Vision* all human history is revolutionary in a very literal sense—another spin of time's Great Wheel—but in 'The Great Day'

[103] *CW1*, 237.
[104] Dáil Debates, 8 December 1922.
[105] Burke, *Writings and Speeches*, vol. 7, 339.
[106] *CW14*, 6.
[107] Yeats to Laura Riding (before 26 April 1936), *CL InteLex* #6541.
[108] Yeats to Maud Gonne McBride, (3 October 1927), *CL InteLex* #5035.
[109] *CW1*, 318.

history simply repeats itself as farce. If the speaker expresses little confidence in revolution, he shows scant respect for those on top (mere beggars upon horseback). In this sardonic vision, one thing seems certain: the lash will go on and the distinction between revolution and counter-revolution—always fairly faint in Yeats—will entirely fade away.

CHAPTER 16

YEATS IN FASCIST ITALY

LAUREN ARRINGTON

'IF something isnt done he'll sink into awful depths of depression and despair … I hope to get him to Rapallo, in fact well or ill I am going to get him there,' George Yeats wrote to her friend, the poet Thomas MacGreevy, in January 1928.[1] Yeats's ailment was psychological as much as it was physical: exhausted from his struggles in the Senate, worn out by theatre business, and depleted from finishing *The Tower*, he was overwhelmed by a sense of 'bitterness'. The word recurs in his letters to his confidantes Olivia Shakespear and Lady Gregory, where he describes Italy as an antidote to 'Irish bitterness' and the 'bitterness of Irish quarrels'.[2] The promise of Italy was so great that soon after W.B. and George arrived in Rapallo, in February 1928, they began to imagine a long-term recurrent migration: 'August to April here & the rest of the year in Dublin, with passing visits to London.'[3] But by the winter of 1930, the shine had worn off; George was starved of intellectual company, and W.B. was drawn back into Irish public life, including plans for experiments at the Abbey. In many ways, Rapallo had lived up to their expectations: the warm climate had restored his body, at least temporarily; Ezra Pound's invigorating friendship had healed his mind, and the idea of Italy had revived his political imagination.

Yeats's seasons in Rapallo, which spanned from 1928 to 1934, coincided with the consolidation of the Italian fascist regime. But unlike Pound, who wholly embraced Mussolini and his government, Yeats's proximity to the increasing totalitarianism of the regime resulted in his turning away from overtly fascist political structures, even while 'aesthetic fascism' continued to inform his work for the rest of his life.[4] Mary Ann Frese

---

[1] Ann Saddlemyer, *Becoming George: the life of Mrs W. B. Yeats* (Oxford: Oxford University Press, 2002), 392; for a discussion of WBY's illness, their journey south, and their first season in Rapallo, see *Life* 2, 352–65.

[2] WBY to Olivia Shakespear, 23 Feb [1928], *CL InteLex* #5079, and WBY to Lady Gregory [24 Feb 1928], *CL InteLex* #5081.

[3] Quoted in *Life* 2, 359.

[4] The nature and extent of Yeats's interest in and commitment to fascism have long been the subject of critical debate. Among the most notable of these is Elizabeth Butler Cullingford's *Yeats, Ireland and Fascism* (New York: New York University Press, 1981). Also important but largely discredited is W. J.

Witt, in her study *The Search for Modern Tragedy*, describes 'aesthetic fascism' as 'On one level ... part of the early modernist belief that innovation in art could lead to revolutionary change in politics. ... On another, it is a product of the aesthetic nature of certain political experiences such as the merging of the self with a crowd representing national identity.'[5] David Lloyd's study of Yeats's late poetry shows how Yeats's use of coercive allegories make the unwitting reader complicit in authoritarian modes of thought.[6] Lloyd sees Yeats's relationship to fascism as a to and fro:

> Though their exultation in violent acts of the will points the way towards a fascist politics, it derives that political solution from a desperation which is by no means capable of offering the consolatory myths of belonging on which fascism relies for its legitimation. If, as Walter Benjamin put it, fascism is the 'aestheticization of politics,' Yeats's writings are profoundly antagonistic to the representational aesthetics in which fascism finds its legitimation. And, on the contrary, the very stridency of both Yeats's poetry and his politics derives from the clarity of his recognition of the aesthetic or poetic foundations of the state.[7]

But early in the Italian fascism regime, aesthetics were not prescribed and were not representational. Early on, Mussolini's authoritarianism appealed to the core of Yeats's attitude to Irish political and cultural life, which can be discerned as early as Yeats and Gregory's 'Manifesto for the Irish Literary Theatre' (1897), in which they claimed the authority to represent Irish national identity. A close study of Yeats's interest in Italian fascism shows the fluidity of his attitude to Mussolini and the regime as well as the steadfastness of Yeats's authoritarian commitment in his aesthetics.

In January 1925, almost exactly three years before their first season resident in Rapallo, W.B. and George had joined Ezra and Dorothy Pound in Sicily, following advice from W.B.'s physician that 'another country and climate' were necessary to improve his health. The tour inspired important aspects of the first iteration of *A Vision* and provided the imagery for some of the images in *The Tower*, including the iconic 'Sailing to Byzantium.'[8]

McCormack's *Blood Kindred: W. B. Yeats: the life, the death, the politics* (London: Pimlico, 2005), which goes so far as to suggest that Yeats supported the Nazi regime because of his refusal to write a letter in support of the release of the writer Carl von Ossietzky from a Nazi camp. For a comprehensive study of Yeats's politics, see Jonathan Allison, ed., *Yeats's Political Identities: selected essays* (Ann Arbor: University of Michigan Press, 1996).

[5] Mary Anne Frese Witt, *The Search for Modern Tragedy: aesthetic fascism in Italy and France* (Ithaca: Cornell University Press, 2011), 2.

[6] See Lloyd's reading of 'Coole and Ballylee, 1931', where Yeats's inventive geography fabricates an elemental connection between the river that runs past Thoor Ballylee and the lake at Coole Park. David Lloyd, 'The Poetics of Politics: Yeats and the Founding of the State', *Qui Parle*, 3:2 (1989), 76–114.

[7] Lloyd, 'The Poetics of Politics', 102.

[8] For an extensive discussion of the source texts, see Catherine E. Paul and Margaret Mills Harper, eds., W. B. Yeats, *A Vision* (1925), hereafter cited as *CW13*; also see Russell Elliott Murphy, '"Old Rocky Face, look forth": W. B. Yeats, the Christ Pantokrator, and the Soul's History (The Photographic Record)', in *YAACTS* XIV (1996), ed. Richard Finneran, 69–117.

On their Sicilian holiday, Yeats and Pound worked companionably alongside one another, and the memory of that winter—itself a revisiting of the three winters that Yeats
and Pound had spent at Stone Cottage—inspired George's belief in January 1928 that
proximity to Ezra would draw W.B. out of his malaise.

Italy was attractive for other reasons: three years before the Sicilian tour, Yeats had
considered the ways that Italy might serve as a model for post-revolutionary Ireland. In
November 1922, a week after Mussolini's March on Rome, Yeats had written, 'The Ireland
that reacts from the present disorder is turning its eyes towards individualist Italy.'[9] He
thought that the tactics displayed in the early years of Mussolini's regime might inspire a
unified Irish culture after the devastating divisions of the Irish Civil War.

Thomas MacGreevy, who visited the Yeats family in Rapallo, recorded in an unpublished essay his understanding of Yeats's impression of the Italian regime: 'About 1923
or 1924 he told me he believed that Mussolini represented the rise of the individual
man as against what he considered the anti-human party machine.'[10] Yeats's distrust of
party politics stemmed from the fall of Charles Stewart Parnell, and in speeches from
the mid-1920s right through the 1930s Yeats frequently draws equivalencies between the
Parnellite Split and the Irish Civil War. Yeats's interest in Mussolini's regime as an antidote to political disorder is evident in remarks made at the Tailteann Games, a sporting
competition and occasion of cultural display that was held in 1924 to coincide with the
Paris Olympics and was intended to broadcast the image of a stable post-independence
state. At the Tailteann banquet, Yeats quoted Mussolini, proclaiming 'as a great popular
leader has said to an applauding multitude, "We will trample upon the decomposing
body of the Goddess of Liberty".'[11] In drafts of this speech, Yeats referred to the 'industrial unrest which had nearly sabotaged the opening of the Games', hinted at a parallel
that he saw in the Irish and Italian political crises, and proposed what he believed was an
Italian solution. He wrote: 'We have exchanged revolver shots for strikes, illegal violence
for the legal violence of a small minority that has claimed the right to deprive of the
necessities of life and health many thousands.'[12]

The Italian National Fascist Party had banned, at its inception in 1921, the right to
strike; this move was a reaction against the nearly two thousand industrial strikes and
two hundred peasant strikes that occurred in 1920.[13] Yeats referred to this policy in his
speech at the Tailteann banquet, when he cited Mussolini's authoritarianism as a cure for
'nineteenth-century liberalism' and proposed that the task for the Irish government was

---

[9] WBY to H. J. C. Grierson, 6 November [1922], *CL InteLex* #4202; see also Paul Scott Stanfield,
'The Irish Free State and the European Crisis', in David Holdeman and Ben Levitas, eds., *W. B. Yeats In
Context* (Cambridge: Cambridge University Press, 2010), 57–68, 58.

[10] Thomas MacGreevy, 'W. B. Yeats: a Generation Later', Trinity College Dublin (TCD) MS 8000/
6 (12).

[11] *Life 2*, 265.

[12] *Life 2*, 265.

[13] For the wave of strikes, socialist protests, clashes with police, and subsequent attacks on
socialists by Fascist squads, see Christopher Duggan, *The Force of Destiny: a History of Italy since 1796*
(London: Penguin, 2008), 421–5.

'not the widening of liberty, but recovery from its errors: that they will set their hearts upon the building of authority, the restriction of discipline, the discovery of a life sufficiently heroic to live without opium dreams'.[14] Yeats developed this idea of constructive authoritarianism in his 'Commentary on a Parnellite at Parnell's Funeral', published in *Dublin Magazine* in 1931 and in *Wheels and Butterflies* by Cuala Press in 1934, at the height of his interest in the Irish Blueshirts and after his rejection of Italian fascism as a political model.[15] Although Yeats's time in Rapallo was relatively brief, fascism as he encountered it in Italy was formative to his development of a specifically Irish response to the perceived crisis.

In 1924, Yeats hoped to give Tailteann an Italian inflection by extending an invitation to 'the first Duce', Gabriele d'Annunzio, to attend. D'Annunzio had just been awarded the title Principe di Montenevoso in recognition of his short-lived dictatorship of Fiume, which set the precedent for Mussolini's use of political performance in the regime.[16] Ezra Pound disliked D'Annunzio's oratorical flourishes, but, as Rebecca Beasley notes, Pound was 'clearly encouraged by the sight of a writer as a political leader', and he went so far as to claim that d'Annunzio 'represents art and literature ... he represents the individual human being'.[17] Pound's ideas about the strong political leader as 'artifex' and his vision of an authoritarian government functioning as a modernizing force would be given full articulation in his book *Jefferson and/or Mussolini: L'idea statele, Facism as I have seen it*, published in 1935—the year after Yeats's Cuala Press version of 'Commentary on a Parnellite at Parnell's Funeral'. Yeats also sent Pound an effusive invitation to Tailteann, but Dorothy advised Ezra against accepting, telling him, 'Don't go to Oireland—There's a strike in Dublin'.[18] There were also problems with Pound's passport, which the Irish Minister for External Affairs, Desmond Fitzgerald, attempted to mitigate. For one reason or another, Pound declined the invitation. D'Annunzio never replied.

Despite Yeats's best efforts, there was no Italian delegation at Tailteann, but his positive perception of the right wing of Italian politics underpins *A Vision* (1925), which shows Yeats at an 'idealistic moment in his investment with fascism'; as Catherine Paul and Margaret Mills Harper have argued, Yeats 'had in common with Mussolini his desire to

[14] Stanfield, 'Free State', 58; *Life* 2, 266; Claire Nally, 'The Political Occult: revisiting fascism, Yeats and "A Vision"', in Neill Mann, Matthew Gibson, and Claire Nally, *W. B. Yeats's 'A Vision': Explications and Contexts* (Liverpool: Liverpool University Press, 2012), 331, DOI:10.5949/liverpool/9780983533924.003.0014; and W. B. Yeats, 'From Democracy to Authority', *UP2*, 435.

[15] 'Commentary on a Parnellite at Parnell's Funeral' was republished in *King of the Great Clock Tower: Commentaries and Poems* (Dublin: Cuala, 1935); for Yeats and the Blueshirts, see Elizabeth Butler Cullingford, *Yeats, Ireland, and Fascism* (London: Macmillan, 1981), and Mike Cronin, *The Blueshirts and Irish Politics* (Dublin: Four Courts, 1997).

[16] WBY to Gabriele D'Annunzio, 2 July 1924, *CL Intelex* #4582; for d'Annunzio, see Lucy Hughes-Hallett, *The Pike: Gabriele D'Annunzio: Poet, Seducer and Preacher of War* (London: Fourth Estate, 2013), *passim*.

[17] Rebecca Beasley, *Ezra Pound and the Visual Culture of Modernism* (Cambridge: Cambridge University Press, 2007), 155, 197–8.

[18] Dorothy Pound to Ezra Pound (n.d. [29 July 1924]), Lilly.

infuse actual world events with the power of myth'.[19] This metaphysical aspect of Italian fascism is evident in d'Annunzio's speeches, and as Lucy Hughes-Hallet summarizes, 'Mussolini's inspirations were D'Annunzio's'.[20] She writes of the second Duce: 'Nietzsche filled him with "spiritual eroticism". He had learnt from Sorel. He called himself "an apostle of violence".[21] At the March on Rome, Mussolini had declared:

> let us too, pure in spirit and without rancor, raise our thoughts to Rome, one of the world's few cities of the spirit, because at Rome ... occurred one of the great spiritual wonders that history records ... . Now we aspire to make of Rome the city of our spirit, a city purged, cleansed of all the elements that have corrupted and violated her; we aspire to make of Rome the pulsating heart, the active spirit of the imperial Italy of our dreams.[22]

Giovanni Gentile—whose writing Yeats first encountered during his 1925 visit with the Pounds and who is an important figure in *A Vision*—developed in partnership with Mussolini the idea that the metaphysical state is a necessary counterpart to its materialism.[23] In 'The Philosophic Basis of Fascism', Gentile argued that fascism

> is eminently anti-intellectual ... that is, if by intellectualism we mean the divorce of thought from action, of knowledge from life, of brain from heart, of theory from practice. Fascist anti-intellectualism holds in scorn a product peculiarly typical of the educated classes in Italy: the *letterato* – the man who plays with knowledge and with thought without any sense of responsibility for the practical world. It is hostile not so much to culture as to bad culture ... . The Fascist system is not a political system.[24]

Gentile's work, as well as books by Oswald Spengler, Leo Frobenius, and Wyndham Lewis—all of whom Yeats discussed with Pound in Rapallo—shaped Yeats's ambitions for the organization of Irish civic life along spiritual and material lines.[25] (See Figure 16.1.)

---

[19]   *AVA*, xliv.

[20]   Hughes-Hallett, *The Pike*, 447.

[21]   Hughes-Hallett, *The Pike*, 447.

[22]   Quoted in Walter L. Adamson, 'Modernism and Fascism: the Politics of Culture in Italy, 1903–1922', *American Historical Review*, 359–90, 359.

[23]   Yeats cites Gentile's *The Theory of Mind as Pure Act* in *AVB*: 'our thoughts and emotions have duration and quality' and exist outside of time; although this statement seems banal, Yeats's reading of Gentile (whose philosophy draws from Kant) supports Yeats's idea of the poet's access to universal knowledge and, therefore, the special role that the poet plays in guiding the state; see Harper and Paul, *AVB*, 52 and 350 n.21.

[24]   Giovanni Gentile, 'The Philosophic Basis of Fascism', in *Readings on Fascism and National Socialism*, ed. Alan Swallow (Chicago: Swallow Press, 1952), 48–61.

[25]   Harper and Paul, *CW14*, xxxiii. For Yeats's discussion of the relationship between Spengler and Frobenius, see section XIII of 'The Great Year of the Ancients' in Harper and Paul, *CW14*, 189–90.

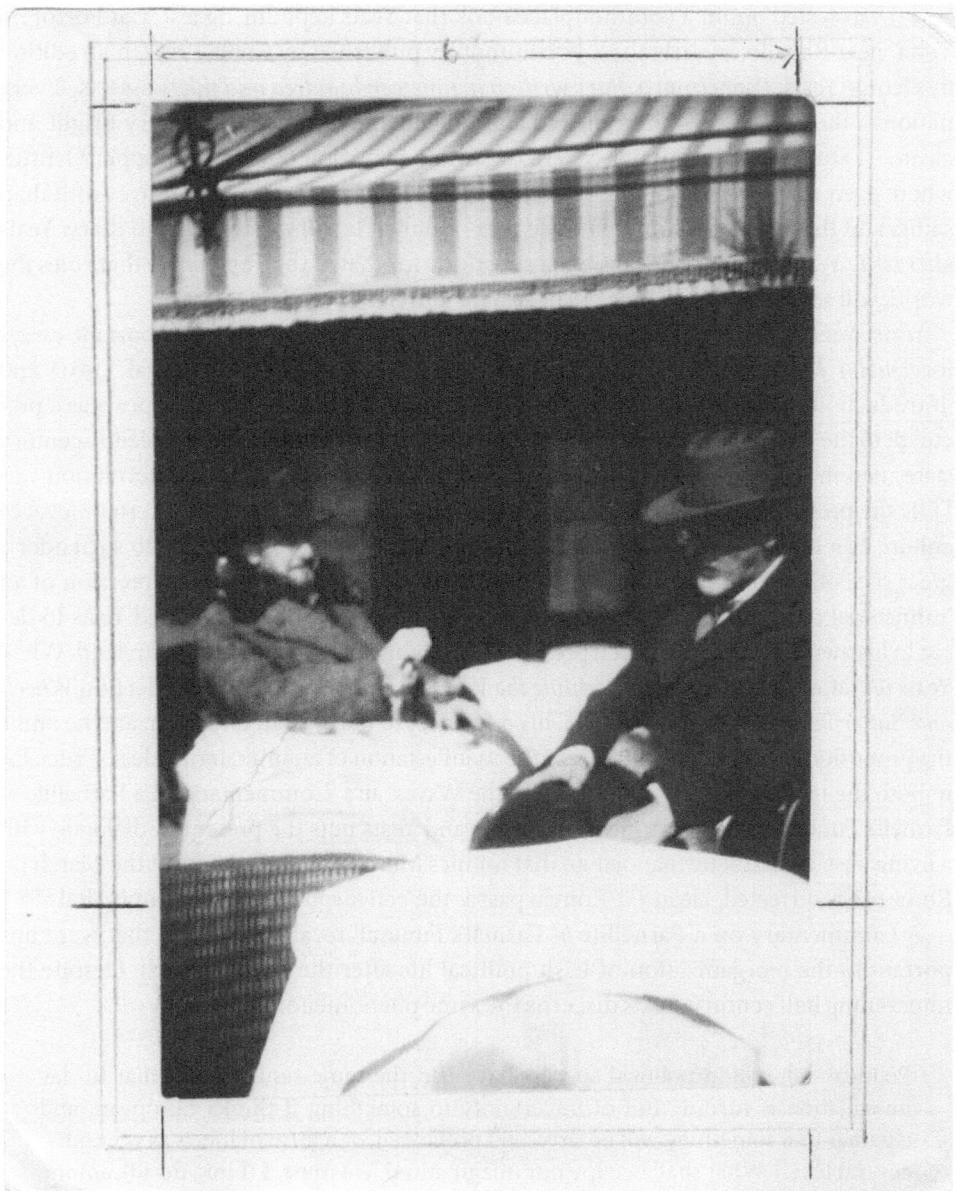

FIGURE 16.1 Yeats and Pound in Rapallo. Courtesy of Harry Ransom Center, University of Texas at Austin.

Yeats's essay 'A Commentary on a Parnellite at Parnell's Funeral' shows how Gentile's scorn for middle-class 'intellectualism' appealed to Yeats's ideas about the organization of politics. In that essay, Yeats equates the 'cellars' (political activists, especially communists) with the 'garrets' (intellectuals divorced from what Gentile describes as the 'practical world'). Yeats's incorporation of Gentile into the second iteration of *A Vision*

(1937) was tested out in a commonplace book that Yeats kept during a stay at Portofino Vetta, near Rapallo, in early 1930. Posthumously published by Cuala Press in an edition by George Yeats, *Pages from a diary written in nineteen hundred and thirty* asserts, 'Every nation is the whole world in a mirror and our mirror has twice been very bright and clear .... Study the educational system of Italy, the creation of the philosopher Gentile, where even religion is studied not in the abstract but in the minds and lives of Italian saints and thinkers, it becomes at once part of Italian history.'[26] In the 1930 diary, Yeats also asks, 'What idea of the State, what substitute for that of the Toga'd race that rules the world, will serve our immediate purpose here in Ireland?'[27]

Yeats went some way toward answering his own question in two important essays for *Dublin Magazine*: 'A Commentary on a Parnellite at Parnell's Funeral' (1931) and 'Introduction to *Fighting the Waves*' (1932), the latter of which uncannily appears as a precursor to the way that Pound compares a contemporary dictator and an eighteenth-century statesman in *Jefferson and/or Mussolini*, where Pound writes, 'The fascist revolution was FOR the preservation of certain liberties and FOR the maintenance of a certain level of culture ... a refusal to surrender certain immaterial prerogatives, a refusal to surrender a great slice of the cultural heritage.'[28] Pound's emphasis on culture as an expression of an 'immaterial prerogative' may have been one of the pressures that compelled Yeats to desist in his own correlation between present-day Italy and eighteenth-century Ireland. When Yeats redrafted 'Introduction to *Fighting the Waves*' for publication in the collection *Wheels and Butterflies* by Cuala Press in 1934, his references to Italy all but disappear, and he omits the proposition that material culture is the manifestation of an immaterial ideal. Crucially, in both the 1932 'Introduction to Fighting the Waves' and 'Commentary on a Parnellite at Parnell's Funeral' historical time is collapsed, and Yeats puts the present in dialogue with a living past: an aesthetic manoeuvre that mimics Mussolini's articulation at the March on Rome of a resurrected, 'cleansed' Roman past as the 'active spirit' of contemporary Italy.[29]

'A Commentary on a Parnellite at Parnell's Funeral' recalls the 'clubs' that were important to the reorganization of Irish political life after the fall of Parnell. Despite the intervening half century, Yeats discerns the same phenomenon in 1931:

> Political failure and political success have had the same result except that to-day imagination is turning full of uncertainty to something it thinks European, and whether that something will be 'arty' and provincial, or a form of life, is as yet undiscoverable .... What shall occupy our imagination? We must, I think, decide among these three ideas of national life: that of Swift; that of a great Italian of his day; that of modern England.[30]

---

[26] W.B. Yeats, *Pages from a diary written in nineteen hundred and thirty* (Dublin: Cuala, 1944), 55.

[27] *Pages from a diary*, 53.

[28] Pound, *Jefferson and/or Mussolini*, 127.

[29] For the architectural recovery projects of the Italian Fascist regime and Ezra Pound's engagement with them, see Catherine Paul, *Fascist Directive: Ezra Pound and Italian cultural nationalism* (Clemson: Clemson University Press, 2016).

[30] *VPl*, 957.

The 'great Italian' goes unnamed: He (and it is a 'he') may be Vico, or he may be a 'contemporary' leader. In *Yeats and Georgian Ireland*, Donald Torchiana goes so far as to say that Vico was the 'precursor of Fascism, according to Yeats.'[31] Yeats's 'Commentary' elaborates:

> Students of contemporary Italy, where Vico's thought is current through its influence upon Croce and Gentile, think it created, or in part created, the present government of one man surrounded by just such able assistants as Vico foresaw. Some philosopher has added this further thought: the classes rise out of the matrix, create all mental and bodily riches, sink back, as Vico saw civilization rise and sink, and government is there to keep the ring and see to it that combat never ends. These thoughts in the next few generations, as elaborated by Oswald Spengler, who has followed Vico without essential change, by Flinders Petrie, by the German traveler Frobenius, by Henry Adams, and perhaps by my friend Gerald Heard, may affect the masses.... and I suggest to the Cellars and the Garrets that though history is too short to change either the idea of progress or the eternal circuit into scientific fact, the eternal circuit may best suit our preoccupation with the soul's salvation, our individualism, our solitude. Besides we love antiquity, and that other idea—progress—the sole religious myth of modern man, is only two hundred years old.[32]

The metaphysical strain in Italian fascism, a strain that is also present in Spengler, Frobenius, and Henry Adams (whose work Pound was also reading in Rapallo), allowed Yeats to postpone choosing between Swift, the 'great Italian', and 'modern England'—the last of which was obviously a rhetorical device that enabled him to focus on parallels between Swift and Italian thought.

Yeats's 'Commentary on a Parnellite' draws explicitly from Croce's *The Philosophy of Giambattista Vico*, which George Yeats gave to him in August 1924.[33] Throughout the couple's philosophical experiments, they toy with the synthesis of paradox. In one of his most controversial late texts, 'The Genealogical Tree of Revolution', Yeats writes that Hegel had resolved the antimonies, enabling 'a diametrically opposed yet related series of propositions, centring on the materialist/idealist polarity .... Fascism, which had once seemed the antithesis of communism, now looked more like its mirror image.'[34] Claire Nally summarizes, 'For Yeats, both political regimes [communism and fascism] represent the suppression of individual freedom and thus are to be rejected.'[35] But Yeats's rejection of fascism and communism in favour of a Swiftian authoritarianism was not

---

[31] Donald Torchiana, *Yeats and Georgian Ireland*, 134.

[32] *VPl*, 963.

[33] See NLI, Yeats Library, 445.

[34] The image of the mirror may owe something to Yeats's reading of Strzygowski, whose 'view of the West [was] as a "mirror" of all other compass points', and Yeats links this to his classification of space and time in *AVB*; see Gibson, 'Timeless and Spaceless', 129. Ezra Pound resolves the antinomies more simply: 'Nowadays two are the men who knew how to "move" to the highest degree, who had the mastery of language which produces action: Il Duce and Lenin'; 'Appunti [Notes]', *Il Mare*, 163–5. I am grateful to Giulia Bruna for her translation of this and other essays from *Il Mare* for my book *The Poets of Rapallo*.

[35] Nally, 'The Political Occult', 341.

immediate. In both the 1931 'Commentary on a Parnellite at Parnell's Funeral' and the 1932 'Introduction to *Fighting the Waves*', fascism is weighed as a real possibility. An Italian inflection is discernible in the latter essay where references to Caesar draw explicitly from Yeats's shared reading with Pound in Rapallo.

In *Decline of the West*, Spengler characterizes Caesar as 'a pure man of fact gifted with immense understanding'.[36] He formulates 'the time of Caesar' as 'the birth [of] the great religions of Salvation' and writes that as a consequence 'the Culture rose to bright day, and what followed continuously throughout one or two centuries was an intensity of religious experience, both unsurpassable and at long last unbearable'.[37] Spengler believed that 'Caesar-men', capable individual leaders, were 'the very elementals of Becoming': the necessary 'powers of the blood, unbroken bodily forces, [that] resume their ancient lordship'.[38] According to Spengler, the 'will' of Caesar was not individualistic in the 'Napoleonic sense' but drew from the 'root-feeling of the Roman soul'.[39] In a long section on 'Caesarism' in his chapter on the 'State and History', Spengler suggests that his terminology refers to what Frese Witt later theorized as aesthetic fascism; Spengler writes, 'By the term "Caesarism" I mean that kind of government which, irrespective of any constitutional formulation that it may have, is in its inward self a return to thorough formlessness.'[40]

In 'Commentary on a Parnellite at Parnell's Funeral', Yeats distinguishes between a political leader who is a vessel for an abstract political virtue and the real, material manifestation of that ideal: 'We can no longer permit life to be shaped by a personified ideal, we must serve with all our faculties some actual thing.'[41] At this juncture in his philosophy Yeats is looking for a coincidence of the abstract and the material: the union of thought and action that was one of Gentile's most important contributions to Italian fascism. In the 'Introduction to *Fighting the Waves*' (1932) Yeats focuses extensively on material culture, imagining that the new Caesar, for whom he claims to write, will define and direct a national culture through public institutions:

> let Caesar talk to the Curator of the Museum; first doubling the Museum's inadequate grant . . . let Caesar command our Irish schools and colleges to teach Berkeley, side by side with more modern philosophy, or side by side with Aquinas as though he were Gaelic, and Kant or Aquinas Greek, and so save us from that popular science that is the opium of the suburbs.[42]

---

[36] Spengler, *Decline of the West*, 52. See also Nally, 'The Political Occult', 333.

[37] Spengler, *Decline of the West*, 299.

[38] Spengler, *Decline of the West*, 361. Nally's 'The Political Occult' first alerted me to the connection between Yeats's Caesar and Spengler's Caesarism. I record that debt here. Nally briefly develops Yeats's reading of Spengler in terms of the 1934 'Commentary on Three Songs', before making a further connection with Yeats's play *Purgatory*.

[39] Spengler, *Decline of the West*, 168–9 n.3.

[40] For a discussion of aesthetic fascism in relation to *Fighting the Waves* and Yeats's proposed collaboration with the Group Theatre in London, see my essay 'Toward a Late Modernist Theater', *Modernism/modernity*, 5:4 (25 Feb. 2021), https://doi.org/10.26597/mod.0186.

[41] *VPl*, 957.

[42] "Introduction to *Fighting the Waves*', *Dublin Magazine* (Apr.–June 1932), 9–10.

Here, Yeats's long campaign for Irish cultural institutions, not only the Abbey Theatre but also a gallery for the Hugh Lane pictures, is revisited in transhistorical terms.

As Yeats was thinking about Gentile and Spengler, he was also reading deeply into Berkeley's philosophy of immaterialism, the idea that thought is the only reality.[43] In Yeats's 1931 introduction to Hone and Rossi's *Bishop Berkeley: his life, writings, and philosophy*, Yeats asserted that Hone and Rossi's treatment 'makes Berkeley stand forth as a very real and solid ... figure'.[44] In their edition, Hone and Rossi emphasized 'Berkeley's return to philosophizing at a time when Berkeley's interests were more and more becoming "practical morality, architecture and scientific curiosities, politics, economic conditions, the Bermuda enthusiasm"'.[45] Berkeley and Gentile appear as dual influences on Yeats's 1932 'Introduction to *Fighting the Waves*', where the material culture of eighteenth-century Ireland—the furnished rooms through which Yeats imagines visitors walking; the mundane objects and costumes of eighteenth-century Irish society—communicates an immaterial idea of the eighteenth century and brings it to life in the present. Here Yeats is also adapting Spengler's idea of Caesar as described in the chapter on 'Philosophy of Politics' in *Decline of the West*, where Spengler concedes: 'Caesar grasped the fact that on the soil of a democracy constitutional rights signify nothing without money and everything with it.'[46] In sum, Spengler thought that materialism was necessary, but it was only a forerunner to what he imagined as a 'final battle between Democracy and Caesarism, between the leading forces of dictatorial money-economics and the *purely political* will-to-order of the Caesars.'[47]

Yeats thought that Pound's treaties on 'money-economics' were the line in the sand that differentiated him from the potential 'Caesar-men'. In 1934, the two poets had a spectacular disagreement over Yeats's new play, *The King of the Great Clock Tower*: a falling-out that signified the end of W.B. and George's visits to Rapallo. In August of that year, Yeats wrote to Olivia Shakespear, enclosing a review of the play and instructing, 'show to Ezra Pound that I may confound him. He may have been right to condemn it as poetry but he condemned it as drama.'[48] In truth, Pound had been more scathing; the previous June in Rapallo, when Yeats shared the play with Pound, Pound's response provoked such a passionate reaction that Yeats recorded the exchange in a notebook:

He condemned it 'Nobody language.' At first I took his condemnation as a confirmation of my fear that I am now too old. I have ~~hardly~~ written little verse for three

[43] For a detailed discussion of Yeats's reading of Berkeley, as mediated by Joseph Hone, who collaborated with Mario Rossi on translations of Berkeley's philosophy, see W. J. McCormack, 'We Irish' in Europe: Yeats, Berkeley and Joseph Hone (Dublin: University College Dublin Press, 2010). Yeats's interpretation of Berkeley informs his 1932 'Introduction to Fighting the Waves' where he collapses the distance between the material object and the idea of the object in the mind of its perceiver; similarly, in Words Upon the Window-pane, Swift articulates the capacity of thought to bring about reality: 'When I rebuilt Rome in your mind it was as though I walked in its Streets.'
[44] Sterling P. Lamprecht, review of Hone, Rossi, and Yeats, Bishop Berkeley: his life, writings, and philosophy, Journal of Philosophy, 29:19 (15 Sept. 1932), 528–30, 528.
[45] Lamprecht, review of Bishop Berkeley, 528.
[46] Spengler, Decline of the West, 374.
[47] Spengler, Decline of the West, 377.
[48] WBY to Olivia Shakespear, 7 Aug [1934], CL InteLex #6080.

years. But 'nobody language' is something I can remedy. I never write in verse, but first in prose to get structure.[49]

In Cave's study of the manuscript materials for *The King of the Great Clock Tower*, he shows how Pound's critique prompted an immediate redrafting: Yeats developed his types into full characters, transforming the King into O'Rourke of Breffny and creating connections between O'Rourke's ancestry and Dervorgilla, who is important to his earlier Noh play *The Dreaming of the Bones*, which was a product of Yeats's and Pound's collaboration during the three winters they spent at Stone Cottage from 1913 to 1916.[50] The revision had the effect of tying *The King of the Great Clock Tower* to the poets' history as collaborators, but—as Cave notes—the changes didn't stick, since they could possibly 'rouse expectations that Yeats was writing to a political agenda; this would seriously jeopardize the communicating of his metaphysical theme about the slain but risen god'.[51] Taking into account Yeats's modelling of his ideas on Spengler, the danger seems less that Yeats was concerned about a specific 'political agenda' and more to do with the concern that naming his characters and limiting his play to a particular set of mythologies would restrict the play's plasticity; in Spengler's terms, *The King of the Great Clock Tower* would no longer embody aesthetic 'formlessness'.[52]

In the version of 'Introduction to *Fighting the Waves*' that was published in *Wheels and Butterflies* (1934), Yeats privileges the kind of formlessness that Spengler associates with cultural purity:

> by the end of the nineteenth century, the principal characters in the most famous books were the passive analysts of events, or had been brutalised into the likeness of mechanical objects. But Europe is changing its philosophy. Some four years ago the Russian Government silenced the mechanists because social dialectic is impossible if matter is trundled about by some limited force. Certain typical books – *Ulysses*, Mrs. Virginia Woolf's *Waves*, Mr. Ezra Pound's *Draft of XXX Cantos* – suggest a philosophy like that of the Samkara school of ancient India, mental and physical objects alike material, a deluge of experience breaking over us and within us, melting limits whether of line or tint; man no hard bright mirror dawdling by the dry sticks of a hedge, but a swimmer, or rather the waves themselves . . . .[53]

Where the 1932 'Introduction' is focused on material artefacts as conduits for a spiritual past, the 1934 'Introduction' praises the way that the spiritual is communicated

---

[49]   Richard Allen Cave, ed. *The King of the Great Clock Tower and A full moon in March: manuscript materials* (Ithaca: Cornell University Press, 2007), xlvi.

[50]   James Longenbach, *Stone Cottage: Pound, Yeats, and Modernism* (Oxford: Oxford University Press, 1988).

[51]   Cave, *KOGCT*, xlvii.

[52]   Cave arrives at the same conclusion, via a different route: 'The strength of *The King of the Great Clock Tower*'s theatrically lies in its heightened abstraction, which enables the play to move effortlessly toward its conclusion through dance, mime, tableau, and choric song'; *KOGCT*, xlvii.

[53]   *CW2*, 703.

materially through great writing that is without temporal or physical limits. Yeats's alterations to 'Introduction to *Fighting the Waves*' reflect his changing attitude to Italian fascism, which are also apparent in the revised *A Vision* (1937), where Yeats asks, 'What discords will drive Europe to that artificial unity—only dry or drying sticks can be tied into a bundle—which is the decadence of every civilization?'[54]

The image of a 'bundle' of 'drying' or 'dry sticks' recurs at key places in Yeats's writing in 1934 and 1935, reflecting his severance of associations with Pound and definitively ending his decade-long fascination with Mussolini's regime. In August 1937, Yeats included in a letter to Dorothy Wellesley his draft of a lyric that explicitly severs his own thought from contemporary politics: 'Though I have bid you turn / From the cavern of the mind; / (There is more to bite upon / In the sunlight and the wind); // I did not say attend / To Moscow or to Rome / Turn from drudgery / Call the Muses home.'[55]

But Yeats did attend to Rome, at least once in a quasi-political capacity, when in early October 1934, he—accompanied by George, in the essential role of translator—was a delegate to the Volta Conference on Theatre.[56] While there, they may have also attended the Exhibition of the Fascist Revolution, which ran for two years from 28 October 1932 to 28 October 1934 and attracted nearly three million spectators.[57] A copy of the English-language exhibition catalogue rests in the Yeats library; there is no record of its acquisition nor any correspondence mentioning the book in the extant W. B. Yeats letters, which suggests that W.B. or George Yeats procured it for themselves.[58]

The Exhibition of the Fascist Revolution exemplifies how the proclaimed capaciousness of the fascist state's aesthetics—articulated by Mussolini and others in the mid 1920s—was, by the mid-1930s, more fixed into recognizably propagandistic and totalitarian forms. As the regime was consolidated, Ruth Ben-Ghiat notes in her study *Fascist Modernities*, 'exhibitions took on a central importance as agents of indoctrination and mass mobilization'.[59] Nominally, artists were still committed to 'formlessness'

[54] *AVB*, 301–2; also see Nally, 'The Political Occult', 340.

[55] WBY to Dorothy Wellesley, 12 Aug [1937], *CL InteLex* Acc #7039. The poem continues for a further two stanzas; in a postscript he writes, 'First stanza goes better thus. (I hate writing for the eye): Because there's more to bite on—In sunlight or in wind,/ I have bid you turn/From the cavern of the mind.' The turn in Yeats's thought away from explicitly totalitarian forms is also indicated in the way that his *Broadside* series with Wellesley in 1936 for Cuala Press lacks the political tenor of his 1935 series with Higgins, discussed further in my book *The Poets of Rapallo* (Oxford University Press, 2021).

[56] Saddlemyer, *Becoming George*, 479. George's skill as a linguist meant she could be critical of WBY's professional translators; Ezra wrote to Dorothy in June 1928, 'W.B.Y.'s translator turned up night before I left Wien. Have write G.Y. to let the feller git on with his work,' Lilly.

[57] Stone gives the figure as 'over 1,800,000 visitors'; see Marla Stone, 'Staging Fascism: The Exhibition of the Fascist Revolution', *Journal of Contemporary History*, 28:2 (April 1993), 215–43, 215, https://www.jstor.org/stable/260709 (accessed 7 Mar. 2019).

[58] I'm grateful to John Kelly for confirming the absence of information about the programme in surviving Yeats correspondence and for confirming the probability of W.B.'s and/or George's attendance at the Exhibition.

[59] Ruth Ben-Ghiat, *Fascist Modernities: Italy 1922-1945* (Berkeley: University of California Press, 2001), 35.

or 'plasticity' in representation, but by 1934 the ideological referents were more clearly discernible.

Ezra Pound visited the exhibition in December 1932, just two months after it opened. He commented briefly in a letter to Olga Rudge that it was an impressive example of 'senso storico' or historical sensibility.[60] Similarly, he wrote to Dorothy Pound, 'Xposition of Xenio rather impressive. Not Art-show, but a history show to inskrukt.'[61] W.B.'s and George Yeats's impression—*if* they attended in person—is irrecoverable from the archive, but despite the paucity of evidence regarding their views on the Exhibition, it *is* possible to reconstruct W. B. Yeats's participation in the Volta Conference and its effect on his ideas about theatre, particularly the notion of heroic drama and its connection to a national culture. His thinly veiled comments at Volta about the Italian state may allude to his impression of the fixed ideology of the Exhibition of the Fascist Revolution; at the very least, he comments on other manifestations of totalitarian aesthetics that were contradicting the 'formlessness' of early Italian fascism.

The Volta Conference on Dramatic Theatre was held from 8 to 14 October 1934, proclaimed in the conference's programme as Year XII of the Fascist regime.[62] The conference was sponsored by the Royal Italian Academy, whose president was Marconi, the pioneer of radio transmission, and it was presided over by Pirandello, who had been awarded the Nobel Prize earlier the same year and was in the midst of a sustained campaign for his own state-subsidized theatre. Marinetti served as the conference's secretary.[63] The lavishly produced programme, preserved in the Yeats Library, outlines five aims for the conference: to put theatre in dialogue with other art forms and media (specifically cinema, opera, and radio); to consider innovations in the architecture and scale of theatre (both 'theatre of the masses' and little theatres); to explore new possibilities for stage design; to consider the role of performance in the moral life of the people; and to consider the idea of a State Theatre—including the history of state theatres' organization throughout Europe, the need for them in the present-day, the content of their programmes, and the possibility for exchanges between state theatres.[64] Major figures in European drama were present, including Yeats's long-term collaborator Edward Gordon Craig, and Ashley Dukes, whom Yeats hoped would be involved in producing a programme of his plays for the Group Theatre in London that same autumn.

[60] A 'rather impressive, if one have of *senso storico*'; quoted in Paul, *Fascist Directive*, 103.

[61] Ezra to Dorothy Pound ('Xmas' [1932]), Lilly.

[62] Reale Accademia D'Italia, *Convegno di Lettere: Il Teatro Drammatico* (Rome: Reala Accademia D'Italia, 1935); hereafter cited in the notes as *Volta*. Yeats Library, NLI.

[63] Lino Pertile writes that the Academy, founded in 1927, 'offered the highest accolades – and a good salary – to Italian scientists, scholars and artists in exchange for support or even simple acquiescence [to the regime]. Again many respected intellectuals, with the exclusion of the Crocean hard core, yielded to the temptation. Marinetti, ironically enough, the old arch-enemy of all academies, was one of the first to be appointed.' Lino Pertile, 'Fascism and Literature', in David Forgacs, ed., *Rethinking Italian Fascism: Capitalism, Populism, and Culture* (London: Lawrence & Wishart, 1986), 162–84, 172–3.

[64] Translations my own.

Yeats's speech at the conference invested his plays with political meaning, proclaiming that his own drama was 'active' and had the power to reunite a divided people. Similar to his Tailteann speech nearly ten years earlier, he referred to the Parnellite Split as a cipher for the Irish Civil War.[65] Yeats asked his audience, 'Had Parnell been betrayed? Who had betrayed him? Families were divided, son against father, brother against brother.' He continued, 'In the midst of that disillusionment, of that bitterness, the Irish imaginative movement began.'[66] He regaled his audience with the story of the riots over *The Playboy of the Western World*: 'Picturesque, poetical, fantastical, a masterpiece of style and music, it roused the populace to fury.'[67] He implied that the Irish National Theatre's history was a long struggle against a 'populace' or 'mob' that had been miseducated by party politics and who lacked a heroic leader. He described a squabble with the Abbey's company over Lady Gregory's play *The Rising of the Moon*: 'The players would not perform it because they said it was an unpatriotic act to admit that a policeman was capable of patriotism. One well known leader of the mob wrote to me, "How can the Dublin mob be expected to fight the police if it looks upon them as capable of patriotism?" '[68] Yeats concluded, 'Every political party had the same desire to substitute for life, which never does the same thing twice, a bundle of reliable principles and assertions.'[69]

Yeats's disparagement of the 'bundle of reliable principles' indicates his rejection of the totalizing iconography of Italian fascism as it was manifested under Mussolini and in Pound's increasingly totalitarian writing. While he dismissed Italian fascism's 'dry sticks', Yeats remained interested in totalizing mythologies, not only the System in *A Vision* but also in the theatre. In a letter to Edmund Dulac in December 1934—about six weeks after Volta—Yeats described *The King of the Great Clock Tower* as 'theatrically coherent, spiritually incoherent'. He told Dulac that his revision was driven by the need to 'work out' a 'blood symbolism' that had 'laid hold upon' him, an impulse that Yeats believed came from 'beyond the will'.[70] This direct echo of Spengler's Caesarism shows that although Yeats no longer espoused the idea of Italian fascism as a political model, and he ultimately rejected Gentile's materialism in favour of Berkeley's immaterialism, Italian fascism in its party-political manifestation and conversations in Rapallo about fascist political thought remained powerful presences in Yeats's late work.

---

[65] See, for example, 'Parnell's Funeral' in *CW1*, 285.

[66] *Volta*, 386. The Civil War as referent in the Volta speech is further underlined by Yeats's discussion of Lady Gregory's heritage: her life spent 'in two Galway houses; the house where she was born, since burnt down in a year of trouble'.

[67] *Volta*, 388.

[68] *Volta*, 391

[69] *Volta*, 391.

[70] WBY to Edmund Dulac [10 Dec. 1934], *CL InteLex* #6145.

CHAPTER 17

THE 1930S

'That day brings round the night'

ALAN GILLIS

'It is time that I wrote my will'—so wrote Yeats in the title poem of *The Tower*, published in 1928. In 1931 he prepared for an 'Edition de Luxe' of his work, then published a *Collected Poems* in 1933 and a *Collected Plays* in 1934. He had almost died in late 1929 from a fever (his health would be poor for the rest of his days). All that came after, for Yeats, was a bonus, and often his output of the 1930s seems consciously written as last work. Indeed, he explored posthumous perspectives through the thirties, creating haunted, spectral personae. But he also indulged in a *carpe diem* approach to old age. One of his last poems was titled 'Why should not Old Men be Mad?'[1] Holding to a doctrine of 'the mask', he felt the artist should explore the opposite of what seems innate or apparent, approaching self and world antithetically. And so, until his death in January 1939, Yeats's last decade was often given to a virulent celebration of energy. He retired as a Senator and from public responsibility in 1928. Giving voice to what he called 'tragic joy', fusing nihilism and affirmation with apocalyptic passion, he sometimes made a point of courting outrage and outrageousness.[2] Yet much of his best work of the decade is lit with grace and humility. Whatever way one looks at him, he demands a second look, for it is supremely difficult to accurately frame Yeats—especially in the 1930s—within a single perspective. Always a poet of paradox, in his last years his contradictions went supernova.

In terms of broad historical context, Ireland in the 1930s was trying to settle in the aftermath of the Easter Rising, the War of Independence, partition, civil war, and the subsequent establishment of a sovereign civic government. But the swift rise of Fianna Fáil represented, for Yeats, a return of the 'Irreconcilables' from the civil war (he had been a supporter of the 'pro-Treaty' side, and of Cosgrave's subsequent government).

---

[1] *VP*, 625.

[2] In Yeats's poem 'The Gyres' we read: 'Irrational streams of blood are staining earth ... We that look on but laugh in tragic joy' (*CW1*, 293).

For Yeats, the party also represented a new Irish hegemony of populist Catholic conservatism, which cemented his passionate opposition towards the dispensation of his day. More broadly still, of course, the thirties are globally synonymous with the rise of vicious and malevolent totalitarian regimes that perpetuated unspeakable crimes against humanity, leading to the global catastrophe of the Second World War. W. H. Auden, in his poem 'September 1, 1939', famously called the 1930s a 'low dishonest decade'.[3] Ireland might casually seem adrift from the more dramatic crises of the era, with its isolationism and trajectory towards neutrality. Yet it was impossible for a twentieth-century nation to escape the global tides of modernity. The brief rise of the fascistic Blueshirt movement in 1933 is the most well-known indicator of 'thirties' politics destabilizing Ireland, but this was merely symptomatic of Ireland's susceptibility to international pressures involving a crisis of capitalism and rise of non-democratic politics from both left and right. And so, it is arguably useful to perceive Yeats as a 'thirties' poet. If the thirties were experienced as a growing crisis, Yeats certainly perceived Ireland to be partaking of the turmoil, and the way in which he explored, reacted to, and pushed back against this sense of a calamitous zeitgeist was fascinating, if idiosyncratic.

The concept of 'thirties poetry' in British literary history centres upon a generation of poets whose most notable figures were W. H. Auden and Louis MacNeice. All such categories are simplifications, but the thirties generation might loosely be defined as the first significant group of British poets after the big modernists (Yeats, Eliot, Pound, and so on), who explicitly responded to the turbulence of their time with left-wing perspectives and a commitment to exploring poetry's relation to social reality and political agency. Yeats was in no way part of this generation, and many of Yeats's political opinions were inimical to Auden et al. Yeats notoriously had a fling with the Blueshirt movement in 1933 and was obsessed with a dialectic between what he called the 'few' and the 'many'. This duality, informed by eugenics and a nostalgia for feudalism that sometimes exploded into fascistic resentment, culminated in an odious if bizarre publication, *On the Boiler*, in which he urged for war against 'the multiplication of the uneducatable masses'.[4]

But MacNeice, whose book *The Poetry of W. B. Yeats* was the first critical monograph on his Irish elder, didn't claim Yeats as an influence on the thirties generation because of any particular ideology. Rather, Yeats was an enabling example because he assumed poetry had a public voice, showing how poetry might push back against the pressures of reality rather than passively reacting to it. MacNeice claimed: 'Yeats suggested by his example that, given a chaotic world, the poet is entitled, if he wishes, to eliminate some of the chaos, to select and systematize.'[5] Yeats was also important to the thirties generation in that he strove against modernist poetry's detachment from the generic man or woman in the street, and because his recourse to folk art paralleled Auden's predilection

---

[3] W. H. Auden, *The English Auden: Poems, Essays and Dramatic Writings 1927–1939*. (1977). Corrected edn (London: Faber & Faber, 1986), 245.

[4] *CW5*, 231.

[5] Louis MacNeice, *The Poetry of W. B. Yeats* (1941), 2nd edn (London: Faber & Faber, 1967), 156–7.

for 'light verse', and the younger poets' interest in adapting verse to popular culture more generally.

Reading Auden's article 'The Public v the Late Mr. William Butler Yeats', published months after Yeats's death in 1939, or MacNeice's book from a few years later, it is striking how these young, liberal, left-leaning and progressive, socially conscious poets were insistent that the estimation of Yeats's value should be separable from any kind of straightforward political message or ideological position he might be identified with.[6] They were not at all interested in condoning his late politics, but as Yeats had done throughout his career in Ireland, they urged against approaching poetry as a mere mouthpiece for ideas and viewpoints, or expressions of pregiven positions.

During the decade Yeats staged several new plays, published a revised edition of *A Vision* (1937) among other prose works, and edited *The Oxford Book of Modern Verse* (1936). These have attracted much scholarship and critical attention. But it remains the case that his work of the thirties is most notable for a series of remarkable lyric poems, from 'Coole Park and Ballylee, 1931', 'Byzantium' and others in *The Winding Stair and Other Poems* (1933), to 'Cuchulain Comforted', 'The Statues', 'Long-legged Fly', 'High Talk', and others in the posthumously published *Last Poems* (1939). The best of his late poems have been hugely influential: the fecundity of debate they have occasioned, from such a wide spectrum of approaches and in relation to so many differing contexts, is a fair indication that they stand as exemplars of achievement for the lyric poem, setting standards of what can be achieved in the form.

Yet not all his late verse is like this. Readers sifting through Yeats's complete verse of the 1930s for the first time might be surprised by how much of it is in the mode of folk songs and street ballads. MacNeice pointed out: 'Many of these poems belong to a peculiar genre—something between epigram and nursery rhyme. Some of them look superficially like light verse, even like nonsense verse; on examination they will be found to carry in concentrated form the same passion and the same ideas that he uttered elsewhere *ex cathedra*.'[7] Perceiving that 'High Modernist' poetry had retreated into academic convolution, Yeats was adamant his own verse should be rooted in older and more popular tradition. This made his work of the decade uneven, but it seems that craggy irregularity became part of the point of his poetic as a whole.

As MacNeice's comments suggest, the line between Yeats's 'high' lyrics and 'folk' verse is hazy. But pragmatically, there is a perceptible difference of mode that would be wrong to discount. Edna Longley has argued: 'Yeats seems to re-immerse himself in folk song whenever his poetry batteries need recharging'. She quotes a letter from Yeats explaining he 'wanted the poems he calls "mechanical little song[s]" to have a verbal music "all emotion and impersonal"'.[8] Some of this verse draws on what is often called 'common measure', in which alternating 4-beat and 3-beat lines create a driving momentum, with end-rhyme adding to the flow:

---

[6] Auden, *The English Auden*, 389–93.
[7] MacNeice, *Poetry of W. B. Yeats*, 140.
[8] Edna Longley, *Yeats and Modern Poetry* (Cambridge: Cambridge University Press, 1992), 162–3.

> O mind your feet, O mind your feet,
> Keep dancing like a wave,
> And under every dancer
> A dead man in his grave.[9]

The final three lines, here, are all 3-beat lines (from 'A Drunken Man's Praise of Sobriety'). Yeats rarely kept to any verse-form model with this populist verse, but instead spun variations on what you might call the spirit of common measure. Like a virtuoso returning to a simple form, what is striking is the versatility of rhythm and stanza Yeats generates in these poems, while broadly sticking to a restrictive template. Sometimes the flow is unexpectedly fleet-footed and fresh, as in 'Sweet Dancer':

> The girl goes dancing there
> On the leaf-sown, new-mown, smooth
> Grass plot of the garden …[10]

Sometimes the syntax is surprisingly tricksy, necessarily affecting the flow, as in 'Crazy Jane grown old looks at the Dancers':

> When she, and though some said she played
> I said that she had danced heart's truth,
> Drew a knife to strike him dead …[11]

Sometimes it is difficult to make sense whatsoever of the imagery and logic, as in 'Crazy Jane Reproved':

> To round that shell's elaborate whorl,
> Adorning every secret track
> With the delicate mother-of-pearl,
> Made the joints of Heaven crack:
> So never hang your heart upon
> A roaring, ranting journeyman.
> *Fol de rol, fol de rol.*[12]

Sometimes the lines run much longer than one might expect, as in 'The Curse of Cromwell':

> He that's mounting up must on his neighbour mount,
> And we and all the Muses are things of no account.
> They have schooling of their own, but I pass their schooling by,

---

[9] *CW1*, 313.
[10] *CW1*, 296.
[11] *CW1*, 260.
[12] *CW1*, 257.

> What can they know that we know that know the time to die?
> *O what of that, O what of that,*
> *What is there left to say?*[13]

This almost goes out of kilter. The first three lines, to this reader at least, are 6-beat lines that fall on the ear as three beats either side of a caesura: 'They have schooling of their own, but I pass their schooling by' (dah-de, dah-de, de-de-dah|de-de-dah, de-dah, de-dah). The fourth line then throws a variation that initially feels like the wheels have come off track, and yet the line is itself a lovely rhythmic unit: 'What can they know that we know that know the time to die?' (de-de-dah-dah, de-dah-dah |de-dah, de-dah, de-dah). Yeats wants to summon zestful energy, create a careening sense of wildness, yet he doesn't generate his chaotic effects through chaotic means.

Longley explains that, in the thirties, Yeats had 'a renewed interest in uniting "music and speech". He thought that the "right balance between sound and word" might help poetry to "get back its public". She cites Yeats who, in a co-written piece with F. R. Higgins, refers to 'the simple metres based on lines of three or four accents, eight or six syllables' as constituting the fundamental 'sing-song of the language'.[14] Idiosyncratic as ever, Yeats wrote to Dorothy Wellesley:

> This difficult work, which is being written everywhere now ... has the substance of philosophy & is a delight to the poet with his professional pattern; but it is not your road or mine, & ours is the main road, the road of naturalness & swiftness and we have thirty centuries upon our side. We alone can 'think like a wise man, yet express ourselves like the common people'. These new men are goldsmiths working with a glass screwed into one eye, whereas we stride ahead of the crowd, its swordsmen, its jugglers looking to right & left.[15]

Notoriously, he wrote 'Three Songs to the Same Tune' with the Blueshirts in mind. In a note, he claimed: 'For the first time in my life I wanted to write what some crowd in the street might understand and sing.'[16] Tellingly, Yeats was elsewhere clear that he detested the crowd in the street. In any case, it is bizarre enough, if the poems were meant to aid a fascist paramilitary march on the streets towards an armed coup, to conceive of them stomping boots while chanting Yeats's chorus:

> *'Who'd care to dig'em,' said the old, old man,*
> *'Those six feet marked in chalk?*
> *Much I talk, more I walk;*
> *Time I were buried,' said the old, old man.*[17]

---

[13] *CW1*, 305.

[14] Longley, *Yeats and Modern Poetry*, 163.

[15] W. B. Yeats, *Letters on Poetry: From W. B. Yeats to Dorothy Wellesley* (Oxford: Oxford University Press, 1940), 64; see also Yeats to Dorothy Wellesley [19 April 1936], *CL InteLex* #6538.

[16] *VP*, 543.

[17] *VP*, 548–9.

Later, embarrassed by his support for the Blueshirts (not because they were fascists, but because they were a shambles), he muddied the waters further by rewriting these songs as 'Three Marching Songs'[18] This 'old, old man' chorus is changed to:

> Robbers had taken his old tambourine,
> But he took down the moon
> And rattled out a tune;
> Robbers had taken his old tambourine.[19]

Both choruses show his willingness to deviate from the driven momentum that normally fuels populist verse. The repetition of the full line slows and swerves the flow, as the echo turns the poem in upon itself, creating an implosive effect. Whatever this indicates about Yeats's fascism, it is an odd manoeuvre given the context of the poems.

A chorus, in a poem, works in the same way as a refrain, and Yeats was very fond of refrains throughout the 1930s. A repeating refrain woven among different stanzas creates a distinct temporal effect: a patterned relation between change and sameness. As the change and variability of stanzas is counterpointed by the repeating refrain, time itself becomes more than mere succession. Temporal experience gains depth and creates an interaction between present and past (between what is happening now in the poem and the return of what has happened before). When the form works successfully, this relation between past and present becomes dynamic. R. P. Blackmur, discussing 'The Apparitions', with the refrain *Fifteen apparitions have I seen: / The worst a coat upon a coat-hanger*, says of the poem's structure: 'Something has been done to the refrain by the progressive interaction between it and the stanzas that has built up a plurisignificance.'[20] The connotations of the refrain modulate in relation to each stanza, but also the refrain affects how we read each stanza, creating multifaceted ramifications.

George Kittredge, in a classic definition of ballads from 1904, claimed they lack 'the instrumentality of a conscious speaker'. He argued: 'the author of a ballad [is] invisible, and, so far as the effect which the poem produces on the hearer is concerned, practically non-existent'.[21] In line with this tendency towards virtual anonymity, refrains are often akin to proverbs, aphorisms, and sayings that represent something like folk wisdom, handed down over generations or used broadly in a community. The same phrase might be used in differing circumstances. They help tie contingency together, linking people to a broader tradition of making sense. The folk saying comes from without, it represents

---

[18] Elsewhere in this book, Lauren Arrington in 'Yeats in Fascist Italy' (Chapter 16) discusses Yeats's intellectual drawing back from fascism during this period.

[19] *CW1*, 335.

[20] *CW1*, 344; R. P. Blackmur, *Language as Gesture: Essays in Poetry* (London: Allen & Unwin, 1954), 111.

[21] George Lyman Kittredge, 'Introduction', in Helen Child Sargent and George Lyman Kittredge, eds., *English and Scottish Popular Ballads* (London: Houghton, Mifflin & Co., 1904), xi.

external wisdom, though it is taken on by the individual, partially internalized in repeating it. In a similar vein, the refrain feels anonymously authored—the emphasis is on communality.

This impersonality is a central facet of Yeats's populist verse. One of the more remarkable aspects of his work is how it suggests our innermost emotions and moods are linked to external sources and archetypes. If I am in love, it will feel profoundly personal; but it is not as if other people haven't also been in love. Though my love is my own, it belongs to a broader tradition of love. It is of the self but transgresses the borders of the self. So it is with all experience, according to Yeats. For a poet so ferociously committed to asserting and defending the sanctity of subjective experience, in a world he perceived to be ruined by the docility of a herd mentality, it is striking how much of his verse ventriloquizes impersonal, communal voices.

On the one hand, then, his folk poems draw from traditions where song and verse are found on the street, in the tavern, around the fire—far from the intimate and interior scenario associated with modern lyric poetry (read alone, in one's own space, involving subtleties and intricacies that engage one's inner sensibility). But on the other hand, it is clear Yeats is manipulating the conventions of folk poetry for complex purposes. And this is most clear in his refrains. MacNeice explains two deviating aspects of Yeats's 'peculiar' use of the technique: 'First the music of his refrain is often less obvious or smooth than that of his verses themselves, being sometimes flat, sometimes halting, sometimes strongly counterpointed.' And secondly, 'his refrains tend to have either an intellectual meaning which is subtle and concentrated, or a symbolist or nonsense meaning which hits the reader below the belt'.[22] From '*Fol de rol, fol de rol*' to '*fol de rol de rolly O*'; from '*I carry the sun in a golden cup, / The moon in a silver bag*' to '*Tall dames go walking in grass-green Avalon*', whatever else one might think of his refrains, one might agree they bring a marked degree of otherness into the heart of Yeats's poetic.[23]

Returning to the paradox that Yeats felt compelled to write populist verse while elsewhere declaring his hatred of the masses, one might suggest his poetry and politics are contradicting one another. He is creating an approximation of popular form to disseminate aspects of his idiosyncratic philosophy and politics, frequently of a nihilist bent; but he seems to be revelling in his messages being mixed or confused, dumb or irrational. It should be noted he is not always serious, and here and there inclines to self-parody.[24] One poem, 'Consolation', finds its speaker 'Struggling for an image on the track / Of the whirling zodiac'.[25] Frequently he is simply venting

---

[22] MacNeice, *Poetry of W. B. Yeats*, 147.

[23] These refrains are respectively from 'Crazy Jane Reproved' (*CW1*, 256), 'The Pilgrim' (*CW1*, 313), 'Those Dancing Days are Gone' (*CW1*, 266), and 'The Statesman's Holiday' (*VP*, 626).

[24] Matthew Campbell's chapter in this book, 'Yeats's Visionary Comedy' (Chapter 38), focuses on the comedic aspect of Yeats, with much to say about this 'folk' strain of his verse.

[25] *CW1*, 272.

antic steam. The level of irony is sometimes difficult to construe, as in 'The Old Stone Cross':

> A statesman is an easy man,
> He tells his lies by rote;
> A journalist makes up his lies
> And takes you by the throat;
> So stay at home and drink your beer
> And let the neighbours vote,
> > *Said the man in the golden breastplate*
> > *Under the old stone Cross.*[26]

We know he opposed the political enfranchisement of the masses, but are the final two lines of this stanza really a serious message to dissuade the crowd from exercising their right to vote? Certainly, the way the refrain then distracts from the message is undeniably odd. Commenting on how poetry in the 1930s had broadly moved its diction and idiom towards common speech, Louis MacNeice pointed out that Yeats was too 'mannered' to fit with this trend. From a different and older generation, Yeats persisted through the thirties with grandiosity and high rhetoric. MacNeice quipped: 'like a figure from a fancy-dress party he looked wrong in the daylight'.[27] But this man with the golden breastplate suggests Yeats enjoyed flaunting a recherché quality. He enjoyed being stylistically off-trend, a poet from another era, almost ostentatiously out of time.

Folk art, through Yeats's pen, became a realm of weirdness, an eruption of the pre-modern into the destabilized present. If many of the poems are strange, especially the refrains, their disturbance is linked to their anonymous communality, plunging subjectivity into uncanny zones—whether ironic, comedic, brutal, or phantasmagoric. Longley argues: '[A]ll Yeats's refrains, eerie or worldly, "nonsensical" or "intellectual", oblique or in-your-face, call up the folk ghost as an unlocated impersonal voice ... There are more roads than one to what Eliot calls "escape from personality".'[28] In disrupting stability, exceeding the boundaries of the known and of the self, prioritizing the body as much as the mind, confusing what's here and now with what is somewhere else and long ago, the poetry's sense of otherness frequently takes on an aspect of negation. Perhaps the most quoted of these folk poems, 'Crazy Jane Talks with the Bishop', announces:

> ... Love has pitched his mansion in
> The place of excrement;
> For nothing can be sole or whole
> That has not been rent.[29]

---

[26] *CW1*, 317.
[27] MacNeice, *Poetry of W. B. Yeats*, 122.
[28] Longley, *Yeats and Modern Poetry*, 165.
[29] *CW1*, 259–60.

At times, Yeats's folk art creates an atmosphere akin to that of the heath in *King Lear*, with Yeats switching perspectives between raging old man and fool, sometimes striving to push sense, and language itself, to breaking point: 'O sea-starved, hungry sea'.[30]

There is a mean streak to much of Yeats's work in the thirties. In part, the unhinged aspects of his verse simply respond to a time out of joint, giving voice to cultural and historical deformation. What we find in some of his thirties work is blood lust, twisted logic, combative rhetoric, rampant prejudice, a fervid divisiveness, a shrill tone, and, overall, verse that gets off on its own mania. In this regard, he created a potent mimesis of the zeitgeist. It would be wrong to say all of this is put on for aesthetic and dramatic purpose; but a lot of it is, and it is ultimately impossible to draw a line between what is performative and what is not.

In early Yeats, the imagination was mostly pitched towards a revelation of otherness that was attractive. The self would be enchanted by a glimpse of a supernatural realm or would yearn for a lover (often these were the same thing), hypnotically pulling the self towards a realm of beauty, timelessness, and magical promise. The desired meeting of self and other would take on an erotic charge, imagined as a consummation that might transform the self. But in Yeats's poetry of the 1930s, the realm of otherness is no longer over there, it is here—the very realm in which one exists. It is no longer a realm of magical promise and seduction, it is now as historical as it is imaginary: a bleak realm of conflict, crisis, and irony. Yeats was always most interested in moments when opposites are close to fusion—not quite in consummation, but close enough that the self might be consumed by its imminence. For early Yeats, this was mostly pitched in a harmonious and organic manner, dripping with the woe and melancholy of desire. In late Yeats, it is apprehended in a more complex and unstable manner. The verse is still transfixed by transformation, or its potential, yet this is frequently now pained and seething. Enchantments are replaced by troubles. The 'antinomies' become 'extremities'.[31] And a world where extremities are perpetually colliding is not a good place.

A tendency to represent the destabilization of the sublime through oxymoron and a theatrical embrace of paradox was perhaps most memorably captured in the 'terrible beauty' of 'Easter, 1916'. And through the thirties Yeats perpetually gravitates towards the combustible moment when oppositions collide, where positive and negative become explosively interchangeable in an ecstasy of creative destruction, or destructive creation. Daniel Albright describes Yeats's 'tragic joy' as 'what a man feels when he feels at once everything that he is capable of feeling—a hypothetical apex of emotion comparable to what Freud called the oceanic process'.[32] This quality of feeling everything at once is especially pitched towards apprehending both the awesome wonder and disgusting futility of life simultaneously and intensely.

---

[30] *CW1*, 303. From 'A Crazed Girl'.

[31] 'Between extremities / Man runs his course; / A brand, or flaming breath, / Comes to destroy / All those antinomies / Of day and night' ('Vacillation', *CW1*, 249–50).

[32] Daniel Albright, ed., *W. B. Yeats: The Poems* (London: Dent, 1990), 768–9.

Nonetheless, as MacNeice argues, 'within Yeats, just as there was a grain of salt in his early enthusiasms—"Part of me looked on mischievous and mocking" —so his latter-day bitterness, cynicism, disgust, weariness, are qualified, never final'.[33] It is not the case that his rebarbative side is exclusive to his populist verse, while the more cultivated poems reveal his balanced and nuanced side. The complex sequence 'Blood and the Moon' refers to 'this pragmatical, preposterous pig of a world'[34]; 'Irrational streams of blood are staining earth' in 'The Gyres'.[35] 'A Bronze Head' imagines a 'supernatural' and stern eye looking out at the world:

> On this foul world in its decline and fall;
> On gangling stocks grown great, great stocks run dry,
> Ancestral pearls all pitched into a sty,
> Heroic reverie mocked by clown and knave,
> And wondered what was left for massacre to save.[36]

There is plenty of toxicity in the cultivated poems. Yet it is also the case that positive and less sensationalist aspects of his poetic are integral to his achievement. These more affirmative aspects of Yeats are bound up with the aesthetic experience of reading him; and while many of these aspects are already found in the vitality of the folk poems, it is unsurprising that his more equipoised and complex poems most readily demonstrate further qualities. Yeats's formal prowess draws from his language an extraordinary range of effects and tones: he generates more pounding resonance than any other poet of his era; but alongside surging emotion, he is a poet of suppleness, a lyricist of the most intricate ambivalences and balances. These effects supercharge the significance of his writing, but their imaginative and affective scope is only partially reproduceable outside of the poems themselves.

Of course, Yeats's 1930s work has generated much scholarship and critical attention.[37] Indeed, he has been so well served by literary critics and historians, it is almost a problem. The closer one leans in, the more rich and strange he becomes. But something of the point

---

[33] MacNeice, *Poetry of W. B. Yeats*, 137.

[34] *CW1*, 238.

[35] *CW1*, 293.

[36] *CW1*, 340.

[37] Recommended in-depth studies of Yeats in the 1930s include Terence Brown's *The Life of W. B. Yeats: A Critical Biography* (Dublin: Gill & Macmillan, 1999); Elizabeth Cullingford's *Yeats, Ireland and Fascism* (London: Macmillan, 1981), and *Gender and History in Yeats's Love Poetry* (Cambridge: Cambridge University Press, 1993); Roy Foster's *W. B. Yeats, A Life Volume II: The Arch-Poet, 1915–1939* (Oxford: Oxford University Press, 2003); Marjorie Howes's *Yeats's Nations: Gender, Class and Irishness* (Cambridge: Cambridge University Press, 1996); Edna Longley's *Yeats and Modern Poetry* (Cambridge: Cambridge University Press, 1992); Lucy McDiarmid's *Saving Civilization: Yeats, Eliot, and Auden Between the Wars* (Cambridge: Cambridge University Press, 1984); Michael North's *The Political Aesthetic of Yeats, Eliot and Pound* (Cambridge: Cambridge University Press, 1992); Paul Scott Stanfield's *Yeats and Politics in the 1930s* (Basingstoke: Macmillan, 1988); and the present author's *Irish Poetry of the 1930s* (Oxford: Oxford University Press, 2005).

of Yeats goes missing if we don't allow for a certain limit to knowledge and recognize the centrality of the reading experience, regarding his work. When it comes to his poetry, the nature of the imagery, the rhythm and sound, and the way constituent parts come together in the dynamism of the whole are integral yet are subjectively apprehended. There is always a quality to his verse—dramatic or ambiguous, excessive or incomplete—that calls for imaginative engagement on the part of the reader. Given Yeats's formal range and thematic scope, no one poem fully represents his poetic, yet scrutiny of an example might nonetheless offer insights as useful as those generated by a broader survey of his sprawling oeuvre. Basic and obvious features of a poem can sometimes be neglected by critics, who understandably may not wish to spend their time pointing out basic and obvious things. But the artfulness of a poem, and thus much of the point of a poem, can go missing unless we occasionally look afresh at fundamental features.

Certainly, one might find many things to discuss in one of Yeats's most anthologized lyrics of the 1930s, the enigmatic 'Long-legged Fly,' which begins:

> That civilisation may not sink,
> Its great battle lost,
> Quiet the dog, tether the pony
> To a distant post.
> Our master Caesar is in the tent
> Where the maps are spread,
> His eyes fixed upon nothing,
> A hand upon his head.
>
> *Like a long-legged fly upon the stream*
> *His mind moves upon silence.*[38]

Immediately, one notes there is almost nothing to distinguish this 'high' lyric from Yeats's folk poems, based as it is on the easeful lilt and bounce of common measure and featuring a refrain that is somewhat 'out there' in counterpoint to the stanzas. While the refrain isn't nonsensical or surrealistic, a likely response to reading it might nonetheless be, 'eh?' With Yeats, it is important to remember his strangeness is often intended and might be central to the purpose and design of the poem.

To be sure, the three main stanzas are clear enough. The poem links three epochal figures from Western history, myth, and art: Julius Caesar, Helen of Troy, and Michelangelo. Undoubtedly, this is a poem of vast scale. Yet it is also a mere lyric of thirty short lines, which takes about one minute to read. Meanwhile, although the stanzas combine to suggest an epic scope, the refrain focuses on something that might be considered small and inconsequential. A kind of zooming in and out between big things and small things is a central facet of the poem. Convention suggests the refrain is key to how the three stanzas are linked. But it is worth noting that the poem merely

---

[38] *CW1*, 339.

juxtaposes its three stanzas. Nowhere does it state they are linked. Yeats is manipulating our expectation that the differing parts of a lyric might interrelate. The poem invites us to speculate on how they might come together. And given the protagonists of its three stanzas, we are being asked to consider a great deal.

The poem immediately announces how high the stakes are: 'That civilization may not sink'. Although this relates to Caesar not being disturbed during his quiet moment, it also implicates our reading of the entire poem. Left to our own devices, we might all think up multiple connections between Julius Caesar, Helen of Troy, and Michelangelo. But what is unlikely is that any reader would think of a long-legged fly upon a stream. By confronting us with such oddness, the poem is inviting us to contemplate anew what exactly holds civilization together: what weaves history, myth, and art into coherence?

The opening lines deftly announce the poem's 'zoom in' effect. How do we save civilisation?

> That civilisation may not sink,
> Its great battle lost,
> Quiet the dog . . .

It is the reader who is being invited to quiet the dog. This imperative places us 'at the scene': we are involved, able to influence. If we let Caesar be distracted, we might become partially responsible for something drastic happening to civilization as we know it. This deepens the way we are pulled in to interpret, or make sense of, the poem as a whole. Moreover, the wry bathos of the shift from the first two lines to 'quiet the dog'—that slightly comedic discombobulating anticlimax—also foreshadows the poem's repeating shift from 'big' consequential stanza to the refrain's peculiar minutiae. On being invited to help stop civilization from sinking, we subconsciously puff ourselves up, primed for significance. Being told to quieten the dog is then quite a let-down. The naturalism of the speech, the tempo of the lines, the sureness of syntax, almost hide the extent to which this is quite an abrupt transition. Further, that we're told to tether the pony to a 'distant post' accentuates the importance of silence to the stanza by tying it to remoteness. Although the stanza's opening invites the reader to feel involved, our involvement is to be quiet, stay away, take the pony (and ourselves) into the distance. Then again, in our silence, lack of action, isolation, we mirror Caesar.

One can see Yeats is exploring ripple effects, but a key to the poem is its involvement of the reader: if you don't quiet the dog, its barking might vex Caesar into a poor decision, which could lead to a shift of fortune for the Roman Empire; if you allow Helen to discover you are gawking at her, she might be surprised enough to fall over and break her nose, or at least become self-aware and lose some quality of gracefulness, some aloof sensual quality fundamental to her particular beauty that will be key to those topless towers being burnt; if you don't shut that door, Michael Angelo might get distracted by real children and mess up his ideal representation of the human form, perhaps making some tiny figurative inflection that could eventually change the course of art history. The potential part we play might be infinitesimal, but Yeats's poem is insistent it could none-theless be crucial.

If the chains of cause and effect in these stanzas are so slight as to be almost incred-ible, one can nonetheless acknowledge a kind of naturalistic logic is at work. This is then stretched by the more extreme 'zoom-in' to the fly in each refrain. Here, the poem shifts to a more outlandish form of interconnection. The popular metaphor behind the naming of the 'butterfly effect' within chaos theory—how a hurricane might be linked to the flapping of a distant butterfly's wings weeks earlier—masks an enormous amount of quantum complexity. But at heart it still traces cause and effect, seeking to map how all things are interrelated. However, with chaos theory, the links become so intricately multifactorial and non-linear that they exceed our habitual frames of reference and per-ception. Meanwhile, Yeats's poem shifts from the metonymic procedure of the stanzas to a leap occasioned by the metaphoric procedure of the refrain's simile. Using the terms of Roman Jakobson, the poem shifts from the horizontal to the vertical. Here, the implica-tion of cause and effect is spliced with a vertiginous expansion of perceptual possibility. Yet the refrain's leap of metaphor remains bound up with the poem's overall emphasis on metonymic chains of cause and effect. How small does something need to be before it might be considered inconsequential? Where do the chains of cause and effect begin and end?

The shift from stanza to refrain is not just from 'big' to 'small'; rather, with the first line of the refrain we are abruptly transited 'elsewhere'; and then, with the refrain's second line, the effect of this spatial transition is redoubled as we move into realms of inward-ness and abstraction ('mind' and 'silence'). All of this is easily underestimated, not least because of Yeats's virtuosic easefulness, where the prosody and momentum of his poem have the effect of making a mind-boggling leap seem naturalistic. One thinks of the opening of Wallace Stevens's 'Thirteen Ways of Looking at a Blackbird':

> Among twenty snowy mountains,
> The only moving thing
> Was the eye of the blackbird.[39]

The poem's syntactic continuity appears to simulate a continuous visual perspective, a sleight of hand that almost masks the radical shift of scale, impossible for human eye-sight. The point of this, one might speculate, is to tacitly assert the boundlessness of the lyric's domain: this small body of words has the capacity to exceed limits, to traverse horizons.

As Don Paterson argues, one of the most fundamental (and often overlooked) aspects of the lyric poem is its dependency upon an a priori assumption that 'a poem is a small thing that stands for a larger thing'.[40] Obviously, Yeats in this poem is manipulating this convention with aplomb. Indeed, although the zoom-in effect from stanza to refrain is

[39] Wallace Stevens, *Collected Poetry & Prose* (New York: Library of America, 1997), 74.
[40] Don Paterson, *The Poem: Lyric, Sign, Metre* (London: Faber & Faber, 2018), 19.

central to the poem, the stanzas themselves are already playing notable games with time and scale. In the second stanza, the issue is not just young Helen's dance. All of Homer, probably all of poetry, and possibly an entire cosmic-mythic system linking sexuality to violence, and further linking personal desire to vast historical conflicts and cycles, are at stake. In the third stanza, the issue is not just the Sistine Chapel's ceiling but the course of art itself, and how aesthetics effect culture and history, which in turn seems to be bound up with sexuality, psychology, and social order. And yet, Yeats merely gives us intimate and quiet moments, banal in themselves. The stanzas invite us to deduce the macro narrative from the given scene. Already, a relationship between 'big' and 'small' is in play, yet, crucially, the bigger narrative is *not there* but merely implied.

In an essay on 'Yeats's Stillnesses', Francis O'Gorman discusses how Yeats distils broader narratives into a single image. He writes:

> There is a resistance to narrative here, even though each image belongs in a narrative: what is offered is a moment, a fixed instant, which we are asked to assume sums up a life or part of it while remaining itself: memorable, exemplary. The messy complexities and contradictions of real human existences are poetically stilled.[41]

Our three stanzas are perfect encapsulations of this technique. Each gives us an image, and some directions of how to approach that image. We are invited to zoom out and speculate how each intimate and everyday image might relate to a bigger vista, while we are also asked to follow the zoom-in to the refrain. The poem thus explores the relation between image and broader narrative or context; but more than this, a further relation between motion and stillness is very much at the heart of 'Long-legged Fly', as it pulls the vast trajectories of each stanza towards the vanishing point of 'silence'.

Moving towards the refrain, we might ask ourselves: what does a long-legged fly upon a stream symbolize? Most readers will quickly feel some kind of Zen quality is being invoked. But a long-legged fly is a strange enough symbol in this regard. In one of Yeats's other key poems of the late 1930s, 'Lapis Lazuli', the chaos and violence of history are famously contrasted with the unchanging calm of an image of three Chinese men. Describing this image of the 'Chinamen', we are told: 'Over them flies a long-legged bird / A symbol of longevity'.[42] Is there a correlation between long-legged bird and long-legged fly? Certainly, both are associated with a serene, unruffled calm that contrasts with the maelstrom of historical action. But if 'longevity' is a quality of our fly, this feels somewhat arbitrary. And although the sense that there might be arcane meaning behind Yeats's symbols is part of the fun of reading him, it should be remembered that Ezra Pound's advocacy of the 'natural object' was something Yeats was perfectly adept at, when he wanted to be.[43] Our long-legged fly perhaps finds Yeats purposively playing

---

[41] Francis O'Gorman, 'Yeats's Stillness', *Cambridge Quarterly*, 49:2 (2020), 127.

[42] *CW1*, 295

[43] In the hugely influential 'A Retrospect' describing the ethos of 'Imagism', Pound exhorted, 'the natural object is always the adequate symbol'; *Literary Essays of Ezra Pound*, ed. T. S. Eliot (New York: New Directions, 1968), 5.

with differing kinds of figuration. We can't help but seek some symbolic key to the meaning of the fly, tracing its possible link to the 'longevity' of another poem, and so on; yet we might also keep in mind the simpler possibility that the key feature of the fly comes from the 'natural object'—namely, that it is very small and often perceived to be insignificant. Ultimately, that we can't say for sure what the fly symbolizes is a crucial part of its significance.

Of course, we are not just dealing with a fly but with a 'long-legged fly upon a stream', which is similar to how the mind of Caesar and Helen and Michelangelo, at the moment depicted in each stanza, 'moves upon silence'. In this refrain, the word 'upon' makes silence seem a palpable thing, turning nothingness into a spatialized object. The nature of silence invokes a sense of stillness, an association amplified by the reverie of Caesar. Daniel Albright suggests the poem explores how 'violent, world-transforming acts begin in a strange stillness'.[44] Yet what is interesting is that a long-legged fly upon a stream could only ever seem still from a distance. While the poem zooms in from broad perspectives to the minutiae of its refrain, it nonetheless holds the refrain's image at arm's length. Up close, the stream would be moving. While the image connotes that the fly is restful 'upon' the stream, as if on a windowpane, a fly upon a stream would more likely be in a flurry of activity, energetically working to ensure it doesn't submerge.

For a poem that seems to be straining for calm, there is much attention to motion: 'Move most gently if move you must'. The rhythmic repetition of 'move' pre-empts the 'to and fro' movement of Michelangelo's paintbrush in the next stanza, itself echoed by the sound of the mice. Caesar apprehends 'nothing', the poem gestures towards 'silence', yet everywhere there is a stilling for silence rather than silence, quiet movement rather than stillness. Moreover, there is a subtle chiastic inversion going on here. The parallelism of the two lines suggests that fly and mind are linked, as are stream and silence. But this sense of simile, where line A and line B are the units being compared, is complicated by a more fluid sense that the four terms dissolve into each other. The stream invokes a stream of consciousness and thus becomes 'mind'; and so, as 'stream' gives way to the 'silence' below it, mind and consciousness stream into blankness. The refrain gives us a definite sense of structure, but also of motion.

One remembers Frank Kermode's claim in *Romantic Image* that, at heart, the 'reconciliation of opposites ... is the purpose of the Yeatsian symbol'.[45] At some level, Yeats with this refrain seems to be gesturing towards a strange symbiosis of movement and stillness.[46] O'Gorman contextualizes Yeats's still image effects with painting and sculpture, claiming: 'Yeats gives to movement the illusion of the stationary'.[47] What is striking is how such a sensual effect might be linked to his broader world view. O'Gorman argues: 'Within Yeats's concept of the circularity of history, too—of the perning of the

---

[44] Albright, *Yeats, Poems*, 830.

[45] Frank Kermode, *Romantic Image* (1957) (Oxford: Routledge, 2002), 52.

[46] In chapter 19 of this book, Adam Piette also discusses the paradox of movement and stillness in 'Long-legged Fly'.

[47] O'Gorman, 'Yeats's Stillness', 137.

gyres—there is always movement. Yet it is movement, considered in one way, back to the same place: a perpetual cycle of return; a mobile stillness, as it were.'[48]

One can see how a text-based close reading of a Yeats poem swiftly involves his other poems, his entire 'system', and also anything and everything else that might be relevant. Where an individual poem stops, and where context begins, is not hard and fast. The reading of poetry involves moving back and forth between what exactly is in a poem, and wherever it reaches out to. It is a kind of testing of subjectivity and objectivity against one another. Returning to the symbolism of the fly, one might persist in seeking symbolic meaning. In *The Penguin Dictionary of Symbols*, we are told 'small flying insects' have been 'regarded as the souls of the dead revisiting Earth'; also that the fly for some cultures is a 'symbol of unity'; and further, 'Their ceaseless buzzing, whirling around and stinging make flies unbearable. They breed from corruption and decay, carry the germs of the foulest diseases and breach all defences against them. They symbolize a ceaseless quest.'[49] All such meanings are possibly germane. At the same time, a potentially definitive symbolism might be derived from the refrain's likely source in Coleridge's *Biographia Literaria*:

> Most of my readers will have observed a small water-insect on the surface of rivulets, which throws a cinque-spotted shadow fringed with prismatic colours on the sunny bottom of the brook; and will have noticed, how the little animal *wins* its way up against the stream, by alternate pulses of active and passive motion, now resisting the current, and now yielding to it … This is no unapt emblem of the mind's self-experience in the act of thinking.[50]

Then again, the idea that 'thinking' is somehow key to the poem doesn't quite fit. Yvor Winters once argued: 'The refrain indicates that all three persons are engaged in deep thought over important action, but Helen is not depicted as thinking — she is depicted as unthinking.'[51] Winters claimed this was a mistake by Yeats, but the error might have been his own in presuming the poem's 'deep thought' is akin to purposive thought. Caesar and Michelangelo might, rather, be in a trance-like contemplative state akin to daydreaming, oblivious to their surroundings. In this sense, the refrain could indicate a meeting of conscious and subconscious realms, a momentary stilling of self-consciousness and will, which could perfectly parallel a dancer's likely headspace.

In contemporary poetics, both Don Paterson and Glyn Maxwell have recently discussed how the white of the page, when we read a poem, is integral to it. This blank space might be associated with the void, or with the absolute; crucially, it is a visual

---

[48] O'Gorman, 'Yeats's Stillness', 125.

[49] Jean Chevalier and Alain Gheerbrant. *The Penguin Dictionary of Symbols*, trans. John Buchanan-Brown (London: Penguin, 1996), 541, 396–7.

[50] Albright, *Yeats, Poems*, 831.

[51] Yvor Winters, 'The Poetry of W. B. Yeats', *Twentieth Century Literature*, 6:1 (April 1960), 3–24, 21.

equivalent of silence. Paterson writes: 'Silence is the poet's ground. Silence delineates the formal borders of the poem.'[52] Maxwell argues:

> Poets work with two materials, one's black and one's white. Call them sound and silence, life and death, hot and cold, love and loss: any can be the case but none of those yins and yangs tell the whole story. What you feel the whiteness *is right now* — consciously or more likely some way beneath that plane — will determine what you do next. Call it this and that, whatever it is *this time*, just don't make the mistake of thinking the white sheet is nothing. . . . For a poet it's half of everything.[53]

One can see that Yeats is delving into this zone where one basic element of poetry meets its other. Albright calls the refrain an image of 'preternatural sensitivity to imperceptible vibrations', which might be another ideal way of describing the poetic act.[54] Just as Michelangelo uses scaffolding to undertake his painting, the entire poem can be seen as scaffolding upon the white of the page. To 'zoom out' from the refrain and back through the stanzas: like a mind upon silence, all thought, all endeavour, all form, and all reality is pitched upon a void.

Relating the poem to Yeats's 'system'—the gyres and cyclic philosophy creating the 'mobile stillness' described by O'Gorman—one need merely note that Yeats perceived all reality to constitute an antinomy of two realms, subjectivity and objectivity, the balance between the two constantly in motion. The way in which he described these two realms is complex and not always clear, but the core antinomy 'subjectivity / objectivity' might be rephrased as 'self / soul', 'individuality / community', 'form / formlessness', or 'temporal / spatial'. Meanwhile, it seems clear that the fly and mind of our refrain might equate to subjectivity, while stream and silence might equate to objectivity. In other words, our refrain could be said to encapsulate the heartbeat of Yeats's entire cosmic system.

As the folk poems have already indicated, for Yeats, where subjectivity meets objectivity is a multifaceted juncture: where day meets night, man meets woman, individual meets society, order meets chaos, being meets non-being, life meets death, something meets nothing. In *A Vision*, Yeats explains, 'whereas subjectivity—in Empedocles "Discord" as I think—tends to separate man from man, objectivity brings us back to the mass where we begin'.[55] That much of his career was given to the assertion of subjectivity, which he perceived to be an inherently discordant force, might explain the wilful attestation and urge towards divisiveness in much of his late verse. Yet 'Long-legged Fly' approaches the same phenomenon with Zen-like equilibrium. The edgy 'energy' of the folk verse is transposed into calm animation.

---

[52] Paterson, *The Poem*, 19.
[53] Glyn Maxwell, *On Poetry* (London: Oberon Books, 2012), 11.
[54] Albright, *Yeats, Poems*, 831.
[55] *CW14*, 53.

For Yeats, all things change and collapse into their opposite. He writes in *A Vision*, 'I ... must think all civilisations equal at their best; every phase returns, therefore in some sense every civilisation.'[56] This, of course, sits uneasily with his insistent political baiting about the masses and the elite. Yeats's wilful paradoxicality would make him infuriatingly inconsistent, to the extent that one might accuse him of bad faith, if he was a politician. But for poetry, the idea of a doublethink, of a deep embrace of contradictoriness, is a different matter. Yeats argued: 'Style and its opposite can alternate, but form must be full, sphere-like, single.'[57] Because we can only ever experience and perceive the world subjectively, the truth of reality is always beyond us. We are fundamentally wired to be partial and divisive. But 'sphere-like' form ensures poetry combines subjective with objective elements into dynamic figurations of 'mobile stillness', and thus provides a means of intimating reality more fully than otherwise possible.

In 'Easter, 1916' some famous lines describe a 'living stream':

> The horse that comes from the road,
> The rider, the birds that range
> From cloud to tumbling cloud,
> Minute by minute they change;
> A shadow of cloud on the stream
> Changes minute by minute;
> A horse-hoof slides on the brim,
> And a horse plashes within it;
> The long-legged moorhens dive,
> And hens to moor-cocks call;
> Minute by minute they live[.][58]

These beautiful rhythms and repetitions, which evoke a harmony of stability and change, reality as a musical balance, are also nascent in the interwoven repetitions, rhymes, and easeful metre of 'Long-legged Fly'. Whatever a 'long-legged moorhen' might symbolize, it is clear that 'long-legged' things, for Yeats, are associated with a state of peaceful order and composed equilibrium. In 'Easter, 1916', this state of grace is ruptured by its opposite, an unchanging stone, which disrupts the beautiful with the sublime to create the 'terrible beauty' that will obsess Yeats through most of his final two decades. But 'Long-legged Fly' offers a different perspective on Yeats's poetics of change. Interanimating antinomies here are not apocalyptic, but the pulse at the heart of normality.

The critic Robert Hodges once claimed Yeats meant 'Long-legged Fly' entirely ironically. He claimed the preposterous nature of the third stanza could only mean that Yeats wanted us to perceive the poem as a 'satire on historical hindsight'.[59] He argued: 'Yeats

---

[56] *CW14*, 152.
[57] *CW5*, 193.
[58] *CW1*, 181.
[59] Robert R. Hodges, 'The Irony of Yeats's "Long-legged Fly', *Twentieth Century Literature*, 12:1 (April 1966), 27–30, 30.

is here satirizing a popular and silly notion usually expressed that the course of history would have been quite different if Cleopatra's nose had been an inch shorter or longer.'[60] The maddening thing, but also the magnificent thing, about Yeats at his best is that Hodges might well be right, even though one can muster so much evidence to suggest otherwise. The reading of a poem is a dance of subjectivity with objectivity, and there will always be an open-ended element to the process.

To conclude, Yeats was hell-bent on provoking us into apprehensions that reality might be malleable, that change was central to reality. And since the world can only ever be subjectively fathomed, Yeats felt that poetry, by providing a wilfully subjective and imaginative means of perceiving the world differently, gives us a greater stake in reality, potentially giving us more agency with regards to how our ever-changing world is shaped and formed. And yet, his work also insists upon the limits to this, which per-haps suggests why Yeats's poetry might still be essential to us today—warts and all. The erosion of objectivity, the lack of checks upon our certitudes, leave us lacking proper measure in the midst of change. Poetry in the face of the world's accelerating crises may well be like a mere fly upon the fast-moving surface of things. But Yeats's work suggests that might not be nothing.

---

[60] Hodges, 'Irony', 28.

CHAPTER 18

....

W. B. YEATS: THE SENATE
AND THE STAGE

....

ADAM HANNA

In 1922 W. B. Yeats was appointed to the sixty-member upper chamber of the Irish Free State's legislature, the Senate, by the President of the Executive Council, W. T. Cosgrave; he was to serve as a senator until 1928. Of all the speeches Yeats gave in these six years, his long speech on divorce has become his best known, perhaps even his most notorious, act as a senator. In particular, his claim during this speech that the minority from which he claimed descent were 'no petty people' has come, in the popular imagination, to define his time in the Senate.[1] However, an analysis of his entire record in the upper house of the Irish legislature shows how atypical this belligerent glorification of his caste was. Rather, Yeats's senatorial record shows him to be the vindicator not so much of Protestant Ireland as of the country's various historic inheritances.

On two occasions Yeats spoke about the preservation of ancient monuments, and on three about the necessity of maintaining the structures and proportions of historic buildings, especially those in which the Irish government was considering locating its parliament.[2] The preservation of buildings and ancient monuments is therefore the subject on which Yeats spoke most frequently in the Senate, with his speeches on this matter representing 12 per cent of his total speaking time (the highest figure for any single subject). He spoke at almost equal length on measures to preserve and promote the Irish language, sidestepping fierce contemporary debates over whether the State should support archaic or contemporary spoken Irish by advocating the funding of both research into

---

[1] W. B. Yeats gave this notorious speech on 11 June 1925; it is collected in *SS*, 99. Yeats versified some of the ideas from this speech in his poem 'The Three Monuments' (*The Tower*, 1928, in *CW1*, 231).

[2] Yeats's Senate record shows that he spoke on the preservation of ancient monuments on 3 August 1923 (*SS*, 56) and 10 June 1925 (*SS*, 88). He spoke on the protection of more modern buildings (including old parliament building in College Green, the Four Courts, and the Royal Hospital, Kilmainham) on 15 March 1923 (*SS*, 36); 11 July 1923 (*SS*, 53); and 1 May 1924 (*SS*, 66). In addition to these speeches, Yeats made a number of speeches on fire precautions at the National Museum, which I discuss later in this chapter.

ancient manuscripts and 'the living tongue'.[3] The frequency with which Yeats spoke on issues relating to linguistic and material preservation, and the length at which he did so, indicate the strength of his interest in the maintenance of the monuments of Ireland's past during the tumultuous years when he was a senator. Yeats's concern in his Senate speeches with the fate of the country's monuments is paralleled in the preoccupations of *The Tower* (1928), a volume which opens with a memorable reflection on the contrast between the rooted monuments of ancient wisdom and the onward pull of heedless, changeful life.[4] In the opening stanza of 'Sailing to Byzantium', old men and monuments stand at either side of the teeming, abundant country that is described at its centre:

> That is no country for old men. The young
> In one another's arms, birds in the trees,
> —Those dying generations—at their song,
> The salmon-falls, the mackerel-crowded seas,
> Fish, flesh, or fowl, commend all summer long
> Whatever is begotten, born, and dies.
> Caught in that sensual music all neglect
> Monuments of unageing intellect.[5]

The meaning of the poem is shaped by the placement of its images: old men and monuments hover at both extremes of the stanza, peripheral to its real action yet crucial to its framework. In between these embodiments of venerability are 'the young', the shining shoals of fish and the flocks of birds, which fill the stanza's heaving, swirling centre. This poem, like the other twenty poems that make up *The Tower*, evinces an admiration for the human achievement represented by cultural and physical monuments. These include 'learned Italian things / And the proud stones of Greece'; Phidias's famous ivories; ingenious golden grasshoppers and bees; stately houses; the works of the great, the good, and the wise; and, of course, the poet's own tower. These things, however, are repeatedly contrasted with what might erode and eclipse them: the depredations of historic chaos, the so-called 'mockers' that deride their majesty, inheritors who are unworthy of their great inheritances, and, more than anything, the ever-encroaching demands of self-delighting, self-generating life. A cyclical vision underlies *The Tower*, where each completed development, whether creative or destructive, is shown to be the originating point of the counter-energy that will, eventually, lead to the fulfilment of its own opposite. This central tension means that *The Tower* both mourns and celebrates the fact that, as Yeats later wrote, 'All things fall and are built again'.[6]

---

[3] Philip O'Leary describes this debate in *The Prose Literature of the Gaelic Revival, 1881-1921: Ideology and Innovation* (University Park: Penn State University Press, 1994).

[4] The preservation of monuments from heedless encroachments or neglect was also a matter of personal interest to Yeats during his years in the Senate, being engaged as he was in restoring a medieval tower near Coole Park in County Galway.

[5] *CW1*, 197.

[6] *CW1*, 300.

Yeats's appointment to the Senate was recognized by contemporaries as an endorsement of the place of poets in Irish national life. At the time Yeats's appointment was announced, the *Freeman's Journal* remarked that it restored the 'ancient relationship' between the Irish bard and councils of State, citing Yeats's own play *The King's Threshold* as evidence for the existence of this relationship.[7] In the play, a bard in pre-Norman Ireland starves himself, an act that is sanctioned by the country's Brehon laws. This is because various advisors to the king seek to move him from his position as royal counsellor. It was perhaps ironic that, in referring to the 'ancient' rights of poets to sit at 'councils of State', the *Freeman's Journal* echoed a change that Yeats had made to his 1903 play as recently as his 1920 revision.[8]

In this revision of the play, the blame for the reduction in the status of Seanchan, the affronted bard, is laid at the door of

> Bishops, soldiers, and Makers of the Law –
> Who long had thought it against their dignity
> For a mere man of words to sit amongst them
> At the great council of the State ...[9]

In the 1903 version of the play, however, the great councils of State are not mentioned: the dispute is over whether Seanchan could sit at the King's 'own table'. The later version of the play reflects the tensions that arise when the poet takes on the mantle of earthly authority. It reflects Yeats's intimations at the very outset of the Irish Free State that there would be tensions between his role as an imaginative artist and his involvement in the work of 'the great council of the State'.

Yeats had absorbed a resurgent idea of the societal role of the poet as a young man. In the decades when Ireland was moving towards the establishment of its first Dublin-based government in over two hundred years, the idea that verbal and temporal power were linked was in the air. Yeats read of the temporal authority of bards in Sophie Bryant's book *Celtic Ireland*, which he reviewed for *The Scots Observer* in 1890.[10] In this book, Bryant presented both law and literature as central to life in Celtic Ireland; and at the centre of this law-and-literature-loving society was the bard: 'The bard is in the place of honour higher than the warrior, and he has a definite duty to the society that supports and honours him', wrote Bryant.[11] Yeats would have come across similar ideas in the

---

[7] Bernard G. Krimm, *W. B. Yeats and the Emergence of the Irish Free State, 1918–1939: Living in the Explosion* (New York: Whitston Publishing Company, 1981), 60.

[8] CW2, 122.

[9] CW2, 122.

[10] In Sophie Bryant's *Celtic Ireland* (London: Kegan Paul, Trench & Co., 1889), the author presented both law and literature as central to life in Celtic Ireland (x and 144).

[11] Bryant, *Celtic Ireland*, xi. Ronald Schuchard reiterated these points in 2008, writing that Yeats had an 'intuitive awareness of the bardic poet's responsibility to the imaginative and aesthetic life of his culture and of his essential role in creating the images, shaping the values and restoring the dignity of a beleaguered nation' (in *The Last Minstrels: Yeats and the Revival of the Bardic Arts* (Oxford: Oxford University Press, 2008), xxi).

Proceedings of the Ossianic Society for 1857 (which he drew on for his play *The King's Threshold*), with its translation of the Middle Irish tale *Immtheacht na Tromdaimhe* as 'The Proceedings of the Great Bardic Institution'.

Yeats's speeches in the Senate, like many of the poems collected in *The Tower*, were written in part during the embattled early years of the Free State, and reflect the violent conditions of this time. His senatorial career also involved chairing the committee that designed the first coinage of the Irish Free State, and sitting on another that examined the state of Irish education. The speeches he delivered as a senator also demonstrate an unexpected interest in the mechanisms of the Irish legal system. He told his fellow senators during a debate on judge's costumes that 'I cannot imagine any place where innovation is more necessary than in the outward image of the law'.[12] He also spoke on the necessity of an independent judiciary, on the dangers of increasing the rights of state security forces to enter private homes, and (on two occasions) on the importance of keeping politics out of prison inspections in an unstable post-civil war environment.[13] This interest in law was perhaps the concomitant of the danger and destruction that accompanied the civil war period.[14] During this war the windows of Yeats's Dublin house were shot out, and thirty-seven of his fellow senators had their houses destroyed by explosions and fires.[15] Yeats's poetry and Senate speeches show how fires were rippling and flashing through his imagination in the immediate wake of two of Ireland's rival jurisdictions going to war with each other.

The records show that the safety of national treasures from fire became an obsession for Yeats in the early 1920s, and his Senate record contains a series of speeches on the necessity of fire precautions at the National Museum, which houses irreplaceable artefacts from Ireland's distant past. The museum was in great danger of being burned down as it adjoins Leinster House, the meeting place of the senators. These circumstances added urgency to Yeats's many Senate speeches on the necessity of protecting the Irish State's material and intellectual inheritances.[16] Images of the destructive capacities of fire recur in the volume *The Tower*, both in ancient and contemporary contexts. 'Nineteen Hundred and Nineteen' opines that 'Incendiary or bigot could be found' to light a fire on the Acropolis.[17] Later in the volume, 'Meditations in Time of Civil War' bears witness to a time in which 'A man is killed, or a house burned, / Yet no clear fact to be discerned'. 'Two Songs from a Play' concludes with a hauntingly vivid image of fiery destruction: 'Whatever flames upon the night / Man's own resinous heart has fed'.[18]

---

[12] *SS*, 125.

[13] These are recorded in *SS*, respectively, on 61, 33, 54, and 60.

[14] This time is explored in Gemma Clark, *Everyday Violence in the Irish Civil War* (Cambridge: Cambridge University Press, 2014).

[15] The shooting-out of Yeats's windows and the destruction of the other Senators' houses are described in *Life* 2, 230.

[16] *SS* shows Yeats spoke on the risk of fire on four occasions: 4 June 1924 (67), 19 June 1924 (77), and twice on 16 July 1924 (82 and 85). These speeches include an extraordinary passage in which he repeats the words 'fireproof door' five times in the space of a single paragraph (84).

[17] *CW1*, 211.

[18] *CW1*, 208 and 217.

However, the Yeats of the *Senate Speeches* and the Yeats of the poems do not always align so neatly in their interests. Rather, reading the two side by side gives an insight into how the tensions and contradictions that arose from his own dual role of poet and legislator came to preoccupy Yeats following his appointment to the Senate. A significant theme from the masterwork of his senatorial years, *The Tower* (1928), is the disjunction between work that is widely recognized as useful and the more mysterious functioning of his own irresponsible craft of poetry: 'something that all others understand or share' set against his love of 'daemonic images'.[19] Though what use that wider society has for the arts is a pertinent question for any artist, Yeats's position as a legislator brought ideas of the social role of the artist home to him with special intensity. In a digression in an imagined dialogue between 'Peter', a Senator, and 'Paul', a Deputy, that Yeats published in 1924, he speaks through his protagonists: one says that 'creation moves in a continual uncertainty', while his interlocutor replies, 'I cannot see any means whereby a Parliament can pass uncertainty into law'.[20] The divisions between creative and legislative activity that these protagonists touch on form a significant strand in Yeats's thinking during his tenure as a senator.

Yeats's sense of the disjunction between his work as a poet and his role as a lawmaker is signalled by an unusual speech he gave on 10 June 1925, in which he noted that he was the first person to quote poetry in the Senate. This was during a debate on a less-than-poetical subject, the Shannon Electricity Bill 1925. A year before he composed 'Sailing to Byzantium', his contributions to this debate show that the themes of this poem were already in his mind: 'there are many monuments which we should respect and which will become of great importance to this country', he told his fellow senators.[21] The legislation that was being debated that day paved the way for the setting up of the Ardnacrusha hydroelectric station on the River Shannon, a project that Yeats, reviewing the first decade of Irish self-government six years later, recalled as being among the great successes of the new State. It is a piece that goes against any simplistic idea of Yeats as the spokesman for the past against the hated encroachment of modernity. When he thought of 'the legislation of those ten years', he wrote, he thought of

> the electrical works at Ardna-crusha. These works are successful ... They were the Government's first great practical success, a first object-lesson in politics. ... My six years in the Irish Senate taught me that no London Parliament could have found the time or the knowledge for that transformation.[22]

Yeats's contributions to the debates on the bill that brought this project about, however, are more ambiguous in tone than this satisfied note would suggest. Characteristically, he

---

[19] *CW1*, 210.
[20] *CW10*, 176.
[21] *SS*, 88.
[22] *CW10*, 231.

worried about the ancient ruins and monuments near the River Shannon that might be affected by these developments.

Speaking of the ruins of Clonmacnoise, an ancient monastery on the banks of the river, Yeats recited lines from T. W. Rolleston's late nineteenth-century translation of bardic verses that had been composed in praise of it:

> In a quiet, watered land, a land of roses
> Stands Saint Kieran's city fair,
> And the warriors of Erin, in their famous generations,
> Slumber there.[23]

Yeats stated that his reason for quoting these lines was that, if the ruins were protected from the works that were under consideration, visitors would be drawn to Clonmacnoise. He also stated that Rolleston's poem could be influential in attracting visitors to the ruins, which would be beneficial for the local economy. By quoting the poem, Yeats may have wished to remind his fellow legislators of the great literary and historic inheritances of modern Ireland. However, the oddities that surround his delivery of this quotation in the Senate that day raise questions about how he viewed himself as a poet in a legislative body, and about the place of the creative imagination in a modern polity.

In his speech, Yeats followed his quotation with a double-edged reflection: 'I think I am the first person who has quoted a poem in the Senate. I only do so because I am sure the poem will be, to use the appropriate words, "a definite asset".'[24] Whatever his motivations in quoting the poem, the critics who have commented on this event agree that his description of the poem as 'a definite asset' carries a tang of acidity.[25] This comment makes it possible to see Yeats's quotation from poetry in another light: he might have wished to highlight the absurdity of his task, compelled as he was to argue for the value of Ireland's ancient monuments in the economically minded terms in which the business of the Senate was typically conducted. The Senate records show that Yeats would have heard Ireland's seas and rivers described as 'a national asset', or similar, on three occasions on that day alone.[26] In saying this, Yeats raises a question about the

---

[23] *SS*, 89.

[24] *SS*, 89.

[25] Philip L. Marcus takes this view in *Yeats and Artistic Power* (Syracuse, NY: Syracuse University Press, 2001), 134, as does Geraldine Higgins in *Heroic Revivals from Carlyle to Yeats* (Basingstoke: Palgrave Macmillan, 2012), 146. Marcus's view that he quoted these lines to disparage them is, however, unlikely. He earlier described them as 'the Gaelic lyric come close to perfection' (*Early Articles and Reviews: Uncollected Articles and Reviews written between 1886 and 1900*, ed. John Frayne and Madeleine Marchaterre (New York: Scribner, 2004), 282). In the early 1920s Yeats recorded that 'after five and twenty years I continually murmur to myself [Rolleston's] lyric, "In the quiet watered land, a land of roses"' (*Mem*, 51).

[26] Senate Proceedings for 10 June 1925, available at http://debates.oireachtas.ie/Senate/1925/06/10/printall.asp.

role of literature in a world governed by laws of rational political economy, and gives a hint that he suspects that poetry and legislatures may not mix.

This was a serious concern for a poet for whom the foundation of the Free State had recently held out the possibility of a new concord between practical and aesthetic life. The excitement in Yeats's letters from the time around his appointment to the Senate is focused on this idea. He had high hopes that the arrival of an Irish State heralded the collapse of distinctions between the 'artistic' and the 'practical': 'Dublin is reviving after the Civil War', he had written hopefully in early 1924. 'People are trying to found a new society' in which 'politicians want to be artistic, and artistic people to meet politicians'.[27] Yeats did what he could to help along a marriage between artistic and practical life in the Free State, telling the Senate that it was 'very important for the future industrial prosperity of this country that art teaching should be brought into relationship with industry'.[28] He formed a Senate committee that attempted to set up a 'Federation of the Arts', through which Irish industry would be influenced by aesthetic ideals.

Yeats's attempts to bring practical work and art into alignment in the Free State were linked to his developing philosophy. Initially, his appointment to the Irish legislature may have appeared to him as an indication that Irish society was moving towards the fulfilment of his ideal of 'Unity of Being'. Yeats's first reference to this concept was in an essay of 1919, in which he expresses a wish to 'begin another Epoch by recommending to the Nation a new doctrine'.[29] Though his ideas on what constituted 'Unity of Being' are vague, they are perhaps best thought of as a continuation of the drives towards harmonization and synthesis that animated his work since the earliest days of his career.[30] His descriptions of the state of Unity of Being (though ironically heterogeneous in nature) have certain overlapping features: Unity of Being is a condition that could at times be embodied by people and by societies, and involves a grand idea that subordinates all other ideas to it. This central idea links all social classes in societies that achieve this condition, and provides the animating spirit behind all their productions, from their arts to their practical wares. A line from 'The Trembling of the Veil', written in 1920, records his hope that modern Ireland 'might be the first [society] in Europe to seek unity as deliberately as it had been sought by theologian, poet, sculptor, architect from the eleventh to the thirteenth century'.[31] These are vaunting hopes for what might be achieved in post-conflict Ireland. Yeats's ironic commendation of a poem to the Senate as a 'definite asset' just five years later, however, indicates that his initial high hopes had become tinged with scepticism.

---

[27] Yeats to Edmund Dulac, 28 January [1924], *CL InteLex* #4462.

[28] *SS*, 63–4. Yeats made similar points in a speech on the stained glass industry (*SS*, 80–1).

[29] *CW5*, 46.

[30] Yeats recollected in his essay 'If I Were Four-and-Twenty' that 'one day when I was twenty-three or twenty-four this sentence seemed to form in my head, without my willing it, much as sentences form when we are half-asleep: "Hammer your thoughts into unity". For days I could think of nothing else, and for years I tested all I did by that sentence.' *CW5*, 34.

[31] *CW3*, 167–8.

Something of Yeats's attitudes towards the possibility of 'Unity of Being' in Ireland, and of the limited role that poetry might play in its achievement, can be inferred from his reflections on Byzantium in *A Vision* (1925):

> I think that in early Byzantium, and maybe never before or since in recorded history, religious, aesthetic and practical life were one, and that architect and artificers – though not, it may be, poets, for language had been the instrument of controversy and must have grown abstract – spoke to the multitude and the few alike.[32]

This desire for a unified culture (he goes on to describe it as one where 'building, picture, pattern, metal work of rail and lamp, seem but a single image') was a projection onto ancient Byzantium of an ambition he had harboured since his early twenties.[33] However, as the above passage from *A Vision* makes clear, the poet in a modern society had a problem, one that was rooted in the nature of language itself. The efficacy of poetry, as the quotation above argues, is compromised by the fact that it is written in the same medium as political arguments and the abstractions of legislatures. Previously, Yeats had been at pains to emphasize the distinct origins of poetry and political rhetoric. His 1917 tract *Per Amica Silentia Lunae* contains the famous aphorism, 'we make out of the quarrel with others, rhetoric, but of the quarrel with ourselves, poetry.'[34] Though Yeats saw both rhetoric and poetry as conflictual in nature, arising from quarrels of different sorts, he nevertheless kept public controversy and lyric inspiration separate. By the time he came to write *A Vision*, however, he saw that the quarrel with others that gave rise to rhetoric was erosive to language, the material out of which poetry was made. Yeats came to suspect that the ignoble uses to which language, the raw material of poetry, had been put made it an unsuitable medium for the promotion of a spiritually unified society.[35]

A Vision (1925) is a systematizing philosophical work that Yeats claimed to have written with the guidance of spirit instructors (whose ideas were mediated by the 'automatic writing' of his wife, George Yeats). It has strong thematic links to *The Tower*, in that its central image, a diagram of two rotating, intersecting cones that respectively represent solar and lunar principles, is expressive of the idea that collapse and rebuilding are inevitable and inextricable processes.[36] In this genre-defying work, Yeats uses these cones to attempt no less than a schematization of epochal change. Though the obliquity of the first two chapters of *A Vision* (in which the 'geometry' of these cones

---

[32] *CW13*, 158–9.

[33] In 'Four Years: 1887–1891', an autobiographical work first published in 1922, Yeats recalled how 'I wished for a world where I could discover the tradition' of 'an almost infallible Church of poetic tradition' all around him, 'not in pictures and in poems only, but in tiles round the chimney-piece and in the hangings that kept out the draught' (*CW3*, 115).

[34] *Myth 2005*, 331.

[35] This idea was prompted by a comment by Alex Davis, whose help with this chapter I gratefully acknowledge.

[36] These were, to use Yeats's terms, primary and antithetical gyres. See *CW13*, 13 ff.

is adumbrated) repels attempts at logical analysis, the volume deepens in interest in the third section, 'Dove or Swan'. In this section, Yeats applies the cycles that the first two chapters identify to particular historical societies, and sets out an understanding of both people and eras as compounds of varying proportions of opposing solar and lunar, or objective and subjective, influences. Certain people and societies, the book claims, through a harmonization of these influences, achieve 'Unity of Being'. This state, a combining of contraries into an indivisible single whole, might be compared to the compounded 'single thought' that Yeats believed his gyre-based system made possible. 'They have helped me', he wrote of the mysterious patterns and structures that he set out in *A Vision*, 'to hold in a single thought reality and justice'.[37] This simultaneous envisioning of the actual alongside a future ideal of 'justice' was a tantalizing possibility for a legislator at the outset of the Free State: his legislative work can be seen in part as an attempt to bring about in the world this condition of 'Unity of Being'.

The differences between what Yeats's senatorial role demanded and what his imagination compelled are central to one of the most important poems in *The Tower*, 'Among School Children'. This was inspired by a visit that the 'sixty-year-old smiling public man' paid to a school as part of his work on a Senate committee that was tasked with investigating primary school conditions in the Free State. In its opening lines the speaker seems fully engaged with a nun's account of the systems that modern thinking has decreed are best for education: the poem's protagonist hears how the children learn 'To cut and sew, be neat in everything / In the best modern way'.[38] The legislative concerns of the Irish Free State are evident in this poem, which Yeats started writing in May 1926, the same month that the School Attendance Act of 1926 passed into law.[39]

However, there is a hint of something dissociative in this senatorial behaviour: after all, the speaker's description of himself as 'A sixty-year-old smiling public man' indicates that he is not seeing himself from his own perspective but from that of the children in the school he is visiting. As the poem continues, the speaker's detachment from his position in time and place increases. The first stanza break signals a leap in perspective as his public duties are forgotten and the interior world takes primacy:

> I dream of a Ledaean body, bent
> Above a sinking fire, a tale that she
> Told of a harsh reproof, or trivial event
> That changed some childish day to tragedy[.][40]

---

[37] W. B. Yeats, *A Vision* (London: Macmillan, 1937), 25.

[38] *CW1*, 219.

[39] Though Yeats was sympathetic to Montessori education, the chief advisor to the Irish government on educational matters, Timothy Corcoran SJ, was strongly opposed to its exploratory ethos, and instead stressed the need for discipline in schools. From Maura O'Connor, 'The Theories on Infant Pedagogy of Dr. Timothy Corcoran, Professor of Education, University College, Dublin', *Irish Educational Studies*, 23:1 (2004), 35–47.

[40] *CW1*, 220.

What follows is an associative chain of images relating to the poet's experiences of love, philosophy, and ageing, combined with a lifetime's questions over the nature of memory and reality. This digressive poem is in stark contrast to Yeats's Senate contributions to the debates around the School Attendance Bill, in which there was nothing fantastical or abstract. In these speeches he shows himself to be a passionate advocate for the improvement of primary education for children from all social backgrounds.[41] Yeats's adoption of a public role came at the same time as his increased interest in discontinuous selfhood; the poem 'Among School Children' dramatizes the differences between his social self, as he performed it in the Senate, and the imaginative self he gave voice to in his poetry.

The differences between Yeats's artistic and social selves can be seen in the different responses in his Senate record and his poetry to the same historical conditions. With the passing of the Enforcement of Law Bill 1923, the Free State government legislated to increase the powers of the army and police to enter private property. Yeats, in one of many Senate interventions in which he asserted the importance of individual liberty, initially spoke out against this Bill. However, he eventually signalled his reversal and capitulation to government plans by telling his fellow senators an anecdote that centred on how a process server who visited his tower needed the protection of seven or eight Free State soldiers.[42] Part V of 'Meditations in Time of Civil War', 'The Road at My Door', describes a similar (or possibly the same) event. Though the interests of Yeats the legislator are in protecting the innocent and keeping the peace, the envious response of Yeats the poet is very different:

> A brown Lieutenant and his men,
> Half dressed in national uniform,
> Stand at my door, and I complain
> Of the foul weather, hail and rain,
> A pear-tree broken by the storm.
>
> I count those feathered balls of soot
> The moor-hen guides upon the stream,
> To silence the envy in my thought;
> And turn towards my chamber, caught
> In the cold snows of a dream.[43]

The tumult of the world beyond the tower is represented by soldiers and by storms, hail, and rain. Yet, rather than deplore these unsettled conditions and the necessity for repressive measures that they entail, as he does in his Senate contributions, the speaker of the poem envies the men who have arrived at his door and imagines himself in their place. His description of himself turning towards his chamber, 'caught / In the cold

---

[41] *SS*, 96 and ff.
[42] *SS*, 34.
[43] *CW1*, 208.

snows of a dream', reflects the chilly solitude of the writing life and also, perhaps, his own daydreams of being out in the field and exposed to the elements as the soldiers are. The divergences between the uses to which Yeats put his experiences as a legislator and as a poet give us the opportunity to reflect on his full complexity and contradictoriness.

The floor of the Senate, as his speeches show, was a kind of stage for Yeats. He had plenty of experience of these, having been involved in theatrical ventures since the 1890s and been a founding director of the Abbey Theatre since 1904. During his tenure as a senator he remained a director of the Abbey, and his lives in theatre and government circles intersected in 1925 when his successful lobbying of the Free State government resulted in the theatre becoming the only one to receive a state subsidy in the English-speaking world.[44] He continued writing for the stage in these years: his dramatic work includes *The Player Queen* (1922) and a version of Sophocles's *King Oedipus* (1928). One of Yeats's most notable pieces of theatre work during his time in the Senate came during the first run of Sean O'Casey's *The Plough and the Stars* in February 1926. On the opening night, Yeats led members of the Executive, including Kevin O'Higgins and Ernest Blythe, into the packed theatre.[45] On the fourth night of the run, he furiously told noisy protestors, who were enraged by the play's irreverent depictions of Dubliners during the Easter Rising, that 'You have disgraced yourselves again'.[46] On this occasion, his pugnaciousness on the stage matched his often challenging and contrarian stances on the Senate floor.

On the afternoon of 22 July 1926, Yeats confronted his fellow senators with a proposal in the Senate whose purpose, at least at an aesthetic level, was intended to draw a line under Ireland's legal past. He recommended that Irish High and Supreme Court judges should give up the grey wig and black gown that they shared with their contemporaries in the English legal system, and wear instead a new Irish-designed costume of black velvet cap and red gown. Yeats was opposed, however, by several senators, who rejected the idea that the legal reality of the new state required new symbols.[47] These senators argued that the Irish people had a residual respect for existing institutions, and that this respect should be drawn on to bolster the authority of the new state. Senator Sir John Keane, a barrister who, like Yeats, had been one of Cosgrave's appointees to the Senate, illustrated his conservative argument with a pointed quotation from poetry:

> How but in custom and in ceremony
> Are innocence and beauty born?
> Ceremony's a name for the rich horn,
> And custom for the spreading laurel tree.[48]

---

[44] Chris Morash, *A History of Irish Theatre, 1601–2000* (Cambridge: Cambridge University Press, 2002), 163.

[45] Krimm, *W. B. Yeats and the Emergence*, 122.

[46] *Life* 2, 305.

[47] Though Yeats's idea was voted down, the Irish government later selected robes for office that Yeats had been instrumental in having designed (*SS*, 132).

[48] *SS*, 129.

These were, of course, lines from W. B. Yeats's own 'A Prayer for my Daughter', first published in 1919; their quotation by Keane put Yeats in the presumably uncomfortable position of hearing his own poetry quoted against him. As is often the case in disputes over style, behind the argument between the two senators was a matter of substance. Had the official Irish legal system so lost its legitimacy during the revolutionary period 1912–23 that even its symbols needed to be done away with and replaced? Or, rather, were there elements of the past that offered desirable grounds for future developments? Did the post-revolutionary moment call for the allaying power of tradition in order to speed the re-establishment of a functioning society, or did it, rather, represent a brief opportunity in which the outmoded might be superseded by something newer and finer? Yeats himself wrestled with just such questions of transience and supersession—of 'what is past, or passing, or to come', as he wrote in 'Sailing to Byzantium', a poem which he drafted in the months that followed this debate.[49] The Senate debates of these years over what changes Irish self-government would bring parallel the thematic preoccupation with change in *The Tower* and in *A Vision*.

Both *The Tower* and *A Vision* are testaments to the obsession with the system-building and structure-making that were a part of the work of the Senate; Yeats described his Senate work as 'the slow exciting work of creating the institutions of a new nation'.[50] *The Tower* was written during a period in which many of the legal and institutional structures in which Irish society operated fell and were built again, and it reflects both of these phases. In particular, Yeats's ambivalent attitude to his new role as a legislator contributes to the volume's strong thematic preoccupation with divided, multiple selfhood. *The Tower* is not just a lament for a former time, it is a paean to the very fact of change; it is not only a hymn to self-assertion but a reflection on just what a fugitive and fluid thing a self can be. Even if Unity of Being was impossible in the modern state, then, as 'Among School Children' shows, Yeats's renewed consciousness of division within himself enabled him to make great poetry out of a state of disjunction.

---

[49] *CW1*, 192.
[50] W. B. Yeats to Olivia Shakespear, 28 June [1923], *CL InteLex* #4342.

CHAPTER 19

'CAST A COLD EYE'

Death in wartime

ADAM PIETTE

YEATS thought long and hard throughout his life on war and peace, and brought that contradiction into relation with the antinomy of love and hate, especially in his lifelong dreaming and yearning and feeling about Maud Gonne and the violence of her politics.[1] Those antinomies—love/hate, war/peace—structured his own struggle with and exploration of the differences and conflicts between his own vocational subject position as lyric poet in the nationalist-individualist, Romantic-bardic tradition, and the man of action, the warrior, the Cuchulain of his psychic dreamwork. This chapter will look at the very late Yeats, the Yeats of *Last Poems and Plays*, and the reception of that volume and the representation of Yeats's achievement in the aftermath of his death, in the context of the Second World War and late 1940s.

The chapter will first consider the reception of his late work in the aftermath of his death in January 1939, looking in particular at the reaction of his fellow modernists, and then the judgements made on his lifetime achievement by Irish writers of different persuasions. The aim is to measure one sense to Yeats's epitaph, 'Cast a cold eye': that sense relating to how his generation, his living readership at the moment he died, the most celebrated poet in the world, Nobel Prize winner, spirit of his country, read and reacted to his late work at a time of international crisis and world war. The second section will consider another thrust to Yeats's epitaph: his injunction to those passing by to treat death lightly: 'Cast a cold eye, / On life, on death'.[2] *Last Poems* dwells on a paradox that entranced Yeats, the cold clarity, quiet ecstasy and momentary-eternal peace felt by the warrior at the instance of death. We might think of this strange death experience as an aspect of what psychoanalysis defines as the death drive, an internal psychological attraction to death deep in the psyche. For Freud, the death drive was an

---

[1] For a useful account of the Romantic mystique of war in Yeats's early youth, see Samuel Hynes, 'Yeats's Wars', *Sewanee Review*, 97:1 (Winter 1989), 36–55.

[2] 'Under Ben Bulben', *CW1*, 328.

internal movement of the mind towards an earlier still state, towards destruction, and yet at the same time, as Lacan argued, towards the quietude of an immortality or endlessness of that very movement towards death.[3] This essay will consider Yeats's poetics as a means of pacifying the war instinct as death drive, as a conjuring of a Shakespearean interim as Nietzschean joy. It will suggest that pacification is itself a mode of the death drive and finds form in the idea of the lyric epitaph as engraved last words. The last section will venture out into the darkness of death as a mystery in late Yeats, attending to the epitaph's injunction 'Cast a cold eye' as addressed to the dead, to the passing horseman of the next historic phase, and also to all future readers as mortal beings. This final section will seek to winkle out from the verse the lineaments of prophecy as foreboding, as weird contact with the war dead of the future.

Yeats's Reception in Wartime: 'Cast a cold eye'

In his provocative treatise of late 1938, *On the Boiler*, Yeats played fast and loose with the relations of a nation to the state-sponsored violence of warfare. *On the Boiler* advocates a military caste capable of defending Ireland from 'the disciplined uneducated masses of the commercial nations'.[4] Yeats imagines the caste will form not only in times of national defence but also in order to check the population explosion of disorderly lower classes—a 'prolonged civil war' of the future is more likely than the submission of the masses, and will be led by heroic cavalrymen in tanks: 'the victory of the skilful, riding their machines as did the feudal knights their armoured horses'.[5] War in this sense was to be welcomed as a bloodletting that would ensure national renewal and racial transformation from democracy to oligarchical rule by an aristocratic clerisy trained in arms. War as the means to this end is a unifying, stratifying, and ideological crucible. *On the Boiler* quotes Michael Robartes, Yeats's magus alter ego, in *A Vision*:

> Dear predatory birds, prepare for war ... Test art, morality, custom, thought, by Thermopylae; make rich and poor act so to one another that they can stand together

---

[3] See Jacques Lacan, *The Four Fundamental Concepts of Psychoanalysis* (1964) (London: Hogarth Press, 1977), and Sigmund Freud, 'An Outline of Psycho-Analysis', *International Journal of Psycho-Analysis*, 21 (1940), 31: 'So long as [the destructive instinct] operates internally, as a death instinct, it remains silent; we only come across it after it has become diverted outwards as an instinct of destruction. ... When the super-ego begins to be formed, considerable amounts of the aggressive instinct become fixated within the ego and operate there in a self-destructive fashion.'

[4] *On the Boiler*, CW5, 241. Irish neutrality was written into the 1922 Constitution, and is alluded to in the section where Yeats critiques British sovereignty, praising the Irish mind's 'detonating impartiality'; CW5, 243.

[5] CW5, 231.

there. Love war because of its horror, that belief may be changed, civilization renewed. We desire belief and lack it. Belief comes from shock and is not desired.[6]

It is this reactionary dream of a future military caste that drew Yeats to flirting with General O'Duffy's Blueshirts, traceable in the three marching songs in *Last Poems*. The longer poems are more ambiguous, however, about the valency of just war as a trigger of authoritarian revolutionary change. In particular, 'Under Ben Bulben', the poem that stages the imaginary compositional and cultural frame around Yeats's own epitaph, stages warfare as apocalyptic, destructive, fearful, but irrepressibly ambivalent. Roy Foster traces the poem's image of the warrior 'at peace' at the moment before death, caught in a moment that both sustains a positive vision of war's transformative powers (with the allusion to John Mitchel's 1854 *Jail Journal* and the prayer in 'Under Ben Bulben', 'Send war in our time, O Lord!') and the sheer chaotic destructiveness of war.[7] Foster writes:

> the idea of impending war hangs behind [the poem]. Early drafts included references to bombs falling upon 'hateful cites' and to apocalyptic visions of horsemen riding out of mountainsides – along with the idea that an eternal moment of peace was contained at the heart of conflict, as of sexual love.[8]

The poem comes as the culmination of a long career as national poet that saw Yeats negotiate, trim, evade, blast, rhetoricize, inspire, and be impassioned by the wars of his time, from the Great War through the Easter Rising, the Anglo-Irish War of Independence, and the Irish Civil War through to the looming Second World War. The warrior's moment of peace at the time of his death might be figured as the lyric poem itself, as a language object of calm quiet fixity in tumultuous times. Equally, it might stand as a literally empty gesture, a dreamlike extinguishing or emptying out of the man of action that needled and disgraced Yeats throughout his life, whether it be the Oisin or Cuchulain figure, the Maud Gonne love object, the irregular soldier he is envious of in 'Meditations in Time of Civil War', the 'Caesar – or Cataline' expected round the corner in his Blueshirt phase, the ambiguous lure of the subject position implied by the gift of Sato's sword.[9] The late poems sing as much the extinguishing of the man and woman of action as they do the temptations of violence, succumbing to and resisting martial energies and authoritarian gestures of violent power in an oscillation impossible to order into tidy dialectic, or even into the voluminous complexities of the grids, gyres, and cycles of *A Vision*.

---

[6] W. B. Yeats, *W. B. Yeats's Robartes-Aherne Writings*, ed. Wayne Chapman (London: Bloomsbury, 2018), 21–2.

[7] *CW 1*, 326 and 511 n.

[8] *Life 2*, 635.

[9] Daniel Albright, ed., *W. B. Yeats, The Poems* (London: Dent, 1990).

This is as much as to say that war accompanies Yeats as a question, a temptation, a challenge not only to the vocation, where there is conflict between lyric poetry as an art of peace and epic poetry as martial, heroic, and nationalist allegiance and witness to violent change, but also to the man, the pastoral dreamer and lover caught up in aesthetic visions of erotic objects of desire at the same time as drawn to the action demanded by the time of revolution. And it is war that, consciously or not, shaped the immediate reception of Yeats's last posthumous collection among the outpouring of responses across the world once his death was announced, and subsequently when the Second World War broke out in September 1939.

The death of Yeats had a creepy repetitiousness. His last poems were published and reviewed after IRA bomb attacks on London, Manchester, Coventry, Birmingham, Liverpool: the S-Plan campaign that hit targets between January 1939 and March 1940—as though replaying the entanglement of Yeats's poetry with the Easter Rising during the Great War. The response to Yeats's death in the wartime that ensued was muted in the coteries of London modernists, partly as a result of the S-Plan attacks, Irish neutrality, and Yeats's interwar flirtation with eugenics and fascism. Auden dramatized this in his spring 1939 article in *Partisan Review* written soon after the attacks and Yeats's death, 'The Public v. the Late Mr William Butler Yeats'. The orthodox Marxist view comes first with the public prosecutor criticizing Yeats's 'feudal mentality' and fascist warmongering on the basis of the quotation of Mitchel's 'send war in our time' in 'Upon Ben Bulben': 'In the last poem he wrote, the deceased rejects social justice and reason, and prays for war. Am I mistaken in imagining that somewhat similar sentiments are expressed by a certain foreign political movement which every lover of literature and liberty acknowledges to be the enemy of mankind?'[10]

In Auden's essay the counsel for the defence puts up a more spirited array of arguments and stands close to Auden's own view, praising Yeats as a 'man of action' in the 'field of language', with a 'true democratic style'.[11] Notwithstanding, the piece does insist on the famous argument that poetry makes nothing happen, the idea which Auden was to make the central claim of his elegy for Yeats: 'The case for the prosecution rests on the fallacious belief that art ever makes anything happen, whereas the honest truth, gentlemen, is that, if not a poem had been written, not a picture painted, not a bar of music composed, the history of man would be materially unchanged.'[12] This influential line on Yeats draws Auden towards echoing the aesthetic arguments proffered by New Critics at the time that erased the real war contexts from the verse;[13] then it uses that very aestheticism against Yeats. In his review of *Last*

[10] W. H. Auden, 'The Public v. the Late Mr William Butler Yeats' (*Partisan Review*, Spring 1939), in Edward Mendelson, ed., *The English Auden: Poems, Essays and Dramatic Writings 1927–1939* (London: Faber & Faber, 1977), 389–93, 391.

[11] Ibid., 393.

[12] Ibid., 393.

[13] In a 1941 special issue of the New Criticism journal *The Southern Review*, Howard Baker argued that 'Sailing to Byzantium' is about the aestheticization of the world; 'Domes of Byzantium', *Southern Review*,

Poems, Auden criticizes the rehashing of old themes in the last collection as an exercise in sound patterns, with Yeats succumbing to the aesthetic temptation: 'always more concerned with whether or not a phrase sounded effective, than with the truth or the honesty of its emotion'. The work was consummate lyric writing, however, in its deployment of a simple, sensuous and passionate diction—Auden damning with faint praise.[14]

Eliot's 'Little Gidding', the first great poem of the Second World War, aims to prise the poet Yeats away from entanglements with history and war into the zone of the uncanny. Eliot writes as receiver of Yeats's theory of history as repetitive wartime violence both psychological and cultural, situating the poem's scene in a ghostly wartime space of Nietzschean recurrence: 'At the recurrent end of the unending'. Eliot's persona hails the ghost of Yeats as though he were Dante hailing Virgil:

> the sudden look of some dead master
> Whom I had known, forgotten, half recalled
> Both one and many; in the brown baked features
> The eyes of a familiar compound ghost
> Both intimate and unidentifiable.
> So I assumed a double part, and cried
> And heard another's voice cry: 'What! are you here?'[15]

The double part being played and the cycle of knowing, forgetting, and half-recall are symptomatic not only of the plural roles over long and war-traumatized times the dream poem asks its characters to play (Yeats as himself and Virgil and all precursors; Eliot as himself and Dante and all descendants) but also of the purgatorial double wartime of the Second World War, the double movement of gyre-like history and its recurrences, and the interplay of repeated acts of violence. The double part here mimics Yeats's, suspended between two wartimes as ghost of the interwar, 'spirit unappeased and peregrine / Between two worlds become much like each other'. 'Unappeased' is a strange and vivid choice given its association with appeasement of Nazi Germany before the war. Eliot takes that political meaning and ghosts it away, and joins forces with the New Critics in this depoliticization, leaving us with the much more powerful vision of Yeats as presiding ghost and creative intelligence, as a death figure at the threshold between the worlds of life and afterlife. What is unappeased is as insubstantial yet powerfully supernatural as the wind-spirit Sidhe of

7:3 (Winter 1941), 639–52. R. P. Blackmur urged readers to censor out the silly magic in Yeats and get to the real matter of the poems on the page; 'Between Myth and Philosophy: Fragments and Yeats', 407–25. Allen Tate asked them to 'censure [Yeats] for possessing "attitudes" and "beliefs" which we do not share'; 'Yeats' Romanticism: Notes and Suggestions', 591–600.

[14] 'Yeats: Master of Diction', 1940 review reproduced in *Yeats: Last Poems – A Casebook*, ed. John Stallworthy (London: Macmillan, 1968), 47–9.

[15] T. S. Eliot, *Collected Poems* (London: Faber, 1974), 204.

Yeats's 1896 poem 'The Unappeasable Host', conjured and conjuring presence from another world.

The Irish responses to Yeats's death are as polarized as Auden's and Eliot's responses. They depend on the allegiance and the history of friendships and political journeys through the war-torn history of Ireland post-Rising, turning on Yeats's espousal of Ascendancy culture as central to the story of independence. The orthodox Catholic view was severe. As J. J. Hogan put it in an obituary review in the Jesuit journal *Studies: An Irish Quarterly Review*, Yeats was

> specially the poet of the Anglo-Irish. But he has lived in Ireland and taken part in every Irish cause and quarrel for nearly forty years. He has fallen in with nationalist movements, and has fallen out with them and lashed them from the Anglo-Irish, the planter's, side.[16]

'Yeats's politics', he goes on, 'are so simple as to be almost negative.'[17] There is a recognition of the importance of war as a trigger for change in Yeats, but here understood as the Irish wars from the Rising through the War of Independence and the Irish Civil War expressed in these patronizing terms: 'War, and the Irish war, and their consequences, and the shortening of his years, wrought the change. He was brought to question and doubt his simple reading of life; to face the problems of Good and Evil, of heaven and hell.' Most intriguing of all, Hogan argues that Yeats may have been right to fear the influence of his poems, historically, which brings us back to the strange figure of Yeats as a harbinger of heroic death:

> Quite early, he shows himself excited by the thought of revolution in *The Old Pensioner* –

> Lads are making pikes again
> For some conspiracy.

> The play *Cathleen Ni Houlihan* might be called the culmination of the Gaelic patriotic *aisling*. *September 1913*, his poem on John O'Leary's death, a rebuke to calculating moderation, was also a thrilling call to the bloodshed that was in store –

> Was it for this the wild geese spread
> The grey wing upon every tide …?

> It leads to *Easter 1916*, *A terrible beauty is born* – leads to it as one poem leads to another, and perhaps actually led many men to their death. Poetry such as that

---

[16] J. J. Hogan, 'W.B. Yeats', *Studies: An Irish Quarterly Review*, 28:109 (Mar. 1939), 35–48, 41.
[17] Ibid., 42.

of *The Nation* makes men demonstrate, but because of poems like those, or *The Dreaming of the Bones*, men will die. Yeats himself wondered much, in these last years, how much of our history was his doing.[18]

Hogan wishes the late politics away, the better to concentrate on the haunting figure of Yeats as a poet at the radical threshold between life and death. That sense of Yeats's influence over the deaths of Irishmen in the Easter Rising and as a figure at the threshold is articulated as another way of downplaying the Yeats of the 1920s and 1930s who identified with the Anglo-Irish class.

Nationalist and republican responses were harsher still. Aodh de Blácam, in a poisonous reminiscence, 'Yeats as I knew him', in *The Irish Monthly* in March 1939 wrote: 'how great a man he would have been, how great a poet, if he had been constant to the dream of his youth and to the fire that was kindled in him again by the deeds of the men of Easter Week.'[19] The anger with Yeats's Ascendancy values continued in Blácam's review of Hone's biography in 1943: 'So, when Yeats talked of Two Irelands, he was pleading for the continuance of an alien ascendancy that never struck roots. All this was inconsistent with his own better genius, his true love of Ireland.'[20]

But it is Louis MacNeice's 1941 study *The Poetry of W.B. Yeats* that stands as the most eloquent defence and judgement of the Irish Yeats; from as non-partisan point of view as was possible at that time, the book was written as a wartime response to his life's work from a poet-critic whose own identity as an Ulster Protestant merged with a poet's vision of the presiding genius of Irish poetry. It is also as a member of the Auden group that he was most valuable in his contesting of Auden's powerfully normative view of Yeats's poetry:

[Auden says] the case for the prosecution [in 'The Public v. Mr W. B. Yeats'] rests on the fallacy that art ever makes things happen. ... It is an historical fact that art *can* make things happen and Auden in his reaction from a rigid Marxism seems in this article to have been straying in towards the Ivory Tower. Yeats did not write primarily in order to influence men's actions but he knew that art can alter a man's outlook and so indirectly his actions. He also recognized that art can, sometimes intentionally, more often perhaps unintentionally, precipitate violence.[21]

The book, too, is a powerful reading of Yeats's attention to warfare and violence from the Easter Rising on. Yeats, MacNeice writes, was 'caught in two minds' about the

[18] Ibid., 42–3.
[19] Aodh de Blácam, 'Yeats as I knew him', *Irish Monthly*, 67:789 (Mar. 1939), 204–12, 211.
[20] 'Yeats Reconsidered', *Irish Monthly*, 71:839 (May 1943), 209–17, 216.
[21] Louis MacNeice, *The Poetry of W. B. Yeats* (London: Faber & Faber, 1941), 225.

rebels: 'The rebels were in the tradition of Wolfe Tone – a tradition whose decline he had deplored – but he could not be sure that their sacrifice was necessary.' That state of being caught in two minds chimes with Eliot's vision of Yeats as peregrine spirit between two worlds, and MacNeice saw, too, how war was a trigger for the creative two-mindedness: '[Yeats] repeatedly recognizes the creativeness of violence (see *Blood and the Moon*).' 'Also,' MacNeice later states, 'in *Blood and the Moon* he blesses "the bloody, arrogant power" of men of action and envies the shedders of blood.' For MacNeice, Yeats identified violence with Maud Gonne and her impatience with the Celtic Twilight:

> I suspect that he had an unconscious revenge in throwing the twilight on her in his love poems. In his 'white woman with numberless dreams' it is a little difficult to recognize the notorious agitator who had thought Parnell 'had failed when he repudiated violence' and who plotted with a Belgian to blow up British troops during the Boer War.

Gonne's political violence is identified, too, with the rise of fascism as a cult of violence: MacNeice reads 'The Second Coming' as about the advent of fascism, the 'blood-dimmed tide' representing 'that upsurge of instinctive violence' associated with fascist mob-mania. The relish in the lines about this advent in the poem is 'attributable to the fact that Yeats had a budding fascist inside himself'.[22]

But at the same time, just as Yeats was caught in two minds by the Easter Rising, so too are the late poems caught in two minds about political violence, for MacNeice, despite the relish and temptation. MacNeice returns again and again to Yeats on death as a double matter, not as an end to life but as an intersection with a timeless and constructed joy or zest for life, a threshold event that MacNeice compares to Rilke, whom he quotes: 'Only from the side of death (when death is not accepted as extinction, but imagined as an altogether surpassing intensity), only from the side of death, I believe, is it possible to do justice to love'.[23] This Rilkean sense of the loving, joyful, and timeless threshold experience is very close to Yeats's celebration of the liminal state, a death drive poetics.[24]

For MacNeice, Yeats's legacy is to have created a plain style capable of merging contemporary and mythological subjects in idioms tried and tested by an imagination that has been through the wars; and he believed that Yeats, as a persona and as a various-sided set of voices and attitudes, spoke to his generation's obsession with and fear of violent death as destruction of being as the Second World War loomed and broke upon the world.

---

[22] Ibid., 42–3, 143, 82, 132.
[23] Ibid., 185.
[24] MacNeice may have been aware that the Ben Bulben epitaph was provoked by Yeats's reading of essays on Rilke's views on death (see Albright, *W. B. Yeats, The Poems*, 814 n.)

THE MOMENT OF DEATH: 'CAST A COLD EYE / ON LIFE, ON DEATH'

The reception of Yeats's poetry shows a dynamic of contestation of its political premises due in no small measure to the outbreak of the Second World War, and it is characterized by efforts either to depoliticize the work or to challenge its belief systems. At the same time, the poets, led by Eliot, Auden, and MacNeice, attempted to redeem Yeats's reputation by affirming the aesthetic power of the plain style of the late period (Auden), to identify the iconic force of Yeats's representation of the threshold between life and death (Eliot and MacNeice), and to reaffirm the importance of the work as a means of capturing war experience and violence at revolutionary moments of international crisis. Yeats's haunting poems about old age and limit experiences at the brink of death stand as icons for the mid-century imaginary: he speaks *as* death to the wartime generation, as a harbinger of a potentially redemptive idea of death despite war's violence. *Last Poems and Plays* returns again and again in different guises to the figure of the 'wild old man in the light' ('The Wild Old Wicked Man', *CW1*, 32), the frenzy of the 'old man's eagle mind' ('An Acre of Grass', *CW1*, 302), Browning's 'old hunter talking with gods' ('Are You Content?' *CW1*, 322),[25] the grandfather singing under the gallows of the third marching song (*CW1*, 335), Crazy Jane, old Cuchulain. The figure of the old seer and sage as beggarman, mad lustful dancer, prophet at the edge of reason, here in this world and yet not, an absent presence: this is the figure of Yeats himself, his elderly identity parsed and dramatized into a spectrum of roles and routines. The figure stands as a prophetic ghost at the edge of wartime culture, like a guardian spirit or charm against war's destruction. It is this liminal Yeats at the old ghost's threshold that bewitched his generation, and many Irish writers after; the Yeats of 'The Tower', the figure who has passed through the 'wreck of body, / Slow decay of blood, / Testy delirium / Or dull decrepitude', the death of friends and lovers, till all of these

> Seem but the clouds of the sky
> When the horizon fades;
> Or a bird's sleepy cry
> Among the deepening shades.[26]

The verse has a quite beautiful rhythm to it, with the first of the three stresses of three of these lines light as a catch in the breath, not a dying fall, a dying rise:[27] '<u>Seem</u> but the **clouds** of the **sky**. / <u>When</u> the ho**ri**zon **fades** / ... / <u>Among</u> the **deep**ening **shades**'.

---

[25] Browning's hunter represents his childhood self-identifying with the heroes found in his father's books in *Pauline*. See, Albright, *W. B. Yeats, The Poems*, 802–3 n.

[26] 'The Tower', *CW1*, 200. Samuel Beckett bases a late play on this poem, ... *but the clouds*.

[27] Hinted at lightly through the stressed element in 'horizon'.

The three to two shape of this chimes with the way the rhymes (two) are supplemented by a third internal rhyme word or half-rhyme (three), so 'sky' / 'cry' has 'horizon' and 'fades' / 'shades' picks up 'bird's'. The lines have a triplet internal rhyme audible across their surface: 'seem' in the first quoted, 'sleepy' / 'deepening' in the third and fourth, splitting one / two in terms of distribution, whilst lengthening syllable by syllable from one to two to three, so bringing to the ear the two / three play. The sense of the lines, that it is the sheer length of time spent at scholarly or writerly work that will eventually enable the poet to pass through decrepitude and the deaths of others, vanishes in the last lines as time itself becomes evanescent, the present moment just a vanishing of cloud and bird cry as night falls.

The two / three play is there semantically—clouds + sky then horizon; bird + cry then shades—and gives us a metaphysical code for what is happening at another level: the poet's 'I' and his soul are at work ('Now shall I make my soul, / Compelling it to study') as a double act that engenders a third bodiless energy, the body become cloud-like, or become pure voice, a cry as the soul enters into the company of the dead (the secondary meaning of 'Among the deepening shades'). The relation of body and soul becomes a third thing, the voice at the threshold, just as the relationship of lyric, the I-voice speaking whilst the reader overhears, engenders a third force, the words on the page as textual afterlife, the threshold he survives in, beyond cry, body, grave.

Yeats returns to this theme in *Last Poems* with 'Long-legged Fly', and associates the voice at the threshold with the man of action suddenly stilled:

> Our master Caesar is in the tent
> Where the maps are spread.
> His eyes fixed upon nothing,
> A hand under his head.
> *Like a long-legged fly upon the stream*
> *His mind moves upon silence.*[28]

The image captures the man of action as he contemplates nothing, a nirvana deathlike state of being: the eyes are fixed on nothing, and yet the Coleridge allusion of the fly on the stream, *Biographia Literaria*'s image of the water insect and its 'cinque-spotted shadow fringed with prismatic colours on the sunny bottom of the brook' assumes that the image is an emblem of 'the mind's self-experience in the act of thinking'.[29] The hand under the head summons Rodin's thinker. The nothing, with this self-experience in mind, is the shadow fringed with colour on the sunny bottom of the brook: Caesar is fixed in radical thinking upon his own shadow, the death shadow, just as the poem on

---

[28] *CW1*, 339.
[29] The allusion first noted by W. E. Rogers in his 1975 *Concerning Poetry*; cf. Albright, *W. B. Yeats, The Poems*, 831 n. Alan Gillis notes the allusion in his chapter in this volume, 'The 1930s' (Chapter 17), which features a fine discussion of 'Long-legged Fly' in terms of its ballad and folk energies, its zoom effects, and their relationship to what Gillis calls 'the boundlessness of lyric's domain'.

the page reads as a text moving upon the silence of post-mortem ontology. Caesar in his tent summons up memories of Brutus seeing the ghost of Caesar in his tent in the fourth act of *Julius Caesar*, the scene itself recalling the second act and Brutus steeling himself to the murder of Caesar: 'Between the acting of a dreadful thing / And the first motion, all the interim is / Like a phantasma or a hideous dream'.[30] Caesar in his tent in Yeats's poem is haunted by the future, becoming like his murderer when spooked by his ghost, and like his murderer too in being stuck in the dreadful interim, caught in two worlds, two minds. Note how in Yeats's lines 'Nothing' stands alone in no rhyming relationship to other line endings, emphasized by the acoustics of 'tent' / 'spread' / 'head'. It connects to nothing, it seems, except that it does begin to move into relation with the word '*silence*' because of the shared 'upon'—Caesar's eyes are fixed *upon* nothing whilst the mind moves *upon* silence. Silence and nothingness, during this fixity and stilled moment, this phantasmatic interim, signals death: not death as fixity and stillness, but as a lonely movement above or upon the nothingness and silence of non-existence and endless death. Brutus's acting and motion in this allusive revision are not a before and after, but a during, the moving of the mind in the interim, an idea that blossoms into being with the quite extraordinary way 'moves' expands when one reads the lines ('*Like a long-legged fly upon the stream / His mind moves upon silence*')—chiming with the moments in the other stanzas of the poem: Helen dancing a tinker's shuffle in the street, whilst the narrator asks us to 'Move most gently if move you must / In this lonely place'; Michelangelo with his hand that 'moves to and fro'. This lonely place is the zone of the death drive at the limit of war's violence, an active creative zone of the mind moving between endless surviving and never-ending dying, the lonely place of the poem on the page by the poet who has died.[31]

The movement and cry at this threshold is staged in *The Death of Cuchulain* when Emer dances round the head of the warrior (the stage directions describe six heads of the warriors who wounded Cuchulain, set in a row at the backcloth as parallelograms):

> She so **moves** that she seems to rage against the heads of those that had wounded CUCHULAIN, perhaps makes **movements** as though to strike them, going three times round the circle of the heads. She then **moves** towards the head of CUCHULAIN; it may, if need be, be raised above the other on a pedestal. She **moves** as if in adoration or triumph. She is about to prostrate herself before it, perhaps does so, then rises, looking up as if listening; she seems to hesitate between the head and what she hears. then she stands **motionless**. There is silence and in the silence a few faint bird notes.[32]

As in 'The Tower' and 'Long-legged Fly', this is the lonely place where the dead listen and sing as a bird cries in the silence. Emer's dance is the movement of the mind at

---

[30] Shakespeare, *Julius Caesar* II.i, ll. 63–5.

[31] The emphasis on the death drive ambivalence in the man of action could be seen as part of the revision of Spenglerian and Fascist Caesarism that Lauren Arrington tracks in her 'Yeats in Fascist Italy' chapter in this volume (Chapter 16).

[32] *CW2*, 553; italics in original, bold my emphasis.

threshold, a movement that is double, caught in two minds as in a hesitation or interim ('[hesitating] between the head and what she hears'). Emer moves as a violent act, as an act of aggression (her raging against the heads, as though to strike them). She also moves towards the lost other, driven by elegiac love, easily confused as the triumph of the victor. But that movement is interrupted and turns into a listening, attending to the lonely space as sounding place for the repeated notes of the creatures of that realm— these movements are both ambiguous, caught between two drives, love and death, and compulsively iterative, as with the three times she moves round the circle. The dance triggers an abstracting of the space, so the six warriors and Cuchulain's head become parallelograms, quadrilaterals that surround the two figures of Cuchulain and Emer. Cuchulain's head is also spiritualized into a parallelogram (a daring comic manoeuvre on Yeats's part, deliberately risking ridicule), inviting us to see Emer as making four moves, the three moves round the circle, then the move to Cuchulain. Repetition is core to the double drive structuring the dance but also the *mise en scène*.

Yeats may be thinking here of Freud's theory of the death drive as set out in the 1920 *Beyond the Pleasure Principle*—as featuring a fusion of erotic and thanatological elements, as in masochistic and sadistic feelings. The death drive is also characterized by the compulsion to repeat and becomes dominant in cultures that have suffered the violent losses of war. The compulsive drive is made up of libidinal desires that conflate destructiveness as release, as in a warrior's zest for killing or the calm stoicism of a Thomas MacDonagh before execution ('I am ready to die and I thank God that I die in such a holy cause'), and also a dreaming of death as immortality, as in Zizek's précis of Lacan's definition of the death drive:

> The Freudian death drive has nothing whatsoever to do with the craving for self-annihilation, for the return to the inorganic absence of any life-tension; it is, on the contrary, the very opposite of dying – a name for the 'undead' eternal life itself, for the horrible fate of being caught in the endless repetitive cycle of wandering around in guilt and pain. The paradox of the Freudian 'death drive' is therefore that it is Freud's name for its very opposite, for the way immortality appears within psychoanalysis, for an uncanny excess of life, for an 'undead' urge which persists beyond the (biological) cycle of life and death.[33]

We can see in Yeats's figure of the threshold poet—the undead head of Cuchulain, the wild old men or Crazy Janes at the frontier of life and death, caught up in a dance of patterns, as with the sound repetitions analysed earlier, or in the abstract shapes formed by Emer's dance—the lineaments of the death drive as uncanny excess, a fusion of destructiveness and immortality. That immortality is an endlessness of play of the warring mind's movements at the threshold, at the limit of war's violence: and the threshold, for Yeats, is the constructed afterlife and textual space where art listens, sings, shapes, patterns, repeats, and acts.

---

[33] Slavoj Zizeck, *The Parallax View* (London: MIT Press, 2006), 61.

ADDRESSING THE DEAD: 'CAST A COLD EYE / ON LIFE, ON DEATH. / HORSEMAN, PASS BY!'

Yeats's epitaph took a while to be realized: the war intervened and kept the body locked in a coffin in France and moved from cemetery to ossuary in 1944; the family had to wait beyond the end of the war for Yeats's body to be transported to its rest in Drumcliff cemetery.[34] It is perhaps unfitting to imagine his body unappeased and peregrine in France waiting for return home beneath the gravestone.[35] It is a little uncanny if we read poems from the last collection as taking on other significances, as though addressed to the future war dead he would be accompanied by as the years rolled on between 1939 and 1948. The epitaph itself can be read as addressed to all those who read the poem, or who visit the graveside, as textual and engraved lines set up deliberately to accompany each other: we read the poem knowing the lines exist as stone epitaph; and we read the epitaph knowing it is the ending of 'Under Ben Bulben'. But its syntax insists, in fact, that Yeats is addressing the dead, the horseman being one of the ghost warriors the family servant Mary Battle saw in the childhood home coming out of the mountains.[36] It may also be a tank commander come home from the Second World War that Yeats knew would break out, one of 'the skilful, riding their machines as did the feudal knights their armoured horses' of *On the Boiler*.[37] The horsemen stand too for the future horde, the forerunner of whom is Yeats as prophet, triggering the next phase of history. But they also represent the ghosts of the heroes of 1916: this is the sense of the repeated refrain '*From mountain to mountain ride the fierce horsemen*' of the 'Three Songs to the One Burden'—the roaring tinker, the reclusive Henry Middleton, and the Abbey player Sean Connolly, first to be shot in the Easter Rising.[38] So the epitaph is addressed to a liminal figure representing the dead of the past, of the Rising, but also the dead of the future, the horde sensed in the mountains around the lonely place of the act of threshold witness. Patrick Pearse invoked Cuchulain at the Post Office, and that entanglement of 'warriors' is remembered by the Singer at the very end of *Last Poems and Plays*:

> What stood in the Post Office
> With Pearse and Connolly?

[34] *Life 2*, 657–8.

[35] There was considerable controversy surrounding the return of Yeats's body to Ireland, and even speculation that the bones returned were not Yeats's at all (MacNeice's view). This has some basis in fact—see the story in *The Irish Times* (13 August 2020), 'WB Yeats: Papers confirm bones sent to Sligo were not poet's', https://www.irishtimes.com/culture/books/wb-yeats-papers-confirm-bones-sent-to-sligo-were-not-poet-s-1.2288662.

[36] T. R. Henn has a good account of the allusive network of references the horsemen have, including the myth of Dhoya, the Fomorian giant and his horses, Rosicrucian legend of the dead leader, etc.; 'Horseman, Pass By!', in Jon Stallworthy, ed., *Yeats: Last Poems: A Casebook* (Macmillan, 1968), 115–21.

[37] *CW5*, 231.

[38] *CW1*, 328–30.

> What comes out of the mountain
> Where men first shed their blood,
> Who thought Cuchulain till it seemed
> He stood where they had stood?[39]

This mythologizing of the rebellion takes shape from the Oliver Shepherd statue that figured the Easter Rising dead as the wounded Cuchulain; and also Pearse's own sense of his mission (influenced by Yeats and Standish O'Grady) as reviving the 'hero-spirit' of 'Fearghus, Conchubar, Cuchulain, Fion, Oisin, Oscar'.[40] Here the death drive honours the Easter Rising dead in the form of repetition of rhetorical questions: 'What stood ...' / 'What comes out ...' / 'Who thought ...' (recalling Eliot's 'Who is the third who walks always beside you?'), here curiously emphasized by the six capital Ws that open these lines, accompanied closely by the hs: What With What Where Who.[41] The aspirated 'wh-' of Irish English chimes with the 'ch' of Cuchulain, as though the hero-spirit is also a breath-spirit inspiring and exhaling the lines. The rhetorical question becomes a rhetorical accent, a special stress along the words signalling repetition as shaping movement, as war-dead hero-spirit, as acoustic hauntedness. The feelings being tracked in the lines acknowledge the eerie Gothic sensationalism involved: the 'Who' is first a 'What', a Thing that first stands with Pearse and Connolly, then where they had stood, as though a memory image once they have passed on, a moment ago, or as an icon or statue marking those who have passed away across the threshold (partly the Shepherd statue, which is itself comprised of Cuchulain tied to the standing stone which is his own monument). The lines shelter obliquities and mysteries neverthe-less: for the 'What' which resolves into the 'Who' that is Cuchulain is in the interim a potential they: 'What comes out of the mountain / Where men first shed their blood'. They figure Mary Battle's Queen Maeve and the Sidhe, firstly.[42] They then figure the heroes of Easter 1916; in the drafts for these lines, Yeats had first written: 'He seemed to have come down his mountain / To stand where they stood / To stand in the post office / Where they must shed their blood.'[43] 'What comes out of the mountain / Where men first shed their blood' fuses Cuchulain and Ben Bulben with Pearse/Connolly and the Post Office; and then mythologizes them as a standing stone severed head in a stone

---

[39] *CW2*, 554.
[40] 'Dying Cuchulain', created in 1911, installed in the GPO in Dublin to commemorate the Easter Rising dead at de Valera's request in 1935; Qu. Reg Skene, *The Cuchulain Plays of W.B. Yeats: A Study* (London: Macmillan 1974), 19.
[41] T. S. Eliot, *The Waste Land, Collected Poems 1909–1962* (London: Faber & Faber, 1974), 77. It is of interest that, in the drafts for these lines, Yeats is clearly working to preserve a 'wh-' opening. For the 'Where men first shed their blood' line, we have 'Who [= when? where?]' before the choice of 'where'; Phillip L. Marcus, '"Remembered Tragedies": The Evolution of the Lyric in Yeats's *The Death of Cuchulain'*, *Irish University Review*, 6:2 (Autumn 1976), 190–202, 195.
[42] The second-sighted servant of Yeats's uncle George Pollexfen had visions of the Sidhe, the faery spirits associated with the Neolithic burial mounds and mountains. Yeats tells the story of her encounter with Queen Maeve, their Faerie Queen, in his memoir, *Autobiographies, CW3*, 212.
[43] *CW3*, 194.

circle of other severed heads, perhaps linking the Sidhe story to Com Cruach and the sacrificial rites associated with the Killycluggin Stone in County Cavan (itself a stylized form of severed head).[44] This puts a different reflection on the stone motif of 'Easter, 1916': 'The stone's in the midst of all', and 'Too long a sacrifice / Can make a stone of the heart'.[45] In *The Death of Cuchulain*, the parallelograms also figure as headstones, and Cuchulain's head is 'about to sing' in the moments before he is decapitated. The singer we hear in the last section at the Irish fair, figuring contemporary poetry and drama that is both song and speech, both myth-making and of this world, is the singing head of Cuchulain, man of war singing of the dead, singing as the collective. In temporal terms, then, the dead horsemen of the Sidhe are the ancient Irish of the mounds, the heroes of Irish independence, and the future war dead of the next historic phase. The mountain where men shed their blood may be taken to be war itself.

Returning to 'Under Ben Bulben', the Sidhe appear in the second strophe of the first section as 'That pale, long-visaged company'.[46] The 'gist of what they mean' is then itemized: in the second section we are told they mean every man and woman who dies is resuscitated, so the Sidhe signify all mortals in cycles of reincarnation. In the third section, they mean the war dead, specifically those who die and experience the weird calm interim: 'For an instant stands at ease', a fine use of the military command at drill. The man of war is transformed, 'his heart at peace'. The fourth section articulates another meaning of the Sidhe: the artists who attempt to give shape and form to paradise, a peaceful afterlife 'where a soul's at ease'.[47] The fifth section identifies the Sidhe as national poets, singing the Irish as ideally a fusion of peasant and aristocracy, but more clearly signifying a species continuity across seven centuries, binding the people together across time and space. Finally, the Sidhe resolves down to one man, Yeats the poet laid to rest in Drumcliff, lying among his people, at peace after a lifetime of many wars, including the Second World War where he lay, in France, and among the crowd of voices of love and loathing, elegiac and judgemental, guarded by the contentious spirits of Eliot, Auden, MacNeice. The horseman, once the 'gist of what [horsemen] mean' has been articulated—the ancient peoples of prehistory, the human species moving through reincarnation cycles, the war dead, the artists of the afterlife, the poets of the Irish people, the dead Yeats among his poet-critics—signifies as the collective singer of Cuchulain's keening song beyond the wars of history, beyond the cycles of life and death that shape the death drive as cold destruction, and into the lonely space of the interim where the endlessness of the death drive as immortality and textual survival can be dreamt as peace.

---

[44] 'Black out; Heaven blazing into the head'; 'Lapis Lazuli', *CW1*, 300; Yeats is laid to rest under 'bare Ben Bulben's head'; *CW1*, 335; *Poems*, 375.

[45] *CW1*, 181.

[46] *CW1*, 325.

[47] *CW1*, 326.

PART III

FROM THE GLOBAL TO THE INTERPLANETARY

CHAPTER 20

···

TAGORE, POUND, AND WORLD ENGLISH

···

JUSTIN QUINN

IN 1912 a poet arrives from India in London and feels alienated from the city and its inhabitants.[1] Although he is from Kolkata's elite, he spent ten years in a rural area of what is now Bangladesh and there educated himself in the folk traditions of that place. Immersed in the local, he has nevertheless also dreamed of a literature that connects people around the globe, one that is based on their common divinity. But now in London he is faced, it seems, with intractable difference: 'It is not possible to know this humanity, or enter into the heart of another place.'[2] Such an admission is difficult for him, given the intensity of his previous hope. He knows hardly anyone in the city and he himself is unknown as a writer. His literary work is intimately connected with his distant home, which he is pining for. He thinks that the people seem to be mere phantoms.

Then he looks up an old friend who helps the poet find better lodgings, and also politely enquires about his poems. He writes in Bengali and while on a steamer ship from India he has made some prose translations of his work, which he has undertaken only 'in order to have the pleasure of going over them again', considering them 'schoolboy exercises.'[3] The poet gives him the prose translations. The friend is enthusiastic and arranges a literary evening, to which several well-known writers come, among them one particularly famous one. These people are also excited about the work, though the poet doubts their sincerity. Of these English versions he would later say: 'In my translations I timidly avoid all difficulties, which has the effect of making them smooth and thin', even going as far as to describe the process as similar to forging money.[4] Only gradually

[1] Justin Quinn would like to acknowledge receipt of funding to enable him to work on this chapter from the Grant System for Academics (GRAK) at the Faculty of Education, University of West Bohemia, Czech Republic.
[2] Quoted by Edward Thompson in *Rabindranath Tagore: Poet and Dramatist* (Oxford: Oxford University Press, 1926), 221. Further details given here of this visit are from the same source, 221–2.
[3] Ibid., 221.
[4] Ibid., 264.

does Rabindranath Tagore accept that his listeners in London are in earnest: they are enormously engaged by his work. The famous poet W. B. Yeats works with the Bengali on the translations and also energetically promotes his reputation, with the help of a younger, lesser-known poet. The following year Tagore is the first non-European to win the Nobel Prize in Literature, and, as one critic has remarked, he did so 'primarily for his works in English'.[5]

It is an extraordinary series of events. Although the Nobel Prize was only twelve years in existence, it was becoming one of the main instruments for imagining how literature might move beyond national boundaries. For a writer to move from near-total anonymity to global fame within a year indicates that exceptional forces were at work, forces that did not perhaps wholly arise from the Bengali's poems themselves.

How is a writer's fame produced and how is it measured? In 1912 W. B. Yeats was possibly the most distinguished poet of his age. In Ireland, although a contentious figure, the arguments only further galvanized his standing: no matter what one thought of him, he was central to debates about Irish culture, as well as being, less contentiously, considered an outstanding poet. In London, his network was multilayered and complex, composed of politicians, cultural figures, and occultists. His fame there was in large part due to his role as a cultural ambassador, through his poems and public engagements representing the Irish imaginary to an English audience. He consolidated the same role further afield in 1903–4, during a lecture tour of the United States. The English language was not yet a global lingua franca, yet its catchment area was vast, and Yeats could make fair claim to being its most famous poet. In the early 1910s, his reputation as a poet of the fin de siècle was indisputable. But such past glory did not guarantee contemporary interest. Yeats was in danger of becoming a museum exhibit. To avoid this, Yeats became a curator, writing memoirs and poems that canonized his friends and associates from the preceding era, while giving himself a new freedom of movement. As James Longenbach remarks, 'he began to lecture about his dead companions fixing them at a point in history that only he himself had transcended'.[6] This retrospective movement, which became so central to his imagination in the 1910s, also gave him a strong forward momentum, joining him to a younger generation.

The younger figure in the episode above is the US poet Ezra Pound, aged 27, who had arrived in London four years earlier, and was busy building his own reputation. Pound's poetry had been deeply influenced by Yeats and his associates of the 1890s, so it was natural that he would seek the older poet in London. From 1909 on, he was in regular social contact with Yeats. But there was a complication: while obviously drawn by Yeats's fame, that fame was, it seemed, inseparably linked with the 1890s, and Pound now was trying to ditch this. Then, as A. Walton Litz describes, 'sometime before midsummer 1910, he saw or heard some of Yeats's newest work that would appear in *The Green Helmet and*

[5] Radha Chakravarty, 'Translating Tagore: Shifting Paradigms', in Debashish Banerji, ed., *Rabindranath Tagore in the 21st Century: Theoretical Renewals* (New Delhi: Springer India, 2015), 25.

[6] James Longenbach, *Stone Cottage: Pound, Yeats and Modernism* (New York: Oxford University Press, 1988), 14.

Other Poems (September 1910)' and remarked in a letter a few months later, 'That is the spirit of the new things as I saw them in London.'[7] Yeats was pursuing the same goal as Pound.

The generational difference was also important as, for Yeats, Pound linked him with the younger generation of poets. Winning his admiration might be the first step toward a healthy posterity. Longenbach remarks that, 'To Yeats, Pound was most valuable as a great admirer during a time when Yeats himself was enormously insecure about the quality of his work.'[8] Yeats's uncertainty is not to be wondered at: he was breaking the style that had established his fame in the preceding decades, and trying to forge a new idiom. Pound would later coin the slogan 'Make it new!', and this was exactly what Yeats was attempting to do. As Longenbach established many decades ago, Yeats did not look to Pound for instruction in forging this new style; rather, the young poet was more of a sounding board and promoter, apart from his role as Yeats's secretary during three winters, when the two were secluded in a house named Stone Cottage in Ashdown Forest, from 1912 to 1915.

In his turn Pound received two benefits: first, he was able to observe a master up close, confronted with the same dilemma as he was, transforming his poetic idiom; and second, he was able to impress others by his intimacy with one of the most famous poets of the age. Longenbach helpfully sums up the situation: 'Pound increased his own prestige by associating with Yeats and saved himself the necessity of indulging in hack journalism to support himself; Yeats had the pleasure of having his greatest admirer close at hand and saved his eyesight by having the admirer read to him.'[9]

There is a further aspect of this commerce in renown that was taking place between Yeats and Pound. Writers' fame can also be aggrandized when they bestow it on others. On the most worldly of levels, Yeats was testing the value of his own stock when he put so much capital behind Tagore. The award of the Nobel Prize in Literature in 1913 perhaps prefigured the award of 1923, which was made to Yeats. Pound energetically joined Yeats in praising Tagore in print, and Longenbach remarks that he had 'selfserving reasons for joining Yeats to "boom" Tagore so strenuously: by doing so, he emphasized his position as the single poet of the younger generation with whom Yeats would associate.'[10] A cynical observer might feel that the Bengali poet was incidental to all this activity.

That the whole encounter was a congeries of misrecognitions and withholding is borne out by later remarks. Yeats would later curse Tagore for producing 'sentimental rubbish' after the early books (which Yeats had been involved with, and which are themselves quite sentimental).[11] For his part, Tagore, as he watched his English reputation

---

[7] A. Walton Litz, 'Pound and Yeats: The Road to Stone Cottage', in George Bornstein, ed., *Ezra Pound Among the Poets* (Chicago: University of Chicago Press, 1985), 132. Pound's letter is also quoted here.

[8] Longenbach, *Stone Cottage*, 20.

[9] Ibid., 29.

[10] Ibid., 25.

[11] In a letter of May 1935 to William Rothenstein, Yeats wrote, 'Damn Tagore', as he produced only 'sentimental rubbish' after his first few books; Yeats added that 'Tagore does not know English, no Indian knows English' (quoted in Chaudhuri, 'The English Writings of Rabindranath Tagore', 112).

tank after 1920, would characterize his engagement with anglophone culture as a mistake (using the figure for self-translation mentioned above):

> When I began this career of falsifying my own coins I did it in play. Now I am becoming frightened of its enormity and am willing to make a confession of my misdeeds and withdraw into my original vocation as a mere Bengali poet. I hope it is not yet too late to make reparation.[12]

Having had such a flimsy basis for his initial enthusiasm, Yeats should have blamed only himself for his disillusionment. Tagore, likewise, cuts an absurd figure, ruing how his self-translations betrayed their originals. At the time some observers did feel that Tagore's achievement (at least in English) was incommensurate to their praise, but he was not merely a random unknown figure that the US and Irish poets decided upon: certain features of the work and the man slotted into broader cultural preoccupations and projects.[13] Both poets were in the grip of a vaster dream.

What were this dream's features? First, Tagore's journey itself to London was important, as it marked for him the vast distance—cultural, geographic—between Bengal and England. If Londoners, who seemed like phantoms, turned out in the end to be made of the same flesh and blood as he was, and also turned out to have, on a fundamental level, the same preoccupations as he did, then there was hope for a literature of the world. Likewise Yeats, for most of his career, had proclaimed oral traditions as central to his imagination: 'Folk-art is, indeed, the oldest of the aristocracies of thought, . . . and because it has gathered into itself the simplest and the most unforgettable thoughts of the generations, it is the soil where all great art is rooted.'[14] He connected with such soil through the oral traditions of Ireland, and this had been the central project of the Celtic Revival during the 1890s, not only in Yeats's own work but in that of a range of scholars, artists, writers, sportspeople, and politicians. In doing so, he figured himself as turning away from the 'mere chronicle of circumstance, or passionless fantasies, and passionless meditations' to which most literature had now been reduced. Other folk traditions had by now faded in vitality, but 'the Celtic, the Celtic alone has been for centuries close to the main river of European literature. It has again and again brought "the vivifying spirit" "of excess" into the arts of Europe.'[15]

Commuting between London and Dublin for most of his career, Yeats generally conceived of his idea of the Celtic in contrast to the main contours of English culture (though there were important exceptions to this, among them the poetry of William Blake and the Arts and Crafts Movement later in the nineteenth century). If the British

---

[12] Quoted in Thompson, *Rabindranath Tagore*, 264.

[13] See, for instance, Marianne Moore's 'To William Butler Yeats on Tagore': 'the jewel that always / Outshines ordinary jewels, is your praise.' Marianne Moore, *New Collected Poems*, ed. Heather Cass White (New York: Farrar, Straus and Giroux, 2017), 278.

[14] *Myth 2005*, 91.

[15] 'The Celtic Element in Literature', in *CW4*, 136.

Empire insisted that its colonial subjects were mostly infantile, Yeats countered that the Irish were not children, but were mistaken for such only because they were closer to this vivifying spirit. They offered an organic wholeness of imagination in contrast to the fractured, technical civilization represented in this instance by Britain. This appeal to an idealized primordial phase in contrast to the corrupted present of advanced civilization was a familiar manoeuvre in cultural debates throughout most of the twentieth century.

The dimensions of this argument were, for Yeats, configured by Ireland, Britain, and, further off, Europe. At the time he encountered Tagore, however, he was broadening his purview to the world itself. Yeats had picked up the idea of the 'world soul', or *Anima Mundi*, from his earlier study of Emanuel Swedenborg, but from the 1910s he began to explore it more specifically through Japanese Noh theatre (a common interest with Pound), and through Tagore also. If he could sense the 'vivifying spirit' in the work of a writer so distant, then it might be taken as confirmation of an even vaster foundation, a kind of world soul, that had previously been unimagined. A better reasoner would insist on finding hundreds of such indices before drawing such a conclusion, but Yeats, although he had never visited India and was monolingual, had no such scruples. Even though he builds the following passage on hypotheses, he gathers an impressive rhetorical force:

> If the civilization of Bengal remains unbroken, if that common mind which – as one divines – runs through all, is not, as with us, broken into a dozen minds that know nothing of each other, something even of what is most subtle in these verses will have come, in a few generations, to the beggar on the roads.[16]

The sense of excitement is powerful. Tagore's work promises to link cultural elites and beggars on the road, hooping a civilization together in contrast to the splintered, specialized sprawl that the US and Europe have created for themselves. We need Tagore, because he reminds us of the origins from which we have strayed:

> A whole people, a whole civilization, immeasurably strange to us, seems to have been taken up into this imagination; and yet we are not moved because of its strangeness, but because we have met our own image, as though we had walked in Rossetti's willow wood, or heard, perhaps for the first time in literature, our voice as in a dream.[17]

The poems are strange to us because they come from a distant culture of which we know little; this exoticizes them. If he had left it at that, Yeats would merge into the pantheon of nineteenth-century orientalism, but the counter-manoeuvre swings thought in a different direction, toward the description of a world soul. Tagore met him halfway in this, also dreaming of such a global community, as he himself moved from an apprehension of the irreconcilable otherness of Londoners to a joyful celebration of connection.

[16] *CW5*, 167.
[17] *CW5*, 168.

Pound brought up the rear, proclaiming a new era of the world soul in *Poetry*: 'I speak with all gravity when I say that world fellowship is nearer for the visit of Rabindranath Tagore to London.'[18]

The major difficulty for world literature then, as now, is translation. Even in his dealings with Irish culture, Yeats was at a disadvantage because, despite his efforts, he had no Irish, and so everything was communicated through translators and interpreters. If he had had mastery of a different language, he might have been aware of the difficulties, unconscious deceptions, enthusiastic misrecognitions, and strategic omissions that movement from one language to another always entails. However troubled, then, his engagement with Irish language culture, this was multiplied by myriads when he picked up Tagore's poems. May Sinclair was present on that first evening when Tagore read in London, and she remarked that it was 'an event of supreme importance … An experience too subtle, too profound, and too personal to be readily translatable into language.'[19] This seems like praise, but it contains within it all the trouble to come.

Leaving aside the broader question of translatability, we might consider the narrower issue of English itself as a medium for this inchoate World Literature. Yeats displays little or no awareness of how compromised his communications with Tagore were—both on personal and literary levels—because they are through English. He artfully omits the Empire as a factor in his meeting of minds with the Bengali poet. Colonization is suppressed, as any such emphasis would throw a problematic light on Yeats, casting him as, in essence, a British poet in the imperial metropolis, giving an audience to an unknown writer from a distant and little-known colony, and consequently blessing him with favours. English has only become a global lingua franca in the last few decades, and with this change many people have become hyper-aware of how, as one critic has remarked, 'the history of world literature is inseparable from the rise of English as global literary vernacular and is in fact to some extent *predicated* on the latter'.[20] But in Yeats's time English was purely an imperial lingua franca, and Yeats's own conflicts of interest left him in a poor position to gauge how this might affect his judgement. Moreover, his promotion of the idea of world literature became a way for him to sidestep empire.

The best account to date of this aspect of Yeats is Barry Shiels's *W. B. Yeats and World Literature: The Subject of Poetry* (2016). There he argues that through his work with Irish antiquarian material he came 'to invent a "common" English applicable to no particular locale – and spoken by no particular person'.[21] This 'common English', Shiels argues, has more generally served to found a global literary lingua franca. He remarks:

> For a monoglot Yeats notched-up a surprising number of important translation credits. As well as the Irish folklore considered in the last chapter, and two

[18] Ezra Pound, 'Tagore's Poems', *Poetry* 1:3 (Dec. 1912), 94.

[19] May Sinclair, 'The *Gitanjali*; or Song-Offerings of Rabindra Nath Tagore', *North American Review*, 197 (May 1913), 659.

[20] Aamir R. Mufti, *Forget English! Orientalisms and World Literature* (Cambridge: Harvard University Press, 2016), 11.

[21] Barry Shiels, *W. B. Yeats and World Literature: The Subject of Poetry* (Farnham: Ashgate, 2016), 129.

late translations (of translations) of the Oedipus plays, he worked to improve Rabindranath Tagore's translation of *Gitanjali* (1912), offered advice to Ezra Pound on the Ernest Fenollosa manuscript for the twin 1916 publications *Certain Noble Plays of Japan* and *Noh or Accomplishment: A Study of the Classical Stage of Japan*, and '[p]ut into English' a new abridged version of the *Upanishads* with Shri Purohit Swāmi (1937).[22]

In relation to the last-mentioned, he continues:

> What distinguishes the Yeats and Shri Purohit version … is its presumptuousness. Showing no need for parenthetical explanation and with a clear emphasis on brevity and simplicity, their edition compresses the scholarly apparatus which we might expect to accompany such a technical feat of translation. Theirs is not a translation into English from another language, but an original production of world English.[23]

The world soul under construction by Yeats and Pound would need a medium, and engaging with literary texts from such distant places allowed them to stress-test this world English. Yeats and Pound, then, were preoccupied with the same question, but they came up with two different answers. That is, they produced two very different kinds of poetry in response to this challenge.

If Yeats tried to smooth Tagore's poems so that they slid easily into this new poetic idiom of world English, then the Bengali poet, as we saw above, met him halfway. Yeats wrote almost exclusively in what were then conventional poetic forms, but he did not insist that the writers mentioned above be press-ganged into such patterns. Here is no. 35, from Tagore's *Gitanjali*:

> Where the mind is without fear and the head is held high;
> Where knowledge is free;
> Where the world has not been broken up into fragments by narrow domestic walls;
> Where words come out from the depth of truth;
> Where tireless striving stretches its arms towards perfection;
> Where the clear stream of reason has not lost its way into the dreary desert sand of dead habit;
> Where the mind is led forward by thee into ever-widening thought and action –
> Into that heaven of freedom, my Father, let my country awake.[24]

For our purposes, and examining its internal evidence only, it is impossible to guess the text's provenance. This is achieved on two levels. First, lexically: no words are used here that

---

[22] Ibid., 101.

[23] Ibid., 129.

[24] Rabindranath Tagore, *Gitanjali: Song Offerings*, with an introduction by W. B. Yeats (New York: Macmillan, 1915), 27–8.

connect the text to a particular variety of English.[25] Whereas Yeats would occasionally use Irishisms in his poems, here there are no markers of local usage, even though English had long been domesticated in India at this stage. Second, semantically: the paraphrasable content deals largely in abstractions (mind, knowledge, truth, etc.) that have no connection with a particular locale; the 'desert sand' is metaphorical, and the 'country' mentioned in the final line has no nationalist slant (Tagore was anti-nationalist). This English is built to travel.

Pound's practice as a translator was less domesticating. Alex Davis remarks that 'Pound's translations and appropriations ... break open rather than attempt to "seal" borders between authors and cultural traditions', and this might seem to align him with Yeats's treatment of Tagore and others. However, Davis continues: 'Pound's work recognizes the alterity, the "difference", of his sources ... even as they are made anew in the target context.'[26] This is because Pound is concomitantly forging a modernist idiom of the fragment, that is, a literary work that achieves its effect through stylistic medley rather than homogeneous idiom (of the kind we see above in the passage from *Gitanjali*).

Yeats's own subsequent poetry was not so insistent on its erasures. He did not, after his engagement with Tagore and others, begin writing in an etiolated global poetic idiom. The pre-eminent collection of the 1920s, *The Tower* (1928), has much local lore. But if there are obscure references, they are obscure for Irish and global reader alike (for example, Robert Artisson and Lady Kyteler in 'Nineteen Hundred and Nineteen' or Jacques Molay in 'Meditations in Time of Civil War'): they are carefully curated and strategically employed as part of larger general arguments (quite often about civilizational themes). The Irish Civil War of 1922–3 is a good example of Yeats's use of a complex political conflict in Ireland to make larger points. Does this reduce to universalism? The critical dispensation of the mid-twentieth century praised texts for their ability to assert common general truths based on local matters (for example, William Faulkner addresses the human condition through his treatment of socially disadvantaged white people in Mississippi). Yeats himself may well have had such universalist aims, but anglophone monoglots often think in such terms: such claims only hold for the linguistic and cultural zone of English (and often not even that).

Also, Yeats continued using rhyme and metre after the 1910s, and often thought of this as a salutary resistance to the affordances of free verse. That choice complicated ideas of modernism in the mid-twentieth century, which thought of Pound's above-mentioned aesthetic of the fragment as the only adequate response to the age. Use of conventional form was figured as somehow retrograde. Yet Yeats, along with Robert Frost, Paul Valéry, Rainer Maria Rilke, and others clearly wrote poetry of their own century, and so exceptions were made to include them in the modernist canon. Whether the term 'modernist' lost a lot of its descriptive force at this point is debatable.

---

[25] Here I leave aside the question of whether this passage itself is written in a particular variety of English. Imperial linguistic practice tends to erase the terroir of its own idiom, which itself has very local roots. For a good account of this, see Raymond Williams's 'The Growth of 'Standard English'', in *The Long Revolution* (London: Chatto & Windus, 1961).

[26] Alex Davis, 'Collaborator: Ezra Pound, Translation, and Appropriation', *Modernist Cultures,* 14:1 (2019), 32, 17–35.

One result of these questions of periodization and style was a subsequent division of poetry in the twentieth century into experimental and conventional. Irish poetry, English poetry, and US poetry, to take three examples, were all, in sundry ways, reduced by this binary. In the US, the Poundian aesthetic of the fragment became, in effect, nationalized by Donald Allen's anthology *The New American Poetry 1945–1960* (1960). As Stephan Delbos remarks, 'Allen created a consensus about innovative poetry as specifically American while at the same time suggesting that formal poetry was old fashioned and tied to the British tradition', locating radical experiment in 'a conservative, national framework'.[27] As a corollary, in Ireland and England experimental poetry was marginalized. Yeats was inarguably Ireland's greatest poet, and his formal choices were taken as representative for the national canon; such a critical characterization then rendered poets who excelled in other modes as eccentric.

Yeats's and Pound's responses to the question of translation, and the way their poetic styles developed in the following decades, mark a fateful division in anglophone poetry in the twentieth century, one that was subsequently consolidated by a cultural nationalism in the period after World War II. If that has come loose in the last two to three decades, then one reason may be that critical paradigms are increasingly transnational rather than national. As one realizes that one is no less a US poet if one writes sonnets, one further realizes the redundancy of placing a national label on a poet who writes in a global lingua franca. The dream of a globalized culture was strong in the late 1990s and early 2000s, but it has taken many hits since. We are not circling back to the idea of the 'world soul', which was so important for Yeats and Pound in the early 1910s.

Much critical debate about the anglophone poetic tradition has dwelt upon the fork in the road that occurred in the 1910s, from which point Yeats went on to write some of the greatest poems in the English language, drawing on all the force of six centuries of formal orthodoxy, while Pound conceived *The Cantos*, a sprawling and, for some, incoherent assemblage of fragments of world culture. But these oeuvres no longer represent the ends of the spectrum; both are bracketed now as 'high modernism', its highness propped up by imperialism (for all of Yeats's nationalist credentials), first of Britain, and then of the US during the Cold War.

For if both Yeats and Pound were open to and generous toward work from distant lands, then ultimately it was so that they could fit it into the anthologizing projects of their poetry. What does this mean? In Pound's case, it is evident even from a cursory reading of *The Cantos*: that work effectively samples from a wide range of sources, and the drama of their coherence is thought of as an expression of the drama of the coherence of a world culture (or even just European culture). *The Cantos* may be a ragged kind of anthology, but it is an anthology none the less. Shiels, again, is illuminating:

> Individual poems which reference multiple poetic traditions and place anachronistic and 'second-hand' lines deliberately side-by-side along with translations and diverse

---

[27] Stephan Delbos, unpublished doctoral thesis, *Behind Enemy Lines:* The New American Poetry *and the Cold War Anthology Wars* (Prague: Charles University, 2017), 5–6.

registers of speech and writing achieve a seminal mobility between their diminished formal autonomy and the grandiosity of their historical ambition. This is the accomplishment of canonical modernist works such as T. S. Eliot's *The Waste Land* or Ezra Pound's *The Cantos*....[28]

Perhaps the apotheosis of this approach is the later anthology of world poetry edited by Jerome Rothenberg, *Technicians of the Sacred: A Range of Poetries from Africa, America, Asia, Oceania, and Europe* (1968). In its introduction it maps artefacts from oral cultures around the world onto the avant-garde poetic techniques (chiefly influenced by Pound) that are championed in Donald Allen's anthology. There is a blurring taking place here between the anthologizer and poet, and it is one that accrues great cultural power. Cultural artefacts that have come from a great distance (Tagore or the shamanistic chants in Rothenberg's anthology) are incorporated by this aesthetic, thus aggrandizing its purview and status.

And what of Yeats? In what way is it possible to consider his poetry an anthology in these terms? Certainly, a page of the *Last Poems* looks unlike a page of *The Cantos*. If we are to think of the latter as an anthology of sorts, then it is a chaotic one, more like an arena in which different voices come and go. In contrast, Yeats's poems for the most part use a single voice and, as remarked above, employ conventional rhyme and metre. Still, Shiels continues the quote above thus:

> This is the accomplishment of canonical modernist works such as T. S. Eliot's *The Waste Land* or Ezra Pound's *The Cantos*, but also ... of Yeats's poems from *The Wind Among the Reeds* through to his *Last Poems*, all of which explore, or perhaps expose, the textuality of the reference book. Instead of simply collating (and quantifying) different historical and geographic forms, and charting formal morphologies, the world literature anthology ... must be revealed in this light as itself a modern form *par excellence*, and its processes of 'distant reading' considered a paradoxical form of textual development from within.[29]

We might consider a stanza from 'The Statues' to see how this works:

> One image crossed the many-headed, sat
> Under the tropic shade, grew round and slow,
> No Hamlet thin from eating flies, a fat
> Dreamer of the Middle Ages. Empty eyeballs knew
> That knowledge increases unreality, that
> Mirror on mirror mirrored is all the show.
> When gong and conch declare the hour to bless
> Grimalkin crawls to Buddha's emptiness.[30]

[28] Shiels, *W. B. Yeats and World Literature*, 22.
[29] Ibid., 22–23.
[30] *CW1*, 337.

Whereas *The Cantos* incorporates substantial tranches of medieval Chinese history, Yeats reduces analogous material to dense synopsis, so dense in fact that here it is rendered almost incomprehensible. What both Pound's and Yeats's poems share, *pace* their stylistic differences, is that they emerge from reference works and textbooks. That is how they carry out 'distant reading' of far-flung civilizations. The poets transform this material into lines of poetry, and this poetry then is subsequently decoded (by academic pedagogy and criticism, like the chapters of this book) through the use of reference works and textbooks. In a curious sense, the poems are nodes along the journeys made by information about, in this case, Greece and Asia among other referents; they grow out of encyclopaedias and similar works, and drift back toward them after they have been published. The work processes texts from far-flung extremes and suspends them temporarily in a particular jaunty arrangement that we call a poem.

A large part of the cultural prestige of such works then resides in their ability to 'distant read' cultures and incorporate observations in syncretic texts. What the works of such high modernism do not want is to be 'distant read' themselves. Whereas Yeats and Pound, in July 1912 listening to the Bengali poet read in William Rothenstein's house, are happy to acknowledge the way that Tagore's texts can express what they believe to be general truths about humanity's place in the cosmos, they are not engaged by texts that might incorporate figures such as the Irish and US poets, and their literary culture, in their own texts. They do not themselves want to be relativized and anthologized. The logic of this argument might seem tenuous, as we have no examples of situations in which either Pound or Yeats emphatically rejected such texts. What we do have are the poems of Tagore and those of anglophone high modernism, and from these it is plain that Tagore's work is valued precisely for the way it does not relativize, synthesize, and anthologize; it must be pure of those manoeuvres. Yeats may well lament how modern culture has lost a unity of being, but in doing so he consolidates his own cultural superiority and that of the nascent world language that he expresses himself in.

Earlier I quoted Alex Davis as he characterized Pound's attitude to translation as recognizing the alterity of foreign texts. However, he goes on to concede Marjorie Perloff's point that while '[c]ontemporary multilingual poetics owes much to Pound ... there is never any doubt but that the voice [in *The Cantos*] that orchestrates these ingenious variations is a well-versed and expert English speaker'.[31] Linguistic expertise, whether in one's own or in other languages, is always linked to power; what both Pound and Yeats suppress is how their own cultural prestige depends on English as a colonial language and later (for our reading of them) on English as a global lingua franca, which raises accompanying questions of the world literature anthology, whether this is in the poems themselves, or in how we arrange about ourselves the literature of the planet.

---

[31] Quoted in Davis, 'Collaborator', 34.

CHAPTER 21

··

AFRICA

··

NATHAN SUHR-SYTSMA

THE narrator of *Ethiopia Unbound* (1911) opines that he 'should like to see *Ethiopian Leagues* formed throughout the United States much in the same way as the *Gaelic League* in Ireland for the purpose of studying and employing Fanti, Yoruba, Hausa, or other standard African language, in daily use.'[1] Widely regarded as the first African novel in English, published in London, where its West African author J. E. Casely Hayford had trained as a lawyer, the book makes repeated references to the Gaelic League, whose efforts to revive public interest in the Irish language the narrator treats as a model for how Africans might reclaim their own languages. Writing in what was then called the Gold Coast (present-day Ghana), Casely Hayford goes so far as to quote from James O. Hannay's 'The Gaelic League' (1905): 'Ten years ago, we had in Ireland a people divorced, by half a century of education conducted along alien lines, from their own proper language and culture.'[2] Given the tension between what the Gaelic League saw as 'The Necessity of De-Anglicising Ireland' (the title of a watershed lecture by Douglas Hyde in 1892) and W. B. Yeats's efforts to craft an Irish literature in English, it may not be surprising that, when a spirit appeared to Yeats on 9 May 1912 at a seance near London, claiming 'he was the Guide of Mr Yeats, had been with him a great many years', it he did not speak Ireland's ancestral language.[3] What is unexpected, however, is that this spirit guide, speaking through the medium's 'long tin trumpet' with 'a strong Irish accent', identified himself as an African—or at least, that is how Yeats would begin to think of him when he discovered that 'Leo, the writer and explorer' was best known as 'Leo Africanus.'[4]

---

[1] J. E. Casely Hayford, *Ethiopia Unbound: Studies in Race Emancipation* (London: C.M. Philips, 1911), 175.
[2] Casely Hayford, *Ethiopia Unbound*, 176. Later, the Anglican clergyman's name is accidentally Gaelicized as James O'Hannay (195).
[3] Edith K. Harper's notes, quoted in Steve L. Adams and George Mills Harper, eds., 'The Manuscript of "Leo Africanus"', in *YA*, 19 (2013), 307, previously published in *YA* 1 (1982).
[4] WBY's notes, quoted in 'The Manuscript of "Leo Africanus"', 308.

In his record of this encounter, Yeats seems to have forgotten that he had encountered the same spirit almost exactly three years earlier, at a seance in Sandymount, Dublin, on 3 May 1909.[5] His notes on that occasion include, 'I am trying to call Leo' and Leo's reply that 'I have been to you before (Africa name)'.[6] Pursued intermittently over the eventful decade of 1909–19, Yeats's engagement with Leo Africanus involved not only audible voices at seances but also automatic writing, ordinary reading, and, at one point, a metallic homunculus. Its culmination, arguably, was an 'exchange' of letters. In the summer of 1915, Yeats notes that Leo, through a medium's automatic writing, had 'asked me to write him a letter addressed to him as if to Africa giving all my doubts about spiritual things and then to write a reply as from him to me. He would control me ~~if he could~~ in that reply so that it would be really from him.'[7] Late in 1915, while at Stone Cottage with Ezra Pound, Yeats complied. As he reported to Alexandra Schepeler the day after Christmas, 'I am writing a letter to Leo Africanus, my "daimon" & reading Landor', the author of *Imaginary Conversations*.[8]

Who was Leo Africanus? At some point after 9 May 1912, Yeats consulted *Chambers Biographical Dictionary*, suspecting the medium had done the same.[9] Here's what he would have found:

> **Leo Africanus** (properly ALHASSAN IBN MOHAMMED ALWAZZAN), a Cordovan Moor, who from 1492 travelled in northern Africa and Asia Minor. Falling into the hands of Venetian corsairs, he was sent to Leo X. at Rome, where he lived twenty years, and accepted Christianity, but returned to Africa and his old faith, and died at Tunis in 1552. He wrote (1526) an account of his African travels in Italian (first printed 1559), long the chief source of information as to the Soudan. Dr R. Brown re-edited John Pory's translation of 1600 (Hakluyt Soc. 1896).[10]

Reflecting the paucity of evidence about Leo's life, a later edition, in other ways identical, informs the reader that its subject 'returned to Africa and (perhaps) his old faith'.[11] The account of his travels, *La Descrittione dell'Africa*, edited by Giovanni Battista Ramusio and attributed to 'Giovan Lioni Africano', was in fact published in 1550. Pory, whom one scholar has recently called 'America's first racist', titled it

---

[5] *Life 1*, 465, 614 n.33.

[6] 'The Manuscript of "Leo Africanus"', 290.

[7] 'The Manuscript of "Leo Africanus"', 302.

[8] Yeats to Aleck Schepeler, 26 December [1915], *CL InteLex* #2838, quoted in Wayne K. Chapman, '"Something Intended, Complete": Major Work on Yeats Past, Present, and Yet to Come', in Matthew Gibson and Neil Mann, eds., *Yeats, Philosophy, and the Occult* ([Clemson, SC:] Clemson University Press, 2016), 33. James Longenbach discusses Pound and WBY's reading of *Imaginary Conversations* in *Stone Cottage: Pound, Yeats, and Modernism* (New York: Oxford University Press, 1988), 187–9.

[9] 'The Manuscript of "Leo Africanus"', 313.

[10] David Patrick and Francis Hindes Groomes, eds., *Chambers Biographical Dictionary: The Great of All Times and Nations* (London: W. & R. Chambers, 1911 [1897]), 584.

[11] William Geddie and J. Liddell Geddie, eds., *Chambers Biographical Dictionary: The Great of All Nations and All Times* (London: W. & R. Chambers, 1929), 584.

A Geographical Historie of Africa and attributed it to 'John Leo a More'.[12] Pory's translation of Leo Africanus's text, which had been 'transmitted to him through at least two layers of Western European translators', likely informed Shakespeare's *Othello, the Moor of Venice* (1604) and authorized racist tropes in Ben Jonson's *The Masque of Blackness* (1605).[13]

The edition Yeats acquired, published 'during the "scramble for Africa"' as *The History and Description of Africa* (1896), was attributed to 'Al-Hassan Ibn-Mohammed Al-Wezaz Al-Fasi, a Moor, baptized as Giovani Leone, but better known as Leo Africanus', the final term 'suggest[ing] both Latinate scholarship and his representative status'.[14] Ninety years later, Amin Maalouf's novel *Léon l'Africain* (1986), translated into English as *Leo the African* in the UK and *Leo Africanus* in the US, brought a vividly imagined version of this fascinating figure to a wider readership. Amidst the rise of postcolonial studies and increasing attention to race in early modern literature during the 1990s, literary scholars in turn became interested in Leo Africanus, 'a name', scholars observe, 'that he never gave himself'.[15] Published at the peak of this wave of interest, Natalie Zemon Davis's speculative biography of the traveller identifies his rightful name, signed on a manuscript in the Vatican Library, as 'al-Hasan ibn Muhammad ibn Ahmad al-Wazzan', to which he appended 'al-Fasi', meaning from Fez, where he spent his formative years, and at other times 'al-Gharnati', meaning from Granada, his birthplace.[16] Following his baptism in 1520, he was named 'Joannes Leo after the pope who sprinkled water on him', although Davis prefers the 'name he gave himself in Arabic after his conversion: Yuhanna al-Asad' (John the Lion).[17] This chapter will refer to the historical figure as al-Wazzan (pre-conversion) or al-Asad (post-conversion), the European construction thereof as Leo Africanus, and Yeats's spirit guide as 'Leo'.

The first volume of the 1896 edition, after enumerating both the virtues and the vices of the Africans, ends with its author telling two stories that reflect on his subject position.

---

[12] Ibram X. Kendi, 'On John Pory, America's First Racist', *Black Perspectives* (21 March 2016), https://www.aaihs.org/john-pory-americas-first-racist/.

[13] Bernadette Andrea, 'The Ghost of Leo Africanus from the English to the Irish Renaissance', in Patricia Clare Ingham and Michelle R. Warren, eds., *Postcolonial Moves: Medieval through Modern* (New York: Palgrave Macmillan, 2003), 199. Andrea draws on the work of Moroccan scholar Oumelbanine Zhiri, particularly her *L'Afrique au miroire de l'Europe: Fortunes de Jean Léon l'Africain à la Renaissance* (Geneva: Droz, 1991), 82–3. On Africanus and *Othello*, see John C. Hawley, 'Colonizing the mind: "Leo Africanus" in the Renaissance and today', in Graeme Harper, ed., *Colonial and Postcolonial Incarceration* (New York: Continuum, 2001), 57–9.

[14] Andrea, 'The Ghost of Leo Africanus', 202; Leo Africanus, *The History and Description of Africa*, trans. John Pory [1600], ed. Robert Brown [1896], 3 vols. (New York: B. Franklin [1963?]); Oliver Hennessey, 'Talking with the Dead: Leo Africanus, Esoteric Yeats, and Early Modern Imperialism', *ELH* 71:4 (Winter 2004), 1025.

[15] Andrea, 'The Ghost of Leo Africanus', 196, translating Zhiri, *L'Afrique*, 49.

[16] Natalie Zemon Davis, *Trickster Travels: A Sixteenth-Century Muslim Between Worlds* (New York: Hill & Wang, 2006), 15.

[17] Ibid., 65.

He is like an executioner who refuses to spare a convicted criminal, his erstwhile friend, the allotted number of lashes; he is like 'a most wily bird' who goes to live in the sea to avoid paying tribute to the king of the birds and then, when required to pay tribute to the king of the fishes, returns to the air, repeating this feat as necessary.[18] 'For mine owne part, when I heare the Africans euill spoken of, I wil affirme my selfe to be one of Granada: and when I perceiue the nation of Granada to be discommended, then will I professe my selfe to be an African.'[19] According to one scholar, 'Leo's wily adaptability' is part of what drew the novelist Amin Maalouf, a Lebanese Christian living in Paris, to him.[20] To that same scholar, Yeats's exchange of letters with Leo is 'a truly fascinating reminder of how bizarre Yeats really was'.[21] But this exchange might instead serve as a reminder of the poet's own 'wily adaptability'.

In *W.B. Yeats and World Literature*, Barry Sheils claims that the poet's recourse to 'international reference points' in Europe, Asia, and the Americas worked, 'at least partially, to release his poetry from a political sphere dominated by the island's contested sovereignty and the discourse of "de-anglicisation" most often associated with his contemporaries Douglas Hyde and D.P. Moran'.[22] Conspicuously missing from Sheils's list is Africa. Granted, whereas Yeats travelled in continental Europe, met Rabindranath Tagore from India and Yone Noguchi from Japan, and lectured across America during the 1910s, he neither met an African intellectual such as Casely Hayford nor visited the continent.[23] Yet Africa still occupies a place in his thought and his reception. Whereas most scholars have considered Yeats's attempt to write 'as if to Africa' in terms of the poet's early modern antecedents and intertexts, what might we learn from looking forward to how Yeats has been read—and continues to be read— by African writers? Beginning with the Leo Africanus episode and continuing to Yeats's afterlife in African letters, this chapter touches on debates about where Yeats fits in discourses of coloniality and decolonization, about how to interpret his esoteric and occult interests, and about the global reception of the Irish Literary Revival. As W. H. Auden so famously wrote in his elegy for Yeats, 'he became his admirers'.[24] This chapter contends that, in Auden's sense, Yeats has become not just European, Asian, or American, but also African.

---

[18] Africanus, *History*, 1:188–9. For discussions of this passage, see Jonathan Burton, '"A Most Wily Bird": Leo Africanus, *Othello* and the Trafficking in Difference', in Ania Loomba and Martin Orkin, eds., *Post-Colonial Shakespeares* (London: Routledge, 1998), 43–63, especially 52–4, and Davis, *Trickster Travels*, 109–13.

[19] Africanus, *History*, 1:190.

[20] Hawley, 'Colonizing the mind', 64.

[21] Ibid., 61.

[22] Barry Sheils, *W. B. Yeats and World Literature: The Subject of Poetry* (Farnham: Ashgate, 2015), 10.

[23] On Tagore and Noguchi, see, respectively, *Life 1*, 469–73, and Nathan Suhr-Sytsma, 'Haiku Aesthetics and Grassroots Internationalization: Japan in Irish Poetry', *Éire-Ireland* 45:3&4 (Fall/Winter 2010), 249–50.

[24] W. H. Auden, *Selected Poems*, expanded edn, ed. Edward Mendelson (New York: Vintage International, 2007), 89.

'As if to Africa': Leo Africanus and 'The Second Coming'

Less than a decade after the poet's death in 1939, Leo Africanus was introduced to readers of Yeats by Richard Ellmann's *Yeats: The Man and the Masks*. Attesting to the existence of an unpublished manuscript, Ellmann referred somewhat confusingly to Leo Africanus as 'the Italian geographer and traveler' and as 'a dead poet from Fez'.[25] Over subsequent decades, isolated scholarship considered this mysterious figure, but it was not until 1982 that 'The Manuscript of "Leo Africanus"' was edited and made accessible to curious Yeatsians. The biographies of W. B. and George Yeats by Terence Brown, R. F. Foster, Brenda Maddox, and Ann Saddlemyer published around the turn of the millennium set Leo Africanus within the context of the Yeatses' relationships and psychological states. Foster's biography, for instance, treats 'Leo' as 'an imaginary *alter ego*', a phrase that he repeats.[26] A series of essays in the early 2000s that offered postcolonial readings of the Yeats–'Leo' exchange has been followed by chapters in monographs devoted to Yeats's 'Occult Nationalism', on the one hand, and his 'lifelong engagement with otherness and the Orient', on the other.[27] For Bernadette Andrea, criticizing the 'psychologism' of Foster's account while echoing Hazard Adams's reading of Yeats as 'antithetical nationalist', 'Yeats's "correspondence" with Leo Africanus—in the dual sense of an exchange of letters and an identification between two ambivalently colonial subjects—foregrounds … his antithetical postcoloniality.'[28] This correspondence has also been read, more sceptically, as a sign of Yeats's orientalism, Africanism, or even, since Leo was a Catholic convert, the poet's attitudes toward Irish Catholicism.[29] Another model, that of discursive possession, may be even more apt, as explored below.

Spiritualism forms the third of the 'four quadrants' of Yeats's occult interests: in roughly chronological order, theosophy, magic, spiritualism, and Hindu mysticism.[30] Yeats's fascination with occult knowledge and practice involved him with the Dublin Hermetic Society and Esoteric Section of the Theosophical Society in the late 1880s; in 1890, he broke with the Theosophical Society and was initiated into the Hermetic Order of the Golden Dawn. Before leaving the Golden Dawn in 1901, he would have met Robert W. Felkin, 'an Arabist and an authority on African anthropology', the author of

---

[25] Richard Ellmann, *Yeats: The Man and the Masks* (New York: Macmillan, 1948), 195, 197.

[26] *Life 1*, 427, 465.

[27] For the monographs, see, respectively, Claire Nally, *Envisioning Ireland: W. B. Yeats's Occult Nationalism* (Bern: Peter Lang, 2010) and Nicholas Meihuizen, *Yeats, Otherness and the Orient: Aesthetic and Spiritual Bearings* (Oxford: Peter Lang, 2018), 1.

[28] Andrea, 'The Ghost of Leo Africanus', 206, 209.

[29] See, respectively, Hawley, 'Colonizing the mind', 61; Hennessey, 'Talking with the Dead', 1021; and Nally, *Envisioning Ireland*, 137–42.

[30] Margaret Mills Harper, 'Yeats and the Occult', in *The Cambridge Companion to W. B. Yeats*, ed. Marjorie Howes (Cambridge: Cambridge University Press, 2006), 144–66 at 150.

such articles as 'Notes on the Waganda Tribe of Central Africa'.[31] In 1909, he returned to the seance room and the spiritualist pursuits in which he had previous dabbled, prompted by his friendship with Everard Feilding, then an honorary secretary of the Society for Psychical Research, of which Yeats himself was an associate member from 1913 to 1928.[32] The Yeatses' biographers stress the poet's predisposition to believe; Foster attributes to Yeats 'a certain credulity', Maddox states that 'Yeats knew that he was credulous', and Saddlemyer reports George's later admission to Ellmann that 'Yeats was very credulous at most séances'.[33] For Brown, Yeats's examination of automatic writing by Elizabeth Radcliffe was 'marked by the blend of credulity and the exacting instinct for evidence ... which would characterize Yeats's traffic with spirit messengers for much of the rest of his life', not least through the automatic writing that his new wife, George Yeats, began while on their honeymoon.[34]

It was a session of automatic writing with yet another woman, Felicia Scatcherd, that had prompted Yeats to write 'a letter addressed to [Leo] as if to Africa'. As he recalls the prompt in that letter, 'You were my opposite. ... [Y]ou said if I would write a letter to you as if you were still living among your Moors or Sudanese, & put into it all my difficulties and afterwards answer it in your name you would overshadow me in my turn & answer all my doubts.'[35] These doubts and a cognate scepticism or incredulity make for a frequent refrain in Yeats's letter to 'Leo'. Even so, he does not seem to entertain the possibility of a conscious hoax, assuming all the while that, even if 'Leo' is not actually the surviving spirit of the historical fifteenth- to sixteenth-century writer, there is either some kind of spirit with access to sitters' minds or at worst a 'secondary personality' of the medium. 'So,' quips Brown, 'even this apparently sceptical entry carried its weight of occult credulity.'[36] The poet's doubts are counterbalanced by moments of tentative belief: 'perhaps you still lived, & were really speaking to me', his evidence, in this case, being that 'Leo' demonstrated seemingly 'excellent' Italian with another sitter.[37]

Indeed, language has a leading and vexed role to play in this drama. When 'Leo' appeared in 1912, had he spoken with 'a slight Irish accent, not unlike Mr Yeats's own', as Edith K. Harper thought, or 'a strong Irish accent' that may have been 'not quite true', as Yeats's own notes had it?[38] In his letter, Yeats settles on 'a slight Irish accent ... a little more marked than my own'.[39] Yeats tried repeatedly to have 'Leo' attest

[31] *Life 1*, 465. For Felkin's article, see *Proceedings of the Royal Society of Edinburgh* XIII (November 1884–July 1886), 699–770.

[32] Terence Brown, *The Life of W. B. Yeats: A Critical Biography* (Dublin: Gill & Macmillan, 1999), 192.

[33] *Life 1*, 466; Brenda Maddox, *George's Ghosts: A New Life of W. B. Yeats* (London: Picador, 1999), 12; and Ann Saddlemyer, *Becoming George: The Life of Mrs W. B. Yeats* (Oxford, Oxford University Press, 2002), 58.

[34] Brown, *Life*, 194.

[35] 'The Manuscript of "Leo Africanus"', 311.

[36] Brown, *Life*, 194.

[37] 'The Manuscript of "Leo Africanus"', 314.

[38] Ibid., 307, 308.

[39] Ibid., 313.

to his authenticity through Arabic, whether by naming himself in Arabic or 'writing through some mediums [*sic*] hand a sentence of Arabic'.[40] The final section of 'Leo's' letter defers any such definitive proof: 'Yet do not doubt that I was also Leo Africanus the traveller, for … I can still remember the sand, & many Arab cities, … & could I but find fitting medium, I could still write my Arab Tongue.'[41]

Even if he could not speak or write Arabic, 'Leo' was not, of course, wholly imaginary. In his letter addressed to 'Leo', Yeats writes of Pory's *Geographical Historie of Africa*, 'I have beside me as I write the translation of the only work of yours extant today – from this one assumes that you still exist –' and Yeats's image of the traveller as 'a young man studying & making verses in the town of Fez' shows that he read at least into the second volume of Brown's 1896 edition.[42] Foster asserts that the 'personality' invented for 'Leo' by Yeats, 'which would, by contraries, define his own … owes a good deal to Robert Brown's introduction', specifically the 'long section on the author's character'.[43] Yet some of what Yeats read there, such as Brown's comment on Africanus's 'suppleness', defines the poet outright.[44] Yeats likely gleaned the notion that Africanus had been a poet from Pory's note 'To the Reader', which counts among the traveller's other works 'diuers excellent Poems, and other monuments of his industrie, which are not come to light'.[45] In a brief section Pory translated as '*Of the African poets*', al-Asad had written, 'In Fez there are diuers most excellent poets, which make verses in their owne mother toong. Most of their poems and songs intreat of loue.'[46] This third-person description of poets was apparently then projected by Pory—and by Yeats—onto the author himself. It is not out of the realm of possibility, however, that the historical al-Wazzan was a poet. Davis presents him as such, even as she notes that the composition of poetry was neither a professional occupation nor romantic avocation but, rather, a religious and diplomatic instrument: 'Al-Wazzan had learned poetic forms at the madrasa—important religious teachings might well be in verse—', and with 'his uncle, a skilled poet', to emulate, 'the metered verse he composed and declaimed to rulers in the course of his visits took the form of *al-madh*, that is, the Arabic panegyric.'[47]

Neither Yeats's identification with Africanus as poet nor his Irish cultural nationalism prevented the correspondence from 'partaking thoroughly of the conventional othering strategies of early modern English imperial discourse', writes Oliver Hennessey, not least 'in what is perhaps the most surreal episode of Africanus's response, the description of his consciousness after death'.[48] 'Leo' narrates his return to Fez, where '[m]y

---

[40] Ibid., 316. Cf. 295, 303.
[41] Ibid., 334.
[42] 'The Manuscript of "Leo Africanus"', 311, 312. Andrea observes that 'Leo's evocative description of Leo Africanus in Fez' consists of 'a tissue of quotations from Pory's translation' ('The Ghost of Leo Africanus', 207).
[43] *Life 1*, 466.
[44] Brown, in Africanus, *History*, 1:l.
[45] Pory, in Africanus, *History*, 1:5.
[46] Africanus, *History*, 2:455.
[47] Davis, *Trickster Travels*, 22, 50.
[48] Hennessey, 'Talking with the Dead', 1032.

life as a shade seemed to move more slowly than that of the living whose movements seemed to me incredulously quick, as the movements of flies over a river had seemed to me when alive'. Such slow movement should not be mistaken for peace, however; 'Leo' the shade relives scenes of sexual rivalry ('When a student I had won to me a friends mistress') and violence ('I was in a desert, & quarrelling with a bedouin I killed him'). 'Leo' then compares the difference between his life and after-death experiences to that between Michelangelo drawing a live model in his studio and the work he did 'upon the scaffolding in the Sistine Chapel' (completed half a dozen years before al-Wazzan arrived in Rome), an intimation of what Nicholas Meihuizen calls 'Yeatsian post-mortem theory as captured later in *A Vision*', in which 'visions after death undergo . . . an aestheticization'.[49] 'Leo' continues, 'I did not seem to wholly wake, for side by side with the streets of Fez, or desert I seemed to see another world that was growing in weight & vividness, the double of yours, but vaster & more significant'.[50] Attempting to make sense of this textual crux, Hennessey proposes that 'Leo' 'conflates Fez and modern Ireland', and ultimately that Yeats's 'vision of Ireland . . . allows room for and appropriates some of the mysticism, violence, and sexuality that Pory's readers projected onto early modern Africa'.[51] For Gauri Viswanathan, though, 'another world' is not a version of Ireland but what we might now term the Global South, 'a world much larger than the one dominated by the West'.[52] A reading less bound to the empirical globe might see in 'another world' a foreshadowing of the 'Spiritus Mundi' that 'Leo', inspired by the seventeenth-century Cambridge Platonist Henry More, later describes as 'that world, your century has named the unconscious', or 'the place of images & of all things [that] have been or yet shall be'.[53]

Beginning with Ellmann, several biographers and critics have linked the Leo Africanus correspondence with 'Ego Dominus Tuus', published as a proem to *Per Amica Silentia Lunae* (1918), in which one of the two speakers, Ille, calls to his 'anti-self'.[54] Readers of Yeats have been more reluctant, however, to connect Africanus with a more famous blank verse poem from the late 1910s, 'The Second Coming', composed in January 1919. The most widely circulated African text of the modern era, Chinua Achebe's *Things Fall Apart* (1958), takes its title, of course, from that poem's third line: 'Things fall apart; the centre cannot hold'.[55] With this title, Achebe's novel appropriates Yeats's poem and reorients its meaning from the continental European apocalypse envisaged by Yeats, embodied locally in the violence of the Irish War for Independence by the time

---

[49] 'The Manuscript of "Leo Africanus"', 325; Meihuizen, *Yeats, Otherness and the Orient*, 156.

[50] 'The Manuscript of "Leo Africanus"', 325.

[51] Hennessey, 'Talking with the Dead', 1033, 1036.

[52] Gauri Viswanathan, 'Spectrality's secret sharers: Occultism as (post)colonial affect', in Walter Goebel and Saskia Schabio, eds., *Beyond the Black Atlantic: Relocating modernization and technology* (London: Routledge, 2006), 139.

[53] 'The Manuscript of "Leo Africanus"', 328, 329.

[54] *CW1*, 163. See Ellmann, *Yeats*, 197–8; Longenbach, *Stone Cottage*, 191; *Life 1*, 519; Brown, *Life*, 237–8; Hennessey, 'Talking with the Dead', 1035; Harper, 'Yeats and the occult', 159; and especially Meihuizen, *Yeats, Otherness and the Orient*, 141–69.

[55] *CP*, 189.

of its publication in November 1920, to the apocalypse wrought by British missions and imperialism on Igbo society in the same period.[56] One critic associates the 'rough beast' of its penultimate line with the Lion of Judah as a symbol of Et\hiopia and thus 'the emergence of Third World peoples as a power to be reckoned with'.[57] Although this dubious reading, like Achebe's canny allusion, says more about the era of decolonization than about Yeats's intentions, there *is* another African lion with a claim on the poem: Leo Africanus.

'The Second Coming' breaks after its initial octave, then resumes for fourteen lines, beginning with the following:

> Surely some revelation is at hand;
> Surely the Second Coming is at hand.
> The Second Coming! Hardly are those words out
> When a vast image out of *Spiritus Mundi*
> Troubles my sight: somewhere in sands of the desert
> A shape with lion body and the head of a man[.][58]

For Helen Vendler, picking up on Seamus Deane's interpretation of the poem as 'an aborted sonnet that is then reborn as a full one', what at first seems a sonnet turns into a sort of ' "monstrous" form'.[59] The apparition of a part-human, part-animal 'shape' in the desert is prefigured by an incident narrated by 'Leo' from his time as a shade: 'Once I was alone in the desert, watching a – rabbit rolling in the hot sunlight, … & presently my shape resembled his.'[60] A human shade-turned-rabbit may seem a far cry from the 'menacing mythological sphinx-shape' Vendler sees in the poem.[61] 'Leo' goes on to describe a method of 'Cabalists', perhaps informed by al-Asad's description of 'a certaine Cabalisticall rule called Zairagia' or *za'iraja*,[62] which makes for an even more plausible subtext: 'One letter, that at the head let us say might correspond to the sun & so have a lions head to represent it, while this might be a mans body [*sic*].'[63] As Meihuizen points out, 'The reference to a "lions head" and "mans body" exists in fascinating inverted tension with the "lion body and the head of a man" of "The Second Coming".'[64] Yet whether Yeats's inspiration here is traced to the Great Sphinx of Giza or the *za'iraja* of Fez, an image of northern Africa forms the uncanny counterpoint to the initial octave's 'anarchy'.

---

[56] On the poem's composition and publication, see Brown, *Life*, 270–1.

[57] R. F. Fleissner, 'The Second Coming of Guess Who?: The 'Rough Beast' as Africa in <u>The Second Coming</u>', *Notes on Contemporary Literature* VI:5 (November 1976), 8.

[58] *CW1*, 189.

[59] Helen Vendler, *Our Secret Discipline: Yeats and Lyric Form* (Oxford: Oxford University Press), 169–70.

[60] 'The Manuscript of "Leo Africanus"', 326.

[61] Vendler, *Our Secret Discipline* 171.

[62] Africanus, *History*, 2:459, and Davis, *Trickster Travels*, 114–16.

[63] 'The Manuscript of "Leo Africanus"', 333.

[64] Meihuizen, *Yeats, Otherness and the Orient*, 163.

The famous rhetorical question that concludes 'The Second Coming'—'And what rough beast, its hour come round at last, / Slouches towards Bethlehem to be born?'[65]— tends to be understood as exemplifying Yeats's cyclical philosophy of history. Noting that the Italian Renaissance—Pope Leo X had been Giovanni de' Medici—would emerge as one of the 'brief periods of human perfection' in the system of *A Vision*, Hennessey suggests that 'Yeats allowed himself to legitimize Africanus by involving them both in a transhistorical cycle, with Africanus configured as the poet when the cycle was beginning its degenerative downturn, and Yeats situated at the time for change, witnessed in the violent struggle for Irish independence.'[66] Africanus's place in Yeats's philosophy of history makes even more plausible a reading of 'The Second Coming' in terms not only of European apocalypse but also of world-historical change.

If 'Leo' functioned as Yeats's 'daimon' or 'anti-self' throughout the mid-1910s, his role in the production of *A Vision* was not so much antithetical as oppositional. In the Script generated by George Yeats's automatic writing after their marriage in October 1917, 'Leo' quickly emerged as 'a malignant and untrustworthy spirit', indeed, 'the most difficult of a category of spirits called Frustrators', bearing little-to-no trace of Africanus.[67] According to Brenda Maddox, who emphasizes George's conscious agency, ' "Leo's" intrusion into the Script was signified by his astrological sign or by a rash of triangles drawn like daggers on Georgie's pages'.[68] Given that Leo Africanus had manifested through female mediums, including the automatic writing of Elizabeth Radcliffe, adds Hennessey, 'one might speculate that George was killing off the traces of a rival'.[69] 'Leo' was last heard of in March 1919, although some scholars suggest that 'Yeats's exchange with Leo Africanus propels' the poet toward *A Vision* or even that Leo Africanus is textually reincarnated in *A Vision* as Michael Robartes.[70]

How should we assess the Yeats–'Leo' correspondence? One of the first commentators, Arnold Goldman, finds only one person in the room: 'Writing in the first person as Leo, Yeats is writing fiction', altering neither his handwriting nor the style of the narrator.[71] For readers inspired by postcolonial theory, however, there is both a historical depth and a political charge to Yeats's experiment. In the wake of Edward W. Said's *Orientalism* (1978), which argued that Europeans constructed 'the Orient' as Europe's mirror image in the service of political domination, John C. Hawley reads Yeats's Leo Africanus as a self-interested projection, a 'highly strung' instance 'of orientalization'.[72] 'What if Africanus is identified as a historically existing African, rather than a highly mystified

---

[65] *CW1*, 190.

[66] Hennessey, 'Talking with the Dead', 1029–30.

[67] 'The Manuscript of "Leo Africanus" ', 304.

[68] Maddox, *George's Ghosts*, 81.

[69] Hennessey, 'Talking with the Dead', 1037.

[70] 'The Manuscript of "Leo Africanus" ', 306; Andrea, 'The Ghost of Leo Africanus', 207; Hennessey, 'Talking with the Dead', 1037.

[71] Arnold Goldman, 'Yeats, spiritualism, and psychical research', in George Mills Harper, ed., *Yeats and the Occult* (Toronto: Macmillan, 1975), 108–29, at 119.

[72] Hawley, 'Colonizing the mind', 61.

Arab?' asks Hennessey, who reads 'Yeats's transactions with Leo as "Africanist"', in Toni Morrison's sense of the 'range of views, assumptions, readings, and misreadings that accompany Eurocentric learning about [African peoples]'.[73] Yet the Africanist paradigm, like the orientalist one, still relies on what Wendy Laura Belcher terms an 'appropriation model of encounter' between European and African discourse.[74] Dissatisfied with the assumption that Europeans have always controlled their encounters with the rest of the world, Belcher proposes a model of *discursive possession*—'African possession *of* Europe, not *by* it'—that adapts 'the paradigm of spirit possession' to textual discourse, thus 'enabl[ing] us to read European texts ordinarily classified as orientalist (i.e., as examples of appropriation) as also exhibiting aspects of African thought'.[75] Belcher contends, in a sentence that is particularly resonant for the case of Leo Africanus, 'The scholar may say that the possessed are actively pretending to be an alter ego, acting out a fantasy, but the scholar should say that the discourse of the other is what allows one to become other'.[76]

Could we venture to say that Yeats is animated or even possessed by African discourse? Among Yeats scholars, Margaret Mills Harper comes closest to rethinking assumptions about the autonomous European author. For Harper, Yeats's writing of letters to and from Leo Africanus 'would put him at the borderland between traditional Western authorship, presided over by the strong myth of the stable self, and the uncharted territory of writerly mediumship with its resonances of femininity, darkness, the irrational, and the non-Western'.[77] 'Leo's' promise to 'overshadow' Yeats as he wrote does not just suggest what Harper calls 'the exotic Other'.[78] This promise echoes the angel Gabriel's words to Mary in Luke 1:35, 'the power of the Highest shall overshadow thee', which would make Yeats analogically at once feminine and the bearer of the divine Word. Yeats certainly accords a kind of agency to Africanus, even if his and George's biographers have read such acknowledgement as evidence of his credulity. Take, for instance, his comment on the existence of *A Geographical Historie*—'from this one assumes that you still exist'—or 'Leo's' assertion, 'You are in the presence of the dead more than you can know'.[79] It is as if Yeats is registering the power of discourses from the past to animate his own thought and writing regardless of his conscious intent.

In what sense *A Geographical Historie* constitutes African discourse is another question. What its author meant by Africa was 'divided into four parts, that is, Barbary, Numidia, Libya, and the Land of the Blacks', which did not extend to much of what we now conceive of as central and eastern Africa, let alone its southern cape.[80] ' "Africa"

---

[73] Hennessey, 'Talking with the Dead', 1021; Toni Morrison, *Playing in the Dark: Whiteness and the Literary Imagination* (Cambridge, MA: Harvard University Press, 1992), 7.

[74] Wendy Laura Belcher, *Abyssinia's Samuel Johnson: Ethiopian Thought in the Making of an English Author* (New York: Oxford University Press, 2012), 2.

[75] Ibid., 1, 7.

[76] Ibid., 15.

[77] Harper, 'Yeats and the Occult', 158–9.

[78] 'The Manuscript of "Leo Africanus"', 311; Harper, 'Yeats and the Occult', 159.

[79] 'The Manuscript of "Leo Africanus"', 311, 329.

[80] Davis, *Trickster Travels*, 128. Cf. Africanus, *History*, 1:123.

sometimes slips or narrows under Yuhanna al-Asad's pen,' notes Davis, 'as when "the Africans" become merely the ancient inhabitants—that is, the Berbers—of northwest Africa,' while 'Ethiopia belongs to Asia' in this schema.[81] Jonathan Burton, arguing against other Shakespeare scholars' treatment of Africanus 'as a toady for European ideology', asserts, 'What distinguishes Africanus's text from other accounts of Africa is ... the ability substantially to add to and transform contemporary discourses about Africa.'[82] In Burton's estimation, Africanus's *Geographical Historie* cites numerous African poets, cosmographers and historiographers' in order to supplement the Eurocentric notions of Africa circulating in the early modern era.[83] Such a historicist reading does not, though, erase passages that cast some Black people as questionably human. Citing a passage describing 'inhabitants of Libya' and 'Negros' who 'leade a beastly kinde of life, being vtterly destitute of the vse of reason, of dexteritie of wit, and of all artes', Ibram X. Kendi refers to *A Geographical Historie* as 'Leo Africanus's thoroughly racist book'.[84] Such passages, in some cases intensified by al-Asad's Italian editor Ramusio, may have reinforced Yeats's image of Africa from turn-of-the-century imperial adventure fiction or Conrad's *Heart of Darkness*.[85] If he reached Brown's third volume, though, he would also have found an account of what is now northern Nigeria, in which the large city of 'Cano' (Kano) is portrayed as a town with chalk walls, where '[t]he inhabitants are rich merchants and most civill people'.[86] Mediated, arguably garbled, by centuries of European editing and translation, a very 'long tin trumpet' of textual history, African discourse may nonetheless have reached Yeats's receptive ears. As he learned from his occult pursuits, any spirit worth the name requires the offices of a medium.

'OUT OF THE ABYSS': YEATS'S AFRICAN RECEPTION

As Omaar Hena observes, 'contemporary global anglophone poets'—that is, poets writing in English from around the globe—'recurrently look to Ireland to contend with the contradictions of modernity'.[87] Like their counterparts in other parts of the

---

[81] Davis, *Trickster Travels*, 128, 129.

[82] Burton, ' "A Most Wily Bird" ', 46.

[83] Ibid., 54.

[84] Africanus, *History*, 1:187; Kendi, 'On John Pory', n.p.

[85] Davis, *Trickster Travels*, 145. Pory, in turn, intensified anti-Muslim sentiments in his translation of the text (Davis, *Trickster Travels*, 155–6).

[86] Africanus, *History*, 3:830.

[87] Omaar Hena, 'Ireland's Afterlives in Global Anglophone Poetry', in Jefferson Holdridge and Brian Ó Conchubhair, eds., *Post-Ireland? Essays on Contemporary Irish Poetry* (Winston-Salem, NC: Wake Forest University Press, 2017), 340.

decolonizing world, African poets have found Yeats, in particular, difficult to ignore. How have African writers contributed to Yeats's legacy, even if 'by contraries'? Speaking at the University of Cambridge in the mid-1970s, the Nigerian writer Wole Soyinka complained,

> A demand which I once made in a paper that the writer in our modern African so- ciety needs to be a visionary in his own times has, I find, been often interpreted as a declaration that this is the highest possible function for the contemporary African writer. The misunderstanding has to do with the elevated status which the European mind inclines to give to works of a mystical or visionary persuasion – witness the way in which the dotty excursions of W. B. Yeats into a private never-never land are reverently exegetised![88]

Whereas Yeats had been reacting against a British society that he strategically characterized as too materialist and rational, Soyinka thought it necessary to empha- size that in 'modern African society'—a rather broad canvas—'the mystical and the visionary are merely areas of reality like any other'.[89] A decade later—and seventy-three years after Yeats—Soyinka would claim the Nobel Prize in Literature, the first African writer to do so.

Would it have changed Soyinka's view of Yeats to know that the poet's 'private never-never land' was littered with shards of discourse from Soyinka's own Yoruba culture? In 1912, the same year that Leo Africanus accosted Yeats in an Irish accent, Leo Frobenius's *Und Afrika Sprach* appeared in Berlin, translated into English the following year as *The Voice of Africa*. Introduced to Frobenius's later *Paideuma* (1921) by Pound in 1929, Yeats made notes on *The Voice of Africa* in search of 'African corollaries for his own phases of the moon, and the months of the Great Year'.[90] Matthew Gibson, who has recently brought these notes to light, argues that Yeats drew on both of Frobenius's books in adopting the symbolism of 'the Cavern and the Roads/Altar' for *A Vision* (1937).[91] A German explorer and 'ethnologist', Frobenius visited Yorubaland in 1910–11 and details its deities, such as 'Shango' the 'Kingly Thunder-God', a key figure in Soyinka's oeuvre.[92] Yeats may also have seen in Frobenius references to Leo Africanus, with whom Frobenius shared dubious beliefs about the Hamitic origins of some African peoples, and some even more problematic theories. *The Voice of Africa*'s first volume concludes with a chapter suggesting that Yorubaland was once home to Atlantis, and although Yeats may not

---

[88] Wole Soyinka, *Myth, Literature and the African World* (Cambridge: Cambridge University Press, 1976), 65.

[89] Ibid.

[90] Matthew Gibson, 'Yeats's Notes on Leo Frobenius's *The Voice of Africa* (1913)', in Gibson and Mann, *Yeats, Philosophy, and the Occult*, 309.

[91] Ibid., 307–8.

[92] Leo Frobenius, *The Voice of Africa: Being an Account of the German Inner Africa Exploration Expedition in the Years 1910–12*, trans. Rudolph Blind, 2 vols. (London: Hutchison and Co., 1913), 1: 204.

have read the second volume, it concludes with a chapter entitled 'Byzantium'.[93] Might Yeats's reading of Frobenius have inspired his own great poem of that title[94], written in 1930?

In a recent reflection on contemporary African writing, the US-based Nigerian writer Chris Abani assumes a more political reading of Yeats as the forerunner of mid-twentieth-century African poets who forged 'nationalist myths' and in whom Abani hears 'the epic echo, the larger-than-life conflations, much like, say, Yeats was doing as Ireland fought for its independence'.[95] These poles of Yeats's reception—Soyinka's 'silly Willy' and Abani's national icon—are also at play in Said's landmark statement about 'Yeats and Decolonization', first published as a Field Day pamphlet in 1988. There Said, a Palestinian intellectual schooled partly in Egypt, proposes that Yeats should be considered not only among English-language poets and European modernists but also as a 'great *national* poet' like others of the 'colonial world' including Aimé Césaire from Martinique, Pablo Neruda from Chile, and Léopold Sédar Senghor from Senegal.[96] Struggling to explain Yeats's occult investments, Said locates in the conflict of 'Irish nationalism with the English cultural heritage' the source of 'tension, and one may speculate that it was the pressure of this urgently political and secular tension that caused him to try to resolve it on a "higher," that is, non-political level'.[97] Yet for Viswanathan, in a reading of Yeats's spiritualism that gently rebukes Said, her one-time PhD advisor and then colleague at Columbia, 'the otherworldliness of the occult, and its premium on secrecy and silence' was not so much an escape from the political as the source of 'alternative possibilities for imagining colonial relations outside a formal hierarchical framework'.[98] Fin-de-siècle occultism, she has argued, 'challenged the received developmental narratives of western knowledge and salvaged obliterated histories, cultures, and beliefs'.[99]

While 1958, the year *Things Fall Apart* first appeared in hardback in London bookshops, is one landmark in the African reception of Yeats, and indeed in the salvaging of devalued 'histories, cultures, and beliefs', another is 1965, which brought a cluster of publications to mark the centenary of Yeats's birth. Suheil Bushrui, like Said a Palestinian-born scholar, who had done his PhD work on Yeats and was teaching at the University of Ibadan, Nigeria, highlighted Leo Africanus in an essay arguing that Yeats's 'interest in [Arabia and the Arabs] in fact stands on the same level as his interest

[93] Frobenius, *Voice*, 1:319–49 and 2:615–49.

[94] *CW1*, 248-9.

[95] Kwame Dawes and Chris Abani, 'Introduction in Two Movements', in Kwame Dawes and Chris Abani, eds., *New-Generation African Poets: A Chapbook Box Set (Tano)* (Brooklyn, NY: Akashic Books, 2018), 14.

[96] Edward W. Said, *Culture and Imperialism* (New York: Vintage, 1994), 220. The best overview of ensuing debates remains Jahan Ramazani's 'W. B. Yeats: A Postcolonial Poet?', in his *The Hybrid Muse: Postcolonial Poetry in English* (Chicago: University of Chicago Press, 2001), 21–48.

[97] Said, *Culture and Imperialism*, 227.

[98] Viswanathan, 'Spectrality's secret sharers', 136.

[99] Ibid., 139.

in Indian philosophy, Japanese drama, occult practices, magic and theosophy'.[100] Bushrui describes seeing in George Yeats's possession a copy of *A Geographical Historie of Africa*, the author of which WBY adopted as 'his opposite, his "mask" ', 'the man of action he was always trying to become'.[101] Like al-Wazzan four and a half centuries earlier, Bushrui travelled throughout Africa and Europe, as well as the Middle East. From studies in Egypt and England to teaching posts in Sudan and Nigeria, his career reveals the outlines of a mid-twentieth-century Commonwealth academic circuit. This circuit regularly drew bright students from the colonies or former colonies—including Ireland—to British universities and then returned them to colonial or newly independent universities. In the process, Irish poetry and ideas of Irishness circulated through English-speaking educational institutions around the globe.

Ibadan was, in fact, something of a centre for writing about Yeats in the 1960s. With Desmond Maxwell, a Trinity-educated Irishman also teaching in Ibadan, Bushrui co-edited *W. B. Yeats, 1865–1965: Centenary Essays on the Art of W. B. Yeats*, published by Ibadan University Press (1965). Alongside the eponymous essays were poems by Laurence Lerner, a South African émigré teaching in Sussex after stints in the Gold Coast and Belfast; James Simmons, a Northern Irish poet who befriended Wole Soyinka at the University of Leeds and was then teaching in Zaria, not so far from the city of Kano depicted by al-Asad; and Christopher Okigbo, a contemporary of Achebe and Soyinka whom many still consider the most notable anglophone African poet of the twentieth century despite his premature death at age 37.[102] As this author has written about elsewhere, Okigbo's remarkable poem 'Lament of the Masks' opens the volume not just by alluding to Yeats's work but by addressing the Irish poet as a Yoruba notable.[103] In Jahan Ramazani's words, 'the relation of his poem to Yeats's verse is more affiliative than corrosive'.[104]

Why would an African poet, let alone such an accomplished one, affiliate with Yeats? There is a circumstantial reason, of course: Maxwell, the Irish professor at Ibadan, asked Okigbo to write a poem to mark the centenary. On a more existential level, however, as Okigbo put it to an interviewer that same year, 'The modern sensibility which the modern African poet is trying to express, is by its very nature complex, and it is a complex of values .... Some of these values we are talking about are Christian, some are non-Christian, and I think that anybody who thinks it is possible to express consistently only one line of values, indigenous or exotic, is probably being artificial'.[105] Okigbo's comment

[100] Suheil B. Bushrui, 'Yeats's Arabic Interests', in A. Norman Jeffares and K. G. W. Cross, eds., *In Excited Reverie, A Centenary Tribute to William Butler Yeats, 1865-1939* (London: Macmillan, 1965), 280–1.

[101] Ibid., 284, 285.

[102] On Okigbo's life and death, see Obi Nwakanma, *Christopher Okigbo 1930-67: Thirsting for Sunlight* (Woodbridge: James Currey, 2010).

[103] Nathan Suhr-Sytsma, *Poetry, Print, and the Making of Postcolonial Literature* (Cambridge: Cambridge University Press, 2017), 1–4.

[104] Jahan Ramazani, *A Transnational Poetics* (Chicago: University of Chicago Press, 2009), 103.

[105] Cosmo Pieterse and Dennis Duerden, eds., *African Writers Talking* (London: Heinemann, 1972), 144.

about the fusion of Christian with non-Christian values suggests why he might have been attracted to Yeats, whose fascination with pre-Christian mythology and the occult would have seemed a welcome alternative to the kind of mission Christianity so dominant in colonial and postcolonial Nigeria. As Hena surmises, 'Okigbo likely saw in Yeats the cosmopolitan modern poet-figure *par excellence*, one who also sought to forge a uniquely national consciousness against colonial rule by elevating local mythology and folklore into high art.'[106]

When a cadre of young military officers, including a friend of Okigbo from university, launched a coup against the unpopular government of Nigeria's First Republic in January 1966, Okigbo turned to Yeats to react to this public event. The telegram he fired off to a contact in London—'HURRAH FOR REVOLUTION LET THE CANNON SHOOT'—alludes to an inexact version of Yeats's late poem 'The Great Day' that Okigbo had encountered in an article on the Yeats centenary in *The Times Literary Supplement*.[107] Okigbo's late poem 'Come Thunder', part of the posthumously published sequence *Path of Thunder*, partakes of the eerie apocalyptic atmosphere of 'The Second Coming':

> And the secret thing in its heaving
> Threatens with iron mask
> The last lighted torch of the century ...[108]

It is closely related, as well, to Yeats's great sequences in *The Tower* about the founding conflicts of the Irish state. Okigbo, however, did not climb to a tower-top and write about 'Monstrous familiar images', as in 'Meditations in Time of Civil War'[109]. If Yeats had once taken Leo Africanus as anti-self, Okigbo did the same with Yeats and became himself 'the man of action' Yeats never quite managed to be. When the newly proclaimed Republic of Biafra was attacked in July 1967 by federal Nigerian troops, supported by Britain, Okigbo took up arms in defence of Biafra and a university library he had helped to build. He was killed in action within the first three months of the war.

Anglophone poets confronting sociopolitical conflict or outright war in other parts of Africa, too, have found themselves in dialogue with Yeats's poetry. Set in Durban, South Africa, amidst the struggle to dismantle the apartheid system, Sally-Ann Murray's 'Easter, 1989' is framed by the narrator's attempt to teach Yeats to a sleepy first-year class. Alluding to 'Easter, 1916'—though without its consistent trimeter—Murray's poem juxtaposes Yeats's effort to comprehend the Easter Rising and its leaders' 'sacrifice'[110]

---

[106] Hena, 'Ireland's Afterlives in Global Anglophone Poetry', 348–9.

[107] Suhr-Sytsma, *Poetry*, 135.

[108] Christopher Okigbo, *Labyrinths with Path of Thunder* (London: Heinemann Educational Books, 1971), 66. See Alexander C. Irvine, 'Postcolonial Generations: Yeats and Okigbo', in Deborah Fleming, ed., *W. B. Yeats and Postcolonialism* (West Cornwall, CT: Locust Hill Press, 2001), 136–9; Ramazani, *Transnational Poetics*, 108; and Suhr-Sytsma, *Poetry*, 137–8.

[109] *CW1*, 209.

[110] *CW1*, 182.

with the narrator's effort to comprehend the imminent sacrifice of a political detainee on hunger strike for being held without charge:

> minute by minute Durban
> streams into the room as I speak
> of metaphor and history,
> romantic myths and Irish pride.
> Minute by minute while Sandile
> Thusi dies.[111]

Proceeding to reflect on Thusi's plight, the media coverage of his mother, and a protest march on his behalf, the poem ends with no revelation of 'terrible beauty'[112]: 'But what has changed so utterly? the students ask. / Yeats has no real answers for the class.'[113] As 'Durban' may call to the ear its absent analogue, Dublin, observes Meihuizen, 'by presenting a series of slightly out-of-focus parallels with Yeats's poem [Murray] in fact undermines any sense of consanguinity derivable from such parallels'.[114] Any parallel between the Irish and South African liberation struggles is necessarily complicated by the fact that, in the Second Boer War, Irish nationalists including Yeats supported the anti-British Afrikaners, who would in later decades engineer the apartheid state. There may be a hidden consanguinity, however, in that Yeats reserved publication of 'Easter, 1916' until the height of the Irish War of Independence, when the Sinn Fein mayor of Cork, Terence MacSwiney, was on a hunger strike in Brixton Prison. The *New Statesman*, which had been sympathetic to MacSwiney, published the poem on 23 October 1920, two days before MacSwiney's death and two weeks before 'The Second Coming' appeared in the *Nation*.[115] Like Murray, in other words, Yeats intended his poem to sound in solidarity with an imprisoned hunger striker. Unlike MacSwiney, Thusi broke his hunger strike, taking communion on Easter Monday as 'Easter, 1989' registers with a brief glimpse two weeks into the narrative future. Amplifying the gravity of Murray's poem in some ways, the Yeatsian intertext also underscores that this South African case represents a turning back from final martyrdom.

   Two decades later, Syl Cheney-Coker, who was forced to leave his Freetown home in 1997 amidst Sierra Leone's decade-long civil war, finds balm for his post-conflict society in Yeats. Cheney-Coker's poem 'Out of the Abyss' wears the first line of Yeats's early poem 'Into the Twilight' as its epigraph: 'Out-worn heart, in a time out-worn'.[116]

---

[111] Sally-Ann Murray, *Shifting*, in *Signs: Three Collections of Poetry*, ed. Douglas Reid Skinner (Cape Town: Carrefour Press, 1992), 79. See also Geraldine Higgins's Chapter 13 in this volume.

[112] *CW1*, 184.

[113] Murray, *Shifting*, 80.

[114] Nicholas Meihuizen, 'Yeats, Revolution and South Africa', *Theoria*, 81–82 (October 1993), 156, 157.

[115] *Life 2*, 182, 150.

[116] *CW1*, 55.

Exchanging the decadent 'out-worn' for the twenty-first-century 'worn-out', the poem opens,

> We emerged, worn-out, from this abyss, a broken country:
> the women less tender; the men wounded, their children gone crazy,
> and the innocents raving naked on the night's brutal highways.

The poet explicitly compares the 'young mother' Sierra Leone with Ireland—'Your mother Eire is always young', Yeats had written[117]—before continuing,

> Worn-out, we await new ceremonies: ancestral, spiritual,
> so that we can be reborn, or simply turn our inhuman clock.

Some of Cheney-Coker's lines, such as 'I need Yeats' guiding light to show us a new path', border on the bathetic. Yet the poem as a whole seems an admirable endeavour to fuse the idealistic nationalism of the early Yeats with the wisdom of the older Yeats, who saw the other side of civil war, so as to imagine a national future for Sierra Leone.[118]

Not all African invocations of Yeats are born of conflict. Tade Ipadeola, whose epic poem *The Sahara Testaments* garnered the Nigeria Prize for Literature in 2013, was introduced to Yeats as a youngster by his father, a school principal.[119] The fourth chapter of *The Sahara Testaments* bears an epigraph by Yeats: 'Only the wasteful virtues earn the sun ...'.[120] In *Responsibilities* this line, which the poet attributes to his 'boyish lips', precedes an apology to his ancestors, dated January 1914:

> *Pardon that for a barren passion's sake,*
> *Although I have come close on forty-nine,*
> *I have no child, I have nothing but a book,*
> *Nothing but that to prove your blood and mine.*[121]

It is not so much the contents of Yeats's verse—Ipadeola is the parent of children as well as books—as its form that seems to have drawn this Nigerian poet. Against the grain of much contemporary African poetry, in which traditional form is a rarity, *The Sahara Testaments* features hundreds of ingeniously rhymed quatrains. Indeed, Ipadeola's work makes of poetic form itself a wasteful but worthwhile virtue.

In 2018, Dublin-based Irish-language publisher Coiscéim issued *Titeann rudaí as a chéile*, a translation of Achebe's *Things Fall Apart* by Irene Duffy Lynch into Irish. Who could have foreseen that Yeats's famous phrase would return to Ireland in its ancestral

---

[117] *CW1*, 55.
[118] Syl Cheney-Coker, *Stone Child (and Other Poems)* (Ibadan: HEBN Publishers, 2008), 27.
[119] Tade Ipadeola, interview with the author, Iowa City, September 30, 2019.
[120] Tade Ipadeola, *The Sahara Testaments* (Lagos: Hornbill, 2012), 65.
[121] *CW1*, 101.

language via a Nigerian writer? Perhaps Casely Hayford, the West African writer who saw the revitalization of non-anglophone African and Irish linguistic cultures as a shared project, could have. African writers and postcolonial scholars alike have rightly challenged misconceptions of Yeats as an exclusively European poet. Achebe, Soyinka, Okigbo, Murray, Cheney-Coker, Ipadeola, and many others have not written back to Yeats so much as made him their contemporary. The *Times Literary Supplement* article in which Okigbo encountered a version of Yeats's 'The Great Day' ends with the sentiment that 'Yeats cannot be buried in the "Celtic twilight", the "Irish literary tradition"— he is a living poet and a world poet, still beckoning our minds.'[122] If so, he is a living poet as much for writers in Africa as for those in Europe.

---

[122] [Derwent J. May,] 'Under Ben Bulben', *Times Literary Supplement*, 21 January 1965, 47.

CHAPTER 22

···

ASIAS

···

JAHAN RAMAZANI

As literary and cultural studies have been transnationalizing themselves, a persistent question has been how to view the West's imaginative extensions elsewhere—artists like Matisse and Kandinsky, composers like Stravinsky and Stockhausen, novelists like Forster and Woolf, poets like Yeats, Eliot, and Pound.[1] Given the asymmetries of power and wealth, should we see these as acts of imperial theft, akin to the pilfering of antiquities from poorer or colonized parts of the world for display in homes and museums? Or do they exemplify humane engagements with non-Western cultures? Are they more like the brazen appropriation of Native American names and mascots by US football teams, or are they respectful exercises in self-education that defy age-old demeaning stereotypes? Now that identitarian conceptions of cultural property are being vigorously debated, it may be time to reopen these questions.[2] Of all world regions that the modernists engaged, Asia had, as Christopher Bush indicates, the broadest impact on the development of literary modernism—South Asia on Eliot, East Asia on Pound, and so forth.[3] Among his contemporaries, Yeats was the only major poet who developed a multifaceted interest in East, South, and West Asian cultures; as such, he deserves a prominent role in reconsiderations of Euro-modernism's non-Western engagements. Scholarship on Yeats and Asia has usually focused on either his Indian or his Japanese investments—understandably so, given their longevity and depth—but what about the West Asian coordinates that have received less attention? What happens if we pluralize Yeats's Asias and consider them together—South, East, and West? Is his

[1] For opportunities to try out earlier versions of this essay, I thank Seán Golden (Barcelona, 'Yeats and Asia', symposium of the International Yeats Society), Matthew Campbell and Lauren Arrington (Sligo, Yeats International Summer School), and Andrew McGowan (W. B. Yeats Society of New York). I cite much of the pertinent scholarship on either side of the question in *A Transnational Poetics* (Chicago: University of Chicago Press, 2009), 184, 201–2.

[2] See, e.g., Kwame Anthony Appiah, 'Whose Culture Is It, Anyway?', *Cosmopolitanism: Ethics in a World of Strangers* (New York: W. W. Norton, 2006), 115–35.

[3] Christopher Bush, 'Modernism, Orientalism, and East Asia', in Jean-Michel Rabaté, ed., *A Handbook of Modernism Studies* (West Sussex: Wiley-Blackwell, 2013), 193–208.

Asian-facing poetry orientalist, anti-orientalist, or both? And how can his poetry help us rethink the paradigm of orientalism?[4]

'ASIATIC VAGUE IMMENSITIES'

The only place where the word 'Asiatic' appears in Yeats's poetry is the second stanza of his late poem 'The Statues' (1939). I begin here, with what may be the most troubling representation of the East in his poetry. Having credited the mathematical calculations of Pythagoras with helping to shape the desires embodied in Greek art, this poem sculpted in ottava rima grants still more significance to ancient Greek artists than to philosopher-mathematicians:

> No; greater than Pythagoras, for the men
> That with a mallet or a chisel modelled these
> Calculations that look but casual flesh, put down
> All Asiatic vague immensities,
> And not the banks of oars that swam upon
> The many-headed foam at Salamis.
> Europe put off that foam when Phidias
> Gave women dreams and dreams their looking-glass.[5]

In the phrase 'All Asiatic vague immensities' Yeats not only recalls the vastness of the Persian fleet vanquished by a smaller Greek force but also imputes to Iranian culture an amorphous grandiosity. He sees the soft power of Greek philosophy and the arts as even more fundamental than the Greek city states' naval victories over the Persians. As he puts it in *On the Boiler*, Europe was born 'when the Doric studios sent out those broad-backed marble statues against the multiform, vague, expressive Asiatic sea'.[6] In the poem, more important than arrows and spears but no less sharp are artistic instruments—mallets and chisels—that carve stone into human form.

As someone whose parentage is mostly Persian, I've long felt uncomfortable about this stanza, since it aligns with and updates the notion that my ancestors were the original 'barbarians'—their unintelligible speech sounding to the ancient Greeks like an echoic and nonsensical *barbarbar* that marked them as the uncivilized other, especially after the Greco-Persian wars. If I may be forgiven a personal point of reference, while Yeats was writing this poem, his nearly exact contemporary in Iran, my maternal great-grandfather, Keikhosrow Shahrokh (1864–1939), who served in

---

[4] I write briefly about Yeats, Eliot, and Pound as orientalist and anti-orientalist in *A Transnational Poetics*, 109–14. See also Joseph Lennon, 'W. B. Yeats's Celtic Orient', in *Irish Orientalism: A Literary and Intellectual History* (Syracuse: Syracuse University Press, 2004), 247–89.

[5] *CW1*, 337.

[6] *CW5*, 249.

parliament as the elected representative of Zoroastrians, had recently completed the mausoleum for Iran's tenth-century epic poet Ferdowsi in ancient Iranian architectural style. Having been inspired by an Achaemenid architectural vocabulary, he would likely have rejected Yeats's contrast between ancient Greek sculptural precision and its supposed Persian opposite. For those who have seen the meticulously carved stonework and formal patterning still visible at Persepolis after two and a half millennia, the contrast between Greek precision and a 'vague' Persia may well seem distortive. Moreover, as those carvings and the intricate metalwork of the time also indicate, ancient Persian and Greek art also had strong mutual influences, despite the stanza's harsh dichotomies. Yeats's enjambment of the phrase 'put down' emphasizes Greek form's heroic defeat of Persian formlessness. His figurative language metonymically associates Persia with the 'many-headed foam' of the sea. When that word is repeated—'Europe put off that foam'—it suggests the inferior, shapeless, nondurable qualities of Iranian culture.

Such views are hardly unique to Yeats. The Persians have been receiving bad press in the West ever since the ancient Greeks wrote the victors' history, not long after the battle at Salamis. To understand this broad cultural 'put down', the almost inevitable framework, if one that Yeats's work can help us reconsider, is Edward Said's orientalist critique. According to Said, orientalism produces and reinforces a series of oppositions by which the West defines itself: orientals 'are always symmetrical to, and yet diametrically inferior to, a European equivalent'.[7] Yeats dichotomizes the heroic, individualized, antithetical West and the Asiatic, formless, many-headed, primary East. He doesn't go so far as to call the Persians, in Said's words for orientalist stereotyping, 'backward, degenerate, uncivilized, and retarded', but their defeat confirms their weakness and cultural inferiority, while the Greeks are artistically, militarily, and philosophically superior. Moreover, as Said writes, orientalism tends 'to wipe out any traces of individual' persons or 'narratable life histories'.[8] The Persians here are an undifferentiated, formless mass ('the Persian hordes at Salamis', Yeats calls them in *On the Boiler*), the Greeks possessed of form and individuality (Pythagoras, Phidias, dreaming women).[9]

Having begun with the hardest case, seen through Said's telling but homogenizing model, I want to show that it's relatively atypical of Yeats and inconsistent with many of his Asian-facing poems, which more sympathetically perform their relation to various Asian cultures. Witness Yeats's comments across his career about Asia: although he often associates the West with materialism, individualism, and realism, the East with spirituality, spontaneous religion, and immateriality, he nevertheless also frequently suggests

---

[7] Edward W. Said, *Orientalism* (New York: Random House, 1978), 72. On the West's often ambivalent fascination with Persian poetry and culture, see Hamid Dabashi, *Persophilia: Persian Culture on the Global Scene* (Cambridge, MA: Harvard University Press, 2015), and John D. Yohannan, *Persian Poetry in England and America: A 200-Year History* (Delmar, NY: Caravan Books, 1977).

[8] Said, *Orientalism*, 207 and 229.

[9] *CW5*, 249.

a) that Ireland and Asia have a common ancestry; b) that East and West have influenced one another over thousands of years; and c) that whether they came about through shared ancestry or influences, the resemblances between Ireland and Asia are profound. He remarks, for example: 'We have borrowed directly from the East and selected for admiration or repetition everything in our own past that is least European, as though groping backward towards our common mother.' He later adds:

> It pleases me to fancy that when we turn towards the East, in or out of church, we are turning not less to the ancient west and north; the one fragment of pagan Irish phil-osophy come down, 'the Song of Amergin', seems Asiatic; that a system of thought like that of these books, though perhaps less perfectly organised, once overspread the world, as ours today; that our genuflections discover in that East something ancestral in ourselves....[10]

Such claims build on what Joseph Lennon shows was a long-lived discourse linking Ireland to 'the Orient'; for modern Irish intellectuals like Yeats, these Celtic–Oriental connections had usefully 'subversive, antimodern, and (often) anticolonial resonances'.[11] Even though some such ideas have been debunked as opportunistic or self-exoticizing pseudohistory, Yeats's general view finds support in subsequent research. Scholars have explored the contacts between Asians and migrant Celts living as far east as Asia Minor, poetic techniques shared across Indo-European languages, and 'orientalizing' elements in Celtic art that may result from Persian, Scythian, or, perhaps most likely, inter-mediary Greco-Etruscan influences.[12] In typically orientalist fashion, Yeats is projecting the reality of the East backward in time, freezing it in the distant past; but in this, the East vitally resembles Celticism in his imagination. Asia and ancient Ireland represent twin alternatives to the degradations of modernity. As John Rickard argues, Yeats saw them both as repositories of the visionary mindset—antiscientific, antimaterialistic, spiritual—that he wanted to revive in Ireland.[13]

Even 'The Statues' puts its orientalism into play with contrary views. Whereas orientalism—both the ideology and Said's account of it—tends to dichotomize, Yeats crams into the poem's third stanza hundreds of years of art history in which East and West cross and even fuse. As a result of the Greek Empire's extension into West and South Asia, Hellenistic sculptural forms 'crossed' into a 'tropic' region and were indigenized

---

[10] *CW5*, 134 and 173-74.

[11] Lennon, *Irish Orientalism*, 250.

[12] See, e.g., Calvert Watkins, *How to Kill a Dragon: Aspects of Indo-European Poetics* (Oxford: Oxford University Press, 1995); Anna June Pagé, 'The Description of Dond Cúalnge in the LL "Táin Bó Cúalnge" and Indo-European Catalogue Poetry', *Proceedings of the Harvard Celtic Colloquium*, 32 (2012): 229–56; N. K. Sandars, 'Orient and Orientalizing in Early Celtic Art', *Antiquity*, 45 (1971): 103–12; and Ruth and Vincent Megaw, 'The Nature and Function of Celtic Art', in Miranda J. Green, ed.,*The Celtic World* (New York: Routledge, 1996), 347.

[13] John Rickard, 'Studying a New Science: Yeats, Irishness, and the East', in Susan Shaw Sailer, ed., *Representing Ireland: Gender, Class, Nationality* (Gainesville: University Press of Florida, 1997), 94–112.

there in sculptures and other depictions of the Buddha. Yeats recalls Greco-Buddhist sculptures that are both idealist and realist, precise and patterned, such as those of the Gandharan style in Central Asia and the northern areas of the subcontinent. The orientalist oppositions may still be at work—the Western individuality and interiority of Hamlet-like figures set against 'Buddha's emptiness'. But even if the fusion involves a slackening of Greek individuation, it reveals an important truth that reaches its full expression in the East:

> Empty eyeballs knew
> That knowledge increases unreality, that
> Mirror on mirror mirrored is all the show.[14]

Here the Buddhist embrace of the fundamental reality of emptiness represents an alternative to the Western knowledge system celebrated earlier in the poem, based on calculation, measure, and character. Yeats counterbalances his Euro-classicist idealization. The Buddha's empty eyeballs, even if traceable back to Greece, are more akin to those of the meditating Hindu ascetics on Mount Meru, who strip away all illusions and see into 'the desolation of reality'.[15] In the final stanza of 'The Statues', Patrick Pearse's revolutionary heroism recalls Attic Greece, but this Western individuality is paradoxically thrown up out of the depths of a 'formless', Asiatic modernity.[16] 'We Irish', the poem declares, but were it not for the iambic pentameter, it might just as well have said 'We Asiatic Europeans', or 'We Greco-Indian-Persian Irish', or 'We Eastern Westerners'. The poem, as Helen Vendler shows, is Yeats's most agitated and unbalanced use of the graceful ottava rima stanza—witness the irregularities and asymmetries, the imperfect rhymes and heterogeneous proper names.[17] As such, a poem that hails the importance of 'plummet-measured' form is itself exemplary of the disruptions of formlessness within form, of the 'Asiatic vague immensities' overbrimming a well-wrought urn. Understood within its own terms, the poem's distorted form and its conceptual torsions and self-disruptions ironically seem party at least as much to the 'many-headed' East as to a measured, calculating West. Although the poem begins with an opposition between inferior Persian vagueness and salvific Greek form that seems to validate Said's model of orientalism, it puts counterdiscursive pressure on it in its form-disrupting form, its endorsement of an Asian conception of reality's vacancy, and its art-historical understanding of the blurred cultural lines between East and West.

---

[14] *CW1*, 337

[15] *CW1*, 289. For a source of the image in Diasetz Suzuki's *Essays in Zen Buddhism*, see Matthew Gibson, '"What Empty Eyeballs Knew": Zen Buddhism in "The Statues" and the *Principles* of *A Vision*', *YA*, 11 (1995): 141–56.

[16] *CW1*, 337.

[17] Helen Vendler, *Our Secret Discipline: Yeats and Lyric Form* (Cambridge, MA: Belknap Press of Harvard University Press, 2007), 270–2.

Persia, Byzantium, and Form

Elsewhere Yeats contradicts this poem's seeming consignment of the East in general and Persians in particular to many-headed formlessness. In *A Vision* he credits the Persians, seemingly the enemies of form in 'The Statues', with being the creators of form, above all the formal vocabularies that are central to Byzantium. Yeats follows William Morris in seeing Byzantine art as synthesizing Eastern (including Persian) design and mystery with Western classicism and, as noted by Elizabeth Bergmann Loizeaux, in being 'especially attracted by the Persian-influenced use of continuous line', or what Yeats calls, in *A Vision*,

> that decoration which seems to undermine our self-control, and is, it seems, of Persian origin, and has for its appropriate symbol a vine whose tendrils climb everywhere and display among their leaves all those strange images of bird and beast, those forms that represent no creature eye has ever seen, yet are begotten one upon the other as if they were themselves living creatures.[18]

As in 'The Statues', Persian form may press against the limits of form—'decoration which seems to undermine our self-control'—but at the same time the vines delineate space. In keeping with the work of the Austrian art historian he repeatedly cites in *A Vision*, Josef Strzygowski, Yeats understands the nonrepresentational lines, patterns, and creatures in Byzantine art to be of Persian origin.[19] The passage's self-replicating, nonmimetic forms ('forms ... begotten one upon the other') anticipate the lines in 'Byzantium' about self-generative forms, 'flames begotten of flame'. Independent of the natural world, they require no fuel ('no faggot feeds'), are unaffected by meteorological events ('Nor storm disturbs'), and in their glorious self-sufficiency have no direct effect outside the imaginative or spiritual realm ('An agony of flame that cannot singe a sleeve').[20] The multiply and ecstatically echoic diction and sounds in 'Byzantium' evoke a patterning that surpasses nature. *Pace* 'The Statues', Yeats's Byzantium poems build on the idea of nonrepresentational, vitalizing, self-replicating Persian forms as embedded in Byzantine art and as reflected in their own intricate stanzaic patterning.

---

[18] *CW14*, 204. See also T. McAlindon, 'The Idea of Byzantium in William Morris and W. B. Yeats', *Modern Philology*, 64:4 (1967), 307–19; Elizabeth Bergmann Loizeaux, *Yeats and the Visual Arts* (New Brunswick, NJ: Rutgers University Press, 1986), 133. Loizeaux sees Yeats's assimilation of Byzantine to Pre-Raphaelite art as also drawing on John Ruskin, Arthur Symons, Oscar Wilde, and Edward Burne-Jones.

[19] On Yeats and Strzygowski, see Russell Murphy, 'Josef Strzygowski and Yeats: "A Starlit or a Moonlit Dome,"' *College Literature*, 13:1 (1986), 106–11; Russell Elliott Murphy, '"Old Rocky Face, look forth": W. B. Yeats, the Christ Pantokrator, and the Soul's History (The Photographic Record)', *Yeats*, 14 (1996), 69–117; and Daniel Albright, 'Yeats, *A Vision*, and Art History', *The Yeats Journal of Korea*, 36 (2011), 5–29.

[20] *CW1*, 248.

Nor is this fusion of Greco-Roman with Persian art visible to Yeats only in Byzantium at the middle or end of the first millennium. Despite the civilizational dichotomy in 'The Statues', he discovers a cross-cultural blend even in Attic Greece itself: 'With Callimachus pure Ionic revives again, as [Adolf] Furtwängler has proved, and upon the only example of his work known to us, a marble chair, a Persian is represented, and may one not discover a Persian symbol in that bronze lamp, shaped like a palm, known to us by a description in Pausanias?'[21] Callimachus's lamp fashioned for the Acropolis is indeed known to us from Pausanias, but neither the Greek geographer nor Furtwängler describes a Persian carved on a marble chair: Yeats learned of this elsewhere and sees the palm-like shape—which the Greek account says is meant to draw away the lamp's smoke—as Persian.[22] Callimachus's Ionic art exemplifies for Yeats a melding of Persian and Greek, East and West. When he returns to Callimachus in 'Lapis Lazuli', he again praises the lamp-and-palm chimney assembly, but more specifically, under Furtwängler's influence, he says the marble is as fluid as metalwork:[23]

> No handiwork of Callimachus,
> Who handled marble as if it were bronze,
> Made draperies that seemed to rise
> When sea-wind swept the corner, stands;
> His long lamp chimney shaped like the stem
> Of a slender palm, stood but a day;
> All things fall and are built again
> And those that build them again are gay.[24]

In this poem's five-part structure, Callimachus is the geocultural hinge between West and East. Between two stanzas set in Europe and two in China, Yeats places the Persianized Greek art of Callimachus. The poem's eastward transition is fully legible only if we're aware of the putative Persianness of Callimachus's art.

Returning to Byzantium, we can flesh out the story of its nonmimetic forms 'of Persian origin', with 'a vine whose tendrils climb everywhere and display among their leaves all those strange images of bird and beast'. Yeats saw Byzantine mosaics with such designs in his visits to Ravenna in 1907 and Sicily in 1925.[25] Although his vision of Byzantium as

---

[21] *CW14*, 196–7.

[22] On Yeats's mixing up of source material, see William H. O'Donnell, 'The Art of Yeats's "Lapis Lazuli"', *Massachusetts Review*, 23:2 (1982), 363. See *Pausanias's Description of Greece*, ed. and trans. James George Frazer (London: Macmillan, 1898), 1: 39, 1.26.6–7 and 1.27.1. But the Persian figure is mentioned, e.g., in Stanley Casson, *Catalogue of the Acropolis Museum* (Cambridge: Cambridge University Press, 1921), 2: 278.

[23] See F. A. C. Wilson, 'The Statues', in Jon Stallworthy, ed., *Yeats: Last Poems, A Casebook* (London: Macmillan, 1968), 170–2.

[24] *CW1*, 295.

[25] See Murphy, 'Old Rocky Face, look forth', and Giorgio Melchiori, 'The Dome of Many-Coloured Glass', in *The Whole Mystery of Art: Pattern into Poetry in the Work of W. B. Yeats* (London: Routledge, 1960), ch. 6.

a site of the blending of East and West is frequently acknowledged, less fully embraced is the idea of a specifically Persian influence. Indeed, at least one critic is exasperated by the idea, saying that 'Yeats is too dependent on Strzygowski's obsession with the supposed Persian origin of Byzantine art'.[26] Strzygowski knew that a claim for Iranian and Mesopotamian influences on the Byzantine Empire was sure to meet resistance, because of 'the deplorable narrowness with which students concentrate their gaze upon Rome and the Mediterranean. They do not think it worth their while to search the East for traces of Christian art, and indeed meet my pioneer work with a hostility which is the measure of their prejudice.' But he sought to 'call attention, in the representational art of Italian mosaics, to an older influence which, in my opinion, must be connected with Iran, and more particularly with Mazdean [that is, Zoroastrian] ideas'.[27] Yeats's embrace of Strzygowski's Iran-centred analysis of early Christian art makes this art historian's account particularly worthy of attention, as we explore a perhaps surprising Asian undercurrent in Yeats's work. Although Strzygowski's eccentrically morphological work may have exaggerated some Persian elements in Byzantine art, recent scholarship has begun to recognize that, despite his appallingly racist political views, Strzygowski helped lead the way to a newly globalized kind of art history. As the historian Suzanne Marchand puts it, he challenged 'Eurocentrism' and attacked the 'classicizing elitism' of the art historical establishment, which 'failed to give the Orient sufficient credit for its independent inventions'.[28]

Yeats indicates that he is well aware of the Iranian conceptual basis that Strzygowski identifies in semi-abstract forms, suggesting of his 'copy of an old Persian carpet that its winding and wandering vine had once that philosophical meaning, which has made it very interesting to Josef Stryzgowsky [sic] and was part of the religion of Zoroaster'.[29] In Strzygowski's view, pre-Islamic Iran affords Byzantine art what he calls its 'anti-representational' forms that are rooted in the Zoroastrian idea of *hvarenah* or 'glory' in ancient Iran (also transliterated *khvarenah* or *khwarnah*, and in Middle Persian *khvarrah* or *xwarrah*), the propulsive force of life associated with the creator god, Ahura Mazda. As indicated by a hymn in the Avesta, it represents, according to Strzygowski, 'the might and majesty of departed spirits', akin to the generative power of departed spirits arriving from across the sea in Yeats's 'Byzantium'. Further, *hvarenah* 'is the power

---

[26] Brian Arkins, *Builders of My Soul: Greek and Roman Themes in Yeats* (Savage, MD: Barnes & Noble, 1990), 182.

[27] Josef Strzygowski, *Origin of Christian Church Art*, trans. O. M. Dalton and H. J. Braunholtz (Oxford: Clarendon Press, 1923), 195 and 172. On Iran and Ireland, see H. E. Chehabi and Grace Neville, eds., *Erin and Iran: Cultural Encounters between the Irish and the Iranians* (Boston: Ilex Foundation, 2015).

[28] Suzanne L. Marchand, 'The Rhetoric of Artifacts and the Decline of Classical Humanism: The Case of Josef Strzygowski', *History and Theory*, 33:4 (1994), 111, 119. See also her 'Appreciating the Art of Others: Josef Strzygowski and the Austrian Origins of Non-Western Art History', in Piotr Otto Scholz and Magdalena Anna Dlugosz, eds., *Von Biala nach Wien: Josef Strzygowski und die Kunstwissenschaften* (Vienna: European University Press Verlagsgesellschaft, 2015), 257–85, and *German Orientalism in the Age of Empire: Religion, Race, and Scholarship* (Cambridge: Cambridge University Press, 2009), 403–10.

[29] *VPl*, 805.

that makes running waters gush from springs' and even 'governs the courses of sun, moon, and stars'. But how is *hvarenah* visually depicted? Its landscapes are 'based upon significance and form, not ... upon natural objects exactly reproduced'.[30] Here again we recall the self-sufficiency of the nonmimetic forms in 'Byzantium', self-begotten and self-begetting, as well as Yeats's lifelong symbolist adherence to a theory of art that refused subordination to nature ('Art is art because it is not nature,' Yeats repeatedly quoted Goethe).[31]

And what form specifically does this Iranian death-derived life source take in art? A miraculous bird is prominent among these unnatural beasts. 'The bird Varegan' (or *vareghna*), writes Strzygowski, 'is the vehicle of Hvarenah': 'The glory flew forth in the likeness of a bird', he quotes from an ancient text, supernatural fowl that resembles other magical Iranian birds such as Simorgh and the *senmurv*.[32] Just as Yeats conceives the continuous vine as Persian, he would also have known from Strzygowski that a bird made by Grecian goldsmiths in sixth-century Byzantium to 'keep a drowsy Emperor awake' may have borne 'Persian' traces[33]—the element in Byzantine art, as quoted above, that includes 'all those strange images of bird and beast, those forms that represent no creature eye has ever seen, yet are begotten one upon the other as if they were themselves living creatures'. So too the emphatically non-naturalistic bird of 'Byzantium' may recall the Persian prototype that Strzygowski emphasizes:

> Miracle, bird or golden handiwork,
> More miracle than bird or handiwork,
> Planted on the starlit golden bough,
> Can like the cocks of Hades crow,
> Or, by the moon embittered, scorn aloud
> In glory of changeless metal
> Common bird or petal
> And all complexities of mire or blood.[34]

Yeats famously conjures this magic bird partly in rebuttal to Sturge Moore's complaint that the bird of 'Sailing to Byzantium' hardly escaped natural form. But when we tell the story of the second Byzantium poem's origins, perhaps we should also remember Strzygowski's concept of the nonmimeticism of Persian art. How to square the circle of the seeming contradiction of birdlike natural forms that are somehow beyond nature? This is at the heart of Strzygowski's discussion. Gibbon's *Decline and Fall of the Roman Empire*, which Yeats bought with his Nobel money, reinforces the at least partly Persian derivation of Yeats's metallic birds. Exemplifying how the Abbasid caliphs 'aspired to

---

[30] Strzygowski, *Origin of Christian Church Art*, 118–19.

[31] W. B. Yeats, *The Letters of W. B. Yeats*, ed. Allan Wade (London: Rupert Hart-Davis, 1954), 440; Yeats to F. J. Fay, 28 August [1904], *CL InteLex*; *CL3*, 641–4.

[32] Strzygowski, *Origin of Christian Church Art*, 121.

[33] *CW1*, 194.

[34] *CW1*, 248.

emulate the magnificence of the Persian kings', Gibbon quotes a Syrian account of the splendours of the Baghdad court—a model in turn for the Byzantine court—including 'a tree of gold and silver … on which, and on the lesser boughs, sat a variety of birds, made of the same precious metals', while the mechanical 'birds warbled their natural harmony'.[35]

As we've seen, Yeats found in Strzygowski's analysis of Persian influences on early Christian art Zoroastrian symbols such as the vine, 'free from the familiar realism of Roman work', and an 'Iranian decorative style' that lacks a 'representational element'. In his description of Byzantine mosaics such as those Yeats visited in Ravenna and Sicily, Strzygowski attributes the 'general scheme' to Iranian influences: 'Hvarenah motives in the form of a vase between birds, or of whole landscapes with sheep or stags by the side of a shepherd and flanked by palms', or, as at the tomb of Galla Placidia in Ravenna, a cross with a starry background, features that 'seem to indicate an Eastern origin, and the supposition is confirmed by the decoration of the adjacent barrel-vaults' and 'apses', with vine-scrolls, 'acanthus scrolls and figures of stags at watersprings', and 'colours suggested by bird's plumage'. Similarly, the Church of San Vitale in Ravenna also has *hvarenah* symbols in the roof mosaic's converging tree designs forming a circle, 'the inter-mediate spaces being filled with continuous scrolls enclosing a large number of birds and animals'. For Strzygowski, other nonrepresentational elements, such as interlaced geometric patterns and scrollwork in capitals, are 'distinctively Iranian'.[36] Although not all of Strzygowski's claims can be substantiated, recent art historians such as Matthew P. Canepa have traced the influence of Persian ornamental art especially through silk textiles to Byzantine edifices of the sixth and seventh centuries such as Hagia Sophia and San Vitale (key models for the Byzantium poems), including features such as medallions, lozenges, ovals with wings, the *senmurv*, birds in roundels, vegetal and geo-metric motifs and patterns, and the pomegranate and palmette and spiky acanthus in symmetrical and semi-vegetal arrangements, all covering the architectural surface in Persian fashion.[37] In Yeats scholarship, it is often noted that Yeats's Byzantium may well

[35] Edward Gibbon, *The Decline and Fall of the Roman Empire* (London: Jones and Co., 1828), ch. 52, 3:516. On the Baghdad–Byzantium connection, see A. Clare Brandabur, 'Arabic Sources of Yeats' Byzantium Poems', *Time's Fool: Essays in Context* (Newcastle upon Tyne: Cambridge Scholars, 2016), 323–38, 325–6. For a synopsis of possible sources of Yeats's Byzantine birds, see Archibald A. Hill, 'Method in Source Study: Yeats' Golden Bird of Byzantium as a Test Case', *Texas Studies in Literature and Language*, 17:2 (1975), 525–38.

[36] Strzygowski, *Origin of Christian Church Art*, 122, 133–6, and 147. So too, when Yeats refers in *A Vision* to 'a romanesque stream perhaps of bird and beast images', he recalls, as Paul and Harper note, Strzygowski's discussion of Iranian influences on Romanesque art, such as 'the vinescroll with enclosed animals': comparison 'reveals that fusion of Iranian and Greek art which succeeded the displacement of the late Roman times, and led gradually to the development of Byzantine art on the Mediterranean, of "Romanesque" in the West, and to the complete triumph of Iranian art in the world of Islam'; *CW14*, 206; *CW13*, 305 n.82; Strzygowski, *Origin of Christian Church Art*, 112–14.

[37] See Matthew P. Canepa, *The Two Eyes of the Earth: Art and Ritual of Kingship between Rome and Sasanian Iran* (Berkeley: University of California Press, 2009), 205–23, and 'Textiles and Elite Tastes between the Mediterranean, Iran and Asia at the End of Antiquity', in M-L Nosch, Zhao Feng and L. Varadarajan, eds., *Global Textile Encounters* (Oxford and Havertown, PA: Oxbow Books, 2014), 1–14. See

recall sites in Ravenna, Sicily, and Constantinople (Istanbul), and, as we've noted, it is a commonplace that Byzantium for Yeats represents a fusion of East and West. But to specify an important aspect of that Easternness as Iranian is to give the generality more precise intercultural force.

ARABIAN MULTICULTURALISM

Except for the Byzantium poems, the place name *Byzantium* appears in only one other of Yeats's poems, 'The Gift of Harun Al-Rashid' (1924). Although I've been focusing on the pre-Islamic, Zoroastrian elements of Persian culture believed to be manifest in Byzantine art, Persian culture is also known to have been a central influence on Arab Muslim culture, particularly during what is often called the Golden Age of Islam, which reached its apex under the rule of Abbasid caliph Harun Al-Rashid (786–809). (Harun closely followed, for example, the Sasanian royal precedent when he presented dazzling gifts to Charlemagne.[38]) Yeats's poem is a dramatic monologue, spoken by the doctor and translator Kusta ben Luka (or Qusta ibn Luqa al Ba'lbakki), which enfolds an epistolary poem, recounting a letter he has written to the caliph's treasurer, which includes a dialogue poem, a 'colloquy' between Harun and Kusta.[39] These frames within frames, genres within genres, recall the layering of the Persian queen Scheherazade's recitations in the poem's prototype, *A Thousand and One Nights*, the amalgam of largely West and South Asian narratives that Yeats said most moved him after Shakespeare.[40]

also Matteo Compareti, 'Evidence of Mutual Exchange between Byzantine and Sogdian Art', in Antonio Carile et al., eds., *La Persia e Bisanzio* (Rome: Accademia Nazionale dei Lincei, 2004), 865–922; A. Shapur Shahbazi, 'Byzantine-Iranian Relations' (1990), in *Encyclopædia Iranica*, http://www.iranic aonline.org/articles/byzantine-iranian-relations (accessed 12 Dec. 2016); and D. Talbot Rice, 'Persia and Byzantium', in A. J. Arberry, ed., *The Legacy of Persia* (Oxford: Clarendon Press, 1953), 39–59. Rice sees Persian influences in decorative motifs such as the peacock feather, the sacred tree, the vase with symmetrical plants, horse trappings and riders' ribbons, a man struggling with beasts on either side, the winged gryphon in a circle, even Justinian's high soft boots and Theodora's two-pointed crown in the Church of San Vitale, as well as the elliptical arch, adorning niches, and squinches for the transition from square base to dome; 45–9.

[38] Canepa, *Two Eyes of the Earth*, 225.

[39] The poem had prefaced book II of the 1925 *Vision* under the title 'Desert Geometry or the Gift of Harun Al-Raschid', *CW13*, 97–102. See Daniel A. Harris, 'The "Figured Page": Dramatic Epistle in Browning and Yeats', *Yeats Annual* 1 (1982): 133–94. For an overview of Yeats's interest in Arab lore and his Arab-related poems, see S. B. Bushrui, 'Yeats's Arabic Interests', in A. Norman Jeffares and K. G. W. Cross, eds., *In Excited Reverie: A Centenary Tribute to William Butler Yeats, 1865–1939* (London: Macmillan, 1965), 280–314.

[40] 'Clearly derived from the Arabic source', Susan Bazargan notes, 'are the references to marble fountains, "goldfish in the pool," "slender bride[s]," "jasmine bough," "the peacock and his mate," and of course the Djinn'; see her 'W. B. Yeats: Autobiography and Colonialism', *Yeats: An Annual of Critical and Textual Studies*, vol. 13 (1995): 201–24, 209–10. She believes that Yeats's erasure of Scheherazade and idealist refashioning of Harun is 'an act of colonial appropriation', 212.

Harun's caliphate in the long eighth century was a time of relatively peaceful coexistence between Byzantium and the Muslim world. Accordingly, Yeats's semi-historical narrative refers to the intercultural exchange between Baghdad and Byzantium, as Kusta instructs an unnamed messenger to carry 'this letter' past the caliphs' dark banners inscribed with calligraphy:

> Pass books of learning from Byzantium
> Written in gold upon a purple stain,
> And pause at last, I was about to say,
> At the great book of Sappho's song; but no,

he corrects himself, out of fear that a love-obsessed young reader of Sappho might drop the letter on the floor. Instead,

> Pause at the Treatise of Parmenides
> And hide it there, for Caliphs to world's end
> Must keep that perfect, as they keep her song,
> So great its fame.[41]

Early foundational Greek works that are later known only in fragments are still whole in the caliph's eighth-century library. In a note originally accompanying the poem, Yeats wrote,

> I do not think it too great a poetical licence to describe Kusta as hesitating between the Poems of Sappho and the Treatise of Parmenides as hiding places. Gibbon says the poems of Sappho were extant in the twelfth century, and it does not seem impossible that a great philosophical work, of which we possess only fragments, may have found its way into an Arab library of the eighth century.[42]

Although it may be a stretch to locate these two particular works there, they are synecdochic of the abundance of ancient Greek works in medieval Muslim libraries.

Islamic learning was crucial to the preservation and transmission of ancient Greek texts—an 'Eastern' detour that Yeats foregrounds but that is sometimes forgotten in narratives of the seemingly unbroken line of transmission of the Western heritage. The Golden Age of Islam saw the development of institutions of scientific, medical, philosophical, and cultural learning such as the House of Wisdom, founded in Baghdad by Harun Al-Rashid, which brought together Muslim, Christian, and Jewish scholars. In both the poem and his note to it, Yeats refers to the historical execution of Harun's vizier Jaffar (or Jaffer), in 803, saying he had been 'head of the family of the Barmecides' (or Barmakids), an important family of advisors now thought to have been of Persian

---

[41] *CW1*, 445.
[42] *VP*, 829.

Buddhist origin in the caliph's court.[43] Add to this cross-cultural mix Kusta's reference in the poem to the 'great Harun Al-Rashid', born in Rey, Iran, near Tehran, as sometimes being 'occupied / With Persian embassy or Grecian war'[44]. And in the poem's first printing, the letter's addressee, later fictionalized as Abd Al-Rabban, meaning the rabbi, was Faristah, a Persian name meaning angel, the equivalent of Angelo.[45] Arab, Persian, Greek, Jewish, Muslim, Buddhist, Byzantine—this is a world of cross-cultural intersections. As if to mark his difference while imaginatively entering a world under Muslim rule, Yeats speaks through the mask of the Christian narrator Kusta, someone who has 'accepted the Byzantine faith'.[46] In these cross-cultural references, and in the poem's central dialogue between Christian and Muslim, Yeats conveys something of the spirit of a medieval Muslim world in which peoples of different faiths (Muslim, Jewish, Christian), working across different languages (Arabic, Persian, Greek), collected and advanced world thought and culture. Postcolonial scholars such as Robert J. C. Young have rightly conceptualized medieval Cordoba as such a transnational and transcultural site under Islam.[47] But Abbasid Baghdad came several centuries earlier. Like Byzantium, and like Cordoba, Yeats's Baghdad exemplifies an East–West cosmopolitanism that is far from an Orient presumed 'backward, degenerate, uncivilized, and retarded'. As in Byzantium, as in Gandharan Asia and in Callimachus's Greece, and as in medieval Ireland, Yeats sees in Harun Al-Rashid's Golden Age Arabia an East–West dialogue of civilizations.

No doubt Yeats is engaged in a kind of orientalist projection, as evident in what both Jon Stallworthy and Roy Foster call the 'fancy dress' he bestows on himself and his automatic-writing wife.[48] The supposed dialogue is creakily artificial. He gets some facts and dates wrong, as he later acknowledged: it might have been difficult for two men alive at different times, Harun Al-Rashid (766–809) and Kusta ben Luka (820–912), to converse in the flesh, let alone for Harun to find Kusta a wife.[49] And in this poem, as in his two poems written in the voice of specifically Muslim versions of biblical figures, 'Solomon to Sheba' and 'Solomon and the Witch', the newly married Yeats goes to Muslim Asia in part because it provides an opening to relatively free and frank references to sexual relations—in his case, between husband and wife.[50] Elsewhere he adapts Scheherazade's remark in Powys Mathers's *Arabian Nights*: 'it is not shameful to talk of the things that lie beneath our belts.'[51] Yeats activates linkages of the Muslim

[43] *VP*, 828.
[44] *CW1*, 445.
[45] See Jon Stallworthy, *Between the Lines: Yeats's Poetry in the Making* (Oxford: Clarendon Press, 1963), 80. Mazen Naous remarks on 'the rabbi' in 'The Turn of the Gyres: Alterity in "The Gift of Harun Al-Rashid" and *A Thousand and One Nights*', in Tatiana Kontou and Sarah Willburn, eds., *The Ashgate Research Companion to Nineteenth-Century Spiritualism and the Occult* (Farnham: Ashgate, 2012), 204.
[46] *CW1*, 447.
[47] Robert J. C. Young, 'Postcolonial Remains', *NLH* 43:1 (2012) 19–42.
[48] Stallworthy, *Between the Lines*, 86; *Life* 2, 603.
[49] He characteristically appeals to 'poetic licence'; see *CW14*, 54.
[50] On the Solomon and Sheba of the Arabs, see Bushrui, 'Yeats's Arabic Interests', 308–11.
[51] Yeats, *Letters*, 832; Yeats to Ethel Mannin, 4 March [1935], *CL InteLex*, #6194.

East with sexuality and sensuality that are, Said shows, intrinsic to orientalism. By reimagining himself as the Arab Solomon—a prophet who can speak with animals and control djinns and the wind—and his new wife as a 'dusky' 'Arab lady' who lies with him 'under the wild moon', he reinforces associations of a racialized East with magic and non-rational communication.[52]

At the same time, in 'Solomon and the Witch', Solomon's philosophical disquisition on the painful difference between one's 'imagined image' and the 'real image' of the beloved, and on the extraordinary blessing of unifying these two images when Choice merges with Chance, suggests a robust conception of the intellectual capacities of the Muslim Asia. Moreover, this poem ends with a remarkable assertion of female sexual desire and agency: 'O! Solomon! let us try again'.[53] Later, in the poem 'His Bargain', Yeats echoes the Persian poet Hafez's variation on the Sufi idea of erotic love as also mystical love of the divine, specifically in the form of a covenant with the beloved's tresses, or what Yeats calls 'A bargain with that hair / And all the windings there'.[54] In the Arabian poems, despite the received image of Solomon and Sheba in the West as Judaeo-Christian icons, Yeats embraces the Arab Islamicization of them. And despite the popular image of Yeats's poetry as focused almost entirely on Ireland, one of the longest poems he wrote in maturity—'The Gift of Harun Al-Rashid'—reimagines the intellectual learning and cultural splendour of the Abbasid era as a context within which to dramatize the beginnings of his marriage. Ireland is understood not in isolation but in a series of parallels and connections with the Byzantine Empire, Abbasid Arabia, India, Japan, and other Asian civilizations.

PERSPECTIVIST INDIA

Albeit written largely within English, Irish, and Euro-classical traditions, Yeats's poetry also engages, as we've been seeing, a variety of Asian cultural spheres. 'I have always sought to bring my mind close to the mind of Indian and Japanese poets,' he declares in *Per Amica Silentia Lunae*.[55] The donning of 'fancy dress' in his Arab poems, written in middle age, harkens back to the staginess and costuming of some of Yeats's earliest published poems, dramatic monologues and dialogues set in India: 'Anashuya and Vijaya' (earlier titled 'Jealousy'), 'The Indian upon God' (earlier 'From the Book of Kauri the Indian— / Section V. On the Nature of God', then 'Kanva, the Indian, on God'), and 'The Indian to His Love' (earlier 'An Indian Song'). The latter two were published in

---

[52] *CW1*, 138, 176.

[53] *CW1*, 176–8.

[54] *CW1*, 264. On the various incarnations of this image from Hafez in Yeats, see Oliver Scharbrodt, ' "From Hafiz": Irish Orientalism, Persian Poetry, and W. B. Yeats', in Chehabi and Neville, *Erin and Iran*, 73–7.

[55] *CW5*, 16.

The Dublin University Review in 1886, when Yeats was only 21 years old, not long after he met and fell under the spell of the Bengali Brahmin theosophist Mohini Chatterjee in Dublin—a figure who reminds us of the crucial role of theosophy and the occult in making possible Yeats's cross-cultural vision, particularly theosophy's absorption and adaptation of aspects of Indian philosophy.[56] These early 'Indian' poems, though often dismissed as apprentice work, can be seen as important stepping stones in Yeats's poetic development. To consider that three of the first eight poems Yeats published were meant to be South Asian in setting, voice, and thought is to become aware of India's foundational significance for his life work.

Take 'The Indian upon God', a poem spoken in the voice of an Indian named Kauri in the original version, a name Yeats took from Kalidasa's Sanskrit play *Shakuntala*. Scholars have differed over the extent to which the poem sets forth specifically Indian religious tenets, suggesting that Yeats may have drawn on a passage in the Bhagavad Gita about the limitlessness of the divine's manifestations or on a creation story in the Brihadaranyaka Upanishad—the same Upanishad that inspired a key part of the last section of Eliot's *Waste Land*.[57] Perhaps more simply, the poem tries out a concept of the multiplicity of gods—each made in the image of the believer—an idea that can be seen as closer to the so-called polytheisms of South Asia than to Christian monotheism. Walking along the water in a state between sleep and waking, the Indian speaker listens to what various creatures profess about their deities. A moorfowl imagines that an eternal moorfowl created the world and holds it in its bill. A lotus projects God in its own image and sees the water as but '*a sliding drop of rain between His petals wide*'. And a roebuck conceives of God as '*The Stamper of the Skies*'; he alone ventures the argument from design: '*how else, I pray, could He / Conceive a thing so sad and soft, a gentle thing like me?*'. Last comes the peacock. Figures of repetition—polysyndeton ('*and ... and*') and conduplicatio ('*made the ... made the ... made my*')—thrum in a heptameter that builds toward the splendour of the ending:

> Who made the grass and made the worms and made my feathers gay,
> He is a monstrous peacock, and He waveth all the night
> His languid tail above us, lit with myriad spots of light.[58]

Like the others, this culminating image shifts in scale between small and vast, minute and cosmic. Albeit the great peacock is a fourth example of religious projection, it is also a meta-example, in that his many colours and '*myriad spots of light*', like this poem,

---

[56] On the importance of theosophy's boundary-crossing internationalism, including the role in Yeats's thinking of the Moroccan-born spirit Leo Africanus, see Gauri Viswanathan, 'Spectrality's Secret Sharers: Occultism as (Post)colonial Affect', in Walter Goebel and Saskia Schabio, eds., *Beyond the Black Atlantic: Relocating Modernization and Technology* (Abingdon: Routledge, 2006), 135–45, and Bushrui, 'Yeats's Arabic Interests', 280–5.

[57] Sankaran Ravindran, *W. B. Yeats and Indian Tradition* (Delhi: Konark Publishers, 1990), 31–3.

[58] *CW1*, 13–14.

evoke the beauty and multidimensionality of creation within which all these living things conceive distinct worlds.

The poem dramatizes perspectivism, or *Perspektivismus*, as Nietzsche called it—the idea that all conceptualizations come from particular perspectives. But it's Yeats's encounter with Asia, long before he became a deep reader of Nietzsche, that helps instil his perspectivism. After all, the imaginative extension of a young Anglo-Irish poet into South Asian thought is itself an exercise in cultural perspectivism. Hence the poem's meditation on the plurality of images of divine creation can be seen as corresponding to Yeats's willingness to don 'fancy dress', to ventriloquize the East through an Indian persona, to try out a foreign perspective.[59] As Richard Ellmann observed, although the poem can be read as either debunking or affirming the multiplicity of religious projections, it does neither but rather keeps both possibilities in play.[60] If, as I'm trying to suggest, the early engagement with the East is foundational for what will emerge as Yeats's celebrated multiperspectivism, then it becomes harder to consign him to a derogatory orientalism. Yeats learned how to be multiple, how to fashion an art that holds discrepant perspectives in play, in part because of his divided allegiances as an Anglo-Irish writer to both English and Irish culture, akin to many other postcolonial writers with split affiliations.[61] But he also learned how to be multiple in part because of his self-reflections through non-Western cultures, and if there has ever been a culture of multiplicity, of syncretism, it is surely to be found in multireligious, multicultural, multilingual India. Too often we think of Eliot and Pound as the leading syncretists, comparativists, or perspectivists and see Yeats as the nationalist, even though his poetic eye is also—to quote an Indian poet he influenced, A. K. Ramanujan—'a rainbow bubble'.[62]

REFLECTING EAST ASIA

Often what that poetic eye beholds is its mirror reflection. In his forays into the East, Yeats signals a self-consciousness about his cross-cultural self-extension, in contradistinction to a blindly appropriative orientalism. In addition to Persia, Arabia, Byzantium, and India, East Asia was, of course, a fertile site for his imaginative development, perhaps especially in his much-discussed adaptations of the formal vocabulary

---

[59] On Yeats's self-consciousness about the poem's projection, see Lennon, *Irish Orientalism*, 261.

[60] Richard Ellmann, *The Identity of Yeats*, 2nd edn (New York: Oxford University Press, 1964), 54.

[61] Jahan Ramazani, 'W. B. Yeats: A Postcolonial Poet?' in *The Hybrid Muse: Postcolonial Poetry in English* (Chicago: University of Chicago Press, 2001), 21–48.

[62] A. K. Ramanujan, 'Mythologies 2', in *The Collected Poems of A. K. Ramanujan* (Delhi: Oxford University Press), 226. Helen Vendler states that Yeats attempted 'to write as a European' and even 'to write poetry as a citizen of the world'; 'he brought Irish verse (as Joyce brought Irish prose) out of insularity and into European culture'; see her 'Yeats as a European Poet: The Poetics of Cacophany', in A. Norman Jeffares, ed., *Yeats the European* (Gerrards Cross: Colin Smythe, 1989), 20–33, 33.

of Noh drama.[63] In his lyric poems as well, there are sporadic Chinese and Japanese engagements. Elsewhere I argue that the use of the verb 'imagine' and the enjambment of 'I' as a pivot in 'Lapis Lazuli' ('and I / Delight to imagine them seated there') signal the poem's awareness that its Western imagination is playing with and projecting onto a Chinese carving.[64] Similarly, in 'A Dialogue of Self and Soul', Self describes the magnificent Japanese sword not so much as a weapon ready to do violence but as a mirror, and this conjunction of the image of self-reflexivity with deliberate projection and fabrication ('I set' the sword and other images, he declares) suggests the poem's self-consciousness about its cultural crossing:

> The consecrated blade upon my knees
> Is Sato's ancient blade, still as it was,
> Still razor-keen, still like a looking-glass
> Unspotted by the centuries;
> That flowering, silken, old embroidery, torn
> From some court-lady's dress and round
> The wooden scabbard bound and wound,
> Can, tattered, still protect, faded adorn.[65]

'My Self' is looking into the looking glass of a Japanese artefact, and in this regard the poet sees himself making it into a symbol—of enduring secular life, of the conjunction of masculine and feminine, and so forth. In the description of the cloth wound around the scabbard, moreover, the winding of an additional internal rhyme into the octave's double envelope rhymes ('torn', 'round', 'bound and wound', 'adorn') is a sonic correlative to the mirror effects earlier attributed to the Japanese sword.[66]

'Visuality is central to Japanism', according to Christopher Reed, and 'must be crucial to intersections of cultures that do not share a written or spoken language'.[67] Hence, it seems, the importance of Sato's sword. But similar effects can be seen in a textually mediated poem that Yeats wrote in December 1936 and placed immediately after 'Lapis Lazuli' in *New Poems* (1938). In 'Imitated from the Japanese', as Edward Marx has shown, Yeats adapts three haiku by the beloved Japanese haiku grandmaster Kobayashi Issa (1763–1827) as translated by Yeats's friend Yone Noguchi, who helped introduce haiku into English-language poetry.[68] Yeats's three-stanza poem implicitly contrasts the poet's

---

[63] See, e.g., the recent discussion in Carrie Preston, *Learning to Kneel: Noh, Modernism, and Journeys in Teaching* (New York: Columbia University Press, 2016), 63–101.

[64] Ramazani, *Transnational Poetics*, 112.

[65] *CW1*, 235.

[66] On Sato's sword and cross-cultural exchange, see Aoife Assumpta Hart, *Ancestral Recall: The Celtic Revival of Japanese Modernism* (Montreal: McGill-Queen's University Press, 2016), 263–72, 309–10, 379–80. See also the documents, some with a bearing on Sato's sword, collected in Shotara Oshima, *W. B. Yeats and Japan* (Tokyo: Hokuseido Press, 1965).

[67] Christopher Reed, *Bachelor Japanists: Japanese Aesthetics and Western Masculinities* (New York: Columbia University Press, 2017), 26.

[68] Edward Marx, 'No Dancing: Yone Noguchi in Yeats's Japan', *YA* 17 (2007), 51–87, 83–6.

chronological ageing with spring's endless and joyous (if melancholy-inducing) recurrence, echoing haiku's frequent seasonal setting in a transient nature (*kigo*) and aesthetic principles such as compression, comparison, alternation, and contrast (*kireji*). Topoi recognizable from haiku tradition include loneliness (*sabi*), lightness (*karumi*), poetic eccentricity (*fukyo*), ascetic freedom (*wabi*), and deep, mysterious beauty (*yugen*).[69] Whereas in modern Japan and the West the haiku has often been treated as a stand-alone poem, it was traditionally linked with other haiku, almost as if each haiku were, as Adam L. Kern puts it, 'one instalment—or "stanza"'. Yeats's linked verses might look odd to those of us habituated to the isolated three-line poem, but their verbal, formal, and thematic linkage brings them closer to traditional haiku, in which, as Kern says, 'the link (*tsukeai*) is the thing'.[70] Pre-modern haiku sequences were collaboratively produced, each poet writing in response to preceding haiku. Yeats's poem is collaborative in a different sense, written in close association with Noguchi ('Imitated from …'), who in turn drew together and translated three of Issa's haiku from different sources.

In homage to the minimalism of haiku, Yeats restricts his lexical palette to a bare handful of repeated words. But, in so doing, he makes the tripartite poem even more heavily recursive than either Issa's three haiku or Noguchi's rendering of them, in ways that may suggest the self-consciousness and heightened formality seen in 'A Dialogue of Self and Soul'. Four of the poem's nine lines begin with the anaphora 'Seventy years', three with a swinging trisyllabic rhythm: 'Seventy years have I lived'.[71] In the middle stanza 'Spring' occurs at the end of one line and again near the beginning of the next: '(Hurrah for the flowers of Spring / For Spring is here again.)' Except for the half-rhyme of 'again' and 'man', the rest of the rhyme scheme resounds with sonic and lexical replication (*ab ac bcbdd*). Even within a line like 'No ragged beggar man' ('Seventy years have I lived / No ragged beggar man'), we can see repetition: the middle words are nearly mirrorlike anagrams of each other. At midline, even the letters 'd' and 'b' mirror each other. This poetic reflexivity doesn't exempt Yeats from orientalism, but it seems at a considerable remove from the kind of unselfconsciously appropriative logic that Said ascribes to orientalism. In potentially awkward traversals of the East/West divide, it harnesses and makes fruitful use of lyric's capacities for rich self-awareness.

Here again it's worth attending even more specifically to the way the East—though Yeats sometimes dismisses it as 'formless', at other times celebrates it as rich in form—informs his forms. Although Yeats doesn't follow the syllabic patterning of haiku (only loosely followed in pre-modern Japan), he plays on haiku's syllabic alternations and stays close to its middle, seven-syllable line. His accentual equivalent for the brevity of the haiku line is trimeter lines that trade off iambs and anapaests. Whereas Noguchi's translations of Issa appear as three three-line haiku, Yeats rearranges the sequence as

[69] See Yoshinobu Hakutani, *Haiku and Modernist Poetics* (New York: Palgrave Macmillan, 2009), 1–16, and Adam L. Kern, introduction and glossary to *The Penguin Book of Haiku* (London: Penguin, 2018), xxiii–lxxi, 399–415.
[70] Kern, *Haiku*, lxxiv and 3.
[71] *CW1*, 295–6. Ensuing references are to the same pages.

two couplets followed by a quintet (or quintain). The first couplet is in lines of seven syllables, followed by a stanza with lines of eight and six syllables. These first two stanzas might well look like violations of what is taken in the West to be the three-line, 5-7-5 norm, but each is in fourteen syllables—as it happens, exactly like the less-well-known, pre-modern haiku form known as *tanku*.[72] Yeats follows these two *tanku*-like couplets with a five-line stanza in lines of 7, 6, 7, 7, and 8 syllables. This stanzaic structure—again far from the three-line Western haiku norm—resembles another related form, the *tanka*, the dominant form of Japanese poetry or *waka* for over a millennium. The *tanka* is a 'short verse' of thirty-one syllables in five measures (5-7-5-7-7), with allowances for additional syllables—a form that Noguchi and the Imagists had helped bring into English.[73] Often *tanka* pivots between its haiku-like, 5-7-5 upper part and its 7-7 lower part. By virtue of rhyme and repetition, Yeats's stanza also bifurcates: the first and third lines of his thirty-five-syllable stanza are identical, forming a haiku-like upper part (rhymed *bcb*), before closing with a couplet (*dd*). The Japanese form's structure has been seen as arising from 'a complex interplay between the classical East Asian ideal of symmetry on the one hand and a desire for its complementary opposite in the form of an asymmetric (and therefore indigenous) structure on the other'.[74] Even if Yeats isn't deliberately engaging the Japanese *tanka* or *tanku*, he develops parallel forms that balance symmetric with asymmetric structures, setting two stanzas of two lines against one of five, and in the final quintet, three lines against a couplet. This structural mixture helps accentuate the poem's tonal mixture of joy ('Hurrah') with regret ('never have I danced'), triumph ('Seventy years') with melancholy (also 'Seventy years'). The septuagenarian poet may never have danced with joy, but in lamenting this lack, he sets his verse forms dancing.

ORIENTALIST, ANTI-ORIENTALIST, OR . . .?

After this reconsideration of some Eastward-reaching moments in Yeats's poetry, where are we on the questions of the extent to which his poetry is and isn't orientalist and of whether we should see his Eastern excursions as appropriative theft or productive cross-cultural engagement? More broadly, can we glean any insight from his example that could be useful for the future development of transnational literary studies? One way to approach these questions is to place Yeats's work between the divergent disciplinary

[72] Kern, *Haiku*, 222, 412.

[73] Gustav Heldt, 'Waka', in *The Princeton Encyclopedia of Poetry and Poetics*, 4th edn, ed. Roland Greene, Stephen Cushman, Clare Cavanagh, Jahan Ramazani, and Paul Rouzer (Princeton: Princeton University Press, 2012), 1528. See also Mark Morris, 'Waka and Form, Waka and History', *Harvard Journal of Asiatic Studies*, 46:2 (1986): 551–610, and Yoshinobu Hakutani, 'Ezra Pound, Yone Noguchi, and Imagism', *Modern Philology*, 90:1 (1992): 46–69.

[74] Heldt, 'Waka', 1528.

frameworks of orientalism and world literature.[75] In Said's model of orientalism, Western forays into the East are often seen as inherently prejudicial and deprecating, because Westerners can't see the East except through the skewing imbalances of power and wealth. In the world literature model, these political and historical differences are less prominent, because of the emphasis on transit, translation, and circulation from one culture to another. In my view, a challenge for transnational literary studies is to navigate a path between the sensitivity to power and historical injustice in orientalist critique and the neutral tracking of cultural dissemination and reproduction in 'world literature'. My hope is that the foregoing analysis demonstrates one way of negotiating those differences between these models, which usefully correct each other's excesses. As Stefan Helgesson writes, we should take advantage of 'the potential for a mutually enriching exchange' between the two approaches.[76]

Although I've been trying to counterbalance the one-sidedness of Said's orientalist model, in *Orientalism* Said himself briefly anticipates a nuanced approach by carving out an exception for two writers, Gérard de Nerval and Gustave Flaubert. According to Said, 'they produced work that is connected to and depends upon the kind of Orientalism we have so far discussed, yet remains independent from it'. The same could be said of Yeats, who, like these writers, reimagined the Orient as a space of possibility. As in Said's end-of-career work on what the Palestinian scholar called 'late style', in which idiosyncrasy and unresolved tensions are crucial to artistic creation, he says of these two French writers: 'What mattered to them was the structure of their work as an independent, aesthetic, and personal fact, and not the ways by which, if one wanted to, one could effectively dominate or set down the Orient graphically. Their egos never absorbed the Orient, nor totally identified the Orient with documentary and textual knowledge of it (with official Orientalism, in short).'[77] Although Yeats's representations of the Orient have little of the corporeality, decrepitude, and experiential immediacy that Said sees in the work of these French writers, he too engages various Asias through an emphatically personal prism without seeking domination or documentation. Just as Said differentiates these French writers from most of the Englishmen who write ultimately in the service of strengthening the British Empire, so too Yeats's Anglo-Irishness, even with his living much of his life in the imperial centre of London, places him on a different footing in relation to the so-called East from that of many British orientalists. Said famously argues in 'Yeats and Decolonization' that Yeats is a 'poet who during a period of anti-imperialist resistance articulates the experiences, the aspirations, and the

---

[75] See Barry Sheils, *W. B. Yeats and World Literature: The Subject of Poetry* (Farnham: Ashgate, 2015). Unlike world literary scholars such as David Damrosch and Pascale Casanova, Sheils emphasizes the material imbrication of Yeats's work in a world economic system.

[76] Stefan Helgesson, "Postcolonialism and World Literature: Rethinking the Boundaries," *Interventions*, 16:4 (2014), 484.

[77] Said, *Orientalism*, 181. See also Edward Said, *On Late Style: Music and Literature against the Grain* (New York: Pantheon Books, 2006). In addition, see Wayne K. Chapman's 'Late Style', Chapter 40 in this volume.

restorative vision' of a colonized people.[78] To the extent that Yeats's identifications are at least semi-anticolonial, they connect him with parts of the world that have been on the receiving end of empires.

Bearing this exception in mind, let's take a last look at Yeats in relation to the standard features of orientalism. As we saw in a stanza in 'The Statues', Yeats is complicit in the orientalist othering of the East as formless, many-headed, weak, sensual, and unintellectual, as opposed to the West's individualism, formalism, and antithetical strength. But even though he sometimes thought 'East and West seem each other's contraries', his poetry also complicates and even confutes these oppositions and the very strategy of dichotomizing.[79] It's hard to view Yeats's work as merely making, in Said's terms, 'more rigid the sense of difference between the European and Asiatic parts of the world'.[80] As we've seen, Yeats foregrounds cross-cultural blending and interplay in his Asian-oriented poetry, as in the Irish-Asiatic and Greco-Indian fusions in 'The Statues', the mingling of Persian and Western forms in the Byzantium poems, of Greek and Persian, Christian and Muslim learning and culture in the Arabian poems. The East may be different, alien, 'other' in various ways, but it's also an important dimension of the West—Asiatic ancient Greece, Asiatic early Christianity, Asiatic ancient and modern Ireland, and so forth. Poetry's capacity for syncretic layering provides a particularly useful structure by which to embody these convergences.

What of the orientalist idea of the East as formless? Various parts of Asia also provide strong formal vocabularies that figure in Yeats's work: the Persian nonmimetic line, vine, patterning, colour, and non-naturalistic beasts in his Byzantium; the Arab interest in measurement, mathematics, and geometry that are a recurrent theme in his Arabian poems (as well as his semi-imaginary Arab tribe of the Judwalis, meaning diagrammatists); the South Asian structures of multifacetedness and plurality that are presupposed in some of Yeats's earliest poems; the East Asian compression and alternations that he loosely adapts from haiku and related forms.[81] Also, even though there is some overlap among Yeats's Asias—as is perhaps fitting, given the amount of trade, migration, and artistic and religious circulation across the continent—these regions are also each reimagined with some distinctness as well, in contrast to the view that, in Said's words, 'Orientals were almost everywhere nearly the same.'[82] Even when Yeats claims that meditative practices of East Asia and India have largely similar aims, he is alert to the differences in 'technique' they employ.[83]

What of the idea of orientalism as negatively prejudicial? In Yeats's poetry, Eastern worlds are often intellectually, sensually, culturally robust sites of wisdom and insight

---

[78] Edward W. Said, 'Yeats and Decolonization', in *Culture and Imperialism* (New York: Knopf, 1993), 220; I develop and complicate the argument in 'W. B. Yeats: A Postcolonial Poet?' and in 'Poetry and Decolonization', ch. 7 of *A Transnational Poetics*, 141–62.

[79] *CW5*, 134.

[80] Said, *Orientalism*, 204.

[81] For the Judwalis, see Busrui, 'Yeats's Arabic Interests', 295.

[82] Said, *Orientalism*, 38.

[83] *CW5*, 177–8.

and cross-cultural integration: witness the empty-eyed Buddhism and *contemptus mundi* Hinduism of north India in poems such as 'The Statues' and 'Meru'; the vitalizing Zoroastrian forms integrated with Christian and classical elements in Yeats's Byzantium; the multicultural libraries and Solomonic-and-Sheban wisdom of the Arabian poems; the prismatic refractions of divinity in the multitheistic Indian poems; and the cultural stability, social hierarchy, asymmetric symmetry, and renunciatory ethos in poems that invoke East Asia.

Finally, what of orientalism's deindividualizing of the East, reducing it and its people, as Said says, to ' "attitudes," "trends," statistics', leaving it 'dehumanized'? As we've seen, Yeats repeatedly speaks through named Arab, Indian, and other masks, and while we can surely see stereotyping in these poetic performances, he is also demonstrating that literature can, as Said puts it, speak 'more or less directly of a living reality', instead of just absorbing these different cultures into blanket abstractions. Hence Yeats's avoidance of what Said calls the orientalist's substitution of texts 'for any actual encounter with the real Orient'.[84] I've been focusing on Yeats's poetry, but it's worth remembering that, even though his desires to travel to Japan and India were never fulfilled, Yeats befriended and collaborated with a number of Asians—Mohini Chatterjee, Rabindranath Tagore, Shri Purohit Swami, Yone Noguchi, Junzo Sato, Michio Ito, Shotara Oshima, and others whose relationships with him have been extensively discussed in Yeats scholarship.[85] We all know that friendships can coexist with prejudices, but, on the evidence of his letters, essays, poems, and collaborative projects, it's clear that Yeats was intellectually open to these Asian friends and that, in some cases, he made important contributions to their careers as well as their texts, just as they did to his.[86] More significant than Yeats's partly distortive presuppositions about 'other' cultures—and it bears repeating that we all have them, however unconscious—is that he took Asian cultures seriously: he engaged them, performed them, learned from them, and made poetry and theatre enmeshed with them—reasons to keep him at the centre of discussions of modernism's global bearings.

---

[84] Said, *Orientalism*, 291 and 80.

[85] An incomplete sampling of the scholarship would include Amrita Ghosh and Elizabeth Brewer Redwine, eds., *Tagore and Yeats: A Postcolonial Re-envisioning* (Leiden: Brill, 2022); Ashim Dutta, *Mystic Modernity: Tagore and Yeats* (New York: Routledge, 2022); Ragini Mohite, *Modern Writers, Transnational Literatures: Rabindranath Tagore and W. B. Yeats* (Clemson: Clemson University Press, 2021); Preston, *Learning to Kneel*; Hart, *Ancestral Recall*; Sheils, *W. B. Yeats and World Literature*; Sirshendu Majumdar, *Yeats and Tagore: A Comparative Study of Cross-Cultural Poetry, Nationalist Politics, Hyphenated Margins and the Ascendancy of the Mind* (Bethesda, MD: Academica Press, 2013); Hakutani, *Haiku and Modernist Poetics*; Foster, *Life 1* and *Life 2*; Sankaran Ravindran, *W. B. Yeats and Indian Tradition*; Masaru Sekine and Christopher Murray, *Yeats and Noh: A Comparative Study* (Gerrards Cross: Colin Smythe, 1990); and Richard Taylor, *The Drama of W. B. Yeats: Irish Myth and the Japanese Nō* (New Haven: Yale University Press, 1976).

[86] See, for example, Justin Quinn's Chapter 20 in this volume, 'Tagore, Pound, and World English'.

CHAPTER 23

THE SCIENTIFIC
REVOLUTION

KATHERINE EBURY

W. B. Yeats's uniquely difficult combination of science and pseudo-science has previously led to a critical neglect of his investment in bridging what C. P. Snow would term, twenty years after the poet's death, the 'Two Cultures'. In assessing the critical history of Yeats and science, it is important to be alert to the fact that the first article to directly address the topic, even before the Two Cultures debate in 1959, is inauspiciously entitled 'William Butler Yeats and the Hatred of Science' (published in 1953). There, Charles I. Glicksberg argues that 'in order to believe his own hieratic truth, the poet must perforce deny the truths of science, repudiate the Age of Enlightenment, throw off the dead weight of rationalism'.[1] Glicksberg's diagnosis of Yeats's hostility to science, however excessive, is nonetheless in keeping with the poet's generative ambivalence about the value of science throughout his life. Indeed, when Yeats directly names scientists, scientific philosophers, and mathematicians in his poetry and autobiographical writings—such as John Locke in 'Fragments', Isaac Newton in 'At Algeciras', and Pythagoras in 'The Statues', as well as Charles Darwin, T. H. Huxley, and John Tyndall in the *Autobiographies*—he is often particularly focused on sceptically critiquing those he has identified as his antagonists. However, Yeats appealed to an older tradition of scientific philosophy, before the creation of disciplinary boundaries, including thinkers such as Democritus and Nicholas of Cusa, and he also created several of his own fictional polymaths, such as Michael Robartes, Owen Ahearn, Giraldus, and Kusta Ben Luka, to represent his ideal of the philosopher-scientist. Yeats is much quieter on the subject of the real modern scientists and popularizers, such as Arthur Eddington and Alfred North Whitehead, whom he read in the 1920s and who sympathetically influenced his later works; even in *A Vision*, when Yeats's preferred scientists are often directly praised,

---

[1] Charles I Glicksberg, 'William Butler Yeats and the Hatred of Science', *Prairie Schooner*, 28 (1953), 29–36 (29–30).

this insight is usually confined to a footnote. While Yeats's aesthetic and world view may superficially appear very idiosyncratic if we stay within disciplinary boundaries, I will show in this chapter—by offering first a critical history and then an analysis of Yeats's career before and after the Einsteinian revolution—that once we begin to do interdisciplinary work his poetry and his thought take a more natural place within 1920s and 1930s scientific culture and, more broadly, within the history of ideas.

Yeats and the Two Cultures: the Critical History

Yeats's frequently expressed antagonism to science explains why many of the current critical guides to his work do not include a chapter on his interests in science.[2] But, as the above sketch of Yeats's engagement with science across his life shows, his work shares characteristics with an earlier set of debates around literature and science which preceded the Two Cultures. Firstly, in Yeats's youth, the Darwinian scientist T. H. Huxley, a figure much admired by Yeats's father, had argued in 'Science and Culture' (1880) for the value of a scientific education over a classical and literary education. Huxley was answered by Matthew Arnold in 'Literature and Science' (1882). Unlike Snow a generation later, Arnold is receptive to the importance of modern science and considers the work of scientists—including Galileo, Newton, and Darwin—to be 'literature' (just not 'belles-lettres'); he nonetheless argues for the value of the humanities, concluding that

> the great majority of mankind, all who have not exceptional and overpowering aptitudes for the study of nature, would do well, I cannot but think, to choose to be educated in humane letters rather than in the natural sciences. Letters will call out their being at more points, will make them live more.[3]

At the same time, Huxley, and other late Victorian scientists such as Tyndall, 'maintained the scientific perspective provided a unique access point to culture' and promoted the scientist as 'peculiarly modern arbiters of culture'.[4] In short, this debate represented, both on Huxley's side and Arnold's, a genuine effort at interdisciplinary thinking despite their jostling for position. Yeats can be said to be influenced by this debate as he frequently borrows the authority of science and scientists when grappling with literary

---

[2] See, for example, *The Cambridge Companion to W. B. Yeats*, ed. Marjorie Howes (Cambridge: Cambridge University Press, 2006), and *W. B. Yeats in Context*, ed. David Holdeman and Ben Levitas (Cambridge: Cambridge University Press, 2010).

[3] Matthew Arnold, 'Literature and Science', in *Prose of the Victorian Period*, ed. William E. Buckler (Boston: Houghton Mifflin, 1958), 499.

[4] Bernard Lightman, 'Science and Culture', in Francis O'Gorman, ed., *The Cambridge Companion to Victorian Culture* (Cambridge: Cambridge University Press, 2010), 12–43, 39.

and philosophical problems, as we will see later in more detail. As an autodidact in both literature and science, with his highest education in the Metropolitan School of Art, Yeats is unlikely to have felt the same territorial spirit in education. Nonetheless, for example, Charles Armstrong has persuasively read this Victorian debate about a classical (as opposed to a scientific) education into the sceptical depiction of Greek thought in Yeats's 'Among Schoolchildren'.[5]

This debate about culture was rekindled in the 1920s by I. A. Richards's *Science and Poetry* (first published 1926, reissued 1935), a text which asked, 'How is our estimate of poetry going to be affected by science? And how will poetry itself be influenced?'[6] Richards's book is thus an early provocation to consider poetic and scientific creativity in the same breath. While, ultimately, Richards is too careful and defensive to offer an early ideal of a methodology of literature and science, as this attitude leads him to miss valuable objects of study in both poetry and in science, his work does offer a valuable historicist way out of the excessive quality of both Snow's and Leavis's later formulation of 'Two Cultures' and provides a framework for thinking about how Yeats might have perceived the relationship between poetry and science.[7] Indeed, Richards's combination of an emphasis on Romanticism and the use of an authority borrowed from science to support his poetics is in itself deeply Yeatsian. But Richards does not appear to recognize this similarity in himself, writing instead in general, detached terms of Yeats's work, claiming that 'The resort to trance, and the effort to discover a new world-picture to replace that given by science, are the most significant points for our purpose in Mr. Yeats's work'.[8]

Richards's misrecognition of Yeats and failure to see his investments in the new physics, as opposed to the mainly materialist science focused on in *Science and Poetry*, was followed by an even greater neglect of Yeats's example within the 'Two Cultures' debate; Snow only writes of Yeats's personality and his politics,[9] and F. R. Leavis's choice to

[5] Charles I. Armstrong, *Reframing Yeats: Genre, Allusion and History* (London: Bloomsbury, 2013), 108.

[6] I. A. Richards, *Poetries and Sciences: A Reissue of Science and Poetry (1926, 1935) with Commentary* (New York: Norton, 1970), 21. Though I cannot prove that Yeats definitely read Richards, his book was broadly influential on modernists and had been reviewed by T. S. Eliot as 'a book which everyone interested in poetry ought to read', while Richards's own discussion of Yeats makes this an important reference point (Frances Dickey et al., eds., 'Literature, Science, and Dogma. A review of Science and Poetry, by I. A. Richards', in *The Complete Prose of T. S. Eliot: The Critical Edition: Literature, Politics, Belief, 1927–1929* (Baltimore: Johns Hopkins University Press, 2015), https://muse.jhu.edu/ (accessed 7 Sept. 2019).

[7] Richards, *Science and Poetry*, 49.

[8] Richards, *Science and Poetry*, 72.

[9] Snow lists Yeats among modernists, such as Pound and Lewis, who were, according to a more liberal scientist friend of his, 'not only politically silly, but politically wicked', even though his personal view is that Yeats was 'according to friends whose judgement I trust, … a man of singular magnanimity of character, as well as a great poet' (C. P. Snow, *The Two Cultures* (Cambridge and New York: Cambridge University Press, 2008), 7–8). This exchange takes place within Snow's wider positioning of the scientific culture as more optimistic and socially liberal, alongside a 'temporary phase' in which the literary culture is more conservative, if not regressive (7–8); Snow keeps this political critique of literature rigorously

respond with an *ad hominem* attack in *Two Cultures: The Significance of C. P. Snow* leaves Yeats completely out of the picture.[10] More useful is Lionel Trilling's measured response to both Snow and Leavis, which uses Snow's critical reading of the politics of Yeats and modernism to highlight his ideological naïvety about science: he argues that, for Snow, 'the future that the scientists have in their bones is understood to be nothing but a good future … to entertain the idea that the future might be bad is represented as being tantamount to moral ill-will'.[11] Trilling accuses Snow of maintaining a belief in science as progress which is unchanged since Huxley and which the modernist generation of literary artists such as Yeats could not subscribe to, and which a newer generation of writers (such as Orwell) justifiably rejected outright after Auschwitz and Hiroshima.[12] In short, this unsatisfactory and antagonistic debate, which Yeats's example often haunts unproductively, extinguished much of the potential for considering poetry in relation to science contained in both Arnold's and Richards's example. Furthermore, it left the question of Yeats's relation to science to be eventually remedied by much later critical work.

A first wave of work on Yeats and the scientific revolution began in the 1990s and the second wave is current in Yeats studies.[13] The real catalyst for a serious reconsideration of Yeats's engagement with science was the sensitiveness and boldness of Daniel Albright's reading of Yeats, alongside T. S. Eliot and Ezra Pound, in *Quantum Poetics: Yeats, Pound, Eliot, and the Science of Modernism* (1997). Albright's work focused on 'the appropriation of scientific metaphors by poets' via these poets' pursuit of an 'irreducible minima of poetry' through the new physics concept of wave-particle duality.[14] Since Albright's groundbreaking book, there has been a boom of literature and science approaches within and beyond modernist studies, with particular landmarks being the founding of the European Society for Literature, Science and the Arts (2000) and the British Society for Literature and Science (2005); the founding of the *Journal of Literature and Science* (2007); and, most recently, the publication of *The Cambridge Companion to Literature*

---

apart from Cold War social anxieties about the politics of science and atomic weaponry. In a later addition to the Rede Lecture, when the essay was published in book form, Snow addressed accusations of being 'oblivious of politics' in his bias toward science because 'I did not relate the lecture to the cold war, as it was being waged in 1959: or, more sinister still, that I did not accept the cold war as the prime absolute of our age, and of all ages to come'; but he remains unable to pivot his reflections fully around to that question (97–8).

[10] F. R. Leavis, *Two Cultures?: The Significance of C. P. Snow* (Cambridge: Cambridge University Press, 2013).

[11] Lionel Trilling, 'Science, Literature and Culture: A Comment on the Leavis-Snow Controversy', *Higher Education Quarterly*, 17:1 (1962), 9–32 (16).

[12] Trilling, 'Science, Literature and Culture', 10, 16.

[13] Some valuable slightly earlier work also exists, such as Ted R. Spivey's 'W. B. Yeats and the "Children of the Fire": Science, Poetry, and Visions of the New Age"', *Studies in the Literary Imagination,* 14:1 (1981), 123–34, and Barton Friedman's 'Dissolving surfaces: Yeats's the wind among the reeds and the challenge of science', *Yeats: An Annual of Critical and Textual Studies,* 7 (1989), 57–90.

[14] Daniel Albright, *Quantum Poetics: Yeats, Pound, Eliot, and the Science of Modernism* (Cambridge: Cambridge University Press, 1997), 1.

and Science (2018).[15] This change in methodology has entered into Yeats studies via excellent scholarship by critics including Rónán McDonald on Yeats and the natural sciences, Aoife Lynch on the new physics, as well as some of my own work on Yeats's science in fields including physics, cosmology, and criminology.[16] Additionally, Yeats's interest in eugenics has always been amply explored because of its biopolitical dimensions, as have his engagements with anthropology and psychoanalysis.[17] This work on Yeats's science exclusively has been complemented by broader studies on the Irish Revival such as Gregory Castle's *Modernism and the Celtic Revival* (2001) and Sinéad Garrigan Mattar's *Primitivism, Science, and the Irish Revival* (2004), which have highlighted Yeats's scientific interests through comparison to his contemporaries, showing how he 'plundered the very science he decried, reading widely and comparatively'.[18]

Looking ahead and identifying developing trends, there is also potential to investigate Yeats as a writer who was distinctively influenced by ecology, animal studies, and the non 'human turn. Yeats gains a unique value when the concept of the Anthropocene is highlighted in his work; the firmest foundation for this critical turn is provided by Garrigan Mattar's recent focus on Yeats in relation to the new animism, as well as Cóilín Parsons's developing project on Yeats, alongside other modernists, as a planetary thinker.[19] Garrigan Mattar shows, in particular, how 'Yeats too was engaged in reassessing the tricky question of animism by challenging contemporary negotiations

---

[15] An American network devoted to literature and science, now called The Society for Literature, Science and the Arts, had been established much earlier in 1985.

[16] Rónán McDonald, 'Accidental Variations: Darwinian Traces in Yeats's Poetry', in John Holmes, ed., *Science in Modern Poetry: New Directions* (Liverpool: Liverpool University Press, 2012), 151–66, and 'The "Fascination of What I Loathed": Science and Self in W. B. Yeats's Autobiographies', in Maria DiBattista and Emily Ondine Wittman, eds., *Modernism and Autobiography* (Cambridge: Cambridge University Press, 2014), 18–30; Aoife Lynch, 'Yeats and the Mask of Science', Études Irelandises, 40:1 (2015), 273–84, and 'The Black Swan: Yeats and the Science of the Unknown', *Irish University Review*, 47:2 (2017), 350–9; Katherine Ebury, *Modernism and Cosmology* (Houndmills: Palgrave Macmillan, 2014); '"A new science": Yeats's *A Vision* and relativistic cosmology', *Irish Studies Review*, 22:2 (2014), 167–83; 'Ghost, Medium, Criminal, Genius: Lombrosian Types in Yeats's Art and Philosophy', in Matthew Gibson and Neil Mann, eds., *Yeats, Philosophy and the Occult* (Clemson: Clemson University Press, 2016); 'Science, the Occult, and Irish Drama: Ghosts in Yeats and Beckett', in Kathryn Conrad, Cóilín Parsons and Julie McCormick Weng, eds., *Science, Technology, and Irish Modernism* (Syracuse: Syracuse University Press, 2019), 229–47.

[17] This remains a very rich field, but see David Bradshaw, 'The Eugenics Movement in the 1930s and the Emergence of on the Boiler', *YA*, 9, (1992): 189–215; Donald J Childs, 'Class and Eugenics', in *W. B. Yeats in Context* (Cambridge: Cambridge University Press, 2010), 169–78; and Melissa Dinsman, 'Politics, Eugenics, and Yeats's Radio Broadcasts', *International Yeats Studies*, 3:1 (2018), 65–80; Alan Graham, 'Sassenachs and their syphilization: The Irish Revival, Deanglicization, and Eugenics', in Conrad et al., *Science, Technology, and Irish Modernism*, 203–14. On Freud's influence on Yeats's poetics, particularly in the period of *Per Amica Silentia Lunae*, see William J. Wenthe, '"It Will Be a Hard Toil": Yeats's Theory of Versification, 1899–1919', *Journal of Modern Literature*, 21:1 (1997), 29–48.

[18] Sinéad Garrigan Mattar, 'Yeats, Fairies, and the New Animism', *New Literary History*, 43:1 (2012): 137–57, 143.

[19] Garrigan Mattar, 'Yeats, Fairies, and the New Animism', 137–57. Cóilín Parsons's work on Yeats was presented at the Yeats School 2018 under the title '"Had I the heavens' embroidered cloths": Yeats's Planetary Imagination'; see Cóilín Parsons, 'Planets', Chapter 24 in this volume.

of the concept that were (as Bruno Latour diagnoses now, and as Yeats realized then) the product of a post-Enlightenment, anthropocentric insistence in the primary "materialism" of the cosmos'. She finds productive connections between Yeats's thinking and our contemporary moment via thinkers such as Marilyn Strathern, Tim Ingold, and Latour.[20] Therefore, Yeats's scientific interests ultimately all fit with his claim to be amongst 'the last romantics' in 'Coole Park and Ballylee, 1931'; Yeats shows a scientific and poetic concern with how mystical insights might be gleaned from a better understanding of the nature of reality.

YEATS BEFORE EINSTEIN

As the diversity of critical activity demonstrates, across Yeats's long life there were many developments in science, as well as one major revolution, which shaped his career through both antagonism and sympathy. Born in 1865, and thus much older than many of the modernist generation, Yeats's childhood took place in the immediate aftermath of the publication of Darwin's *On the Origin of Species* in 1859, and his early education was shaped by his father, the painter John Butler Yeats, and his enthusiasm for Darwinism and the Huxley perspective on the importance of learning science. In his *Autobiographies*, as Rónán McDonald has described, Yeats depicts his father spoiling his childhood simple Christian faith through his belief in materialism, as well as pressuring his son to become a scientist rather than a poet. Yeats describes how he briefly becomes obsessed with an ambition to be a naturalist, with 'a theory of my own, which I cannot remember, as to the colour of sea anemones'.[21] By contrast, Yeats's mother's family, the Pollexfens, offered Yeats a counter to his father's associations with the city and with science; childhood visits to Sligo took Yeats close to a romantic view of nature and to traditional folk beliefs.

Yeats's flirtation with a career as a naturalist is a phase in his development that he remains extremely nostalgic for, even after his adolescent rebellion into occult beliefs. For example, in the late poem 'At Algeciras—A Meditation Upon Death' (1928), Yeats intertwines science and nature in his recollections of his childhood:

> Often at evening when a boy
> Would I carry to a friend —
> Hoping more substantial joy
> Did an older mind commend —
> Not such as are in Newton's metaphor,
> But actual shells of Rosses' level shore.[22]

---

[20] Garrigan Mattar, 'Yeats, Fairies, and the New Animism', 137–8.
[21] *CW3*, 77.
[22] *CWI*, 246.

This memory represents this phase of ambition to be a naturalist, with the child Yeats going to his friend for the 'more substantial joy' of a scientific understanding of the shells, but the location of the memory in Sligo (the beach at Rosses Point) already signals the turn towards a more mystical understanding of death expressed in subsequent stanzas of 'At Algeciras'. In childhood, the shells were 'actual', which Yeats apparently means as a rebuke to Newton's metaphorical shells, but the beauty of the Newton quotation that the poet has buried within his dense allusion is central to the poem. In the original reflection, quoted in the mathematician Selig Brodetsky's 1927 biography of Newton (which Yeats must have read soon before composing the poem), the scientist sums up his life's work in terms of creativity and play and also reflects on the depths of scientific knowledge that have escaped him:

> I do not know what I may appear to the world but to myself I seem to have been only a boy playing on the sea-shore, and diverting myself in now and then finding a smoother pebble or a prettier shell than ordinary, whilst the great ocean of truth lay all undiscovered before me.[23]

In contrast to Newton, Yeats confronts death, figured in the poem in the 'narrow straits' and 'mingled seas' of separation between Europe and Africa, with a cautious claim to a knowledge that bridges the mystical and the scientific. The poem closes by reflecting on what the poet, 'if questioned' by the Great Questioner, 'Can with a fitting confidence reply'.[24]

Yeats's emphasis on his 'actual shells' in 'At Algeciras' reflects his retention of an empirical methodology and epistemology, even in rejecting materialism and claiming occult knowledge; as a young man he would soon learn to time the speed of fairy apparitions using his watch and, in adulthood in the 1890s, would be expelled from the Theosophical Society for establishing a paranormal research bureau inside it because of what McDonald terms his 'abiding obsession with verification'.[25] Indeed, Yeats would always seek out the work of scientists who shared his idealist and/or spiritualist beliefs, including the criminologist Cesare Lombroso, the anthropologist Andrew Lang, the chemist and physicist William Crookes, and the astronomer Arthur Eddington, in the hope of securing experimental proof for his world view. This combination of an empiricist epistemology and an idealist philosophy was perhaps unusual, but is not unique to Yeats: it was found, as we will see, among many scientists, even later in the twentieth century.

Beyond evolutionary theory, early Yeats's poetic imagination was also shaped by a fin de siècle period of apocalyptic thinking influenced by concepts of entropy and thermodynamics alongside eugenic ideas of degeneration; the details of this discredited science, captured most powerfully in science fiction narratives such as H. G. Wells's

---

[23] Selig Brodetsky, *Sir Isaac Newton: A Brief Account of his Life and Work* (London: Methuen, 1927), 153.

[24] *CW1*, 246.

[25] McDonald, 'The "Fascination of What I Loathed", 18–30, 27.

The Time Machine, pictured the slow decay of human biology alongside the gradual death of the sun. The key thinker who popularized these ideas was Max Nordau, who expressed in his 1892 work *Degeneration* that 'In our days there have arisen in more highly-developed minds vague qualms of a Dusk of the Nations in which all suns and all stars are gradually waning, and mankind with all its institutions and creations is perishing in the midst of a dying world'.[26] Yeats's own response to this sense of crisis was captured in his 1899 collection *The Wind Among the Reeds*, where difficult human relationships are set alongside an anticipation of solar and stellar destruction in poems such as 'The Secret Rose', 'He Hears the Cry of the Sedge', 'He Tells of the Perfect Beauty', 'The Valley of the Black Pig', and 'He Wishes his Beloved Were Dead'. Concepts of entropy and degeneration had a long-lasting effect on Yeats's imagination, as far as poems such as 'The Second Coming' (1919), 'Nineteen Hundred and Nineteen', and *Meditations in Time of Civil War* (1928). Further, the gradual discrediting of this science—as scientists discovered a much wider universe, and a correspondingly large sense of cosmic time—also revealed to Yeats that at times the distinction between science and pseudoscience was artificial. This idea of being mistaken and betrayed by a fashion for entropy was powerfully expressed by Wells in his 1931 preface to a new edition of *The Time Machine*: 'the geologists and astronomers [of the 1890s] told us dreadful lies about the "inevitable" freezing up of the world – and of life and mankind with it … they impressed this upon us with the full weight of their authority, while now Sir James Jeans … waves us on to millions of millions of years.'[27] This principle of upheavals, revolutions, and even reversals in science, rather than the alternative of a narrative of gradual scientific progress, certainly fits with Yeats's belief in the power of sudden reversals as a historical force. This is most prominently expressed in *A Vision* through the concepts of alternating gyres and of primary and antithetical. For Yeats, science happens by means of sudden breakthroughs, like the annunciations he associates with historical change. As he put it in the second edition of *A Vision*,

> What if Christ and Oedipus or, to shift the names, Saint Catherine of Genoa and Michael Angelo, are the two scales of a balance, the two butt-ends of a seesaw? What if every two thousand and odd years something happens in the world to make one sacred, the other secular; one wise, the other foolish; one fair, the other foul; one divine, the other devilish?'[28]

Awareness of the misuse of entropy in the 1890s left Yeats sensitive to fashions in science and hopeful that currently discredited branches of science, such as the occultism which he was invested in throughout his life, might be vindicated, just as older forms of science could be discredited by newer work.

[26] Max Nordau, *Degeneration* (New York: D. Appleton & Co., 1895), 2.
[27] H. G. Wells, *The Time Machine* (New York: 1931), ix–x.
[28] *AVB*, 21–2.

YEATS AFTER EINSTEIN

The final revolution to affect Yeats's poetic world view, the Einsteinian one, with its ramifications in both the small scale (via quantum theory) and the vast macrocosmic world of the whole cosmos (via relativity theory) would contribute to a radical undermining of the imperial tradition of Newtonian science in which Yeats had had his early education and which he had resisted in his writing ever since. As we see from Yeats's letters about relativity to T. Sturge Moore, although they disagreed on many philosophical issues, both men felt that Einstein's theory had disproved, rather than nuanced, the Newtonian world view.[29] From the vindication of Einstein's general relativity by Eddington's eclipse expeditions in 1919, which occurred during Yeats's automatic writing project with George Yeats from 1917 onwards, Yeats would be more in harmony with mainstream science than he had been since boyhood. Indeed, though Yeats did occasionally express sympathy with Wyndham Lewis's critique of Einstein in *Time and Western Man*, he was generally far more receptive to the new physics than other reactionary modernists. Further, as I previously described, Yeats had already experienced a battle between his father's predominantly English scientific world view and the path towards the Irish Revival offered by his mother's roots, which promised a deeper knowledge of the West of Ireland.

As critics such Garrigan Mattar have described, English science had frequently been used to 'other' Irish people and to exclude them from a technological modernity. Yeats's conflicted relationship with science is thus latently anti-imperial. The more outward-looking, global European science of Einstein and Heisenberg, which also found a place for non-Western attitudes, was bound to be far more appealing to him. Indeed, Einstein's and Heisenberg's relaxed approach to the intersection of spiritual, scientific, and artistic creativity had been influenced by visits to India and meetings with Yeats's colleague Rabindranath Tagore. Tagore first met Einstein in 1926 and they exchanged visits at least four times in 1930, while he also exchanged ideas with Heisenberg in 1929.[30] Further, aside from this engagement with Eastern thought, as initially explored by Peter J. Bowler, a further set of scientific popularizations of relativity, associated most prominently with

---

[29] Katherine Ebury, '"A new science": Yeats's *A Vision* and relativistic cosmology', *Irish Studies Review*, 22:2 (2014): 167–83.

[30] In *Uncommon Wisdom*, Fritjof Capra summarizes what Heisenberg and Tagore discussed, based on his own conversation with the scientist: 'In 1929 Heisenberg spent some time in India as the guest of the celebrated Indian poet Rabindranath Tagore, with whom he had long conversations about science and Indian philosophy. This introduction to Indian thought brought Heisenberg great comfort, he told me. He began to see that the recognition of relativity, interconnectedness, and impermanence as fundamental aspects of physical reality, which had been so difficult for himself and his fellow physicists, was the very basis of the Indian spiritual traditions. "After these conversations with Tagore," he said, "some of the ideas that had seemed so crazy suddenly made much more sense. That was a great help for me."' (*Uncommon Wisdom: Conversations with Remarkable People*, (London: Flamingo, 1987), 43)

Eddington and James Jeans, would also use Einstein's theories to support a renovated branch of Christian philosophy which Bowler calls 'new idealism'.[31]

In this context we should remember that Yeats explained the first edition of *A Vision* via an Eastern origin myth of Giraldus and the Judwalis, a fiction which he added to obscure George's participation. In this story, Yeats created Giraldus as a fictional polymath, who, as Neil Mann suggests, is partially based on Giordano Bruno, and who influences the thought of Yeats's earlier creation, Michael Robartes, via a book called *Speculum Angelorum et Hominum*. Robartes's investigations of the book's insights eventually lead him to an Arab tribe, the Judwalis, who draw diagrams on the desert reflecting Yeats's gyres, and who follow the philosophy of the real historical scientist, philosopher, and translator Kusta ben Luka, whom Yeats also writes about in 'The Gift of Harun Al-Rashid'. This origin myth of Yeats's philosophical and scientific system ultimately fits with concepts of the new physics as non-Western, utilized by both those supportive of and hostile to Einstein's perspective. For example, in *Time and Western Man*, Lewis rejects relativity through an emphasis on its foreignness and with reference to Einstein's Jewish background, while, as we have seen, scientists of the new physics were receptive to Eastern religions and proud of the similarities between their modern science and older modes of thought.

Alongside this mainstream of quite rigorous popularizations of the new physics via concepts from non-materialist—and often non-Western—spiritual traditions and writings, there was also a more idiosyncratic attempt to 'prove' the truth of occult beliefs through concepts borrowed from the new physics which Yeats sometimes participated in himself.[32] After Einstein's general relativity was supported by several sets of experimental proofs in the late 1910s and early 1920s, Yeats was keen to use relativity as support for his own poetic cosmology: for example, his friend Oliver St John Gogarty noted in his diary Yeats's description of the first edition of *A Vision* as 'a mixture of Einstein and myth' and that he believed that Einstein's curved universe proved his concept of gyres.[33] In poetry such as 'Meditations in Time of Civil War', Yeats rejects 'mechanical shapes' for his poetic world-building, while in 'Chosen' from *A Woman Young and Old* (composed in 1926–7 soon after the first edition of *A Vision*, but not published until *The Winding Stair* in 1929), Yeats expresses the inspirational power of Einsteinian curved geometry in relation to both astronomy and astrology. For the female speaker of the poem, 'The Zodiac is changed into a sphere' in a moment of sexual and epistemological annunciation:

> The lot of love is chosen. I learnt that much
> Struggling for an image on the track

---

[31] Peter J. Bowler, *Science for All: The Popularization of Science in Early Twentieth Century Britain* (Chicago and London: University of Chicago Press, 2009), 97.

[32] For example, a 1922 article, "Ghosts and the Scientist: The Aura Under Physical Tests", discusses a likely new age of paranormal research which would involve a new understanding of electromagnetism borrowed from the new physics (*The Manchester Guardian*, 26 October 1922, 4).

[33] *Life* 2, 280 n.106, 717.

Of the whirling Zodiac.

…

I struggled with the horror of daybreak,
I chose it for my lot! If questioned on
My utmost pleasure with a man
By some new-married bride, I take
That stillness for a theme
Where his heart my heart did seem
And both adrift on the miraculous stream
Where—wrote a learned astrologer—
The Zodiac is changed into a sphere.[34]

In a note to the poem, Yeats wrote that here he 'symbolised a woman's love as the struggle of the darkness to keep the sun from rising from its earthly bed. In the last stanza … I change the symbol to that of the soils of man and woman ascending through the Zodiac. In some Neoplatonist or Hermetist—whose name I forget—the whorl changes into a sphere at one of the points where the Milky Way crosses the Zodiac.'[35] After the popularization of the new physics, there is a renewed interest in occult light, especially starlight, in Yeats's poetry. This fits with the way that light is both problematized in quantum theory and held up as a standard of measurement in relativity theory. In poems from across the 1920s, celestial light combines astrological and astronomical properties in its visionary qualities, such as 'An Image from a Past Life' (1921), where 'elaborate starlight' reflected in a river shows up a warning ghost with 'starry eddies' in her hair;[36] 'The Tower' (1928), where the poet's imagination is governed by 'the day's declining beam' to conjure images from the past;[37] 'A Dialogue of Self and Soul' (1929), where this dialogue is structured partly by 'the breathless starlit air / … the star that marks the hidden pole.'[38] In short, after Einstein's revolution, stars become central to Yeats's poetry for the first time since *The Wind Among the Reeds*.

Beyond this sympathetic response to the new physics, it is also noteworthy that Yeats's most direct poetic responses to scientists he is broadly hostile to—including Newton in 'At Algeciras', as well as his invocations of John Locke in 'Fragments'—generally *post-date* the Einsteinian revolution. Yeats appears to have felt empowered to challenge traditional science by this new paradigm. In *The Tower* (1928), a collection of poems particularly influenced by relativity in its emphasis on the transformative power of light, Yeats includes 'Fragments', a two-part poem that confidently takes to task Locke's Enlightenment scientism by reconfiguring the biblical story of the origin of Eve in Adam's rib to suggest his philosophy gave birth to the Industrial Revolution: 'God took the spinning-jenny / Out of his side.' The first fragment has the confidence of a fable, or

---

[34] *CW1*, 272–3.
[35] Yeats, 'Author's Note to "Chosen"', *CW1*, 503 n.
[36] *CW1*, 178–9.
[37] *CW1*, 195.
[38] *CW1*, 234.

a piece of nonsense writing, but the second fragment locates the riposte to Locke within Yeats's automatic writing project with George and thus to the *Vision* project which was inspired both by this occult practice and by their shared scientific reading.

> Where got I that truth?
> Out of a medium's mouth.
> Out of nothing it came,
> Out of the forest loam,
> Out of dark night where lay
> The crowns of Nineveh.[39]

The specific reference to Nineveh in the second fragment places Yeats's rejection of a particular form of modernity within the framework of Eastern wisdom, but it is also likely occasioned by modern archaeological science, as new excavations were taking place at this famous site under Reginald Campbell Thompson from 1927 onwards.

In late poems, including 'The Statues' and 'News for the Delphic Oracle' (both 1939), Yeats reconsiders the value of science for art more broadly, moving a little beyond Einstein and the new physics after the publication of the second edition of *A Vision* in 1937. But this is not a critique of science, as it goes alongside Yeats's reassessment of his own emphasis on geometry throughout the 1920s and early 1930s. In this last phase, Yeats compares scientific and philosophical principles to the more disordered force of human passions in a way anticipated by his earlier poem 'Chosen'. Towards the very end of his life, Yeats's scientific epistemology is especially eroticized, and ideas often have a primary meaning in their connection to sexuality. In 'The Statues' Yeats expresses a complex dissatisfaction with, and desire for, the 'plummet-measured face' in a world in which Eastern thought ('Asiatic immensities', 'Buddha's emptiness') tends to dominate, in contrast to 'a filthy modern tide':

> Pythagoras planned it. Why did the people stare?
> His numbers, though they moved or seemed to move
> In marble or in bronze, lacked character.
> But boys and girls, pale from the imagined love
> Of solitary beds, knew what they were,
> That passion could bring character enough,
> And pressed at midnight in some public place
> Live lips upon a plummet-measured face.[40]

Similarly, in 'News for the Delphic Oracle' (1939), Pythagoras is even more sexualized; 'There sighed amid his choir of love / Tall Pythagoras', within a poem which famously ends with an explosion of sexual energy, as 'nymphs and satyrs / Copulate in the foam'.[41]

---

[39] *CW1*, 214.
[40] *CW1*, 336.
[41] *CW1*, 338.

In these two poems, Pythagoras, perhaps because located in the ancient world, becomes a hybrid, neutral figure of the artist and the scientist who bridges the Two Cultures within a strange economy of knowing and desiring.

In fact, what we have perhaps missed so far in studying Yeats is how his approach to science fits into a historical context in which the cosmos was 'remagicalized' by the Einsteinian revolution to lend support to an occult world view, in direct contrast with Richards's view that the most important ramification of modern science was 'the transference from Magical View of the world to the scientific'.[42] Richard's belief that this was true explains his resistance to Yeats's work but also marks Richard's own understanding of science as fundamentally dated. During Yeats's great poetic and philosophical flowering in the 1920s and 1930s, there was a strong intellectual fashion for exploring connections between magic and science in books such as Lewis Wallace's *Cosmic Anatomy* (1921), while the eight volumes of Lynn Thorndike's *A History of Magic and Experimental Science* project began appearing from 1923. Yeats was influenced by this fashion and participated in it—he had copies of the first two volumes of the Thorndike work in his personal library.[43]

While the radical potential of Yeats's combination of Eastern and occult philosophy with the new physics had previously been neglected in literary studies, aspects of it were kept alive by a specific strain of popular science exemplified initially by the pioneers of the new physics themselves, such as Einstein's *Cosmic Religion* (1931) and Werner Heisenberg's *Physics and Philosophy* (1958), which reflected their engagement with Eastern mysticism, and developed by 'New Age' scientific publications including Fritjof Capra's *The Tao of Physics* (1975) and Gary Zukav's *The Dancing Wu Li Masters* (1979). This intellectual movement had previously been anticipated by a sceptical Bertrand Russell in a 1926 article, where he nonetheless accepted that concepts from relativity 'may hereafter be utilized in India to make a bridge between religion and science'.[44] In sum, Yeats's engagement with the scientific revolution of the new physics—as magical, as idealist, as non-Western—is in many ways in harmony with the scientific culture in the period and beyond, especially with a print culture of popularization. This goes far beyond the limited views of both art and science expressed in the different 'Two Cultures' debates, between Huxley and Arnold in the 1880s and Snow and Leavis in the 1960s, which determined the terms of critical debate during the twentieth century. As an undergraduate student, I was taught that Yeats's world view was 'silly', in the words of W. H. Auden, but twenty-first-century critical resources and methods can prepare a new generation of students to engage more productively with his unique creative appropriation of science.[45]

---

[42] For the 'remagicalized' cosmos, see John Bramble, *Modernism and the Occult* (Houndsmills: Palgrave Macmillan, 2015), 97. Richards, *Science and Poetry*, 50

[43] Edward O'Shea, *A Descriptive Catalogue of W. B. Yeats's Library* (New York: Garland, 1985), 284.

[44] Bertrand Russell, 'Relativity in Dialogue Form', *The Observer*, 17 January 1926, 5.

[45] W. H. Auden, 'In Memory of W. B. Yeats' (1940), in *Collected Poems*, ed. Edward Mendelson (New York: Vintage, 1991), 227–28, 245–7.

CHAPTER 24

··

PLANETS

··

CÓILÍN PARSONS

W. B. and George Yeats paid a visit in 1929 to childhood friends and neighbours in Sligo: the Coopers, who lived in Markree Castle. When the Yeatses visited, the castle was in the hands of Bryan Cooper, first a Unionist MP (and the youngest MP ever to lose his seat, at 26), then a TD in Dáil Éireann after independence, and a sometime playwright for the Abbey Theatre. Bryan Cooper's son, Peter, remembers the visit as having been 'a great nuisance'. Yeats, Cooper remembers, 'was deposited by his long-suffering wife, with instructions not to let him go out in the wet grass in his slippers, and she then disappeared off to Galway with the children'. Yeats appears to have attempted (unsuccessfully) to endear himself to Mrs Cooper by writing a poem and reading it to her. She was also unmoved by his declaration that in coming to Markree he had 'realized the ambition of my life . . . as we have always looked on the Coopers and Markree Castle as greater than the Royal Family and Buckingham Palace'.[1]

Any reader of Yeats will recognize the characteristic blend of bragging, humility, and hyperbole in this comparison of Markree to Buckingham Palace, but in one sense Yeats was not entirely off track: for a time in the nineteenth century, Markree could boast of great standing in the world. The prevailing dreadful weather notwithstanding, Markree was the site of an astronomical and solar observatory recognized by the Royal Astronomical Society as 'undoubtedly the most richly furnished private observatory known'.[2] Edward Joshua Cooper, who inherited the estate in 1830, built a refractor telescope (one with glass lenses through which the observer looked, rather than a mirror) with a 13.3-inch lens, bought from Cauchoix of Paris. It was, for a few years, the largest refractor lens in the world, and in 1845 it was joined in Ireland by the Earl of Rosse's

---

[1] The scene is described in *Life 2*, 390.

[2] 'Report of the Council to the Thirty-first Annual General Meeting', *Monthly Notices of the Royal Astronomical Society*, 11:4 (1851), 104–5. Markree has another, more indirect, claim on Yeats lore—the original name of the estate is Mercury, and the planet Mercury has had, since 1975, a crater on it named after W. B. Yeats. For details of the original name see the Landed Estate Registry website of the National University of Ireland, Galway, https://landedestates.ie/property/141 (accessed 31 Jan. 2020).

Leviathan, the largest reflecting telescope in the world for decades. The Markree lens was in constant use (although to little scientific advantage) until 1902, when the observatory fell into disuse and the lens and its telescope were sold to a Jesuit seminary in Hong Kong. There they were damaged by bombing in 1941, and sold in 1947 to Manila Observatory, in the Philippines, where they remained in use at least until the late 1980s.[3]

The Markree lens was the most sophisticated technology available in the 1830s, but it was set upon a rickety wooden mount, which made accurate observation difficult. Thomas Romney Robinson, director of the Armagh Observatory, suggested that Cooper have a more substantial mount made by an instrument maker in Dublin, Thomas Grubb.[4] This was Grubb's first astronomical commission, and he used it to prove his capacity, allowing him to win ever larger contracts. Grubb and his son Howard would go on to become one of the best-known telescope makers in the world, sending their lenses, tubes, and mounts to Wellington, Melbourne, Kolkata, Hyderabad, Johannesburg, Cape Town, Vienna, London, and many more cities besides. One of the Grubb company's lenses was used by Arthur Eddington to perform the first experimental test of the theory of general relativity, during which Eddington proved that gravitational fields can cause warps in space-time.

In this meandering and expanding story—of Yeats and his regard for Markree and its connection to the often forgotten primacy of Irish scientists in astronomical research in the nineteenth century—lie the poles of the argument in the pages that are to follow: an admiration for aristocracy, a geography that spans our own planet and others, and a fascination for astronomy and astrology. This chapter looks forward from Yeats to the discourse of planetarity that has swept through certain corners of literary and cultural criticism in the twenty-first century, from environmental humanities to postcolonial studies and beyond. In doing so, it wagers that we have something to learn from Yeats, given his lifelong interest in trying to figure the size and shape of our imagined and material universe, about how we have imagined the planet since the beginning of the twentieth century. Our current-day planet-thinking might be given depth and definition by asking how it is that we came to know about our planet as it passed clearly into view in the early part of the twentieth century. In other words, this chapter asks what planetary thinking looks like when glimpsed squarely through the lens of what we now know as modernism. As Edwin Hubble proved definitively in 1924 that the Milky Way is just a galaxy among galaxies (as Kant had surmised), and as measurements during the opposition of the asteroid Eros in 1931 finally confirmed the size of our own solar system, how did we make sense of these revelations about the shape of our universe?

Yeats doesn't have the answer to these questions, but he is invested in thinking through the philosophical, spiritual, and political implications of thinking about and with the

---

[3] These details are drawn from a brief description of the history of Markree Observatory in Michael Hoskin, 'Archives of the Dunsink and Markree Observatories', *Journal for the History of Astronomy*, xiii (1982), 149–50. See also http://www.europa.com/~telscope/tsfrance.txt (accessed 31 Jan. 2020).

[4] On the history and output of the Grubb company, see Ian S. Glass, *Victorian Telescope Makers: The Lives and Letters of Thomas and Howard Grubb* (Bristol: Institute of Physics, 1997).

planet and the stars. As Katherine Ebury points out, Yeats had a lifelong interest in the stars, but their appearance in his work ebbs and flows throughout his career. They are, Ebury writes, 'key images' in the early work, all but disappear in Yeats's middle phase, and 're-emerge as part of the spectacular late-flowering associated with the *Vision* project'.[5] In this late phase, Yeats's interest turns to post-Einsteinian thinking about space and time, and 'much of the curved mystic geometry of *A Vision* and the poetry that it inspired seems sourced in the non-Euclidian geometry which under-pinned relativity theory'.[6] There is no doubt that Yeats was as interested as anyone else in this period (think Hardy, Woolf, Joyce, and more) in a science that was making breathless headlines.

But Yeats's astronomical interests were not limited to following the fashions of scientific research. His are derived from but not dependent on the new science, which is how he can stand for a new philosophical approach to the planet in the early decades of the twentieth century, one that runs from an emergent pattern of environmental thinking to a fully developed system for thinking about history and the future at the scale of the planet that we see in *A Vision*. Wrapped up in all of this is an idiosyncrasy that is all Yeats's own, with occult and esoteric origins, and shot through with a planetary consciousness. If Yeats can be thought of as a theorist of planets and stars, they are certainly 'dishevelled wandering stars'—chaotic, of no fixed meaning, yielding no easy insight.[7] They cohere in that they point to an attempt, even if incomplete, to imagine a new world from the ruins of our own.

* * *

To think about the first of the various ideas of the planet that exercised Yeats's mind—the planet in the environmental sense, as a home towards which humans have a duty of care—we could look at 'The Lake Isle of Innisfree', which trades in many of the generic expectations of the Romantic nature poem. This, indeed, is what makes the poem so satisfying. 'The Lake Isle' is not only very clearly about a fantasy of living in and with nature, where evening is 'full of the linnet's wings', but also deeply local—it partakes of an ethics of dwelling that any reader would recognize as a feature of nature poetry. Its nostalgic memory of nature from the 'pavements grey' of London, of the country from the city, also locates it as the latest in a long line, from Virgil to Wordsworth and on.[8] But its relationship to the particulars of place are complicated. Jahan Ramazani, remarking on the geographical extension of the poem, from Walden Pond to Fleet Street in London, writes that 'it can be difficult to keep a poem fastened exclusively to one place; even as it evokes a single site, it darts in multiple directions. As any one poem is enmeshed with

---

[5] Katherine Ebury, *Modernism and Cosmology: Absurd Lights* (Basingstoke: Palgrave Macmillan, 2014), 54. See also Katherine Ebury, '"A New Science": Yeats's *A Vision* and Relativistic Cosmology', *Irish Studies Review*, 22:2 (2014): 167–83; and Aoife Lynch, 'The Black Swan: Yeats and the Science of the Unknown', *Irish University Review* 47:2 (2017), 350–9.

[6] Ebury, *Modernism and Cosmology*, 43.

[7] *CW1*, 43.

[8] *CW1*, 39.

other poems, and as any one place is bound up with other places, the combination of the two ... multiplies entanglements with numerous unseen places elsewhere.'[9] In short, the locality on which the poem seems to stake its claim is unsettled. In addition, the lake isle is so romanticized as to be difficult to take seriously as a description of the material reality of an island in Lough Gill, and the real may have been far from Yeats's mind when he was composing the poem—in 'Reveries over Childhood and Youth' he writes that he could not remember whether he had chosen to write about the island because of its beauty or because of an affecting story of doomed lovers attached to it.[10] Many years later the unreality of the place became even clearer, as it was in danger (according to Lily Yeats) of becoming both a shrine to Yeats and a tourist attraction of questionable taste. Lily wrote to W.B. in 1938 to tell him that the Land Commission was taking over the estate around Innisfree, and soon, she joked, 'there will be put up notices - this way to the Bee Glade ... and interfering with the bee will be severely dealt with ... The beans must not be eaten. They are the property of the Land Commission.'[11] The poem is built on a sense of the particularity of the local and a desire for an escape into nature, but its commitment to either of those aspects is not in any way indisputable. The geography of the lake isle is both larger and more material than Yeats would have the reader believe.

But, for all that, the poem's commitment to planetary and environmental ethics might actually be strengthened. There is no necessary connection between an attachment to place and an environmental outlook. As Pat Sheeran argued in the early days of ecocritical work in Irish letters, in Ireland there was 'a paradox to be faced: a professed— and sincere—allegiance to places together with an actual, almost total inability to care or cope with them.'[12] The Irish, Sheeran implies, doth protest too much, singing the praises of the local without making meaningful efforts to protect those landscapes and habitats that are so well documented in the topographical tradition. Though much has changed in the area of environmental protection and ecocriticism since Sheeran wrote his withering critique in the late 1980s, his disaggregation of place-based thinking and environmental ethics still holds. Now more than ever, in fact, the scale of environmental thinking appears to be shifting from the local to the planetary, as Ursula Heise argues in her book *Sense of Place and Sense of Planet*. Heise recognizes and questions the environmental movement's 'investment in a particular kind of "situated knowledge", the intimate acquaintance with local nature and history that develops with sustained interest in one's immediate surroundings.'[13] It is often fed by a phenomenological outlook, or by a Heideggerian investment in dwelling and habitation, associating 'spatial closeness, cognitive understanding, emotional attachment, and an ethic of responsibility and

---

[9] Jahan Ramazani, 'The Local Poem in a Global Age', *Critical Inquiry*, 43:3 (2017), 677.

[10] *CW3*, 85.

[11] Quoted in Patrick Sheeran, 'The Narrative Creation of Place', in Timothy Collins, ed., *Decoding the Landscape: Contributions Towards a Synthesis of Thinking in Irish Studies on the Landscape* (Galway: University College Galway Centre for Landscape Studies, 2003), 152.

[12] Patrick Sheeran, '*Genius Fabulae*: The Irish Sense of Place', *Irish University Review*, 18:2 (1988), 194.

[13] Ursula K. Heise, *Sense of Place and Sense of Planet: The Environmental Imagination of the Global* (Oxford: Oxford University Press, 2008), 30

"care".'. The problem with this position is that it assumes that 'engagements with intimately known local places can be recuperated intact from the distortions of modernization'.[14] If there is any poem that plays knowingly on that fantasy and its impossibility, it is 'The Lake Isle', with its rootedness in the 'roadway' and the 'pavements grey'. Like any good pastoral, its composition and its desires are intertwined with the city and its promise of modernity.

Heise's invocation of the planet is an invitation for the environmentalist to exceed the narrow bounds of place-based thinking with which 'The Lake Isle' flirts; and on this reading the poem falls short of the demands of a new environmentalism. If we look elsewhere, though, in the later work, we find Yeats working with significantly larger scales, reaching astronomical heights in the attempt to imagine a vastly different future rather than simply enlarging the scale of his attention. In doing so, Yeats turns from a planet that is within his grasp (even if slipping away) to one that exists on the plane of imagination and on the horizon of a new world.

This planet foreshadows the work of Gayatri Chakravorty Spivak, for whom planetary consciousness is a profoundly political condition, an alternative way to conjure an entire world system while also attempting to think beyond it and to resist the siren call of globalization, which has been our most effective and devastating form of world-making. For Spivak, planetarity opposes the global scale of environmental thinking, whose planetary scale leads only to an 'alternate description of the globe, susceptible to nation-state geopolitics'. New modes of thinking cannot simply be old ones made bigger. Indeed, planetarity is 'a word set apart from notions of . . . the earth, the world, the globe, globalization, and the like in their common usage', more a thought experiment than an ontological description of a world.[15] Grasping this new planetarity is not an easy prospect, and the language in which Spivak expresses it is itself resistant:

> I propose the planet to overwrite the globe. Globalization is the imposition of the same system of exchange everywhere. In the gridwork of electronic capital, we achieve that abstract ball covered in latitudes and longitudes, cut by virtual lines, once the equator and the tropics and so on . . . The globe is on our computers. No one lives there. It allows us to think we can aim to control it. The planet is in the species of alterity, belonging to another system; and yet we inhabit it, on loan.[16]

To be a planetary thinker, in Spivak's proposition, is to attempt to imagine an entirely alternative world, from a position of impossibility and an awareness of the necessary failure of the project. And, importantly, this imagination must be suffused with the understanding that, 'if we imagine ourselves as planetary subjects rather than global agents … alterity remains underived from us, it is not our dialectical negation, it contains us as much as it flings us away'.[17]

---

[14] Heise, *Sense of Place*, 33, 54
[15] Gayatri Chakravorty Spivak, 'Planetarity', *Paraphrase*, 38:2 (2015), 290–1.
[16] Gayatri Chakravorty Spivak, *Death of a Discipline* (New York: Columbia University Press, 2003), 72.
[17] Ibid., 73.

The word and the idea of planetarity are figured as untranslatable, not in any ordinary sense of the term, but in a philosophical account of the impossible: 'we must persistently educate ourselves into the peculiar mindset of accepting the untranslatable, even as we are programmed to transgress that mindset by "translating" it into the mode of "acceptance"'.[18] We must, in a sense, imagine a future that is not derived from the present, and think, as Spivak insists, 'for a future reader'.[19] The term that Spivak borrows from Derrida to describe this speculative futurity is 'teleopoiesis'—creating with aspiration, with a sense of the future to come. Derrida writes that 'the teleopoiesis we are speaking of is a messianic structure ... We are not yet among those philosophers of the future, we who are calling them and calling them the philosophers of the future, but we are in advance their friends'.[20]

All of this is, I should say (and contra Yeats), deeply utopian, inspired by the Marxist tradition. But, along with Yeats, it draws from an occult and difficult vocabulary to figure a new planet and imagine alternatives to the world we live in. Imagining our shared planetary future happens at the limit of our thinking, at the point at which the world we see and feel we know is no longer adequate to the future. The desire to call out to the future, to try to imagine its shape, even with no clear evidence, is not what we see in a poem like 'To Ireland in the Coming Times', despite the name—that poem's turn to 'Davis, Mangan, Ferguson' as lodestars of the future, along with its explicit concerns for nation building and for reputation building, mean that the future horizon of the poem is patterned entirely on a reconstituted past.[21] Although, as Matthew Campbell argues, the perpetually rewritten poem is 'in temporal and textual motion across at least thirty-two years', its future thinking is not yet teleopoietic—for that, we have to turn to Yeats's later writings.[22]

* * *

We have shifted rapidly from the bee-loud glade to planetary consciousness, and it is time to bring it back down to earth. At its core, whether explicitly environmental or politically utopian, planet-thinking involves the radical decentring of the human or the individual as the agent of history, whether natural or collective. It is an attempt to think about distance and difference from a position of humility, a position defined above all by a sense of the impossibility and yet the imperative of action. Yeats, I want to say, strives towards a planetary consciousness, and it is expressed in a project more maligned than read—*A Vision*, his systemic magnum opus from 1925, revised and expanded over many years, and reissued in a substantially different version in 1937. In this chapter I will concentrate on the 1925 version, not because the 1937 one is less important, but because the overall structure and shape of the system in its 1925 iteration maps out the cosmology

---

[18] Spivak, 'Planetarity', 292.
[19] Spivak, *Death of a Discipline*, 93.
[20] Spivak, *Death of a Discipline*, 31.
[21] *CW1*, 50.
[22] Matthew Campbell, 'Yeats in the Coming Times', *Essays in Criticism*, 53:1 (2003), 16.

that Yeats heavily reworked for the later edition. Begun in 1917, just after Yeats's marriage to George Hyde-Lees and the revelation of automatic writing, *A Vision* occupied almost twenty years of the Yeatses' life. Not expecting much of an audience for the book, Yeats agreed to a print run of just 600. This was a prescient move.

One of *A Vision*'s greatest interpreters, Margaret Mills Harper, calls it 'part cosmology, part apocalypse, part psychoanalysis, part poetry, and part confusion'. It is, she continues admiringly, 'full of wildly a-priori assumptions, unproven assertions, gross generalizations, and ahistorical pronouncements about grand narratives of history and the human condition'.[23] To this confusing cocktail of attributes, Katherine Ebury adds a series of disciplines in which *A Vision* dabbles: 'astrology, occult philosophy, theory of history and poetic symbology'.[24] In short, it is a tangled web of all of George and W.B.'s preoccupations, one piled on top of the other, and each in some way competing with the next. In this lie both its genius and its opacity. Undergirding this complex, moving system is not just an occult fantasy (though that is there) but a radical political vision built on the shape of an idea that allows us to think beyond human time and human scales. It is an experiment in what Michael Wood calls 'the time that mattered most to the poet for much of his life: the long, "sidereal" time of his metaphysical system, of his scheme of other worlds and other lives, the effect of his patient quest for conversations with the dead'.[25] *A Vision* turns to astronomical time and planetary scales to outline a world profoundly decentred from the here, the now, the visible, and the material.

In very broad outline, *A Vision* comprises four books, with ancillary materials in both the 1925 and 1937 versions. The first book, 'What the Caliph Learned', lays out the initial story of the emergence of the system, which we learn from a dialogue between Owen Ahearne and Michael Robartes. Here we see the explication of the Great Wheel, a system of division of not just historical times but human types into the twenty-eight Phases of the Moon, loosely based on the ancient Arabic Mansions of the Moon. Book 2, 'What the Caliph refuses to learn', lays out a complex and somewhat tedious geometry of gyres. The final book, 'The Gates of Pluto', traces the stages of existence, between birth and death. The third book is the one given most attention, as it sketches out Yeats's philosophy of history, based on 2,150-year cycles, more or less, each one of them one-twelfth of a Great Year (every 26,000 years), or the astronomical point at which the planets reset themselves in relation to each other—what is called the precession of equinoxes.[26] Each 2,150-year cycle is an era, divided roughly into two 1,050-year cycles, or civilizations. Cycles are either primary/objective (democratic) or antithetical/subjective (corresponding to autocracy). The antithetical cycle of the Greeks, for example,

---

[23] Margaret Mills Harper, 'Yeats and the Occult', in Marjorie Howes and John Kelly, eds., *The Cambridge Companion to W. B. Yeats* (Cambridge: Cambridge University Press, 2006), 160.

[24] Ebury, *Modernism and Cosmology*, 42.

[25] Michael Wood, *Yeats and Violence* (Oxford: Oxford University Press, 2010), 48–9.

[26] On the genealogy of Yeats's interest in the concept of the Great Year, see Matthew Gibson, 'Yeats, the Great Year, and Pierre Duhem', in Matthew Gibson and Neil Mann, eds., *Yeats, Philosophy, and the Occult* (Clemson, SC: Clemson University Press, 2016), 171–223.

was followed by the primary Christian era, which will be followed by its own antithetical and autocratic era, which Yeats appears at times eagerly to await. Each cycle is divided into twenty-eight phases, no matter the length of the cycle—so each moment occurs at a different phase in various cycles.

It is easy to get lost in the minutiae and lose a sense of the whole, so here I want to emphasize the integrity of *A Vision* as a system—as a description of a world that works on a vast scale that precedes and will outlive the mere four score years of humankind. Here is how Yeats's dedication to the 1925 version explains the system:

> I had a practical object. I wished for a system of thought that would leave my imagination free to create as it chose and yet makes all that it created, or could create, part of the one history, and that the soul's. The Greeks certainly had such a system, and Dante ... and I think no man since. Then when I had ceased all active search, yet had not ceased from desire, the documents upon which this book is founded were put into my hands, and I had what I needed, though it may be too late. What have found indeed is nothing new, for I will show presently that Swedenborg and Blake and many before them knew that all things had their gyres; but Swedenborg and Blake preferred to explain them figuratively, and so I am the first to substitute for Biblical or mythological figures, historical movements and actual men and women.[27]

Yeats translates the mythological into the historical, but doesn't do away with the totalizing vision of myth. Although *A Vision* has long been derided as occultist or spiritualist mumbo jumbo, Elizabeth Butler Cullingford argues that it is 'essentially poetic in conception, [and it] shares ... acute sensitivity towards the forces which have created and are creating contemporary history ... *A Vision* is Yeats's attempt to understand the calamitous events of that time, and also to predict the future.'[28] Its esoteric provenance has, on the whole, occluded its status as a work in the philosophy of history, an area in which it carves out a niche for large-scale cycles across space and time. It is a masterpiece of synthetic history and, as Daniel Albright claims, not 'ancillary' to modernist literature, but an important part of modernism's achievement.[29]

These recognitions of *A Vision*'s place as not just a storehouse of images to be plundered by the poet and his readers but a deeply imaginative text in its own right ask us to approach it not necessarily for its rather impacted and contradictory content but for its vast ambition and form—its sweep across millennia that is both deeply (because necessarily) impersonal and profoundly intimate given its provenance in the marriage bed of the Yeatses. It oscillates between the private knowledge of its producers and the great public scales of history it proclaims. Yeats might not appreciate the comparison to such a prominent figure in popular fiction, but *A Vision* dashes through epochs in a way

---

[27] *CW13*, liv–lv.
[28] Elizabeth Butler Cullingford, *Yeats, Ireland, and Fascism* (Basingstoke: Palgrave Macmillan, 1981), 121.
[29] Daniel Albright, *Quantum Poetics: Yeats, Pound, Eliot, and the Science of Modernism* (Cambridge: Cambridge University Press, 1997), 5.

that H. G. Wells, for example, does in his monumental *The Outline of History* (1920). The effect can be dizzying:

> After Plato and Aristotle, the mind is as exhausted as were the armies of Alexander at his death, but the Stoics can discover morals and turn philosophy into a rule of life. Among them doubtless ... we may discover the first benefactors of our modern individuality.[30]

The swift and seamless transitions from phase to phase in Yeats's writing, though their engine is historical strife, makes for a planet on which all phases exist at once, nascent or dormant, echoing and shadowing each other, even if occluded in everyday life. The effect can also be, as Katherine Ebury points out, both chaotic and absurd, a combination produced when the scale of the planets encounters the scale of the human.[31] As rigid as the system might seem at times, driven by the relentless movement of the planets, it also careens here and there, teetering between order and chaos.

This is part of a whole series of ways in which the individual, the here, and the now are suspended between other voices and places. Decentring the author is an unusual move in Yeats, but, as Mills Harper writes, Yeats discovered that 'the relationship between writer and text that is authorship is more than usually unstable in this book'.[32] Its genesis in automatic writing, and as collaboration between George and W.B., mitigate any sense of the individual genius of the poet-creator. The poet as generator of meaning has been displaced, not just by his wife's virtuosity, but by a whole host of mediums and controls—of voices from before, beyond, and around human life. Yeats had, of course, long been working on this form of distanced creation, and perhaps his most famous 'Daimon', or spirit, was the one most perfectly expressive of the geographical and temporal extension of this entire system—Leo Africanus. Africanus was a geographer of Africa from the fifteenth century who was Andalusian, of Berber extraction, with whom W.B. began communicating in 1914, and who brought Yeats the doctrine of split self that would be so key to the delicate balances of primary and antithetical that structure *A Vision*.[33]

The point is not just that *A Vision* is a vast system—there are many of those—but that it is predicated on a whole series of decentrings, diffusing agency and subjectivity across time and space. Its very mechanism focuses on the contradiction or competition between (but not negation of) the self and the anti-self. It decouples human history from progress, offering an alternative that is both liberating and somewhat terrifying. And it reaches, at its very best, towards an expansive and inclusive geography, binding together

---

[30] *CW13*, 153

[31] Katherine Ebury, *Modernism and Cosmology: Absurd Lights* (Basingstoke: Palgrave Macmillan, 2014), 41.

[32] *CW13*, xxiii.

[33] For a thorough discussion of Leo Africanus as historical and mythologized figure, see Nathan Suhr-Sytsma's 'Africa', Chapter 21 in this volume.

disparate times and places. For all its vastness, however, it never becomes entirely untethered from the human; the human eye is always the focalizing force. In this way we could think about this as limited planetary horizon—it grasps towards a vision of the planet on which we live as wholly part of an external astronomical system, yet pulls back again and again to the scale of the human actor through which this system exerts itself. The timescales teeter between the four score years of human life and the millennia and millions of years of sidereal time. While Yeats attempts to think these scales together, he doesn't quite manage to bring their absurd difference into balance.[34]

* * *

Unusually for Yeats, and with great difficulty, he tried to move at the end of Book III and in some other places from a description of the past to an imagination of the future. Yeats had a gift for anticipating a distant apocalyptic future in his poetry (think only of 'The Second Coming' or 'Nineteen Hundred and Nineteen'), but here he attempts to rein in his penchant for the end of days.[35] Yet the future we see in *A Vision* is a future that is marked not by a detailed population of its contours but by its unknowability—not in the ordinary sense that we cannot know the future, but in the sense that we will know the future only by its unknowability. At the end of Book IV, Yeats admits the difficulty of the task, writing that 'Much of this book is abstract, because it has not yet been lived'.[36] The phrase may seem offhand or a little too glib, but the fact caused Yeats some anguish. In a long passage that appears in the manuscript and typescript, but not the final printed version of the 1925 edition, he gives us a hint of the difficulty of the problem:

> Hitherto I have described the past or but the near future, but now I must plunge beyond the reach of the senses . . . Though I think that I too can describe the mind of the future, I must, if I am not to make the description so abstract that it is unintelligible, imagine circumstance [*sic*] which will be at least as unlike the future as the water clock [of Alexandria] is unlike my watch.[37]

Characteristically obtuse in its phrasing, this observation brings us back to Spivak's description of planetarity as reaching towards a future horizon that is, properly speaking, unavailable to us and which we must yet imagine. Yeats's analogy compares his watch

---

[34] For a discussion of these competing and overlapping timescales, and the challenges to historians of thinking them together, see Dipesh Chakrabarty, 'The Planet: An Emergent Humanist Category', *Critical Inquiry*, 46 (2019): 1–31. Chakrabarty claims that a truly planetary historicity emerges along Earth System Science in the 1960s and 1970s, but we can see glimmers of it in Yeats's work as he grapples with overlapping and competing timescales in *A Vision*.

[35] Malcolm Sen has argued that we might rather read 'Nineteen Hundred and Nineteen' as a proleptic description of our current world of anthropogenic climate change rather than some vaguely imagined distant future. Malcolm Sen, '"Dragon-Ridden" Days: Yeats, Apocalypse, and the Anthropocene', *International Yeats Studies*, 4:1 (2020), 111–24. See also Justin Quinn, 'W.B. Yeats and the End of the World', *International Yeats Studies*, 4:1 (2020), 59–72.

[36] *CW13*, 206.

[37] *CW13*, 317.

and the clock of Alexandria, but we could also turn to the challenge of contemporary planetary scientists in their search for life on other planets—they must find ways to search for life forms that have never before been seen. As a result, when Yeats turns to prophesy, it can appear soupy and vague:

> I foresee a time when the majority of men will so accept an historical tradition that they will quarrel, not as to who can impose his personality upon others but as to who can best embody the common aim, when all personality will seem an impurity—'sentimentality', 'sullenness', 'egotism'—something that revolts not morals alone but good taste. There will be no longer great intellect for a ceaseless activity will be required of all; and where rights are swallowed up in duties, and solitude is difficult, creation except among avowedly archaistic and unpopular group will grow impossible.[38]

* * *

> But *A Vision* is, of course, a deeply problematic text on which to balance a claim that Yeats can be a model for planetary thinking. This is, in fact, what draws me to the very idea of reading him in this way. What links together Ursula Heise's ecocritical planet and Gayatri Spivak's politically utopian planet is a commitment to a radical, leftist politics; these are works whose desires are closer to the Occupy movement than Yeats will ever be. Yeats wrote in 1919, as he and George were working on *A Vision*, 'What I want is that Ireland be kept from giving itself ... to Marxian revolution or Marxian definitions of value in any form'. It was this fear, expressed in *A Vision*, that was the 'motive force' behind 'The Second Coming'.[39] It is at once a poem that declares its planetary scale but does not link that to a politics of advancement or radical change. In the same way, *A Vision* is a corrective to the progressive structure of the Hegelian dialectic.[40] The system is always moving but is cosmically at a standstill, repeating itself over and over again.

The result of this anti-progressivist impulse could easily be a tale of decline and decay— that would suit a particular environmentalist narrative as well as fascist imaginings of social decline in the 1920s and 1930s. Indeed, Nicholas Allen has carefully traced Yeats's delight in reading Oswald Spengler's *The Decline of the West*, an enabling text for a good deal of fascist thought in the 1920s and 1930s, and finding in it an historical system that closely mirrored *A Vision*. For Allen, Spengler and Yeats both are seeking new forms of authority in the aftermath of empire, and they both nod to autocratic rule, or what Spengler calls 'Caesarism'.[41] Picking up on this autocratic streak already in 1929, AE wrote of 'A Packet for Ezra Pound' (which forms a part of the 1937 *Vision*):

> The virtue of the soul is to be free, and Mr. Yeats' spirits condemn us all to a cyclic progression, which is like the judgment of a mad dictator willing it that men should

---

[38] *CW13*, 175.

[39] Cullingford, *Yeats, Ireland, and Fascism*, 117.

[40] Ibid, 122–3.

[41] Nicholas Allen, 'Yeats, Spengler, and *A Vision* after Empire', in Richard Begam and Michael Valdez Moses, eds., *Modernism and Colonialism* (Durham, NC: Duke University Press, 2007), 209–25.

be imprisoned in one cell after another in a great prison, from which there is no escape, and in the imprisonments there is no justice only a kind of destiny willed by a
divinity as indifferent as that Setebos brooded upon by Caliban.[42]

What AE points to here is what has long exercised critics of systemic thinking—the
question of determinism and, in this case, Viconian repetition. To what extent is Yeats's
system tolerant of either free will or historical change?

This was an area of some difficulty for Yeats himself as he was working on *A Vision*. As
Michael Wood points out, in 'Nineteen Hundred and Nineteen' (written in 1921) Yeats
writes that 'the Platonic Year / Whirls out new right and wrong, / Whirls in the old instead', suggesting that history is a circular, closed system.[43] There is at this early stage of
Yeats's development of *A Vision* a rigid determinism in his system, but by the time the
first version is published in 1925 the Platonic Year takes on a more flexible aspect as a
symbol that 'refutes randomness and asserts the enduring principle of order, or perhaps
simply the possibility of such a principle'.[44] This loosening of the rigidity of the system
is described in Yeats's own dedication in 1925, in which he writes of looking for 'a system
of thought that would leave my imagination free to create as it chose and yet makes all
that it created, or could create, part of the one history, and that the soul's'.[45] *A Vision* was
meant, Yeats wrote to Edmund Dulac, as 'a last act of defence against the chaos of the
world, & I hope for ten years to write out of my renewed security'.[46] In all of this con-
tortion over the question of determinism we see a tension in Yeats's thinking between a
system that acts as a 'mad dictator' (in AE's evocative formulation) and a loose enabler,
one that is very much formed in the mind of its author.

I only gesture to the problem here, but it is significant—at the heart of Yeats's generative, expansive, planetary system there is a deeply troubling drive to authoritarianism
and proto-fascism, which will erupt in *On the Boiler*. In this system too we will find a
profound historical violence that is delicately effaced in much of the poetry.[47] But it is
not the case that Yeats therefore cannot be a planetary thinker. We learn from Yeats that
there is nothing inherently radical about thinking at the scale of the planet, and we are
challenged to recalibrate the critical language of planetarity accordingly. It's not as if we
can suddenly say that we have moved beyond a certain politics by invoking planetary
consciousness—the notion, as Matthew Taylor puts it, that 'our ethics enlarge with our
sense of scale'.[48] What makes planetary consciousness possible, in a meaningful way, is

---

[42] AE [George Russell], 'A Packet for Ezra Pound', *The Irish Statesman*, 7 September 1929, 11–12,
https://yeatsvision.com/G553.html.

[43] *CW1*, 208.

[44] Michael Wood, *Yeats and Violence* (Oxford: Oxford University Press, 2010), 54.

[45] *CW13*, liv–lv.

[46] Quoted in Neil Mann, 'A Vision: Ideas of God and Man', in *Yeats Annual No. 8*
(Basingstoke: Macmillan, 1991), 158.

[47] Wood, *Yeats and Violence*, 57–8.

[48] Matthew A. Taylor, 'At Land's End: Novel Spaces and the Limits of Planetarity', *Novel*, 49:1
(2016), 116.

the technology of armies and empires. Yeats could be so immersed in the *Upanishads* because of over a century of orientalist work by William Jones and many more, published and disseminated by a printing industry that spanned a good deal of the globe. That is to take just one example of how expansive empathy can also be complicit in appropriation. I want neither to laud nor to condemn Yeats, but to recognize his place in the emergence of planetary consciousness in the 1920s, and his work in tying human history to planetary scales, in reorienting the time and space of the poet away from the individual and the local or national and out into a vast, unexplored hinterland. Ultimately, what do we learn about Yeats when we think about him in relation to the planet, and what do we learn about planetarity?

On the one hand, late Yeats can show us the way to a new language of planetary consciousness, moving away from the second-wave environmentalist rhetoric of catastrophic decay and depredation that structures how we think about nature, a rhetoric that has proven to be all too limited. If a third wave of ecocriticism has emerged, it moves beyond an attention to place, nature, or even planet, beyond the simple critique of those scales of thinking, and towards a greater attention to forms of thinking. Timothy Morton's book *Ecology without Nature* provides something of a signpost here, in its critique (alongside Heise) of 'deep ecology', asking instead for what he jokingly, with a sense of irony, calls 'really deep ecology':

> I have not been writing against a deep green view, if to be deep green means to take seriously the idea of philosophical reflection. Ironically, to contemplate deep green ideas is to let go of the idea of Nature, the one thing that maintains an aesthetic distance between us and them, us and it, us and 'over there' ... We must deal with the idea of distance itself. If we try to get rid of distance too fast, in our rush to join the nonhuman, we will end up caught in our prejudice, our concept of distance, our concept of 'them'. Hanging out in the distance may be the surest way of relating to the nonhuman. Instead of positing a nondualistic pot of gold at the end of a rainbow, we could hang out in what feels like dualism ... This is the ultimate rationality: holding our mind open for the absolutely unknown that is to come.[49]

Yeats is, like Spivak, too much of a humanist to be the harbinger of a new non-human philosophy—we cannot simply transpose Morton's ideas onto him—but we can find an affinity through Yeats between Morton's thought and Spivak's, and point to Yeats as one of our progenitors of the teleopoietic, the striving to reach out to as yet unknown futures and try to divine their shape. To hang out in the distance and to inhabit the strange and yet-to-come; this is the work of *A Vision*, if nothing else. This is not to say that Yeats has somehow seen it all in advance, but to recognize that, as Spivak reminds us, the task of the critic who is oriented towards the planet is 'to find moments in ... earlier texts that can be reinscribed for ... planetarity'.[50] Yeats may be reinscribed for planetarity, but it

---

[49] Timothy Morton, *Ecology Without Nature: Rethinking Environmental Aesthetics* (Cambridge, MA: Harvard University Press, 2007), 205.

[50] Spivak, *Death of a Discipline*, 92.

is a cautionary tale, in which we recognize the perils of planetary thinking alongside its advantages.

It comes down, in the end, to distance and to observatories. Yeats marked with pencil the following passage from his copy of Vol. 1 of Spengler's *Decline of the West*: 'Neither Plato nor Aristotle had an observatory. In the last years of Pericles, the Athenian people passed a decree by which all who propagated astronomical theories were made liable to impeachment … This last was an act of the deepest symbolic significance, expressive of the determination of the Classical soul to banish distance, in every respect, from its world-consciousness.'[51] We have no indication of why it was marked, but it seems that Yeats is on Spengler's side here, seeing the classical love of the here and the now, of place over space, as a sign of philosophical weakness rather than strength. *A Vision* grapples with distance and difference and reaches, tentatively and with all its flaws, towards a system for thinking beyond and against the ordinary scales of poetic creation and historical imagining.

---

[51] Allen, 'Yeats, Spengler, and *A Vision*', 216.

CHAPTER 25

YEATS'S VISIONARY POETICS

NEIL MANN

FACED with W. B. Yeats's interest in the occult and involvement with magical orders, many readers react with something like the incomprehension summed up by W. H. Auden as 'mediums, spells, the Mysterious Orient—*how* embarrassing'.[1] Yeats's esoteric interests may be tolerated for the artistry and the art they fertilized, but are often otherwise viewed askance. Yeats himself recognized some of the embarrassment provoked by what might appear 'popular spiritualism', yet added that 'Muses resemble women who creep out at night and give themselves to unknown sailors and return to talk of Chinese porcelain … except that the Muses sometimes form in those low haunts their most lasting attachments'. If Yeats's Muses were slumming in the docks of occultism, they certainly formed lasting attachments and drew great inspiration from these haunts.

Yeats was in search of spiritual meaning for his whole life, and he claimed that his first impulse had been to use literature as the schema for understanding the world. Naturally 'very religious', he found 'the simple-minded religion of my childhood' impossible and had therefore 'made a new religion, almost an infallible Church of poetic tradition … passed on from generation to generation by poets and painters with some help from philosophers and theologians'.[2] But the poetic tradition was the heterodox spirituality of William Blake and Percy Bysshe Shelley, in whose work Swedenborgian Christianity and Platonic atheism were expressed in myth and symbol. Such interests led to theosophy,[3] but, after a few years of involvement with the Theosophical Society in Dublin and London, he entered the Order of the Golden Dawn, which schooled its students in the traditional Western mysteries.[4] Though it is usually identified as a

---

[1] W. H. Auden, 'Yeats as an Example', *Kenyon Review*, 10:2 (Spring, 1948), http://kenyonreview.org/kr-online-issue/weekend-reads/w-h-auden-656342 (accessed October 2019).

[2] *CW3*, 115.

[3] See *Life 1*, 45–52.

[4] The period of WBY's involvement is over thirty years. According to his autobiography *The Trembling of the Veil*, he joined the order 'in May or June of 1887' (*CW3*, 160), but the invitation to his first initiation (pasted into NLI MS 36,276/2) gives 7 March 1890. His association with its successor, the Stella Matutina, appears to have petered out after 1924.

magical group, the Golden Dawn's outer order focused on teaching its members 'occult philosophy': structured through progressive initiations, the training organized all aspects of creation through the cabalistic diagram of the Tree of Life, a simple fundamental schema that is capable of endless elaboration, a powerful tool and memory device for organizing the eclectic, syncretic compendium of material. One of Yeats's fellow students stated that 'the Order was my university. In it were collected, classified and edited the great traditions of occultism and mysticism.'[5]

Yeats's commitment to the order survived both disillusionment, when its supposed origins were revealed as partly invented, and also the schisms that splintered the first order into separate factions. He remained involved with the successor group called Stella Matutina and sponsored George Hyde-Lees when she joined it in 1914; she had reached almost as high a level of initiation as he had by the time that they married. Husband and wife therefore shared a large store of common interests and knowledge, much of it evident in the system that emerged in their collaboration.

A VISION: MARRIAGE, AUTOMATIC SCRIPT, AND VERSIONS

> On the afternoon of October 24th 1917, four days after my marriage, my wife surprised me by attempting automatic writing. What came in disjointed sentences, in almost illegible writing, was so exciting, sometimes so profound, that I persuaded her to give an hour or two day after day to the unknown writer, and after some half-dozen such hours offered to spend what remained of life explaining and piecing together those scattered sentences. 'No' was the answer, 'we have come to give you metaphors for poetry.'[6]

The automatic writing began in October 1917 as George Yeats's attempt to distract her husband on their honeymoon and reassure him that he had not made a mistake in marrying her. Both of them knew people who could apparently let spirits communicate by controlling their writing hand, and W. B. Yeats set some store by this technique.[7] George Yeats later said that she faked a few lines to say that he had done the right thing, after which 'she suddenly felt her hand grasped and driven irresistibly. The pencil began to write sentences she had never intended or thought, which seemed to come as from another world.'[8]

---

[5] Dorothea Hunter, draft letter to Richard Ellmann, 15 November 1946, quoted in Warwick Gould, '"The Music of Heaven": Dorothea Hunter', *YA*, 9, 142.

[6] *CW14*, 7.

[7] In 1913, Elizabeth Radcliffe's automatic script had apparently confirmed that Yeats's lover was not pregnant as she claimed, which proved true, a case he found conclusive; see *Life 1*, 488–9.

[8] Ellmann, *Yeats: The Man and the Masks*, xv. These appear to be George Yeats's own words; see Warwick Gould, ed., '"Gasping on the Strand": Richard Ellmann's W. B. Yeats Notebooks', *YA*, 16 (2005), 315.

Whether readers take the 'automatic script' that emerged as the product of spirits, of unconscious telepathy, of George Yeats's unconscious, or her own fabrication depends largely on their world view, and it does little or nothing to change the many pages of question and answer the couple produced, which now take up over a thousand printed pages in the three volumes of Yeats's 'Vision' Papers.[9] If the early stages were a collaboration in which George Yeats's answers carried most authority, both contributed to the process of sifting and extracting the concepts, and the actual exposition of the system was almost exclusively the work of W. B. Yeats. And, while he writes of spirits and 'instructors' communicating the material, he could treat such terminology as a convenient metaphor rather than literal truth, and in any form of mediumship he saw dramatization by the medium, writing in a draft:

> All ghosts controls, communicators, materialisations, poltergeists, apparitions, instructors, are personnifications [sic], dramatisations of what would otherwise remain unknown ... . Whenever I speak of spirits having form or voice it must be understood that such dramatisations are implied.[10]

The voices that appear in the automatic script—with names that range from Thomas of Dorlowicz, Dionertes, and Carmichael to Frazzlepat, Leaf, and Apple—are comparable to the figures in a drama or novel; as the character of a play has a provisional identity or independence within the confines of the work and discussion about it, the 'voices' have a provisional identity within the creation of the system, without that necessarily implying any objective reality.[11] A draft introduction noted that A Vision 'would be different if it had not come from those who claim to have died many times and in all they say assume their own existence', a statement that leaves many possibilities open.[12]

Indeed, in his earliest drafts Yeats embedded the presentation of the system within a 'phantasmagoria' of fictional characters and narratives, a mythic construct that would give colour to ideas and possibly a plausible provenance that would enable his wife's role to be hidden.[13] In his first sketches Yeats used two characters from stories he had

---

[9] Yeats's 'Vision' Papers, George Mills Harper (general editor), assisted by Mary Jane Harper; vol. 1 and vol. 2, ed. Steve L. Adams, Barbara J. Frieling, and Sandra L. Sprayberry; vol. 3, ed. Robert Anthony Martinich and Margaret Mills Harper (London and Iowa City: Macmillan and University of Iowa Press, 1992). The script as such took place between October 1917 and March 1920 (vols. 1 and 2); 'sleeps' which superseded them took place between 1920 and 1924 (vol. 3, 8–124). A number of further sleeps later in the 1920s are not included in these volumes.

[10] CW14, 281–2, Appendix II; a draft for A Vision B, NLI 36,272/6/2a, corrected typescript, titled 'Book III', pages numbered 5–7.

[11] See Neil Mann, A Reader's Guide to Yeats's 'A Vision' (Clemson, SC: Clemson University Press, 2019), 34. Hereafter ARGYV.

[12] This quotation appears in a series of drafts from 1928 to 1929, including NLI MS 36,272/11a, [p. 1], cited in ARGYV, 40–1.

[13] In a 1922 note to the poems, Robartes and Aherne 'take their place in a phantasmagoria in which I endeavour to explain my philosophy of life and death' (VP, 821; CW1, 604). George Yeats 'didn't want him to print her share in Vision—their "first and only serious quarrel". She didn't want myths either. Myths began very early—Giraldus by Jan. 1918, when Dulac did the woodcut'; 'Ellmann's W. B. Yeats Notebooks', YA, 16 (2005), 318.

written in the 1890s, Michael Robartes and Owen Aherne, with Robartes acting as the discoverer of teachings which he recounts to Aherne, a scenario preserved in the poem 'The Phases of the Moon'.[14] Robartes has supposedly learned the system he propounds from two sources: the first is a European book from the 1590s, which exists in a single mutilated copy, written by Giraldus; this doctrine coincides in all major points with his second source, the oral doctrines of an Arab sect or tribe, who attribute them ultimately to a ninth-century scholar, Kusta ben Luka, and his now lost book. While Giraldus is deliberately made untraceable,[15] Kusta ben Luka is given a complex story, and most of the fictions concern him and the small tribe of followers that Robartes has lived with in order to learn the doctrines.[16] Although the dialogue between Robartes and Aherne was abandoned as the means of presenting the system itself, the surrounding fictions frame the earliest published accounts of the system in notes to poems and plays.[17] They are still prominent in the first version of *A Vision*, dated 1925 and entitled in full *A Vision: An Explanation of Life Founded upon the Writings of Giraldus and upon Certain Doctrines Attributed to Kusta ben Luka*.[18] It was divided into four books, the first two of which take their names from the stories about Kusta ben Luka and his Caliph—'What the Caliph Partly Learned' and 'What the Caliph Refused to Learn'—and accounts based on the Yeatses' own experiences are fictionalized in terms of Robartes and the Judwalis or Kusta ben Luka and the Caliph.[19]

Yeats later claimed this 'first version of' *A Vision* filled him 'with shame', presenting 'an unexplained rule of thumb that somehow explained the world' without its conceptual foundation.[20] In *A Vision A*, Yeats has extracted a coherent scheme from the material in the automatic script, but it is still only partially mastered. It has a consequent immediacy, and the expositions of human character and the cycles of history are presented in dense prose that suggests as much as it states (and these sections survive largely intact into the second version). The style has an allusiveness reminiscent of *Per Amica Silentia Lunae*, and the system is seen partially through the filter of myth, with elements that are

[14] These early drafts are collected in George Mills Harper and Margaret Mills Harper, with Richard W. Stoops, Jr., eds., *Yeats's 'Vision' Papers*, vol. 4 (London: Palgrave Macmillan, 2001).

[15] In the revised version of the story used in *A Vision B*, Michael Robartes emphasizes that he has 'made a fruitless attempt to identify my Giraldus with Giraldus of Bologna' (*CW14*, 29).

[16] Kusta ben Luka is a historical figure, though Yeats makes little use of his real life, creating a story of a Caliph of Baghdad with elements of the *Thousand and One Nights*. The name of the fictional tribe, the Judwalis, is said to mean 'diagram-makers', and they are modelled on a small Middle Eastern sect such as the Druze or Yazidis.

[17] The fictions that Yeats published—including notes to poems and plays—are collected in Wayne K. Chapman's *W. B. Yeats's Robartes–Aherne Writings* (London: Bloomsbury, 2018), along with some unpublished material.

[18] Printed privately in an edition of 600 copies by T. Werner Laurie, London, it actually came out in January 1926.

[19] 'Desert Geometry or The Gift of Harun al-Raschid' fictionalizes the Yeatses' marriage as that of Kusta ben Luka and his young mediumistic bride (*CW13*, 97–102), while interjections in the text of 'The Gates of Pluto' dramatize some of their experiences with supernatural phenomena as Robartes's in Baghdad or Arabia (*CW13*, 196, 202, 203–4).

[20] For 'shame' see *CW14*, 15; and for 'unexplained rule of thumb,' see *CW14*, 59.

animist and even magical. For instance, the figure of the *Daimon* presides over life in female form, a figure of opposition and a persecuting angel; the spirits in non-human incarnations act as messengers and muses; the afterlife is viewed as a fitful sleep in which dreams of the past alternate with a waking state; and the book ends with an appeal to restore mythology to philosophy and to conceive every element of the universe—physical and mental—as embodied in distinct spirit forms.[21] All of these elements were removed or attenuated in the second version of the book, giving *A Vision B* (1937) a more technical and abstract character.[22]

The major reasons for the shift are both external and internal, yet connected: the new version gives evidence of wider philosophical reading, which contributed to a conviction that the spiritual *Principles* were far more central than he had realized: 'I had misinterpreted the geometry, and in my ignorance of philosophy failed to understand distinctions upon which the coherence of the whole depended.'[23] Despite having spent almost seven years preparing *A Vision A*, Yeats claimed not to have read much philosophy and, in a move almost guaranteed to feed any dissatisfaction that he may have felt with the book he had just produced, he appears to have started to supplement his reading on philosophy before he had even received the proofs of *A Vision A*.[24] He told Thomas Sturge Moore, brother of the philosopher G. E. Moore:

> I could not read philosophy till my big book was written — those who gave me material forbid me to do so, they feared I think that if I did do so I would split up experience till it ceased to exist. When it was written (though the proofs had yet to come) I started to read. I read for months every day Plato & Plotinus. Then I started on Berkeley & Croce & Gentile. You introduced me to your brothers work & to Russell & I found Eddington & one or two others for myself.[25]

The account that he published three years later in *A Packet for Ezra Pound* (1929) varies slightly but has the same contours,[26] and the second version of *A Vision* definitely bears the signs of this reading programme, both in the references made and the approach used.[27] New terms are used to describe the concepts, such as 'antinomy', borrowed

[21] The *Daimon* is said to be of opposite sex to its human companion, but Yeats writes from a male perspective, so that the *Daimon* is consistently female in 1925 *Vision*.

[22] Thomas Parkinson suggests that, as it lacks the philosophical material that Yeats added to *A Vision B*, 'The A version was not so much metaphysical in its arguments as psychological, historical, astrological, and personal' ('That Extraordinary Book', *YA*, *1* (1982), 195–206, 197).

[23] *CW14*, 15.

[24] The first drafts date from early in 1918; although they were very far from being drafts of *A Vision* itself, some material from early drafts such as 'The Discoveries of Michael Robartes' survives into the published version. Though critics tend to be sceptical about this claim, Yeats's earlier philosophical reading was evidently in areas that appealed to him, and he was far less widely read in the broader philosophical tradition.

[25] Yeats to T. Sturge Moore, 14 March [1926]; *CL InteLex* #4850.

[26] See *CW14*, 15–16, which reprints *A Packet for Ezra Pound* with a few changes, but not here.

[27] Drafts from the late 1920s include a significant number of references to other philosophers that were pruned from the final version.

from Kant. Looking at *A Vision A*, Yeats could appreciate both the coherence he had achieved and the weaknesses that were revealed, so that *A Vision B* is more considered, as well as being contextualized within a more philosophical framework.[28] Further from the thought and style of *Per Amica Silentia Lunae*, it lacks some of the immediacy of *A Vision A* but is more fully realized and consistent. The most compelling sections remain the two that are repeated almost unchanged from *A Vision A*: the examination of the twenty-eight phases of incarnation and the survey of European history. In the other books, where *A Vision A* often presents the underlying ideas in a tenuously connected zigzag of sections, *A Vision B* gives a more sequential and logically developed exposition. Furthermore, a whole book is added to expand on the traditions of the Great Year in the ancient world, which does not extend the system significantly but gives a broader historical and cultural context for the concepts, with greater scholarship.[29]

Unlike the female angel of *A Vision A*, the *Daimon* of *A Vision B* is nowhere described clearly, and it is sexless and closer to being an archetype than an antagonist; the agency of the supernatural incarnations is not mentioned; and the afterlife is outlined as a process and in sparer detail. The final appeal to restore mythology to philosophy is replaced in the second version by an ambiguous question about where to focus the spiritual vision, framed as choosing between Heracles the shade and Heracles the divine hero.[30] Other changes, such as the fuller explanation of the geometry and the clearer outline of the afterlife, certainly make the basis of the system more intelligible, but the supposedly crucial treatment of the spiritual *Principles* lacks a cogent explanation of their nature and purpose, concentrating on technical detail.[31] The system gains in clarity and consistency, but many readers actually have only marginal interest in the system per se and are mainly looking for insight into Yeats's poetry and drama or for a work of comparable intrinsic interest, and *A Vision* may therefore disappoint. Though most of Yeats's writing from 1918 onwards is informed by the system to some extent, the connection between *A Vision* and the poetry is often buried deep.

---

[28] Barbara Croft gives a full comparison of the two versions in *'Stylistic Arrangements': A Study of William Butler Yeats's 'A Vision'* (London: Associated University Presses, 1987).

[29] Yeats had relied heavily on articles in Hastings's *Encyclopaedia of Religion and Ethics* for *A Vision A*, and these were significantly supplemented by the early volumes of Pierre Duhem's *Le système du monde* (10 vols.; Paris: Hermann, 1913–59) in *A Vision B*, as well as elements taken from Yeats's very partial readings in the works of Josef Strzygowski and Leo Frobenius; see Matthew Gibson, 'Yeats, the Great Year, and Pierre Duhem', in *Yeats, Philosophy and the Occult* (Clemson, SC: Clemson University Press, and Liverpool: Liverpool University Press, 2016), and '"Timeless and Spaceless"?—Yeats's Search for Models of Interpretation in Post-Enlightenment Philosophy, Contemporary Anthropology and Art History . . .', in *W. B. Yeats's 'A Vision': Explications and Contexts* (Clemson, SC: Clemson University Press, 2012).

[30] The essay 'Swedenborg, Mediums, and the Desolate Places', written in 1914 (see following section), had closed with the same figure of the dual afterlives of Heracles (*CW*5, 72–3).

[31] If Yeats hoped to explain the importance of these *Principles*, perceptive and well-disposed critics have found them to be simply unnecessary doubles of their ephemeral counterparts, the *Faculties*; see Helen Vendler, *Yeats's Vision and the Later Plays* (Cambridge: Harvard University Press, 1963), 26; Donald Torchiana, 'Yeats and Croce', *YA, 4* (1986), 3–12, at 6; Graham Hough, *The Mystery Religion of W. B. Yeats* (Brighton: Harvester, 1984), 110.

ANTECEDENTS: YEATS'S ESOTERIC PROSE

A Vision does not emerge from nowhere and, although it contains ideas that Yeats might not have accepted had he not believed them to come from spirit voices, little in it would surprise a reader familiar with his preoccupations. Yeats had been open about his esoteric interests earlier, declaring in 1901 his belief 'in the practice and philosophy of what we have agreed to call magic, in what I must call the evocation of spirits ... in the visions of truth in the depths of the mind when the eyes are closed', their connection to a universal 'single mind' and 'one great memory', and his conviction that 'a certain evil, a certain ugliness ... comes from the slow perishing through the centuries of a quality of mind that made this belief and its evidences common over the world'.[32] Part of his interest in folklore and Irish tradition was the attempt to recover this 'quality of mind' and make 'this belief' possible again.

Other essays of this period, such as *Discoveries* (1906), declare or allude to his mystical thinking on symbolism and poetic evocation, and in the following decade he was writing and lecturing on ghostly phenomena and life after death. The years between 1912 and 1914 showed a heightened interest in the evidence of seances as he worked on essays for Lady Gregory's *Visions and Beliefs in the West of Ireland*, titled 'Witches and Wizards and Irish Folk-Lore' and 'Swedenborg, Mediums, and the Desolate Places' (1914; published 1920).[33] In the latter, Yeats writes that he 'was comparing one form of belief with another ... discovering a philosophy', as he 'pieced together stray thoughts written out after questioning the familiar of a trance medium or automatic writer ... or arranged the fragments into some pattern, till I believed myself the discoverer of a vast generalization', connecting the mediums of Soho or Holloway in London with the country people of the West of Ireland, and 'constantly comparing my discoveries with what I have learned of mediaeval tradition among fellow students, with the reveries of a Neoplatonist, of a seventeenth-century Platonist, of Paracelsus or a Japanese poet'.[34]

In 1917 he was preparing a 'long psychic essay "The Alphabet"' that was 'more or less suplimentary [*sic*] to' the two essays he had written for *Visions and Beliefs in the West of Ireland*.[35] The title of 'An Alphabet' indicates the work's fundamental nature, and it was the most systematic setting forth of his thought to that date. For publication, however, it was given a more allusive Latin title, *Per Amica Silentia Lunae*—literally, 'through the friendly silences of the moon'—and it comprises two parts, again titled in Latin, 'Anima Hominis' and 'Anima Mundi'—'the Soul of Man' and 'the Soul of the World'. The opening of 'Anima Mundi' echoes what he had written in 'Swedenborg, Mediums, and

---

[32] *CW4*, 25.

[33] See Neil Mann, 'Yeats, Dream, Vision, and the Dead', in *Yeats, Philosophy, and the Occult*, esp. 131–9. George Yeats told Richard Ellmann that 'About 1914 Yeats' talk of spirits became so constant as to alienate his friends'; see 'Ellmann's W. B. Yeats Notebooks', *YA, 16* (2005), 317.

[34] *CW5*, 48.

[35] WBY to Augusta Gregory, 1 April [1917], *CL InteLex* #3209.

the Desolate Places': 'I have always sought to bring my mind close to the mind of Indian and Japanese poets, old women in Connaught, mediums in Soho, lay brothers whom I imagine dreaming in some mediaeval monastery the dreams of their village, learned authors who refer all to antiquity', and again he found the common memory or 'what we have begun to call "the subconscious"'. He states that he has 'delighted in all that displayed great problems through sensuous images, or exciting phrases', viewing the artist's grounding of philosophical questions in sensuous and striking language as key.[36]

In the automatic writing Yeats was impressed by the way that the script would 'have some pictorial symbol relating to' a given topic, which would relate back 'to the main symbol', encapsulating a great problem in a concrete or geometric image.[37] In a draft, Yeats entertained the idea that the automatic script and *A Vision* could be said to have grown out of *Per Amica Silentia Lunae*:

> In Per Amica Silentia Lunae I have described the whole of human life as a man's attempt to become the opposite of himself or to create the opposite of his fate, and if I were to judge by accepted psychology I would describe this system as an elaboration by my wife's subconsciousness of those few crude sentences.[38]

Yeats, of course, does not judge by accepted psychology, but he sees this as a matter of interpretation or metaphor. Certainly *A Vision* develops from *Per Amica Silentia Lunae*, recasting and reformulating its ideas, along with those behind the earlier essays as well. In *Per Amica*, however, the presentation is tentative and suggestive and its scope apparently limited, whereas *A Vision's* scope is more obviously ambitious and its presentation more assertive. Many will prefer the more poetic mode of *Per Amica Silentia Lunae*, that 'nothing affirmeth, and therefore never lieth', though others may be unsatisfied by allusive hinting that never affirms.[39] While the system of *A Vision* is not, therefore, a radical departure from Yeats's own earlier thought, it has greater clarity and precision, proposing definite categories.

In seeking to recover the 'quality of mind that made' belief in magic and the Great Memory possible and widespread, 'Swedenborg, Mediums, and the Desolate Places' and *Per Amica Silentia Lunae* draw on the seventeenth-century Cambridge Platonists, whom Yeats saw as perhaps the last proponents of an outlook that stretched back to Plato, resisting their century's scientific revolution and the rising tide of Cartesian philosophy.[40]

---

[36] *CW5*, 16.

[37] Draft for *A Vision B*, NLI 36,272/24, TS corrected in ink and pencil, 'Book III The Completed Symbol', [p. 22]. He also writes how the 'instructors, who use geometrical figures as I do words, have a dozen ways of expressing those marriages and conflicts which constitute all existence, and of relating those that last but a few years or months to those that last for centuries' [p. 1].

[38] Typescript draft 'The Double Vortex', 1928, cited in Connie Kelly Hood, 'The Remaking of *A Vision*', *YAACTS, 1* (1983), 49, and 'A Search for Authority: Prolegomena to a Definitive Critical Edition of W. B. Yeats's *A Vision (1937)*', unpublished PhD thesis, University of Tennessee (1983), 42–3.

[39] Sir Philip Sidney, *The Defence of Poesie* (London: Ponsonby, 1595), 102.

[40] For 'quality of mind', see *CW4*, 25.

Their approach, in particular Henry More's use of such concepts as *Anima Mundi*, was consonant with Yeats's occult interests, conceiving of a natural world that conforms to simple ideas of harmony and proportion rather than the precision of scientific observation. Similarly, Yeats saw the philosophy presented in *A Vision* as a return to pre-Cartesian forms of thought, saying in a draft that 'it resembles nothing of philosophy from the time of Descartes but much that is ancient'.[41]

TAPPING THE SOUL'S OWN HISTORY

Yeats spent the last twenty years of his life immersed in the symbol system of *A Vision*, wrestling the information that emerged from his wife's automatic writing and trance speech in 'sleep' into a coherent form. Though its first purpose was personal—the script had told him that the purpose was 'to give you metaphors for poetry'—much of his labour was devoted to making it possible to present the system publicly to others.[42]

To himself, *A Vision* represented a framework to provide inspiration and a context for poetry. Yeats addressed Moina Mathers, who had been with him in the Order of the Golden Dawn, in the 'Dedication' to *A Vision A*, explaining his purpose in pursuing his earlier esoteric interests:

> I wished for a system of thought that would leave my imagination free to create as it chose and yet make all that it created, or could create, part of the one history, and that the soul's .... Then when I had ceased all active search, yet had not ceased from desire, the documents upon which this book is founded were put into my hands, and I had what I needed, though it may be too late.[43]

As he conceived it, the system of *A Vision* would enable him therefore to root his poetry in the human soul's own nature and history, providing a symbolic matrix that he trusted to guarantee the validity and value of what he wrote from it. He told Augusta Gregory, 'for the first time I understand human life', and stated to Edmund Dulac that the system meant 'a last act of defense against the chaos of the world & I hope for ten years to write out of my renewed sense of security'.[44] He had those ten years and more, and wrote with a vigour and fertility rare in a poet's old age.

He also wanted to communicate this revelation to other people. William Blake had created an elaborate mythology that is presented poetically, and in the 1890s Yeats had

---

[41] This sentence appears in a series of drafts from 1928 to 1929, including NLI MS 36,272/11a, p. [1], cited in *ARGYV* 41.

[42] *CW14*, 7.

[43] *CW13*, liv–lv.

[44] WBY to Augusta Gregory, 4 January [1918], *CL InteLex* #3384; WBY to Edmund Dulac, 23 April [1924]; *CL InteLex* #4525.

attempted to expound the meaning of that myth in systematic form.[45] He also wrote an essay on 'The Philosophy of Shelley's Poetry' in 1900, organizing Shelley's symbolism and drawing out overarching principles. In 1932, he told Olivia Shakespear that, when he was young, 'I wanted to feel that any poet I cared for — Shelley let us say — saw more than he told of, had in some sense seen into the mystery', and for the same reason he wanted to offer his vision of the mystery: 'The young men I write for may not read my "Vision" — they may care too much for poetry — but they will be pleased that it exists.'[46]

While the system's purpose was, therefore, in the first instance at least, to provide Yeats with a creative foundation that was personally inspiring and universal enough to make his poetry speak to others, the purpose of the published book of *A Vision* is to offer that system for those who want the background to the poetry. It is not intended for the majority of readers, who will not be interested in where the poetry comes from as much as the poetry itself, but Yeats considered that those who wanted to see what underpinned the poetic vision would find clarification and explanation in *A Vision*. For most it will be enough 'that it exists', otherwise it is 'intended for students of Plotinus, the Hermetic fragments & unpopular literature of that kind'.[47] Pressing the revised version on his prospective publisher, Harold Macmillan, in 1934, Yeats said, 'It is a book which will be very much wanted by a few people — I get letters already asking for it — but will puzzle the bulk of my readers'; at the same time, he emphasized: 'I want it to be taken as a part of my work as a whole, not as an eccentricity. I have put many years of work into it.'[48]

A Vision in Outline

The outline here is necessarily brief and superficial, but the interested reader can find helpful guides to the intricacies, both general treatments and examinations of specific aspects.[49] The basis of the system is reflection and opposition: 'the ultimate reality, symbolised as the Sphere, falls in human consciousness ... into a series of antinomies'.[50] Though the primal state may be an ideal unity, all of manifest reality and creation is dualistic, and the antinomies include the One and the Many, God and humanity, monotheism and polytheism, *Daimon* and human, race and individual soul, soul and self, objectivity and subjectivity, concord and discord, democracy and aristocracy, female and

[45] W. B. Yeats and Edwin John Ellis, eds., *The Works of William Blake Poetic, Symbolic, and Critical*, 3 vols. (London: Bernard Quaritch, 1893).

[46] WBY to Olivia Shakespear, [9] February [1932], *CL InteLex* #5444.

[47] WBY to Ignatius McHugh, 26 May [1926], *CL InteLex* #4874.

[48] WBY to Harold Macmillan, 9 March 1934, *CL InteLex* #6019.

[49] See particularly Mann, *ARGYV*, and http://www.yeatsvision.com; Mann, Gibson, and Nally, eds., *W. B. Yeats's 'A Vision': Explications and Contexts*; and the articles in the regular section of the *Yeats Annual*, 'Mastering What is Most Abstract'.

[50] *CW14*, 137.

male, dark and light, sun and moon.[51] The poles pull in opposite directions and there is constant motion between them, whether it is towards unity—the unifying, centripetal, homogenizing force is labelled solar or *primary*—or towards multiplicity—the separating, centrifugal, individuating force is labelled lunar or *antithetical*. The two movements are the gyres, the spiral motion from the minimum of one element to its maximum and then back, while its opposite goes through the inverse process. Each life is an example of this cycle, as well as containing many cycles of varying dimensions and being contained within larger cycles of death and rebirth. This is summed up in the couplets from 'Under Ben Bulben':

> Many times man lives and dies
> Between his two eternities,
> That of race and that of soul,
> And ancient Ireland knew it all.[52]

The two eternities of the unified race and the individual soul's separateness are symbolized particularly by sun and moon, or more usually by new moon (full sun) and full moon. Yeats sees the soul as progressing from one pole to the other as the moon progresses from new to full and back again, and each symbolic stage or day is a life in his reincarnational scheme, so that there are twenty-eight incarnations in a cycle. This is the cycle set forth by Michael Robartes in 'The Phases of the Moon':

> Twenty-and-eight the phases of the moon,
> The full and the moon's dark and all the crescents,
> Twenty-and-eight, and yet but six-and-twenty
> The cradles that a man must needs be rocked in:
> For there's no human life at the full or the dark.[53]

The tension necessary to life is said to be lacking at the two extremes, the dark moon (Phase 1) and the full moon (Phase 15), but these are supernatural existences that have special characteristics. In *A Vision*'s scheme these twenty-eight phases or states make up a wheel: 'This wheel is every completed movement of thought or life, twenty-eight incarnations, a single incarnation, a single judgment or act of thought. Man seeks his opposite or the opposite of his condition, attains his object so far as it is attainable, at Phase 15 and returns to Phase 1 again.'[54]

---

[51] The clearest form is probably a Table of Opposites; see *ARGYV*, 66–8, and Northrop Frye, 'The Rising of the Moon', in *Spiritus Mundi: Essays on Literature, Myth, and Society*, 245–74, at 256–7. Some of these pairs may appear the opposite to traditional associations, but sun, dark, and female are all regarded as *primary*, while moon, light, and male are regarded as *antithetical*.

[52] *CW1*, 325.

[53] *CW1*, 164.

[54] *CW14*, 60.

The cycle also applies to long periods of time, particularly eras of one thousand or two thousand years each, where the stages of Phase 1 and 15, the new and the full moon, mark particularly important junctures in history. Phase 1 is associated with new beginnings, the initiation of a religious era, such as Christianity, or a social order, such as the consolidation of medieval Christendom, while Phase 15 is associated with perfected expression, seen in idealized conceptions of the Athens of Phidias, the Byzantium of Justinian, or Renaissance Italy. This large-scale cycle relates to a Great Year of 26,000 years, tied to ancient and modern conceptions of astronomical ages, divided into twelve months, with alternating 'annunciations' roughly every two thousand years. Yeats imagines the annunciation that established the *antithetical* polytheism of classical Greece as the rape of Leda by the god Zeus in the form of a swan; its counterpart over two thousand years later was the annunciation that ushered in an age of *primary* monotheism when the Virgin Mary was overshadowed by the Holy Ghost in the form of a dove: hence the title of the book that considers history, 'Dove or Swan'.[55] Some two thousand years later, in our own time, Yeats foresees an imminent annunciation, which lies behind the vision of the 'rough beast' in 'The Second Coming', appearing after 'twenty centuries of stony sleep'.[56] This new period will be a swing of the pendulum back to *antithetical* polytheism and in 'The Gyres' he invokes 'Old Rocky Face', the ancient Greek Oracle of Delphi, to validate the return to the old that is also new, so that 'all things run / On that unfashionable gyre again'.[57]

The individual human being is a microcosm and thus embodies the antinomies, specifically in the form of the spiritual *Principles* and the transactional *Faculties*. The *Faculties* are temporary reflections of the *Principles*, existing only for a particular lifetime, while the *Principles* continue after death. The afterlife is first a judgement of the preceding life, as the title 'The Soul in Judgment' indicates, but the soul sits in judgement on its own life. This is followed by preparation for rebirth, with the whole process lasting at least as long as a lifetime. After completing many lives and cycles, the spiritual being will escape reincarnation into a state referred to as the *Thirteenth Cone*, going beyond the twelve cones or months of temporal existence.

The *Principles* divide into the two solar or permanent *Principles*, *Celestial Body* and *Spirit*, the soul's continuity, and the two lunar or regenerating *Principles*, *Passionate Body* and *Husk*, which are the desire for life and experience. At birth these four are reflected into the *Faculties*, translating into practical interfaces for dealing with the world. *Celestial Body* and *Spirit* reflect as *Body of Fate* and *Creative Mind* respectively, while *Passionate Body* and *Husk* reflect as *Mask* and *Will*. *Will*, the basis of individual choice, is the *Faculty* that is regarded as determining the bias of life. People are broadly divided into those whose *Will* is predominantly objective—in a *primary* phase, where dark

---

[55] The swan element is made clear in the poem 'Leda' and the opening paragraphs (*CW14*, 194–5), but Yeats leaves the reader to extrapolate the rest.

[56] *CW1*, 187.

[57] *CW1*, 293.

predominates—and those whose *Will* is predominantly subjective—in an *antithetical* phase, where light predominates. The objective person, for instance, might be motivated by the calls of law, duty, or 'cheering crowds', while subjective motivation would be 'A lonely impulse of delight'.[58]

One final figure needs mentioning: the *Daimon*, partly a survival from Yeats's formulations of the anti-self in *Per Amica Silentia Lunae*, and partly a dramatization of the system's reflective doubling. The *Daimon* is a companion spirit that stage-manages the life of the human being, a guardian angel who brings crisis in order to heighten life, precipitating pain as often as joy. Yeats's conception of the *Daimon* changed with time, and by the time of the second version of *A Vision* he came to see the *Daimon* less as the opposite of the human and more as the complement, the total archetype out of which a fragment manifests in space and time as a particular life and person.

Many readers of *A Vision* are struck by the diagrams, which vary from stark geometric figures of intersecting triangles and figures within circles, to representations of the moon's phases with zodiacal symbols, and even a full woodcut illustration of the Great Wheel (see Figure 25.1), all hinting at cosmic geometry or astrological dimensions which are not really present in the work. Yeats seems to have relished the technicalities of the movements of the *Faculties* and *Principles* within their gyres, giving rules for finding the place of each element in its cycle with respect to the others, along with complex and tortuous interrelations of subsidiary influence. He was quick to say, however, that such elements were mainly intended for his 'old fellow students' of hermetism and theosophy, people who would have the cast of mind to deal with 'what is most technical and explanatory' and to 'master what is most abstract there' by making 'it the foundation of their visions' and meditations; then, he announced, 'the curtain may ring up upon a new drama'.[59] Other readers were advised just 'to dip here and there in the verse and into my comments upon life and history'.[60]

The System in the Poetry

Yeats published a new 'Introduction to The Great Wheel' of *A Vision* in *A Packet for Ezra Pound* (1929), explaining openly the system's origin in automatic writing and stating that he would 'never think any thoughts but these, or some modification or extension of these; when I write prose or verse they must be somewhere present though not it may be in the words'.[61] The thoughts may provide inspiration to the poet, but poems are made of words, sounds, and images. Yeats himself saw the importance of the skeleton but the beauty of the flesh: 'We can (those hard symbolic bones under the skin) substitute for a

---

[58] 'An Irish Airman Foresees His Death', *CW1*, 135.
[59] *CW13*, lv.
[60] *CW13*, lv.
[61] *CW14*, 325.

FIGURE **25.1** Edmund Dulac, *The Great Wheel (for W. B. Yeats)*, 1927. © The Estate of Edmund Dulac. All Rights Reserved, DACS 2022.

treatise on logic the Divine Comedy, or some little song about a rose, or be content to live our thought.'[62]

The 'symbolic bones' obtrude occasionally in earlier work where the system is least digested and perhaps only partly understood. Concerning three poems from 1918 and 1919—'The Phases of the Moon', 'The Double Vision of Michael Robartes', and 'Michael Robartes and the Dancer'—Yeats himself notes that 'To some extent I wrote these poems as a text for exposition', while a poem such as 'The Four Ages of Man' versifies the categories of *A Vision*'s 'Four Contests of the Antithetical within Itself'.[63] Sometimes, within the automatic script's exchanges, Yeats explicitly quizzed the 'instructors' about aspects of plays such as *The Only Jealousy of Emer* or *Calvary*, but most of the creative inspiration derives from the ferment of ideas and metaphors that the Yeatses were processing as they pieced together the script's ideas. Generally the system provides seed material

---

[62] *CW14*, 18.
[63] For WBY's comment, see *CW1*, 288; *CW14*, 75.

or a deep foundation for the poetry, and most of Yeats's poems after 1918, including the most celebrated works, bear some trace of the system, some very distinctly and others less clearly.

The more fully the reader knows the system from which the ideas come, the further the ramifications and sources reach. The following brief considerations seek to show how two important poems have roots in *A Vision*'s system, one very clearly, and the other rather more subtly: 'The Second Coming' and 'A Dialogue of Self and Soul'. Though the poetry communicates even when the conceptual origins are unknown, its meaning is extended by understanding these layers of complexity.

A. Norman Jeffares noted that 'to understand "The Second Coming" in its full Yeatsian significance requires a reading of *A Vision*'.[64] Yet, as many readers will testify, the poem's impact is strong even without that fuller significance. Its power derives from the imagery, the language, and the traditions used, inextricably entwined with ideas about history informed by the system. The opening lines, 'Turning and turning in the widening gyre / The falcon cannot hear the falconer', put the gyre of *A Vision* to the fore, embodied in a concrete image from the natural world.[65] The system provides the metaphor, expressing the breakdown of social order, but the circling falcon clothes the gyre in image. Similarly, the abstract anarchy 'loosed upon the world' is made sensuous in 'The blood-dimmed tide is loosed' and 'The ceremony of innocence is drowned', the first visually potent and the second more vaguely religious. Societal breakdown prompts certainty that 'some revelation is at hand; / Surely the Second Coming is at hand', using the language of the Christian Last Judgement or millenarian apocalypse.

Even without further knowledge of *A Vision*, the reader will realize that any conventional expectations about the Second Coming of Christ are subverted, with the appearance of the 'vast image' of a sphinx-like being in a sun-scorched desert 'out of *Spiritus Mundi*',[66] the collective memory or imagination. It draws on personal visionary experiences Yeats had experienced years earlier, including one of 'a desert and a black Titan raising himself up' and another of 'a brazen winged beast that I associated with laughing, ecstatic destruction', which was 'Afterwards described in my poem "The Second Coming"'.[67] The poem is also located within Western and Christian culture: even if Yeats is not envisaging Christ's Second Coming, the mention of Bethlehem recalls the birth of Christ two thousand years ago, but the 'rough beast' possibly alludes to the Beast in the Apocalypse or Revelation of St John. Furthermore, it is the sensuous language, describing the 'slow thighs' of the sphinx and the way that

---

[64] A. N. Jeffares, 'Yeats's "The Gyres": Sources and Symbolism', *Huntington Library Quarterly*, 15:1 (November 1951), 89. Yeats himself provided a concise and useful summary of key elements of the system to support the poem in *Michael Robartes and the Dancer* (1921).

[65] *CW1*, 187 (all subsequent quotations from the poem are from this reference).

[66] A concept akin to *Anima Mundi*, *Spiritus Mundi* is generally taken to be a lower manifestation (the Latin terms *spiritus* [spirit] and *anima* [soul] both derive from concepts of breath, and which is the 'higher' varies according to context).

[67] *CW3*, 161; *CW2*, 723. For a reading of this poem in context of 'Leo Africanus', see Nathan Suhr-Sytsma's essay 'Africa', Chapter 21 in this volume.

the 'rough beast' 'slouches', that fixes these phrases in our heads and makes the poem so widely quoted.

Though the poem certainly alludes to all these ideas, most readers realize that there is a larger myth or concept informing the poem and its details, and the mystery acts as an invitation to explore further. The note that Yeats provided in 1921 gives some help, as does A Vision itself, though in neither case is the explanation presented simply or directly. The central concept derives from the two-thousand-year religious cycle described in A Vision's 'Dove or Swan', apprehending the imminent arrival of a new anti-thetical religious dispensation to replace the primary Christian dispensation of the last two millennia.[68] As outlined earlier, Yeats paralleled the Christian annunciation with its pagan predecessor, and sees the pendulum returning to that pagan mode but in a different and unforeseeable form. The poem implies that the antithetical pagan world has had 'twenty centuries of stony sleep', though these have been 'vexed to nightmare by a rocking cradle', and A Vision indicates that antithetical forces have lain dormant, so that their return is 'not so much a breaking out of new life as the vivification of old intel-lect', a concept Yeats associates with a sphinx.[69]

If 'The Second Coming' invites readers to explore its hinterland in A Vision, 'A Dialogue of Self and Soul' is less obviously tied to the system. It comes from the period when Yeats was most intensely engaged in trying to understand the spiritual aspect of the human being as embodied in the Principles, and this is certainly part of the poem's genesis. Yet, as David Ross notes, ' "A Dialogue of Self and Soul" is one of Yeats's most flawlessly executed poems', and it stands on its own without need for extraneous com-mentary.[70] The external references are more personal to Yeats himself; though it is unnecessary to know about the physical sword, silk, and tower that Yeats refers to, awareness of Junzo Sato's gift and Thoor Ballylee can intensify appreciation. Similarly, it does not require a knowledge of Yeats's system to understand the positions set out by 'Self' and 'Soul', but such knowledge may deepen and extend the poem's significance.

In the dialogue of the poem's first part, readers will immediately recognize that the Self is bound to earthly life, while the Soul aspires to spiritual ascent. The Soul summons 'to the winding ancient stair' focusing always on moving upward to the top, the dark night and starry sky, the Pole Star's still point; the Self looks downwards to sitting knees where the sword lies, emphasizing the physical and sensuous, the blade's edge and steel surface, the embroidered silk wound around the wooden scabbard.[71] The Soul rejects the love and war these objects represent and repeats its desire to still the wandering mind and to end repeated incarnation in 'ancestral night', while Self focuses on actual

[68] CW1, 493 n.

[69] CW14, 153–4. In 'The Double Vision of Michael Robartes', 'A Sphinx with woman breast and lion paw' 'Gazed upon all things known, all things unknown, / In triumph of intellect' (CW1, 171), connected in A Vision with a Jupiter–Saturn conjunction and 'introspective knowledge of the mind's self-begotten unity, an intellectual excitement'.

[70] David A. Ross, Critical Companion to W. B. Yeats: A Literary Reference to His Life and Work (New York: Facts on File, 2009), 82.

[71] CW1, 234-6 (all subsequent quotations from the poem are from this reference).

ancestors, flowers, and rebirth. The Soul speaks for the spiritual *Principles*, which dominate after death when experience is absorbed as understanding and are symbolized, from the natural perspective, by darkness; the Self speaks for the waking *Faculties*, which engage with the physical world and, from the natural perspective, are symbolized by light.[72] The Soul therefore desires to ascend to the 'starlit air' and questions, 'Who can distinguish darkness from the soul?'

The Self asserts its 'emblems of the day against the tower / Emblematical of the night', a samurai sword and a piece of embroidered silk wrapped round the scabbard, identified by the Soul as 'Emblematical of love and war'. Life is the constant tension of the two, of the concord and discord of *A Vision*. The Self, identifying with both, claims 'as by a soldier's right / A charter to commit the crime [of death and birth] once more'. Within the scope of the poem, the idea of reincarnation can be taken either on its own terms or as a metaphor for love of life.

The Soul closes the poem's first half with a beatific vision of 'fullness', in which the polarities of love and war merge, something that is impossible in life.[73] This is presented in terms of the *Principle* of *Spirit* or intellect being unable to distinguish opposites: 'intellect no longer knows / *Is* from the *Ought*, or *Knower* from the *Known*', referring to the four attributes of the *Four Faculties*—the core of selfhood, *Will* or Is, and its guiding goal, *Mask* or the Ought; the mental centre, *Creative Mind* or Knower, and its goal of physical reality, *Body of Fate* or the Known.[74]

The tension between the Self and Soul establishes the dialogue of the poem's first half, giving way to Self's monologue in the second half. While the Soul's silence is presented as the wordlessness of completion, Yeats's bias is evident in giving Self the stage. Self takes the viewpoint of a subjective or *antithetical* person, as Yeats viewed himself, who seeks return to life rather than release from the wheel. This is despite the indignities of growing up and ignominies of slander, epitomized as 'the frog-spawn of a blind man's ditch'. The supremely tactile image of the blind man with his hands in a ditch of frog-spawn, full of potential life, also alludes to the parable presented in *The Cat and the Moon*, in which Yeats dramatized 'the mind in relation to the body as a lame man upon a blind man[']s back', where the *Passionate Body* and *Husk*, the *Principles* that seek experience and incarnation, are portrayed as the blind man, who carries the *Principles* that can 'see', *Spirit* and *Celestial Body*, the lame man.[75] Here we see the contrast of the Soul's tendency to become motionless, set against the Self's need to move but its blindness.

---

[72] The *Principles* are, however, light when seen from their own ideal perspective (*CW14*, 140), such that, in the broadest sense, incarnate life is treated as the dark hours from dusk to dawn or the months of autumn and winter, while the life after death is treated as the light hours from dawn to dusk and the months of spring and summer (see *CW14*, 58–9, and *ARGYV* esp. ch. 11).

[73] 'Such fullness in that quarter overflows / And falls into the basin of the mind' uses imagery of flow/overflow and stream/basin that Yeats associates repeatedly with the *antithetical* or subjective, the Full Moon or, here, the Beatific Vision (see *CW1*, 235).

[74] *CW14*, 54. Yeats also related Is, Ought, Knower, and Known to the *Principles* themselves; see n. 73 below.

[75] In a notebook, Yeats writes of the play, 'picturing as in some obscure & grotesque tapestry the dependence upon one another of Will (*Husk* & *Passionate Body*[)] & Thought (*Spirit* & *Celestial Body*)',

The poem's final stanza suggests the process of the afterlife outlined in 'The Soul in Judgment', where there is no judge except the soul itself understanding its own life, by following 'to the source / Every event in action or in thought'.[76] In 'The Man and the Echo' Yeats refers to this as the 'spiritual intellect's great work'; the remorseful thoughts that plague him in sleepless worry while alive, are rightly pursued after death, until he 'stands in judgment on his soul / And, all work done, dismisses all / Out of intellect and sight / And sinks at last into the night'.[77]

At the close of the first half of 'A Dialogue of Self and Soul', the Soul comments that 'Only the dead can be forgiven', and purification for both Self and Soul is to 'Measure the lot; forgive myself the lot', consequently 'casting out remorse'. Dismissing all remorse in self-forgiveness, 'So great a sweetness flows into the breast' that it enables true blessedness, engaging with the world through love. This contrasts with the Soul's overflowing fullness that strikes 'deaf and dumb and blind … That is to say, ascends to Heaven'. Unlike Yeats, George Russell (AE) declared himself 'on the side of Soul, but know that its companion has its own eternal claim, and perhaps when you side with the Self it is only a motion to that fusion of opposites which is the end of wisdom'.[78] There is potentially here a meeting of the subjective way of Self with the objective way of Soul, the positive way and the negative way of the mystics: 'Hatred of God may bring the soul to God', as the hermit Ribh suggests.[79]

CONCLUSION

As these two poems show, many aspects have their roots in the details of the system, though the poetry certainly has many other levels and elements, and the same is true, in varying degrees, of almost all the poetry and drama that appeared after 1917. The system that emerged in the automatic script and that Yeats outlined in *A Vision* was vital to his creative impetus, but Yeats was poet enough to avoid using it in ways that created an obstacle to readers, seeking 'sensuous images, or exciting phrases', to create the 'little song about a rose' rather than versified abstractions, except perhaps in a few cases.[80] The exoteric form of the work of art is accessible to all and communicates through understandable words and imagery, though the esoteric rationale or skeleton underlies it and

---

the blind mind and the lame man respectively. In cancelled text, the *Principles* themselves are referred to as: '*Spirit & Celestial* Body, the Knower & the Known, upon the *Husk & Passionate Body*, the Is & the Ought' (Rapallo Notebook A, NLI 13,578 [37r–38r], pages numbered 10–11).

[76] *CW14*, 159 ff; cf. 'In the *Return* … the *Spirit* must live through past events … to trace every passionate event to its cause until all are related and understood, turned into knowledge, made a part of itself' (*CW14*, 164).

[77] *CW1*, 346.

[78] *Letters to W. B. Yeats*, eds. Richard J. Finneran et al, 2 vols (London: Macmillan, 1977), 2, 560..

[79] *CW1*, 286.

[80] *CW5*, 16; *CW14*, 18.

provides further levels of meaning. Yeats seeks to explore the 'one history, and that the soul's', and, wherever the map comes from, its usefulness lies in reflecting something of the soul that can speak to any reader and that reflects human experience.[81]

In his letter to Macmillan, Yeats insisted that *A Vision* should 'be taken as a part of my work as a whole, not as an eccentricity. I have put many years of work into it.' He noted in that same letter, 'It is a book which will be very much wanted by a few people ... but will puzzle the bulk of my readers', and *A Vision* continues to fascinate a minority of readers for its own sake, whether as an occult world view or as a coherent symbol system that offers an insight into one of the twentieth century's most creative literary minds in English or any language.[82]

[81] *CW13*, lv.
[82] *CL InteLex* #6019; see n. 48 above.

PART IV

GENRES AND MEDIA

CHAPTER 26

....

ROMANTICISM AND AESTHETICISM

....

CHARLES ARMSTRONG

IN two of his mature poems, W. B. Yeats more or less explicitly identifies with Romanticism. In both instances, however, he specifies that this is a case of his being among the last survivors of a dying breed or movement. These are complex gestures, which signal his allegiance to Romanticism but also imply a complex relationship. In 'September 1913', originally published in *The Irish Times* on 8 September 1913, Yeats expresses his disappointment at the lack of local Irish support for a new art gallery, which had been made possible by Hugh Lane's willingness to donate a number of artworks. The refrain of the poem declares (with a slight variation in the fourth and final stanza): 'Romantic Ireland's dead and gone, / It's with O'Leary in the grave.'[1] Alongside the Wild Geese enumerated in the third stanza (Edward Fitzgerald, Robert Emmet, and Wolfe Tone), the Fenian John O'Leary is here cast as representative for a heroic Irish nationalism that has been sidelined by the newly powerful, penny-pinching middle classes. Although Yeats's own role is not directly thematized, he is evidently on the side of a more generous, expansive ethos that has now been eclipsed for good—unless the poem's philippic might succeed in stirring a rearguard action. Nineteen years later, in *Words for Music Perhaps*, Yeats uses an elegiac celebration of Lady Gregory to once more invoke a passing Romantic legacy. In 'Coole Park and Ballylee, 1931', first published in 1932, the final stanza makes the following affirmation:

> We were the last romantics—chose for theme
> Traditional sanctity and loveliness;
> Whatever's written in what poets name
> The book of the people: whatever most can bless
> The mind of man or elevate a rhyme;
> But all is changed, that high horse riderless,

---

[1] *CW1*, 108.

> Though mounted in the saddle Homer rode
> Where the swan drifts upon a darkening flood.[2]

Once more the passing of Romanticism is evoked, Yeats now unequivocally being cast as among the last representatives of a vanishing breed. At first sight, though, this also appears to be an idiosyncratic interpretation of Romanticism. 'Traditional sanctity and loveliness' might be taken as rather saccharine values, out of tune with the turbulence and complexity of a manifold and tumultuous movement. On the other hand, the emphasis on the 'mind of man' points towards a transcendental tendency, crucial to the Romantic legacy both for him and more mainstream accounts. Earlier in the poem, in the first stanza, Yeats has asked, 'What's water but the generated soul?'[3] As will be demonstrated further on, this image—accompanying the use of the swan, as in 'The Wild Swans at Coole', as a natural emblem that brings out the speaker's mortality—is closely linked with Yeats's earlier dealings with English Romanticism.

Together 'September 1913' and 'Coole Park and Ballylee, 1931' amount to a significant summary of Yeats's relationship to Romanticism. As George Bornstein points out, these two uses of the term 'romantic' indicate how 'Yeats saw literature and politics as intertwined, even when he opposed the reduction of literature to mere opinion'.[4] Further, one might add, these poems show that his is an interpretive gesture, which not only takes over Romantic tenets but actively makes sense of and selects among the Romantic canon. The bifurcation between a nationalistic heritage and a more literary emphasis on beauty and transcendentalism is a significant one, which is also central to his interpretive gesture. Furthermore, these poems both display Yeats's strong sense of identification with a movement, the most significant epoch of which had played out a century earlier. Not only a custodian of a long-lost movement, he also presents himself as a survivor. Although the filthy modern tide may impatiently have sidelined the heritage of Romanticism, Yeats stands forward as witness to the neglected but constant value of that heritage. Seen from this perspective, he is a survivor in much the same sense that he is a survivor of the late nineteenth-century protest against Victorian values. This chapter will show how a Decadent and aestheticist inflection was important to Yeats's relationship to Romanticism: his aestheticism may have been touched by Romanticism, but inversely Yeats's Romanticism was also more than a little coloured by the context of Victorian aestheticism. The first section will dwell on how Yeats's early writing drew on Shelley and Blake, with particular emphasis given to his reflections on symbolism. Subsequently, the complex interaction between aestheticism and Romanticism in Yeats's work will be addressed, and how Yeats's apparent leaving behind both of these movements early in the twentieth century actually led them to be surreptitiously reintroduced in differing ways. The final section looks at how Yeats,

---

[2] *CW1*, 245.

[3] *CW1*, 244.

[4] George Bornstein, 'Yeats and Romanticism', in Marjorie Howes and John Kelly, eds., *The Cambridge Companion to W. B. Yeats* (Cambridge: Cambridge University Press, 2006), 19.

late in his career, drew upon the Romantics for not only philosophical insight but also formal inspiration.

Shelley, Blake, and Symbolism in the Early Work

Yeats's early poetry shows evidence of the formative influence of William Blake and Percy Bysshe Shelley, who were to remain lifelong touchstones. The influence of these poets is mediated by the Victorian environment in which Yeats found himself. His father, the painter John Butler Yeats, communicated early on a passion for dramatic set pieces by Byron and Shelley, such as in *Manfred* and 'the first speeches of the *Prometheus Unbound*'.[5] Although John Butler Yeats's close friend Edward Dowden was not overly enthusiastic about Shelley in private, his biography of the Romantic poet also provided an early impetus for Yeats. In the Pre-Raphaelite environment which John Butler Yeats frequented, Blake was a special interest, cultivated by, for instance, William Michael Rossetti and Algernon Swinburne. The young Yeats draws on Romantic precedent in developing a visionary brand of poetry, where the poet attempts to attain a transcendental experience beyond the remit of prosaic, everyday life. Already in early verse drama such as *The Seeker*, *The Island of Statues*, *Mosada*, and *Love and Death*, Yeats engages in a Shelleyan quest for transcendence that typically involves an encounter with death through an ambivalent, muse-like female character.[6] This explains Yeats's enduring love for Shelley's *Alastor*, and will remain an important strain in his work, recurring in, for instance, *The Shadowy Waters* and *The Herne's Egg*. Imagination is a key value, as Yeats endorses Blake's interpretation of the poet as an imaginative genius who must penetrate to the timeless human truth hidden below the surface. Yet Yeats's scepticism about language and the poet's necessary historical embeddedness leads to qualification and irony, such as in 'To the Rose upon the Rood of Time', where the poet calls upon vision, only to demur:

> *Come near, come near, come near—Ah, leave me still*
> *A little space for the rose-breath to fill!*
> *Lest I no more hear common things that crave;*
> *The weak worm hiding down in its small cave,*
> *The field-mouse running by me in the grass,*
> *And heavy mortal hopes that toil and pass;*
> *But seek alone to hear the strange things said*
> *By God to the bright hearts of those long dead,*
> *And learn to chaunt a tongue men do not know.*[7]

---

[5] *CW*3, 80.
[6] See George Bornstein, *Yeats and Shelley* (Chicago and London: University of Chicago Press, 1970), ch. 2.
[7] *CW*1, 31.

For Blake, the eternal speaks directly to the imaginative poet through the minute particulars of our existence: he can, if inspired, 'see a world in a grain of sand. / And a heaven in a wild flower, / Hold infinity in the palm of your hand, / And eternity in an hour'. In Yeats's poem, however, the moment breaks apart from the eternal, and the 'common things' are valuable even when distinct from the rose's sacred realm.[8] The impossibility of sustained transcendence will be key to Yeats's later insistence upon a tragic dimension. Furthermore, the danger of 'chaunt[ing] a tongue men do not know' is acutely felt by Yeats, who in this respect would always see Blake's esoteric obscurity as something of a warning.

Around 1900 Yeats devotes several essays to discussions of the aims and possibilities of the poetic word. These discussions of symbolism not only are key expressions of a Yeatsian poetics but also are in close dialogue with Blake and Shelley.[9] Yeats shows himself as a well-read critic of Romantic poetry in a way that builds upon his work on an 1893 edition of Blake's writings, with an extensive critical commentary, co-written with Edwin John Ellis. But Yeats is interested in doing more than merely mapping out the oeuvres of these two writers. Instead, he engages in a complex negotiation with their legacies, both endorsing some features and distancing himself from others. At the beginning of 'William Blake and his Illustrations to *The Divine Comedy*', Yeats defines the symbol as 'the only possible expression of some invisible essence, a transparent lamp about a spiritual flame, while allegory is one of many possible representations of an embodied thing, or familiar principle, and belongs to fancy and not to imagination'.[10] The distinction between fancy and imagination reveals a Romantic lineage, being an opposition decisively articulated in Samuel Taylor Coleridge's *Biographia Literaria*. At the same time, though, Yeats is concerned with later developments, declaring Blake to be 'certainly the first great *symboliste* of modern times'[11] in the original Savoy version of the essay. When Yeats declares that 'no symbol tells all its meaning to any generation' in another essay of the time, 'Symbolism in Painting', he is making a nod towards the suggestiveness and polysemy that is a distinctive feature of French Symbolism.

In 'The Philosophy of Shelley's Poetry', Yeats interprets Shelley's symbolism as having one constant and indivisible signified: Intellectual Beauty. Caves, rivers, fountains, and the Morning and Evening Star are all interpreted as subtle 'metaphors' for Intellectual

---

[8] For Hazard Adams, the worldly, tragic dimension in Yeats represents a crucial difference between Yeats and Blake, despite their widespread agreement. See Hazard Adams, *Blake and Yeats: The Contrary Vision* (New York: Russell & Russell, 1968 [1955]), 194.

[9] For readings of Yeats and symbolism, see Matthew Campbell, 'Yeats and the English Romantic Symbolists', in David Holdeman and Ben Levitas, eds., *W. B. Yeats in Context* (Cambridge: Cambridge University Press, 2010); and David Dwan, 'Important Nonsense: Yeats and Symbolism', *New Literary History*, 50:2 (Spring 2019), 219–43.

[10] *CW4*, 88.

[11] *CW4* n.1, 379–80.

Beauty.[12] Yeats uses the Neoplatonist Thomas Taylor's interpretation of Porphyry's 'The Cave of the Nymphs' as a source, mentioning how Taylor 'contends that fountains and rivers symbolise generation, and that word nymph "is commonly applied to all souls descending into generation"'.[13] This motif is casually picked up in the eighth line of 'Coole Park and Ballylee, 1931', quoted earlier. At the same time, that poem's proposed link between Romanticism and tradition is qualified by Yeats's position in both this essay and his contemporary interpretations of Blake. For Yeats finds both Shelley and Blake wanting in their relations with tradition. It is known that the young Yeats 'devoted considerable energy to refuting' Matthew Arnold's famous dismissal of Shelley, in a review of Edward Dowden's biography of the poet, as a 'beautiful and ineffectual angel, beating in the void his luminous wings in vain'.[14] But even if his wording is different, Yeats makes a not unrelated criticism of the ineffectual nature of Shelley's verse. Already in 'The Philosophy of Shelley's Poetry', we find the following:

> Intellectual Beauty has not only the happy dead to do her will, but ministering spirits who correspond to the Devas of the East, and the elemental spirits of medieval Europe, and the Sidhe of ancient Ireland, and whose too constant presence, and perhaps Shelley's ignorance of their more traditional forms, give some of his poetry an air of rootless phantasy.[15]

Versions of this criticism will resurface in Yeats's later denigration of the cosmopolitanism of *Prometheus Unbound*. Despite Yeats's manifest admiration for the Romantic poet, Shelley ultimately comes up short in his estimation, due to his being a 'rootless' figure whose symbols are not sufficiently grounded in tradition. This explains the surprisingly dismissive final note in 'The Philosophy of Shelley's Poetry', where we are told that Shelley 'was born in a day when the old wisdom had vanished and [he] was content merely to write verses, and often with little thought of more than verses'.[16]

A related criticism is evident in Yeats's interpretation of Blake at this time. Repeatedly through his career, Yeats ponders upon the value and communicability of Blake's symbolism. In 'William Blake and the Imagination' there is much praise, but that praise is mixed with a gesture of wary distancing:

> when one reads Blake, it is as though the spray of an inexhaustible fountain of beauty was blown into our faces, and not merely when one reads the *Songs of Innocence*, or the lyrics he wished to call 'The Ideas of Good and Evil', but when one reads those 'Prophetic Works' in which he spoke confusedly and obscurely because he spoke things for whose speaking he could find no models in the world about him. He was

[12] *CW4*, 63.
[13] *CW4*, 63.
[14] See Bornstein, *Yeats and Shelley*, 5; the Arnold quotation is given on p. 40.
[15] *CW4*, 58.
[16] *CW4*, 72.

a symbolist who had to invent his symbols; and his counties of England, with their correspondence to the tribes of Israel, and his mountains and rivers, with their correspondence to parts of man's body, are arbitrary as some of the symbolism in the *Axël* of the symbolist Villiers de L'Isle-Adam is arbitrary, while they mix incongruous things as *Axël* does not. He was a man crying out for a mythology, and trying to make one because he could not find one to his hand.[17]

The essay goes on to contrast Blake's mythology with the more grounded narratives that might have been created if he were born in 'Ancient Norway, or Ancient Wales, or Ancient Ireland'.[18] Like Shelley, Blake is ultimately rootless and cannot completely compensate for the fact that he is cut off from the ancient wisdom of a national tradition.

Implicitly, Yeats is contrasting the nationalist grounding of his own verse with the position of these two exemplars. His own brand of Romanticism includes not only the intellectual, transcendental One he inherits from Blake and Shelley but also the 'Romantic Ireland' of nationalists such as John O'Leary, celebrated in 'September 1913'. There are several ironies involved here. Not only is Yeats accusing his own, personal tradition—for Blake and Shelley are indeed key figures in whose lineage Yeats consistently casts himself—of lacking tradition; he is also accusing Blake and Shelley of being cosmopolitan from the vantage point of a movement that itself was decidedly international. Yeats's romantic nationalism is no parochial invention, but rather partakes in a tendency that was general to Europe. As Joep Leerssen has affirmed, 'Romanticism and nationalism, each with their separate, far-flung root-systems and ramifications, engage in a tight mutual entanglement and *Wahlverwandschaft* [i.e. elective affinity] in early-nineteenth-century Europe.'[19] From this international movement Yeats acquired not only the idea that symbolism could be rooted in a particular national locality but also an emphasis on folklore and the idea of a national theatre. The long process that would lead to the establishment of the Abbey Theatre is part of a European history of drama that finds a parallel in how Goethe and Schiller launched a German theatre and Ibsen and Bjørnson were instrumental in establishing a national Norwegian theatre.[20]

Yeats had a 'rich imaginative dialogue with a specifically Irish romanticism'.[21] This was a strand of Romanticism that not only granted him a national narrative and a local mythology but also explored the linguistic affordances of a specifically Anglo-Irish context. If Yeats could somewhat patronizingly refer to Blake's 'explicit if not very poetical rhyme',

---

[17] *CW4*, 86.

[18] *CW4*, 86.

[19] Joep Leerssen, 'Notes toward a Definition of Romantic Nationalism', *Romantik: Journal for the Study of Romanticisms*, 2:1 (2013), 28.

[20] On Yeats's view of Ibsen and Bjørnson as exemplars for his own Irish project, see *CW8*, 65; Yeats also uses Finnish nationalist Romanticism for his own purposes—see Anne Karhio, '"Strange Woods and Seas": W. B. Yeats, the Kalevala and Repurposing Folk Literature', in Fionna Barber, Heidi Hansson, and Sara Dybris McQuaid, eds., *Ireland and the North* (Oxford: Peter Lang, 2019).

[21] Claire Connolly, 'Counting on the Past: Yeats and Irish Romanticism', *European Romantic Review*, 28:4 (2017), 473.

this is because he looked elsewhere for formal models he could himself develop.[22] Poets such as Thomas Moore, James Clarence Mangan, and William Allingham all played a role here, as did the nationalist verse of the Young Ireland movement. The latter is, however, an ambivalent influence for Yeats. Although there appears to be a grudging admission of the rhetorical power of the Young Ireland ballads, which Yeats himself taps into in 'Easter, 1916,' explicitly political verse is not something he would ever unequivocally endorse.

AESTHETICISM AND YEATS'S BECOMING MODERN

In 'The Philosophy of Shelley's Poetry', Yeats has related reservations regarding Shelley's political verse. He is at pains to distinguish this verse from straightforward radicalism, instead emphasizing what he sees as the deeper foundations of Shelley's reformist bent. At the heart of everything lies Intellectual Beauty, in a way which echoes Yeats's *The Wind Among the Reeds* volume and poems such as 'He Remembers Forgotten Beauty' and 'The Lover Tells of the Rose in his Heart'. In the latter text, the poet defends his own idealization of transcendental beauty against all marring contrasts:

> All things uncomely and broken, all things worn out and old,
> The cry of a child by the roadway, the creak of a lumbering cart,
> The heavy steps of the ploughman, splashing the wintry mould,
> Are wronging your image that blossoms a rose in the deeps of my heart.[23]

Such passages represent a high point in Yeats's early-career aestheticism, where all impurities and distractions from a rarefied sense of harmony are avoided or derided. Although aestheticism is a concept and a movement that is hard to distinguish fully from related tendencies such as Pre-Raphaelitism, Decadence, and Symbolism, it is precisely a cultivation of pure beauty to the exclusion of any other determinate goal that constitutes its clearest tendency.[24]

In her account of aestheticism in the visual arts, Elizabeth Prettejohn has identified aestheticism with a pursuit of 'art for art's sake'. This notorious slogan is, however, not, she claims, to be identified with formalism or any articulated theory. Rather, aestheticism is the articulation of a 'problem ... that does not predetermine its own answer'.[25]

---

[22] *CW*4, 90; on Yeats's formal use of the Irish tradition, see Matthew Campbell, *Irish Poetry under the Union, 1801–1924* (Cambridge: Cambridge University Press, 2013).

[23] *CW*1, 56.

[24] See for instance the linked treatment of Decadence and Aestheticism in Sean Purchase, *Key Concepts in Victorian Literature* (Basingstoke: Palgrave Macmillan, 2006), 37–41.

[25] Elizabeth Prettejohn, *Art for Art's Sake: Aestheticism in Victorian Painting* (New Haven and London: Yale University Press, 2007), 2.

At the heart of this understanding lies the Kantian definition of the aesthetic as founded on the beautiful, the latter being understood as a purposiveness without any determinate purpose or conceptual content. As Prettejohn points out, a 'fully fledged justification for literary Aestheticism (in all but the word) can be found as early as 1831, in Arthur Henry Hallam's review of Tennyson's *Poems*'.[26] Looking back, in the essay 'Art and Ideas' (published in 1914), Yeats would declare: 'When I began to write I avowed for my principles those of Arthur Hallam in his essay upon Tennyson.'[27] The 'aesthetic school' that was founded in that essay distinguished between different Romanticisms, choosing Shelley and Keats over Wordsworth because the former 'intermixed into their poetry no elements from general thought, but wrote out of the impression made by the world upon their delicate senses'. A poetry of sense impressions is contrasted with a poetry that emphasizes 'moral maxims, or some received philosophy'.[28] Implicit here is the Kantian division (systematically put forth in his three critiques) between the true, the good, and the beautiful.

Yeats saw in Hallam's essay a renunciation of the popular, which would also be key to his understanding of Decadence. But the emphasis on taste (implicit in the reference to the 'delicate senses') and the beautiful is also important in how it paves the way for an emphasis on the common ground of different arts. The 'aesthetic' is a meeting place for the arts, an environment in which they can mingle and exchange freely. The currency of that exchange is the symbol, which Yeats understands as the basic mode of artistic expression. This is illustrated by how 'Symbolism in Painting' and 'The Symbolism of Poetry' are sibling essays in *Ideas of Good and Evil*. The interplay between the visual and verbal arts is also crucial for Yeats's early suggestions (developed more fully in *A Vision*) of the existence of a collective memory. In *Four Years*, he retrospectively accounts for the germ of the ideas as follows:

> I had made a new religion, almost an infallible Church of poetic tradition, of a fardel of stories, and of personages, and of emotions, inseparable from their first expression, passed on from generation to generation by poets and painters with some help from philosophers and theologians. I wished for a world where I could discover this tradition perpetually, and not in pictures and in poems only, but in tiles round the chimney-piece and in the hangings that kept out the draught.[29]

Although the religious trappings of this conception are in tension with the secular cast of much of British aestheticism, the implicit privileging—despite Yeats's desire for a broader remit—of the common ground shared by painting and poetry is more typical. In 'Magic' (1900), Yeats would explicitly state that the 'one great memory, the memory of Nature herself . . . can be evoked by symbols'.[30]

---

[26] Prettejohn, *Art for Art's Sake*, 11.
[27] *CW4*, 251. For another account of Hallam's influence on Yeats, see *CW3*, 361–2.
[28] *CW4*, 251.
[29] *CW3*, 115.
[30] *CW4*, 25.

If we return to 'Art and Ideas', it is a strikingly tentative essay, very much marked—as is much of Yeats's prose—by the nuances, qualifications, and elaborations characteristic of Walter Pater's aestheticist style. Yeats would later describe Pater's *Marius the Epicurean* as being written in 'the only great prose in modern English'.[31] 'Art and Ideas' does, however, let on that something has changed since Yeats could dismiss, in the style of Hallam, the reference to any kind of heterogeneity in verse. In the interim he had published the poems that would end up in *The Green Helmet and Other Poems* (1910) and *Responsibilities* (1914), volumes that would introduce a tougher and more topical voice to Yeats' poetry. What had happened? Richard Ellmann once wrote that Yeats in the 1890s had built up a world that 'is not really an independent world at all, but a skillful evasion, neither here nor there'.[32] For George Bornstein, the turning away from that constructed world went hand in hand with a critique of Shelley, albeit one that erroneously projected into Shelley's work all the limitations of Yeats's own late Victorian verse: 'To become Yeats, he had to repudiate Shelley'.[33] This perceived dismissal of Romanticism and aestheticism has been seen to be linked with the appearance of a modernist Yeats, typically seen as being given birth through Ezra Pound's skilful midwifery. Yet James Longenbach, in particular, has challenged that narrative, showing that key elements of Yeats's new poetics not only predated any meeting with Pound but were in place very soon after the turn of the century.[34]

A key milestone in Yeats's metamorphosis is his letter to John Quinn on 15 May 1903. There Yeats writes disparagingly of his own *Ideas of Good and Evil*, describing it as 'too lyrical, too full of aspirations after remote things, too full of desires'. This might be construed as a growing suspicion of infinite, Romantic yearning. Against such writing he pitches 'that sort of thought that leads straight to action, straight to some sort of craft', before designating these opposed forces as being identical to Nietzsche's Dionysian and Apollonian tendencies.[35] While Nietzsche undoubtedly had a major impact on Yeats, though, he was not entering into completely uncharted territory. For Yeats, Nietzsche's writings are fathomable, to a certain degree, as a strand of Romanticism. We can see this in a somewhat earlier letter to Lady Gregory, where Yeats claims that 'Nietzsche [*sic*] completes Blake & has the same roots'.[36] This grafting of a later influence onto a Romantic precedent is typical, as Yeats frequently interprets post-Romantic developments via the examples set by not only Blake and Shelley but also other key Romantics.

This is particularly true of Yeats's complex relationship to the offshoot of aestheticism frequently termed as 'Decadence' or 'Fin de siècle'. When Yeats in 'Coole Park and Ballylee, 1931' describes himself as being among 'the last romantics', he is surreptitiously

---

[31] *CW3*, 235.
[32] Richard Ellmann, *Yeats: The Man and the Masks* (New York and London: Norton, 1948), 165.
[33] Bornstein, *Yeats and Shelley*, 113.
[34] See James Longenbach, *Stone Cottage: Pound, Yeats and Modernism* (New York and Oxford: Oxford University Press, 1988).
[35] WBY to John Quinn, 15 May [1903], *CL InteLex*; *CL3*, 372.
[36] WBY to Lady Gregory, 26 December 1902, *CL InteLex*; *CL3*, 284.

blurring the lines between the 1890s and Romanticism. This tendency is evident already in 'Friends of My Youth', a 1910 lecture that constitutes a first stab at the kind of memoir that later will result in *The Tragic Generation* (1922). There Yeats ponders over the fate of his colleagues, describing them as 'a strangely accursed generation: two went mad, two died of drink, one committed suicide'.[37] To make sense of this mysterious falling away of a whole generation, Yeats suggests the cause may lie

> in the work itself. They were lyric poets, that only. Life existed for them in a few intense moments that when they were gone left darkness behind them. They had no causes, no general interests to fill up the common day, and then, look back through all the lyric poets of the world, how few of them have been happy or fortunate, Keats, Shelley, Villon, Burns, the peasant poets of my own country, all who have put into lyric poetry an exceedingly personal expression. Is that perhaps the explanation of all? [A poet such as this] knows there is nothing that sings but passion and that the greatest passions are one's own. He would give nothing but pure flame. … the lyric poet who sings his own passions must be always in the blue heart of the flame.[38]

The final image echoes Pater's famous recommendation, in the conclusion to *The Renaissance*, to pursue the 'poetic passion' of art, and to 'burn always with this hard, gemlike flame'.[39] But the precedent within which Yeats frames the tragedy of the Decadents is dominated by Romantic lyricism. Between the lines, he is surely drawing on the fact that Keats, Shelley, and Byron died in such quick succession as a parallel for the sudden demise (in one way or another) of key 1890s figures such as Oscar Wilde, Aubrey Beardsley, Ernest Dowson, and Lionel Johnson. In *The Tragic Generation* Yeats will add Coleridge to this lineage, stating that he and Dante Gabriel Rossetti 'sought this new, pure beauty, and suffered in their lives because of it'.[40] An implicit difference from Romantic precedent is, however, suggested in Yeats's repeated insistence that the Decadents were intrinsically traditional. In a 1936 BBC broadcast, for instance, he states that the poets of the Rhymers' Club 'thought always that style should be proud of its ancestry, of its traditional high breeding, that an ostentatious originality was out of place whether in the arts or in good manners'.[41] This is clearly in line with the Ascendancy-inflected romanticism celebrated in 'Coole Park and Ballylee, 1931', but less so with British Romanticism.[42]

---

[37] Joseph Ronsley, 'Yeats's Lecture Notes for "Friends of My Youth"', in Robert O'Driscoll and Lorna Reynolds, eds., *Yeats and the Theatre* (London and Basingstoke: Macmillan, 1975), 80.

[38] Ronsley, 'Yeats's Lecture Notes for *Friends of My Youth*', 80.

[39] Walter Pater, *Selected Writings*, ed. with an introduction and notes by Harold Bloom (New York: Columbia University Press, 1974), 62 and 60.

[40] *CW3*, 242.

[41] *CW5*, 92.

[42] For a nuanced statement of how British Romanticism did not dismiss traditional genres, but developed and bent them into new shapes, see David Duff, *Romanticism and the Uses of Genre* (Oxford: Oxford University Press, 2009).

Decadents and Romantics did share a focus on the poetic self, though, and the latter concept is crucial to the reinvention Yeats pursued after *The Wind Among the Reeds*. His poetry after that high point of late Victorianism develops a more personal stance, albeit one that often is highly rhetorical and self-conscious. It is a complex and overdetermined phenomenon, inflected by various traditions—including, as Wayne Chapman has shown, by Renaissance poets such as Ben Jonson.[43] Romanticism plays an important role, too. As Michael O'Neill has pointed out on a general basis, 'Yeats, deeply schooled in Romantic poetry, especially that of Blake and Shelley, inherits from them a fascination with the representations of the self in poetry'.[44] In the 'Friends of My Youth' lecture, Yeats insists that 'the culture of the Renaissance was based not on self-realization, on a knowledge of things, on things reflecting themselves in the soul, but upon the deliberate creation of a great mask'.[45] Lest we believe this turn to a constructed form of self is a simply anti-Romantic turn, though, Yeats is quick to add another frame of reference: 'Wordsworth was dull as compared with Shelley and Byron, because these men had the theatrical quality which enabled them to project an image of themselves.'[46] This 'theatrical' subjectivity impinges upon Yeats's concept of the mask. An overly literal genealogy of this concept, however thorough, risks overlooking its relationship to Romanticism.[47] The way in which the mask mediates between self and daemon in Yeats's esoteric musings reflects various Romantic distinctions between a bare or naïve self and a more fully developed, self-conscious one (evident, for instance, in the Hegelian distinction between the self *an sich* and *für sich*, i.e. 'in itself' and 'for itself'). A more specific conceptual precedent, which we know Yeats was very much influenced by, lies closer at hand in Shelley's dialectic between self and epipsyche. For instance, the fatal dream vision of the youth in 'Alastor', which will lure him into disaster, is an ominous, erotic precursor for Leo Africanus and various other counterparts to the Yeatsian self:

> A vision on his sleep
> There came, a dream of hopes that never yet
> Had flushed his cheek. He dreamed a veiled maid
> Sat near him, talking in low solemn tones.
> Her voice was like the voice of his own soul

---

[43] See Wayne K. Chapman, *Yeats and English Renaissance Literature* (Basingstoke: Macmillan, 1991).

[44] Michael O'Neill, '"Something Intended, Complete": Yeats and the Remodelled Self', in *Romanticism and Victorianism on the Net*, Issue 51, August 2008. Accessed on 11 October 2019 at: https://www.erudit.org/en/journals/ravon/2008-n51-ravon2473/019261ar/

[45] Robert O'Driscoll, 'Yeats on Personality: Three Unpublished Lectures', in Robert O'Driscoll and Lorna Reynolds (eds.), *Yeats and the Theatre* (London and Basingstoke: Macmillan, 1975), p. 39.I have removed various italics in O'Driscoll's transcription of the letter, since these have been added by O'Driscoll himself to mark Yeats's revisions of an earlier draft.

[46] O'Driscoll, 'Yeats on Personality: Three Unpublished Lectures', 39.

[47] See for instance Warwick Gould, 'The Mask before *The Mask*', in *YA*, no. 19, 2013. Gould 2013. Gould quotes from the 'Friends of My Youth' lecture early on in his article, but does not dwell on its Romantic lineage – soon moving, instead, to a section titled 'The Fin de Siècle Mask'.

> Heard in the calm of thought; its music long,
> Like woven sounds of streams and breezes, held
> His inmost sense suspended in its web
> Of many-coloured woof and shifting hues.[48]

LATER DEVELOPMENTS: OTHER ROMANTICS AND POETIC FORMS

Shelley was far from alone among the Romantics in exploring the dialectic of self and other. Coleridge pursued this theme, too. In both his verse and his more philosophical texts, Coleridge provided the foremost articulation in British Romanticism of the distinction between organic and mechanical unities, and the former concept arguably provides the most important precedent for Yeats's conception of Unity of Being (even if Yeats mentioned other sources, such as Dante and Goethe). Yeats does not quote Coleridge's verse often, but the unfinished fragment 'What is Life?' shows up in Yeats's 1934 introduction to Bhagwan Shri Hamsa's *The Holy Mountain*:

> Resembles life what once was deemed of light,
> Too ample in itself for human sight?
> An absolute self – an element ungrounded –
> All that we see, all colours of all shade,
> By encroachment of darkness made?[49]

Yeats's quotation alerts us to the fact that Coleridge's ideas about the extremity of being, where the opposition between subject and object breaks down, bears a fundamental connection with the impossible unities of Phases 1 and 15 in the systematics of *A Vision*. It is also symptomatic that Yeats draws upon Romantic precedent in elucidating Eastern thought: much of Yeats's dealings with Buddhist and Hindu metaphysics late in his career can be interpreted as a covert return to the transcendental idealism of the Romanticism of his youth.

Keats's notion of Negative Capability is a form of surpassing the self that is addressed in complex fashion in various works of Yeats's oeuvre. In Keats's letter to Richard Hobhouse on 27 October 1818 he develops his famous critique of what he saw as 'the Wordsworthian or egotistical sublime, which is a thing *per se* and stands alone'. This conception he contrasts with his own ideal, wherein a 'poet is the most unpoetical of any thing in existence, because he has no identity, he is continually in for—and filling—some

---

[48]   *Alastor*, ll. 149–57, in *Percy Bysshe Shelly: The Major Works*, ed. Zachary Leader and Michael O'Neill (Oxford: Oxford University Press, 2003).

[49]   *CW5*, 149. This quotation is discussed in Matthew Gibson, *Yeats, Coleridge and the Romantic Sage* (Basingstoke: Macmillan, 2000), 83–5.

other body'. Keats goes on to envisage a more anxious aspect of this state of sympathetic imagination:

> It is a wretched thing to confess, but not one word I ever utter can be taken for granted as an opinion growing out my identical nature – how can it, when I have no nature? When I am in a room with people, if I ever am free from speculating on creations of my own brain, then not myself goes home to myself but the identity of everyone in the room begins so to press upon me, that I am, in a very little time, annihilated – not only among men, it would be the same in a nursery of children.[50]

This scenario might be compared to the opening of the first section of Yeats's *Per Amica Silentia Lunae*, where Yeats reflects on his disappointment, when he comes home 'after meeting men who are strange to me', at how 'all my natural thoughts have been drowned by an undisciplined sympathy'.[51] This is contrasted with Yeats's conception of poetic creativity, which turns out to be the product of the poet's mask rather than his empirical self. In 'Ego Dominus Tuus' Yeats ungenerously dismisses Keats as a sensualist who made 'luxuriant song' but remained a 'coarse-bred son of a livery-stable keeper'.[52] Although Yeats appears to resist the 'undisciplined sympathy' of Keats and his Negative Capability on principle, several poems—including 'The Song of the Old Mother', 'Paudeen', 'To a Squirrel at Kyle-na-no', and 'Man and the Echo'—gain much of their power from a breakdown of this resistance.

If Keats remained a poet whom Yeats never fully endorsed, his relationship to Byron was more fluctuating. By the second decade of the twentieth century, Yeats's own attempts to construct a public self in his verse, often drawing upon his own love life, made Byron an obvious template. But the most important influence from Byron was of a formal kind. Through the conduit of his friendship with the scholar Herbert Grierson, Yeats discovered the possibilities of the ottava rima stanza, which was to become the spine of several of his key poems. Here Helen Vendler's interpretation of the form as being 'stately and ceremonious in motion', and marked by 'grandeur', does not do full justice to its possibilities.[53] A poem such as 'Sailing to Byzantium' is indeed marked by grandeur. In its pursuit of a constructed, artistic transcendence, an 'artifice of eternity', it also has an aestheticist heritage. But the irony of its concluding stanza, where Yeats pretends he would be happy to be a toy bird entertaining 'a drowsy Emperor', displays a tongue-in-cheek sense of play that is ultimately just as Byronic as Byzantine.[54]

While Byron, alongside Shelley, was contrasted with the boredom of Wordsworth in 'Friends of My Youth', this does not mean that Yeats could safely ignore the latter. For

---

[50] John Keats, Letter to Richard Hobhouse, 27 October 1818, in John Keats, *Selected Letters,* ed. Jon Mee (Oxford: Oxford University Press, 2002), 148.

[51] *CW5,* 4.

[52] *CW1,* 162.

[53] Helen Vendler, *Our Secret Discipline: Yeats and Lyric Form* (Oxford: Oxford University Press, 2007), 36.

[54] *CW1,* 193–4.

Yeats, Wordsworth may have been tainted by the brush of Edward Dowden's admiration and a heterogeneity that did not gel with Yeats's early aestheticist ideals, but still he provided him with an important example and lessons to be learnt. During their second winter together in Stone Cottage, in early 1915, Wordsworth was one of the poets Ezra Pound would read aloud to Yeats.[55] This return to Wordsworth makes sense in light of Yeats's attempt to cultivate a richer sense of self in his poetry, and one can find the poetic results of it in the way a poem such as 'The Fisherman' rewrites 'Resolution and Independence'. Harold Bloom is also surely right when he claims that the title poem of *The Wild Swans at Coole*, in its implicit contrast between the poet's distanced view on nature and a former, more naïve immersion, displays a 'pattern' that 'is inherited indirectly from *Tintern Abbey*'.[56] Other examples could be added, suggesting that the mature Yeats also is making use of deeper patterns, in the sense of the underlying dynamics of what M. H. Abrams dubbed the Greater Romantic Lyric.[57] According to Abrams, Coleridge and Wordsworth created an influential template in the final years of the eighteenth century by twisting the loco-descriptive poem into a more elevated, meditative form akin to the ode. One of the key modes of this lyric form is Coleridge's so-called 'conversation poem': in lyrics such as 'Frost at Midnight' and 'This Lime-Tree Bower My Prison', Coleridge's speaker pursues a freely wandering exchange with a close friend or family member, which also includes references to the physical setting. Although Yeats does not simply reproduce these tendencies, his later poetry tends to fuse various poetical forms in an incremental process that both reminds one of, and partially appropriates, the example of the Greater Romantic Lyric. Key examples are 'The Tower', 'In Memory of Major Robert Gregory', and 'The Municipal Gallery Revisited', all of which mix meditation, familiarity, and spatial exploration with the depths of the memoried self.

Yeats also drew on the Romantics for a different kind of poem—the apocalyptical lyric. While a poem such as 'The Second Coming' draws upon his earlier thought in dramatizing a symbol, both verbal and visual, 'out of *Spiritus Mundi*', it is also unthinkable without Romantic precedent.[58] When compiling the character sketches that people the pages of the 'Great Wheel' section of *A Vision,* Yeats would interpret both Blake and Shelley as antithetical artists closely similar to his own self-understanding. Certainly, they are never left completely behind in his verse, and commentators have shown how 'The Second Coming' appropriates them both. Another figure lurks, however, behind the scenes. In an early draft of the poem, Yeats alludes to Edmund Burke's defence, in *Reflections on the Revolution in France*, of the deposed Marie Antoinette: 'For this / Marie

---

[55] See Longenbach, *Stone* Cottage, 42–3; John Kelly, *A W. B. Yeats Chronology* (Basingstoke: Palgrave Macmillan, 2003), 176–7.

[56] Harold Bloom, *Yeats* (New York: Oxford University Press, 1970), 191.

[57] See M. H. Abrams, 'Structure and Style in the Greater Romantic Lyric', in F. W. Hillis and Harold Bloom, eds., *From Sensibility to Romanticism: Essays Presented to F. A. Pottle* (New York: Oxford University Press, 1965).

[58] *CW1,* 187.

Antoin ette [*sic*] has / Most brutally died, & no / Burke has cried / With his voice.'[59] Draft material shows that one of Yeats's original ideas in writing this poem was to interpret the deposing of Empress Alexandra, and the violence of the Russian Revolution, in light of the events to which Burke responded. Thus 'The Second Coming' uses the crucial, historical event of the Romantic era, the French Revolution, as a template for his understanding of contemporary change. At the same time, though, the final version subtly erases these references, making the poem into a flexible, unrooted prophecy, which can be applied to a great variety of cataclysmic events. If Yeats himself draws on Blake and Shelley here, he is also drawing on Burke, a figure slightly tangential to the traditional conception of the Romantic canon.

Yeats tends to present Burke as part of his eighteenth-century Ascendancy heritage rather than as a figure imbricated in Romanticism. Burke's example thus shows how the borders of Romanticism are permeable, and how figures not always conceived of as central to the canon can play an important role. This account of Yeats's relationship to Romanticism has largely emphasized the 'big six' of the traditional canon, even as it has gestured towards the political and literary nationalist forms of Romanticism with which Yeats supplemented his appropriation of the British poets. In bringing these strains in dialogue with Victorian aestheticism, something of the fluidity and complexity of Yeats's dealings with literary tradition has been elicited. As I have shown, Yeats interprets and identifies with Romanticism, but he is also highly selective. Although it is a powerful presence, Romanticism is no univocal thing in his writings but, rather, interacts in constantly changing ways with other historical tendencies and movements. If Yeats's portrayal of himself as a survivor of Romanticism—as one of 'the last romantics'—has some truthfulness about it, it is perhaps in part because of the subtlety, breadth, and power which he deploys in this interaction.

[59] W. B. Yeats, *Michael Robartes and the Dancer: Manuscript Materials*, ed. Thomas Parkinson with Anne Brannen (Ithaca: Cornell University Press, 1994). For an interpretation that brings out the roles played by Blake, Shelley, and Wordsworth in both drafts and the final version, see Patrick J. Keane, *Yeats's Interactions with Tradition* (Columbia: University of Missouri Press, 1987), 72–105.

CHAPTER 27

···

RITES AND RHYMES

···

CLAIRE NALLY

In an article published in 1987, Hugh Kenner addresses what he characterized as the 'three deaths' of Yeats—the first entombment being the poet's work prior to 1909, followed by *The Tower* in 1928, and his final volume, *Last Poems*, in 1939, the table of contents for which he settled upon his deathbed. Kenner directly links this funereal phenomenon with Yeats's occult practices, stating, 'it was not an outlandish idea; to go and come back was theosophical routine'.[1] Nonetheless, despite some occasional and insightful interventions, the subject of death remains a relatively under-theorized aspect of Yeats's work, with notable exceptions being Jahan Ramazani's book *Yeats and the Poetry of Death* (1990) and Roy Foster's lecture from 2006 ' "Now Shall I Make My Soul": Approaching Death in Yeats's Life and Work'. Foster suggests that death is 'perhaps a peculiarly Irish subject'.[2] Later critical approaches to Yeats and the subject of death, such as those by Hawk Chang (2019) and Marjorie Howes (2014) offer sophisticated readings of the relationship between the poet's biography, later poems, and the subject of mortality. In a departure from these excellent studies, this chapter addresses death in the context of Yeats's early occultism: his membership of the Golden Dawn, the influence of Rosicrucianism, and his abandoned project, the Castle of Heroes, which was a form of Celtic Mystery religion. This reading aims to contextualize examples of prose stories from *The Secret Rose* (1897) and early poetry in *The Wind Among the Reeds* (1899), alongside the occult practices with which Yeats was engaged at the time. Such a perspective argues that this part of Yeats's oeuvre was an exercise in death and rebirth as much as his later work. Poems such as 'A Dream of Death', and 'The Man who Dreamed of Faeryland' register death as an ongoing thematic concern, whilst short stories, such as 'The Death of Hanrahan the Red' and 'The Rose of

---

[1] Hugh Kenner, 'The Three Deaths of Yeats', *Yeats: An Annual of Critical and Textual Studies*, 5 (1987), 87–94, 87.

[2] R. F. Foster, ' "Now Shall I Make My Soul": Approaching Death in Yeats's Life and Work', *Proceedings of the British Academy,* 151 (2007), 339–60, 339.

Shadow', map occult influences and symbols onto a wider experience of mortality and supernaturalism.

In many ways Yeats's early work also points towards the breadth and reach of his later occultism in *A Vision* (1925 and 1937), with its ambition to account for, and penetrate, history, human existence, personality, the realms of the living and the dead. This chapter reads Yeats's work through the theory of 'continuing bonds', which has evolved over the past twenty years to displace Freudian ideas of melancholia as a pathological 'problem' to be fixed. Thus the idea of mourning has shifted from maintaining the need of the bereaved to 'recover', emphasizing the benefit of maintaining ongoing connections with the dead. In so doing, Yeats's poetry and prose represent a navigation of the tension between the survival of loss, and what Catriona Clutterbuck describes as a 'cultural theoretical approach to grief, which defends ongoing *un*resolved melancholic attachment to our lost objects as the engine of our capacity for collective political dissent'.[3] In addressing how death and mortality intersect with Yeats's early work, nationalist politics, and occult practice, this chapter also acknowledges how far Yeats enacts a fantasy of renewal (and rebirth).

CONTINUING BONDS AND IRISH FUNERARY CULTURE

Ireland has been constructed throughout its history as a repository of the dead. As Witoszek and Sheeran note, 'The funerary tradition ha[d] been reinforced by the memory of the Great Famine and its accompanying horrors.' Irish funerary practice and belief are also influenced by a particular model of Catholicism, which has an 'emphasis on the spiritual rather than the material, its incessant *memento mori* and its exaltation of sacrifice'.[4] Yeats's later poems, such as 'Parnell's Funeral', explore this in relation to political martyrdom, and most notably, 'Easter, 1916' addresses the value of such sacrifice: 'was it needless death after all?'[5] Whilst critics such as Ramazani have traced Yeats's engagement with death to broader cultural practice, it is very much the Irish manifestation of death culture that will be addressed here.[6] Considered in these specifically Irish terms, the land and its dead are indivisibly (and perhaps conventionally)

[3] Catriona Clutterbuck, '"The Art of Grief": Irish Women's Poetry of Loss and Healing', in Fionnuala Dillane et al., eds., *The Body in Pain in Irish Literature and Culture* (Basingstoke: Palgrave Macmillan, 2016), 237.

[4] Nina Witoszek and Pat Sheeran, *Talking to the Dead: A Study of Irish Funerary Traditions* (Amsterdam, Rodopi, 1998), 38–9.

[5] *VP*, 393. For an example of Yeats's rhetorical construction of questions, see Geraldine Higgins's 'Talking back to history: From "September 1913" to "Easter, 1916,"' Chapter 13 in this volume.

[6] Jahan Ramazani, *Yeats and the Poetry of Death: Elegy, Self-Elegy and the Sublime* (New Haven: Yale University Press, 1990), 7.

connected, and this can be traced through Yeats's early verse. One way in which the dead are rendered visible to the living is through a manifestation of 'continuing bonds'. This theory has been successfully applied to late twentieth- and twenty-first-century writers tracing contact with the dead 'in the psychic life of the country'.[7] Whilst not strictly elegiac in the formal sense, the poems and prose analysed in this chapter nonetheless suggest that recovering the dead is indissolubly correlated with ideas of nationhood, ritual, and myth.

In conceptualizing Yeats's early work through the lens of continuing bonds, this essay draws upon the work of Silverman and Klass, who maintain that '[continuing bonds] re-examines the idea that the purpose of grief is to sever the bonds with the deceased in order to free the survivor to make new attachments. We offer an alternative model based on the mourner's continuing bonds with the deceased.'[8] Rejecting the pathologization of 'appropriate' forms of response to the dead, Silverman and Klass suggest that 'Memorializing, remembering, knowing the person who has died, and allowing them to influence the present are active processes that seem to continue throughout the survivor's life ... We are not talking about living in the past, but rather recognizing how bonds formed in the past can inform our present and future.'[9] This is in contradistinction to Freud's theory of melancholia on grief and loss. In Freud's definition, mourning and melancholia may be encountered as a reaction to abstractions such as the loss of nation. Mourning is considered a normative response, where the grieving subject enacts separation from the deceased, and eventually full detachment signifies the subject's recovery (decathexis). In melancholic states, however, not just the world but the self become empty and devoid of meaning, and Freud characterizes this as 'an open wound' which should be healed and ultimately overcome, with the replacement of a new object of affection.[10] This theory has influenced clinical practice in terms of 'appropriate' responses to bereavement, and has been extensively revised by the model of 'continuing bonds' which complicates the clear distinction between mourning and melancholia.

The 'continuing bonds' theory also emphasizes how this is a collective enterprise: as a cultural activity, it influences the social environment and practices in the wider community, especially through ritual. The deceased can be feared as well as welcomed, and this has influenced many 'tie-breaking ceremonies' which help to mitigate the power of the dead over the living. Where rituals are absent, communities, and even individuals, invent them: 'we need to look anew, in the historic Western tradition and in the traditions of other peoples, for rituals that facilitate continuing bonds with the

---

[7] Clutterbuck, 'The Art of Grief', 235.

[8] Phyllis R. Silverman and Dennis Klass, *Continuing Bonds: New Understandings of Grief* (New York: Routledge, 1996), 3.

[9] Silverman and Klass, *Continuing Bonds*, 17.

[10] Sigmund Freud, 'Mourning and Melancholia' (1917 [1915]), in *The Standard Edition of Complete Psychological Works of Sigmund Freud*, trans. James Strachey and Anna Freud, vol. xiv (London: Hogarth Press, 1957), 255.

dead and absent'.[11] In re-evaluating the model of 'continuing bonds', Klass and Steffen suggest that pre-First World War literature can exemplify a pre-Freudian attachment to the dead.[12]

Similarly, many ancient cultures, including the Celtic (mythologized in the nineteenth-century Celtic Twilight), emphasize an ancestral attachment to the dead, evoked through ritual. Witoszek and Sheeran explain that, 'Whilst it is ultimately impossible to reconstruct with any accuracy the degree to which the dead or a cult of ancestors informed the world model of the Celts, all the extant evidence points to just such a conclusion.'[13] In terms of these Celtic practices, Arnold and Gibson note that there might be evidence of a cult of ancestors in the European archaeological record.[14] Similarly, as Renata MacDougal says,

> Ritual actions, such as funerary rites, gained power (often understood as magico-religious results), from their grounding in a common belief system, derived from underlying mythic scenarios, particularly those that delineated the shape of the cosmos. The conception of terrestrial, celestial and subterranean planes, inhabited by human as well as supernatural beings, is essential to our understanding of the fate and destination of humans after death.[15]

Yeats's poetry and prose, inflected by occult practice, attempts something of a fictional reconstruction in this regard. Therefore this chapter proposes that Yeats's experimentation with Rosicrucianism, the Golden Dawn, and especially his own project, the Castle of Heroes, involved not only a recovery of the lost nation through ritual and symbol but a pre-Freudian, nineteenth-century example of continuing bonds. In some ways, his early occult investigations might also imply an attempted recovery of the lost love object, Maud Gonne, with whom he collaborated on the Castle of Heroes project. At the end of his life, Yeats commented to Gonne that 'we should have gone on with our Castle of Heroes, we might still do it'.[16] Despite never being realized, the Castle of Heroes is also a clear example of how important the recovery of the ancestral dead seemed to be, and how this permeated not only his poetry and prose but the spiritual(ist) endeavours throughout his life.

[11] Silverman and Klass, *Continuing Bonds*, 21.

[12] Dennis Klass and Edith Maria Steffen, eds., *Continuing Bonds in Bereavement: New Directions for Research and Practice* (New York: Routledge, 2018), 3.

[13] Witoszek and Sheeran, *Talking to the Dead*, 38.

[14] See also Bettina Arnold and D. Blair Gibson, eds., 'Introduction', in *Celtic Chiefdom, Celtic State: The Evolution of Complex Systems in Prehistoric Europe* (Cambridge: Cambridge University Press, 1995), 6–8.

[15] Renata MacDougal, 'Ancient Mesopotamian Remembrance and the Family Dead', in Klass and Steffen, *Continuing Bonds in Bereavement*, 268.

[16] Maud Gonne, 'Yeats and Ireland', in Stephen Gwynne, ed., *William Butler Yeats: Essays in Tribute* (1940; New York: Kennikat Press, 1965), 24. See also Lucy Shepard Kalogera, 'Yeats's Celtic Mysteries', PhD thesis, Florida State University (March 1977), 42.

The Castle of Heroes, Rosicrucianism, and the Golden Dawn

Yeats's occult experimentation is well documented, but perhaps less visible in many of these conversations and critiques of the poet's interest in the arcane is the visibility of an attempted dialogue with the dead and how this permeates both his early verse and prose. Such a conversation with the other world is also common in the various rituals and practices associated with the Golden Dawn and, relatedly, through Yeats's familiarity with Rosicrucianism. In a short essay from 1895, the poet rehearses the 'old tradition' associated with Father Christian Rosencrux: '[his] followers ... wrapped his imperishable body in a noble raiment and laid it under the house of their Order, in a tomb containing all the symbols of all things in heaven and earth, and in the waters under the earth, and set about him inextinguishable magical lamps, which burnt on generation after generation ....'[17] Yeats uses this image to draw some broader conclusions about the imagination and how the modern world has forgotten its 'ghostly voice'. In dismissing the 'age of criticism', Yeats affirms that the 'supersensual world' is imminent, one in which humanity once more understands that 'the external world is no more the standard of reality'.[18] There is much here to elucidate a reading of Yeats's work in the period: his reflection on the use of symbols, ritual, and voice; on the centrality of the dead and the other world in occult practice; and how this is explored in the work of the imagination. He clearly articulates here the later idea from *A Vision* that the spirits 'come to bring you metaphors for poetry'.[19] Yeats explains with some certainty the emergence of a new mode of perception, where conventional everyday reality is displaced by a new ontology of the spirit world.

Yeats was initiated into the Hermetic Order of the Golden Dawn on 7 March 1890, and it attracted him because of its emphasis on the practice of ritual magic. Founded by three Freemasons (Samuel Liddell MacGregor Mathers, William Robert Woodham, and William Wynn Westcott), it was guided by principles of Freemasonry, the Kabbala, and Rosicrucianism. Notably, Mathers was one of the ruling Chiefs from *Societas Rosicruciana in Anglia,* and even the name of the magical order, the Golden Dawn, was a reference to Rosicrucianism.[20] The ten 'grades' or levels of adept in the Golden Dawn also mapped onto that of Freemasonry and *The Societas Rosicruciana in Anglia*, and within this schema existed the Third Order, entities who were discarnate or beyond the

---

[17] *CW4*, 144.
[18] *CW4*, 145.
[19] *CW14*, 7. See also *Life 1*, 106: 'this seems to have been a half-conscious motivation from early on'.
[20] Alex Owen, *The Place of Enchantment: British Occultism and the Culture of the Modern* (Chicago: University of Chicago Press, 2004), 52.

mortal coil. In 1892, Mathers developed what constituted 'a secret elite within a secret elite', which would emphasize practical magic.[21] This Second Order (*Rosae Rubeae et Aureae Crucis* or R. R. et A. C.) enjoyed an entrance ritual which is of particular import here, deriving from the myth of the Rosicrucian order. The opening of Rosencrux's tomb or vault (to which Yeats refers in his essay) signifies in broad terms a revelation, or 'the great formation of Occultism in the West'.[22] Likewise for the Second Order Ritual in the Golden Dawn, a replica tomb was constructed, 'known in the Order as the Vault of the Adepts ... The Vault was a seven-sided chamber eight feet high, and its interior was adorned with a complex array of Cabbalistic, astrological, and alchemical symbols, each painted in accordance with the symbolic importance accorded specific colours.'[23] Following an initial appeal, the Adept's request to be admitted to the Second Order is denied, and (s)he returns dressed in black to be symbolically crucified. The process delineates more generally 'the candidate's journey from darkness into light', something which the Golden Dawn grades traced from neophyte onwards.[24] It was a descent into darkness, and a spiritual rebirth. The importance of this material becomes more visible when we reflect on the content of Yeats's Irish nationalist occult project, the Castle of Heroes.

In an article published after Yeats's death, Maud Gonne explained the motivation behind the Castle of Heroes:

> One of our early dreams was a Castle of the Heroes. It was to be in the middle of a lake, a shrine of Irish tradition where only those who had dedicated their lives to Ireland might penetrate; they were to be brought there in a painted boat across the lake and might only stay for short periods of rest and inspiration. It was to be built of Irish stone and decorated only with the Four Jewels of the Tuatha de Danaan, with perhaps a statue of Ireland, if any artist could be found great enough to make one, which we doubted.[25]

As Kalogera has noted, this is Yeats's attempt at an Irish 'national religion', which would provide the ritual to communicate with forgotten and lost generations, but also to compensate for the loss (and renewal) of the nation.[26] It was also a means whereby he could work closely with his (lost) unattainable love object, Maud Gonne, who left the Golden Dawn due to its links with the British Empire.[27]

---

[21] Owen, *The Place of Enchantment*, 71; *Life 1*, 105.

[22] Francis King, ed., *Ritual Magic of the Golden Dawn* (Vermont: Destiny Books, 1987), 105. See Yeats's poem 'The Mountain Tomb' (*VP*, 311) for a poetic version of this entombment.

[23] Owen, *The Place of Enchantment*, 71.

[24] Owen, *The Place of Enchantment*, 70.

[25] Maud Gonne, 'Yeats and Ireland', 22–3.

[26] Kalogera, 'Yeats's Celtic Mysteries', 43.

[27] See George Mills Harper, *Yeats's Golden Dawn* (London: Macmillan, 1974), 19–20.

Poetry and the *Theatrum Mortis*

An intersection of occult practice and Yeats's poetry also identifies a specifically Irish tradition, emphasizing a clear link between theosophy and the dead, which Witoszek and Sheeran define as the *theatrum mortis*. Yeats's occult sensibilities in the 1880s and 1890s maintained a dialogue between the living and the dead, which continued throughout his life, in his experiments with spiritualism, and the work of *A Vision* (1925 and 1937). In the early work, this *theatrum mortis* became visible in Yeats's repeated emphasis on the distinction between the material and the immaterial worlds:

> In the Irish *Theatrum Mortis,* the land below watches the land above. The poetic evocations ... hint at the existence of a powerful realm bordering on the world of the living. Images of a 'land coming to consciousness by jumping in graves', the house as coffin, and the grave as 'Irish stage' point to a kernel situation which might be stated in structuralist terms as an opposition between the world of the living and the world of the dead. Such an opposition is only pertinent up to a point, however. For if the dead constitute an invisible audience which observes and judges the doings of the living, they frequently trespass on the stage of this world. Their ghostly presence is acknowledged by a rich repertoire of symbolic actions – behavioural, gestural and verbal – staged and performed for their benefit. As we shall see, the division into 'actors' (the living) and 'spectators' (the dead) gives these actions a quintessential theatrical cast.[28]

Resonant of the Hermetic doctrine 'As Above, So Below', the *theatrum mortis,* like the occult ritual, stages a negotiation of two worlds, the spiritual and the mundane. Both depend upon a 'rich repertoire of symbolic actions' including incantation and performance, which engage the living and the dead in dialogue and community. We might think how in *Crossways* (1889) this Irish *theatrum mortis* is represented through the lost child who journeys to the realm of the fairies ('The Stolen Child'), and through poems in *The Secret Rose* (1897). We also find this theatre of the dead continuing in *The Wind Among the Reeds* (1899). A poem such as 'The Hosting of the Sídhe' has Niamh repeatedly calling 'Away, come away' and 'Empty your heart of its mortal dream'.[29] Readers also bear witness to the rise of an immortal army ('The Valley of the Black Pig') and an affecting confrontation between fairy and mere mortal ('The Unappeasable Host'). Such poems identify the nuanced ways that the figures of fairy lore are conjured in Yeats's early occult experimentation, and how emphatically this relates to an ongoing conversation with the dead.

In the context of Yeats's occult practice and its links with the dead generations, the early poetry can be read as an exercise in 'continuing bonds'. One clear example of this

---

[28] Witoszek and Sheeran, *Talking to the Dead*, 21–2.
[29] *CW1*, 55.

link with the dead is 'The Valley of the Black Pig', first printed in *The Savoy* (April 1896), and included in *The Wind Among the Reeds*. Featuring imagery commonly associated with the early Yeats and the Celtic Twilight ('dews drop slowly', 'dreams gather'), the poem is marked by an ambiguity and the indeterminacy of vision occurring at twilight: 'when day sinks drowned in dew'.[30] Alongside occult imagery, the poem outlines how the supernatural 'unknown perishing armies' will rise and free Ireland from its colonial yoke. The 'grey cairn on the hill' features as a memorial to the forgotten and dead generations, or indeed more literally as a burial mound, whilst the labouring peasantry enact a ritualistic and deferential 'bow' before the 'Master of the still stars and the flaming door'. Matthew Campbell has identified not only the apocalyptic content of the poem but also its curious timelessness: 'This door is threshold and not achievement. It is flaming, but not yet broken down. The poem faces impasse: it can go no further, being caught out of time'.[31] This timeless threshold might very well be identified as the performative impulse rehearsed in occult practice: bowing down to these symbols brings into being the circumstance of the poem or, rather, the revolutionary call to arms. As a bridge or gateway between this world and the next (or the living and the dead), the 'flaming door' as a motif is especially resonant when paired with Yeats's early essay 'The Broken Gates of Death' (1898), where he says, 'Sometimes a spell, like the spell of fire, even where used by accident, is thought to have brought the dead home'.[32] As a symbolic gateway, the 'flaming door' is part of the dialogue between the living and the ancestral dead.

Yeats was later to outline how far the dead become embroiled in the wish fulfilment of the living in 'Swedenborg, Mediums, and the Desolate Places' (1914), an article which carefully develops his thinking on the dead:

> Sometimes our own minds shape that mysterious substance, which may be life itself, according to desire or constrained by memory, and the dead no longer remembering their own names become the characters in the drama we have ourselves invented.[33]

The poem as wish fulfilment is a gesture towards national revival, both on the level of a reinvigorated Ireland and the more literal revenants of the ancient army, but it also navigates the symbolic death and resurrection so common in occult practice (as well as Christianity), performed in the Golden Dawn's Second Order ritual (discussed above). The comparable ritual in the Celtic Mysteries, 'The Opening of the Gates', marks the passage into greater initiation and indeed vision, something which the 'flaming door' of the poem also implies.[34] 'The Valley of the Black Pig' stages a ritual as much as it presents a poem.

[30] *CW1*, 65–6.
[31] Matthew Campbell, 'Yeats in the Coming Times', *Essays in Criticism*, 53:1 (2003), 26.
[32] *CW9*, 394.
[33] *CW5*, 63.
[34] See Kalogera, 'Yeats's Celtic Mysteries', 234.

In the 1901 essay 'Magic', Yeats suggests that occult vision can be evoked through the use of symbols, and that these can be used to tap into the great mind and the great memory.[35] It is noteworthy, therefore, that Yeats's own gloss on the poem identifies an old man from Sligo, 'who would fall entranced upon the ground from time to time, and rave out a description of the battle'.[36] If the poem is indelibly linked to trance or vision, then it is possible to think of the 'unknown perishing armies' as poetic symbols which will enact Ireland's freedom, but also as being summoned from the other world.[37] Yeats says as much in 'Magic'—'there is no reason to doubt that men could cast intentionally a far stronger enchantment, a far stronger glamour, over the more sensitive people of ancient times, or that men can still do so where *the order of life remains unbroken*.'[38] This idea of an unbroken connection across the generations, performed through occult symbol and the revivification of the military heroes of Celtic myth, has much in common with 'continuing bonds'. As MacDougal explains, cultural memory maintains a powerful presence in dialogues with the dead: 'Remembering as an act required renewal … this includes the more distant ancestral past of cultural memory as well as remembered memory, which applies to the living who had actual remembrances of interactions and events with the more recently deceased.'[39] By comparison, Yeats's construction of the peasantry maintained that rural people had an unbroken cultural link across centuries, similar to this notion of the ancestral past.[40]

The companion poem to 'The Valley of the Black Pig', entitled 'The Unappeasable Host', likewise emphasizes the intersection of death, the occult, and Yeats's early work. The poems were originally published with the subtitle 'Two Poems concerning Peasant Visionaries'.[41] On the surface, the poem simply represents a speaker who encounters the seemingly malevolent fairy folk, utilizing common Gothic tropes such as 'narrow graves calling', 'The doors of Hell', and a 'whimpering ghost'.[42] However, by the end of the poem the children of the Tuatha Dé Danann have also been identified as 'comelier than candles at Mother Mary's feet', juxtaposed favourably with one of the foremost icons of Catholicism. Yeats is representing both a folkloric and an occultist idea of the fairy folk, which were related concepts but identifiable from different traditions. As Yeats explains in an early review, 'Clearly the occultist should have his say as well as the folklorist.'[43]

---

[35] *CW4*, 25–41.

[36] *VP*, 808–10.

[37] See Kalogera, 'Yeats's Celtic Mysteries', 46–7, for Yeats's use of symbols in the Celtic Mysteries, a technique he learned from MacGregor Mathers.

[38] *CW4*, 34; italics mine.

[39] MacDougal, 'Ancient Mesopotamian Remembrance', 270.

[40] Deborah Fleming, *A Man Who Does Not Exist: The Irish Peasant in the Work of W. B. Yeats and J. M. Synge* (Ann Arbor: University of Michigan Press, 1995), 1, notes that 'Yeats saw the peasants as inheritors of "Celtic" tradition, whose folklore and legends were essential for the development of a national literature'.

[41] *VP*, 161.

[42] *CW1*, 58.

[43] *CW9*, 75.

The late Victorian and folkloric concept of the fairies suggested that they were 'neither harmless nor playful ... at their worst, they were simultaneously anarchic, spoiling and ruining products of human culture, and parasitic, living off their hosts while they destroyed them'.[44] However, much of the occult work of the late nineteenth century sought to reconcile fairies with philosophical and theosophical beliefs. What emerges is a Platonic concept that 'fairies were the spirits of the recent dead, awaiting incarnation in new bodies or transportation to new astral planes'.[45] In this reading of 'The Unappeasable Host', the speaker finds the fairies persuasive and compelling because, although dead (hence the way in which the poem uses Gothic imagery associated with the Host), they are also identifiable as ancestral and familial. Indeed, in this context, the poem performs some of Yeats's major thematic and occult concerns at this time. For instance, he records the various experiments associated with the Celtic Mystery rites in *Autobiographies,* where he explains that he and his uncle, George Pollexfen, would employ images in order to achieve vision or trance-like states (sometimes, the visions recorded were also those of the servant Mary Battle).[46] In one such vision, Yeats identifies the initiation rites of Cauldron, Stone, Wand, and Sword, the latter of which Yeats associates with Danu (or Bridget), a Celtic goddess of the Tuatha Dé Danann.[47]

The importance of these figures to the Castle of Heroes project cannot be overestimated. Both the rituals and the visionary material are peppered with ideas drawn from myth, and clearly have a religious/theosophical resonance as well as a folkloric one. Therefore, 'The Unappeasable Host' is an occult poem in the same way as those more overt pieces such as 'The Two Trees'. Related to the wider Castle of Heroes project, these poems become examples of occult and ritualistic performativity, of 'continuing bonds' with the ancestral dead. Likewise, the speaker's simultaneous alarm and bewitchment in the presence of such supernatural entities becomes even more poignant if we think of the confrontation in the poem as not just a dialogue with the fairy kingdom, but with the deceased. The speaker identifies how she hears 'the narrow graves calling my child and me'. This vocative appeal from a supernatural realm is made all the more emotional because the Danann children are playful and seemingly content. As an example of 'continuing bonds', the speaker nurses a living child whilst grieving for and managing a dialogue with dead infants. Additionally, as Matthew J. Spangler has convincingly argued, the poem's repetition of the phrase 'desolate winds' on three occasions emphasizes the nature of oral performance: 'it creates a repetitive rhythm as similar sounds define the aural contours of the poem; the spoken language, then, becomes a tapestry of interwoven sounds, foregrounding the musical aurality of language

[44] Carole G. Silver, *Strange and Secret Peoples: Fairies and Victorian Consciousness* (Oxford: Oxford University Press, 1999), 150.

[45] Silver, *Strange and Secret Peoples*, 40.

[46] *CW3,* 207–11.

[47] See Kalogera, 'Yeats's Celtic Mysteries', 147, and the Occult Papers of W. B. Yeats (National Library of Ireland), Accession No. 5554, MS 36, 261/1.

itself ... this particular use of repetition is common in ballads and oral literature.'[48] Indeed, Sean Pryor suggests that 'during the 1880s and 1890s Yeats wrote poems which do expressly claim a divine or otherworldly voice ... [taking] the form of charms, spells or incantations ... The identification of poetry with magic, incantation and religious rituals was widespread during the last decades of the nineteenth and the first decades of the twentieth century.'[49]

If this emphasis on orality is apparent in occult practice, it is also noteworthy that repetition is a key theme. Israel Regardie notes that the student of the Golden Dawn benefits from 'regular repetition' in Grade Ceremonies, and, within the realm of ritual, repetition is also used as invocation.[50] Yeats translated such practices into his verse, as he pithily identified in an early review essay, 'Bardic Ireland'—'A poem and an incantation were almost the same'.[51] Yeats's later essay 'Speaking to the Psaltery' (1902), describing his experiments with Florence Farr and voice, made this even more apparent, and linked the idea of trance or vision with sound: 'In chanting a poem, Yeats withdrew into an approximation of the magical process in which he created the poem, into the visionary trance in which its images and rhythms arose–recreating the rhythmic breathing and pauses, recovering the cadence achieved through the many subtle repetitions of line ....'[52] Such poetry emerges as an extension of Yeats's occult work, in both the Golden Dawn and the Castle of Heroes, but it is also the work of the bereaved and of memory—an account of those who have lost nation and loved ones, and who seek an ongoing channel of communication with those who are absent.

THE ROSE AND THE SKELETON

Whilst Yeats's poetry provides one key element in thinking about the occult and its relationship to death, his short stories are equally striking in this context. In *The Secret Rose* (1897) Yeats explained in his dedication to A. E. that these stories represent 'but one subject, the war of spiritual with natural order'.[53] In these stories, recourse to supernatural

[48] Matthew J. Spangler, '"Haunted to the Edge of Trance": Performance and Orality in the Early Poems of W. B. Yeats', *New Hibernia Review*, 10:2, (Summer 2006), 140–56, 153.

[49] Sean Pryor, *W. B. Yeats, Ezra Pound, and the Poetry of Paradise* (Abingdon: Routledge, 2016), 54, 59, 60.

[50] Israel Regardie, *The Golden Dawn: An Account of the Teachings, Rites and Ceremonies of the Order of the Golden Dawn* (Minnesota: Llewellyn Publications, 1986), 5th edn, 135. Regardie also notes that the Magical Formulae for the Neophyte Grade should be repeated three times: see 383.

[51] *CW9*, 110.

[52] Ronald Schuchard, *The Last Minstrels: Yeats and the Revival of the Bardic Arts* (Oxford: Oxford University Press, 2008), 135.

[53] Warwick Gould, Philip Marcus, and Michael Sidnell, eds., *The Secret Rose, Stories by W. B. Yeats: A Variorum Edition* (London: Macmillan, 1992), 233.

or spiritual knowledge often fails, or comes at a price: the inaccessible rose which Yeats invokes in 'To the Rose upon the Rood of Time' ('Come near, come near–Ah, leave me still') represents 'beauty … mystic rapture [and] the spiritual life to which Yeats' heroes try and often fail to gain access'.[54] But it is also paired with death and rebirth, powerfully established through the book cover design of *The Secret Rose*. Richard Ellmann explains that the cover was devised by Althea Gyles, and was 'intended to make the book resemble a grimoire'.[55] Warwick Gould has drawn some comparisons between this book cover design and that of the ritual book contained in the story, 'Rosa Alchemica', saying that '[Gyles] turns the Ritual Book of the Order of the Alchemical Rose into Yeats's personal talisman, or grimoire'.[56] Indeed, self-reflective books, or (unattainable) arcane knowledge, featured frequently in the early stories, with 'The Book of the Great Dhoul and Hanrahan the Red' (1897) being another example of the phenomenon.[57]

At the centre of the blue and gold embossed design is the Rosicrucian symbol of a rose joined to a cross and, at the base of the tree, a prostrate skeleton. Ellmann identifies the symbology as 'the conjunction of Rose and Cross, and of man and woman, in the midst of the serpentine folds of the Tree of Life. The three roses at the top represent the three principal states of being (Sephiroth) of the Kabbalistic Tree, and the skeleton at the bottom represents the lowest state of being or nature'.[58] However, it is worth noting that the skeletal image also references the idea of ritual death and rebirth which is the cornerstone of initiation. In Yeats's account of the Celtic visions he shared with his uncle George Pollexfen during 1897–8, the poet narrates, 'he saw a skeleton of gold with teeth of diamonds and eyes of some unknown and dim precious stone'.[59] Kalogera notes that 'The skeleton concentrates the "essence" of life from which the candidate is reborn following the ritual "death" of initiation'.[60] As such, the skeletal image of the cover links directly not only to the symbols of Golden Dawn rites but also to the experiments with the Celtic Mysteries. Through such self-conscious referents and images the reader of Yeats's book becomes as much a ritual participant in the stories as any of the characters. Symbolic rebirth is performed as the reader encounters the pseudo-grimoire, whilst Red Hanrahan (or a figure such as Owen Aherne) provide a narrative double of readerly experience.

---

[54] *VP*, 101. Heather Ingham, *A History of the Irish Short Story* (Cambridge: Cambridge University Press, 2009), 66.

[55] Richard Ellmann, *The Identity of Yeats* (London: Macmillan, 1954), 64–5.

[56] Warwick Gould, 'Yeats and his Books', *Essays in Honour of Eamonn Cantwell: Yeats Annual, 20* (2016), 36–7.

[57] The story was also published as 'The Devil's Book' (1892). See Gould et al., The Secret Rose, Stories by W. B. Yeats: A Variorum Edition, 185.

[58] Ellmann, The Identity of Yeats, 65. William H. O'Donnell concurs. See his 'Yeats as Adept and Artist: *The Speckled Bird*, *The Secret Rose*, and *The Wind among the Reeds*', in George Mills Harper, ed., *Yeats and the Occult* (London: Macmillan, 1975), 63.

[59] Kalogera, 'Yeats's Celtic Mysteries', 142.

[60] Kalogera, 'Yeats's Celtic Mysteries', 142. See also Mircea Eliade, *Rites and Symbols of Initiation: The Mysteries of Birth and Rebirth* (New York: Harper & Row, 1958), 92.

As Ingham notes, 'The Red Hanrahan stories are based on the eighteenth-century Kerry poet, scribe and hedge schoolmaster, Eoghan Rua Ó'Suílleabháin', but his attraction for Yeats was based in a fictionalized identity of 'the Irish peasant as dreamer and man of action'.[61] The story of particular interest here, 'The Book of the Great Dhoul and Hanrahan the Red', was excised from the subsequent 1905 edition. Despite this, the story captures the cross-fertilization of occultism, death, and Yeats's work in a number of ways. The story describes Hanrahan's invocation of Cleena/Cleona through the dark magic of the entirely fictional *Grimoire of Pope Honorius*:

> Last of all, his eyes lit on a receipt for making the spirits appear, by writing their names on paper with the blood of a bat and encircling their names with certain squares and triangles and many-pointed stars, drawn also with the blood, and then burning the paper calling the names aloud the while.[62]

It is also noteworthy that the hem of Cleena/Cleona's 'saffron robe' aligns her with the Rosicrucian tradition: 'he saw the silk stitches in the border of the little embroidered roses that went round and about the edge of her robe'. As with Yeats's early poetry, a performative invocation is notable here. The reiteration of writing and vocalizing a name suggests the ritualistic summoning of a spirit. Such an emphasis on folkloric motifs of death has been submerged in Yeats's later emendations, as he replaced 'Cleona ... the Queen of the Munster Sheogues' with the more accessible 'Cleena of the Wave' in the 1897 published version.

Cleona (or Clíodhna) is actually the Queen of the Banshees, and, as Yeats records in *Irish Fairy Tales*,

> [John] O'Donovan, writing in 1849 to a friend, who quotes his words in the *Dublin University Magazine*, says: 'When my grandfather died in Leinster in 1798, Cleena came all the way from Ton Cleena to lament him; but she has not been heard ever since lamenting any of our race, though I believe she still weeps in the mountains of Drumaleaque in her own country, where so many of the race of Eoghan More are dying of starvation.'[63]

Thus Cleona/Cleena is not simply a beautiful fairy woman in yellow, whom Hanrahan conjures as a love interest; rather, she is a fairy spirit that Yeats directly associated with the Great Famine. The occult book provides the possibility of dialogue with the other world and in turn reflects upon stories associated with mourning and ritual and how these functioned in Ireland. Indeed, a dialogue with these particularly funereal Sheogues (fairies) is restored the following day through the traditional offering of sustenance:

---

[61] Ingham, *History of the Irish Short Story*, 67.
[62] Gould et al., *The Secret Rose, Stories by W. B. Yeats: A Variorum Edition*, 189–92. Such lavish description is excised from the later version, 'The Devil's Book'.
[63] CW6, 180.

he got another pan and filled it with milk, and put it, with a griddle-cake, under the haunted thorn-tree on the hill above his cabin. All day he longed for night, and when night came he wrote the words anew, and the Lady of the Shee came again.[64]

This part of the story identifies a broad anthropological tradition which maintains the 'continuing bonds' between the living and the dead. Having conjured Cleena/Cleona through forbidden and occult knowledge, Hanrahan bids the fairy woman return. This too has clear connotations in terms of navigating a relationship between the living and the dead. MacDougal identifies the 'provision of food' as influential in ancient litera-ture in maintaining continuing bonds, and Witoszek and Sheeran note that this is also a feature of the Irish wake.[65] Dennis Klass observes that ancestor rituals have occurred in most cultures: 'Incense and food are offered daily to the dead, morning and evening. The rituals maintain the continuity of the ties between the living and the dead.'[66] At the same time, Joseph Lennon has demonstrated that *The King's Threshold* (1904) and *The Countess Cathleen* (1892) relate to a broader consideration of hunger, hospitality, and the Great Famine in Yeats's work.[67] Cleena/Cleona thereby becomes a metonym for the Famine—as a banshee, and an ancestral fairy goddess.

Hanrahan's encounter with Cleena/Cleona culminates with her rejection. Hanrahan explains: 'I tell you that it was not you, but the fairy Woman that I loved. She had no sorrows, she had not to foight wid people, she would not grow ould and git grey hairs like these that are comin' on my head. O, I have lost the Woman o' the Shee!'[68] This is worth unpicking in some detail. In some ways, Cleena/Cleona's transformation into a mortal woman signifies renewal and a return to the normative everyday world. It is thereby akin to the various occult rituals with which Yeats was familiar: she has returned from the other world, and is reborn into mortality, at which Hanrahan despairs (it is noteworthy that he highlights decay of the body and sorrow as his justification). But the revenant is also uncomfortable, and, as in 'The Unappeasable Host', such entities seemingly prompt ambivalent responses. Cleena/Cleona points to the limits of metaphor in terms of the Great Famine. As Morash has observed, 'the primary referent of the word "famine" is "death". To write the Famine is, in the first instance, to write about death on a massive, almost unimaginable scale. Indeed, the Famine's hold on our imaginations remains un-affected by the running debate over the numbers of the dead … the Famine dead whose defining characteristic is their absence.'[69] Cleena/Cleona is unsustainable as any form of vision because she is unimaginable: in part this is because she is other-worldly and

[64] Gould et al., *The Secret Rose, Stories by W. B. Yeats: A Variorum Edition*, 191.

[65] MacDougal, 'Ancient Mesopotamian Remembrance', 267; Witoszek and Sheeran, *Talking to the Dead*, 26–7.

[66] Dennis Klass, 'Continuing Bonds, Society, and Human Experience: Family Dead, Hostile Dead, Political Dead', *Omega*, 70:1 (2014–15), 99–117, 102.

[67] Joseph Lennon, '"Dreams that hunger makes": Memories of Hunger in Yeats, Mangan, Speranza, and Irish Folklore', *Irish University Review*, 47:1 (2017), 62–81.

[68] Gould et al., *The Secret Rose, Stories by W. B. Yeats: A Variorum Edition*, 193.

[69] Christopher Morash, *Writing the Irish Famine* (Oxford: Clarendon Press, 1995), 4.

conjured through unholy knowledge, but she is also a metonym for the uncalibrated or unmeasurable loss of the Famine. Her continuing absence is necessary and perhaps the only testament to the loss and grief experienced by the nation.

CONCLUSION

While several eminent critics have identified Yeats's relationship with death, which begins in his early work and continues until the final poems and *Under Ben Bulben,* this chapter has steered a different path in accentuating how far Yeats's early experiences of occult inform and underpin the navigation of death in his work. Through both magical practice and ritual encountered in the Golden Dawn, Rosicrucianism, and in his own experiments with Maud Gonne, George Pollexfen, and the Castle of Heroes, Yeats was able to articulate an ancient tradition of 'continuing bonds' with the dead. Such a communion was not without its ambiguities or ambivalences, as demonstrated in such poems as 'The Unappeasable Host', but it was also an idea which Yeats invoked when writing about the Irish Revival and the renewal of the nation ('The Valley of the Black Pig'). In his use of imagery, symbol, and repetition, Yeats mapped the conventions of occult ritual onto his poetry, and, similarly, his interests in fairy lore and folkloric belief became entwined with a very different form of the dead, through the memory of the Famine. Here Yeats explores the complexities of literary representation, and the limits of symbolism when encountering absent presences. Ultimately such a reading of these texts challenges the received legacy of Freudian melancholia, through a representation of Ireland's *theatrum mortis*, and foregrounds a concerted attachment to and conversation with the ancestral dead.

CHAPTER 28

··

MODERNIST
ACCOMMODATIONS

··

TOM WALKER

READERS of *The Dial* in the early 1920s would have been well acquainted with the recent work of W. B. Yeats. Ezra Pound became the New York magazine's man on the ground in Europe in 1920. Thereafter, his old friend's work featured extensively. That November's issue, for example, carried ten poems: 'Michael Robartes and the Dancer', 'Easter, 1916', 'Under Saturn', 'Sixteen Dead Men', 'The Rose Tree', 'On a Political Prisoner', 'Towards Break of Day', 'Demon and Beast', 'A Meditation in Time of War', and 'The Second Coming'. A letter sent by Yeats in March 1921 to *The Dial*'s editor and co-owner Schofield Thayer recounts Pound having passed on Thayer's ambition for the periodical to be 'the American exponent of Mr Yeats [*sic*] religious & other notions'. Yeats in turn promised to 'take' Thayer—a payer of generous fees—at his 'word'.[1] Soon after, the June to August issues serialized 'Four Years, 1887–1891', the first part of *The Trembling of the Veil* (1922), a memoir dedicated to another wealthy New York patron, John Quinn. This was followed that September by 'Thoughts Upon the Present State of the World', the poetic sequence later retitled 'Nineteen Hundred and Nineteen'. Further autobiographical prose extracts featured in the May to September issues of 1922. The November 1922 issue included the whole of the play *The Player Queen*. During 1923, the magazine carried the sequence 'Meditations in Time of Civil War' in June, as well as a further autobiographical fragment in July. Four more poems ('Leda and the Swan', 'The Gift of Harun Al-Rashid', 'The Lover Speaks', 'The Heart Replies') and an explanatory note appeared in June 1924. 'The Bounty of Sweden', Yeats's account of his recent experiences collecting the Nobel Prize, was printed in September 1924.

---

[1] W. B. Yeats to Schofield Thayer, 26 March [1921], *CL Intelex* #3889.

The Dial is now most readily recalled in relation to the publication in November 1922 of T. S. Eliot's *The Waste Land*. (See Figure 28.1.) Central to Lawrence Rainey's *The Institutions of Modernism: Literary Elites and Public Culture* (1998), for instance, is an account of the machinations behind this event, described as 'the crucial moment in the transition of modernism from a minority culture to one supported by an important

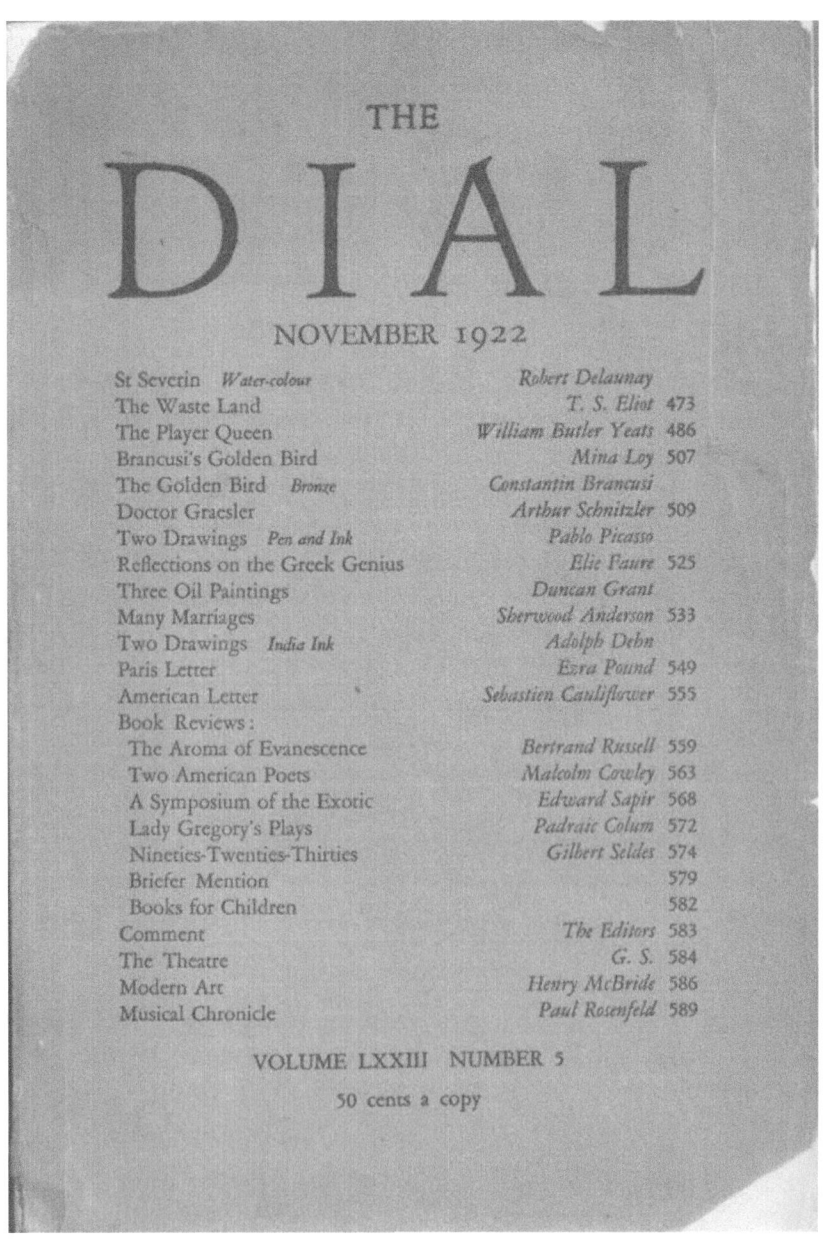

FIGURE 28.1 Cover of *The Dial*, November 1922.

institutional and financial apparatus.[2] However, *The Waste Land* is followed by *The Player Queen*—with the play taking up more space than the poem.[3]

If *The Dial* has persuasively been viewed as preparing 'the path for the canonization of modernism' in enabling 'writers such as T. S. Eliot, Ezra Pound, Marianne Moore, William Carlos Williams, D. H. Lawrence, Hart Crane, Wallace Stevens, and others to achieve recognition as leaders of what Pound called "the modern movement"', Yeats was a presence within this process too.[4] Indeed, something more than presence is acknowledged in Padraic Colum's review of the 1921 *Selected Poems* (published in New York by Macmillan), which hails Yeats's post-1904 lyrics as 'making for us all a rare, an austere standard of perfection.'[5] Moreover, Yeats's place in *The Dial* was not unprecedented. In 1917–19, Pound had served as the foreign editor for *The Little Review*, another key modernist magazine (one of whose benefactors was John Quinn). It is now best remembered for publishing the first episodes of James Joyce's *Ulysses*, but also during this period printed plenty of Yeats's recent work—including carrying seven poems in both the May and June issues of 1917.[6]

Yeats's prominence in *The Dial* and *The Little Review* might seem unsurprising. As far back as 1899, his work had been described as having 'found for itself a new form, a form really modern' in a review by Arthur Symons of *The Wind Among the Reeds* (1899). There Symons—then a close poetic confidant and later described by Yeats as 'the best critic of his generation'[7]—insightfully outlines this volume's innovations:

> Probably, to many people, accustomed to the artificiality which they mistake for poetical style, and to the sing-song, which they mistake for poetical rhythm, Mr Yeats' style will seem a little bare, and his rhythm, at its best, a little uncertain. They will seem astonished, perhaps not altogether pleased, at finding a poet who uses no inversions, who says in one line, as straightforward as prose, what most poets would dilute into a stanza, and who, in his music replaces the aria by the recitative. How few, it annoys me to think, as I read over this simple and learned poetry, will realise the extraordinary art which has worked these tiny poems, which seem as free as waves, into a form at once so monumental and so alive! Here, at last, is poetry which has found for itself a new form, a form really modern, its rejection of every artifice, its return to the natural chant out of which verse was evolved; and it expresses with a

---

[2] Lawrence Rainey, *Institutions of Modernism: Literary Elites and Public Culture* (New Haven: Yale University Press, 1998), 91.

[3] *The Dial*, 73:5 (November 1922), 473–85, 486–506.

[4] Christina Britzolakis, 'Making Modernism Safe for Democracy: *The Dial* (1920–1929)', in Peter Brooker and Andrew Thacker, eds, *The Oxford Critical and Cultural History of Modernist Magazines, Volume II: North America 1894–1960* (Oxford: Oxford University Press, 2012), 85–102, 85.

[5] Padraic Colum, 'Mr Yeats's Selected Poems', *The Dial*, 71:4 (October 1921), 464–8, 468.

[6] See Claire Hutton, 'Yeats, Pound, and the *Little Review*, 1914–1918', *International Yeats Studies*, 3:1 (2018), DOI: https://doi.org/10.34068/IYS.03.01.03.

[7] W. B. Yeats to Rhoda Symons [13 October 1908], *CL Intelex* #973.

passionate quietude, the elemental desires of humanity, the desire of love, the desire of wisdom, the desire of beauty.[8]

Symons's review highlights the challenge that Yeats's early work offered to contemporaneous readers' formal and stylistic expectations. As Yopie Prins describes of rhythm more specifically, amid a proliferation of poetic forms and critical debate about prosody, the Victorians came to conceptualize poetic metre 'as a formal grid or pattern of spacing, created by the alternation of quantifiable units'—an abstraction of poetic rhythm into a metrical law that was in turn 'enforced by the rules of scansion and recitation taught in schools'.[9]

A poem such as what was then titled 'Mongan Laments the Change that has Come Upon Him and his Beloved' does not easily fit such rules:

> Do you not hear me calling, white deer with no horns!
> I have been changed to a hound with one red ear;
> I have been in the Path of Stones and the Wood of Thorns,
> For somebody hid hatred and hope and desire and fear
> Under my feet that they follow you night and day.
> . . .
> I would that the Boar without bristles had come from the West
> And had rooted the sun and moon and stars out of the sky
> And lay in the darkness, grunting, and turning to his rest.[10]

Its first line might be taken as settling into an iambic groove. But with an unstressed hyperbeat coming into play with the 'ing' of 'calling', and a further stressed hyperbeat appearing at the end of the line with 'horns', things soon go awry. The second line seems to start with three unstressed syllables (a scarcely conceivable tribrach perhaps) and to end with three stressed syllables (possibly an only slightly more conscionable molossus). By the end of the poem, within a poetic voice that symbolically suggests various instabilities and etherealities, no clear pattern of alternating stressed and unstressed syllables has emerged. There seems, rather, to be some kind of accentual verse in play, with five stresses irregularly distributed in most lines. Moreover, in searching out any one line's rhythm, a reader is repeatedly tempted unusually to emphasize certain syllables ('they' in the fifth line, say), so offending the supposed proprieties of quantity— that much-debated Victorian notion, carried over from Greek and Roman prosody, that syllables in English have a specific length of articulation.[11] Indeed, Yeats's father had

---

[8] Arthur Symons, 'Mr. Yeats as a Lyric Poet', *Saturday Review of Politics, Literature, Science and Art*, 87:2271 (6 May 1889), 553–4.

[9] Yopie Prins, 'Victorian Meters', in Joseph Bristow, ed., *The Cambridge Companion to Victorian Poetry* (Cambridge: Cambridge University Press, 2005), 89–113, 90.

[10] *CW1*, 61.

[11] On this and related Victorian literary critical debates, see Meredith Martin, *The Rise and Fall of Meter: Poetry and English National Culture, 1860–1930* (Princeton: Princeton University Press, 2012), 16–47.

earlier pointed to the uncertainties of his son's ear in exactly such terms, writing in 1884 to Edward Dowden that the 'bad metres arise very much from his composing in a loud voice manipulating of course the quantities to his taste'.[12]

Critics have ascribed such deviations to Yeats's and others' forging of a sonically distinctive Irish-English poetry—what Thomas MacDonagh labelled as 'the Irish mode', reflective of the 'less pronounced hammering of stressed syllables' in 'English as we speak it in Ireland'.[13] They have also viewed Yeats, along with other poets during the 1890s, as trying so to transcend the burdens of Victorian poetry. Against descriptive and discursive verbosity, and the carrying of abstract ideas and high-minded moralization, Yeats has been described as attempting 'an English version of Mallarmé's "pure poetry", in which "the poet's voice must be still and the initiative taken by the words themselves"'—as the French poet had proposed in his essay 'The Crisis of Poetry' (1896).[14] Yet the paternal criticism quoted above also features in Hannah Sullivan's account of how Yeats 'began as a more experimental prosodist than he ended'.[15] Although Yeats after 1899 continued to employ speech-like syntax and eschew conventional poetic diction—as well as more often addressing contemporary subject matter through an increasingly concrete symbolism—free, new, and modern were not epithets the poet would embrace. Nor would they seem wholly apposite in relation to the work he produced. This includes the poems printed in *The Dial*. For example, the opening section of 'Thoughts Upon the Present State of the World' contains Yeats's first use of ottava rima—a stanza form that would thereafter proliferate, including in two sections of 'Meditations in Time of Civil War'. Looking back on his career in the late 1930s, Yeats justifiably cast himself as having been compelled 'to accept those traditional metres that have developed with the language. Ezra Pound, [W. J.] Turner, [D. H.] Lawrence wrote admirable free verse, I could not. ... I must choose a traditional stanza, even what I alter must seem traditional'.[16]

This move towards traditional metres and forms was, moreover, already in play at the moment when younger poets and critics were articulating a self-consciously modern anglophone poetics advocating the opposite. In his 'Lecture on Modern Poetry' (c.1908–9), T. E. Hulme argued that a modern 'introspective' spirit that 'has found expression in painting as Impressionism will soon find expression in poetry as free verse ... Regular metre to this impressionist poetry is cramping, jangling, meaningless, and out of place'.[17] Longenbach notes that, on first reading Yeats's 'No Second Troy' and 'Reconciliation' in 1910,

---

[12] *Letters of John Butler Yeats*, ed. Joseph Hone (London: Faber & Faber, 1999), 53.

[13] Thomas MacDonagh, *Literature in Ireland: Studies Irish and Anglo-Irish* (Dublin: Talbot Press, 1916), 65. For an overview of the Irish mode, see Matthew Campbell, *Irish Poetry under the Union, 1801–1924* (Cambridge: Cambridge University Press, 2013), 21–47.

[14] Ronald Bush, 'Modernist Poetry and Poetics', in Laura Marcus and Peter Nicholls, eds, *The Cambridge History of Twentieth-Century English Literature* (Cambridge: Cambridge University Press, 2004), 232–50, 238.

[15] Hannah Sullivan, 'How Yeats Learned to Scan', *YA*, 21 (2018), 3–37, 12.

[16] *CW5*, 204–16, 213.

[17] T. E. Hulme, *Selected Writings*, ed. Patrick McGuinness (Manchester: Carcanet, 1998), 64–5.

Pound enthused: 'he and I are now as it were in one movement with *aims* very nearly identical'. Somewhat complexly, however, the younger poet would soon launch imagism, of which 'the third of its famous principles ("compose in the sequence of the musical phrase, not in sequence of a metronome") would be supported by the Yeats of the 1890s more readily than the more metrically vigorous Yeats of "Reconciliation".'[18] The older poet was not only an inspirational precursor but also an engaged, independent-minded contemporary.[19] Furthermore, any sense of modernist poetic history as a teleology towards formal freedom is complicated by the conscious turn made in 1917 by Pound and Eliot towards 'rhyme and regular strophes' as a 'counter-current' to the by then, for them, dangerous prevalence of free verse.[20]

Yeats has, therefore, proved central yet tricky to accommodate within accounts of modernist poetry. Daniel Albright depicts Yeats and modernism as ghosts haunting one another, before turning to the comparison made in *A Vision* of the gyres to the visual abstraction of Wyndham Lewis and Brancusi, to argue: 'Yeats fights Modernism as hard as he can, only to find himself acknowledging that he is Modernist to the marrow of his bones'—a paradox Albright finds 'itself typical' of modernism.[21] For George Bornstein, *The Tower* (1928) is 'paradigmatic of modernism', in its condition of bibliographic and textual instability.[22] By contrast, Ronald Schuchard describes that volume as 'an anti-modernist text ... consciously constructed as a counter-monument to *The Waste Land* and *Ulysses*'.[23] Denis Donoghue on balance holds that 'Yeats was modern, but not a modernist'—a distinction he partially illuminates via a comparison with music, whereby 'Debussy, Schoenberg, Alban Berg, and Webern' made different sounds to 'Rachmaninov, Mahler, Richard Strauss, or even Stravinsky'.[24] Edna Longley, meanwhile, bracingly poses: 'If "modern poetry" can seem oxymoronic to Yeats, perhaps "Yeats and modernism" should seem so for criticism.'[25] This leads into an attempt to extricate Yeats from that very story of modernist poetry, which she critiques as a retrospective critical paradigm that has damagingly dominated the anglophone literary academy since the late 1960s. Or as Anne Fogarty less polemically describes, Yeats 'may be viewed as an instigator and central practitioner of modernist poetry but, on another level, he is of note because he deviates from, or implicitly

---

[18] James Longenbach, *Stone Cottage: Pound, Yeats, and Modernism* (Oxford: Oxford University Press, 1988), 17–18; James Longenbach, 'Modern Poetry', in David Holdeman and Ben Levitas, eds, *Yeats in Context* (Cambridge: Cambridge University Press, 2010), 320–9, 324.

[19] On Yeats's ongoing playing of this role, see Tom Walker, '"our more profound Pre-Raphaelitism": W.B. Yeats, Aestheticism and *Blast*', in Philip Coleman, Kathryn Milligan, and Nathan O'Donnell, eds., *Blast at 100: A Modernist Magazine Reconsidered* (Amsterdam: Brill, 2017), 79–92.

[20] Ezra Pound, 'Harold Monro', *The Criterion*, 11:45 (July 1932), 581–92, 590.

[21] Daniel Albright, 'Yeats and Modernism', in Marjorie Howes and John Kelly, eds, *The Cambridge Companion to W. B. Yeats* (Cambridge: Cambridge University Press, 2006), 59–76, 63, 75.

[22] George Bornstein, *Material Modernism: The Politics of the Page* (Cambridge: Cambridge University Press, 2001), 80.

[23] Ronald Schuchard, '*The Tower*: Yeats's Anti-Modernist Monument', *YA*, 18 (2013), 121–50, 124.

[24] Denis Donoghue, 'Yeats, Trying to be Modern', *New England Review*, 31:4 (2010), 131–44, 144.

[25] Edna Longley, *Yeats and Modern Poetry* (Cambridge: Cambridge University Press, 2013), 35.

unsettles, any historiographical or conceptual map of modernism that we might want to adopt'.[26]

Whether seeking to connect Yeats with or disassociate him from modernism, though, most critical assessments have broadly followed a traditional understanding of modernism 'primarily in formalist terms as a loose affiliation of movements coalescing around certain aesthetic rebellions, styles, and philosophical principles and resisting the aesthetics of immediate precursors in the arts and literature'.[27] However, recent decades have seen attempts to reckon with modernism in other terms. The emphasis placed on questions of publication, publicity, and patronage by Rainey's *Institutions of Modernism* has proved seminal within a broader move towards historicist, materialist, and sociological perspectives in the so-called 'New Modernist Studies'.[28] The publication practice pursued by Yeats from the early 1900s on, whereby initial limited-edition publications from his sister's Dun Emer/Cuala Press were followed by trade editions, is pointed to in passing by Rainey as having been adopted, via Pound, as a strategy 'by the emerging English avant-garde'.[29] Scholars such as Bornstein have, moreover, explored how the shifting textuality and materiality of Yeats's publications were as much a part of his modernism as developments in style and subject matter. But the perspectives of the 'New Modernist Studies' might also highlight that, however dissatisfying the term and the critical history that has led to its widespread use, Yeats has been a significant presence within modernism's institutionalization—as attested to by the poet's prominence in *The Little Review* and *The Dial*.

Related to this institutionalization is the prominence from the 1890s onward of critical advocacy for poetical progress, novelty, and modernity as regards form and style, sometimes linked to a need for poetry to reconnect to life. Unstable and polarizing, this discourse of novelty and modernity can simplify the nature of what is actually taking place in any one poem, but it serves to signal, whether assented to or opposed, some form of entanglement with what has come to be called modernism.[30] It can be seen in Symons's appraisal of *The Wind Among the Reeds*. It is present in the terms of Hulme's polemic, as well as Pound's sense in 1910 that Yeats 'has come out of the shadows & has declared for life ... has found within himself spirit of the new air'.[31] It is also at work in the stories Yeats's poetry starts to tell about itself, such as in the casting off of 'embroideries' and

---

[26] Anne Fogarty, 'Yeats, Ireland and Modernism', in Alex Davis and Lee M. Jenkins, eds, *The Cambridge Companion to Modernist Poetry* (Cambridge: Cambridge University Press, 2007), 126–46, 126.

[27] Susan Stanford Friedman, 'Planetarity: Musing Modernist Studies', *Modernism/modernity*, 17:3 (September 2010), 471–99, 474.

[28] This shift was influentially outlined in Douglas Mao and Rebecca L. Walkowitz, 'The New Modernist Studies', *PMLA*, 123 (2008), 737–48.

[29] Rainey, *Institutions of Modernism*, 100.

[30] This discourse is illuminated as regards the oppositions frequently made in the period between the old and the new, poetry and rhetoric, and the hard and the soft in Robert Scholes, *The Paradoxy of Modernism* (New Haven: Yale University Press, 2006).

[31] Longenbach, *Stone Cottage*, 17.

'old mythologies', and turn towards 'walking naked' staged in 'A Coat' (written in 1912).[32] Here one cannot tidily assess whether Yeats's work does thematically or formally change in such a fashion, and whether or not this makes him a modernist. Rather, the provisional assertion of change places the poet in relation to the negotiations and debates of a modernism now conceived as a network or institution, rather than formal or ontological category. As David Holdeman argues, such narratives of progress are also furthered by intricate developmental ordering within Yeats's books and the self-dramatization they offer of his poetic and bibliographic revisionism.[33]

Expansions in the study of modernism and nineteenth-century literature have also seen reconsiderations of questions of periodization. Comparative and transnational perspectives, as well as critical returns to a more fully historicized formalism, have called into question modernists' apparent resistance to the aesthetics of their predecessors. Subsequently, scholars have stressed the connections between aestheticism, decadence, and modernism. Vincent Sherry, for example, has sought to uncover the suppressed decadent sensibility at work in literary modernism.[34] Other scholars have highlighted the continuities between Victorian and modernist poetics, such as when Garrett Stewart describes the 'freeing' of 'poetry from the shackles of diction' as 'one main historical agenda … inherited by the Victorians and pressed further, in turn, by modernist experiment'.[35] Against broader shifts in literary historiography, Yeats's Romanticism, Victorianism, aestheticism, and decadence can no longer be considered as straightforwardly working in opposition to his modernism. Also important are reconsiderations of the location and politics of modernism. Yeats's Irish cultural nationalism was long viewed as problematic to his participation in a modernism conceived of as metropolitan and apolitical. But, as Fogarty describes, the emergence of 'a plurality of competing and geographically diverse alternative modernisms' has seen Yeats's modernism reconceived as being partly 'the outcome of his engagement with the Irish literary revival'. Now 'his recuperation and construction of an Irish literary tradition and his discovery of the

---

[32] CW1, 127.

[33] David Holdeman, *Much Labouring: The Texts and Authors of Yeats's First Modernist Books* (Ann Arbour: The University of Michigan Press, 1997), 20–2.

[34] Vincent Sherry, *Modernism and the Reinvention of Decadence* (Cambridge: Cambridge University Press, 2015). On the continuities between aestheticism, decadence, and modernism, also see Kate Hext and Alexander Murray, eds, *Decadence in the Age of Modernism* (Baltimore: Johns Hopkins University Press, 2019); and Miranda B. Hickman, *The Geometry of Modernism: The Vorticist Idiom in Lewis, Pound, H.D. and Yeats* (Austin: University of Texas Press, 2005), 27–88.

[35] Garrett Stewart, 'Diction', in Matthew Bevis, ed., *The Oxford Handbook of Victorian Poetry* (Oxford: Oxford University Press, 2013), 93–111, 97. On the interrelations between nineteenth-century and early twentieth-century poetics, also see Carol T. Christ, *Victorian and Modern Poetics* (Chicago: University of Chicago Press, 1984); Linda C. Dowling, *Language and Decadence in the Victorian Fin de Siècle* (Princeton: Princeton University Press, 1986); Jason David Hall and Alex Murray, eds, *Decadent Poetics: Literature and Form at the British Fin de Siècle* (Basingstoke: Palgrave Macmillan, 2013); Joseph Phelan, *The Music of Verse: Metrical Experiment in Nineteenth-Century Poetry* (Basingstoke: Palgrave Macmillan, 2012); Marion Thain, *The Lyric Poem and Aestheticism: Forms of Modernity* (Edinburgh: Edinburgh University Press, 2016).

importance of folklore and oral verse' can be apprehended as underpinning 'his experi-mentation with poetic form'.[36] Moreover, an investment in the peripheral or national has itself been perceptively linked to how Yeats participates in the cosmopolitan institution-alization of modernist literary value.[37]

In the face of this thicket of modernisms and of Yeatses, there is no one answer to how Yeats and modernism can be accommodated. But a basis for understanding Yeats's de-velopment and its relationship to the cultural history of its time can be located by tracing how Yeats kept the 1890s in play beyond the end of that decade, yet remained an essen-tial contemporary presence into the 1920s, for Pound, Colum, and others. A striking element of Yeats's work from around 1900 on is not that he stops being a Victorian or an aesthete or a decadent or a cultural revivalist, but that he simultaneously joins himself to and separates himself from his past. A related achievement is Yeats's placing of his poetry in repeated dialogue with a sense of the contemporary and the modern. He acquires an amazing ability in his middle and late work insistently to address his time, even via in-credibly abstruse material. He does not straightforwardly become a modern or a mod-ernist; rather, his work recurrently marks its proximity yet distance from a sense of the present as an epoch, including the other artistic products of that epoch. Yeats does so through a generically diverse body of mythologizing life-writing that establishes his work as an ongoing process of self-making. Such a body of writing, moreover, links ra-ther than polarizes his shifting use of language and form, and a more sociological sense of modernism as a burgeoning institution or network.

Soon after encountering 'Reconciliation', Pound used part of its opening line ('Some may have blamed you –') as an epigraph to 'The Fault of It'—a poem that in turn reworks Yeats's words: 'Some may have blamed us that we cease to speak / Of things we spoke of in our verses early'. Longenbach describes this inscription of influence as marking a shift: 'What was for Yeats a personal transformation became, in Pound's adoption of its metaphors, the beginning of the large conundrum we now call modernism: Yeats's "I" became Pound's "we".'[38] This captures Pound's recurrent fervour for fostering a collective movement of cultural renewal, such as through his editorial work. But it risks sidelining how Yeats during the 1900s and into the early 1910s started to place himself within this 'large conundrum' on decidedly personal terms.

'Reconciliation' can be read not just as offering a song of self but as telling (like 'A Coat') a self-reflexive story about Yeats's work.[39] Having first replayed the stock address to the indifferent object of desire of Renaissance lyric, its second line brings into view the broader poetic oeuvre, 'verses', and its audience, 'that they cared for'. One has only to think of Shakespeare's sonnets to recognize that a love poem that is self-conscious about the act of writing is a feature of the tradition on which Yeats is drawing.[40]

---

[36] Fogarty, 'Yeats, Ireland and Modernism', 127–8.

[37] See Barry Shiels, *W. B. Yeats and World Literature: The Subject of Poetry* (Farnham: Ashgate, 2015).

[38] Longenbach, 'Modern Poetry', 323.

[39] *CW1*, 91.

[40] For example, the closing couplet of Sonnet 86: 'But when your continuance fild up his line, / Then lackt I matter, that infeebled mine'.

As Jahan Ramazani describes, Yeats's 'poetic self-expositions intensify during his middle period … partly because he is returning to Renaissance and Neoclassical models, in which the part of poetry is often an overt subject'.[41] Rather than being merely generic, however, Yeats maps such a conceit more precisely onto the contours of his career. The poetic voice refers to his writing of poetic drama drawing on ancient Irish myth: his turn during the 1900s, in disempowered despair, towards songs 'about kings, / Helmets, and swords, and half-forgotten things', which he implores the addressee to join him in now hurling 'into the pit'—a theatrical pun. It also offers an autobiographical source— a lover's abandonment ('you went from me') and the sublimation of desire ('like memories of you')—for the turn to these themes. Moreover, this is an episode whose real-life co-protagonist, Maud Gonne, is alluded to (a revelation already anticipated in the poem: 'now / We'll out') via a pun in the penultimate line: 'since you were gone'.[42] It is hard to conceive of a reading of this poem that would not either draw on or draw one into some wider engagement with Yeats's work, career, or (by then somewhat public) personal life.

The poem also parallels this story of change to its use of style and form. The opening two lines are in iambic pentameter. But in the third and fourth lines these give way to longer thirteen- and eleven-syllable lines offering a less distinct pattern of rhythmic stress: 'When, the ears being deafened, the sight of the eyes blind / With lightning you went from me, and I could find'. This deviation occurs when the poem's voice describes the passing of his previous poetic mode—a mode in which such lines were prevalent. The rest of the poem returns to iambic pentameter. It also moves away from the use of enjambement and towards matching syntax to line length:

> … – but now
> We'll out for the world lives as long ago;
> And while we're in our laughing, weeping fit,
> Hurl helmets, crowns, and swords into the pit.
> But, dear, cling close to me; since you were gone,
> My barren thoughts have chilled me to the bone.

The resulting coincidence between rhyme and punctuation underlines the form. Yet order does not readily equate to reconciliation. The closing couplet offers an appeal to the addressee that is ostensibly intimate ('dear'), but also bitterly reiterates the asperities she has caused and that are now reflected in the poet's style—such as in the jarring half-/ sight rhyme of the closing couplet. There will be no return to the past or to past poetic modes. A sense of the speaker's will, strongly asserted through argument and formal control, is ironically shaded by what the speaker cannot control: the will of the addressee

---

[41] Jahan Ramazani, 'Self-Theorizing Poetry: Yeats's *Ars Poetica* in *The Green Helmet and Other Poems*', *YA*, 16 (2005), 53–69, 55.

[42] Ramazani links this encryption of Gonne's name to 'other comparable puns on the Innominata, such as Petrarch's on *Laura/l'aura/lauro*': Ramazani, 'Self-Theorizing Poetry', 64.

('gone') and the inexorable nature of time, including, of course, human mortality ('bone'). It is hard to conceive of a reading of this poem that would not in some way link its dramatic use of form and style, again, to Yeats's wider work, career, or personal life.

Some of the means of making such links were provided in this poem's original print context. As first published by the Cuala Press in *The Green Helmet and Other Poems* (1910), 'Reconciliation' sits as the fifth in an eight-poem sequence titled 'Raymond Lully and his Wife Pernella'. This obscure, unglossed title was a mistake. As a later erratum slip relayed, 'By a slip of the pen when I was writing out the heading of the first group of poems, I put Raymond Lully's name in the room of the later Alchemist, Nicholas Flamel.'[43] Readers of Yeats were perhaps unlikely to recall that he had mentioned 'Flamel, who with his wife Pernella achieved the elixir many hundreds of years ago' in his 1896 story 'Rosa Alchemica'—first published in *The Savoy* and more recently collected in Volume 7 of his 1908 *Collected Works*.[44] They also could not have known that back in the early 1890s Yeats may have spoken to Gonne of Flamel and Pernella while forming plans for their joint 'lives devoted to mystic truth', or have known that it was Gonne who alerted him to the error in the Cuala edition.[45] Nevertheless, some kind of occult or mystical implication is put into play through the title, connecting the sequence to the poet's earlier work, when his esoteric mysticism was to the fore. The title might also, as Albright suggests, insinuate that 'spiritually—alchemically—[Gonne] is Yeats's own wife, though flesh and society refuse to confirm this occult truth', or at least suggest a focus on a specific male–female relationship.[46] This posits a relationship between the sequence's poems and Yeats's earlier love poetry, including the recurrent, unnamed (yet widely known) addressee of such poems. In the particular case of 'Reconciliation' and the poem that is bibliographically presented as its partner, 'No Second Troy' (in being printed on the same page and in being the same length), this points back to the two twelve-line love poems similarly paired in *The Wind Among the Reeds*: 'Mongan Laments the Change that has Come Upon Him and his Beloved' and 'Michael Robartes bids his Beloved be at Peace'.[47] Yeats inscribes his present mode within the formal parameters of his earlier visionary love poetry.

The ironies of such signposts and links are considerable. As Holdeman describes, whereas even such 'a strikingly naturalistic, dramatic poem' as 'Adam's Curse' from *In the Seven Woods* (1903) ends with a symbolic vision of a shell, by the 1910 volume 'readers may turn over many a shell without uncovering a single esoteric symbol'.[48] Yeats's

[43] *VP*, 253.

[44] *Myth* 2005, 282.

[45] The apparent earlier identification of his and Gonne's relationship with this alchemical marriage seems to have been taken at face value by many critics. But it was only noted in 1915 and went unpublished in Yeats's lifetime: *Mem*, 49. Previous to this, it was Gonne who wrote, 'Tell me, are you quite sure that Pernella was the wife of Raymond Lully? My memory is so bad but I think Pernella was the name of the wife of Nicholas Flamel' (Gonne to Yeats [September 1910], *G-YL*, 294–5).

[46] W. B. Yeats, *The Poems*, ed. Daniel Albright (London: J.M. Dent, 1994), 502.

[47] *CW1*, 61, 63.

[48] Holdeman, *Much Labouring*, 162.

sequence offers a now distinctly disenchanted poetry. It opens with the obscure 'His Dream', in which the speaker's singular, visionary position upon the stern of a ship aligns the lyric 'I' to Forgael from *The Shadowy Waters* (1894–1906), Yeats's sole, protracted attempt to write a full-blown symbolist play. In the poem, this isolated viewpoint gives way to a joining in, against the speaker's initial will, with the 'ecstatic' crying of 'the sweet name of Death' by 'a crowd'—which offers a figure for a rowdy theatre audience.[49] Ramazani describes the poem as offering an 'idealized version of the poet's relation to the public', with 'his revelatory words soon' being 'taken up by the crowd, until public and poet emerge in one harmonious chorus'.[50] More circumspectly, Marjorie Howes describes how its 'crowd embodies the erotic promise and threat of the dissolution of the subject in the Rose poems and *Cathleen ni Houlihan*'.[51] Through the medium of a parabolic dream, ironically enough, the initial voyage of visionary idealism is disturbingly circumscribed by the irrational realities of the social sphere. This allows the poetic speaker to partake in the collective aesthetic experience of tragedy. However, the poem does not as such offer its readers the tragic or even a tragedian; rather, it casts the speaker as a self-conscious, uneasy co-spectator. The poet as empowered seer is dissolved into the frenzied crowd.

The poems that follow rail against such a crowd but also find their few comforts firmly in a disillusioned temporal realm. For instance, the closing couplet of 'Peace' offers a sense of the complexity of finding peace in this realm. It first performs ('Ah, but') and describes ('peace that comes at length') the coming of peace as an extended temporal process. It then depicts the arrival ('Came when') of a personified 'Time' as an action that had distinct (as in before and after) physical consequences ('had touched her form').[52] Moreover, this use of 'form' as a metonym for the female body stands in contrast to the word's atemporal usages earlier in the poem, such that time is now not only touching a physical shape but also so materializing an abstract ideal. The idea of love poetry representing an alchemical marriage (so occult and eternal), suggested by the sequence's title, stands against a temporally contingent reality. What mystery there is lies in the semi-divine, semi-inhuman nature of the female subject and addressee ('being what she is'), hence the several implicit references to Helen of Troy and Homer in the sequence: 'Was there another Troy for her to burn?'[53] Depicted is not so much a spiritual union as the speaker becoming attuned to the terms of his alienation from his beloved's otherness.

This adjustment is dramatized implicitly and explicitly within the sequence and the wider volume as necessitating nothing less than the wholesale alteration of his past poetic and its underpinning world view. It also seems to take place unavoidably in the

---

[49] *CW1*, 89.

[50] Ramazani, 'Self-Theorizing Poetry', 58.

[51] Marjorie Howes, *Yeats's Nations: Gender, Class and Irishness* (Cambridge: Cambridge University Press, 1996), 97.

[52] *CW1*, 92.

[53] *CW1*, 91.

public sphere and in the here and now. The next part of the volume is another sequence, 'Momentary Thoughts', which, as its title suggests, contains several topical and provisional responses to the present. These include the poem then titled 'Upon a Threatened House', which responds to contemporaneous land agitation in Ireland and its possible effects on Lady Gregory's Coole Park. Like several poems in this collection, and more again in Yeats's next, *Responsibilities* (published in two different versions by Cuala and Macmillan in 1914 and 1916), it is a poem that addresses a contemporary social or political issue in a manner that explicitly considers it in relation to the condition of cultural production—in this case what would allow for the high achievement of 'a written speech / Wrought of high laughter, loveliness and ease'.[54] To relate this to the preceding sequence, and so too to Yeats's earlier work, is to start to discern a drama in which a sense of poetry as analogous to an alchemical marriage (such as in being a visionary and private effusion) is brought into tension with a vision of art itself as a socially formed and embattled practice—'a written speech', fostered amid a socially stratified space of leisure.

Holdeman relates the lack of esoteric symbolism in *The Green Helmet and Other Poems* to other shifts in Yeats's style. He points to the 'slangy diction, speechlike rhythm, and enjambed syntax' to be found in 'The Fascination of What's Difficult' (the final poem in the 'Raymond Lully and his Wife Pernella' sequence). He notes the limited use of mythology in the volume, eschewing all references to Irish myth except in the closing titular play, and only infrequently referring to classical myth (such as the few, straightforward references to Helen of Troy and Homer mentioned above). He also describes this absence of symbolism and myth as reflecting Yeats's keen engagement around this time with early seventeenth-century English lyric.[55] The volume's poetics and the changes they enact can be placed too in a longer story of how Yeats altered his presentation of the self to embrace a poetics of personality.

In the Seven Woods was subtitled 'Being Poems Chiefly of the Irish Heroic Age'. However, its opening title poem opens with a bald lyric 'I' ('I have heard') that is contemporarily placed in space (the Seven Woods being within the Coole Park estate) and time (the poem is dated 'August, 1902'), and which also makes topical references to excavations on the Hill of Tara ('Tara Uprooted') and the coronation of Edward VII ('new commonness / Upon the throne').[56] On turning to the Heroic Age in the following poem, 'The Old Age of Queen Maeve', Yeats soon switches (in self-chastisement) from the narrative back to the lyric voice:

> O unquiet heart,
> Why do you praise another, praising her
> As if there were no tale but your own tale
> Worth knitting to a measure of sweet sound?[57]

---

[54] *CW1*, 95.
[55] Holdeman, *Much Labouring*, 163.
[56] *CW1*, 77.
[57] *CW1*, 387.

Such switches are continued in the next poem, 'Baile and Aillinn', 'in which Yeats interlards a tripartite narrative of the doomed lover with lyric passages, but in his voice rather than theirs'—a difference emphasized by using red ink for the lyric voice.[58] Out of the further nine poems in the volume, four begin with the pronoun 'I'. A note following the poems in the book (which ends with the play *On Baile's Strand*) reiterates the identi-fication of the lyric 'I' with the real-life poet: 'I made some of these poems walking about among the Seven Woods, before the big wind of nineteen hundred and three blew down so many trees, & troubled the wild creatures, & changed the look of things; and I thought out there a good part of the play which follows.'[59] Pseudonymous mythological and eso-teric names, such as Mongan and Michael Robartes, were then stripped out of the titles of almost all the poems from *The Wind Among the Reeds* when they were reprinted in a revised form in *The Poetical Works of W. B. Yeats* (1906), published by Macmillan in New York. A sense of Yeats's works as offering a multifaceted representation of the artist was then further suggested in the use of different visual portraits as frontispieces to four volumes of the 1908 *Collected Works*.

As such a paratextual manoeuvre indicates, the poetry's presentation of the 'I', along-side various other stylistic, formal, and thematic shifts, did not just intrinsically change in the 1900s and 1910s. Rather, this change was repeatedly flagged and theorized in the poetry itself and through a range of other related texts. For instance, the note to *In the Seven Woods* quoted above continues: 'The first part of [*On Baile's Strand*] came to me in a dream, but it changed much in the making, foreshadowing, it may be, a change that may bring a less dream-burdened will into my verses.'[60] Such a note invites a reader comparatively to consider whether this 'less dream-burdened will' is at work in the poetry contained in the volume. It also signals the possibility of relations between Yeats's poetry and his drama.[61]

On a larger scale, Yeats's prose reflections on his past and present career and work, and its relationship to cultural history (including a sense of the contemporary as a distinct phase in such a history), also burgeoned in the 1900s and 1910s. Several pieces collected in *The Cutting of an Agate* (1912) occupy a hybrid zone between criticism, memoir, and diary, through which the poet is presented self-reflexively questing towards a poetics of personality. The second section of 'Discoveries', for example, first published in 1906 and

[58] Alex Davis, 'Edwardian Yeats: *In the Seven Woods*', *Études Anglaises*, 68:4 (2015), 454–67, 464.
[59] *VP*, 814.
[60] *VP*, 814.
[61] It is beyond the scope of this chapter to consider such relations in any detail. Yeats's immersion in the writing and production of drama through the 1900s has often been used as means to explain his shift towards a more dramatic and tragic poetic, going back to Thomas Parkinson, *W. B. Yeats, Self-Critic: A Study of his Early Work* (Berkeley: University of California Press, 1951). But in the context of this chapter, it might more particularly be noted that *In the Seven Woods*, *The Green Helmet and Other Poems*, and both the Cuala Press and Macmillan versions of *Responsibilities* (1914, 1916—which both contain *The Hour-Glass*), resonantly end with plays that dramatize the heroic-visionary quest of an individual against a broader social background. They so implicitly offer the poet in the lyric portion of each collection as a figure also to be regarded in such terms.

subtitled 'Personality and the Intellectual Essences', initially grounds its reflections in Yeats's own experience in the theatre and through this with a specific, contemporary cultural enterprise and audience: 'My work in Ireland has continually set this thought before me: "How can I make my work mean something to vigorous and simple men whose attention is not given to art but to a shop, or teaching in a National School, or dispensing medicine?"' From here Yeats broadens out to consider the challenges faced by literature more generally in terms of a loss of personality: 'In literature, partly from the lack of that spoken word which knits us to normal man, we have lost in personality, in our delight in the whole man—blood, imagination, intellect, running together—but have found a new delight, in essences, in states of mind, in pure imagination, in all that comes to us most easily in elaborate music.' This distinction is developed as a point of difference between the personalities of actual artists. They represent the dilemma of achieving personality and offering 'the whole man', which he associates with Villon and (in a modern diminished form) Burns, while not leaving behind 'the traditions of modern imagination' that have cast up 'now a Shelley, now a Swinburne, now a Wagner'.[62] Yeats so implicitly dramatizes himself as a figure within a cultural history that has led down to a specifically modern dilemma. In a 1913 letter to his father, the poet more explicitly, though privately, relates such oppositions to developments in his own work:

> Of recent years instead of 'vision' meaning by vision the intense realization of a state of ecstatic emotion symbolized in a definite imagined region I have tried for more self portraiture. I have tried to make my work convincing with a speech so natural & dramatic that the hearer would feel the presence of a man thinking & feeling. There are always the two types of poetry — Keats the type of vision, Burns a very obvious type of the other, too obvious indeed. It is in dramatic lyric expression that English poetry is most lacking as compared with French poetry. Villon always & Ronsard at times create a marvellous drama out of their own lives.[63]

Active self-making in Yeats's thought and work around this time has long been recognized by critics.[64] Placing Yeats centre stage in a history of anglophone modernist poetry, Ron Bush well describes how 'like Nietzsche, he began to insist that poets, rather than attempting to *realise* themselves in their lives and verse, constantly battle to *overcome* themselves through the aid of a deliberately created theatrical mask – a projected image of the passionate self'.[65] Bush quotes some of Yeats's articulations of this idea of the poet, including his famous maxim from his treatise much concerned with his related doctrine of the mask, *Per Amica Silentia Lunae* (1917), that 'We make out of the quarrel with others, rhetoric, but of the quarrel with ourselves, poetry'.[66] Bush then relates such statements to how Yeats's poetry from the 1910s onward earned its authority within

---

[62] *CW4*, 191–215, 195.
[63] W. B. Yeats to J. B. Yeats, 5 August 1913, *CL Intelex* #2232.
[64] See Claire Lynch, 'Self Making', Chapter 1 in this volume.
[65] Bush, 'Modernist Poetry and Poetics', 239.
[66] *Myth* 2005, 331.

modern poetry by offering a compelling drama of self-conflict that also managed to embody complex truths and beliefs. Carol T. Christ similarly sees Yeats as falling in with modernist poetry's search for objectivity and knowledge, but paradoxically through dramatizing a mediating ego: 'Reflection and reminiscence give Yeats access to a psychological and moral range that extends poetry's power. He incorporates these diverse modes though a theory of personality and imagination that unites image and discourse in a dramatic event.'[67]

However, like the broader phenomenon that has come to be described as modernism, Yeats's cultural work is not just that of being a lyric poet—though his poetry does much cultural work. He is, of course, concurrently a dramatist and theatre director, and a writer of criticism and other prose, and a public figure. Across such texts and practices his 'theory of personality', as it comes to the fore around 1910, does not simply facilitate the achievement and authority of his modernist poetry from the mid-1910s on. Rather, the generically various texts that put forward, dramatize, and mythologize such theories also inculcate Yeats's central place within his cultural moment. This includes his poetry itself, including of course its use of form and style. A measure of its success in doing so on the ground and at the time is suggested in yet another of the key US modernist periodicals, Harriet Monroe's *Poetry*. Its February 1916 issue carried no fewer than nine poems by Yeats: 'The Dawn', 'On Woman', 'The Fisherman', 'The Hawk', 'Memory', 'The Thorn Tree', 'The Phoenix', 'There is a Queen in China', and 'The Scholars'. These were accompanied by an editorial comment on 'The Later Yeats' by Mary Colum, beginning:

> Yeats in his later work, all things considered, is really the most characteristic poet of modern Europe. He has, more than any other continental writer, that virile pessimism which has haunted Europe for the last quarter of a century; he celebrates, subtly and strangely, that aristocratic idea which in our day has again become paramount in Europe, and his work has in full measure the pride and anger which are the only two of the seven deadly sins which produce great literature. Great literature, like great wars, always derives from somebody's pride or somebody's anger.
>
> The later Yeats may be said to begin with the publication by the Cuala Press, in 1910, of *The Green Helmet and Other Poemexs*, and continues with further developments in the volume *Responsibilities* published last year. This later work differs from his early work in vocabulary, and in an impassioned directness of expression acquired through years of working for the theatre. It is an attempt to get nearer the ordinary things of life, an attempt to grapple with common and topical interests—city councils, political intrigues, music hall dancers, and so on. The nearer he gets to these things, the more tragic and personal does he become, so that the joyousness, as of a man out on a great adventure, which characterized the work of his youth, is all gone, but in its stead there is the virility of one 'who has come unto his strength'.[68]

---

[67] Christ, *Victorian and Modern Poetics*, 82
[68] Mary M. Colum, 'The Later Yeats', *Poetry: A Magazine of Verse*, 7:5 (February 1916), 258–60, 258.

Yeats's work as the embodiment of his artistic personality has already, and very much on its own terms, become cast as a protagonist in a broader cultural drama. In striving to become a personality and in telling his reader he is striving to become a personality, Yeats has seemingly managed to transform himself into a representative figure within what is coming to be perceived as a cultural epoch. If modernism was on its way to blossoming, Yeats and his work were already placed within its boughs.

CHAPTER 29

....

ILLUSTRATING YEATS

....

JACK QUIN

A FAMILY OF ILLUSTRATORS

....

In 1931, Lady Gregory recalled the lavish book covers that stood out on her old bookcase, 'filled as it is with Yeats bounty from end to end', at her home in the Coole Park estate. According to Gregory, the 'earlier volumes shine and glitter through the glass; golden designs, by a genius, of leaves and birds and the mystic rose'. The later Yeats volumes, she noted, 'have become quieter in tone; Macmillan and pale green, and Laurie's grey *Vision* and *Trembling of the Veil*'.[1] The genius illustrator of Yeats's early work was Althea Gyles, who produced elaborately gilded wrap-around covers with interweaving reeds, rose stems, and petals for *The Secret Rose* (1897), *Poems* (1899), and *The Wind Among the Reeds* (1899). The later Macmillan volumes in muted colours were less lavishly illustrated; nevertheless, they featured iconic cover designs by Thomas Sturge Moore and Charles Ricketts, or arresting illustrations by Edmund Dulac and Norah McGuinness set alongside the text. The later volumes imprinted an iconography of the elder poet at the height of his powers with a mastery over his recurring symbols. George Bornstein has noted that, as Yeats gained a greater command of his poetic voice, he also 'gained more control over the physical form of his text, he expanded his concerns to include size, book covers, page layout, and other material features', as he moved publishers from Charles Kegan Paul to T. Fisher Unwin, to the Cuala Press, and to Macmillan.[2] In terms of illustration, Yeats revised and refined his aesthetic preferences from photomechanically reproduced narrative paintings to Celtic interlace designs, symbolist flora and fauna, to line work inspired by Byzantine mosaics, and finally abstract and geometrical renderings that aligned with his self-made mythography of gyres and historical

---

[1] Augusta Gregory, *Coole*, completed from the manuscript and edited by Colin Smythe with a foreword by Edward Malins (Dublin: Dolmen, 1971), 39.

[2] George Bornstein, 'Publishers and the material text', in David Holdeman and Ben Levitas, eds., *W. B. Yeats in Context* (Cambridge: Cambridge University Press, 2010), 376–84, 376.

cycles. Yeats's choice of illustrators and collaborators throughout his career deepens our understanding of his metamorphic aesthetics of word and image.

Yeats was not averse to judging a book by its cover, or indeed to judging a writer's oeuvre by their collective book covers and illustrations. In a letter to Charles Ricketts thanking him for his cover design for *Later Poems* (1922), published by Macmillan, Yeats added:

> My own memory proves to me that at 17 there is an identity between an authors [*sic*] imagination and paper and book-cover one does not find in later life. I still do not quite separate Shelley from the green covers, or Blake from the blue covers and brown reproductions of pictures, of the books in which I first read them. I do not separate Rossetti at all from his covers.[3]

Following the example of William Blake and Dante Gabriel Rossetti—both painters as well as poets—Yeats wanted to create 'total books' by collaborating closely with his illustrators. Rossetti's talismanic projects were supposed to unite text and book design, word and image, with the poems or prose stories bound and glossed with representations of their latent symbolism. While Yeats did not illustrate his own work like Blake and Rossetti, he was an art school student in Dublin. From 1884 to 1887 he attended the Dublin Metropolitan School of Art and the Royal Hibernian Academy. When it came to selecting an illustrator for the cover of his 1895 *Poems*, he admitted to his second publisher, T. Fisher Unwin, that his art school training made him 'opinionated and probably crotchety over this question of design'.[4]

The illustration of Yeats's poetry and prose often complicates the narrative of a total book aesthetic; while Yeats exerted increasing control over the physical appearance of his books, he was not a poet-illustrator. The totalizing influence of the author was confronted with imaginative translations of word into image; visual misprisions of his work by different artists for different readerships and contexts. This chapter shows how illustrations offer a material trace of contemporary readers' reception of Yeats's writing, not only in the interpretative bindings and images themselves but also through book reviews of the period, which evaluate the pictures in relation to the prose stories or poems.

Yeats grew up among a family of illustrators as much as painters. His father, John Butler Yeats, was not a successful draughtsman despite his best efforts to illustrate for various London newspapers in the 1880s and 1890s. His soft pencil drawings with marked gradations from faint to dark hatching were generally ill-suited to newspaper reproduction.[5] Nevertheless, the popularization of more expensive photomechanical reproduction methods allowed John Yeats to prepare paintings and

---

[3] Yeats to Charles Ricketts, 5 November [1922], *CL InteLex* #4200.
[4] Yeats to T. Fisher Unwin, 10 April [1895], *CL InteLex*; *CL1*, 462.
[5] Hilary Pyle, *The Different Worlds of Jack B. Yeats: His Cartoons and Illustrations* (Dublin: Irish Academic Press, 1994), 16.

sketches as illustrations for his son's books. W. B. Yeats's brother, Jack, also started out as a draughtsman when the family moved to Bedford Park in the late 1880s, and was soon earning more money than any member of his family through his newspaper illustrations.[6] Consequently, the early frontispieces and illustrations of Yeats's poems and prose were largely a family affair. Jack Yeats's first published illustration of his brother's work appeared in the 1888 Christmas edition of the *Vegetarian*, for the poem 'A Legend'. The early pen drawing demonstrates an eye for visual narrative, capturing the gestures and outlines of the country people named in his brother's poem. Hilary Pyle notes that Jack Yeats's illustrations for the *Vegetarian* show the formative influence of Aubrey Beardsley and George Cruikshank on the artist.[7] It wasn't until the 1890s that Jack developed his characteristic angular drawings of scenes and people with hatching and a sharp linearity to the works that meant they were frequently mistaken for wood engravings. In the 1880s and 1890s, W. B. Yeats actively sought illustration work and commissions for his brother, including the illustration of his own poems and prose, commissions that forced Jack Yeats to learn on the job from time to time. For example, WBY recommended the services of his brother to the editor Frederick Langbridge in September 1893 to illustrate a story he had prepared for *The Old Country: A Christmas Annual*.[8] This was the first of only two occasions when Jack Yeats used gouache for an illustration, accompanying his brother's prose story 'Michael Clancy, The Great Dhoul, and Death'.[9]

When WBY switched publisher from Charles Kegan Paul to T. Fisher Unwin in 1892, he had greater influence over the physical appearance of his books. The move coincided with his editorial role on *The Works of William Blake* (1893), the supreme poet-illustrator and benchmark for the total book.[10] Yeats persuaded Fisher Unwin to allow an illustrated frontispiece of 'The Death of Cuchullin' by Edwin Ellis to adorn his second volume of poems, *The Countess Kathleen and Various Legends and Lyrics* (1892). Ellis was a long-time friend of John B. Yeats and had worked alongside WBY as co-editor of the three-volume *The Works of William Blake*. Ellis also illustrated the mythic personages Oisin, Niamh, and St Patrick for Fisher Unwin's printing of *The Wanderings of Oisin Dramatic Sketches, Ballads & Lyrics* in May 1892. In keeping with the anecdotal tradition in illustrated works of the nineteenth century, these early illustrations by Ellis, Jack Yeats, and John Yeats faithfully represented certain narrative moments in WBY's descriptive and generally Celtic narrative poems. However, at the turn of the century, as WBY began to find poetic symbols adequate to his researches in occultism, Rosicrucianism, and the Irish Revival, he also sought the services of illustrators from alternative aesthetic schools.

---

[6] Hilary Pyle, 'Jack B. Yeats's Illustrations for His Brother', *YA*, 11, 77–86, 78.
[7] Pyle, 'Jack B. Yeats's Illustrations for His Brother', 11, 79.
[8] Yeats to Frederick Langbridge [late September 1893], *CL InteLex*; *CL1*, 361.
[9] Pyle, 'Jack B. Yeats's Illustrations for His Brother', 11, 81–2.
[10] Bornstein, 'Publishers and the material text', 377.

ALTHEA GYLES AND SYMBOLISM

WBY's first illustrated book cover was designed by the British artist Herbert Granville Fell for his collected *Poems* (1895). The publisher T. Fisher Unwin and Yeats had originally hoped to commission Charles Shannon for the cover design, but the poet admired several illustrations by Fell which he had seen on display at an exhibition in London of bookbinding and drawings organized by the Royal Institute of Painters in Water Colours from September to October 1894.[11] Fell's gilt cover depicts a winged angel, probably St Michael who appears in 'The Countess Cathleen', fully armoured and enveloped in an aureole from the midriff. At the feet of the angel is a serpent impaled by St Michael's sword, and the scene is bordered by roses and thorns which, as Warwick Gould has noted, resemble the outline of a harp.[12] The cover design overflows with symbolic suggestiveness in a style that corresponds with French decadent art of the fin de siècle. By 1899, however, Yeats was keen to abolish Fell's cover from the new issue of poems as he felt the design was 'facile' and meaningless; he later wrote to John Quinn that he 'hate[d] this expressionless angel' on the 1895 cover.[13] Yeats's selection of new artists and livery to redecorate his collected poems and prose would become a recurring theme as he sought to exorcize earlier styles and experiment with new aesthetic trends.

After Granville Fell's sole cover, Yeats fostered a much more fruitful period of collaboration with the Irish artist Althea Gyles. The opulent fin de siècle books decorated with elaborate foliage and blocked in gold by Charles Ricketts at the Vale Press, and Laurence Housman's work at Macmillan, were important influences for Gyles. Her first commission for Yeats was a wrap-around design for *The Secret Rose* (1897) book of stories, where she combined the Rosicrucian symbol of a rose in interlacing thorns with the Kabbalistic symbol of the Tree of Life, which stems from the skeleton of a knight on the cover. The knight's horizontal spear functions as the bottom of the frame for the elaborate illustration. Warwick Gould notes that the intricate knotwork appears to draw on international precursors like the Sacramentary Fleury, and knotwork on a Spanish Quran that Gyles might have seen reproduced in the British Museum.[14] Closer to home, *The Evergreen*, a Celtic Revival biannual magazine from 1895 to 1897, edited by William Sharp and printed in Edinburgh, featured a stylized tree on each cover, with elaborate entangled branches and roots on the covers of the final two issues. Kristin Mahoney notes that the Gyles cover integrated multiple mythic visual resources 'into a complex web of Celtic occultism'.[15] Yeats, after all,

---

[11] *CL1*, 462 n.1.

[12] Warwick Gould, 'Yeats and his Books', *YA*, 20, 3–70, 31–2.

[13] *CL2*, 357.

[14] Gould, 'Yeats and his Books', 35.

[15] Kristin Mahoney, *Literature and the Politics of post-Victorian Decadence* (Cambridge: Cambridge University Press, 2015), 125.

dedicated the book to George Russell, writing that '[s]o far ... as this book is visionary it is Irish'.[16]

Gyles's wrap-around cover drew its inspiration most directly from a passage in page proofs to Yeats's 'Rosa Alchemica'. The short passage was added to the story after it appeared in *The Savoy* (April 1896), but it was deleted before the story was reprinted in the 1897 edition of *The Secret Rose*:

> In the box was a book bound in vellum, and having *a rose-tree growing from an armed anatomy, and enclosing the faces of two lovers painted on the one side, to symbolize certainly the coming of beauty out of corruption, and probably much else*; and upon the other, the alchemical rose with many spears thrusting against it, but in vain, as was shown by the shattered points of those nearest.[17]

In Yeats's story this description of a vellum-bound book refers to a manuscript of the Order of the Alchemical Rose, where the imaginary book supposedly explained the rituals and doctrines of the secret society. Gyles subsequently illustrated the front cover of *The Secret Rose* with a tree growing from the armed skeleton of a knight, with the faces of two lovers encircled in thorns; on the back cover she embellished a rose with a ring of spears pointing towards it, and an inner ring of spears crossing each other's paths, suggesting that the spears have split and shattered. The cover design encapsulates Lorraine Janzen Kooistra's assertion that in illustrated books of the 1890s the 'visual and verbal texts "*read*" each other' and 'many fin-de-siècle illustrators set out to be interpretive readers of the texts they embellished'.[18] Deirdre Toomey suggests that '[i]t is perhaps an indication of just how satisfied Yeats was with the design that he cut the passage' from the 1897 edition of *The Secret Rose*.[19] In either case, the cover demonstrates that Gyles was an illustrator interested in multilayered verbal-visual mediations of the same charged symbol, particularly the rose symbol. John B. Yeats's halftone reproductions of watercolours within *The Secret Rose* seemed conventional and somewhat outdated when compared to Gyles's striking talismanic cover. Susan Yeats was the model for her father for a number of the illustrations involving female subjects.[20] Walter Crane, among others, criticized the tradition of photomechanically reproduced paintings as book illustrations prevalent in the late nineteenth century as 'simply pictures without frames', bearing no formal relation to the type and layout of the printed page. Crane preferred line work or woodcut book decorations that emerged from shared processes of book designing and printing as the type and letterpress of the book.[21] Early reviewers of

---

[16] *The Secret Rose, Stories by W. B. Yeats: A Variorum Edition*, eds. Phillip L. Marcus, Warwick Gould and Michael J. Sidnell (Ithaca & London: Cornell University Press, 1981). 233.

[17] Quoted in *Secret Rose*, 274.

[18] Lorraine Janzen Kooistra, *The Artist as Critic: Bitextuality in Fin-de-Siècle Illustrated Books* (Aldershot: Scolar Press, 1995), 2, 3.

[19] *Secret Rose,* 275 n.14.

[20] Gould, 'Yeats and his Books', 33.

[21] Walter Crane, *Of the Decorative Illustration of Books Old and New* (London: George Bell & Sons, 1896), 146.

The Secret Rose commended the book cover by Gyles, while the inside illustrations by John B. Yeats received comparatively little attention.[22]

Unlike WBY, Althea Gyles was not a formal initiate of the Hermetic Order of the Golden Dawn; however, *The Secret Rose* cover attests to her immersion in occult and Rosicrucian thought.[23] The elaborate weave or matrices of thorns accord with esoteric thought on *apotropaic* (from the Greek for 'to ward off') interlace. In early medieval Europe knotwork and interlace patterns were understood to contain protective magical properties that could stave off malign spells and confuse or misdirect the evil eye.[24] Beyond the decorative value of interlace, Yeats and Gyles were clearly invested in the concealing, apotropaic function of these patterns. In 'Symbolism in Painting', an essay first published as the introduction to *A Book of Images, Drawn by W. T. Horton and Introduced by W. B. Yeats* (1898), Yeats articulated a model for symbolist painting and line drawing inspired, in part, by his shared occult leanings with the British illustrator William Thomas Horton. He also cited the black-and-white art of Beardsley and Ricketts, the lithographs of Charles Shannon, and the paintings of Blake and Whistler that departed from conventional portraiture and landscape. In his celebration of various symbolic artists Yeats alluded to an older apotropaic tradition of interlaced or entangled forms:

> All art that is not merely story-telling, or mere portraiture, is symbolic, and has the purpose of those symbolic talismans which medieval magicians made with complex colours and forms, and bade their patients ponder over daily, and guard with holy secrecy; for it entangles, in complex colours and forms, a part of the Divine Essence.[25]

The publication of *The Secret Rose* in the previous year, with the entangled organic forms on Gyles's cover, no doubt informed Yeats's turn backwards to a mystic and symbolic phase of art that preceded the representational phase of narrative painting and Victorian portraiture that held sway in the present.[26]

In the same year, Yeats extended his thinking about symbolist art through a critical interpretation of Gyles's line work. In an article for *The Dome*, entitled 'A Symbolic Artist and the Coming of Symbolic Art', he cited a number of line drawings by Gyles including *Lilith* and *The Knight upon the Grave of His Lady*. He noted her emphasis on intricate and interweaving patterns, tessellated armour, and the elaborate animal scales in *Lilith*. All the while, Yeats alluded to Gyles's *The Secret Rose* cover and forthcoming book commissions to propose a wider reconsideration of the decorative arts, including illustration, within the standards of the high art forms. Comparing her art to the prints of Whistler and Beardsley, he asserted:

> Pattern and rhythm are the road to open symbolism, and the arts have already become full of pattern and rhythm. Subject pictures no longer interest us, while pictures

---

[22] *VSR*, 277–8.
[23] Gould, 'Yeats and his Books', 37.
[24] James Trilling, *The Language of Ornament* (London: Thames & Hudson, 2001), 134–45, 135.
[25] *CW3*, 108–12, 109.
[26] Ian Fletcher, 'W. B. Yeats and Althea Gyles', *Yeats Studies*, 1 (1971), 42–79, 47.

with patterns and rhythms of colour, like Mr. Whistler's, and drawings with patterns and rhythms of line, like Mr. Beardsley's in his middle period, interest us extremely. Mr. Whistler and Mr. Beardsley have sometimes thought so greatly of these patterns and rhythms, that the images of human life have faded almost perfectly[.][27]

In a dismissal of traditional subject painting, Yeats alludes indirectly but admiringly to Gyles's symbolist art. Yeats was also beginning to distance himself from the portraiture and narrative focus of his father's illustrative work in this period. 'The Madness of King Goll' was illustrated by John B. Yeats's reproductive print of King Goll tearing the strings from a harp when it appeared in *The Leisure Hour*, in September 1887, and was later reproduced in *A Celtic Christmas*, in 1898. John B. Yeats used his son WBY as the model for the King Goll portrait, but the verisimilitude of author and character irked WBY in later years. He wrote in a letter of 1892 that the illustration had been 'done from me and is probably like though it was not intend[ed] as a portrait. Be sure I would never have had myself painted as the mad "King Goll" of my own poem had I thought it was going to turn out the portrait it has. I was merely the cheapest and handiest model to be found.'[28]

With the 1899 issue of *Poems*, which replaced Granville Fell's angel with another design by Althea Gyles of a golden rose on a cross, WBY quickly earned twenty or thirty times the income of all his previous books combined.[29] No longer restrained financially to seek the illustration work of family members, he exerted a greater control over the visual and material appearance of his books, preferring symbolist cover designs over reproduced narrative paintings and sketches within the texts. John B. Yeats through his training and practice was tied to the real world; his images were descriptive and figurative, adhering to the pictorial conventions of the Pre-Raphaelites in graphic art, while typically including emotive elements. By comparison, the decorative stylizations of Beardsley and Gyles departed from nature and figurative resemblance to create a palpable artifice from spiritual or metaphysical forms: unbridled constructions of a new visual language of Symbolism.

CUALA PRESS

The change in fashion from decadent and lavishly illustrated books of the fin de siècle to the modern and minimalist designs of private presses in the early 1900s is encapsulated in an account by the bibliophile W. G. Blaikie Murdoch upon seeing Cuala Press books for the first time in the London home of avowed symbolist Arthur Symons:

> [I]t was Symons, in fact, who originally showed me the Cuala books. In his study the walls were a faint delicate green ... on the oak mantelpiece stood some little gems

---

[27] W. B. Yeats, 'A Symbolic Artist and the Coming of Symbolic Art', *The Dome* (December 1898), 234.

[28] Yeats to John McGrath [19 January 1893], *CL InteLex*; *CL4*, 939.

[29] Quoted in *The Letters of W. B. Yeats*, ed. Allan Wade (London: Rupert Hart-Davis, 1954), 156.

by Tanagra sculptors ... we chanced to begin talking about the art of book production ... The Vale and Kelmscott productions were duly applauded, while I referred
enthusiastically to those of the Eragny Press ... then, going to one of his bookshelves,
Symons produced a Cuala volume, which delighted me at once, inasmuch as it
disclosed qualities foreign, or largely foreign, to the books of those other hand-
presses aforesaid. That is to say, it was wholly simple, its beauty of a restful, unob-
trusive, almost severe kind, so that the slim, graceful volume seemed to harmonize
faultlessly with the room enshrining it.[30]

In Blaikie Murdoch's account, the refined and unembellished Cuala Press volume
contrasts exquisitely with William Morris's florid, medieval-inspired books for the
Kelmscott Press and similar productions from Charles Ricketts's Vale Press and
Lucien Pissarro's Eragny Press. The Dun Emer Press and later the Cuala Press under
Elizabeth Corbet Yeats ('Lolly' to her friends and family) created direct and refined
volumes where a deliberate lack of obtrusive textual ornaments and illustrations
emphasized the centrality of the text, in line with the principles of Emery Walker
and T. J. Cobden-Sanderson at the Doves Press. Reginald Blomfield, an architect and
contributor to Morris's Arts and Crafts Exhibition Society, proposed that the illustrator working in an Arts and Crafts tradition should exercise 'self-restraint' and even
a 'self-abnegation' in service to his craft. In accord with Walter Crane's pronouncement, illustrations should be primarily decorative, and the illustrator must show deference to the author if the art of book illustration is to 'again attain to a permanent
value'.[31] Blomfield, Crane, and Cobden-Sanderson resisted the adoption of paintings
as illustrations through fashionable halftone or photolithographic processes, while
making an argument for the holistic design of the book and the centrality of the type.
By the turn of the century these Arts and Crafts debates about the utility of decoration
and illustration were also apparent in the design aesthetic of the Dun Emer Press and
later the Cuala Press in Ireland.

As early as 1890, W. B. Yeats had noted another potential failing of the London 'book
beautiful' tradition, namely the prohibitive costs of each lavishly decorated book. In
WBY's only exhibition review he acknowledged the apparent contradiction in Morris's
vision of art as egalitarian while surveying an 1890 display of the Arts and Crafts
Exhibition Society at the New Gallery, Regent Street. His review for the *Providence
Sunday Journal* admired the Kelmscott and Chiswick Press book designs, but not
unreservedly:

> These Cobden Sanderson books are, however, simple and artistic, but also not
> cheap. One expects illuminated pages like G.E. Renter's six specimen sheets of

[30] W. G. Blaikie Murdoch, 'The Cuala Press', *Bruno's Weekly* (26 August 1916), 942–4, 942; see also
Gifford Lewis, *The Yeats Sisters and the Cuala* (Dublin: Irish Academic Press, 1994), 116–28.

[31] Reginald Blomfield, 'Of Book Illustration and Book Decoration', in *Arts and Crafts Essays: by
Members of the Arts and Crafts Exhibition Society*, Preface by William Morris, new Introduction by Peter
Faulkner (Bristol: Thoemmes Press, 1996) 237–48, 248.

Morris's romance, *The Roots of Mountains* to be as dear as you please, but there seems to be no reason why the cover of books should not be designed by good artists and yet remain not altogether beyond the purse of the poor student for whom, after all, books chiefly exist.[32]

Yeats admired the bookbindings and illumination of Morris and Cobden-Sanderson's cohort, remarking that 'the art of the old world has been revived in our day'.[33] However, Morris's vision of art as the possession of society at large was never fully realized at the Kelmscott Press. The exorbitant costs of fine illustrated books from a private press seemed to be at odds with his egalitarian doctrine.[34]

The Dun Emer Press under Elizabeth Corbet Yeats reflected the layout and type of Emery Walker and T. J. Cobden-Sanderson's Doves Press much more than Morris's Kelmscott.[35] Cobden-Sanderson was resistant to the florid illustrations and textual ornaments employed by Morris, writing in the Doves Press catalogue raisonné (1908) that the principles of the book beautiful required a greater commitment to 'the arrangement of the whole book, as a whole, with due regard to its parts and the emphasis of its divisions, than by the splendour of ornament, intermittent, page after page'.[36] Illustrations could become interruptions to the reader; decorations could be disruptive in the act of reading. Cobden-Sanderson's emphasis on the layout of text on the page was a conscious privileging of the printed word above intermittent illustration or ornamentation:

> I dislike the dislocation of the verses apparent in his [Kelmscott] books of poems, for the sake of decorated margin or initial letter. In such case the verse, which as I have said, has an organic structure of its own, is broken up anyhow, is perfectly destroyed and with it its message to the eyes and to the mind.[37]

By the same token, elaborate illustrations should not disrupt the organic wholeness of the text, or encroach upon 'the immediate Typographical environment, the medium of communication amid which it appears', writes Cobden-Sanderson. 'It should have a set frame or margin to itself, demarcating it distinctly from the text, ... and the illustrative content itself should be formal and kept under so as literally to illustrate, and not to dim the rest of the subject matter left to be communicated to the imagination by the aid of symbolism alone.'[38] Illustrations should be faithful

---

[32] W. B. Yeats, 'The Arts and Crafts: An Exhibition at William Morris's', *CW7*, 108–10, 109.

[33] *CW7*, 110.

[34] Adrian Paterson, 'On the Pavements Grey: W. B. Yeats, William Morris, and the Suburban Paradise', in Tom Herron, ed., *Irish Writing London Vol. 1* (London: Bloomsbury, 2013), 34–53.

[35] Liam Miller, *The Dun Emer Press, later the Cuala Press* (Dublin: Dolmen, 1973), 21.

[36] Quoted in Miller, *The Dun Emer Press, later the Cuala Press*, 20.

[37] T. J. Cobden-Sanderson, 'The Book Beautiful: Calligraphy, Typography, Illustration', quoted in Marianne Tidcombe, *The Doves Press* (London: British Library, 2002), 10.

[38] Ibid.

to their textual subject matter and in keeping with the overall typographic design of the book.

Elegant typography and minimalist decoration on the printed page were carried over from the Doves Press to Dun Emer and the Cuala Press. The first prospectus of Dun Emer Press is similar to the language in Cobden-Sanderson's lecture on the illustrated book, and follows the design principles learnt from Emery Walker: 'A good eighteenth century fount of type which is not eccentric in form, or difficult to read has been cast ... The pages are printed at a Hand Press by Miss E.C. Yeats, and simplicity is aimed at in their composition.'[39] On the advice of Walker, Lolly Yeats bought a hand-operated Albion press and fourteen-point Old Style Caslon typeface. In the prospectus, an emphasis on printmaking by hand and sourcing local Irish materials was connected to the press's elegant and minimalist aesthetic of the printed page, including paper made at Saggart Mill, County Dublin, from linen rags without bleaching chemicals.

WBY's *In the Seven Woods* (1903) with Dun Emer Press lacked illustrations, and in an inscription to John Quinn's copy of the book Yeats commented: 'This is the first book of mine that is a pleasure to look at – a pleasure whether open or shut.'[40] Robert Gregory provided a frontispiece device for WBY's *Stories of Red Hanrahan* (1904), depicting the four aces from a pack of cards spread across the four provinces of Ireland. Robert Gregory's later devices in red—the 'Charging Unicorn', the 'Bell, waterfall and fish'— and Elinor Monsell's wood engraving 'Lady Emer and tree' were reproduced in multiple books, creating a coherent design identity for Dun Emer and Cuala Press publications. The blank space of the thick-framed illustrations was almost as significant as the spare renderings of symbolic animals and nature within them, complementing the elegant and unadorned pages of text. As Andrew A. Kuhn has noted, the Cuala Press deliberately avoided many of the conventional visual tropes of the Celtic Revival—shamrocks, wolfhounds, elaborate interlace—as well as the iconography of the English Arts and Crafts Movement.[41] The sparsity of decoration was perhaps a palate-cleanser for W. B. Yeats after the opulent book covers of the 1890s. By the late 1890s he found Granville Fell's cover facile and meaningless, and by the early 1900s Yeats and Lady Gregory dissociated themselves from Althea Gyles when she began an affair with the publisher and pornographer Leonard Smithers.

WBY published poems in Cuala Press's early *Broad Sheets* (1902–3), a precursor to the Press's *Broadsides* of 1908–15. Both series printed poems and hand-coloured illustrations on popular themes from Celtic myths to the Wild West, pirate adventures, and the circus. WBY's contributions to the *Broad Sheets* included 'Spinning Song'— later entitled 'There are Seven that pull the thread'—and 'Cathleen, the Daughter of

---

[39] Quoted in Miller, *The Dun Emer Press, later the Cuala Press*, 29.

[40] Quoted in *Wade*, 67.

[41] Andrew A. Kuhn, 'The Irish Arts and Crafts Edition: Printing at Dun Emer and Cuala', in Vera Kreilkamp, ed., *The Arts and Crafts Movement: Making it Irish* (Chestnut Hill: McMullen Museum of Art/Boston College, 2016), 153–63, 158.

Houlihan' alongside line drawings by Pamela Colman Smith and Jack Yeats. However, the poet did not exercise the same control over his illustrated poems in these pamphlets as he typically ensured with his book printings.

Indeed, the *Broad Sheets* and later *Broadsides* complicate our understanding of illustration practice in WBY's work, and the nature of collaboration between poet and illustrator, word and image. While illustrations are traditionally understood in literary studies as the faithful translation of a text into graphic form, carried out alongside or shortly after the author's work, Jack Yeats occasionally chose old line drawings to go alongside poems; several of his drawings were executed years before their printing in *A Broadside*.[42] Coming full circle from WBY's critique of the costly Kelmscott books in the 1890s, from 1915 the Cuala Press sold individual illuminated sheets of WBY's poems at a premium to boost sales, an irony that one reviewer for the *Daily News* (18 June 1925) noted at an exhibition in Central Hall, Westminster, where an illuminated copy of 'He Wishes for the Cloths of Heaven' was priced at three shillings and sixpence. The reviewer sardonically quoted Yeats's poem, 'But I, being poor, have only my dreams', before balking at the price: 'you must be a little richer than your dreams to buy it.'[43]

T. Sturge Moore and Norah McGuinness

A case for refinement and graphic minimalism instilled through the books of the Dun Emer and later Cuala Press aligned with WBY's growing interest in geometry and the aesthetics of Byzantine mosaics in the 1920s, as he collaborated with Norah McGuinness and Thomas Sturge Moore on some of his most iconic book covers for Macmillan. McGuinness studied at the Dublin Metropolitan School of Art when Harry Clarke, the renowned stained-glass artist and illustrator, taught black-and-white graphic art. McGuinness's early work emulated Clarke's sharp linear style and carefully constructed compositional arrangements.[44] Her economy of decoration for the cover of *Stories of Red Hanrahan and the Secret Rose* (1927) contrasts markedly with Althea Gyles's 1897 cover, preferring sparse, strictly delineated, and symmetrical planes without interlace or elaborate decorative patterns. McGuinness's cover features two symmetrical circumpuncts, a five-petalled flower motif, and a knight holding a vertical sword which integrates with the gold borderline of the frame. These simplified emblems bore a closer

---

[42] Pyle, *The Different Worlds of Jack Yeats*, 34.

[43] Quoted in Gifford Lewis, *The Yeats Sisters and the Cuala*, 169. A Cuala Press advertisement brochure (*c*.1915) listed four illuminated poems by Yeats: 'The Lover Pleads', 'Innisfree', 'Had I the Heavens', and 'The Lover Tells of the Rose'; TCD CUALA 49A/13.

[44] Angela Griffith, 'Marketing the "*Elixir of Life*" and Re-imagining Irishness: Harry Clarke's Illustrations for Messrs John Jameson & Son', and Kathryn Milligan, 'Harry Clarke and *The Dublin Magazine*', both in Angela Griffith, Marguerite Helmers, and Roisin Kennedy, eds., *Harry Clarke and Artistic Visions of the New Irish State* (Dublin: Irish Academic Press, 2019), 155–79, 181–201.

proximity to wall designs and mosaics than to the elaborate, apotropaic talismans of Gyles's gilt cover from thirty years before. With the inside illustrations in particular, as Karen Brown has noted, McGuinness's work attempts to 're-enact the function of iconographic Byzantine church wall paintings', mimicking the stylized faces and figures, exaggerating the flatness of the plane through geometric forms and a rejection of naturalism.[45] The harrowing realism of John B. Yeats's illustration of 'The Crucifixion of the Outcast' from three decades earlier is replaced with a pared-down crucifixion scene that emphasizes geometry and symmetry over any apparent depiction of suffering on the cross. Yeats similarly imagined a paring down of violent scenes into measure and balance in Byzantine mosaics in his 1925 *A Vision*:

> I think if I could be given a month of Antiquity and leave to spend it where I chose, I would spend it in Byzantium … I think I could find in some little wine shop some philosophical worker in mosaic who could answer all my questions, the supernatural descending nearer to him than to Plotinus even, for the pride of his delicate skill would make what was an instrument of power to Princes and Clerics and a murderous madness in the mob, show as a lovely flexible presence like that of a perfect human body. … The painter and the mosaic worker, the worker in gold and silver, the illuminator of Sacred Books were almost impersonal.[46]

Yeats's reveries for an imagined Byzantium in the 'Dove or Swan' section of *A Vision* preceded his commissioning of Byzantine-inspired illustrations from McGuinness to adorn his book of stories. The emphasis on the mosaic worker's 'delicate skill' and a 'lovely flexible presence' in response to violent or chaotic scenes seems to accord with the simplified rendering of a hunt, the severed head, and the crucifixion achieved in McGuinness's illustrations.

Robert S. Nelson has shown that the cover image of the knight wielding a sword is remarkably similar in pose, armour, and weaponry to an enamel book cover of St Michael the Archangel in the Treasury of San Marco, Venice.[47] The enamel was illustrated in black and white in O. M. Dalton's *Byzantine Art and Archaeology* (1911), a copy of which was owned by Yeats.[48] In December 1926, Yeats wrote to Frederick Macmillan that he and McGuinness 'spent the evening looking through photographs of Sicilian mosaics and the like, and she went away full of the idea'.[49] As Nelson surmises, what Yeats and McGuinness understood to be a Byzantine book cover was deliberately adapted to gloss his old stories, reintroduced to the reader with 'Sailing to Byzantium' placed as a preface poem, effectively creating a modern version of a deluxe Byzantine manuscript. Nelson

---

[45] Karen Brown, *The Yeats Circle: Verbal and Visual Relations in Ireland, 1880–1939* (Farnham: Ashgate, 2011), 63–87, 71

[46] *CW13*, 158–9.

[47] Robert S. Nelson, *Hagia Sophia, 1850–1950: Holy Wisdom Modern Monument* (London: University of Chicago Press, 2004), 129–54, 133.

[48] Edward O'Shea, *A Descriptive Catalog of W. B. Yeats's Library* (New York: Garland Pub. Co., 1985), 71–2.

[49] Yeats to Frederick Macmillan, 14 December 1926, *CL InteLex* #4959.

also attributes the frontispiece arrangement of Cathleen and the four women with sacred objects to a sixth-century ivory book cover that is illustrated in Dalton just before a bookmarked page in Yeats's copy.[50] The poet and illustrator even attempted to replicate the mosaic figures of sages on a gold field by requesting gold as a background colour for two plates in the book, including McGuinness's frontispiece. The colour would have clearly invoked lines from the poem 'Sailing to Byzantium' on Byzantine mosaics: 'O sages standing in God's holy fire / As in the gold mosaic of a wall'.[51] The choice of colour was not feasible for Macmillan, who felt the gold illustration would be too bright, preferring the toned-down yellow backdrop to Cathleen in the 'Red Hanrahan' illustration, and the yellow cross for 'The Crucifixion of the Outcast'.[52] Yeats was disappointed by the initial technique of colour reproduction used for McGuinness's plates, which he felt ruined some of the designs. He suggested to McGuinness that, rather than compromise with the muted patterns of colours, she should do without colour on all designs but the frontispiece: 'You work by suggestion not only in your colour but your design. Your hand and finger convention, for instance, would not go with pattern which by its very nature is the opposite of suggestion. A tudor rose, in decoration, for instance, must be completely realized in its convention like a letter of the alphabet.'[53]

Yeats visited Ravenna in 1907, and as early as 1908 he stated an admiration for the abstract patterning of Byzantine illustration work through the voice of Owen Aherne in 'The Tables of the Law': 'the Byzantine style, which so few care for to-day, moves me because these tall, emaciated angels and saints seem to have less relation to the world about us than to an abstract pattern of flowing lines that suggest an imagination absorbed in the contemplation of Eternity.'[54] If Yeats accepted that few cared for the strong linear but austere figures in Byzantine book illuminations in 1908, the modernist turn towards abstraction and primitivism offered an opportunity for a Byzantine Revival by the 1910s and 1920s. Tellingly, the above passage, which was printed in 1908 and 1914 printings of 'The Tables of the Law', was removed from later printings of the story, including the *Stories of Red Hanrahan and the Secret Rose* (1927). Similarly to the deleted passage from *The Secret Rose* that mirrored Althea Gyles's 1897 cover, perhaps Yeats could see the full materialization of his earlier ambitions for Byzantine patterns of abstract flowing lines approaching transcendence in McGuinness's illustrations. Yeats was re-embellishing his book with latent but vindicated aesthetic styles in a new context and for new readers.

The stylized, Byzantine-inspired illustrations in 1927 were nevertheless interpreted by contemporary critics to be somewhat unmoored from the text of the prose stories. In the *Dublin Art Monthly*, Oliver Sherry (George Edmund Lobo) admired McGuinness's illustrations for radically updating Yeats's well-known prose stories. 'Her fluidity of line ignores ordinary standards of illustration', Lobo remarked; '[McGuinness] expresses

[50] Nelson, *Hagia Sophia*, 133; O'Shea, *Descriptive Catalog*, 71.

[51] *CW1*, 193.

[52] *The Secret Rose*, 282–3.

[53] Ibid., 283.

[54] Ibid, 154.

the subjective effect of the tales upon the artist's emotional nature'. The suggestion that McGuiness's illustrations were subjective, visual misprisions of the poet's early work is something that Lobo praises: 'The pictures are as haunting, in an entirely different way, as the prose itself, and it would seem as if the artist had brought something fresh to the stories themselves, given them a meaning beyond the scope of mere words.'[55] This was in keeping with McGuiness's mentor, Clarke, who was never a mere translator of the texts he illustrated.

McGuinness's line work is just one example of illustration offering a live record of contemporary readers' reception of Yeats's writing, not only in the pictures themselves that were executed several decades after the original text but also through the critical reviews evaluating the pictures in relation to their poems or prose stories. Furthermore, the illustrated Yeats provides a material trace of his aesthetic development for readers of the poet when read alongside his correspondence with illustrators, his arrangement and revision of poems, and his subsequent writing on art, where readers might otherwise encounter Yeats's work solely through collections and anthologies. For example, following the initial publication of 'Sailing to Byzantium' in Cuala's *October Blast* but preceding its appearance in *The Tower*, the placement of Yeats's ottava rima poem as a frontispiece alongside McGuinness's fresh illustrations appears to inaugurate a new *ars poetica* on the old foundations of his Celtic Revival prose stories from the 1890s. This new poetic voice and aesthetic outlook would be developed further through his collaborations with Thomas Sturge Moore on *The Tower* and *The Winding Stair* covers.

T. Sturge Moore's gold-blocked blue cloth Macmillan covers from the 1910s through the 1930s established a unity of design, dimensions, and livery to Yeats's books that complemented the early Gyles covers, while seeming quieter in tone and decoration, as Warwick Gould has noted.[56] Many of Sturge Moore's covers take as their starting point the mundane conventions of bookbinding in which a central panel is delineated by a variety of ruled lines, angular devices, and symmetrical flanking panels, establishing a structural consistency to the covers learnt from Charles Ricketts's blocking and framing for modern bindings. Ricketts also created covers with abstract and geometric arrangements of lines and borders that provided versatile, if thematically unspecific, bindings for Yeats's *Selected Poems* (1929) and the US edition of *Collected Poems* (1933).[57] Sturge Moore's originality emerges from the way he incorporates the framing elements into more dynamic and symbolic arrangements of lines to create a perch for the hawk for the cover of *Responsibilities* (1916), monolithic vertical panels flanking and mirroring Thoor Ballylee for the cover of *The Tower* (1928), or chequered panels that achieve a floor-tile effect and reflect the shading on the spiral staircase for the cover of *The Winding Stair and Other Poems* (1933).

---

[55] G.E.L. [Oliver Sherry], 'W.B. Yeats Illustrated', Dublin Art Monthly (January 1928), 17, 20–3, 23.
[56] Gould, 'Yeats and his Books', 50.
[57] *Wade*, 165–7, 174–6.

Sturge Moore was a close reader of Yeats's poetry as well as a close collaborator for the book cover illustrations. Yeats's correspondence with Sturge Moore over the confusing metaphysics of 'Sailing to Byzantium' motivated his later writing of the poem 'Byzantium'. The artist was 'sceptical as to whether mere liberation from existence has any value or probability as a consummation. ... Your *Sailing to Byzantium*, magnificent as the first three stanzas are, lets me down in the fourth, as such a goldsmith's bird is as much nature as a man's body.'[58] Sturge Moore seemed troubled by the inherent paradox of an 'artifice of eternity'.[59] The question of whether the afterlife might permit visual representations if these would merely construct a *paradis terrestre* troubled Yeats as well, who acknowledged Moore's objection that 'a bird made by a goldsmith was just as natural as anything else'; the query showed Yeats that 'the idea needed exposition'.[60]

Yeats intended to entitle *The Winding Stair* simply *Byzantium*. A preliminary sketch of the book cover by Sturge Moore, bearing the title 'Byzantium' rather than 'The Winding Stair', depicts the accumulated symbols of Yeats's Byzantium poems, including Hagia Sophia, the crescent moon, the gyre, the boy riding a dolphin, the bird in flames, and the bird perched on a golden bough.[61] (See Figure 29.1.) The three animal images are preserved in the final dust jacket of *The Winding Stair and Other Poems* (1933), although the boy riding a dolphin was adapted, and the stylised flames and bird blend into one another in the top right-hand corner on the finished cover.

TOTAL BOOKS

When reflecting on his poetic development in the 1890s in *The Trembling of the Veil* (1922), Yeats reached for another visual arts analogue in the form of modern paintings in an art gallery, and introduced a thinly veiled caricature of J. M. Synge to illustrate his point about Irish aesthetic leanings being at odds with Continental art trends and yet instinctively attuned to the elements of French Symbolism. Despite the onward march of modern art movements, Yeats imagined a nonplussed Aran Islander, 'who had strayed into the Luxembourg Gallery, turning bewildered from Impressionist and Post-Impressionist, but lingering at [Gustave] Moreau's *Jason*, to study in mute astonishment the elaborate background, where there are so many jewels, so much wrought stone and moulded bronze'.[62] There is a primitive and decorative sensibility to Yeats's imagined

---

[58] *W. B. Yeats and T. Sturge Moore: Their Correspondence, 1901-1937*, ed. Ursula Bridge (London: Routledge and Kegan Paul, 1953)., 162.

[59] *CW1*, 194.

[60] *TSMC*, 164.

[61] See Gould, 'Yeats and his Books', 54.

[62] *CW3*, 248.

FIGURE **29.1** Sturge Moore sketch for the Cuala Press edition of Yeats, 'Byzantium'. Reproduced by permission of the Senate House Library, University of London.

Irishman, a predilection for tactile, material things over the modish paintings lining the gallery walls. Yeats is also juxtaposing a fine-art representational mode in the foreground, the nude figures of Jason and Medea, with the properties of the decorative arts and abstracted patterns in the background. He reads volumetric depth in Moreau's symbolist painting by emphasizing the jewels, stones, bronze medallions, and gold set into a pillar behind the couple. The ornate column in the painting is topped with a sphinx statuette, forming a link with Moreau's *Orpheus and the Sphinx* painting, and a decapitated ram's head which has been read as a symbolic compression of Jason's attainment of the Golden Fleece with the help of Medea. Moreau's decorative and symbolic excesses in

And walk among long dappled grass,
And pluck till time and times are done
The silver apples of the moon,
The golden apples of the sun.
                    W. B. Yeats.

FIGURE **29.2** Cuala Press illustration to 'The Song of Wandering Aengus'. Reproduced by permission of the Board of Trustees, Trinity College Dublin.

paintings from the mid-1860s were widely criticized for subordinating the narrative action of well-known Greek myths.[63] By the same token, Yeats felt that by the 1890s he 'had gone a great distance from my first poems, from all that I had copied from the folk-art of Ireland'.[64]

---

[63] Peter Cooke, *Gustave Moreau: History Painting, Spirituality and Symbolism* (London: Yale University Press, 2014), 57.
[64] *CW3*, 247–8.

In Yeats's curious painting analogy from *The Trembling of the Veil*, the mythic hero narratives of his lengthy early poems faded in importance to the charged symbols and rhythms of his later lyric poems, just as the anachronistic Aran Islander in the gallery prefers the patterns and rhythms of the moulded decorations lying behind the bodily forms. Similarly, in the graphic art of the symbolist and decadent illustrators Yeats had most admired in the 1890s—Whistler, Beardsley, and Althea Gyles—he felt that 'the images of human life ... faded almost perfectly' in the contemplation of elaborate patterns and rhythms.[65] In the 1920s, Yeats was memorializing his writings of the 1890s with new livery and graphic designs that also pointed backwards to a compressed history of aesthetics—of neo-Byzantinism and abstract but systematic patterns—latent in his early writing but expounded in his later verse and prose.

In Yeats's lifetime illustrated literature evolved in material format, artistic practice, and style in response to technological developments and changes in aesthetic fashions both literary and visual. Yeats was deeply engaged in the illustration of his work, using his poetry and prose to develop an aesthetic model or models of illustration and even returning to his poetic subjects and remaking them through his extensive correspondence and collaboration with illustrators. He wrote at length about the graphic arts and book design, particularly in the late 1890s. As he could more fully appreciate by the 1920s, Symbolism was a vital antecedent to twentieth-century art—abstraction, primitivism, and even non-objective art. In *The Trembling of the Veil*, he aligns himself with the shift from narrative poems and representational, narrative painting towards the decorative and symbolist aesthetics of an earlier time. As his collaborations with Norah McGuinness show, textual ornament and illustration afforded Yeats an opportunity to step backwards in history to an abstract or symbolic phase of art that was antiquated in relation to a succeeding representational phase, and yet strikingly modern and refreshing. Nevertheless, the decoration of old poems and prose, from the Cuala Press illuminated sheets to McGuinness's line work in *Stories of Red Hanrahan and the Secret Rose*, opened Yeats's oeuvre to commentaries and interpretations beyond his control—whether in the illustrations themselves or the readers encountering newly bound and decorated books to read or reread Yeats's bounty from end to end.

[65]   W. B. Yeats, 'A Symbolic Artist and the Coming of Symbolic Art', *The Dome* (December 1898), 234.

....

CHAPTER 30

FAMILY BUSINESS AT DUN EMER AND CUALA

Collaboration, contention, and creativity

....

ELIZABETH BERGMANN LOIZEAUX

WHEN the slim, white volume *In the Seven Woods* was published by Dun Emer Press in August 1903, it suggested a new development in Yeats's poetry: in its evocations of an Irish heroic past and personal lost love, it was more conversational, more direct syntactically, 'less dream-burdened',[1] Yeats hoped, an entry into the more immediate, engaged mode of his middle and late years. As the first book published by the Dun Emer Press, it also marked the start of a remarkable family business that ran from 1902 to 1986, first as part of Dun Emer Industries (1902–8), founded by Evelyn Gleeson and Henry Augustine with Yeats's sisters, Elizabeth Corbet Yeats (Lolly or Lollie) and Susan Mary Yeats (Lily), then under Lolly and Lily (1908–40) and other family members (1940–86) as Cuala Industries or, later, Cuala Press. Over the course of its history, Dun Emer/Cuala involved, in one way or another, most of the family for three generations, including Lolly, Lily and WBY's brother, the painter Jack, their father John Butler Yeats (selections of whose letters the press published), WBY's wife George (who took the enterprise in hand at various times of crisis and ran it after Lolly's death), and, in the press's revival in the 1970s and 1980s, WBY's children and grandchildren. Under Lolly's direction, with WBY as literary editor, the press published 77 books in its regular series, 108 broadsides, 38 books and pamphlets published on commission, and more than 200 cards, bookplates, calendars, and prints, along with other promotional material.[2] Lily oversaw the design and production of hundreds of embroidered pictures, curtains, cushions, cradle quilts, and other pieces. Jack, the youngest sibling, always slightly at a distance from the family, provided designs for embroidery and dozens of popular illustrations for the press. With Dun Emer/Cuala's attention to creating

---

[1] W.B. Yeats, *In the Seven Woods* (Dundrum: Dun Emer Press, 1903), 25.

[2] Richard Kuhta, *Elizabeth Corbet Yeats: The Other Yeats in the Irish Literary Renaissance* (Canton, NY: St. Lawrence University, 1994), 9.

beautiful everyday objects made by hand, and its insistence on Irish labour, materials, design, and writers for its press, it brought William Morris's Arts and Crafts Movement to Ireland to feed the Revival. With its intention to train and provide work for women, it advanced the growing movement for women's independence.

Yeats's remarkable remaking of himself as the twentieth century opened—his 'movement downwards upon life'—was, at heart, a probing, driven effort to place poetry rightly in the world, to press the range of its power to affect individual people and a broader public where they lived.[3] It required a new relation to the lyric self, new ways of expressing the political. It also involved complexly interrelated explorations of the *forms* words might take in the world so they could enter the lives of people and, as he said, 'go with us'.[4] From writing and staging plays to experimenting with musically spoken verse with actress Florence Farr and musician Arnold Dolmetsch, his remaking was an extraordinarily inter-artistic and collaborative undertaking.[5] With the founding of Dun Emer, he gained the arenas of the printed book and embroidery—along with a business—all necessarily requiring many hands.

From its start, the Dun Emer/Cuala enterprise was fraught with misunderstandings, financial confusion, and the clash of difficult personalities. Intertwined with these were energy, creativity, intelligence, and family solidarity. Art that needed to provide a living for its makers brought urgency and commitment to the enterprise, along with clashes over the relative weight of art and commerce. Collaboration that involved family in the making of art and the running of a business brought family dynamics into both, along with enduring loyalty. For WBY, what the physical embodiment of his work should look like in a new century, and how it might be brought into the world through collaboration with family members whose personalities and priorities differed, was the abiding challenge and chance in his lifelong commitment to the family business.

Until the 1990s, WBY's vantage largely shaped accounts of Dun Emer/Cuala. Biographical accounts depict its drain on his patience and resources. He appears as its hero, keeping the enterprise true to high artistic standards and bailing it out of financial difficulty, beleaguered by what was understood as Lolly's practical ineptitude. In the 1990s, new perspectives began to complicate this account, as feminist criticism brought more informed and expanded views of the women who ran Dun Emer/Cuala and textual studies brought to the fore the role of fine presses, including Lolly's, in the development of literary and visual modernism.[6] Lily's work is less known than her

---

[3] *CL Intelex* #343.

[4] Yeats, 'Art and Ideas', *CW4*, 256.

[5] David Holdeman points to collaboration as necessary to accomplishing what Yeats wanted (*Much Labouring: The Texts and Authors of Yeats's First Modernist Books* [Ann Arbor: University of Michigan Press, 1997], 52–3); Adrian Paterson sees a Yeats 'impelled to collaboration' ('"Stitching and Unstitching": Yeats material and immaterial', *Review of Irish Studies in Europe* 2, no. 1 (March 2018), 178).

[6] For feminist perspectives, see, for example, Joan Hardwick, *The Yeats Sisters: A Biography of Susan and Elizabeth Yeats* (London: Pandora, 1996); Kuhta; Gifford Lewis, *The Yeats Sisters and the Cuala* (Dublin: Irish Academic Press, 1994). For textual studies and modernism, see, for example, George Bornstein, *Material Modernism: The Politics of the Page* (Cambridge: Cambridge University Press, 2001); Holdeman, *Much Labouring*; Clare Hutton, 'Toward a Modernism of the Book: From Dun Emer to Shakespeare and Company', in *A History of Irish Modernism*, edited by Gregory Castle and Patrick

siblings' and has been little regarded in relation to WBY's, but it is well worth attention.[7] I have written elsewhere about Jack Yeats's remarkable and extensive contributions to Dun Emer and Cuala Presses, including his illustrations to his brother's poems for the 1935 and 1937 Cuala *Broadsides*, the only time the two brothers collaborated.[8] Jack is also discussed elsewhere in this volume.[9] What follows here explores the early days of Dun Emer/Cuala focusing on the nature of the relationships that shaped the business from its start, then takes a closer look at examples of WBY's collaborations with each of his sisters.

FAMILY DYNAMICS AND WOMEN'S WORK AT DUN EMER AND CUALA

In early 1902 Evelyn Gleeson, suffragist, Irish nationalist, and admirer of William Morris, set about establishing a women's craft cooperative in Dublin with advice and backing from family friend and advisor, botanist Augustine Henry. They enlisted the talents of two of Gleeson's fellow members of the London Irish Literary Society, Elizabeth and Lily Yeats. What the sisters saw in the invitation was, above all, the promise of steady, suitable employment. As unmarried women with uncertain prospects and no family money, they needed to support themselves and other family members, including, always, their talented, improvident artist father. Money to feed the family 'swalley hole' was desperately tight. In the new venture, Lily would use her skills learned from six years (1888–94) working in the embroidery workshop of Morris & Co. under Morris's daughter, May. Lolly might put her considerable resourcefulness and experience as an artist to learning how to use a hand press. Rigorously trained in modern pedagogical methods, she had successfully taught painting and had written four well-received books on brushwork. She was warmly encouraged in the new enterprise by Emery Walker (1851–1933),

---

Bixby (Cambridge: Cambridge University Press, 2019), 128–41; Jerome McGann, *Black Riders: The Visible Language of Modernism* (Princeton: Princeton University Press, 1993). For Cuala/Dun Emer in Irish literary and cultural history, see, for example, Robin Skelton, 'Twentieth-Century Irish Literature and the Private Press Tradition: Dun Emer, Cuala, & Dolmen Presses 1902–1963', *The Massachusetts Review* 5, no. 2 (Winter 1964), 368–77; Karen Brown, *The Yeats Circle, Verbal and Visual Relations in Ireland, 1880–1939* (Farnham: Ashgate, 2011); and Vera Kreilkamp, ed., *The Arts and Crafts Movement: Making It Irish* (Chestnut Hill: Boston College McMullen Museum, 2016).

[7] Hardwick's brief note on Lily's embroidery techniques is helpful (251–2). Lily's work has been shown recently in '[In]visible: Irish Women Artists from the Archives', 19 July 2018–3 March 2019, National Gallery of Ireland. See also Cynthia Fowler, 'Transatlantic Textiles: Ireland's Dun Emer Textiles in America During the First Decade of the Twentieth Century', *Textile History* 50, no. 2, 163–186, doi: 10.1080/00404969.2019.1646622, https://www.tandfonline.com/loi/ytex20.

[8] Elizabeth Bergmann Loizeaux, 'The Art of Resistance: Jack Yeats, W.B. Yeats and the Cuala Press Broadsides', *YAACTS* 11 (1994), 144–85.

[9] See Nicholas Allen, 'The Writings of Jack Yeats', Chapter 8 in this volume.

inspiration and advisor for Morris's Kelmscott Press (1891–8) and founding partner in the famous Doves Press (1900–17). WBY would lend his growing reputation and literary connections as the press's literary advisor, soliciting and selecting work for Lolly to print.

The nationalist goals of Gleeson's cooperative also appealed and spoke to the sisters' longing to return to Ireland after their years in London. Named Dun Emer (Emer's Fort) after the wife of Irish hero Cuchulain, renowned for her skilled needlework, the new enterprise would 'find work for Irish hands in the making of beautiful things .... Everything as far as possible, is Irish: the paper of the books, the linen of the embroidery and the wool of the tapestry and carpets. The designs are also of the spirit and tradition of the country.'[10] Irish language lessons for the staff were part of the plan. WBY immediately saw an opportunity to brand the press as *the* publisher of new Irish writing of the highest literary merit to advance his vision of an Irish cultural revival.[11] With few exceptions, the Dun Emer/Cuala Press list would be exclusively Irish: John Millington Synge, George Russell (AE), Douglas Hyde, Lady Gregory, Oliver Gogarty, Frank O'Connor, and others. Thirty-one books written by Yeats himself appeared from 1903 to 1944.[12] Nationalist aims also found immediate expression in the first work Lily undertook at Dun Emer, a set of embroidered sodality banners for Loughrea Cathedral, founded in 1897, the architectural 'jewel in the crown of the Celtic Revival'.[13] Most of the designs for the banners' central figures were created by contemporary Irish artists, among them Jack Yeats and AE.[14] Many incorporated the names of the saints in Irish lettering.

By December 1902, the Yeats family was installed outside Dublin near the large, airy house that Evelyn Gleeson had let to house the cooperative, and Lolly had purchased an Albion hand press from a provincial printer, and a set of 14-point Caslon Old Style type. In the course of 1903, Lolly not only learned to print but trained two local teenagers to help, and published both *In the Seven Woods* (July, 325 copies), and *The Nuts of Knowledge* by AE. By September, *In the Seven Woods* had sold out, a promising start.

But even so early in their association, all was not well among the three women principals of Dun Emer. Too much was left to vague good feelings around the ideal of a craft cooperative and not enough to carefully working out the specific, realistic understanding among the partners that such a collaboration requires. What cooperation might mean in practical terms does not seem to have been discussed among those involved, nor did it reliably guide the operation as a working value in either the financial arrangements or the making of tapestries, embroideries, and books. While considering themselves equal partners, the Yeats sisters were positioned more like employees in the structural organization of Dun Emer. They received a guaranteed income, brought no

---

[10] The first prospectus for Dun Emer Industries (1903), quoted in full in Liam Miller, *The Dun Emer Press, Later the Cuala Press* (Dublin: Dolmen, 1973).

[11] For an account of Yeats as literary editor of Cuala, see Warwick Gould's Chapter 41, 'Editing Yeats', in this volume.

[12] See Dun Emer/Cuala bibliography up through 1972 in Miller, *The Dun Emer Press*, 103–31.

[13] http://www.loughreacathedral.ie.

[14] See Hilary Pyle, *Yeats: Portrait of an Artistic Family* (London: Merrell Holberton, 1997), 166.

funding themselves to the enterprise, and thought, mistakenly, that Gleeson and Henry had ready reserves to support it. There were no hours of work specified in the founding articles, and no set limits on what each member, 'independent in her own department', could spend on supplies and other expenses. As a friendly investor, Henry understood the cooperative as 'an interesting scheme and experiment' worth the risk.[15] Unaware of the provisional nature of the enterprise and not seeing what 'cooperative' might suggest about their own obligations, the Yeats sisters optimistically dived in.

Quickly, Gleeson came to resent the sisters' assumption of equal status and independent decision-making. The sisters pushed back. In one petty, illustrative incident, Lolly, as she prepared the press for its first publication, ignored Gleeson's opinion of the proposed pressmark ('pretty' but 'feeble'), had it engraved anyhow, then refused to show Gleeson the result.[16] By the end of its first year in operation, despite the success of In the Seven Woods, none of the divisions showed a profit once the supplies and the Yeatses' guaranteed salaries were deducted. Relations disintegrated. In 1904, with AE's mediation, Dun Emer split into two enterprises: Dun Emer Guild to be run by Gleeson, and Dun Emer Industries to be run by the Yeats sisters. With two Dun Emers now competing fiercely for customers, complete separation was inevitable. In 1908, while Lily was in New York selling their wares, Lolly impulsively moved the sisters' operations into a cottage nearby. She had to leave behind the heavy Albion press for the moment, giving Gleeson the opportunity for a dramatic move of her own. Holding it hostage, she demanded that the sisters relinquish the Dun Emer name. Cuala Press and Industries was thus born and named after the ancient baronry where their business was now housed and would remain until 1923.

Peace, however, was still not to be had. Tension among Lily, Lolly, and WBY had caused disruption from the start and now continued to flare periodically. Forced by circumstance to live together throughout their lives, the sisters did not get on. In family biographer William Murphy's account, Lily listened well, was calm and attentive, and was the favourite of her father and WBY. Lolly, in contrast, talked constantly, was restless, irascible, defensive, 'unstable' at times, and difficult to live with. She had, he judged, 'a severe personality disorder, an extreme neurosis', a 'psychopathy'.[17] Biographies of the sisters by Gifford Lewis and Joan Hardwick offer a more sympathetic portrait of Lolly. 'Elizabeth became the maddening focus of irritation for Lily and WBY,' Lewis writes. Yet, she goes on, 'Elizabeth was the first woman to run a private art press, her work was acclaimed throughout the world of printing and publishing.'[18] One might also point out that Lily's lively letters to her father made common cause with him against Lolly in a way that was surely undermining. John Butler Yeats and Lily, Hardwick notes, 'agreed to destroy "dangerous" letters exchanged between them … In this way a less pleasing side of both father and daughter has been quietly eradicated.'[19]

[15] Quoted in William M. Murphy, Family Secrets: William Butler Yeats and His Relatives (Syracuse: Syracuse University Press, 1995), 96.

[16] Murphy, Family Secrets, 112.

[17] Murphy, Family Secrets, 176, 364.

[18] Lewis, Yeats Sisters, 4.

[19] Hardwick, vi.

While the sisters irritated each other, both also chafed under WBY's authoritative interference in their business and artistic practice. In the early days of Dun Emer, Lily allied herself with her sister: 'Willy was full of "Do this, you must do that," etc., "a press man is absolutely necessary," and so on,' she wrote to their father. Lily wanted Jack to design embroideries for her, but Willy, she claimed, had 'pets' he wanted to commission. The results were designs that she judged 'ridiculous' and 'quite commonplace'. Willy, she charged, 'threatened us and bullied generally'.[20]

Lolly's tussles with WBY over control of the press became a constant feature of their relationship. Looking back over eighty years, WBY's daughter Anne—painter, designer, and later director of Cuala—wryly described the familial power dynamics of birth order, gender relations, and personality that shaped their collaboration: 'He probably interfered. He did interfere. He liked having a press at his command. Who wouldn't? [Elizabeth] would have wanted the press to be hers. She'd finally found something that was hers and along comes her brother and interferes ... [and] father knew how to get his way.'[21] 'I don't want a dictator for my press, but a literary advisor—Have you any advise [sic] to give [?],' Lolly wrote to Emery Walker in 1906 in the midst of a dispute over the publication of AE's *By Still Waters*, typical of battles large and small.[22] Lolly, desperate to make money, blamed WBY for not providing the press enough titles to keep it busy, a frequent problem. Asserting what she saw as her prerogative as head of the press, she independently asked AE to make another selection of poems, and immediately set it up in type. WBY was furious, judged the selection inferior, refused to let it be published, and when Lolly did not back down, resigned as literary advisor. Jack urged her to remain firm. JBY jumped in, remonstrating with his eldest son: 'Why *do you write such offensive letters?* ... You treat Lollie as if she was dirt. She is as clever a woman as you are, and in some respects much cleverer .... After all *the press is Lollie's business* and it means our means of living. And she has often other things to consider besides the literary excellence of a particular book.'[23] While self-interest certainly speaks here, JBY, stepping back, recognized that similarity sparked contention: WBY and Lolly were both 'clever' and driven. Giving with one hand while taking with the other, he had written to Lolly, 'You have every bit as much intellect as Willie–only you have not his serene self-confidence. And [not] having this you have not his patience ....You are here [in intellect] quite as strong as Willie, only you don't exercise it.'[24] But 'serene self-confidence' made all the difference.

The push and pull of perceived aesthetic standards and financial necessity played out within the context of a social revolution in gender roles with which Lily and, especially,

---

[20] Quoted in Murphy, *Family Secrets*, 103.

[21] Quoted in Kuhta, 11, brackets his.

[22] Quoted in Kuhta, 20. For this and later disputes over editorial selection, see also Simone Murray, 'The Cuala Press: Women, publishing, and the conflicted genealogies of "feminist publishing"', *Women's Studies International Forum* 27 (2004), 489–506.

[23] Quoted in William M. Murphy, *Prodigal Father: The Life of John Butler Yeats* (1839–1922) (Ithaca: Cornell University Press, 1978), 304.

[24] Quoted in Murphy, *Prodigal Father*, 241.

Lolly struggled. Anne Yeats described her aunts: 'Lolly was restless, fidgety, always talking, always fidgeting with her jewelry. She wasn't a very good listener ... [and she was] hard to be around. Lily was boring, sedentary, always sitting, stationary .... Lolly was more interesting ... an interesting irritant [who] didn't get along with her brother at all ... and, oddly, didn't get along with Lily, goodness no .... Aunt Lily was ill for so long ... couldn't go anywhere or do anything ... always sitting, with some sewing in her lap ... [but] she was a good listener. THAT's why the Yeats men liked her. She sat and listened to them. [As a result] they went to her before Lolly. Lily was the favorite.'[25]

Although Dun Emer was founded as a feminist enterprise, neither sister fully embraced the transformed social order feminism envisioned; neither was able to, or wanted to, cut free of established patterns, old dependencies and self-conceptions, perhaps especially because family and the business on which they counted for their livelihood were so intertwined. There was no place fully apart from the family circle in which to try out new ways of being. Lily largely sidestepped head-on confrontation. She was often ill with a long-undiagnosed thyroid problem, around which she had to work. She loved the pleasures of domestic life and had longed for marriage and children. A peaceful household mattered to her. That embroidery was comfortably 'women's work' suited her.

Within the world of fine press printing, Lolly was a pioneer. The British Women's Printing Society, where Lolly had trained for a month to prepare for her new career, was founded in 1876 with the aim, in part, to demonstrate that the demanding physical labour of printing could be done and done well by women. She enjoyed the work and the socializing that selling it entailed. Although her sister and WBY found her difficult, Lolly was a dedicated mentor who inspired the loyalty of the women who worked for her, including Esther Ryan (employed for thirty-seven years) and Maire Gill (thirty-two years).[26] In her own mind, she acceded often to 'Willie's' whims, desperately seeking his recognition and approval.

Given the family dynamics that shaped her business, there was little hope that Lolly could gain the experience and confidence necessary to exercise the occasional editorial control she wanted. WBY explained the 1906 'difference of opinion with my sister' to Katharine Tynan: 'She would like me to go on editing various books, she on her part to put in others when the fancy pleased her, and this I won't have, as it means I know the gradual lowering of the standard of quality.'[27] The now-lost agreement that finally resolved the dispute gave WBY clear editorial approval rights while acknowledging Lolly's interests. Lolly felt she'd won something, but with her financial need to keep the press busy characterized as 'when the fancy pleased her' and the compromise allowing her to choose some titles rejected outright, business went on as before. Despite his defence of her interests in 1906, JBY devastatingly responded to a similar incident in

---

[25] Quoted in Kuhta, 11, brackets his.
[26] Lewis, *Yeats Sisters*, 182. For a more qualified view of Lolly as pioneer, see Murray.
[27] WBY to Katharine Tynan Hinkson (24 Aug [1906]), *CL Intelex* #461.

1914, 'were he not the Editor your press would fail'.[28] Following Lolly's death in 1940, a year after WBY's, Lily commented on Cuala's fate had Lolly lived longer: 'Lolly could not have run the Press alone. She had no judgment in the choice of books. Willy did all that.'[29] The frustrations WBY encountered at the Abbey and described in 'The Fascination of What's Difficult' repeated themselves in his work with his sister at the press.

* * *

> The fascination of what's difficult
> Has dried the sap out of my veins, and rent
> Spontaneous joy and natural content
> Out of my heart.[30]

Little questioning the necessity of the day's war, his role in fomenting it, or the effect of this brand of collaboration on others, Yeats names its human cost so evident in his and sometimes JBY's and Lily's relations with Lolly.

Accolades accrued to Dun Emer/Cuala during its lifetime and after. Both Lolly and Lily won numerous awards at the arts and crafts shows where they exhibited.[31] By the 1930s, Cuala's books were sought after by collectors and selling for large sums. The American bibliophile William Ransom encouraged Lolly to write a history of the press he deemed so significant.[32] By century's end, it was considered by some 'the most important private press in the history of printing in Ireland'.[33] The polymath modernist literary critic Hugh Kenner went considerably farther, reportedly declaring of the long-lived enterprise 'that the most beautiful printing in modern times is being accomplished by a small Dublin firm called the Cuala Press'.[34]

In the Seven Woods: WBY and Lolly Remaking and Making

How did such success emerge from the contentious collaboration of WBY and Elizabeth Corbet Yeats? Much has been written about the year-long production of Dun Emer

---

[28] Quoted in Hardwick, 181.
[29] Quoted in Murphy, *Family Secrets*, 261.
[30] *CW1*, 93.
[31] See, for example, Lewis, *Yeats Sisters*, 106, 166–7.
[32] Hardwick, 236.
[33] Kuhta, 9.
[34] In an unpublished talk to the Grolier Club around the time Cuala officially closed. Cited in Murphy, *Family Secrets*, 453–4 n.182.

Press's first volume, *In the Seven Woods*, out of which came the beginnings of WBY's transformation into a modern poet, the establishment of Lolly's life's work as a printer, and the launching of an important fine press.[35] Its consequences are so significant that it is worth another look here.

Lolly later lamented to her father, 'it is no joke publishing with Willy's finger in the pie', but when the siblings got down to it, creative determination took over, perhaps sharpened by the tensions between them, each digging in.[36] Under the immediate need to assemble a book, in the summer and fall of 1902 WBY burst into creative activity. He sorted through the few poems he had written since *The Wind Among the Reeds* (1899), retreated to Coole to work on new poems, and, by filling in with dramatic work, assembled enough pages to merit the goodly sum (10s. 6d.; approximately £63 today) that would be charged for this 'specially beautiful and expensive first edition'. He seemed energized by the recognition that even the contents 'will depend to some extent on the general look of the book'.[37] He assessed his evolving aesthetic: 'The close of the last century was full of a strange desire to get out of form to get to some kind of disembodied beauty and now it seems to me the contrary impulse has come'.[38] Full of high hope, steamrolling ahead, he involved himself in nearly every aspect of this chance to get language into beautiful form: weighing in on materials, colours, binding; suggesting changes to the wording of the press's name in the volume's opening pages; commenting on the pressmark that had been such a bone of contention with Gleeson ('impossible');[39] and drafting the press's first prospectus. From December 1902, when Lolly produced the first few rough pages of proofs until the book's final printing on 17 July 1903, Yeats, intent on self-transformation, constantly revised the contents of the volume, their order, and the poems themselves.

Lolly, too, was remaking herself. She, too, was ambitious for this book and bent on success, artistic and commercial. The many surviving page proofs, annotated by WBY, Walker, and Lolly, demonstrate her sheer persistence as she tried and tried again to get the printing clear and the look of the page satisfying, guided by Walker's firm expertise.[40] There are over thirty pulls of the first gathering she printed, dozens of pulls of subsequent gatherings, and unknown numbers that were tossed away at the time. While WBY's revisions required much frustrating and time-consuming setting up 'in fifty

---

[35] See, especially, David Holdeman's two comprehensive and insightful accounts of the volume, to which I am greatly indebted: David Holdeman, ed., *"In the Seven Woods" and "The Green Helmet and Other Poems": Manuscript Materials by W. B. Yeats*, (Ithaca and London: Cornell University Press, 2002) and *Much Labouring*. I also thank Holdeman for his generosity in sharing with me, while coronavirus closed the archives, his copies of the proofs of *In the Seven Woods* from Stony Brook University's copies of material in the National Library of Ireland, and in offering me his take on what they show about the collaboration of the siblings.

[36] Quoted in Lewis, *Yeats Sisters*, 114.

[37] *CL3*, 298, 297.

[38] *CL3*, 369.

[39] Quoted in *Life 1*, 300.

[40] Holdeman, email to author, 1 May 2020.

ways'—the difficulty of which he seemed serenely unaware—they gave Lolly additional practice. She learned to work with the paper size (too small and irregular) in relation to the type (too large), puzzling through with Walker where to begin poems and how to set the long lines that wouldn't all fit on a page. She dealt with uneven printing and blots of ink squish. Struggling initially, she learned how to use 'furniture' to hold a block with an image firmly in place, only to determine, in the end, not to use images.[41] She learned the difficult process of printing colour, putting the page through the press separately for each colour, perfectly aligned; a single colour, red, possibly suggested by Walker, was decided upon as ambitious enough for some parts of this first book.

As David Holdeman has shown in his definitive treatments of this volume, much of the back and forth between Lolly and Walker on the proofs concerns the desire for a 'unified page'—achieved by arranging the print closer to the gutter than to the outer edges of the page, so that a coherent field of print surrounded by pleasing proportions of white space presents itself in the centre of the open book.[42] The proofs are full of Walker's guiding instructions to close up spaces between titles and poems, narrow the margins at the gutter, or widen those at the outer edges. Images for a pressmark and colophon were tried and rejected as unworkable, given space and their look on the page. Lolly and Walker, it is clear, 'were seeking real artistic mastery, not just competence'.[43]

A working method for collaboration among the three developed: Lolly printed, sent the proofs to Walker, who corrected, offered tips, made suggestions, and returned them for Lolly to revise and print again. On the first gathering she printed, they seem to have gone back and forth between the two of them before sending the gathering to WBY for his comment. Reading WBY's inscrutable handwriting had always been a challenge for typesetters, and Lolly had an advantage here.[44] Still, some difficulty with his corrections seems to lie behind his testy (if reasonable) request to Lolly: 'If you have the slightest doubts as to the meaning of any of my corrections you must send me yet another "revise". You make my work harder by not sending me my own ~~corrected~~ proof with corrections with the "revise". I have to do double work.'[45] As the process stretched on through multiple revisions and she advanced in skill and confidence, Lolly sent proofs simultaneously to WBY and Walker. Her requests for WBY's response are straightforward and make an effort to be clear about the process, as on one proof of the front matter: 'Very rough. Have you suggestions. I have sent this also to Mr Walker for suggestions.'[46]

---

[41] Gifford Lewis, '"This terrible struggle with want of means": Behind the Scenes at the Cuala Press' in *The Oxford History of the Irish Book, Volume V: The Irish Book in English, 1891–2000*, edited by Clare Hutton (Oxford: Oxford University Press, 2011), 532. https://doi.org/10.1093/acprof:os obl/9780199249114.003.0023.

[42] Holdeman, *Much Labouring*, 40–1.

[43] Holdeman, email to author, 1 May 2020.

[44] Lewis, *Yeats Sisters*, 64.

[45] William Butler Yeats Microfilmed Manuscript Collection, Special Collections Department, Stony Brook University (SBU 1201461 NLI 30073).

[46] SBU 1400040 (NLI 30246).

Necessarily, WBY's initial ideas were tempered by what was possible, given the materials and equipment, and by the assertions of Lolly's developing professional and artistic sense, guided by Walker. At one point WBY directed changes to the capitalization of titles in the table of contents and wanted page numbers to follow the titles immediately, removing the justified right margin.[47] At another, he suggested the title page and preliminaries be eliminated altogether.[48] Apparently wanting blue or grey for endpapers and cover (no green, he'd explained to John Quinn[49]), he high-handedly noted on one proof, 'Surely all you have to do would be to put the paper in solution of indigo. I know nothing about paper dyes, but I thought the process simple.'[50] The preliminaries remained; the justified right margin for the table of contents was kept, maintaining the balance of print and white space on the page as a whole; WBY's suggestions for capitalization were accepted; and, while Lolly later added coloured covers to her repertoire, this first cover was undyed linen with the title printed in red on a rectangle of plain white paper.

In the summer of 1903, the printing of the first book done and lessons learned, Dun Emer Press published its first prospectus setting out its principles and announcing its first titles (Figure 30.1). Yeats drafted it; Lolly and Walker revised. A comparison of the draft and the published prospectus, with a look at revisions along the way, gives a window into the collaboration with Walker and Lolly that shaped Yeats's evolving sense of the physical book and established the press's aesthetic and commercial principles.

The draft's prototext is the 1900 tract *The Ideal Book or Book Beautiful* by book-binder T. J. Cobden-Sanderson, who, like Walker, had been deeply involved in Morris's Kelmscott Press. Published in 1900 as a statement of principles for the new Doves Press, founded by Walker and Cobden-Sanderson, it offers tribute to 'the great revival in printing which is taking place under our own eyes' in Morris's work, while offering a general cautionary tale about elaborate decoration, Kelmscott's hall-mark.[51] Cobden-Sanderson observes the 'usurpation' that occurs when 'a beauty of decoration once started on its way' moves on 'to the making of pictures', and thence to the 'danger ... of sacrificing the thing signified to the mode of its signification'.[52] 'The moral is', he concludes, 'that every artist, in contributing to the Book Beautiful, must keep himself well in hand and strictly subordinate both his art and his ambition to the end in view.'[53] 'The whole duty of Typography', it follows, 'is to communicate to the imagination, without loss by the way, the thought or image intended to be communicated by the Author. And the whole duty of beautiful typography is ... to win access for that communication by the clearness & beauty of the vehicle.'[54] Not

[47]   SBU 1400043 (NLI 30246).

[48]   Quoted in *Life 1*, 300.

[49]   *CL*3, 361.

[50]   *Life 1*, 300.

[51]   T. J. Cobden-Sanderson, *The Ideal Book or Book Beautiful: A Tract on Calligraphy, Printing, and Illustration & on the Book Beautiful as a Whole* (Hammersmith: Doves Press, 1900), 6. https://hdl.handle.net/2027/uc1.31175035226466., 6.

[52]   Cobden-Sanderson, 3, 4.

[53]   Cobden-Sanderson, 5.

[54]   Cobden-Sanderson, 6.

THE DUN EMER PRESS

THOUGH many books are printed in Ireland, book printing as an art has been little practised here since the eighteenth century. The Dun Emer Press has been founded in the hope of reviving this beautiful craft.

A good eighteenth century fount of type which is not eccentric in form, or difficult to read has been cast, and the paper has been made of linen rags and without bleaching chemicals, at the Saggart Mill in the county Dublin. The pages are printed at a Hand Press by Miss E. C. Yeats, and simplicity is aimed at in their composition.

The first book printed has been 'In the Seven Woods' a new volume of poems, chiefly of the Irish Heroic Age, by W. B. Yeats. The edition is limited to 325 copies, and the book will not be republished in this form. It is now ready, price ten shillings and six pence a copy payable in advance. The next book will be 'The Nuts of Knowledge' a book of new and old lyrical poems by A. E. The price will be seven shillings and sixpence a copy. Subscribers names will be received by Miss E. C. Yeats at the Dun Emer Press, Dundrum, Co. Dublin.

Other books are in preparation, an Irish prose story by Mr G. Bernard Shaw; Dr Hyde's famous translations of the Love Songs of Connacht; some translations by Lady Gregory of heroic and mediaeval Irish poems; and a book on speaking to the Psaltery, with music, and a description of the art by Mr Arnold Dolmetsch and others. Other books will be announced shortly.

FIGURE 30.1 W. B. Yeats, Dun Emer Press Prospectus, proof of final version (1903), the Henry W. and Albert A. Berg Collection of English and American Literature, New York Public Library, Astor, Lenox, and Tilden Foundations.

focused on what would later be understood as the difficulties of knowing authorial intent and the impossibility of transparent mediation, he thus set a course-correcting direction for the Doves Press: 'if the Book Beautiful may be beautiful by virtue of its writing or printing or illustration, it may also be beautiful, be even more beautiful, by the union of all to the production of one composite whole, the consummate Book Beautiful.'[55]

To Yeats, who was struggling with excessive gestures in acting style and dramatic scenic effects in the theatre, and proposed rehearsing the actors in barrels 'that they might forget gesture and have their minds free to think of speech for a while', this was certainly a sympathetic theory of the book.[56] In his draft prospectus for Dun Emer (Figure 30.2), he immediately picked up the twinned concepts of 'access' and 'clearness': 'a good eighteenth century fount of type which is not eccentric or difficult to read has been cast and simplicity has been aimed at in the composition of the pages.'[57] Yeats had witnessed Lolly's and Walker's laborious refining for access (readability) and simplicity in the successive annotated page proofs for *In the Seven Woods*. Thus were set two tenets of Yeats's evolving sense of a modern movement into form consonant with his new ambition as a poet 'to express myself without waste, without emphasis'.[58] A Dun Emer book would also give its authors' works an Irish habitation with its paper, 'made entirely from linen rags at the Saggart Mills ... without the use of bleaching chemicals'. The details Yeats chose express the intimacy of the local and the authenticity of the down to earth and unadorned he wanted for his new poetic language and found in *In the Seven Woods* in such poems as 'In the Seven Woods', 'The Folly of Being Comforted', and 'Adam's Curse'.

In the draft, nothing is said of Elizabeth Corbet Yeats's role beyond collector of subscriptions. The published prospectus asserts her hand, heightening claims for her craft as an art, calling out its 'beauty'. The 'art of printing' thus becomes 'book printing as an art', which is now distinguished from 'the many books printed in Ireland', suggesting along the way that Ireland is a literary nation ripe for a revival of this art 'little practised here since the 18th century'. The book's printer is now named, her act of printing made more vivid, and the handcraftedness of her products called out: 'The pages are printed at a Hand Press by Miss E. C. Yeats.' The insertion of Lolly's name precipitated a rearrangement of the sentence so that she is now suggested as the agent of that passively expressed 'simplicity is aimed at'. Securing the linguistic link to Cobden-Sanderson's book beautiful, and calling to mind the Arts and Crafts Movement as context, the prospectus names printing 'this beautiful craft', a resounding end to the first paragraph.

What strikes most about Lolly's and Walker's revisions on proofs along the way are the dynamics between Lolly and her partners (see Figures 30.3, 30.4, 30.5, and 30.6). The open, looping hand is Lolly's; the smaller hand in darker ink is Walker's. We can see Lolly deferentially, sometimes nervously, posing questions of her collaborators, even on small details. 'Will I put your name in full,' she asks WBY. 'Also shall I put Dr Douglas Hyde.' 'Should we not have a heading?' she asks Walker, a question to which the obvious

---

[55] Cobden-Sanderson, 8.

[56] *CW8*, 12.

[57] William Butler Yeats collection MS 43, Special Collection/University Archives, Ellen Clarke Bertrand Library, Bucknell University, Lewisburg, PA.

[58] *CL3*, 122. See Holdeman on the multivalencies of 'simplicity' for Yeats (*Much Labouring*, 32–40).

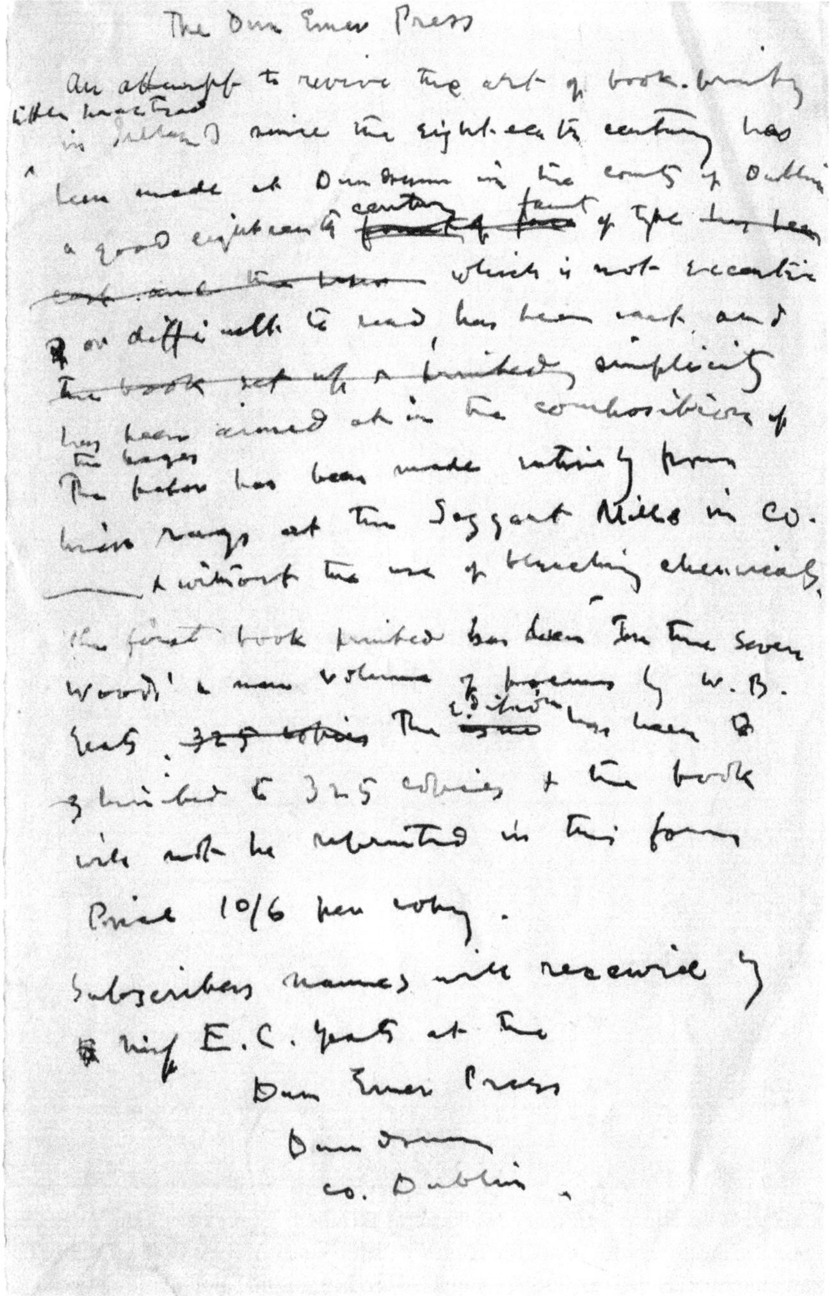

FIGURE 30.2 W. B. Yeats, Dun Emer Press Prospectus, draft. Courtesy of Special Collections/ University Archives, Ellen Clarke Bertrand Library, Bucknell University, Lewisburg, PA.

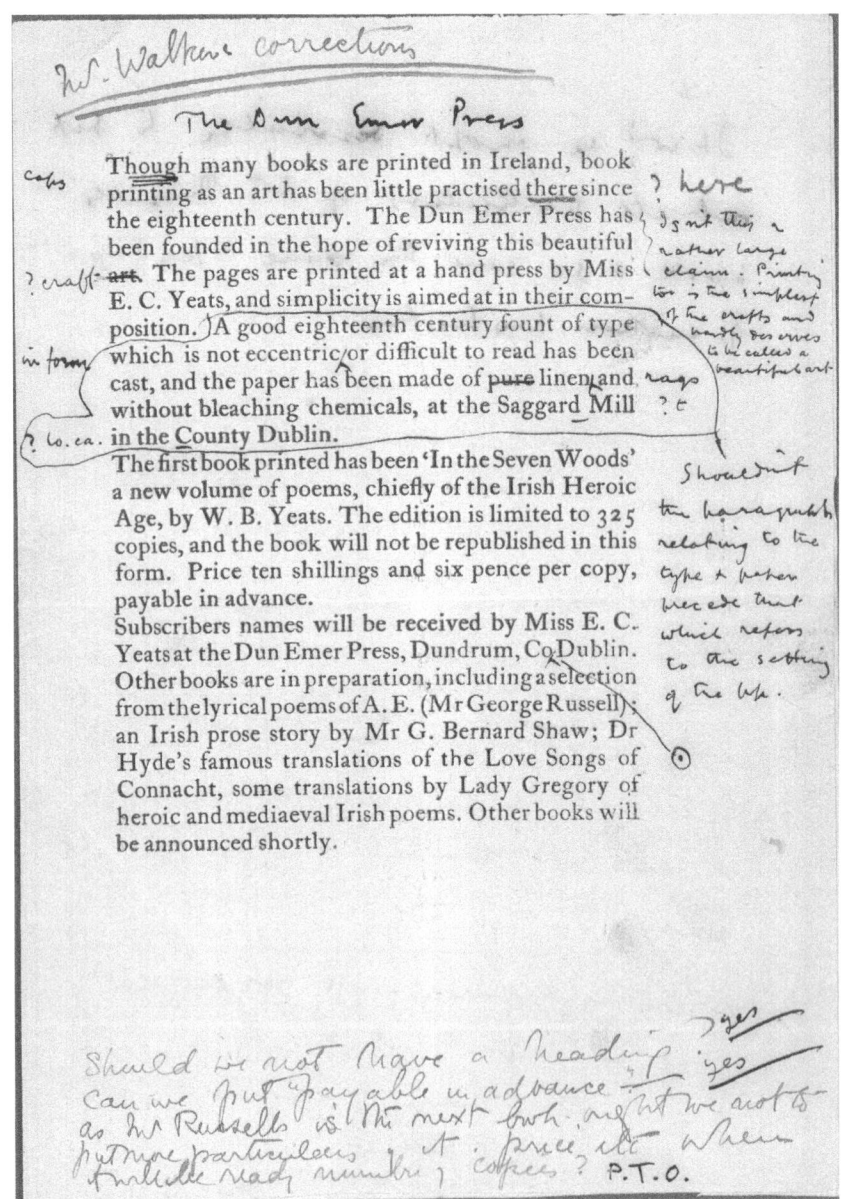

FIGURE 30.3 Annotations by Emery Walker and Elizabeth Corbet Yeats on W. B. Yeats, Dun Emer Press Prospectus, proof recto; the Henry W. and Albert A. Berg Collection of English and American Literature, New York Public Library, Astor, Lenox, and Tilden Foundations.

answer for a stand-alone prospectus must be 'yes'. Walker, in turn, repeatedly shows his patient efforts to launch his pupil into greater independence, making a suggestion in the form of a question ('Shouldn't the paragraph …'), using a modal verb ('it would be most sensible'), qualifying his thoughts ('At least I think that is best'), and ratifying hers with a 'yes'. So he gently passes the decision-making power back into her hands.

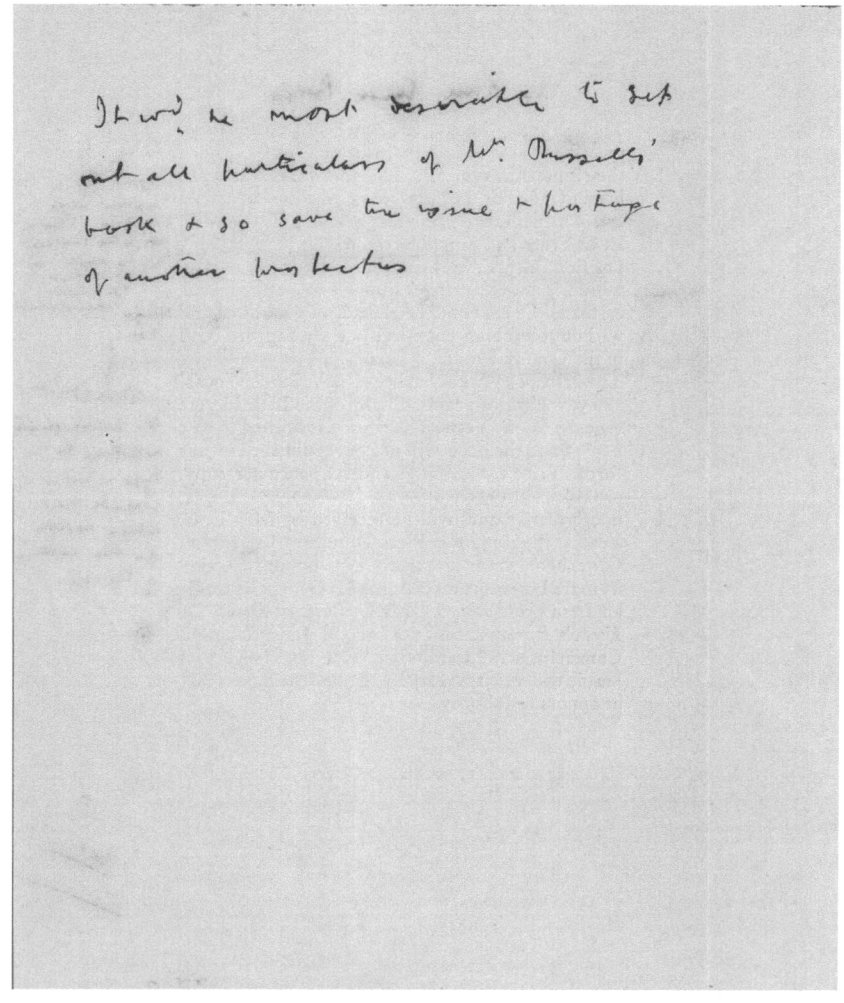

FIGURE 30.4 Annotation by Emery Walker on W. B. Yeats, Dun Emer Press Prospectus, proof verso; the Henry W. and Albert A. Berg Collection of English and American Literature, New York Public Library, Astor, Lenox, and Tilden Foundations.

Lolly, like her brother, and despite (perhaps because of) her lack of confidence, could also overstep in claiming her own. In response to the first paragraph's double emphasis on the 'art of printing', Walker demurs twice on proofs Lolly pulled, questioning whether too much has been made of her role as it is inserted into the prospectus. 'Isn't this a rather large claim,' he asks. Acting, as so often, on the principle of the Book Beautiful that every artist must 'subordinate both his art and his ambition to the end in view', he nudges printing back into properly balanced service to the whole: 'Printing too is the simplest of the crafts and hardly deserves to be called a beautiful art.' He lets stand 'printing as an art', presumably for the distinction it makes between Dun Emer and commercial printing, but

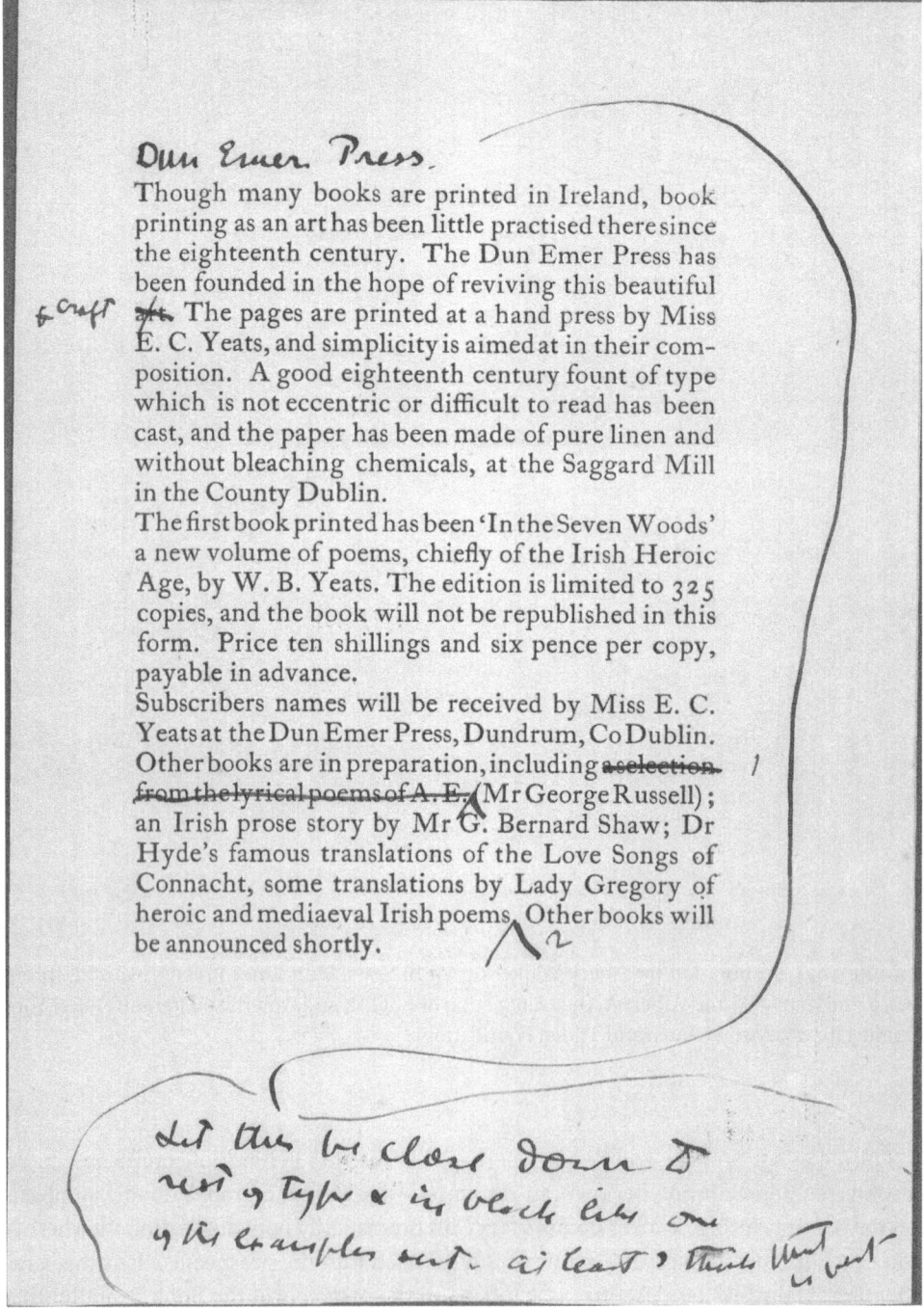

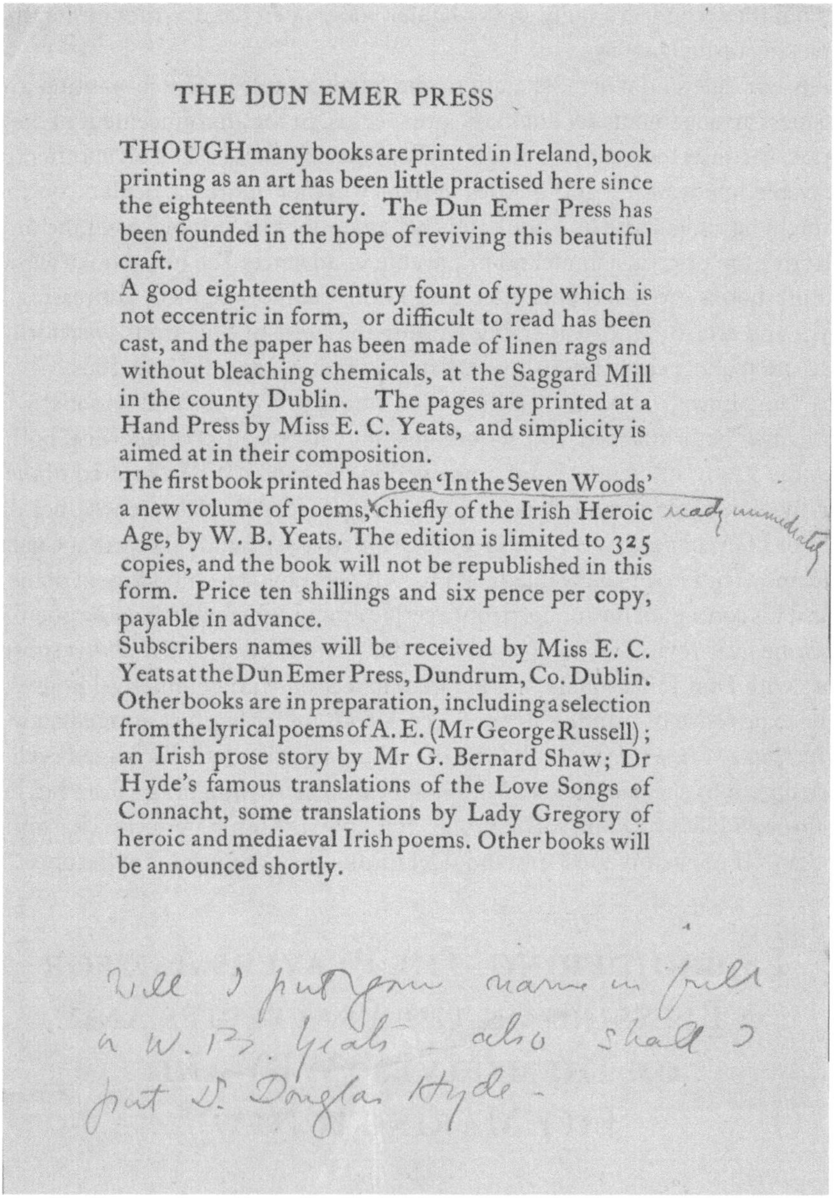

THE DUN EMER PRESS

THOUGH many books are printed in Ireland, book printing as an art has been little practised here since the eighteenth century. The Dun Emer Press has been founded in the hope of reviving this beautiful craft.

A good eighteenth century fount of type which is not eccentric in form, or difficult to read has been cast, and the paper has been made of linen rags and without bleaching chemicals, at the Saggard Mill in the county Dublin. The pages are printed at a Hand Press by Miss E. C. Yeats, and simplicity is aimed at in their composition.

The first book printed has been 'In the Seven Woods' a new volume of poems, chiefly of the Irish Heroic *ready immediately* Age, by W. B. Yeats. The edition is limited to 325 copies, and the book will not be republished in this form. Price ten shillings and six pence per copy, payable in advance.

Subscribers names will be received by Miss E. C. Yeats at the Dun Emer Press, Dundrum, Co. Dublin. Other books are in preparation, including a selection from the lyrical poems of A. E. (Mr George Russell); an Irish prose story by Mr G. Bernard Shaw; Dr Hyde's famous translations of the Love Songs of Connacht, some translations by Lady Gregory of heroic and mediaeval Irish poems. Other books will be announced shortly.

Will I put your name in full a W. B. Yeats — also shall I put D. Douglas Hyde —

FIGURE 30.6 Annotations by Elizabeth Corbet Yeats, on W.B. Yeats, Dun Emer Press Prospectus, proof; the Henry W. and Albert A. Berg Collection of English and American Literature, New York Public Library, Astor, Lenox, and Tilden Foundations.

crosses out the second 'art'. Lolly, in her lighter, more open hand, writes in '?craft', tentatively picking up his language.[59]

If Lolly was deferential in most matters, she was anxiously urgent in wanting to clarify the business arrangements set out in the prospectus. In the announcement of the press's first book, she inserted 'ready immediately' on one proof and asked on another, 'can we put "payable in advance"', and queries Walker whether 'more particulars' on the next book might be added. The first book thus becomes not just 'printed', as in the draft, but 'now ready'; the price is named and is 'payable in advance'. The next book (with price) and future books are listed and their well-known authors named, addressing Lolly's concerns and also, not inconsiderably, lending the sense of a vigorous, meritorious enterprise and making clear the Irishness of subject matter as well as materials.

Thus Dun Emer projected itself into the future with W.B. and Elizabeth Corbet Yeats's names both attached and its heritage and its vision of modernity both clear. Walker, the steady, influential hand, remained in the wings. WBY declared *In the Seven Woods* 'the first book of mine that is a pleasure to look at—a pleasure whether open or shut'.[60] For Lolly, *In the Seven Woods* set the distinctive style and quality that Cuala Press books came to be known and valued for. For WBY, its physical embodiment of his words advanced his concept of the modern more certainly and coherently than the poems, most of which he later revised. It so pleased him that he published nearly all his subsequent volumes with Dun Emer/Cuala first before publication with commercial houses. Lolly, with the experience of printing *In the Seven Woods* under her belt, immediately set up AE's *The Nuts of Knowledge* with the aim of making what she had discovered even better. In December 1903 she had the satisfaction of hearing hard-won praise from her brother, albeit through Lily to whom WBY wrote: 'Tell Lolly I think it perfectly charming. It is better than "The Seven Woods" and should, I think, advance the fame of the press.'[61]

Embroidering 'The Players Ask for a Blessing on the Psalteries and on Themselves': WBY and Lily Making It New

I said, 'A line will take us hours maybe;
Yet if it does not seem a moment's thought,
Our stitching and unstitching has been naught.[62]

---

[59] The order of the annotated proofs is not entirely clear, but it seems that Walker confirms Lolly's tentative "?craft" (Figure 30.3) with his "craft" (Figure 30.5).

[60] In the copy he sent to John Quinn, quoted in Miller, *The Dun Emer Press*, 33.

[61] *CL3*, 495.

[62] 'Adam's Curse', *CW1*, 80.

When it came to the business of the family business, WBY had less confidence in the embroidery section than he did in the press. In early 1904, he bluntly replied to Lily's appeal for funds to invest in Dun Emer, as Gleeson was pressing the sisters to do: 'The printing looks like a good investment but I can only say about the embroidery that if I were a rich man I would require the opinion of some man like Image or Lewis Davis or Ricketts or Whall as to the excellence of the design.' Although he condescended to and fought with Lolly, he judged her 'business like within certain limits & a strong soul'. He confided to Lady Gregory, 'If Lolly were by her self how gladly I would give it. I feal [sic] loyalty to an idea very keenly & could sacrifice a great deal for a cause.' He already had control of the books the press produced, but had no such purchase on the embroidery. And Lily, he understood, didn't readily 'take advice', because, he thought, she was influenced by their father (who also didn't take advice and had supported her side against his interference in Dun Emer).[63] He had experienced Lily's resistance when he had tried to intervene in her work on the Loughrea banners by independently soliciting designs from his 'pets', as Lily had called them.[64] She 'rejected' the designs, to WBY's acute embarrassment.[65] Rather than a cause he could sacrifice for, he now conceived the embroidery business as one of his 'family duties'.[66]

And yet, as 'Adam's Curse', published in *In the Seven Woods*, makes clear, stitching and unstitching served WBY as an important metaphor for the patient, persistent work of poetry. He couldn't quite let go of the embroidery, always in sight in his sister's lap, by setting it aside in a category of family duty separate from his own craft. Connecting his past to his present, embroidery gave his modernizing experiments in verse their genealogy in Morris's vision of handcrafted beauty. Fulfilling family duty for the rest of his life, he drummed up clients, bought pieces from Lily, and praised and encouraged her. From 1914 until his death, he also periodically returned to his first gambit commissioning designs for her from contemporary artists, sometimes, importantly, to illustrate his own early poems.

The theme running through these commissions was his expressed desire to get her designs that would sell; the sub-theme was modernizing her work with designs from artists who appealed to monied patrons of the modern, those who liked Bakst and supported Diaghilev, artists on the cutting edge, in 'esoteric vogue'.[67] In terms not unlike those he used about his own early work, he judged Lily's early embroidery at Cuala 'to[o] sear a ghost of long past colours & forms'.[68] Assuming a superior sense of what was required, he aimed to keep Lily's needle 'reasonably busy', 'improve' her embroidery, and save her talent from 'being wasted' by setting her to make 'work[s] of art' from

[63] *CL3*, 547–8.
[64] *CL3*, 406, 410. On WBY and the Loughrea banners, see Hardwick, 129–31.
[65] *CL Intelex* #2509.
[66] *CL3*, 548.
[67] The phrase refers to Henry Taylor Lamb. *CL Intelex* #2826, 2509.
[68] *CL Intelex* #4359.

designs by Henry Taylor Lamb, Brigid O'Brien, and Diana Murphy, among the 'new s[c] hool', and by some of his favourites in the 'old schools', including Beatrice Elvery (Lady Glenavy) and Sturge Moore, designer of book covers and illustrations for some of his work.[69]

Yeats served as self-appointed go-between and arbiter, identifying and negotiating with the designers, informing Lily of his plans, vetting the designs, asking for revisions, getting the designs to Lily. He paid up-front costs for the artist, embroidery materials, and Lily's time, to be paid back when Lily sold the piece. Through these arrangements, WBY aimed to 'lift' Cuala's embroiderers 'into a world where people pay great prices and where workers aim at making their work the best of its kind in the world'. 'I won't go ahead at all unless it's going to be a work of art,' he warned.[70]

Unlike Lolly, however, Lily wasn't ambitious in the ways her brother envisioned for her. She wouldn't be bullied, but she also didn't directly seek a collaboration of equals, as Lolly did. Perhaps because ill health left her exhausted, perhaps because she preferred to keep the peace, perhaps because she discovered she could steer her own path simply by embroidering as much or as little as she could or wanted to, and certainly because she needed money, she accepted her brother's plans, at least some of the time. With Diana Murphy and maybe other designers she established a warm working relationship. 'I like working your designs very much,' she told Murphy in a 1937 letter that reports progress on one piece and seeks advice on how best to handle the corners of another illustrating Yeats's 'Innisfree'. Murphy apparently offered suggestions as Lily worked the designs, something WBY did as well. Lily thoughtfully explained choices she made in her 'translation into needlework' and willingly undertook the 'alterations' Murphy suggested.[71] A kind of patronage model had thus evolved as the means by which WBY collaborated with Lily: WBY periodically revived his ambitious interventions and she, knowingly, with consultation, embroidered the designs he gathered and approved—along with those she designed or acquired for herself.

WBY seems to have first taken the opportunity to commission embroideries illustrating his own words in December 1915 when he asked Sturge Moore to design a table centre, a gift to Olivia Shakespear, to illustrate 'the infinite fold' from *The Countess Cathleen*.[72] He informed Lily through their cousin Ruth, an indirect form of communication he often used with his sisters, perhaps for efficiency, perhaps as more likely to get a positive response. Other commissions followed for 'The Players Ask for a Blessing

[69] *CL Intelex* #2826, 2556, 7033, 2509, 2802. Lamb enlisted in World War I shortly after discussing the commission with Yeats; the project was put aside. Letters to Emery Walker and Lily in November 1915 also refer to a 'big piece of embroidery of my sisters from a Russian design' which 'greatly impressed' Ann Gregory 'when she heard the name of the designer'. *CL Intelex* #2798, 2802.

[70] *CL Intelex* #2509.

[71] Lily Yeats to Diana Murphy, 19 November 1937, Box 1, Folder 50, Boston College collection of Yeats family papers, MS 1986.054, John J. Burns Library, Boston College.

[72] Unfortunately, I have not been able to trace this piece.

on the Psalteries and Themselves', discussed below (c.1929–31 and 1935, designed by Brigid O'Brien); Tir n'an Og (The Land of Youth), 'The Lake Isle of Innisfree', 'The Happy Townland', 'Sailing to Byzantium' or 'Byzantium' (1936–7, Diana Murphy), and 'The Song of Wandering Aengus' (1939, Michael Rothenstein).[73] Most of the commissions follow the financial collapse of the Cuala embroidery business in 1931 and its closure in January 1932. Lily continued on at home, however, making money from her signed embroidered pictures and other items. WBY's commissions lent his name and the popularity of his early verse to address Lily's economic need.

The commissions also served as ways of remaking his own early work, another kind of revision, quite literally revising it in a modern, visual language. Lily and the designers' illustrations might also be called 'remediations': WBY's written word transformed into a design transformed into an embroidered work of art. This was another kind of publication, another way Yeats's work could enter the world. The year before he broached the idea of an illustration for 'the infinite fold', Yeats had reinterpreted the Pre-Raphaelites as a foundation for his modernizing efforts in his underappreciated 1913 essay 'Art and Ideas'. Putting aside 1890s aestheticism, he called resoundingly for a reintegration of art and ideas and an attendant reunification of the arts with each other and with daily life as 'means of power' that artists had mistakenly 'put away' in their effort to purge art of Victorian moralizing. He envisioned that reintegration as 'all the arts play[ing] like children about the one chimney', a harkening back to Morris and an expansion and new articulation of the idea of the arts coordinated in service of the 'book beautiful' that he'd taken on from Walker and Cobden-Sanderson. Shall we thus rediscover, he asked, 'our more profound Pre-Raphaelitism, the old abounding, nonchalant reverie?'—a characterization of Pre-Raphaelite reverie not readily visible in their work but according with Yeats's own developing sense of himself.[74]

The designs Yeats commissioned continued this work of remaking the past for the present by reimagining Morris's Pre-Raphaelite legacy in embroideries that made his early poems new. He intended his commissions to use the 'means of power' he had identified. He 'postponed' Diana Murphy's first design for the 'Lake Isle of Innisfree', for example, instructing her that, unlike it, her next design must be a 'recognizable representation of the poem': 'I do not mean that it should be naturalistic or a mere illustration, but that it should make the onlooker think of the poem, and when he reads the

[73] On 28 December 1938 Yeats reported that he was expecting a fourth design from Murphy, picturing 'an ideal country', probably from either 'Sailing to Byzantium' or 'Byzantium', both of which he had suggested as subjects. I have not been able to trace whether this design was completed; CL Intelex #7370. For Rothenstein, see CL Intelex #7359. For the image, see the listing of Sotheby's sale of the Yeats family collection, 27 September 2017: https://www.lotsearch.net/lot/susan-mary-lily-yeats-the-golden-apples-of-the-sun-the-silver-apples-of-28390081?searchID=828060 (accessed 3 May 2020). WBY suggested 'Byzantium' and 'Sailing to Byzantium' as subjects for embroidery design to Michael Rothenstein as well as Murphy.
[74] CW4, 255, 256.

poem think of the embroidery.'[75] This was an ambitious brief indeed: a design powerful enough not only to recall the poem, but to be recalled when the poem was read, in ongoing dynamic interrelation—the arts playing about one chimney.

Some years apart, Brigid O'Brien, a talented young artist and neighbour of the Yeatses in Dublin, designed two distinctively different illustrations to 'The Players Ask for a Blessing on the Psalteries and Themselves', published in *In the Seven Woods*. Lily embroidered them. These embroideries offer an unusual opportunity to see WBY's poems made new, twice. In 1929 WBY commissioned O'Brien to design Stations of the Cross for Lily to embroider and sell in the market for ecclesiastic decoration.[76] Sometime between then and 1931, he commissioned the illustration to 'The Players Ask' (Figure 30.7), done in similar style.[77] The impetus for the second illustration (Figure 30.8), dated 1935, is unclear. The Tuscan background reflects O'Brien's year (1933) in Italy, where WBY had previously spent winters convalescing from illness and remaking his poetry.

That WBY should commission an embroidery design for 'The Players Ask for a Blessing on the Psalteries and Themselves' is hardly surprising, uniting as this piece does the arts of poetry, image, and music. It celebrates his experiments with the actress Florence Farr's chanting verse to a stringed instrument, the psaltery, made for her by musician and musicologist Arnold Dolmetsch. Yeats wrote the poem as he, Dolmetsch, and Farr, who had embroidered beside Lily in May Morris's workshop, were preparing to launch their 'new art' on 10 June 1902 in the hall of Clifford's Inn, the former meeting place of Morris's Art Workers' Guild.[78] Yeats lectured on 'Speaking to Musical Notes', pausing in mid talk for a demonstration by Farr and two accompanying musicians.[79] In his 1902 essay 'Speaking to the Psaltery', he described the relation between words and music he so desired, one that did not distort the words for the sake of the music, one that could give to words their musicality.[80] His efforts in theatre, printing, and musical

[75] *CL Intelex* #7034. Yeats used Murphy's designs in his polemical *On the Boiler* (Cuala Press, 1939) to offer up, again, his vision of beauty by noting his 'one reservation' about her designs: 'Miss Murphy's forms are deliberately thick and heavy, and I urge upon her the exclusion of all exaggerations, a return to the elegance of Puvis de Chavannes' (*CW5*, 249).

[76] Yeats commissioned three Stations of the Cross from Brigid O'Brien Ganly (1909–2002). By 1931, Lily was embroidering them and WBY was critiquing both the designs and her work. See *CL Intelex* #5501. The three Stations were exhibited at the 1932 Eucharist Week show of Irish art, where they were purchased by Genevieve Brady, who commissioned the remaining eleven. She donated them to what is now the Jesuit Center in Wernersville, PA, USA, opened in 1930 in grounds and buildings donated by Brady and her husband. See *CL Intelex* #5692 and http://thespiritblowswhereitwill.blogspot.com/2016/03/needlepoint-stations-of-cross-at-jesuit.html.

[77] See Christian Dupont, 'Embroidered Cloths', *Irish Arts Review* 35 (Spring 2018). https://www.irishartsreview.com/embroidered-cloths/. As chair of the committee to select designs for the Free State's new coinage, from 1925 to 1927 Yeats had worked closely with O'Brien's father, Dermod O'Brien, President of the Royal Hibernian Academy.

[78] Linda Parry, *William Morris Textiles* (London: Weidenfeld and Nicolson, 1983), 31.

[79] For a compelling account of the evening, see Ronald Schuchard, *The Last Minstrels: Yeats and the Revival of the Bardic Arts* (London: Oxford University Press, 2008), 68–73.

[80] *CW4*, 12–14.

FIGURE 30.7 Lily Yeats/Brigid O'Brien, 'Three Musicians' (c.1930); John J. Burns Library, Boston College. Courtesy of Museum Textile Services.

speech were of a piece. Two of the musicians in the earlier embroidery play lutes, the third holds a kind of lyre, perhaps the 'beautiful instrument, half psaltery, half lyre' made by Dolmetsch that Yeats describes in the essay.[81] In the second embroidery, the lead musician holds a Dolmetsch psaltery, though upside down. If Yeats commissioned this piece, he probably did not review the final design.

Unlike other poems published in *In the Seven Woods*, Yeats hardly revised 'The Players Ask' for subsequent publication. It was perhaps ripe for some kind of revision when, in 1928–9, around the time he commissioned Brigid O'Brien for the first piece, Yeats was remaking himself again in a fury of creative composition which included the sequence 'Words for Music Perhaps'. This resurgence of interest in the relation between words and music was fuelled by his new friendship with George Antheil (introduced by Pound) in Rapallo that winter; the August 1929 production of *Fighting the Waves*, an adaptation of *On Baile's Strand* with music by Antheil; and, in 1934, shortly before the creation of the

---

[81] *CW4*, 14. Thanks to Victor Coelho for help identifying this instrument.

FIGURE **30.8** Lily Yeats/Brigid O'Brien, 'Three Musicians' (1935); John J. Burns Library, Boston College. Courtesy of Boston College Media Technology Services.

second embroidery, the appearance on his doorstep of the avant-garde 'Californian musician' and instrument maker Harry Partch.[82] All recalled the energy and modernizing experiments of 1902–3: the 'new art', the founding of Dun Emer, the publication of *In*

<hr />

[82] *CL Intelex* #5229 and #6126. For Yeats and Antheil, see Adrian Paterson, 'Words for Music Perhaps: W.B. Yeats, Music, and Meaninglessness', in Katherine O'Callaghan, ed., *Essays on Music and Language in Modernist Literature* (London: Routledge, 2018), 140–58.

the Seven Woods where 'The Players Ask' and *On Baile's Strand* first appeared. Now, in revised and new work, Yeats pursued the 'avant-garde and esoteric' with renewed enthusiasm.[83] The physical vibrancy of the central female figure in the first embroidery and its general sense of abundance accord with the new-found sexual energy of his late poetry. The reduced colour palette of the second piece and its hard edge might illustrate or find analogue in the musical sensibilities of Antheil and Partch.

The embroideries display Lily's talent and versatility as she put what she learned from May Morris to modern designs. Features of the earlier, colourful piece derive from Morris: the shades of blues, pinks, greens, and golds of the Kelmscott bed-hangings that Lily had helped embroider, the arrangement of upright figures across the field, and the device of verse on a scrolling ribbon familiar from such Morris tapestries as *The Orchard,* literally uniting word to image, the embroidery explicitly recalling the poem. But this is a sparer design than Morris's, simpler in its effect, worked on a plain green silk background free of Morris's lush floral patterns. The decorative sleeves of the left-hand musician's robes are more modern, more like Bakst's costumes for the Ballets Russes that Yeats had commended to Lily as exemplar of the kind of modern design she needed, but even simpler, less extravagant. Closer to home, they recall the 'eyes' on the wings of Edmund Dulac's costume design for the Hawk in *At the Hawk's Well* (1916). Working in silk thread, Lily skilfully plied the darning stitch, familiar from Morris's work, to create the solid ground of the figures, the banner, and the landscape, varying their length and direction to create the wonderful sense of movement in the robes, hair, and fingers of the players. She outlined the figures and marked the folds in their clothing in black stem and outline stitches, giving them volume and solidity, and she heightened the rich texture of the skirt of the female figure with large dots worked in a satin stitch across a vertical grain of darning stitches.[84] Lily had struggled depicting faces. Whether she pursued the remedy Yeats advised—consult a London expert—is unlikely, but here she's got them: each is distinctively expressive.[85] Absorbed in their music, the male musicians possess the inward gaze of many of the figures designed for Morris's textiles. The female musician seems to be glancing up at her audience directly, not too burdened by dream to make contact. Their bodies, especially hers, are full of vibrant energy and movement rarely seen in Morris. They picture the 'old abounding, nonchalant reverie,' a gaiety and fullness of life, whose recovery Yeats had called for in 'Art and Ideas'.

Brigid O'Brien's 1935 design, which Lily worked largely in black silk thread on a tan ribbed ground, offers a radically different vision.[86] Gone is exuberance, gone is nonchalance, gone is rich colour. This highly stylized vision of the musicians—stately, dignified, monumental—is more art deco, coming into its own in the 1930s, than Morris. The figures bear resemblance to an art deco frieze, and to deco's forebears, those 'forms a

---

[83] See *Life 2*, 385–90, for an account of this period.

[84] For a brief account of Lily's time at Morris & Co. and the stitches she learned, see Hardwick, 66.

[85] *CL Intelex* #2509.

[86] While Sotheby's identified the monogram in the lower left of this embroidery as WBY's, it is most likely 'bB' contained in a circle for *Brigid O'Brien.* 'BB' in a circle also appears along with Lily Yeats's signature on the Stations of the Cross O'Brien designed.

stark Egyptian thought' as Yeats described them, especially in the profile view of the two male musicians and in the female musician's boldly stylized hair.[87] The central vertical white stripe of the female musician's stiff gown does not bend to any female curves. This gown will not slip off the shoulder to reveal a strap beneath; nor is there a frilly petticoat that might kick up as she plays. Her gown crops out to the right, mountainous, solid, like stone. For her stitchery, Lily chose to update blackwork, a Renaissance embroidery technique that had regained popularity in the 1920s. Amidst the predominant black, the touches of colour stand out starkly: the gold hair, red psaltery and lips, and, especially, the electric aquamarine eyes of the central figure, perhaps signal of some liveliness in her playing, certainly visual sparks in an otherwise sober palette.

Both embroideries foreground the poem's three speaker-musicians and literally move offstage or to the background the poem's main interpretive challenge: who are the 'masters of the glittering town' whom the three musicians call upon to 'bless the hands that play'? The masters play a 'shrilly trumpet', which the musicians implore them to lay down, presumably to hear their own more melodious 'notes'. Whether the masters will heed the plea is uncertain, 'drunken' as they are 'with the flags that sway / Over the ramparts and the towers, / And with the waving of your wings'. The first musician fears the masters 'linger by the way': 'One gathers up his purple gown, / One leans and mutters by the wall– / He dreads the weight of mortal hours.' The second musician counters, 'O no, O no! they hurry down / Like plovers that have heard the call', unafraid to cross into earthly life. The third musician identifies them as 'kinsmen of the Three in One'.[88] Given such visual material, an illustrative embroidery could have depicted the masters, expanding on the poem's details, perhaps offering a visual opinion on the nature of these kinsmen of the divinity, so full of the showiness of their own wings and the town's flags, and playing so shrilly. Instead, Brigid O'Brien and Lily Yeats leave that central question standing, and depict the musicians we hear, but do not see, in the poem. Poem and embroidery, word and image are united by the poem's shared closing lines and their evocations of music. Each piece also supplies what the other does not: in complementary depiction, the poem's speaking musicians envision the masters in the background, the embroideries envision the musicians in the foreground—embroidery recalling poem, poem recalling embroidery.

Despite their quality and interest, Lily's embroideries are little known. Yeats's ambition that the poem would recall embroidery was not fulfilled, except for those few readers who know these two examples of Lily's work. Partly, the status of decorative work, as distinct from 'art', done as it most often was by women, is to blame; partly, the physical fragility of most of Lily's work, domestic items that wear out with use. But partly, her own lack of ambition may have pushed her into the margins of the serious collecting and preservation of decorative arts that began in the early twentieth century. From another perspective and ironically, had Yeats gotten what he wanted and directed most of Lily's work as he did Lolly's, her work might, like Lolly's, have been associated more closely with his and carried forward.

[87] 'Under Ben Bulben', *CW1*, 326.
[88] *CW1*, 84.

CUALA AFTER WBY

In an outburst of energy and annoyance, in 1937 WBY resolved to reckon with 'the great problem of my life, put off from year to year, and now to be put off no more; and that is to put the Cuala Press into such shape that it can go on after my death, or incapacity through old age, without being a charge on my wife'.[89] He sent Lolly a statement on the 'Future of the Press', announcing his intention to propose a reorganization and listing his plans for the next several publications.[90] 'Reminding Lolly that he had already spent "more than £2,000" on rescuing Cuala', George's biographer Ann Saddlemyer recounts, 'Willy would bulldoze his plans through the following summer', effectively putting George in charge.[91]

Under this arrangement Lolly ran Cuala Press for just another two years. She died in 1940, following WBY by just a year. George fully assumed Cuala's operation. The press's last book, *Stranger in Aran* by Elizabeth Rivers, was published in 1945. The press continued to publish hand-coloured prints and greetings cards until George's death in 1968. In 1969, WBY's children, Michael and Anne Yeats, revived Cuala Press with Thomas Kinsella and Liam Miller of Dolmen Press, with the aim of continuing the press's original intention to 'search for new work by Irish writers'.[92] It ran until 1986, in its later years offering additional occasional work to young family members and their friends hand-colouring prints.

Yeats understood that his effort to 'make it new' required collaboration, Adrian Paterson argues. Paterson's subtle reading of Yeats's penultimate poem, 'Cuchulain Comforted', suggests Yeats knew that peaceful communal making is a heavenly, not an earthly, vision.[93] Yeats was not good at collaboration, if 'good' means enabling others, making the efforts of the group more than the sum of their parts, in other words, making the process of creating the analogue of Cobden-Sanderson's vision of the arts in relation to the Book Beautiful, and his own vision of the arts playing around the same chimney. Yeats did, however, possess in spades the undersung quality essential to successful collaboration: persistence. So did Lolly to an extraordinary extent, Lily in her way, Jack, George, and the Yeats children. 'Inside the family', WBY's son Michael recalled of Cuala, 'one's attitude to it was ambivalent. On the one hand its very existence presented a constant threat of some financial disaster, on the other hand it was an enterprise of such literary and artistic importance that everyone was willing to endure a good deal of family tension and inconvenience in order to preserve it.'[94]

---

[89] *CL Intelex* #7056.

[90] Enclosed in *CL Intelex* #7118.

[91] Ann Saddlemyer, *Becoming George: The Life of Mrs. W. B. Yeats* (Oxford: Oxford University Press, 2002), 519, 555–6.

[92] Miller, *Dun Emer Press*, 99.

[93] Paterson, '"Stitching and Unstitching"', 177.

[94] Michael Yeats, 'Preface', in Miller, *Dun Emer Press*, 8.

CHAPTER 31

....

YEATS IN THE MEDIA

....

EMILIE MORIN

Yeats is trendy: that much is clear from the frequency with which his poetry, name, and face crop up, in expected and unexpected places. The twenty-first century has done peculiar things to Yeats so far, transforming him into a revolutionary who 'made some noise', in Bob Geldof's words,[1] and into the social media star #Yeats, author of 'The Second Coming' and owner of Twitter accounts spouting poetry lines at random. The cultural capital carried by the work has increased with every passing year, bolstered by large-scale physical and virtual celebrations such as the National Library of Ireland's Yeats exhibition, launched in 2006, and Yeats 2015. Yeats's name sells, and commands attention and respect: an Irish military vessel and a luxury cruise ship bear his name, and domestic Yeatsiana—postcards, mugs, tissue-box covers, teddy bears—has become a genre in itself. When the work passed into the public domain, busy editorial hands were quick to disseminate it on virtual platforms: Amazon issued cheap Kindle editions of Yeats's works, including more obscure texts such as *Rosa Alchemica*, and his poems were granted a place of pride on poetry apps, Wikipedia, and poetry websites such as famouspoetsandpoems.com or poemhunter.com. 'The Second Coming' (a strong favourite in the hundreds of songs invoking Yeats's poetry, which range from light opera to indie rock through to heavy metal)[2] has become ubiquitous: it was cited so profusely throughout 2016—the year that saw Donald Trump's election, the Paris and Brussels terror attacks, and the UK's Brexit vote—that Fintan O'Toole coined the concept of 'the Yeats test', arguing that references to Yeats's poem on social media and in the online press provide an 'index of how bad the world has

---

[1] *A Fanatic Heart: Bob Geldof on W. B. Yeats*, scripted by Bob Geldof, directed by Gerry Hoban, 98 mins, BBC4/Peninsular TV/RTÉ/BBC Arts, 2016.

[2] For representative examples see Roselinde Supheert, *Yeats in Holland: The Reception of the Work of W. B. Yeats in the Netherlands Before World War Two* (Amsterdam: Rodopi, 1995), 134 n.1; Nick Tabor, 'No Slouch', *The Paris Review*, 7 April 2015, https://www.theparisreview.org/blog/2015/04/07/no-slouch/; El Hunt, 'Sleater-Kinney: Things Fall Apart', *DIY*, 9 August 2019, http://diymag.com/2019/08/09/sleater-kin ney-things-fall-apart-the-center-wont-hold-interview-cover-august-2019.

become', and concluding, '[T]he more quotable Yeats seems to commentators and politicians, the worse things are.'[3]

There is only a short step between Yeats's prevalence in contemporary media and the dissemination of his work during his lifetime. Indeed, his world was always the world of mass media, and his work was widely reproduced from early on, via official as well as unofficial channels.[4] He was the solemn poet published by Macmillan and one of the dramatists of the American Little Leather Library, whose miniature volumes were added to cereal packets or sold at Woolworths across the US for a few cents.[5] His poetry was presented to the readers of *The New York Times*, the *New Statesman*, and a wide range of newspapers and magazines of different political persuasions. He was a prolific journalist and reviewer; his opinions on literature appeared across the political spectrum, from *The Irish Homestead* to *The Manchester Playgoer* through to *Harper's Weekly*. He was also an easily irritated Irish citizen who enjoyed crafting letters to the editor of *The Irish Times*, and a poet courted by the BBC, who transformed his lifelong reflection on the performance of poetry into a broadcasting success.[6] Patterns of dissemination sometimes criss-crossed: for instance, *The Land of Heart's Desire*, reproduced in a large number of unlicensed editions, was also a radio favourite and the first play by Yeats that the BBC broadcast in the early years of public radio, in 1924 and 1925, while Yeats's editorial work on *The Oxford Book of Modern Verse 1892–1935* provided the basis for three of his radio programmes from 1936 and 1937.[7]

The media relied on Yeats and he, too, relied on the media: his journalism generated the income he needed in the early part of his career,[8] and he initially saw radio as little more than a source of royalties.[9] The BBC felt that it could never go wrong with Yeats: his

---

[3] Fintan O'Toole, '"Yeats Test" Criteria Reveal We Are Doomed', *Irish Times*, 28 July 2018, https://www.irishtimes.com/opinion/fintan-o-toole-yeats-test-criteria-reveal-we-are-doomed-1.3576078.

[4] See, for example, Warwick Gould, 'Predators and Editors: Yeats in the Pre- and Post-Copyright Era', in *Textual Monopolies: Literary Copyright and the Public Domain*, ed. Patrick Parrinder and Warren Chernaik (London: Office for Humanities Communication Publication, 1997), 69–82; George Bornstein, *Material Modernism: The Politics of the Page* (Cambridge: Cambridge University Press, 2001); Yug Mohit Chaudhry, *Yeats, The Irish Literary Revival and the Politics of Print* (Cork: Cork University Press, 2001); Warwick Gould, 'Yeats in the States: Piracy, Copyright and the Shaping of the Canon', *Publishing History*, 51 (2002): 61–82; David Dwan and Emilie Morin, eds., *Yeats and Mass Communications*, special issue of *International Yeats Studies* (2018).

[5] The play chosen was *The Land of Heart's Desire*. See the Online Archive of California's description at https://oac.cdlib.org/findaid/ark:/13030/c86d604k/; Colin Smythe, '*The Land Of Heart's Desire*: Some Hitherto Unrecorded Printings – "Work In Progress,"' *YA*, 19, 361–2.

[6] See Ronald Schuchard, *The Last Minstrels: Yeats and the Revival of the Bardic Arts* (Oxford: Oxford University Press, 2008), 191–218; Emily C. Bloom, *The Wireless Past: Anglo-Irish Writers and the BBC, 1931–1968* (Oxford: Oxford University Press, 2016), 27–63.

[7] For unlicensed editions of *The Land of Heart's Desire*, see Smythe, 'The Land Of Heart's Desire', 351–68; for BBC broadcasts, see Emilie Morin, "W. B. Yeats and Broadcasting, 1924–1965," *Historical Journal of Film, Radio and Television*, 35:1 (2015), 145–75; for *The Oxford Book of Modern Verse* and radio, see Schuchard, *The Last Minstrels*, 373; Bloom, *The Wireless Past*, 42.

[8] For a full examination of Yeats's relation to journalism see David Dwan, *The Great Community: Culture and Nationalism in Ireland* (Dublin: Field Day, 2008).

[9] WBY to the Secretary of the Society of Authors, 18 August 1923, *CL Intelex* #4361.

poetry and plays provided fodder for special Irish and St Patrick's Day programmes long before he took to radio. His ideas about the voice, too, were cited as useful cues for speakers eager to find a reading style suited to radio's demands: an image from 'Speaking to the Psaltery'—'the subtle monotony of voice which runs through the nerves like fire'—was recast in the 1929 *BBC Handbook* as a definition of 'the perfect harmony of voice, rhythm, and expression which interprets and vitalises a poem'.[10] When Yeats became personally involved in broadcasting, his programmes were a boon, and he was quickly portrayed as someone who had turned the radio tide in favour of poetry. In a listing for his 'Reading of Poems' of June 1935, the *Radio Times* advertised Yeats as the poet who spoke to 'everyone, from the simple lover of haunting word-music who cherishes "The Lake-Isle of Innisfree" to the mystic and metaphysician who can follow him into the secret recesses of *The Tower* and *The Winding Stair*'.[11] Two years later, 'In the Poet's Pub' was presented as a triumphant illustration of 'the poetry of the people', and as the conclusive proof that 'poetry can still be popular, even in England, when it is made exciting'.[12] This was not idle praise: some of Yeats's radio programmes had a public impact during his lifetime and did something to democratize public poetry reading. In England notably, 'In the Poet's Pub' pre-empted a regrowth of interest in using pubs as spaces for poetry and public readings. In June 1937, the *Manchester Guardian* advertised a 'new experiment in social service'—'an enlargement of the scope of public-houses by using them for verse-speaking, drama, and readings of good prose'—and offered two prizes for prologues that might be read at such occasions.[13] A subsequent report stated that thirty poetry recitals and plays had been performed in twenty-four Greater London pubs in November and December 1938.[14] A column in *The Irish Times* speculated that these English attempts to bring poetry back into the pub may have arisen from 'the broadcast arranged by Mr. W. B. Yeats a year or so ago for the BBC', nonetheless arguing that '[t]here was in [Yeats's] BBC programme not the slightest hint that it had been devised to bring culture to the masses, or that there was in it any desire to do good to anyone'.[15]

At the BBC, the recordings from the 1930s made Yeats an inescapable household name: from the 1940s to the 1960s snippets from Yeats's readings were replayed regularly to illustrate programmes dedicated to his work as well as general discussions of poetry, the sound of words, and the craft of the poet. Occasionally, the BBC used Yeats's voice to showcase the powers of new technologies: in 1939, on the occasion of the sixth anniversary of the BBC recording service, British journalists were invited to Broadcasting House to listen to a series of discs including recordings of Gladstone, Tennyson, Shaw, Trotsky, Gandhi, Hitler, and Yeats reciting 'The Lake Isle of Innisfree'—a poem about

---

[10] *CW4*, 15; Anon., 'The Broadcasting of Poetry', in *BBC Handbook 1929* (London: British Broadcasting Corporation, 1929), 234.

[11] *Radio Times*, 7 June 1935, 54.

[12] *Radio Times*, 16 April 1937, 54.

[13] 'Poet's Pub', *Manchester Guardian*, 23 June 1937, 8.

[14] 'Miscellany edited by "Lucio"', *Manchester Guardian*, 7 January 1939, 8.

[15] A. E. M., 'Poets' Pub: Verse in the Tavern', *Irish Times*, 19 March 1938, 7.

listening and sonic textures, now emblematic of early radio.[16] Yet it is as a dramatist, rather than as a poet, that Yeats first made his reputation on the BBC airwaves in the days when theatre programmes mostly consisted of straight readings of stage plays.[17] *The Land of Heart's Desire*, for example, was broadcast on six occasions by the BBC stations between 1924 and 1928. *The Shadowy Waters*, Yeats's translation of Sophocles' *King Oedipus*, and *The Hour Glass* also held strong appeal during the 1920s and 1930s. Experimental television followed suit: adaptations of *The Words upon the Window Pane* were televised in 1937, 1938, and 1939, and *The Shadowy Waters* and *Deirdre* in 1938; further performances were televised after the war—*The Words upon the Window Pane* in 1946, and *The Player Queen* and *The Land of Heart's Desire* in 1946 and 1948 respectively. By 1942, Yeats was one of the five playwrights represented by the British League of Dramatists whose plays featured most frequently in BBC programmes; the other stars were John Galsworthy, H. Granville Barker, J. M. Synge, and Oscar Wilde.[18] This need for Yeats was expressed clearly in the pages of the *Manchester Guardian* that same year: 'One wishes the BBC would do more of Yeats' was the response to Barbara Burnham's radio adaptation of *The Words upon the Window Pane*.[19] In the 1950s and 1960s, Yeats's plays became strangely topical; in the *Radio Times*, Frederick Bradnum, who had planned a series of radio adaptations of Yeats's plays, presented *The Player Queen* as a 'prophetic' play, which 'says that evil can triumph in the contemporary world, and … shows this happening'.[20] For Bradnum, Yeats's drama, with its language 'so exact and so coloured that it should carry the imagination without effort to the play's own world', was naturally radiogenic.[21]

The BBC's continued interest in Yeats opened up a new public for his work—large, amorphous, and defined by wave frequencies rather than national borders. This radio audience was never simply British or simply Irish: radio's public was always transnational and widely practised distant listening throughout the 1920s and 1930s, with listeners from beyond the British Isles tuning in to BBC programmes.[22] Newspapers and

---

[16] 'Voices for the Future', *Observer*, 12 March 1939, 21. The BBC recordings of Yeats, which mostly consist of fragments that survived a warehouse fire during the Blitz, were collected in the British Library's 2013 Spoken Word CD 'I Will Arise', and feature on websites such as PennSound. The two snippets of film footage of Yeats that remain (the amateur film discovered by Ann Saddlemyer of Yeats in Algeciras in 1928 and the clip of Yeats shot by a television crew in Stockholm in 1923) have been less widely used; see Lance Pettitt, '"Reversing the Cinematograph?": Yeats, Autobiography, and the Medium of Film', *Éire-Ireland*, 52:1&2 (2017), 228–9.

[17] Between 1924 and Yeats's centenary, the BBC broadcast seventeen of Yeats's plays, offering a more comprehensive range of adaptations than Radio Athlone and Radio Éireann.

[18] M. E. Barber to M. T. Candler, 16 July 1942, BBC Written Archives Centre, Caversham, Yeats copyright file 2.

[19] 'Broadcasting Review', *Manchester Guardian*, 18 July 1942, 8.

[20] *Radio Times*, 15 January 1954, 25, 6.

[21] Ibid.

[22] For radio's transnational public, see Simon J. Potter, *Wireless Internationalism and Distant Listening: Britain, Propaganda, and the Invention of Global Radio, 1920–1939* (Oxford: Oxford University Press, 2020).

magazines across Europe listed the offerings of international radio stations, including BBC stations, in their radio programmes' ad hoc selections. *Radiocorriere*, the magazine of the Italian broadcasting authority, for example, published comprehensive programmes throughout the 1930s, including stations based anywhere from Norway to Algeria and from Britain to Poland; Yeats's 'Poems about Women' and 'In the Poet's Pub' featured in its listings, along with BBC adaptations of *The Land of Heart's Desire* and *The Words upon the Window Pane*.[23] The correspondence of the BBC Copyright Department hints at the wide reach of Yeats's work; it refers, notably, to a 1944 adaptation of *On Baile's Strand* by V. K. Narayana Menon, translated into Hindi by an unnamed BBC staff member for the Eastern Service to India, and to other broadcasts from early 1945: a repeat of Burnham's radio adaptation of *The Words upon the Window Pane* on the Empire Service, scheduled for further repeats on the BBC's African, North American, Pacific, and General Overseas services; and a Hindi version of *Deirdre*, in a translation by A. K. Qureshi, broadcast on the Eastern Service to India.[24] Yeats would have greeted these developments enthusiastically: he was aware that radio had the power to open up a whole other public to him and dreamed of new promised lands for broadcasting—Cairo, 'where the wireless is in Irish hands',[25] Delhi, where 'the vernacular tongues of India [are broadcast as] sung or spoken poetry',[26] and India more generally, in the wake of the enthusiasm expressed by Lionel Fielden of All India Radio towards his broadcast 'My Own Poetry'.[27]

This sense that Yeats's plays are inherently suited to broadcasting, and conform to radio's mission to entertain a large audience, was specific to the BBC and to that particular moment: the plays have not been granted such public attention since, and today Yeats's prevalence in the media revolves closely around his poetry and around the process of reading his poems aloud. The website for Yeats 2015 illustrated this very well, giving a central place to the 1937 BBC recording of Yeats reading 'The Lake Isle of Innisfree', and to 'Your Yeats', a large SoundCloud archive of freely submitted recordings.[28] The archive features numerous moving and powerful poetry readings, staged or seemingly off the cuff, performed by Yeats enthusiasts from all walks of life as well as poets such as Paula Meehan and scholars such as Margaret Mills Harper. These many performances rely upon the assumption that, to be a good reader of Yeats's poetry, one does not need to be a poet or an actor; one merely needs to be sensitive and affectionate towards the

---

[23] See *Radiocorriere*'s online archive, http://www.radiocorriere.teche.rai.it/Default.aspx.

[24] Z. A. Bokhari to Miss Alexander, BBC Copyright, 21 July 1944, BBC WAC, Yeats copyright file 2; Mary T. Sharpe to BBC Copyright, 30 November 1944, BBC WAC, Yeats copyright file 2; Helen Beddall to Miss Alexander, 27 January 1945, BBC WAC, Yeats copyright file 3.

[25] WBY to Patrick McCartan, 22 January [1937], *CL Intelex* #6786.

[26] *CW6*, 193.

[27] See Bloom, *The Wireless Past*, 62 n.39. Yeats reported to Edmund Dulac in July 1937 that 'Lionel Felden, head of Indian broadcasting told Hilda Matheson that the broadcast ['My Own Poetry'] was perfect, would have interested India & that 'the music was exactly right' (*CL Intelex* #7006). Fielden had previously acted as Matheson's assistant at the BBC.

[28] https://soundcloud.com/yeats2015 (accessed 11 May 2020).

work. Yeats's own poetry readings for the BBC certainly encouraged the perception that glitches in the human voice and the hazards of reading are part of the art of poetry. He concluded 'Modern Poetry' by pre-empting all manner of criticisms of his 'rhythmical' reading: 'I may be a bad reader; or read badly because I am out of sorts, or self-conscious; but there is no other method.'[29]

Recent film documentaries, likewise, have focused on the process of reading Yeats, and have given a pride of place to recordings of Yeats reading 'The Lake Isle of Innisfree'—so much so that the poem has become an expected component in representations of his life on screen, along with views of the Sligo coast and sunshine rippling over water at sunset. For Lance Pettitt, the recordings of 'The Lake Isle of Innisfree' have provided an answer to an old problem faced by film-makers—how to 'voice' Yeats and his poetry.[30] The Yeats documentary, as Pettitt shows, has a substantial history, beginning with official state commissions such as John D. Sheridan and Georg Fleischmann's *W. B. Yeats: A Tribute* (1950), funded by the Cultural Relations Committee of Ireland, and Patrick Carey's *Yeats Country* (1965), sponsored by the Irish Department of External Affairs. More recent instalments are better known: Alan Gilsenan's film-poem *A Vision* (2014), Sean O Mordha's *W. B. Yeats: Cast a Cold Eye* (1989), Maurice Sweeney's *No Country for Old Men* (2012), and Bob Geldof's *A Fanatic Heart: Bob Geldof on W. B. Yeats* (2016). The latter three films were developed in dialogue with Yeats scholarship: O Mordha's documentary is a piece of research featuring illuminating interviews with Anne and Michael Yeats; Sweeney's film presents a series of detailed commentaries by scholars and by poets such as Seamus Heaney and Paul Muldoon, while Geldof's documentary features extensive interviews with Roy Foster and a posse of celebrity readers performing Yeats in music studios, pubs, and actors' changing rooms. Some of Geldof's readers are long-standing Yeats fans; others feature as novices, presumably selected because they would benefit from discovering Yeats in Geldof's opinion. Many contributors (Van Morrison, Sting, Shane MacGowan, or Noel Gallagher) appear to share little with their subject other than their Irish roots. There is much artfully tousled hair in the Yeatsian fashion, a good dash of testosterone, and Geldof haranguing an imaginary crowd from the stage of the Abbey Theatre, pretending to be Yeats himself, and speculating about how he might have assisted 'Willie and the boys'. Without a doubt, Geldof's documentary, which carefully animates Yeats's life through a series of photographs, painted portraits, and close-ups of his face, is the most successful in transforming Yeats into a fashionable contemporary icon. Textual scholarship becomes hip too: Geldof's journey through Yeats's life is also the journey of the scholar, to the National Library of Ireland, through Yeats's library and through some of his manuscripts.

Geldof's portrait of a figure at the cutting edge of his and our time becomes less idiosyncratic and less Geldofian once we take into account Yeats's involvement in popular media and his genuine interest in the new worlds opened up by modern technologies of

---

[29] *CW5*, 102.
[30] Pettitt, 'Reversing the Cinematograph?', 216–43, 229.

communication. 'This broadcasting may change the oratory of the world,' he surmised in 1931, in an interview published on the occasion of his first poetry reading on air.[31] Radio and cinema, he argued, would help 'the dramatic art [to] come back in a new form,' for '[b]etween broadcasting and the "talkies" … a man can be present, as it were, at the ends of the earth'. He joked about the similarity between broadcasting and 'addressing the Senate in Dublin', because one is speaking to 'an audience which is only just not there', and observed that the 'remarkable experience' of speaking on the wireless 'would be wonderfully good for politicians'. 'Such a lot of rhetoric could not be flung directly' at a solitary listener, he concluded, failing to anticipate radio's rise as a prime tool for propaganda. Six years later, he expressed similar warmth towards the vast market created by the gramophone record, commenting with optimism on its possibilities for sung poetry: 'We may be at the start of an historic movement.'[32]

Yeats became a master of mass communication by design, thanks to his immense industriousness, and by accident. The press articles he wrote dealt with the esoteric subjects that fascinated him—in the early years, fairies, Irish witch doctors, and all manner of folklore—and he seemed more comfortable dabbling in interviews with spirits and mediums than with journalists. In any case, he consistently looked upon journalists with contempt.[33] '[T]he Lord deliver us from Journalists,' he wrote to Katharine Tynan after visiting W. E. Henley.[34] 'The shallowest people on the ridge of the earth,' he complained in a sequel.[35] He had a particularly low opinion of 'the journalists, who wish to be men of letters & the men of letters who have become journalists', and deplored how 'the spirit of literature' had been defeated by 'the spirit of the press, of hurry, of immediate interests'.[36] His own journalism, from his perspective, was a minor endeavour and something other than journalism. He described the review *To-Morrow*, spearheaded by Iseult Gonne, Francis Stuart, F. R. Higgins, and Cecil Salkeld, as 'about the only cause for which I am prepared to turn journalist'; this was an attempt, he explained, to 'test all art & letters by the doctrine of the immortality of the Soul', and to 'criticize the church not from the side of unbelief but from that of a more intense beleif' [*sic*].[37] The newspapers—'slow to care for work that does not appeal to the ordinary interests'—could not be relied on to open up new vistas, he argued on another occasion.[38] He staunchly believed that one should 'form [one's] own opinions without asking any journalist to form them'.[39]

Somewhat paradoxically, radio seemed free of the trappings of the press, more welcoming to thought and the imagination. He tried to represent the mysteries of broadcasting to his listeners by recasting the studio as an extension of the lecture

---

[31] 'A Poet Broadcasts', *Belfast News-Letter*, 9 September 1931, 6.
[32] WBY to Moya Llewelyn Davies, 31 January 1937, *CL Intelex* #6793.
[33] See Dwan, *The Great Community*, 18–19, 160–6, 169–200.
[34] WBY to Tynan [? 22–28 September 1888], *CL Intelex*.
[35] WBY to Tynan, 25–30 August [1888], *CL Intelex*.
[36] WBY to Edmund Gosse, 12 April [1910], *CL Intelex* #1331.
[37] WBY to Lady Gregory, 28 June [1924], *CL Intelex* #4578.
[38] WBY to Annie Horniman [10 December 1906], *CL Intelex* #498.
[39] WBY to Harold G. Rugg, 5 September 1911, *CL Intelex* #1717.

hall, the theatre, and the pub—all the spaces in which it is socially acceptable to engage in an extended monologue.[40] He became a reflective broadcaster quickly, using
radio to give some of his poems a first airing, occasionally revising his poetry in light
of his studio experience, and affirming his eagerness to understand the impact of recording and broadcasting upon the voice and upon sound.[41] He was interested in the
platform that radio offered for staged conversations, delivering an interview on Radio
Athlone in 1935 and pondering a debate with Edmund Dulac and a programme with
Walter Starkie, both of which were cancelled at a later stage. He wrote poetry broadcasts
that did not involve him as a speaker—the 'Abbey Theatre Broadcast' and a programme
read on the occasion of his seventieth birthday.[42] Other plans—a television appearance
that would have involved Yeats reading his poetry—were never realized.[43] In late 1938,
George Barnes also invited Yeats to write a brief Christmas or New Year message for the
National Programme alongside other BBC favourites John Masefield, Walter de la Mare,
and E. M. Forster. Yeats, then in poor health, turned down the invitation by telegram, on
the grounds that if he were to 'write whatever [he] would "most like to say to the country
as a whole" or to my own family as a whole, it would be altogether unprintable'.[44] It is
unclear what he found most unpalatable—the idea of speaking to the United Kingdom
as a whole, instead of speaking to the vast radio community he liked to address in his
broadcasts, or the idea of writing a four-and-a-half-minute message, or else the prospect
of finding himself without the rhetorical layers afforded by his poetry broadcasts. It is
certain, however, that his interest in radio was unabated: he was still pondering radio
work and radio possibilities a few days before his death.[45] He relished radio's directness
and immediacy, but only if the setting gave him enough space to elaborate on his views,
and only if he could flesh out the artistic persona that he had crafted for the BBC.

On the airwaves, Yeats enjoyed presenting himself as a naïve, earnest soul unsuited
to the demands of modern media and discovering the wonders of the wireless for the
first time. All of this was artifice, and although he did use his BBC programmes to

[40] See also Charles I. Armstrong, 'Pub, Parlour, Theatre: Radio in the Imagination of W.B. Yeats',
in Matthew Feldman, Erik Tonning, and Henry Mead, eds., *Broadcasting in the Modernist Era*
(London: Bloomsbury, 2014), 23–37.

[41] 'For Anne Gregory', 'Roger Casement', 'Come on to the Hills of the Mourne', 'Sweet Dancer',
and 'The Curse of Cromwell' were broadcast before appearing in print, while 'The Pilgrim', originally
destined to be broadcast as part of 'In the Poet's Parlour' before its publication, was replaced by 'Imitated
from the Japanese'. See Bloom, *The Wireless Past*, 29; Schuchard, *The Last Minstrels*, 383. After his studio
experience, he rewrote, for example, the first line of 'Sailing to Byzantium' for Clinton-Baddeley; *CW10*,
409 n.524. For the impact of recording on the voice and sound, see WBY to Barnes, 24 February 1937, *CL
Intelex* #6821.

[42] Schuchard, *The Last Minstrels*, 359.

[43] Schuchard, *The Last Minstrels*, 395; Yeats to Edith Shackleton Heald, 14 November [1937], *CL
Intelex* #7116.

[44] Barnes to WBY, 8 December 1938, BBC WAC; Yeats to Barnes, 13 December [1938], *CL Intelex*
#7351. Masefield, de la Mare, and Forster accepted the invitation; James Stephens replaced Yeats.
The programme, entitled 'Here's Wishing', was broadcast on 26 December 1938. See *Radio Times*, 23
December 1938, 48.

[45] WBY to Clinton-Baddeley, 23 January 1939, *CL Intelex* #7375.

experiment with performance styles, his broadcasts also show an aversion to risk: when including texts by other writers, he prioritized poets who had already been deemed radiogenic by the BBC (the extent to which his choices were guided remains unclear). 'Modern Poetry', a recasting of Yeats's introduction to *The Oxford Book of Modern Verse*, gives a pride of place to Cecil Day-Lewis, Edith Sitwell, T. S. Eliot, and Dorothy Wellesley, all of whom had read for radio in recent memory. The more experimental programmes broadcast in 1937—the 'Abbey Theatre Broadcast', 'In the Poet's Pub', and 'In the Poet's Parlour'—centre upon prominent radio poets, offering selections that are closely aligned in spirit with the history of BBC literary programming. Indeed, most of the poets chosen by Yeats for these programmes—except Frederick York Powell, J. E. Flecker, and Lionel Johnson—had long acted as the figureheads of modern poetry on BBC airwaves too, and not simply in his *Oxford Book of Modern Verse*.[46] Texts by James Stephens, Hilaire Belloc, G. K. Chesterton, Henry Newbolt, and Walter de la Mare had been radio staples since the mid-1920s, and had been read by seasoned performers who also read Yeats's poetry and plays on radio (for example, Carleton Hobbs and the long-forgotten Nadja Green and Nesta Sawyer). Several poets selected by Yeats had been invested in broadcasting long before his own turn to radio in 1931. Stephens had made his debut on the airwaves in 1928; Belloc and Chesterton in 1925 (both had featured in well-publicized radio debates with Shaw); Newbolt in 1930. Walter de la Mare conceived a BBC broadcast on Keats in 1937, read by others. The BBC endeavours of Sylvia Townsend Warner and Edith Sitwell were smaller in scale, in keeping with radio's conservatism and predilection for male voices: Townsend Warner read English ballads in 1926; Sitwell performed a reading from *Macbeth* in 1928.

Among the BBC's literary stars, Yeats was easier to accommodate than some. He read poems that had been tried and tested by other BBC speakers—for example 'The Fiddler of Dooney', 'He Wishes for the Cloths of Heaven', and 'The Lake Isle of Innisfree'.[47] He conformed to the BBC's rehearsal protocols, unlike Forster, who refused to engage in formal rehearsals.[48] Yeats was keen to please his audience—by, for example, reading his 'most popular poems', as he explained in 'Poems about Women', or by beginning his 'Reading of Poems' with 'The Lake Isle of Innisfree' ('if you know anything about me, you will expect me to begin with it').[49] He could be relied upon to deliver the goods without protest and, in that sense, he provided a welcome antidote to Shaw, whose own relationship to the BBC was deeply fraught (Shaw, nicknamed the BBC's 'Grandest Inquisitor', was eager to be 'as nasty as possible', in the opinion of BBC production staff).[50] Contrary to Shaw, Yeats seemed to care remarkably little about how his work was used, either in

---

[46] *CW*5, 102.

[47] See Morin, 'Yeats and Broadcasting', 13–14; Emily Bloom, 'Broadcasting the Rising: Yeats and Radio Commemoration', *International Yeats Studies*, 3 (2018): 30 n.7.

[48] Mary Lago, Linda K. Hughes, and Elizabeth MacLeod Walls, eds., 'General Introduction', in *The BBC Talks of E. M. Foster, 1929–1960* (Columbia: University of Missouri Press, 2008), 7–8.

[49] *CW*10, 243, 224.

[50] L. W. Conolly, *Bernard Shaw and the BBC* (Toronto: University of Toronto Press, 2009), xiv–xv.

radio programmes or on experimental television; his stature also meant that blanket copyright agreements with the Society of Authors remained possible from early on, even when cross-institutional relations became strained.

Prominent BBC minds who reflected on radio's relation to literature became personally invested in his work. Yeats enthusiasts included C. A. Lewis, author of one of the earliest books on radio, *Broadcasting from Within* (1924); Charles Siepmann, Director of Talks from 1932 onwards (both conceived readings from Yeats's works, broadcast in 1924 and 1936 respectively); and Hilda Matheson, whom Yeats admired greatly, and who acted as the BBC's Director of Talks from 1927, when the Talks Department was created, until her resignation in 1932. Yeats met Dorothy Wellesley—whom John Kelly calls his 'surrogate Lady Gregory'—in 1934, shortly after the beginning of her relationship with Matheson.[51] At the BBC, Matheson had been the driving force behind the development of literary programming and scripted talks, and one of a handful of people seeking to conceptualize radio broadcasting and its possibilities for literature and poetry.[52] It was through Matheson that George Barnes approached Yeats in the autumn of 1936 to deliver more poetry programmes and reflect on ways of 'extending the audience for broadcasts of poetry'.[53] Matheson no longer worked for the BBC then, but had retained strong ties to radio broadcasting through her radio journalism for *The Observer*, the *New Statesman*, and other publications.

Like Yeats, who enjoyed crafting metaphors to represent radio's capacity to reach multitudes, and often borrowed from his experience of psychical research to come to terms with radio's novelty, Matheson thought of broadcasting as more than a technology.[54] In a landmark book from 1933, she described broadcasting as 'a harnessing of elemental forces', and 'a means of enlarging the frontiers of human interest and consciousness', part of a cultural revolution that 'may end in some form of thought transference of which we now have no conception'.[55] With her extensive experience of radio, her mind 'full of folk tunes', and her numerous contacts among contemporary poets, she was an ideal interlocutor for Yeats and a precious source of help.[56] It seems likely that Yeats discussed the granular details of his broadcasts with Wellesley too, since Wellesley also had a fine understanding of radio's potential for poetry and was a well-practised radio anthologist. The anthology of broadcast poetry that she compiled for the Hogarth Press and the BBC in 1930, for a series of readings planned that year and focusing on

---

[51] John Kelly, *A W. B. Yeats Chronology* (Basingstoke: Palgrave Macmillan, 2003), xv; *Life 2*, 528.

[52] Fred Hunter, 'Hilda Matheson and the BBC, 1926–40', in Sybil Oldfield, ed., *This Working Day World: Women's Lives and Culture(s) in Britain, 1914–1945* (London: Taylor & Francis, 1994), 169–74; Kate Murphy, *Behind the Wireless: A History of Early Women at the BBC* (London: Palgrave Macmillan, 2006), 169.

[53] Jeremy Silver, 'George Barnes's "W. B. Yeats and Broadcasting"', 1940, with an Introductory Note', *Yeats Annual*, 5, 189.

[54] For WBY's radio and psychical research, see Emilie Morin, '"I Beg your Pardon?": Yeats, Audibility, and Sound Transmission', *YA* 19, 191–219.

[55] Hilda Matheson, *Broadcasting* (London: Thornton Butterworth, 1933), 14–15.

[56] WBY to George Yeats, 14 June [1936], *CL Intelex* #6575.

poets born after 1880, had grown out of 'certain conversations on the broadcasting of poetry' as well as her awareness that the poems would be 'read aloud' and that each reading required 'some unity'.[57] Edith Shackleton, with whom Yeats became romantically entangled at the end of his radio years, when his ties to Wellesley were still strong, was another radio pioneer, who had contributed to the BBC's short-lived 'Women's Hour' and given talks on career options for women in 1923 and 1924; a few years later, she pondered the need for an imaginative approach to radio sound in a piece for the *Radio Times*, where, lingering on 'The Lake Isle of Innisfree', she cited Yeats and Robert Louis Stevenson as good radiophonic sound-hunters.[58]

Matheson seems to have been directly involved in shaping Yeats's approach to broadcasting. She is mentioned affectionately in many letters praising her insight and professionalism. Yeats's correspondence records, notably, her extensive involvement in rehearsals for 'Modern Poetry', the 1936 instalment in the series of BBC National Lectures inaugurated in 1929, and her attendance at rehearsals in April 1937, when he was preparing 'In the Poet's Parlour' and had just broadcast 'In the Poet's Pub'. He wrote to George Yeats in October 1936, for example: 'I did not go to London for rehersal [*sic*] as two B.B.C were coming here. Last night Miss Matheson rehersed me. … I have spent the last two days adding three pages —asked for by BBC to Broadcast & this afternoon Miss Matheson does the typing'.[59] Yeats had long been aware that radio did not enable the faithful transmission of textured sound; to George Yeats, in 1931, he reported hearing that 'Ezra's opera was bad on the wireless; certain instruments failed to get through'.[60] Later, he expressed his disappointment with the 'Abbey Theatre Broadcast' in no uncertain terms. Matheson would have been sympathetic with his concerns; her monograph on radio reveals her sensitivity to microphone's demands upon the voice, and ventured the guess that radio would eventually develop its own performers and thrive upon improvements in microphone technology. She strongly believed in the importance of rehearsal and advocated utmost simplicity, arguing that poetry broadcasts were most successful when poems were 'read quite simply by a number of specially selected readers, devoid of theatricality of voice or manner'.[61] Radio, she asserted, should preserve the special sense of intimacy fostered by the microphone, and could create intimacy like no other media if the right mode of delivery were adopted. There are natural affinities between some of her arguments and Yeats's views on reading and on intimacy as 'the mark of fine literature'.[62]

The model of intimacy that Yeats prioritized on the airwaves was confessional. Clearly, he was aware that confession—or the semblance thereof—makes for good radio; he used

[57] Dorothy Wellesley, ed., *A Broadcast Anthology of Modern Poetry* (London: Hogarth Press, 1930), 5. Her estranged husband Gerald spoke on the BBC airwaves too and contributed an essay on 'The Decoration of the Studios' to the 1933 *BBC Year-Book*.

[58] Edith Shackleton, 'What a Woman Would Like to Hear', *Radio Times*, 17 August 1928, 273–4.

[59] WBY to George Yeats [9 October 1936], *CL Intelex* #6667.

[60] WBY to George Yeats, 17 November [1931], *CL Intelex* #5537.

[61] Matheson, *Broadcasting*, 127.

[62] WBY to J. B. Yeats, 7 August [1910], *CL Intelex* #1403.

some of his broadcasts to recast his career, invoking discoveries made and wrong turns taken with a simplicity of expression that contrasts with the ornate allusiveness of his *Autobiographies*. His BBC broadcasts take great pains to craft the image of an honest and simple artist, able to convey the principles of his art in honest and simple form. The language remains plain; the idea of putting 'the natural words in the natural order' becomes a leitmotif, with the radio broadcast providing a concrete illustration that the poet can indeed speak in everyone's idiom.[63] In his brief prefatory commentaries, he explained why he felt that his early poetry was inferior whenever he read from it; 'Poems about Women' contrasts the work of a maturing mind, able to 'know what I felt, to stand outside myself as it were and look at myself' with the folly and exuberance of youth ('when we are young we do not know what we feel, we cannot stand outside ourselves and look at ourselves, we live in dreams and express ourselves in a kind of mythology').[64] The bizarre audience that he summons for this art of simplicity is, characteristically, out of time and out of place, and encompasses the scholar, the potboy, and a stray mountain dweller and fisherman.[65]

Yeats's BBC broadcasts and mode of delivery bolstered the perception that the authorial voice is the key to a challenging and nebulous body of work; that the author's thoughts, captured in the studio, can provide a way into the work. Invoking poets' radio work, and the voices of Yeats, T. S. Eliot, Dylan Thomas, and Louis MacNeice in particular, Philip Larkin suggested, in 1962, that after silent reading 'comes a moment with any poem we have really taken to ourselves when we want to hear its author read it', to 'confirm our conviction that he would quicken the pace here, throw away an irony there, or perhaps our curiosity is just for what his voice can add, something we cannot define until we hear it'.[66] The first radio critics who heard Yeats's BBC readings felt the same and believed that his voice brought something unique. In 1931, for example, the *Belfast News-Letter* reviewer expressed delight at how Yeats had 'imbued every word with colour and life' and at the 'tiny narrative' he had crafted around each poem's creation.[67] The following year, the *Manchester Guardian*'s radio critic praised Yeats's 'very individual' voice and delivery, venturing a guess that 'after this perhaps no poems should be read except by their authors'.[68] Thereafter, the memory of Yeats's voice lingered in the pages of the *Manchester Guardian*; in 1935, Audrey Moran, hired to read a programme scripted by Yeats, was deemed a pale imitation of the author ('it is always difficult to avoid remembering how he did it; comparison is almost bound to creep in'),[69] while in 1943 Yeats's voice was once more evoked as the standard for broadcast poetry: 'Once again we see that poetry is best read either by the poet (remember W. B. Yeats) or by an actor

---

[63] See, notably, *CW10*, 219, 249; WBY to Margot Collis, (early July 1935), *CL Intelex* #6278; WBY to Dorothy Wellesley, (6 April 1936), *CL Intelex* #6531.

[64] *CW10*, 238, 239.

[65] *CW10*, 219, 252.

[66] Philip Larkin, 'Masters' Voices', *New Statesman*, 2 February 1962, https://www.newstatesman.com/culture/2015/04/archive-philip-larkin-voices-poets (accessed 25 July 2019).

[67] 'A Poet Broadcasts', *Belfast News-Letter*, 9 September 1931, 66.

[68] M.C., 'Week-end Broadcast', *Manchester Guardian*, 11 April 1932, 10.

[69] 'Yesterday's Broadcast', *Manchester Guardian*, 14 June 1935, 10.

who uses the voice with full range.'[70] As soon as vinyl records were disseminated, however, and Yeats's voice could be played again and again on a record player, newspaper reviewers began to feel that the Yeatsian chant had lost its magic and had aged more quickly than the poetry.[71] The 1959 vinyl record released by Spoken Arts, featuring some BBC recordings of Yeats as well as readings by Micheál Mac Liammóir and Siobhan McKenna, was greeted unfavourably as a 'dry, dogmatic Anglo-Irish chant filter[ing] through the din of the old recording like a voice from beyond the grave in Drumcliff churchyard'.[72] The review spurred a reader called George Potts, who had heard Yeats reading his poetry in Oxford in the early 1920s, to write to the editor and relate a conversation he had witnessed. To the question 'Why, Mr Yeats, do you read your poetry in that sing-song voice?' Yeats replied solemnly: 'That is how Shakespeare read his poetry.' When pressed to elaborate, he replied, 'To that question I would tell you the story of the Scotsman who strictly maintained that Shakespeare was a Scot.' Pressed further, he answered, 'The ability of the man warrants the assumption.'[73]

The anecdote will be familiar to readers of Yeats's BBC broadcasts: 'Reading of Poems' recalls the same exchange, but in a heightened form, invoking Homer instead of Shakespeare. Yeats's interlocutor is here a professional elocutionist, to whom Yeats explains that he is reading his poetry in precisely this way because he is taking his orders from Homer and 'all poets from Homer up to date'.[74] Like his idiosyncratic versions of Shakespeare and Homer, the persona that Yeats crafted through his involvement in public media is strewn with paradox. His engagement with modern media was a large-scale rhetorical experiment: he clung to his professed inexperience and naïvety like talismans, yet affirmed that he carried an authority conferred by the whole history of literature. He transferred his experience from one medium to another, taking his experience as poetry anthologist, public reader and jack-of-all-trades journalist into the radio studio. His career benefited from precisely the kind of benevolent assumptions about ability that he liked to float when invoking Shakespeare and Homer: it is, indeed, thanks to all the newspaper editors and radio executives willing to believe in his unlikely talent that the poet so gifted for ornate and allusive metaphor was transformed into a gifted and prominent mass communicator.

[70] 'Broadcasting Review', *Manchester Guardian*, 28 December 1943, 6.

[71] In a review of the 1965 centenary record, Terence de Vere White argued that Clinton-Baddeley's and Michael Gwynn's readings, which emulated Yeats's chanting, were 'a little turgid, as if the wind was blowing against the speaker'. T. de V. W., 'Yeats Readings', *Irish Times*, 16 April 1965, 8.

[72] W. L. Webb, 'The Poet's Voice on Record', *Guardian*, 13 November 1959, 7.

[73] George C. Potts, 'Yeats's Voice', *Guardian*, 17 November 1959, 8.

[74] *CW10*, 229. Yeats had long used this anecdote to '[disarm] in advance those members of an audience whose modern ears were sceptical of or objected to his bardic chanting', as Ronald Schuchard notes. Schuchard, *The Last Minstrels*, 341.

PART V

PLAYING YEATS

CHAPTER 32

....

EARLY PLAYS

Gender, genre, and queer collaboration

....

SUSAN CANNON HARRIS

THIS chapter examines Yeats's initial turn toward drama through his theatrical collaborations with women. Through his work with Laura Armstrong, Maud Gonne, and Florence Farr, Yeats discovered theatre as a practice that would enable him to pursue one of his most cherished and burning desires: the transcendence of individual subjectivity through shared consciousness. I will argue that Yeats first turned toward drama *in order to* experience a kind of collaboration that was not available to him through literary societies like the Rhymers' Club. As I will show, the persistent recurrence of desire between women in Yeats's earliest plays—from his first play, *Vivien and Time*, in 1884 to *The Land of Heart's Desire* ten years later—is an expression of the transformative effect of these theatrical collaborations.

'Theatrical collaboration' means working on any and all aspects of the production process: commissioning (more informally, asking for) a play, organizing its production, appearing in it as a performer, and so on. Theatrical collaboration includes but is not limited to co-authorship, which—partly because Yeats and Gregory's writing partnership has (belatedly) begun to attract an appropriate amount of scholarly interest—I do not intend to take up in this chapter. Lady Gregory is now acknowledged as the co-author of three of Yeats's revival dramas: *Cathleen ni Houlihan* (1902), *The Pot of Broth* (1904), and *The Unicorn from the Stars* (a substantial revision of Yeats's 1902 *Where There Is Nothing*); but it's possible that we still underestimate her contribution to 'Yeats's' revival dramas. As early as 1964, Daniel J. Murphy argued that Gregory had 'a share in all of Yeats's plays' between *Cathleen ni Houhlihan* and *At the Hawk's Well*, noting that Gregory testified to helping with 'the plot and the construction of some of the poetic plays'.[1] It is safe to say, at any rate, that many of the plays produced under Yeats's name between 1902 and 1916 were not written by him alone.

---

[1] Daniel J. Murphy, 'Yeats and Lady Gregory: A Unique Dramatic Collaboration', *Modern Drama*, 7 (1964), 322–8, 323, 328.

A decade before his writing partnership with Gregory began, Yeats started writing plays and 'dramatic sketches'. Most were created *for* and *with* women whose contributions are less easily categorized than Gregory's, but no less important. Nearly all of the plays completed in the decade between Yeats's first amateur production in 1884 and his failed attempt to join London's free theatre movement in 1894—*Vivien and Time* (1884), *The Island of the Statues* (1885), *Mosada* (1886), *The Seeker* (1886), *The Countess Cathleen* (begun by 1889, published in 1892, first produced in 1899), and *The Land of Heart's Desire* (1894)—were undertaken in collaboration with women who were interested in or involved with theatre before they met Yeats. Laura Armstrong, who according to Elizabeth Brewer Redwine was 'responsible for [Yeats's] initial serious interest in drama', organized the production of *Vivien and Time* and played the title role; Armstrong was also the model for the protagonists of *The Island of Statues* and *Mosada*.[2] Maud Gonne, who trained for a career as a professional actress, suggested that Yeats write *The Countess Cathleen* and tried to organize a production of it a decade before the Irish Literary Theatre staged it.[3] Florence Farr, who acted in Ibsen and Shaw in the early 1890s and played the bard Aleel in the ILT's production of *Countess Cathleen*, commissioned and produced *The Land of Heart's Desire* for a season she organized at London's Avenue Theatre in 1894.[4]

Yeats scholars have been happy to celebrate these women in the capacity of 'muse'— the love object who inspires the artist to create the work. Conventionally, the muse is understood to be necessary to the artist's process but also external to it; the poet is presumed to be the sole author and owner of the work that her inspiration generates. Decades after Elizabeth Butler Cullingford's *Gender and History in Yeats's Love Poetry* challenged this reductive conception of the muse/poet relationship, it continues to reassert itself in Yeats scholarship.[5] I argue that these women were integral to the creation of Yeats's early plays and, indeed, of Yeats the playwright.

Because it anticipates production, drama always tends toward collaboration. Collaborating with the women who introduced him to drama's non-literary aspects was what first turned Yeats toward playwriting. Drama initially mattered to Yeats as the path toward a new experience of embodiment which he discovered with Laura Armstrong, and then strove (with mixed success) to replicate with Maud Gonne and Florence Farr. Specifically, Yeats's experience of theatrical collaboration taught him that it was possible, outside the rarefied world of magical societies, to challenge the materialist

[2] Elizabeth Brewer Redwine, '"She Set Me Writing My First Play": Laura Armstrong and Yeats's Early Dramas', *Irish University Review*, 35:2 (2005), 245–58, 245.

[3] David R. Clark and Rosalind E. Clark, 'Sailing from Avalon: Yeats's First Play, *Vivien and Time*', *Yeats: An Annual of Critical and Textual Studies* 5 (1987), 1–86, 8.

[4] See Susan Cannon Harris, 'Desiring Women: Irish Playwrights, New Women, and Queer Socialism, 1892–1894', in Susan Cannon Harris, *Irish Drama and the Other Revolutions: Playwrights, Sexual Politics and the International Left, 1892-1964* (Edinburgh: Edinburgh University Press, 2017).

[5] Recent examples include Joseph M. Hassett, *W. B. Yeats and the Muses* (Oxford: Oxford University Press, 2010), and Adrian Frazier, *The Adulterous Muse* (Lilliput Press, 2016).

understanding of human consciousness as limited by the physical boundaries of the individual human body.

That Yeats's theatrical collaborations with these women were bound up with romantic and/or erotic desire for them is not surprising; in the poetic tradition that Yeats was joining, as Pondrom writes, 'erotic love for another person' has long been 'one of the most consistent symbolic means of figuring ontological certainty, or union with an Absolute'.[6] But we should not assume for that reason that the *only* role that Armstrong, Gonne, and Farr played here was to generate an erotic frustration that Yeats could productively sublimate. These women were not merely interpellated into Yeats's dramatic career; they initiated it and oriented it.

'To fail in plotting is to die'

In an 1889 letter to Katharine Tynan, Yeats identified the moment at which he first turned toward drama. Denying Tynan's insinuation that he was 'taken up with Maud Gonne', Yeats compares Gonne to his first theatrical collaborator, Laura Armstrong. They are linked in this retelling not only by Yeats's semi-disavowed erotic 'interest' in them, but also by their interest in drama:

> [Gonne and I] had some talk as to the possibility of getting my 'Countess O'Shea' [later *The Countess Cathleen*] acted by amateurs in Dublin and she felt inclined to help, indeed suggested the attempt herself if I remember rightly. I hardly expect it will ever get outside the world of plans. As for the rest she had a borrowed interest, reminding me of Laura Armstrong without Laura's wild dash of half insane genius. Laura is to me always a pleasant memory she woke me from the metallic sleep of science and set me writing my first play. Do not mistake me she is only as myth and a symbol. ... 'Time and the Witch Vivien' was written for her to act. 'The Island of Statues' was begun with the same notion, though it soon grew beyond the scope of drawing room acting. The part of the enchantress in both poems was written for her.[7]

Redwine writes that Yeats scholars have often 'dismiss[ed]' Armstrong's 'influential relationship with the young writer as a flirtation'.[8] Gonne and Farr, to some degree, shared this fate; but as Redwine has noted, Armstrong has evoked a particularly pungent contempt.[9]

---

[6] Cyrena Pondrom, 'T. S. Eliot: The Performativity of Gender in *The Waste Land*', *Modernism/modernity* 12 (2005), 425–41, 439.

[7] Quoted in Clark and Clark, 'Sailing from Avalon', 8.

[8] Redwine, 'She Set Me Writing', 245.

[9] As Redwine, 'She Set Me Writing', 245, puts it, 'R. F. Foster calls her "pretty, unstable, and already spoken for," David Clark labels her a "tantalizing witch," and Keith Alldritt sums her up as "a flirt and a tease"'.

For example, in Armstrong's sole surviving letter to Yeats, she invites him to read his poetry to her: 'I like yr poems more than I can say—but I should like to hear you read them—I have not nearly finished with them.'[10] Clark and Clark cite this letter only to mock its writer, dismissing her interest in Yeats's literary work as pretextual: 'Obviously, the poetry held little interest except as a means of dangling the poet!'[11]

This is 'obvious' only if we assume that romantic and/or sexual fulfilment was all Yeats wanted from Armstrong, and all she 'dangled' before him. In fact, this letter shows Armstrong telling Yeats something that would change the direction of his literary career: that his poetry could be more compelling in performance than on the page. Read aloud, even for an audience of one, poetry becomes a collaborative experience. Armstrong expresses a desire to *participate* in Yeats's poetry instead of merely absorbing it; and Yeats appears to have welcomed and shared that desire. When he tells Tynan that 'Time and the Witch Vivien' was 'written for [Armstrong] to act', he admits that he turned from poetry to drama *in order to* give Armstrong an opportunity for more active participation. Armstrong then introduced Yeats to the kinds of non-literary collaboration required to turn a text into a performance and to turn poetry into theatre. Whereas poetry can be written, as Yeats put it, in 'a loneliness that is like the loneliness of death' (quoted in Foster, xxvii), no theatrical event ever takes place there.[12] With *Vivien and Time*, Yeats may well have been pursuing love and/or sex; but he was also pursuing collaboration for its own sake, and *Vivien and Time* is at its most powerful when it both enacts and represents that collaboration.

Vivien and Time immediately reveals Yeats's deep antipathy towards the generic demands of literary drama—including and especially plotting. In the 1880s and1890s, London critics judged new plays primarily on plot, and specifically on the elegance and ingenuity with which the playwright executed a formulaic combination of technical and structural features, including the management of entrances and exits, the linking of scenes, and the final dénouement—in which all mysteries were explained, conflicts resolved, villains expelled, and stability restored. This type of 'construction' was pioneered in Paris by Eugène Scribe and embraced in London, where it was known as the 'well-made play'.[13] Most of the Irish playwrights trying to make it in London in the 1890s—Oscar Wilde, George Bernard Shaw, John Todhunter, George Moore—struggled with this straightjacket; but before escaping from it, they did prove to the London critics that they *could* construct a serviceable well-made plot.[14]

---

[10] Armstrong, qtd. in Clark and Clark, 'Sailing from Avalon 40.
[11] Clark and Clark, 'Sailing from Avalon 5.
[12] *Life1*, xxvii.
[13] Harris, Irish Drama and the Other Revolutions, 33.
[14] Oscar Wilde produced three successful well-made plays before blowing up the formula in the hyper-constructed *The Importance of Being Earnest*. George Bernard Shaw successfully adapted the well-made plot for ideological purposes in *Widower's Houses* and other plays before dismantling it in *John Bull's Other Island*. George Moore's *The Strike at Arlingford* is uneven, but Moore was clearly attempting a well-made plot even if he only created an adequately made one. John Todhunter's heart belonged to verse drama; but his most critically successful play was the prosaic 1893 New Woman drama, *The Black Cat*.

Yeats never even made an attempt. Plot is not a strength for Yeats in any genre, and *Vivien and Time* shows why. Tennyson's poem 'Merlin and Vivien' provided the play's title character.[15] Its plot is lifted from 'Snow White'.[16] Vivien asks the bard Clarin to say whether she or her companion Asphodel is most beautiful; Clarin chooses his beloved Asphodel. After confirming with her magic mirror that Asphodel is 'the fairest in the land', Vivien orders Asphodel's execution.[17] As in 'Snow White', the assassins take pity on their victim and allow Asphodel to go into hiding. As in 'Snow White', Vivien visits her victim's hiding place in disguise, tricking her into contact with an enchanted object (in this case, a flower) which puts her into a deathlike trance.

Instead of building on the foundations of this fairy tale plot, however, Yeats wreathes its bones in the misty coils of a different kind of story. A properly constructed play would use Scene 1 to establish Clarin and Asphodel's love, which Vivien will later tragically thwart. But Yeats gives no indication that Asphodel has any feelings for Clarin; and Clarin is 'so weak that the women end up courting each other' (24). Redwine correctly identifies Asphodel and Vivien as the play's primary couple. Instead of expressing his own feelings in Scene 1, Clarin sings 'a ballad bought ... From a lean pedlar with a bag and scythe':

> Two shining drops of gracious dew
> Two sprigs of rosemary and rue
> > Two loving friends there are
> > None fairer in story
> > But yonder is hoary
> Time on a whirling star
> > Falling are the golden sands
> > In the glass in his old, old hands. (18–19)

Vivien evidently understands that she and Asphodel are the 'two loving friends' whose days together are numbered; after ordering Asphodel's death, Vivien remarks that 'When the rosemary's dead the rue shall live / So much more in the sun' (20). Asphodel also gets the message: '[K]now you not / Our only enemy is withered time / Here in the Castle Joyeuse, Sir Clarin?' (19). In the final scene of Act 2, the 'lean pedlar' does appear, complete with hourglass, as Father Time. Vivien loses to Time at dice and chess, and dies. Clarin finds Vivien dead, and expires. Asphodel awakens from her trance, remembering that 'a queen once loved me—loved—yes, loved!' (35). She is beset by 'fairy voices' promising reunion with Vivien: 'Soon like us you'll find her / And dwell with her above' (36). Asphodel begins 'her wanderings', and the play ends.

---

[15] For a thorough investigation of Yeats's relationship with 'Merlin and Vivien', see Chene Heady, 'I Am Weary of That Foolish Tale', in Karl Fugelso and Carol L. Roobinson, eds., Studies in Medievalism XVI (Woodbridge: Boydell & Brewer, 2008), 67–82.

[16] Clark and Clark, 'Sailing from Avalon', 9–10.

[17] *Vivien and Time,* in Clark and Clark, 'Sailing from Avalon', 20 (subsequent page references in main text.)

Instead of constructing a single edifice, Yeats has taken an archetypal romance plot and mashed it up with one which is queer in multiple ways: it focuses on same-sex love, it refuses to develop, and it never resolves. The end is not so much a dénouement as a dis-integration. Clarin and Asphodel never reunite. Neither ever confronts Vivien. Time's defeat of Vivien doesn't follow from the play's prior *events*; it simply fulfils the prophecy of that opening ballad. Clarin justifies his otherwise inexplicable death by recalling an-other prophecy of Time's in which it was fated (35). Asphodel's final scene is severely anticlimactic; but it fulfils the terms of Vivien's curse. The action of *Vivien and Time* is defined not by Aristotelian logic but by magical thinking.

When it comes to plot, then, it is fair to say that Yeats's heart wasn't in it. Where we *do* see investment is in *Vivien and Time*'s magical climax, which allegorizes Yeats's collab-oration with Armstrong. Poetry is frequently recited or sung in *Vivien and Time*, but it only comes to ferocious life in Act 1 Scene 2, when Vivien inveigles a page into helping her cast the spell that dooms Clarin to wander restlessly till the end of his days. When casting spells as Vivien, Armstrong demonstrates for the spectators what working with her taught Yeats: that performance supercharges poetry, activating its latent sensational and affective power.

The spell is written in Merlin's book; but instead of reading it herself, Vivien asks the page to read it to her, observing in an aside that 'these charms of Merlin's have most might / When said by sinless children's lips' (21). Vivien describes the spell to the page as 'the wild poem of a wild old man', presumably referring to Merlin (22). But the drawing-room audience knew then as well as we do now that the man who actually wrote this poem is Yeats. By asking the page to cast the spell, then, Armstrong-as-Vivien re-enacts the request she made in her letter to Yeats and dramatizes its transformative effect on Yeats's poetry. Neither reader nor hearer can do magic alone. The page tries to open the book, but Vivien has to do it for him, just as she has to command him to continue—'Read, read!'—when he becomes alarmed by his own incantation (21).

It is not by reading this poem aloud, but by *causing it to be read to her*, that Vivien activates both its power and her own. As Yeats's verses are spoken in Armstrong's presence, their imagery becomes reality. The page calls on the unnamed power to 'wrap' the spell's target 'like flame;' a 'blue flame' leaps from the book's pages (21). The page wishes for Clarin's body to 'burn' and his 'whole brain' to 'melt'; the book becomes 'fiery hot' (21). Yeats's poem becomes both sensationally effective (as theatre) and tragically efficacious (as magic). This is the power of theatrical collaboration: the author, the per-former, and the spectator together turn poetry into theatre and both into magic.

This fusion of poetry and magic through collaboration with a woman is the first it-eration of a process that will recur throughout Yeats's career, culminating in his collab-oration with George Yeats on the automatic script. Yeats's letter to Tynan shows that by 1889 he had already initiated the process with Gonne; and indeed, Yeats dedicated *The Countess Kathleen* (1892) to Gonne, 'at whose suggestion it was planned out and begun some three years ago' (*Countess Kathleen and Various Legends and Lyrics*). Gonne withdrew her cooperation, however, and would not collaborate with him in another theatrical project until *Cathleen ni Houlihan* in 1902.

The afterlife of *Vivien and Time* shows how much Yeats learned from his collaboration with Armstrong about why drama mattered to him. When, five years and several plays later, Yeats revised *Vivien and Time* for publication as 'Time and the Witch Vivien', he eliminated the 'Snow White' plot along with Clarin and Asphodel. 'Time and the Witch Vivien' excludes everything but Vivien's final confrontation with Time. 'Time and the Witch Vivien' revises and expands an exchange in which the original Vivien, told to name a new stake for her next game with Time, decides to play for 'triumph in my many plots'. 'Defeat is death', Time replies, and Vivien agrees: 'To fail in plotting is to die' (33). In 'Time and the Witch Vivien', just before she dies, Vivien returns to the idea that plot is life:

> I must be careful now. I have such plots—
> Such war plots, peace plots, love plots—every side;
> I cannot go into the bloodless land
> Among the whimpering ghosts.[18]

Yeats's reference to 'the bloodless land' underlines the fact that, with the love plot torn out, *Vivien and Time* becomes—like the *mugen*-noh dramas that would captivate Yeats when he discovered them in 1913—a ghost play whose only 'plot' is 'the manifestation of a spirit'. *Vivien and Time* thus shows that in the 1880s Yeats was already looking for some of the things that he eventually found in Noh drama—including, along with ghosts and hauntings, permission to jettison 'construction' altogether.[19]

In Vivien's plea we see Yeats's anxiety about abandoning plot so early in his career. Vivien imagines failure at plotting as disembodiment—the 'bloodless' existence of those whose mind–body connection has disintegrated. Crossing from the world of flesh and blood into the land of the bodiless is precisely what many of Yeats's early protagonists most ardently desire (the Old Knight in *The Seeker*, Forgael in *The Shadowy Waters*, Maire in *The Land of Heart's Desire*). But in *Vivien and Time*, wandering through the material world in search of an insubstantial dream is a curse for Clarin and Asphodel. And in 'Time and the Witch Vivien' the woman who cursed them fears that abandoning these generic 'war plots, peace plots, love plots' means her own undoing; that parted from her body and its manoeuvres, she will be no more than a 'whimpering ghost'.

While Yeats's difficulty with 'construction' manifests in *Vivien and Time* as incoherence, in 'Time and the Witch Vivien' it appears as a moment of phenomenological terror. By 1889 Yeats understood that his investment in drama lay, not in plot, but in the way performance disrupts embodiment. In *Vivien and Time*'s immediate successors—*The Island of Statues*, *Mosada*, and *The Seeker*—we see how Yeats's turn toward drama was bound up with his desire for a kind of embodiment which most of his contemporaries would have considered impossible, and how that desire pulled his early plays out of line.

---

[18] *VP*, 722.
[19] Clark and Clark, 'Sailing to Avalon,' 47–48

LINES OF DESIRE

To show how Yeats's sexual pursuits, his magical activities, and his theatrical explorations intertwined, I will approach this group of plays through the concept of 'orientation' that Sara Ahmed develops in *Queer Phenomenology*. Ahmed emphasizes desire as *directional*—as both determining and determined by the field of spatial relationships that defines the subject's position in the world. Ahmed restores the spatial content of the term 'sexual orientation', reminding us that 'orientation' is 'a directional metaphor drawn from magnetism and navigation'.[20] No command is more insistently repeated in Yeats's early plays than the one issued by the fairies of 'The Stolen Child': *come away*. Like his protagonists, Yeats as a playwright is drawn *away* from all the things that might have brought him success on the London stage, extending himself not so much *into* the world as *through* the world and *toward* the immaterial world that he believed existed in, above, behind, and around it.

Yeats's idealism is usually defined in philosophical terms: idealists hold that the material world is an inadequate shadow of the immaterial forces that move it. Idealism can also, following Ahmed, be defined as an orientation—a mode of 'extend[ing] through our bodies into the world'. Everyone must 'face' the concrete world in order to act; but unlike materialists, idealists face objects not to attain them but to move *through* them. Ahmed argues that the 'repetition of bodily actions over time' reinforce social norms by defining what Ahmed calls 'the bodily horizon, a space for action, *which puts some objects and not others in reach*' (their emphasis).[21] Ever seeking that which was out of reach, Yeats was always swerving away from the 'bodily horizon' of a triumphantly materialist Victorian culture.

Vivien and Time is the first of several early plays in which an apparently straight line of desire veers off course. *The Island of Statues* begins with two shepherds contending for the love of the fair Naschina; by Act 2, Naschina has donned men's clothing to woo the island's powerful enchantress. Redwine attributes this to Armstrong's dominant personality, which inspired Yeats to '[challenge] gender roles' by giving the women all the agency: 'Naschina and the Enchantress challenge each other's power while the male characters stand by frozen and silent.'[22] But the same veering-off recurs in plays written after Armstrong's exit. *The Seeker, The Countess Cathleen,* and *Land of Heart's Desire* deviate from conventional romance plots to produce queer situations made queerer by Gonne and Farr's involvement. In *The Countess Cathleen*, Yeats creates another bard alter ego—initially named Kevin, eventually named Aleel—full of hopeless love for an unattainable woman; but instead of a male actor, Yeats cast Florence Farr as his alter ego.

---

[20] Norton Rictor, quoted in Sara Ahmed, *Queer Phenomonology: Orientations, Objects, Others* (Durham, NC: Duke University Press, 2006), 69.

[21] Ahmed, Queer Phenomenology, 66–8.

[22] Redwine, 'She Set me Writing', 248.

The restless Maire Bruin of *The Land of Heart's Desire* was written with Maud Gonne in mind; Farr, who commissioned and produced that play, also requested that Yeats include a part for her 11-year-old niece. Yeats accordingly created the Fairy Child; and, as a result, the call to *come away* manifests in *Land of Heart's Desire* as a seduction played out between two female figures.[23]

Desire in Yeats's early plays is thus never straight—either in the sense of being 'in line' with norms, or in the sense of proceeding directly toward a destination. According to Ahmed, 'queer' derives from 'the Indo-European word "twist"'.[24] In the epilogue of *The Island of Statues*, published in the *Dublin University Review* in 1885 and reprinted in *Crossways* (1889) as 'The Song of the Happy Shepherds', the shepherd shares the secret of his eponymous happiness: never travel on a direct route toward a desired object. To seek, like the petrified suitors of *The Island of Statues*, is death; to find, like the horrified knight of *The Seekers*, is disgrace. The shepherd instead diverts his hearers into a cul-de-sac: 'Go gather by the humming sea / Some twisted, echo-harboring shell, / And to its lips thy story tell.' This would seem to guarantee the end of the story, which will repeat inside this echo chamber, decay, and die. But directing words toward death—as the shepherd does when he heads off to sing to a grave hoping to 'please the hapless faun' buried there—is what turns them into dreams and visions: 'And still I dream he treads the lawn, / Walking ghostly in the dew' (51–3).

If 'Song of the Happy Shepherd' offers a utopian, or at least an Arcadian, perspective on Yeats's literary orientation, *The Seeker*, also published in the *Dublin University Review* in 1885, dramatizes the punishments visited upon those who follow their desires 'offline'. In *The Seeker*, three shepherds are having an idyllic night around the campfire when they are approached by an 'Old Knight' who has reached the end of 'three score years of dream-led wandering'. The shepherds warn him not to enter the nearby wood, which they know to be inimical to life: 'The very squirrel dies that enters there.' The Old Knight pushes past them and into Scene II, approaching 'a ruined palace' containing a 'motionless Figure'. He accuses the Figure of luring him away from the objects toward which he *should* have been moving: sexual and martial prowess. 'Thou knowest', he charges, 'how from 'mid the dance / Thou call'd'st me forth. And how thou madest me / A coward in the field.' Having reached the source of the voice that enchanted him, the Old Knight affirms his faith in his queer journey: 'I murmured not, / Knowing that thou hadst singled me with word / Of love from out a dreamless race for strife ... Through joys unhuman, and to thee.' He finally touches his object—and finds what he least expected:

> KNIGHT: A bearded witch, her sluggish head low bent
> On her broad breast! Beneath her withered brows
> Shine dull unmoving eyes. What thing art thou?
> I sought thee not.

[23] See Harris, *Irish Drama and the Other Revolutions*, 39–44.
[24] Ahmed, *Queer Phenomenology*, 67.

FIGURE: Men call me Infamy.
  I know not what I am.
KNIGHT: I sought thee not.
FIGURE: Lover, the voice that summoned thee was mine.[25]

The Knight dies, presumably of chagrin.

The Seeker, which contains early versions of many key elements of *At the Hawk's Well*, reveals Yeats's apprehensions about where his literary orientations might lead him. In addition to losing all the prizes given to ordinary knights who happily dance with their ladies and slaughter their enemies, the Knight has found not glory but annihilation. It is not accidental that Infamy appears as a gender-nonconforming woman. The Knight's spasm of disgust is a reverse *blazon*, in which he itemizes the ways in which Infamy's body negates conventions of female beauty (it is 'broad', not slender; 'withered', not young; 'sluggish', not lithe). The Old Knight's queer journey leads not to an Enchantress or to a Countess or to the land of faery, but to disgrace.

Significantly, the Figure cannot name herself; she can only speak the name 'men' have given her. 'Infamy's' female but unfeminine body incarnates what desire is supposed to lead straight men away from: the corpulent, the coarse, the infertile, the menopausal. *The Seeker* is thus a nightmare vision in which Yeats's literary orientations bring him to ruin. And yet, even here, Yeats suggests that the Knight's final mistake might have been to recoil from the shock of discovery, instead of leaning into it:

FIGURE: What, lover, die before our lips have met?
KNIGHT: Again, the voice! The voice! [Dies.][26]

By the time he and Gregory wrote *Cathleen ni Houlihan*, Yeats had discovered the sovereignty myth, which allows the seeker to have his infamy and his immortality too; at the moment of attainment the hag becomes a 'young woman with the walk of a queen'. But in *The Seeker* Infamy remains a hag—possibly because the Knight, despite a lifetime spent cultivating a distaste for his own culture's norms, tragically fails the final test and refuses to embrace the queer object of his desire.

Were it not for *The Seeker*'s 1885 publication date, we could see 'Infamy' as an ambivalent representation of Florence Farr, the most gender-nonconforming of Yeats's theatrical collaborators—and (as the performer who incarnated the masculinized bisexual heroine of John Todhunter's *The Comedy of Sighs*) the woman held responsible for bringing 'infamy' to at least one of the Irish playwrights who loved her.[27] But since at this point Yeats hadn't met Farr (or Gonne, or Gregory), we should perhaps understand *The Seeker* as a representation of Yeats's fear of exposing to his readers desires which might be labelled as shameful—and not only for the usual reasons. Yeats's erotic desires for these nonconforming women

[25] *VPl*, 1263.
[26] *VPl*, 1263.
[27] Harris, *Irish Drama and Other Revolutions*, 44–55.

were inseparable not only from his turn toward drama but from another transgressive desire in which Gonne and Farr, as members of the Order of the Golden Dawn, were also
collaborators. Theatrical collaboration offered Yeats his first taste of the kind of mystical
shared experience that he would pursue through his magical studies.

THE MAGIC OF THE THEATRE

It's easy enough to read *Vivien and Time*'s spell scene as an allegory of Yeats's sexual
awakening, what with all the heat and the fire consuming Clarin's imagined but absent
male body. But if Yeats's assertion that Armstrong 'woke me from the metallic sleep of
science' is euphemistic, then he is explicitly linking his sexuality to his rejection of scientific materialism. Yeats's awakening thus appears as a change of direction; and one of
the things toward which Yeats is travelling is the activation of poetry's latent sensory and
metaphysical power. This activation manifests in Yeats's early plays as magic; and the objective of this magic is to allow its participants to share consciousness.

In *Mosada*, the spell-casting scene of *Vivien and Time* returns with a difference. By
June 1886, when *Mosada* was published, Yeats had found like-minded people with
whom to pursue his magical interests. Yeats joined the Dublin Hermetical Society in
June 1885; by April 1886 it had become the Dublin Theosophical Society and Yeats was
familiar with Mohini Chatterji and Madame Blavatsky. Through his friendship with
George Russell (AE), Yeats followed lines laid down by Romantic idealism toward a
more mystical idealism. As Foster puts it, 'Russell, particularly, was possessed by a sense
that the visible world was "like a tapestry blown and stirred by winds behind it"'; and
'[t]he dream of lifting that tapestry bound the two students together'.[28]

The influence of these early forays is legible in *Mosada*—as is Yeats's fear that his
magical explorations will lead to infamy. In *Mosada*, Yeats sloughs the Arthuriana of
Vivien and Time and the aestheticism of *The Island of the Statues* and *The Seeker* and
continues the turn toward Asia initiated by his encounter with theosophy. The 'eastern-
hearted' Mosada, a 'Moorish lady' living in a Spanish village, has been separated from
her lover Gomez. The visions through which Mosada seeks Gomez are produced in collaboration with a boy named Cola—again, ostensibly because magic requires the participation of an 'innocent'. As in *Vivien and Time*, neither can create the vision alone;
Mosada does the incantation and burns the herbs that create the smoke in which Cola
sees visions. Mosada 'beckon[s]' the 'phantoms' to their chamber, describing them until
Cola perceives them: 'Your lute hung in the window sounded! / I feel a finger drawn
across my cheek!' Only after Cola senses them can Mosada feel the spirits' presence: 'The
phantoms come; ha! ha! they come, they come! / I wave them hither, my breast heaves
with joy.'[29] Together, they form a complete embodied subject: Cola experiences the

[28]   *Life 1*, 46–9.
[29]   *VPl*, 1266–8.

phantoms as external sensory perceptions, and Mosada experiences them internally, as emotions generated by her own heart.

Just as this split subject is about to be magically unified, the 'Officers of the Inquisition' burst in to arrest Mosada. Only after Mosada has taken poison do we discover that the local head of the Inquisition, the monk Ebremar, is Mosada's lover Gomez. The remorse-stricken Ebremar implores her to look at him. Refusing to direct her attention toward Gomez/Ebermar's earthly form, however, the dying Mosada strains for the vision of Gomez that she was denied, and finally sees it with her own eyes: 'Yonder he treads / The path o'er-muffled with the leaves.'[30] The real Gomez is actually holding her; but the man himself is evidently not the primary object of her desires. What she has pursued all along was not fulfilment but desire itself—a desire strong enough to pierce the veil.

George Russell, looking back on this time, offers an autobiographical context for this collaboration: at this time, '[Yeats] was not clairvoyant and had to use other peoples spiritual eyes to see for him'.[31] Looking forward toward Yeats's later discovery of Irish myth and cultural nationalism, however, we can see in Mosada's vision-quest an early attempt at generating shared consciousness through performance. Julian Dean argues that by the opening of the Abbey Theatre in 1904 Yeats had fully worked out, and committed to, a theory of theatre as magic—and specifically, of theatre as a means of using symbols to enlist performers and spectators in the creation of a collective vision. 'In doing so,' Dean contends, 'Yeats sought to thrust Ireland into Unity of Being.' 'Unity of Being' had a specific magical significance for Yeats, who imagined it as 'a musical in-strument so strung that if we touch a string all the strings murmur faintly'.[32] But the desire for this kind of sympathetic vibration has animated other avant-garde dra-matic movements; and Richard Schechner's embrace of Victor Turner's idea of ritual as producing *communitas*—a shared liminal state in which participants are freed from social structures—built the dream of shared consciousness into modern performance theory. Even Bertolt Brecht, materialist curmudgeon that he was, talked about the 'emo-tional infection' of spectators by actors as one of theatre's distinctive features. Though Yeats has not yet discovered, as Dean argues he will in *On Baile's Strand*, how to use his esoteric knowledge to harness and expand the power of nationalism into 'a trans-national, planetary form of subjectivity', these early theatrical collaborations did show Yeats how theatre might help him escape from the lonely confines of his own skull.[33]

Yeats rejected the materialist understanding of human consciousness as limited by the boundaries of the human body. The apparently conflicting impulses towards lofty isola-tion *and* organization noted by Foster appear in this light as complementary expressions of Yeats's desire to extend his own consciousness *beyond* those boundaries.[34] The solitary

[30] *VPl*, 1277.

[31] Quoted in *Life 1*, 49.

[32] Julian Dean, 'The "Supernatural Artist" and the Tarot Fool: Transnational Esotericism in W. B. Yeats's *On Baile's Strand*', *Modern Drama*, 63:1 (2020), 2–3.

[33] Ibid., 4.

[34] *Life 1*, xxvii.

pursuit of esoteric knowledge was undertaken in the hope of discovering secrets that would allow Yeats's own consciousness to contain the whole of the created universe. But Yeats was also driven to pursue this knowledge in the company of others. Yeats's writing about magic is full of anecdotes in which he and his fellow participants share thoughts, simultaneously experiencing the same vision.

Yeats's desire to escape the limits materialism placed on human consciousness determined the direction of his magical studies. In 'Magic' (1901), Yeats names belief in shared consciousness as the first of three 'doctrines' that are 'the foundations of nearly all magical practices':

(1) That the borders of our minds are ever shifting, and that many minds can flow into one another, as it were, and create or reveal a single mind, a single energy.
(2) That the borders of our memories are as shifting, and that our memories are a part of one great memory, the memory of Nature herself.
(3) That this great mind and great memory can be evoked by symbols.[35]

Given the convergence of Yeats's own preoccupations and the priorities of literary criticism, it is not surprising that commentary on 'Magic' tends to focus on Yeats's third doctrine. The ordering of Yeats's list, however, suggests that doctrines 2 and 3 rest on an understanding of the individual human consciousness as fluid, porous, and protean—and not a discrete unit tethered to and sealed within a single body.

Yeats's memoirs betray a desire to experience shared consciousness *for its own sake*. In 'Magic's opening anecdote, we see Yeats testing the vision to assure himself, not just that it is 'real', but that it is shared. Yeats documents moments when his vision anticipated the seer's narration: 'sometimes I saw what she described before I heard her description'. The timing reassures Yeats that their minds are 'flowing into each other': they experience the vision simultaneously, while the seer's use of speech to communicate it lags behind. Later, Yeats, 'wishing to find out how far we had one vision among us', conceals one detail of his vision, and is gratified to hear it confirmed by the seer. Shared visions matter not only as 'proof of the supremacy of the imagination' but as proof of 'the power of many minds to become one, overpowering one another by spoken words and by unspoken thought till they have become a single intense, unhesitating energy'.[36]

In all these anecdotes, Yeats merges with the consciousness of another person or people in order to reach the 'great mind and great memory' that unites humans with the cosmos. Yeats recalls that in the first years of his relationship with Gonne,

I had a crystal and showed many how to see in it, and an even larger number to see visions according to the method of my Order. A very considerable proportion

[35] CW4, 25.
[36] CW4, 33, 43.

would pass into trance and see what I called up as vividly as ever with the eye of the body. Looking back now I recognize that these visions often repeated to my own thoughts—often some woman would see a marriage with a beautiful woman.[37]

In this anecdote, as in others told long after the fact, Yeats does not represent the sharing of consciousness as mutual; he projects his own consciousness into the participant. Taken on Yeats's terms, this is a story about how a man's sexual desire, as it 'flows into' the mind of another woman, generates an image of lesbian fulfilment. We as readers might nevertheless question Yeats's assertion that this unnamed 'woman' is sharing Yeats's *Liebestraum* instead of enjoying her own.

Yeats's selection of women as theatrical collaborators is linked, in the same way, to the persistence of desire between women in these early plays. In creating a shared vision with Armstrong, Gonne, or Farr, Yeats imagines his own desire extending into the female characters he creates with and for them, directing them toward his own objects. In the process, he creates a fantasy of shared consciousness which is mutual and harmonious precisely because it is not troubled by gender difference. Kelsey Williams has documented Yeats's early interest in Michael Field, a poet and playwright who was the joint creation of Katharine Bradley and Edith Cooper. For Bradley and Cooper, to collaborate was 'to immerse themselves in a collective political consciousness'. Yeats discovered their work in 1884–5, at around the time of *Vivien and Time* and *The Island of the Statues*.[38] Thus, one of his earliest models for collaboration was a pair of women enmeshed in both shared consciousness and mutual desire.

We can understand the queer lines of desire in these plays as an expression not only of Yeats's desire *for* Armstrong, Gonne, and Farr but of a wish to identify *with* them— to merge his consciousness with their own. In Armstrong-as-Vivien, in Naschina, in Mosada, and in Farr-as-Aleel, we see Yeats's theatrical collaborators recruited in service of this fantasy, enabling Yeats to desire a woman *as* and *from the position of* another woman. Yeats articulates this fantasy explicitly much later in his career, in a 1936 letter to the poet Dorothy Wellesley. After deploring the 'rage and lust' that populate his most recent poetry, Yeats lingers over a moment when he, in gazing upon a woman he desires, becomes one: '[W]hen you crossed the room with that boyish movement, it was no man who looked at you, it was the woman in me. It seems that I can make a woman express herself as never before. I have looked out of her eyes. I have shared her desire.'[39]

---

[37] *Mem*, 70.
[38] Kelsey Williams, '"Copied without loss": Michael Field's Poetic Influence on the Work of W. B. Yeats', *Journal of Modern Literature*, 40 (2016), 130, 132.
[39] *CL1*, 868–9.

Conclusion

Yeats's theatrical collaborations suggest that although his most powerful desires travelled toward women, he experienced them not as straight but as transgressive and deviant. Yeats was neither the first nor the last playwright to find in theatre a means of exploring such desires; and one of the things that made this exploration possible was the way in which theatrical collaboration brought him into intimate relationship with women who modelled not only the courage to transgress but a version of female masculinity which he strove to adopt as his own. In 'Emotion of Multitude', Yeats strives to articulate some of the ways in which his theatrical collaborations with women have liberated him not only from gender norms but from generic norms.

Recognizing the pursuit of shared consciousness as central to his magical practice, Yeats finally theorizes his aversion to 'the clear and logical construction which seems necessary if one is to succeed on the Modern Stage'.[40] The problem, he asserts, is that none of the work put into plotting helps anyone transcend individual subjectivity. Scribean construction can deliver 'everything of high literature', Yeats says, 'except the emotion of multitude'. Characteristically, Yeats does not define this emotion; but the examples given evoke a feeling of communion with the 'great mind and great memory' of which Yeats speaks in 'Magic'.[41] Greek drama produces the 'emotion of multitude' through the chorus, whose allusive odes call up a cloud of ghosts to witness the specific 'well-ordered fable' being acted out by the principals. Ibsenite realism connects spectators to the 'great mind' through 'vague symbols' like the wild duck, which 'set the mind wandering from idea to idea, emotion to emotion'. In contrast, 'construction' is a product of 'the mere will', which cannot 'do the work of the imagination'.

Yeats describes the contrast in terms of the gender symbolism that governed his magical explorations; construction belongs to 'the nature of the sun', but his own desire is for the 'vague many-imaged things that have in them the strength of the moon'. He closes, abruptly, with an unanswered question: 'Did not the Egyptian carve it on emerald that all living things have the sun for father and the moon for mother, and has it not been said that a man of genius takes the most after his mother?'[42] Whether it has or not, Yeats is saying it now: his own dramatic genius derives not from his literary fathers but from the women with whom he learned the practice of theatre.

Much of this would shift with the end of the Irish Literary Theatre and the beginning of Yeats's collaboration with Gregory in an intentionally nationalist project. Lauren Arrington has argued that Yeats recognized Gregory as another nonconforming woman, whose literary gifts were 'associated with masculine power', and who enjoyed giving 'conventionally masculine traits to female characters'. The worlds of *Cuchulain*

---

[40] *CW4*, 160.
[41] *CW4*, 25.
[42] *CW4*, 159–60.

of Muirthemne and *Gods and Fighting Men*, from which Yeats's revival plays derive so many of their plots, '[do] not merely critique the "masculinist" values of society but also [offer] scenarios in which more fluid identities are at play'.[43] If she shared Armstrong, Gonne, and Farr's contempt for gender roles, however, Gregory had a strong affinity for genre rules. In *Spreading the News* and *Hyacinth Halvey*, Gregory demonstrates that she understands and enjoys 'construction' in a way that Yeats himself never would. The line extending from Armstrong through Gonne to Farr thus takes a sharp turn when it reaches Gregory. Yeats's rejection of Aristotelian drama with *At the Hawk's Well* should, after our investigation of these early plays, no longer appear to us as an unprecedented innovation but as an extension of the line Yeats was pursuing—through his collaborations with Armstrong, Gonne, and Farr—in the years before he met Gregory.

[43] Lauren Arrington, '"I myself delight in Miss Edgeworth's novels": Gender, Power and the Domestic in Lady Gregory's Work', in Marjorie Elizabeth Howes, ed., *Irish Literature in Transition, 1880–1940* (Cambridge: Cambridge University Press, 2020), 204, 207.

CHAPTER 33

....

A COUNTRY OVER WAVE

Japan, Noh, kyogen

....

AKIKO MANABE

YEATS's encounter with Japan, influenced by intellectuals from various countries, created a completely new art form, removed from the established Western tradition. Ezra Pound and Ernest Fenollosa had an enormous impact on Yeats's work.[1] The Japanese artists Michio Ito, Torahiko Kori, and Tamijuro Kume, whom Yeats met in London, all played crucial roles in cultivating his awareness of Japan. This chapter will evaluate Yeats's reception of Japanese culture and its impact on his experiments with traditional Noh and kyogen theatre, collectively referred to as nogaku, which were simultaneously developed during the fourteenth century. I will also discuss how Yeats integrated both Noh and kyogen in his dramaturgy. In turn, Yeats's Noh-influenced plays brought about change in the traditional Japanese theatre, which had observed the same traditions for over 600 years. I will conclude with a consideration of how Japan responded to Yeats's work as well as how East and West have interchangeably influenced each other to create new theatrical art forms.

In the Irish theatre periodical, *Samhain*, in 1904 Yeats wrote:

> I will write of Irish country-people and make them charming and picturesque ... then they had better be satisfied with the word 'provincial'.... A writer is not less National because he shows the influence of other countries and of the great writers of the world. No nation since the beginning of history, has ever drawn all its life out of itself.[2]

---

[1] Seán Golden has done a detailed study of Yeats's encounter with Japan; his insight into Fenollosa as an art historian is worth noting, since previous studies mostly focused on Fenollosa's literary contribution. See Sean Golden, 'W. B. Yeats: From Sligo to Nōh via Ernest Fenollosa', *Moving Worlds: A Journal of Transcultural Writings*, 16:2 (2016), 37–49.

[2] *CW8*, 63.

Through his encounter with Japan Yeats created works which are simultaneously 'national', international, and universal. Creation of a new art out of a traditional established art form of an exotic culture is a typically modernist practice. Such examples can be found in Pound's *Cantos*, T. S. Eliot's *The Waste Land*, and James Joyce's *Ulysses* and *Finnegans Wake*. These modernists were of the conviction that they were the end of a line of Western culture in a tradition dating back to ancient Greece or even earlier, and that it was their responsibility to continue this tradition by creating their own art to hand over to future generations. Furthermore, they believed this tradition was on the verge of extinction, reflected in writing such as Pound's pronouncement about 'Uncle William' Butler Yeats 'labouring a sonnet of Ronsard', 'Quand vous serez bien vieille', to make his own poem entitled, 'When You Are Old'.[3] Here Pound also reminds his daughter Mary, 'mia pargoletta', to pass on the tradition:

> and there was also Uncle William
> > labouring a sonnet of Ronsard
> ...
> > Quand vous serez bien vieille
> > > remember that I have remembered,
> mia pargoletta,
> > and pass on the tradition
> there can be honesty of mind
> > without overwhelming talent
> I have perhaps seen a waning of that tradition[4]

Pound saw this contemporary poet he highly respected 'labouring' for as long as 'two months on ten lines of Ronsard'.[5] By adding his own voice to the voice of the sixteenth-century French poet Pierre de Ronsard, Yeats created a kind of palimpsest that layers voices beyond time and locale. In this way his art tried to contain elements of 'good' art permeated through the long annals of world history, achieving a true sense of world literature—like the *Cantos* or *Finnegans Wake*. Contributing to this tradition of world literature, Fenollosa's notes and translation added a crucial new dimension by introducing both Japanese theatre and aesthetics to a Western audience.

---

[3] The creative process of 'When You Are Old' and its first finished version can be found in 'Warwick Gould and Deirdre Toomey, ' "Take Down This Book": *The Flame of the Spirit*, Text and Context', *YA*, 11, 124–37.

[4] Ezra Pound, *The Cantos of Ezra Pound* (New York: New Directions, 1995), 'Canto 80', 505–6. (ellipsis mine).

[5] 'Canto 98', 686. Biographical facts contradict as Yeats wrote 'When You Are Old' on 20 or 21 October 1891, while Pound first met Yeats in 1908. A. Norman Jeffares, *A New Commentary on the Poems of W. B. Yeats* (London: Macmillan [1968], 1984), 32. Gould and Toomey's 'Take Down This Book' certifies that Yeats finished the first version of this poem on 21 October when it was compiled in a manuscript book entitled *The Flame of the Spirit*, dedicated to Maude Gonne, but as their study shows this is 'a perpetually unfinished volume'; the possibility that Yeats was still working on this poem in Stone Cottage remains.

A passage of the *Pisan Cantos* which Pound wrote while he was imprisoned at a Disciplinary Training Centre in Pisa in 1945 recalls the circumstances in which Yeats first encountered nogaku at Stone Cottage in Sussex, when Pound worked as Yeats's secretary during three winters between 1913 and 1916.[6] There, Yeats listened to Pound's translation of Fenollosa's manuscript given to him by Fenollosa's widow, Mary, in 1913.

> The Kakemono grows in flat land out of mist
>   sun rises lop-sided over the mountain
>   so that I recalled the noise in the chimney
> as it were the wind in the chimney
>   but was in reality Uncle William
> downstairs composing
> that had made a great Peeeeacock
>   in the proide ov his oiye
>   had made a great peeeeeeecock in the ...
> made a great peacock
>   in the proide of his oyyee
>
> proide ov his oy-ee
> as indeed he had, and perdurable
>
> a great peacock aere perennius[.][7]

This extract vividly recreates Yeats and Pound's living together at Stone Cottage. The natural landscape, visible from Pound's cage, seemed like 'Kakemono', a Japanese scroll. *sumie*, charcoal brushstrokes, are often drawn on 'Kakemono', with a natural landscape in black ink composed of rocks, mountains, and a river shrouded in 'mist'. In these kinds of drawings, landscapes of the Funan area of ancient China, *Sho-Sho Hakkei (Eight Views of Xiao Xiang)* are often represented. This exotic scenery has inspired Japanese artists through the ages, which Pound's 'Canto 49', called 'Seven Lakes Canto', is based upon. The Funan air is humid, and the artists' dexterous craft represents something that fills the empty air or sky—like something you read between the images of Pound and Yeats. Pound's was a poetics of juxtaposition or superimposition, referred to as the ideogrammic method, which he clearly learned from Fenollosa's manuscripts.[8] This

---

[6] James Longenbach first developed a thorough discussion of Yeats's initial contact with Japanese traditional theatre of Noh and kyogen in his *Stone Cottage: Pound, Yeats, and Modernism* (Oxford: Oxford University Press, 1988).

[7] Pound, 'Canto 83', 533–4.

[8] Ernest Fenollosa, *The Chinese Written Character as a Medium for Poetry*, ed. Ezra Pound (San Francisco: City Light Books, 1968); Ernest Fenollosa and Ezra Pound, *The Chinese Written Character as a Medium for Poetry*, A Critical Edition, ed. Haun Saussy, Jonathan Stalling, and Lucas Klein (New York: Fordham University Press, 2008). Ezra Pound, *ABC of Reading* (New York: New Directions, 1987). The craft of *notan*, 'the use of light and dark in Japanese painting', which Golden takes as an example of Yeats's failure to acknowledge his debt to Fenollosa, in my opinion, contributes to the presentation of the moist air in *sumie*. Golden, 'From Sligo to Nōh', 43–4.

superimposition of images creates more than just the addition of images, since the energy created out of this graphic collision creates something unique that fills the spaces in between, like the air in 'Kakemono'.

The landscape of Pisa, which looked similar to a Japanese 'Kakemono', reminded Pound of the days he spent with Yeats at Stone Cottage exploring Fenollosa's manuscripts of nogaku. Among a collection of Noh plays, Pound and Yeats were drawn to the highly sophisticated form of Noh called *Fukushiki Mugen Noh*—its literal translation being a double-layered dream-fantasy Noh play—that embodies the poetics of superimposition both visually and physically. *Fukushiki Mugen Noh* is divided into two scenes. In the first half, a ghost of the protagonist appears as a living human being, while in the second half the same protagonist dramatically shows his or her real identity as a ghost. The two scenes, just like images in ideogrammic method, are superimposed, collide, and consummate in one final image, usually expressed by the protagonist's intense, passionate dance.[9]

Yeats's dramaturgy of Noh is apparent in the introduction to *Certain Noble Plays of Japan*, where we can trace the essence of a breakthrough Yeats discovered as a dramatist, and how specifically that is embodied in Pound's four Noh translations published in the same book—*Nishikigi, Hagoromo, Kumasaka,* and *Kagekiyo*. We can then examine how these factors are integrated into Yeats's own plays. But before discussing Yeats and nogaku in detail, I will briefly explain the fundamental different characteristics of Noh and kyogen. Noh plays generally deal with serious or tragic matters whose subject is mostly mythological, historical, or based largely on classical Japanese and Chinese literature. Actors sing and dance in gorgeous costumes, with a background chorus chanting, accompanied by four simple traditional instruments—three different types of drums and a flute. One could think of Noh as a traditional Japanese opera or musical—though the stage and the setting are extremely simple compared with performances at La Scala, Broadway, or even the amphitheatres in ancient Greece. While Noh plays generally deal with serious or tragic matters, kyogen plays, by contrast, are generally comical or farcical, performed between individual Noh plays to relax the tense atmosphere.

Noh, *Kyogen*, and Folklore

At the beginning of his Introduction to Certain Noble Plays of Japan, Yeats emphasized two fundamental points, 'beauty' and the 'Irish dramatic movement'. Beauty was among the most striking elements he found in Noh, and also what he saw in Noh could be

---

[9] Yeats was fully aware of the crucial role of the climatic dance in nogaku: 'Instead of the players working themselves into a violence of passion indecorous in our sitting-room, the music, the beauty of form and voice all come to climax in pantomimic dance.' Ernest Fenollosa and Ezra Pound, *Certain Noble Plays of Japan: From the Manuscripts of Ernest Fenollosa*, Chosen and Finished by Ezra Pound, with an Introduction by William Butler Yeats (Churchtown, Dundrum: Cuala Press,1916), I–II. Hereafter, *CNPJ*.

reflected in the new play he planned to contribute to the Irish dramatic movement: 'I have asked Mr. Pound for these beautiful plays because I think they will help me to explain a certain possibility of the Irish dramatic movement.'[10] Here is the definition of Noh by Yeats via Pound and Fenollosa:

> 'Accomplishment' the word Noh means, and it is their accomplishment and that of a few cultured people who understand the literary and mythological allusions and the ancient lyrics quoted in speech or chorus, their discipline, a part of their breeding. The players themselves, unlike the despised players of the popular theatre, have passed on proudly from father to son an elaborate art.[11]

Before Yeats or Pound, Noh had never been defined as an 'accomplishment'—even Japanese people had forgotten the original meaning of Noh—but Yeats's translation touches the core of this traditional Japanese drama.[12] Yeats appreciated Noh as an 'accomplishment', since a Noh or kyogen script is the result of hundreds of years of literary refinement, which forms a sort of palimpsest. For instance, one of the four Noh pieces Pound first translated, *Hagoromo*, which the Kanze School of Noh considered to be one of the masterpieces among some 200 classical Noh plays, begins with a *waki* fisherman quoting from *Manyoshu*, the oldest book of poetry in Japan compiled in the seventh and eighth century, and the entire play is filled with bits and pieces from classical Japanese and Chinese literature and art.[13]

Another important point about *Hagoromo*, besides these allusions to historical myths which might be recognized only by the few, is that its story has parallels that can be found in Japanese folklore and is shared by Japanese people as a collective cultural memory or 'ancient memories'. *Hagoromo*, in fact, provided a solution to Yeats's two seemingly contradictory ideals of creating art which aristocratic or courtly people would appreciate, but which at the same time common people could enjoy. As he wrote in his Introduction,

> [I]t pleases me to think that I am working for my own country. Perhaps some day a play in the form I am adapting for European purposes shall awake once more, whether in Gaelic or in English, under the slope of Slieve-na-mon or Croagh Patrick ancient memories; for this form has no need of scenery that runs away with money nor of a theatre-building.[14]

[10] *CNPJ*, I.

[11] *CNPJ*, XI.

[12] *Noh* originally meant craft of art, and then came to mean plays full of songs and dances performed by actors with their 'craft of art'. This expression first appeared in the record of Kasuga Wakamiya Festival in Nara in 1349. Now it is used to call a Noh play, initially used and established by Motokiyo Zeami in the 14th century. Seki Konishi, Tetsuo Nishi and Hisashi Hata, *Nohgaku Daijiten (Encyclopedia to Nohgaku)* (Tokyo: Chikuma Shobo, 2012), 680–681, my translation.

[13] Motokiyo Zeami, *Hagoromo, Kanzeryu Taiseiban (the Definitive Text for the Kanze School)*, edited and corrected by Sakon Kanze (Tokyo: Hinoki Shoten, 1990).

[14] *CNPJ*, XIX.

The oldest of the *Hagoromo* legends in Japan can be found in *Ohmi Fudoki* (*Ancient Shiga Local History*) compiled in the seventh century. Genealogical records say that descendants of a child born from a celestial *tennin* or a fairy from heaven and a local man have succeeded to the priesthood of Ikagu Jinja Shrine, still located in the nort-eastern part of Shiga Prefecture.[15] What is important for Yeats is that the local legend, or folklore, that local people have accepted as a real life event was turned into a Noh drama. This means Noh can be rooted in folk belief, which corresponds with Yeats's idealization of people: 'I love all the arts that can still remind me of their origin among the common people.'[16]

Yeats imagined the Abbey Theatre's role as that of a people's theatre. Here kyogen can work to accomplish Yeats's ideal, since kyogen's repertoire is frequently based on local folklore, and most of the time kyogen plays relate to the life of contemporary common people. Lighter storylines permeate kyogen, unlike the serious tone of Noh, which is inevitable due to a more serious theatrical genre connected to distinguished or privileged people in the past. Yeats wrote a play out of his encounter with kyogen, *The Cat and the Moon*, which attains this goal. In his notes on the play, Yeats states, 'I intended my play to be what the Japanese call a "Kiogen", and to come as a relax-ation of attention between, let us say, "The Hawk's Well" and "The Dreaming of the Bones".'[17] This play is based on a local legend about St Colman's Well located near Thoor Ballylee in Galway, and the story proceeds with a casually light exchange be-tween the two main characters, an anonymous Blind Beggar and a Lame Beggar, in which Yeats employs a Hiberno-English dialect. In this way, Yeats includes essential elements to kyogen's dramaturgy.

Hagoromo can be categorized with similar legends worldwide, such as the Scottish *selkie* legend of seals and Irish mermaid tales developed with the same storyline.[18] Mary Fenollosa pointed out to Pound its affinity to Irish myth: ' "Hagoromo" ... is a le-gend strangely like the old Celtic one of the mermaid who had her magic sea-garments stolen by a mortal.'[19] The story of *Hagoromo* goes like this: while a celestial woman, *tenninn* or *tennnyo*, leaves her coat over a tree and plays in the water, a local (fisher) man steals her coat. Without the coat she cannot fly back to the moon. After a series of events, she finally gets her coat back and returns to the moon--at least in the Noh version, departing by performing an elegantly stylized final dance by a protagonist called *shite*. The whole drama consummates itself in a delicately exquisite final image

---

[15] Kichiro Akimoto, ed., *Fudoki, Iwanami Koten Bungaku Taikei 2* (*Ancient Local History, Selected Japanese Classic Literature Vol. 2*) (Tokyo: Iwanami Shoten, 1968), 457–9.

[16] *CNPJ*, III.

[17] *VP1*, 805.

[18] Katharine Briggs, *A Dictionary of Fairies: Hobgoblins, Brownies, Bogies and other Supernatural Creatures* (Harmondsworth: Penguin, 1979), 353–5.

[19] Mary Fenollosa's letter to Pound, dated 25 November 1913, in Ezra Pound, *Ezra Pound & Japan: Letters & Essays*, ed. Sanehide Kodama (Redding Ridge, CT: Black Swan Books, 1987), 8.

by having the *shite* dance through a screen into the backstage. The backstage in Noh represents the other world, in this case the moon. This *tennin*'s dance is, in fact, the Noh dance that Yeats and Pound experienced for the first time when Tamijuro Kume performed in London in 1917, marking an essential departure point for their collaboration for creating a new art form.[20] (See Figure 33.1.)

Mastering *kata*, a stylized form of movements, is crucially important to this notion of Noh as 'accomplishment'. Noh actors train themselves so that 'the distance from life which can make credible strange events, elaborate words'; Yeats mirrors this idea of refinement through discipline in his Introduction:

> I hope to have attained the distance from life which can make credible strange events, elaborate words. I have written a little play that can be played in a room for so little money that forty or fifty readers of poetry can pay the price .... In fact with the help of these plays 'translated by Ernest Fenollosa and finished by Ezra Pound' I have invented a form drama, distinguished, indirect and symbolic, and having no need of mob or press to pay its way--an aristocratic form.[21]

When Yeats says 'the distance from life', he does not mean an esoteric eerie world but the distance against a pushing world of vulgar journalism and popular culture. He would like his audience to be able to appreciate 'poetry' with 'the memory of beauty and emotional subtlety' or his art in 'an aristocratic form' which is 'distinguished, indirect and symbolic'.

Noh plays employ 'elaborate words' using *utai* chanting, composed using symbolic and suggestive verses, not realistically direct, and filled with allusion from the classics. *Shite* protagonists are often ghosts, creatures from the other world, or gods. They communicate with people living in this world, called *waki*, usually as travelling priests—the audience accepting these 'strange events' in the usual sense of the world as natural and 'credible' once they are immersed in this special world of Noh. *Shite*, coming from the other world, whether from the land of death, gods, or madness, wear masks, while *waki*, living in the principle of this ordinary world, do not. In his own drama, *The Dreaming of the Bones*, Yeats successfully employs the essence of Noh, where the audience experience Diarmuid and Dervogilla, both of whom wear masks, crossing over 700 years of time to

---

[20] Pound, *Ezra Pound & Japan*, 143; Mary de Rachewilts, A. David Moody, and Joanna Moody, eds., *Ezra Pound to his Parents: Letters 1895–1929* (Oxford: Oxford University Press, 2010), 366. Although Ito was not favourable to Noh when Pound first asked him to teach it, he came to appreciate the form after collaborating with Pound and Yeats. Michio Ito, '*Omoide wo Kataru--Taka no I Shutsuen no Koto Nado* (Momoir--My Appearance at *At the Hawks Well*)', Transcript of his Lecture at Tokyo Women's Christian University given in 1956, in *Hikaku Bunka* 2 (Tokyo: Tokyo Women's Christian University, 1956), 57–76. In Japan a new term, *yousei* (妖精), was created to translate a Western fairy, which the definitive text of *Hagoromo* for Kanze School uses to explain the *tennin* (*Hagoromo*, 1). This demonstrates that, during the past 150 years, Japanese culture has accepted and merged Western culture into its own culture.

[21] *CNPJ*, 1–2.

TAMI KOUMÉ
From photographic study by Arnold Genthe

FIGURE 33.1 Tamijuro Kume, photograph reproduced by permission of the Museum of Modern Art, Kamakura & Hayama, Japan.

speak to a young man, contemporary to Yeats, without any mask on his face, who fought in the Easter Rising in 1916. The Noh is also evident in Yeats's plays involving Cuchulain, in which other-worldly creatures such as the Morrigu, Aoife, and a hawk-like Guardian of the Well act, speak, and dance.

Yeats's Introduction to *Certain Noble Plays of Japan* strives to the universal:

A poetical passage cannot be understood without a rich memory, and like the older school of painting appeals to a tradition ... in rhythm, in vocabulary; for the ear must notice slight variations upon old cadences and customary words, all that high breeding of poetical style where there is nothing ostentatious, nothing crude, no breath of parvenu or journalist.[22]

STAGING NOH

Yeats writes that in order for the audience to appreciate 'slight variations upon old cadences and customary words, all that high breeding of poetical style', the theatre should not be big but 'a room for so little money that forty or fifty readers of poetry can pay the price', as '[I]n the studio and in the drawing-room we can found a true theatre or beauty'.[23] Noh theatre is an intimate theatre that consists of a 6 x 6-metre square stage attached to a passageway called a *hashigakari*. The *hashigakari* connects the square stage, or this world, to the backstage, or the other world. Between the backstage and the *hashigakari* is a simple screen of five colours, each representing different elements in nature, which is manually raised and dropped by two actors, each of whom holds a long bamboo stick. The audience waits for actors to appear on the stage while listening to music. After Yeats's encounter with nogaku, he allowed musicians to open and close a cloth on the stage, which would function similarly to the use of the screen in nogaku. As for stage lighting, Yeats, in the stage direction of *At the Hawk's Well*, says, 'so far as my present experience goes, that the most effective lighting is the lighting we are most accustomed to in our rooms'.[24] In such an intimate space actors on stage and the audience on the floor share what is going on with a sense of unity, with all five senses attuned. This is the ideal theatrical backdrop for Yeats, who searched for such a theatrical space to create a communal unity to stimulate Irish people's sense of nationalism.

Another important characteristic of the Noh stage is its emptiness, without elaborate settings or props. The actors' words combined with restricted acting through the use of *kata* stimulate the audience's imagination, thereby bringing about a background scenery. For instance, there is a kyogen play entitled *Mizukake Muko* (*Son in Law Splashing Water*). On a completely empty stage two men appear, an old man and his daughter's husband. These two men carry a long plough and proceed to splash water, sand, and mud at each other. On stage, there are no props representing water, sand, or mud, and instead the actors simply carry long wooden sticks. However, because of the actors' dexterous movements, somewhat like a pantomime players' gestures, as well as words spoken, including onomatopoeic sounds, the audience can visualize splashing water and sand. When water and mud are mixed and thrown, the actors' slow movements force the audience to imagine the stickiness of the material. This is dependent on the absolutely perfect timing of their exchanges—not only by words, but by actions as well.

[22] *CNPJ*, VIII–IX.
[23] *CNPJ*, I, IX.
[24] *CW2*, 297.

The key to *Nogaku* is imagination, which Yeats valued most highly. As he wrote in *Samhain* in 1901,

> I may say, for I am now perhaps writing an epitaph, and epitaph should be written in a genial spirit, that we have turned a great deal of Irish imagination towards the stage. We could not have done this if our movement had not opened a way of expression for an impulse that was in the people themselves. The truth is that the Irish people are at that precise stage of their history when imagination, shaped by many stirring events, desires dramatic expression.[25]

We can find this same kind of verbal interchange in Yeats's later plays: in *The Resurrection*, for example, all the actions happening outside the stage are brought before the audience's eyes through a dialogue between a Hebrew and a Greek, with a Syrian later joining in. By contrast, the final appearance of a resurrected Christ on stage without speaking a word gives the intense sense of the here and now. Yeats knows full well the power of physicality if used effectively, which reminds us of Pound's poetics: 'Direct treatment of the "thing" whether subjective or objective'.[26] We can see the same kind of poetics in the Noh play *Kumasaka*, one of the four Noh plays in *Certain Noble Plays of Japan*. Here 'things' and 'words' cooperatively exert their power—actors' words lead the audience's imagination to see something invisible on stage as visible in their mind. Kumasaka appears in the first scene as a Buddhist priest, but when the travelling priest goes into the prayer hall, he does not see the Buddha's statues that should be there but instead is surrounded by swords and iron bars, something completely inappropriate for Buddhist temples to have on display. These things speak of Kumasaka's real identity as a thief—not a priest. What is memorable is that there are no props or stage settings to show these things, and they are presented only by the *waki* priest's words.

In *The Resurrection*, the rhythmical onomatopoeic sound of 'Barrum, barrum, barrum' effectively introduces the song followed by the drum taps[27], and this reminds us of the onomatopoeia used frequently in nogaku—as in Pound's translation of *Nishikigi*:

> SHITE: The sound of the loom.
> TSURE: It was a sweet sound like katydids and crickets,
>   A thin sound like the Autumn.
> SHITE: It was what you would hear any night.
> TSURE: Kiri.
> SHITE: Hatari.
> TSURE: Cho.
> SHITE: Cho.

[25] *CW8*, 4.
[26] Ezra Pound, *Literary Essays of Ezra Pound*, ed. with introduction by T. S. Eliot (New York: New Directions, [1918,] 1968), 3.
[27] *CW2*, 487.

CHORUS (mimicking the sound of crickets):
    Kiri hatari cho, cho,
    Kiri, hatari, cho, cho.
    The cricket sews on at his old rags,
    With all the new grass in the field; sho,
    Churr, isho, like the whir of a loom: churr.
CHORUS (antistrophe): Let be, they make grass-cloth in Kefu,
Kefu, the land's end, matchless in the world.[28]

In this ghostly vision, these words and sounds recreate the sound of a loom, repeated endlessly, somewhat implying the passage of time, with a woman never returning love towards the man. The sound of the loom is here associated with an autumn insect's sound—a sound that is traditionally pleasing in Japanese culture. This adds a sad touch of transience represented by the season's change from summer to winter.

Kumasaka and *Nishikigi* take the typical style of *Fukushiki Mugen Noh*. In the first half of *Nishikigi* the *shite* ghost, along with the ghost of the woman he loved, appear on stage, pretending to be a local couple in Kefu, the northern countryside, and in the latter half they appear as their real selves, expressing their true desire—asking the *waki* priest to repose their agonized souls. Thanks to this first encounter with these two *Fukushiki Mugen Noh*, Yeats learned the way to let the dead speak in a way which the audience can accept as 'credible' without awkwardness. The most successful outcome can be seen in *The Dreaming of the Bones*, in which the ghosts of Diarmuid and Devorgilla appear in the scene and express their desire to be relieved of their sins. The scene is set in the present, a couple appearing as a local boy and a girl, asking a stranger who escaped from Dublin to the Aran Islands for their sins to be forgiven. A climactic dance is also employed. The setting is quite similar to *Nishikigi*, but the difference is that *Nishikigi* deals with the universal theme of unrequited love, while Yeats works on a specific theme of his nation's historical destiny whereby the couple could not be saved.

Further developing this theme of letting the spirit or soul of the dead speak, Yeats created an idiosyncratic form by integrating Noh and kyogen together into the traditional Western theatrical practice. Years later, in *A Full Moon in March*, the severed head of the Swineherd sings, and in the farcical kyogen version, *The King of the Great Clock Tower*, a severed head of the Stroller also sings. This is another form of the dead person's voice resurrected, where the actual heads themselves do not speak but the audience are told that the head/face begins to move as if they were speaking:

TheKing: His eyelids tremble, his lips begin to move.
First Attendant [*singing as Head in a low voice*]:   Clip and lip and long for more–
The King: O, O, they have begun to sing.

---

[28] Ernest Fenollosa and Ezra Pound, *The Noh Theatre of Japan: With Complete Texts* of 15 Classic Plays (New York: Dover, 2004), 143–4.

> *Second Attendant* [*laughs softly as Head*]:   He has begun to laugh.
> *First Attendant*:   No; he has begun to sing. (*Full Moon*)[29]

The audience believe through the actors' words that something immovable is moving and hear the voice coming out from another person rather from the Head. In *The King of the Great Clock Tower* the 'lips' sing, while in *Full Moon* 'he' sings. Compared to the earlier version, in which part of the human body functions, in the later play a dead person or a ghost sings, so the function of the head becomes more like a *nochi shite*: the protagonist of the latter scene of Noh who comes back to this world as a ghost.

BLIND MEN AND BEGGAR MEN

Yeats's dramaturgy also works with his poetics in another Noh play that Yeats first encountered through Pound's translation, *Kagekiyo*. Kagekiyo Fujiwara/Taira was among the strongest warriors, whose huge contribution to the Heike clan was much appreciated, especially at the final battle at Dan-no-ura against the Genji clan. After the Heike's complete defeat, he was captured and exiled. His daughter travelled a long way to search for him and finally tracked him down. At first he hid his identity as he felt ashamed of his wretched state of living like a beggar. After his identity was revealed, he told his daughter about his past battles and successes. Unusually for a Noh piece, he just talks and sings without dancing. He explains verbally, using only subtle movements true to the *kata* form. This piece uses both verbal and imaginative theatrics combined with *kata*-style acting to the extreme.

Two important qualities for Yeats are presented in *Kagekiyo*—the blind man and the beggar. Yeats took a strong interest in these types of characters living at the margins of society, including the two Beggars in *The Cat and the Moon*. Kagekiyo blinded himself, since he did not want to see his own wretched state nor the world under the Genji clan's reign. He would rather face the inner darkness of himself. Blind men in Yeats's plays are supposed to be witty and knowledgeable, often appearing alongside fool-like figures who, like the Lame Man in *The Cat and the Moon*, are closer to being innocent and have overtones of the sacred. 'My mother or my nurse said that the blind / Know everything,' Cuchulain tells the Blind Man, who is about to cut off his head in *The Death of Cuchulain*.[30] To this same Blind Man, a Fool in *On Baile's Strand* states, 'There's nobody with two eyes in his head that is as clever as you are.'[31]

The Cat and the Moon brings these two qualities together in one character, similar to Kagekiyo—the Blind Beggar, who knows the way of the world, chooses to be physically blessed rather than spiritually blessed, and disappears backstage after beating his

---

[29] *CW2*, 498 and 507.
[30] *CW2*, 552.
[31] *CW2*, 151.

long-standing companion, the Lame Beggar. Kyogen's central ethos is laughter. People laugh and accept the reality of life, even if it is harsh and cruel. The overall tone and the exchange between two main characters here are light, 'flighty', and warmly comical, so that the audience laugh. In a sense Yeats's 'tragic joy', which ancient glittering gay eyes of 'Chinamen' in 'Lapis Lazuli', while seeing the tragedy of the world, represent is theatrically embodied in *The Cat and the Moon*.

In the Fenollosa manuscript, there is one kyogen, *Kikazu Zato*, in which blind Kikuichi and deaf Taro-kaja are ordered to look after the house while their master is away. *Kikazu Zato* attracted Yeats's attention, and its influence on *The Cat and the Moon* can be traced.[32] They are supposed to compensate for each other's physical weakness, but while being alone in the house together, they mock each other's blindness and deafness, using abusive language and behaviour. Each character's specific physical disability is ruthlessly mocked. Even if the audience is attuned to the cruelty of the laughter, there is still comedy in the absurdity of human nature, because there is no other alternative but to laugh.

Kyogen relates to the life of the common person, rather than the distinguished or privileged people in history which Noh favours. Kyogen characters are anonymous common people, including servants and peasants. They use names like Taro-kaja and Jiro-kaja. *Kaja* means servant, while Taro and Jiro are real names that are often used to point to an Everyman character. These servants are often witty and wise; using their intuition, they plot to trick their masters or make fun of them. They are anonymous but embody strong individual characteristics. Another type often used in the kyogen is the physically challenged character, as in *Kikazu Zato*, who lives peripherally like the two beggars in *The Cat and the Moon*, and their life philosophy is strongly positive.

Yeats in Japan

Yeats's work has been warmly accepted in Japan, and his encounter with nogaku has in turn influenced Japanese nogaku. *At the Hawk's Well* in particular has opened new aspects to the Japanese nogaku world. This is one connection in a long tradition of Irish literature's reception in Japan. At the turn of the twentieth century, leading Japanese literary figures such as Ryunosuke Akutagawa, Konosuke Hinatsu, Hakuson Kuriyagawa, Sei Ito, Kan Kikuchi, Masao Kume, Yaso Saijo, Makoto Sangu, and Bin Ueda were attracted to Irish literature.[33] Many of them were introduced to Yeats's work while they were students of the Greek-born Irish literary scholar/writer Lafcadio Hearn. Hearn

---

[32] Yoko Sato tried to pin down the version of *Kikazu Zato* to which Fenollosa referred. Yoko Sato, 'Fenollosa's Manuscript of *Kikazu Zato*, the Japanese Source of Yeats's *The Cat and the Moon*', *Journal of Irish Studies*, 30 (Tokyo: IASIL Japan, 2015), 27–38.

[33] Akiyo Suzuki, *Ekkyo suru Souzouryoku (Imagination Beyond Borders)* (Suita: Osaka University Press, 2014).

arrived in Japan in 1890 and taught at high schools, Tokyo (Imperial) University, and Waseda University. An important lecture at Tokyo University on Yeats's poem 'The Folk of the Air' and his play *The Land of Heart Desire* led to a correspondence between Hearn and Yeats.[34] We should also note that Fenollosa, who was a colleague of Hearn's in Japan, was indebted to the acute sensitivity of Hearn. Hearn found the poetical quality of the Japanese written character, and Pound's reading in Fenollosa on Chinese characters, led him to create his ideogrammic method.[35]

At the Hawk's Well became known in Japan when Michio Ito performed it first in 1939, with his brother Koreya Senda, who was a famous theatre director. It stimulated Noh scholar Mario Yokomichi to write a new *Fukushiki Mugen Noh* under the title *Taka no Izumi (Hawk's Spring)*, with an old man as a *shite* in the first half and his ghost in the second.[36] In 1967 Yokomichi rewrote it as a poetical drama, *Taka Hime (Hawk Princess)*, using a classical verse form—classical Japanese but without using a Noh or kyogen style of language. At its premier performance the *shite* Hawk Princess was performed by Hisao Kanze, a legendary Noh actor. The script by Yokomichi, along with Noh music composed by Hisao, brought the structure and language of this new Noh play to the highest level. The storyline of *Hawk Princess* is almost the same as *At the Hawk's Well*, though it is specifically set on an isolated island surrounded by a desolate sea. Three characters appear on stage, as in Yeats's play. However, Yokomichi dexterously adjusted the characterization of Cuchulain to suit a Japanese audience. To arouse a Japanese sense of exoticism, Yokomichi had Cuchulain declare himself Prince of Persia, since Yeats's use of Irish mythology does not make sense to a Japanese audience.

Yokomichi's new Noh play marks two subtle yet revolutionary changes. One is that it breaks the barrier between the three roles of actors: *shite-kata*, who plays a protagonist; *waki-kata*, who plays a supporting role; and *kyogen-kata*, who plays kyogen.[37] In the traditional world of nogaku, actors are categorized into these three stereotypes and never cross over. Those who play *shite* only play *shite*, not *waki* or kyogen. However, here, any nogaku player can take the role of Cuchulain, Hawk Princess, or the Old Man. The world of traditional nogaku strictly followed the rigid rules, which were set when nogaku became designated as an official art for the Tokugawa Shogunate, *Shikigaku*, in the early seventeenth century. Even at present the rigid rules are not easily broken.

---

[34] Lafcadio Hearn, 'Some Fairy Literature', in John Erskine, ed., *Life and Literature* (New York: Dodd, Mead, 1917), 324–39.

[35] Ernest Fenollosa, 'On Lafcadio Hearn, *Glimpses of Unfamiliar Japan*', *The Ernest F. Fenollosa Papers: The Houghton Library Harvard University, Japanese Edition Vol. III. Literature*, ed. and trans. with Introduction, Notes, and Appendices by Akiko Murakata (Tokyo: Museum Press, 1987), 103; Fenollosa, *The Chinese Written Character as a Medium for Poetry*; Seiichi Yamaguchi, *Fenollosa: Nihon bunka no Senyo ni Sasageta Isshou (Jou) (Ge) (Fenollosa: Life Dedicated to Japanese Culture I, II)* (Tokyo: Sanseido, 1982).

[36] First performed by Minoru Kita in 1949. Seki Kobayashi, Shozo Matsuda, and Hisashi Hada, eds., *Noh: Honsetsu to Tenkai (Noh: Authoritative Text and its Development)* (Tokyo: Ohfusha, 1977), 211–29.

[37] *Kata* (方),which means 'people in charge of some specific roles', is different from *kata* (型), meaning 'form or style'.

Therefore, although this flexible change in the crossover of roles may seem small, it indeed marked a revolutionary change.

Another of Yokomichi's idiosyncratic experiments can be found in his creation of 'rocks'. By applying Noh's principle to Yeats's original play in his use of rocks, Yokomichi brings Yeats's play to another level. Though their origin is not specified, we are led to believe these rocks were once warriors, just like young Cuchulain, who desires to drink the well's water that brings about immortality. The rocks symbolize the warriors, whose wishes have never been achieved; the warriors have become one with the earth, but their unfulfilled wish still lingers on earth. This representation of unrequited desire follows a Noh motif. Yokomichi also seems to tell us rocks and human beings are not so different; everything that exists in nature is uniform under a universal principle. In the play, the rocks move, sometimes while chanting strange sounds to accompany their movement. This is an extraordinary experiment with the traditional *jiutai*, or chorus. In the traditional Noh play eight chorus singers, wearing formal male kimonos—a black *montsuki* coat and sober-coloured, usually grey, *hakama* pants—sit in two lines, four on each line at the far right side of the stage, all the time the play is performed. They never move around. In *Hawk Princess* eight actors, acting as rocks on the island, wearing a grey half-mask and long big grey kimonos, move around the stage, like a chorus in Western opera. They move slowly in a serenely restricted and stylized *kata*-based way. The rocks function like *shite* in *Fukushiki Mugen Noh*. Unlike *shite*, however, who are often ghosts of famous tragic heroes or historical figures, the rocks are an anonymous representation of all human beings.

Yokomichi was inspired to rewrite *At the Hawk's Well* as a new Noh drama at the urging of his friend, another Noh scholar and playwright, Shizuo Kobayashi, who was killed in battle during the Second World War at the age of 35. In *Hawk Princess*, we hear the prayer for Kobayashi as well as for all the young people killed in war—people whose hope, desire, or life has been cut short. A chorus of rocks sounds like a requiem. While there is no obvious dedication to Kobayashi, the final word of the play is 'Kobayashi', a homonym that also means 'small forest'. The lines go:

> 泉は永遠に涸れ果てて
> 静かなり榛の小林[38]
>
> *Izumi wa Towa ni Kare Hatete*
> *Shizuka nari Hashi no Kobayashi* (phonetic transcription)
>
> Well is dried up eternally
> Silent now are small hazel woods. (my translation)

Yokomichi's new *Noh* play was born out of the encounter with Yeats, who created the original *At the Hawk's Well* because of his encounter with nogaku, and in this way Yeats contributed to a breakthrough in twentieth-century Japanese Noh.

---

[38] Kobayashi et al., *Noh: Honsetsu to Tenkai*, 229.

In 2017, in commemoration of the sixtiethth anniversary of the diplomatic relationship between Ireland and Japan, Gensho Umewaka (Minoru Umewaka IV), a *shite* actor of Kanze School, along with Michael McGlynn, the Irish composer and artistic director of the choral ensemble from Dublin ANÚNA, directed a production of *Hawk Princess* in Tokyo, with Gensho himself playing the role of Hawk Princess with ANÚNA. In a sense, the twenty-first-century encounter was realized 100 years after the first encounter between Japanese and Irish performance art. With its grand stage setting and the use of large-scale sound and light effects, this performance achieved a commercial success that encouraged a renewed interest in Ireland and Yeats. In the same year, two performances of *The Hawk Princess* held at Kyoto Kanze Kaikan Noh Theatre, as well as a performance in 2018 at the Kyoto RHOM Theatre by two *shite* actors of the Kanze School, Kuroemon Katayama and Tetsunojo Kanze, engendered a similar exchange without any special settings or effects. The production in Tokyo was a huge blockbuster performance, while performances in Kyoto followed Yeats's original intention and the principles of Noh more faithfully. In 2017 I produced kyogen performances of *The Cat and the Moon* as another commemoration event for the sixtieth anniversary. Yeats intended the play to be a kyogen, but it had never been performed in Japanese as a kyogen piece until the production staged in 2015 by the Shigeyama Sengoro Troupe, a prestigious kyogen theatrical troupe in Kyoto, with their origin as kyogen players dating back to 1600, in commemoration of the 150th anniversary of Yeats's birth.[39] I asked the Shigeyama Sengoro Troupe to perform at three venues in Ireland—Dublin, Sligo, and Waterford—in 2017, and in all three places our performances were favourably received.[40] Whatever the style of performance or the mode of adaptation, what is important is that Yeats's encounter with Japan has been breathing new life into the classical Japanese tradition of Noh. His works do indeed 'pass on tradition'.

---

[39] Performed at Kobe Gakuin University, 10 November 2015, as part of the 370th Kobe Gakuin University Green Festival, produced by Professor Shigeru Ito. Script translated into Japanese by Tetsuro Sano, and directed by Kaoru Matsumoto. The Blind Beggar by Masakuni Shigeyama the Lame Beggar by Shigeru Shigeyama, and the Saint by Senzaburo Shigeyama.

[40] People involved are the same as in n. 39 above, except for the Saint performed by Kaoru Matsumoto. Dublin at Smock Alley Theatre, 24 July 2017; Sligo at the Factory Performance Space, 27 July; and Waterford at Garter Lane Arts Centre, 29 July. Articles to announce the performance: the *Mainichi Newspaper*, 15 April 2017; the *Yomiuri Shinbun*, 22 June; and *The Irish Times,* 27 July. TV broadcast: 'NHK World News', 29 July, and 'Kyogen' in the NHK TV series, 'Introduction to Traditional Theatre', 24 September. Reviews: the *Mainichi Newspaper*, 9 August 2017, and the *San-in Chuo Shmnpo* by Bon Koizumi, the great-grandson of Lafcadio Hearn, 26 August.

CHAPTER 34

READING THE LATE PLAYS

Sexual unorthodoxies

ZSUZSANNA BALÁZS

IN this chapter, I consider the intersection between violence/power and sexual desire in three of Yeats's late plays—*The Cat and the Moon* (1926), *The King of the Great Clock Tower* (1935), and *A Full Moon in March* (1935),[1] with a focus on sadomasochism (SM) which Elizabeth Freeman has defined as 'an erotic dialectic between two or more people that ostensibly focuses on the ritualized exchange of power'.[2] I contend that, through theatrical representations of sadomasochistic attachments based on reversible power, Yeats's late drama reveals the systemic failures of normative distributions of power, gender, and sexual roles. I first discuss Yeats's unconventional relationship with sexuality, his increasing interest in corporeality, and the importance of literary representations of SM. From there, I apply a dramaturgical approach, focusing on the potentials of the scripts to demonstrate that Yeats's plays convey crucial messages about power, the body, and difference for contemporary audiences as well. The plays discussed here feature clashes between the unruly forces of seduction and the normative force of power and production. Their protagonists are defiant social outcasts (disabled beggars in *CM*, a Stroller in *KGCT*, and a Swineherd in *FMM*), whose clashes with power paradoxically earn them temporary visibility and authority.[3] These socially marginalized characters fail to meet normative standards of bodily being, which becomes an act of resistance, since the characters representing the power of production (the Saint in *CM*, the King in *KGCT*, and the Queen in *FMM*) are

---

[1] I will use the following abbreviations for the plays in the main text: *CM*, *KGCT*, and *FMM*.

[2] Elizabeth Freeman, 'Turn the Beat Around: Sadomasochism, Temporality, History', in Donal E. Hall and Annamarie Jagose, with Andrea Bebell and Susan Potter, eds., *The Routledge Queer Studies Reader* (London: Routledge, 236–62), 238.

[3] Michel Foucault discusses this phenomenon in his 'Lives of Infamous Men', in *Power*, ed. James D. Faubion, trans. Robert Hurley et al., Vol. 3 of *Essential Works of Foucault, 1954–1984* (New York: New Press, 2000), 157–75.

obsessed with bodily perfection. These master–slave relationships appear as sadomaso-chistic mostly due to their reversibility, which also renders them an element of excite-ment and playfulness.

YEATS AND SEXUALITY

Yeats's works are marked by unorthodox forms of sexual desire, which derive largely from his lifelong interest in the occult, the unavailability of Maud Gonne, and his close friendship with sexual radicals such as Florence Farr and Oscar Wilde.[4] In fact, Yeats experienced sadomasochistic practices through his involvement in the Golden Dawn in the 1890s: '[t]he Golden Dawn, like other occult societies, used its religious rites as displaced vehicles for the frustrated eroticism of its members: at his initiation into the 6/5 grade Yeats's hands were tied behind his back, a chain was hung round his neck, he was bound to a cross, and he received the symbolic stigmata.'[5] Yeats's early relationship with sexuality was indeed marked by frustration and feelings of shame and difference: he experienced much anxiety with sexuality, as he 'lacked confidence in his masculinity, and being repeatedly refused weakened his self-esteem'.[6] Due to these anxieties, Yeats became more interested in his friends' unconventional sexualities, including the ambiguous relationship between Edward Martyn and George Moore, which also offers the background for CM's queer bonds. Yeats noticed Martyn's 'se-cret torture', and observed that Martyn's 'intellect has been always thwarted by its lack of interest in life, religious caution having kept him always on the brink of the world in a half-unwilling virginity of the feeling imagining the virginity of his body. ... He had no interest in women, and Moore would accuse him of a frustrated passion for his own sex.'[7]

Yeats's posthumously published Memoirs offers a frank account of his experiences of sexuality, demonstrating that Yeats's relationship with sexual desire was marked by pain and absence.[8] Describing his first masturbation, Yeats indicates his difference from nor-mative masculinity deriving from his unfulfilled desire for Maud Gonne:

> I was tortured by sexual desire and had been for many years. ... Normal sexual inter-course does not affect me more than other men, but that, though never frequent, was plain ruin. It filled me with loathing of myself; and yet at first pride and per-haps, a little, lack of obvious opportunity, and how love kept me in unctuous celibacy.

[4] See Susan Cannon Harris, Irish Drama and the Other Revolutions: Playwrights, Sexual Politics, and the International Left, 1892–1964 (Edinburgh: Edinburgh University Press, 2017), 24.
[5] Elizabeth Butler Cullingford, Gender and History in Yeats's Love Poetry (Cambridge: Cambridge University Press, 1993), 51–2.
[6] Cullingford, Gender and History, 53.
[7] Mem, 253; Mem, 118–19.
[8] Life 2, 66.

When I returned to London in my twenty-seventh year I think my love seemed almost hopeless, and I knew that my friends had all mistresses of one kind or another and that most, at need, went home with harlots. [William Ernest] Henley, indeed, mocked at any other life. I had never since childhood kissed a woman's lips.[9]

This anxiety with sexual desire was transformed into an obsession and experimentation with sexuality by the 1920s and 1930s, and *KGCT* and its revised version *FMM* were the products of Yeats's Steinach operation in April 1934, which was 'actually a simple vasectomy, intended to increase and contain the production of male hormone, thus arresting the aging process and restoring sexual vitality'.[10] As Foster explains, in these years, '[s]ex is an urgent, imperious presence, ultimately unsatisfying unless linked to some kind of revelation'.[11] Desire remained marked by restraint and absence for Yeats, who even reckoned that 'the desire that is satisfied is not a great desire'.[12] Inevitably, the longing for annihilation became intertwined with sexual passion in Yeats's late drama: '[a]ll our lives long, as da Vinci says, we long, thinking it is but the moon that we long [for], for our destruction, and how, when we meet [it] in the shape of a most fair woman, can we do less than leave all others for her? Do we not seek our dissolution upon her lips?'[13] What is more, as Cullingford notes with regard to Yeats's reaction to Villiers de l'Isle-Adam's *Axel*, '[p]resumably the idea that death is preferable to consummation consoled the frustrated Yeats'.[14]

The non-normative desires in Yeats's drama and poetry have long been addressed in Yeats scholarship. Cullingford has explored the androgynous sensibilities of Yeats's life and love poetry and the intersection between love/desire and pain/death, which helps understand Yeats's late drama too. Joseph Valente has highlighted the gender and sexual exorbitancies of Yeats's Cuchulain with regard to *On Baile's Strand* (1907).[15] Harris also notes Cuchulain's non-normative masculinity and discusses the controversial sexual issues of *The Herne's Egg* (1938) as an interrogation of Irish politics' abuse of women's bodies and its regressive approach to sexuality.[16] In her recent monograph, Harris has stressed the connection between Yeats's friendship with sexual radicals and the openness of his drama to a wide range of sexual and gender possibilities.[17] The sadomasochistic aspects of Yeats's works have been mentioned by Cullingford and most recently Alexandra Poulain, who explored the mutual dependence, violence and the asymmetrical power distributions between the two beggars in *CM*.[18] Poulain

---

[9] *Mem*, 71–2.

[10] *Life* 2, 496.

[11] *Life* 2, 503.

[12] Quoted in Cullingford, *Gender and History*, 43.

[13] *Mem*, 88.

[14] *Mem*, 48.

[15] Cullingford, *Gender and History*, 174.

[16] Susan Cannon Harris, *Gender and Modern Irish Drama* (Bloomington: Indiana University Press, 2002), 25, 227–66.

[17] Harris, *Irish Drama*, 50.

[18] Alexandra Poulain, 'Failed collaboration and queer love in Yeats's *The Cat and the Moon* and Beckett's *Rough for Theatre I*', *Ilha do Desterro*, 71:2 (2018); 'Artistic Collaborations', 233–44, 236–7.

has also emphasized the presence of an inherent resistance in Yeats's plays related to queer versions of love and relationships, which 'resists the play's drive towards unity'.[19] Literary and theatrical representations of such unruly relationships help reveal the often silenced histories of sexuality, race, nationalism, and imperialism, as Freeman has explained. Poulain also pointed this out in her 2016 monograph, arguing that the spectacle of the body in pain can help make visible the otherwise invisible violence imposed on marginalized individuals by various power structures.[20] Since the focus of these studies is not explicitly SM, I explore this theme in more detail here to demonstrate the centrality of unorthodox representations of the body, power, and resistance in Yeats's late drama.[21]

Focus on the Body

Yeats's move towards anti-naturalistic, total theatre techniques informed by his interest in Japanese Noh theatre from the early 1910s helped introduce pleasure and corporeality in his plays about power and violence. Eastern total theatre focuses on the body and fosters storytelling with a combination of dance, music, singing, gesture, and movement. Yeats noted how the unusual mingling of singing and violence in KGCT and FMM outraged certain audience members: 'I remember a famous war-correspondent saying in an aggressive voice as he left the hall, "singing is a decadent art".'[22] This physical theatre allows the 'exploration of the more emotionally painful and suppressed aspects of the human psyche, including sadomasochistic sexuality and homoeroticism', as Paul Allain and Jen Harvie have observed regarding the Butoh performances of Tatsumi Hijikata.[23] In fact, Yeats's late drama was strikingly similar to what Kazuo Ohno and Hijikata named as Butoh in 1959: a dark style of performance focusing on corporeality, combining Eastern (mostly Japanese) and Western theatrical conventions, including Jean Genet's and Antonin Artaud's theatre.

As Yeats explained, KGCT was the first version of FMM.[24] By giving the Queen a speaking part and authority, Yeats rendered a more sadomasochistic undertone to FMM in which a woman and a Swineherd can both play powerful authorities. Yeats

[19] Poulain, 'Failed Collaboration', 234.

[20] Freeman, 'Turn the Beat Around', 239; Alexandra Poulain, *Irish Drama, Modernity and the Passion Play* (London: Palgrave Macmillan, 2016), 11.

[21] For discussions of SM in Irish literature see, for instance, David Cotter's *James Joyce and the Perverse Ideal* (New York: Routledge, 2003), and Michael Patrick Lapointe, *Between Irishmen: Queering Irish Literary and Cultural Nationalisms,* PhD dissertation (University of British Columbia, 2006).

[22] *VPl*, 1009.

[23] Paul Allain and Jen Harvie, *The Routledge Companion to Theatre and Performance*, 2nd edn (London and New York: Routledge, 2014), 57.

[24] *VPl*, 1311.

also delays the execution in *FMM*, whereby the Queen lets the Swineherd provoke her for a long time as if enjoying it, whereas in *KGCT* the King kills the Stroller after his first acts of defiance. SM is thus more central to *FMM* by making the passive Queen of *KGCT* an authoritative matriarch, while *KGCT* is more about the tension between the authority of the King and two oppressed bodies who join forces against him in a dance.

By mingling power/violence and *eros*, Yeats's plays reveal both the potentials and vulnerabilities of the body as well as the injustices of historical power relations, both within the Irish context and more globally. Yet such connections between the erotic and the violent are usually pathologized and condemned as ethically unacceptable.[25] Moreover, those who exercise power do not confess to the excitement they derive from it—instead, emotions/pleasure/desire tend to get excluded from the realm of power.[26] This repressive approach to the body characterized Irish nationalism's response to imperial oppression, ending up policing and sterilizing sexual behaviours, especially those of women. Irish nationalism aimed to hide the potentials and vulnerabilities of the body, marginalizing corporeality and materialism for an abstract national ideal in order to reject victimhood and imperial oppression, as '[t]he body is what renders the "Irish national character" vulnerable to imperial coercion'.[27] Yet Yeats's drama prioritizes the body, and the often sadomasochistic undertones reveal the problems with historical distributions of power in society at large, interrogating the normative forces that urge (re)production by curing disabled bodies, policing women's bodies and oppressing the voices of social outcasts.

Even though the reversibility of power inherent to SM can help raise awareness to the manipulative strategies of totalizing political ideologies or institutions, SM is still sexually marginalized and condemned as immoral both by normativity and cultural feminism, which tend to regard SM as a perpetuation of genocidal culture and a reinforcement of conventional sexual roles.[28] But Pat Califia rightly stresses that 'the flesh should not be despised', and the truth of the flesh can be represented mostly through pain.[29] As Geoff Mains notes, the practice and literary representations of SM can help people 'be more aware of the elements of dominance and submission in all relationships'.[30]

---

[25] Staci Newmahr, *Playing on the Edge: Sadomasochism, Risk, and Intimacy* (Bloomington: Indiana University Press, 2011), 126.

[26] Leo Bersani, *Homos* (Cambridge, MA, and London: Harvard University Press, 1996), 87.

[27] Harris, *Gender*, 39.

[28] Jill Dolan, *Presence and Desire: Essays on Gender, Sexuality, Performance* (Ann Arbor: University of Michigan Press, 1993), 181; Freeman, 'Turn the Beat Around', 239; Bersani, *Homos*, 84.

[29] See Dolan, *Presence and Desire*, 185.

[30] Bersani, *Homos*, 84.

SADOMASOCHISM AND
UNRULY TEMPORALITIES

'I shall embrace body and cruelty, / Desiring both as though I had made both', exclaims the Swineherd in *FMM*, who comes from the margins of society to challenge the Queen's authority and seduce power.[31] In the earlier version of the script, the Queen's reply was an acceptance of this erotic power game: 'You cannot help but yield to such desire.'[32] The Swineherd's lines identify the double desire that marks all three plays: sexual desire and the desire for power over the other.

All three plays feature non-normative temporalities and authority figures who urge fast-paced action with pressing questions and commands. These authorities aspire to dominate the bodies of characters who represent a slower, unruly temporality aimed at producing only pleasure, which is, however, worthless for power. As Freeman has observed, sexual deviants are often 'seen as creatures whose very minds had gone temporally awry' and who become '*analogies* for temporal catastrophe'. Freeman thus defines SM 'as the deployment of bodily sensations wherein the subject's "normative timing" is denaturalized and deconstructed'.[33]

In *CM*, the two beggars, especially the Lame Beggar, embody this non-normative time zone. The Blind Beggar is teasing the Lame Beggar because he is flighty and forgets things: 'Nothing stays in my head, Blind Man.'[34] Jack Halberstam has stressed that forgetting advocates for 'certain forms of erasure over memory precisely because memorialization has a tendency to tidy up disorderly histories (of slavery, the Holocaust, wars, etc.)'.[35] Halberstam highlights that memory itself is a ritual of power, as it selects what is important, so forgetting becomes 'a way of resisting the heroic and grand logics of recall and unleashes new forms of memory'.[36] This forgetfulness appears in *FMM* as well where the Swineherd claims 'my memory too is gone, / Because great solitudes have driven me mad', thus countering the fast-paced action that the Queen demands and delaying his promised song until after his beheading.[37]

The Lame Beggar also talks too much, which delays the two men reaching the Well of St Colman: 'Get up. It's too much talk you have.'[38] The two men move together on the stage: their bodies are constantly touching, as the Blind Beggar is carrying the Lame Beggar on his back. The Lame Beggar's forgetfulness and tardiness slow down the Blind Beggar and put him in a fragmented slow time, as they have been together for forty

---

[31] *CW2*, 504.
[32] *VPl*, 983.
[33] Freeman, 'Turn the Beat Around', 238, 236.
[34] *CW2*, 448.
[35] Jack Halberstam, *The Queer Art of Failure* (Durham and London: Duke University Press, 2011), 15.
[36] Ibid.
[37] *CW2*, 503.
[38] *CW2*, 446.

years. Their shared temporal dissonance is interrupted by the Saint, who speaks through the body of the First Musician and who stays invisible for most of the play. The Saint disrupts their slow and playful pace with his pressing question, 'Will you be cured or will you be blessed?'[39] The Blind Man chooses to be cured, thus accepting the homogenizing attempt of the Saint who wants to cure disabled bodies to merge them into the realm of the able-bodied, as Poulain has insightfully explored: Yeats's drama 'posits that normality is always desirable, and yearns to cure disabled bodies rather than accommodate them, physically and symbolically, within the space of social exchanges.'[40] When the Lame Beggar chooses to become blessed and as a reward gets cured as well, the Saint enjoins him with more questions, forcing him to express happiness with his new companion: 'Are you happy?', 'Haven't you got me for a friend?', 'Aren't you blessed?', 'Aren't you a miracle?'[41] These questions urge the Lame Beggar to make up his mind and begin dancing quickly; thus the flighty, slow, and disabled Lame Beggar is not only cured but also manipulated into the fast-paced temporality of the modern capitalist agenda, which tolerates only production-oriented able bodies.

This pressing normative force appears in *KGCT* as well, where the King cannot tolerate the defiant passivity of the Queen any more, and urges her to speak and act. This is also a will to pin her down, suggesting that in her passivity she is useless to society:

> A year ago you walked into this house,
> A year ago to-night. Though neither I
> Nor any man could tell your family,
> Country or name, *I put you on that throne*.
> And now before the assembled court, before
> Neighbours, attendants, courtiers, men-at-arms,
> I ask your country, name and family,
> *And not for the first time*. Why sit there
> Dumb as an image made of wood or metal,
> A screen between the living and the dead?
> All persons here assembled, and because
> They think that silence unendurable,
> Fix eyes upon you.

The King is obsessed with time and presents his authoritarianism as benevolent, stressing that he saved her and put her in a power position. Yet he expected action and transparency in exchange, which the Queen refuses to provide. She has mastery over her passivity, which is a challenge to the authority of the King. When the Stroller arrives to claim a kiss and a dance from the Queen, the King urges him in the same way: 'What is your name?' But the Stroller talks to him as his equal: 'Send for the Queen.' While in *FMM* the Swineherd's confidence is a source of excitement for the Queen, here it

---

[39] *CW2*, 449.
[40] Poulain, 'Failed Collaboration', 236.
[41] *CW2*, 453.

generates anger in the King: 'He seems a most audacious brazen man, / Not caring what he speaks of, nor to whom, / Nor where he stands.' Hence he orders his death but puts the blame on the silent Queen: 'Stand where you are! / Stand! All from the beginning has been lies, / Extravagance and lies. Who is this man? / Perhaps if you will speak, and speak the truth, / I may not kill him. What? You will not speak? / Take him, Captain of the Guard.' The King thus blames the Queen's passive (sexual) behaviour and body for the murder of the Stroller—similar to *Deirdre* (1907), where Conchubar blames Deirdre's disobedience for his execution of Naoise—but the Queen claims agency over her body. What disturbs the King is that the two dissident characters refuse to show submission and act in a very different pace from what he demands. What matters to him is fast-paced action, hence the urging: 'Do something, anything, I care not what / So that you move—but why those staring eyes?'[42]

What clashes here is also the unruly temporality of seduction and the fast-paced modern temporality of production/power/truth, and the ritual of seduction between the Stroller and the Queen destroys the King's mastery. Baudrillard called power a 'figure of anti-seduction *par excellence*', while 'seduction has no power of its own, only that of annulling the power of production.'[43] For power, seduction is useless as it does not produce anything, yet paradoxically it does produce something that destabilizes power itself. When the Queen speaks her first line, the King believes she finally obeys and demands her to sing a song of joy, yet her song draws attention to the patriarchal oppression of women's bodies: 'He longs to kill / My body, until / That sudden shudder / And limb lie still.' Since the King does not know what she means, he suspects mockery: 'I do not know the meaning of those words / That have a scornful sound.' He attempts once more to enforce action from the Queen, demanding that she mock the Stroller's severed head through dance:

> Dance, turn him into mockery with a dance!
> No woman ever had a better thought.
> All here applaud that thought. Dance, woman, dance!
> Neither so red, nor white, nor full in the breast,
> That's what he said! Dance, give him scorn for scorn,
> Display your beauty, spread your peacock tail.[44]

For the King, dance has nothing to do with pleasure: it is a tool which power can use to shame people. He wants the Queen to dance with a specific political purpose—that is the only way dance (and the arts) makes sense to power. What happens here is similar to what Poulain has discerned with regard to *CM*, where queer disabled bodies challenge the production-oriented ethos of bourgeois capitalism through 'an alternative paradigm of failed collaboration as unproductive, highly successful *jouissance*'.[45]

---

[42] *CW2*, 494–7.
[43] Jean Baudrillard, *Seduction*, trans. Brian Singer (Montreal: New World Perspectives, 2001), 15.
[44] *CW2*, 498.
[45] Poulain, 'Failed Collaboration', 239.

The Queen is not only unproductive in the eyes of power but defies conventional attractiveness, which, however, the Stroller applauds. As Newmahr has explained, 'particular SM-related traits often trump conventional attractiveness as social currency'.[46] The Stroller had an image of the Queen's beauty, yet when he sees her, he notes, 'Neither so red, nor white, nor full in the breast / As I had thought. What matter for all that / So long as I proclaim her everywhere / Most beautiful!'[47] This implies a more fluid approach to femininity, but since the King regards her as his possession, he is deeply insulted by the remark and uses it as a justification for his murder of the defiant Stroller.

Instead of helping the King, the Queen joins forces with the Stroller to scorn him, which resonates with Foucault's idea that 'the most intense point of a life, the point where its energy is concentrated, is where it comes up against power, struggles with it, attempts to use its forces and to evade its traps'.[48] The Queen's dance with the head upon her shoulder confuses the King's reality, especially when the First Attendant begins singing as Head. The gesture of placing the head on her shoulder draws a parallel between the Stroller's murder and the abuse of the Queen's body by the King. Similar to the Queen's song, the Head sings about people who feel they have prerogative over certain bodies: 'All those living wretches crave / Prerogatives of the dead that have / Sprung heroic from the grave.' When the Queen kisses the Head, the King, disturbed by this strange attachment, threatens them with physical violence, yet the ritual of seduction is so powerful that he kneels instead of striking, 'laying the sword at her feet'.[49] The Queen thus employs the strategy demanded by the King, but turns it against him.

SWITCHING, SURPRISE, RESTRAINT

The three plays' sadomasochistic dynamics are also maintained by various moments of surprise, the possibility of the oppressed to turn against the oppressors: 'the unexpected element, the *switching* ... which takes the participants by surprise'.[50] Bersani also stresses that the most radical trait of SM is the prioritization of pleasure over power: 'the shocking revelation that, for the sake of that stimulation, human beings may be willing to give up control over their environment.'[51]

The asymmetrical attachments of the three plays appear symmetrical within their asymmetry, as the characters always tease each other mutually, and this reciprocity of insult and manipulation is a sign of mutual attraction towards the other's body. Sadomasochistic power relations in Yeats's late drama also forge a clash between what

---

[46] Newmahr, *Playing on the Edge*, 26.
[47] *CW2*, 495.
[48] Foucault, 'Lives of Infamous Men', 161–2.
[49] *CW2*, 498.
[50] Lynda Hart, quoted in Freeman, 'Turn the Beat Around', 247.
[51] Bersani, *Homos*, 95.

Jean Baudrillard called artificial power and real power. Artificial power is associated with seduction in Baudrillard, which 'is stronger than power because it is reversible and mortal, while power, like value, seeks to be irreversible, cumulative and immortal'.[52] SM is therefore pure theatre, which reveals that power too is reversible and that there is no difference 'between those who enforce power and those who submit to it'.[53] In fact, reversibility connects masochism and sadism: 'When the masochist gets his partner to humiliate him, it is ultimately the partner who is being humiliated by the masochist. From this perspective, masochism can be seen as a subtle form of sadism in which the roles are ironically inverted'.[54]

CM and *FMM* display such unexpected yet delectable changes of agency. In the Blind Beggar–Lame Beggar relationship, the Blind Beggar appears as the domineering party even though he occupies the bottom position carrying his partner on his back. Yet the Lame Beggar talks back and steals from his companion, thus refusing submission. When the Blind Beggar accuses him of leading him in the wrong direction, the Lame Beggar retorts: 'I have brought you the right way, but you are a lazy man, Blind Man, and you make very short strides.' Yet the Blind Beggar's resistance to his partner's mastery is also what revivifies their playful dialogue: 'It's great daring you have, and how could I make a long stride and you on my back from the peep o' day?' When the Lame Beggar starts talking back, their body position changes as the two men stand next to each other suggesting a more even distribution of mastery. When he gets up his companion's back again, he continues teasing the Blind Beggar, who punishes him by pinching his leg: 'But as I was saying, he being a lazy man—O, O, O, stop pinching the calf of my leg.'

The possibility of physical violence that can strike the Lame Beggar anytime appears, paradoxically, an exciting possibility: 'If I speak out all that's in my mind you won't take a blow at me at all?' Anytime the Lame Beggar contradicts him, he threatens him with his stick: 'Is it contradicting me you are? Are you in reach of my arm? [*swinging stick*].' The Lame Beggar's answers suggest an enjoyment of the anger raised in his partner, which he pushes further: 'I'm not, Blind Man, you couldn't touch me at all; but as I was saying—'.[55] Newmahr highlights the importance of such acts of pseudo-violence in sadomasochistic dynamics: it means overwhelming the other by demonstrating that they could hurt them, but the participants are not necessarily fearful or tense, like the two beggars, whose playful dialogue suggests that they play with the possibility of violence as a source of excitement.[56]

But the Saint's abrupt interruption ends their relationship, as he longs for a companion to experience the pleasure of domination. His voice makes both beggars kneel, as they feel they need to show submission to this disembodied voice of power. He offers

---

[52] Baudrillard, *Seduction*, 46

[53] Jean Baudrillard, *Forget Foucault*, Trans. Nicola Dufresne (Los Angeles: Semiotext(e), 2007), 51.

[54] Sergio Benvenuto, *What are Perversions? Sexuality, Ethics, Psychoanalysis* (London: Karnac, 2016), 61.

[55] *CW2*, 446–9.

[56] Newmahr, *Playing on the Edge*, 129.

a partnership proposal first to the Blind Beggar, whereby he reveals his vulnerable side pretending powerlessness: 'I am saint and lonely. Will you become blessed and stay blind and we will be together always?'[57] When the Blind Beggar refuses him, the Saint turns directly to the Lame Beggar, who accepts the companionship. The Lame Beggar aspires to become blessed so that his name would feature in a book, which is also a wish for authority. As Poulain has discerned, this proposal 'mimes the diction of wedding vows', which is later consummated by the symbolic physical union of the Lame Beggar and the Saint.[58]

In order to get full mastery over the Lame Beggar, the Saint pushes the beggars' relationship towards physical violence, which he enjoys as he starts laughing: 'there he is in front of you and he laughing out of his wrinkled face.' When he is cured, the Blind Beggar catches sight of the skin of his black sheep on the Lame Beggar's back, which proves that while he thought he had mastery over him, the Lame Beggar was deceiving him. The Lame Beggar's attitude also changes towards his former companion, as being blessed gives him a sense of power, so when the Blind Beggar accuses him of being flighty, he proudly replies: 'I am that flighty. [*Cheering up.*] But am I not blessed and it's a sin to speak against the blessed?' When the Blind Beggar threatens him with 'I shall know where to hit', the Lame Beggar becomes more authoritarian and at the same time protective: 'Don't lay a hand on me. Forty years we've been knocking about the roads together, and I wouldn't have you bring your soul to mortal peril.'[59] But the Blind Beggar starts beating him, which turns into a fragmented, clumsy dance, which will be countered by the fast-paced dance of the Lame Beggar–Saint formation at the end of the play. While the two beggars accepted each other's respective bodily marginality for forty years, this normative force only tolerates the Lame Beggar as submissive and able-bodied. The Saint soon becomes domineering: he enjoins the Lame Beggar to bend his back so that he could get up, then to bless the road they follow and to dance, thus obtaining full mastery. This relationship is no longer about playful teasing, but the Saint's pleasure of domination over the Lame Beggar's body.

The two beggars' bond is mirrored in the subtextual holy man–old lecher relationship which refers to Edward Martyn's and George Moore's homosocial friendship, as Yeats explains in his notes to the play.[60] The old lecher is 'telling over all the sins he committed, or maybe never committed at all, and the man of Laban does be trying to head him off and quiet him down that he may quit telling them'. Yet the holy man also derives a secret excitement from the old lecher's stories of sexual exploits: 'He wouldn't have him different, no, not if he was to get all Ireland.' In the earlier 1924 version, Yeats included an explicit reference to the romantic nature of their relationship: 'Did you ever know a holy man but had a wicked man for his comrade and his heart's darling?' The equally subtextual relationship between the cat Minnaloushe and the moon—which opens and

---

[57] CW2, 449.
[58] Poulain, 'Failed Collaboration', 237.
[59] CW2, 450–2.
[60] VPl, 808.

closes the play as a song—also implies reversible mastery: the moon manipulates the movements of the cat, whose eyes change according to the phases of the moon, yet the moon might also be willing to give up his mastery: 'Maybe the moon may learn, / Tired of that courtly fashion, / A new dance turn.'[61]

In *FMM*, the surprise element lies in the Swineherd's restraint and defiance: he refuses to praise the Queen's beauty, to sing when the Queen demands it, and rejects submission towards her authority. This restraint is part of the symbols of pain in sadomasochistic relationships, and it is able to generate excitement.[62] The Queen is visibly bored at the beginning of the play: 'Some man has come, some terrifying man, / For I have yawned and stretched myself three times.' What differentiates her authority from *KGCT*'s patriarch is that for her pleasure is more important than truth and production. She merges the realm of politics with pleasure: 'I and my heart decide. We say that song is best that moves us most. No song has moved us yet.' Even though the Swineherd admits he comes from the margins of society and wonders if disabled people can succeed as well ('But what if some blind aged cripple sing / Better than wholesome men?'), the Queen allows him to participate regardless of his background or bodily ability. Yet he speaks to the Queen as her equal and expresses his wish to obtain power: 'And they say / The kingdom is added to the gift.' He uses imperative mode and enjoins the Queen to observe his body carefully: 'Queen, look at me, look long at those foul rags, / At hair more foul and ragged than my rags; / Look on my scratched foul flesh.' This is also an attempt to direct power's attention to the truth of marginalized bodies manifested through the pain of the flesh, thus claiming visibility through the gaze of power.

The Swineherd's attempt to dominate the conversation enrages the Queen, hence she delivers a verbal power demonstration:

> Remember through what perils you have come;
> That I am crueller than solitude,
> Forest or beast. Some I have killed or maimed
> Because their singing put me in a rage,
> And some because they came at all. Men hold
> That woman's beauty is a kindly thing,
> But they that call me cruel speak the truth,
> Cruel as the Winter of Virginity.
> But for a reason I cannot guess
> I would not harm you. Go before I change.
> Why do you stand, your chin upon your breast?

This passage also expresses the Queen's sympathy for the Swineherd; she is both authoritarian and nurturing. But instead of leaving, he depicts their marriage night, positing himself in a position of mastery: 'What gives you that strange confidence? What makes /

---

[61] *CW2*, 446.
[62] Dolan, *Presence and Desire*, 182.

You think that you can move my heart and me?' The Swineherd's answer implies that the Queen has no power over him at all: 'Because I look upon you without fear.' This confidence is both enraging and attractive for the Queen, who, instead of sending him away, demands that he praise her in a song. Yet, to her surprise, the man who has come to seduce her still refuses to do so: 'I tended swine, when I first heard your name. / I rolled among the dung of swine and laughed. / What do I know of beauty?' She demands once again: 'Sing the best / And you are not swineherd, but a king.'[63] Yet he ignores both the Queen's body and power, even though he claimed to come for both: '[*Snapping his fingers*] That for kingdoms!'[64] This is a 'show of rejection' which is in fact 'a *mise-en-scène* directed by the masochist himself' aimed at provoking his own humiliation and through that the humiliation of the other, and this shared defeat of the other causes mutual pleasure as the final erotic dance scene will demonstrate.[65]

The more defiant the Swineherd becomes, the more attraction the Queen expresses towards him, so, instead of punishing him, she promises him her own power: 'I leave this corridor, this ancient house, / A famous throne, the reverence of servants— / What do I gain?' Both characters appear as masochists, longing to experience pain and humiliation. Even though the Queen leaves the throne, which seems like an act of submission, she suddenly regains her mastery and threatens to punish him: 'he came hither not to sing but to heap / Complexities of insult upon my head.' Even when he offers the expected song, he implies that whatever he sings about her beauty will be nonsense: 'But first my song—what nonsense shall I sing?' The Swineherd continues to play with power, goes upstage, and asks defiantly, 'Why should I ask? / What do those features matter?' With his confidence, defiance, and free movement on stage, the Swineherd makes the Queen's power and space his own, ridiculing her authority. He laughs at her and brings up an enigmatic, violent story from the past about a woman who bathed in blood, 'the blood begat', and conceived a child in her sleep.[66] This makes the Queen drop her veil, which seems like an act of submission, but this is when the Swineherd is beheaded off-stage. The Swineherd dares the Queen to hurt him, but with this he punishes the Queen; as Benvenuto writes, 'masochism is a form of protest against the other . . . . Masochism is actually a 'do it yourself' way of punishing the other.'[67] The Swineherd's mastery over his own passivity (his persistent disobedience) becomes a way of mastering authority, which the Queen also achieved in *KGCT*, aptly articulating what Benvenuto describes: 'As in the case of an artist who creates a representation of his own failure, it is in the active representation of the masochist's abjection that his mastery prevails.'[68]

The surprise continues when the Swineherd's head begins to sing after the beheading. The Queen symbolically conveys authority to the Head by lifting it above her head while dancing, then laying it upon her throne and expressing regret for her

[63] *VPl* 502–5.
[64] *CW*2, 983.
[65] Benvenuto, *What are Perversions?*, 61
[66] *CW*2, 502–5.
[67] Benvenuto, *What are Perversions?*, 61.
[68] Benvenuto, *What are Perversions?*, 64

'virgin cruelty': 'I did you wrong.' The sadomasochistic dynamics go on, as the Queen enjoins the Head to sing specifically for her: 'She is waiting for his song', but what she receives is laughter as the Second Attendant laughs as Head. When the Head eventually sings, the song itself suggests a mixture of violence and desire: 'Jill murdered Jack. / Jack had a hollow heart, for Jill / Had hung his heart on high.' The Queen starts dancing to the song, moving away from the Head, 'alluring and refusing', performing the sadomasochistic dynamics of their relationship. She begins laughing and singing, emulating the Swineherd, but the Second Attendant does not understand how violence and love can coexist like this: 'She is laughing. How can she laugh, / Loving the head?' The final phase of the dance reads as a consummation of this violent relationship marked by restraint and attraction: she presses her lips to the lips of the head, her body shivers to very rapid drum taps, then the drum taps cease, and she sinks slowly down, holding the head to her breast.[69] What happens here is an eroticization of unpleasant experiences (the insults of the Swineherd and the traumatic story he brought up before his death), which Benvenuto has identified as one of the main traits of masochism, which 'is also a strategy for deriving pleasure from something that was once extremely unpleasant'.[70]

CONCLUSIONS

The three plays I have discussed above demonstrate that the reversibility of normative distributions of power imbued with pleasure, violence, and playfulness lies at the centre of Yeats's late drama. Such representations reveal the injustices behind conventional power roles and the manipulative strategies of normativity, capitalism, and patriarchy, which aim to oppress everyone who defies their power. Thanks to the element of playful reversibility, the plays portray power as fragile, constructed, performable, and thus destroyable. In the words of Jill Dolan, the importance and the power of sadomasochistic representations in theatre lie in their potential 'to explode the old images of gender and sexuality and to test the limits of what can be seen'.[71] By staging bodies that access the pleasures and truths of the flesh through pain, 'theatre can present the explicit danger of the visual and ... discomfort prompted by looking, forc[ing] people to define morality that keeps them from seeing', which Yeats achieves by representing disturbing, erotic-violent bonds which would otherwise be denied visibility.

[69] CW2, 507–8.
[70] Benvenuto, *What are Perversions?*, 64.
[71] Dolan, *Presence and Desire*, 186.

CHAPTER 35

....

PLAYING YEATS

....

PATRICK LONERGAN

WRITING in 1991, Garry Hynes justified the decision to stage a season of Yeats's plays at the Abbey Theatre by describing him as 'Ireland's foremost avant garde playwright'—as an artist whose work needed to be seen again, 'not because we are sure of its place in the repertoire of modern theatre, but because we are not'. That uncertainty was unlikely to be resolved any time soon, Hynes thought: not until 'methods of performance and reception' adequate to his work were discovered.[1]

Yeats would probably have welcomed the suggestion that his plays' insecure reputation might be due to actors and audiences rather than any flaws in the work itself—but, viewed with the benefit of hindsight, Hynes's remarks might now seem generous, if not inaccurate. She made them in an introduction to the third annual W. B. Yeats Festival, a series that presented fifteen of his plays between 1989 and 1993, and which aimed to answer affirmatively those lingering questions about Yeats's position in the repertoire. But his subsequent production history offers its own verdict: after the final festival in 1993, the Abbey staged a full production of a Yeats play only once more—in 2004 (the theatre's centenary), when *Purgatory* appeared on a triple bill with George Fitzmaurice's *The Dandy Dolls* and Synge's *Riders to the Sea*.

Yet, as Hynes implied, questions about Yeats's place in modern theatre had been asked many times before. At the Abbey itself, his dramas were staged at least once every decade from his death in 1939 until the 1990s—often in productions by emerging directors who wanted to demonstrate their own originality by proving Yeats's stageworthiness. He also inspired the development of two of Ireland's other major theatres, the Gate and the Lyric; and his influence upon less well-known companies is also readily detectable. Yeats's plays have brought many Irish companies to international attention: among the first Irish productions at the Edinburgh Festival were performances of Yeats's drama by recent graduates of Trinity College Dublin in 1956, and, more than fifty years later, the

---

[1] Abbey Theatre Digital Archive at University of Galway (henceforth ATDA). 0810_MPG_01, 6. All Abbey production information is taken from this archive. Garry Hynes was Artistic Director of the Abbey from 1991-93.

Sligo-based theatre company Blue Raincoat gained similar recognition when its version of *On Baile's Strand* was performed on the beach at Coney Island.[2] His plays have regularly appeared in university productions across the United States, and have inspired adaptations into other art forms, often in languages other than English.[3] *The Countess Cathleen*, for example, became the opera *Irische Legende*, which was composed by Werner Egk for a premiere at the Salzburg Festival in 1955; and in 2010 the Paris-based Compagnie du Samovar staged an adaptation of Yeats's 1904 play *The Shadowy Waters* as *Les Eaux d'Ombre*, blending dance, theatre, and spectacle while seeking to remain faithful to the original's status as a dramatic poem.

In summary, it might be tempting to conclude that if there is a tradition of staging Yeats's plays, it is one in which successive generations discover his work as if no one has ever done so before: the plays are performed, sometimes with reverence but often with a healthily iconoclastic commitment to experimentation; they are well received, prompting questions about why they are not better appreciated—and then they are forgotten, until the pattern begins again. The purpose of this chapter, therefore, is not just to trace the production history of Yeats's drama but also to consider why those isolated moments have never coalesced into a distinctive tradition.

Yeats would surely have been disappointed by his plays' invisibility in the modern repertoire—but he might not have been surprised by it. As early as 1913, he had displayed some anxiety about 'the connection of my work ... with the history of the stage', telling Lady Gregory that a proposed London production of *On Baile's Strand* by Florence Darragh might place his reputation on a more certain footing.[4] A decade later, his Nobel Prize lecture displayed a similar desire to highlight his status as a playwright: he claimed that he wanted to celebrate the contributions to the Irish dramatic movement of many 'known and unknown persons', but (as some of those mentioned in the speech later complained) he was also rewriting history so as to assert his own centrality.[5] Even in his final volumes of poetry, he remained keen to remind readers of his work for the theatre, a theme explored in 'the Circus Animals Desertion', 'The Municipal Gallery Revisited', and—now notoriously, due to its claim that *Kathleen ni Houlihan* sent out 'Certain men the English shot' in 1916—'Man and the Echo'.[6]

But perhaps it may be true for Yeats (as for many other modern dramatists, from Chekhov to Beckett and beyond) that his successes were often determined by the quality of his collaborations with others. That was evident from an early stage in his career as a dramatist—revealingly so in the contrasting reception to the premieres of *Diarmuid and Grainne* in 1901 and *Kathleen ni Houlihan* the following year. Both plays were

---

[2] Patrick Lonergan, 'Feast and Celebration', in Nicholas Grene and Christopher Morash, eds., *The Oxford Handbook of Modern Irish Theatre* (Oxford: Oxford University Press, 2017), 637–53, 651.

[3] James W. Flannery, *W.B. Yeats and the Idea of a Theatre* (New Haven: Yale University Press, 1976), 374–7.

[4] WBY to Lady Gregory [18 March 1913], *CL Intelex* #2186.

[5] *CW3*, 410. For the reactions of the Fays see *Life 1*, 378; for Gregory see Judith Hill, *Lady Gregory: An Irish Life* (Dublin: Collins Press, 2011), loc. 7667 (e-book).

[6] *CW1*, 345.

co-written, the former in a tempestuous but openly acknowledged arrangement with George Moore, and the latter in a mostly harmonious partnership with Lady Gregory that Yeats never publicly admitted to (he continued to take sole credit for the play's authorship right up to 'Man and the Echo' in 1939, where it is described rather pointedly as 'that play of mine').[7] *Diarmuid and Grainne* appeared before hundreds of people at the sumptuous Gaiety Theatre; *Kathleen* was staged in a temperance hall, its performance punctuated by the noise of billiard balls from an adjoining room, on a stage so cramped that actors waiting in the wings were terrified to move for fear of knocking over the set.[8] *Diarmuid and Grainne* has an action-filled plot about characters well known from Irish legend; it also featured well-known professional actors. But *Kathleen ni Houlihan* was performed by amateurs and is dramatically inert, with almost all of its consequential action happening offstage. The fact that *Kathleen* is celebrated while *Diarmuid and Grainne* has been mostly forgotten owes much to the people that Yeats worked with on each production.

Diarmuid and Grainne was staged during the third season of the Irish Literary Theatre, and was performed by the company of Frank Benson, the distinguished Shakespearean actor whose popularity with Dublin audiences, it was hoped, would attract large numbers to the Gaiety. That proved a miscalculation. Staging a new Irish play with English performers was always going to be a provocation for some sections of the Dublin audience, but it was also a bad decision on theatrical grounds: the English actors simply could not pronounce their characters' names and seemed generally ill at ease with the material. Even before the play opened, Yeats knew that there were problems: visiting a rehearsal (directed by Moore), he declared to the company that 'the only sensible creature on the stage' was a live goat that Benson was supposed to carry on (moments later, the animal was seen eating some props).[9] James Moran has argued that the production was not quite as catastrophic as is now believed, and Joseph Holloway did record a general attitude that was 'favourable if not enthusiastic'.[10] The production would also prove important for scholars of music, who have shown some interest in the incidental compositions for it by Elgar (later published as his op. 42, *Grania and Diarmid*). Even so, the fact that the play went unpublished until 1951 and was never revived by the Abbey tells its own story.

Kathleen ni Houlihan had none of the advantages of *Diarmuid and Grainne*, yet it appeared at the Abbey 233 times between 1904 and 2010 and has frequently been anthologized.[11] The performance in the lead role by Maud Gonne undoubtedly accounts

---

[7] Thanks to James Pethica's scholarship, Lady Gregory's co-authorship of *Kathleen* is no longer disputed. But it was apparently an open secret in Dublin during Yeats's lifetime: George Moore alluded to it in 1914 in *Salve – Hail and Farewell* (Gerrards Cross: C. Smythe, 1976), 328.

[8] Maire Nic Shuibhlaigh, *The Splendid Years* (Dublin: New Island, 2016), loc. 1352 (e-book); Joseph Holloway, *Impressions of a Dublin Playgoer* (Carbondale: Southern Illinois University Press, 1967), 16

[9] *CW2*, 927.

[10] James Moran, 'Avon Calling: The Influence of Frank Benson on the Irish Theatre', *Irish University Review*, 42:2 (2012), 217–35. See also Holloway, Impressions, 15.

[11] Figures are from Abbey Theatre Digital Archive. No other Yeats play comes near to matching this number.

to some extent for the legendary status of its opening night—but its success must also be attributed to the inclusion in the cast of the performers who later went on to develop the acting style of the early Abbey. One of the people who fought alongside those 'men the English shot' in 1916 was the actress Máire Nic Shiubhlaigh, but in 1902 she was playing the role of Delia in *Kathleen* (she later played the title role twenty-six times at the Abbey, including in its 1904 opening night). Also in the 1902 cast was Willie Fay, who co-directed the play with his brother Frank. Yeats had been inspired to give the play to the Fays when he saw them in Alice Milligan's *Red Hugh* in 1901; their ability to deliver verse in their own Dublin accents so excited him that he came away with 'my head on fire'.[12] As director of the Irish National Dramatic Society, Frank developed performance techniques that were (at least initially) attuned to Yeats's intentions, and which were also a reaction against the style of acting that English actor-managers such as Benson had popularized.[13]

The Fays proved important interpreters of Yeats's drama, doing much to determine the production and reception of his early Abbey plays. Yeats was aware of their importance, telling Willie that his performance in *On Baile's Strand* in 1904 had been a 'masterpiece'.[14] But among Yeats's many talents was a prodigious gift for alienating actors. Nic Shiubhlaigh and others seceded from the Abbey to establish the Theatre of Ireland in 1906 (she returned four years later), but when the Fays departed at the end of 1907, the break was more severe: Willie never came back, and Frank appeared only in a handful of productions between 1917 and 1925—a huge loss for all concerned. It tells us much that, after the Fays' departure, Yeats declared an intention to take exclusive responsibility for tragic and romantic drama at the Abbey—but that no discernible improvement in the company's abilities, or their audiences' interests, occurred. If Yeats's attitude seems redolent of the proverbial bad carpenter who blames his own tools, Frank did not much help his case: in November 1907 he fell asleep on stage during a performance of *The Unicorn from the Stars*, another play that Yeats co-authored with Gregory (though here her contribution was publicly acknowledged).

It is perhaps ironic that, having seen off the Fays due to a belief that his plays were being ill-served, Yeats's interest in writing verse drama for the Abbey began to diminish. One explanation might be his deepening awareness of other elements of theatre, including scenography. As Ben Levitas remarks, Yeats's embrace of Gordon Craig's ideas about lighting suggests an intention to 'redeploy his creative energies' into new areas from 1910 onwards.[15] Craig had donated several of his screens to the Abbey in 1909, and they became the focus of much Yeatsian experimentation, including a rewritten version of *Deirdre* and a new production of *The Hour Glass* in 1911 that appeared alongside Gregory's *The Deliverer*. Craig's screens involved the use of projected light to create

---

[12] *CW3*, 331.
[13] Frank J. Fay, *Towards a National Theatre* (Dublin: Dolmen Press, 1970), 87–8; Eglantina Remport, *Lady Gregory and Irish National Theatre* (London: Palgrave Macmillan, 2018), 128–31.
[14] To W. G. Fay, 13 August [1906], *Unpublished Letters (1905–1939)* (accessed 12 November 2019).
[15] Ben Levitas, *The Theatre of Nation* (Oxford: Oxford University Press, 2002), 191.

mood, and thus marked a shift away from painted backdrops and colourful costuming—and although Craig's style of aesthetic representation is now so often used within the theatre as to be unremarkable, it failed to impress the Dublin audiences of 1911. Craig's 'freak scenery and lighting' was an 'affected failure', wrote Holloway, who saw it as being in no 'way an improvement on the old methods'.[16] Craig would later express regret that Yeats 'went off the rails "looking at the moon"'—but the screens continued to be used at the Abbey for many years.[17]

After 1911, Yeats experienced what Roy Foster describes as a 'wider disillusionment with theatrical forms'.[18] His ongoing difficulty in writing *The Player Queen* (begun in 1907 but not premiered until 1919) provides evidence of that disenchantment—but, as ever with Yeats, the negativity was also turned to constructive use, resulting in a 1916 collaboration with Edmund Dulac and Michio Ito on *At the Hawk's Well*. That play was premiered not at the Abbey but in the London drawing room of Lady Cunard. 'An elite audience was a requirement rather than disadvantage' for the play, notes Foster, implying (accurately) that it would not have found a responsive Dublin audience at that time.[19] However, it did eventually find its way to the Abbey in 1929, when it was staged in the newly opened experimental Peacock space, as part of a trilogy that also included *On Baile's Strand* and *The Only Jealousy of Emer*, now collectively entitled *Fighting the Waves*. That production was choreographed by Ninette de Valois, later to become 'one of the most powerful people in the world in international classical ballet' as the founder of the English Royal Ballet.[20] In Yeats's relationship with her, we again find evidence of his collaborations working best when conducted with people who were accomplished artists in fields other than his own.[21]

But for the most part Lennox Robinson took responsibility for directing Yeats's plays from 1910 onwards, including *The Player Queen*, his two adaptations of Sophocles in 1926 and 1927, and *The Words Upon the Window Pane* (1930). In an essay published shortly after Yeats's death (and thus possibly guilty of some hagiography) Robinson described Yeats's occasional visits to the rehearsal room as 'a joy and an inspiration':

> He would spend half an hour on getting some movement or piece of 'business' to his liking, would cry out in a passion – never in temper – at some clumsiness of mine or on the part of the players ... He brought to bear on the play an instinct and an intelligence vastly superior to our own. He was completely lucid in his explanation of what

---

[16] Holloway, *Impressions*, 148

[17] For Craig's comment, see Michael Holroyd, *A Strange Eventful History* (London: Farrar, Straus and Giroux, 2010), 433.

[18] *Life 2*, 34.

[19] *Life 2*, 35

[20] Elizabeth Schafer, 'An Irish Jig? – Edris Stannus, Ninette de Valois and the English Royal Ballet', in Richard Cave and Ben Levitas, eds., *Irish Theatre in England* (Dublin: Carysfort, 2008), 143.

[21] As discussed in Aoife McGrath's *Dance Theatre in Ireland* (Basingstoke: Palgrave Macmillan, 2013), 47–50.

he wanted, but he nearly always demanded something beyond our capacity and he would patiently try in this way and that way to attain his desired result.[22]

Robinson is not being insincere here, but there does seem to be rather a lot of subtext in this passage. Yeats's presence may indeed have been inspirational, but it must also have been inhibiting—as implied by Robinson's allusions to his moments of 'passion', the excessive time spent on stage business, and the suggestion that Yeats's demands persistently went beyond the company's abilities (which is usually the characteristic of a bad director).

It is also noteworthy that Robinson claims that Yeats rarely gave the actors instruction on verse-speaking—perhaps because he lacked confidence in their abilities to perform it. Writing many years later, Micheál Mac Liammóir offered an explanation for the Abbey's difficulties with verse: 'Look through the long list of the names of players the Abbey has made or helped to make famous ... and you find that they are not romantics, nor symbolists, nor stylists, but realists ... And this, it may be, is one of the Abbey's tragedies.'[23] That assessment is supported by the fact that the most frequently revived of Yeats's late plays was *The Words Upon the Window Pane*, a drama well suited to the realistic acting style of the Abbey company. Documents in the Abbey archive show that it was performed on a set indistinguishable from most Abbey plays of its era, featuring a drawing room with windows and a door, and curtains and furnishing that were somewhere between shabby and genteel. And indeed, as evident from a furniture plot for a 1960s production of the play (probably designed by Tomas Mac Anna, that style of representation remained for decades. (See Figure 35.1.)[24]

But by the 1930s much of the experimental energy in Irish theatre was to be found not at the Abbey but the Gate. Histories of that theatre tend to emphasize its differences from the Abbey—to see it as the 'Sodom' to the Abbey's 'Begorrah', as the Dublin wags of the 1930s had it. That approach is understandable: after all, the title of the Gate's first new Irish play—Denis Johnston's *The Old Lady Says No!* (1929)—was a defiantly mocking response to its rejection by the Abbey (the eponymous 'old lady' was widely understood to be Lady Gregory, but might just as easily have been the theatre itself). And many of those who supported the Gate made a point of distancing themselves from Yeats and Gregory. As Elaine Sisson has documented, one of its four co-founders (with Hilton Edwards, Micheál Mac Liammóir and the actor Gearóid Ó Lochlainn) was Madame 'Toto' Bannard Cogley—a figure whose late-night cabarets featured a send-up of Yeats's speech to the rioters at the premiere of the *Plough and the Stars* (1926), his 'you have disgraced yourselves again' being gleefully caricatured.[25]

---

[22] E. H. Mikhail, *WB Yeats: Interviews and Recollections II* (London: Macmillan, 1977), 257.

[23] Micheál MacLiammóir, *Theatre in Ireland* (Dublin: CRC, 1950), 16–17.

[24] Production information is from ATDA, 1346_SM_0001. Thanks to Abbey archivist Mairead Delaney for information about *Words upon the Window Pane*.

[25] Elaine Sisson, 'Experiment and the Free State', in David Clare, Des Lally, and Patrick Lonergan, eds., *The Gate Theatre, Dublin: Inspiration and Craft* (Oxford: Lang, 2018), 11–28.

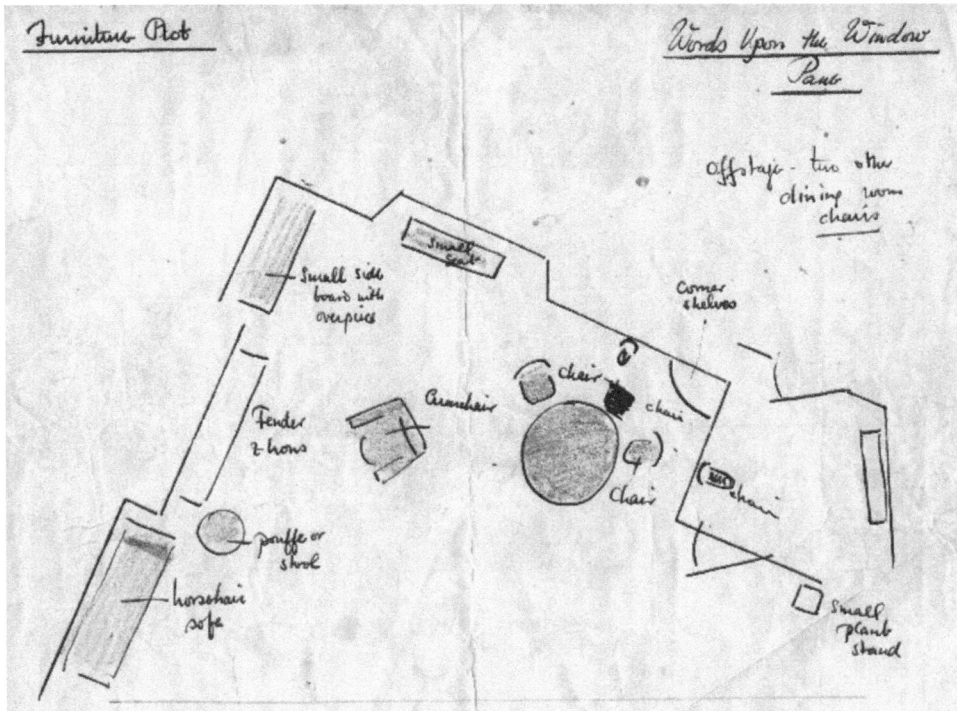

FIGURE 35.1 Furniture plot for *The Words Upon the Window Pane* by W. B. Yeats, directed and designed by Tómas Mac Anna, Abbey Theatre at the Queen's Theatre, 1960; reproduced courtesy of Abbey Theatre Archive.

Yet, unlike many of his peers, Mac Liammóir's attitude to Yeats was characterized more by emulation than mockery. The two met for the first time in 1929, at Lady Gregory's suggestion: Yeats chided the younger man for arriving late but told him that he was 'a magnificent actor' (Mac Liammóir struggled not to weep in response).[26] In 1933, Mac Liammóir showed that the Gate too could be a home for drama based on Irish mythology, when he staged a translation of his own *Diarmuid agus Gráinne*, a play originally written for the national Irish-language theatre An Taibhdhearc. And, in 1940, he wrote *Where Stars Walk*, an original drama that, as Ruud van den Beuken notes, derives its title from Yeats's *The Land of Heart's Desire* (1894).[27] An attempt to both preserve and build upon Yeats's legacy only a year after his death, it was the only original drama presented at the Gate during the Second World War—and it was popular, being revived in 1942 and 1945.

[26] Micheál Mac Liammóir, *All for Hecuba* (Dublin: Progress House, 1960), 69.
[27] Ruud van den Beuken, 'Ancient Ireland Comes to Rathmines', in Clare et al., *Gate Theatre Dublin*, 47–62.

FIGURE 35.2 Micheál Mac Liammóir in *The Countess Cathleen,* 1953, reproduced courtesy of Gate Theatre Digital Archive.

Mac Liammóir's identification with Yeats deepened substantially during later decades. In a 1953 Gate production of *The Countess Cathleen*, he took the role of Aileel, an early Yeatsian alter ego. As revealed in a production image from the Gate's digital archive (see Figure 35.2), [28] Mac Liammóir was attempting not just to play the character but also to channel its author: there is more than a passing resemblance to several portraits of Yeats from the 1890s in Mac Liammóir's hairstyle, stance, and facial expression.

That identification became more direct as Mac Liammóir began to perform *as* Yeats, first in his one-man show *I Must be Talking to My Friends* (1963) and then in *Talking About Yeats* (1965). That pattern of moving from staging Yeats's plays to playing him as a character would be followed by other Irish theatres, as we will see below.

But the major interpreter of Yeats's drama after his death was not Mac Liammóir but Mary O'Malley, whose Lyric Theatre produced all of his plays during a thirty-year period, beginning with *At the Hawk's Well* in its 1951 opening season. [29] Yeats's drama

[28] Gate Theatre Digital Archive at University of Galway, 1877_PH_0001, 1. Gate production information is from this archive.
[29] Lyric production information is from the Lyric/O'Malley archive at University of Galway and the Lyric papers at the Burns Library, Boston College.

was a personal passion for O'Malley, but she also believed that an immersion in his work would allow actors to develop skills that could be employed across a range of theatrical forms: 'if you can act Yeats, you can act anything', she told her company.[30] The theatre of Yeats thus had an enormous impact upon the development of professional acting, directing, and design in Northern Ireland.

Originally from Cork, O'Malley moved to Belfast with her husband, Pearse, in 1948. She had been involved with Austin Clarke's Dublin-based Lyric Players, a group founded in 1944 to promote verse drama. Inspired by Clarke's example, O'Malley founded her own Lyric Players theatre in 1951, with the aim of creating 'a style suitable for dramatic poetry'.[31] Working with an amateur company in a makeshift theatre, first in her husband's surgery and then in their home in Derryvolgie Avenue, Belfast, O'Malley staged more than a dozen of Yeats's plays during the Lyric's first decade. Her success in doing so led to the formation of a professional company in 1960, followed by the opening of a dedicated theatre space in 1968—by which time the Lyric was firmly established as Northern Ireland's major repertory theatre.

There had been attempts to stage Yeats in Belfast before O'Malley, notably by the Ulster Literary Theatre (ULT)—the origins of which lie in an attempt to produce *Kathleen ni Houlihan* in 1902. As Ophelia Byrne explains, its directors expected 'to gain the support of the National Theatre Society in Dublin [and] found most of their Dublin counterparts "most cordial and helpful". Yeats however proved "haughty and aloof"', much to their disappointment.[32] The ULT did eventually stage *Kathleen*, but Yeats's hostility provoked them into developing original work: 'damn Yeats, we'll write our own plays', they declared.[33] In a similar but more constructive fashion, the Lyric's productions of Yeats operated as a kind of bedrock that supported the development of other forms of drama.[34]

O'Malley's productions tended to follow Yeats's originals faithfully. In Figure 35.3 we see masks and costumes for a 1960 production of *At the Hawk's Well* that resemble Dulac's designs; also notable is that the rigid blocking of the actors would necessarily have restricted their movement, thereby placing an emphasis on the recitation of the verse.

That is not to suggest that O'Malley's directing was derivative or old-fashioned, however. The actor Sam McCready, who later became one of the leading Irish interpreters of Yeats's drama, was introduced to his work by O'Malley in the late 1950s when he joined the Lyric players. All of the other actors, he recalls,

> spoke the lines authoritatively and mellifluously but with a feeling of detachment that I found novel and strange—as if they not only inhabited their roles but also

[30] Quoted by Sam McCready, *Baptism by Fire* (Belfast: Lagan Press, 2007), 70.

[31] Ophelia Byrne, *The Stage In Ulster* (Belfast: Linen Hall, 1997), 37.

[32] Ibid.

[33] Eugene McNulty, *The Ulster Literary Theatre and the Northern Revival* (Cork: Cork University Press, 2008), 55.

[34] This link was asserted repeatedly in *The Needle's Eye*, a commemorative magazine published in 1978 by the Lyric. Burns Library Lyric collection, Boston College, MS.2002.020, Box 1, Folder 8.

FIGURE 35.3 *At the Hawk's Well* by W. B. Yeats, Lyric Theatre, Belfast. Lyric Theatre/O'Malley Archive, reproduced courtesy of Hardiman Library, University of Galway.

commented on them at the same time—a kind of Brechtian *verfremdung*. It was a style which I found difficult to reproduce even though Mary spoke the lines for me in a kind of tuneless singsong...

But gradually McCready became more comfortable with the verse, later claiming that 'my love of Yeats was the greatest gift I received from Mary'.[35]

McCready's reference to Brecht is also significant, implying that Yeats's drama was ahead of its time, that audiences needed to be broken free of their habit of interpreting all theatre as if it were pictorially realistic, thus becoming more open to Yeats's use of symbolism and other forms of theatrical 'estrangement' or *Verfremdung*. But O'Malley's success with Yeats was also based on her understanding of his commitment to collaboration: as McCready recounts, she 'followed [Yeats's] lead' in working closely with choreographers, visual artists, and musicians. In an era when the model of the director as lone *auteur* was becoming increasingly common, O'Malley's practice stood out.

As the Lyric moved to its Ridgeway Street premises in 1968, its articles of association committed it to staging one Yeats play every year—something that even the Abbey had never tried to achieve. Perhaps that edict can be interpreted negatively: after all, good plays should not need to become the subject of a mandate. Yet the Lyric often went well

<hr />

[35] McCready, *Baptism by Fire*, 68.

beyond its own regulations: to give just one example, in 1974 they presented *The Hour Glass* and *The Player Queen* together (in a season that also featured the Belfast premiere of *Jesus Christ Superstar*). The theatre also commissioned other directors to work on Yeats, including Sam McCready, James Flannery, and Mary McCracken. Perhaps inevitably, O'Malley's retirement in 1981 led to the end of that tradition: McCready's adaptation *Yeats in Limbo* was staged in 1983, but thereafter Yeats left the Lyric's repertoire.

Could the Lyric have survived without Yeats? Perhaps—but O'Malley's engagement with his ideas led her to make decisions that allowed the theatre to thrive. Just as Yeats had used *Samhain* to provide a theoretical underpinning for his work, so would O'Malley develop a journal called *Threshold* in order to ensure that her audience were primed to receive the kinds of work she was interested in staging. That journal soon became a major force in the cultural life of the whole island. O'Malley also seems to have learned much from Yeats's approach to the politics of theatre production. She did occasionally act on the basis of her sympathy for Irish nationalism, conspicuously so in a damaging row about the playing of 'God Save the Queen' at the Lyric in 1968.[36] But for the most part she embraced Yeats's idea that the theatre must be a space for overcoming divisions: as Lionel Pilkington shows, when appointing honorary directors of the company she ensured an even balance between Catholic and Protestant members, an approach that was later emulated by Brian Friel's Field Day.[37] Her acting company included performers from both communities and, as the Troubles broke out, the Lyric usually enjoyed cross-community patronage, staging new plays from Catholic and Protestant writers alike.

The centrality of Yeats to the Lyric from the 1950s must be compared with his growing peripherality at the Abbey during the same period. There were, however, some important productions—particularly by Ria Mooney, who had acted in the premiere of *Words upon the Window Pane*, and who became the theatre's artistic director in 1948, occupying the role with distinction until 1963. Among Mooney's first productions were a well-received *Kathleen ni Houlihan* in 1948 (featuring Ray McAnally in one of his earliest roles), and a 1950 *Countess Cathleen* that featured Siobhan McKenna in the lead, shortly before the premiere of McKenna's celebrated translation of *Saint Joan*, the play that made her name internationally.[38] Mooney did not explicitly draw a link between staging Yeats and developing young actors, as O'Malley had done—but the evidence from her practice is that she saw the importance of that link, and was keen to act upon it.

Perhaps of greater significance was Mooney's promotion of theatrical experimentation as having value in its own right. In 1937 she had founded the Abbey Experimental Theatre Company, a group dedicated to staging work that would not normally attract an audience. In addition to providing her with opportunities to develop her skills as a director (including in the premiere of two plays by Jack B. Yeats), she also built up

---

[36] For more on O'Malley's nationalism see Fiona Coleman Coffey, *Political Acts: Women in Northern Irish Theatre, 1921–2012* (Syracuse: Syracuse University Press, 2016), 74.

[37] Lionel Pilkington, *Theatre and the State* (London: Routledge, 2001), 186.

[38] Patrick Lonergan, *Irish Drama and Theatre Since 1950* (London: Bloomsbury, 2019), 17–21

an audience that would prove responsive to her later innovations.[39] Those included five productions of *The Dreaming of the Bones*, a play that the theatre had staged only once during Yeats's lifetime (in 1931), but which became one of the most popular revivals during her artistic directorship.

After Mooney, however, the theatre seemed unsure of how to create space for Yeats. That might have been because the link to Yeats sometimes seemed very immediate—perhaps oppressively so. For example, Udolphus Wright had played the role of Patrick in the Abbey's opening night performance of *Kathleen ni Houlihan* in 1904; he stage-managed the same play for Mooney in 1950. Her last production of *The Dreaming of the Bones* in 1962 featured Pat Laffan in the role of the Stranger; Laffan in turn appeared in a staged reading of *The Death of Cuchulain* in 2010. So even a century after the plays premiered, it was still possible to find Abbey actors who had been trained by people who had worked directly with Yeats. That sense of proximity might explain a continuing pattern of excessively reverential productions, such as a 1965 *Deirdre,* which, as shown by the actors' melodramatic facial expressions and authentically 'Celtic' costumes (Figure 35.4), suggests a desire to present the play in a realistic style that would not have served it well.

The opening of a new Abbey building in 1966 did allow for new approaches to the plays, though they appeared infrequently and always in the Peacock space. The director Jim Fitzgerald had made a name for himself when his season of Yeats plays was one of the successes of the first Dublin Theatre Festival, in 1957; the Abbey belatedly recognized his expertise in 1973 when it asked him to present a double bill of *Purgatory* and (appearing for the first and only time in the history of the Abbey) *The Herne's Egg*—both of which were staged in a realistic style due to Fitzgerald's conviction that the 'Celtic Twilight' mode of the originals could be dispensed with.[40] One might argue with that approach, but the productions were well received. Like Mac Liammóir, Fitzgerald also eventually put Yeats on stage, in a 1978 lunchtime play called *Mr Yeats and the Death of Cuchulain.*

The Peacock remained the primary site of Yeatsian production during the 1980s, when Raymond Yeates presented previously neglected works such as *Calvary* (receiving its premiere at the Abbey in 1986) and *The Cat and the Moon*, alongside such better-known plays as *Kathleen ni Houlihan*. Those productions were marketed as a departure from tradition—though, aside from leaving the house lights on, most of the company's techniques (such as using masks and non-Western movement styles) had been employed by Yeats at one time or another.

Those productions established the audience that later turned out for the Yeats Festivals of 1989 to 1993. Led by James Flannery, those productions were generally well received, though they occasionally met with ambivalent or even sneering critical reactions (a headline describing the 1989 Cuchulain cycle as 'Rambo Meets the Sidhe' is a typical

---

[39] The plays were *Harlequin's Positions* and *La La Noo.* Ian R Walsh, *Experimental Irish Theatre* (Basingstoke: Palgrave Macmillan, 2010), 44–6.

[40] ATDA, 4747_MPG_01, 3.

FIGURE **35.4** Geoffrey Golden as Concobar and Edward Golden as Fergus in *Deirdre* by W. B. Yeats, a special performance to mark the Yeats centenary year, Abbey Theatre at the Queen's Theatre, 1965. Reproduced courtesy of Abbey Theatre Archive.

example).[41] The fact that the festivals were sponsored by Coca-Cola also seemed distractingly incongruous for some commentators (see Figure 35.5).

Nevertheless, the series would prove important. The festival model that it developed later become a major force in Irish theatre—evident in the Gate's Beckett Festivals of 1991 and 2006; the joint Abbey, Gate, and Lyric Friel Festival of 1999; the Druid's production of all of Synge's plays in 2005; and indeed a 2009 Yeats Cycle at the Irish Repertory Theatre in New York.

Following the pattern established by Mooney and O'Malley, Flannery provided opportunities for younger artists to establish themselves. Olwen Fouéré, now regarded as one of the great Irish actors of her generation, appeared as Kathleen ni Houlihan in

[41] ATDA, 2502_PC_0001, 38.

FIGURE 35.5 Programme cover for *Sacred Mysteries*, the third annual Yeats International Festival, Peacock Stage, Abbey Theatre, 27 August 1991. Reproduced courtesy of Abbey Theatre Archive.

1989; Raymond Keane, a co-founder of the influential theatre company Barabbas, made his Abbey debut in a 1991 production of *The Shadowy Waters*; and a 1993 production of *The Hour Glass* featured music by Bill Whelan, who, a year later, came to global attention with the premiere of *Riverdance*.

But perhaps the inclusion of those plays within a series of festivals may inadvertently have suggested that there was no audience for Yeats within the ordinary repertoire of the national theatre.[42] In the quarter-century that followed the Coca-Cola series, Yeats's drama largely vanished from the Abbey: there was the centenary production of *Purgatory* (mentioned already), and a series of staged readings in 2010. Other than that, his only appearance (in a recurrence of the pattern already identified) was as a character in original plays: *Down Off His Stilts*, Aideen Howard's compendium of excerpts from his letters (staged at the Peacock in 2014), and Colm Tóibín's *Beauty in a Broken Place*, which was also part of the 2004 centenary production.

Tóibín's play is not much remembered now, but it is notable in the present context for being directed by Niall Henry, the artistic director of Blue Raincoat theatre company. That Sligo-based ensemble has, under Henry's direction, done much to reinvigorate the performance of Yeats since 2013, through a series of site-specific productions that brought *Purgatory* to the top of Knocknarea in 2013, *At the Hawk's Well* to O'Rourke's Table in 2015, *The Cat and the Moon* to the shores of Lough Gill in 2016, and, perhaps most memorably, *On Baile's Strand* to Streedagh Beach at the foot on Ben Bulben in 2013 (and also to Coney Island in the same year). Bringing the scripts into alignment with the landscapes that partially inspired them, those productions were simultaneously innovative (in doing something no one else had attempted) and faithful to Yeats's ideas (he had sometimes imagined his plays being performed outdoors in the west of Ireland).

But they also succeeded because Blue Raincoat had, since its foundation in 1991, developed a style of acting rooted in Ireland but informed by European ideas about performance, especially by such figures as Jacques Copeau, Étienne Decroux, Marcel Marceau, and Jacques Lecoq. As Katherine Worth and Michael McAteer have argued, Yeats's drama was always European in outlook and orientation; as the only Irish ensemble dedicated to similar styles of theatre-making, it was probably inevitable that Blue Raincoat would eventually find its way to Yeats—though it took them more than twenty years to do so.[43] Before that time, they had developed their skills and reputation mainly in productions of European classics; their engagement with the Irish canon came tentatively—first with Thomas Kilroy's *Double Cross* (another Irish play rooted in European traditions), then with Synge, and finally with a series of adaptations of the novels of Flann O'Brien.

The strange voyage of Blue Raincoat, starting with Marcel Marceau in order to end up with Yeats, meant that Henry had developed sufficient confidence to stage his plays

[42] Brian Singleton, 'The Revival revised', in Shaun Richards, ed., *The Cambridge Companion to Twentieth-Century Irish Drama* (Cambridge University Press, 2004), 258–70.

[43] Katherine Worth, *The Irish Drama of Europe* (London: Athlone, 1978); Michael McAteer, *Yeats and European Drama* (Cambridge: Cambridge University Press, 2010).

without undue deference. Most of Yeats's plays are not very good, he bluntly told the *Irish Examiner*: 'On Baile's Strand* is the only really modern play insomuch as it doesn't reek of Yeats', whereas the others are 'a little bit like Rudolf Nureyev dancing fantastically while reading *Hamlet*'—which is to say that there is 'too much going on, nothing to throw things into relief'.[44]

Admirers of Yeats might want to argue with Henry's opinions, but what matters is that they display his determination to find new ways to stage the work. Locating them in a striking landscape, he claims, makes the verse easier to comprehend: 'You have to under-emphasise the lyrical in the play and [thus] ground the thing in its simplicity.' What Henry did, therefore, was to treat the plays as if they were new—to attend not to their reputation but to their capacity to stimulate an audience in the present. That strategy returns us to Garry Hynes's suggestion in 1991 that Yeats's theatre seems perpetually in search of new forms of audience reception.

Will Blue Raincoat's successes—like much that came before them—be forgotten, so that Yeats's plays must again be discovered, as if for the first time, by some future theatre company? Perhaps. But as this outline history has sought to demonstrate, Yeats's plays have rarely left the stage—something that differentiates him from almost all of his contemporaries, with the exception of Synge and O'Casey. That realization brings us back to the question asked at the beginning of this chapter: why has Yeats's presence on the stage never evolved into a recognized tradition?

One answer might be that in his dramaturgy Yeats was perhaps more interested in means than ends: he often expressed a preference for the experimentation of rehearsal over the fixity of meaning that a production before audiences imposed. That approach can be inspiring for practitioners but does not necessarily lend itself well to the modes of academic scholarship that were common during the twentieth century. But perhaps Yeats was again ahead of his time. From the late 1990s, many Irish theatre companies presented work that was labelled 'postdramatic' but which displayed a thoroughly Yeatsian preference for indeterminacy: indeed, one of the best of those productions, Pan Pan's *Playing the Dane* (2012), staged the rehearsal for a production of Shakespeare's *Hamlet* rather than the play itself. The greater integration of such practices into the Irish tradition might create fertile ground for new critical explorations of Yeats's drama, both by scholars and practitioners.[45]

Another factor might be the growing popularity of Beckett in Ireland (and of Irish-themed performances of Beckett internationally) since 1991, the date of the Gate's first Beckett festival. Stephen Watt has persuasively argued that the influence of Beckett upon Irish culture has become so pervasive that even his precursors can now seem 'Beckettian' *avant la lettre*—which means that the Beckettian (as both adjective and aesthetic) may overdetermine audiences' reception of Yeats's plays, in Ireland and

---

[44]   Padraic Killeen, 'Life's a Beach', *Irish Examiner*, 9 July 2014.

[45]   Flannery similarly argued that the innovations of Peter Brook, Artaud, and Grotowski ought to have enabled new approaches to Yeats's drama after 1950. Flannery, *Yeats and the Idea of a Theatre*, 355–67.

internationally.[46] Beckett expressed admiration for some (but not all) of Yeats's drama, but the resemblances between their works are often overstated: an important difference is that Beckett sought to answer with great precision the questions about stagecraft that Yeats preferred to leave open-ended.[47] Nevertheless, would-be producers might justly worry that audiences familiar with *Footfalls* or *Waiting for Godot* might see *At the Hawk's Well* or *Purgatory* as second-rate Beckett rather than first-rate Yeats. That does not mean that Yeats's plays must be set aside, but perhaps they need again to be made strange.

A final explanation might be that traditions must be named and documented—and that this simply has not happened yet with Yeats. There have been many books about Yeats's drama: so many, in fact, that it may sometimes feel as though there is nothing more to be said.[48] But few of those studies consider the life of Yeats's plays beyond their first productions, the work of James Flannery being an important exception. That problem is compounded by the long neglect of female directors such as Ria Mooney and Mary O'Malley within Irish theatre history generally, not to mention the persistence until the early 2000s of a belief that mid-century Irish theatre was unworthy of serious attention. Those blind spots are gradually being identified and redressed, but many important stories remain to be told: not just about Yeats himself but also about the many directors, actors, and audiences who rose to the challenges posed by his theatre.

[46] Stephen Watt, *Beckett and Contemporary Irish Writing* (Cambridge: Cambridge University Press, 2009).

[47] For Beckett on Yeats, see James Knowlson, *Damned to Fame* (London: Bloomsbury, 1995), loc. 4235 (e-book).

[48] An exception is Lauren Arrington's *W. B. Yeats, the Abbey Theatre, Censorship, and the Irish State* (Oxford: Oxford University Press, 2010), which demonstrates that the availability of new archival material can substantially deepen our understanding of Yeats's work.

CHAPTER 36

DANCE

SUSAN JONES

DANCE in Yeats's writing embodies a range of preoccupations, ideas, and states of being, variously referring to shifting historical change, memory, an expansion of consciousness, and giving access to forms of transcendence, expressions of eternality, insanity, or violence. Lyrical movement expresses the mystical in 'The Man who Dreamed of Faeryland': 'glittering summer runs / Upon the dancer by the dreamless wave'. Dance registers the passage of time in 'To the Rose Upon the Rood of Time', with stars 'grown old / In dancing silver-sandalled on the sea'. In 'The Happy Shepherd', dance stands in for the movement of history as the shepherd sings of 'all the many changing things / In dreary dancing past us whirled'. Connections to antiquity and to primeval forces appear in 'To Ireland in the Coming Times', where 'fairies, dancing under the moon' invoke an anthropomorphized 'Druid' Ireland whose heart beats in time with 'the flying feet' of 'her, whose history began / Before god made the angelic clan'. Other dances generate spirituality or epochal destruction: 'dying into a dance /An agony of trance', gesturing to transcendence beyond the body which is nevertheless achieved *through* the medium of the body.[1]

All these examples give dance a metaphorical force, where the dancers' mode of action might be generally termed 'expressivist' (as in Isadora Duncan's abandoned, outward-reaching gestures).[2] An invocation to the inner rhythms of the body to initiate outward expression continues to appear in plays like *The Cat and the Moon* (1917), where the emphasis lies on communication beyond words (the First Musician exhorts the Lame Man to move beyond language, and instead dance).[3] But Yeats's perspective shifts when he discusses dance style in the 1921 Preface to *Four Plays for Dancers*. Here Yeats provides

---

[1] *CW1*, 45, 31, 1, 50–1, 248.

[2] See Mark Franko, *Dancing Modernism/Performing Politics* (Bloomington: Indiana University Press, 1995), 1–25. Franko theorizes Duncan's mode of dance as an expressivist response to inner impulses of energy originating in what she called 'the soul', located in the solar plexus.

[3] See Santosh Paul's analysis of the play in 'The Dancer in Yeats', *Studies: An Irish Quarterly Review*, 65, 258 (Summer, 1976), 113–27.

a distinctive focus on a more inward-looking perspective. He wrote of his invention of an innovative form of drama to fit an intimate, domestic space (such as Lady Cunard's drawing room, where the first performance of *At the Hawk's Well* took place in London in 1916), combining music, poetry, dance, design. He confessed that, were he to produce the plays himself, he would have the most trouble with the dance. But he was clear about the *quality* of movement he required: 'something with a smaller gamut of expression, something more reserved, more self-controlled' than anything he believed existed in stage dancing of the period.[4] Yeats's imagining of a new dance style for the plays hints at dance's potential to create a 'poetics' of impersonality, much closer to the spiritual invocation of ritual. Yeats seems to have been claiming for the dancer, who subsumes her/his subjective personality, the role of medium or conduit of the choreographic idea.

Rather than using dance to metaphorize expressivity through a general outward gesturing of evocative states—mystical joy, excessive terror, violence, erotic energy, insanity—in the plays for dancers Yeats now focuses on the actual style of the dancer, privileging a more controlled performance, ritualized in some way, where movement is more physically contained, succinct, intense, and inward-looking, executed with a sense of composure rather than an overtly histrionic presentation. He now considers the dancer's *mode* of creativity in action, the choreographic style, the technical material of the dance. In this chapter I will explore Yeats's apparent shift to a 'new' kind of dance for the plays and show how it had a longer gestation than we might think. I suggest that the later dance style emerged as a natural development of Yeats's ongoing ideas about the function of the symbol, ceremonial ritual, and a poetics of impersonality. Thus the chapter will consider the development of these three themes and their intersection principally in relation to the choreographic focus of later dance plays such as *At the Hawk's Well* (1916), *The Only Jealousy of Emer* (1919), *Fighting the Waves* (1928), *King of the Great Clock Tower* (1934), and *A Full Moon in March* (1935). Finally, I suggest how Yeats produced an innovative form of theatre that, in spite of his anxieties, found itself in step with debates among contemporary dance practitioners and choreographers of the period.

SYMBOL

Yeats's identification of an appropriate movement style for his plays arose in part from the contemplation of dance as symbol throughout his career. In Yeats's writing, dance always to some degree suggests symbolic form and structure and tends to highlight either dialogue with, or conflict between, opposites. The symbol for Yeats often attempts to reconcile such contraries, encapsulating mood and tone, but in an expression that contains the energy of opposing forces. After all, Yeats preferred the 'wizard frenzy' of

---

[4] W. B. Yeats, *Four Plays For Dancers* (London: Macmillan, 1921), p. v.

the symbol to the extended narrative properties of allegory.[5] In *A Vision* (1925 and 1935), he privileged the tensions of the spiralling gyres and the interconnectedness of opposing energies that likewise provided him with an imaginative formula for creativity. In the plays, dance predominantly suggested the medium through which such conflicts are expressed and/or unified in symbolic form—the hawk, the waves, the dance of the Sidhe. In fact Yeats conceptualized the achievement of such unity as a form of dance itself, as in *Per Amica Silentia Lunae* (1917), where the tension between the 'shades' is represented by the distinctive *figures* of a dance—showing the degree to which the formality and embodiment of the dance is constitutive of the symbolic idea: 'Hitherto shade has communicated with shade in moments of common memory that recur like the figures of a dance in terror or in joy, but now they run together like to like.'[6] What is important here is that Yeats gestures to a sense of containment of opposites, that which produces the symbol. But what is distinctive in the plays, as we shall see from his remarks about the dancers Michio Ito and Ninette de Valois, is Yeats's specific focus on the stylized technique of the dancer in performance, which in itself provides an 'impersonal' yet physical medium for that symbol. This 'mode' is striking because Yeats is considering the dancer *as* the dance, the material of dance as the means through which symbolic form may be achieved.

To some extent Yeats's use of symbolic form to express his philosophical or spiritual concerns was closely related to an ongoing interest in poetic impersonality, filtered through the influences of many writers including Stéphane Mallarmé (1842–98) and his contemporaries. Yeats's direct links to Mallarmé are difficult to pin down, but a point of commonality can be identified in their references to the American solo dancer Loïe Fuller, whose aesthetic innovations in dance in the 1890s (when she moved away from conventional balletic forms) integrated free movement vocabulary with a high degree of design, costuming, and stage technology.[7] Fuller's move away from narrative meaning and her emphasis on the dance as a 'thing in itself' may have provided Yeats with an idea of the dancer as conduit or medium of the poetics of impersonality. Fuller continued to perform until the late 1920s, and, although we have no concrete evidence that Yeats saw her on stage, his biographer Roy Foster indicates that 'it was probably with [Arthur] Symons that WBY saw Loïe Fuller perform, bequeathing him an enduring image.'[8]

It is also possible that Symons had alerted him to Mallarmé's written account of Fuller. In 1893 Mallarmé had published a short but significant essay describing his responses

---

[5] 'Edmund Spenser' (1902), in *CW4*, 275.

[6] See also Adrian Paterson, 'Men of Letters: W.B. Yeats's *A Packet for Ezra Pound* (1929)', *E-rea*, 15:2 (2018), online (accessed 31 March 2021). Paterson observes that *Per Amica* 'captures a sense of self-consciously playful contrariness'. Also *CW5*, 25.

[7] Yeats wrote to Dorothy Wellesley on 4 May 1937 that he was reading Roger Fry's translations of Mallarmé and that they reminded him of the preoccupations he had had at an earlier time in his career. *CL InteLex* #6922.

[8] *Life 1*, 109.

to Fuller's solo performance at the Folies-Bergère in Paris.[9] He described her musical embodiment, entwined in swirling materials (whose circumference was enhanced by the use of long sticks held out beneath the cloth) shimmering in the play of light. She was an 'enchanteresse' engaged in mystical sorcery (208). For Mallarmé, her solo was 'la forme théâtrale de poésie par excellence' (207). Fuller's innovative performance opens up the discussion of a symbolist relationship between dance and literature in the fin de siècle, one which Frank Kermode famously associated in part with Yeats.[10] As Kermode observed, Fuller provided literary modernism, in its early years, with 'an emblem of the Image of art, "self-begotten" in Yeats's favourite word'.[11]

In 'Nineteen Hundred and Nineteen' Yeats refers to Fuller by name, describing her dramatic incorporation of materials and lighting effects into her group of dancers in a way that suggests his familiarity with innovative dance forms in the period:

> When Loie Fuller's Chinese dancers enwound
> A Shining web, a floating ribbon of cloth,
> It seemed that a dragon of air
> Had fallen among dancers, and whirled them round
> Or hurried them off on its own furious path[.][12]

Yeats's reference may have been deliberately inaccurate—since he captures precisely the mood of Fuller's performances, with her vertiginous *chaînée* turns, sometimes travelling, sometimes spinning on the spot, 'enwound' in spiralling materials.[13] In addition, in later works Yeats goes on to draw on solo dancers' interpretations of the popular fin de siècle figure of Salome—whom Kermode suggested as the quintessential symbolist image of the dancer:

> The image is to be all movement, yet with a kind of stillness ... She has the impassive, characterless face of Salome, so that there is nothing but the dance, and she and the dance are inconceivable apart, indivisible as body and soul, meaning and form, ought to be.[14]

---

[9] Stéphane Mallarmé, 'Autre étude de danse: les fonds dans le ballet d'après une indication récent' (1893–6), from *Divagations* (1897), in Bertrand Marchal, ed., *Igitur, Divagations, Un Coup de dés* (Paris: Gallimard, 2003), 206–11.

[10] For further discussion see Susan Jones, *Literature, Modernism, and Dance* (Oxford: Oxford University Press, 2013), 13–43.

[11] Frank Kermode, 'Poet and Dancer before Diaghilev', *Salmagundi*, 33:4 (Spring/Summer 1976), 41 (23–47).

[12] *CW1*, 208.

[13] In April 1919 Loïe Fuller's dancing girls (not Chinese dancers) appeared at the Coliseum in London. In fact Yeats mistakenly identifies Fuller as leader of a troupe of Chinese dancers. Fuller had toured earlier in the century with Sada Yacco, who was Japanese.

[14] Frank Kermode, *The Romantic Image* (1957; London: Fontana, 1971), 99.

Yeats's famous line from 'Among Schoolchildren'—'How can we know the dancer from the dance?'—in part hovers behind Kermode's description, but the characterless face of Salome reminds us of the symbolist/decadent preoccupation with the Herodias/Salome story, and also of the performative impersonality of Fuller's dances.[15] Yeats may have also drawn on the work of the American dancer Ruth St Denis (he supported her tour of Europe in 1908–9), famous for 'Radha' (1906), a radical interpretation of Indian dance, suggesting the abstraction, mood, and quality that may have appealed to Yeats.[16] But the Salome story leads us to Yeats's two late plays, *King of the Great Clock Tower* (1934) and *A Full Moon in March* (1935), and by looking at Mallarmé's poem *Hérodiade*, we can trace the genesis of Yeats's role for the dancer of both plays. Yeats had read Mallarmé's poem in Symons's 1896 translation, and in 1910 he remarked in 'The Tragic Generation' that he was compelled to create 'some Herodiade of our theatre, dancing seemingly alone in her narrow moving luminous circle'.[17] In many ways Yeats unknowingly fulfilled Mallarmé's intentions for his own unfinished *Hérodiade*. Yeats's late works also demonstrate the enduring connection between early symbolist preoccupations with performance dance and his experimental drama of the 1930s.[18]

Both Yeats plays respond to the Salome story and use the motif of beheading. But Salome appears indirectly in Yeats—she is neither named as Salome nor Herodias as subject of his work. And as Bernard O'Donoghue remarked, the beheading motif of the John the Baptist story 'is only an accidental reinforcement of the Celtic cult of the head as trophy noted by Diodorus Siculus', alerting us to the Irish inflections Yeats brought to both these dramas.[19] Terence Brown observed that Yeats himself 'explained the anthropological origins of the severed-head motif in European literature' in the old annual rituals of the mother goddess and the slain god.[20] Yeats's late plays also seem to be related to several contemporary interpretations of Salome.[21] But the Irish inflections in *A Full Moon in March* form part of a series of references to the Salome narrative in the late work, including his last play, *Death of Cuchulain*

---

[15] Popular danced versions of Salome included those by Fuller (1900), Maud Allan's 'Vision of Salome' (1906), and Ida Rubinstein's dance to music by Alexander Glazunov for her 1908 production of Wilde's play.

[16] See Suzanne Shelton, *Divine Dancer: A Biography of Ruth St Denis* (New York: Doubleday, 1981) for information on St Denis's career.

[17] *CW3*, 247.

[18] Gardner Davies edited Mallarmé's previously unpublished sketches for the prospective Hérodiade in Stéphane Mallarmé, *Les Noces d'Hérodiade* (Paris: Gallimard, 1959).

[19] Bernard O'Donoghue, 'To tell the dancer from the dance', review of Sylvia Ellis, 'The Plays of W. B. Yeats: Yeats and the Dancer (1995)', *Times Literary Supplement* (28 April 1995), 11.

[20] Terence Brown, 'W. B. Yeats and Rituals of Performance', in Nicholas Grene and Chris Morash, eds., *The Oxford Handbook of Modern Irish Theatre* (Oxford: Oxford University Press, 2016), 85.

[21] Apart from the allusion to Oscar Wilde's play, Cave also noted Yeats's affinities with various versions of the Turandot story—by Gozzi, Klabund, and Puccini; and with Maeterlinck's 1892 *Pelléas et Mélisande* (lxviii). Cave observes that Yeats had seen Maeterlinck's play performed by Sarah Bernhardt and Mrs Patrick Campbell, noting that 'where Mélisande fades away in pathos, the Queen [of Yeats's plays] comes into the power that attends complete self-possession' (lxix).

(1939), in which an Old Man, the fictional 'author' of the play, suggests that 'Emer must dance, there must be severed heads ... severed heads for her to dance before'.[22] Yeats always claimed that there were some elements of his earlier self in these plays, and in other ways they coincide with his increasing interest, during his late career, in Platonic philosophy.[23]

Yeats's allusions to Mallarmé's *Hérodiade* are in part surprising since they fulfil sketches for the ending of the French poem unpublished during the poet's lifetime. In 1933 Yeats initiated work on *King of the Great Clock Tower*, for which he gave the Irish dancer Ninette de Valois, who later founded the Sadler's Wells Ballet in 1931, the part of the silent Queen because de Valois had not trained as an actress and had refused to take a speaking role. The story is simple—the King has the character called the Stroller beheaded for daring to make advances to his wife, and the play culminates with the Queen's extraordinary dance with the severed head. The first performance of *King of the Great Clock Tower* at the Abbey in 1934 was a great success with the public, although literary figures were not always so kind, and Ezra Pound's criticism spurred Yeats on to a revision of the play.[24] At first Yeats tried to accommodate Pound's critique by characterizing and historicizing the King more fully as the Irish O'Rourke of Breffny—but eventually he rejected this direction. In the final version of *A Full Moon in March* Yeats economized on the form—dropping the part of the King altogether. Instead, a lowly Swineherd is beheaded for his presumption in expressing his passion for the Queen (she has promised to share her kingdom with the man who successfully woos her with his song). We now have a Swineherd and a Queen—and it is the Queen who is responsible for his decapitation. This inversion of power brings the play closer to versions of the Salome figure, but also chimes with Yeats's increasing authoritarianism.

Like *King of the Great Clock Tower*, *A Full Moon in March* requires a dancer, but here the part of the Queen is shared between an actress (Yeats envisioned Margot Ruddock in the part) and a dancer (he hoped de Valois would again take the dancing role). In *A Full Moon in March* the changes to scenario and the division of the speaking and dancing roles of the Queen suggest a radical realignment of Yeats's late thinking towards the idea of dramatic form as an expression of transformation (the Guardian of the Well into the hawk of *At the Hawk's Well* sets a powerful precedent). The final dance of *Full Moon* is in itself a symbol of that transformation. As Cave puts it, Yeats developed 'a shift in the Queen's modes of perception ... extending her awareness beyond the limitations

[22] CW2, 546.

[23] See Brian Arkins, *Builders of my Soul: Greek and Roman Themes in Yeats* (Gerrards Cross: Colin Smythe, 1990).

[24] Samuel Beckett referred to de Valois's dancing as 'uterine scratchings' (Martha Dow Fehsenfeld and Lois More Overbeck, eds., *The Letters of Samuel Beckett 1929–1940* (Cambridge: Cambridge University Press, 2009), 217; Ezra Pound slammed the transcript as 'nobody language' (quoted in Richard Allen Cave, Introduction, in *W. B. Yeats, King of the Great Clock Tower and A Full Moon in March* (Ithaca, NY, and London: Cornell University Press, 2007), xlvi. According to Cave (xlvi), the phrase was recorded by Yeats in his Rapallo Notebook, June 1934).

of ... rank to the extent that she now can apprehend the value of the Swineherd's daring and sacrifice' (xlvii). The role of the Queen, split between actress and dancer, allows his character to appear to be discovering a new mode of living in the body (the dancer as emblem of inner unity)—suggesting the sacrifice of the artist to art. In addition, this shift in the play to the centre of the Queen's consciousness takes us not to the Wilde Salome, but much closer to Mallarmé's manuscript sketches for *Hérodiade*. In *A Full Moon in March*, whose setting is a timeless 'anywhere', agency is given solely to the isolated Queen, who has no husband and whose language and actions remind us of the obsession and cold yet despairing cruelty of the virginal protagonist of Mallarmé's poem. The play's situation is expressed economically through verse, music, song, and dance, incorporating the use of a half-mask for the Swineherd. This lowly character is beheaded after expressing his passion for the Queen, and the action closes with the Queen dancing as she embraces the head, an aspect of the Salome story that appears in Wilde's play, in Heine's poem (*Atta Troll*, 1841), and Laforgue's narrative (*Salomé*, 1887)—the act of kissing the dead lips. Yeats wrote in the Preface to *Full Moon* that his idea for the dance was inspired by Wilde, except that Wilde's dance comes before the beheading, not after it.[25] This is a crucial distinction in that Yeats focuses on the sacrifice to art and its production through suffering (of both the Swineherd, who loses his life, and the Queen, who loses her love—poetry and dance are produced at the moment at which the head is severed).

Yeats's Queen is close in character to Mallarmé's Hérodiade, whose virginity is complicated by her self-isolation and stoical endurance. Yeats's Queen may be a maturer woman, but in commenting on the price of her beauty she echoes the tyranny of Hérodiade: 'Men hold / That woman's beauty is a kindly thing / But they that call me cruel speak the truth, / Cruel as the winter of virginity (*CW2*, 504). Helen Vendler has linked the role of the Queen with Yeats's *A Vision* (1925), where aloof beauty is the 'pre-eminent symbol of the poetic image'. In Phase 14 'the Image is considered as the thing-in-itself', and in Phase 15 it is 'something absorbed into the poetic consciousness'.[26] Like Mallarmé, who used his poem's expression of frigid beauty to explore the painful creation of poetry, Yeats uses the pathological cruelty of the Queen to evoke the woman's tragic status, and to illustrate the ideal of art and impersonality of the artist, whose sacrifice of detachment comes at a terrible price (poetry is created by the Swineherd at the moment of his death—when the severed head sings). But Yeats's stage directions explicitly show the inadequacy of language to communicate these themes as the Queen's dialogue gives way to the expression of the body in a dance whose function is connotative rather than denotative.

The closure intriguingly echoes the mood of Mallarmé's sketches for an uncompleted version of *Hérodiade*, where he intimates that Hérodiade, having had the Baptist destroyed for unnerving her with his uncompromising gaze, commences a solitary

---

[25] *CW2*, 727.
[26] Helen Hennessy Vendler, *Yeats's Vision and the Later Plays* (Cambridge, MA: Harvard University Press, 1969), 145.

dance, the severed head before her. Mallarmé drafted a literary sketch for, 'une sorte de danse /effrayante esquisse /—et sur place, sans / bouger / —lieu nul ('a sort of frighteningly exquisite dance, on the spot without moving—any place').[27] He tantalizingly contemplates a version of *Hérodiade* in which the character's ambiguity (her cold yet desirable beauty, her death-in-life existence) would transcend the words of the poetic drama, to be expressed bodily in a dance resembling one of Fuller's solos, where she swirled repeatedly in one place. Mallarmé's manuscript sketch transforms words into a movement of frenetic energy, a perpetual expression of emotional intensity that remains nevertheless 'fixed' in its spatial and historical moment, 'on the spot' and in 'no place'. Yeats's Queen, in her dance with the head, seems to fulfil this Mallarméan idea, but Yeats developed the role to suit his individual account of the relationship between artifice and eternity, which has been 'absorbed into the poetic consciousness'.[28] Unlike Mallarmé, Yeats emphasizes the human reality of the Queen's conflicted desires (for the man who presumes to woo her, and for her autocratic power), and from this point of view the choreographed action is fundamental to his account. Yeats's stage directions suggest her anagnorisis: 'The Queen dances to drumtaps and in the dance lays the head upon the throne', thereby acknowledging the Swineherd's right to share her kingdom, and the fact that she had fallen in love with him. But her internal antagonism is also expressed by the final dance, which is both erotic and frenetically driven by rhythmic force: 'The Queen in her dance moves away from the head, alluring and refusing.'[29] The stage directions explicitly point to an inward ethical conflict that produces a state bordering on insanity, driven by unfulfilled erotic desire:

> The Queen takes up the head and lays it on the ground. She dances before it—a dance of adoration. She takes the head up and dances with it to drumtaps, which grow quicker and quicker. As the drumtaps approach their climax, she presses her lips to the lips of the head. Her body shivers to very rapid drumtaps. The drumtaps cease. She sinks slowly down, holding the head to her breast. (*CW*2, 508)

Thus the Queen's final dance fulfils its function as bodily expression beyond language. The symbolic form of the dance, reminiscent of Fuller's self-contained solo, is illustrated by the spare physical structure of the movement and unified by space and time in a dehistoricized moment. Encapsulating a Mallarméan resonance, the play focuses on the medium of the dancer's strange but tantalizing performance with its suggestion of movement 'towards' narrative meaning—one that never attains closure. Most striking, perhaps, is the sense of violent expression tragically contained within the 'self-restraint' and impersonality of the style that Yeats had envisioned in 1921.

---

[27] Davies, Les Noces d'Hérodiade, 86.

[28] Vendler, Yeats's Vision, 145.

[29] *CW*2, 507.

CEREMONY

The Queen's dance in the 1935 play shows Yeats's drama focusing increasingly on economy of form, bringing out the impact of contemporary solo dance on Yeats's play. Elsewhere in the dance plays, however, Yeats strove to find the appropriate dance vocabulary and style for the production as a whole (its dialogic, choral, as well as solo elements). For this aspect of Yeats's innovations we need to think more closely about the function of dance in relation to communal ritual and ceremony. Critics customarily cite the stylized movement of the Japanese Noh plays as Yeats's main stimulation for these dramas. But Yeats's interest in ritual and ceremony was far from new, nor was it exclusively sourced in the Noh. We can trace the antecedents of Yeats's research of ritual to much wider preoccupations with Ireland's 'ancient' history, to the rhythms and elemental forces accessed in Druidic/Celtic ceremony. We could also cite the influence of the dramaturg Edward Gordon Craig, who collaborated with Yeats on *The Hour Glass* (1903) and whose ideas of an almost ritualized impersonality in acting are reflected in Yeats's directions for the Old Man in *At the Hawk's Well*: 'His movements, like those of the other persons of the play, suggest a marionette.'[30] Santosh Pall has also observed Yeats's embrace of the ritual practices found in Indian philosophy, with Hindu and Buddhist culture and art, and claims that 'in 1914 Yeats read Patanjali's *Aphorisms of Yoga*'. Yeats wrote the introduction to *Aphorisms*, bringing these elements further into alignment with the later plays.[31] Furthermore, Pall shows how 'Yeats was in personal touch with Ananda Coomaraswamy and possessed a copy of Coomaraswamy's *The Mirror of Gesture* (1917), a treatise on Indian dance and drama'.[32] Yet there is another less obvious source for his later interest in stylized choreography. Yeats's earlier turn to the occult mysteries is of particular interest here because Yeats himself experienced their ceremonies. His personal participation in 'choreographed' ritual during the period of the 1880s and 1890s has often been overlooked as a source for his ideas about the impersonality of the dance style in the plays.

In his essay of 1898 'The Celtic Element in Literature' Yeats imagined 'a supreme ritual' expressed through 'tumultuous dance among the hills or in the depths of the woods', that indicated how 'unearthly ecstasy fell upon the dancers' to suggest a union of earthly reality and spiritual epiphany.[33] And Brown rightly observes that 'Yeats the neophyte playwright had been introduced to the powers of ritual in ways that undoubtedly must have influenced his early dramaturgy by his membership of the Order of the Golden

---

[30] *CW2*, 299; for Edward Gordon Craig's theories see his 'The Actor and the Über-Marionette', *The Mask: Journal of the Art of the Theatre*, 1:2 (April, 1908), 3–15.

[31] *CW5*, 175–80.

[32] Santosh Pall, 'The Dancer in Yeats', *Studies: An Irish Quarterly Review*, 65:258 (Summer, 1976), 117–18 and 216 n.4 (citing Pall's debt to John Kelly for sharing an unpublished letter between Yeats and Coomaraswamy).

[33] *CW4*, 132.

Dawn'.[34] I would argue that this source for ceremonial form may have led in part to his imagining of dance for the dance plays as an embodiment of impersonality, since individual identity may be subsumed through the physical observance of ritual. In the 1880s and 1890s, when Yeats learned about and participated in the symbolic ceremonies of Rosicrucianism, he would have experienced at first hand a form that was highly choreographed. Yeats's uncle, George Pollexfen, first introduced him to the Hermetic Order of the Golden Dawn, and Pollexfen's Notebooks, held in the National Library of Ireland in Dublin, provide an intriguing source for understanding Yeats's personal access to the choreographed aspect of progression through the Order, when the Aspirant would advance by means of examination from one stage to the next. Pollexfen records one instance in which Yeats (as Festina Lente) moved to a higher stage through a two-part examination, in which, during the second part, 'the ceremonials must show effect as well as verbal accuracy'. Pollexfen goes on to describe 'Consecration or Evocation', in which 'A Ceremony on the Formulae of Ritual Z.2 must be performed before examiner and must meet with his approval as to method Execution and effect'.[35] Another notebook contains a more elaborate description of 'The Ceremony of the Vault', where its physical particularities, including the choreographed moves of the three Adepters and Aspirant are recorded in minute detail. Some rites are specifically described in terms of spatial disposition and symbolic gesture:

> 2nd & 3rd Adepters conduct Aspirant to the door of the vault & open it wide ... Kneel with Aspirant at west of altar. Aspirant still with arms crossed, & bearing Crook and scourge. All kneel except Chief Adepter who stands at East side of altar facing them.
>   Chief Adepter: as they enter extends his arms with a cross.

At another point they move 'all together with the saluting sign & bowing head' or 'bow their heads, shield their eyes with their hands'. At yet another moment the timing is specific. The Chief Adepter 'raises his hands, & turns up his face. All others bow their heads'. There is 'A short pause' before the Chief Adepter addresses the Aspirant: 'Rise up now'. Then, 'All rise'. 2nd and 3rd Adepters assist Aspirant to extend his arms like a cross. Then Aspirant re-crosses his arms on his breast & is faced to the West.[36]

The gestures are precise—extension of the arms, bringing them back to the chest, crossing arms over the heart, while floor patterns and pacing is detailed throughout. The specificity of the movement outlined in the rituals shows a formality in choreographic terms that emphasizes modes of comportment, timing, pace, rhythm, all of which combine to deliver the symbolic meaning of spiritual development through the stages of the Order (related to the Christian Mass, but highly distinctive in the forms of gesture and movement within the space).

[34] Brown, 'Rituals of Performance', 75.
[35] NLI MS 36,276/7 WB Yeats (Occult Papers). Examination of Festina Lente (George Pollexfen), 1896. Small notebook (holograph).
[36] NLI MS 36277/1 Hardbound notebook (holograph). Ceremony of the Vault, np.

The influence of these ceremonies may be found in Yeats's work of the 1890s. Yeats especially elaborates on the choreographed constitution of ceremony in his description of the dance in the 1897 short story 'Rosa Alchemica', based on the narrator's experience of witnessing a dance of the Order. We find a focus on the importance of 'learning the steps', and the influence of the rites associated with Yeats's 'Golden Dawn' examinations in his attention to choreographic detail:

> A couple of hours after sunset Michael Robartes returned and told me that I would have to learn the steps of an exceedingly antique dance, because before my initiation could be perfected I had to join three times in a magical dance, for rhythm was the wheel of Eternity, on which alone the transient and accidental could be broken, and the spirit set free. I found that the steps, which were simple enough, resembled certain antique Greek dances, and having been a good dancer in my youth and the master of many curious Gaelic steps, I soon had them in my memory.[37]

The importance of rhythm in the description of actual steps of the dance here suggests that Yeats's focus on dance as symbol of transcendence was combined with the wish to understand the technical specificities of the choreographed movement, since form itself is what for him generated access to that transcendence. The body memory is triggered by the rhythm and formal pattern of the steps—this is the physical material that induces the experience beyond the real. The narrator is drawn into a dreamlike state: 'a mysterious wave of passion, that seemed like the soul of the dance moving within our souls, took hold of me, and I was swept, neither consenting nor refusing, into the midst.'[38] We might apply a psychoanalytic reading of Yeats's dance here, but it is not just a matter of accessing the unconscious through a trance-like state—the fact that the very *choreography* of the dance was important suggests that there is always a formal, rational, or cognitive element (learning the steps) that unlocks the passage between real and spiritual states.

The dance also represents communal expression, or the individual's relationship to community, rather than the focus on the identity of the solo dancer that we see later in *At the Hawk's Well* or *A Full Moon in March*. When Yeats wrote 'Rosa Alchemica', he was probably not yet entirely familiar with Nietzsche, but we can already detect the oppositions of Dionysiac/Apolline drives from *The Birth of Tragedy* (1872) that later gave Yeats another dimension for understanding the 'contraries' of symbolic form, the disruption and reconciliation, and access to the 'Eternal', through ritualized movement.

This balance of drives between the control of ceremonial specificity and the abandonment of identity in the choral dance recurs in the performance of dance in the late plays, especially in *Fighting the Waves* (1928), a prose version of an earlier verse play, *The Only Jealousy of Emer* (1919). The earlier play established the element of ritual in the controlled, rhythmic movements and stillness of the musicians, who fold and unfold the cloths (as in

---

[37] W. B. Yeats, *Mythologies* (London: Macmillan, 1932), 144.
[38] *Myth*, 147.

At the Hawk's Well). The appearance of the Woman of the Sidhe to the Ghost of Cuchulain in mask and costume of metallic hue adds to the ceremonial resonance—as she dances, 'she seems more an idol than a human being'. Yeats insists that her movements and hair must also 'keep the metallic suggestion'.[39] As in the ceremonies of the Golden Dawn, communion with the spiritual is in part represented through movement and material symbol as the rituals of the play act as intercessors to the mystery.

In the later version, however, Yeats attempted something closer still to the theory of the Wagnerian *Gesamtkunstwerk* and to Nietzsche's idea of the chorus. *Fighting the Waves* was first performed in 1928 at the Abbey Theatre, with music by the American modernist composer George Antheil and choreography by de Valois, in which a group of musicians and dancers were integrated into the action, and de Valois took the role of the Woman of the Sidhe. Yeats commented on the fulfilment of several ambitions for the drama, and in particular the use of dance for both solo and choral aspects of the play:

> My Fighting the Waves has been my greatest success on the stage since Kathleen-ni-Houlihan … everyone here is as convinced as I am that I have covered a new form by this consolidation of dance, speech, and music. The dancing of the goddess in her abstract almost non-representative mask was extraordinarily exciting. The play begins with a dance which represents Cuchullan fighting the waves, then after some singing by the chorus comes the play which for its central incident the dance of the goddess and of the ghost of Cuchullan, and then after more singing is the dance of the goddess mourning among the waves. The waves are of course dancers. (*CW*2, 899)

Yeats had been inspired by Hildo Krop's construction of masks for all the characters of a Dutch production of *The Only Jealousy of Emer*, originally one of the Plays for Dancers conceived for 'private' viewing in a drawing room. Yeats concluded that he should rewrite this play 'to fit it for a public stage' and 'to free it from abstraction and confusion',[40] a rather contradictory impulse given that the addition of dance elements made it more abstract. Yet Yeats's extensive corrections to typescripts and proof pages of the Introduction and the text of *Fighting the Waves* show the importance to his rewriting of his focus on the relationship of individual to chorus. His emendations to the typescript show his engagement with the role of dance in constituting the form, the action as well as the poetic content, sometimes providing symbolic expression of the words, sometimes unifying the music and the words in movement or replacing words altogether with the moving chorus. In the first typed version of *Fighting the Waves*, which concluded with Fand, the Woman of the Sidhe's dance of despair at the loss of Cuchulain, Yeats's final stage direction urges the use of percussive cymbals to express 'the dashing of the waves'. In the page proofs to the De Luxe Edition, Yeats added a significant handwritten note: 'as before there may be other dancers who represent the waves', thus dramatizing the scene with the specifically choral element to enhance the symbolic musical accompaniment

---

[39] *CW*4, 325.
[40] Typescript of *Fighting the Waves*, NLI MS 8774 [1], n.d.

of Fand's final solo and to add the ritual element.[41] Yeats's emendations to his play show to some extent the influence of a quasi-Nietzschean aesthetics (drawing on the *Birth of Tragedy* [1872]), and the kind of *chthonic* energy imagined for the dance of 'Rosa Alchemica'. The 'Dionysiac' contributes forcefully to the choral presentation (of waves, of the Sidhe) in *Fighting the Waves*, where the idea of conflict and dissonance dominates the title, music, and choreography. Yet the ceremonial aspect of the play is retained in the way in which stylized dance creates the medium for transformative effect. As we have seen from the previous discussion, Yeats explored further these tensions of Apolline and Dionysiac in the icy attraction but tragic passion of the Queen of *A Full Moon in March*. In her virginal beauty and the instability of her finally demented solo we also see how Yeats developed the dance as introspective symbol—the predominantly agonistic strain expressed as an economic containment of 'wizard frenzy', limited by the formal properties of a solo dance of impersonality.

YEATS'S DANCERS

The new dance style Yeats envisaged in 1921 was principally made possible by his choice of dancers. Yeats was lucky to find the ideal performer of 'impersonality', of precise stylization combined with dramatic presence in two soloists. First he hired the Japanese dancer Michio Ito for *At the Hawk's Well* (1916), and then Ninette de Valois. The received notion is that Yeats's interest in the Noh theatre was exclusively stimulated by Ezra Pound, although Carrie Preston corrects this: 'Rather, the bilingual poet and art critic Noguchi Yone (1875–1947) introduced Yeats to Noh, which contradicts the common story'.[42] Pound introduced Yeats to Ito, a dancer whose knowledge of Noh practices lent itself to Yeats's project for the plays. In 1915 Pound and Yeats were both present for a demonstration of Ito's technique. Pound's description suggests how Ito embodied the perfect vehicle for the form of dance Yeats imagined:

> In the studio and in the drawing-room alone where the lighting was the light we are most accustomed to, did I see him as the tragic image that has stirred my imagination. There where no studied lighting, no stage-picture made an artificial world, he [Itō] was able, as he rose from the floor, where he had been sitting cross-legged or as he threw out an arm, to recede from us into some more powerful life. Because that separation was achieved by human means alone, he receded, but to inhabit as it were the deeps of the mind.[43]

---

[41] *CW4*, 62.

[42] Carrie Preston, *Learning to Kneel: Noh, Modernism, and Journeys in Teaching* (New York: Columbia University Press, 2016), 70.

[43] Ezra Pound and Ernest Fenollosa, *The Classic Noh Theater of Japan* (1917; repr., New York: New Directions, 1959), 153.

Carrie Preston emphasizes Ito's ability to access the 'deeps of the mind' while controlling and sustaining the 'impersonal' style of movement, and she also describes in intimate detail the combination of Noh and kabuki that Ito had absorbed in his early pre-1912 training in Japan:

> Perhaps most significant for the dance lessons that Itō gave Yeats are the common bodily styles and movement techniques shared by Japanese traditional performance forms. Noh, *nihon buyō*, and kabuki all feature the basic bodily posture called *kamae* or *kitachi*, in which the pelvis is tipped forward, in opposition to the lift of the chest and head ... The main locomotor step of all three, and of most Japanese art forms, is the *suriashi* (sliding step). In fact, so much time in a noh play is spent walking down the *hashigakari* entrance bridge or across the stage that noh has been dubbed 'the art of walking'.[44]

Preston provides remarkable insight into the style and posture that Ito absorbed through his training, but it is important to remember that when Ito came to Europe he developed a hybrid method encompassing a variety of techniques learned in Japan and elsewhere. Far from being exclusively a Noh dancer, his training incorporated forms from other Eastern practices, from ballet, and, having spent time studying with Emile Jaques-Dalcroze in Germany at Hellerau, from Dalcroze eurhythmics. Ito created an individual 'system' that he continued to pass on to dancers in the twentieth century and which can be seen on YouTube through the exercises taught to a group of American dancers by a Japanese student of Ito.[45] Here the dancers demonstrate both the 'art of walking' to which Preston refers and the rhythmic counterpoint of arm and leg movements practised in eurythmics. This glimpse of Ito's style reveals precisely the kind of control, use of silences, and rhythmical counterpoint that one can imagine informing his performance of the Hawk, which had enabled him to produce the 'symbolic' form Yeats required of his dance. It is important to remember that Yeats was inspired not so much by an individual technique or method (such as the Noh) as by a more general quality of 'self-control, restraint', a meeting of Eastern and Western practices that focused on the internalized spirituality/mentality Ito embodied. Ito performed the role of the Hawk or the Guardian of the Well in the 1916 production of *At the Hawk's Well*, and this became the first of *Four Plays for Dancers* published in 1921. In the 'Note on the First Performance of *At the Hawk's Well*' accompanying that edition, Yeats makes clear his debt to Ito for providing him with the corporeal aspect of the play: 'and besides in poetical and tragic art, as every "producer" knows, expression is mainly in those movements that are of the entire body'. When Ito left

---

[44] Preston, *Learning to Kneel*, 75.

[45] University of Washington Chamber Dance Company Documentary Collection Vol. 3: The Dances of Michio Ito (recorded 2001), https://www.youtube.com/watch?v=HwNg17bFIUY (accessed 30 April 2021). The compelling combination of 'Noh' walking and Dalcrozian eurythmic counterpoint (where the arms move independently of the rhythms of the legs) begins at 1:10:22.

Europe for New York, Yeats wondered whether he could sustain this mode of dance in his drama:

> Perhaps I shall turn to something else now that our Japanese dancer, Mr. Itow, whose minute intensity of movement in the dance of the hawk so well suited our small room and private art, has been hired by a New York theatre, or perhaps I shall find another dancer. I am certain, however, that ... I have found out the only way the subtler forms of literature can find dramatic expression.[46]

In fact Yeats found an equivalent intensity of movement in Ninette de Valois's dancing. Yeats met de Valois in 1927 and engaged her to choreograph and dance for the Abbey Theatre in 1928, where she proved a powerful and dramatic performer. She had been trained in classical ballet, but was alert to the technical mode of 'contemporary' forms such as European expressionism and the practice of dancing barefoot. She took over Ito's part in *At the Hawk's Well* and, as we saw above, Yeats created for her the part of the Queen in *King of the Great Clock Tower* (1934/5). She created her own choreography and in an interview with G. M. Pinciss, de Valois spoke of her experience:

> I used movement that was highly stylized. The dances were very abstract – masked you couldn't be anything else, anything else would have been out of place. One really did use the simplest gestures possible, rather symbolic movements, really; in fact, one avoided the more full-blooded, realistic theater. It was impossible to play it in a straightforward way. One had to think about it differently, about the style and the spirit behind it.[47]

Later de Valois created the choreography for *Fighting the Waves* and performed the role of Woman of the Sidhe. Yeats was impressed with the intensity of her dancing and her ability to hold herself perfectly still at moments when others were speaking. Cave wrote of de Valois's sensitivity to Yeats's drama: she 'could respond physically to the imagery' as well as to the 'rhythms of verse or prose that were being spoken around her', and, 'by some internal alchemy', could embody their 'aesthetic import'. He concluded that 'dancing, she became symbol'.[48]

CONCLUSION

In 1921, when Yeats envisaged for the dance plays the self-control and restraint of a particular style, he remarkably anticipated T. S. Eliot, who, writing of the Russian dancer

---

[46] *CW2*, 692.

[47] G. M. Pinciss, 'A Dancer for Mr. Yeats', *Educational Theatre Journal*, 21:4 (Dec. 1969), 389, 386–91.

[48] Cave, Introduction to *King of the Great Clock Tower*, xxxi.

Léonide Massine in 1923, contrasted 'the abstract gesture of Massine, which *symbolises* emotion' with the 'untrue, and always monotonous … conventional gesture of the ordinary stage, which is supposed to *express* emotion'.[49] We begin to see how this recurring theme of 'impersonality' comes to fruition in Yeats's later imagining of a new movement style. Yet there is also a significant parallel to draw between his contemporaries' innovations in dance and the dance style he envisaged. While in the 1921 Preface he wrote of having been sceptical about the existence of such a style, his propositions were often in line with debates about experimental dance of the period. The emergence of the solo dancer (like Fuller), whose choreography was largely non-mimetic, and who practised a free, non-balletic vocabulary, illustrates the way in which experiments in stage dancing were in themselves moving away from the idea of the narrative ballet towards the abstraction and suggestiveness of symbolic form.

There are intriguing correspondences that show how Yeats's innovative drama anticipated several aspects and technical currents of modernist dance. Martha Graham's partner and collaborator, the musician and composer Louis Horst, gave a central place to a 'Dance Study in Dissonance' that illustrates a complete physical awareness giving dance a new texture: 'tense, full of potential action, one part pulling against another'.[50] These are the agonistic forces initiated in Nietzsche's *Birth of Tragedy*, but also suggestive of the physical conflict of Cuchulain's fight with the waves. Chicago-based choreographer Doris Humphrey also touched on the inward focus of the dancer. Ernestine Stodelle, a long-standing member of Humphrey's company, wrote extensively of the choreographic work of the 1930s, when Humphrey emphasized the inwardness of the gaze—in a way that Yeats himself anticipated for the dancers of his plays. Stodelle wrote, 'don't look up, look out … the kind of looking out when people are looking beyond themselves but looking inwardly'.[51]

In a typescript of the Introduction to *Fighting the Waves*, when Yeats identified a similarity between the Irish myths and the plays of the ancient Greeks, he wrote of their presentation of God as perfection, 'like some Byzantine dance crowded with the gyres of Dionysus the Areopagite'. He goes on to explain that 'Dionysus meant by the word "gyre" doubtless such spirals as are made by a mounting hawk, but the mosaic workers preferred the level circle of that dance Plotinus attributed to his Third Authentic Existant or soul of the world, our Holy Spirit'.[52] Yeats offers here a somewhat esoteric insight into

[49] T. S. Eliot, 'Dramatis Personae', *The Criterion* 1 (April 1923), in *Complete Prose* 2, 434–5. Eliot here draws on his ideas for 'Tradition and the Individual Talent' (1919).

[50] Louis Horst and Carroll Russell, *Modern Dance Forms in Relation to the Other Modern Arts* (1961; New York: Dance Horizons, 1967), 50.

[51] Doris Humphrey, Programme Note (1935) for *Two Ecstatic Themes* (1931), page 3 of Ernestine Stodelle, Typescript, Notes (1935). Doris Humphrey Archive, Oak Park, Chicago.

[52] W. B. Yeats, Introduction, in Fighting the Waves, 6, typescript with holograph corrections (Dublin: National Library of Ireland, MS 8774 [1], n.d.), 1-6, by kind permission of the National Library of Ireland. For more information on the manuscript version see also W. B. Yeats, '*The Only Jealousy of Emer and Fighting the Waves*': *Manuscript Materials*, ed. Steven Winnett (Ithaca, NY: Cornell University Press, 2004).

his reading of Plotinus, but we find that Neoplatonist texts also provided an important model for a variety of aesthetic enquiries related to choreographic modernism. During the 1920s and 1930s Rudolf Laban's research depended on imagining the body extending to the limits of various Platonic solids. Martha Graham developed techniques that focused on the spiralling of the body, initiated by the breath and movement of the musculature originating at the base of the spine.

Another major source for the embodiment of the spiral form in modern dance originated with the work of Graham's contemporary Doris Humphrey, who, in 'Two Ecstatic Themes' (1931), explored choreographic tensions initiated by a centrifugal force moving through the body. Ernestine Stodelle, a dancer from her company, elaborated on Humphrey's ideas, observing, 'As an exploration of an abstract idea—the spiral form—the dance is a study in pure design.'[53] This aesthetic tension between the spare economic forms of two-dimensional design and the centrifugal movement and energy of the spiral can be found in a variety of modern dance and literary creations: Loïe Fuller's dances, Yeats's gyres, Pound and Lewis's concept of the vortex. But the spiral also expresses a conflict between descent into a modern hell and a post-Romantic struggle for sublimity—something Yeats expresses in his attempts to unify contraries in *Per Amica Silentia Lunae*. Humphrey's modernism of this period falls between a starkly abstract geometricity and a revisionist aspect encompassing the lyricism of a modernist sublime—something akin to Yeats, when we consider the diagrammatic aspects of his occult knowledge and his imaginings of *A Vision* set against the sometimes post-Romantic tone of his poetry. By comparing Yeats's imagining of dance for the plays together with the work of dance modernism, we might extend our analysis of the role of dance in Yeats. The shift in perspective to the inward gaze of the dancing body, the dance as medium of non-linguistic communication, and to a poetics of impersonality symbolized by the dance illustrate Yeats's innovative contribution to a wider context of modernist aesthetics. Interestingly, a questionnaire devised by Eliot Hutchinson, a psychologist who approached Yeats in 1949 to contribute to his study of creative effort (published as *How to Think Creatively*, 1949) leaves us with intriguing evidence of an ongoing preoccupation. One of Hutchinson's questions was, 'Do you feel that some power not yourself is trying to find expression through you, i.e. do you have a feeling of *impersonality* about your work?' Yeats replied that he usually did, but added a note to the effect that it would be impossible to answer these questions without writing an essay.[54]

[53] Stodelle, *Two Ecstatic Themes*, Typescript Notes, 1–2.

[54] Eliot D. Hutchinson, *How to Think Creatively* (Ashville, TN: Abingdon Press, 1949), discussion of impersonality, 78, 117, 166–73. Yeats's holograph comment appears on the New York edition copy currently on display (in June 2021) in the exhibition at the National Library of Ireland, Dublin: *Yeats: The Life and Works of William Butler Yeats*.

PART VI

READING YEATS

....

CHAPTER 37

IMPERFECT FORMS

....

STEPHANIE BURT

In an influential recent definition, Caroline Levine writes that the concept of 'form' includes 'all shapes and configurations, all ordering principles, all patterns of repetition and difference'.[1] For a temporal art such as poetry—dependent (as Yeats liked to stress) on imagined or actual listening—form requires repetition, expectation, and variation, within poems and among them. One anaphora, one rhymed quatrain, one pentameter, prepares the informed reader for what comes next—what may or may not be more of the same.

Yeats often does give more of the same, holding metrical and other formal elements constant in order (as Hannah Sullivan and others have argued) to vary tone, lexical register, sentence shape.[2] 'Stanzaic formality was necessary to him for many reasons,' explained Thomas Parkinson in 1964, 'but chiefly he required it as discipline for the passionate syntax that he accepted as a norm'.[3] We can learn more about poetic form, about Yeats's forms, and about Yeats's notions of perfection and imperfection, repetition and variation, order and disorder when Yeats rejects this norm: from poems in which the metre, or the rhyme scheme, as well as the imaginative logic, change midway through. These poems—most of them lesser known or less often discussed—can help us think about recent models of form, and recent definitions of lyric poetry, as well as helping us view and appreciate the aesthetic effects and choices that set Yeats's poems apart.

The gold standard for discussion of Yeats and form remains Helen Vendler's 2007 monograph *Our Secret Discipline*. Drawing on decades of smaller-scale or more specific work, Vendler devotes chapters to Yeats's most significant lyric and lyric-adjacent metres and forms: ballads and ballad stanzas; sonnets and quasi-sonnets (such as the couplet-free sonnet-like quatrains of 'When You Are Old', or the thirteen interlocking lines of 'The Fascination of What's Difficult'); tetrameter; blank verse; 'rare forms' such

---

[1] Caroline Levine, *Forms* (Princeton: Princeton University Press, 2015), 3.

[2] Hannah Sullivan, 'How Yeats Learned to Scan', *Yeats Annual*, 21 (2019), 21–37, 8.

[3] Thomas Parkinson, *W. B. Yeats: The Later Poetry* (Berkeley: University of California Press, 1964), 201.

as the terza rima of 'Cuchulain Comforted'; and, of course, ottava rima, the signature form of Yeats's final decades. Anyone who wants to learn to read Yeats's 'repertoire of stanza forms and line lengths and rhythmic variants' ought to start there.[4]

If that volume remains the first word on Yeats's forms, it cannot be the last: indeed, the 'ardent and arduous passage from conception to execution' that Yeats's poems ask us to follow also promise a richness in available interpretation that no single study or critic can give.[5] And we can find that richness not only (with Vendler) in the way that Yeats adapted one or another received form, not only (with Vendler) in the way that Yeats repeats his themes, 'writing the "same" poem twice', but also in the way that certain among Yeats's shorter poems revise, or swerve away from, the form that they seem to promise in their first few lines.[6]

For the Yeats of *Responsibilities* and afterwards, a form—no matter how beautiful, how worked up—must include flaws, swerves, changes, dissonances, in order to be aesthetically persuasive: in order to fit, as well as exalt or decry, the world it describes. Sometimes he says so: sometimes he shows us so. One poem that shows so—self-consciously, even anomalously so—is 'The Realists'. Here is the whole poem:

> Hope that you may understand!
> What can books of men that wive
> In a dragon-guarded land,
> Paintings of the dolphin-drawn
> Sea-nymphs in their pearly wagons
> Do, but awake a hope to live
> That had gone
> With the dragons?[7]

The first, introductory exclamation at once instructs 'The Realists' and dismisses them. They seem unlikely to understand: they read or write realistic books, like George Eliot's (a writer the young Yeats dismissed), and so they probably will not understand the hopes, or the wishes, or the passions, or the aspirations of the 'men' in those fantastic, non-realist books, nor the hopes of the people who read them. 'Hope' appears twice, an imperative verb and a noun: the only other significant word that shows up twice is 'dragons', emblem of that hope which the realists ignore. (Malcolm Sen has claimed, implausibly, that Yeats's 'realists' *are* his dragons.[8]) Readers of non-realist books, dreamers of unrealistic dreams, will of course harbour unrealistic hope: a perfect love, or a perfect work of art, or a perfect nobility can be had in no age, certainly not our own.

---

[4] Helen Vendler, *Our Secret Discipline* (Cambridge, MA: Harvard University Press, 2007), 3.
[5] Ibid., 26.
[6] Ibid., 27.
[7] *CW1*, 120.
[8] Malcolm Sen, 'Dragon-Ridden Days: Yeats, Apocalypse and the Anthropocene', *International Yeats Studies*, 4:1 (2020), https://tigerprints.clemson.edu/iys/vol4/iss1/10/.

This hope wrenches the poem out of its apparent form: seven-syllable tetrameter couplets rhymed *abab*, one of Yeats's most common late metres. As Vendler says, 'there is very little they cannot do.'[9] What they 'do' here, however, is to fall apart and become something else. Yeats could have composed a seven-line poem in regular tetrameters ('Do, but keep up hopes to live / That had vanished with the dragons') or an eight-line poem that preserved the metre and regularized the rhyme ('Do, but keep up hopes to live / That we know are dead and gone / With the long-ago-lost dragons').

Yeats's compositional strategy instead tilts the poem, first out of rhythm—the first four lines scan alike—and then out of metre. The realists must be wrenched out of their assumptions, out of their sense of what's possible in this world, in order to see how displaced, how disappointed, even how angered, the fantasists, the dragon-lovers, must be. The verb 'live', in rhyming position, has no adverb, no limiting phrase attached: perhaps the readers of books about dragons, sea-nymphs and pearly wagons, trapped among realists, denied access to fantasy, feel as if they cannot 'live' at all.

A relatively neglected asymmetrical gem in itself, 'The Realists' also opens out into claims we can make about Yeats and form more generally: the poem imagines, but does not itself produce, a fantasy of perfect love, perfect nobility, and heroes who slay (or love) dragons. In the same way Yeats's handling of external form—of stanza shape, of metre and rhyme, of syntax—speaks to the imperfections and compromises that the poet sees as part of life in our world.

'A Coat', like 'The Realists', changes shape midway through, albeit in less drastic ways. 'Yeats never again repeated its total form', says Vendler.[10] The form is a mini-sonnet of sorts, quatrain and a sestet—but one quatrain, not two, and in two- and three-beat lines, not pentameters. The poem seems to doff its own earlier form as Yeats doffs—or rather accedes to losing—his 'coat': the *abba* quatrain, with its polysyllabic half-rhyme (embroideries–mythologies[11]), gives way to the sharp alternating full rhymes of the final six lines, whose shape the first four could not have let us predict. Ambiguity in the first line has become classroom cliché: did Yeats make a coat for his song to wear, or did he make his song into a coat? Are the 'mythologies' surface or substance? Can he subsist without them? Can his song? What sort of 'enterprise' might he envision, naked? And why use a word—'enterprise'[12]—whose connotations of business, practicality, we might expect the poet who wrote 'September 1913' to avoid?

One answer brings in a biblical allusion. Joseph's embroidered, desirable coat, stolen by his foolish brothers, landed him ultimately in Egypt, where his 'enterprise' let him grow rich by interpreting dreams (Genesis 39–41). The poem, like the poet, like the biblical Joseph, falls in order to rise. And the 'song' itself is a less predictable remake of Yeats's earlier commentary on his revisions: 'whenever I remake a

[9] Vendler, *Our Secret Discipline*, 183, 205.
[10] Vendler, *Our Secret Discipline*, 349.
[11] *CW1*, 127.
[12] *CW1*, 127.

song … it is myself that I remake'.[13] The poet remakes the poem; the poem, in a case like this, remakes itself midway through, becoming a tenser, denser, visibly imperfect, and more vulnerable thing. Yeats would even rewrite both 'A Coat' and the 1908 quatrain near the end of his life, as 'An Acre of Grass': 'Myself must I remake / Till I am Timon and Lear'.[14]

All these poems set the uses of art against the shape of the artist's life. So does 'What Then?', where the poet ('he') seems to have achieved, if not a perfect life, a satisfactory one, a Horatian rural retreat with 'plum and cabbage' and 'friends indeed'. He has 'something to perfection brought'. But the poet stays unsatisfied, and so the poem will not complete its 'perfect' shape by revisiting its refrain verbatim. 'What then?' sang Plato's ghost. 'What then?' becomes, instead, 'But louder sang that ghost "What then?"'.[15] Yeats denies himself the completeness that exact repetition could bring. Instead, the ghost of Plato, the philosopher of forms and absolutes, insists that there is an ideal that he and his poems could not attain. Perhaps no human on this Earth could.

Form is always a function of repetition, within a poem or from one poem to the next. In poems about memory or futurity, that repetition itself can carry emotion and meaning: will the next experience resemble, or measure up to, the last? In life the answer is 'never, or not exactly': we cannot step into the same river twice. In poems, the answer can vary with the poet, and with the form of the poem: failed repetition, repetition with variation, can match poets' disappointment with the present, as well as their reconciliation to ways in which time marches on.

Yeats makes that variation, and that repetition, central to his late poem 'Towards Break of Day', whose speaker emerges from a sexual idyll: 'Was it the double of my dream / The woman that by me lay / Dreamed, or did we halve a dream?'[16] Yeats's speaker (perhaps a young man) and his paramour dreamed entirely different dreams, she of a 'marvellous stag' (Arthurian rather than Irish) and he of 'a waterfall/ Upon Ben Bulben side' that seemed, in childhood, magical. Like the adult Wordsworth, this naïve version of Yeats feels disenchanted, and finds, at best, philosophical consolation: 'Nothing that we love over-much / Is ponderable to our touch.'

And that disenchantment with a repeated experience saturates Yeats's bizarrely disrupted, repetition-filled nonce form. 'Towards Break of Day' opens with a tetrameter quatrain, and then continues in seven-line stanzas. It begins, too, with an *AbAb* rhyme, repeating 'dream': Yeats could have repeated this pattern, or appended a couplet to make a six-line stanza. Instead, he opens the next stanza with an unrhymed and unrepeated line-terminal, 'waterfall'; rhymes *cDcDc*, repeating 'dear'; and concludes with another non-rhyming word, 'delight'. Memories, experiences, words repeat themselves, until they do not: perfection, in the present, cannot be attained. Nor can the pattern of that second stanza recur: the third rhymes, instead, *efeggff* if we take 'touched' and 'touch' as

---

[13] *CW1*, 557.
[14] *CW1*, 301.
[15] *CW1*, 302.
[16] *CW1*, 185.

rhymes. No touch, no material experience, no moment can duplicate another. Man—at least this man—loves what vanishes.

But Yeats has more to say. The last stanza holds two non-rhymed terminals, but only one couplet: *bxbhxhh*. The ever-evasive stag of the last line must 'leap / From … steep to steep'. The memories of a magical childhood, like the dreams of a lover, evade the adult in waking life, in an aubade that takes the disruptions and dejections, the imperfections and reconciliations, attendant upon waking and parting into the self-disrupting form. (Auden famously founded 'Lay your sleeping head, my love' on Yeats's 'A Prayer for My Son'; it is hard to believe he did not have this poem in mind too.[17])

In *A Vision*, too, perfected or completed 'forms'—such as those of Phases 1 and 15—do not belong to human life, which instead sees itself in approximations, homeostasis, desire, and cyclical change. 'The ideal forms are only apparent through hope: perhaps [the instructors] mean that we do not in reality seek these forms, that while separate from us they are illusionary.'[18] No wonder Plato's ghost can never be satisfied. In one of Yeats's most famous remarks on verse form, perfection seems achievable: the finished poem 'comes right with a click like a closing box'[19] (Yeats, *Letters on Poetry*, 22). 'The Choice'— that anomalous single-stanza instance of ottava rima—presents a more complex picture. The often-cited poem deserves quoting in full:

> The intellect of man is forced to choose
> Perfection of the life or of the work
> And if it take the latter must refuse
> A heavenly mansion, labouring in the dark.
> When all that story's finished, what's the use?
> In luck or out, the toil has left its mark:
> That old perplexity, an empty purse
> Or the day's vanity, the night's remorse.[20]

James Longenbach, among others, objects to Yeats's famous 'distinction between perfection of the life and of the work … Yeats knew this couldn't be the case'. Instead, Longenbach's later Yeats knew how to 'celebrate the imperfect life … in dialogue with himself'.[21] This Yeats is also Francis O'Gorman's poet who has 'made aesthetic objects out of … let downs', whose 'disappointments are not only part of his life but of poetry's relationship with time'.[22] Disappointment inheres in the shape of this poem as well, a poem that splits up not into six lines, then two (as the form implies), but into four and

[17] Nicholas Jenkins, 'Historical as Munich—Auden at 100: Who Is He Now?', *Times Literary Supplement*, 9 Feb. 2007, 12–15.

[18] W. B. Yeats, *A Vision* (New York: Macmillan, 1967), 191

[19] Yeats to Dorothy Wellesley, 8 September [1935], *CL InteLex* #6335; see also W. B. Yeats, *Letters on Poetry from Yeats to Dorothy Wellesley* (New York: Oxford University Press, 1964), 22.

[20] *CW1*, 246–7.

[21] James Longenbach, *The Virtues of Poetry* (Minneapolis: Graywolf, 2013), 18–19.

[22] Francis O'Gorman, 'Yeats's Disappointments', *International Yeats Studies*, 1:2 (2017), 19.

four: the first 'quatrain' posing a choice of goals, the second declaring neither satisfying, if either is even possible. There may be no place on Earth where, in the terms of an earlier poem, 'body is not bruised to pleasure soul'—the ideal dance-like labour of 'Among Children' may be no goal adults can attain.[23]

Other examples of Yeatsian imperfection, irregular rhymes, and altered repetitions occur inside sequences. 'The Stare's Nest by My Window', the penultimate poem from 'Meditations in Time of Civil War', follows the grim self-isolation, and the regular quinzaines, of 'The Road at My Door', where Yeats seems to 'envy' the men of action. In 'The Stare's Nest' he seeks consolation from non-human nature, from the 'honeybees' who might build a new home, a new community, even a new nation, in the stare's vacated nest, just as Yeats hopes (perhaps vainly) for a new solidarity, a newly trustworthy architecture, to replace or improve the 'loosening masonry' of a divided nation. It is a poem of failed spring, a poem like Coleridge's 'Work Without Hope' or Hopkins's 'Thou art indeed just, Lord' ('Birds build, but not I build'), in which renewed fertility and vitality cannot extend to the poet himself.

Unlike those nineteenth-century sonnets, 'The Stare's Nest' makes its failure political, and plural. '*We* are closed in'. The atrocities of the Irish Civil War continue, as the stare's nest remains unoccupied: bees 'build' in the crumbling walls, but not in that nest. And though the tetrameters remain constant, the rhyme scheme changes: *abaab*, with the *a* rhyme on 'bees' and a hard caesura before the invocation, becomes a bee-less rhyme with no midline stops. Instead of bees, we hear about 'blood': instead of the first stanza's life-giving creatures, Yeats offers two stanzas whose 'enmities' endure.[24]

And then the honeybees return: the fourth stanza really deviates from the pattern the second and third have set (the bees may also point to eighteenth-century figures of industry, as in Mandeville's 'Fable of the Bees' or Oliver Goldsmith's periodical *The Bee*). Unlike the disrupted patterns in the poems discussed above, though—poems that end in ways no reader could have predicted from the beginning—the pattern in 'The Stare's Nest' returns to the one left behind. Paul Muldoon writes that 'the refrain is itself a symbol in Yeats'.[25] Like the first and unlike the second and third, this final stanza incorporates its refrain into its rhymes, not *ababx* but *ababb*: 'O honey-bees … stare'. Perhaps the bees will come, and peace come to Ireland. But the stare—the emblem of initial perfection—has gone.

We have seen, in all these poems that change or remake their external form, a poet who rejects or resists ideas of 'perfection', purity, unworldliness, such ideas as governed his peers in the 1890s, and some of his own early work. Few poems put more energy into that rejection than Yeats's late, and bitter, ballad 'The Old Stone Cross'. Vendler does not describe 'The Old Stone Cross', though its form fits her category of 'consciously worked' ballad stanzas.[26] These six-line stanzas, rhymed *xaxaxa* with a refrain, recount

---

[23] *CW1*, 217.

[24] *CW1*, 204–5; *CW1*, 209.

[25] Paul Muldoon, 'Moving on Silence: Yeats and the Refrain as Symbol', *YA*, 20 (2018): 155–78, 175.

[26] Vendler, *Our Secret Discipline*, 111.

the supposed sayings of a Roman centurion, the sort of man (if not the actual man) who supervised the death of Christ (whose cross, of course, was not stone).

This man is a cynic: he distrusts statesmen and journalists, and will not vote. He parodies the Stoics and Sophocles, calling no man 'happy', no age lucky: all 'engender in the ditch' (unlike Crazy Jane, he dislikes ditches). He saves his most interesting complaint, however, for 'actors', stage drama, and by extension all verbal arts: 'actors lacking music / Do most excite my spleen'. He prefers them musical, perfect, 'unearthly', and resents a play in which they 'shuffle, grunt, and groan', like the doomed figures in Yeats's own late and disturbing play *Purgatory*. He has missed the point of modernism, perhaps. He seems to hate real life. But he has also articulated an aesthetic of smoothness, of musicality, surprisingly close to the one in 'Adam's Curse', where effortless beauty appears as the final goal both of poets and of cosmetics.

Perfect smooth unity, for the heavily ironic Yeats who creates this callous soldier, seems a callous, indeed a cruel, soldier's goal. Better to represent dissatisfaction, to show human beings who can make mistakes. And the stanza itself 'groans' with him: that last segment shuffles half-rhyme ('groan' with 'scene') alongside a line-terminal that might as well be an extra half-rhyme ('human').[27] It sticks out. The soldier's mistake is, perhaps, not expecting perfection but expecting it to last. It is a thing of miracles and moments, as 'Words for Music Perhaps' attests: 'The Dancer at Cruachan and Cro-Patrick' announces 'that there is / Among birds or beasts or men, / One that is perfect or at peace',[28] but this dancer may not be in his right mind. He may be the same person as 'Tom the Lunatic', who speaks magic half-truths, and the whole truth (as Tom acknowledges) is that 'Things out of perfection sail'.[29] 'The Dancer at Cruachan' itself changes up its metrical pattern, throwing its trochaic trimeter to the wind in favour of triple metre in its anomalous last line.

The later Yeats wrote more poems that disrupt themselves, or set up formal expectations that they then fail to meet, in small-scale ways: 'The Collar-bone of a Hare', for example, whose second stanza incorporates repetitions alien to the first, or 'Two Songs of a Fool', neither a pair of sonnets nor a set of six-line stanzas nor a poem with predictable refrains. These poems of self-disrupting form, of imperfection (large or small) at the level of form, are poems that many readers might call minor. They are not the poems that land in anthologies, nor are they poems by which readers first encounter Yeats. Most of his major poems instead adhere to the stanzaic or to the stichic isometric patterns they adopt, finding their magnificent variations in other ways. 'The Second Coming', taken as a whole, makes sense as blank verse, though some readers hear, in the patterns of 'world' and 'hold', the potential *rime riche* of 'hand' and 'hand', hints of a submerged rhyme scheme. Even 'Lapis Lazuli', whose paragraph breaks and rough tetrameters may strike new readers as irregular, keeps to its four-beat quatrains all the way through, concluding in a sonnet-sized stanza marked almost all the way through by

[27] *CW1*, 317–18.
[28] *CW1*, 268.
[29] *CW1*, 268.

its exact rhyme: avalanche–branch, I–sky, play–gay. Even there, however, 'melodies' has to rhyme with 'eyes'.[30]

'Coole Park and Ballylee, 1931'—though in ottava rima throughout—reveals its own internal dissents, its own formal swerves and imperfections, when we reread with attention to its syntax. Like 'Towards Break of Day', like 'Meditations in Time of Civil War', it is a point of dejection, of disappointment, about the way that the present will not repeat or even reflect the past. And—if we look not only at metre but at rhyme and syntax—it, too, becomes a poem of disrupted form.

Ottava rima sets off a final couplet sonically. The sound invites syntactic offsets too: 'O body swayed to music, o brightening glance, / How can we know the dancer from the dance?' 'I must lie down where all the ladders start, / In the foul rag-and-bone-shop of the heart.' 'And therefore have I sailed the seas and come / To the holy city of Byzantium.' Yeats follows that pattern four times in the six stanzas of 'Coole and Ballylee, 1931'. The first stanza, though, does something almost shocking: the waters he follows proceed for seven lines, then 'drop into a hole. / What's water but the generated soul?'[31] This kind of isolated exclamation, or rhetorical question, defies the normal workings of English couplets. It is as if the poet looked up from his project of mimesis, from following land-scape and weather, to ask what he could learn about human life.

The next four stanzas constitute his answer: Coole Park itself, like other ancestral houses and noble estates in Yeats, represented tradition, continuity, ceremony, 'ordering, patterning, shaping' (to quote Levine), all the desiderata Yeats had already invoked in 'A Prayer for My Daughter'.[32] And 'we'—we poets, we aesthetes, we traditionalists, we Irish, we modern humans—cannot have those desiderata now:

> We were the last romantics, chose for theme
> Traditional sanctity and loveliness;
> Whatever's written in what poets name
> The book of the people; whatever most can bless
> The mind of man or elevate a rhyme;
> But all is changed, that high horse riderless,
> Though mounted in that saddle Homer rode
> Where the swan drifts upon a darkening flood.[33]

'All is changed', of course, repeats the refrain of 'Easter, 1916', where everything about Ireland has 'changed, changed utterly'.[34] (Yeats added this echo in revision: *Words for Music Perhaps* had read 'But fashion's changed'.[35]) After that change, a reader familiar

---

[30] *CW1*, 295.
[31] *CW1*, 217, 348, 193, 244.
[32] Levine, *Forms*, 3.
[33] *CW1*, 245.
[34] *CW1*, 180–2.
[35] *VP*, 492.

with ottava rima would expect a concluding couplet, a declaration or a single image to fit the couplet form.

Instead, Yeats offers a concessive—'though'—followed by chaos and solitude: a riderless horse, a single swan, a flood. Why and how could Homer, being blind, ever ride a 'high horse'? The horse would have to know—to remember—where to take its sightless rider, as a horse that always took the same path could. But the path is gone. This water is not 'the generated soul' but the apocalyptic flood, and it overflows its couplet boundary, so that the final image takes up the last three lines. Adding to the sense that things have gone off, that nothing can be perfect or whole any more, this final stanza contains only forced rhymes and off-rhymes: all prior stanzas ended with perfect couplets. 'Loveliness', 'bless', and 'riderless' end with the same vowel–consonant combination, but only 'bless' would ordinarily stress that vowel. Though Parkinson finds that 'off-rhymes were to [Yeats's] mind normal, not violations of convention', they register here as they accumulate; the only other ottava rima poem with a similar set of off-rhymes is 'The Gyres'.[36] 'Coole and Ballylee, 1931', for all its initial composure, envisions and follows the demise of an elegant order, the fall of a world, and Yeats's attempt to represent it faithfully by representing failures, flaws, falls away from 'perfection'.

That fall may also explain why Yeats excised the single stanza that became 'The Choice'. That stanza's ambiguous vision of artists' lives, materially successful but spiritually bereft or vice versa, ends within the track of a single life. 'Coole and Ballylee, 1931' concludes instead with collective effort. It is not the single artist, the single life, the supposedly perfectible solitary human being, who has lost the horse: 'we', all of us, all the last Romantics, cannot maintain the order and the patterns that were 'once more dear than life', and we do not know what if anything can replace them. 'Coole and Ballylee, 1931' is not the only other poem whose syntax defies expectations so abruptly, but it makes an especially clear example. And it presents, writ large, a kind of third answer to the binary Yeats envisioned in 'The Choice'.

What is a perfect life? Yeats does not say: he suggests, instead—ambivalently, even ambiguously, as Vendler's discussion reveals—that neither material success nor its absence, neither acknowledgement nor obscurity, can tell the poet whether he has achieved anything, whether anything will survive the flood. Auden—that author who called human beings 'the inconstant ones', that great student of Yeats who worked so hard to disavow Yeats, objected to 'The Choice': 'perfection is possible in neither'.[37] This life, and its works, and its communities, are a series of more or less frustrating, more or less triumphant, let-downs and imperfections. And Yeats's forms seem to have known as much all along.

* * *

[36] *CW1*, 293; Parkinson, *The Later Poetry*, 198.
[37] Thekla Clark, *Wystan and Chester* (New York: Columbia University Press, 1995), 9.

What can we learn from Yeats's imperfect forms, Yeats' mid- and late-career tributes to imperfection? What can we learn, not only about Yeats, but about poetic form, or about lyric poetry in general?

To begin with, we might learn that form in practice does not usually mean perfect or flawlessly regular form. The self-disrupting, self-destabilizing forms in exceptional poems such as 'The Realists' repeat, at the level of stanza shape and of poem shape, the flexibility that Yeats's peers and juniors recommended at the level of the sentence and the line. Consider Ezra Pound's famous prescription that poets compose 'in the sequence of the musical phrase, not in the sequence of the metronome', published in 1913, near the start of the 'Stone Cottage' period when (as James Longenbach has persuasively argued) Yeats was teaching Pound (more than vice versa) 'how to forge a modern idiom for poetry'.[38]

Benjamin Glaser has argued that Pound and other modernists extend this anti-metronomic attitude into revisions of recognizable metres, and into their metrical theories, 'position[ing] themselves against false freedom' as they explore their 'unease with print mediation and its publics'.[39] For Glaser, Yeats's own 'practice of metre' (unlike Frost's or Eliot's) belongs outside this particular modernist company, since Yeats's metric 'evokes relative continuity and comfort with a longer metrical tradition'.[40] What these poets do with metre, one might say, Yeats sometimes does by remaking (among many other aspects of a poem) stanzaic form.

Yeats's formally irregular poems also let us test broad recent models of how poetry, or modern poetry, or lyric poetry, can work and be and mean. Jonathan Culler claims that lyric—a transhistorical kind of composition, one that may be as old as music or language—presents consistent and easily recognized features, among them musicality and especially rhythmic interest; repetition; hyperbole; address to an absent, non-existent or non-human listener; the 'lyric present, which is a present of enunciation', both an unusual relation to time itself and an anomalous verb tense; and a focus on the 'ritualistic dimension' of the linguistic event, rather than on what language imitates or describes.[41] Culler quotes Yeats's remark, 'Poetry is rhythm', by which he suggests both the rhythm in strings of syllables and the greater patterns of repetition that (for Culler) set lyric apart. Culler also notes the modern tension between 'the singularity of a literary work' and the constraints of genre, by which literary works inevitably resemble one another, and without which we would not be able to interpret, nor to enjoy, nor to recognize them.[42]

---

[38] James Longenbach, *The Stone Cottage: Pound, Yeats and Modernism* (New York: Oxford University Press, 1991), 14.

[39] Benjamin Glaser, *Modernism's Metronome* (Baltimore: Johns Hopkins University Press, 2020), 21, 19.

[40] Glaser, *Modernism's Metronome*, 22.

[41] Jonathan Culler, *Theory of the Lyric* (Cambridge MA: Harvard University Press, 2015), 294, 7.

[42] Culler, *Theory of the Lyric*, 137, 41.

The features of lyric within individual poems, if we remember and value the poems, do not strain against that singularity so much as they make it possible. 'The Realists', for example, keeps its base trochaic rhythm at bay ('HOPE that YOU may ...') and then dispels that rhythm entirely by the last line ('with the DRAGons'). If 'The Realists' constitutes a ritual after all, it is a ritual like the one in Kafka's story 'Leopards in the Temple', one whose disruption, repeated, itself becomes part of the norm. As for magical, other-worldly, unrealistic, or hyperbolic effects, manifested in Culler's lyric present, 'The Realists' does not so much produce those effects as point outside the poem, to show that they remain possible elsewhere. Yeats's eight-line work defends works that manifest dragons, works that propagate magic, without becoming such a work itself: it resembles, say, a study of fantasy novels more than it resembles a fantasy novel itself.

'The Realists'—like many of Yeats's works, even before *The Green Helmet*—retains an irreducible minimum of argument, pointing outside itself to ritual or to uncanny doings in which the reader, and often the poet, cannot take part. Culler might say that the poem is therefore part lyric and part something else. Following Paul de Man's theories of litera-ture in general, some readers might say that the poem demonstrates the impossibility of presence, of truthful and unmediated manifestation, either in lyric poetry, or in lit-erature, or in human life more generally. A more attentive reader of Yeats might say that this kind of self-aware gesture, by which the poem remains marginal to the ritualistic or magical event it honours, might be a property not of poetry, nor of human life, but of Yeats.

Consider, again, 'A Coat': is our poet naked himself, by the end of the poem? Or does he propose to walk naked in the future? Is his song naked, or will his song disrobe after the poem concludes? De Man made heavy weather out of similar ambiguities at the end of 'Among School Children', whose 'authority ... is fully obscured by the duplicity of a figure that cries out for the differentiation that it conceals'.[43] Few readers not wholly devoted to de Man would find the figure duplicitous, or deceptive. Human beings, even outside of Yeats's poems, ask ambiguous questions, questions with no one clear an-swer, all the time. Such questions often take on expressive functions: they demonstrate wonder mingled with incapacity, for example, or bafflement with a soupçon of awe.

To read Yeats's questions that way—in 'The Realists', as well as in 'Among School Children'—is to imagine Yeats as a speaking character, to imagine a persona behind the words, exactly the kind of imagining that de Man and Culler (for different reasons) in their models of (respectively) literary language and lyric ritual, discourage. All three poems ('Among School Children', 'The Realists', and 'A Coat') point with respect to a ritual, even to magical doings, taking place elsewhere, where dragons are real, where people and poems go naked, where the dancer becomes the dance.

Yeatsian 'lyric events', that is to say, tend to take place partly inside, but partly out-side, the reader's own experience of the poem, and the poet's experience as speaker: they are hybrid in this sense far more often than they are hybrid, or self-disrupting, or

---

[43] Paul de Man, 'Semiology and Rhetoric', *diacritics*, 3:3 (1973), 27–33, 30.

two-headed, in their stanzaic shapes (like the poems I began by considering). 'There all the barrel-hoops are knit / . . . There all the gyres converge in one', says Yeats's Ribh: 'there', not 'here'.[44] Of course there are exceptions, such as 'A Dialogue of Self and Soul': in the later Yeats there are exceptions to everything.

Accurate models of lyric—Ribh's among them!—acknowledge the ways in which ritual and mimesis, event and the presentation of an event, disembodied voice and realized character, coexist. Culler emphasizes the former term in each of these binaries as the one that stands out, that makes lyric properly lyric. Yeats, just as often, emphasizes the latter—and the more he wants to show magic at work, the more likely he is (especially after about 1910 and *The Green Helmet*) to create a speaking character who beholds the event in his stead. Ribh stands among the last and clearest among those dramatic creations, and when Ribh gives us ritual ecstasy, the summoning of a god, he does so not by bringing the god to the page (as Pindar or Rilke, Coleridge or Dickinson might) but by looking back on the indescribable event: 'Doubtless I spoke or sang what I had heard / In broken sentences'.[45] The clean pentameter couplets (unusual for late Yeats) work like an airlock, or like a soap molecule, safely and comprehensibly connecting two otherwise incommensurable domains.

Such connections, more than an emphasis on ritual or event, characterize, not lyric, but Yeatsian lyric. And they occur in other poems already considered: for example, in 'Coole and Ballylee, 1931', where the supernatural enters the common world in the past (harmoniously) and at the very end of the poem (menacingly) but not in between. Exactly the kind of extended description, and even the aural mimesis, that Culler discounts, inform the sonic effects that open the poem, as Yeats's phrases 'race', 'run', 'drop, run underground, rise', 'spread to a lake and drop into a hole'. As for 'The Old Stone Cross', Yeats's villainous soldier—himself caught up in the most consequential of supernatural events—appears nostalgic for exactly the kind of ritual, anti-mimetic presence that for Culler lyric as such provides. The centurion grumbles:

> Actors lacking music
> Do most excite my spleen,
> Not knowing what unearthly stuff
> Rounds a mighty scene.

The centurion wants ritual and gets mimesis; he is himself part of the Western world's most famous ritual, even as he remains a dramatic speaker, delivering stanzaic monologue or a protagonist in what Marion Thain calls 'meta-lyric, played out at one remove'.[46]

---

[44] *CW1*, 285.

[45] *CW1*, 291.

[46] Marion Thain, *The Lyric Poem and Aestheticism* (Edinburgh: Edinburgh University Press, 2016), 179.

Yeats's poems, and especially the 'imperfect' sort discussed here, emphasize both sides of a polarity (ritual against mimesis, enactment against description, 'voicing' against character). If these Yeatsian poems count as lyric, they are imperfect lyric, hybrid lyric, lyric with leopards inside, lyric that is constantly doffing, and can never quite remove, its coat. In Vendler's model, the lyric poem is the cry of a soul in space (Rilke's 'Seele im Raum'), 'stripping away ... the details associated with a socially specified self ... In lyric poetry voice is made abstract ... the range of things one would normally know about a voice in a novel one does not know about a voice in a lyric.'[47] How old is Ribh? What colour is his beard, if he has a beard? We do not know; we cannot know. Lyric in Vendler's model is about people, just as much as (if not more than) novels and plays and comic books are about people. In her model its ritual status becomes optional, while its 'abstract' properties—its concision and its musicality—come to the fore. Vendler often takes Yeats as an example; her career-long touchstones have been Keats and Stevens and Yeats, and so, unsurprisingly, her model of how lyric works fits Yeats's poems, even his obviously 'imperfect' poems. Vendler's abstraction is Yeats's 'ice': 'All that is personal soon rots. It must be packed in ice or salt.'[48] Not removed or deleted; salted or iced. Character, persona, whether Yeats's own or a fool's, remain. This kind of abstraction is not the same as the Hegelian universal, 'the universalizing impulse in lyric' (to quote Thain), nor does Yeats pretend it is.[49] A lyric speaker in Yeats may be old or young, Welsh or Nigerian, urban or rural, just not (or not normally) 66 years old, or 82, or a resident of Wintersmith Lane. And people, like poems, are imperfect: we ourselves exist, most of the time, between an outer world and an inner life—we are part abstract and part concrete, part a response to circumstance and part emotion that can be generalized.

That briefer model of lyric fits Yeats's short poems more often, and more justly, and recognizes his imperfections more aptly, than one that separates ritual from dramatization. It accounts more fully for the unanswerable questions that conclude poems such as 'Among School Children': they are abstract, but they embody a feeling, more than they point to any hypocrisy or duplicity within language as such.

And yet a model of lyric that does nothing but present a soul, nothing except embody feeling, might scant the other effects that Yeats's poems—including his 'imperfect' poems—seek. Do they also digress, or divert our attention, from one thing to another, from the given world or the immediate environment to things and people and events elsewhere? Do they also attempt to create events? Don't they try, not only to manifest a voice, but to divert (in the sense of a traffic diversion) our thoughts, and our mind's eye? 'I call to the eye of the mind', Yeats's agent intones in 'At the Hawk's Well': 'Now as at all times I can see in the mind's eye', begins 'The Magi'.[50] What models of lyric, or of poetics, or of modern poetics, encompass such callings?

---

[47] Vendler, *Our Secret Discipline*, 3.
[48] *CW5*, 213.
[49] Thain, *Lyric Poem*, 178.
[50] *CW1* 561; 126.

Two kinds of models, at the least, fit those effects. In the first kind, poetry, or genuine poetry, or perhaps lyric poetry, inheres in a slippage between the given world and another that cannot be apprehended directly: poetry works to move us always away, never towards the already-grasped, always towards the uncanny, or the unknowable. It is at least a shrug, at most a gesture of continual awe, and in between it seeks slippage, uncertainty, motion. Above all it does not admit what it knows, and its knowledge (such as it is) subtends an opposition to rationality, to empiricism, to the visible world, to toothpaste and rocks and news headlines. We can find this model in the early Yeats, most often in his characters: consider 'The Man Who Dreamed of Fairyland', a lovely example of Thain's category 'meta-lyric' (when Thain writes that 'rhythm in the [early] poetry of Yeats seems to lead to symbolic representation of a spiritual realm').[51] The Argentine poet Sergio Chejfec's ideal-typical modern poet 'has a slippery way of thinking'; 'he thinks digression is a mode of being', 'a method of attaining perfection in pursuit of a harmonious cohabitation with reality and poetry'.[52] We can find this anti-mimetic model, too, in T. S. Eliot's remark that 'content' in a poem might be like 'the nice bit of meat' that a burglar carries to distract 'the house dog'.[53] Contemporary American proponents of this model tend to find it in John Ashbery. For the contemporary poet Matthew Zapruder—taking Ashbery as a touchstone—'poetry in general ... required me to give up on looking for a certain kind of meaning'. This giving up involves 'a kind of dreamlike, associative ... drifting ... on the frontier of dreaming', a 'reverie'; 'the preservation of this drifting experience is the purpose and promise of poetry'.[54] Not Ashbery's poetry; not (or not explicitly) lyric poetry; all poetry.

The later Yeats could not possibly have believed that. The experience of drift, of reverie, of removal from the given world becomes in his lyric poems, at most, a half-truth. The dragons have their power because the shopkeepers have theirs: if we knew no shopkeepers we might not treasure the dragons, and once we envision the dragons and the sea-nymphs we are less likely to drift away with them than to envision their allure, or their claws. The naked singer, or the naked song, proposes not flânerie but 'enterprise': he will make something, or accomplish something, for himself or for somebody else. The damaged estate of Coole Park invites reverie— the 'sudden thunder of the mounting swan', the mysterious drift of a white cloud, 'no man knows why'—but it also invites specific commemoration, 'a spot whereon the founders lived and died'.[55] It even invites attention to political history, to the here and now, however abstracted or generalized: the 'darkening flood' at the end of

---

[51] Thain, *Lyric Poem*, 83.

[52] Sergio Chejfec, *Notes Towards a Pamphlet*, trans. Whitney DeVos (Brooklyn, NY: Ugly Duckling, 2020), 20, 24.

[53] T. S. Eliot, *The Use of Poetry and the Use of Criticism* (1933; London: Faber, 1964), 151.

[54] Matthew Zapruder, 'Unlocking the Unconscious Through Poetry,' *Paris Review*, 14 August 2017, https://www.theparisreview.org/blog/2017/08/14/advice-how-to-drift-through-poems/.

[55] *CW1*, 244.

that poem constitutes a menace, and we, the readers, might want to do something about it.

We can see such wants in the oddly constructed and rarely discussed final song in 'A Man Young and Old'. 'His Wildness', manifests neither drift, nor reverie, nor impersonality, nor a reaction to the day's news, but rather the dramatic possibility in a kind of 'cry', a loneliness that demands a personal fantasy and a secondary world:

> Were I but there and none to hear
> I'd have a peacock cry,
> For that is natural to a man
> That lives in memory,
> Being all alone I'd nurse a stone
> And sing it lullaby.[56]

It is another of Yeats's imperfect forms: the whole poem rhymes *abcbcbc adedede*, with the internal rhyme or rime riche that connotes folk song present only before the second *a* (the first magazine publication lacked a stanza break).[57] The rhyme *memory/ lullaby* remains as tenuous as the Old Man's links between past and present. If he recommends life in memory, life in a reverie, he neither recommends nor enacts a refusal to focus.

Indeed, Yeats's Old Man craves focus: he would prefer a well-defined speech act, a kind of relation, to something or someone, to another person—even an imaginary one, a baby in the shape of a stone (it is Yeats at his most Stevensian; the stone baby as interior paramour). If he will sing—and he will sing—he wants, as the song from *Buffy the Vampire Slayer* has it, 'Something to Sing About'. That aboutness, present in Vendler's model of lyric, has been evacuated (understandably) from Zapruder's model, and de-emphasized, to say the least, in Culler's. Another name for aboutness is attention: what we hold, what we examine, what we take, now, in the mind. And another model for poetry—especially for the poetry that we have learned to label as lyric—accounts both for reverie and for 'enterprise': for the clouds as well as the ancestors, the gutters as well as the water, in 'Coole and Ballylee, 1931' for the man who dreamed of Fairyland and the man who would rather nurse a stone. That model is Lucy Alford's, in her study *Forms of Poetic Attention*, and it is as useful here, where I am trying to describe Yeats's poetry in relation to ideas about lyric and form, as it is useless for the purpose of archive-based literary history (such as Thain's).

To Alford, 'what is formed *by* and *in* poetic language is an event of attention generated in the acts of ... reading and writing'; 'a poem might be better understood not simply as a gathering of composed formal features, but as an instrument for tuning and composing the attention'; 'Attention to language as object ... not *only* as conduit of meaning, can be said to characterize the poetic as such'. We may focus our attention on formal features

---

[56] *CW1*, 226.
[57] *VP*, 458.

as such, or on a poetic speaker, or on what that speaker calls to mind. 'The presence of a speaker is one', only one, 'of the effects the poem has been designed to produce'. 'Poetic attention brings about an event', as per Culler, but it also 'positions us in relation to others'. And—crucially—attention, in Alford's model, may be 'transitive' or 'intransitive': a poem may direct our attention either to something outside the poem and outside its speaker, or to itself, or to nothing at all. This last sort of attention, an anti-mimetic or anti-referential as well as 'intransitive' sort, incorporates 'idleness', drift and reverie, when 'attention is allowed to wander' in 'a garden of unstructured time', corresponding to Zapruder's, or Ashbery's, meditative drift.

But Yeats is a poet of transitive attention: there is, almost always, something his poems are *about*, usually (even in short poems such as 'A Coat') more than one thing. The changes and unpredictable formal features in those poems divert, focus or refocus our attention on something, on 'an observation, whether in the eye of the speaker or in the mind's eye', to quote Alford on George Oppen. 'Often the object of the poem's contemplation turns out to be other than its initial semantic object of focus', not the same thing as possessing no object at all.[58]

Yeats's changes in the course of a poem—his swerves away from the exact repetitions that are the mark of perfected form—serve to direct and redirect his own, and his readers', transitive attention. Grammar and assonance in the first stanza from 'Coole and Ballylee, 1931' become directly mimetic, flowing and stopping with the water they show. The same tools redirect our attention to the purely aural aspects in the poem, the 'sound of a stick upon the floor', before resolving into the stately pace of ritual, honouring people not otherwise described: here 'gardens rich in memory glorified / Marriages, alliances and families / And every bride's ambition satisfied'. The rhythms of Yeats's attention change when the poem returns from its most 'elevated' objects of contemplation (or mourning, another category in Alford's taxonomy) to the threatened present, 'where the swan drifts upon a darkening flood'.[59] He is, to quote Alford, 'following the movement of the mind's eye as it opens'—in this case from the observed to the projected, from literal rainstorm to figural apocalypse.[60]

'A Coat', too, tunes and retunes our attention: we may understand its miniaturist workings as melody and countermelody, attention drawn first to the poet's past, to 'embroideries / Out of old mythologies', with polysyllabic 'embroidered' half-rhymes to boot. Then Yeats, so to speak, puts the boot in, rhyming 'take it' with 'naked', changing the kind of attention the poem demands: from past to future, from soft to hard, from memory to an oath-like resolution. 'The Choice' also alters the kinds of attention it offers, not once, like 'A Coat', but back and forth: we attend for three lines to a generality, testing a claim made of abstract nouns ('intellect', 'perfection', 'work') against cases

---

[58] Lucy Alford, *Forms of Poetic Attention* (New York: Columbia University Press, 2020), 3–4, 14, 10, 275, 216–17, 93, 75.

[59] *CW1*, 244–5.

[60] Alford, *Poetic Attention*, 148.

known to us, or taking that claim on faith.[61] Alford (if I understand her labels correctly) calls that kind of attention 'contemplation': we neither wish for a thing, nor lament its passing, but consider its salient examples. We then consider 'a heavenly mansion, raging in the dark', what Alford calls an act of visual imagination, followed by another, 'an empty purse'; then we land again on names that denote, not things, but emotions, bereft of the very images that a perfected poetic 'work' might bring to mind, mourning (or hearing the poet mourn) we know not what ('attending to the departed object', in Alford's terms, as well as 'to the object's absence').[62]

Yeats's imperfections, in other words, become ways to alter or redirect Yeats's own forms of transitive poetic attention: from contemplation to recollection, from diffuse to specific, from apprehension to imagination to longing. Yeats is, of course, not the only poet who redirects attention from one kind to another, one object to another. Rather, he is especially good at it, as other poets—Dickinson, say, or A. R. Ammons—are good at producing exactly one kind per poem. Yeats uses the *concordia discors* in his ottava rima couplets as a means for this kind of redirection, almost as a matter of course. And, he uses other effects of external form, imperfections and mid-poem shifts, similarly: in 'A Coat' and in 'The Choice' and in—to conclude where I began—'The Realists'. Hailing us as readers and listeners, focusing our attention upon ourselves in that single belt of trochaic tetrameter, Yeats then redirects us, not to our own attempts to imagine dragons, but to other, prior readers'. We, too, envision—as the poem's rhythms shift around us— 'sea-nymphs in their pearly wagons' (an act of 'imagination' in Alford's sense). And then we recollect, and we lament: we ourselves, not being fictional characters, cannot 'live ... with the dragons'. We can, however, live with imperfections, and with the feelings, and with the sonic inventions, that we discover in Yeats's imperfect forms.

---

[61] *CW1*, 251.
[62] Alford, *Poetic Attention*, 98–9.

CHAPTER 38

YEATS'S VISIONARY COMEDY

MATTHEW CAMPBELL

> It is called 'wisdom' and this wisdom (personality reflected in a *primary* mirror), is general humanity experienced as a form of involuntary emotion, and involuntary delight in the 'minute particulars' of life. The man wipes his breath from the window pane, and laughs in his delight at all the varied scene.[1]

WHAT on earth does the everyday sensible reader do when faced with a poet who entertained beliefs that are not sensible at all? What to do with William Butler Yeats, a poet who believed in ghosts, attended seances, decided to get married only after consulting his horoscope, and then involved his much younger wife in automatic writing most nights for the first years of their marriage? How does one approach a poet who devoted much of the last twenty-two years of his career to elucidating a world-historical system revealed to him by mysterious communicators who wrote to him through his right-handed wife's left hand—often in mirror writing? And then, how can you read that same writer when he tells his readers not to take the system they have created seriously, and that even for the mediums through which the avatars spoke it was all a bit of a mystery?

Someone who has treated this material very seriously indeed, Margaret Mills Harper, says of the eventual bringing together of this material into the two versions of *A Vision,* published by Yeats in 1925 and 1937, that while he tells the story of his visionary experience, it sometimes looks as if he is inviting the reader into a joke:

> … the tone of 'any excuse however plausible' is the kind of smiling self-deflation which runs throughout *A Vision,* although it has not often been recognized as such. Self-deference is a significant rhetorical strategy in the book, … linked with the narrator/writer's sense that he is not the sole author of his philosophical text and that he does not even understand all of it. The WBY who presents *A Vision* and has a

[1] *CW*14, 122.

secondary role as a character in some of its bewilderingly prominent framing stories and poems is in fact several Yeatses, sliding between subject and object positions, who refer to each other in complex ways that are uncertainly and simultaneously serious and comic.[2]

Harper tells us that Yeats had planned to include the following dedication to the 1937 *Vision*:

> To my wife Who created this system which bores her, who made possible these pages which she will never read & who has accepted this dedication on the condition that I write nothing but verse for a year.[3]

Needless to say, George Yeats requested that he not include this dedication. She may have found the automatic writing physically hard work, but, as countless explorers of the *Vision* papers have told us, she was far from bored, rather an active collaborator, even instigator, of the whole project.

The epigraph to this chapter touches tangentially on Yeats's view of the wise in the twenty-third phase of the moon, for whom wisdom 'is general humanity experienced as a form of involuntary emotion and involuntary delight in the "minute particulars" of life'. The involuntary emotion is laughter. With such wisdom comes a comic or even comedic view of the world. The exemplars of this phase—'The Receptive Man'—are Rembrandt and Synge, and Yeats does not entirely present them without demur. Their 'wisdom' may be a thing to be admired but, if it comes with an attention to 'minute particulars 'and consequently 'laughter', it may also come from a detachment from belief. It is also, as this section of *A Vision* goes on to say, associated with 'technical mastery'. Those artists who show too much technique also show too much involuntary delight at 'minute particulars' (the phrase is derived from Blake[4]) as well as a willingness to shirk higher artistic demands, where the mastery exists for 'laying bare ... general humanity'. The consequences are that the Receptive Man 'laughs in his delight at all the varied scene'.

This chapter explores various aspects of reading Yeats as a sort of comedian or, if not that, someone who wrote a visionary comedy, albeit one passing through 'general humanity' to 'The Fool' of the twenty-eighth phase of *A Vision*: 'his thoughts are an aimless reverie; his acts are aimless like his thoughts; and it is in this aimlessness that he finds his joy' (*CW14*, 135). Primarily, this is the Fool of Shakespeare, and specifically from *King Lear*, but it is a figure seen throughout the various world-artistic cultures and forms with which Yeats experimented, from Mayo to London to Kyoto. In Synge and Shakespeare and the *kyogen* drama, the fool is both mindless and all-knowledgeable. There is, of course, another version of the comedic, that of the Dantean *Commedia*: that great

---

[2] Margaret Mills Harper, *Wisdom of Two: The Spiritual and Literary Collaboration of George and W. B. Yeats* (Oxford: Oxford University Press, 2006), 14.

[3] Draft dedication to *A Vision*, 1937, Yeats MS 23 Nov 31930, cited in Harper, *Wisdom of Two*, 13

[4] *CW14*, 377 n.

foundational Western Christian engagement with other worlds, afterlives, eternity, and the divine was something that Yeats certainly had in mind for much of his career.[5] And, later in life, Yeats reverted often to the example of Jonathan Swift and a sort of classical Fescennine poetry, a satire of the body, often obscene and bawdy.

In all of these versions, comedy comports with serious matter, and Yeats certainly thought of it as such: the idea of *joy* as the most important consummating achievement to which so many of his later poems aspire may be partly the comedic joy of divine knowledge and partly the tragic joy of the Nietzschean hero. But comedy is also something that we can mute down to the sensible, the ethical, the everyday, our feelings about what it is to be in good humour, to have an equable and not obsessive temperament. According to Yeats, this is the 'wisdom' of Synge or Rembrandt, as well as *King Lear* played through a now-forgotten contemporary of whose poetry Yeats spoke highly, William Watson: 'Out of the pool . . . Bubbles the wan mirth of the mirthless fool'.[6]

If we don't immediately think of Yeats as a comic poet, we certainly don't think of William Wordsworth as one. But the critic Matthew Bevis argues just that in a book called, counter-intuitively, *Wordsworth's Fun*. It is an exploration of how we read for irony, innuendo, and insinuation, pratfalls and foolishness, incongruity and insanity, deflation and sometimes just for fun. True seriousness is at issue:

> . . . while the life of a good joke is often in league with the unabashed, the perilous, the tendentious, it may also prompt its audience to consider whether solemnity might sometimes be an act of bad faith, or an avoidance of true seriousness. If, as Schopenhauer suggested, humour is 'the seriousness concealed behind a joke', then Wordsworth is interested in humour—and in what the sharing, getting, and not-getting of jokes may say about us.[7]

The urbane speaker who opens Yeats's great poem for the executed leaders of the Easter Rising admits that he had underestimated them: 'And thought before I had done / Of a mocking tale or a gibe / To please a companion / Around the fire at the club' (*CW1*, 180). But the members of any respectable Dublin club of the time would be as likely to be delivering mocking jibes at William Butler Yeats as Padraig Pearse. When we snigger at the solemnity of our friends or idols, we may be acting in bad faith, but perhaps to take them and ourselves too seriously amounts to the same thing. And if we don't listen out for nuance and self-contradiction or attend to the tone of what is being said as much as to its paraphrasable matter, we are not taking them seriously either.

Yeats, like Wordsworth, knew that to present the perilous or, more likely, the tendentious in an unabashed way is to betray both the comic uncertainties of the minute

[5] For Yeats, Shakespeare, and Dante see the chapters by Edna Longley (Chapter 11) and Hugh Haughton (Chapter 12) in this volume.

[6] Yeats misquotes Watson's epigram on 'The Play of *King Lear*' after the description of the twenty-eighth phase in both versions of *A Vision*. Watson was only absent from *The Oxford Book of Modern Verse* because his executors would not give permission. See *CW5*, 291.

[7] Matthew Bevis, *Wordsworth's Fun* (Chicago: University of Chicago Press, 2019), 7.

particulars of everyday life and the larger implications for an ethical life too certain of what it is saying—or entirely without the tempering of appropriate doses of scepticism. For all his dabbling with the right wing of Irish and European politics, his lifelong fascination with authority and power, the practice of Yeats's poetry is neither authoritarian nor nihilistic: scepticism can be unhealthy, and to apply it too firmly can in itself mean we have missed the point and are thus open to a joke. For readers, as much as poets, attending closely to writing and what is written can be like listening to a voice, albeit an absent one; and voices when present have tone and pitch. By means of raising its pitch a poem can question; by lowering it can emphasise; and by inflection it can raise the matter of the humour that attends much social as well as linguistic intercourse.

Readers of Yeats, like readers of Dante or Wordsworth, need to listen for the comic intonation, look out for the linguistic sense that accompanies its poetic as much as mystical progress, be wary that what seems like an assertion has been phrased as a question and the raising of the voice can make us go back and ponder over the comedy of how we as readers got it wrong. We realize that something else might have been said once the ironic or the querulous have come into play. 'Did she put on his knowledge with his power / before the indifferent beak could let her drop?' 'Now I know' not *that* rough beast, but 'what rough beast, its hour come round at last / Slouches towards Bethlehem to be born?' We might think that Yeats can be very silly sometimes, but we must be wary of laughing too hard when we actually read his poetry, in case the joke might be on us. As Louis MacNeice said, in what is still one of the best books about Yeats, published just two years after the poet died,

> I have met people whose attitude is: 'Yeats was a silly old thing but he was a *poet*.' This is a foolish attitude. No silly old thing can write fine poetry. A poet cannot live by style alone; nor even by intuitions alone. Yeats, contrary to some people's opinions, had a mind. He had also extraordinary force of personality. It is impossible to explain him by merely murmuring about beauty.[8]

Yeats is a poet who can be both silly and fine, one who can allow the fanciful to intrude into the deeply personal and the deeply political. 'You were silly *like us*'[9] (my emphasis), MacNeice's friend W. H. Auden had to say about this saving facet of Yeats's actual poetic process.

This comedic element works in Yeats's poetry and drama, where the humour is allowed to play over both the visionary and the deeply personal, extending rather than ruining it. To take the first of two examples, Yeats's poem 'The Cat and the Moon' was first published in 1919 in *The Wild Swans at Coole* volume, recycled in a different form from *The Cat and the Moon,* a play he wrote in 1917 but didn't publish until 1926. The poem is spread across the play as a sort of chorus but brought together into a single

---

[8] Louis MacNeice, *The Poetry of W. B. Yeats* (London: Faber, 1941), 31.
[9] W. H. Auden, 'In Memory of W.B. Yeats', in *Collected Poems*, ed. Edward Mendelson (London: Faber & Faber, 2007), 246.

integrated lyric in the 1919 collection. These are the second and third 'choruses', which make up the centre of the earlier-published lyric:

> Minnaloushe runs in the grass
> Lifting his delicate feet.
> Do you dance, Minnaloushe, do you dance?
> When two close kindred meet,
> What better than call a dance?
> Maybe the moon may learn,
> Tired of that courtly fashion,
> A new dance turn.
> Minnaloushe creeps through the grass
> From moonlit place to place,
> The sacred moon overhead
> Has taken a new phase.[10]

Leaving aside the phases of the moon, which are invoked at the end here, a historical cat, called Minnaloushe, belonged to Iseult Gonne, Maud Gonne MacBride's daughter. The poem and play come out of the difficult year, 1917, when Yeats proposed first to Maud Gonne after the execution by the British of her estranged husband, John MacBride, in May 1916 and then contemplated marriage to Iseult. When refused by both, his proposal was accepted by George Hyde-Lees. The moon, of course, is a common symbol in astrology or the Tarot, say, but the male cat Minnaloushe and the female moon seem to be cavorting in a symbolic lyric.

Yeats later had this to say about what the relation of cat and moon might mean in a note to the published play, indulging what Harper calls 'smiling self-deflation' in his completely unhelpful gloss:

> Minnaloushe and the Moon were perhaps – it all grows faint to me – an exposition of man's relation to what I called the Antithetical Tincture, and when the Saint mounts upon the back of the Lame Beggar he personifies a great spiritual event which may take place when Primary Tincture, as I have called it, supersedes Antithetical – ... I have altogether forgotten whether other parts of the fable have, as is very likely, a precise meaning, and that is natural, for I generally forget in contemplating my copy of an old Persian carpet that its winding and wandering vine had once had that philosophical meaning, which has made it very interesting to Josef Stryzgowski and was part of the religion of Zoroaster.[11]

In a way this is a tease, challenging the reader to view the symbolism as impenetrable nonsense. In another way the antithetical and primary are key parts of the dialectic of world history in *A Vision*, vital elements of the geometry of horoscopes and lunar

---

[10] *CW1*, 167–8.
[11] *VPl*, 805.

phases. Lyric and play invoke a sort of family story, or a love story, a story of men and women, for which you don't really need to know the biography or the astrology. Though it helps, particularly the role of Iseult Gonne and her cat, and the poem written about a cat which may once have belonged to a child, whom Yeats had known from her birth, but who when she was 22 was a participant in a vacillating half-courtship with the 52-year-old poet.[12]

The story is a family story, or at least a story among families who had known each other for decades, and while there is no evidence that Yeats behaved in an improper or transgressive way, it is a bit funny—as in odd. But there is other much more difficult material in the environs of the poem and the play. As regards the play, Yeats envisaged it as the Japanese form of *kyogen*, not a Noh drama.[13] The *kyogen* is a comic play, and we can see the Zen parable of the cat playing with the reflection of the moon in the lyric and a comic parable of holy man and fool in the play. Elsewhere in the note to the play Yeats suggests it could be played as 'a relaxation of attention between, let us say "The Hawk's Well" and "The Dreaming of the Bones".'[14] Taken together, all three plays move from the heroic to the comic to the tragic, the latter concerning Padraig Pearse and the Rising of 1916.

'The Cat and the Moon', the lyric participant in this nexus of poems, plays, and biographical and historical event, is aware of itself as play, both child's play and play-acting. Its intention is to incorporate the symbol of dance into the symbol of the moon, but it can't help but teeter somewhat. 'Do you dance, Minnaloushe, do you dance?' This is an invitation to the cat to dance, which even children—particularly children—would know to be silly. What is it to 'call a dance'? At balls and gatherings—the social dance—it means the calling of quadrilles or waltzes. The type of dance, though, is not inconsequential: there are no balls here, or 'courtly fashion'. Rather, there will be a new dance, or, as Yeats puts it, 'A new dance turn'. The word 'new' in the 'new dance turn' will be picked up a few lines later in 'The sacred moon overhead / Has taken a new phase', where it refers merely to the astronomical phenomenon of a 'new moon'. The moon is not of course 'new', and its return to its newness every twenty-eight days is in part an astronomer's (or indeed astrologer's) metaphor for prediction as repetition. Fashion, wedded to another version of the new, thinks that nothing like it had existed before. For a moment, the everyday concern with the fashionable and the performative and the moment of play for its own transient sake has taken over in these figures of repetition as recycling. In the poem and the play about the cat and the moon, the focus in that word 'turn' is primarily sense 8b in the OED, as a slang term related to the theatre: 'A short performance, especially one of a number given by different performers in succession; an item in a variety entertainment; an act. Also: a person giving such a performance." It might occur only once in any given performance, but of course the whole performance—including the turn—might happen again on subsequent evenings. It is not a modern word (OED

---

[12] *Life 2*, 55–92.
[13] See Akiko Manabe' Chapter 33 in this volume.
[14] *VPl*, 805.

tracks it back to 1715), but it is sounded here with a certain modernity, or modishness: Minnaloushe or Iseult might even be a star turn, the girl and cat performing an Edwardian pantomime or Japanese *kyogen*.

This might be a small matter, a 'minute particular', if the word 'turn' didn't appear in other senses throughout Yeats's poetry: 'Turning and turning in the widening gyre', for instance, where it seems to presage a more apocalyptically 'new phase' ('The Second Coming', *CW1*, 187). And it appears in one place where the family are involved in one of the most difficult writing tasks that might face a poet: how to match a public duty for the memorial poem with the personal memory of a great and justifiable hatred. John MacBride was not Iseult's father, and although the details are inevitably politicized, and tied up with Maud Gonne's legal case for divorce in 1905, it was alleged that MacBride molested Iseult when she was 9: 'the blackest thing you can imagine', according to Yeats.[15] After the death of MacBride in 1916, as their correspondence shows, while Gonne was in a forgiving mood,[16] Yeats was the one who had to say something in print:

> This other man I had dreamed
> A drunken vainglorious lout.
> He had done most bitter wrong
> To some who are near my heart,
> Yet I number him in the song;
> He, too, has resigned his part
> In the casual comedy;
> He, too, has been changed in his turn,
> Transformed utterly:
> A terrible beauty is born.[17]

MacBride's part in the casual comedy is written throughout in the slang terms of the stage: 'number', 'resigned his part', 'changed in *his* turn' where it is his turn to be named, his turn to be the next to be changed, his turn to take a turn in the casual comedy. John MacBride is an unlikely candidate to be thought of as a comic turn, but, of course, 'Easter, 1916' is a poem about the turning of history and about change, in which even the drunken vainglorious can be transformed utterly. The mocking tale or gibe at the club, reserved for your enemies, has been transformed utterly into terrible beauty. The word 'comedy' appears nowhere else in Yeats's poetry. Here, the 'casual comedy' is of players and painted stage (as if it were no matter that violent revolution and MacBride's execution were not playing in the background). Geraldine Higgins recalls in this book that the Proclamation of Independence that was read and distributed from the steps of the GPO

---

[15] *Life 1*, 330–1. For the fullest account of the allegations, see Caoimhe Nic Dháibhéid, ' "This Is a Case in Which Irish National Considerations Must Be Taken into Account": The Breakdown of the MacBride-Gonne Marriage, 1904–8', *Irish Historical Studies*, 37:146 (2010), 241–64.

[16] Anna MacBride White and A. Norman Jeffares, eds., *The Gonne-Yeats Letters, 1893–1938* (London: Hutchinson, 1992), 372–85.

[17] *CW1*, 181.

on Sackville Street on 24 April 1916 was mistaken for a theatre playbill. MacBride was not actually one of the signatories of the Proclamation, but he died for a document that, Higgins says, 'claims its authority by appealing to the "dead generations" … [and] does not display any doubts through ambiguous figures of speech. A Proclamation by definition has no question marks'.[18] If 'casual comedy' is not the artifice of eternity, it is at least the artifice of history: cat, moon, and revolutionary hero play the ambiguous linguistic game where the heroic and the comic are nevertheless brought together in the joy of elegiac transformation.

* * *

Yeats is not making casual comedy of important historical matter, but the poetry consistently moves back and forward between positions in ways which suggest a comic shuttling. Sometimes it appears that, for all the system-building that goes on in front of the poetry, the actual poetic machinery is tugging in another way. This is as much a matter of the comedy of composition as it is of the critical comedy of trying to make out what the poem is about. Given this critical and scholarly conundrum when reading Yeats, with many readers caught between serious matter and sceptical judgement, MacNeice has a sensible thing to say about Yeats's symbols often not making sense:

> And it must be admitted that, whatever Yeats intended, he did not always handle his symbols precisely; not that this is necessarily to the bad if it is conceded that a poet may not himself know what he is driving at (Coleridge held that a poem gives more pleasure when it is not 'perfectly understood' by the reader; it is at least possible that some poems are more effective because they were not perfectly understood by the poet himself). Yeats, who in A Vision had arranged the universe in pigeon-holes, wished to treat his poetry similarly. But his poetry resisted him. The symbols, which were meant to retain their identity like the separate pieces of a mosaic, are always melting, fusing, becoming equivocal. For Yeats indeed the moon, being the mistress of the world's dialectic, not only contains all opposites but can identify herself now with one set of opposites, now with another.[19]

The casual comedy is creativity, founded not so much in misunderstanding as deliberate un-understanding, a *via negativa* where 'the symbols … are always melting, fusing, becoming equivocal'. MacNeice is one of the first to say of Yeats that it is poetry which resisted the system, as if it contains the ethical as well as aesthetic material which can right the preposterous, the tendentious, or the silly. And this is, in a very particularly Yeats way, an aesthetically redeeming matter, where the elevated symbolism is brought down to earth.

Of course, Yeats's poetry itself could move in the space of a single page from the silly to the extremely unsettling, and as a poetry grounded in visionary experience moved on

---

[18] See Chapter 13 in this volume.
[19] MacNeice, *Poetry of Yeats*, 124–5.

into the 1920s and 1930s the comedy struggles with its efficacy as a vehicle for meaning. For a start, the visionary is something that Yeats believed you could schedule. Many varieties of orthodox religious experience seek transcendence through programmes of meditation or ritual. If Yeats didn't always believe it would happen on tap, as it were, he put himself in the way of such experience through years attending seances: his participation in the theatricality of those events was sometimes credulous, sometimes comic. The credulity could reach extremes, none more so than Yeats's delight in David Wilson's 'metallic medium' that purported to channel voices from the spirit world. Visiting Wilson in 1917, Yeats labelled the machine 'the metallic homunculus'.[20] Many of the experiences about which Yeats wrote in his memoirs, however, were related with less enthusiasm. His first seance, recounted humorously in the *Reveries over Childhood and Youth*, ends up with him in terror, reciting the opening lines of *Paradise Lost* while his 'Catholic friend . . . was saying a Paternoster and Ave Maria in the corner'. The eventual gloss to his sense of being possessed is typically equivocal: 'Was it a part of myself—something always to be a danger perhaps; or had it come from without, as it seemed?'[21]

The Gothic comedy persists through Ezra Pound's celebrated memory of hearing Yeats compose out loud when they shared a house in Surrey, Stone Cottage, in 1913:

> so that I recalled the noise in the chimney
> as it were the wind in the chimney
>   but was in reality Uncle William
> downstairs composing
> that had made a great Peeeeacock
>   in the proide ov his oiye
> had made a great peeeeeeecock in the . . .
> made a great peacock
>   in the proide of his oyyee
>
> proide ov his oy-ee
> as indeed he had, and perdurable
>
> a great peacock aere perennius.

Pound's spelling of Yeats's accent pushes at the limits of the Irish joke, but his is part memory of haunting and part actual haunting, both having fun with the Gothic and explaining away the ghost with relieving laughter. The noise in the chimney 'was in reality Uncle William / downstairs composing'. In Pound's reality, the present of the poem in which he was composing—1948—was imprisonment by the victorious US army in Pisa after the disgrace of his fascist collaboration. Yeats was dead nine years. The apostate is haunted by his dead friend's voice, sharing the joke across the void: 'well those days are gone forever'.[22]

---

[20] *Life 2*, 80
[21] *CW3*, 106-7.
[22] Ezra Pound, *The Cantos* (London: Faber & Faber, 1975), LXXXIII, 533–4.

Yeats's own peacock poem was composed as part of a synthetic visionary experiment, a so-called 'intellectual vision', where the person concentrates on an image or symbol until a vision appears. Pound's version of this is, as James Longenbach says, 'characteristically jocular':

'Intellectual vision' is, acc. Wm. Blake & others, the surest cure for ghosts. You'd better begin by seeing fire, or else by doing that visualization of points that I recommended. Fix a point, colour it, or light it as you like, start it moving, multiply it, etc. Make patterns, colours, pictures, whatever you like. You will end up a great magician & prize exorcist.[23]

Pound printed 'The Peacock' in *Poetry* magazine in May 1914. He placed it on the same page as another poem, 'The Witch' from 1912, making a pair of poems, both in their way about the irreconcilables of art and mammon. When they were republished in *Responsibilities* they were printed by Yeats as numbers I and II. The first poem in the pair is slightly less conducive to comic interpretation:

> The Witch
> Toil and grow rich,
> What's that but to lie
> With a foul witch
> And after, drained dry,
> To be brought
> To the chamber where
> Lies one long sought
> With despair?[24]

This is a visionary parable which can be set alongside Yeats's 'The Magi' and its version of the birth of Christ as 'the uncontrollable mystery on the bestial floor' (*CW1*, 126). That poem had gone back to Yeats's story, 'The Adoration of the Magi', and the latter-day Magi who discover a dying prostitute who has been impregnated with the power of history: 'the Immortals . . . have chosen this woman in whose heart all follies have gathered, and in whose body all desires have awaked; this woman who has been driven out by Time and has lain upon the bosom of eternity.'[25] Later in Yeats this woman will appear as Leda, in 'Leda and the Swan', and as Mary in 'The Mother of God'.

As is the way with visionary or occultist poetry, the trail is initially obscure. But eventually that obscurity must give way, for the contemporary reader at least, to something which is ethically complicated. Perhaps even more so when we learn that in 1916 Yeats attempted to revise the phrase 'a foul witch' with 'some stale bitch' when including the

---

[23] Ezra Pound to Dorothy Shakespeare, 1913, quoted in James Longenbach, *Stone Cottage: Pound, Yeats and Modernism* (Oxford: Oxford University Press, 1988), 49–50.

[24] *CW1*, 121.

[25] *The Secret Rose, Stories by W. B. Yeats: A Variorum Edition*: Ed. Warwick Gould et al (Basingstoke: Macmillan 1992), 169.

poem in *Responsibilities*. His editor at Macmillan objected, and Yeats climbed down in order to avert attracting the notice of the censor: 'much as I desire to see the vocabulary of the seventeenth century restored I prefer to leave martyrdom to the young who desire it'.[26] Whether or not the revision stood, the episode is one of the first examples of how this visionary and, in the genuine sense, *occult* material is provoked into an obsession with the bodily, the risqué, and the obscene. For the critic Elizabeth Butler Cullingford, that can best be thought of in terms of bawdy classical verse, in particular the Latin 'Fescennine'.[27] And that Fescennine had a history in English and Irish poetry from the seventeenth to the nineteenth centuries, most typically in the work of Jonathan Swift and his many adversaries in controversy and obscenity.

* * *

The word 'witch' is associated with a risqué joke, especially in the poems spoken by the figures of Crazy Jane or Tom the Lunatic in the 'Words for Music Perhaps' sequence in *The Winding Stair* (1933), where the experience of sex, love, and ageing leaves one not blessed with wisdom but 'mad as the mist and snow'. An earlier poem, 'Solomon and the Witch', is about a carnal love that is not just a metaphor for transcendence and unity of being but one that can itself attain unity, no matter how momentary. Elsewhere in Yeats—'The Supernatural Songs' or 'A Woman Young and Old'—this unity of being is associated with the love of angels or even of Gods: 'Godhead on Godhead in sexual spasm begot / Godhead'.[28] Yeats knew that self-creation as tautology was silly in the Auden–MacNeice sense, and funny even in a schoolboy sense. In terms of his longer-held desire for transfiguration it is the comedy of a bodiless ecstasy that ghosted the early years of his marriage and its mystic accompaniment of voices from the other world; or, to evoke the title of one poem about alternative loves and sexual imaginings of affairs that might have been, 'images from a past life'. The poem that goes by that title faces terrors, but the joke comes at the end of 'Solomon and the Witch' when gathered into the volume, and thus between the ecstasy and the fear, as it were. It emerges from the unity of the supernatural love of the gods before Eden, both preceding human history and out of nature, and thus beyond both the contingent and the human will: 'Chance being at one with Choice at last ... And this foul world were dead at last'.[29] 'At last / at last', the Yeatsian full repetition (at end-line rhyming position) is of the things that will have no repetition: you can't repeat the thing that comes 'last'. These might be paradoxes, even logical antinomies, and they are conveyed in a kind of non-poetry, or a giving up on rhyme, as if the best that the linguistic and aesthetic medium can offer is repetition as the self-reproduction of unity of being which belongs only to the divine: 'Godhead on Godhead ... begot Godhead'. Human history is a brief hiatus

[26] *Life* 2, 521.
[27] Elizabeth Butler Cullingford, *Gender and History in Yeats's Love Poetry* (Syracuse: Syracuse University Press, 1991), 120.
[28] 'Ribh in Ecstasy', *CW1*, 285.
[29] *CW1*, 177.

between two cockcrows; eternity has been crowed out and then back in again. But for eternity there can be no 'again'.

This is comic, or at least comedy. 'Solomon and the Witch'—as with other dialogue poems and the dialogue between poems—contains voices that are separated because they are on the earth, as well as voices separated by the separation of the earthly and the human itself. They are also separated by gender: they comment on each other within poems, across poems, and across the divide between men and women, Yeats's own marriage, and the sexual history of his images from a past life and a supernatural other. Yeats held these views with the utmost seriousness as a visionary possibility, but they are rendered in these surrounds as the comedy of what is on the one hand 'mere' human life ('All mere complexities, / The fury and the mire of human veins'[30]) and on the other the only life we have, one which refuses to remove itself from our momentary grasping of something which might appear to be transcendence, and stubbornly persists in remaining as the earthly medium through which art and poetry and love must work.

The punchline to the joke in 'Solomon and the Witch' develops thus:

> [']Yet the world ends when these two things,
> Though several, are a single light,
> When oil and wick are burned in one;
> Therefore a blessed moon last night
> Gave Sheba to her Solomon.'
> 'Yet the world stays':
>   'If that be so,
> Your cockerel found us in the wrong
> Although he thought it worth a crow.
> Maybe an image is too strong
> Or maybe is not strong enough.'
>
> 'The night has fallen; not a sound
> In the forbidden sacred grove
> Unless a petal hit the ground,
> Nor any human sight within it
> But the crushed grass where we have lain;
> And the moon is wilder every minute.
> O! Solomon! let us try again.'[31]

Jahan Ramazani says in this volume that 'the newly married Yeats goes to Muslim Asia in part because it provides an opening to relatively free and frank references to sexual relations', also allowing into the poem 'a remarkable assertion of female sexual desire and agency'.[32] Sheba has already had her own one-line riposte to Solomon's

[30] 'Byzantium', *CW1*, 248.
[31] *CW1*, 177–8.
[32] See Chapter 22 in this volume.

other-worldliness, or end-of the-worldliness. When he offers an image for consummation as extinction—'oil and the wick are burned in one'—Sheba responds with what we
might imagine to be a simple gesture from the grass on which the lovers are lying in the
morning: 'Yet the world stays'. Her last lone request, 'O! Solomon! let us try again', with
its two exclamation marks, speaks from the bed to the rather useless philosophizing of
the male lover.

Sheba's is not so much a call from the body as a call back into the conundrum
which is puzzling Solomon, and he is rendered here by Sheba as in a comic pickle.
The worldly, the earthly, the ribald even, are at all times in play: a wick doesn't need
a Freudian analysis to suggest its semantic provenance, since it retains a history in
the vernacular as obscene innuendo—dip your wick—and cockney rhyming slang,
Hampton Wick / prick. In 'Solomon and Sheba' there is no sense that the sex was bad.
Neither indeed, as Cullingford points out, is the candle burnt out. If the 'sexual apocalypse of Yeats's early love poetry is here reframed as comedy ... Desire satisfied is not
desire quenched, but desire continually reborn.'[33] What is being asked of that sex—an
experience which will end the world?—is comically out of proportion. *Spiritus Mundi*,
is, as Yeats says in the note to 'An Image from a Past Life', the 'general storehouse of
images which have ceased to be the property of any personality or spirit'.[34] And to the
comedy of Sheba's reply can be added the storehouse of images that includes symbol
and allegory, the past and current social usage of language and the crudities of its
everyday symbolism into which a less than pure, comic, thought might come. Thus
the lover speaks back from the bed and the poet (as Solomon) continues with the conundrum in poetic regatherings of the question along with its recreation in image and
metaphor and symbol.

What is this aspect in Yeats, this odd ribaldry just when his poems appear to be closest
to expressing his desire for supernatural knowledge, his desire for unity with lives and
loves in the present and the past, as well as a unity of being which every bit of sense he
has (which includes the instincts of his art) tells him cannot be? It is partly a comedy of
disappointment, or law of irony, where what is willed always falls short in the enactment
of it. This is something that Samuel Beckett, for instance, saw in Yeats, and usually saw as
funny. As Marjorie Perloff says in a suggestive and sensitive 2007 essay on Beckett's perhaps unexpected admiration for Yeats (in an essay called 'Beckett's Yeatsian Turn', where
a 'turn' is a modish word for the modish itself, the literary-critical 'new'),

> Beckett was hardly a Yeatsian 'last Romantic'—indeed, he could confront the notion
> of passion only obliquely and parodically—but it was Yeats who, so to speak, gave
> Beckett the permission to explore the aporias, not of sexual failure as such, but of
> the failure to follow one's inclinations which animates such key Beckett plays as
> *Krapp's Last Tape*.[35]

[33] Cullingford, Gender and History,119–20.
[34] *CW1*, 644.
[35] Marjorie Perloff, '"An Image from a Past Life": Beckett's Yeatsian Turn', *Fulcrum*, 6 (2007).

In Beckett, the failure is ultimately played as comedy, and, according to Perloff, the Beckettian pay-off in the use of Yeats is the mock-heroic. In Yeats that involves sometimes downright silly characterizations, such as Maud Gonne as Helen of Troy or Yeats himself as Solomon, later to be speared in Paul Muldoon's parody of the Gore-Booth–Markievicz elegy: 'Two girls in silk kimonos. // Both beautiful, one a gazebo.'[36]

In 'An Image from a Past Life', one half of the dialogue and the marriage—the male half, whether or not he be King Solomon—is presented in a seance with the image, 'A sweetheart from another life floats there.'[37] The other, female, half is both the medium and the present lover (at this stage in Yeats's life, his wife George). What, then, does that other half think when she is not acting as medium for the male? If Yeats himself can appear unwittingly preposterous, being high-minded about earthly loves never coming to satisfaction while suggesting other loves from previous lives, George is simply afraid—of the ghost and for her marriage. Readers of Yeats's poetry and biography, who know about the circumstances of his mediumistic composition in the early years of his marriage and the poet's past loves in *this* life, will see that the poet may be said to have missed the ironies of the situation.[38] The medium—'*She*'—is, after all, the one who sees the ghost of the former lover. As Yeats puts it in his note, he has not misrepresented the (fake) information he has constructed from the messenger Michael Robartes in 'permitting the woman and not the man to see the Over Shadower or Ideal Form, whichever it was' (*CW1*, 645 n).

'*She*' is given the last stanza and expresses terror before 'the hovering thing night brought me'.

> *He.* But why should you grow suddenly afraid
> And start – I at your shoulder –
> Imagining
> That any night could bring
> An image up, or anything
> Even to eyes that beauty had driven mad,
> But images to make me fonder?
>
> *She.* Now she has thrown her arms above her head;
> Whether she threw them up to flout me,
> Or but to find,
> Now that no fingers bind,
> That her hair streams upon the wind,
> I do not know, that know I am afraid
> Of the hovering thing night brought me.[39]

---

[36] Paul Muldoon, '7 Middagh Street', in *Meeting the British* (London: Faber, 1987).

[37] *CW1*, 178.

[38] See, for instance, Brenda Maddox's discussion of George's instruction through the automatic writing that Yeats satisfy her sexually, even given that he was writing poems about former lovers: *George's Ghosts* (London: Picador, 1999), 147.

[39] *CW1*, 179.

'*He*' is solicitous here and offers husbandly protection ('I at your shoulder'), but it is he who is the visionary beneficiary of 'images to make me fonder'. Fonder of whom? Her? Or just happier in himself? This is the only occurrence of the word in Yeats's poetry, and OED tells us that until the nineteenth century 'fond' meant 'Infatuated, foolish, silly. Since 16th c. the sense in literary use has been chiefly: Foolishly credulous or sanguine'. In one of Yeats's earliest pieces of journalism, his 1891 tribute to the recently deceased poet Rose Kavanagh, he quotes Ellen O'Leary on Kavanagh's 'the fond, foolish dreams of fervid youth'.[40]

Ambiguities multiply into irony, as they must in Yeatsian ghost belief. The poem does admit that fear of ghosts and horror and laughter are close kin—we allow ourselves not just a sort of ironic scepticism here, but also the nervous laugh as vent for the shock. Yeats's poems continue to insist that the fear must give way before desire. 'The world stays', Sheba tells Solomon, and the punchline which answers his conundrum is the short or reiterative—'let us try again'. That is in many ways the utterance of a Yeatsian poetic in which for all of his talk of 'a poem which comes right like the click of a closing box',[41] the end of the poem—like consummation as the end of the world—is usually only a presage to trying it all over again. We don't need to insert our own scepticism into this thinking to hear that something is happening with tone of voice.

Given Yeats's insistent play with the ribald, the obscene, the suggestive—whether or not it be 'Freudian'—Elizabeth Butler Cullingford suggests another word for what is going on in these poems. It is one which empowers the woman speaker within them as much as the sniggering of the unbelieving reader:

> The sexual comedy that in classical fescennine verses took the form of the ribald male joking at the expense of the bride is appropriated by Yeats's Sheba. The wedding night frozen into the hieratic structure of the epithalamium is, through her provocative and teasing initiative, here opened up and prolonged into a succession of nights dedicated to sexual and occult exploration. Desire satisfied is not desire quenched, but desire continually reborn.[42]

Cullingford suggests that in these poems Sheba and the sceptical reader can turn 'ribald male joking' back on the male. Yeats himself is doing this, as even the terrors of ghost stories are released into a sort of humour. But at this stage of his career (and marriage), how then did Yeats begin to explore the tonal possibilities of Fescennine comedy while bringing up matter that was so close to his mystical concerns? And how can we as readers discuss this as comedy as we view the poet engaged with an ethical, or even political, negotiation with the women in his bed and in his dreams (and in her dreams)?

* * *

[40] *CW7*, 43.
[41] WBY to Dorothy Wellesley, 8 September 1935, *CL InteLex* #6335.
[42] Cullingford, *Gender and History*, 120.

Cullingford calls the Fescennine 'classical', and if it might in fact have been pre-Roman, it does waver over the 'Augustan'. In the Loeb Library an example can be found as epithalamium, in Claudian's marriage verses for the Emperor Honorius, but this is late in the Roman period, fourth century AD.[43] As such it is epithalamium as the Renaissance (or, for Yeats, Byzantine) poet might understand it, a marriage poem singing to Lords and Ladies of what is past or passing or to come. In English-language verse the mode is associated with the so-called Augustan age, and more particularly with Jonathan Swift. Poet and Church of Ireland clergyman, the Dean of Clogher Jonathan Smedley directed a 1728 squib at Swift called 'A Lilliputian Ode; In Imitation of, and humbly Inscrib'd to, Captain Gulliver; sole Redivivor of the ancient Fescennine'. Smedley tells us that his poem has been composed in imitation of the Fescennine metre, a three-syllable trochaic line, or amphibrach.[44] It ends with the accusation of sinking in tone:

> And Dean *Swift*,
> Left hath us
> *Useful Gift!*
> True BATHOS.

For Smedley, Swift was last in a long line of 'dull imitators of Anacreon'. Swift's friend Alexander Pope had Smedley swimming in the shit in *The Dunciad*, and the word 'bathos', in the sense used by Smedley here, was invented by Pope in *The Art of Sinking* the year before Smedley's squib was written, in 1727.[45]

It might be that this is not quite related to the Yeatsian Fescennine—although the word 'excrement' does make an appearance in 'Crazy Jane Talks with the Bishop' (*CW1*, 260). Yeats can allow himself the *saeva indignatio* with which Swift described himself in his self-written epitaph. Yeats's 1932 version of the epitaph translates both the Augustan poise and satiric anger ('Savage indignation there / Cannot lacerate his breast') as much as the oddness of the self-memorial, something that Swift had been doing much before his death, including the extraordinary—and extraordinarily funny—obituary for himself, 'Verses on the Death of Dr Swift'. What Yeats recreates in his version of the epitaph is not quite what is going on in these poems. Indeed, where we might find Yeats at his most Swiftian—in the late prose invective *On the Boiler* (1938–9)—when Yeats quotes Swift, it is an early poem to William Temple, which turns to a diatribe against those who would tear down 'unity of being'. The extract from the poem to Temple that Yeats quotes ends:

> They purchase Knowledge at the Expense
> Of common Breeding, common Sense,
> And grow at once Scholars and Fools;
> Affect ill-manner'd Pedantry,

[43] See *Claudian, Vol I, Loeb Classical Library*, Vol 135, trans. M. Platnauer (Cambridge: Harvard University Press, 1922), 230–1.

[44] [Jonathan Smedley,] *Gulliveriana: Or, A Fourth Volume of Miscellanies* (London: Roberts, 1728), 265–6.

[45] *The Dunciad*, ll. 279–86, in *The Poems of Alexander Pope*, ed. John Butt (London: Methuen, 1963), 394.

> Rudeness, Ill-nature, Incivility,
>   And, sick with Dregs of Knowledge grown,
>   Which greedily they swallow down,
> Still cast it up and nauseate Company.[46]

In Yeats's quotation of these early lines by Swift to his patron, this is in one way a riposte to the critics (perhaps literary critics). But we can see how Yeats would be attracted to a classic conservative statement of the case. On the one hand, there is the mention of 'common Breeding', which elsewhere in *On the Boiler* vexes many readers of Yeats. And on the other, there is the conservative satire directed at what Swift calls 'Scholars and Fools' and Yeats calls 'the specialists': 'The specialist's job is anybody's job, seeing that for the most part he is made, not born'. 1930s and successive authoritarian populist movements to this day continue to reserve their ire for those sceptical of claims made for unified national cultures: 'culture, unity of being, no longer sufficed, and the specialists were already there'.[47]

A century earlier, in 1859, John Mitchel accused the poetry of James Clarence Mangan of 'Fescennine buffoonery ... purposely spoiling and marring the effect of fine poetry and turning it into burlesque'.[48] His complaint was partly that Mangan did not deliver on the seriousness of Mitchel's own radical mission. If the main purveyors of the Fescennine are conservative, not all comedy is inherently of that position. Yeats's comedy is one half of a dialogue or even antinomy of tone, a bringing down to earth or earthiness to set against the transcendent. Even in the brief moments in Yeats when its mere possibility is considered, unity of being must include the earthly and the divine, the demon and the beast, as well as the attentions of both the well-bred and the specialists. Yeatsian comedy, like Yeatsian history, swivels between destruction and rebuilding, rough beast and renewal. Where the Fescennine starts in the marriage bed, it gives comic colour or tone to something we might call 'sexual politics', and from that we intuit another politics, freighted with longer historical memory: images from a past life.

The Yeatsian comedy of belief in human history is, in one of its antinomies, a working through of tragedy. In this book Hugh Haughton reminds us of Yeats's view of tragicomedy: 'it is in moments of comedy that character is defined, in Hamlet's gaiety, let us say'.[49] The idea returns in 'Lapis Lazuli', a poem which turns around the tragedies of both Hamlet and Lear: 'All things fall and are built again / And those that build them again are gay'. However, 'Lapis Lazuli' does not end with that aphorism, which the poem could satisfyingly have done. Instead its last verse paragraph offers 'A symbol of longevity', the piece of sculpted lapis lazuli and the figures sculpted on it: 'Their ancient, glittering eyes are gay'. The symbol is both cold rock and 'tragic scene'.[50] The ending of 'Lapis Lazuli'

---

[46] 'Ode to the Honble Sir William Temple', *c.*1690, in Harold Williams, ed., *The Poems of Jonathan Swift*, 3 Vols (Oxford: Clarendon Press, 1958), I, 27.

[47] *CW* 5, 235–6.

[48] See my 'Mangan in England', in Sinead Sturgeon, ed., *Essays on James Clarence Mangan* (London: Palgrave Macmillan, 2014), 218.

[49] See Chapter 12 in this volume. The phrase comes from 'The Tragic Theatre' essay in *CW*4, 175.

[50] *CWI*, 294–5.

could not be further from the Swiftian bathos which preoccupied Yeats in these years, but Yeats does leave his reader with a typical equivocation, transfiguring dread while allowing the glittering eyes of the wise, recalling the Receptive Man who 'laughs in delight at all the varied scene'. Theirs is not the mocking tale or gibe at the club, although the sinking of the Swiftian satire remains a tonal possibility. Yeats's later poetry develops to comedy, and it is in the broadest sense a comedy which explores a Dionysian potential which both proceeds by vacillation and *is* vacillation. It is a poetry, Geoffrey Hill observed, of returns and revocations upon itself, as in the poem 'Vacillation', where Yeats contemplates his own remorse: 'something is recalled, / My conscience or my vanity appalled'.[51] Hill comments that the last line 'concedes the element of clownishness in the man who might have preferred to be a hero in remorse'.[52]

By this account it would be a rare moment in a Yeats poem unreservedly to give the reader its author's personal experience of unity of being as transfiguration. Does it happen in 'Vacillation'?

> While on the shop and street I gazed
> My body of a sudden blazed;
> And twenty minutes more or less
> It seemed, so great my happiness,
> That I was blessèd and could bless.

It was an everyday transfiguration. The surrounds were banal, a café in a London shop, and the timing of the experience courts bathos: 'twenty minutes more or less'. 'Vacillation' nevertheless sets itself up between the sinking of remorse and moments of blessedness, and it questions the spoiling and marring of joy by burlesque. Yeats echoes the amphibrachs of the Fescennine metre when he opens the poem by asking, 'What is joy?':

> Between extremities
> Man runs his course;
> A brand or flaming breath,
> Comes to destroy
> All those antinomies
> Of day and night;
> The body calls it death,
> The heart remorse.
> But if these be right
> What is joy?

---

[51] *CW1*, 249–53.

[52] Geoffrey Hill, '"The Conscious Mind's Intelligible Structure"; A Debate', *Agenda*, 9:4 (Autumn/ Winter, 1971), 20. I am grateful to Karl O'Hanlon for conversations on this essay; see also O'Hanlon, '"Noble in his Grandiose Confusions": Yeats and *Coriolanus* in the Poetry of Geoffrey Hill', *English*, 65:250 (2016), 211–33.

CHAPTER 39

YEATSIAN MASCULINITIES

LUCY MCDIARMID

*Michael stepped on to the road incautiously upon which Anne struck him
rather hard on the face & said, 'Michael dont you understand that if you are
killed there will be nobody to continue the family.'*
    Gregory (21 June [1930]) *Talking to the Dead, Talking to the Dead,*

 Some violent bitter man, some powerful man
 Called architect and artist in, that they,
 Bitter and violent men, might rear in stone
 The sweetness that all longed for night and day,
 The gentleness none there had ever known;
 But when the master's buried mice can play.
 And maybe the great-grandson of that house,
 For all its bronze and marble's but a mouse.

            Yeats, 'Ancestral Houses'

 *What makes your work so good is the masculine element allied to much
feminine charm – your lines have the magnificent swing of your boyish body.
I wish I could be a girl of nineteen for certain hours that I might feel it even
more acutely.*

ANNE Yeats was only 11 years old when she impressed on her younger brother the importance of stepping onto the road carefully: if he was killed by a passing car, there would be 'nobody to continue the family'. The possibility that she herself might continue the family wasn't mentioned. Anne appears to have inherited her father's patrilineal model of the Yeatses: male begat male who begat male. Such is the model in 'Pardon, Old Fathers', where Yeats invokes only his male ancestors, and in 'Meditations in Time of Civil War', in which the decline of a generic upper-class landed family is marked by descent from a 'powerful man' to a 'great-grandson' who is 'but a mouse'.[1] By the later 1930s,

Yeats to Dorothy Wellesley (21 Dec [1936])

[1] *CW1*, 100, 200.

Thanks to R. F. Foster, Adrian Frazier, Nicholas Grene, Mella McAuley, Maureen Murphy, Clíona Ó Gallchoir, and Kelly Sullivan for academic help of various kinds.

however, Yeats's notions of what he had once called 'the masculine element' had become somewhat relaxed; it was a quality that could inhere in women also. As Yeats wrote to Lady Dorothy Wellesley, in words that have since become famous, 'What makes your work so good is the masculine element allied to much feminine charm'.

The idea of masculinity is interrogated in poems throughout Yeats's career, at least as early as 'Adam's Curse' (composed in 1901) and as late as 'Cuchulain Comforted' (composed in January 1939). This chapter will use the word 'masculinity' to mean characteristics of people in Yeats's poems whom he identifies as male, and the way those characteristics are enacted, performed, or displayed in appearance, small behaviours, large behaviours, sexualities, or actions of any sort. Like so much else in Yeats's work, the concept of masculinity is in a constant state of revision, variously embodied in generic men working in conventional professions ('bankers, schoolmasters, and clergymen'[2]), in long dead Pollexfens and Yeatses, in Dublin merchants, in literary characters (Hanrahan), legendary figures ('The man drowned in a bog's mire'[3]), Irish heroes (Cuchulain, Parnell, Casement), sometimes women (Wellesley's 'boyish body'), and the poet himself, apologetic, uncertain, proud, defiant, remorseful, and always questioning.

The word 'interrogated' suggests the way Yeats's speakers wrestle with varying notions of masculinity; they correct conventional definitions or resolve ambivalent feelings by constructing new models of masculinity. Some of these formations are unorthodox; some are reluctantly accepted; all are provisional. Subsequent poems begin from entirely different positions and fashion other provisionally acceptable models. As is the case with all types of Yeatsian vacillation, the instability of Yeats's versions of the masculine provides continuing inspiration and continuing anxiety. The sources of anxiety are various: concern about the masculinity of a poet in 'sedentary' labour relative to that of men engaged in more active pursuits; concern about the judgements his male ancestors might deliver on his life's work, were they alive to observe it; concern about his inadequate courtship of Maud Gonne.[4] Various as they are, these anxieties about masculinity are linked in the poems to a larger demographic anxiety about the diminishing power and population of Anglo-Irish Protestants. Invocation of a line of Protestant ancestors, biological or cultural, is a recurrent trope in Yeats's poems. Because it tends to occur in close proximity to malaise about masculinity, this trope suggests the intimate association between personal and larger demographic concerns. The connection is created by poetic means—images, allusions, juxtapositions—and becomes more pronounced in Yeats's later poetry after the establishment of the Irish Free State.[5]

[2] *CW1*, 78.

[3] *CW1*, 201.

[4] For examples of Yeats's use of ' sedentary', see 'A style is found by sedentary toil' (' Ego Dominus Tuus', *CW1*, 162) or ' This sedentary trade' (' The Tower', *CW1*, 203).

[5] Of course, Yeats's demographic and eugenic concerns are nowhere clearer than in his late play *Purgatory* (1938), in which the ' Old Man' kills his son in order to finish ' all the consequence' of improper, cross-class couplings: ' I killed that lad because had he grown up / He would have struck a woman's fancy, / Begot, and passed pollution on' (*CW2*, 543).

Concern about masculinity coincides with other moments of political transition in Ireland. Clíona Ó Gallchoir's 2019 essay '"Whole Swarms of Bastards": *A Modest Proposal*, the Discourse of Economic Improvement and Protestant Masculinity in Ireland, 1720–1738' establishes that the insecure and distinctly Protestant masculinity in Yeats existed in similar form in Anglo-Irishmen of the eighteenth century. As Ó Gallchoir notes, 'in a community experiencing increasing marginalization and disenfranchisement' masculinity is 'invoked', contested, and worried over.[6] Such is also the case in the Gaelic poets Sarah McKibben analyses in *Endangered Masculinities in Irish Poetry, 1540—1780*.[7]

This chapter continues the arguments of those scholars but of necessity narrows its focus, looking exclusively at Yeats's poems, especially the later ones, because it is in poetry that Yeats expresses his ideas of masculinity in their full complexity. Two of the long poems in *The Tower* merit special consideration because they question particular versions of masculinity and engage with its failures. The first section considers poetry exploring the masculinity of the male poet, looking at early poems and at 'Meditations in Time of Civil War'; the second section studies the trope of motion and immobility in 'The Tower' and several late poems; and the final section shows how masculinity is 'comforted' by birds.

THE POET'S MASCULINITY

In several poems written between 1901 and 1923, Yeats considers poets' alleged lesser masculinity; lesser, that is, than the masculinity of men who are not poets. Although the contrast Yeats implies is not so extreme as that 'between normative masculinity and emasculation' described by McKibben, Yeats's references to this inferiority are always contrasted to a 'normative masculinity' that is seemingly superior to his own.[8] In 'Adam's Curse', 'Pardon Old Fathers', and 'Meditations in Time of Civil War', Yeats

---

[6] Clíona Ó Gallchoir, 'Whole Swarms of Bastards': A Modest Proposal, the Discourse of Economic Improvement and Protestant Masculinity in Ireland, 1720–1738', in Rebecca Anne Barr, Sean Brady, and Jane McGaughey, eds., *Ireland and Masculinities in History* (London: Palgrave Macmillan, 2019), 40.

[7] Sarah McKibben, *Endangered Masculinities in Irish Poetry, 1540-1780* (Dublin: UCD Press, 2010). In recent years, other scholars have historicized Irish masculinity: Joseph Valente's *The Myth of Manliness in Irish National Culture, 1880–1922* (Champaign, IL: University of Illinois Press, 2011) is a fierce and enlightening study of 'manliness' in Yeats and his contemporaries. In '"I am a Victorian!" W. B. Yeats, Modern Manliness and the Problems of Work', *Review of English Studies*, NS, 1–23 (November 2019), 1–23, Peter Bland Botham focuses on the 'athletic ideal of the male body' in Yeats's prose and early poems, and in Adrian Frazier's groundbreaking essay 'Queering the Irish Renaissance: The Masculinities of Moore, Martyn, and Yeats', in Anthony Bradley and Maryann Valiulis, eds., *Gender and Sexuality in Modern Ireland* (Amherst: University of Massachusetts Press, 1997), 8–38, the contrastive masculinities of those three writers are defined and analysed. The most important recent work is the collection edited by Rebecca Anne Barr et al., *Ireland and Masculinities in History* (Cham: Palgrave Macmillan, 2019).

[8] McKibben, *Endangered Masculinities*, 7.

devotes particular attention to the difference in the nature of masculine display between poets and other males. The non-poets display powerfully in recognizable forms of activity: all are noticed, visible in the public sphere, labouring in an enterprise with a clear purpose and clear results.

In 'Adam's Curse', anxiety about the poet's masculinity takes the form of irritated defensiveness. The curse on Adam in Genesis was, of course, work ('In the sweat of thy face shalt thou eat bread', in the King James Version); in a poem that foregrounds the labour required for every 'fine thing', including beauty and courtship, the composition of poetry receives the most prominent defence. The speaker's remarks on this subject initiate the conversation:

> "Better go down upon your marrow-bones
> And scrub a kitchen pavement, or break stones
> Like an old pauper, in all kinds of weather;
> For to articulate sweet sounds together
> Is to work harder than all these, and yet
> Be thought an idler by the noisy set
> Of bankers, schoolmasters, and clergymen
> The martyrs call the world."

It would be 'better' to labour at these chores because at least the exhausting physicality would be noticed and appreciated; poets, the speaker says, 'work harder than all these'. The 'noisy' worldly men think poets are 'idlers'. That these are male workers (with the possible exception of the scrubber) is clear from the gendered response of the 'beautiful, mild woman' with the corresponding female work: 'To be born woman is to know'.[9]

In the introductory 'rhymes' to the volume *Responsibilities*, 'Pardon, Old Fathers' (1914), new elements of masculinity appear that dominate Yeats's poetry for the rest of his life. The speaker himself feels inadequate when his mere book is contrasted to the exciting, visible adventures of his male ancestors:

> *Pardon that for a barren passion's sake*
> *Although I have come close on forty-nine,*
> *I have no child, I have nothing but a book,*
> *Nothing but that to prove your blood and mine.*[10]

An active, flamboyant bunch, these ancestors are caught at their most memorable moments: '*Old Dublin merchant "free of ten and four"… And country scholar, Robert Emmet's friend.*' However obscure the phrase '*free of ten and four*', it sounds energetic because it's something the '*Old Dublin merchant*' is free of.[11] To have been '*Robert*

---

[9] *CW1*, 80.

[10] *CW1*, 101.

[11] In a note, Yeats writes that he was told after he had written the poem that the phrase was actually 'free of the eight and six' but it would take 'more rewriting than I have a mind for' to fix it (*VP*, 816–17).

'*Emmet's friend*' places the next ancestor in the centre of the Irish Protestant rebel tradition, and his '*hundred-year-old memory to the poor*' credits him with civic prominence. The merchant and rebel are joined in the unfortunate remark that they left Yeats '*blood / That has not passed through any huckster's loin*'. This comment calls attention to the ancestors' generative success and also hints at the reproductive anxiety central to Yeats's notion of masculinity.[12]

The varieties of masculinity in Yeats's ancestors also include the other (that is, 'wrong') political side, those fighting against 'James and his Irish', but as Yeats's first biographer, Joseph Hone, points out, Yeats had to revise the lines about the soldiers at the Boyne, because he originally believed they fought *with* James.[13] (He didn't have to change the nicely alliterative line 'Beside the brackish waters of the Boyne'.) The dramatic eccentricity of Yeats's great-grandfather, he who 'leaped overboard / After a ragged hat in Biscay Bay', completes the list of men who were visibly active in their time. Because Yeats's maternal grandfather, William Pollexfen, was 'the daily spectacle that stirred / My fancy', Yeats addresses him directly, hoping to receive 'pardon' for not having contributed to the family line. The reference to that 'barren passion' reinforces the superiority of the ancestors' loins and hints at the urgency Yeats feels (in 1914) to 'continue the family', as Anne Yeats put it. The syntactic balance of reproductive anxiety with vocational insecurity ('I have no child, I have nothing but a book') shows two of the forms the pervasive demographic anxiety could take. The measure of masculinity is right there in the title, 'Old Fathers'. Yeats himself is not yet a father.[14]

Juxtaposed to the male bloodline of the old fathers with their brief but robust résumés is a male cultural kinship characterized by an entirely different kind of masculinity. 'The Grey Rock' (1912–13), which follows immediately in *Responsibilities*, was written earlier than 'Pardon, Old Fathers', but its placement suggests a contrastive set of values in its celebration of another male group of which Yeats forms a part.[15] They are the Rhymers, the poets with whom Yeats 'learned [his] trade', and so for them a book of poems doesn't require apology. Their masculinity is not so extravagant and visible as

---

[12] As Yeats wrote in a throwaway witticism in one of his autobiographies, 'Lady Gregory once told me what marriage coarsened the Moore blood, but I have forgotten' (W. B. Yeats, 'Dramatis Personae, 1896–1902', in *The Autobiography of W. B. Yeats* [New York: Collier Books, Macmillan, 1965], 269).

[13] Joseph Hone, *W. B. Yeats, 1865–1939* (London: Macmillan, 1942), 2. See Valente, *The Myth of Manliness*, 240–1, for a lively discussion of the politics of this poem.

[14] In the context of 'Pardon, Old Fathers', the famous remark in 'September 1913' that 'Romantic Ireland's dead and gone' (*CW1*, 107–8) can be understood as a complaint that the Protestant contribution to Irish history, the martyrs Edward Fitzgerald, Robert Emmet, and Wolfe Tone, has been forgotten. The Protestant men who 'weighed so lightly what they gave' have been replaced by the Catholic merchants who put their fingers on the scale to weigh heavily, as they 'add the halfpence to the pence'. They 'were born to pray and save;' their petty materialism and their Catholicism are linked. The poem can be read as a conflict of sectarian masculinities. The occasion that inspired this occasional poem, the Dublin Corporation's vote against the Ha'Penny Bridge site for the Municipal Gallery of Modern Art, is never mentioned, so most readers have no idea of its connection. For Yeats, the Corporation's rejection of the Anglo-Irish *Sir* Hugh Lane's choice of site was one more sign of his tribe's diminishing influence. The conflict is not over religion; it is over the cultural domination of the Ireland Yeats sees coming into being.

[15] See *Responsibilities: Poems and a Play* (Dundrum: Cuala Press, 1914).

that of the blood kin, but Yeats honours it, addressing them directly, as he did his 'old fathers'. These 'tavern comrades'

> *... never made a poorer song*
> *That you might have a heavier purse,*
> *Nor gave loud service to a cause*
> *That you might have a troop of friends.*
> *You kept the Muses' sterner laws,*
> *And unrepenting faced your ends,*
> *And therefore earned the right – and yet*
> *Dowson and Johnson most I praise –*
> *To troop with those the world's forgot,*
> *And copy their proud steady gaze.*[16]

The poets' masculinity differs from that of merchants, rebels, soldiers, and skippers. Though they are not leaping overboard for old hats or fighting beside 'the brackish waters of the Boyne', their fidelity to poetry, to 'the Muses' sterner laws', deserves a eulogy. Their virtues—not writing bad poetry to get rich, not serving an undeserving cause to become popular, remaining stern, steady, and proud—are not visible or dramatic qualities. The Rhymers are praised for a masculine display that couldn't be seen. They are left, however, to 'troop with those the world's forgot'.

Setting these masculinities against one another, the flamboyant, physically active ancestors, and the decadent, almost forgotten poets of the Cheshire Cheese, Yeats creates a distinction that appears in another form in 'Meditations in Time of Civil War' (1922–3). There, the poet-speaker confronts the normatively masculine soldiers and is driven to reconsider his own masculinity and vocation. It's worth noting that the title does not state that the poem is *about* the Civil War; the meditations take place *in a time of* Civil War. Yet the poem's title, its preoccupations, and the sequence of its sections make clear that the Civil War and its proximity to the Yeats family in their tower precipitated a crisis of masculinity. The poem begins with a narrative of family decline, from the 'violent bitter man' who 'Called architect and artist in' to the mousey great-grandson ('Ancestral Houses'). It closes with the speaker, closely identified with Yeats himself (the tower, the daughter, son, wife, and 'old neighbour', Lady Gregory), accepting the personal if not the social rightness of his vocation. The poem is therefore framed by the interrogation of masculinities, and the Civil War soldiers, who appear only in the middle of the poem, are subsumed to that issue. The speaker does not engage with Civil War politics because his interest lies elsewhere, in the varying types of masculinity performed by the 'rich man', the mousey man, the generations of Sato's ancestors, the soldiers, and the 'rage-driven' troop of men who appear in the mist as part of the speaker's tower-top vision.[17] In 'Meditations', more than in any other poem by Yeats, notions of the masculine are invoked, studied, and brooded on.[18]

---

[16] *CW1*, 104.

[17] *CW1*, 200, 206, 204, 206.

[18] For a meticulous analysis of the various poetic forms used in ' Meditations in Time of Civil War', see Helen Vendler, *Our Secret Discipline: Yeats and Lyric Form* (Cambridge, MA: Harvard University Press, 2007), 231–6.

Contrasting masculinities in 'Meditations' are distinguished metaphorically in terms of indoor and outdoor sites. In 'Ancestral Houses', the poem's first section, a macho ancestor is credited with the artistic patronage that gets the house built on his extensive grounds; he is responsible for the 'flowering lawns' and 'planted hills':

> Some violent bitter man, some powerful man
> Called architect and artist in, that they,
> Bitter and violent men, might rear in stone
> The sweetness that all longed for night and day . . .

Troubled that this creative energy might not last, the speaker fears that the luxury of 'leveled lawns and graveled ways' may 'take our greatness with our violence'. The scion of the family is imagined as so weak that he has become a participle in a domestic interior:

> The pacing to and fro on polished floors
> Amid great chambers and long galleries, lined
> With famous portraits of our ancestors[.]

The effete descendant has no need to go outside; all the landscaping was taken care of two generations earlier. In this interior space, he admires the superior masculinity of his ancestors, who look down at him from the gallery walls. The luxury of the great chambers and the polished floors explain why 'buildings that a haughtier age designed' might 'take our greatness with our bitterness'.[19] According to Mrs Yeats, the house that inspired these stanzas was Garsington, where Ottoline Morrell and her family were living when the Yeatses visited, but the setting might just as well have been an Anglo-Irish Big House.[20]

To distinguish his own landscape, and hence his masculinity, from that of the 'rich' family, Yeats in 'My House' describes a landscape that has not been tamed and prettified; he writes, 'An acre of stony ground' where 'the symbolic rose can break in flower', as if it blossoms without horticultural aid. It is a rather rugged Irish place, with rain, wind, thorns, a water hen and cows, but no ornamental peacock. And to counter the notion that indoor work is a form of idleness, Yeats emphasizes the rough-hewn architecture, as if physical exertion were required to reach the room, and the presence of stone in his 'chamber', as if the exterior landscape extended there (no 'polished floors'):

> A winding stair, a chamber arched with stone,
> A grey stone fireplace with an open hearth,
> A candle and written page.[21]

[19] *CW1*, 200–1.
[20] *Life 2*, 217–18, 707.
[21] *CW1*, 201.

As in 'Adam's Curse', Yeats feels the need to emphasize that he is working hard: 'Il Penseroso's Platonist toiled on / In some like chamber', and 'Benighted travelers / From markets and from fairs / Have seen his midnight candle glimmering'. The word 'toiled' attaches to Yeats himself, of course, and the implication of the next lines, with the pun on 'Benighted', is that the people who do agricultural work go home at night for rest, while the poet himself is still up, toiling at poetry. The labour that elsewhere Yeats describes as 'sedentary' is here shown to be so vigorous that he hopes his domestic interior and landscape serve as 'emblems of adversity' to inspire his 'bodily heirs'.[22]

With the phrase 'bodily heirs', the eugenic concern of 'Ancestral Houses' associates itself with Yeats, and that concern continues in the next section's focus on the seemingly successful masculinity of Sato's family.[23] In 'My Table', a section situated in the most professionally significant part of Yeats's domestic site, 'Sato's gift, a changeless sword' lies by the poet's 'pen and paper' so that 'it may moralise / [My] days out of their aimlessness'. What happened to that midnight candle? Maybe Yeats is not toiling so hard as 'Il Penseroso's Platonist' after all. The sword, however, is linked to a five-hundred-year line of male artists, a line that demonstrates how creative indoor work can be a performance of masculinity:

> A marvellous accomplishment,
> In painting or in poetry, went
> From father unto son
> And through the centuries ran[.][24]

No barren passions here, it seems, and also no mothers and daughters: it is masculine creativity that did not decline. The sword on Yeats's table 'lies' there to inspire the same energy in himself, but his workspace appears as a *nature morte*, with still objects but no labour.

The mousey grandson haunts Yeats's imagination: 'And what if my descendants lose the flower?' Yeats asks in the next section ('My Descendants'). He can vouch for his own worth ('Having inherited a vigorous mind / From my old fathers') because he is now an old father himself, and with luck the 'woman and a man' who descend from him will create another five-hundred-year line of vigorous, creative people, like those in Sato's lineage.[25] With the exception of the 'woman' (Anne Yeats, who knew at age 11 that her brother Michael was destined to 'continue the family'), the first four sections of the poem are haunted by male lineages, the violent, bitter powerful man and his grandson, the 'bodily heirs', Sato's male ancestors, and Yeats's 'old fathers'.

---

[22] *CW1*, 202.

[23] Yeats joined the Eugenics Education Society in 1937, but his approach to family lineage was consistent with eugenic notions before his membership in the society (*Life* 2, 629).

[24] *CW1*, 202–3.

[25] *CW1*, 202–3.

When, then, with the fifth section, 'The Road at My Door', the Civil War soldiers enter the poem, they enter as men whose masculinities may be understood in the context of all the men invoked up to this point. Both are rough and hearty: the 'affable Irregular' is a 'heavily-built Falstaffian man' who

> Comes cracking jokes of civil war
> As though to die by gunshot were
> The finest play under the sun.

His Free State counterparts, 'A brown Lieutenant and his men', are carefully positioned: they 'Stand at my door' while the poet makes small talk about the weather and his pear tree. The three elegant stanzas, with their subtle off-rhymes, embody two examples of masculinity—soldier and poet. The final stanza of this section revises the significance of the poet-speaker's domestic interior:

> I count those feathered balls of soot
> The moor-hen guides upon the stream,
> To silence the envy in my thought;
> And turn towards my chamber, caught
> In the cold snows of a dream.[26]

The envy in the speaker's thought is inspired by the fully fleshed masculinity of the soldiers: they are outside while he is at his door. When the speaker turns 'toward his chamber', he leaves them to the war, while is 'caught / In the cold snows of a dream'. His domestic interior has become associated with escape from the rough male world of men of action, and he has lost agency, 'caught' in the dream. He has made small talk about the 'foul weather', but the soldiers are outside in it: for him, weather is metaphorical, 'the cold snows of a dream'.[27]

The sixth section ('The Stare's Nest at My Window') devastatingly corrects the concept of masculinity in all the previous sections. Who would feel 'envy' of the soldiers when 'Last night they trundled down the road / That dead young soldier in his blood'?[28] It's not all about cracking jokes and bad weather; it's about the murder of a young man who was some family's male descendant. Nor is he the only casualty: 'A man is killed, or a house burned'. These events, too, are displays of masculinity. When Yeats writes, 'We had

---

[26] *CW1*, 204

[27] Joseph Keene Chadwick, in *Interventions and Continuities in Irish and Gay Studies* (Honolulu: College of Languages, Linguistics, and Literature, 2002), is interesting on this section: 'The isolation and envy felt by the speaking *I* of "The Road at My Door"... derive not primarily from the ostensibly contemplative nature of the poet's vocation ... but rather from the insecurities of his class and sectarian position as a member of the diminished remnant of a once-dominant group.'

[28] *CW1*, 209.

fed the heart on fantasies, / The heart's grown brutal with the fare', one of the fantasies may be about the 'greatness' of violent, bitter men and their magnificent houses.

And so Yeats turns away from masculinity to the mother bird feeding her chicks, a comforting sight to contemplate.

> The bees build in the crevices
> Of loosening masonry, and there
> The mother birds bring grubs and flies.[29]

The bees are building a house without being rich, violent, or bitter. Both sets of creatures are concerned only with the present moment; the birds are not preoccupied with generations of future chicks, nor the bees with bodily heirs who might inherit the hive. And while the bees build, the Yeats family is without agency in their house: 'We are closed in, and the key is turned / On our uncertainty.'

The apocalyptic visions in the final section ('I See Phantoms of Hatred and of the Heart's Fullness and of the Coming Emptiness') show what the fantasies 'we' fed the heart on look like when their brutality is realized. Every form of masculinity idealized or even touched on in the earlier parts of the poem makes a final appearance in the snowy, misty sky: violent, bitter men, Sato's ancestors (the 'glittering sword out of the east'), soldiers in opposed armies, 'the sweetness that all longed for', effete slippered Contemplation, hearts full of fantasies.[30] When Yeats writes, 'I turn away, and shut the door, . . .', and enters his domestic interior once more, he cannot return to contemplation of Sato's sword, having now understood its violent implications, or anything like the 'self-delighting reverie' of the poet pleased with his toil by the light of the midnight candle.[31]

There 'on the stair', in an interstitial space, not quite in his 'chamber' where pen and paper await him, but with the shut door just behind him, Yeats pauses to confront directly the 'envy in his thought' that he had not altogether explained earlier. Plain words, free from the hallucinatory, apocalyptic language ('Their legs long, delicate and slender, aquamarine their eyes'), indicate that the speaker is attempting to free himself from fantasies:

> I turn away and shut the door, and on the stair
> Wonder how many times I could have proved my worth
> In something that all others understand or share;
> But O! ambitious heart, had such a proof drawn forth
> A company of friends, a conscience set at ease,

---

[29] *CW1*, 204–5.
[30] *CW1*, 205; *CW1*, 204; see Chadwick's excellent discussion on the relation of the apocalyptic stanzas to the 'social hierarchy' of the Ascendancy (*Interventions and Continuities*, 48–58).
[31] *CW1*, 206.

> It had but made us pine the more. The abstract joy,
> The half-read wisdom of daemonic images,
> Suffice the ageing man as once the growing boy.[32]

There are no judgemental ancestors and no inferior offspring. The only lifespan that concerns Yeats is his own, from 'growing boy' to 'ageing man'. Perhaps the sight of the birds and the bees with their devotion to the present moment was salutary. Or maybe Yeats has remembered the Rhymers, who never '*gave loud service to a cause / That [they] might have a troop of friends*'.[33] He does not mention the Civil War. Like Sato's male ancestors, it has served its purpose, offering a different form of masculinity for the poet-speaker to consider, confront, and reject. In the final lines he imagines but does not yet reach his workspace and the 'half-read wisdom' of the open book. His work is in progress; he will soon return to the book he had left open.[34] Some of the labour that gives his life indoors value and meaning is about to begin. As Nicholas Grene writes eloquently, Yeats here 'accepts with rueful resignation the inadequacies of the poet's engagement with the world'.[35] That resignation allows Yeats to acknowledge a little of the envy he may still feel, as well as the longing for that 'company of friends'.[36] The verb 'Suffice' situates the poet—provisionally—apart from ideals, apocalypse, and anxiety.

MASCULINITY IN MOTION

In 'The Tower' (composed in 1925) and many subsequent poems, Yeats privileges the masculinity of Protestant males. There is a eugenic subtext to their apparent superiority: they are retrospectively endowed with an intellectual power that is troped as physical vigour. An understanding of the way motion and energy feature in 'The Tower', especially in the curious sequence of thirteen stanzas in the centre of the poem and the unheralded appearance of Burke and Grattan in the final section, shows the demographic foundation of Yeats's anxieties about masculinity. 'Pardon, Old Fathers', in its apology for 'a barren passion', linked romantic failure and reproductive anxiety with a cast of potentially judgemental male ancestors; the later poems attribute physical prowess and intense movement to the notably Protestant men in a long male line.

'Meditations' interrogates the value of writing poetry, 'only a book', in a genealogical context. 'The Tower' considers the other part of Yeats's flawed masculinity, the barren

---

[32] *CW1*, 206.

[33] *CW1*, 104.

[34] For an illuminating analysis of Yeats's use of ' half' as a prefix, see Nicholas Grene, *Yeats's Poetic Codes* (Oxford: Oxford University Press, 2008), 220–6.

[35] Grene, Yeats's Poetic Codes, 225.

[36] For one of the best analyses of the final section of 'Meditations', see Daniel A. Harris, *Yeats: Coole Park and Ballylee* (Baltimore and London: Johns Hopkins University Press, 1974), 183–4: '… the retrieval of any constructive purpose from the debris of civil war represents a tangible gain' (184).

passion, and redeems his failure by creating a cultural lineage defined by flawless masculinity. The framing outer sections, written in quatrains rhyming *ABAB*, are set in Sligo and invoke mountain climbing and fly fishing. In the opening section, masculine display is associated with sporting activities. As in 'Adam's Curse', Yeats associates writing poetry with physical exertion. In spite of 'Decrepit age',

> Never had I more
> Excited, passionate, fantastical
> Imagination, nor an ear and eye
> That more expected the impossible –
> No, not in boyhood when with rod and fly,
> Or the humbler worm, I climbed Ben Bulben's back
> And had the livelong summer day to spend.[37]

The active imagination is linked with climbing and fishing because of their temporal coincidence: the speaker's imagination in old age is more intense than it was at a time 'when'. There is no suggestion that Yeats's poetic composition and mountain climbing were simultaneous, but the vivid description of a summer day in Sligo in the 1870s adheres to the concept of an energetic imagination and endows it with a quality of youthful, boyish vigour.

The inner section, situated in Galway and written (as Helen Vendler has pointed out) in Cowley stanzas (*AABBCDDC, 55545445 iambs*), is distinct in form, setting, tone, and perspective; it is both more oblique in approach and more intimate in concern.[38] The focus on physical energy and movement continues in the central section in a more complex form.

The series of vignettes that constitute the second section of 'The Tower' involve a repeated narrative formation, an interaction between a *belle dame sans merci* and her male victim. The distinct, consistent, but gradually diminishing presence of powerful women (Mrs French, Mary Hynes, Hanrahan's unnamed love interest, and finally the 'woman lost') shifts the stanzas' emphasis to the lover's masculinity. Daniel Albright writes that there is 'a kind of defiant randomness about the sequence which may forever resist complete elucidation', but I believe elucidation is possible.[39] The emotional and imagistic logic that determines the vignettes' sequence connects this section metaphorically with the framing parts of the poem.

---

[37] *CW1*, 194.

[38] See Vendler's discussion of the Cowley stanza in ' The Tower' and elsewhere in Yeats's poems (*Our Secret Discipline*, 292–5).

[39] Daniel Albright, *The Myth against Myth: A Study of Yeats's Imagination in Old Age* (Oxford: Oxford University Press, 1972), 13. Harris, *Coole Park and Ballylee* 184-200, argues plausibly that ' The Tower' is (as Yeats explicitly announces at the opening) about the poet's imagination, and his close reading is persuasive. Such an interpretation, however, does not preclude a reading that sees masculinity as the unannounced subject.

The characters who populate this part of 'The Tower' are local figures summoned by Yeats as he stands at the top of the tower looking out to the places they lived. The original purpose is to ask them a question about old age, but at the end, as Daniel Harris writes, he asks another question that he 'initially has no intention of asking'.[40] All episodes are variations of the first one, a charming, gothic, and slightly comic story:

> Beyond that ridge lived Mrs. French, and once
> When every silver candlestick or sconce
> Lit up the dark mahogany and the wine,
> A serving-man, that could divine
> That most respected lady's every wish,
> Ran and with the garden shears
> Clipped an insolent farmer's ears
> And brought them in a little covered dish.[41]

The logic of the sequence lies in a narrative retrogression in the pattern formed by the separate vignettes. The basic narrative line is enchantment (by a woman, by beauty, magic, poetry, drink), a sudden movement from indoors to outdoors, and then some form of destructive action: over the course of the stanzas Yeats's interest moves back from the action to the actor's state of mind. In the second episode, inebriated men leave a pub in the middle of the night to see if they can find Mary Hynes, the woman whose beauty is celebrated in Raftery's 'famous Máire ní Eidhin'.[42] 'And one was drowned in the great bog of Cloone.'[43] Reminded by the blind Raftery of the allegedly blind Homer, Yeats mentions Helen of Troy (who 'has all living hearts betrayed') and then gives a fragment of his own story about Red Hanrahan, who is tricked into following a pack of cards changed into hounds and a hare.[44] As many critics have shown, the anacoluthon that interrupts the story of Hanrahan ('And followed up those baying creatures towards – / O towards I have forgotten what – enough!') cuts it off at the point when Hanrahan followed the hounds toward a double failure, a failure to ask about the four symbols of Pleasure, Power, Courage, and Knowledge revealed to him by the women of Slieve Echtge, and later, a failure to find Mary Lavelle.[45] The women's condemnations echo through several of the stories: 'He is weak . . . He is afraid . . . He had not courage.'[46]

---

[40] Harris, Coole Park and Ballylee, 188.

[41] CW1, 195.

[42] According to Maureen Murphy, the poem is titled 'Máire ní Eidhin nó an Pabhsaw Gléigeal' in Hyde's Amhráin agus Dánta an Reachtabhraigh, but is called 'Máire ní Eidhin' in Ciarán Ó Coigligh's Raiftearaí (2000).

[43] CW1, 195.

[44] CW1, 196.

[45] CW1, 196.

[46] The definitive analysis of this stanza may be found in Deirdre Toomey, 'Labyrinths: Yeats and Maud Gonne', in Deirdre Toomey, ed., Yeats and Women (London: Macmillan, 1997), 1–39. Toomey discusses (among many aspects of background) the original literary version of his Hanrahan story that Yeats was probably referring to (8) and the manuscript of the poem (22–5).

The serving-man gets five lines, but Hanrahan's story is cut off before we hear where he went; we never see him outdoors. Beginning with an emphasis on performance of actions, Yeats moves toward a more psychological concern with the obsessed imagination. As the women gradually fade from the scenes, implied but not present, the men's role becomes more dominant. In each successive episode, agency is increasingly attributed to the man: what transpires is not the fault of the 'belle dame' but of the man. The interior space that these stanzas move toward is the haunted, paralysed masculine imagination, shown most dramatically in the male sleeper in the tower surrounded by nightmare male ghosts in the last vignette:

> And certain men-at-arms there were
> Whose images, in the Great Memory stored,
> Come with loud cry and panting breast
> To break upon a sleeper's rest.[47]

The sequence of these carefully chosen little narratives moves subtly but deliberately to the paralysed mind of a man haunted by the sounds of his desires and reminded of his failure to act with sufficient courage to satisfy them.

When, in the final stanza, Yeats asks Hanrahan not a question about old age but a more profound and significant one—'Does the imagination dwell the most / Upon a woman won or a woman lost?'—the pronoun 'you' in the answer is ambiguous, linking Yeats to the character he created:

> If on the lost, admit you turned aside
> From a great labyrinth out of pride,
> Cowardice, some silly over-subtle thought
> Or anything called conscience once ...[48]

'Admit' is the key word; catharsis comes with the acknowledgment of a refusal to face a failure. The poem's narrative centre is emotional paralysis and the consequent failure of masculine action. In the not random but deliberate sequence of episodes, agency shifts from Mrs French, who has the 'insolent farmer's' ear cut off, to Hanrahan, who 'turned aside / from a great labyrinth out of pride ...', to the sleeper who was unable to act, and to the ambiguous 'you' who 'turned aside ...'[49] Deirdre Toomey's research has located the precise occasion when Yeats 'turned aside' from a full commitment to Maud Gonne.[50] Even with the event unspecified, however, the power that remembering it affords can be felt in the poem.

---

[47] *CW1*, 196.
[48] *CW1*, 197.
[49] See also the discussion of the middle section by Harris, *Coole Park and Ballylee*, 184–93.
[50] Toomey, 'Labyrinths', 2–8.

Roman numerals and extra spaces separate the three sections of this poem, marking clearly the different forms, tones, and approaches to masculinity.[51] Helen Vendler has pointed out the significance of Yeats's use of Roman numerals to indicate a change in 'station', that is, 'physical or mental location'.[52] In this case, between sections II and III, Yeats moves from a specific Galway landscape to a Sligo landscape; he mentions mountains, as in the first section, but not Ben Bulben. That extra space on the page is temporal as well as locational and suggests that the speaker has a chance to assimilate the significance of his admission.

When, then, Yeats returns strong and determined in the third section ('It is time that I wrote my will; / I choose upstanding men'), he is no longer summoning images of masculine paralysis but returning with energy to the activities associated with 'boyhood' on the mountainside of Ben Bulben.[53] The sometimes metaphorical, sometimes literal, emphasis on bodily vigour and motion provides continuity throughout the poem. Its significance is psychological in the second section but demographic and eugenic in the third. The tone, the energy, and the rhetorical force of the final section have been read as a result of the 'liberation' afforded by the admission at the end of the middle section and the consequent release from emotional paralysis.[54] Yeats gains renewed authority and confidence in two ways: by creating male heirs whose athletic prowess becomes a requirement of the Yeatsian legacy—'young upstanding men / Climbing the mountainside, / That under bursting dawn / They may drop a fly'—and by reminding himself of the Irish Protestant tradition at a time when it dominated Irish culture and politics.[55] This lineage perpetuates a genealogy consisting only of men, a cultural kinship that Yeats brings into being by announcing it here. The pride that the young anglers will inherit forms part of a male Anglo-Irish legacy,

> The pride of people that were
> Bound neither to Cause nor to State,
> Neither to slaves that were spat on,
> Nor to the tyrants that spat,
> The people of Burke and Grattan[.][56]

Burke and Grattan's surprise appearance at the poem's end shows how the overall demographic anxiety about Anglo-Irish political power and population produces

---

[51] Daniel Harris interprets the entire poem in terms of the choice 'between an art which accepts the body and no art at all ... [the poem] is Yeats's most self-demanding revaluation of the imagination' (Coole Park and Ballylee, 185–6). Harris's reading of ' The Tower' is not incompatible with an emphasis on masculinity; the two readings supplement one another.

[52] Vendler, Our Secret Discipline, 29–30, 280.

[53] CW1, 198.

[54] See Harris, quoting T. S. Eliot on ' the use of memory ... for liberation' (Coole Park and Ballylee, 193).

[55] CW1, 199.

[56] CW1, 198.

and incorporates concerns about masculinity in all its forms. Placing himself in this extended kinship of proud Anglo-Irish men, identifying with their strengths of body and character, Yeats is no longer speaking (as he did in the first section) as a solitary man whose energies are thwarted by old age. The strong stresses of the trimeter express this explicitly Protestant pride aggressively in the face of the dominant Catholicism of the Irish Free State.[57]

In the later Yeatsian imaginary, many subsequent examples of masculinity descend from the men in the third section of 'The Tower': they are physically active like the young men, and they are public figures like Burke and Grattan.[58] Masculinity becomes increasingly kinetic in the poems written after 1926: motion is the defining mark of a privileged masculinity. The tower's stair is revisited in a few lines in 'Blood and the Moon' (composed in 1927), a poem inspired in part by the assassination of Kevin O'Higgins, Cumann na nGaedheal Minister for External Affairs and Minister for Justice, and also Yeats's good friend.[59] Here, the stair is charged with an almost hysterical energy as the poem announces a male cultural ancestry composed of eighteenth-century Anglo-Irish intellectuals ('an Irish-Georgian quartet', Foster calls them), who have managed to manoeuvre their way up the stair of the tower, described in such a way that to mount it seems an athletic feat:[60]

> I declare this tower is my symbol; I declare
> This winding, gyring, spiring treadmill of a stair is my ancestral stair;
> That Goldsmith and the Dean, Berkeley and Burke have travelled there.[61]

Goldsmith et al. 'have travelled there' because they are fellow travellers, Yeats's cultural ancestors, chosen from the century when (in Yeats's view) they were most dominant.[62] The winding 'ancestral' stair, like strands of DNA, connects them metaphorically, but the description of the stair and the verb 'travelled' suggest a masculine vigour that the 'ageing man' of 'Meditations' didn't have.

The defiant Protestant men who serve as muses for Yeats in the 1930s are associated with bodily movement as well as transgressive sexuality. The few ancient remaining

---

[57] A longer, more detailed analysis of the poem such as Harris gives (*Coole Park and Ballylee*, 193–200) devotes time to the rest of the third section, in which Yeats reclaims his imagination ('Death and life were not / Till man made up the whole / Lock, stock and barrel / Out of his bitter soul' [*CW1*, 198]). See also Vendler's discussion of the trimeter (*Our Secret Discipline*, 197–202).

[58] Another example of the (biological) ancestral roll call in the late poems is 'Are You Content?', in which the male Protestant ancestors are also featured in terms of their physical activity: 'He that in Sligo at Drumcliff / Set up the old stone Cross, / That red-headed rector in County Down, / A good man on a horse' (*CW1*, 322).

[59] As Foster points out, O'Higgins is here 'posthumously co-opted' into the 'Ascendancy tradition' (*Life* 2, 346).

[60] *Life* 2, 346.

[61] *CW1*, 237.

[62] But see Clíona Ó Gallchoir (op. cit.) for the insecurities felt by many of the eighteenth-century writers whom Yeats claims as cultural ancestors.

Parnellites are urged to 'Stand upright on your legs a while'. Parnell is a 'proud man', and 'No prouder trod the ground.'[63] Edward VIII is differentiated from those who 'sat' on 'thrones from China to Peru' because he refused the throne: he wouldn't 'keep his lover waiting'.[64] And in the best-known lines about this famously transgressive man, '*The ghost of Roger Casement / Is beating on the door*'.[65] Sexuality in this period of Yeats's poetry is anti-Catholic even when it is not explicitly Protestant: the generic women who proudly report their sexual adventures explicitly defy the Catholic Church. The title of 'A Last Confession' mocks the Catholic ritual of that name, and Crazy Jane defies the bishop; their sexuality, like the men's, is hedonistic and not reproductive.

Birds

Throughout his career Yeats wrote poems in which truth is revealed by stripping away what covers it: 'Now I must wither into the truth …'; 'there's more enterprise / In walking naked'; 'But when this soul, its body off / Naked to naked goes …'; 'I must lie down where all the ladders start'.[66] 'Cuchulain Comforted' is one of those stripping poems, and what is stripped are the trappings of masculinity, the obsession with wounds and violence; and then, finally, gender. Masculine display is removed, superseded, and transformed.

Three weeks before his death, Yeats woke up in the middle of the night from a dream that he dictated to his wife. With few changes, the words in the prose transcript became the poem 'Cuchulain Comforted' (originally titled 'Cuchulain Dead').[67] The new form is Dantean terza rima, used because Cuchulain is imagined at the stage of the afterlife Yeats called 'the Shiftings', in which 'the dead person experience[s] the opposite of the emotional and moral code he had adopted during his life on earth'.[68] In the poem, all the vigour, energy, and occasionally violent masculine display Yeats associated with men who were not poets is stripped away from his most important heroic figure. 'Cuchulain Comforted' is about the demasculinizing of the hero.

In the simple ritual that transpires, Cuchulain arrives 'among the dead' with six mortal wounds, more than the average man would require. He is called 'Violent and famous', and he is not walking: he 'strode'. When he leans against a tree, it is 'As though to meditate on wounds and blood'. He is still in male hero mode: wounds, violent, strode, blood. The Shrouds are 'bird-like things', timid and gentle, and one of them 'let fall / A bundle of linen'. A few more only 'Come creeping up because the man was still'. The 'linen-carrier'

---

[63] *CW1*, 309.

[64] *CW1*, 316.

[65] *CW1*, 306–7.

[66] The quotations are from 'The Coming of Wisdom with Time' (*CW1*, 94), 'A Coat' (*CW1*, 127), 'A Last Confession' (*CW1*, 275), and 'The Circus Animals' Desertion' (*CW1*, 348).

[67] For Mrs Yeats's transcription of the words her husband dictated to her, see *Life* 2, 646. See Vendler for an analysis of the prose text's transformation into terza rima (*Our Secret Discipline*, 370–5).

[68] Vendler, Our Secret Discipline, 371.

tells Cuchulain, 'Your life can grow much sweeter if you will / Obey our ancient rule and make a shroud.'[69] A 'sweet' life is not what a violent and famous hero has ever wanted, and making shrouds is not one of his skills.

Everything about the Shrouds implies a fear of masculinity and a preference for the unmasculine. Peter Bland Botham has shown how in Yeats's prose sewing is associated with the feminine, especially with his mother, Susan Pollexfen.[70] The Shrouds give Cuchulain precise directions for this craft:

> 'We thread the needles' eyes, and all we do
> All must together do.' That done, the man
> Took up the nearest and began to sew.

Then the Shrouds identify themselves to Cuchulain as 'Convicted cowards all ...' and begin to sing.

> They sang, but had nor human tunes nor words,
> Though all was done in common as before;
> They had changed their throats and had the throats of birds.[71]

In the prose draft dictated to Mrs Yeats in the middle of the night, the line is, 'they did not sing like men or women but like linnets'.[72] In the poem, Cuchulain is 'he', but the Shrouds are only 'we'. No longer human, the Shrouds have become genderless birds. In this very late poem, to imagine a counterweight to strong, visible, noisy masculinity, the hero Cuchulain with six mortal wounds, it wasn't enough to change the species: Yeats had to get rid of gender also. And gender in this poem is marked by wounds and weapons. The other line transcribed from his dream makes that clear: 'You would be much more comfortable if you would me a Shroud to wear it instead of the arms.' At the end of the sequence I've been discussing, then, Yeats write a poem about demasculinizing a famous Irish warrior hero, not making him effeminate or a quieter male, but getting rid of both gender and species altogether. Of course, because any version of masculinity is provisional in Yeats's poems, his *final* last poem, 'The Black Tower', covers its male figures in masculinity, albeit a rough and desperate kind: their money is spent and 'their wine gone sour', but they 'Lack nothing that a soldier needs, / ... all are oath-bound men'.[73]

As in Oisín Kelly's statue of the Children of Lir at the Garden of Remembrance in Dublin, this avian metamorphosis marks the death of a hero. Another kind of bird is often found in poems where Yeats turns away from the recurrent anxiety, the

---

[69] *CW1*, 332.
[70] Bland Botham, 'I am a Victorian', 3–6.
[71] *CW1*, 332.
[72] *Life* 2, 646.
[73] *CW1*, 331.

defensiveness, and the errors of masculinity.[74] As early as 'Easter 1916' he rejects 'Hearts with one purpose alone' in favour of a small rural scene of avian courtship: 'The long-legged moor-hens dive, / And hens to moor-cocks call'.[75] In 'Meditations in Time of Civil War', he counts the chicks that 'The moor-hen guides upon the stream' to silence his envy of the soldiers at his door. His realization that people are being killed quite near where he lives, that the body of a 'young soldier' has been 'trundled down the road' outside the tower—those realizations are framed by his reference to 'the stare's nest' in the wall of the tower, 'and there / The mother birds bring grubs and flies'.[76] Creating his male genealogy and summoning his male heirs in the third section of 'The Tower', Yeats mentions the daws that 'drop twigs layer upon layer' and then,

> The mother bird will rest
> On their hollow top,
> And so warm her wild nest.[77]

The birds Yeats turns to when he is writing about masculinity are not decorative birds like the peacock or large birds in flight like swans, but smaller, immediately visible birds, ones close by whose activities he can see, especially nest-building birds, nurturing mother birds, birds that are part of families, reproducing in spontaneous, intuitive, unanxious ways, not feeling judged by their ancestor birds, birds without loins, non-sectarian birds, not worried about the accomplishments of future generations of chicks, just doing their reproductive thing. Because masculinity, for Yeats, is never stable, always uneasy, threatened or threatening, never permanently good or permanently satisfying, he turns to birds courting, building nests, feeding chicks or guiding them upon the stream. Like Cuchulain, he is comforted.

---

[74] For more on the Irish birds of 1916, see Lucy McDiarmid, ' The Avian Rising: Yeats, Muldoon, and Others', *International Yeats Studies*, 1:1 (2016), Article 10, https://doi.org/10.34068/IYS.01.01.09. See also, Kelly Sullivan, 'Yeats's Birds: Recognizing the Animal," *Modernist Cultures* 16.1 (Spring 2021), 114–37.

[75] *CW1*, 181.

[76] *CW1*, 204–5.

[77] *CW1*, 199.

CHAPTER 40

....

LATE STYLE

....

WAYNE K. CHAPMAN

THE tragicomedy of life is outlined in verse. With epigrammatic succinctness, the logic is laid out in the opening stanza of the poem 'Vacillation':

> Between extremities
> Man runs his course;
> A brand, or flaming breath,
> Comes to destroy
> All those antinomies
> Of day and night;
> The body calls it death,
> The heart remorse.
> But if these be right
> What is joy?[1]

Paradoxically, the 'brand' that destroys the life of one's body also brings, in chance moments to the poet, a blaze of absolute joy: 'so great my happiness, / That I was blessed and could bless.'[2] The logic is coincident with that of 'Quarrel in Old Age', on the subject of love wasted on Maud Gonne, in that Yeats would declare in a letter to Olivia Shakespear of 3 January 1932: 'Live Tragically but be not deceived ... I shall be a sinful man to the end, and think upon my death-bed of all the nights I wasted in my youth.'[3] The vacillating poet (at 67 and recovering from illness) had begun to strike a characteristic attitude found in his poems of the early 1930s and after.

In this chapter, the words 'later' and 'late' are informed by the taxonomy of Thomas Parkinson in his pioneering book *W. B. Yeats, the Later Poetry* (1964), which still inspires

---

[1] *CW1*, 249–50.
[2] *CW1*, 253.
[3] Yeats to Olivia Shakespear, 3 January 1932, *CL InteLex* #5556. Olivia Shakespear, not Maud Gonne, was the greater love of Yeats's life, according to Ronald Schuchard, 'Yeats and Olivia Revisited: A Pathway to *The Winding Stair and Other Poems*', *South Atlantic Review*, 77:1-2 (2014), 99–140.

by excellent example and generally out of enthusiasm for Yeats's creative life from 1917 onward, beginning with the 'personalist and elegiac poems' of *The Wild Swans at Coole* (1919).[4] According to Parkinson's practical division of the oeuvre, the poetry collected in the 'definitive (to 1922) Macmillan edition of *Later Poems*' was one of the 'crucially rewarding events' of Yeats's life (58). As it is usual to divide Yeats's canon into at least three parts—early (to 1899), middle (or transitional, 1900–16), and late (or mature, 1917–39)—I prefer Parkinson's simpler, bipartite division into 'Early' and 'Later' poetry in connection with style, because the project at hand requires the selection of texts that compare favourably with the most recent poems published in *Later Poems* than most of those written prior to 1917 or published before 1922. For this study, the term 'late' shall mean the subsection of Yeats's later poems published after *The Tower* and *The Winding Stair* and that first iteration of the *Collected Poems* (1933). In particular, the focus shall include the lyrics first published by the Cuala Press as *New Poems* (1938), *On the Boiler* (1939), and *Last Poems and Two Plays* (1939), and the posthumous states of these lyrics as they occurred in Macmillan's standard edition of *Last Poems and Plays* (1940). Thus, for comparison, the designation 'late' correlates with the term 'last' in Jon Stallworthy's early genetic study *Visions and Revisions in Yeats's Last Poems* (1969) and the still helpful essay anthology he edited before that, *Yeats, Last Poems: A Casebook* (1968).[5] Except for 'The Sorrow of Love', the poems treated in Stallworthy's first book, *Between the Lines: W. B. Yeats's Poetry in the Making* (1963), are all 'later' poems, by Parkinson's definition.

From the late-1920s to 'Vacillation', Yeats's health was so bad that, essentially, he was in a fight for his life. Nevertheless, remarkably, in 'A Dialogue of Self and Soul'—a parody of Marvell's 'A Dialogue between the Soul and the Body' in which the Body (like 'my Self' in Yeats's poem) is given rhetorically the last word—the debate concludes both emphatically and conditionally: 'I am content to live it all again / And yet again, if it be life ...', a life that is recursive yet progressive, abundant, and without remorse:

> I am content to follow to its source
> Every event in action or in thought;
> Measure the lot; forgive myself the lot!
> When such as I cast out remorse
> So great a sweetness flows into my breast
> We must laugh and we must sing,
> We are blest by everything,
> Everything we look upon is blest.[6]

[4] Thomas F. Parkinson, *W. B. Yeats, the Later Poetry* (Berkeley and Los Angeles: University of California Press, 1964). Parkinson's first book, *W. B. Yeats, Self-Critic: A Study of His Early Verse*, was issued in 1951 by the same publisher.

[5] Stallworthy's two studies were published in Oxford, at the Clarendon Press, with the anthology of essays *Yeats, Last Poems: A Casebook* (London: Macmillan, 1969), bearing short reviews and mostly reprinted 'recent studies' by Stallworthy, Curtis Bradford, T. R. Henn, J. R. Mulryne, A. N. Jeffares, F. A. C. Wilson, Arra Garab, and Peter Ure.

[6] *CW1*, 236.

In pursuit of health by a better climate than Ireland offered, in 1927 to 1933 Yeats's movements around the Mediterranean are marked, like 'a fever chart', by poems written in 'Algeciras, Seville, Cannes, Rapallo, Rome, Portofino Vetta [before] returning to London, Dublin, [and] Coole ..., recording the valleys and peaks of despondency and joy'.[7] Together, the poems of *The Tower* (1928) and *The Winding Stair* (1933), some few lyrics of which were jumbled in the same manuscript notebooks, have given us his two best books, triumphs of genius and will in the execution of major poems and the design of intricate sequences such as 'A Man Young and Old', 'A Woman Young and Old', and the exceptionally worldly 'Words for Music Perhaps', a medley of male and female voices featuring Crazy Jane and her circle.[8]

This chapter considers the poetry Yeats wrote *after* those poems in light of stated aims and mitigating circumstances; and it examines the fundamentals of *late style* in terms of some competing arrangements of texts that have made ambiguity and contradiction incident to the interpretation of the poet's life.

In Yeats's prose, the onset of this stage of development in his poetic canon roughly coincides with the making of his so-called 'true' and 'fictional' prologues *A Packet for Ezra Pound* (1929) and *Stories of Michael Robartes and His Friends* (1931), which were eventually incorporated into the almost completely revised edition of *A Vision* in 1937.[9] At first, in the unpublished 'Discoveries of Michael Robartes', which Yeats composed in the form of a dialogue between two characters closely aligned with himself, his philosophy came to account for life and history, generally, as matters of serious and comic import. One's experience acknowledges the primary and antithetical oscillating forces of the 'antinomies' (or the 'extremities') between which a man's or a woman's life will run its course. The drama of one's experience, viewed in the

---

[7] Schuchard, 'Yeats and Olivia Revisited', 99.

[8] 'A Man Young and Old' was collected from two segmental units in *October Blast* (Cuala Press, 1927) entitled 'The Young Countryman' (I–IV) and 'The Old Countryman' (I–VI), retitled by its constituents, and reprinted in *The Tower* (Macmillan, 1928). 'A Woman Young and Old' derives from a named sequence in *The Winding Stair* (Fountain Press, 1929), then reprinted with similar lyrics from *Words for Music Perhaps and Other Poems* (Cuala Press, 1932), but differentiated from the latter sequence in Macmillan's *The Winding Stair and Other Poems* (1933). Finally, Yeats altered the arrangement of the male sequence so that it aligned, poem for poem, with the female one in *Collected Poems* (Macmillan, 1933). See Wayne K. Chapman, '"Metaphors for Poetry": Concerning the Poems of *A Vision* and Certain Plays for Dancers', in Neil Mann, Matthew Gibson, and Claire Nally, eds., *W. B. Yeats's A Vision: Explications and Contexts* (Clemson, SC: Clemson University Press, 2012), 239–44; see also Schuchard, 'Yeats and Olivia Revisited', 126–34, on the significance of Olivia Shakespear in these poems; and Joseph M. Hassett, *W. B. Yeats and the Muses* (Oxford: Oxford University Press, 2010), 157–66, on 'memories of love and lyrics for imaginary people'. For jumbled manuscripts in the Rapallo notebooks, see Wayne K. Chapman, 'Yeats's White Vellum Notebook, 1930–1933', *International Yeats Studies*, 2:2 (spring 2018), 41–60.

[9] The 'true account' of biography and history and the 'fictional account' in 'the guise of nonsense' are terms Elizabeth Müller coins in 'The Mask of Derision in Yeats's Prologue to *A Vision* (1937), *YA*, 19 (2013) 128–32; see W. B. Yeats, *W. B. Yeats's Robartes-Aherne Writings: Featuring the Making of His 'Stories of Michael Robartes and His Friends'*, ed. Wayne K. Chapman (London: Bloomsbury Academic, 2018), xiv–xlvii.

aggregate, was neither wholly tragic nor comic. Though possibly a little of both, this drama was only not to be a 'fool's Tragedy'.[10]

Based on fundamental principles, then, 'What is joy?' (a) It is the *feeling* or emotion of extreme pleasure or felicity arising from the body; but, to allow conventional ambiguity, also (b) an abstract state or manifestation from beyond the natural, as in 'the place of bliss, paradise, heaven' (OED). Consequently, by definition, *poetry* must be the *art* made from the poet's quarrelling with himself: 'We make out of the quarrel with others, rhetoric, but of the quarrel with ourselves, poetry.'[11] So when the work is *finished,* it becomes not simply a thing *made,* but something more significant than everyday life as 'we sing amid our uncertainty'. Poetry was the means by which Yeats, as *vates,* might live up to the significance of his 'First Principle' in 'A General Introduction for my Work':

> The poet writes always of his personal life[;] in his finest work out of its tragedy ... he never speaks directly as to someone at the breakfast table, [as] there is always a phantasmagoria .... He is never the bundle of accident and incoherence that sits down to breakfast; he has been reborn as an idea, something intended, complete.[12]

The poet, Yeats adds, might acknowledge his accidence but never his incoherence, for, with his complicit audience, he is an agent of artistic creation more important than himself or any one of them: 'He is part of his own phantasmagoria and we adore him because nature has grown intelligible, and by so doing a part of our creative power .... The world knows nothing because it has made nothing, [whereas] we know everything because we have made everything.'[13]

Chronologically, 'The First Principle' was also the first part of Yeats's 'General Introduction', written for the eventually abandoned 'Coole' and 'Dublin' Editions *de Luxe,* in dual productions by Macmillan and Charles Scribner's Sons. Yeats began writing this theme in spring 1937 and continued it (with two shorter introductions, for his essays and plays) into 1938. When he died several months later, this timely account of his objectives remained in an envelope, inscribed in his handwriting: 'Contents of Morrocco Book (large) January 4, 1938'. For a time, corrections followed on a few typescripts, even as he composed the final poems of his lifetime.[14]

Style involves the elements of craftsmanship that are influenced by a subject. The agency of the writer as *poietes* is implied. For such an artist, style is the product of the marriage of content and form, matter and manner, as dictated by the marketplace,

---

[10]   Yeats to Olivia Shakespear (3 January 1932), *CL InteLex* #5556; *L,*790

[11]   *Myth 2005,* 331.

[12]   *CW5,* 204.

[13]   *CW5,* 204–5. See Michael J. Sidnell, *Yeats's Poetry and Poetics* (London: Macmillan Press, 1996), 97–107.

[14]   Edward Callan, *Yeats on Yeats: The Last Introductions and the 'Dublin' Edition,* New Yeats Papers XX (Mountrath, Portlaoise: Dolmen Press, 1981), 15. This critical edition of Yeats's introductions is recommended for 'A General Introduction' and letters between the publishers and Yeats's agent from Nov. 1935 to Jan. 1951.

tradition, or the poet's predilections. An Irish subject matter, which Yeats addresses in the second part of his late essay 'A General Introduction for my Work', was fraught with paradox and frustration:

> I remind myself that though mine is the first English marriage I know of in the direct line, all my family names are English; that I owe my soul to Shakespeare, to Spenser and to Blake, perhaps to William Morris, and to the English language in which I think, speak, and write; that everything I love has come to me through English. My hatred tortures me with love, my love with hate ... Gaelic is my national language, but it is not my mother tongue.[15]

However, 'Style and Attitude', the third part of that essay, provides a key to understanding Yeats's later poetry, in particular when he recalls having led English poetry to a language that 'comes most naturally when we soliloquise', as 'I tried to make the language of poetry coincide with that of passionate, normal speech'. 'It was a long time before I had made a language to my liking', he says, but

> I began to make it when I discovered some twenty years ago [i.e. around 1917] that I must seek, not as Wordsworth thought, words in common use, but a powerful and passionate syntax, and a complete coincidence between period and stanza. Because I need a passionate syntax for passionate subject-matter I compel myself to accept those traditional metres that have developed with the language ... What moves me and my hearer is a vivid speech that has no laws except that it must not exorcise the ghostly voice ...[16]

In 'An Introduction for my Plays' also written in 1937, he adds:

> As I altered my syntax I altered my intellect ... I had begun to get rid of everything that is not, whether in lyric or dramatic poetry, in some sense character in action; a pause in the midst of action perhaps, but action always its end and theme.[17]

Perhaps it should be said that Jon Stallworthy and Thomas Parkinson were themselves poets and studied Yeats's poetry from the standpoint of its making, rather than from the methodology of traditional poetics or descriptive stylistics, as such studies were common in that generation and as impressive, even elegant, analytical exercises of the kind occasionally still appear in the scholarship of Helen Vendler and Brian Devine.[18] It was Parkinson, though, who has built the most on Yeats's account of what he strove

---

[15] *CW5*, 211–12.

[16] *CW5*, 212–14.

[17] *CW2*, 24.

[18] Examples are Helen Vendler, *Our Secret Discipline: Yeats and Lyric Form* (Cambridge, MA: Belknap Press of Harvard University, 2007), and Brian Devine, *Yeats, the Master of Sound* (Gerrards Cross: Colin Smythe, 2006).

to achieve syntactically. Unnecessarily edited by Parkinson to form an unpublished essay by Yeats, a few dated entries in a small white vellum notebook begun 7 April 1921 produced at least 'a long sequence of rumination'[19] along the lines that Yeats developed in 'A General Introduction for my Work'. Radically simplified below, the gist of his three diary entries of 7, 24, and 26 April 1921 presents the idea as a discovery in its eureka moment:

> I have been wondering why I like a lyric that sings, rather than talks, to go to an old rhythm ... Today for the first time after months of wondering I have hit it. If a poem talks, ... we have the passionate syntax, the impression of the man who speaks, the *actual* man[,] no abstract poet ...; but if it sings[,] we want the impression of a man either actually singing, or at least murmuring it over, and not as a show, a perform-ance, but at some moment of emotion .... We tolerate, or enjoy an artificial syntax and a rhythm *which* is neither speech, nor anything suggesting a song because our thought is artificial .... The revolt against impersonal eloquence ~~and impersonal form~~ climaxed at the end of [the] last century and that against impersonal form at the beginning of this.[20]

In light of this testimony, the style of 'talking' or 'singing' in verse by finding or invoking 'passionate syntax' belongs to a theory of writing articulated during Yeats's 'later' period and especially applied to the late poems of 1936-9.[21]

Recently, scholarship has accommodated itself to the term 'late style', coined by phil-osopher Theodor Adorno and popularized by literary critic Edward Said in his last book, *On Late Style: Music and Literature Against the Grain*.[22] The terminology is the product of an inductive procedure applied to last works of music and literature such as the compositions of Beethoven and Goethe, or, in Said's case, of Strauss, Mozart, Genet, Cavafy, Mann, and others, with Yeats cited once for coining the expression for life's be-ginning as 'the uncontrollable mystery on the bestial floor'.[23] Although Marjorie Howes examines a selection of Yeats's poems with respect to Said's notion that 'late style' is 'art produced under the sign of approaching death and defined not through "harmony" and "resolution" but through "intransigence, difficulty, and unresolved contradiction"',

[19] NLI, 13,576; Parkinson, *W. B. Yeats, the Later Poetry*, 186. Cf. pp. 184–6 with my transcription and treatment of entries (quoted here) in *Yeats's Poetry in the Making: 'Sing Whatever Is Well Made'* (London: Palgrave Macmillan, 2010), 9–13, 291–2. On Parkinson's chapter 'The Passionate Syntax' and his acquaintance with Yeats's manuscripts before they became the property of the National Library of Ireland, see Wayne K. Chapman, 'George Yeats, Thomas Parkinson, and the Legacy of the Archive', *New Thresholds in Yeats Studies: Yeats Annual*, 22 (forthcoming).

[20] NLI, 13,576, ff. 2–4.

[21] In 1934 Yeats wrote little poetry; the dozen 'Supernatural Songs' in *A Full Moon in March* (Nov. 1935) constituted most of his lyric output with Macmillan, coincident with his spiritualist translations and Indian essays. In 1935 he wrote almost no poetry, a lull before resurgence.

[22] Edward W. Said, *On Late Style: Music and Literature Against the Grain*, foreword Mariam Said, intro. Michael Wood (New York: Vintage Books, 2007). Edward Said died in 2003.

[23] 'The Magi', *CW1*, 126.

Said's enquiry 'into the relationship between bodily condition and aesthetic style' has been more faithfully replicated in Beckett studies.[24] In late Yeats, there is complicating ambiguity, if not actual ambivalence, in the conflict between the writer's 'bodily condition' and his aesthetic principles. In the idiom of 'late style', an artist's life (which is about to end) and his art (which aspires to the condition of finished work) are in a state of *tension*. 'Late style', according to Said, 'is what happens if art does not abdicate its rights in favour of reality'.[25] Unlike Shakespeare, Bach, and Matisse, who appear to exhibit 'a new spirit of reconciliation and serenity' in their late work, Beckett, for example, 'adopts an ironic attitude toward both aging and also toward the inevitable end with, and *in*, death'.[26] However, Yeats would seem to have it both ways in his late poems. There is no end, and yet there is an end. Committed as ever to achieving perfection in art, he spurns 'all that makes a wise old man' and embraces the contradiction of seeming, 'though I die old, / A foolish, passionate man'.[27] His irony registers differently, more or less, from poem to poem, but especially depending on how his latest texts have been presented in the posthumous editions.

The last collection of verse that Yeats lived to see printed at the Cuala Press was optimistically entitled *New Poems* (as in latest, not last). Finished in April and published in May 1938, it was reviewed favourably because of the perceived 'continuing vigour' of a master of plain language, clean diction, and 'ruminative', 'delightful' poetry more like 'excellent prose' than 'wilfully rhymed' verse. It exhibited, according to Winfield Townley Scott, the 'half-mad balladry of lusty living'.[28] In the key of passionate intensity, 'The Gyres' makes a shaky and strange beginning for talking in ottava rima verse, in the volume succeeded by the more stately elegy 'The Municipal Gallery Revisited'. The note of hysteria associated with an approaching apocalyptic turn to 'blood and mire', away from the values of 'workman, noble and saint', is carried to a self-reflexive, compound mask named, effacingly, 'Old Rocky Face', after a remembered phrase in Ben Jonson's 'My Picture Left in Scotland' as well as after a noted passage on the Delphic Oracle in

---

[24] Marjorie Howes, 'Yeats's Graves: Death and Encryption in *Last Poems*', in Marjorie Howes and Joseph Valente, eds., *Yeats and Afterwords: Christ, Culture, and Crisis* (Notre Dame: University of Notre Dame Press, 2014), 217. Howes recommends Jahan Ramazani, *Yeats and the Poetry of Death: Elegy, Self-Elegy, and the Sublime* (New Haven: Yale University Press, 1990), as the 'most sustained and accomplished exploration of Yeats's engagement with death' (Howes, 'Yeats's Graves', 231). Her definition of 'late style' is from Said, *On Late Style*, 7; Steven Matthews, 'Beckett's Late Style', in Steven Barfield, Philip Tew, and Matthew Feldman, eds., *Beckett and Death* (London: Continuum, 2009), 188–205.

[25] Said, *On Late Style*, 9.

[26] Matthews, 'Beckett's Late Style', 188. For Adorno, subjective power in late works of art makes 'the irascible gesture with which it takes leave of the works themselves' and 'cast[s] off the appearance of art. Of the works ... it leaves only fragments behind, and communicates itself ... through the blank spaces from which it has disengaged itself. Touched by death, the hand of the master sets free the masses of material that he used to form; its tears and fissures, witnesses to the finite powerlessness of the I confronted with Being, are its final work' (quoted in Said, *On Late Style*, 11).

[27] 'A Prayer for Old Age', *CW1*, 283.

[28] Winfield Townley Scott, 'Yeats at 73', *Poetry*, 53:2 (Nov. 1938), 84–8; repr. in Stallworthy, ed., *Yeats, Last Poems*, 28–31—the only review of *New Poems* published before Yeats died.

Yeats's library.[29] Tag questions raised repeatedly in 'The Gyres' (beginning 'What matter ...?') are echoed later in the poems 'What Then' and 'Are You Content?' (a dozen poems later and then, for symmetry, at the very end), in lyric assessments of the poet's life's work to that point.[30] 'Lapis Lazuli' and 'Imitated from the Japanese', the second and third poems in the collection, are exquisite models of craftsmanship after the artefacts that they contemplate (carven stone and poem). In 'Lapis Lazuli', as in 'The Gyres', the messengers take on the tragic scene in a long view of history and a short view of life. The call to 'Rejoice!'[31] on the one hand, and the surprising, ironic disclosure that the 'ancient, glittering eyes'[32] of the ascending 'Chinamen' are gay, on the other, leads to the speaker's sad admission amid springtime's celebration of his seventy years in 'Imitated from the Japanese', that 'never have I danced for joy'.[33]

Dancing, then, is a link that introduces the first of two poems in memory of a foolish, tragic affair with a young actress and poet, Margot Ruddock Collis. The songs 'Sweet Dancer' and 'A Crazed Girl' participate with more than a dozen lyrics that make up the 'half-mad balladry of lusty living' observed by Townley Scott.[34] Many of these works were barely sublimated acts of creation undertaken with Lady Dorothy Wellesley during their collaboration as contributing editors of *Broadsides: A Collection of New Irish and English Songs* (Cuala Press, 1937). Wellesley became an intimate friend from June 1935 to January 1939, when she stood vigil with her partner, Hilda Matheson, at Yeats's deathbed in the south of France. She was probably chief among the 'rich women' of whom Auden disapproved in lines 32–4 of his famous elegy 'In Memory of W. B. Yeats': 'You were silly like us: your gift survived it all; / The parish of rich women, physical decay, / Yourself'.[35] Moreover, Yeats seems to have delighted in his own naughtiness, to judge by one of his contributions to *Broadsides* that he expanded into a whole sequence in *New Poems*. Inspired by Wellesley's poem 'The Lady, The Squire, and the Serving-maid' and its illicit

[29] *CW1*, 293; among Yeats's 'Lovers of horses and women', old Rocky Face is reminiscent of Jonson's self-effacing reference to his pox-marked 'rockie face' in two sources. See Wayne K. Chapman, *Yeats and English Renaissance Literature* (London: Macmillan Press, 1991), 228 n. 44. George Yeats noted in a copy of *Last Poems and Plays* (1940) that 'Cleft in the Rock' glossed a passage on p. 8 of Rev. Thomas Dempsey's *The Delphic Oracle: Its Early History, Influence and Fall* (Oxford: Blackwell, 1918); see Chapman, *Yeats's Poetry in the Making*, 225, 243.

[30] *CW1*, 302 and 321.

[31] *CW1*, 293.

[32] *CW1*, 295.

[33] *CW1*, 296.

[34] The poems bear nearly identical inscriptions by George Yeats in her copy of *Last Poems*: 'Margot Collis at Barcelona, May 1936' (Chapman, *Yeats's Poetry in the Making*, 243). See W. B. Yeats and Margot Ruddock, *Ah, Sweet Dancer: A Correspondence*, ed. Roger McHugh (London: Macmillan, 1970), 90–102, 116–22.

[35] The longer version of Auden's poem is reprinted in Stallworthy, ed., *Yeats, Last Poems*, 25–7, as well as Auden's review of *Last Poems and Plays*, 'Yeats: Master of Diction', 47–9. Kathleen Raine's introduction to *Letters on Poetry from W. B. Yeats to Dorothy Wellesley* (1964) and selected correspondence are also reprinted by Stallworthy, 50–72. Yeats's awareness of Wellesley's sexual preference is noted in a redacted part of the *Letters* on Roger Casement and the homosexuality of Charles Ricketts and T. E. Lawrence (Yeats to Dorothy Wellesley, 2 December [1936], *CL InteLex* #6737).

triangle of a courtly lady, her chambermaid, and their male lover, Yeats's 'The Three Bushes' is attributed in subtitle to a fictitious source: 'the "Historia mei Temporis" of the Abbé Michel de Bourdeille' (or bordello). The imaginary fable of rose trees grown to one root became a sequence of songs in 1938, consisting of seven poems: 'The Three Bushes', 'The Lady's First Song', 'The Lady's Second Song', 'The Lady's Third Song', 'The Lover's Song', 'The Chambermaid's First Song', and 'The Chambermaid's Second Song'. Yeats's other contributions to *Broadsides* (1937) that were distributed over *New Poems* are 'The Curse of Cromwell', 'Come Gather Round Me, Parnellites', 'The Pilgrim', and 'Colonel Martin'. In an effort to shock Wellesley during their poetic competition, a particularly ribald story was added in proof copy to the fictional front matter of *A Vision* (1937).[36] But their momentary rivalry led to hurt feelings when Yeats intervened to rewrite her poem for *Broadsides*. Her 'Lass, Is Your Heart Dead' appeared in March, 'The Judas Tree' in July, and Yeats's expropriated version of 'The Lady, The Squire, and the Serving-maid' in September; thereafter her signed version was printed in full on an 'ERRATA' sheet, beneath the caption, 'The words and music of "The Lady, the Squire and the Serving Maid" were incorrectly printed in the September number. The correct versions are as follows …'. On 20 November 1937, he had approved her 'amendations' [*sic*] and confided to her, 'I thought my problem was to face death with ga[i]ety [but] now I have learnt that it is to face life'.[37]

Penance for overstepping his place as co-editor took three additional forms: (1) an explanation, if not quite an apology, for taking an overzealous interest in her poetry; (2) a poem commendatory, entitled 'To a Friend' (later 'To Dorothy Wellesley'), written for *New Poems*; and (3) the selection and praise of her poetry beyond compare in the contemporary *Oxford Book of Modern Verse* (1936), edited by Yeats. Grudgingly conceding his exceptional engagement with her work—to much the same degree as had been his practice with Margot Collis, perhaps—he appealed to Wellesley's spirit of erotic adventure: 'Ah my dear how it added to my excitement when I re-made that poem of yours to know it was your poem. I re-made you and myself into a single being. We triumphed over each other and I thought of [Shakespeare's] *The Turtle and the Phoenix*.'[38] Similarly, Deborah Ferrelli thinks that '"To Dorothy Wellesley" allowed Wellesley to be internalized by Yeats at the same time as she was internalized in the ballads'.[39] He wore his impotence with charm and false bravura in 'The Wild Old Wicked Man', as philandering had become one of his metaphors for writing and poetry had become a substitute for sex. His apologia was a cavalier lyric called 'The Spur':

> You think it horrible that lust and rage
> Should dance attendance upon my old age;

---

[36] See Chapman, *W. B. Yeats's Robartes-Aherne Writings*, 340–59.

[37] Yeats To Dorothy Wellesley (20 November [1937]), *CL InteLex* #7122.

[38] Yeats to Dorothy Wellesley (21 July [1936]), *CL InteLex* #6619; quoted in Stallworthy, ed., *Yeats, Last Poems*, 68. He refers to *The Phoenix and the Turtle*, Wellesley's favourite poem.

[39] Deborah Ferrelli, 'W. B. Yeats and Dorothy Wellesley', *YA*, 17 (2007), 258.

> They were not such a plague when I was young;
> What else have I to spur me into song?[40]

He explored the difference between being dead and dead drunk in 'A Drunken Man's Praise of Sobriety'. Fluency and productivity had spiked, as he told another intimate friend, Ethel Mannin, while invalided to a wheelchair: 'It is a curious experience to have an infirm body & an intellect more alive than it has ever been. One poem leads to another as if I were smoking cigarettes & lit them from each other! Nothing now interrupts the chain.'[41] Echoing 'The Gyres' in 'What Then?', the premature declaration that he had finished a life's work, 'According to my boyish plan; || ... Something to perfection brought', is questioned by Plato's ghost, his master: *'But louder sang that ghost "What then?"'*[42]

To be sure, there is an undercurrent of discontent running through these poems as Yeats seems on the verge of complete, artistic fulfilment. In 'A Model for the Laureate', the ballad ends with a hollow refrain as the Muse is mute to fools:

> That waxen seal, that signature,
> For things like these what decent man
> Would keep his lover waiting?
> Keep his lover waiting?[43]

In 'The Municipal Gallery Revisited', Parkinson detects 'a sense of quotation' akin to Eliot's 'pedantry' and criticizes Yeats for merely 'certify[ing] meanings already habitual' and 'playing upon agreements already established with the audience'.[44] Then, in 'Are You Content', *New Poems* concludes by calling upon the Old Fathers from the Prologue of *Responsibilities*, hoping that, 'Infirm and aged I might stay / In some good company, / I who have always hated work'; as before, he acknowledges that he is neither content nor entirely worthy of their company.[45]

The turmoil inherent in completing his life's work produced more ambiguity for the late style of Yeats due to the intervention of his wife and editors at Macmillan to rearrange the order of his poems after he died on 28 January 1939. In effect, an alternate narrative had been created for readers, although Yeats had left instructions on the order of the poems to be published in *Last Poems and Two Plays* (Cuala Press, 1939), as there were, by then, nineteen uncollected poems to precede the new plays, *The Death of Cuchulain* and *Purgatory*. For the impression of late style, order matters. For a long time, the additional poems were only published in authorized order in the Cuala Press edition

---

[40] *CW1*, 312.
[41] Yeats to Ethel Mannin, 1 August [1936], *CL InteLex* #6627.
[42] *CW1*, 302.
[43] *CW1*, 317.
[44] Parkinson, *W. B. Yeats, the Later Poetry*, 170–1; see Chapman, *Yeats's Poetry in the Making*, 205.
[45] *CW1*, 322.

(indicated by number in the list below) but were scrambled in 1940 when Macmillan joined them with the thirty-five lyrics of *New Poems* (1938).

Titles according to their appearance in *Last Poems and Plays* (Macmillan, 1940) and interjections from *On the Boiler* (Cuala Press, 1939):

2.   Three Songs to the One Burden
6.   In Tara's Halls
7.   The Statues
8.   News for the Delphic Oracle
5.   Three Marching Songs
9.   Long-legged Fly
10. Bronze Head
11. A Stick of Incense
13. John Kinsella's Lament for Mrs. Mary Moore
12. Hound Voice
14. High Talk
15. The Apparitions
16. A Nativity
     [Why Should Not Old Men Be Mad—from *On the Boiler*]
     [The Statesman's Holiday—from *On the Boiler*]
     [Crazy Jane on the Mountain—from *On the Boiler*]
18. The Circus Animals' Desertion
19. Politics
17. The Man and the Echo
4.   Cuchulain Comforted
3.   The Black Tower
1.   Under Ben Bulben

Eventually, Curtis Bradford transcribed the list of contents Yeats authorized for *Last Poems*, noting that Macmillan's inclusion of 'nonchalant' songs from *New Poems* 'somewhat obscured the grimness of Yeats's Last phase' because, 'framed as it is by "Under Ben Bulben" and *Purgatory*, [that phase is] a grim and desperately earnest book' wherein 'moments of relaxation', as in 'High Talk', are fleeting and 'usually highly ironic'.[46] The three interjected poems from *On the Boiler* might be taken to be 'nonchalant' lyrics in keeping with Yeats's exaggerated projection of himself in the guise of 'the great McCoy' recalled from childhood (*CW5*, 220), a satirical persona like Daniel O'Leary in *Stories of Michael Robartes and His Friends* and the Old Man who stage-manages *The Death of Cuchulain*. Hence the three poems introduce a prolonged 'moment of relaxation' prior

---

[46] Curtis Bradford, *Yeats's 'Last Poems' Again*, No. VIII of *Dolmen Press Yeats Centenary Papers*, ed. Liam Miller (Dublin: Dolmen Press, 1966): 259–60; the essay, revised, is reprinted in Stallworthy, *Yeats, Last Poems*, 75–97. Bradford's assumptions are challenged by Phillip L. Marcus, 'Yeats's "Last Poems": a Reconsideration', *YA*, 5 (1987), 3–14; Yeats's list of contents is reproduced there as Plate 1.

to the transposed finale of poems 1, 3, and 4 from the Cuala edition. Since 1983, collected editions of Yeats's poetry have moved the *On the Boiler* lyrics to the end matter of an 'Additional Poems' or to a section of 'Poems from *On the Boiler*' placed between *New Poems* and a *Last Poems* of 1938–9—otherwise, all arranged in Cuala order.[47]

A commercial and aesthetic recommendation at Macmillan was accepted by Mrs Yeats; and, as a result, the 'Last Poems' familiar to two generations began with 'The Gyres' and finished dramatically with 'Under Ben Bulben' and the three-line epitaph: 'Cast a cold eye / On life, on death. / Horseman, pass by!'[48] The memorial effect would have been diminished had the poem occurred, instead, as the thirty-sixth of fifty-four or fifty-seven lyrics (with or without the songs from *On the Boiler*). Furthermore, to transition from 'The Circus Animals' Desertion' and 'Politics', in the 1939 Cuala arrangement, to conclude with 'Under Ben Bulben', two additional poems were also moved to create atmosphere: 'Cuchulain Comforted' and 'The Black Tower', poems 4 and 3 in the limited edition. It was a tactical manoeuvre in anticipation of the play below and as Yeats's actual last poem, 'The Black Tower', was completed several days before he died. Narrative perspective was sacrificed in the manoeuvre, according to Bradford, who preferred to read in the Cuala order an authorial intention that the speaker should be interpreted to be Yeats as 'discontented artist' who is already dead and 'speaking to us from the tomb'.[49] In any case, this thesis seems of little consequence when one considers that the poet who wrote the poems was very much alive when he made them. Of greater merit on the question of late style is whether dislocation damaged the musical aspects of theme and variation.

In that respect, the body of sixteen lyrics from 'Three Songs to the One Burden' through 'A Nativity' proceed as if seamlessly from *New Poems* (picking up from 'Are You Content'), with minor modulations due to very local transpositions. The gulf between the former and 'In Tara's Halls' is filled by a common subject, namely the decay of Irish traditions viewed, inversely, by a roaring tinker, a reclusive Middleton cousin, an Abbey player on the exploits of 1916's heroes, and an abdicating king in the ancient house of Tara. 'The Statues' and 'News for the Delphic Oracle' juxtapose Greek laws of proportion in sculpture (art) and mythological treatments of the mystery of generation (life), with links backwards and forwards to other poems—for example, to reflections on Maud Gonne in 'Among School Children' and 'A Bronze Head', on the one hand, and aspects of 'The Delphic Oracle on Plotinus', 'The Gyres', and (ironically) 'A Nativity', on the other.

---

[47] See, respectively, W. B. Yeats, *The Poems*, ed. Richard J. Finneran (London: Macmillan, 1983); and *Yeats's Poems*, ed. A. Norman Jeffares, with appendix by Warwick Gould (London: Papermac, 1989).

[48] *CW1*, 328. T. R. Henn notes that in the phrase 'cold eye' 'coldness is a favourite term for [Yeats's] own ideal of perfection in art', to which he refers in 'Vacillation' and elsewhere. Henn also says that, to give public notice in the poem, Yeats 'decided to be buried at Drumcliffe when he noted the crowd of "A.E." 's enemies at "A.E." 's funeral' in Dublin. T. R. Henn, 'Horseman, Pass By!' in Stallworthy, ed., Yeats, *Last Poems*, 116.

[49] Bradford, 'Last Poems' Again, 261; also, in Stallworthy (ed.), *Yeats, Last Poems*, 77. Moreover, Marcus, 'Yeats's "Last Poems" ' (12), asserts that Yeats *never did* prepare a "Last Poems" section' or '*a paradigm for a collected edition*' (emphasis his).

With a displacement of three places from (2), the disorderly 'Three Marching Songs' (5) precedes the irregular ballad 'Long-legged Fly' (9)—with Helen/Maud Gonne (dancing pivot) between primary Caesar (man of action) and antithetical Michael Angelo (contemplative artist)—with the poem 'A Bronze Head' (10) arriving in due course. After that, the mocking, gay gravity of the cluster 'A Stick of Incense', 'Hound Voice', and 'The Apparitions' is modified by a single transposition (11, 13, 12, 14, 15) to alternate with two poems of mocking, grave gaiety, 'John Kinsella's Lament for Mrs. Mary Moore' and 'High Talk', the latter introducing the comic creatures of the critical inquisition that Yeats, again mockingly, conducts in the great self-elegy 'The Circus Animals' Desertion'.

The impression made by poems 17, 18, and 19 in Cuala order (that is, 'The Man and the Echo', 'The Circus Animals' Desertion', and 'Politics') is that of regret rather than remorse. An old man's joy, grown deep to fill an empty heart, gives strength needed to the 'mystery and fright' of 'the increasing Night' in 'The Apparitions'.[50] In 'The Man and the Echo', the worst apparition is confronted as if it were an oracular voice issuing from 'a cleft that's christened Alt' on the slope of Knocknarea near Sligo. Yet, as an echo, it answers the worst fears of the man, who bears Yeats's history, lying awake at night, pondering questions of conscience 'until I / Sleepless would lie down and die'—to which the Echo, naturally, answers, 'Lie down and die'. True to this Jacobean device, Man reasons that his pursuit of answers to such questions is to prepare for 'the judgment on his soul' when, 'all work done', he 'sinks at last into the night', followed directly by Echo's grim reply: 'Into the night'. And so the poem ends with the cry of a 'stricken rabbit', without answer to the question 'Shall we in that great night rejoice?'. Distraction is only momentary, however, for the poet's contemplation of a 'work so great' that it may cleanse 'man's dirty slate' carries over to 'The Circus Animals' Desertion' and a selective review of Yeats's collected work as both a feigned and real exercise to address writer's block.[51] That wonderful poem, which, as James Pethica says, 'about creative incapacity and the loss of poetic inspiration — typifies the kinds of imaginative swerve and irresolutions' that Yeats experienced in completing his last volume of poetry. From 'The Circus Animals' Desertion', as Pethica argues based on manuscript evidence, 'resolute seizure of poetic possibility out of apparent bankruptcy' became 'the keynote' of *Last Poems and Two Plays* (1939) in strategic position as the 'penultimate poem rather than its "start" as initially planned in [November] 1937'.[52]

Yeats averted disaster to produce a masterpiece only because he had the sense to leave the poem for the better part of a year until the theme he sought emerged or, rather, a resolution of old themes arose, by suggestion, from the *disjecta membra* of jottings preserved on his desk blotter. Finally, to reject gaiety as an unsatisfactory conclusion after review of themes and shortcomings in part II of the poem, a solution came in September 1938, when he wrote an entirely new stanza for part III from the blotter's 'doodlings, jottings,

[50] *CW1*, 344.

[51] *CW1*, 345–6.

[52] W. B. Yeats, *'Last Poems': Manuscript Materials*, ed. James Pethica (Ithaca and New York: Cornell University Press, 1997), xxx, xxxiii; see also Chapman, *Yeats's Poetry in the Making* 27.

and other fragments of verse, as if literalizing the emergence of poetry ... out of the fragments of experience just as valuable raw materials are recycled out of the uncompromising welter of rubbish in the "rag and bone" trade'.[53] Masterful images from *anima mundi* grow 'in pure mind', but the Platonic ladder is gone, leaving no option but to 'lie down where all the ladders start / In the foul rag and bone shop of the heart', a sobering image of a man about to commit himself to the grave.[54]

Still, *life* and *art* were not finished sparring because the poem 'Politics' compromises the gesture of *ars moriendi* by pulling back toward passionate life. Pethica notes several degrees of ambiguity that are introduced by the final lyric, essentially a love poem, which 'leaves it unclear whether [1] Yeats is simply articulating without irony his wish for immersion in desire and emotion, [2] is instead laughing at himself ... [by] undercutting the achievement of self-knowledge ... or [3], as seems most likely, is deliberately leaving these possibilities in provocative tension'.[55] Another distinction, on the side of art, is in the difference between talking in ottava rima and singing in doubt. In any case, closure for the poetry, as for our discussion of Yeats's late style in a time of world catastrophe, puts a vernacular spin on death for a distracted man whose memory of past joy must prepare him for a possibly long darkness:

> How can I, that girl standing there,
> My attention fix
> On Roman or on Russian
> Or on Spanish politics?
> Yet here's a travelled man that knows
> What he talks about,
> And there's a politician
> That has both read and thought,
> And maybe what they say is true
> Of war and war's alarms,
> But O that I were young again
> And held her in my arms.[56]

---

[53] Pethica, '*Last Poems*', xxxiii
[54] *CW1*, 348.
[55] Pethica, '*Last Poems*', xxxv–xxxvi
[56] *CW1*, 348.

CHAPTER 41

EDITING YEATS

WARWICK GOULD

YEATS died in 1939 with two limited collected editions in train, both soon to be shelved for the duration of the Second World War, the 'Edition de Luxe', later the 'Coole Edition', with Macmillan, London, and the so-called 'Dublin Edition' with Scribner, New York. Of these, only the materials for the 'Coole Edition' were advanced enough to be issued, albeit in much modified form, in the Macmillan two-volume signed and limited *The Poems* (1949), the so-called 'definitive edition', and in Macmillan's uniform edition of the major, but by no means complete, prose works (1955–62). These Macmillan books drew their authority from their textual base, standing type set from before the war including, in many cases, Yeats's own instructions and corrections, as well as from the associated editorial guidance of Yeats's two most trusted delegates, his wife George Yeats and Thomas Mark, his publisher's reader at Macmillan. Subsequent examination of the letters and proofs in the Macmillan Archive at the British Library confirmed the nature of these claims while exposing to debate certain decisions taken after Yeats's death as to the canon, arrangement, and order of the contents.

This chapter focuses upon the achievements of major editorial projects undertaken during the past sixty-five years. For editorial endeavours in respect of Yeats's published works—specifically the Macmillan/Scribner *Collected Works* (1984–)—as set into the context of contemporary editorial theory, the reader is referred to 'Conflicted Legacies: Yeats's Intentions And Editorial Theory'.[1] The present chapter begins with a summary of that essay's findings and takes as its overall focus the editorial pressures upon, and achievements of, the other major editorial projects undertaken during the past eighty years.

---

[1] See 'Conflicted Legacies: Yeats's Intentions and Editorial Theory', in *Yeats's Legacies: YA 21: A Special Issue*, ed. Warwick Gould (Cambridge: Open Book Publishers, 2018), 479–541. See https://doi.org/10.11647/OBP.0135.13. Full details of all works cited will be found in the bibliography below.

The approaching end of Yeats's European copyrights[2] occasioned a good deal of thought in the late 1970s towards new scholarly editions which might extend those copyrights, particularly given the strenuous activity in other areas of Yeats research, including the two-volume *W. B. Yeats: A Life, I: The Apprentice Mage* and *II: The Arch-Poet*, by R. F. Foster (Oxford and New York: Oxford University Press, 1997 and 2003). The principal precipitate of this editorial ferment is the Macmillan/Scribner *Collected Works* (1984–), an unfinished project compromised by UK/US publishers' rivalries. Its late co-General Editor, Richard J. Finneran, was also the editor of volume one, which first appeared as *The Poems: A New Edition* (1983). An extended *TLS* controversy in 1984 disputed his editorial decisions as to the canon, arrangement, order, text, as well as the policies and quality of the annotation. That volume, however, very much set the standard for subsequent volumes, many of which have a very uneven relation to author/publisher/agent archives. The controversy resulted in entrenched views as seen in Finneran's *Editing Yeats's Poems: A Reconsideration* (1990), which attracted further confutation. Another was the emergence of rival scholarly editions such as A. Norman Jeffares's *Yeats's Poems* (1989, 3rd rev. edition 1996—conceived very much with his *A New Commentary on the Poems of W. B. Yeats* (1984) in mind—and *The Poems,* edited by Daniel Albright (1990). Full bibliographies of these controversies will be found in the works cited below, but it is worth pointing out that, at bottom, it was Finneran's dislike and distrust of biography and bio-bibliography (and so his desire to supervene over the evidence of the archives left by George Yeats and Thomas Mark of Macmillan) which was at issue. Daniel Albright found 'Finneran's revulsion against biography' to be an editorial 'policy':

> The consequence of this policy is that the protagonist of 'An Irish Airman foresees his Death' is not identified as Major Robert Gregory; the statue discussed in 'A Bronze Head' is not identified as an image of Maud Gonne; and so forth. Professor Finneran is right to note that Yeats had some purpose in omitting such names from the text of his poems, but if an annotator tells us anything, he should tell us those names. If one assumes that ignorance is helpful to interpretation, then any annotation whatsoever is harmful to the text . . .
>   We all know that annotation requires such rigor of selection that one might say that to annotate is to omit. But I cannot approve of the tone that Professor Finneran takes when he says, at the beginning of his notes, that he is not going to mention that 'Upon a Dying Lady' was based on the death of Mabel Beardsley (p. 613). It is as if he were pleased to withhold a fact that most readers would consider relevant.[3]

In the light of its editorial strictures against reliance on the Macmillan Archive and against biographically based annotation, the editors of *Mythologies* withdrew their

[2] See Warwick Gould, 'Predators and Editors: Yeats in the pre- and post-Copyright Era', in Patrick Parrinder and Warren Chernaik (eds.), *Textual Monopolies* (London: Office for Humanities Communication/Centre for English Studies, 1997), 69–82.
[3] *The New York Review of Books*, 32. 12, 18 July 1985, in reply to 'Naming the Dying Lady', a letter by Karl Beckson protesting against Daniel Albright's review, 'The Magician', *NYRB* 31 January 1985.

volume from the *Collected Works* series and published it separately in 2005.[4] This is a fully annotated, final text edition, based on proofs corrected and passed by Yeats, and of which he had written that he did not need to see them again, remarking that Macmillan's reader, Thomas Mark, could finish them off better than he could.[5] A dual approach for this final text edition was required: while *The Celtic Twilight* lacked and still lacks a variorum edition, the augmented and revised edition of *The Secret Rose, Stories by W. B. Yeats: A Variorum Edition* had been available since 1992.[6] The *Mythologies* textual appendices provide condensed textual histories in narrative form and, in the case of the stories of *The Celtic Twilight*, selected passages of important, if superseded, text from its numerous lifetime editions. The appendices detailing the textual histories of the *Secret Rose* and *Red Hanrahan* stories, however, cross-refer to *The Secret Rose, Stories by W. B. Yeats: A Variorum Edition*.

Disentangled both from the challenges in editorial theory of the late twentieth century and from issues raised by electronic alternatives to codex-based editing, certain features of Yeats's approach to writing and publishing emerged from these controversies to set the editorial horizon for his published works, whether in print or digital media:

- Yeats believed in authorial intention.
- He was an inveterate post-publication reviser: such revision was self-editing.
- As a self-shaping author who tailored and marketed his work with intended audiences in mind, he was a professional.

[4] To date, no *Mythologies* volume has appeared in the *Collected Edition*.

[5] On 5 July 1932, W. B. Yeats wrote to his editor, Harold Macmillan, 'The volume called "Mythologies" I need not see again. Your reader can complete the revision better than I could' (B.L. Add. MS 55003 f. 129). With these words, Yeats delegated to his trusted publisher's reader at Macmillan, Thomas Mark, the completion of the work remaining to be done on *Mythologies AND The Irish Dramatic Movement*, a single volume, set in 1931. The contents of *Mythologies AND The Irish Dramatic Movement* were separated after Yeats's death by Thomas Mark with the approval of George Yeats, the poet's widow and executrix, and their decision was accepted at the outset by the General Editors of the *Collected Works*. William H. O'Donnell included *Per Amica Silentia Lunae* in *Later Essays* (1994), while O'Donnell and Douglas N. Archibald chose the 1955 published text of *Autobiographies* as copy-text for their 1999 edition of that work in the same series. For their edition of *The Irish Dramatic Movement* in the *Collected Works* series (2003), the late Mary FitzGerald and Richard Finneran chose, however, to set aside Yeats's delegation of the completion of his work, despite these precedent volumes. Further, as co-General Editor of the series, Finneran took the view that the editorial guidelines for the series could no longer accommodate the implications of Yeats's acts of delegation. The *Collected Works* could not tolerate what he saw as an inconsistency between the approaches adopted for *Mythologies* and for *The Irish Dramatic Movement*. Its editors therefore withdrew *Mythologies* from the series and were grateful to accept the invitation of the Yeats Estate and Yeats's publishers to publish it separately. Publication outside the *Collected Works* offered, too, a climate of annotation hospitable to sustained consideration of Irish folkloric material, oral sources, social history, and the occult traditions of thought in which Yeats worked: see also *Myth 2005*, xxii.

[6] Edited by Warwick Gould, Phillip L. Marcus, and Michael J. Sidnell (Cornell, 1981; 2nd edition revised and enlarged, Macmillan, 1992). This volume superseded some early attempts to collate, on uncertain principles, Yeats's occult romance *The Tables of the Law* and his *Stories of Red Hanrahan*, in *Yeats Studies: an international journal: 1, Yeats and the 1890s*, ed. Robert O'Driscoll and Lorna Reynolds (Shannon: Irish University Press, 1971), 87–118, 119–74.

- He therefore sought to collaborate with the publishing process, and, as his fame grew, worked closely with trusted publishers' readers.
- He was happy to delegate certain editorial decisions, always retaining a right of veto.

II

Scholarly editing of Yeats's published works began with Peter Allt and Russell K. Alspach's *The Variorum Edition of the Poems of W. B. Yeats* (New York: The Macmillan Company, 1957), followed by *The Variorum Edition of the Plays of W. B. Yeats*, edited by Russell K. Alspach, assisted by Catherine C. Alspach (London and New York: Macmillan, 1966). These sustained and irreplaceable masterpieces of collation allow the reconstruction of all states of Yeats's published poems and plays,[7] and inspired the two further variora, *John Sherman & Dhoya* (1969) and *The Secret Rose, Stories by W. B. Yeats: A Variorum Edition* (1981, revised and enlarged, 1992).[8]

Cornell University Press had pioneered computer-generated concordances with its Matthew Arnold concordance (1959). Stephen Maxfield Parrish, assisted by the programmer James A. Painter, then based their *A Concordance to the Poems of W. B. Yeats* (1963) on the Allt and Alspach *Variorum Edition*. The now extraordinary tale of its handmade assemblage is told in the *Concordance's* introduction (v–xxxvii). Eric Domville's two volume *A Concordance to the Plays* followed from the same press in 1972. Remarkably, here were the essential forerunners of digital editing being put to the purposes of producing print editions, with little further awareness of the value of the digital by-products of their production processes. William H. O'Donnell assembled a computer-generated *Literatim Transcription of the MSS of William Butler Yeats's 'The Speckled Bird'* (1976), while compiling reading texts of the novel for limited and trade publication, a rare conjunction of punch-card computer editions and the end of hand-printing at Anne Yeats's revived Cuala Press (1970–8).[9]

---

[7] Recent criticism of the alleged difficulty of using these variora with their on-page, below-the-line collations largely derives from pre-post-digital impatience with print-based codical editing. See, e.g., George Bornstein's protest that the *Variorum's* format is 'confusing ... almost no one other than scholarly editors themselves can construe such apparatus' in Bornstein's *Material Modernism: The Politics of the Page* (Cambridge: Cambridge University Press, 2001), 53, 44, a view with which my own students do not concur.

[8] I pass over Donald R. Pearce's edition of *The Senate Speeches of W. B. Yeats* (Bloomington: Indiana University Press, 1960; London: Faber & Faber, 1961).

[9] *Literatim Transcription of the Manuscripts of William Butler Yeats's* The Speckled Bird (Delmar, NY: Scholars' Facsimiles and Reprints, 1976); *The Speckled Bird* (Dublin: Cuala Press, 1974), *The Speckled Bird: with variant versions* (Toronto: McClelland & Stewart, 1977). O'Donnell's efforts to edit the novel culminated with *The Speckled Bird by William Butler Yeats: An Auto-biographical Novel with Variant Versions: New Edition, incorporating recently discovered manuscripts*, edited and annotated by William H. O'Donnell (Basingstoke: Palgrave Macmillan, 2003).

Before Cornell University Press turned its attention to facsimile publication of Yeats's manuscripts with facing page typographical transcriptions, there had been two enterprising experiments elsewhere.[10] *Druid Craft: the Writing of* The Shadowy Waters, *Manuscripts of W. B. Yeats: transcribed, edited & with a commentary* by Michael J. Sidnell, George P. Mayhew, and David R. Clark had come from the University of Massachusetts Press in Amherst (1971) as the first volume in a projected 'Manuscripts of W. B. Yeats' Series, with Clark as the General Editor. He moved the series to Northern Illinois University Press in DeKalb, no doubt under the financial pressures faced by university presses producing to high standards complex texts for limited audiences. Again, only one volume was produced, in 1977, *The Writing of* 'The Player Queen': *Manuscripts of W. B. Yeats transcribed, edited & with a commentary* by Curtis Baker Bradford (d.1969).

As the words 'writing' and 'commentary' in these titles and in that of a third, breakaway volume, David R. Clark and James B McGuire's *The Writing of* 'Sophocles King Oedipus' (1989), suggest, their conception of the editorial act and its responsibilities is rather more expansive and rewarding to readers in respect of editorial commentary and biographical detail than that of the Cornell volumes, the first of which was Phillip L. Marcus's edition of 'The Death of Cuchulain': *Manuscript Materials, Including the Author's Final Text* (1982).[11] The ambition to establish 'the Author's Final Text' was compromised. Yeats's full participation in commercial publishing processes, including his editorial delegation of some textual decisions to George Yeats and his publisher's reader, Thomas Mark, was not fully understood, and the establishment of final texts was dropped after 1986 in silent concession that editing involves input from others as works pass through presses.[12] Even after their own concordances and four variora had been published, two of them devoted to prose works, Cornell's 'Yeats Editorial Board' still had no full appreciation of Yeats's settled habit of post-publication revision nor the multivolume contexts—e.g. the *Collected Works* of the 1920s—in which major revisions took place. The Board's firmly conservative but otherwise vague editorial horizons were set out in the first volume, Marcus's edition of 'The Death of Cuchulain': *Manuscript Materials*:

> The volumes in this series will present the manuscripts of W. B. Yeats's poems (all extant versions), plays (complete insofar as possible), and other materials (including selected occult writings) from the rich archives of Senator Michael B. Yeats, the National Library of Ireland, and elsewhere. The primary goal of the editors is to

---

[10] Richard J. Finneran states that the plans for the Cornell series date back to a meeting of scholars at Senator Michael Yeats's house in the spring of 1977: see The Tower *(1928): Manuscript Materials by W. B. Yeats*, ed. Richard Finneran with Jared Curtis and Ann Saddlemyer (Ithaca and London: Cornell University Press, 2007), xii.

[11] That the 'Making' model continues to yield excellent results is displayed in the recent *W. B. Yeats's Robartes–Aherne Writings: Featuring the Making of his "Stories of Michael Robartes and His Friends"* ed. Wayne K. Chapman (London: Bloomsbury Academic, 2018).

[12] Sandra Siegel's edition of Purgatory: *Manuscript Materials, Including the Author's Final Text* (1986)was the second volume issued, and the last to make this claim.

achieve the greatest possible fidelity in transcription. Photographic facsimiles will be used extensively to supplement the texts.

The series will include some important unpublished works of high literary quality, and individually and as a whole the volumes will help to illuminate Yeats's creative process. They will be essential reference works for scholars who wish to establish definitive texts of the published works. They will contain many passages of biographical interest as well as passages that will be helpful in interpreting other works by Yeats. The emphasis throughout will, however, be on the documents themselves, and critical analysis will be limited to discussion of their significance in relation to the published texts; the editors assume that publication of the documents will stimulate critical studies as a matter of course.[13]

Of the introductory commentaries in the volumes of poetic MSS, James Pethica's for 'Last Poems': *Manuscript Materials*, is more extensively and appropriately based in biographical material. The Cornell Yeats Series (1982–2014) offers various lessons.[14] Perceptions of Yeats's hand vary significantly from editor to editor, and reflect the extent to which editors either checked their readings against original manuscripts or relied upon the 'dude ranch' default set of printouts in the State University of New York at Stony Brook from poorly timed and exposed microfilms and fiches made at Michael Yeats's house. Even when editors relied on much better-quality microfilm from, for example, Harvard or the National Library of Ireland, they were working from a monochrome surrogate, and in many cases comparison of their transcription with inferior reproductions on facing pages is far from reassuring. Very few of the Cornell volumes transcribe Yeats's prose introductions and notes in their appendices, again compromising his view of what it was to edit a volume of his own poems, or to re-edit it as a volume unit in a collected volume.

The Cornell Series' Editors had initially envisaged a daunting set of multiple sub-series of volumes—Poems, Plays, Prose, and Family Papers—each offering volume-by-volume facsimile reproduction of Yeats's manuscripts with facing page typographical transcription. A factor in its deferral of—and, finally, its failure to commission—volumes of Yeats's prose manuscripts is that so many extant prose manuscripts are to be found in his working notebooks, for example the so-called PIAL and Rapallo notebooks, where his compositional process utilizes the whole verso–recto spreads, a format difficult to replicate in manageably sized, facing-page transcriptional codices. At the time of writing, work is proceeding on several such manuscripts and notebooks.

---

[13] See W. B. Yeats, The Death of Cuchulain: *Manuscript Materials, Including the Author's Final Text* (Ithaca and London: Cornell University Press, 1982), [v]. The statement was tightened in subsequent volumes with the elimination of the words about biographical and helpful passages, the replacement of 'definitive texts of the published works' with 'authoritative texts', and the wholesale extirpation of 'and critical analysis will be limited to discussion of their significance in relation to the published texts': see, e.g., the statement in James Pethica's edition of 'Last Poems': *Manuscript Materials* (Ithaca and London: Cornell University Press, 1997), [v].

[14] See http://www.sfu.ca/~curtis/CornellYeats/.

Attritional forces such as the increasingly difficult climate for research funding in the United States has led to the project's apparent abeyance since 2014. Overall, its thirty-three volumes contain the manuscripts of twenty-nine plays, with thirteen of the volumes containing manuscripts of the poems, constitute a remarkable achievement in a facing-page print format on the verge of supersession by the digital medium.

III

Occult Yeats and the Birth of Digital Yeats

George Mills Harper broke ground for the editing of Yeats's occult manuscripts in his edited volume for the Yeats Studies Series, *Yeats and the Occult* (1975), which opened with his own survey, 'Yeats's Occult Manuscripts', in which Harper emphasizes the contexts of occult papers by others in which Yeats's own occult manuscripts, properties, tarot cards, and other paraphernalia were then to be found.[15] That volume included 'Preliminary Examination of the Script of Miss E[lizabeth] [R]adcliffe', edited by George Mills Harper and John S. Kelly, 130–71; ' "A Subject of Investigation": Miracle at Mirebeau', edited by George Mills Harper 172–89; and Walter Kelly Hood's presentation, 'Michael Robartes, Two Occult Manuscripts', 204–24. The first issue of *Yeats Annual* in 1982 opened with 'The Manuscript of Leo Africanus', edited by Steve L. Adams and George Mills Harper, and this, the most mysterious of Yeats's dialogues, was reprinted in *Yeats's Mask: Yeats Annual 19* (2013). Almost all of the *Yeats Annuals* contain manuscript material, such as ' "Laying the Ghosts"?—W. B. Yeats's Lecture on Ghosts and Dreams', edited by Peter Kuch in *Yeats Annual 5*, and David R. Clark's presentation of 'The Poets and the Actress' dialogue in *Yeats Annual 8*.

Somewhat surprisingly, the same trade press, Macmillan (London), took up the large-scale publishing of recondite manuscript material from Yeats's *Vision* papers, and did so initially on what I have termed the 'writing' or 'making' model with *The Making of Yeats's "A Vision": A Study of the Automatic Script*, by George Mills Harper (1987). This was followed eventually by the four volumes of *Yeats's Vision Papers* (1992–2001). Other trade presses established series—the Catholic University of America Press's Irish Dramatic Texts Series is a good example—but found market penetration difficult. *Where there is Nothing* and *The Unicorn from the Stars* as well as *The Herne's Egg* appeared in that series, the first including freshly edited manuscript material from the Macmillan Archive.[16]

---

[15] On the dispersal of the Yeats family collections at two sales of 2017, see the Editor's Introduction, 'The Poetry of the Thing Outlived', in *Yeats's Legacies: YA 21*, xxxv–lxviii, https://doi.org/10.11647/OBP.0135.01.

[16] See *Where there is Nothing* by W. B. Yeats; *The Unicorn from the Stars* by W. B. Yeats and Lady Gregory, edited with an introduction and notes by Katharine Worth; and *The Herne's Egg*, edited with an introduction and notes by Andrew Parkin (both Washington: Catholic University of America Press; Gerrards Cross: Colin Smythe, 1987 and 1991 respectively).

The W. B. Yeats Collection edited by Richard J. Finneran was issued as a single, subscription-based CD collection in 1998. Including twenty-two volumes, it is based on 'the major work … in all genres'. The claim that 'usually the last known [text] to have been approved by Yeats, has been included' is far from true because 'where available, the scholarly editions in the Scribner/Macmillan Collected Edition of the Works of W.B. Yeats … have been used'. While '[t]he entire text of each work has been included' including '[a]ny accompanying text written by the author and forming an integral part of the work' and 'images appearing in the text', the keyboarding is poorly executed, and proofreading standards are deplorable. For the first time, keyword, Boolean, and wild-card searches became possible on Yeats's published writings, but various sections of Yeats's texts prove in fact to be unsearchable in this dataset for a number of reasons, one of which is that numerous prefaces, notes, and prose items are missing from the Chadwyck-Healey corpus. Moreover, some materials have been included twice, and inconsistencies abound. Serious rights questions have also not been addressed, and the project would seem to be characterized by its lack of sound editing. Nevertheless, in a more general sense it claimed *ab initio* to 'protect both the rights of the Yeats Estate and the integrity of Yeats's texts in electronic form'.[17] However uneasily, the digital era for Yeats had arrived, even if Finneran's envisaged Yeats Hypermedia Archive came to nothing.

IV

EDITING YEATS'S CORRESPONDENCE

If the above penumbra of editions beyond the Cornell Series reveals a widespread if tacit disquiet with Cornell's old New Critical abjuration of editorial commentary, the Clarendon/Oxford University Press's *The Collected Letters* (1986–) under the General Editorship of Professor John Kelly offers the starkest possible contrast in terms of its conception of the editorial task and the extent and place of editorial commentary within it, particularly of that which draws on bio-bibliographical and biographical sources. Each volume sets out the series' principles of transcription and editorial conjecture and emendation. A history of the project would reveal the evolution of the concept of a letter, be it a telegram, a draft, a contract, a lost letter to which a reference can be found or of which a recollection or summary exists, and even a ghost or implied lost letter as evidence by other correspondence.

When reviewed volume by volume in order of their publication, it is observable that the annotation, though always pertinent to the letter under consideration, steadily grows

---

[17] http://collections.chadwyck.com/marketing/products/about_ilc.jsp?collection=yeats. For a detailed review see Warwick Gould, 'Yeats Digitally Remastered: *The W. B. Yeats Collection* ed. Richard J. Finneran: A Review Essay', *Yeats and the Nineties: YA 14* (2001), 334–49.

into a narrative commentary. This commentary is generously supplemented by further narrative appendices on individuals, and Irish political and theatrical movements and institutions. *The Collected Letters* is rewriting the Irish literary, theatrical, and to some extent political history of Yeats's time, and from the bottom up.

Given the tasks of collecting and extensively annotating the texts, progress is necessarily slow in the *Collected Letters,* but five volumes are now published, bringing Yeats's letters down to the end of 1910. Further volumes are in preparation as a print-based product, as is a two-volume *Selected Letters.* With the *Collected Letters* project, the Yeats Estate largely put a stop to piecemeal editing of Yeats's letters, but it seems to have allowed certain collections of Yeats-related correspondences to flourish, on a model stretching back to 1940, when Lady Dorothy Wellesley had published her correspondence with Yeats.[18]

In 2003, Oxford University Press granted to the InteLex Corporation permission to issue *The Collected Letters* as a subscription-based CD in its Past Masters Series (later a web-accessible database: see http://www.nlx.com/home). This included the first three volumes of the edited and annotated letters as published, plus beta texts of all collected, transcribed, but unedited letters 1904–39. The object of this online publication was to establish and to protect the copyright in Yeats's letters. The series has been inadequately maintained and so far has failed to take in the fully annotated, updated, and corrected texts of volumes 4 and 5.

V

'NEW THRESHOLDS, NEW ANATOMIES'

Editorial horizons are rightly constraining, but editors dream of what lies beyond them.[19] In 2016, Yeats's and Edwin John Ellis's *The Works of William Blake: Poetic, Symbolic and Critical: A Manuscript Edition, with Critical Analysis* outstandingly showed the way forward. Edited by Arianna Antonielli and Mark Nixon, it was published by Firenze University Press in hard copy and electronic forms, with full reproduction of original thickets of holograph in which Ellis's and Yeats's hands rewrite the other's work. With their presentation of perhaps the most complex prose manuscript Yeats was ever involved with, Antonielli and Nixon signal the approaching end of large-scale codex-based manuscript editions.

---

[18] A representative example is Ian Fletcher's edition of Yeats's 'Letters to Herbert Horne, Ernest Radford and Elkin Mathews', in *Yeats Studies No. 1: Yeats and the 1890s* (1971), 203–8. Numerous examples of Yeats-related correspondence will be found in the appended bibliography.

[19] My heading is from Hart Crane's 'The Wine Menagerie': see *The New Oxford Book of American Verse,* chosen and ed. Richard Ellmann (New York: Oxford University Press, 1976), 654.

There is vital editorial work in progress, especially, as indicated above, upon Yeats's notebooks. But certain anthologies and reading texts prepared during the 1970s now required re-editing, more extensive annotation, updating in the light of recent biographical scholarship, and the editing of Yeats's letters. I have in mind the following volumes and editorial projects:

- A. Norman Jeffares's *W. B. Yeats: The Critical Heritage,* published as a direct (i.e. typewriter-set) edition in the Routledge & Kegan Paul Critical Heritage Series amid the tight publishing constraints of the 1970s. This could be augmented, in an annotated edition.
- E. H. Mikhail's enterprising selection, *W. B. Yeats: Interviews and Recollections* (London: Macmillan, 1977) could now be overhauled and vastly expanded.
- Just as *A Critical Edition of Yeats's* A Vision *(1925),* edited by George Mills Harper and Walter Kelly Hood (1978), has been superseded by *A Vision: The Original 1925 Version,* edited by Catherine E. Paul and Margaret Mills Harper (2008) as volume XIII of *The Collected Works,* so Denis Donoghue's indispensable reading text entitled Yeats's *Memoirs: Autobiography—First Draft: Journal* could now be re-edited to incorporate a vast amount of new knowledge excavated during the editing of Yeats's letters and the writing of new biographies of Maud Gonne and Olivia Shakespear, and perhaps in a manner closer to a *literatim* presentation of the manuscript.
- Yeats's lectures and speeches—including, of course, his *Senate Speeches*—could now be collected and annotated, following the latest bibliographical listings by K. P. S. Jochum. Because Yeats's lectures in America were reused but at the same time revised according to audience and occasion, the manuscripts are far from clear: newspaper reports are often the best guide as to what was said on a particular occasion.[20] The regrettably unpublished PhD thesis by the late Karin Margaret Strand, 'W. B. Yeats' American Lecture Tours' (Northwestern University, 1978), remains the point of departure for further enquiry.
- *Letters to W. B. Yeats* (1977) was another imaginative commission of Tim Farmiloe, Thomas Mark's successor as Yeats's editor at Macmillan, who commissioned so many pioneering editions at that firm in the 1970s. Such letters could be freshly collected and keyed to the Oxford and InteLex presentations of Yeats's letters.
- Family letters, especially those of John Butler Yeats to his son, first published in Cuala volumes and then in Joseph Hone's more generous 1944 selection, should be fully published in annotated form, as above.

---

[20] Early attempts to edit Yeats's lectures and lecture notes were on something of a piecemeal basis, but Robert O'Driscoll and Lorna Reynolds collected O'Driscoll's own editorial effort on 'Yeats on Personality: Three Unpublished Lectures' and Joseph Ronsley's 'Yeats's Lecture Notes for "Friends of my Youth"' in their *Yeats and the Theatre* (Toronto: Maclean-Hunter Press, Macmillan of Canada, 1975), a volume in their short-lived Yeats Studies Series: see 4–59, 60–81. Richard Londraville followed suit with 'Four Lectures by W. B. Yeats' in *YA* 8, 1991, 78–122.

The greatest challenge now, however, would be to create and sustain a digital platform which will close the gap between the editing of MSS and the editing of post-publication texts, and provide commentary up to the highest standards of the annotation of the letters. Such a fully integrated knowledge site—something along the lines of the *Bichitra Tagore Online Variorum,* with scanned images reflecting the iconicity of cover designs and printed pages in Yeats's books – would be required..[21] The entry point would a revised and updated online edition of Wade and Alspach's *A Bibliography of the Writings of W. B. Yeats* (1968), from which all MSS and printed states would be clickable. It should contain scanned pages (with transcriptions of holograph) and all periodicals, books, and other printed materials, the letters, speeches, lectures, interviews and newspaper reports, as well as collaborative works including translations made by Yeats, a search engine, an online collator, a user-oriented concordance, and, indispensably, that most venerable of editorial interventions, full editorial textual and annotational commentary.

There are as many means of editing Yeats as there are imagined audiences for his work, but future *scholarly* editing of his work should apply Yeats's own sense of a hierarchy of his audiences, and the various opportunities this implied for his editorial self-shaping.[22] In short: Yeats as an editor and self-editor continues to clarify the task for those who might take the editing of his work into the digital future.

BIBLIOGRAPHY

The arrangement is as follows: principal editions of the works of W. B. Yeats edited by others are given in approximately chronological order, followed by modern editions of works by Yeats, and then scholarly studies in alphabetical order by author and chronological order.

Texts by Yeats as Edited by Others

Yeats, W. B., *The Variorum Edition of the Poems of W. B. Yeats* (1957), ed. Peter Allt and Russell K. Alspach (New York: The Macmillan Company, 1957). To be cited from the corrected third printing of 1966.

Yeats, W. B., *The Senate Speeches of W. B. Yeats,* ed. Donald R. Pearce (Bloomington: Indiana University Press, 1960; London: Faber & Faber, 1961).

Yeats, W. B., *The Variorum Edition of the Plays of W. B. Yeats,* ed. Russell K. Alspach, assisted by Catherine C. Alspach (London and New York: Macmillan, 1966). To be cited from the corrected second printing of 1966.

---

[21] The Bichitra Online Variorum was created at the School of Cultural Texts and Records, Jadavpur University: (http://bichitra.jdvu.ac.in/index.php). It does not yet include most letters, speeches, and translations other than those made by Tagore.

[22] I have not considered in this essay the explosion in popular trade and set text publishing which followed the exit of Yeats from European copyright restrictions.

Yeats, W. B., *John Sherman & Dhoya*, edited, with an introduction, collation of the texts, and notes by Richard J. Finneran (Detroit: Wayne State University Press, 1969).

Yeats, W. B., Manuscripts of W. B. Yeats Series, General Editor, David R. Clark. 1. *Druid Craft: The Writing of the Shadowy Waters, Manuscripts of W. B. Yeats: transcribed, edited & with a commentary* by Michael J. Sidnell, George P. Mayhew, and David R. Clark (Amherst: University of Massachusetts Press, 1971); 2. *The Writing of* The Player Queen: *Manuscripts of W. B. Yeats transcribed, edited & with a commentary* by Curtis Baker Bradford (d.1969) (DeKalb: Northern Illinois University Press, 1977).

Yeats, W. B., *Memoirs: Autobiography—First Draft: Journal*, transcribed and edited by Denis Donoghue (London: Macmillan, 1972; New York: Macmillan, 1973).

Yeats, W. B., *A Critical Edition of Yeats's A Vision (1925)*, ed. George Mills Harper and Walter Kelly Hood (London: Macmillan, 1978).

Yeats, W. B., *The Secret Rose, Stories by W. B. Yeats: A Variorum Edition*, ed. Warwick Gould, Phillip L. Marcus, and Michael J. Sidnell (Cornell University Press, 1981; London: Macmillan, 1992). To be cited from the second edition, revised and enlarged.

Yeats, W. B., 'The Cornell Yeats', General Editors Phillip L. Marcus, Stephen Parrish, Ann Saddlemyer, Jon Stallworthy (1982–2014). 33 volumes, 20 of plays, 13 of poems. The first volume was *The Death of Cuchulain: Manuscript Materials, Including the Author's Final Text by W. B. Yeats* ed. Phillip L. Marcus (Ithaca and London: Cornell University Press, 1982). Other volumes cited above include Sandra Siegel's *Purgatory: Manuscript Materials, Including the Author's Final Text* (1986) and *The Tower (1928): Manuscript Materials by W. B. Yeats*, ed. Richard Finneran with Jared Curtis and Ann Saddlemyer (2007).

Yeats, W. B., *The Collected Works of W. B. Yeats* (formerly *The Collected Edition of the Works of W. B. Yeats*) under the general editorship of the late Richard J. Finneran and the late George Mills Harper. This series began with *The Poems: A New Edition* (New York: Macmillan Publishing Company, 1983; London: Macmillan London Ltd, 1984), replaced by *The Poems: Revised* (New York: Macmillan Publishing Company, 1989; London: Macmillan, 1989), replaced by *The Poems:* Second Edition (New York: Scribner, 1997), all ed. Richard J. Finneran. A total of fourteen volumes have been published.

Yeats, W. B., *The Collected Letters of W. B. Yeats: Volume I, 1865–1895*, ed. John Kelly and Eric Domville; Volume II, 1896–1900, ed. Warwick Gould, John Kelly, Deirdre Toomey; Volume III, 1901–1904, Volume IV, 1905–1907 and Volume V: 1908–1910, ed. John Kelly and Ronald Schuchard (Oxford: Clarendon Press, 1986, 1997, 1994, 2005, 2018).

Yeats, W. B., *Where there is Nothing* by W. B. Yeats, *The Unicorn from the Stars* by W. B. Yeats and Lady Gregory, edited with an Introduction and Notes by Katharine Worth (Washington: Catholic University of America Press; Gerrards Cross: Colin Smythe, 1987).

Yeats, W. B., *The Writing of Sophocles' King Oedipus*, ed. David R. Clark and James B McGuire (Philadelphia: American Philosophical Society, 1989).

Yeats, W. B., *Yeats's Poems* (London: Macmillan, 1989, 1996), ed. A. Norman Jeffares, to be cited from the third, revised edition, 1996.

Yeats, W. B., *The Poems* (London: J. M. Dent & Sons Ltd, 1990) ed. Daniel Albright.

Yeats, W. B., *The Herne's Egg*, edited with an introduction and notes by Andrew Parkin (Washington: Catholic University of America Press; Gerrards Cross: Colin Smythe, 1991).

Yeats, W. B., *Yeats's Vision Papers* (London: Macmillan, 1992; Palgrave, 2001), ed. George Mills Harper (General Editor, assisted by Mary Jane Harper): *Vol.1: The Automatic Script: 5 November 1917–18 June 1918*, ed. Steve L. Adams, Barbara J. Frieling, and Sandra L. Sprayberry; *Vol. 2: The Automatic Script: 25 June 1918–29 March 1920*, ed. Steve L. Adams,

Barbara J. Frieling, and Sandra L. Sprayberry; *Vol. 3: Sleep and Dream Notebooks, Vision Notebooks 1 and 2, Card File*, ed. Robert Anthony Martinich and Margaret Mills Harper (all 1992); Vol. 4: *'The Discoveries of Michael Robartes' Version B ['The Great Wheel' and 'The Twenty-Eight Embodiments']*, ed. George Mills Harper and Margaret Mills Harper, assisted by Richard W. Stoops, Jr. (2001).

Yeats, W. B., *The W. B. Yeats Collection,* ed. Richard J. Finneran (Cambridge: Chadwyck-Healey, 1998). Subscription-based CD issue followed by online version in the Chadwyck-Healey Literature Series: http://collections.chadwyck.com/yeats/htxview?template=basic. htx&content=frameset.htx.

Yeats, W. B., InteLex Corporation Past Masters Series: *The Collected Letters of W. B. Yeats. Electronic Edition* (Charlottesville: InteLex Corporation, 2002 [*sic*, i.e. 2003]). First issued 2003 as a CD, later a web-accessible database: http://www.nlx.com/home.

Yeats, W. B., *Mythologies*, ed. Warwick Gould and Deirdre Toomey (Houndmills: Palgrave Macmillan, 2005).

Yeats, W. B., *W. B. Yeats's Robartes-Aherne Writings: Featuring the Making of his 'Stories of Michael Robartes and His Friends'*, ed. Wayne K. Chapman (London: Bloomsbury Academic, 2018).

Yeats, W. B., and Edwin John Ellis, *The Works of William Blake: Poetic, Symbolic and Critical: A Manuscript Edition*, *with Critical Analysis*, ed. Arianna Antonielli and Mark Nixon, with a preface by Warwick Gould (Print, PDF, XML).

Yeats, W. B., *The Poems of W. B. Yeats*, Volume 1 1882–1889, Volume Two 1890–1898, ed. Peter McDonald (London & New York: Routledge, 2021). Volume 3 (1899–1910) is announced for 3 May 2023.

Editions of Yeats-associated Correspondence, Reviews, Lectures, Interviews, and Selected Occult Papers and Dialogues, in Chronological Order of Publication

Letters on Poetry from W. B. Yeats to Dorothy Wellesley, ed. Dorothy Wellesley (London and New York: Oxford University Press, 1940), reissued in 1964 with an introduction by Kathleen Raine.

Letters to his Son W. B. Yeats and Others 1869–1922 by J. B. Yeats, edited with a Memoir by Joseph Hone and a Preface by Oliver Elton (London: Faber & Faber, 1944).

W. B. Yeats and T. Sturge Moore: Their Correspondence, 1901–1937, ed. Ursula Bridge (London: Routledge & Kegan Paul; New York: Oxford University Press, 1953).

'Ah, Sweet Dancer': W. B. Yeats | Margot Ruddock, A Correspondence, ed. Roger McHugh (London and New York: Macmillan, 1970).

'Letters to Herbert Horne, Ernest Radford and Elkin Mathews' ed. Ian Fletcher, *Yeats Studies No. 1: Yeats and the 1890s* (1971), 203–8.

Letters from Bedford Park: A Selection from the Correspondence (1890–1901) of John Butler Yeats, edited with an introduction and notes by William M. Murphy (Dublin: Cuala Press, 1972).

'Preliminary Examination of the Script of E[lizabeth] R[adcliffe]' ed. George Mills Harper and John S. Kelly, in *Yeats and the Occult*, ed. George Mills Harper (Toronto: Macmillan of Canada; Niagara Falls, New York: Maclean-Hunter Press, 1975), 130–71.

'"A Subject of Investigation": Miracle at Mirebeau', ed. George Mills Harper, in *Yeats and the Occult* (1975), 172–189.

'Michael Robartes: Two Occult Manuscripts' ed. Walter Kelly Hood, in *Yeats and the Occult* (1975), 204–24.

W. B. Yeats: The Critical Heritage, ed. A. Norman Jeffares (London: Henley; Boston: Routledge & Kegan Paul, 1977).

Letters to W. B. Yeats, ed. Richard J. Finneran, George Mills Harper, and William M. Murphy, with the assistance of Alan B. Himber (London: Macmillan; New York: Columbia University Press, 1977), 2 volumes.

W. B. Yeats: Interviews and Recollections, ed. E. . Mikhail (London: Macmillan, 1977), 2 volumes.

The Correspondence of Robert Bridges and W. B. Yeats, ed. Richard J. Finneran (London: Macmillan, 1977; Toronto: Macmillan of Canada, 1978).

'The Manuscript of "Leo Africanus"', ed. Steve L. Adams and George Mills Harper, in *Yeats Annual No. 1,* ed. Richard J. Finneran (London: Macmillan, 1982), 3–47; repr. *Yeats Annual 19: Yeats's Mask,* ed. Margaret Mills Harper and Warwick Gould (Cambridge: Open Book Publishers, 2013), 289–335, https://www.openbookpublishers.com/htmlreader/978-1-78374-017-8/Essay-12.xhtml#Leo-Africanus.

The Letters of John Quinn to W. B. Yeats, ed. Alan B. Himber, with the assistance of George Mills Harper (Ann Arbor: UMI Research Press, 1983).

'"Laying the Ghosts"?—W. B. Yeats's Lecture on Ghosts and Dreams', ed. Peter Kuch, in *Yeats Annual 5,* ed. Warwick Gould (Houndmills: Macmillan, 1987), 114–35.

'Olivia Shakespear: Letters to W. B. Yeats', ed. John Harwood, in *Yeats Annual No. 6,* ed. Warwick Gould (London: Macmillan, 1988), 59–107.

'Four Lectures by W. B. Yeats, 1902–04', ed. Richard Londraville, in *Yeats Annual No. 8,* ed. Warwick Gould (Houndmills: Macmillan, 1991), 78–122. The same volume contains David R. Clark's presentations of the occult dialogue '"The Poet and the Actress" (123–43) and '"The Irish National Theatre": An Uncollected Address by W. B. Yeats' (144–54).

The Gonne-Yeats Letters 1893–1938: Always Your Friend, ed. Anna MacBride White and A. Norman Jeffares (London: Hutchinson, 1992).

'Florence Farr: Letters to W. B. Yeats, 1912–17', ed. Josephine Johnson, in *Yeats Annual 9: Yeats and Women,* ed. Deirdre Toomey (Houndmills: Macmillan, 1992), 216–54.

Letters to W. B. Yeats and Ezra Pound from Iseult Gonne 'A Girl that knew all Dante once', ed. A. Norman Jeffares, Anna MacBride White, and Christina Bridgwater (Houndmills: Palgrave Macmillan, 2004).

W. B. Yeats and George Yeats: *The Letters,* ed. Ann Saddlemyer (Oxford: Oxford University Press, 2011).

Editorial Studies and Tools

The Bichitra Online Tagore Variorum, School of Cultural Texts and Records, Jadavpur University (http://bichitra.jdvu.ac.in/index.php) (updated 2016).

Bornstein, George, What is the Text of a Poem by Yeats?', in Bornstein and Ralph G. Williams, eds., *Palimpsest: Editorial Theory in the Humanities* (Ann Arbor: University of Michigan Press, 1993), 167–93.

Bornstein, George, *Material Modernism: The Politics of the Page* (Cambridge: Cambridge University Press, 2001).

Bornstein, George, and Theresa Tinkle, eds., *The Iconic Page in Manuscript, Print, and Digital Culture* (Ann Arbor: University of Michigan Press, 1998).

Bradford, Curtis B. *Yeats at Work* (Carbondale and Edwardsville: Southern Illinois University Press, 1965).

'Editing Yeats', letters in reply in ensuing controversy, *Times Literary Supplement,* 4345 (10 August 1984), 893, and (21 September 1984), 1055.

Finneran, Richard J., *Editing Yeats's Poems* (London: Macmillan, 1983).

Finneran, Richard J., *Editing Yeats's Poems: a Reconsideration* (London: Macmillan, 1990).

Finneran, Richard J., 'Text and Interpretation in the Poems of W. B. Yeats', in George Bornstein, ed., *Representing Modernist Texts: Editing As Interpretation* (Ann Arbor: University of Michigan Press, 1991), 17–48.

Gould, Warwick, 'The Editor Takes Possession', Times Literary Supplement, 4239 (29 June 1984), 731–3. A review article on Richard J. Finneran, ed., *The Poems of W. B. Yeats: A New Edition* (London: Macmillan; New York: The Macmillan Press, 1984)

Gould, Warwick, 'Appendix Six: The Definitive Edition: a History of the Final Arrangements of Yeats's Work', in A. Norman Jeffares, ed., *Yeats's Poems* (London: Macmillan, 1989), 706–49. Third, revised edition (London: Macmillan, 1996). This textual rationale of the edition was revised in 1991 and 1996, employing new evidence, occasioning textual revision of some poems, and other alterations.

Gould, Warwick, 'Yeats Deregulated', in *Yeats Annual No. 9: Yeats and Women*, ed. Deirdre Toomey (Houndmills: Macmillan, 1992), 356–72. (Review essay on Hazard Adams, *The Book of Yeats's Poems*; Richard J. Finneran, *Editing Yeats's Poems a Reconsideration*; Finneran, ed., *The Poems of W. B. Yeats (Revised)* and *The Collected Poems: A New Edition*; Augustine Martin, ed., *The Collected Poems of W. B. Yeats;* Daniel Albright, ed., *The Poems of Yeats.*)

Gould, Warwick, 'W. B. Yeats and the Resurrection of the Author', *The Library*, 16: 2 (June 1994), 101–34. Developed from the Cecil Oldman Memorial Lecture in Bibliography and Textual Criticism, University of Leeds, 17 March 1993.

Gould, Warwick, 'Predators and Editors: Yeats in the pre- and post-Copyright Era', in Patrick Parrinder and Warren Chernaik, eds., *Textual Monopolies* (London: Office for Humanities Communication/Centre for English Studies, 1997), 69–82.

Gould, Warwick, 'Yeats Digitally Remastered: *The W. B. Yeats Collection* ed. Richard J. Finneran: A Review Essay', in *Yeats and the Nineties: Yeats Annual 14*, ed. Warwick Gould (Houndmills: Macmillan, 2001), 334–49.

Gould, Warwick, 'Yeats in the States: Piracy, Copyright and the Shaping of the Canon', *Publishing History*, 51 (Summer 2002), 61–82.

Gould, Warwick, 'W. B. Yeats on the Road to St Martin's Street, 1900–17', in Elizabeth James, ed., *Macmillan: A Publishing Tradition* (Basingstoke and New York: Palgrave/IES, 2002), 192–217.

Gould, Warwick, 'Contested Districts: Synge's Textual Self', in Andrew Nash, ed., *The Culture of Collected Editions* (Basingstoke and London: Palgrave Macmillan/IES, Nov. 2003), 128–53.

Gould, Warwick, 'Stitching and Unstitching': Yeats, Bibliographical Opportunity, and the Life of the Text', in Brian G. Caraher and Robert Mahoney, eds., *Ireland and Transatlantic Poetics: Essays in Honor of Denis Donoghue* (Newark: University of Delaware Press, 2007), 129–56.

Gould, Warwick, 'Yeats and his Books', in *Yeats Annual 20: Essays in Honour of Eamonn Cantwell* (Cambridge: Open Book Publishers, 2017), 3–70; http://dx.doi.org/10.11647/OBP.0081.02.

Gould, Warwick, 'Conflicted Legacies: Yeats's Intentions and Editorial Theory', in *Yeats's Legacies: Yeats Annual 21: A Special Issue*, ed. Warwick Gould (Cambridge: Open Book Publishers, 2018), 479–541; https://doi.org/10.11647/OBP.0135.13.

Harper, George Mills, 'Yeats's Occult Papers', in *Yeats and The Occult*, ed. George Mills Harper (Toronto: Macmillan of Canada; Niagara Falls, New York: Maclean-Hunter Press, 1975), 1–10.

Harper, George Mills, *The Making of Yeats's 'A Vision': A Study of the Automatic Script* (London: Macmillan; Carbondale and Edwardsville, IL: Southern Illinois University Press, 1987).

Jeffares, A. Norman, *A New Commentary on the Poems of W. B. Yeats* (London: Macmillan, 1984).

Jochum, K. P. S., *W. B. Yeats: A Classified Bibliography of Criticism*, second edition revised and enlarged (Urbana and Chicago: University of Illinois Press, 1990); an online version, updated to 2017 and enlarged, is in progress.

Kelly, John, 'Books and Numberless Dreams', in A. Norman Jeffares, ed., *Yeats, Sligo and Ireland*, Irish Literary Studies 6 (Gerrards Cross: Colin Smythe, 1980), 232–53.

McDonald, Peter, 'Yeats's Canons', *Essays in Criticism*, 60:3 (July 2010), 242–64, https://doi.org/10.1093/escrit/cgq008; https://academic.oup.com/eic/article/60/3/242/539954.

McDonald, Peter, 'Editing Yeats: The Widening Gyre', *Essays in Criticism*, 68:4 (October 2018), 415–27, https://o-doi-org.catalogue.libraries.london.ac.uk/10.1093/escrit/cgy021.

O'Shea, Edward, *Yeats as Editor*, New Yeats Papers XII (Dublin: Dolmen Press, 1975).

Richard J. Finneran, *Editing Yeats's Poems* (London: Macmillan, 1983); A. Norman Jeffares, *A New Commentary on the Poems of W. B. Yeats* (London: Macmillan, 1984).

Sidnell, Michael J., 'Unacceptable Hypotheses: The New Edition of Yeats's Poems and its Making', *Yeats Annual No. 3*, ed. Warwick Gould (London: Macmillan, 1984), 225–43.

Smythe, Colin, 'A. L. Burt's 1898 edition of *Irish Fairy and Folk Tales*, in Warwick Gould and Edna Longley, eds., *Yeats Annual 12: That Accusing Eye: Yeats and his Irish Readers* (Houndmills: Macmillan, 1996), 248–52.

Wade, Allan, *A Bibliography of the Writings of W. B. Yeats*, third edition, rev. Russell K. Alspach (London: Rupert Hart-Davis, 1968).

POSTSCRIPT

CHAPTER 42

....

YEATS AND CONTEMPORARY POETRY

Twelve Speculative Takes

....

VONA GROARKE

1. IN WHICH WBY GOES, IN FACT, TO LIVE ON INNISFREE

Sans electricity, plumbing, a mirror, a roof over his head, his wife and children, wine, dapper suits, neckties, lady friends, any friends, a typewriter, music, a postal service, visitors, an audience, masks, swords, conversation, politics, theatres, bills, the Cuala Press, his father's creditors, art, handmade furniture, tarot cards, telephone, gold enamelling.

Avec greatcoat, slippers, notebooks, pen and ink, volumes by Nietzsche, Shakespeare, Rilke, Synge, Blake, Shelley, *Ulysses*, a hive, candles in tall candlesticks, a mirror, unction for his bothersome knee, a pipe and a week's worth of tobacco, a selection of seeds, a time frame, a project, an idea.

When word gets out that he has decamped, people start to send him gifts, and soon there is call for a rowboat operated by a local man of few words and abundant eyebrows to make the trip out twice a week. Within a month, he is furnished with creature comforts such as truffles and port and even copies of the *Sligo Champion,* which he reads down to the very last word of upcoming auctions and obituaries. (He is charmed to note on page 4 of one issue a small, bordered article titled 'Local Poet W.B. returns to reside on Sligo island', featuring a quote he has no recollection of furnishing or idea as to whom he might have furnished it, but which nonetheless reads, 'I find the peace and quiet here inspirational'.)

Other reading material to be sent to him includes a sizeable donation of ecopoetry books from a magazine editor who thinks Yeats might find them interesting and stimulating, and wonders if he might find the time to review a selection of the accompanied slim volumes, in 700 words.

Yeats has never before heard of ecopoetry and initially wonders if it might be a spelling error for 'ego poetry', which he thinks is a fair (if rather too damning) description of much work he has encountered.

But no. Upon probing, he discovers that ecopoetry (or 'eco-poetics', a term which several of the blurbs on these collections insist on using) is poetry with an ecological bent. A magazine editorial says as much, informing him that this dedicated issue of this robust and necessary publication will specifically feature poems concentrating on the relationship between humanity and nature. 'Ah', he thinks, settling down to an evening's reading beside his improvised camp fire, propped on a surprisingly accommodating mossy rock: humanity and nature? This is his subject, he thinks, as he looks around at the shelter he improvised from twigs bound together with his good silk socks, and the rabbit (which had fallen in the hole he'd dug, must have broken a leg and died, obligingly: at any rate, he does not remember killing it, though he has read up on how this is to be accomplished and is certain he could manage it, if he had to) cooking fitfully over a fire yet to take, and which still resists his every effort to coax it into warmth.

In fact the rabbit is a hare (a creature in which he has invested magical, even sacred, possibilities), but Yeats, innocent of this fact, cannot be expected to care. He wishes for a dinner of meat. He wishes he'd come better prepared, with a sturdy tent, ample provisions, something to drink, and a hearty bar of soap. He wishes he had more serviceable clothes; his greatcoat is soaked through. He wishes he knew more about how nature actually works. He wishes, in fact, he were home.

It's not even peaceful. He's anxious about practicalities—how tentative his shelter is (a light breeze would expose him entirely), how his life proceeds at home without him, how long he must stay on this crabby island, how dull island living is, how his surprising new beard suits him well.

Nature. He sighs (and his sigh trembles the ferns around him and sets the linnets a-flutter, and overrides, for once, the lake with that relentless drone that he thinks he will never, ever manage to excise from his brain). Nature, he thinks, is too much and much too little for him.

He wonders if the books might help. There might be something useful there about identifying edible plants or species of bird (he'd like those birds he sees to be linnets—such a pretty name—but they could easily be thrushes or sparrows. Or robins). (He's certain they're not seagulls. He'd know a seagull anywhere. Of course he would.) There might be something about surviving in an environment that doesn't seem either to require or cherish your continued vigilance. Plus, he feels he has fallen behind in his reading of contemporary poets and would like to bring himself up to date. Lacking the British Library now, he falls upon ecopoetry with enthusiasm; with appetite, even.

His first action is to remove any pages with the words 'eco-poetics': these he intends to return to nature in a cheekily appropriate way.

Then he gets to reading.

He is surprised by how literal these poems are: they read a river as a river and a blade of grass as grass (not as synecdoche or as metaphor). Or do they? He likes it when they appear to watch themselves arriving at their own conclusions by stealth and craftily. He likes the way he can see the world in the best of them, and how vivid it is, how present, how alive. He appreciates having his attention drawn to particular details, a stone, a raindrop, a sheaf of wheat, a spider, even that blade of grass. The ecopoems do make him feel more at home on Innisfree: there is less of him and more of the island, and that is how he likes it to be when he is reading poems, so that he gives himself (almost) the slip.

But certain aspects confuse him. He finds he doesn't understand why these are *eco*poems. He doesn't favour the splicing of poetry according to subject matter and he's not sure how he could possibly categorize his own work in this way. Naturepoems. Ecopoems. Lovepoems. Sexpoems. Deathpoems. Politicspoems. Artpoems. Selfpoems. Worldpoems. Poems that are good for reading aloud. Poems that want to be small and quiet. Poems he knows not what they want and dare not ask for fear they would take umbrage and take off.

He has enjoyed the reading, but finds he scarcely wants to think at all about ecopoems. He determines he will not write the review, for what would he say other than that 'some of these are good poems, and some of these are not'? The difference couldn't be one of theme, surely? And yet, he acknowledges, he has written poems he wished to send out in the world as a happening, a cause to stir up a result, with a particular target in sight, and meant to strike it true.

For what is the value of ambivalence, if a point is to be made? He observes that the ecopoems, the best of them, have no truck with either ambivalence or detachment. They identify cataclysm and seem determined to remind the world of its responsibility to prevent it. He is, despite himself, moved.

He recites 'The Lake Isle of Innisfree' to the indeterminate birds. He wonders if he might call it an ecopoem? He hardly can say what it is about, except maybe loneliness and homesickness, neither of which he would wish to be accused of campaigning for, despite the poem's convincingly pleasing ways of going about winning over the reader, which he now finds bothersome. It seems to him to have strange truth in it that doesn't float right to the surface, quite, but is banked underneath other ways of being a poem, that yet yields when pressed to do so. No one, he thinks, would be spurred to action of any kind by 'The Lake Isle of Innisfree'.

Perhaps things have gone beyond pleasingness, he thinks: perhaps that is the point. The world is such that it requires only clarity now; clear thinking and direction. Poetry as easy to understand as lake water is, that enacts its concern and activism without embarrassment, ambivalence, reticence, or qualm. The idea appeals to him so much, he begins to inscribe pointed words with a sharp twig in the soil under his feet.

But when he wishes to move from this single spot, he finds his feet scuff the words so they are illegible, and he can't, for the life of him, afterwards remember how they went.

2. In Which WBY Receives a Rejection Letter

MiAsMa

Dear William,

Thank you for submitting your poems to us. We have read them with interest and while we find much to admire there, we don't think they're for us.

If you've read our online content, you'll know we tend to favor poems that challenge form in a more interrogative/speculative, and less ideational/imitative way. Yours we found a little sleek and oddly mannerly. We also had concerns about your use of rhyme, a poetic device which we at *MiAsMa* question for its static inevitability and its assumption of much of the authoritative positions of late-stage capitalism.

We are, of course, sorry to disappoint, but we wish you a good home for your poems, and all the best in your future career.

Yours sincerely,

Chris Stubbs & I.M. Skarr
The Editors

MiAsMa Undergraduate Journal of Arts and Letters
Hillman University,
Fountainhead, CA

3. In Which an Intern Records in Her Diary Meeting WBY at PoetryShowTime

Sept 21 11:00   Met Professor Yeats at train station, easy to pick him out on account of that cockatoo's spiel of white hair. Friendly but distant. Maybe that's just me, I was nervous. I LOVE, love, love his poems: could hardly believe I was shaking his hand and carrying his bags. Think maybe someone more senior from the festival should have gone. A Welcome Committee. Speeches. Bouquets. Brass band playing Salley Gardens. Freedom of the town. In the taxi, he didn't say much. Gave him his welcome pack with his lanyard and meal vouchers. Went through his itinerary for tonight. He didn't like the 20:30 slot, too late to eat afterwards, he said; too early for dinner before. His voice is beautiful! Told him a dinner was planned for 22:00, but not sure if he heard. He seemed too warm in his tweed jacket and overcoat but not inclined to take it off. I didn't dare suggest it. Hardly knew what to be saying to him. Mostly just looked at his hands. He has very wise old hands. Then he asked me if I was a poet. Me! I didn't know what to say, I mean, *Yes* obvs but also really really (considering who I was talking to) really *No*.

Got him to hotel, different one to where most speakers are staying, fancier—one star more. Suppose he didn't know that though. Was about to say goodbye when he asked if I could recommend an event in the afternoon for him to attend. I showed him the programme and he put his finger on one at 13:15, said, Perfect, he'd go to that, so, and then have lunch and a nap before the evening festivities. Could I accompany him? On his nap? Really? *Jesus Christ*, but he must have read my mind, said he 'hated dining alone', and if I could spare him those few hours, he'd be grateful for my time. *My* time? Bloody hell! So I said yes of course, and arranged to meet him back there at 13:00, to proceed to the reading from there.

They weren't too pleased back in the festival office. I was supposed to meet Julian Barnes at the station at 13:00 and Billy Collins at 15:00 and Ruth Padel at 17:30. Mike said *he'd* take care of Yeats instead but I said he was expecting *me* and might be put out if someone new showed up. No way was I going to miss this!

12:45   Fifteen minutes early. I spent the time flicking the edges of my copy of his Collected Poems, wondering if I'd get up the nerve to ask him to sign it. Of course I didn't in the end. Would have been like asking the Pope if he had a clean tissue on him. Left my bag open though, hoping he'd see it and offer, but he mustn't have. He was all chat on the walk to the venue, how long had I worked for the festival, did I grow up here, did I sing (asked me that twice), had I been to India, did I get my cat earrings there, (they were surprising), did I intend to marry, did I grow my own vegetables, (they were awfully good for you), and so on. Didn't seem too bothered about me answering, but I was glad enough not to have to think of things to say. Sprightly enough too, no old-man dawdling. Box Office weren't expecting us: I said I needed two comps, the woman said I'd have to pay because they'd not been logged in advance, but then the manager behind her saw Prof Y and brought the tickets out himself and said, 'Welcome to our humble theatre' and practically bowed (hilarious—the same man is well known to all us female interns as an arrogant shit and dropper of the hand). I let Prof Y choose the seats, he sat right up the front, on account of bad eyesight, I suppose.

3 poets reading, all women. First wore a complicated orange dress and read poems mostly about insects while doing odd, clicky things with her hands. I think maybe she was making insect gestures, but since insects don't really have hands, I didn't get it. Prof Y seemed to enjoy it though, clapped loudly when she was finished then leaned over to me, whispered 'a waspish performance, wouldn't you say?' except it wasn't really a whisper and I was kind of mortified in case anyone else would hear.

I thought the second poet was brilliant: she was sharp and clever and the poems about the bigger picture had me in the palm of their hand. I looked over at him to see if he was as struck as I was. His eyes were closed, I'm not sure if he was riveted or asleep.

The third poet was middle-aged and a bit strealish, as my mother would say. It's not everyone can pull off a turquoise, pleather pinafore. She introduced her sequence about money by saying she would perform the way money did, getting more and more shouty as it went on. And it was a long sequence. No napping off there. You'd have to be stone deaf.

Afterwards, he said it was a lovely event and had brought him up nicely to lunchtime.

14:15   Which he ate delicately, like his fingers were made of carved ice, liable to snap. Talked the whole time, I wanted to write everything down, but was afraid it would be bad manners. I do remember he said poetry would save us all, even all the poets. At least I think that's what he said: he was eating banoffi pie at the time, and his words curdled into it a bit.

15:00   I walked him back to the hotel and he kissed my hand and thanked me for keeping time along with him. I said I was looking forward to his reading, and he asked if there was any poem I'd like him to read for me. For me!!! I said 'The Second Coming' and he said, 'Oh'. I'm not sure what he meant by that. Anyway he didn't read it. I suppose he forgot. Everyone loved him anyway. He was very theatrical, his hands all about his head like seagulls ready to swoop and his voice, that voice, going over the lines like an antique rolling pin made of black marble with a vein of gold all the way along. It was <u>something</u>. The whole day was something. If they ever make a film of it, I'll be played by Saoirse Ronan and Colin Farrell (in old man make-up, like Benjamin Button) would *so* make a good him.

4. In Which WBY Discusses Prosody with a Panel of Early Career Creative Writing Academics

'Questions? Anyone? Yes, the small man in the back row. Speak up, please.'
–'Mr Yeats, Why do you use so many questions in your poems?'
–'Do I?'
–'Yes. Often at the end of your poems.'
–'Have you examples, by any chance?'
–'I have. "The Second Coming". "Among School Children". "Nineteen Hundred and Nineteen". "Leda and the Swan". "No Second Troy". "Stream and Sun at Glendalough". "Girl's Song".'

–'Would you call that a great many?'

–'I could go on. "A Nativity". "Sixteen Dead Men". "The Wild Swans At Coole". "Upon a House" …'

–'Do I have many poems that don't end in question marks?'

–'In fact, you do. But in *The Green Helmet and Other Poems*, you have five poems in a row that all end in question marks.'

–'Do I now?'

–'You do. I'm wondering if you were conscious of that, and what you were hoping to achieve?'

–'By ending poems with questions?'

–'Yes.'

–'That I hoped to achieve poems that end in questions, wouldn't you say?'

–'Well, yes. But could you say a little more about your decision-making process?'

–'Why don't you ask the poems?'

–'Oh … Because the poems can't answer me.'

–'Well there you are. You see?'

–'Ok …'

–'Are you quite sure it's the same question mark at the end of each?'

–'I'm sorry?'

–'Don't you think there might be different kinds of question mark, to suit different kinds of question?'

–'Could you say a little more about that?'

–'No. Except that some questions are hopeful of answers, and some have learned to abandon hope before they come into being, don't you agree?'

–'Do you mean us to infer that you use the question mark purely as a rhetorical device?'

–'Purely?'

–'Solely.'

–'Would you say so?'

'Perhaps another question, please, on a different topic? Yes, the lady in the yellow dress.'

–'I'd like to ask about repetition in your poems. It seems to me that you double up words and phrases deliberately, to create a kind of echo chamber within which the poem listens to its rhetorical devices and repeats them, in a kind of closed circuit of proposal and either refusal or adherence. Is this an ironic or self-reflexive comment on a world which insists on directing response, and on drawing attention to the means of that direction?'

–'Could you repeat the question?'

Laughter.

–'Well, for example, in "Sailing to Byzantium" you have "hammered gold and gold enamelling".'

–'Perhaps I wish to draw attention to the reflective qualities of gold.'

–'But in "The Tower" you have "O heart, O troubled heart": is the repeated noun an active intensifier, in place of the adjective that would usually be asked to do this kind of heavy lifting?'

–'I think the adjective "troubled" does quite a bit of the heavy lifting, as you call it, here.'

–'I'm also thinking of "Mere dreams, mere dreams!" in "Meditations in Time of Civil War". And of "The fire that stirs about her, when she stirs" in "The Folly of Being Comforted". You could have chosen synonyms or any one of a range of alternatives, but you didn't. Why not?'

–'A scale has but eight notes at its disposal, and yet we don't tire of music because it must repeat them.'

'Thank you, Mr Yeats. I think I saw a hand up here. Ah yes, the man in the suit…'

–'I'd like to probe the subject of beauty in your poems, not just their preoccupation with idealized notions of physical perfection, but also (and these are not, I think, unrelated), the surface beauty of your poetry, the glossy sheen of rhythm and rhyme that is, in itself, a tightened bow. Do you regret that your work offers no challenge to the culturally and socially normative, or to the formally secure?'

–'The unbeautiful is the unresolved. The poetic act enjoys the power of resolution, for even the most lumpen subject matter.'

–'Transformative, therefore, rather than observational?'

–'The poet must do more than record. He must mediate.'

–'By imposing ego?'

–'There must be sincerity.'

–'Why must there?'

–'Because without it, the investment is minor and the poem is compromised.'

'We have time for just a couple more. The woman in the green waistcoat. No, let's have all the remaining questions now and ask Mr Yeats to choose which one he'll answer for a finish.'

–'Why poetry? Why not prose?'

–'Do you agree that the personal is political?

–'What now, do you think, are the responsibilities of the committed poet?'

–'Could you speak to the distinction between the didactic and the poetical impulse?'

–'If you could change any of your poems now, what edits would you make and to which poems?'

–'Can you honestly stand over your preference for metre in an age defined by chaos, nihilism, and cynicism?'

–'What is your favourite critical study of your work?'

–'How would you teach your most difficult poems, for example "The Statues"?'

–'Must the poet objectify herself in a poem; isn't there any alternative way of distinguishing between sensibility and craft? In other words, can you tell us: how can we know the dancer from the dance?'

–'What do you think is your relevance to contemporary poetry?'

'Right. Thanks everyone. Rich pickings, I'm sure you'll agree. Mr Yeats, which will you plump for? Mr Yeats? Mr Yeats? Have we finished? Oh, I see.'

5. In Which WBY Receives a Letter from a Rape Victim Concerning 'Leda and the Swan'

Dear Mr Yeats,

'Feathered glory', really?

You are not without imagination: some of it, you come close—'terrified fingers', the indifference, the helplessness. And I appreciate that you've given yourself the advantage of a removal from realism, which (presumably) gives you free rein over recorded, actual experiences of rape. It's a swan, not a man, I get it. A swan who is actually Zeus, a god (another convenient distancing step away from gritty realism?). And it's a mythological figure, Leda—not a flesh and blood woman. Not a daughter, mother, sister, aunt, niece, grandmother, great-grandmother, girlfriend, wife or friend. Not a teenager who thinks this is just what happens, what can you do. Not a pensioner who has just heard the sound of a breaking window downstairs. Not a woman walking home alone. Not a woman whose husband has just come, fast and furious, through the door. Not a child in darkness, desperately pretending she's asleep. Not a woman at a party saying no, no, and no again to a chain of men who will not hear.

But still. Even a poem about a mythological figure being raped by a god-swan has some responsibility, surely, to conjure the moment with something like fidelity, so the poem is convincing and has impact, rather than draining through our fingers into feathery insignificance?

So here's the truth: even in your poem, Leda wasn't seduced: she was raped.

You can't pretty that up. Someone should tell you, I think, about what using words such as 'caressed', 'holds', and 'feel' brings to a poem about rape. A rapist violates a woman's body in order to feel, for a moment, powerful. It's an act of violence and brutality, often as revenge for a slight or insult someone (usually not the woman) has visited on the man. There's really nothing sexy about it, not even for the man, but certainly not for the woman.

Rape is not sexual intimacy. I can't believe I have to tell you this.

Or say that, for my own part, I felt no 'strange heart beating' where it lay: I was too busy trying not to be killed. Aestheticize that all you want, but in the end, rape is a grubby, brutal, appalling, shaming, fearful affair, not a second of beauty or calm or reflection in it. If you tell it true.

You don't mention Zeus in your poem; you go to trouble to have us believe in that swan as a real swan, its physical presence, the white rush of it, its great wings, the 'brute blood of the air'. Fine, I say: it's a swan, a raping swan. But what knowledge might a swan have (no matter how powerful), that is more than a woman does? Surely, the swan would be putting on Leda's knowledge, since it has to be more than his?

One thing to have a character in a poem by you be raped; another to strip her of knowledge as well as power.

If she were a woman, I'd want to go to her in the white space into which your poem drops her, so coldly and finally. I know that white space, was dropped in it myself, where there is no consequence, no aftermath (forget about justice or punishment commensurate with the crime), just an absolving silence occasionally punctuated by the screams that will wake her in the night for many years.

If Leda were a woman, dropped into that awful hole of trauma, pain and relentless recall, I'd like to help her out of it. What I wouldn't want is to consign her to the knowledge you imagined into her.

What is the knowledge a person puts on from the experience of having been raped? It can only be this: what it is to have been raped. The rapist knows nothing whatsoever about this, and neither, Mr Yeats, do you.

Poor Leda, victim twice over, once in the doing, once in the telling. But that's an old story here. It was ever thus.

So in a way, your poem (despite itself?) tells it just as it is: no account of rape that isn't the victim's knows enough to avoid big lies. Even if they are beautifully put, they remain lies nonetheless.

Yours sincerely,

(Name withheld)

6. In Which Is Read WBY's Judge's Comments on the National Political Poetry Prize (the Poet Himself Being Unable to Attend)

I have been asked to read the entries for this year's National Political Poetry Prize and from them to choose a winner I deem worthy of the prize.

I know it is customary at such times to say how much I enjoyed the task, how excellent most entries were and how difficult it was to choose a winner. I offer no such customary words.

In all, one thousand nine hundred and nineteen entries were passed on to me. I cannot say if this represents the full number of entries, though I suppose it may have been. I cannot think of there having been additional poems so bad (or indeed so good) as to be deemed by a sifting committee unsuitable for even mild exposure to my judgement or my taste.

I do not intend to waste your time here justifying my eventual decisions or defending (as I know some of you would have me do), my right to so decide. Instead, I wish to draw more general conclusions about what it means to write political poetry in this day and age, and about why so many of the entries I read seemed unequal to the task.

But first, it is necessary for us to consider what we mean by 'political poetry'. Is it poetry about current political matters (as so many entries determined), or is it poetry that, by expression of certain, firmly held and partisan beliefs, perhaps wishes to affect a particular political stance and, quite possibly, consequent change? In other words, is political poetry *about* politics, or is it poetry that enacts itself in something of the way politics would wish to do?

I have spent much of my life, as you may know, engaged in some campaign or other for the right encouragement of noble national ideals in our Irish state.

Respect for tradition, a finely tuned moral conscience, integrity, simplicity of national expression, an affirming aesthetic—all are central to what I believe should be this country's purest idea of itself. Along with certain crucial negative determinations—an abhorrence of the coarse, pedantic, rhetorical, sentimental, provincial, mercenary, trivial and sectarian.

This is what I think of as proper political ambition—the seeking after a heroic and passionate conception of life. I would have our people's politics be one of love, and not squalid hates and envies. And I would commend to you the politics that commits itself to the antithesis of the petty or trifling. Would that all our politicians held fast to the idea of a national feeling as intense as it is pure and good! Then we might have political poems intent on probity and rectitude, on justice and decency.

I consider moral integrity to be fundamental to the inner workings of a good political poem. Therefore, let me declare that an entry entitled, for example, 'The Billygoat That Ate the Ballot Paper' or 'They're All a Shower of Crooks' has set itself a difficult task in trying to win me over. Equally, an entry that is no more or less than political manifest disguised as 'poetry' is unlikely to impress me. Take, for instance, the following poem:

> What Ireland needs is a revolution, I'll tell it to you straight
> in order to fix all the national woes and set the country right
> again, after decades of austerity that have destroyed the state,
> making the poor poorer, the rich richer, blood-sucking fat cats.

A strident and forceful expression of political allegiance, perhaps, but not very much to do with poetry. As the competition is directed at Political Poetry, I decided to insist on there being some poetry in the poetry. I sought language that understood how to distinguish itself from other discourse, especially of the political kind.

Of course there are many ways of admiring a poem. For example, entranced as I was by the beguiling language of the entry that opens:

> It is time to talk of reticence, bloodlines and honeybees,
> time to salve the injured dream, to soothe the injured soul,
> to bolster all credulity and to determine faith.
> To cauterize estrangement, and to slip between.

… I was unable to quite relate the content to the subject of this particular competition. Likewise, I tended to overlook poems that relied for their energy and persuasion chiefly on references to contemporary events, without any sense of the span or scope of historical context. Therefore, references to brown envelopes, whistle-blowing, Garda corruption, phone tapping, campaign funding, specific policies and unspecified 'shenanigans' made scant impression on me. I decided to have no truck with this man's gripe or this woman's disappointment. I sought, instead, a poem to outlast its political relevance, this year's headlines.

Ladies and gentlemen, it is time to announce this year's winner.

Or it would be, if there were one.

But I'm sorry to say I found no entry worthy of the prize. The poems, I'm afraid, were either too small or too big. Nothing fitted. Nothing convinced. Nothing made me want to knock on the door of government so that I might present the winning poem and watch it, thusly enlightened and educated, ennoble itself by fresh vision and generous purpose. By passionate intensity.

And what is the point of a political poem if it is not to ennoble politics? What value, the snide poem that knows much more about its ambitions than any reader will? I wish never to read another poem written out of bitterness, quarrel, righteousness, ennui, or despair. And I reserve the right to refuse to award any such poem a prize.

Therefore, I have decided that this year's prize will be held over until next year, when a new prize for Apolitical Poetry will be launched, judge to be announced (not me).

Perhaps, since the political poems fell so wide of the mark, it may fall to Apolitical Poetry to remind us why we must be in love with life, as any prize-winning poem ought to do. I do not want to know how good a poet thinks himself to be: I ask only for a poem to be well made, compassionate, and true. I seek a poem to defend humanity against tyranny and egotism, that is all.

Give me such a poem, my friends, and I will gladly award for you the €250 prize.

7. In Which People Post Comments on Recordings on YouTube of WBY Reading His Own Poetry

HeidiSnoark58
Profoundly exquisite! Thank you for posting—I love how mellifluous he is, how he wrings every gram of beauty from each word. I wish more modern poetry was like this!

Infilltr8
This really helped me with my term paper.

JimMore12
I had to stop listening because I couldn't bear for this to come to an end.

SuzieQuinTro
He doesn't sound Irish to me.

ParkanAbole
We owe a deep of gratitude.

novachok98
I dunno.

SuzieQuinTro
He sounds German.

pieterdieter
definitely not German.

LifeisforLivers
Sounds like a priest. A holy man. Some sort of prophet. Someone who has some insight on this crazy shitbag of a world and what it's coming to and what we've done to it. We've ruined it. Late stage capitalism, fake news, far-right, plastic beaches, NRA—it's all fucking crazy now. Nobody knows anything. Yeats knew. He wasn't scared of being right. We need poetry more than ever now.

GirlyGirlGirl
What's true here? Just interested … Doesn't sound to me like anything to do with the world I live in.

GorgeJorge
Bit of a ride, yeah?

brightonrock
Think he's got a stone in his mouth he's trying not to swallow.

Rakshanda
What a blessing to be able to hear his voice! I cry.

ClaraLara
This isn't poetry. It says nothing about the real world, about anything happening now. Just another straight old white rich dude hogging the mic. Expecting to be listened to. There's much better stuff available if you know where to look. Poems with something to say for themselves.

JJOkay
Okay.

MarlenaDickTrick
Claralara, if you don't like it, why do you listen?

ClaraLara
Know your enemy, is why.

MarlenaDickTrick
How is Yeats your enemy?

luckyduck
This is shit. Is just old poems is all.

ClaraLara
Trying to make a new world, MarlenaDickTrick. One where people of all colours, creeds, races, orientation and identity can also have their say. Not this one, where so many are pushed outside the door and never allowed back in.

Dogstar22
Like who? Like yourself, maybe? But seems like it's a big room if it has you in it.

LucyMcGinn
I love Ireland, home of my ancestors. Someday I'll visit, that's my dream. Yeats sounds like I think Ireland will look—lush and poetic and ancient.

ClaraLara
Like anyone who isn't white, rich and has a penis, basically.

MarlenaDickTrick
Sounds about right to me!

Scratchthat
Great hatred, little room.

Dogstar22

No Yeats, so. Or will you make an exception for dead poets?

NextReadyArmy

LifeisforLivers and ClaraLara, you're both totally naïve. If you think poets or prophets will defend you when the shit hits the fan, forget it. There are no safe places, only prepared people. Don't come screaming to me for help when there's a madman holding your children hostage. Learn to defend yourself. Do It Now.

IndiePop

Wha'?

ClaraLara

Language is power. We need to rescue language from fascists and the patriarchy, get poetry back to the people, where it belongs.

Dogstar22

People. But just female ones.

ClaraLara

Female-identifying, actually.

Buzzwell

FOAD.

Chris B. Danagher

What has any of this to do with Yeats?

Scratchthat

Well, you could say Yeats wasn't above shifting identities when it suited him. Irish Nationalist—Professional literary Irishman in the drawing rooms of London. Dreamer—Campaigner. Lover—Virgin. Poet—Politician. Mystic—Gardener. Shape-shifter, all his life.

Chris B. Danagher

Revisionism!

BobDillon

Ireland is dark, damp and expensive, LucyMcGinn. Try Croatia or Poland, much better value. Better beer also.

IndiePop

Boring. Came here for bantz. Check out my blog on IndiePop@A1Poet #bestintheworld.

laughingstock

Gardener? What next: Golfer? Ringmaster? Coroner? Pastry-chef?

jb613jb
poety so beutifull. Wish I write like you.

misticmig
Yeats knew things through his visions no one else has ever known. A great seer.

Scratchthat
He was like a full orchestra, was Yeats. So many ways to sing a Yeats poem, from the gentle to the loud. He could be a cello or a trumpet, depending on the poem.

Claralara
Couldn't be a woman, though. With a woman's agency.

oracleinnit
Is it true he used beat up Maud Gonne?

Scratchthat
No.

Noncewords
I heard that too. And her daughter. Burned her clothes?

Claralara
Wouldn't surprise me. His poems reek of patriarchy.

Scratchthat
Oh for god's sake. IT'S NOT TRUE.

jeremyisinthelimo
We studied him in school.

Dogstarrr
If it isn't true, maybe it should be.

BobDillon
You people are insane.

mugsgame
Yeah, difficult bugger, as I recall. Easy to learn off but hard to say what the meaning was.

laughingstock
poetry makes nothing happen. Even a poet said that.

Scratchthat
But Yeats was actually pretty good at making things happen.

mugsgame
Yeah, like the Nobel Prize? They knew to look after their own.

Carn8ionRose
Everyone so crazy mad. Why so crazy mad? Listen is good. Nice words. Soft. Fix stuff. Sweet.

songforlovers
gotta ♥ Yeats!

8. The Poets' Society Press Release

THE POETS' SOCIETY

Press Release

Concerned about the falling standards of craft in our profession, the Poets' Society will now require aspiring members to complete a test. From this day, it will not be possible to obtain full membership of the Poets' Society without the successful completion of this test, which will be administered by our staff and a panel of reputable poets. Affiliate membership will be available to any applicant, which may be converted into full membership at any time, once the test has been passed.

We regret that such a step has been judged necessary, but it has become increasingly clear to us that contemporary poetry is now liable to be appreciated more for its 'relevant' content than for its stylistic flair. We cannot preside over a culture where subject matter consistently trumps craft, or where poetic success is to be a matter of readers' emotive response rather than any more substantial appreciation of a poem's accomplishments. In short, we are bored with sincerity. We are tired of being shouted at, tired of poems that chase the latest headline, or corral themselves into tiny patches of representational rhetoric without sufficient attention to the subtle arts by which good poems succeed in a lasting way.

And we are done with poetry philistines who say that to be meaningful is to be necessary.

Our test will, we hope, serve as a corrective to patterns of creeping depletion and coarsening.

We seek to encourage deep reading, attention to craft, and sincere engagement with poetic tradition and skill. Our hope is that a new generation of poets will leave aside their fixed thematic positions and aspire instead to an art that is more refined, ambitious, and ingenious.

To this end, our test will offer a poem by W. B. Yeats, since he it was who instructed that poets must 'learn their trade'. We will ask applicants to respond in the following five ways:

- scan the poem both metrically and rhythmically, using a recognizable visual scheme
- identify the poem's metre, according to counted feet (monometer, tetrameter, hexameter, etc.)
- mark the poem's use of caesura, anapaests, trochees, headless and pyrrhic feet, masculine and feminine endings
- explain (max 500 words) why all of this (or none of this, possibly) matters to the Yeats poem
- explain (max 500 words) why all of this (or none of this) matters to your own poems.

Not everyone can be a poet. Not even everyone who understands how poetry works can be a poet. But just as we expect musicians to be able to read musical notation and to show mastery of their instruments, we expect poets to know their craft. Without it, how can we know what a poem is, or why this poem is better than that, or parse why it has somehow succeeded?

In response to this test, we anticipate increased demand for membership to the Poets' Society. Application forms may be found at singwhateveriswellmade.com.

9. Yeats and the Ordinary: Colloquium Programme

Yeats and the Ordinary

A One-Day International Colloquium

June 24, 2023
University of Hunsang, South Korea
Butler Hall

Programme

8.30–9.00	Registration and Coffee

9.00–10.15 *Plenary Session No 1*
Professor Yoko Kim (Yonsei University)
'Pans, Pots and Poetry, and Everything in Between: Keeping House in the poems of W.B. Yeats'

10.15–10.45 *Coffee Break*

10.45–12.15 *Breakout Session 1:*

Group A

Jason Jacobs (University of Birmingham)	'Solid Air': The Poetry of Doors and Windows in the later work of Yeats
Mairead Ni Cheallaigh (Sligo I.T.)	'Two Heavy Trestles': Yeats's Determinedly Unmagical Furniture
Gordan Moran (Boston College)	A Crazy Salad? Food and Drink in the Poetry of W.B. Yeats

Group B

Claudio Moroni (Florence)	Hare, Hound, Horse and Hawk: Creature Comforts in the poems of Yeats
Sebastien Inglewood (Kings)	'Biddy's Halfpennies': gender roles in the twentieth century service economy
Anita Holt (Saarbrücken)	What are children doing in the poems of W. B. Yeats?

12.15–13.30 *Lunch*

13.30–15.00 *Breakout Session 2:*

Group A

Elizabeth Barker (University of Brighton)	Big House -v- Little House: 'Great hatred, little room'?

Yves Dommartin (Nice Institute of Letters)	Fishermen and Stilt-walkers: Real Jobs for Fictional Characters - Yeats's poems and the workplace
Aoife Burke (NUIG)	The Word on the Street: direct speech and the vernacular in Yeats's dramatic monologues

Group B

Akido Akanado (University of Toyko)	Gardening and other Leisure Activities in the poems of Yeats
Chad Kodell (Alabama State)	'The Real World': Yeats's proper nouns and the uncanny.
Jiwoo Soo-wook (Seoul University)	'A goldfish swimming in a bowl': the metaphoric valence of domesticity in Yeats

15.00–5.15	*Coffee Break*	
15.15–16.45	***Breakout Session 3***	
	Group A	

Elena Cruz (Salamanca University)	Silk kimonos and grey Connemara cloth: stuff and nonsense in the clothes of Yeats's poetry
Andy Burke (U.F. Gainesville)	Why is there no pub to be found in all of Yeats?
Jeremy Northington (Loughborough)	Selling Yeats in the Age of Trump

Group B

Zhang Chi (Beijing University)	No Ordinary Love: tension between the ideated and quotidian in the love poems of Yeats
Arnav Arnand (Delhi)	'Beautiful Lofty Things': Patrician Yeats
Rita Schrier (Clermont)	Yeats and Music Hall: Proletarian Past-times and Delights

16.45–18.00	***Plenary Session No. 2***	
	Bahk Seulgi (Pusan National University)	'Being Transported: Vehicular Traffic in the Poetry of Yeats'
18.15–19.30	Colloquium Concludes with Reception, Poonguan Visitor Hall	
20.00–24.00	Emerald Bar, Four Ages Hotel, downtown Hungsang (bus provided):	WBY Impersonation Contest (No masks, please!).

10. INKLING PRESS ADDENDUM

Inkling Press

25 W 13th Street, New York, NY 10020
Tel: +11 212 344 2598: email: books@inkling.com

Addendum to PUBLISHING AGREEMENT

made this 30th day of February, 2023 between **W.B. Yeats** of Shrangri-La Cottage, 98 Cusp Street, Dublin 4, Ireland (hereinafter called the **Author** of the one part) and **Inkling Press**, (hereinafter called the **Publisher** of the other part) whereby it is mutually agreed as follows concerning a Work at present entitled *Lastest Poems*.

1. Morality Clause
   The Publisher can terminate the agreement if the Author or The Work fails to uphold standards reasonably accepted in the industry, or becomes the subject of public disrepute, contempt, complaints or scandal.

2. Book Marketing
   a) The Author holds responsibility for researching the marketability of his book and helping to advertise it upon publication.
   b) The Author should plan to actively use social media and other avenues to be consistent with advertisement of his or her books, such as the Amazon author page, Twitter, Facebook, Google Plus, Instagram, and participating in blogs/forums. Authors should be open to doing local readings and book-signings.
   c) Inkling Press will also submit press releases, create an author page and title page, advertise the book in social media, and work with book-signing venues.
   d) Inkling holds no guarantee for the book's sales.

3. Termination
   The Author may not claim any breach on the grounds of 'publisher abuse', unless this can be proven beyond doubt and only if the grounds are judged sufficiently significant: 'hurt feelings' or 'rude emails' will not be considered sufficient grounds for termination.

This Agreement Addendum will be binding upon the Author, and Publisher, their heirs, successors & assigns.

Signed _____   Signed _____
         for the Author   for the Publisher

Witnessed by _____   Witnessed by _____

Dated _____

1 Office Use Only

?
Good speaker: strong potential for festival circuit, radio interviews etc. Inclined to go on a bit? Coach re soundbites? Cut the singing, deffo.

Proust Questionnaire? Mag feature inside home, décor, pic at writing desk for Sun supplements? Bedroom? Wife allow?

Ding-dong with Germaine Greer? Panel guest on HIGNFY?

Advise on clothes. Lose the bow tie? Jeans? Organise re-tweet campaign, around birds, maybe? He likes birds... Melvyn Bragg? TV? In U.S. – Conan? (Irish thing?)

celeb endorse? Needs classy- Obama? Meryl? Stephen Fry?

Opportunity for brand tie-ins and product placement? Use of proper nouns?

Note incident of Irish woman with handbag: avoid repeat? Monitor book signing line…

Place in movie, Actor reading book. Robert Pattinson? Will Smith? Jennifer Lawrence? Idris Elba? Colin Farrell?

Lines as Ad Copy? Galleries? Ireland? Greece? Nice pics..

Reviews: Broadsheets, yes. Monitor Goodreads / Amazon? TLS? LRB? Poetry Uxminster?

Enter for Prizes – risky? Cld be runner-up? Too old, white, male?

Reputation for crankiness? Wife's? No pushover…. Allocate intern to keep both sweet

11. In Which a Disgruntled Creative Writing Student Writes to WBY, to Ask for Help

Dear Professor Yeats,

I'm a second year M.A. student of Creative Writing (Poetry) at the University of Winnington. My results for semester 1 put me at 66%, similar to my previous grades on this programme. As I'm sure you'll understand, I'm not happy with that.

Having paid the (significant) course fees; having fulfilled all set assignments on time and to the best of my ability; having attended all scheduled workshops and seminars; having completed all recommended reading, and having participated, knowingly, in class discussions, I don't understand why my grade isn't in the top ten percentile which I believe my poetry merits.

As a celebrated, bestselling, Nobel Prize-winning poet who consistently ranks in the top 10 per cent of 'Best Modern Poets' polls, I'm hoping you can help me to improve my grade.

Our course leader has set us an exercise this week to write a letter to a poet of our choice, outlining why their work matters to us. And so, I'm writing to you. Bur rather than wasting time on an abstract letter, I want to actually send you mine via your website 'Contact Me' option, as I don't really see the point of wasting time on writing what no one much will ever read, and because I think writing is about communication and writing a letter you don't send is like talking to yourself in a dark, empty room.

I attach a sample of my work, three poems for your perusal. 'Instant Coffee', 'The Furry Underneath of Solitude', and 'In a Tube Station at 5am'. Can you read them please and tell me what (if anything) is wrong with them? It need not take long, just a quick email pointing out what's good and suggesting changes to make them even better? Then I could submit these poems for my final portfolio and with your help achieve the grade that has been so far denied me. Your opinion would definitely outrank my poetry professor's so if you judge them complete and satisfactory, I'll be able to tell her that my work has more merit than she's able to recognize.

I honestly think she's down on me because I'm the only man in her class. I think you'll understand my difficulty as you really seem to go into the whole issue of masculinity in contemporary society. And you understand rejection. ('Why should I blame her that she filled my days / With misery'? But why should I not? Does she not deserve it? Call a spade a spade, I say. And let it do its digging.) 'Tread softly'? Not a chance.

I proposed writing my end of term essay on 'W.B. Yeats and Incel', but my professor said I should limit myself to close readings of three of your poems. Typical short-sightedness! I'm sorry I'm not in your class, as I really think you'd get it. 'That is no country for old men'. Definitely not, or for young men either, if she gets her way. Typical femoid.

So, will you help me? Would you be willing to put your considerable experience behind someone who's just starting out, having to battle through the morass of prejudice and fear that seems to sum up my course and so much of contemporary society? So far as I can see, your whole life was about battling through one morass or another, so I really think this is something that will appeal to you.

Yours in hope,

Chris Cummings
Poet

12. WILD SWAN ADVERT

Wild Swan

'Intellect approved'

Tired of hearing that the falcon cannot hear the falconer?

That a terrible beauty is born?

About the filthy, modern tide?

We present

Wild Swan

– a computer programme that swoops down on and gobbles
Yeats phrases from politicians' speeches.

Never again will you have to read a misquoted line of Yeats!

No more fumbling wits! No more weasel's tooth!
No more barbarous tongue!

Only $9.99

Checks, Money Orders, Paypal, Cash – easy payment options

INDEX

Gosse, Edmund 69
Graham, Martha 585
'Great Day, The' (Yeats) 234–35
Great Famine, the 426, 428
Greco–Persian wars 330 –31
Greek culture 330–39, 340–41, 349
Greene, George 52, 54
Green Helmet and Other Poems, The (Yeats)
    aestheticism 407
    modernism 439–42, 444
    Pound response 300–1
    revolution 223
Gregory, Isabella Augusta (Lady Gregory)
    Abbey Theatre 59, 65–66, 69, 70, 554–55,
        556, 558–59
    Ascendency 223, 230
    collaboration 49, 59, 69–70, 137–38, 144
    Coole 58, 62, 67, 68, 158, 192, 440–41, 446–47
    correspondence 14–15, 67, 70, 192, 236
    co-writing role 63–66, 507, 516, 521–22,
        554–55, 555n.7
    death 58, 67
    Dun Emer 467
    folklore 25, 29–30, 60–61, 68, 118–19, 120–21,
        384
    Gonne 61
    Robert Gregory, 69, 206–7, 212–13
    'Manifesto for the Irish Literary Theatre' 237
    mythopoeic shaping by Yeats 59, 67–70
    nationalism 69–70
    nonconforming woman 521–22
    patron 59–63, 158, 165–66, 197
    playwright 63–65, 137, 249, 521–22, 556–57
    Romanticism 399
    Vision 62–63, 69, 386
    writings on the Rising 192–84
Gregory, Robert 69, 76, 159, 204–7, 211–14, 215, 455
Gregory, William 59, 60
'Grey Rock, The' (Yeats) 628–29
Grierson, Herbert 158, 411
Grubb, Thomas and Howard 365
Gyles, Althea 424–25, 446–47, 449–52
'Gyres, The' (Yeats) 389, 649–50, 654

H

Hagoromo (Noh drama) 526, 527–29
Hail and Farewell (Moore) 6, 140

Hall, Sydney 45
Hamlet (Shakespeare) 167–68, 173, 175, 180–81,
    182, 183, 568, 622–23
Hardy, Thomas 43
Harrison, Henry 146
Harun Al-Rashid 339, 341–42
Harvey, Paul 60, 61
Heald, Edith Shackleton 146–47
Heaney, Seamus 176–77, 183, 497
Hearn, Lafcadio 535–36
Heath, Lady 201–3
Heffernan the Blind, William 35
Hegel, G. W. F. 93–94, 172, 226–27, 243–44
Heisenberg, Werner 359–60, 359n.30
Henry, Niall 565–68
Henry V (Shakespeare) 172–73
Heptaplus (Pico della Mirandola) 93–94
Heraclitus 219
Herne's Egg, The (Yeats) 401, 541–42, 564, 663
Hérodiade (Mallarmé) 574–59, 576–61
heroic, the
    Cuchulain 115–16, 118, 132–33, 174–75
    death 286, 293–95
    masculinity 640–42
    Nietzsche 608
Hicks, Cuthbert 205–6
Higgins, F. R. 254
Higginson, Thomas Wentworth 74
'High Flight' (Magee) 204, 205–6
Hijikata, Tatsumi 542
Hindi language 495–96
Hindu mysticism 314–15
'His Bargain' (Yeats) 342
history. See also *A Vision*, system of history/
    symbols
    cyclical 142, 146–47, 264–65, 285–86, 319
    folklore 116–18
    legends 116, 132–33
    vs. logic 232
    1930s 250–51
    poetry 167–68, 184, 185–86
    Pound on 248
    revolution 216
    time collapsed 242
    time travel/manipulation 184
    war 285–86, 295
History of Ireland (S. J. O'Grady) 122–23, 125